Queensland
a Lonely Planet Australia guide

Mark Armstrong

Queensland

1st edition

Published by
   Lonely Planet Publications
   Head Office: PO Box 617, Hawthorn, Vic 3122, Australia
   Branches: 155 Filbert St, Suite 251, Oakland, CA 94607, USA
                    10 Barley Mow Passage, Chiswick, London W4 4PH, UK
                    71 bis rue du Cardinal Lemoine, 75005 Paris, France

Printed by
   SNP Printing Pte Ltd, Singapore

Photographs by

Mark Armstrong	Mark Norman
Great Barrier Reef	David Sherman
Marine Park Authority	Paul Steel
Richard I'Anson	Tony Wheeler
R & V Moon	Steve Womersley

Front cover: Cruising the Whitsundays (Mark Armstrong)
Title page: Old Court House, Ravenswood (Mark Armstrong)

This Edition
   January 1996

**Although the authors and publisher have tried to make the information as
accurate as possible, they accept no responsibility for any loss, injury or
inconvenience sustained by any person using this book.**

National Library of Australia Cataloguing in Publication Data

Armstrong, Mark, 1961-.
   Queensland.

   1st ed.
   Includes index.
   ISBN 0 86442 318 7.

   1. Queensland – Guidebooks.
   I. Title. (Series: Lonely Planet Australia Guide).

919.430463

text & maps © Lonely Planet 1996
photos © photographers as indicated 1996
climate charts compiled from information supplied by Patrick J Tyson, © Patrick J Tyson, 1996

Mark Armstrong

Mark was born and raised in Melbourne and studied at Melbourne Uni. Amongst other things, he has worked in computer sales and marketing, as a restorer of old houses, as a fencing contractor and in the hospitality industry. He lived in Barcelona for a couple of years and has travelled in South-East Asia, Europe and North America. In 1992 he wrote *Where to Wine, Dine and Recline in Central Victoria* before beginning work for Lonely Planet on the *Victoria* and *Melbourne* guides. He has also contributed to *Australia – a travel survival kit* and updated *Islands of Australia's Great Barrier Reef* and the Spain chapter of *Mediterranean Europe on a shoestring*.

From the Author

Mark would like to thank everyone who helped out along the way, particularly the national park rangers and staff at the tourist offices throughout the state. Thanks also to John Noble for the use of his extensive research notes on Queensland, to Paul & Hope Hayes (Cairns) for yet another dose of fine hospitality, to Byron Kurth and Vicki Hepner (Port Douglas), to Jim Albury for the after-hours tour of the Australian Workers Heritage Centre in Barcaldine, to Frank for the tour of the Gemfields and pointing out the difference between a sapphire and a lump of gravel, and to John Meckiff for his companionship on the trip from Cairns to Cape York.

And thanks to everyone at LP, especially Steve Womersley and Lindsay Brown for patient editing and Marcel Gaston & Co for design stuff and all things cartographic.

From the Publisher

Steve Womersley and Lindsay Brown edited this book and Marcel Gaston co-ordinated the mapping and design. Simon Bracken and Paul Clifton designed the cover. Thanks go to Jane Fitzpatrick and Mary Neighbour for their help with proofing and to Ann Jeffree, Andrew Tudor, Andrew Smith, Matt King and Tamsin Wilson who all helped with mapping, and to Tamsin and Reita Wilson, Ann Jeffree and Marcel for illustrations. Thanks also to Adrienne Costanzo and Valerie Tellini for their help checking artwork and to Bruce Cameron for his information for disabled travellers in Queensland.

This Book

Although this is a new book, some sections of it have been adapted and expanded from other Lonely Planet books. The Cape York, Gulf Savannah and Outback chapters are based on the corresponding sections from Lonely Planet's *Outback Australia*, which were written by Ron & Viv Moon and Denis O'Byrne. The sections on Queensland's Barrier Reef islands are based on *Islands of Australia's Great Barrier Reef*, originally written by Tony Wheeler and updated by Mark Armstrong. Some sections have also been expanded from the Queensland chapter of *Australia – a travel survival kit*, originally written by Tony Wheeler and subsequently updated by numerous people including John Noble and Susan Forsyth, Hugh Finlay and Mark Armstrong.

Warning & Request

Things change – prices go up, schedules

change, good places go bad and bad places go bankrupt – nothing stays the same. So if you find things better or worse, recently opened or long since closed, please write and tell us and help make the next edition better.

Your letters will be used to help update future editions and, where possible, important changes will also be included in a Stop Press section in reprints.

We greatly appreciate all information that is sent to us by travellers. Back at Lonely Planet we employ a hard-working readers' letters team to sort through the many letters we receive. The best ones will be rewarded with a free copy of the next edition or another Lonely Planet guide if you prefer. We give away lots of books, but, unfortunately, not every letter/postcard receives one.

Contents

INTRODUCTION 11

FACTS ABOUT QUEENSLAND 15

History 15
Geography 30
Climate 32
Flora 33
Fauna 36

National Parks 40
State Forests 42
Government 42
Economy 43
Population & People 44

Arts & Culture 46
Religion 51
Language 53

FACTS FOR THE VISITOR 55

Visas & Embassies 55
Documents 56
Customs 56
Money 57
When to Go 59
What to Bring 60
Tourist Offices 61
Useful Organisations 62
Business Hours 66
Holidays 66
Cultural Events 66

Post & Telecommunications ... 67
Time 70
Electricity 70
Weights & Measures 70
Books 70
Maps 74
Media 74
Film & Photography 75
Health 76
Women Travellers 80
Gay & Lesbian Travellers 80

Dangers & Annoyances 80
Work 84
Emergency 85
Outback Survival 85
Activities 85
Highlights 90
Accommodation 91
Food 96
Drinks 98
Entertainment 99
Things to Buy 101

GETTING THERE & AWAY 104

Air 104
Land 112

Sea 115
Warning 116

GETTING AROUND...117

Air 117
Bus 117
Train 118
Car 120

Motorcycle 126
Bicycle 127
Hitching 128
Boat 129

Local Transport 129
Tours 129

BRISBANE..131

Orientation 131
Information 133
Brisbane Walks 140
Views 141
Museums............................ 141
Galleries............................. 141
City Centre 142
City Botanic Gardens 147
Historic Houses 147
Queensland Cultural Centre .. 147
South Bank Parklands 148
Beaches 149
Mt Coot-tha Park 149

Brisbane Forest Park.............. 149
Wildlife Sanctuaries 151
Australian Woolshed.............. 152
Spring Hill 152
Fortitude Valley, New Farm &
Kangaroo Point...................... 152
Petrie Terrace & Paddington .. 153
University of Queensland....... 155
Activities............................... 157
Organised Tours.................... 161
Festivals................................ 162
Work..................................... 163
Places to Stay........................ 164

Places to Eat......................... 174
Entertainment......................... 184
Things to Buy........................ 191
Getting There & Away 194
Getting Around 196
Moreton Bay....................... 199
The Bayside 199
North Stradbroke Island......... 201
Moreton Island...................... 205
St Helena Island.................... 206
Coochiemudlo Island.............. 206
Bay Isles............................... 207
Bribie Island.......................... 207

GOLD COAST 209

Theme Parks 215	Broadbeach & Mermaid	Tamborine Mountain 232
Southport & Main Beach 215	Beach 224	Springbrook Plateau............... 233
South Stradbroke Island 217	Burleigh Heads 226	Canungra 234
Surfers Paradise..................... 218	Coolangatta 229	Lamington National Park........235
	Gold Coast Hinterland..... 232	Mt Lindesay Highway 236

SUNSHINE COAST 237

Caboolture 239	Noosa 248	**Sunshine Coast Hinter-**
Glass House Mountains.......... 240	Tewantin 255	**land 258**
Caloundra 241	Cooloola Coast 256	Nambour 259
Maroochydore, Alexandra	Pomona 257	Maleny 259
Headland & Mooloolaba 243	Eumundi................................258	Mapleton 260
Peregian Beach &	Yandina 258	Palmwoods 261
Coolum Beach 246		

DARLING DOWNS 262

Ipswich 264	Texas 273	Bunya Mountains National
Ipswich to Warwick 264	Goondiwindi 273	Park 282
Warwick 264	West of Goondiwindi 274	Kingaroy 282
Allora 268	Toowoomba 274	Nanango.................................283
Killarney 268	Toowoomba to Miles 277	Murgon..................................283
Warwick to Stanthorpe 268	Miles.....................................278	Gayndah 284
Stanthorpe 269	North from Miles 279	Mundubbera 284
Granite Belt Wineries 271	Roma 279	Eidsvold 284
Girraween National Park 272	Roma to Charleville 81	Monto 285
Sundown National Park 273	**South Burnett**	Cania Gorge National Park 285
Inglewood 273	**Region 281**	Monto to Rockhampton 285

FRASER COAST... 286

Gympie 286	Hervey Bay 293	Woodgate National Park 306
Rainbow Beach 290	Fraser Island 300	Gin Gin..................................306
Tin Can Bay.......................... 291	Childers 304	Bundaberg..............................306
Maryborough 292	Woodgate 305	Bundaberg Beaches................311

CAPRICORN COAST 313

Gladstone Area 315	Mt Morgan 336	Capella 348
Miriam Vale 315	Rockhampton to	Clermont 348
Agnes Water &	Baralaba 338	Clermont to Mackay 349
Seventeen Seventy................. 315	Yeppoon 338	Gemfields 349
Local National Parks 317	Yeppoon to Byfield 339	Springsure 352
Gladstone 317	Yeppoon to Emu Park 340	Rolleston 352
Gladstone Harbour Islands 321	Great Keppel Island 341	Carnarvon National Park 352
Around Gladstone 321	Other Keppel Bay Islands 344	Injune 353
Southern Reef Islands 322	Rockhampton to Sarina 345	Rolleston to Banana – the
Rockhampton Area 327	**Capricorn Hinterland 346**	Dawson Highway....................353
Rockhampton 327	Rockhampton to Emerald 346	Banana to Miles – the
Around Rockhampton 335	Emerald 347	Leichhardt Highway 353
Bouldercombe 336	Around Emerald 348	Biloela 354

WHITSUNDAY COAST 356

Mackay Area **358**
Sarina.................................358
Sarina Beach 358
Sarina to Mackay...................359
Mackay 359
Mackay's Northern Beaches .. 367
Brampton Island 368
Carlisle Island 369
Other Cumberland Islands 370
Cape Hillsborough National
Park 370

Newry Island Group 370
Eungella National Park 371
Whitsundays Area **373**
Laguna Quays 378
Proserpine 378
Airlie Beach 379
Conway National Park 387
Cedar Creek Falls & Conway
Beach 388
Long Island 388
Hook Island 389

Daydream Island 390
South Molle Island 391
Hamilton Island 391
Hayman Island 394
Lindeman Island 395
Whitsunday Island 396
Other Whitsunday Islands 396
Northern Whitsunday
Islands 397
Bowen 397
Collinsville 401

NORTH COAST 402

Ayr To Townsville **404**
Home Hill 404
Ayr 404
Alva Beach 405
Australian Institute of Marine
Sciences.................................405
Mt Elliot National Park 406
Townsville 406
Magnetic Island 421
**Townsville to Charters
Towers** **429**

Ravenswood...........................429
Charters Towers 430
**Townsville to Mission
Beach** **434**
Mt Spec National Park 434
Paluma 434
Jourama Falls National
Park 435
Ingham 435
Around Ingham 435
Orpheus Island 436

Other Palm Islands 437
Cardwell 437
Hinchinbrook Island 441
Islands Near Hinchinbrook 445
Tully 446
Mission Beach Area 446
Dunk Island 451
Bedarra Island 453
Other Family Islands 453
Mission Beach to
Innisfail 454

FAR NORTH QUEENSLAND 456

Innisfail to Cairns **459**
Innisfail...................................459
Around Innisfail 460
West from Innisfail 461
Josephine Falls 462
Bramston Beach 462
Babinda 462
Babinda Boulders 463
Gordonvale 463
Gordonvale To Yungaburra 463
Yarrabah Aboriginal
Community 463
Cairns **464**
History 465
Orientation 465
Information 465
Things to See 468
Activities 469
Organised Tours 471
Festivals 474
Places to Stay 474
Places to Eat 480
Entertainment 483
Things to Buy 484
Getting There & Away 485

Getting Around 487
Islands off Cairns **488**
Green Island............................488
Fitzroy Island 490
Frankland Islands 490
Atherton Tableland **491**
Kuranda 492
Kuranda To Mareeba 495
Mareeba 495
Mareeba To Chillagoe 496
Chillagoe 498
Tolga 500
Atherton 500
Lake Tinaroo 501
Yungaburra 501
Lakes Eacham & Barrine 502
Peeramon 503
Malanda 503
Around Malanda 503
Millaa Millaa 504
Mt Hypipamee National Park . 504
Herberton 504
Ravenshoe 505
Ravenshoe to Undara or
Charters Towers 505

Cairns to Port Douglas ... **506**
Northern Beaches....................506
Ellis Beach to Port
Douglas 509
**Port Douglas to Cape
Tribulation** **509**
Port Douglas 509
Mossman 520
Mossman to Mt Molloy 521
Mossman to Daintree..............521
Daintree..................................522
Daintree to Cooktown via the
Creb Track 524
Cape Tribulation Area.............525
Places to Stay – Daintree
River to Cape Trib 530
Places to Stay – Cape Trib......531
North to Cooktown **534**
Cape Tribulation to Cooktown
– the Coast Road.....................534
Cairns to Cooktown – the
Inland Route............................536
Cooktown................................538
Lizard Island 544
Islands around Lizard Island... 547

CAPE YORK PENINSULA 549

The Route **558**
Cape York Sampler 558

North of Cooktown 558
Cooktown to Musgrave 560

Lakeland to Laura 562
Laura to Musgrave................. 564

Musgrave to Coen 565
Coen to Archer
River 567
Archer River to Iron Range
National Park 568
Archer River to Weipa 569

Weipa 570
Archer River to Wenlock
River 572
Wenlock River to Jardine
River 572
Jardine River to Cape York 575

**Thursday Island & the
Torres Strait 579**
Thursday Island 580
Other Islands 582

GULF SAVANNAH..584

Eastern Gulf Region 588
Undara Lava Tubes 588
Mt Surprise 589
The Savannahlander 589
Einasleigh & Forsayth 590
Cobbold Gorge 590
Mt Surprise to Georgetown ... 591
Georgetown 591

Croydon 591
The Gulflander 592
Normanton 592
Normanton to Karumba 594
Karumba 594
Western Gulf Region 596
Northern Territory Border to
Burketown 596

Burketown 597
Burketown to Normanton 599
Burketown to Camooweal 600
Lawn Hill National
Park 601
Cloncurry to Normanton 602
Gulf Islands 602

OUTBACK QUEENSLAND 604

**Charters Towers to
Camooweal – the Flinders
& Barkly Hwys.................. 605**
Charters Towers to
Hughenden 606
Hughenden 608
Porcupine Gorge National
Park 608
Richmond 609
Julia Creek............................. 609
Julia Creek to Cloncurry 610
Cloncurry 610
Cloncurry to Mt Isa 611
Mt Isa.................................... 612
Camooweal 618
Camooweal Caves National
Park 618
Camooweal to
Threeways 618

**Cloncurry to Cunnamulla
– the Matilda Highway 619**
Cloncurry to Winton 619
Winton 620
South of Winton 623
Winton to Longreach 623
Longreach 624
Longreach to Windorah – the
Thomson Developmental
Road 628
Longreach to Barcaldine 628
Barcaldine 629
Barcaldine to Hughenden 631
Barcaldine to Alpha – the
Capricorn Highway 631
Alpha 632
Alpha to Rockhampton 632
Blackall..................................632
Isisford 633

Idalia National Park 634
Blackall to Charleville 634
Charleville..............................635
Charleville to
Cunnamulla 638
Cunnamulla 638
West of Cunnamulla...............639
The Channel Country 639
Mt Isa to Boulia 639
Boulia 639
Boulia to Winton 640
Bedourie 640
Birdsville 640
Around Birdsville 642
Betoota 643
Windorah 643
Quilpie 643
Quilpie to Charleville 644
Cunnamulla to Innamincka 644

GLOSSARY 646

INDEX 653

Maps 653   Text 653

Map Legend

BOUNDARIES

.... State Boundary
.... Tropics

ROUTES

.... Freeway
.... Highway, Major Road
.... Other Sealed Road
.... Major Unsealed Road
.... Unsealed Road or Track
.... City Road
.... City Street
.... Four Wheel Drive Track
.... Railway
.... Underground Railway
.... Tram
.... Walking Track
.... Ferry Route
.... Bridge

AREA FEATURES

.... Park, Gardens
.... Built-Up Area
.... Pedestrian Mall
.... Market
.... Cemetery
.... Reef
.... Beach or Desert
.... Rocks
.... Mountain Ranges

HYDROGRAPHIC FEATURES

.... Coastline
.... River, Creek
.... Intermittent River or Creek
.... Lake, Intermittent Lake
.... Salt Lake
.... Canal
.... Swamp

SYMBOLS

✪ CAPITAL		...........................National Capital
◉ Capital		...........................Regional Capital
◍ CITY		.... Major City
● City		.... City
● Town		.... Major Town
● Town		.... Minor Town
■		...........................Place to Stay
▼		.... Place to Eat
▼		...........................Pub, Bar, Nightclub
✉	☎	...........................Post Office, Telephone
❶	❷	...........................Tourist Information, Bank
◔	℗	...........................Transport, Parking
🏛	♦	...........................Museum, Youth Hostel
⌂	⚲	Caravan Park, Camping Ground
✚	⊟	...........................Church, Cathedral
■	⚑	...........................Shrine, Golf Course

✪	★	...........................Hospital, Police Station
✈	✛	...........................Airport, Airfield
▭	✿	...........................Swimming Pool, Gardens
❖	🐾	...........................Shopping Centre, Zoo
◔	⚕	Embassy, Winery or Vineyard
←	A25	. One Way Street, Route Number
	∴	...... Archaeological Site or Ruins
🏛	⚑	...........................Stately Home, Monument
⚐	⚓	...........................Beach, Cafe
◠	⌂	.... Cave, Hut or Chalet
▲	✳	... Mountain or Hill, Lookout
⚒	⚓	...........................Lighthouse, Shipwreck
)(	◎	...........................Pass, Spring
»»	∺	...................Rapids, Waterfalls
		...... Cliff or Escarpment, Tunnel
		...........................Railway Station

Note: not all symbols displayed above appear in this book

Shark bites in shallows

By MICHAEL REID

A shark attacked a man in shallow water at Ohope Beach in the eastern Bay of Plenty yesterday.

The man, aged in his late 20s, stumbled into the shark as he walked out of the water.

The man was too shaken to describe his ordeal, but his neighbour, Mr Maurice Eggleton, said the shark attacked him repeatedly and wounded him in the abdomen and the left leg.

"He was walking out of the water when he actually hit the thing with his leg," said Mr Eggleton.

"It swung him around, came out of the water and bit him above the water line, around his stomach area.

"Then he managed to swipe it off him and made for the beach, but it bit him again."

The second lunge caught the man in the leg.

Last night the man was in Whakatane Hospital where his condition was described as satisfactory.

"He was very shocked. It frightened the hell out of him," said Mr Eggleton.

"He's a good strong man . . . that's what saved him. It would have been curtains for a kiddie."

The man described the shark as a silver grey colour, about 1.5m long.

Sergeant Dave Archibald, of Whakatane, said that bronze whaler sharks are known to bathe and breed in the area, but it would be difficult to say if it might have been a bronze whaler.

He said the attack appeared to have been a defensive bite, not a feeding attack.

PLANT NOW

ourite for fragrance
Top quality bulbs from
d's leading
assured
ccess.

ll Talks Bulbs

are a very versatile bulb and
ed to add colour and
n all sorts of garden
Naturalise them
es, plant them in
keries and along

Bill Ward,
Palmers
Garden
Show

Introduction

Queensland is Australia's second-largest state. It's a vast and often surprising place that is widely known as the 'Sunshine State' – an alluring land of blue skies, holidays and brighter tomorrows.

Queensland's popularity as a tourism destination is easily understood. Apart from the fact that the sun (almost) always shines, the state is blessed with an abundance of natural riches. Three areas – the Great Barrier Reef, the majestic Fraser Island and the Wet Tropics rainforests of the Far North – have been inscribed on the World Heritage List. In addition, there are dozens of stunning national parks which encompass a tremendous diversity of landscapes – from the red-sand wilds of the Simpson Desert to the dense greenery of the coastal forests, and from the oasis-like beauty of the Carnarvon Gorge to the ancient volcanic lava tubes at Undara.

The major resorts are sprinkled all the way up the east coast, and travellers have a choice between the hustle and bustle of places like the Gold Coast and Cairns and the smaller and more sophisticated 'boutique style' towns like Port Douglas and Noosa Heads. These developed resort towns contrast dramatically with Queensland's magnificent wilderness areas, which include places like the Cape York Peninsula, the Gulf Savannah, Hinchinbrook Island, and the vast and empty expanses of the mystical outback.

The Great Barrier Reef is sprinkled with coral cays and continental islands, and it isn't too difficult to find an island to suit your particular fantasy, whether you want to string a tent between two palm trees on a deserted

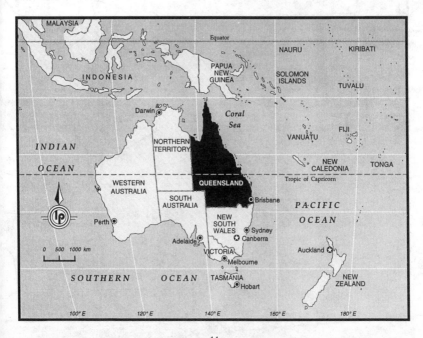

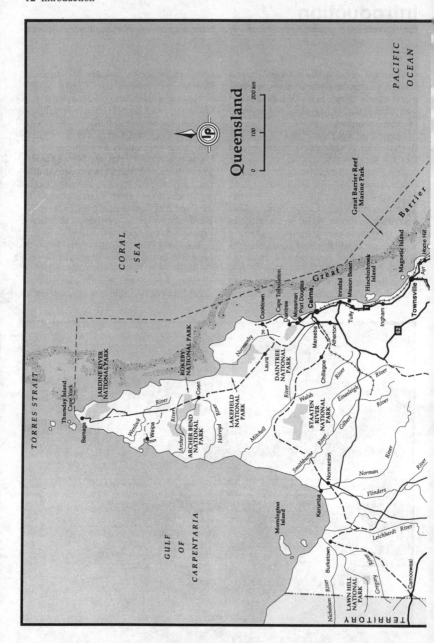

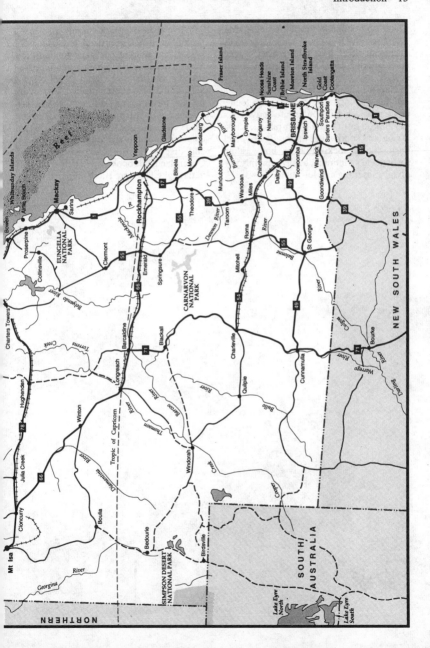

island or indulge yourself on a luxurious island resort. Or if you'd rather stay on the mainland, there's a veritable armada of operators offering trips out to the reef and its islands from the coastal towns.

Plenty of people head for Queensland wanting nothing more than a banana lounge and a beach, but if you're into activity you can choose from white-water rafting, scuba-diving and snorkelling on the Barrier Reef, bushwalking, rock climbing, horse riding, surfing and swimming, bungy jumping, sky-diving, abseiling and lots more.

While there is a not-entirely-inaccurate perception that Queensland has laid itself bare at the altar of packaged tourism, the Sunshine State still has plenty to offer independent travellers who want to get off the well-and-truly beaten track. We're all looking for something different, so whether you just want to recline by the pool in the shade of a palm tree while sipping on multi-coloured cocktails or strap on a backpack and discover the undiscovered side of Queensland, this book should help point you in the right direction. Have fun.

Facts about Queensland

HISTORY
The Aborigines

It is believed that the ancestors of the Aborigines journeyed from South-East Asia to the Australian mainland at least 40,000 years ago, possibly much earlier. During the last Ice age, land bridges connected Malaysia to Indonesia and Australia to New Guinea, but watercraft would still have been needed to reach Australia. These people may have made the perilous 120-km sea journey across the Timor Sea to Australia, or they may have island-hopped across to Papua New Guinea and travelled overland into Australia. Either way, northern Queensland would have been their main entry point.

Although much of Australia is today arid, the first migrants found a much wetter con-

Queensland
Chapters

0   250   500 km

Gulf of
Carpentaria

CAPE YORK
PENINSULA

FAR NORTH
QUEENSLAND

CORAL

SEA

PACIFIC

Great

Barrier

Reef

GULF SAVANNAH

NORTH
COAST

OCEAN

N
O
R
T
H
E
R
N

T
E
R
R
I
T
O
R
Y

WHITSUNDAY
COAST

OUTBACK QUEENSLAND

CAPRICORN COAST

FRASER
COAST

SUNSHINE COAST

BRISBANE &
MORETON BAY

GOLD COAST

SOUTH
AUSTRALIA

DARLING DOWNS

NEW SOUTH WALES

tinent, with large forests and many inland lakes teeming with fish. The fauna included giant marsupials such as three-metre-tall kangaroos, giant koalas and wombats, and huge, flightless birds. The environment was relatively non-threatening – only a few carnivorous predators existed.

With such favourable conditions, archaeological evidence would suggest that the descendants of these first settlers colonised the whole of the continent within a few thousand years.

As the last Ice age ended around 15,000 to 10,000 years ago, sea levels rose and the Aborigines were isolated on the continent. Many of the inland lakes dried up and vast deserts formed, and the majority of the inhabitants lived in the coastal areas.

By the time the Europeans arrived, it's estimated that there were at least 300,000 Aborigines living in Australia and around 250 different languages were spoken, many of them mutually unintelligible. Queensland was the most densely populated area, supporting as many as 100,000 to 120,000 Aborigines, embracing about 200 tribal groups of between 500 and 1500 people each. The Cape York Peninsula alone may have supported up to 30,000 people.

Early European settlers considered the Aborigines to be a backward race of people. This assumption was based on the definition of civilisation being the progression from a hunter-gatherer society to an agricultural one. Failure to cultivate plants and crops and domesticate animals was seen as a failure to progress – but these theories are now being widely questioned on the basis that the Aboriginal people had no need for agriculture. The land they lived in supplied them in abundance, and their survival and prosperity were a result of their deep understanding of a very rich environment. In his book *Triumph of the Nomads*, Geoffrey Blainey writes that the average Aborigine, as far as food, health, warmth and shelter are concerned, probably enjoyed as good a standard of living as the average European in 1800.

Their semi-nomadic existence was a defining feature of their adaptation to the Australian landscape. This is amply evidenced by the fact that they were able to survive in areas Europeans would later consider to be uninhabitable.

Before his disappearance, the explorer Ludwig Leichhardt would write of the Aborigines:

They seem to have tasted everything from the highest top of the bunya tree and the seaforthia and cabbage palm, to the grub which lies in the rotten tree of the bush.

Coastal tribes lived on an amazingly wide variety of plants and vegetables, supplementing their diet with fish, turtles and dugong from the sea. Shellfish were collected and eaten on the beaches – evidence of these feasts in the form of huge shell middens have been found all along the Queensland coast, at places like Weipa, Fraser Island and Double Island Point. Inland tribes were expert game hunters, using nets to catch kangaroos, spears to kill emus and boomerangs to bring down birds. They also built stone dams in rivers to trap fish. In the arid north-west, the Kalkadoons dug wells up to 10 metres deep to supply themselves with water. The rainforests supplied wild berries and other plants, and even the coastal mangroves provided them with food such as water-lily tubers and seeds, mangrove pods, crabs and shellfish.

They also had inter-tribal barter systems and well-developed trading routes which followed the major river systems in what is now Queensland. Cape York tribes were in regular contact with Torres Strait Islanders.

Ross Fitzgerald noted in his *History of Queensland* that the European settlers brought with them a notion of progress which upset the equilibrium between humans and nature, and which in turn ushered in the destruction of Aboriginal culture.

Because of the fragmented nature of Aboriginal society, which was based on family groups with an egalitarian political structure, a co-ordinated response to the European colonisers was not possible.

Despite the presence of the Aborigines, the newly arrived Europeans considered the new continent to be *terra nullius* – a land belonging to no-one. Conveniently, they saw no recognisable system of government, no commerce or permanent settlements and no evidence of land ownership. Thus, when Governor Phillip raised the Union Jack at Sydney Cove in 1788, the laws of England became the laws governing all Aborigines on the Australian continent. All land in Australia was from that moment the property of the British Crown.

If the Aborigines had had a readily recognisable political system and had resisted colonisation by organised force of arms, then the English might have been forced to recognise a prior title to the land and therefore legitimise their colonisation by entering into a treaty with the Aboriginal landowners.

At a local level, individuals resisted the encroachment of settlers. Warriors including Pemulwy, Yagan, Dundalli, Pigeon and Nemarluk were, for a time, feared by the colonists in their areas. But, although some settlements had to be abandoned, the effect of such resistance was only to temporarily postpone the inevitable.

Without any legal right to the lands they once lived on, some Aborigines were driven from their lands by force, and some succumbed to exotic diseases. Other Aborigines voluntarily left their lands to travel to the fringes of settled areas to obtain new commodities such as steel and cloth, and experience hitherto unknown drugs such as tea, tobacco, alcohol and narcotics.

By the early 1900s legislation designed to segregate and 'protect' Aboriginal people was passed in all states. The legislation imposed restrictions on the Aborigines' right to own property and seek employment, and the Aboriginals' Ordinance of 1918 even allowed the state to remove children from Aboriginal mothers if it was suspected that the father was non-Aboriginal. In these cases the parents were considered to have no rights over the children, who were placed in foster homes or childcare institutions. Many Aborigines are still understandably bitter about having been separated from their families and made to grow up apart from their people. An advantage of the Ordinance was that it gave a degree of protection for 'full-blood' Aborigines living on reserves, as non-Aborigines could enter only with a permit, and mineral exploration was forbidden.

The process of social change was accelerated by WW II, and 'assimilation' became the stated aim of post-war governments. To this end, the rights of Aborigines were subjugated even further – the government had control over everything, from where Aborigines could live to whom they could marry. Many people were forcibly moved to townships, the idea being that they would adapt to the European culture, which would in turn aid their economic development. The policy was a dismal failure.

In the 1960s the assimilation policy came under a great deal of scrutiny, and White Australians became increasingly aware of the inequity of their treatment of Aborigines. In 1967 non-Aboriginal Australians voted to give Aborigines and Torres Strait Islanders the status of citizens, and gave the federal government power to legislate for them in all states. The states had to provide them with the same services as were available to other citizens, and the federal government set up the Department of Aboriginal Affairs to identify the special needs of Aborigines and legislate for them.

The assimilation policy was finally dumped in 1972, to be replaced by the government's policy of self-determination, which for the first time enabled Aborigines to participate in decision-making processes.

In 1976 the Aboriginal Land Rights (Northern Territory) Act gave Aborigines in that region indisputable title to all Aboriginal reserves (about 20% of the Territory) and a means for claiming other Crown land. It also provided for mineral royalties to be paid to Aboriginal communities. This legislation was supposed to be extended to cover all of Australia, but the removal of the reformist Labor government in 1975 put paid to that prospect.

Mabo & the Native Title Act Only in the last couple of years did the non-Aboriginal community, including the federal government, come to grips with the fact that a meaningful conciliation between White Australia and its indigenous population was vital to the psychological well-being of all Australians.

In May 1982, five Torres Strait Islanders led by Eddie Mabo began an action for a declaration of native title over the Queensland Murray Islands. They argued that the legal principle of *terra nullius* had wrongfully usurped their title to land, as for thousands of years Murray Islanders had enjoyed a relationship with the land that included a notion of ownership. In June 1992 the High Court of Australia rejected *terra nullius* and the myth that Australia had been unoccupied. In doing this, it recognised that a principle of native title existed before the arrival of the British.

The High Court's judgment became known as the Mabo decision, one of the most controversial decisions ever handed down by an Australian court. It was ambiguous, as it didn't outline the extent to which native title existed in mainland Australia. It received a hostile reaction from the mining and other industries and resulted in some fairly hysterical responses with non-Aborigines fearing their precious backyards were suddenly going to be subject to Aboriginal land claims, but was hailed by Aborigines and Prime Minister Paul Keating as an opportunity to create a basis for reconciliation between Aboriginal and non-Aboriginal Australians.

To define the principle of native title, the federal parliament passed the Native Title Act in December 1993. Contrary to the cries of protest from the mining industry, the act gives Australian Aborigines very few new rights. It limits the application of native title to land which no-one else owns or leases, and to land with which Aborigines have continued to have a physical association. The act states that existing ownership or leases extinguish native title, although native title may be revived after mining leases have expired. If land is successfully claimed by Aborigines under the act, they will have no veto over developments including mining. Despite (or because of) its complexity, it will no doubt take a number of years and court cases before the implications of the Native Title Act are fully understood.

European Exploration

Historians believe that Portuguese sailors were the first Europeans to sight the Australian coast early in the 16th century, although because of the secrecy that shrouded maritime discoveries of that time there are no records of these voyages.

In 1606 the Spaniard Torres is known to have sailed through the strait between Cape York and New Guinea, that still bears his name, although there's no record of his actually sighting the Australian continent. During the same year the Dutch explorer Willem Jansz sailed the *Duyfken* into the Gulf of Carpentaria, charting part of the Queensland coastline. In 1623 another Dutchman, Jan Carstensz, landed at Cape York and explored a little, but like Janz before him, he considered the land inhospitable and unsuitable for settlement. His journal records his impressions:

In our judgment this is the most arid and barren region that could be found anywhere on earth; the inhabitants, too, are the most wretched and poorest creatures that I have ever seen in my age or time.

This dismal continent was forgotten until 1768, when the British admiralty instructed Captain James Cook to lead a scientific expedition to Tahiti, to observe the transit of the planet Venus across the Sun, and then begin a search for the Great South Land. On board his ship *Endeavour* were also several scientists including an astronomer and a group of naturalists and artists led by Joseph Banks.

After circumnavigating both islands of New Zealand, Cook set sail in search of the Great South Land, planning to head west until he found the unexplored east coast of the land known as New Holland.

On 19 April 1770 the extreme southeastern tip of the continent was sighted and named Point Hicks, and when the *Endeavour* was a navigable distance from shore Cook turned north to follow the coast and search for a suitable landfall. It was nine days before an opening in the cliffs was sighted and the ship and crew found sheltered anchorage in a harbour they named Botany Bay.

During their forays ashore the scientists recorded descriptions of plants, animals and birds the likes of which had never been seen, and attempted to communicate with the few native inhabitants, who all but ignored the first White people to set foot on the east coast. Cook wrote of the Blacks: 'All they seemed to want was for us to be gone.'

After leaving Botany Bay, Cook continued north, charting the coastline and noting that the fertile east coast was a different story from the inhospitable land the earlier explorers had seen to the west. He named a number of places as he sailed up the coast of Queensland, including Morton Bay (an 'e' was added later by the editor of his journal), the Whitsundays and Cape Tribulation. The *Endeavour* struck a reef off shore from Cape Tribulation and was badly damaged on 11 June 1770.

After heaving various heavy items overboard, including an anchor and six cannons, the *Endeavour* was freed from the reef. A sail was hauled under the hull to plug the hole, and the ship limped up the coast to the Endeavour River, landing at the site of present-day Cooktown. It took six weeks to repair the ship, during which time Cook and the scientists investigated their surroundings further, this time making contact with the local Aborigines.

Unlike Carstensz, Cook was quite taken with the indigenous people and wrote:

They may appear to some to be the most wretched people upon the earth: but in reality they are far more happier than we Europeans...They live in a tranquillity which is not disturbed by the inequality of condition...they seem to set no value upon anything we gave them, nor would they ever part with anything of their own...

After repairing the *Endeavour*, navigating the Great Barrier Reef and rounding Cape York, Cook again put ashore at Possession Island around the tip of Cape York to raise the Union Jack, rename the continent New South Wales and claim it for the British in the name of King George III.

James Cook was resourceful, intelligent, and popularly regarded as one of the greatest and most humane explorers of all time. His incisive reports of his voyages make fascinating reading, even today. By the time he was killed, in the Sandwich Islands (now Hawaii) in 1779, he had led two further expeditions to the South Pacific.

Convicts & European Settlement

Following the American Revolution, Britain was no longer able to transport convicts to North America. With jails and prison hulks already overcrowded, it was essential that an alternative be found quickly. In 1779 Joseph Banks suggested New South Wales as a fine site for a colony of thieves, and in 1786 Lord Sydney announced that the king had decided on Botany Bay as a place for convicts under sentence of transportation.

Less than two years later, in January 1788, the First Fleet sailed into Botany Bay under the command of Captain Arthur Phillip, who was to be the colony's first governor. Disappointed in Botany Bay, Phillip immediately moved the colony to Port Jackson, present-day Sydney Harbour.

The Second Fleet arrived in 1790 with more convicts and some supplies, and a year later, following the landing of the Third Fleet, the population had increased to 4000.

Little of the country was explored during those first years; few people ventured further than the Sydney Cove settlement, and by 1800 there were still only two small White settlements – the one at Sydney Cove and the other on Norfolk Island to the east.

Then a great period of White discovery started as the vast inland was gradually explored and the coastline extensively charted. In 1799 Matthew Flinders left Sydney in the *Norfolk* to explore the northern coast and search for useful ports and rivers, and landed at Bribie Island north of Moreton Bay. He sailed north as far as Fraser Island before returning to Sydney. In 1802 Flinders continued his explorations in the *Investigator*, and became the first person to circumnavigate the Australian continent.

Moreton Bay Penal Colony

By 1822 the penal colonies at Norfolk Island and Port Jackson were overcrowded, and it was suggested that a new settlement be established to store the more recalcitrant convicts. John Oxley, the surveyor general of New South Wales, was sent north to investigate the Moreton Bay area as a prospective site. He explored the bay and sailed up the Brisbane River, and on his return recommended Redcliffe Point as the site for the new colony. Oxley returned in 1824 with a settlement party led by Lieutenant Henry Miller. There were about 35 convicts in the party, with a regiment of guards and several civilians, including the botanist Allan Cunningham and Assistant Surveyor Robert Hoddle (who would later lay out the city of Melbourne).

The new settlement only lasted several months at Redcliffe Point. The site was soon considered unsuitable, due to a combination of factors including the lack of a safe anchorage and fresh water, swampy land and trouble with local Aboriginal tribes. In May 1825 the settlement was moved up the Brisbane River to the site of present-day Brisbane, which offered a safe harbour, fertile land and fresh water from a string of water holes. The second shipment of convicts arrived soon after, and construction of the new settlement began in earnest. Regular shipments of 30 to 40 convicts would follow in succeeding years, although the colony was never really the success it was intended to be. Being so far away from Sydney, it was very difficult to administer, and it never accommodated more than about 1100 convicts.

Moreton Bay was a brutal and isolated place of punishment. Several hundred convicts escaped in the early years, but most returned to the colony within a few weeks, unable to cope with life in the bush. A few never returned – some died of thirst or hunger and some were killed by Aboriginal

tribes, but others were adopted and lived with the tribes for many years.

Gradually, explorers ventured west from Moreton Bay into the hinterland. Coal and limestone deposits were found in the vicinity of present-day Ipswich, and in 1827 Allan Cunningham discovered the vast, grassy plains of the Darling Downs. The following year he returned and found the gap through the mountains of the Great Dividing Range which now bears his name. Patrick Leslie and his brothers became the first permanent settlers on the Darling Downs when they arrived in 1840, after a difficult overland journey from the south. Within another couple of years the entire district had been taken up by free settlers.

British authorities gradually lost interest in the penal system. Brisbane's convict era ended in 1839, when the last of the convicts were moved from Moreton Bay back to Sydney. Three years later the Moreton Bay area was opened up to free settlers, and the fertile lands around the Brisbane River were also quickly taken up.

White Exploration of Queensland

By the 1840s most of Queensland's vast interior was still unexplored by Whites, but a dramatic series of expeditions, some ill-fated, gradually opened it up.

Ludwig Leichhardt In 1843 the enigmatic Prussian explorer Ludwig Leichhardt arrived in Brisbane after trekking overland from Sydney, and soon announced plans to continue his overland trek to the newly established outpost of Port Essington, 3000 km away near present-day Darwin. Despite his eccentricities and notorious incompetence as an explorer, Leichhardt and his party completed the journey – in 15 months, twice as long as planned. The only casualty of this trip was the young botanist John Gilbert, who was killed by Aborigines.

Leichhardt returned to Sydney in 1846 as a hero. Almost immediately, he mounted another expedition, this time to cross the continent from east to west, but the party

Eccentric explorer Ludwig Leichhardt

turned back after only six months. Other members of the expedition cited Leichhardt's lack of leadership and planning, together with bad weather and illness, as the reasons for the failure. Undeterred, Leichhardt mounted yet another expedition and recruited six new men, all of whom were inexperienced in outback travel. The party set out from the Darling Downs in April 1848 and were never seen again. Their disappearance remains one of the great mysteries of Australian exploration.

Major Thomas Mitchell In 1845 the surveyor general of New South Wales, Major Thomas Mitchell, led a government-backed expedition from Orange (200 km inland from Sydney) into central Queensland, searching for an inland route to the Gulf of Carpentaria. When he received the news that Leichhardt's first expedition had already

arrived in Port Essington, Mitchell abandoned his plans and turned back.

Edmund Kennedy Second in command of Mitchell's expedition was Edmund Kennedy, the assistant surveyor. In 1848 Kennedy was given what turned out to be an impossible mission, that of trekking overland from Rockingham Bay (south of present-day Cairns) to the top of the Cape York Peninsula. The ship HMS *Rattlesnake*, which was to explore the coast and meet Kennedy at the top of the Cape, dropped his party of 13 men, 27 horses, 100 sheep and three cartloads of stores and equipment at Tam O'Shanter Point (at present-day Mission Beach). The expedition almost immediately struck trouble when their heavy supply carts could not be dragged through the swampy ground around Tully. The rugged land, harsh climate, lack of supplies, hostile Aborigines and missed supply drops all took their toll and nine of the party of 13 died. Kennedy himself was speared to death in an attack by Aborigines when he was only 30 km from the end of the fearsome trek. His Aboriginal servant, Jacky Jacky, was the only expedition member to finally reach the supply ship.

Burke & Wills In 1860 the stage was set for the greatest act in the White exploration of Australia. Some would say today that it was the greatest folly, but the Burke and Wills expedition was the largest, most lavish and best equipped expedition that set out to solve the riddle of inland Australia.

The lure of being the first to cross the continent was only part of the story. In 1859 the wonder of the telegraph line had reached India and was soon to head for Darwin. Depending on the route forged across the continent by an explorer, an overland telegraph line would finish either in Adelaide or Melbourne.

With much fanfare Robert O'Hara Burke led an expedition north out of Melbourne on 20 August 1860. Chosen by a committee of the Royal Society, Burke was neither an explorer nor surveyor, had no scientific

Robert O'Hara Burke

William John Wills

training, had never led an expedition of any kind, had never set foot out of Victoria since arriving there just a few years previously, and was considered to be, if anything, a very poor bushman. He also ignored the advice of earlier explorers to enlist the help of Aboriginal guides. So much for committees.

Leaving most of his group at Menindee (New South Wales), Burke and his new second-in-command, William John Wills, pushed north to Cooper Creek where they set up a depot. From there Burke chose Wills, Charles Grey and John King to accompany him to the Gulf of Carpentaria, leaving the depot and the remainder of the expedition on 16 December 1860. At the height of summer, these men set out to walk 1100 km through central Australia to the sea! It says something of their fortitude and sheer guts that they made it, reaching the mangroves that barred their view of the Gulf of Carpentaria on 11 February 1861. Camp No 119, near present-day Normanton, was their northernmost camp and can be visited today.

Turning their backs on the sea, the rush south became a life-and-death stagger with Grey dying at a place later called Lake Massacre, just west of the Cooper Creek depot.

When Burke, Wills and King arrived at the depot they were astonished to find that the men there had retreated to Menindee that very morning! The famous 'Dig Tree', arguably the most historic site in inland Australia, still stands on the banks of Cooper Creek in Queensland, near the border with South Australia. The name relates to the message carved into its trunk by the departing men: 'DIG 3FT N.W. APR 21 1861'.

Trapped at Cooper Creek the explorers wasted away, dying on the banks of this desert oasis. Only King, who had been befriended by some Aborigines, was alive when the first of the rescue parties arrived in September 1861.

These rescue expeditions really opened up the interior to Whites, with groups from Queensland, South Australia and Victoria crisscrossing the continent in search of Burke and Wills. Howitt, McKinlay, Landsborough and Walker were not only better explorers than Burke, but experienced bushmen who proved that Europeans, cattle and sheep could survive in these regions.

William Landsborough Landsborough, a successful stockman, gold miner and pastoralist, was chosen by the Victorian government to lead one of the expeditions that went in search of Burke and Wills.

Landsborough's party left Brisbane on the *Firefly* in August 1861 and sailed to the Gulf of Carpentaria. Landsborough travelled south along the Gregory River as far as the Barkly Tableland before returning to his depot on the Gulf, then followed the Flinders River south to the site of present-day Hughenden. At a station further south, he heard that Burke and Wills had perished, and he continued south all the way to Melbourne.

Ironically, Landsborough's party became the first to cross Australia from north to south. In his search, Landsborough had discovered Queensland's rich inland grazing areas. His reports of the country as being the finest pastoral land he had ever seen were responsible for a minor rush to settle the area. Many southern settlers who heard his reports rounded up herds of cattle and overlanded to central and northern Queensland, opening up areas previously unknown to the Europeans.

The Jardines In 1863 John Jardine was made the first government magistrate of the settlement of Somerset on the tip of the Cape York Peninsula. He considered the Cape to be commercially viable cattle country, and commissioned his sons, Frank and Alick, both then aged in their 20s, to overland a mob of cattle from Rockhampton to the new settlement.

Their epic journey took 10 months, and they arrived at Somerset in March 1865. Along the way they overcame lack of water, skirmishes with Aborigines, flooded rivers and a maze of swamps and waterways.

Frank Jardine later took over from his father as government magistrate at Somerset, where he died in 1919 after building an empire of cattle farming and pearl fishing.

Other Explorers There were many other explorers responsible for opening up Queensland's vast interior to White settlement. They included George Elphingstone Dalrymple, who in 1859 led an expedition inland from Rockhampton and discovered the rich pastoral districts of the Burdekin Valley, and later founded a port settlement at Bowen. In 1872 William Hann spent five months exploring the Cape York Peninsula and named many of the Cape's major rivers. Hann found traces of gold in the Palmer River, leading to a major gold rush to the area in 1873.

In 1855-56 Augustus Gregory had blazed a trail from the Victoria River, near the border of Western Australia and the Northern Territory, across the top of the continent and down through Queensland's coastal hinterland to Moreton Bay. He was appointed Queensland's first surveyor general in 1859.

Separation & Growth

At the end of 1859 the colony of Queensland finally won separation from New South Wales. Brisbane became the capital, and the first governor was Sir George Bowen. At this time there were only about 28,000 Europeans in the colony, but separation ushered in one of Queensland's major periods of growth and prosperity.

Initially, this growth was based on the steady development of the pastoral industry. Pioneer squatters who had started out in the Darling Downs gradually moved into other parts of Queensland. Landholdings grew larger and larger, and the small-scale settlers found it increasingly hard to compete with huge pastoral companies, such as the Northern Australian Pastoral Company, many of which were backed by overseas funds. The number of sheep grazing in Queensland went from eight million in 1870 to more than 20 million in the 1890s; the number of cattle rose from one million in 1870 to over six million by the 1920s.

By the 1860s Brisbane had shed its convict background and developed into a handsome provincial centre, although it wasn't until the 1880s that the central business district was transformed by the construction of many fine public and commercial buildings.

The rapid growth of the colony came at a hefty price to both the landscape and the people who had lived in harmony with it for thousands of years. The early White settlers saw the land and its resources as theirs to be exploited ruthlessly and as quickly as possible. The pastoral industry quickly exhausted vast areas of natural grasslands; wholesale clearing of the native forests followed, and cut timber was either burnt or left to rot. Sawmilling operations cut huge swathes through the forests, supplying the timber-hungry building, mining and railway industries. As early as the 1880s, many of the cedar and pine species in Queensland's coastal ranges were almost exhausted.

The Aborigines, who were looked upon as little more than animals, were ruthlessly pushed off their tribal lands as the settlers continued to take up land for farming, and later mining. Tribal boundaries, hunting rights and sacred grounds were all ignored in the land grab. Particularly in northern Queensland, many tribes resisted forcefully, and a virtual frontier war was waged for years. With their spears and clubs, the Aborigines were no match for the well-armed settlers, many of whom carried Colt revolvers and breech-loading or repeating rifles.

Although some settlers tried to maintain friendly relations with the tribes, others hunted Aborigines for sport or killed them with gifts of flour laced with arsenic. Many Europeans were themselves killed in this ongoing guerrilla war, but the Aborigines ultimately lost almost every battle, and every White death was followed by brutal reprisals. Estimates suggest that while four to five hundred Europeans were killed in the struggle, Aboriginal losses were anywhere from five to fifteen thousand.

The notorious Native Mounted Police force was responsible for some of the bloodiest massacres in Australian history. Made up of Aborigines from disrupted tribes, they were a virtual paramilitary force of Black troopers who were used against their own people. With their skills in tracking and bushcraft combined with the use of European weaponry, they were a terrifyingly effective force against Queensland's Aborigines until they were abolished in 1900.

One of the most infamous episodes of the time was the Hornet Bank Massacre in 1857. Led by two deserters from the Native Mounted Police, a group of Aborigines from the local Jiman tribe attacked a remote station on the Dawson River, killing a widow, seven of her children and three shepherds. A revenge 'posse' was made up of squatters and members of the Native Mounted Police. The reprisals that followed continued for six weeks, at the end of which not one Jiman was left in the Dawson valley.

Transport & Communications

Queensland's vast distances made it imperative for the colony to develop effective networks of transport and communications. Wool exports soon made up a major proportion of Queensland's economy, but the wool and other products had to be transported to the southern markets. The pastoralists' earliest forms of transport were timber wagons drawn by teams of bullocks. Cobb & Co coaches started operating in Queensland in 1865, and as holder of the mail-run contract it was the main overland transport operator until its last horse-drawn coach ran in 1924.

From the coast, cheaper sea transport was used to move wool and other supplies to and from Sydney. The development of ports quickly spread up the coast; between 1860 and 1885 there were 14 new coastal ports established, with the main ones being at Gladstone, Rockhampton, Bowen, Townsville, Burketown and Normanton.

At the same time the construction of an extensive railway network commenced. The first line from Brisbane into the Darling Downs was completed in 1867, an inland line from Rockhampton to Longreach in 1892, and the line from Brisbane to Rockhampton in 1897. The coastal link which connected Brisbane to Cairns wasn't completed until 1924; until then, Queensland transport still relied mainly on its coastal ports.

Communications were also vital. Brisbane was connected to Sydney by the telegraph in 1861, and the lines were rapidly extended further along the coast, with connections reaching across to Normanton on

The Chinese in Queensland

During the gold-rush era, Chinese prospectors poured into Queensland in their thousands. At one stage of the Palmer River gold rush, there were 11,000 Chinese miners and only 1500 Europeans. The Chinese were diligent workers, but they kept largely to themselves and were strongly resented by the Europeans. They were stereotyped as immoral and diseased heathens and subjected to racist attacks. Leading prospector James Venture Mulligan expressed his anti-Chinese feelings in a letter to the *Queenslander* in 1874:

'They follow up in swarms with odious filth, get the best gold, never give the miner the opening and chance to fall back on old ground where a man could get a little if he did not succeed in other directions.'

Workers also came to resent the presence of the Chinese, especially during the recession of the 1890s when they were blamed for taking the jobs of others and lowering wages by working cheaply. Anti-Chinese leagues were formed, and the government was eventually pressured into placing restrictions on the economic activities of the Chinese, and finally, restricting further migration. In the 1870s the Chinese made up almost 6% of Queensland's population, but as the gold ran out and they were continually hounded and repressed by racist policies, many left during the 1880s and 90s, and by the turn of the century they made up less than 2% of the population. Of those who remained, the majority worked in rural industries such as sugar cane production and banana plantations, and came to be valued as workers. ∎

the Gulf by 1872, and to the top of Cape York by 1887.

Qantas (the Queensland & Northern Territory Aerial Service), now Australia's major airline, was first registered for business in Winton in 1920. It opened its first office in Longreach soon after and commenced its first regular mail run between Charleville and Cloncurry in 1922.

Gold & Mining

The discovery of gold in Queensland in the 1860s and '70s brought about the most significant social and economic changes. The first major find was at Gympie in 1867; more than 15,000 diggers rushed the site. In 1872 the rich Charters Towers goldfields were discovered; the town grew so quickly and so dominated life in northern Queensland that it came to be known as 'The World'. Mt Morgan, which became the richest of Queensland's mines, was discovered near Rockhampton in 1882.

In 1873 the legendary Palmer River gold rush began. William Hann found traces of gold there in 1872, and a party of diggers led by James Venture Mulligan travelled to the river soon after. Their reports of a rich alluvial field prompted a major rush, despite the inhospitality of the region. Hector Holthouse's book *River of Gold* paints an amazing picture of the Palmer River days.

Many of these early mining towns were frenetic, chaotic places, filled with larrikin diggers who drank and gambled in wild frenzies. They were also places of great contrasts: between those lucky few who struck it rich and the battlers, many of whom ended up broke, or worse still, dead. Accidents and disease claimed a heavy toll – as you'll see if you visit any of the gold towns' cemeteries, many died young.

Between 1860 and 1915 more than £81 million worth of gold was recorded to have been won in Queensland, reaching a peak of £2.8 million in 1900.

Gold wasn't the only mineral to feed the Queensland economy. Extensive deposits of tin were found at places like Stanthorpe, Herberton and Irvinebank. Rich copper deposits were discovered at Cloncurry, Chillagoe, Mt Garnet and Mt Molloy, and coal-mining provided the main source of energy for the railways, mines and factories.

Sugar & the Plantation Economy

After early experiments with cotton plantations, sugar cane production quickly became the colony's major industry. The first plantation was established at Moreton Bay in 1864,

The Kanakas

Based on the convenient 19th-century concept that Europeans were inherently unsuited to work in the tropics, Queensland's early squatters used Indian and Chinese labourers and German contract workers to do much of the hard work on the land. As the sugar industry grew, these cheap labour sources came into short supply, and a new source of labour had to be found.

Robert Towns, the founder of Townsville, had previously been a South Seas trader and had the idea to import Islanders to work on his cotton plantation south of Brisbane. In 1863, his ship the *Don Juan* returned from the Solomons with 67 Islanders, who were employed for either six or 12 months at 10 shillings a month. These men were the first of Queensland's Kanakas.

Desperate for labourers, Queensland's sugar pioneers followed Towns' need, and soon found that Islander labour was easy to import, cheap and reliable. Initial workers were contracted for three years and paid £6 a year, with full board and a return passage. As the demand for labourers grew, a fleet of 'recruiting' boats operated between the islands and the mainland. Not all of these recruiters operated scrupulously, and the process of collecting, transporting and delivering them came to be known as 'blackbirding' – a nice euphemism for kidnapping.

The term 'Kanaka' was derived from a Hawaiian word for 'man', but its use to describe these Islanders came to be contemptuous and condescending. The Kanakas were 'recruited' from various Melanesian islands, including the Solomons, New Guinea, the New Hebrides and the Torres Strait Islands.

Voluntary workers or not, the 'Kanakas' worked long hours in sometimes appalling conditions, and their mortality rate was up to five times higher than for Europeans. By the late 1860s, those who recognised the immorality of exploiting the Islanders began to voice their criticism, but mainly because of Queensland's growing economic reliance on the sugar industry, the practice continued.

In 1868, the Queensland government responded to pressure by passing the Polynesian Labourers Act (the act was incorrectly named; the Kanakas were Melanesian, not Polynesian). The act required all employers to register their recruits and guarantee to return them within three years, and led to the placement of government agents on all recruiting vessels.

Despite these changes, pressure to abolish the practice grew. The missionary William Gray travelled to Queensland to inspect the plantations, and later wrote: '...I went to Queensland determined to keep my mind open...I would now say what I would not have said before I went...that the Kanaka Labour Traffic is veiled slavery'. The British government denounced the practice, as did the *Sydney Morning Herald*. Yet Queensland's politicians refused to bow to the pressure, and the large plantations owners of the north were increasingly being compared to those of the American South during the slave-owning days.

By the 1880s there were about 14,000 Kanakas working in Queensland. Despite the harsh conditions, some of the Islanders adapted to life in Queensland. Many learned English and developed basic skills; some were converted to Christianity, but others were more captivated by the evils of alcohol. Settlers began to complain of 'social problems', and a growing anti-Kanaka movement developed in the Labor movement as workers began to resent the exclusive use of Islander labour by many plantation owners.

Restrictions on recruiting vessels were tightened after 1884 by Samuel Griffith's government, which had campaigned on a platform of abolishing Kanaka labour. A number of recruiters were later charged with kidnapping and murder, but ruled by internal economic pressures, Griffith never upheld his campaign policy. It wasn't until Federation in 1901 that the Federal government passed the Pacific Island Labourers Act and terminated the use of Islander labour, by which time more than 60,000 Islanders had worked in the canefields of Queensland. As a result of the racist White Australia policy, only about 1600 Kanakas were allowed to remain in Queensland after 1906. ■

and over the next decade cane plantations spread like wildfire up the fertile coastal belt. By the late 1860s the plantations had reached the Mackay district, and then spread further north to the delta of the Burdekin River, to Bowen, and to the Mulgrave and Johnston rivers. A feature of Queensland's early sugar cane industry was its use and exploitation of cheap imported labour.

Labour vs Capital

The last part of the 19th century was a time

of social upheaval in Queensland, characterised by a series of clashes between labour and capital which at times bordered on civil war, but which would eventually lead to the election of the world's first (albeit brief) labour government.

By the 1880s many of the goldfields had been exhausted and the labour markets were flooded with diggers. Wages dropped and working conditions were tightened, and a worldwide recession led to the collapse of the Queensland economy.

In this climate, a number of radical weekly newspapers emerged, including the *Boomerang* and the *Worker*. These papers had wide appeal to their working-class audiences and featured articles and stories which began to espouse alternative theories of social organisation. At the same time the labour movement initiated the formation of craft and labour unions to represent seamen, factory workers, miners and shearers.

The first major battlefront was in the Darling Downs. In an attempt to break the hold of the shearers' unions, the newly formed Darling Downs Pastoralists' Association employed non-union labour at Jondaryan Station. During the subsequent strike, the Queensland Shearers' Union appealed to the waterside workers and seamen's unions for support, and the refusal of the maritime workers to handle the Jondaryan wool won a settlement in favour of the shearers. However, the maritime strike eventually ended in October 1890 with the defeat of maritime workers' unions all along the east coast.

Further major confrontations took place in 1891 and 1894 on the immense pastoral stations of central and western Queensland. During the famous shearers' strike near Barcaldine in 1891, the strikers responded to the use of non-union labour by forming themselves into armed camps, rioting and sabotaging property belonging to the pastoralists. The government supported the pastoralists and sent in more than 1400 soldiers armed with machine guns and field artillery to confront the strikers. Twelve of the strike leaders were arrested without war-

rants, and 10 of them were later convicted of conspiracy and sentenced to three years jail with hard labour. The strike was ended a couple of weeks later, defeated by the close relationship between the government and the pastoralists, a lack of funds and the massive supply of unemployed labour that was willing to take the strikers' places.

Support for the parliamentary Labor Party, which had been formed in 1890, continued to grow throughout the 1890s. In the elections of 1899, disputes between Queensland's governing Liberal and Conservative factions allowed the Labor Party, led by Andrew Dawson, to form the world's first Labor government. Dawson's government lasted only six days – he was defeated after the Liberals and Conservatives managed to reconcile their differences.

The 20th Century
Federation to WW I Despite the fact that many people had agitated for the division of Queensland into three separate states throughout the 1890s, Queensland eventually voted to join the other states and became part of the Commonwealth of Australia on 1 January 1901. At that time Queensland's population was around 500,000.

Despite Federation, Australia's loyalty to Britain remained. Queensland was the first colony to offer troops to Mother England when the Boer War broke out in South Africa. Between 1899 and 1902 almost 3000 Queenslanders served in South Africa.

In 1901 the Immigration Restriction Bill, known as the White Australia policy, was passed by the federal parliament to prevent the immigration of Asians and Pacific Islanders. Prospective immigrants were required to pass a dictation test in a European language. The language in which the test was given could be as obscure a tongue as the authorities wished. The dictation test was not abolished until 1958.

The desire to protect the jobs and conditions of White Australian workers that had helped bring about the White Australia policy also had some positive results. By 1908 the principle of a basic wage sufficient

The first Qantas office, in Longreach

to enable a male worker to support himself, a wife and three children had been established. By that time also, old age and invalid pensions were being paid.

WW I to WW II Like the rest of Australia, Queensland greeted the outbreak of WW I with naive enthusiasm; Queensland-born Prime Minister Andrew Fisher pledged that 'Australians will stand beside our own to help and defend her to the last man and our last shilling'.

The most infamous of the WW I battles in which diggers took part was that intended to force a passage through the Dardanelles to Constantinople. Australian and New Zealand troops landed at Gallipoli only to be slaughtered by well-equipped and strategically positioned Turkish soldiers. Ever since, the sacrifices made by Australian soldiers have been commemorated on Anzac Day, 25 April, the anniversary of the Gallipoli landing.

While support for Australia's involvement in the war remained strong, efforts to introduce conscription led to bitter argument, both in parliament and in the streets. In Queensland, the radical Labor Party (led by the brilliant barrister T J Ryan) won govern-

ment in 1915 with a platform of anti-conscription policies.

Labor went on to dominate Queensland politics for the next 42 years. Ryan remained as premier until 1919, introducing a series of social and industrial reforms including compulsory voting, improved safety and working conditions, workers' compensation and an Arbitration Court. Ryan resigned in 1919 to enter federal politics, and Edward Theodore (also known as 'Red Ted') took over.

The aviation era of the 1920s brought a number of significant changes to Queensland. Qantas was formed in 1920 to provide the first air transport service for the outback. John Flynn, a minister from the Australian Inland Mission, established the first Flying Doctor Service base at Cloncurry, and, in conjunction with Alfred Traeger's pedal wireless, gave the stations of the remote outback access to medical services. Brisbane's Charles Kingsford Smith made the first trans-Pacific flight in the *Southern Cross* in 1928, and went on to set dozens of other flying records before he disappeared in a crash off the coast of Burma in 1935. Bert Hinkler from Bundaberg also made a series of record-breaking solo flights, including his famous 15½-day flight from England to

Australia in the single-engined *Avian Cirrus* in 1928. Hinkler was killed in 1931 when his plane crashed in the Italian Apennine Mountains during another attempt at the England-Australia record.

There was great economic expansion in the 1920s and in 1923 incredibly rich copper, lead, silver and zinc deposits were discovered at Mt Isa, leading to a new phase in Queensland's resource boom.

All this came to a halt with the Great Depression, which hit Australia hard. In 1931 almost a third of breadwinners were unemployed and poverty was widespread. Swagmen became a familiar sight once more, as thousands of men took to the 'wallaby track' in search of work in the country. By 1932, however, Australia's economy was starting to recover, a result of rises in wool prices and a rapid revival of manufacturing.

WW II & the Post-War Years In the years before WW II, Australia became increasingly fearful of Japan. When war did break out, Australian troops fought beside the British in Europe, but after the Japanese bombed Pearl Harbor, Australia's own national security finally began to take priority.

Singapore fell, the northern Australian towns of Darwin and Broome and the New Guinean town of Port Moresby were bombed, the Japanese advanced southward, and still Britain called for more Australian troops. This time the Australian prime minister, John Curtin, refused. Australian soldiers were needed to fight the Japanese advancing over the mountainous Kokoda Trail towards Port Moresby. In appalling conditions, Australian soldiers confronted and defeated the Japanese at Milne Bay, east of Port Moresby, and began the long struggle to push them from the conquered Pacific territories.

During the war, large areas of Queensland were transformed into military camps, and a string of air bases was built all the way from Brisbane to the top of Cape York. Thousands of American troops were garrisoned in various places in Queensland, including Cape York, the Atherton Tableland and Townsville and the United States Navy established a base in the Coral Sea. Townsville was damaged by bombs from Japanese flying boats, and attempts were made to bomb Cairns. The defeat of the Japanese in the Coral Sea in May 1942 was one of the major turning points of the war.

Australia's appreciation of its own vulnerability had been sharpened immeasurably by the Japanese advance. One result of this was the post-war immigration programme, which offered assisted passage not only to Britons but also to refugees from eastern Europe in the hope that the increase in population would strengthen Australia's economy and contribute to its ability to defend itself. 'Populate or Perish' became the catch phrase. Between 1947 and 1968 more than 800,000 non-British migrants came to live in Australia, although Queensland received a smaller proportion of migrants than the other states (see the Population & People section later).

The post-war years also saw Queensland begin its shift from a rural to an industrial economy as the state's vast resources of raw materials were increasingly exploited. Labor's long rule came to an end in 1957 when internal conflict led to the formation of the breakaway Queensland Labor Party by then-premier Vincent Gair. Divided, Labor was defeated by the Country and Liberal parties who formed a coalition and pooled their votes. They ruled until 1983 when the National Party won government in its own right. (Before the 1974 elections, the Country Party had changed its name to the National Party.)

The Country/Liberal Party's first premier, George Nicklin, ruled from 1957 to 1968. He was succeeded by Jack Pizzey, who died soon after taking over, opening the way for the Country Party's charismatic Sir Johannes Bjelke-Petersen (universally known as Joh) to become premier. Aided by a gerrymandered electoral system, Joh went on to become Queensland's longest serving premier, ruling the state with his 'progress'-oriented policies for 19 years. Economically, his policies were a huge success, attracting overseas investment to fund a major mining and industrial boom. New mines were developed, railways were built and shipping facilities were constructed to export Queensland's resources.

Recent Developments Joh and his right-wing Nationals were also Australia's most controversial state government. Whether it was views on rainforests, Aboriginal land rights, the public's right to hold demonstrations or even whether condom machines should be allowed in universities, you could count on the Queensland government to take the opposite stand to just about everybody else. Under the Nationals, the state also had more than its fair share of corruption scandals. In 1987 Joh's own party decided he was a liability and replaced him. Since the defeat of the Nationals in the 1989 state election, it seems everyone from the former commissioner of Queensland police to Joh himself

has appeared in court on charges relating to some sort of shady deal. Today, Queensland has a Labor government led by Premier Wayne Goss.

Queensland's rapid economic growth, its favourable climate and Joh's 1977 decision to abolish death duties have all been factors in attracting a massive wave of internal migration. Since 1980 over half a million Australians from other states have packed up and moved to Queensland. Brisbane came of age after hosting several major international events in the 1980s, including the 1982 Commonwealth Games and Expo '88, and is now a modern cosmopolitan city.

Australia found itself in recession again in the early 1990s, although Queensland wasn't as hard hit as the southern states. With its booming tourism industry and continuing growth, the future looks to be blue skies all the way for the Sunshine State. The question of how that growth is managed is currently the major challenge facing Queensland.

The most recent state government elections were held in July 1995. Tipsters predicted that the incumbent Labor government would win easily, with their leader Wayne Goss enjoying a popularity rating of up to 70%, but on the day the government came perilously close to losing to the Liberal/National coalition. The government finally scraped back in with a one-seat majority, winning several seats by no more than a handful of votes. The surprise result was in part a swing back to Queensland's conservative past, and in part a backlash against the Goss government's failure to deliver on promised reforms. The environment was a major election issue, and a proposal to build the South Coast Motorway directly cost the government four seats.

GEOGRAPHY

Australia is the world's sixth largest country. Its area is 7,682,300 sq km, about the same size as the 48 mainland states of the USA and half as large again as Europe, excluding the former USSR. It is approximately 5% of the world's land surface. Lying between the

Sir Joh Bjelke-Petersen

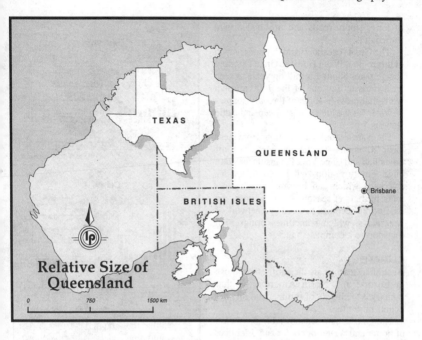

Relative Size of Queensland

TEXAS

QUEENSLAND

Brisbane

BRITISH ISLES

0   750   1500 km

Indian and Pacific oceans, Australia is about 4000 km from east to west and 3200 km from north to south, with a coastline 36,735 km long.

Queensland, Australia's second-largest state, has an area of 1,727,200 sq km, making up about 22% of the Australian continent; at its widest point, it is about 1500 km from west to east, and stretches for over 2000 km from north to south, with a coastline 5208 km long.

Queensland has a series of distinct regions. As with the rest of the east coast, the Great Dividing Range, the mountain range which continues down through New South Wales and Victoria, runs generally parallel with the coastline of the Coral Sea. The coastal strip between the mountains and the sea is the basis for Queensland's booming tourist trade, with its beaches, bays, islands and, of course, the Great Barrier Reef. Much of the coastal region is green and productive with lush rainforests, endless fields of sugar cane and stunning national parks.

The Great Dividing Range is most spectacular in the Far North – at several places, the mountains actually run right down to the coastline, and the Bellenden Ker Range, which is south of Cairns, has Queensland's highest mountain, Mt Bartle Frere (1657 metres). The McPherson Ranges, in the south-east corner, contain some of the state's most spectacular areas, including the pleasant and mountainous Lamington and Springbrook national parks.

Running to the west of the mountain range are the tablelands – vast areas of flat agricultural land with rich volcanic soils. These areas, which include the Darling Downs in the south and the Atherton Tablelands in the Far North, are some of Australia's most fertile and productive.

Finally, there's the vast inland area, the barren outback, which fades into the Northern Territory further west. Rain can temporarily make this arid area bloom but basically it's a place of sparse population –

of long, empty roads and tiny and distant settlements.

The Great Artesian Basin lies under much of this region. Water from the Great Dividing Range takes about 2.5 million years to seep westwards to any one of the 7500 artesian wells that provide some of the only sources of water for the area's huge sheep and cattle stations.

There are a couple of variations from these basic divisions. In the far northern Gulf Savannah and Cape York Peninsula there are huge, empty regions cut by countless dry riverbeds which can become swollen torrents in the wet season. At such times, the whole area becomes covered by a network of waterways, which sometimes brings road transport to a complete halt.

CLIMATE

Australian seasons are the antithesis of those in Europe and North America, so that January is the height of summer and July the depths of winter.

The Queensland seasons are more a case of hotter and wetter or cooler and drier than of summer or winter. The Tropic of Capricorn crosses Queensland about a third of the way up, running through the major city of Rockhampton and the outback town of Longreach. As such, the northern two-thirds of the state is technically within the tropics, but only the extreme north lies within the monsoon belt. Although the annual rainfall there looks adequate on paper, it comes in more or less one short, sharp burst. This has prevented the Top End from becoming seriously productive agriculturally.

November-December to April-May is the wetter, hotter half of the year, while the real Wet, particularly affecting northern coastal areas, is January to March. Cairns usually gets about 1300 mm of rain in these three months; Tully, 100 km south of Cairns, is the wettest place in Australia, with a drenching 4400 mm of rain each year!

Summer is also the season for cyclones, and if one hits, the main road north (the Bruce Hwy) can be blocked by the ensuing floods.

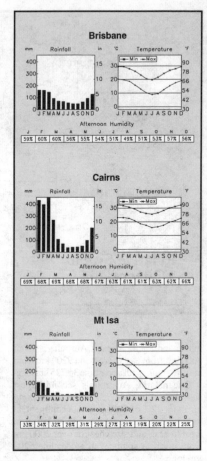

By comparison, the south-east and inland areas have relatively little rain – though they still have a wet season. Brisbane and Rockhampton both get about 450 mm of rain from January to March. Further north, Mackay receives about 1250 mm, Townsville 850 mm, Innisfail 1800 mm, and Weipa, on the Cape York Peninsula, 1300 mm in these months. Just halfway across the southern part of the state, Cunnamulla receives only about 400 mm in the whole year, while Birdsville, in the south-west corner, receives the least amount of rain with a only 150 mm a year.

Except inland or upland at night from about May to September, it rarely gets anything like cold. Temperatures in Brisbane peak somewhere in the 20°C-29°C range just about every day of the year. In Cairns the daily maximum is usually between 25°C and 32°C whereas around the Gulf, few days in the year fail to break the 30°C mark. Over at Birdsville you can expect 33°C or more every day from November to March, but rarely more than 20°C from June to August.

FLORA

Despite vast tracts of dry and barren land, much of Queensland is well vegetated. Plants can be found even in the arid regions, although many of them flower and grow erratically.

Origins

Australia's distinctive vegetation began to take shape about 55 million years ago when Australia broke from the southern supercontinent of Gondwanaland, drifting away from Antarctica to warmer climes. At this time, Australia was completely covered by cool-climate rainforest, but due to its geographic isolation and the gradual drying of the continent, rainforests retreated, plants such as eucalypts (gum trees) and acacias (wattles) took over and grasslands expanded. Eucalypts and acacias were able to adapt to warmer temperatures, the increased natural occurrence of fire and the later use of fire for hunting and other purposes by Aborigines. Now many species benefit from fire and even rely on it to crack open their tough seed casings.

The arrival of Europeans two centuries ago saw the introduction of new flora, fauna and tools. Rainforests were logged, new crops and pasture grasses spread, hoofed animals such as cows, sheep and goats damaged the soil, and watercourses were altered by dams. Irrigation, combined with excessive clearing of the land, gradually

The famed Australian eucalypt

resulted in a serious increase in the salinity of the soil.

An interesting book on Australian flora is *Field Guide to Native Plants of Australia* (Bay Books). Brisbane's Mt Coot-tha Botanic Gardens features Australia's arid-zone plants, Cairns' Blecker Botanic Gardens has an interesting Aboriginal plant use area, and Townsville's Anderson Park features rainforest plants and palms from the Cape York Peninsula and the tropical north.

Eucalypts

Large eucalypts, or gum trees, are one of the most distinctive features of the Australian landscape, and the smell of burning eucalyptus leaves and twigs is guaranteed to make any expatriate Aussie homesick. The gum tree features in Australian folklore, art and literature. All varieties flower, and the wood is prized and its oil used for pharmaceuticals and perfumed products.

There are around 560 species of the eucalyptus genus in Australia but only 60 or so are found in the arid zone, where, not surprisingly, most are rather stunted. However, some species can grow into huge trees that make a spectacular sight in their dry setting. **Mallee**, a multi-stemmed form of gum, is very common, and the roots of fallen mallees will burn seemingly forever in a campfire.

Usually called river gums or red gums, **river red gums** are generally confined to watercourses where their roots have access to a reliable supply of moisture. Given good conditions they can grow to 40 metres high and may live for 1000 years. This species is fairly easily identified from its habitat and its smooth, often beautifully marked grey, tan and cream bark. River gums are found throughout Australia, and in the outback wherever there is suitable habitat. They have a bad habit of dropping large limbs, so while they may be good shade trees it's certainly not wise to camp under them.

The **ghost gum** is a great favourite thanks to its bright green leaves and glossy white bark. Although these often majestic, spreading trees are common in tropical northern Australia, it's around Alice Springs where they've achieved most of their fame through the work of artists such as Albert Namatjira.

A common feature of watercourses, swamps and flood plains right through the outback's drier areas are **coolabahs**. They are typically gnarled, spreading trees with a rough, dark-brown bark and dull, leathery leaves. Coolabahs can grow to 20 metres high and often provide excellent shade. All eucalypts are hardwoods and this species is said to have the hardest timber of all. It is also very strong and termite-resistant, which made it extremely useful for building fences and stockyards in the days before steel became more readily available.

Acacias

The Australian species of the acacia genus are commonly known as wattle – and they are common indeed. There are 660 species in Australia. They tend to be fast-growing, short-lived and come in many forms, from tall, weeping trees to prickly shrubs. Despite their many differences, all wattles have furry yellow flowers shaped either like a spike or a ball. If you see a plant with a flower like this you'll know it's a wattle.

Most species flower during late winter and spring. Then the country is ablaze with wattle and the reason for the choice of green and gold as Australia's national colours is obvious. Wattle is Australia's floral emblem.

Probably the most widespread of the arid-zone wattles is the **mulga**, which occurs in all mainland states except Victoria. Although young mulga can look a little like small pines, the adults, which are 10 metres tall at their best, are more of an umbrella shape with a sparse crown of narrow grey leaves. Mulga sometimes forms dense thickets (the explorer John McDouall Stuart complained how the scrub near Alice Springs tore his clothes and pack saddles to bits) but usually is found as open woodland. Mulga leaves are very resistant to water loss, and the tree's shape directs any rain down to the base of the trunk where roots are most dense. With these attributes mulga is a great drought survivor, but being good fodder for stock puts it at risk from overgrazing.

Mangroves

Once considered to be swampy wastelands, mangrove forests are now highly valued for the essential role they play in coastal ecosystems. Mangroves grow in dense thickets along the Queensland coast and tidal estuaries, and they help to stabilise shorelines and provide a safe habitat for a huge range of fish, birds, crabs, prawns and other wildlife.

They are unique in that they have adapted to live in saltwater and are able to filter the salt out of the water they take in, expelling the residue through their leaves. Their tangled root systems enable them to 'breath' at low tide, and they can store oxygen in their spongy tissues for use during high tides. Mangroves are fascinating areas to explore, particularly at low tide, but don't forget to wear insect repellent – they also support huge populations of mosquitoes and sand-flies.

Rainforest

Almost all of the remnants of the tropical rainforest which covered the Australian continent millions of years ago are found in north Queensland. While the early European settlers cleared most of these forests for farming and timber milling, they ignored some of the less accessible areas of the coastal mountains and ranges. These tropical forests today provide a fascinating insight into a rich ecosystem of plants and animals, and are one of the major drawcards for visitors to the state.

Poincianas & Jacarandas

These spectacular and colourful trees are common sights in Queensland. The poinciana is a flamboyant tropical tree which you'll see throughout the Far North, particularly on the Cape York Peninsula. In full bloom they resemble an enormous flaming umbrella, and are covered with a stunning blaze of red-orange flowers.

Originally from Brazil, the Jacaranda is equally famous for its spectacular spring bloom of lavender-purple flowers. Jacarandas can grow up to 12 metres high, and with their dark branches they have a somewhat oriental appearance.

Moreton Bay Fig

These majestic evergreen trees were widely planted throughout Australia last century in avenues, parks, gardens, schools and other public places. They are particularly impressive, with broad, buttressed trunks, wide glossy leaves and purple-green fig-like fruits (popular with fruit bats). They can grow to enormous sizes, with their dense canopies often spreading out to cover an area the size of a small house. They are great climbing trees, but because of their size, their aggressive root systems and the mess made by their fruit, they have fallen from favour somewhat as garden trees.

Bottle Trees

These trees are similar in appearance to the African baobab tree, with their small bushy heads and swollen, pregnant-looking bases. They are widely found in the semi-arid areas of central Queensland and have been planted in avenues in quite a few towns in the outback (see the Roma section in particular).

Bottle trees can tolerate long periods of drought, and although it's a myth that they contain drinkable water in their bases, their fibrous interior pith does absorb and store moisture. During severe drought, pastoralists have been known to cut down bottle trees and feed this pith to their cattle.

Bunya Pine

The bunya is a native pine tree found in the Bunya Mountains National Park north of Brisbane, and in north Queensland. They grow best in rich soil and moist valleys, and like the Moreton Bay Fig they have been planted ornamentally in many public places. Their branches are long and slender, growing out from the trunk in whorls with the foliage generally bunched at the end of the branches.

Bunya pines produce a large pineapplesized nut every three years which contains edible seeds which are delicious either raw or roasted. The bunya nuts were prized by local Aboriginal tribes, who would hold feasts and ceremonies every three years when the nuts ripened, inviting tribes from other areas and holding elaborate celebrations.

Note that bunya nuts drop to the ground when they are ripe, and because of their size and weight this can be particularly dangerous if you happen to be sitting or walking underneath the tree at the time.

Spinifex

One of the hardiest and most common desert plants is spinifex, the dense, dome-shaped mass of long, needle-like leaves that you find on sandy soils and rocky areas. There are many species of spinifex but most share an important characteristic: in dry times their leaves roll into tight cylinders to reduce the number of pores exposed to the sun and wind. This keeps water loss through evaporation to a minimum, but even so, most plants will succumb during a really bad drought. Spinifex grasslands are very difficult to walk through – the explorer Ernest Giles called the prickly spinifex 'that abominable vegetable production'. They cover vast areas of central Australia and support some of the world's richest populations of reptiles.

Saltbush

Millions of sheep and cattle living in the arid zone owe their survival to dry shrubby plants called saltbush, which get their name from their tolerance to saline conditions. Saltbush – there are 30 species – is extremely widespread and can be dominant over vast areas.

Wildflowers

After good autumn rains the normally arid inland explodes in a multicoloured carpet of vibrant wildflowers that will take your breath away. The most common of these ephemerals, or short-lived plants, are the numerous species of daisy. Others include docks (which came to Australia in camel-saddle stuffing last century), parakelias, pussy tails and pea flowers.

In a miracle of nature, the seeds of desert ephemerals can lie dormant in the sand for years until exactly the right combination of temperature and moisture comes along to trigger germination. When this happens, life in the desert moves into top gear as the ephemerals hurry to complete their brief life cycles and woody plants likewise burst into bloom. The sandhills, plains and rocky ridges come alive with nectar-eating birds and insects, which adds up to a bumper harvest for predators as well. Everywhere the various forms of wildlife are breeding and rearing their young while food supplies are abundant. For nature lovers this is definitely the best time to tour the inland. Although the Top End can't match the visual spectacle of the desert in full bloom, it nevertheless has many spectacular wildflowers.

Weeds

By the 1920s the introduced **prickly pear** had choked millions of hectares of central Queensland before an effective biological control was found in the form of the cactoblastic moth. Today, in tropical Australia, weeds such as **mimosa bush** are threatening huge areas, while **salvinia** has begun to choke several waterways. Introduced weeds can destroy wildlife habitats as well as make pastoral and cropping land unusable. Australia-wide, their cost in environmental and economic terms is impossible to calculate.

Preventing the Spread of Weeds Studies have shown that motor vehicles are a major culprit in the spread of weeds. The implications of this are obvious when you consider the millions of vehicles that travel Australia's roads and tracks each year. The question is: how can you avoid being responsible for an outbreak?

First, you need to be able to identify the various weeds as well as their seeds and seed capsules. This is easy: get hold of a weeds pamphlet from a state department of primary production or shire office. Second, if possible avoid driving through weed infestations – pay particular attention to quarantine signs, which should be observed to the letter. Third, immediately after leaving an infested area, give your vehicle a thorough check for seeds and pieces of plant which may propagate. It's a good idea to carry out such checks on a regular basis, regardless of whether you think you've been near weeds. As well, always carefully check the dog, your clothing, tent and bedding for burs and seeds whenever you go walking or camping in the bush.

FAUNA

Australia is blessed with a fascinating mix of native fauna, which ranges from the primitive to the highly evolved – some creatures are unique survivors from a previous age, while others have adapted so acutely to the environment that they can survive in areas which other animals would find uninhabitable.

Australian fauna is distinct, partly because the Australian land mass is one of the most ancient on earth, and also because the sea has kept it isolated from other land masses for more than 50 million years. In this time the continent has suffered no major climatic upheavals, giving its various indigenous creatures an unusually long and uninterrupted period in which to evolve in isolation.

Since the arrival of Europeans in Australia 17 species of mammal have become extinct and 28 more are currently endangered. Many introduced non-native animals have been allowed to run wild and have caused a great deal of damage to native species and to Australian vegetation. Introduced animals include foxes, cats, pigs, goats, camels, donkeys, water buffalo, horses, starlings, blackbirds, Indian mynahs, cane toads and, best known of all, the notorious rabbit. Foxes and cats kill small native mammals and birds, rabbits denude vast areas of land, pigs carry disease and introduced birds take over the habitat of local species.

Mammals

Kangaroos The extraordinary breeding cycle of the kangaroo is well adapted to Australia's harsh, often unpredictable environment.

The young kangaroo, or joey, just millimetres long at birth, claws its way unaided to the mother's pouch where it attaches itself to a nipple that expands inside its mouth. A day or two later the mother mates again, but the new embryo does not begin to develop until the first joey has left the pouch permanently.

At this point the mother produces two types of milk – one formula to feed the joey at heel, the other for the baby in her pouch. If environmental conditions are right, the mother will then mate again. If food or water is scarce, however, the breeding cycle will be interrupted until conditions improve.

Although kangaroos generally are not aggressive, males of the larger species, such as reds, can be dangerous when cornered. In the wild, boomers, as they are called, will grasp other males with their forearms, rear up on their muscular tails and pound their opponents with their hind feet, sometimes slashing them with their claws. Such behaviour can also be directed against dogs and, very rarely, people. Kangaroos being pursued by dogs will sometimes hop into deep water and drown the dogs with their strong forearms.

There are now more kangaroos in Australia than there were when Europeans arrived, a result of the better availability of water and the creation of grasslands for sheep and cattle. Certain species, however, are threatened because their particular environments are being destroyed. In all there are about 45 species.

About three million kangaroos are culled legally each year in Australia, but probably as many more are killed for sport or by those farmers who believe the cull is insufficient to protect their paddocks from overgrazing.

Large kangaroos can be a hazard to people driving through the outback – hitting a two-metre kangaroo at 110 km/h is no joke.

The unusual-looking Lumholtz's tree-kangaroo is unique to the rainforest areas of Far North Queensland. It is short and stocky with a long round tail, pale grey fur and a dark-coloured face, and its front limbs are longer than those of other kangaroos. It's a skilful tree-climber, and feeds by night on leaves and fruits in the canopies of rainforest trees, but can also be seen walking or hopping along the ground.

Possums There is an enormous range of possums in Australia – they seem to have been able to adapt to all sorts of conditions, including those of the city, where you'll find them in parks, sometimes tame enough to eat from your hand. Look for them at dusk. Some large species are found in suburban roofs and will eat cultivated plants and food scraps.

Certain possums are small and extremely timid, such as the tiny honey possum, which is able to extract nectar from blossoms with its tube-like snout. Others are gliders, able to jump from tree top to tree top by extending flaps of membrane between their legs.

Wombats Wombats are slow, solid, powerfully built marsupials with broad heads and short, stumpy legs. These fairly placid and easily tamed creatures are also legally killed by farmers, who object to the damage done to paddocks by wombats digging large burrows and tunnelling under fences.

Koalas Koalas are distantly related to the wombat and are found along the eastern seaboard. Their cuddly appearance belies an irritable nature, and they will scratch and bite if sufficiently provoked.

Koalas carry their babies in pouches but later the larger young cling to their mother's back. They feed only on the leaves of certain types of eucalypt and are particularly sensitive to changes to their habitat.

Today many koalas suffer from chlamydia, a sexually transmitted disease causing blindness and infertility.

Platypuses & Echidnas The platypus and the echidna are the only living representatives of the most primitive group of mammals, the monotremes. Both lay eggs, as reptiles do, but suckle their young on milk secreted directly through the skin from mammary glands.

The amphibious platypus has a duck-like bill, webbed feet and a beaver-like body. Males have a poisonous spur on their hind feet. Recent research has shown that the platypus is able to sense electric currents in the water and uses this ability to track its prey.

Echidnas are spiny anteaters that hide from predators by digging vertically into the ground and covering themselves with dirt, or by rolling themselves into a ball and raising their sharp quills.

Dingoes Australia's native dog is the dingo, domesticated by the Aborigines and thought to have arrived with them 40,000 years ago. Dingoes now prey on rabbits and sometimes livestock, and are considered vermin by many farmers.

Birds
Emus The only bird larger than the emu is the African ostrich, which is also flightless. The emu is a shaggy-feathered bird with an often curious nature. After the female emu lays the eggs, the male hatches them and raises the young.

Parrots & Cockatoos There is an amazing variety of these birds. The noisy pink and grey galahs are among the most common, although the sulphur-crested cockatoos have to be the noisiest. Rainbow lorikeets have one of the most brilliant colour schemes and in some parks they're not at all backward about taking a free feed from visitors.

Kookaburras A member of the kingfisher family, the kookaburra is heard as much as it is seen – you can't miss its loud, cackling laugh, usually at dawn and sunset. Kookaburras can become quite tame and pay regular visits to friendly households.

Lyrebirds The lyrebird, found in moist forest areas, is famous for both its vocal abilities and its beauty. Lyrebirds are highly skilled mimics, which copy segments of other birds' songs to create unique hybrid compositions. During the courting season, with his colourful fern-like tailfeathers spread like a fan, the male puts on a sensational song-and-dance routine to impress potential partners.

Magpies The black-and-white magpie (no relation to the European bird of the same name) has a distinctive and beautiful warbling call. Magpies can be aggressively territorial when nesting (around September). Being 'swooped' by a magpie is an unnerving experience, as it dives at you silently from behind.

Black-necked Stork (Jabiru) The black-necked Stork is Australia's only stork, and is quite common in north Queensland. It's a slender red-legged bird which grows up to 1.2 metres tall. Its head, neck, tail and wings are a brilliant green-black, while its body is white. The female's eyes are yellow, the male's brown. This bird is often referred to as the Jabiru, which most people assume is its Aboriginal name. Jabiru is actually a Portuguese name for the South American stork, so its use has been incorrectly if widely adopted in Australia.

Brolga Another bird you'll often see in north Queensland is the graceful brolga. Brolgas feed on frogs, insects and small reptiles and are usually found near wetlands or beside lakes or rivers, although it's not unusual to see them wandering around the streets of small outback towns like Normanton. The brolga is a crane which grows up to 1.2 metres tall and is pale grey with a red head, a green bill and grey legs. The brolga is a part of many Aboriginal legends and its elegant dances are imitated in the ceremonial dances of numerous tribes.

Birds of Prey Being on top of the feathered food chain, the various eagles, goshawks, kites, harriers, falcons and kestrels are usually the most commonly seen of all outback birds. Largest of all is the **wedge-tailed eagle**, which you'll often notice feeding on road kills. With a wingspan approaching three metres they soar high on the thermals while scanning the ground for prey such as rabbits and young kangaroos. Their eyesight is so keen that they're thought to be able to see a rabbit quite clearly from a distance of 1.5 km. On remote coasts, watch for ospreys and white-bellied sea eagles.

Reptiles

Snakes There are many species of snake in Queensland, all protected. Many are poisonous, some deadly, but very few are at all aggressive and they'll usually get out of your way before you even realise that they are there. See the Dangers & Annoyances section of the Facts for the Visitor chapter for ways of avoiding being bitten and what to do in the unlikely event that you are.

Lizards There is a wide variety of lizards, from tiny skinks to prehistoric-looking goannas that can grow up to 2.5 metres long, although most species you'll meet in Queensland are smaller. Goannas can run very fast and when threatened will use those big claws to climb the nearest tree – or perhaps the nearest leg!

Bluetongue lizards, slow-moving and stumpy, are children's favourites and are sometimes kept as pets. Their even slower and stumpier relations, shinglebacks, are common in the outback.

Crocodiles There are two species: the large **saltwater**, or estuarine crocodile and the smaller **freshwater** variety. 'Salties' are found in coastal areas north of Mackay, though there have been occasional sightings further south. Contrary to their name, salties aren't confined to saltwater; they inhabit estuaries, and following floods may be found many km from the coast. They may even be found in permanent freshwater more than 100 km inland. Salties, which can grow to seven metres, will attack and kill humans.

'Freshies' are smaller than salties – anything over four metres should be regarded as a saltie. Freshies are also more finely constructed and have much narrower snouts and smaller teeth to suit their fish diet. Though generally harmless to humans, freshies have been known to bite in defence of their nests, and children in particular should be kept away from them.

Both species of crocodiles were once hunted almost to extinction, but since they were proclaimed a protected species they have become prolific in northern Queensland. So far, very few tourists have been killed by salties and attacks still make headlines.

There are simple rules to avoid being

Freshwater crocodile, or 'freshie'

Saltwater crocodile, or 'killer' – keep clear

attacked and the most important one is to stay out of the water whenever you're in their territory. This can be rather difficult after a hot, muggy day's travel along a dusty track, but you'll just have to put up with it until the next safe bath. Observe the guidelines contained in park brochures and you'll be quite safe.

Fish & Crabs

Barramundi Found throughout coastal and estuarine waters of the Gulf Savannah and Cape York, the barramundi is a highly prized sports fish which has great fighting qualities. Once it takes a lure or fly, it fights like hell to be free. As you try to reel one in, chances are it will play the game for a bit, then make some powerful runs, often leaping clear of the water and shaking its head in an attempt to throw the hook.

Landing the barra is a challenge, but it's only half the fun; the other half is eating it! The barramundi is a prized table fish, although the taste of the flesh does depend to some extent on where the fish is caught. Those caught in saltwater or tidal rivers are generally found to have the sweetest flavour; those in landlocked waterways can have a muddy flavour and soft flesh if the water is a bit murky.

Lungfish The lungfish is a unique and rare prehistoric relic which is found in a handful of rivers in Queensland. It has a skeleton of cartilage, a tail that is more like a continuation of its body, and a pair of limb-like fins. It lives in fresh water and normally breathes through its gills, but if the water is stagnant and the level of oxygen in the water drops too low, it can surface and breath air through its lung! It can also survive out of water for a couple of days if it is kept moist.

Mud Crabs The mud crab, also known as the mangrove crab, is commonly seen on restaurant menus throughout Queensland. These crabs can grow up to two kg in weight and are amongst the most prized of the state's seafood delicacies, and if they are fresh and cooked correctly, are absolutely delicious. Before they find their way into the kitchens,

mud crabs live in the mud flats and tidal waters, especially those lined with mangroves. They are fished for with baited crab pots or hoop nets.

Introduced Species

The Acclimatisation Society was a bunch of do-gooders in the Victorian era who devoted themselves to 'improving' the countries of the British Empire by introducing plants and animals. On the whole, their work was a disastrous blunder.

Exotic animals thriving in Queensland include rabbits, cats (big, bad, feral versions of the domestic moggie), pigs (now bristly black razorbacks with long tusks), goats, brumbies (wild horses) and cane toads. All these have been disastrous for the native animals, as predators and as competitors for food and water.

Probably the biggest change to the ecosystem has been caused by another exotic animal: the sheep. To make room for sheep there was wholesale clearing of the bush, and the plains were planted with exotic grasses. Many small marsupials became extinct when their habitats changed, and major reasons for the incarceration and massacre of Aborigines were that they hunted sheep and resisted the theft of their land by graziers.

Disruption of Aboriginal land-management meant that there was no longer regular burning of the bush and plains, causing less frequent but disastrous bushfires which fed on the accumulated growth. This meant change for an ecosystem which depended on regular low-intensity fires for germination.

NATIONAL PARKS

Queensland has some 220 national parks – protected wilderness areas of environmental or natural importance. While some just cover a single hill or lake, others are large wilderness areas. Many islands and stretches of the coast are national parks, including Fraser Island, Hinchinbrook Island, Moreton Island, Lizard Island, and most of the Whitsundays group. Cape York Peninsula contains some of the state's best and most remote parks, including the Lakefield, Rokeby and Iron Range national parks. And inland, some of the most spectacular parks are Lamington, on the forested rim of an ancient volcano on the New South Wales border; Carnarvon, with its 30-km gorge south-west of Rockhampton; Lawn Hill, an oasis-like river gorge in the remote north-west corner; and rainforested Eungella, near Mackay, which is swarming with wildlife.

The international World Heritage List, which includes the Taj Mahal, the Pyramids and the Grand Canyon, currently includes three of Queensland's most significant areas: the Great Barrier Reef, the Wet Tropics areas of the coastal north, and Fraser Island. In recent years, various bodies have lobbied to have the Cape York Peninsula included on the list.

Queensland's national parks are managed by the Queensland National Parks & Wildlife Service (QNP&WS), which is part of the Department of Environment & Heritage. The QNP&WS operates the following main regional information centres:

Naturally Queensland Centre (the QNP&WS head office) (☎ (07) 3227 8185), 160 Ann St, Brisbane

South-West/Central Regional Office (☎ (076) 39 4599), 158 Hume St, Toowoomba

Central Coast Regional Office (☎ (079) 36 0511), corner of Yeppoon and Norman Sts, North Rockhampton

North Queensland Regional Office (☎ (077) 21 2399), Great Barrier Reef Wonderland, Townsville

Far North Regional Office (☎ (070) 52 3096), 10 McLeod St, Cairns.

Another major office is the Whitsundays Regional Office (☎ (079) 46 7022), Shute Harbour Rd, Airlie Beach. It's worth calling at one of these to find out what's where, and to get the rundown on camping in the national parks.

There are also information centres and/or ranger stations in many of the parks, as well as QNP&WS offices in many towns. The park rangers themselves are often the best sources of info – they usually know their parks like the backs of their hands, and can tell you which are the best walking areas, which camping grounds are crowded and what birds and wildlife to look out for, etc.

Cane Toads

One of the most enduring aural memories of the thousands of km I drove through Queensland was the regular 'crunch-squelch' as I ran over yet another cane toad. That may sound sadistic but these gruesome, horny toads are everywhere – constantly swerving to avoid them would be impossible, not to mention dangerous. Besides, I figured I was making a small contribution to the Queensland environment by running a few of the bastards over.

Ironically, cane toads were deliberately imported into Queensland from South America in 1935 in an attempt to combat the sugar-cane beetles, whose larvae had devastated Queensland's sugar industry. The experiment was an ecological disaster. The cane toads were supposed to be a predator of the beetles, but they soon realised it was much easier to dine on native insects, frogs and other unsuspecting goodies than worry about trying to catch flying beetles. And when they weren't gorging themselves, the toads spent their time having sex. They are prolific breeders, with the females laying up to 35,000 eggs in a single spawn. Before too long they had spread throughout Queensland in plague proportions, and in recent years have moved into parts of northern New South Wales. The toads have had a devastating effect on native animals – they have a poisonous gland on their shoulders, and their venom kills most of the birds, snakes and mammals that eat them.

Despite their ugliness and ecological impact, Queenslanders have developed an almost grudging respect for the toads and their survival instinct. Cane toad races are a regular feature at quite a few pubs and backpackers' hostels throughout Queensland – definitely one of the weirdest forms of gambling you'll come across.

There has even been a film made about them. If you want to learn more, hire the video *Cane Toads – An Unnatural History*, an offbeat and comical 1988 documentary that takes an in-depth look at the plague upon Queensland. ■

Public access to the parks is encouraged, so long as safety and conservation regulations are observed. Many parks have camping grounds with water, toilets and showers and there are often privately run camping grounds, motels or lodges on the park fringes. Sizeable parks usually have a network of walking tracks, ranging from short discovery strolls to longer treks such as the three to five-day walk on Hinchinbrook Island.

To camp in a national park – whether in a camping ground or in the bush – you need a permit which you can either get in advance (by writing or calling in at the appropriate QNP&WS office) or from the ranger at the park itself. Many camping grounds also have self-registration booths, so if the rangers aren't around you can fill in a registration form and leave your permit fee in an envelope, which the rangers will collect later.

Until recently, camping fees varied for each site, depending on the facilities provided, but nowadays the fees system has been standardised. With the exception of Moreton and Fraser islands, camping fees at *all* national park sites are $3 per night per person for anyone over the age of four. Some of the more popular camping grounds fill up at holiday times, so you may need to book well ahead; you can usually book sites six to 12 weeks ahead by writing to the appropriate office. Lists of camping grounds are available from QNP&WS offices.

The QNP&WS publishes a series of handy booklets called *Discover National Parks*, which have useful information about Queensland's national parks and state forests, including brief descriptions of the parks, suggestions for things to do, camping details and how to get to the parks. They cost $2.50 each and are available from bookshops and QNP&WS offices. Another booklet, *Camping in Queensland* ($3.50), contains useful info on more than 100 national parks, state forests and lakeside reserves with camping facilities throughout the state, including rates.

The Department of Environment and Heritage publishes *Shades of Green: Exploring Queensland's Rainforests*, an attractive large-format paperback with colour photos and brief notes on the state's rainforest national parks and state forests.

STATE FORESTS

Queensland also has a large number of state forests – timber reserves which are selectively logged – and public reserves around reservoirs and water-catchment areas. These areas can be just as scenic and wild as national parks, depending of course on how recently the area has been logged. There are plenty of opportunities for recreation in the reserves – scenic drives, camping (free), bushwalking, trail-bike riding, 4WDing, etc.

You can get information on state forest camping sites and facilities from tourist offices or from the Forest Services section of the Department of Primary Industry (☎ (07) 3234 0158), on the 5th floor at 160 Mary St, Brisbane. Other forestry offices are at Fraser Rd, Two Mile, near Gympie; 52 McIllwraith St, Ingham; Gregory St, Cardwell; and also at 83 Main St, Atherton.

GOVERNMENT
Australian Government

Australia is a federation of six states and two territories, and has a parliamentary system of government based on the Westminster model. There are three tiers of government: federal, state and local. Under the Constitution, which came into force on 1 January 1901 when the colonies joined to form the Commonwealth of Australia, the federal government is mainly responsible for the national economy and Reserve Bank, customs and excise, immigration, defence, foreign policy, and post and telecommunications. The state governments are chiefly responsible for health, education, housing, transport and justice. There are both federal and state police forces.

In the federal parliament, the lower house is the House of Representatives, the upper house the Senate, and the government is led by a prime minister. Elections for the House of Representatives are held at least every three years; senators serve six-year terms,

An Australian Republic
An issue set to dominate Australian political debate for the rest of the 1990s is the question of whether Australia should become a republic, as increasing numbers of people feel the continued constitutional ties with Britain are no longer relevant. With Sydney hosting the 2000 Olympic Games, many people feel it would be fitting that the games be opened by the constitutional head of the new Republic of Australia. The issue is far from decided and there is still a deal of soul-searching to be done, but change seems inevitable. ■

with elections for half of them every three years.

Australia is currently a constitutional monarchy. The head of state is the Governor-General, and each state also has its own governor. Technically, the Governor-General and governors are the representatives of the British monarch – while the respective governments appoint them, these decisions must be ratified by the monarch.

Queensland Government

Queensland's state government is based in Brisbane. Queensland is the only state without an upper house – it was abolished in 1922. Instead, the decisions of the Legislative Assembly (the lower house) are ratified by the Executive Council, which comprises the cabinet ministers and the governor. Elections for the lower house are held at least every three years; voting is by secret ballot and is compulsory for everyone 18 years of age and over.

Queensland's three main political parties are the Liberal Party, the Australian Labor Party (ALP), and the National Party (formerly the Country Party). The Liberal Party is traditionally conservative, representing the interests of free enterprise, law and order and family values; the Australian Labor Party is traditionally socialist, having grown out of the workers' disputes and shearers' strikes of the 1890s; and the National Party is traditionally the party of rural interests, having originally formed to represent conservative farmers' unions.

During this century, the distinctions between the major parties have become more and more blurred, as political expediency and holding onto office have increasingly taken priority over traditional party values.

Currently the Labor Party, under the premiership of Wayne Goss, governs Queensland.

ECONOMY

Queensland is richly endowed with natural resources. Until the mining boom of the 1960s, Queenslanders were largely dependent on agricultural and pastoral production for most of their wealth.

Agriculture still plays a major economic role, employing around 10% of the state's workforce. Sugar cane is the major crop, and Queensland produces about 95% of Australia's sugar and exports more than two million metric tonnes of raw sugar annually. Other major crops include wheat, sorghum, maize, barley and sunflower seed. A thriving fruit industry supplies most of Australia's tropical fruits, such as mangoes, bananas, pineapples and pawpaws, as well as producing many other fruits, such as apples, pears, peaches, apricots etc.

The pastoral industry has always been one of the state's economic mainstays, and raising beef cattle for meat is the largest rural industry. Wool growing is also important, although less so in recent years.

Since the 1960s, the mining sector has been at the forefront of the Queensland economy. Coal from the huge open-cut mines of central Queensland is the state's major export, with international shipping facilities at Hay Point (near Mackay), Abbot Point (near Bowen), and Gladstone. Northwest Queensland is mineral-rich, and the copper, zinc, silver and lead mine at Mt Isa is one of the world's largest underground mines. On the Cape York Peninsula, Weipa has the world's largest bauxite mine. Gold-mining has also undergone a resurgence in recent years. The Kidston mine in north Queensland is the state's richest, and old

Traditional Aboriginal Culture

Early European settlers and explorers usually dismissed the entire Aboriginal population as 'savages' and 'barbarians', and it was some time before the Aborigines' deep, spiritual bond with the land, and their relationship to it, was understood by White Australians.

Society & Lifestyle Traditionally, the Aborigines were tribal people living in extended family groups or clans, with clan members descending from a common ancestral being. Tradition, rituals and laws linked the people of each clan to the land they occupied and each clan had various sites of spiritual significance on their land and places to which their spirits would return when they died. Clan members came together to perform rituals to honour their ancestral spirits and the creators of the Dreaming. These traditional religious beliefs were the basis of the Aborigines' ties to the land they lived and thrived on for thousands of years before the coming of the Europeans.

It was the responsibility of the clan, or particular members of it, to correctly maintain and protect the sites so that the ancestral beings were not offended and would continue to protect the clan. Traditional punishments for those who neglected these responsibilities was often severe, as their actions could easily affect the well-being of the whole clan – food and water shortages, natural disasters or mysterious illnesses could all be attributed to disgruntled or offended ancestral beings.

Many Aboriginal communities were almost nomadic, others sedentary, one of the deciding factors being the availability of food. Where food and water were readily available, the people tended to remain in a limited area. When they did wander, however, it was to visit sacred places to carry out rituals, or to take advantage of seasonal foods available elsewhere. They did not, as is still often believed, roam aimlessly and desperately in the search for food and water.

The traditional role of the men was that of hunter, tool-maker and custodian of male law; the women reared the children, and gathered and prepared food. There was also female law and ritual for which the women were responsible.

Environmental Awareness Wisdom and skills obtained over millennia enabled Aborigines to use their environment to the maximum. An intimate knowledge of the behaviour of animals and the correct time to harvest the many plants they utilised ensured that food shortages were rare. They never hunted an animal species or harvested a plant species to the point where it was threatened with extinction. Like other hunter-gatherer peoples of the world, the Aborigines were true ecologists.

Although Aborigines in northern Australia had been in regular contact with the farming peoples of Indonesia for at least 1000 years, the farming of crops and the domestication of livestock held no appeal. The only major modification of the landscape practised by the Aborigines was the

mines at places like Charters Towers, Ravenswood and Mt Morgan are being reworked successfully.

Nowadays the manufacturing sector is playing an increasingly important economic role. The area around Brisbane is the main industrial centre, with textile, metal, food processing, car assembly and many other industries.

Other major industrial centres include Ipswich, Townsville and Gladstone, and sugar refineries are found throughout the north.

As this book indicates, Queensland is also incredibly rich in natural 'tourism' resources. In recent decades tourism has been the fastest growing sector of the economy and is now one of the state's major sources of income.

POPULATION & PEOPLE

Queensland has a population of over three million people, making up about 18% of the total Australian population. Around 80% of people live in urban areas, and the majority of Queenslanders live along the fertile coastal strip between Brisbane and Cairns. The other parts of the state are sparsely populated.

Queensland is notable for being the Australian state with the largest proportion of its people living outside its capital city. The south-east corner of the state is Queensland's selective burning of undergrowth in forests and dead grass on the plains. This encouraged new growth, which in turn attracted game animals to the area. It also prevented the build-up of combustible material in the forests, making hunting easier and reducing the possibility of major bush fires. Dingoes were domesticated to assist in the hunt and to guard the camp from intruders.

Environmental Practices Similar technology – for example the boomerang and spear – was used throughout the continent, but techniques were adapted to the environment and the species being hunted. In the wetlands of northern Australia, fish traps hundreds of metres long made of bamboo and cord were built to catch fish at the end of the wet season. In the area now known as Victoria, permanent stone weirs many kilometres long were used to trap eels, while in the tablelands of Queensland finely woven nets were used to snare mobs of wallabies and kangaroos.

The Aborigines were also traders. Trade routes crisscrossed the country, dispersing goods and a variety of produced items along their way. Many of the items traded, such as certain types of stone or shell, were rare and had great ritual significance. Boomerangs and ochre were other important trade items. Along the trading networks which developed, large numbers of people would often meet for 'exchange ceremonies', where not only goods but also songs and dances were passed on.

Cultural Life The simplicity of the Aborigines' technology contrasts with the sophistication of their cultural life. Religion, history, law and art are integrated in complex ceremonies which depict the activities of their ancestral beings, and prescribe codes of behaviour and responsibilities for looking after the land and all living things. The link between the Aborigines and the ancestral beings are totems, each person having their own totem, or Dreaming. These totems take many forms, such as caterpillars, snakes, fish and magpies. Songs explain how the landscape contains these powerful creator ancestors, who can exert either a benign or a malevolent influence. They tell of the best places and the best times to hunt, and where to find water in drought years. They can also specify kinship relations and correct marriage partners.

Ceremonies are still performed in many parts of Australia; many of the sacred sites are believed to be dangerous and entry is prohibited under traditional Aboriginal law. These restrictions may seem merely the result of superstition, but in many cases they have a pragmatic origin. One site in northern Australia was believed to cause sores to break out all over the body of anyone visiting the area. Subsequently, the area was found to have a dangerously high level of radiation from naturally occurring radon gas. In another instance, fishing from a certain reef was traditionally prohibited. This restriction was scoffed at by local Europeans until it was discovered that fish from this area had a high incidence of ciguatera, which renders fish poisonous if eaten by humans. ■

most crowded region, and more than 60% of the total population live within 150 km of Brisbane. Brisbane has more than 1.4 million residents; the Gold Coast, Toowoomba and the Sunshine Coast are the south-east's other major population centres.

Of the string of cities along the east coast, Maryborough, Hervey Bay, Bundaberg, Gladstone, Rockhampton, Mackay, Townsville and Cairns have populations of more than 20,000. In contrast, the mining town of Mt Isa is the only place in the interior to top this figure.

There are about 48,000 Aborigines and about 3500 Torres Strait Islanders living in mainland Queensland, most of whom live in the north of the state. In addition, there are another 10,000 Torres Strait islanders living on the islands between Cape York and Papua New Guinea.

As with the rest of Australia, Queensland has an incredibly diverse population. The first European settlers to arrive were predominantly of English, Scottish or Irish descent. At first, these settlers had access to convict labour, but with the closure of the Moreton Bay penal colony in 1842 they were forced to find alternative sources of labour. The solution was to begin importing cheap labour from other countries – Indian and Chinese coolies, Melanesians (known as Kanakas), and German contract workers – to work the land, a pattern which continued until WW I.

From the mid-1800s, a series of large-scale migration programmes and promotional campaigns were instigated to boost Queensland's White population, which by 1861 numbered a mere 30,000. Britons and Germans were the main targets of these programmes, but many Irish, Scandinavians and Italians packed up and moved to Queensland, lured by various incentives including sponsored passage or free land on arrival.

The discovery of gold in Queensland provided an even greater incentive, and people from all around the world poured into Queensland during the 1870s, including thousands of Chinese miners. By 1876, the Chinese comprised 6% of Queensland's population, but far from being welcomed into the young colony, the Chinese were vilified and portrayed as immoral heathens. Hounded by racist attitudes and policies, the majority of them left in the 1880s.

By 1891, the state's population had risen to 394,000; by 1921 it was 756,000. At this stage, the majority of Queenslanders were still of English, Scottish and Irish descent, although a significant number of Italians were working in the sugar industry of north Queensland. Germans, Scandinavians, Russians, and Spaniards comprised the other significant minority groups.

Throughout these growth periods, Queensland's immigration policies led to ongoing racial tensions, with xenophobic Anglo workers resenting having to compete with cheap imported labour. As a result, Queensland's Labor government developed policies biased towards Anglo-Celtic migrants.

After WW II, Australia's mass migration policies transformed the country from a predominantly Anglo-Celtic culture into the multi-cultural society it is today.

Thousands of Jewish survivors of the Holocaust came to Australia, along with people from Italy, Greece, Turkey, Lebanon and Yugoslavia. More recently there have been large influxes of Asians, particularly Vietnamese after the Vietnam War.

Queensland, however, received only about 8% of new immigrants after WW II, with the state government actively discouraging immigrants from moving to urban centres and 'cluttering up the labour market'. As a result, Queensland has a less diverse cultural mix than other states – for example, Brisbane's Italian and Greek communities make up less than 2% of the population, as opposed to over 7% in Melbourne. A large proportion of Queensland's non-Anglo people still live in rural areas.

In recent years, Queensland's major source of human resources has been internal migration. Since 1980, more than half a million Australians have moved to Queensland from other states, seeking a new life in the land of sunshine and dreams.

ARTS & CULTURE

In the epilogue to his 1982 *A History of Queensland*, local historian Ross Fitzgerald lamented 'the cultural wasteland that is Queensland'. Fitzgerald thought the blame for Queensland's cultural malaise lay with a range of factors, including the authoritarianism and anti-intellectualism of the then National/Liberal Party government, the historically low value that had been placed on education in Queensland, and the low levels of overseas migration that meant that 'Queenslanders have been less exposed than other Australians to the clash and challenge of new and heterodox ideas'.

Times have changed somewhat. The National Party finally fell from grace, and with them went much of the repressiveness and intolerance that characterised their reign.

The current state Labor government has restored the civil liberties which were taken away by the former Bjelke-Petersen government, such as the right to assembly, and done much to stimulate and encourage artistic and cultural developments. Nevertheless, it has to be said that Queensland retains strong elements of its conservative past, and that in many ways it is still well and truly entrenched in the cultural mainstream.

Cinema

The Australian film industry began as early as 1896, a year after the Lumière brothers opened the world's first cinema in Paris. Cinema historians regard an Australian film, *Soldiers of the Cross*, as the world's first 'real' movie. It was originally screened in 1901, cost £600 to make and was shown throughout America in 1902.

The next significant Australian film, *The Story of the Kelly Gang*, was screened in 1907, and by 1911 the industry was flourishing. Over 250 silent feature films were made before the 1930s when the 'talkies' and Hollywood took over.

In the 1930s film companies like Cinesound sprang up. Cinesound made 17 feature films between 1931 and 1940, many based on Australian history or literature. *Jedda* and *Forty Thousand Horsemen*, directed by Cinesound's great film maker Charles Chauvel, were highlights of this era of locally made and financed films which ended in 1959, the year of Chauvel's death.

Before the introduction of government subsidies during 1969 and 1970, the Australian film industry found it difficult to compete with US and British interests. The New Wave era of the 1970s, a renaissance of Australian cinema, produced films like *Breaker Morant*, *Picnic at Hanging Rock*, *Sunday Too Far Away*, *Caddie* and *The Devil's Playground*, which appealed to large local and international audiences. Since the '70s, Australian actors and directors like Mel Gibson, Judy Davis, Greta Scacchi, Paul Hogan, Bruce Beresford, Peter Weir, Gillian Armstrong and Fred Schepsi have gained international recognition. Films like *Gallipoli*, *The Year of Living Dangerously*, *Mad Max*, *Malcolm*, *Crocodile Dundee I* and *II*, *Proof*, *The Year My Voice Broke*, *Strictly Ballroom*, *The Piano*, *Muriel's Wedding* and *Priscilla – Queen of the Desert* have entertained and impressed audiences worldwide.

Queensland has a growing film industry based around the Warner-Roadshow studios at Movie World on the Gold Coast, and has also become a popular location for overseas productions. Films which have been made or shot in Queensland in recent years include *Streetfighter*, a version of a popular martial arts video game, starring Kylie Minogue and Jean-Claude Van Damme; *Escape from Absalom*, a futuristic action-adventure set on a prison island, starring Ray Liotta; *Rough Diamonds*, in which an ex-pop star and her 13-year-old daughter leave Brisbane and travel to the outback where they meet a singing cattle breeder (Jason Donovan); *Travelling North*, based on a David Williamson play and starring Leo McKern and Julia Blake; *The Fringe Dwellers*, based on the novel of the same name by Nene Gare; and *Broken Highway*, made by independent writer-director Laurie McGuinness and starring Claudia Karvan and Aden Young.

Parts of the hit films *Muriel's Wedding* and *Crocodile Dundee I* were also shot on location in Queensland.

Painting

Most of the major developments in the Australian art world since White settlement have taken place in Sydney and Melbourne. Queensland has played only a minor role, although there are a number of excellent galleries which exhibit the works of Australian artists. In particular, the Queensland Art Gallery in Brisbane is well worth visiting and has an excellent Australian collection.

In the 1880s a group of young artists, known as the Heidelberg School, developed the first distinctively White Australian style of painting, working from a bush camp near Melbourne. In Sydney a contemporary movement worked at Sirius Cove on Sydney Harbour. Together these painters were known as the Australian Impressionists, and the main artists were Tom Roberts, Arthur Streeton, Frederick McCubbin, Louis Abrahams, Charles Conder, Julian Ashton and, later, Walter Withers.

In the 1940s, another revolution in Australian art took place at Heide, the home of John and Sunday Reed in suburban Melbourne. Under their patronage a new generation of young artists redefined the direction of Australian art. They included some of Australia's most famous contemporary artists – Sir

Sidney Nolan, Albert Tucker, Joy Hester and Arthur Boyd.

Lloyd Rees is probably the best-known artist to have come out of Queensland. Others include Ian Fairweather, Godfrey Rivers, Davida Allen (famous for her obsessive portraits of the actor Sam Neill) and Bill Robinson, who won the 1995 Archibald Prize for portraiture with his quirky *Portrait of the Artist With Stunned Mullet*.

Queensland is a rich centre of traditional and contemporary Aborignal art. Judy Watson and Gordon Bennett have both won the rich Moet & Chandon Prize for contemporary artists.

Although Tracey Moffatt is now based in Sydney, her work is also worth looking out for. See the Bisbane chapter for details of galleries featuring Australian art.

Literature

While Tom Roberts and his mates were developing a distinctively Australian art style, there were a number of writers doing similar things with the written word.

Two of the most widely acclaimed early Australian writers were A B ('Banjo') Paterson and Henry Lawson. Paterson, a lawyer who grew up in the bush and contributed ballads and poems to the Sydney *Bulletin*, was an optimistic writer who romanticised life in the Australian bush and outback. His poems include the classics *Clancy of the Overflow* and *The Man from Snowy River*. Henry Lawson brought a much more bleak outlook to his work, and was more of a social commentator and political thinker than Paterson. His greatest legacy is his short stories of life in the bush, which seem remarkably simple yet manage to capture the atmosphere perfectly – *The Drover's Wife* and *A Day on a Selection* are good examples. Lawson published a number of short-story collections, including *While the Billy Boils* (1896) and *Joe Wilson and His Mates* (1901).

Steele Rudd, a contemporary of Paterson and Lawson's, was born in Toowoomba in 1868. With his classic sketches of the hardships of early Queensland life and the enduring characters he created like 'Dad & Dave' and 'Mother & Sal', Rudd became one of the country's best loved comic writers. A new Dad & Dave film has just been made, featuring Leo McKern, of *Rumpole of the Bailey* fame.

Rolf Boldrewood's classic *Robbery Under Arms* tells the tale of Captain Starlight, Queensland's most notorious bushranger and cattle thief. Neville Shute's famous novel *A Town Like Alice* is partly set in Burketown, in the Gulf Savannah.

The prolific Ion Idriess was one of Australia's most popular early writers, and most of his stories were set in the outback. They include *Flynn of the Inland*, the story of the man who created the Flying Doctor Service; *The Cattle King*, a portrayal of the life of wealthy pastoralist Sydney Kidman; and *Nemarluk: King of the Wilds*, about an Aboriginal resistance fighter in the Top End.

Ray Lawler's play *Summer of the Seventeenth Doll*, about two north Queensland cane cutters and their girlfriends, was first performed back in 1955. With its portrayal of mateship and the ethos of the stereotypical bushmen, 'The Doll' is considered to be a watershed in Australian drama.

Miles Franklin was one of Australia's early feminists. Her best-known book, *My Brilliant Career*, was written at the turn of the century when the author was only 20. On her death she endowed an annual award for an Australian novel; today the Miles Franklin Award is the most prestigious in the country.

Eleanor Dark wrote her historical trilogy *The Timeless Land*, *Storm of Time* and *No Barrier* in the 1940s. These covered the period from 1788 to 1914, and were highly unusual at the time for the sympathetic treatment they gave to the Aboriginal culture.

Patrick White was a prolific writer who won the Miles Franklin Award twice, for *Voss* (1957) and *Riders in the Chariot* (1961), and the Nobel Prize for *The Eye of the Storm* (1973). The main character in Voss is said to have been loosely based on the eccentric explorer Ludwig Leichhardt. Other contemporary Australian writers of note

MARK ARMSTRONG

DAVID SHERMAN

TONY WHEELER

Top: Cattle grid on the road to Birdsville
Middle: The lush sub-tropical Lamington National Park
Bottom: Peaceful & remote Lizard Island

Top: Legends Lodge, Chillagoe
Left: Lady Elliot Lighthouse, Lady Elliot Island
Right: North Queensland Architecture, Cairns

include Peter Carey, Thomas Keneally, Tim Winton and Elizabeth Jolley.

Queensland has produced plenty of outstanding writers of its own. In particular, Brisbane's University of Queensland has for many years been one of Australia's richest literary breeding grounds.

David Malouf is one of Queensland's most internationally recognised writers. Born in Brisbane to Lebanese immigrants, his novels include the evocative *Johnno* and *12 Edmondstone Street*, tales of an Australian boyhood set in the Brisbane of the 1940s and 1950s. Malouf's other works include *The Great World* (perhaps his best), *Fly Away Peter* and *An Imaginary Life*.

Australia's best-known Aboriginal poet and writer, Oodgeroo Noonuccal (Kath Walker) was born on North Stradbroke Island in 1920, and buried there in September 1993. Her 1964 book *We Are Going* was the first published work by an Aboriginal woman; her other works include *My People*.

Thea Astley's 11 published novels include *Hunting the Wild Pineapple*, set in the rainforests of north Queensland, and *It's Raining in Mango*, a historical saga which traces the fortunes and failures of one pioneer family from the 1860s to the 1980s. Expatriate writer Janet Turner Hospital was born in Melbourne but moved to Brisbane aged seven, and attended school and university there. Her works include *The Ivory Swing*, *The Tiger in the Tiger Pit*, *Charade* and the wonderful *The Last Magician*, parts of which are set in the rainforests of Queensland.

Ipswich-born Thomas Shapcott is an editor and one of Australia's most prolific writers. His recent books include *The White Stag of Exile*, set in Brisbane and Budapest around the turn of the century.

Rodney Hall, who attended school in Brisbane but now lives in NSW, is another major Australian literary figure and his masterpiece, the *Yandilla Trilogy*, is one of the great epics of Australia's colonial era. It comprises the novels *Captivity Captive*, *The Second Bridegroom* and *The Grisly Wife*.

Nancy Cato writes popular historical and romantic works which include *All the Rivers Run*, which was made into a TV series. Another of Cato's works, *Brown Sugar*, is billed as 'a story of love and inter-racial passions set against the backdrop of the Queensland sugar industry'. Hmmm.

Journalist Hugh Lunn has written a number of popular books on and about Queensland. They include his humorous two-part autobiography *Over the Top With Jim* and *Head Over Heels*.

In recent years, Brisbane has produced a new wave of promising young writers. Helen Demidenko, who studied Classics and English at the University of Queensland, wrote a remarkable first novel, *The Hand That Signed the Paper*, which tells the story of a Ukrainian peasant who enlists in the Nazi Death Squads. This novel won the prestigous 1995 Miles Franklin award. Andrew McGahan, a university dropout, wrote his controversial first novel *Praise* in about two months – it shows, but he won the prestigious Australian Vogel Literary Award. Set in the seedy underbelly of Brisbane's Fortitude Valley, *Praise* is a tale of sex, unemployment, sex, drugs and more sex. Verano Armanno's *Romeo of the Underworld* is another contemporary novel set in the Valley. Another prominent young writer is Matthew Condon, whose novels include *The Motorcycle Cafe* and *Usher*.

Architecture

Queensland's architectural beginnings were of the humblest kind. Many of the first settlers to arrive in the colony lived itinerant lives, and their homes reflected this. Canvas tents and tarpaulins, slab-timber cabins and bark huts were the most common types of early dwelling, and even by the time of the first census in 1861, more than 50% of housing was classified as 'temporary'.

As the colony became more established, towns grew and settlers settled, and temporary dwellings were gradually replaced by more permanent structures, the majority of which were built from locally sawn timber. Brick was used in a handful of areas which had local clay deposits, but timber was by far the most common building material. Early houses were even roofed with shingles or bark sheets, although galvanised iron soon took over and became the ubiquitous roofing material.

These early squatters' houses built from timber and iron became the model for the classic 'Queenslanders', the distinctive buildings which you'll still see all throughout the state. Queenslanders (we're talking houses, not people...) are generally square in shape and raised off the ground by stumps or poles, with a high-pitched iron roof and broad, shady verandahs on at least two, and often four sides. There are various advantages to having the houses raised off the ground; the under-house ventilation keep the houses cooler and reduced humidity; pests such as termites can be controlled by protecting the stumps with tar or creosote; and using stumps of varying heights allows the houses to be built on hillsides.

Queenslanders are found in all parts of the state, and while the designs vary idiosyncratically from place to place, the general format remains the same. From the lonely houses surrounded by cane fields in the north, to the clusters of timber houses in Brisbane's hill suburbs, these buildings remain an enduring image of Queensland for most travellers.

On the other hand, for a time many locals grew to be less than enchanted with them as homes, and considered them to be ugly, pest-ridden woodpiles that were hard to keep clean. In recent years there has been something of a turnaround in attitudes, and Queenslanders are now widely appreciated as a unique part of the state's architectural heritage. These days many people renovate and restore their old homes instead of tearing them down and replacing them with modern, functional and dull brick blocks.

Apart from lots of old Queenslanders, almost every town in Queensland has a number of impressive public buildings. First and foremost would have to be the country pub, perhaps the most important of all public facilities and traditionally the centrepoint of a town's social life. Town halls, railway stations, courthouses, post offices, banks and masonic lodges are also worth looking out for – you can read much about each town's history from a study of its public buildings.

Most of Queensland's more impressive public buildings date back to the boom years of the mid to late-1800s (the height of the Victorian era), or to the period between the turn of the century and WW I (the Federation era). Some of the state's finest Victorian architecture is found in the old gold-mining towns, places like Charters Towers, Ravenswood, Cooktown, Gympie and Mt Morgan, while the immense pastoral wealth of the Darling Downs built towns like Roma, Toowoomba and Warwick. Brisbane, as the capital, seat of government and economic centre, also has its fair share of prominent Victorian-era buildings.

By the 1890s many of the goldfields had begun to decline, and a world-wide recession had brought Queensland's economy to its knees; together, these factors brought Queensland's first construction boom to a grinding halt.

As the turn of the century and Australia's pending federation approached, a new style of architecture known as Federation began to evolve. It featured simplicity of design and less ornamentation, and produced buildings more suited to the Australian climate and environment.

Much of Queensland's contemporary architecture is much less noteworthy. Rabid developers and a short-sighted obsession with 'progress' have produced such architectural eyesores as the high-rise concrete jungles that engulf the Gold Coast and parts of the Sunshine Coast, and several other booming tourist centres are in danger of following suit. On a more positive note, Queensland's growing ecotourism industry seems to have led to a trend in resort developments that attempt to blend in with their environment and achieve a degree of stylistic integrity. Places like the Kingfisher Bay Resort on Fraser Island, the Bedarra Island Resort, the Lugger Bay Rainforest Apartments at South Mission Beach and the Coconut Beach Rainforest Resort at Cape Tribulation come to mind.

Music

Queensland is the birthplace of Australia's most famous song. Banjo Patterson wrote the lyrics to *Waltzing Matilda*, Australia's unofficial national anthem, early in 1895 while he was visiting his fiancée at an outback station near Winton in central Queensland.

Queensland hosts a wide range of music festivals throughout the year, featuring everything from jazz and blues to chamber music and alternative rock. Two of the best known music events are the Maleny-Woodford Folk Festival, held annually between Christmas and New Year, and the Brisbane Biennial International Music Festival, held every odd year from late May to early June.

Plenty of towns in Queensland host regular bush dances featuring folk and country bands – bush dances are great fun, and an excellent way to meet the locals and gain an insight into Australian music. Country & Western line dancing has also become incredibly popular in recent years.

Indigenous music is one of the Australian music industry's great success stories of recent years. Yothu Yindi, with their land rights anthem *Treaty*, is the country's best known Aboriginal band, but Queensland has produced some outstanding indigenous musicians of its own. Christine Anu is a Torres Strait Islander who was born in Cairns. Her debut album/CD *Stylin' Up* blends Creole-style rap, Islander chants and traditional languages with English – highly recommended listening.

Brisbane's pub-rock scene may not have produced the same wealth of bands that have come out of Sydney and Melbourne, but a couple of Australia's all-time greatest bands had their beginnings in the Sunshine State. The Go Betweens started out in Queensland, and many of their songs like *Cattle and Cane* evoke a strong sense of place. Their best albums include *Tallulah* and *Before Hollywood* – great driving music while you're travelling around Queensland.

The Saints, considered by many people to be one of the seminal punk bands, started out in Brisbane in the mid-1970s before moving onto bigger things in Sydney, and later London. Despite the fact that they no longer talk to each other, Chris Bailey and Ed Kuepper have gone on to become legends of the Australian music scene.

More recently, Brisbane bands like Custard and Regurgitator have shot to prominence in the alternative music scene.

Alternative Lifestyles

Under the National Party, Queensland considered itself to be one of Australia's great bastions of conservatism. The leader of the Nationals, Sir Joh Bjelke-Petersen, had a reputation as a wowser, and considered all

Ferals in the Forests

Ferals, the alternative lifestylers who live deep in the dark rainforests of Far North Queensland, are the hippies of the 1990s – with a couple of fundamental differences. The long hair, flares, tie-dyed clothes and peace signs of the 1960s and '70s have been replaced by shaven or dreadlocked hair, ragged rainbow-coloured clothes, bare feet or heavy work boots, and pierced noses, ears and belly-buttons. And instead of peace, love and understanding, ferals espouse radical environmentalism.

Ideologically, ferals reject contemporary culture and see city life as the ultimate urban nightmare. They consider the mass-production, mass-consumption doctrines that drive modern society to be totally unsustainable in the long term. Rather than seeing themselves as dropouts, ferals consider their lifestyle to be the way of the future, and that their rejection of materialism is the only way modern society will ever progress to a point where life on earth is sustainable.

Ferals live in communal, semi-nomadic tribal groups. Most of them are vegetarians who live off unemployment benefits and avoid using mass produced goods or fossil fuels and they see themselves as the protectors of the forests they live in. You'll often see them wandering barefoot around places like Cairns and Mossman, where they come to collect supplies and their unemployment benefits. ■

that hippie nonsense that went on down in the southern states to be totally unsuitable for Queenslanders. The notorious 1976 raid on the 'hippie commune' at Cedar Bay, in the rainforests north of Cape Tribulation, was one of many examples of Joh's refusal to accept anyone or anything beyond the mainstream.

Attitudes have changed substantially since then, although Queensland still has nothing to compare to the alternative lifestyle communities that have flourished in northern New South Wales since the late 1960s. There are several alternative lifestyle towns in the Sunshine Coast Hinterland, places like Maleny, Mooloolah and Eumundi, and several of Brisbane's inner suburbs have a distinctly alternative flavour. The mountain village of Kuranda near Cairns has always attracted its fair share of hippies, but in recent years Kuranda has been turned into a mainstream tourist attraction based on its 'alternative charm and character' – most of which has been destroyed by the flood of commercial tourism.

The rainforests of Far North Queensland are home to the state's best known communities of alternative lifestylers – the Ferals.

RELIGION

A shrinking majority of people in Queensland are at least nominally Christian. Most Protestant churches have merged to become the Uniting Church, although the Church of England has remained separate. The Catholic Church is popular (about a third of Christians are Catholics), with the original Irish adherents now joined by the large numbers of Mediterranean immigrants.

Non-Christian minorities abound, the main ones being Buddhist, Jewish or Muslim.

Traditional Aboriginal cultures are either irreligious or are nothing but religion, depending on how you look at it. Is a belief system which views every event, no matter how trifling, in a nonmaterial context a religion? The early Christian missionaries certainly didn't think so. For them a belief in a deity was an essential part of a religion, and anything else was mere superstition.

Sacred Sites Aboriginal sacred sites are a perennial topic of discussion. Their presence can lead to headline-grabbing controversy when they stand in the way of developments such as roads, mines and dams. This is because most other Australians still have great difficulty understanding the Aborigines' deep spiritual bond with the land.

Aboriginal religious beliefs centre on the continuing existence of spirit beings that lived on Earth during the Dreamtime, which occurred before the arrival of humans. These beings created all the features of the natural world and were the ancestors of all living things. They took different forms but behaved as people do, and as they travelled about they left signs to show where they passed. Most Australians have heard of rainbow serpents carving out rivers as they slithered from A to B. On a smaller scale you can have a pile of rocks marking the spot where an ancestor defecated, or a tree that sprang from a thrown spear.

Despite being supernatural, the ancestors were subject to ageing and eventually they returned to the sleep from which they'd awoken at the dawn of time. Some sank back into the ground while others changed into physical features including the moon and stars. Here their spirits remain as eternal forces that breathe life into the newborn and influence natural events. Each ancestor's spiritual energy flows along the path it travelled during the Dreamtime and is strongest at the points where it left physical evidence of its activities, such as a tree, hill or claypan. These features are sacred sites.

The ancestors left strict laws that determine the behaviour of people and animals, the growth of plants, and natural events such as rain and the change of seasons. Although all living things are considered to be conscious beings with their own language and way of life, they are still required to live in accordance with their ancestors' laws.

Every person, animal and plant is believed to have two souls – one mortal and one immortal. The latter is part of a particular ancestral spirit and returns to the sacred sites of that ancestor after death, while the mortal soul simply fades into oblivion. Each person is spiritually bound to the sacred sites that mark the land associated with his or her ancestor. It is the individual's obligation to help care for these sites by performing the necessary rituals and singing the songs that tell of the ancestor's deeds. By doing this, the order created by that ancestor is maintained.

However, the ancestors are extremely powerful and restless spirits and require the most careful treatment. Dreadful calamities can befall those who fail to care for their sites in the proper manner. As there is nowhere beyond the influence of an angry ancestor, the unpleasant consequences of either disrespect or neglect at a single site may stretch far and wide.

Some of the sacred sites are believed to be dangerous and entry is prohibited under traditional Aboriginal law. These restrictions often have a pragmatic origin. One site in northern Australia was believed to cause sores to break out all over the body of anyone visiting the area. Subsequently, the area was found to have a dangerously high level of radiation from naturally occurring radon gas. In another instance, fishing from a certain reef was traditionally prohibited. This restriction was scoffed at by local Europeans until it was discovered that fish from this area had a high incidence of ciguatera, which renders fish poisonous if eaten by humans.

Unfortunately, Aboriginal sacred sites are not like Christian churches, which can be desanctified before the bulldozers move in. Neither can they be bought, sold or transferred. Other Australians find this difficult to accept because they regard land as belonging to the individual, whereas in Aboriginal society the reverse applies. In a nutshell, Aborigines believe that to destroy or damage a sacred site threatens not only the living but also the spirit inhabitants of the land. It is a distressing and dangerous act, and one that no responsible person would condone.

Throughout much of Australia, when pastoralists were breaking the Aborigines'

subsistence link to the land, and sometimes shooting them, many Aborigines sought refuge on missions and became Christians. However, becoming Christians has not, for most Aborigines, meant renouncing their traditional religion. Many senior Aboriginal law men are also devout Christians, and in many cases ministers.

LANGUAGE

Australia contains many surprises for those who think all Aussies speak some weird variant of English. For a start many Australians don't even speak Australian – they speak Italian, Lebanese, Vietnamese, Turkish or Greek.

Those who do speak the native tongue are liable to lose you in a strange collection of Australian words. Some have completely different meanings in Australia than they do in English-speaking countries north of the equator; some commonly used words have been shortened almost beyond recognition. Others are derived from Aboriginal languages, or from the slang used by early convict settlers.

There is a slight regional variation in the Australian accent, while the difference between city and country speech is mainly a matter of speed. Some of the most famed Aussie words are hardly heard at all – 'mates' or 'pals' are more common than 'cobbers'. If you want to pass for a native, try speaking slightly nasally, shortening any word of more than two syllables and then adding a vowel to the end of it, making anything you can into a diminutive (even the Hell's Angels can become mere 'bikies') and peppering your speech with as many expletives as possible. Lonely Planet publishes *Australia – a language survival kit*, an introduction to both Australian English and Aboriginal languages, and many of the words contained in the Glossary in the back of this book may also help.

Aboriginal Language

At the time of contact there were around 250 separate Australian languages spoken by the

600 to 700 Aboriginal 'tribes', and many of these languages were as distinct from each other as English and French. Often three or four adjacent tribes would speak what amounted to dialects of the same language, but another adjacent tribe might speak a completely different language.

It is believed that all the languages evolved from a single language family as the Aborigines gradually moved out over the entire continent and split into new groups. There are a number of words that occur right across the continent, such as *jina* (foot) and *mala* (hand), and similarities also exist in the often complex grammatical structures.

Following European contact the number of Aboriginal languages was drastically reduced. At least eight separate languages were spoken in Tasmania alone, but none of these was recorded before the native speakers either died or were killed. Of the original 250 or so languages, only around 30 are today spoken on a regular basis and are taught to children.

Aboriginal Kriol is a new language which has developed since European arrival in Australia. It is spoken across northern Australia and has become the 'native' language of many young Aborigines. It contains many English words, but the pronunciation and grammatical usage are along Aboriginal lines, the meaning is often different, and the spelling is phonetic. For example, the English sentence 'He was amazed' becomes 'I bin luk kwesjinmak' in Kriol.

There are a number of generic terms which Aborigines use to describe themselves, and these vary according to the region. The most common of these is Koori, used for the people of south-east Australia. Murri is used to refer to the people of Queensland, Nunga for those from coastal South Australia, and Nyoongah is used in the country's south-west.

Facts for the Visitor

VISAS & EMBASSIES

Once upon a time, Australia was fairly free and easy about who was allowed to visit the country, particularly if you were from the UK or Canada. These days, only New Zealanders get any sort of preferential treatment, and even they need at least a passport. Everybody else has to have a visa.

Visa application forms are available from Australian diplomatic missions overseas and some travel agents. There are several different types of visas, depending on the reason for your visit.

Australian Embassies

Australian consular offices overseas include:

Canada
  Suite 710, 50 O'Connor St, Ottawa K1P 6L2 (☎ (613) 236 0841); also in Toronto and Vancouver
China
  15 Dongzhimenwai Dajie, San Li Tun, Beijing (☎ (1) 532 2331)
Denmark
  Kristianagade 21, 2100 Copenhagen (☎ 3126 2244)
France
  4 Rue Jean Rey, Paris, 15e (☎ (1) 40 59 33 00)
Germany
  Godesberger Allee 107, 5300·Bonn 1 (☎ (0228) 81030); also in Frankfurt and Berlin
Greece
  37 Dimitriou Soutsou, Ambelokpi, Athens 11512 (☎ (01) 644 7303)
Hong Kong
  Harbour Centre, 24th floor, 25 Harbour Rd, Wanchai, Hong Kong Island (☎ (5) 73 1881)
India
  Australian Compound, No 1/50-G Shantipath, Chanakyapuri, New Delhi 110021 (☎ 60 1336); also in Bombay
Indonesia
  Jalan Thamrin 15, Gambir, Jakarta (☎ (21) 323109); also in Denpasar
Ireland
  Fitzwilton House, Wilton Tce, Dublin 2 (☎ (01) 76 1517)
Italy
  Via Alessandria 215, Rome 00198 (☎ (06) 832 721); also in Milan

Japan
  2-1-14 Mita, Minato-ku, Tokyo (☎ (3) 5232 4111); also in Osaka
Malaysia
  6 Jalan Yap Kwan Seng, Kuala Lumpur 50450 (☎ (03) 242 3122)
Netherlands
  Camegielaan 12, 2517 KH, The Hague (☎ (070) 310 8200)
New Zealand
  72-78 Hobson St, Thorndon, Wellington (☎ (4) 73 6411); also in Auckland
Papua New Guinea
  Independence Dve, Waigani, Port Moresby (☎ 25 9333)
Philippines
  Bank of Philippine Islands Building, Paseo de Roxas, Makati, Manila (☎ 817 7911)
Singapore
  25 Napier Rd, Singapore 10 (☎ 737 9311)
South Africa
  4th floor, Mutual & Federal Centre, 220 Vermuelen St, Pretoria 0002 (☎ (012) 325 4315)
Sweden
  Sergels Torg 12, Stockholm C (☎ (08) 613 2900)
Switzerland
  29 Alpenstrasse, Berne (☎ (031) 43 0143); also in Geneva
Thailand
  37 South Sathorn Rd, Bangkok 10120 (☎ (2) 287 2680)
UK
  Australia House, The Strand, London WC2B 4LA (☎ (0171) 379 4334); also in Edinburgh and Manchester
USA
  1601 Massachusetts Ave NW, Washington DC, 20036 (☎ (202) 797 3000); also in Los Angeles, Chicago, Honolulu, Houston, New York and San Francisco

Tourist Visas

Tourist visas are issued by Australian consular offices abroad; they are the most common and are generally valid for a stay of up to six months within a 12-month period. If you intend staying less than three months, the visa is free; otherwise there is a $30 processing fee.

When you apply for a visa, you need to present your passport and a passport photo, as well as signing an undertaking that you have an onward or return ticket and 'sufficient funds' – the latter is obviously open to interpretation. Like those of any country, Australian visas seem to have their hassles, although the authorities do seem to be more uniform in their approach these days.

Working Visas

Young visitors from Britain, Ireland, Canada, the Netherlands and Japan may be eligible for a 'working holiday' visa. 'Young' is fairly loosely interpreted as around 18 to 26 years, and 'working holiday' means up to 12 months, but the emphasis is supposed to be on casual employment rather than full-time, so you are only supposed to work for three months. Officially this visa can only be applied for in your home country, but some travellers report that the rule can be bent.

See the section on Work later in this chapter for details of what sort of work is available and where.

Visa Extensions

The maximum stay allowed to visitors in Australia is one year, including extensions.

Visa extensions are made through the Department of Immigration & Ethnic Affairs offices in Australia and, as the process takes some time, it's best to apply about a month before your visa expires. There is an application fee – either $50 or $100, depending on the extension length – and even if they turn down your application they can still keep your money! Some offices are very thorough, requiring things like bank statements and interviews. Extending visas is a notoriously slow process, so allow plenty of time.

If you want to extend your stay, contact the Department of Immigration & Ethnic Affairs. Their Queensland head office is at 100 Edward St in Brisbane (☎ (07) 3360 5111); there are other offices at 19 Aplin St in Cairns (☎ (070) 31 4055) and 143 Walker St in Townsville (☎ (077) 72 6811).

If you're trying to stay longer in Australia, the books *Temporary to Permanent Resident in Australia* and *Practical Guide to Obtaining Permanent Residence in Australia*, both published by Legal Books, might be useful.

Foreign Embassies & Consulates

Canberra is home to most foreign embassies, but many countries maintain consulates in Brisbane as well – see the Brisbane chapter for addresses.

DOCUMENTS

Foreign driving licences are valid for the first three months of your visit to Australia. If you're staying for longer, it's worth obtaining an International Driving Permit (IDP) from your local automobile association before you leave – you'll need a passport photo and a valid licence. IDPs are valid for one year.

While you're there, ask your automobile association for a letter of introduction or other proof of membership, which will give you reciprocal rights to the services of the Royal Automobile Club of Queensland (RACQ), including free maps, breakdown services and technical advice.

Carrying a student card will entitle you to a wide variety of discounts throughout Queensland. The most common of these is the International Student Identity Card (ISIC), a plastic ID-style card with your photograph. These are issued by student unions, hostelling organisations or 'alternative-style' travel agencies.

It's also worth bringing your youth hostel membership card (HI, YHA etc) if you have one. As well as entitling you to various discounts, your card is also valid for membership of YHA Queensland for the duration of your stay.

CUSTOMS

When entering Australia you can bring most articles in free of duty, provided that Customs is satisfied they are for personal use and that you'll be taking them with you when you leave. There's also the usual duty-free per-person quota of one litre of alcohol, 250 cigarettes and dutiable goods up to the value of A$400.

With regard to prohibited goods, there are

two areas you need to pay particular attention to. Number one is, of course, dope – Australian Customs has a positive mania about the stuff and can be extremely efficient when it comes to finding it. Unless you want to make first-hand investigations of conditions in Australian jails (not very good), don't bring any with you. This particularly applies if you are arriving from South-East Asia or the Indian subcontinent.

Problem two is animal and plant quarantine. You will be asked to declare all goods of animal or vegetable origin – wooden spoons, straw hats, the lot – and show them to an official. The authorities are naturally keen to prevent weeds, pests or diseases getting into the country – Australia has so far managed to escape many of the agricultural pests and diseases prevalent in other parts of the world. Fresh food is also unpopular, particularly meat, sausages, fruit, vegetables and flowers. There are also restrictions on taking fruit and vegetables between states.

Weapons and firearms are either prohibited or require a permit and safety testing. Other restricted goods include products (such as ivory) made from protected wildlife species, non-approved telecommunications devices and live animals.

And when you leave, don't take any protected flora or fauna with you. Australia's unique birds and animals fetch big bucks from overseas collectors, and Customs comes down hard on animal smugglers. Penalties include jail sentences and huge fines.

There are duty-free stores at the international airports and their associated cities. Treat them with healthy suspicion. 'Duty-free' is one of the world's most overworked catch phrases, and it is often just an excuse to sell things at prices you can easily beat by a little shopping around.

MONEY
Currency
Australia's currency is the decimal system of dollars and cents (100 cents to the dollar) and has been since 1966 when the old system of pounds, shillings and pence was phased out. There are $100, $50, $20, $10 and $5 notes and $2, $1, 50c, 20c, 10c and 5c coins. It's easy to confuse the new plastic $5 and $10 notes, which look much more alike than did the old paper ones (which you still sometimes see). The 2c and 1c coins have been taken out of circulation, although prices can still be set in odd cents. Shops round prices up (or down) to the nearest 5c on your *total* bill, not on individual items.

There are no notable restrictions on importing or exporting currency or travellers' cheques except that you may not take out more than A$5000 in cash without prior approval.

Exchange Rates
Over the years the Australian dollar has fluctuated quite markedly against the US dollar, but in recent years it seems to have stabilised somewhat, generally fetching between US$0.68 and US$0.73. Approximate exchange rates are as follows:

Canadian dollars	C$1.00	=	A$1.01
Deutsche marks	DM1	=	A$0.99
Dutch guilders	Dfl1	=	A$0.88
Hong Kong dollars	HK$10	=	A$1.78
Japanese yen	¥100	=	A$1.56
New Zealand dollars	NZ$1	=	A$0.93
Pound Sterling	UK£1	=	A$2.19
Singapore dollars	S$1	=	A$0.99
US dollars	US$1	=	A$1.38

Changing Money
Changing foreign currency or travellers' cheques is no problem at almost any bank. There are also foreign exchange booths at Brisbane and Cairns international airports which are open to meet all arriving flights. The Westpac Bank also has branches at the airports.

You will also find foreign exchange booths in the city centres of Brisbane, Cairns and some other major cities. These places are OK for emergencies – they have more convenient opening hours than the banks, but their rates generally aren't as good.

Travellers' Cheques
American Express, Thomas Cook and other

well-known international brands of travellers' cheques are all widely used in Australia. A passport will usually be adequate for identification; it would be sensible to carry a driver's licence, credit cards or a plane ticket in case of problems.

Commissions and fees for changing foreign currency travellers' cheques seem to vary from bank to bank and month to month. It's worth making a few phone calls to see which bank currently has the lowest charges. Some charge a flat fee for each transaction, which varies from $2.50 (Commonwealth Bank) to $6.50 (ANZ Bank), while others take a percentage of the amount changed – Westpac charges 1% with a minimum charge of $10.

Major currencies like pounds sterling, US dollars and Swiss francs can be readily exchanged, but you'll be better off if you buy Australian dollar travellers' cheques. These can be exchanged immediately at the bank cashier's window without being converted from a foreign currency and incurring commissions, fees and exchange rate fluctuations.

Credit Cards

The most commonly accepted credit cards in Australia are Visa and MasterCard. American Express, and to a lesser extent Diners Club, are also widely accepted, although some establishments don't (or would rather not) accept them because of the higher fees they charge. The Australian-only Bankcard is also common, although less so in recent years.

Credit cards are a convenient alternative to carrying cash or large numbers of travellers' cheques. With the advent of electronic banking and the proliferation of automatic teller machines (ATMs) throughout the country in recent years, a credit card, preferably linked to your savings account, is now an ideal way to travel. Visa, MasterCard and American Express cards are most commonly accepted in ATMs – most machines will display the symbols of the credit cards that it accepts. Cash advances are also available over the counter from all banks.

If you plan to rent cars while travelling

around Australia, a credit card makes life much simpler; they're looked upon with much greater favour by rent-a-car agencies than nasty old cash, and many agencies simply won't rent you a vehicle if you don't have a card.

Local Bank Accounts

If you're planning to stay longer than just a month or so, it's worth considering other ways of handling money that give you more flexibility and are more economical. This applies equally to Australians setting off to travel around the country.

Most travellers these days opt for an account which includes a cash card, which you can use to access your cash from ATMs found all over Australia. You put your card in the machine, key in your personal identification number (PIN), and then withdraw funds from your account. Westpac, ANZ, National and Commonwealth bank branches are found nationwide, and the Bank of Queensland has branches throughout the state. It is possible to use the machines of some other banks: Westpac ATMs accept Commonwealth Bank cards and vice versa; National Bank ATMs accept ANZ cards and vice versa. Most reasonably sized towns have at least one place where you can withdraw money from a 'hole in the wall'. There is a limit on how much you can withdraw from your account. This varies from bank to bank but is usually $400 to $500 per day.

If you're planning to travel to the more remote outposts, say Cape York or the Gulf Savannah, it may be worth opening a Commonwealth Bank passbook account; the Commonwealth has fewer branches than the other nationwide banks, but all post offices and postal agencies throughout Australia also act as agencies for the bank. You can either use a passbook with a blacklight signature or a card, although some of the more remote postal agencies only accept passbook accounts.

Many businesses, such as service stations, supermarkets and convenience stores, provide Electronic Funds Transfer at Point of Sale (EFTPOS), and at places with this facility you can use your bank cash card to pay for services or purchases direct, and sometimes withdraw cash as well. Bank cash cards and credit cards can also be used to make local, STD and international phone calls in special public telephones, found in most towns throughout the country.

Opening an account at an Australian bank is not all that easy these days, especially for overseas visitors. A points system operates and you need to score a minimum of 100 points before you can enjoy the privilege of letting the bank take your money. Passports, driver's licences, birth certificates and other 'major' IDs earn you 40 points; minor ones such as credit cards get you 20 points. Just like a game show really! However, if visitors apply to open an account during the first six weeks of their visit, then just showing their passport will suffice. Once you've opened your account, it takes about a week to get your card. Some of the banks will only forward the card to an address; you can't go back to the branch to pick it up.

If you don't have an Australian Tax File Number, interest earned from your funds will be taxed at the rate of 48% and this money goes straight to our old mate, the Deputy Commissioner of Taxation.

Foreign Banks

Quite a few foreign banks also have branches in Queensland. These include the Banque Nationale de Paris (☎ (07) 3229 2361), at 10 Eagle St, Brisbane; the Hong Kong Bank of Australia (☎ (07) 3835 7888), at 123 Eagle St, Brisbane; and the Bank of New Zealand (☎ (07) 3231 1222), at Level 7, 345 Queen St, Brisbane.

Costs

Compared with the USA, Canada and European countries, Australia is cheaper in some ways and more expensive in others. Manufactured goods tend to be more expensive – on the other hand, food is both high in quality and low in cost.

Accommodation is also very reasonably priced. In virtually every town where backpackers are likely to stay there'll be a backpackers' hostel with dorm beds for around $12 to $15 and double rooms for around $30, or a caravan park with on-site vans for around $25 for two people. Most pubs in country towns also have cheap accommodation for around $15 per person, and an average motel room will cost between $40 and $60 a night.

The biggest cost in any trip to Australia is going to be transport, simply because it's such a vast country. If there's a group of you, buying a second-hand car is probably the most economical way to go.

Tipping

In Australia tipping isn't 'compulsory' the way it is in the USA or Europe. A tip is more a recognition of good service than an obligation, and the amount you tip is usually weighted according to how good the service has been. It's only customary to tip in restaurants, and only then if you want to. If you do decide to leave a tip, 5% to 10% of the bill is considered reasonable. Taxi drivers don't expect tips, although if you tell them to keep the change, they're unlikely to argue with you.

WHEN TO GO

The winter months are Queensland's busiest time for tourism – it's the place all of the Mexicans (a banana-bender's term for anyone from south of the border) head for to escape the cold southern winters. The main tourist season stretches from April to November, and the official high-season is from June to September. As with elsewhere in the country, the Easter and Christmas breaks are also considered to be high-season.

Queensland doesn't really have what most of us would call a winter. Even in mid-July, when people in the southern states are snuggling up in front of open fires and heading for the ski slopes, you'll find people swimming at Queensland's beaches. Winter is the perfect time to visit – the extreme heat and stifling humidity of summer have been replaced by warm sunny days and surprisingly cool – even cold – nights. The cooler weather also deters the bushflies, sandflies and mosquitoes, which in the warmer months can be an absolute nightmare. In particular, the April to November period is the best time for visits to Far North Queensland, the outback and the Top End.

Summer in Queensland can be unpleasantly hot and humid; more so the further north you go. In the Far North, summer is the wet season and the heat and humidity can make life pretty uncomfortable, and once the monsoonal rains of the Wet arrive, most parts of the Cape York Peninsula and the Gulf of Carpentaria, and much of the outback, are often inaccessible except by light aircraft. To make matters worse, swimming in the sea is not possible anywhere north of Rockhampton due to the deadly 'stingers' (box jellyfish) which frequent the waters at this time (see the Dangers & Annoyances section later in this chapter). On the other hand, if you want to see the Top End green and free of dust, be treated to some spectacular electrical storms and enjoy the best of the barramundi fishing while all the other tourists are down south, this is the time to do it. See the activities section of this chapter for details on the closed season for Barra fishing.

Of course, Queensland covers a huge and diverse area, and as you would expect the climate varies significantly from one end to the other. For more specific information, see the Climate section in the Facts about Queensland chapter.

Apart from the climate, the other major factor you'll need to take into consideration is the school holidays. Australian families take to the road (and air) en masse at these times and a significant proportion of them head for the Sunshine State – many places are booked out, prices rise and things generally get a bit crazy.

School holidays vary somewhat from state to state, and from year to year. The Australian school year is divided into four terms; the main holiday period is the Christmas break, which lasts from mid-December until late January. The Christmas holidays are definitely the high-season in Queensland, particularly in southern Queensland and on the Barrier Reef islands. The other two-week breaks are roughly from early to late April (depending on when Easter falls), from late June to mid-July and from late September to early October.

WHAT TO BRING

With its tropical climate and relaxed attitudes, Queensland's unwritten dress code is 'cool and casual'. Apart from swimwear, the most useful items of clothing are shorts and T-shirts, cotton dresses and tops, perhaps a sarong – in general, light and loose-fitting clothing. Most people dress informally – even businesspeople seldom wear suits and ties – although many resorts, pubs and restaurants specify shirts for men and ban bare feet and thongs, especially in their dining areas. The only places where you'll need a jacket for dinner are at the fancier restaurants at places like Hayman Island and in Brisbane's five-star hotels. Most of the more up-market nightclubs also have 'smart casual' dress codes, as do the casinos.

You are unlikely to need anything warmer than a long-sleeved shirt, although if you're visiting southern Queensland or you're there during the winter months, it's worth bringing a light jacket or a jumper (sweater, pullover) for the occasional chilly evening. Wet weather gear – an umbrella or perhaps a waterproof poncho – will prove handy for those tropical downpours, which are regular occurrences during the summer months and in the rainforests of the Far North.

You need to be aware of the dangers of UV radiation in Queensland. Partially due to a hole in the ozone layer, Australians have the highest incidence of skin cancer in the world. A broad-brimmed sunhat, good sunglasses and effective sunscreen are all essential, especially for fair-skinned folks from cooler climates. Snorkelling without wearing a T-shirt and sunscreen is an especially good way to get sunstroke. Like safe sex, safe sun is an important health consideration – in both cases, use protection.

Another important item is insect repellent. In tropical Queensland, it sometimes seems like the mosquitoes, sandflies and various other insects are queuing up to bite you – a good repellent will usually (but not always) help alleviate the problem. If, like me, you're particularly 'attractive' to insects, it may also be worth investing in a mosquito net. Antihistamine tablets (preferably the kind that don't make you drowsy) are the most effective way to relieve insect bites, particularly those of sandflies (which can drive even the sanest of us over the edge – 'Aaagghhhh!').

When it comes to footwear, 'reef sandals' are all the go in Queensland at the moment. Reef sandals are sturdy rubber-soled sandals with Velcro straps. Cooler than shoes and with good grip, you can wear them just about anywhere – on the beach (hot sand is a summer hazard), in most pubs and clubs, and on boat trips. While sandals are OK for shorter walks, if you're planning to do any serious bushwalking a pair of strong and comfortable walking shoes or boots are essential. You'll also need footwear for walking around the reefs and islands – old running shoes or reef sandals are ideal.

TOURIST OFFICES

There are a number of information sources for visitors to Queensland and you can easily drown yourself in brochures and booklets, maps and leaflets.

Local Tourist Offices

There are plenty of places throughout Queensland willing to provide tourists with information, although it's worth noting that most of these places aren't strictly independent.

There are 14 major regional tourist associations in Queensland, each with their own tourist information centre. These offices are generally extremely helpful and can provide a good range of information on their respective regions, although they will generally only provide you with information on businesses that are paid-up members of the association. Offices are found in the following cities: Brisbane, Surfers Paradise (Gold Coast), Maroochydore (Sunshine Coast), Toowoomba and Warwick (Darling Downs),

Maryborough (Fraser Coast), Gladstone, Blackall (Outback), Rockhampton (Capricorn Coast), Bundaberg, Mackay, Airlie Beach (Whitsundays), Townsville (North Coast) and Cairns (Far North Queensland). See the information sections under individual towns for addresses, phone numbers and opening hours.

There are also hundreds of privately run 'tourist information centres' which are basically booking agents. These places can also be helpful, but bear in mind that they make a commission on whatever tours or accommodation they book for you.

The Royal Automobile Club of Queensland (RACQ) offices are another very helpful source of information about road and weather conditions, and they can also book accommodation and tours. For information on national and state parks, contact one of the QNP&WS's offices. See the following Useful Organisations section for more details on both of these groups.

Interstate Tourist Offices

The Queensland Tourist & Travel Corporation is the government-run body responsible for promoting Queensland interstate and overseas. Their offices act primarily as promotional and booking offices, not information centres, but are worth contacting when you're planning a trip to Queensland. There are QT&TC Travel Centre offices in the following places:

Australian Capital Territory
    25 Garema Place, Canberra City 2601 (☎ (06) 248 8411)
New South Wales
    75 Castlereagh St, Sydney 2000 (☎ (02) 9232 1788)
    Shop 2, 376 Victoria Ave, Chatswood 2067 (☎ (02) 9412 3000)
    Shop 11, Mayfair Mall, St George St, Parramatta 2150 (☎ (02) 9891 1966)
    Shop 3, 133-135 King St, Newcastle 2300 (☎ (049) 26 2800)
South Australia
    10 Grenfell St, Adelaide 5000 (☎ (08) 212 2399)
Victoria
    257 Collins St, Melbourne 3000 (☎ (03) 9654 3866)

Western Australia
    Shop 6, 777 Hay St, Perth 6000 (☎ (09) 322 1777)
Queensland
    Corner of Adelaide and Edward Sts, Brisbane 4000 (☎ (07) 3221 6111)

Overseas Reps

The Australian Tourist Commission (ATC) is the government body intended to inform potential visitors about the country. ATC offices overseas have a useful free magazine-style booklet called *Travellers' Guide to Australia* which is a good introduction to the country, its geography, flora, fauna, states, transport, accommodation, food and so on. They also have a handy free map of the country. This literature is intended for distribution overseas only; if you want copies, get them before you come to Australia. Addresses of the ATC offices for literature requests are:

Australia
    80 William St, Woolloomooloo, Sydney, NSW 2011 (☎ (02) 9360 1111)
Germany
    Neue Mainzerstrasse 22, D6000 Frankfurt/Main 1 (☎ (069) 274 00 60)
Hong Kong
    Suite 6, 10th floor, Central Plaza, 18 Harbour Rd, Wanchai (☎ 802 7700)
Japan
    8th floor, Sankaido Building, 9-13, Akasaka 1-chome, Minato-ku, Tokyo 107 (☎ (03) 3582 2191)
    4th floor, Yuki Building, 3-3-9 Hiranomachi, Chuo-Ku, Osaka 541 (☎ (06) 229 3601)
New Zealand
    Level 13, 44-48 Emily Place, Auckland 1 (☎ (09) 379 9594)
Singapore
    Suite 1703, United Square, 101 Thomson Rd, Singapore 1130 (☎ 255 4555)
South Africa
    c/-Mrs Dee Mets, 6th floor, Petrob House, 343 Surrey Ave, Randburg 2125, Johannesburg (☎ (011) 787 6300)
UK
    Gemini House, 10-18 Putney Hill, London SW15 (☎ (0171) 780 2227)
USA
    Suite 1200, 2121 Avenue of the Stars, Los Angeles, CA 90067 (☎ (213) 552 1988)
    31st floor, 489 Fifth Ave, New York, NY 10017 (☎ (212) 687 6300)

Canadian travellers should contact the offices in New York or Los Angeles; those from France, Ireland or the Netherlands should contact the London office.

The Queensland Tourist & Travel Corporation (QT&TC) also has its own overseas representatives, so for information specifically about Queensland, contact one of the following offices:

Germany
    Neuhauser Str 27/4th floor, 80331 Munich 2 (☎ (089) 260 9693)
France
    16 Rue Pierret, F-92200 Neuilly Sur Seine (☎ (1) 4747 6215)
New Zealand
    9th floor Quay Tower, 29 Customs St West, Auckland (☎ (09) 309 6421)
Hong Kong
    Room 2209, 22nd floor Harbour Centre, 25 Harbour Rd, Wanchai (☎ 827 4322)
Japan
    Suite 1301, Yurakucho Denki Building NW, Yurakucho 1-chome, Chiyoda-Ku, Tokyo 100 (☎ (03) 3214 4931)
Singapore
    101 Thomson Rd, 07-04 United Sq, Singapore 1130 (☎ 253 2811)
USA
    Northrop Plaza Suite 330, 1800 Century Park East, Los Angeles CA 90067 (☎ (310) 788 0997)
    QT&TC 25th floor, 100 Park Ave, New York 10017 (☎ (212) 687 7810)
UK
    Queensland House, 392 The Strand, London WC2R OLZ (☎ (0171) 780 2227)
Taiwan
    Suite 2601, 26th floor International Trade Building, 333 Keelund Rd, Section 1, Taipai 10548 (☎ (2) 723 3196)

USEFUL ORGANISATIONS
Automobile Associations

Australia has a national automobile association, the Australian Automobile Association, but this exists mainly as an umbrella organisation for the various state associations and to maintain international links. The day-to-day operations are all handled by the state organisations who provide an emergency breakdown service, literature, excellent maps and detailed guides to accommodation.

The state organisations have reciprocal

arrangements amongst the various states in Australia and with similar organisations overseas. So, if you're a member of the National Roads & Motorists Association (NRMA) in New South Wales, you can use RACQ facilities in Queensland. Similarly, if you're a member of the AAA in the USA or the RAC or AA in the UK, you can use any of the state organisations' facilities. But bring proof of membership with you.

The Royal Automobile Club of Queensland (RACQ) is the Queensland motoring association – they produce a particularly useful set of regional maps to Queensland which are free to members. Their offices also sell a wide range of travel and driving products, including good maps and travel guidebooks, and as mentioned earlier, can book tours and accommodation and advise on weather and road conditions. The RACQ's head office (☎ (07) 3361 2444) is in Brisbane at 300 St Pauls Tce in Fortitude Valley (although their office beside the Brisbane GPO in Queen St may be more convenient). There are other offices all around the state and almost every town has a garage affiliated with the RACQ – see the information sections of the individual towns for details of these.

Queensland National Parks & Wildlife Service (QNP&WS)

This organisation is responsible for the management of Queensland's national parks. There are information offices and rangers' stations throughout the state, and all provide good advice and information about the respective parks. See the National Parks section in the Facts about Queensland chapter for details.

Australian Conservation Foundation

The Australian Conservation Foundation (ACF) is the largest nongovernment organisation involved in conservation. Only about 10% of its income is from the government; the rest comes from memberships and subscriptions, and from donations (72%), which are mainly from individuals.

The ACF covers a wide range of issues,

including the greenhouse effect and depletion of the ozone layer, the negative effects of logging, preservation of rainforests, the problems of land degradation, and protection of the Antarctic. It frequently works in conjunction with the Wilderness Society and other conservation groups.

With the growing focus on conservation issues and the increasing concern of the Australian public in regard to the environment, the conservation vote has now become increasingly important to all political parties.

The ACF's Brisbane office (☎ (07) 3844 5011) is at 131 Melbourne St in the West End, just south of the city centre across the Brisbane River.

Wilderness Society

The Tasmanian Wilderness Society was formed by conservationists who had been unsuccessful in preventing the damming of Lake Pedder in south-west Tasmania but who were determined to prevent the destruction of the Franklin River. The Franklin River campaign was one of Australia's first major conservation confrontations and it caught the attention of the international media. In 1983, after the High Court decided against the damming of the Franklin, the group changed its name to the Wilderness Society because of its Australia-wide focus on wilderness issues.

The Wilderness Society is involved in issues concerning protection of the Australian wilderness, such as forest management and logging. Like the ACF, government funding is only a small percentage of its income, the rest coming from memberships, donations, its shops and merchandising. In Brisbane, the Wilderness Society has a shop and office (☎ (07) 3221 3695), at 97 Albert St in the city.

Australian Trust for Conservation Volunteers

This nonpolitical, nonprofit group organises practical conservation projects (such as tree planting, track construction and flora and fauna surveys) for volunteers to take part in. Travellers are welcome and it's an excellent way to get involved with the conservation

Access for Disabled Travellers in Queensland

Queensland's level of disability awareness is encouraging. In practice, the level of accessibility is generally quite high and all new facilities must satisfy the standards set down by law.

There are a number of organisations that can supply information and advice to disabled travellers planning to visit Queensland. NICAN (National Information Communications Awareness Network), PO Box 407, Curtin, ACT 2605 (☎ (06) 285 3713 or toll-free 1800 806 769), produces information fact sheets on accessible accommodation and recreation and sporting facilities for people with disabilities. ACROD (Australian Council for the Rehabilitation of the Disabled) offers similar services and has an office in Brisbane at 1 Park Rd, Milton (☎ (07) 3367 1605).

Also in Brisbane, the Office of Disability (a branch of Queensland's Department of Family Services) operates the Disability Information and Awareness Line (☎ (07) 3224 8031 or toll-free 1800 177 120, 9 am to 5 pm, Monday to Friday), a telephone information and referral service for all people with disabilities. Other organisations which could be contacted are the Independent Living Centre (☎ (07) 3394 7471) (equipment and care), the Community Disability Alliance (☎ (07) 3260 7133) (physical access to buildings) and the Paraplegic and Quadriplegic Association (☎ 008 810 513).

The Disability Information and Awareness Line (DIAL) (☎ 1800 177 120/TTY 2248021; fax 224 8037) can provide advice and guidance and can refer you to service providers.

For a full list of other useful organisations, look under 'Disabled Persons' Support Organisations' in the *Yellow Pages* telephone directory.

Airport access in Queensland is good with both Brisbane and Cairns airports having suitable facilities for disabled travellers. Qantas and Ansett cater for people with mobility difficulties and encourage them to travel.

Interstate travel on buses and trains is not yet a viable option for the wheelchair user. The Brisbane City Council's Disability Services Coordinator, GPO Box 1434, Brisbane, Qld 4001 (☎ (07) 3225 4416), has produced the excellent *Access Brisbane* brochure, with a range of information about buildings, services, restaurants, hotels and some accommodation in Queensland. They also produce a *Mobility Map* of the city centre, showing an accessible route, parking and toilets. Queensland Railways (☎ (07) 3235 2222), at 305 Edward St in the city, has produced the *City Train Accessibility Guide* brochure, showing accessible stations.

In Far North Queensland, the Cairns City Council has produced a *Cairns City Mobility Directory* – you can obtain a copy by writing to the Cairns Access Committee, PO Box 859, Cairns, Qld 4870.

---

movement and, at the same time, visit some of the more interesting areas of the country. Past volunteers have found themselves working in places such as Tasmania, Kakadu and Fraser Island.

Most projects are either for a weekend or a week and all food, transport and accommodation is supplied in return for a small contribution to help cover costs. Most travellers who take part in ATCV join a Banksia Package, which lasts six weeks and includes six different projects. The cost is $650, and further weeks can be added for $105.

Contact the head office (☎ (053) 33 1483 or toll-free on 008 032 501), at PO Box 423, Ballarat, Vic 3350, or the Queensland office at Old Government House (in the grounds of the Queensland University of Technology) in George St, Brisbane (☎ (07) 3210 0330).

Willing Workers on Organic Farms (WWOOF)

WWOOF is a relatively new organisation in Australia, although it is well established in other countries. The idea is that you do a few hours' work each day on a farm in return for bed and board. Some places have a minimum stay of a couple of days but many will take you for just a night. Some will let you stay for months if they like the look of you, and you can get involved with some interesting large-scale projects.

Becoming a WWOOFer is a great way to meet interesting people and to travel cheaply. There are about 200 WWOOF associates in Australia, mostly in Victoria, New South Wales and Queensland. As the name says, the farms are supposed to be organic but that isn't always so. Some places aren't even

The international wheelchair symbol for parking in allocated bays is generally recognised throughout Queensland. These car stickers are available from local councils upon production of a medical certificate.

Avis and Hertz offer hire cars with hand controls at no extra charge. The vehicles can be picked up at major airports; the agencies require 24-hours notice. Most of the taxi companies in the major cities and towns have modified vehicles which take wheelchairs. In Brisbane, contact Ascot Taxis (☎ (07) 3831 3000), Black & White Taxis (☎ (07) 3238 1000) or Yellow Cabs (☎ (07) 3391 0191). In Cairns, Black & White Taxis (☎ (070) 51 5333) has five vans with hydraulic lift access at the rear and one stretch cab.

Accommodation in Queensland is generally good, and most of the newer places must now include facilities for people with disabilities to comply with regulations. Contact tourist information centres for lists of accessible accommodation and tourist attractions – see Tourist Offices earlier in this chapter.

The RACQ's *Accommodation Guide* to Queensland includes symbols indicating accommodation which is 'Independently Accessible' and 'Accessible With Assistance'; however always check with the accommodation proprietors to ensure that facilities will be suitable for you. The guide is available from all RACQ offices. A number of the YHA's hostels have accessible accommodation; contact the YHA Membership & Travel Centre (☎ (07) 3236 1680), at 154 Roma St, Brisbane, Qld 4000.

An increasing number of accommodation places have wheelchair-accessible units. On the Gold Coast these include the *Labrador Holiday Units* (☎ (07) 5537 4766) and the Teneriffe Holiday Units (☎ (07) 5531 6575). Also on the Gold Coast, Movie World, Sea World and Currumbin Sanctuary encourage disabled visitors. In Cairns there is the *Tropicana Motel* (☎ (070) 51 1729).

Many tour operators can also cater for people with disabilities. In Cairns, for example, Great Adventures encourages disabled people to travel on their trips out to the Barrier Reef by offering a discount to the wheelchair traveller's companion, and will take you snorkelling to see the coral. The Kuranda Scenic Railway can accommodate wheelchair passengers and some of the tour operators to the rainforest areas of the Daintree and Cape Tribulation will take you on their vehicles, although they are not specifically accessible vehicles.

Sporting Wheelies has offices throughout Queensland, with information on accessible diving trips, sporting and recreation facilities. Contact their Brisbane office (☎ (07) 3252 5242), or for regional information, their Townsville office (☎ (077) 21 4881).

Bruce M Cameron

farms – you might help out at a pottery or do the books at a seed wholesaler. There are even a few commercial farms which exploit WWOOFers as cheap harvest labour, although these are quite rare. Whether they have a farm or just a vegie patch, most participants in the scheme are concerned to some extent with alternative lifestyles.

To join WWOOF (☎ (051) 55 0218) send $25 and a photocopy of your passport data page to WWOOF, Buchan, Vic 3885, and they'll send you a membership number and a booklet which lists WWOOF places all over Australia.

National Trust

The National Trust is dedicated to preserving historic buildings in all parts of Australia. The Trust actually owns a number of buildings throughout the country which are open to the public. Many other buildings are 'classified' by the National Trust to ensure their preservation.

The National Trust also produces some excellent literature, including a fine series of walking-tour guides to Brisbane and some of Queensland's more historic towns. These guides are often available from local tourist offices or from National Trust offices and are usually free whether you're a member of the National Trust or not.

Membership of the trust is well worth considering, however, because it entitles you to free entry to any National Trust property for your year of membership. The National Trust's Brisbane office is at Old Government House (in the grounds of the QUT) in George St (☎ (07) 3229 1788).

Australian & New Zealand Scientific Exploration Society (ANZSES)

ANZSES is a nonprofit organisation which undertakes scientific expeditions into wilderness areas of Australia. Each year over 100 volunteers are sent into the field, always under the guidance of an experienced leader.

The organisation offers volunteers the opportunity to participate in the collection of scientific data and the experience of living and working in remote areas of Australia generally not accessible to the average traveller.

Recent studies have included flora and fauna gathering west of Coober Pedy and in Witjira National Park (outback South Australia), Eungella National Park, Cedar Bay National Park, Fraser Island, Sturt National Park (NSW), south-west Tasmania and far-east Gippsland (Vic).

The ANZSES postal address and phone number is PO Box 174, Albert Park, Vic 3206 (☎ (03) 9690 5455).

BUSINESS HOURS

Business hours are from 9 am to 5 pm, Monday to Friday. Most shops in Queensland are open on weekdays from around 8.30 or 9 am until 5 pm and on Saturday mornings, and most of the larger towns and cities will have at least one night a week when the shops stay open until 9 pm – usually Thursday or Friday. In the larger centres and tourist resorts – notably Brisbane, the Gold and Sunshine Coasts and Cairns – shopping hours are more flexible. In these places, many larger stores stay open later and all day on Saturday, although on Sunday you still won't find many shops open anywhere.

Banks are open from 9.30 am to 4 pm on weekdays, and until 5 pm on Friday.

There are plenty of exceptions to these standard hours. Most of the larger cities have 24-hour convenience stores, and supermarkets are often open until quite late at night. On the other hand, in the more remote areas shopping hours are often more desultory – small-town general stores seem to set their hours according to demand, opening later during the tourist season and closing whenever they feel like it during the off season.

Pubs open their doors at 10 am and close at 10 or 11 pm, later on Friday and Saturday. Many pubs either close on Sunday or open for 'Sunday sessions' from perhaps noon to 2 pm and 5 pm to 8 pm. Most service stations are open daily from around 7 am until around 9 pm, but there are lots of 24-hour roadhouses along the major routes and in the larger centres. If you're desperate for petrol late at night, you'll find that in most towns at least one of the service stations has a night bell.

HOLIDAYS

The Christmas holiday season is part of the long summer school vacation and the time you are most likely to find accommodation booked out and long queues. Easter is also a busy holiday time, and there are three other shorter school holiday periods during the year. See the earlier When to Go section.

The main public holidays in Queensland are:

New Year's Day
1 January
Australia Day
26 January
Easter
Good Friday and Easter Saturday, Sunday and Monday (March or April)
Anzac Day
25 April
Labour Day
1st Monday in May
Queen's Birthday
2nd Monday in June
Christmas Day
25 December
Boxing Day
26 December

CULTURAL EVENTS

Queensland's major annual festivals and events include the following:

January to February
Australia Day – this national holiday, commemorating the arrival of the First Fleet in 1788, is observed on 26 January.
International Cricket – one-day internationals,

Test matches and Sheffield Shield games are played at the Brisbane Cricket Ground in Woolloongabba.

Australian Skins – this big-money golf tournament is played over two days at Laguna Quays Resort on the Whitsunday Coast.

March

IndyCarnival – a four-day festival centred around the Indy Car Grand Prix car race around the barricaded streets of Surfers Paradise.

Surf Life-Saving Events – several major life-saving championships are held on the Gold Coast over the summer months, including the classic Iron Man and Iron Woman events.

April

Anzac Day – This is a national public holiday, on 25 April, commemorating the landing of Anzac troops at Gallipoli in 1915. Memorial marches by the returned soldiers of both world wars and the veterans of Korea and Vietnam are held all over the country.

May to June

Brisbane Biennial International Music Festival – held biennially (odd years), this festival features Australian and international musicians and styles – jazz, rock, indigenous, classical and world music.

Queensland Day – this festival celebrates the achievement of Queensland's independence as a state on 6 June 1859.

July

Gold Coast International Marathon – this event attracts thousands of runners from around the country. A half-marathon and 10-km walk are also held.

August

Brisbane International Film Festival – the festival features films from Australia and the Asia-Pacific region.

Brisbane Ekka – held at the RNA Showgrounds in Brisbane, this is Queensland's largest agricultural show. Many other towns in Queensland also have agricultural shows at this time of year.

Mt Isa Rodeo – this is one of the country's richest rodeos.

September

Birdsville Races – the tiny town of Birdsville hosts the country's premier outback horse-racing event on the first weekend in September.

Warana Festival – Brisbane's annual arts festival is held over 10 days in late September.

Carnival of Flowers – Toowoomba's gardens are on display for eight days, with a flower show, a parade and a Mardi Gras.

October

Oktoberfests – Traditional beerfests with food, plenty of beer and live entertainment for all ages are held in several towns in Queensland.

Fun in the Sun – this is Cairns' main annual festival, and features a carnival, street parades and musical events.

November

Melbourne Cup – Australia's premier horse race is run in Melbourne on the first Tuesday in November. The whole country shuts down for three minutes or so while the race is run, and many country towns schedule race meetings to coincide with it – in Cape Tribulation, the locals race their horses along the beach.

December

Maleny-Woodford Folk Festival – this is one of the country's best folk festivals, featuring local and international musicians, arts and crafts markets and other entertainment and activities. It's held over five days between 28 December and New Year's Day.

These are just a few of the festivals held throughout Queensland. See the Festivals section of the Brisbane chapter for full details of festivities in the capital city. In addition to the events mentioned here, almost every community in Queensland has at least one annual festival of its own, and these are often unique and quirky celebrations. As you travel around Queensland, it's worth keeping your ear to the ground to find out about special events that might coincide with your visit. You might find anything from rodeos and bush race meetings to cooee championships and cockroach races – and these festivals are a great way to meet the locals. A couple of years ago a friend and I arrived in Karumba (a remote fishing town on the Gulf of Carpentaria) one Saturday night only to find that the annual Barra Ball, a wild celebration at the end of the barramundi fishing season, was in full swing at the local hall. I had such a good time, I ended up in the base hospital the next day – but that's another story...

POST & TELECOMMUNICATIONS
Postal Rates & Hours

Australia's postal services are relatively efficient but not too cheap. It costs 45c to send a standard letter or postcard within Australia, while aerograms cost 70c.

Air-mail letters/postcards cost 75c/70 to New Zealand, Singapore and Malaysia, 95c/90 to Hong Kong and India, $1.05/95c to the USA and Canada, and $1.20/1 to Europe and the UK.

Generally, post offices are open from 9 am to 5 pm Monday to Friday, although hours vary from place to place. You can often get stamps from newsagencies or from Australia Post shops, found in large cities, on Saturday mornings.

Receiving Mail

All post offices will hold mail for visitors and some city GPOs have very busy poste restantes. Cairns GPO poste restante, for example, can get quite hectic. You can also have mail sent to you at the American Express offices in big cities if you have an Amex card or carry Amex travellers' cheques.

Telephone

Australia's phone system was until recently owned and run by the government-owned Telecom (now Telstra), but these days the market has been deregulated with a second player, Optus, now offering an alternative in the major cities, but only for long-distance and international calls. The system is efficient and, equally important, easy to use. Local calls from public phones cost 40c for an unlimited amount of time. You can make local calls from gold or blue phones – often found in shops, hotels, bars, etc – and from payphone booths, which are often solar powered in the more remote parts of Queensland.

It's also possible to make long-distance (STD – Subscriber Trunk Dialling) calls from virtually any public phone. Many public phones accept the Telstra Phonecards, which are very convenient. The cards come in $5, $10, $20 and $50 denominations, and are available from retail outlets such as newsagents and pharmacies which display the Phonecard logo. You keep using the card until the value has been used in calls. Otherwise, have plenty of 10c, 20c, 50c and $1 coins, and be prepared to feed them through at a fair old rate.

Some public phones are set up to take only bank cash cards or credit cards, and these too are convenient, although you need to keep an eye on how much the call is costing as it can quickly mount up. The minimum charge for a call on one of these phones is $1.20.

Many businesses and some government departments operate a toll-free service, so no matter where you are ringing from around the country, it's a free call. These numbers have the prefix 1800 (or the old toll-free prefix 008) and we've listed them wherever possible throughout the book.

Phone numbers with the prefixes 018, 015 or 041 are mobile or car phones. Many companies, such as the airlines, have six-digit numbers beginning with 13, and these are charged at the rate of a local call. Often they'll be Australia-wide numbers, but sometimes they are applicable only to a specific STD district. Unfortunately there's no way of telling without actually ringing the number.

Other odd numbers you may come across are nine-digit numbers starting with 0055. These calls, usually recorded information services and the like, are provided by private companies, and your call is charged in multiples of 25c (40c from public phones) at a rate selected by the provider (Premium 70c per minute, Value 55c per minute, Budget 35c per minute).

Rates for STD calls are charged according to distance, and rates vary depending on when you call. In ascending order of cost, the three different price brackets are:

Economy – from 6 pm Saturday to 8 am Monday; and from 10 pm to 8 am every night
Night – from 6 to 10 pm Monday to Friday
Day – from 8 am to 6 pm Monday to Saturday

International Calls From most STD phones you can also make ISD (International Subscriber Dialling) calls. Dialling ISD you can get through to overseas numbers almost as quickly as you can access local numbers and if your call is brief it needn't cost very much.

All you do is dial 0011 for overseas, the country code (44 for Britain, 1 for the USA or Canada, 64 for New Zealand), the city code (171 or 181 for London, 212 for New

New Telephone Numbers

Australia is running out of telephone numbers! In response to this problem, the Australian Telecommunications Authority (AUSTEL) began to implement a new numbering plan in June 1994. Progressively over the next four to five years, every number in Australia will gain an extra one or two digits, so that all telephone numbers will eventually have eight digits.

AUSTEL is also merging the country's 54 STD area codes into four codes covering larger areas. When the changes are implemented, all of Queensland will have an 07 area code. Regional numbers which are currently six digits will have two extra digits added to their old number to make an eight digit number, and their new area code will be 07.

After a number is changed, there will be a six-month period when both the old and new numbers will be accessible, followed by a further three-month period when a recorded message will refer callers back to the *White Pages* information section.

The changes will not affect the cost of calls – STD calls will still be charged according to time and distance.

In Queensland, the first numbers were changed in mid-1995. Numbers in the Brisbane and Moreton Bay areas, which originally had the area code 07, retained the same area code but had a '3' added to the front of every seven-digit number. For example, (07) 123 4567 became (07) 3123 4567. Numbers in the Gold Coast area which had the area code 075, now have the area code 07, and '55' has been added to the front of their numbers. For example, (075) 98 7654 became (07) 5598 7654.

The next numbers to be changed in Queensland will be those with the 074 area code (February to April 1997), followed by 070 (April 1998), 079 (June 1998), 076 (June 1998 to February 1999), 071 and 077 (March 1999).

You can call AUSTEL's information hotline for further information (☎ 1800 888 888 between 8 am and midnight daily), or look in the *White Pages* directory for a complete update. If you're having trouble getting through to a number, call directory assistance on ☎ 013 (for a local number) or ☎ 0175 (for a number elsewhere in Australia) – these calls are free.

In this book, all phone numbers for the Brisbane metropolitan area, Moreton Bay and the Gold Coast are the new numbers, as these areas had already been changed in 1995. All other numbers given in this book are the pre-change numbers. ■

York, etc), and then the telephone number. And have a Phonecard, credit card or plenty of coins to hand.

To use Optus rather than Telstra (which may or may not be cheaper – the two are constantly trying to undercut one another), dial 1 or 1456 before the ISD country code or STD area code. The prefix differs according to preferential dialling: you dial 1456 to access Optus from a Telstra phone; those who have not yet subscribed through a ballot dial 1; and Optus subscribers dial normally (0011 etc).

Optus is only available from private phones in certain areas.

A standard Telstra call to the USA or Britain costs $2.50 a minute (\$2 off peak); New Zealand is $2.10 a minute (\$1.40 off peak). Off-peak times, if available, vary depending on the destination – see the front of any telephone book for more details. Sunday is often the cheapest day to ring. With the competition offered by Optus, Telstra often has discount specials to various destinations, although many of these are only available from private phones.

Country Direct Country Direct is a service which gives travellers in Australia direct access to operators in 42 countries, to make collect or credit card calls. For a full list of the countries hooked into this system, check any local telephone book. They include:

Canada (☎ 1800 881 150)
France (☎ 1800 881 330)
Germany (☎ 1800 881 490)
Japan (☎ 1800 881 810)
New Zealand (☎ 1800 881 640)
the UK (☎ 1800 881 440 for BT and 1800 881 417 for Mercury)
the USA (☎ 1800 881 011 for AT&T, 1800 881 212 for IDB WorldCom, 1800 881 100 for MCI and 1800 881 877 for Sprint).

Operator Assistance Some useful numbers include:

Emergency (free call)
    ☎ 000 from any phone in the country

Directory assistance (free call)
  ☎ 013 for a number in the area you are in
  ☎ 0175 for a number elsewhere in Australia;
  ☎ 0103 for an overseas number
Reverse Charges – Domestic
  ☎ 0176 from a payphone;
  ☎ 011 from a private phone
Reverse Charges – International
  ☎ 0107 from a payphone;
  ☎ 0101 from a private phone

Interpreter Service If you have trouble communicating in English, a free translating and interpreting service is available over the telephone in 23 different languages. To access it, call ☎ 13 1450 from anywhere in Australia, 24 hours a day.

Fax
You can send faxes from any post office, either to another fax or to a postal address. Faxes to another fax machine anywhere in Australia cost $4 for the first page and $1 for each subsequent page. Faxes to postal addresses within Australia cost the same, and will be delivered by the postal service, usually the next day. If your fax/post items are urgent, they can be delivered on the same day for $8 if you send them before 1 pm; or within two hours (by courier) for $16 if you send them before 3 pm.

Overseas faxes cost $10 for the first page and $4 for each subsequent page. The same fax/post system is used for overseas postal addresses (this system has replaced international telegrams). International fax/post items costs $16 for each delivery.

As well as post offices, you can also send faxes from many local businesses such as secretarial services and photocopying shops, and these places are usually much cheaper than the post offices.

TIME
Australia is divided into three time zones. Queensland is on Eastern Standard Time (as are New South Wales, Victoria and Tasmania), which is 10 hours ahead of UTC (Greenwich Mean Time).

The other time zones in Australia are Central Standard Time (Northern Territory, South Australia), which is 9½ hours ahead of GMT/UTC or half an hour behind Eastern Standard Time; and Western Standard Time (Western Australia), which is eight hours ahead of GMT/UTC or two hours behind Eastern Standard Time.

At noon in Queensland it's 2 am in London, 9 am in Bangkok, 2 pm in Auckland, 3 am in Rome, 6 pm the previous day in Los Angeles and 9 pm the previous day in New York.

Lamentably, Queensland is on Eastern Standard Time all year, while the rest of Australia sensibly switches to daylight saving time over the summer months. With the exception of Western Australia all the other states buy themselves an extra hour of summer daylight by putting their clocks forward one hour from the last Sunday in October until the last Sunday in March.

ELECTRICITY
Voltage is 220-240 V and the plugs are three-pin, but not the same as British three-pin plugs. Users of electric shavers or hair dryers should note that, apart from in fancy hotels, it's difficult to find converters to take either US flat two-pin plugs or the European round two-pin plugs. Adaptors for British plugs can be found in good hardware shops, chemists and travel agents. You can easily bend the US plugs to a slight angle to make them fit.

WEIGHTS & MEASURES
Australia went metric in the early '70s. Petrol and milk are sold by the litre, apples and potatoes by the kg, distance is measured by the metre or km, and speed limits are in km per hour (km/h). Nevertheless, lots of people still refer to the old imperial units, especially older folks and people from country areas. You're still more likely to hear someone described as six foot tall rather than 183 cm, tyre pressures are given in pounds per square inch, fuel consumption is referred to as miles per gallon, and boat lengths are given in feet etc.

For those who need help with metric there's a conversion table at the back of this book.

BOOKS

In almost any bookshop in the country you'll find a section devoted to Australiana with books on every Australian subject you care to mention. If you want a souvenir of Australia, such as a photographic record, there are numerous coffee-table books available. There are also plenty of glossy picture books specifically on Queensland and its various regions – the reef, the outback, the islands, the national parks. A range of these are available from bookshops, souvenir shops and most post offices. Bookshops are listed in the information section under individual towns and cities.

Apart from bookshops, it's also worth trying places like the Wilderness Society shops and Government Printing Office shops. In Brisbane, the QNP&WS's Naturally Queensland office sells a good range of books, posters and calenders with environmental themes, as does the Billabong Bookshop.

Most books are published in different editions by different publishers in different countries. As a result, a book might be a hardcover rarity in one country while it's readily available in paperback in another. Fortunately, bookshops and libraries search by title or author, so your local bookshop or library is best placed to advise you on the availability of the following recommendations.

Aborigines

The Australian Aborigines by Kenneth Maddock is a good cultural summary. The award-winning *Triumph of the Nomads*, by Geoffrey Blainey, chronicles the life of Australia's original inhabitants, and convincingly demolishes the myth that the Aborigines were 'primitive' people trapped on a hostile continent. They were, in fact, extremely successful in adapting to and overcoming the difficulties presented by the climate and resources (or seeming lack of them) – the book's an excellent read.

For a sympathetic historical account of what's happened to the original Australians since Whites arrived, read *Aboriginal Aus-*

Much has been written about Aborigines and their relationship to the land

tralians by Richard Broome. *A Change of Ownership*, by Mildred Kirk, covers similar ground to Broome's book, but does so more concisely, focusing on the land rights movement and its historical background.

The Other Side of the Frontier, by Henry Reynolds, uses historical records to give a vivid account of an Aboriginal view of the arrival and takeover of Australia by Europeans. His *With the White People* identifies the essential Aboriginal contributions to the survival of the early White settlers. *My Place*, Sally Morgan's prizewinning autobiography, traces her discovery of her Aboriginal heritage. *The Fringe Dwellers* by Nene Gare describes just what it's like to be an Aborigine growing up in a White-dominated society.

Don't Take Your Love to Town by Ruby Langford and *My People* by Oodgeroo Noonuccal (Kath Walker) are also recommended reading for people interested in Aborigines' experience.

The late Bruce Chatwin's book *The Songlines* tells of his experiences among central Australian Aborigines and makes more sense of the Dreamtime, sacred sites, sacred songs and the traditional Aboriginal way of life than 10 learned tomes put together. Along the way it also delves into the origins of humankind and throws in some pithy anecdotes about modern Australia.

The Queensland Tourist & Travel Corporation produces an excellent 30-page brochure called *A Guide to Experiencing Aboriginal and Torres Strait Islander Culture*, which covers culture and art, and lists galleries and shops, festivals and tour operators. It's free and available from most regional information centres, or phone the QT&TC on ☎ (07) 3833 5400.

Australian History

For a good introduction to Australian history, read *A Short History of Australia*, a most accessible and informative general history by the late Manning Clark, the much-loved Aussie historian. Robert Hughes' bestselling *The Fatal Shore* is a colourful and detailed account of the history of transportation of convicts. Geoffrey Blainey's *The Tyranny of Distance* is a captivating narrative of White settlement.

Finding Australia, by Russel Ward, traces the story of the early days from the first Aboriginal arrivals up to 1821. It's strong on Aborigines, women and the full story of foreign exploration, not just Captain Cook's role. There's lots of fascinating detail, including information about the appalling crooks who ran the early colony for long periods, and it's intended to be the first of a series.

The Exploration of Australia, by Michael Cannon, is coffee-table book in size, presentation and price, but it's a fascinating reference book about the gradual European uncovering of the continent.

Cooper's Creek, by Alan Moorehead, is a classic account of the ill-fated Burke and Wills expedition which dramatises the horrors and hardships faced by the early explorers.

The Fatal Impact, also by Moorehead, begins with the voyages of James Cook, regarded as one of the greatest and most humane explorers, and tells the tragic story of the European impact on Australia, Tahiti and Antarctica in the years that followed Captain Cook's great voyages of discovery. It details how good intentions and the economic imperatives of the time led to disaster, corruption and annihilation.

To get an idea of life on a Kimberley cattle station last century, *Kings in Grass Castles* and *Sore in the Saddle*, both by Dame Mary Durack, are well worth getting hold of. Other books which give an insight into the pioneering days in the outback include *Packhorse & Waterhole* by Gordon Buchanan, son of legendary drover Nat Buchanan who was responsible for opening up large areas of the Northern Territory; *The Big Run*, a history of the huge Victoria River Downs cattle station in the Northern Territory; and *The Cattle King* by Ion Idriess, which details the life of the remarkable Sir Sidney Kidman, the man who set up a chain of stations in the outback early this century.

Queensland History

If you're specifically interested in the history of Queensland, Ross Fitzgerald's *A History of Queensland* is a comprehensive, well-researched and sometimes controversial study. It was published in two volumes in the early 1980s – *From the Dreaming to 1915: A History of Queensland*, and *A History of Queensland: From 1915 to the 1980s*, and it can be difficult to find copies in bookshops, although most Australian libraries have it.

River of Gold, by Hector Holthouse, is a 'factional' account of the wild days of Cooktown and the Palmer River gold rush in the 1870s. As he explains in his author's note, Holthouse has used a little artistic licence to fill in the gaps in his research, but the result is a fascinating read and gives an impressive insight into the period.

Glenville Pike is a local writer who has produced more than 20 books based on Queensland's colourful history. They include *Queensland Frontier* (tales of the explorers and pioneers who opened up Queensland), *The Men Who Blazed the Track* (another account of the Palmer River gold rush) and *Queen of the North* (a history of Cooktown). His books are widely available in bookshops throughout Queensland.

Queensland Politics

For an insight into the decline and fall of Queensland's National Party, pick up a copy of award-winning journalist Evan Whitton's *The Hillbilly Dictator*. Subtitled 'How Democracy and the Rule of Law in Queensland were subverted, and injustice and corruption elevated to the commonplace', Whitton's book is a fascinating study of the 1987-89 Fitzgerald Inquiry and the 250 trials for police and political corruption that followed.

Fiction

You don't need to worry about bringing a few good novels from home for your trip to Australia; there's plenty of excellent recent Australian literature. See the Literature section of the Facts about Queensland chapter for some suggestions.

Travel Guides

Burnum Burnum's Aboriginal Australia is subtitled 'a traveller's guide'. If you want to explore Australia from the Aboriginal point of view, this large and lavish hardback is the book for you.

The RACQ publishes a comprehensive *Accommodation Guide* to Queensland which lists caravan parks, motels, resorts and hotels – it lists their facilities, prices and rates them out of five stars. It also lists some (but not many) pubs and hostels. The guide is available from all RACQ offices and costs $2 for members and $8 for nonmembers.

In conjunction with the QT&TC, the RACQ also publishes a series of motoring holiday guides to Queensland. There are four guides in the series, covering South-East Queensland, Central Queensland, North Queensland and the Matilda Highway. These large format paperbacks are well produced and feature colour photos, touring maps, suggested excursions and sights and attractions, as well as some extracts from the *Accommodation Guide* and travelling tips.

They cost $12.50 for members and $15 for nonmembers and are available from RACQ offices and some bookshops.

The Queensland Experience by Jan Bowen (about $25) covers Queensland region by region, offering historical backgrounds, recommendations and personal anecdotes. It could be a handy primer to read before you go – it lacks hard information but is quite descriptive.

Queensland Getaways by Warwick Randall (about $15) describes more than 50 interesting holiday escapes throughout Queensland, from mountain guesthouses and island resorts to outback cattle stations and five-star hotels.

The Australian Bed & Breakfast Book (about $14) lists B&B places throughout Australia, although bear in mind that they have all written their own reviews.

For trips into the outback in your own vehicle, it's worth investing in a copy of Lonely Planet's award-winning *Outback Australia*. There are a number of other books about vehicle preparation and driving in the outback, including Brian Sheedy's *Outback on a Budget*, *Outback on your Doorstep* and *The Centre on a Budget*, and Peter & Kim Wherrett's *Explore Australia by Four-Wheel Drive*.

There is a cornucopia of books published which deal with the Great Barrier Reef. One of the best souvenirs of the reef is the *Reader's Digest Book of the Great Barrier Reef* – it's colourful, expensive and nearly as big as the Barrier Reef itself. Lonely Planet's *Islands of Australia's Great Barrier Reef* covers the reef, the islands, diving and accommodation in greater detail than the book in your hand.

For travel elsewhere in Australia, Lonely Planet publishes *Australia – a travel survival kit*, as well as guidebooks to the states of Victoria, New South Wales and Western Australia, as well as city guides to Sydney and Melbourne. Other state guides are forthcoming.

See the Activities section later in this section for guides to specific sports and activities.

Children's Books
Some Australian classics to look out for are *The Magic Pudding* by Norman Lindsay, *Snugglepot & Cuddlepie* by May Gibbs and *Blinky Bill* by Dorothy Wall.

MAPS
The RACQ publishes a good series of regional road maps which show almost every driveable road in the state – these are free to RACQ members, and to members of affiliated motoring organisations. There are also plenty of road maps published by the various oil companies – Shell, BP, Mobil etc, and these are available from service stations. Commercially available city street guides, such as the Gregory's Brisbane street directory and UBD's *Queensland Cities and Towns* street directory, are also useful.

Queensland's Department of Lands produces the Sunmap Tourist Maps which, together with commercial maps by companies including Hema, Gregory's and UBD, are available from most newsagents and many bookshops in Queensland. World Wide Maps & Guides (☎ (07) 3221 4330) (formerly Hema Maps), on the corner of George and Adelaide Sts in Brisbane, has one of the best selections of maps in the state.

Tourist information centres also have good maps available, usually free, although often pretty inaccurate. These include city centre maps, historical walking guides and regional touring maps, usually with the area's major tourist attractions highlighted.

For bushwalking and other activities which require large-scale maps, the topographic sheets put out by the Australian Surveying & Land Information Group (AUSLIG) are the ones to get. Many of the more popular sheets are available over the counter at shops which sell specialist bushwalking gear and outdoor equipment. AUSLIG also has special-interest maps showing various types of land use, population densities and Aboriginal land. For more information, or a catalogue, contact AUSLIG (☎ (07) 3233 7600 or toll-free on 1800 800 173) at Level 6, 313 Adelaide St, Brisbane, Qld 4000.

MEDIA
Newspapers & Magazines
The *Courier Mail*, Brisbane's major daily newspaper, is available almost everywhere in Queensland. It's a reasonably serious but somewhat parochial broadsheet.

The Australian, a Murdoch-owned paper and the country's only national daily, is also widely available. It makes better reading for non-Queenslanders, with good national and international news coverage, although it is definitely ultra-conservative. The *Weekend Australian* includes several excellent review sections.

Many of the larger towns and cities produce their own papers, some daily and some weekly. Major regional dailies include the *Cairns Post*, the *Townsville Bulletin* and the *Gold Coast Bulletin*. The *Sunday Mail* is a bulky but lightweight broadsheet (a somewhat oxymoronic, but accurate, description) that appears on Sunday.

Weekly magazines include an Australian edition of *Time* and the *Bulletin*, a conservative and long-running Australian news magazine which includes a condensed version of *Newsweek*. International papers such as the *International Herald Tribune*, the *European* and the *Guardian* are available from larger newsagencies, particularly in the more heavily touristed areas.

Radio
The Australian Broadcasting Corporation (ABC) is government-funded, commercial-free and by far the largest broadcaster in the country. There are two main services, Radio National, which can be heard just about everywhere (sometimes on AM and sometimes via FM relays), and the regional/metropolitan services, which are generally only available around major centres.

Fine Music is the ABC's classical music station and Triple J is its 'youth network'. Triple J has recently gone national and can be heard in most of the larger centres in Queensland. It specialises in alternative music and young people's issues and has some interesting talk shows.

Outside Brisbane, which has more than 15 AM and FM radio stations, you'll usually be able to pick up one or more of the ABC stations, a local commercial station or two and often a local public station which will broadcast a lot of announcements about interesting local events in addition to a pretty diverse range of music and news. Some of the ABC's programmes are well worth finding. In particular, the morning AM and evening PM programmes are the best radio news services. *The Traveller's Guide to ABC Radio* is a handy brochure which will help you find the respective stations wherever you are – it's available from ABC centres, bookshops and some information centres.

In summer, huge slabs of the ABC's airtime are taken up with broadcasts of international cricket matches, and in the winter Australia's overseas Test matches are often broadcast, especially the Ashes series from England. The regional ABC stations broadcast horseracing from around the country on Saturday afternoons.

TV

There are five main TV networks in Queensland: the government-funded ABC, the multi-cultural and multi-lingual SBS (Special Broadcasting Service, UHF) and the three commercial networks, channels 7, 9 and 10. All of these can be received in Brisbane. Most regional areas receive the ABC and at least one commercial network, but in the more remote areas you might only be able to pick up the ABC. SBS is only available in Brisbane, the Gold and Sunshine coasts, the Darling Downs, Townsville, Cairns, Mt Isa and Longreach.

The commercial networks have fairly similar programming formats, with the usual diet of news and current affairs, sport, soap operas and sit-coms, and an overdose of American talk shows during the day. The ABC produces some excellent current affairs shows and documentaries as well as showing lots of sport, slightly heavier news and sit-coms (mostly British). The ABC also makes some excellent comedy and drama programmes. SBS is fairly eclectic, but screens

some of the best programmes on TV, including an excellent international news service (in English) nightly at 6.30 pm, serious current affairs programmes, interesting documentaries and great foreign films (with English subtitles where necessary).

FILM & PHOTOGRAPHY

If you come to Australia via Hong Kong or Singapore it's worth buying film there, but otherwise Australian film prices are not too far out of line with those of the rest of the Western world. Including developing, 36-exposure Kodachrome 64 or Fujichrome 100 slide film costs around $25, but with a little shopping around you can find it for around $20 – even less if you buy it in quantity.

There are plenty of camera shops in all the big cities and standards of camera service are high. Developing standards are also high, with many places offering one-hour developing of print film. While print film is available from just about anywhere (a roll of 36-exposure Kodak or Fuji print film should cost under $10, not including processing), slide film can be harder to find. Camera shops in the larger cities are usually the best bet for Kodachrome or Fujichrome.

For the best results, try to take most of your photos early in the morning and late in the afternoon when the light is softer. As the sun gets higher, colours appear washed out. You must also allow for the intensity of reflected light when taking shots on the Barrier Reef or at other coastal locations – a polarising filter will help eliminate much of this glare, and also saturate colours. Remember that film can be damaged by heat, so allow for temperature extremes and do your best to keep film as cool as possible, particularly after exposure. Other film and camera hazards are dust in the outback and humidity in the tropical regions of the Far North.

Cheap disposable underwater cameras are widely available at most beach towns and resorts. These are OK for snapshots when snorkelling or shallow diving and can produce reasonable results in good conditions, but without a flash the colours will be washed out. These cameras won't work below about five metres because of the water pressure. If you're serious about underwater photography, good underwater cameras with flash unit can be hired from many of the dive shops along the coast.

As in any country, politeness goes a long way when taking photographs; ask before taking pictures of people. Note that many Aborigines do not like to have their photographs taken, even from a distance.

HEALTH

Australia is a remarkably healthy country considering that such a large portion of it lies in the tropics. Tropical diseases such as malaria and yellow fever are unknown, diseases of insanitation such as cholera and typhoid are unheard of, and even some animal diseases such as rabies and foot-and-mouth disease have yet to be recorded.

So long as you haven't visited an infected country in the past 14 days (aircraft refuelling stops do not count) no vaccinations are required for entry. There are, however, a few routine vaccinations that are recommended worldwide whether you're travelling or not, and it's always worth checking whether your tetanus booster is still up to date.

Medical care is 1st class and only moderately expensive. A typical visit to the doctor costs around $35. If you have an immediate health problem, contact the casualty section at the nearest public hospital or a medical clinic.

Visitors from the UK, New Zealand, Malta, Italy, Sweden and the Netherlands have reciprocal health rights in Australia, and can register at any Medicare office.

Travel Insurance

Ambulance services in Australia are self-funding (ie they're not free) and can be frightfully expensive, so you'd be wise to take out travel insurance. Make sure the policy specifically includes ambulance, helicopter rescue and a flight home for you and anyone you're travelling with, should your condition warrant it. Check the fine print: some policies exclude 'dangerous activities' such as scuba diving, motorcycling and even trekking. If such activities are on your agenda, you don't want that policy.

Medical Kit

Doctors and hospitals are few and far between in the more remote reaches of Queensland. If you're heading off the beaten track, at least one person in your party should have a sound knowledge of first-aid treatment, and in any case you'll need a first-aid handbook and a basic medical kit. Some of the items that should be included are:

Aspirin or Panadol – for pain or fever
Antihistamine (such as Benadryl) – useful as a decongestant for colds, allergies, to ease the itch from insect bites or stings or to help prevent motion sickness. Antihistamines may cause sedation and interact with alcohol so care should be taken when using them
Kaolin preparation (Pepto-Bismol), Imodium or Lomotil – for stomach upsets
Antiseptic such as Betadine, which comes as impregnated swabs or ointment, and an antibiotic powder or similar 'dry' spray – for cuts and grazes
Calamine lotion or old-fashioned Tiger Balm – to ease irritation from bites or stings
Eye drops
Sterile gauze bandages (50 and 75 mm)
Triangular bandages – to support limbs and hold dressings in place
Assortment of other bandages and Band-aids – for minor injuries
Adhesive tape, cotton wool, tissues
Elastic or crêpe bandages – for sprains and snake bite
Scissors, tweezers, safety pins and a thermometer (note that mercury thermometers are prohibited by airlines)
Insect repellent, sunscreen, chapstick, perhaps water purification tablets
Pencil and note pad

Optional items include:

Cold and flu tablets
Mylanta tablets, or similar, for indigestion
Ear drops (Aquaear if you're heading for the tropics)
Rubber-pointed eye probe, eye wash
Vinegar for jellyfish stings
Temporary tooth-filling mix to replace fillings, loose caps
Toothache drops
Burn cream
Cream/ointment for bruises and swelling due to injury
Strepsils or similar
Methylated spirits

Airsplint – for broken limbs, or immobilising limbs after snake bite

St John Ambulance Australia has a selection of first-aid kits for car drivers, motorcyclists and bushwalkers, ranging in price from $45 to $85. They include a first-aid handbook and are well worth considering as a base kit to which you can add some of the above items. They're available at St John offices and at the motoring organisations.

Don't forget any medication you're already taking, and include prescriptions with the generic rather than the brand name (which may not be available locally).

Health Precautions

Travellers from the northern hemisphere need to be aware of the intensity of the sun in Australia. Those ultraviolet rays can have you burnt to a crisp even on an overcast day, so if in doubt wear protective cream, a wide-brimmed hat and loose-fitting cotton clothing that gives maximum skin coverage. Loose clothes allow the air to circulate around your skin and you'll find cotton to be much more comfortable and cooler than synthetics. Smother all exposed areas of skin with a sunscreen (protection factor 15 or higher). Australia has the world's highest incidence of skin cancer, a fact directly connected to exposure to the sun. Be careful.

Good sunglasses are a must, but make sure they're treated to absorb ultraviolet radiation – if not, they'll actually do more harm than good by dilating your pupils and making it easier for ultraviolet light to damage the retina.

If you wear glasses or contact lenses, take a spare pair and your prescription. A Medic Alert tag is worth having if your medical condition is not always easily recognisable (heart trouble, diabetes, asthma, allergic reactions to antibiotics etc).

The contraceptive pill is available on prescription only, so a visit to a doctor is necessary. Doctors are listed in the *Yellow Pages* phone book or you can visit the outpatients section of a public hospital. Condoms are available from chemists, many convenience stores and often from vending machines in the toilets of pubs.

Basic Rules

Heat You can expect the weather to be hot throughout Queensland between October and April, and travellers from cool climates may feel uncomfortable even in winter. 'Hot' is a relative term depending on what you're used to. The sensible thing to do on a hot day is to avoid the sun between mid-morning and mid-afternoon. Infants and elderly people are most at risk from heat exhaustion and heatstroke (see below).

Water People who first arrive in a hot climate may not feel thirsty when they should; the body and 'thirst mechanism' often need a few days to adjust. The rule of thumb is that an active adult should drink at least four litres of water per day in warm weather, more when walking or cycling. Use the colour of your urine as a guide: if it's clear you're probably drinking enough but if it's dark you need to drink more. Remember that body moisture will evaporate in the dry air with no indication that you're sweating.

Tap water is safe to drink in the settled parts of Queensland, but in the outback it may be bore water that's unfit for human consumption – check with the locals. Bore water is often OK even if it tastes unpleasant, but children's stomachs in particular may have trouble coping with the high mineral content. (Note how soap often won't lather in outback showers.) There's nothing you can do short of actually distilling the water – or carrying your own supply of drinking water. Outback residents normally save valuable rainwater for drinking and use bore water for other purposes.

Always beware of water from creeks, rivers or lakes, as it may have been infected by cattle or wildlife. The surest way to disinfect water is to boil it thoroughly for 10 minutes. Simple filtering won't remove all dangerous organisms, so if you cannot boil water, treat it chemically. Chlorine tablets (Puritabs, Steritabs or other brand names) will kill many but not all pathogens. Iodine is very effective and is available in tablet form, such as Potable Aqua, but follow the directions carefully and remember that too much iodine can be harmful.

If you can't find tablets, tincture of iodine (2%) can be used. Two drops per litre or quart of clear water is the recommended dosage, and the treated water should be left to stand for 30 minutes before drinking. Flavoured powder will disguise the taste of treated water and is a good idea if you're travelling with children.

Salt Sweating will also lead to loss of salt. Excessive salt loss manifests itself in headaches, dizziness and muscle cramps. Salt tablets are not a good idea as a preventative, but will quickly restore the balance if you show symptoms of salt loss. Add salt to your food to prevent this happening – a teaspoon a day should normally be enough in hot climates. If you're on a low-salt diet, check with your physician before you leave.

Food If you don't vary your diet, are travelling hard and fast and therefore missing meals, or simply lose your appetite, you can soon start to lose weight and place your health at risk, just as you would at home.

If you rely on fast foods dished out by roadhouses and local takeaway shops, you'll get plenty of fats and carbohydrates but little else. Remember that overcooked food loses much of its nutritional value. If your diet isn't well balanced, it's a good idea to take vitamin and iron pills. Fruit and vegetables are a good source of vitamins and they're more readily available than you'd expect.

Health Problems

Prickly Heat Prickly heat is an itchy rash caused by excessive perspiration trapped under the skin. It usually strikes people who have just arrived in a hot climate and whose pores have not yet opened sufficiently to cope with greater sweating. Keeping cool, bathing often, using a mild talcum powder or even resorting to air-conditioning may help until you acclimatise.

Heat Exhaustion Dehydration or salt deficiency can cause heat exhaustion. Take time to acclimatise to high temperatures and make sure you get sufficient (nonalcoholic) liquids. Think of your salt level too. Wear loose clothing and a broad-brimmed hat.

Anhydrotic heat exhaustion, caused by an inability to sweat, is quite rare. Unlike the other forms of heat exhaustion it is likely to strike people who have been in a hot climate for some time, rather than newcomers.

Heatstroke This serious, and sometimes fatal, condition can occur if the body's heat-regulating mechanism breaks down and the body temperature rises to dangerous levels. Long, continuous periods of exposure to high temperatures can leave you vulnerable to heatstroke. You should avoid excessive alcohol or strenuous activity when you first arrive in a hot climate.

The symptoms are feeling unwell, not sweating very much or at all and a high body temperature ($39°C$ to $41°C$). When sweating has ceased, the skin becomes flushed and red. Severe, throbbing headaches and lack of co-ordination will also occur, and the sufferer may become confused or aggressive. Eventually the victim will become delirious or convulse. Hospitalisation is essential, but meanwhile get the patient out of the sun, remove their clothing, cover them with a wet sheet or towel and fan them continually.

Fungal Infections Hot-weather fungal infections are most likely to occur on the scalp, between the toes or fingers (athlete's foot), in the groin (jock itch or crotch rot) and on the body (ringworm). You get ringworm (a fungal infection, not a worm) from infected animals or by walking on damp areas, like shower floors.

To prevent fungal infections, wear loose, comfortable clothes, avoid artificial fibres, wash frequently and dry carefully. Always wear plastic sandals or thongs in showers you can't completely trust. If you do get an infection, wash the infected area daily with a disinfectant or medicated soap and water, and rinse and dry well. Apply an antifungal powder or cream like the widely available Tinaderm. Try to expose the infected area to air or sunlight as much as possible, wash all towels and underwear in hot water and change them often.

Motion Sickness Eating lightly before and during a trip will reduce the chances of motion sickness. If you are prone to motion sickness, try to find a place that minimises disturbance – near the wing in aircraft, near the centre in cars and buses. Fresh air and looking at a steady reference point like the horizon usually help, whereas reading or cigarette smoke don't. Commercial anti-motion-sickness preparations, which can cause drowsiness, have to be taken before the trip commences; when you're feeling sick it's too late. Ginger is a natural preventative and is available in capsule form.

Diarrhoea Two major causes of diarrhoea are drinking mineralised bore water and stopping or camping at places that have been frequented by travellers with a poor understanding of hygiene. Knowing where the flies have been before they crawl over your face and food is enough to make you find somewhere else to camp. It's always a good idea to carry plenty of safe drinking water in the car, particularly if you have little children in tow – adults can usually cope better with changes in water. Various forms of gastroenteritis sometimes occur, and one of the more common ways by which it is passed around is on contaminated money.

Worms These parasites are common in outback animals. The steak that you buy at the butcher's or get served in the roadhouse will be perfectly safe, but kangaroo or wild goat that hasn't been checked by the proper authorities can be risky, especially if undercooked.

Worms may also be present on unwashed vegetables, and you can pick them up through your skin by walking in bare feet.

Infestations may not show up for some time, and though they are generally not serious, if left untreated they can cause

severe health problems. A stool test is necessary to pinpoint the problem, and medication is often available over the counter.

Tetanus This potentially fatal disease is difficult to treat but is preventable with immunisation. Tetanus occurs when a wound becomes infected by a germ which lives in the faeces of animals or people; so clean all cuts, punctures, or animal bites. Tetanus is also known as lockjaw, and the first symptom may be discomfort in swallowing, or stiffening of the jaw and neck; this is followed by painful convulsions of the jaw and the whole body.

Sexually Transmitted Diseases Abstinence is the only 100% preventative against STDs, but using condoms is also effective (though not against pubic lice known as crabs).

Gonorrhoea and syphilis are the most common of these diseases; sores, blisters or rashes around the genitals, discharges or pain when urinating are common symptoms. Symptoms may be less marked or not observed at all in women. Syphilis symptoms eventually disappear completely but the disease continues and can cause severe problems in later years. The treatment of gonorrhoea and syphilis is by antibiotics.

Unfortunately there is no cure for herpes and there is also currently no cure for HIV/AIDS. Remember that it is impossible to detect the HIV-positive status of an otherwise healthy-looking person without a blood test.

There are numerous other sexually transmitted diseases, for most of which effective treatment is available. If you suspect anything is wrong, go to the nearest public hospital or medical clinic.

Cuts & Scratches Skin punctures can easily become infected in hot climates and may be difficult to heal. Treat any cut with an antiseptic solution and Mercurochrome. Where possible, avoid bandages and Band-aids, which can keep wounds wet. Coral cuts are notoriously slow to heal, as the coral injects a weak venom into the wound. Avoid coral cuts by wearing shoes when walking on reefs.

Women's Health

Poor diet and even contraceptive pills can lead to vaginal infections when travelling in hot climates. Maintaining good personal hygiene, and wearing skirts or loose-fitting trousers and cotton underwear will help to prevent infections.

Yeast infections (thrush), characterised by a rash, itch and discharge, can be treated with a vinegar or even lemon-juice douche or with yoghurt. Nystatin suppositories are the usual medical prescription. Trichomonas is a more serious infection; symptoms are a discharge and a burning sensation when urinating. If a vinegar-water douche is not effective, medical attention should be sought. Flagyl is the prescribed drug. In both cases, male sexual partners must also be treated.

Some women experience irregular periods when travelling because of the upset in routine. Don't forget to take time zones into account if you're on the pill. If you run into intestinal problems, the pill may not be absorbed. Ask your physician about these matters before you go.

WOMEN TRAVELLERS

Queensland is generally a safe place for women travellers, although it's probably best to avoid walking alone late at night in any of the major cities. Sexual harassment is rare, although the Aussie male culture does have its sexist elements. Don't tolerate any harassment or discrimination.

Female hitchhikers should exercise care at all times. See the section on Hitching in the Getting Around chapter.

GAY & LESBIAN TRAVELLERS

Historically, Queensland had a poor reputation when it came to acceptance of gays and lesbians, but the situation has changed significantly since the fall of the right-wing National Party government in 1990. Previously repressive attitudes and laws have been relaxed, and homosexuality was decriminalised in Queensland in 1991.

Brisbane has an increasingly lively gay and lesbian scene centred around the inner-city suburbs of Spring Hill and Fortitude Valley, with quite a few nightclubs, pubs and a couple of guesthouses. See the Brisbane chapter for more information on gay and lesbian culture there. There are also gay and lesbian-only accommodation places in some of the more popular tourist centres including Cairns, the Gold Coast and Noosa Heads. Elsewhere in Queensland, however, there's still a strong streak of homophobia and violence against homosexuals is not unknown.

Publications such as Brisbane's *Brother Sister* magazine list contact points, accommodation places and other gay and lesbian groups throughout Queensland.

DANGERS & ANNOYANCES
Theft

Queensland is a relatively safe place to visit, but it's better to play it safe and take reasonable precautions, especially in some of the larger centres. Unfortunately, Cairns has a bad reputation for theft, with more than a few travellers having been robbed at hostels there.

Most accommodation places have somewhere they can store your valuables, and it's always worth taking advantage of this service. Don't leave hotel rooms or cars unlocked, and don't leave your money, wallets, purses or cameras unattended or in full view through car windows, for instance.

If you are unlucky enough to have something stolen, immediately report all details to the nearest police station. If your credit cards, cash card or travellers' cheques have been taken, notify your bank or the relevant company immediately (most have 24-hour 'lost or stolen' numbers listed under 'Banks' or 'Credit Card Organisations' in the *Yellow Pages* telephone directory).

Swimming

It seems unnecessary to mention it, but don't ever go swimming if you have been drinking alcohol. Swimming after a heavy meal is also unwise.

GREAT BARRIER REEF MARINE PARK AUTHORITY

MARK ARMSTRONG

PAUL STEEL

DAVID SHERMAN

GREAT BARRIER REEF MARINE PARK AUTHORITY

A	B
	C
D	E

A: Goanna, Cape Kimberley
B: Humpback whale, Hervey Bay
C: Saltwater crocodile, check those teeth

D: King Parrot, Lamington National Park
E: Star fish *(pentagonaster dubeni)*

MARK ARMSTRONG

TONY WHEELER

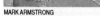

DAVID SHERMAN

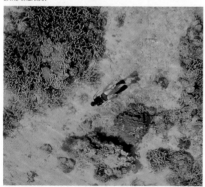
GREAT BARRIER REEF MARINE PARK AUTHORITY

RICHARD I'ANSON

A	B
C	
D	E

A: Aboriginal rock art, Jowalbinna Station Cape York Peninsula
B: Opheus Island sunset
C: Rainforest detail

D: Diving through the reef
E: Boats & Pelicans at sunrise, Tin Can Bay

Surf Beaches There are surf beaches all along the coast of southern Queensland as far north as Fraser Island. Many of these, especially along the Gold Coast and Sunshine Coast, are patrolled by surf life-saving clubs, and many people need to be rescued from the surf every year. Patrolled beaches are indicated by a pair of yellow and red flags. If possible, always swim between the flags. If you get into trouble in the water, raise one arm above your head to catch the attention of the lifesavers.

If you happen to get caught in a rip and are being taken out to sea, the first (and hardest) thing to do is not panic. Raise your arm until you have been spotted, and then swim parallel to the shore – *don't* try to swim back against the rip, you'll only tire yourself.

Sharks Shark attacks are extremely rare in Australia, especially along the warm waters of the Great Barrier Reef where the sharks are very well fed.

The closest you're likely to come to a shark is in the local fish & chip shop, unless you're scuba diving. Tiger sharks and whaler sharks are found on the reef but generally on drop-offs from the outer reef. They are a negligible danger.

Box Jellyfish The potentially deadly box jellyfish, also known as the sea wasp or 'stinger', occurs in Queensland's coastal waters north of Rockhampton during the summer months. The danger period varies from year to year and place to place, but is generally from around November to April, and swimming is definitely not advisable during these times. These creatures are usually found close to the coast, especially around river mouths – they aren't often found further out on the reef or islands, although they can drift out to some of the islands that are closer to the mainland.

The jellyfish's stinging tentacles spread several metres away from the sea wasp's body; by the time you see it you're likely to have been stung. If someone is stung, they are likely to run out of the sea screaming and collapse on the beach, with weals on their body as though they've been whipped. They may stop breathing. Douse the stings with vinegar (available on many beaches or from nearby houses), do not try to remove the tentacles from the skin, and treat as for snake bite. If there's a first-aider present, they may have to apply artificial respiration until the ambulance gets there.

Some coastal resorts erect 'stinger nets' which provide small areas for safe swim-

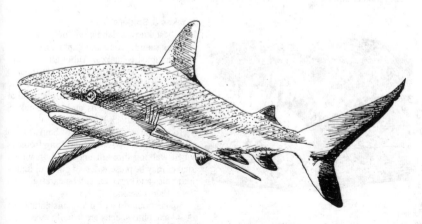

Whaler Shark – delicious with salt and vinegar

ming, but elsewhere, stay out of the sea when the sea wasps are around. If you're in doubt, check with a local, and if you're still in doubt, don't swim – it's not worth the risk.

Crocodiles In north Queensland, saltwater crocodiles can be a real danger and have killed a number of people (travellers and locals). They are found in river estuaries and large rivers, sometimes a long way inland, so before diving into that inviting, cool water find out from the locals whether it's croc-free. See the section on crocodiles in the Fauna section of the Facts about Queensland chapter for more details.

Coral Cuts Coral can be extremely sharp, and you can cut yourself by merely brushing against the stuff. Even a small cut can be very painful and take a long, long time to heal. The best solution is not to get cut in the first place – avoid touching coral. Wash any coral cuts thoroughly and douse them with a good antiseptic.

Fish Poisoning Ciguatera poison is a poison which seems to accumulate in certain types of fish due to the consumption of certain types of algae by grazing fish. The poison seems to concentrate the further up the food chain it goes so it isn't the original algae-eating fish which poses the danger, it's the fish which eats the fish which eats the algae-eating fish! The danger is remote but erratic and recovery, although usually complete, is very slow. Chinaman-fish, red bass, large rock cods and moray eels have all been implicated.

Don't consider dining on pufferfish unless you're a Japanese *fugu* fan.

Other Marine Dangers There are quite a few other potential hazards lurking in the waters of the Barrier Reef, although the dangers are slight and in most cases it's simply a matter of not picking up things which are best left alone.

Butterfly cod and stonefish both have a series of poisonous spines down their back, which can inflict a serious and even fatal wound. Blue-ringed octopus and Barrier Reef cone shells can also be fatal, so don't pick them up. If someone is stung, apply a pressure bandage, monitor breathing carefully and conduct mouth-to-mouth resuscitation if breathing stops.

Also watch out for the scorpion fish, which has venomous spines; stingrays, which can inflict a nasty wound with their barbed tails; and sea snakes, which are potentially deadly, although they are more curious than aggressive.

Snakes & Spiders

The best known danger in the Australian outback, and the one that captures visitors' imaginations, is snakes. Although there are many venomous snakes there are few that are aggressive, and unless you have the bad fortune to stand on one it's unlikely that you'll be bitten. Taipans and tiger snakes, however, will attack if alarmed.

To minimise your chances of being bitten always wear boots, socks and long trousers when walking through undergrowth where snakes may be present. Don't put your hands into holes and crevices, and be careful when collecting firewood.

Snake bites do not cause instantaneous death and antivenenes are usually available. Keep the victim calm and still, wrap the

Moray eels inhabit the Great Barrier Reef

Funnel-web spider   Redback spider

bitten limb tightly, as you would for a sprained ankle, and then attach a splint to immobilise it. Then seek medical help, if possible with the dead snake for identification.

Don't attempt to catch the snake if there is even a remote possibility of being bitten again. Tourniquets and sucking out the poison are now comprehensively discredited.

Australia has a couple of nasty spiders too, including the funnel-web, the redback and the white-tail, so it's best not to play with any spider. Funnel-web spiders are mostly found in New South Wales and their bite is treated in the same way as snake bite. For redback bites apply ice and seek medical attention.

Insects
Flies In the cities the flies are not too bad; it's in the country that it starts getting out of hand, and the further 'out' you get the worse the flies seem to be.

In central Queensland the flies start to come out with the warmer spring weather (late August) and last through until winter. They are such a nuisance that virtually every shop sells the Genuine Aussie Fly Net (made in Korea), which is rather like a string onion bag but is very effective. It's either that or the 'Great Australian Wave' to keep them away.

Repellents such as Aerogard and Rid go some way to deterring the little bastards.

Mosquitoes Mozzies can be a problem, especially in the warmer tropical and subtropical areas. Fortunately malaria is not present in Australia, although its counterpart dengue fever is a significant danger in tropical areas.

Dengue fever is a non-fatal but incurable disease transmitted by the *Aedes aegypti* mosquito. The symptoms are fairly indistinct – typically a high fever, malaise or a rash will be present. There is no immunisation or tablets that prevent the disease, so the only form of prevention is to avoid being bitten by mosquitoes.

Mosquitoes are most active at dusk, and also at night, but there are some precautions you can take to avoid being mauled. The first is to use a good insect repellent such as Rid. Slap it on all over – during the day, at dusk and at night before you go to bed. Wearing long, loose clothing will at least reduce the amount of flesh a mozzie has to choose from. it's also worth considering investing in a mosquito net or a packet of mosquito coils, which will burn all night and keep most rooms mozzie-free. Alternatively, you'll rarely be bitten if you sleep under a reasonably fast ceiling fan.

Ticks & Leeches The common bush-tick (found in the forest and scrub country along the eastern coast of Australia) can be dangerous if left lodged in the skin, as the toxin the tick excretes can cause paralysis and sometimes death. Check your body for lumps every night if you're walking in tick-infested areas. The tick should be removed by dousing it with methylated spirits or kerosene and levering it out, but make sure you remove it intact. Remember to check children and dogs for ticks after a walk in the bush.

Leeches are common, and while they will suck your blood they are not dangerous and are easily removed by the application of salt or heat.

On the Road

Cows and kangaroos can be a real hazard to the driver. A collision with one will badly damage your car and probably kill the animal. Unfortunately, other drivers are even more dangerous, particularly those who drink. Australia has its share of fatal road accidents, particularly in the countryside, so don't drink and drive and please take care. The dangers posed by stray animals and drunks are particularly enhanced at night, so it's best to avoid travelling after dark. See the Getting Around chapter for more on driving hazards.

Bushfires

Bushfires happen every year in Queensland. Don't be the mug who starts one. In hot, dry, windy weather, be extremely careful with any naked flame – no cigarette butts out of car windows, please. On a day of Total Fire Ban (listen to the radio, watch the billboards on country roads or front pages of daily newspapers), it is forbidden even to use a camping stove in the open. The locals will not be amused if they catch you breaking this particular law; they'll happily dob you in, and the penalties are severe.

If you're unfortunate enough to find yourself driving through a bushfire, stay inside your car and try to park off the road in an open space, away from trees, until the danger's past. Lie on the floor under the dashboard, covering yourself with a wool blanket if possible. The front of the fire should pass quickly, and you will be much safer than if you were out in the open. It is very important to cover up with a wool blanket or wear protective clothing, as it has been proved that heat radiation is the big killer in bushfire situations.

Bushwalkers should take local advice before setting out. On a day of Total Fire Ban, don't go – delay your trip until the weather has changed. Chances are that it will be so unpleasantly hot and windy, you'll be better off anyway in an air-conditioned pub sipping a cool beer.

If you're out in the bush and you see smoke, even at a great distance, take it seriously. Go to the nearest open space, downhill if possible. A forested ridge is the most dangerous place to be. Bushfires move very quickly and change direction with the wind.

EMERGENCY

In the case of a life-threatening situation, dial ☎ 000. This call is free from any phone and the operator will connect you with the police, ambulance or fire brigade.

For other telephone crisis and personal counselling services (such as sexual assault, poisons information or alcohol and drug problems), check the front pages of the local telephone book.

Medical Emergency

In an emergency, call an ambulance (☎ 000) or go to the casualty ward of the nearest public hospital. Foreigners (except those from the UK, New Zealand, Malta, Italy, Sweden and the Netherlands, who have reciprocal health rights in Australia) are charged at least $160 for a visit to casualty, and you'll be billed to your home address.

OUTBACK SURVIVAL

If you're planning to travel in remote parts of Queensland, be sure to prepare adequately for your trip by finding out such things as what the temperatures are likely to be when you visit the area, whether drinking water is available, which are the best maps of the area and what sort of vehicle is required in the area. Expert advice never goes astray either – the police and national park rangers are good sources of information in the outback.

Always carry plenty of water – around 20 litres for each person is considered a reasonable amount, but store it in more than one container just in case. Before heading off to a remote area, notify someone responsible of what you are doing and where you are going, and always remember to check in again once you have reached your destination – an unnecessary search and rescue operation will be very expensive for you.

If your vehicle breaks down, the general rule is *never* wander off and leave the vehicle – a car is much easier to spot from the air than a person. To help aerial searchers, you can lay out a large TVU (the recognised ground-to-air signal for help) in any material that contrasts with the ground.

A minimum of three people is recommended for remote-area bushwalking – if someone is injured, one person can wait with them while the other goes for help.

WORK

If you come to Australia on a 12-month 'working holiday' visa you can officially only work for three out of those 12 months, but it is absolutely *verboten* to be working on a regular tourist visa. To receive wages in Australia you must be in possession of a Tax File Number, issued by the Taxation Department. Forms are available from post offices and you'll need to show your passport and visa.

The best prospects for casual work include labouring, bar work, waiting on tables or washing dishes, nanny work, fruit picking, telephone sales and collecting for charities.

With a national unemployment rate of 10%, it is now much more difficult to find a job than it once was – legal or otherwise. Gone are the days when you could rock in to practically any town or city and find some sort of paid casual work.

Many travellers who have budgeted on finding work return home early, simply because the work they hoped to find just isn't available. If you are coming to Australia with the intention of working, make sure you have enough funds to cover you for your stay, or have a contingency plan if the work is not forthcoming. Having said that, it *is* still possible to find short-term work, it's just that the opportunities are far fewer than in the past.

The Commonwealth Employment Service (CES) has over 300 offices around the country, and the staff usually have a good idea of what's available where. Try the classified section of the daily papers under Situations Vacant, especially on Saturday and Wednesday.

The various backpackers' magazines, newspapers and hostels are good information sources – some local employers even advertise on their notice boards.

Fruit and vegetable picking is probably the most common source of employment for travellers in Queensland. While this sort of work is often readily available and quite a few travellers make good money at it, it is usually physically exhausting, back-breaking work, with long hours and short breaks. The heat and humidity also take their toll, and lots of people only last a couple of days out in the fields.

Crops in Queensland include mangoes, bananas, pineapples, tomatoes, pears, apples, stone fruits and lychees. Harvest times vary for the different crops, but there is usually some type of picking work available year-round.

There are numerous 'workers' hostels' which have been set up in Queensland to cater specifically to local farmers who need itinerant labour – ie backpackers. Most of these places are quite reputable and well run, although there are a few places with less than favourable reputations, so a little caution is needed. If you think you're being exploited, get in touch with a CES office.

For details of workers' hostels, see the accommodation listings for Stanthorpe, Bundaberg, Bowen, Innisfail, Childers and Tully.

ACTIVITIES

There are plenty of activities you can take part in while travelling around the state. You can go scuba diving and snorkelling on the Great Barrier Reef, the world's largest underwater theme park. Bushwalking is cheap and you can do it anywhere – there are many fantastic walks in the various national and state parks. If you're interested in surfing, you'll find some great beaches and surf in southern Queensland. You can go horse riding in many places – from the coastal beaches, rainforests and mountains of the hinterland to the wilds of the outback. You can cycle all around Queensland; for the athletic there are long, challenging routes and for the not-so-masochistic there are plenty of great day trips.

Bushwalking

This is a popular activity in Queensland year-round. There are bushwalking clubs in the state and several useful guidebooks. Lonely Planet's *Bushwalking in Australia* describes 23 walks of different lengths and difficulty in various parts of the country, including three in Queensland.

50 Walks; Coffs Harbour & Gold Coast Hinterland by Tyrone Thomas is a good reference book for bushwalkers which includes maps and walking track notes to some of the best walks in Queensland's south-east corner – places like Tamborine Mountain, Springbrook National Park, Binna Burra and O'Reilly's, and Cunningham's Gap.

Tyrone Thomas has also written *50 Walks in North Queensland*, which covers the area from Cape Hillsborough (near Mackay) up to Cape Tribulation and inland as far as Chillagoe. Most of these walks are beach walks or through the rainforest areas of the World-Heritage-listed Wet Tropics areas.

100 Walks in South Queensland by Tony Groom and Trevor Gynther covers a wide range of walks around Brisbane, the Gold and Sunshine coasts and Moreton Bay. It's out of date and out of print now, but is still available in a few bookshops.

Bushwalks in the Toowoomba Region by N McKilligan and I Savage is a small but very comprehensive guide to the best walks in this area, and includes mud maps, track notes and notes on natural history. *Bushwalking in South-East Queensland* (Bushpeople Publications, $23), is a large-format paper back guide with colour photos and comprehensive walking-track notes to the south-east.

One of the best ways to find out about local bushwalking areas is to contact a local bushwalking club, such as the Brisbane Bushwalkers Club (☎ (07) 3856 4050), at 2 Alderley Ave, Alderley, or look in the *Yellow Pages* under 'Clubs – Bushwalking'. Outdoor shops such as Mountain Designs and Paddy Pallin are also good sources of information.

National parks and state forests are some of the best places for walking. Almost every national park either has walking trails or offers wilderness walking. You can get full information on walking in national parks and state forests from their respective offices. There are excellent bushwalking possibilities in many parts of the state, including on several of the larger coastal islands such as Fraser and Hinchinbrook. National parks on the mainland favoured by bushwalkers include Lamington in the McPherson Ranges, Main Range in the Darling Downs, Cooloola just north of the Sunshine Coast, the Carnarvon Gorge in central Queensland, Eungella just west of Mackay and Bellenden Ker south of Cairns, which contains Queensland's highest peak, Mt Bartle Frere (1657 metres). See the individual sections for details.

Diving & Snorkelling

The Great Barrier Reef provides some of the world's best diving and there's ample opportunity to learn and pursue this activity. The Queensland coast is probably the world's cheapest place to learn to scuba dive in tropical water – a five-day course leading to a recognised open-water certificate usually costs somewhere between $250 and $450 and you almost always do a good part of your learning out on the Barrier Reef itself. These courses are now very popular and almost every town along the coast has one or more

Turtles are often spotted by divers on the
Great Barrier Reef

diving schools. The three most popular
places are Airlie Beach, Cairns and Townsville.

Important factors to consider when choosing a course include the school's reputation,
the relative amounts of time spent on
pool/classroom training and out in the ocean,
and whether your open-water time is spent
on the outer reef as opposed to reefs around
islands or even just off the mainland. The
outer reef is usually more spectacular. Normally you have to show you can tread water
for 10 minutes and swim 200 metres before
you can start a course. Some schools also
require a medical which will usually cost
extra.

For certified divers, trips and equipment
hire are available just about everywhere. You
usually have to show evidence of qualifica-
tions. You can snorkel just about everywhere
too. There are coral reefs off some mainland
beaches and around several of the islands,
and many day trips out to the Barrier Reef
provide snorkelling gear free.

During the wet season, usually January to
March, floods can wash a lot of mud out into
the ocean and visibility for divers and
snorkellers is sometimes affected.

Bicycling

There are possibilities for some great rides
in Queensland. See the Getting Around
chapter for information on long-distance
cycling. Available from most bookshops,

Pedalling Around Southern Queensland, by
Julia Thorn (about \$15), has tour notes and
mud maps for 25 bike rides in and around
Brisbane, the Gold Coast and the
Toowoomba region.

There are companies that offer cycling
tours in various places, including Cairns,
Townsville and Brisbane. It might also be
worth contacting one of the local cycling
clubs like the Brisbane Bicycle Touring
Association (☎ (07) 3358 4590), at 25
Abbott St, New Farm, Brisbane 4000. For
other areas, look under 'Clubs – Bicycle' in
the *Yellow Pages*.

White-Water Rafting, Sea-Kayaking &
Canoeing

The Tully and North Johnstone rivers
between Townsville and Cairns are the big
ones for white-water rafting. You can do day
trips for about \$100 to \$120, or longer expeditions. See the Cairns and Mission Beach
sections for details.

Sea-kayaking has become popular in
recent years, and there are numerous operations along the coast that offer paddling
expeditions through the calm Barrier Reef
waters, often from the mainland out to off-
shore islands. See the Cairns, Mission
Beach, Cape Tribulation, and Hinchinbrook
Island sections for details.

Coastal Queensland is full of waterways
and lakes so there's no shortage of canoeing
territory. You can rent canoes or join canoe
tours in several places – among them Noosa,
Townsville and Cairns.

Surfing

From a surfer's point of view, Queensland's
Great Barrier Reef is one of nature's most
tragic mistakes – a 2000-km-long breakwater! The reef protects almost the entire
Queensland coast from ocean swells, and
about the only waves you'll see along the
coast are those whipped up by passing boats
or strong winds. Many a surfer has driven
along the coast past all those picture-perfect
points and coves thinking, 'if only...'.

Thankfully, the reef finishes down near
Gladstone, and there are some great surf

beaches in southern Queensland. The Gold Coast has some of the best of these, including a classic right-hand point break at Burleigh Heads, although you have to be prepared for crowds. Near Brisbane, North Stradbroke Island also has good surf beaches, as does Moreton Island. The Sunshine Coast also has lots of good beach breaks and a few rocky points – at Noosa Heads, Tea Tree Bay in the national park is a favourite with long-board riders, especially during the cyclone swells of summer. Further north, Fraser Island often has good surf along its east coast, although not too many people surf here due to the large numbers of sharks in the water. Queensland's most northern surf beaches are at Agnes Water and the town of Seventeen Seventy, just south of Gladstone.

You can hire second-hand boards from almost any surf shop along the coast. For beginners, though, boogie-boarding or body-surfing are probably better propositions – standing up on a surfboard is much harder than it looks, and when it's crowded things can get pretty aggressive out in the water. If you're keen, there are a couple of learn-to-surf schools in Surfers Paradise and at Noosa Heads.

Surfing Australia's East Coast by Aussie surf star Nat Young is a slim, cheap, comprehensive guide to the best breaks from Victoria to Fraser Island. He's also written the *Surfing & Sailboard Guide to Australia* which covers the whole country. Surfing enthusiasts can also look for the expensive coffee-table book *Atlas of Australian Surfing*, by Mark Warren.

Swimming

The very word 'Queensland' conjures up visions of magnificent beaches – endless stretches of sun-bleached sand with turquoise-blue waters lapping at the shore, backed by palm trees swaying gently in the breeze; idyllic little coves where you can shed all your clothes and worries, then swim out to explore a garden of underwater coral; fabulous surf-beaches with perfectly formed waves, enticingly held erect by a light off-shore breeze...

Indeed, Queensland has all of these and more, but don't expect to find perfect (or even decent) beaches everywhere. The good surf beaches are restricted to southern Queensland, and once you get north of Gladstone, many of the mainland beaches are spoiled by mudflats and mangroves. Even the sandy beaches on the mainland are often quite shallow and less than idyllic, and in the summer months you can't swim in the coastal waters of north Queensland due to box jellyfish (see the earlier Dangers & Annoyances section). The Barrier Reef is undeniably one of nature's most magnificent creations, but one of the drawbacks is that it acts as a breakwater, creating thousands of km of still water along the coast.

Fortunately, there are hundreds of islands dotted along the reef, ranging from tropical coral cays to continental islands. This is where you'll find all those great beaches – and half of the fun is getting out to them and discovering them.

Inland, there are many rivers and lakes where you can cool off, and almost every country town has its own Olympic-sized swimming pool.

Sailing & Other Water Sports

Sailing enthusiasts will also find plenty of opportunities to practise their sport and many places which hire boats, both along the coast and inland. Airlie Beach and the Whitsunday Islands are probably the biggest centres and you can find almost any type of boating or sailing you want there. Waterskiing is often available too. There are water sports hire places in all the coastal resorts and on most of the islands, from where you can hire catamarans, sailboards, jet skis, canoes, paddle boats and snorkelling gear.

Hang-Gliding, Paragliding & Gliding

Hang-gliding is popular at many places along the Queensland coast, including the Lamington National Park in the south-east corner and Eungella National Park near Mackay. You can take tandem flights, or enrol in a learn-to-fly course. Paragliding outfits can be found at many beach resorts.

There are more than a dozen gliding clubs throughout the state, many of which will take you up to experience this pure form of flying. Contact the Queensland Soaring Association on ☎ (07) 3378 0294 (after hours) to find out where the nearest clubs are.

Bungy Jumping & Skydiving
There are plenty of opportunities for adrenalin-junkies to get a hit in Queensland. Bungy jumping is big in places like Surfers Paradise, Airlie Beach and Cairns. The tandem skydiving craze has swept Queensland in recent years, and for around $250 you can do a tandem jump from around 10,000 feet. Surfers Paradise, Cairns, Mission Beach, Hamilton Island, Airlie Beach and Great Keppel Island all offer tandem jumps.

Horse Riding & Trekking
Horse riding is another activity available all along the coast, from one-hour strolls to gallops along the beach to overnight (or longer) treks. Check with backpacker hostels and tourist offices to find out what's available.

Rockclimbing & Abseiling
Believe it or not, Brisbane is a good place to learn rockclimbing. There are a couple of indoor rockclimbing centres, and you can graduate to The Cliffs, a series of 18-metre rock faces along the southern banks of the Brisbane River. A number of operators offer climbing and abseiling instruction in Brisbane and other popular climbing areas such as the Glass House Mountains – climbing and outdoor shops are good sources of info. Look under Outdoor Adventure Activities in the *Yellow Pages*.

Fishing
As you'll soon realise, fishing is incredibly popular in Queensland in all its forms – surf fishing in places like North Stradbroke Island and Fraser Island, line fishing in the clear tropical waters of the Barrier Reef, big-game fishing at places like Hamilton, Hayman and Lizard islands, and barramundi fishing in the coastal and estuarine waters of Far North Queensland. The 'barra' is Australia's premier native sport fish, partly because of its tremendous fighting qualities and partly because it's delicious! Note that the minimum size for barra is 50 cm in Queensland – there are also bag limits, and the barra season is closed from 1 November to 31 January. There are quite a few commercial operators offering sports-fishing trips in the Far North.

The waters of the Barrier Reef are teeming with colourful fish, and the coral trout is the most prized catch and makes sensational eating. Not all of the reef's fish are edible, however, so make sure you have properly identified your catch before you toss it in the pan. See the Dangers & Annoyances section earlier. The reef is also divided into different zones which impose certain restrictions on what you can and can't do in each area. Zoning maps are available from most tourist offices along the coast, or from offices of the Great Barrier Reef Marine Park Authority or the National Parks & Wildlife Service.

Made famous by the likes of actor Lee Marvin, Lizard Island in the Far North is Queensland's big-game fishing capital. The heavy-tackle season runs from September to December, and the annual Black Marlin Classic on Halloween night (31 October) is a major attraction. Hamilton Island also hosts the Billfish Bonanza each December. There are also innumerable good freshwater and estuarine fishing spots around the state.

Fossicking
There are lots of good fossicking areas in Queensland – see the *Gem Fields* brochure, published by the Queensland Government Travel Centre. It tells you the places where you have a fair chance of finding gems and the types you'll find. You'll need a 'miners right' before you set out.

Most of Queensland's gemfields are in fairly remote areas. Visits to these areas can be adventurous, great fun and maybe even profitable, and even if you don't strike it lucky you're bound to meet some fascinating characters. Queensland's main fossicking areas are the gemfields around Sapphire and

Rubyvale (about 300 km inland from Rockhampton), the Yowah Opalfields (deep in the southern outback, 150 km west of Cunnamulla) and the gemfields around Mt Surprise and Georgetown (about 300 km south-west of Cairns) – see those sections for more detailed information.

HIGHLIGHTS

Mention Queensland and most people immediately think of endless sunshine and blue skies, the wonders of the Great Barrier Reef, island resorts and beaches, and the rainforests of North Queensland. Well, there's all of that, and much, much more...

Taking it from the top, the **Cape York Peninsula** is one of Australia's last great adventure trips. All the roads through the Cape are dirt and there are numerous river crossings, so you need a 4WD to get all the way to the top. The diversity of landscapes on the Cape is amazing. It's one of the last frontiers, a rugged place of crocodiles and barramundi, remote national parks, rainforested mountains, tropical savannah, Aboriginal rock art and lonely roadhouses – and without doubt, one of Queensland's greatest experiences.

The **Gulf Savannah**, in the north-western corner of Queensland, is also largely the domain of the adventure traveller. It's a remote, hot, tough and sparsely populated region, and most visitors come for the fishing (sensational!) or are 4WD travellers on their way somewhere. The Gulf also has two of Queensland's most spectacular natural attractions – the **Lawn Hill National Park**, an oasis-like river gorge in the north-west; and the **Undara Lava Tubes**, a series of ancient and enormous volcanic tubes about 260 km south-west of Cairns.

Far North Queensland is a relatively small area, but it's jam-packed with tourist drawcards. Centred around **Cairns**, this area has it all – the reef and islands, the rainforests, **Cape Tribulation** and the **Daintree**, the **Atherton Tablelands** – and you don't have to travel far inland to sample the outback. North of Cairns, **Port Douglas** is one of the

state's most fashionable resort towns. Further north again is **Cooktown**, on the fringe of Cape York – and a great place to visit if you want to sample what North Queensland was like pre-tourism.

On the **North Coast** between Cairns and Townsville, **Hinchinbrook Island**, is a majestic island national park and unspoiled wilderness. The Thorsborne Trail, a 32-km walking track along the island's east coast, takes a memorable three to five days. Townsville has the **Great Barrier Reef Wonderland** with its excellent aquarium, and inland from Townsville you can visit the old **goldmining centres** of Charters Towers and Ravenswood. There are some great little national parks along the coast between Townsville and Mission Beach, including Mt Spec and Jourama Falls. Bedarra Island, off shore from Mission Beach, is perhaps the best and most exclusive of the **island resorts** along the coast, and if you can afford the $500-plus a night, don't miss it.

The lush green continental islands of the **Whitsundays** contrast idyllically with the deep blue-green waters which surround them, and the Whitsundays is one of the best areas for pleasure boating and diving. There are some great resorts out on the islands, ranging from simple backpackers' cabins on Hook Island to the indulgence of five-star luxury on Hayman Island. **Eungella National Park**, inland from Mackay, is one of the few places where you can see platypus in the wild – it's also a great spot for bushwalks, camping and hang-gliding.

On the **Capricorn Coast**, north-east of Rockhampton, **Great Keppel Island** is one of the most attractive and popular islands along the coast. There's a resort owned by Qantas, plus a few more affordable options, and Keppel's beaches are just great. Further south are the **Southern Reef Islands** – Lady Elliot and Heron islands offer some of the best diving along the reef. Inland from Rockhampton is the spectacular **Blackdown Tableland National Park**, and the rugged gemfields around Sapphire and Rubyvale are also well worth a visit. A couple of hundred km south of Sapphire is the **Carnarvon**

National Park, another oasis-like gorge and a wonderful place for bushwalking.

Back on the coast is **Fraser Island**, the world's largest sand island and one of the state's true gems. Fraser is simply stunning. Between August and mid-October, you can join one of the many **whale-watching** tours which operate out of nearby **Hervey Bay**.

The south-east corner of Queensland is the state's most densely populated area, and a popular one for tourism. **Brisbane** is often overlooked by travellers, but it's a surprisingly cosmopolitan city with a lively inner-city area, and there's an amazing diversity of attractions within a couple of hours' drive of the state capital. One hour north of Brisbane is the **Sunshine Coast**, with a string of busy resort towns along the coast (including trendy Noosa Heads), and an attractive hinterland packed with surprises.

The **Gold Coast** is the most heavily developed tourist area in Queensland – it might not be to everybody's taste, but its beaches, restaurants, nightclubs and theme parks attract millions of visitors every year. A short drive inland from the Gold Coast are the wonderful **Springbrook and Lamington national parks** – great places for bushwalking, camping and generally communing with nature. The **Darling Downs**, south-west of Brisbane, also has some great national parks. The area around Stanthorpe is one of the only places in Queensland where it really does get cold – they even celebrate winter by holding the Brass Monkey festival! Stanthorpe is also the centre of the state's only winery district. Warwick and Toowoomba are both attractive cities, with plenty of historic buildings.

Queensland's vast **outback** offers a completely different experience to the hedonistic pleasures of the coast. The outback towns all have their own particular character – places like **Birdsville**, with its famous pub and annual race meeting; Longreach, with the **Stockman's Hall of Fame**; Mt Isa, with its enormous mine brooding darkly over the town; and the dozens of little places like Stonehenge, where you can meet the entire population while you're sitting on a bar

stool. And between the towns? Endless wide open spaces, the monotony of the lonely roads, huge road trains spewing trails of dust, slow-moving cattle and sheep, graceful emus and brolgas...

ACCOMMODATION

Queensland is very well equipped with a wide range of accommodation alternatives, with everything from backpackers' hostels and caravan parks to five-star hotels and island resorts.

A typical town of a few thousand people will have a basic motel at around $40/45 for singles/doubles, an old town centre hotel with rooms (shared bathrooms) at, say, $15/25, and a caravan park – probably with camp sites for around $10 and on-site vans or cabins for $25 to $30 for two. If the town is on anything like a main road or is bigger, it'll probably have several of each. If there's a group of you, the rates for three or four people in a room are always worth checking. Often there are larger 'family' rooms or units with two bedrooms.

The RACQ produces a comprehensive accommodation directory to Queensland – see the earlier Travel Guides section for details.

Camping & Caravanning

Camping in the bush is for many people one of the highlights of a visit to Australia. In many state and national parks camping is free, although the more popular places charge a fee – usually $3 per person. In lots of places in the outback or the bush, you won't even need a tent – swags are the way to go, and nights spent around a campfire under the stars are unforgettable.

You can also pitch your tent in one of the hundreds of caravan parks which are scattered across Queensland. The news on these places is both good and bad. The good news is that Queensland has plenty of caravan parks and they are quite cheap, with tent sites costing around $10. The bad news is that they cater predominantly for caravanners, and usually have no cooking facilities or communal dining areas for tenters – you just get a tent site and toilet, shower and laundry facilities. There are plenty of exceptions, however, and many of the better caravan parks now have swimming pools, shops and campers' kitchens.

Caravan parks are generally on the outskirts of towns, which means they can be a long way from the centre of big towns. Brisbane is the worst city in Australia in this respect because council regulations actually forbid tents within a 22-km radius of the centre. Although there are some sites in Brisbane within that radius, they're strictly for caravans – no campers allowed.

Many caravan parks also have on-site vans which you can rent for the night. These give you the comfort of a caravan without the inconvenience of actually towing one of the damned things. On-site cabins are also widely available, and these are more like a small self-contained unit. They usually have one bedroom, or at least an area which can be screened off from the rest of the unit – just the thing if you have small kids. Cabins also have the advantage of having their own bathroom and toilet, although this is sometimes an optional extra. They are also much less cramped than a caravan, and the price difference is not always that great – say $25 to $30 for an on-site van, $30 to $40 for a cabin.

Mobile Homes

The advantages of travelling in a Kombi, campervan or station wagon are that it's cheap – you don't have to pay for a bed – and you can sleep wherever you happen to be, without having to worry about booking a room. Queensland is one of the only states that allows people to sleep in roadside stops, and these can be found along many of the major highways.

The main disadvantage is trying to find a shower in the morning! One option is to head for a caravan park – they charge between $1 and $3 for a hot shower, although many parks refuse to allow non-guests to use their facilities. Other options are roadhouses,

gymnasiums, squash courts and town swimming pools. Along the coast, some towns have public toilet blocks with coin-operated hot showers.

Youth Hostels

Australia has a very active Youth Hostel Association (YHA). YHA hostels provide basic accommodation, usually in small dormitories or bunk rooms although more and more of them are providing twin rooms for couples. The nightly charges are rock bottom – usually between $10 and $14 a night in a dorm, around $25 for a single room and $30 for a twin or double.

With the increased competition from the proliferation of backpackers' hostels, almost all YHA hostels have done away with the old fetishes for curfews and doing chores, but still retain segregated dorms. Many even take non-YHA members, although there may be a small 'temporary membership' charge. To become a full YHA member in Australia costs $24 a year (there's also a $16 joining fee, although if you're an overseas resident joining in Australia you don't have to pay this). You can join at a state office or at any youth hostel.

The YHA has recently introduced the Aussie Starter Pack, whereby Australian residents joining the YHA will receive two vouchers worth $8 each to use at a hostel in their state. International visitors joining the YHA at a hostel will receive their first night at that hostel for free. The scheme has standardised the additional nightly fee charged to non-YHA members at $2 per night. Non-members will receive an Aussie Starter Card, to be stamped each night by the YHA. Full membership is given when the card has 12 stamps.

Youth hostels are part of an international organisation, the International Youth Hostel Federation (IYHF, also known as HI, Hostelling International), so if you're already a member of the YHA in your own country, your membership entitles you to use the Australian hostels. Hostels are great places for meeting people and great travellers' centres, and in many busier hostels the foreign visitors will outnumber the Australians.

The annual *YHA Accommodation Guide* booklet, which is available from any YHA office in Australia and from some YHA offices overseas, lists all the YHA hostels around Australia with useful little maps showing how to find them. YHA members are eligible for discounts at various places and these facilities are also listed in the handbook.

You must have a regulation sheet sleeping bag or bed linen – for hygiene reasons a regular sleeping bag will not do. If you haven't got sheets they can be rented at many hostels (usually for $3), but it's cheaper, after a few nights' stay, to have your own. YHA offices and some larger hostels sell the official YHA sheet bag.

All hostels have cooking facilities and 24-hour access, and there's usually some communal area where you can sit and talk. There are usually laundry facilities and often excellent notice boards. Many hostels have a maximum-stay period – because some hostels are permanently full it would hardly be fair for people to stay too long when others are being turned away.

The YHA defines its hostels as 'simple', 'standard' or 'superior'. They range from tiny places to big modern buildings, from historic convict buildings to a disused railway station. Most hostels have a manager who checks you in when you arrive and keeps the peace. Because you have so much more contact with a hostel manager than the person in charge of other styles of accommodation he or she can really make or break the place. Good managers are often great characters and well worth getting to know.

Accommodation can usually be booked directly with the manager or through a Membership & Travel Centre. The YHA handbook tells all. Not all of the 140-plus hostels listed in the handbook are actually owned by the YHA. Some are 'associate hostels', which generally abide by hostel regulations but are owned by other organisations or individuals. You don't need to be a YHA member to stay at an associated hostel. Others are 'alternative accommodation' and do not totally fit the hostel blueprint. They might be motels which keep some hostel-style accommodation available for YHA members, caravan parks with an on-site van or two kept aside, or even places just like hostels but where the operators don't want to abide by all the hostel regulations.

The Australian head office is in Sydney, at the Australian Youth Hostels Association, 10 Mallett St, Camperdown, NSW 2050 (☎ (02) 9565 1699). Queensland's YHA Membership & Travel Centre (☎ (07) 3236 1680) is at 154 Roma St, Brisbane, Qld 4000.

Backpackers' Hostels

Queensland also has plenty of backpackers' hostels. The standard of these places varies enormously: There are run-down inner-city pubs which have been 'converted' to hostels by shoving a few bunks in the bedrooms; former motels where each unit, typically with four to six beds, will have fridge, TV and bathroom, and there is often a pool; and modern, purpose-built hostels with all the mod-cons. These latter places are often the best places in terms of facilities, although sometimes they can simply be too big.

In some places, backpackers are often employed to do the day-to-day running of hostels and usually it's not too long before standards start to slip. The best places are often the smaller hostels where the owner is also the manager.

Backpacker hostels also vary enormously in terms of their atmosphere – some of the bigger places along the coast are heavily party-oriented, with late-night entertainment, drinking games and trips to pubs and clubs, but there are plenty of smaller, quieter, more intimate places.

With the proliferation of hostels has also come intense competition. Hop off a bus in any town on the Queensland coast and chances are there'll be at least three or four touts from the various hostels, all trying to lure you in. To this end many have introduced inducements, and virtually all have courtesy buses. Even the

YHA hostels have had to resort to this to stay in the race in some places.

Prices at backpackers' hostels are generally in line with YHA hostels – typically $10 to $12, although often $14 to $15 in the more popular places. Again, singles and doubles are often available for around $25/30, and quite a few places now offer private rooms with their own bathrooms – typically around $35 to $45 a double.

There's at least one organisation (VIP) which you can join where, for a modest fee (typically $20), you'll receive a discount card (valid for 12 months) which will save you $1 a night, and a list of participating hostels. This is hardly a great inducement to join but you do also receive useful discounts on other services, such as bus passes, so they may be worth considering.

As with YHA hostels, the success of a hostel largely depends on the friendliness and willingness of the managers. One practice that many people find objectionable – in independent hostels only, since it never happens in YHAs – is the 'vetting' of Australians and sometimes New Zealanders,

Backpacking in Queensland

Backpacking in Queensland is a breeze. Once you've slotted yourself into the backpacking mainstream, you don't even have to think about where to go or what to do. There's a well-worn backpackers' circuit, which basically runs up the coast between Brisbane and Cairns, with a choice of stops that includes the Gold Coast, Noosa Heads, Hervey Bay/Fraser Island, Rockhampton/Great Keppel Island, Airlie Beach and the Whitsundays, Magnetic Island, and Mission Beach.

When you get off the bus in each place, there will be a courtesy coach waiting to take you to your hostel (which you pre-booked before you left the last place). Once you've settled in, you can find out about tours on offer, and even book them through the hostel. Lots of the hostels also have their own bars and provide meals, so you don't even have to worry about going out and exploring an unfamiliar town. And after a while, you'll start seeing familiar faces and renewing acquaintances with the same people you met at the other hostels.

This system provides some tremendous advantages, and many an international visitor has marvelled at how easy this travelling caper is. Gone are the bad old days of actually having to carry your backpack around while you search for a bed, or having to deal with the locals...

The trend in Queensland in recent times is that backpackers' hostels seem to be getting bigger and bigger. There are plenty of benefits these larger hostels can provide, and the facilities are often much better than at the smaller, old-fashioned places. There are also several hostel 'chains' along the coast. The owner of one long-running chain recently told me that he reckoned all backpackers were 'sheep', and they all wanted exactly the same thing anyway. His vision for the future was of a linked network of huge, 200 to 300-bed hostels decked out with all the mod-cons – pool, spa, air-con, gymnasium, restaurant, packaged tours – with, presumably, a constant stream of backpackers moving mindlessly from one place to the next. For those of us who thought backpacking was about independent travel, it's a depressingly mass-market scenario – one that threatens to cross that thin grey line between independent travel and packaged tourism.

Anyhow, for those of you who do want to get off the beaten track, Queensland offers some fantastic alternatives. While the 'mainstream' destinations are popular precisely because they have so much to offer, there are plenty of other great areas just waiting for you to discover – and that's where this book comes in. They may be out of your way or a little harder to get to – you might even have to take a local bus service, or do some walking, or find a lift – but remember the immortal last words of Ludwig Leichhardt, one of Queensland's first independent travellers, who said, 'The effort of exploring is often rewarded by the joy of discovery'. Sadly, Leichhardt and his entire exploration party disappeared in the outback in 1848, faithfully pursuing that aphorism to the very end.

Queensland's current network of backpackers' hostels is well established and operates incredibly efficiently – it's a cheap, convenient and fun way to travel around. But if you start to get that sheepish, anonymous feeling, it can sometimes help to find somewhere quiet, take a few deep breaths and chant to yourself; 'I am an individual. I am capable of making my own decisions. I am an individual...' ■

who may be asked to provide a passport or double ID which they may not carry. Virtually all city hostels ask everyone for some photo ID – usually a passport – but this can also be used as a way of keeping unwanted customers out.

Some places will actually only admit overseas backpackers. This happens mostly in cities and when it does it's because the hostel in question has had problems with some locals treating the place more as a dosshouse than a hostel – drinking too much, making too much noise, getting into fights and the like. Hostels which discourage or ban Aussies say it's only a rowdy minority that makes trouble, but they can't take the risk on who'll turn out bad. If you're an Aussie and encounter this kind of reception, the best you can do is persuade the desk people that you're genuinely travelling the country, and aren't just looking for a cheap place to crash for a while.

Colleges
Several of the university colleges in Brisbane, and some of the regional university towns, offer inexpensive accommodation during vacation periods. See the Brisbane chapter for details.

Guesthouses & B&Bs
These are the fastest growing segment of the accommodation market. New places are opening all the time, and the network of accommodation alternatives throughout the country includes everything from restored miners' cottages, converted barns and stables, renovated and rambling old guesthouses, up-market country homes and romantic escapes to a simple bedroom in a family home. Many of these places are listed throughout the book. Tariffs cover a wide range, but are typically in the $40 to $100 (per double) bracket.

Farm & Station Stays
Australia is a land of farms (known as 'stations' in the outback) and one of the best ways to come to grips with Australian life is to spend a few days on one. Many farms offer accommodation where you can just sit back and watch how it's done, while others like to get you more actively involved in the day-to-day activities. With commodity prices falling daily, mountainous wool stockpiles and a general rural crisis, tourism offers the hope of at least some income for farmers, at a time when many are being forced off the land.

The standard of accommodation varies enormously. Some places have just bunged a couple of dongas (transportable huts, often used in mining towns) in the yard and will charge perhaps $20 a night; at others, you can pay $150 a double to stay in a historic country homestead which has been restored to provide a luxurious taste of a bygone era. Most places fall somewhere between these two extremes.

Quite a few farmstays are included in this guidebook. The QT&TC also produces a brochure called *Farm & Station Holidays*, which lists many of the places with accommodation – it's available from regional information offices or from the QT&TC. You can book most farmstays through the RACQ's Travel Service (☎ (07) 3361 2390 or toll-free 1800 777 888), and they can put together packages which include transport and accommodation. You can also make bookings through travel agents.

Pubs
Outside of Brisbane, Cairns and a few of the larger centres, hotel accommodation means pub accommodation. Although the grandest buildings in country towns are often the pubs, the standard of accommodation rarely lives up to the architecture. Many pubs would prefer not to offer accommodation, but in the past the licensing laws required them to do so.

Pub rooms are usually clean but pretty basic, with not much more than a bed, a wardrobe and sometimes a wash-basin. The bathrooms are almost always shared. Despite the lack of luxury, it's worth considering staying in pubs rather than motels. Apart from the saving in cost (around $15/25 a single/double is average for basic pub accommodation), staying at 'the pub' means that you have an entrée to the town's social life. Rather than watching networked TV all night in a motel room, you're likely to spend some time in the bar and, as you'll already be known to the bar-person, you won't have trouble meeting people. The smaller the town, the friendlier the pub will be.

The two essentials in choosing a pub room are to get one which isn't directly above the noisy bar (not a problem if you plan to be in the bar until closing time), and to check that the bed is in reasonable condition.

A big plus with pubs is that the breakfasts (sometimes included in the tariff, but increasingly it's an extra charge) can be quite enormous.

Motels

If you want a more modern place than a pub, with your own bathroom and other facilities, then you're moving into the motel bracket. Prices vary, and with motels (unlike hotels), singles are often not much cheaper than doubles. The reason is quite simple – in the old hotels many of the rooms really are singles, relics of the days when single men travelled the country looking for work. In motels, the rooms are always doubles. Costs for budget motel rooms are usually around $40 a night, although you can sometimes find rooms for $30. The more up-market motels, and those in the busier centres, charge anywhere from $50 to $80 a night.

Hotels

As well as pubs, the other end of the hotel spectrum is well represented, in Brisbane, the Gold Coast and Cairns at least. There are many excellent four and five-star hotels and quite a few lesser places where standards vary widely. Outside the capitals, quality accommodation is offered by the more expensive motels or beach resorts.

Serviced Apartments

Serviced apartments are pretty much restricted to Brisbane. However they offer hotel-style convenience with cooking facil-ities and a bit more room to move than a hotel room. They are becoming increasingly popular in the upper price brackets, with the cheaper ones very attractive for families travelling on a budget.

Holiday Flats

Holiday flats, found mainly in beachside towns, are geared to family holidays, so they fill up at peak times and often have minimum rental periods of a week. Outside peak times you might be able to let one by the night. Standards and prices vary enormously, but if you have a group they can be very affordable and might even be cheaper than hostels outside peak season.

Resorts

As you would expect, Queensland has all sorts of holiday resorts – they range from up-market five-star places with golf courses, pools and spas, gymnasiums, fleets of windsurfers, catamarans and jet skis, diving schools and restaurants and bars; to clusters of old-fashioned cabins on lonely islands on the reef. There are hundreds of places to choose from, and many of them are included and described in this guide.

Other Accommodation

There are lots of less conventional accommodation possibilities. You don't have to camp in caravan parks, for example. There are plenty of parks where you can camp for free, or roadside rest areas where short-term camping is permitted.

In the cities, if you want to stay longer, the first place to look for a shared flat or a room is the classified ad section of the daily newspaper. Wednesday and Saturday are the best days for these ads. Notice boards in universities, hostels, certain popular bookshops and cafes, and other contact centres are good places to look for flats/houses to share or rooms to rent.

FOOD

The culinary delights can be one of the real highlights of Australia. Time was – like 25 years ago – when Australia's food (mighty steaks apart) had a reputation for being like England's, only worse. Well, perhaps not quite that bad, but getting on that way. Miracles happen and Australia's miracle was immigration. The Greeks, Yugoslavs, Italians, Lebanese and many others who flooded into Australia in the '50s and '60s brought, thank God, their food with them. More recent arrivals include the Vietnamese, whose communities are thriving in several cities.

So in Australia today you can have excellent Greek moussaka (and a bottle of retsina to wash it down), delicious Italian saltimbocca and pastas, or good, heavy German dumplings; you can perfume the air with garlic after stumbling out of a French bistro, or try all sorts of Middle Eastern and Arab treats. The Chinese have been sweet & souring since the gold-rush days, while more recently Indian, Thai and Malaysian restaurants have been all the rage. And for cheap eats, you can't beat some of the Vietnamese places.

Tropical Fruits & Nuts
Queensland produces a wonderful variety of tropical fruits, all of which are widely available in supermarkets and grocery shops throughout the state. As you travel around, you'll notice that there are also plenty of roadside stalls in Queensland selling produce straight off the trees or out of the ground. The list of what's available is long and delicious, and includes mangoes, lychees, bananas, avocados, rambutans, watermelons, figs and oranges. Roadside stalls are worth looking out for – not only is the produce fresher than what you'll find anywhere else and (usually) better value, but you'll also get to meet the people who grow the stuff.

If you haven't tried macadamia nuts yet, you're in for a memorable treat. These small, circular nuts grow on macadamia trees which are native to the rainforest areas of Queensland. The nuts themselves are richly flavoured and encased within a tough protective shell. You can buy them raw in the shell, or roasted and salted in bags or jars. ∎

Self Catering
Throughout Queensland you'll find a superb range of fresh and affordable produce, all locally produced – vegetables, tropical fruit, beef and lamb, great seafood, bread and much more. There are food markets in most of the larger cities. Most supermarkets have a fruit-and-vegetable section as well as meat and seafood departments. Alternatively, there are the smaller, more personalised neighbourhood shops – butchers, grocers, fishmongers and bakeries – and you can also buy some fresh produce in many milk bars and convenience stores. Then there's a myriad of smaller speciality shops like organic grocers, health-food shops and exotic delicatessens.

In the smaller towns, your choices will be somewhat more limited – there might just be a supermarket, a butcher and grocer, although in the really small towns there is often just a general store with lots of canned food on the shelves and freezers full of frozen food.

Takeaway Food
There are plenty of choices when you're looking for food on the run. In Brisbane and the larger cities, you'll find all the major fast-food chains – McDonald's, KFC, Pizza Hut, etc – all in prominent positions and blatantly signposted.

On a more local level, you'll find plenty of milk bars, and most of them sell things like meat pies, pasties, sausage rolls, sandwiches and milk shakes. Then there are the speciality sandwich bars, delis and health-food shops – all worth looking out for if you're after something fresh and tasty. Another good alternative is to look for a bakery – with fresh bread, pies, pastries and cakes – and the local fruit shop.

Most shopping centres also have a fish & chip shop (which also do hamburgers, souvlakis, etc) and a pizzeria (for pastas and pizzas). And keep an eye out for the more exotic Indian, Lebanese, Turkish, Malaysian, and other takeaways which are usually good and give value for money.

On a less tasty note, on the highways you'll constantly encounter roadhouses and anonymous cafes with stuff they call food sitting under hot lights waiting for unsuspecting travellers – don't eat it, you'll only encourage them. On the other hand, I've had some of the best hamburgers I've eaten at the small, remote roadhouses of the outback, the Gulf and Cape York – enormous, old-fashioned burgers that will keep you going all day.

Pub & Club Food

Every town in Queensland has at least one pub – in fact, there are plenty of 'one-pub towns' that are just that – a pub, and nothing else.

Eating in a pub can be a great experience, as long as you choose the right pub. While the quality of food can vary enormously, it's usually fairly basic and unimaginative, but often very good value. Pub menus all start to look fairly similar after a while – steaks, roasts, seafood and pasta dishes are the standard fare, although there are plenty of exceptions. The normal eating times are from noon to 2 pm and from 6 to 8 pm, but lots of pubs don't serve meals on Sunday.

Most pubs serve two types of meals: counter meals are served in the bistro (or dining room), and are usually in the $8 to $14 range (you'll often find a self-serve salad bar with bread, condiments, etc); bar meals are served in the public bar and eaten at the bar.

Pub Names

Historically, Queensland's publicans weren't terribly imaginative when it came to naming their establishments. A popular on-the-road game is to lay bets on the name of the first pub you'll see as you drive into a town. You can just about bet your bottom dollar that it will be called the Royal, the Commercial, the Criterion, the Railway, the Imperial, the Union or the Prince of Wales. Then again, it might have just been named after the town.■

They are usually simplified versions of the bistro meals and cost around $4 to $7.

Almost every town in Queensland also has at least one club serving meals – RSLs (Returned Servicemen's Leagues Clubs), bowls clubs and rugby league clubs are the most common. These places usually have simple pub-style food, but because they make so much money through their poker machines, the meals are often a bit cheaper than what you'll get in a pub. Visitors are welcome in most clubs – you have to sign in, and there are usually basic dress regulations.

Cafes & Restaurants

In Brisbane and the larger centres, you'll find plenty of cafes and restaurants offering a huge range of cuisines and styles, but in smaller country towns you might just find and old-fashioned cafe, a pub and a Chinese restaurant.

Most of the popular tourist destinations have at least a couple of good places to eat. Brisbane, Port Douglas, Noosa Heads and Cairns are the best restaurant centres in Queensland.

DRINKS

Tap water is clean and drinkable in most parts of Queensland, with the exception of some of the more remote outback towns. Bottled water is also widely available, as are plain and flavoured mineral waters. Most shops stock a wide range of soft drinks, fruit juices and flavoured milk; a milk shake from a local milk bar is a bit of an Aussie institution. Cafes and delis often make smoothies (a milk shake with added fruit, yoghurt, honey, nuts, etc) and squeeze fresh juices.

Most cafes and restaurants in places like Brisbane, the Gold and Sunshine coasts, Cairns and Port Douglas serve cappuccinos, espressos and macchiatos that will satisfy any caffeine addict. 'Real' coffee is much harder to come by in other areas, although most of the larger towns have at least one good Italian cafe where you can get a fix.

Queensland is also the home of Australia's most famous spirit, the distinctive Bundaberg Rum, a dark rum made from raw molasses (which is a by-product of the local sugar industry).

Beer

There's a bewildering array of beer available in bottleshops, pubs, bars and restaurants. There are local beers like XXXX (pronounced fourex), interstate beers like VB (Victoria Bitter), Foster's and Toohey's; boutique beers like Redback; and international beers like Steinlager and Budweiser. Local beers have an alcoholic content of around 4.9% alcohol, and popular light beers, like XXXX Light, Toohey's Blue and Foster's Special range from 2% to 3.5%. A few boutique or brewery pubs brew their own beers, and Guinness is usually found on draught in Irish pubs.

Beer comes in bottles (750 ml), stubbies (375 ml), and cans (375 ml). When ordering at the bar you ask for a 'glass' (200 ml) or a 'pot' (285 ml). With the increasing popularity of light beers you might be asked by the person behind the bar if you want a 'light' or a 'heavy'. If in doubt, take local advice, which will readily be offered!

Wine

If you don't fancy the beer, then turn to wines. European wine experts now realise just how good Australian wines can be – exporting wine is a multi-million dollar business. Wines need not be expensive. You're entering the 'pretty good' bracket if you pay over $10 for a bottle and very drinkable wines can be found for much less.

Some of Australia's best known wine producing areas are the Hunter Valley in NSW, the Barossa Valley and Coonawarra in South Australia, the Margaret River district in Western Australia and the Yarra Valley near Melbourne, but there are dozens of others, each with its own enthusiastic promoters and producing its own distinct styles. Queensland's climate is generally too warm to produce good wines, although there is a small but growing wine district based around the town of Stanthorpe in the cool-temperate mountains of south-east Queensland, with more than 15 boutique wineries which can be visited. See the Darling Downs chapter for details. There are a couple of other wineries in Queensland, including in the Atherton Tablelands, the Sunshine Coast and around Kingaroy, and there's a fruit winery outside of Bundaberg.

It takes a little while to become familiar with Australian wineries and their styles, but it's an effort worth making. All over Queensland, you'll find restaurants advertising that they're BYO. The initials stand for 'Bring Your Own' and it means that they're not licensed to sell alcohol but you are permitted to bring your own with you. This is a real boon to wine-loving but budget-minded travellers, because you can bring your own bottle of wine from the local bottleshop or from that winery you visited last week and not pay any mark-up. There might be a small 'corkage' charge (typically 60c to $1 per person) if you bring your own.

ENTERTAINMENT
Cinema

Although the cinema took a huge knock from the meteoric rise of the home-video market, it has bounced back as people rediscover the joys of the big screen.

In the big cities there are commercial cinema chains, such as Village, Hoyts and Greater Union, and their cinemas are usually found in centres which will have anything from two to six screens in the one complex. Smaller towns have just the one cinema, and many of these are almost museum pieces in themselves. Seeing a new-release mainstream film costs around $12 ($7.50 for children under 15) in the big cities, less in country areas and less on certain nights at the bigger cinema chains.

In Brisbane you'll find art-house and independent cinemas, and these places generally either screen films that aren't made for mass consumption or specialise purely in re-runs of classics and cult movies.

Drive-in cinemas used to be found all over Australia. They're a dying breed now, although there are still quite a few towns in Queensland where you can watch a movie from the comfort of your own car.

Pubs, Nightclubs & Live Music

There's certainly no shortage of pubs in Queensland, and many of them feature live music or DJs, especially on Thursday, Friday and Saturday nights and Sunday afternoons. You might see a local guitarist strumming his stuff, a local rock or jazz band trying to make a name for themselves, or a major national or international act on tour. Some of the larger cities, including Brisbane, Cairns and Townsville, have free music and entertainment magazines which list local gigs. Otherwise, look in the local papers or enquire at information offices. Cover charges usually apply, especially for well-known bands. Pubs usually stay open until around midnight or 1 am.

Most reasonably sized towns also have at least one nightclub. These places vary enormously, from grungy pick-up joints to up-market clubs with dress codes and cover charges. Nightclubs are generally licensed until 5 am, although they'll close earlier during the week if there's no-one around.

This book provides comprehensive information on lots of pubs, clubs and venues – look under the Entertainment section for each town.

Spectator Sports

If you're an armchair – or wooden bench – sports fan, Queensland has plenty to offer.

Football Australians play at least four brands of football, each type being called 'football' by its aficionados. All codes are played over winter, with seasons from about March to September.

Rugby is the main game in Queensland, and it's rugby league, the 13-a-side working-class version, that attracts the crowds. The ARL's (Australian Rugby League) Winfield Cup competition produces the world's best rugby league – fast, fit and clever. Queensland currently has four sides in the ARL – the Brisbane Broncos, the South Queensland Crushers, the North Queensland Cowboys and the Gold Coast Seagulls (although the Seagulls are based in Tweed Heads, NSW).

At the time of writing the ARL (backed by media magnate Kerry Packer) was involved in a to-the-death struggle with Rupert Murdoch and his concept for an international 'Super League', a battle which looks destined to change the face of rugby league for ever. Stay tuned.

Rugby union, the 15-a-side game for amateurs, is less popular but gained ground when Australia won the World Cup in 1991.

Australian Rules, a fast and spectacular indigenous game based on elements of Gaelic football, is also played throughout the state, although unlike their counterparts in Victoria, South Australia and Western Australia, most Queenslanders are pretty indifferent when it comes to Aussie Rules. The Brisbane Bears, Queensland's only side in the AFL (Australian Football League), play their home games at the Gabba (the Brisbane Cricket Ground in Woolloongabba, a suburb of Brisbane).

Soccer is a bit of a poor cousin: it's widely played on an amateur basis but the national league is only semiprofessional and attracts a fairly small following. It's slowly gaining popularity thanks in part to the success of the national team. At the local level, there are ethnically based teams representing a wide range of national origins.

Cricket During the other (non-football) half of the year there's cricket. International Test and one-day matches are played at the Gabba every summer. There is also an interstate competition (the Sheffield Shield) and numerous local grades.

Other Sports Basketball is growing in popularity as a spectator sport and there is a national league. Queensland has three sides in the NBL (National Basketball League) – the Brisbane Bullets, the Townsville Suns and the Gold Coast Rollers.

Surfing competitions are held at a couple of places including North Stradbroke Island and at Burleigh Heads on the Gold Coast; there are also numerous surf life-saving carnivals which take place on the beaches of southern Queensland over the summer months.

There's also yacht racing, some tennis and motor racing. The Australian IndyCar Grand Prix is held in Surfers Paradise every March. Major golf tournaments include the Coolum Classic, held on the Sunshine Coast in December, and an international 'skins' tournament at Laguna Quays on the Whitsunday Coast each February.

Queensland Cricket's Holy Grail

For Queensland's cricket followers, 1995 will be joyfully remembered as the year the drought finally broke. Queensland's failure to win the Sheffield Shield, the annual trophy awarded to the state which wins the domestic 1st-class cricket competition, was one of the longest-running droughts in the history of sport.

Queensland joined the Sheffield Shield competition back in 1926, but despite the fact that there were only four teams (nowadays there are six), they managed to remain winless for almost 70 years. In the meantime Western Australia, who joined the competition in 1947, had won 12 times. But it wasn't just Queensland's failure to win that was remarkable, it was the way they went about not winning. The 'banana-benders' made it into six Shield finals – and found a different way to lose them all.

Winning the Shield become an obsession in Queensland. So much so that they even tried to 'buy' a victory, importing a string of big-name players over the years. Ian Botham and Graeme Hick from England, Viv Richards, Wes Hall and Alvin Kallicharran from the West Indies, Majid Khan from Pakistan, and interstate players Alan Border, Jeff Thomson and Greg Chappell were all enlisted to try and help break the dreaded drought – to no avail.

But the 1994-95 season changed all that. With a new name (the Queensland Bulls), a new coach, a new captain (Australian vice-captain Ian Healey), and with recently retired Australian captain and all-time cricketing legend Alan Border playing for the side full time, the Queensland Bulls finally broke through for their historic first Shield victory, thrashing South Australia in the final at the 'Gabba' in Brisbane. ∎

Rodeos are held at dozens of places throughout the state. Some of the biggest rodeos are held at Mareeba in the Far North, Warwick in the Darling Downs, and Mt Isa and Longreach in the outback.

Gambling

Australians love to gamble, and hardly any town of even minor import is without a horse-racing track or a Totalisator Agency Board (TAB) betting office. You can place a bet on the horses, the trots (harness racing) and the dogs (greyhound racing), and you'll also find TAB agencies inside plenty of Queensland's pubs. Poker machines can be found inside most pubs and all licensed clubs – bowling clubs, RSL clubs, rugby league clubs are everywhere.

Townsville, the Gold Coast and Brisbane all have casinos and Cairns' casino is due to open in 1996.

THINGS TO BUY
Aboriginal & Torres Strait Islander Art

Top of the list of real Australian purchases would have to be art and craft items produced by Aboriginal and Torres Strait Islander artists.

Aboriginal art is a traditional and symbolic art form. In ancient times, the main forms of art were body painting, cave painting and rock engraving, and it's only recently that Aboriginal artists have begun painting in more portable formats and using Western art materials like canvas and acrylic paints.

These works have quickly gained wide appreciation. The paintings depict traditional Dreamtime stories and ceremonial designs, and each design has a particular spiritual significance. These works capture the essence of the Australian outback, and make a wonderful reminder of a trip to Australia.

Prices of the best works are way out of reach for the average traveller, but among the cheaper artworks on sale are hand-painted boomerangs and didgeridoos, ceramics, art works on paper, bark and canvas, prints, baskets, small wood carvings, and some very beautiful screen-printed T-shirts produced by Aboriginal craft co-operatives – and a larger number of commercial rip-offs. It's worth shopping around and paying a few dollars more for the real thing.

Some places worth visiting are Queensland Aboriginal Creations, FireWorks Gallery and the Geerbaugh Cultural Centre in Brisbane, Barambah Emu Farm in Murgon, the Dreamtime Cultural Centre in Rockhampton, the Edward River Crocodile Farm south of Cairns, and the Deeral Aboriginal and Torres Strait Islander Corporation's shops in Cairns and Babinda. See the brochure *A Guide to Experiencing Aboriginal and Torres Strait Islander Culture*, available from most regional tourist information centres, for more information.

Crafts

You'll find many shops and galleries displaying crafts by local artists, as well as goods from almost every region of the world. The local craft scene is especially strong in the fields of ceramics, jewellery, stained glass and leathercraft. There are also hundreds of markets throughout Queensland where you can buy the work of local craftspeople. These include the Southbank, Riverside and Eagle St Pier markets in Brisbane; the Eumundi markets on the Sunshine Coast; and the Kuranda markets near Cairns.

Antiques

A large proportion of antiques on the Australian market are imported from Europe, especially England. Instead, look for early Australian colonial furniture made from cedar or huon pine; Australian silver jewellery; ceramics – either early factory pieces or studio pieces (especially anything by the Boyd family); glassware such as Carnival glass; and Australiana collectables and bric-a-brac such as old signs, tins, bottles etc. Look for genuine Australian pieces – the value of antiques is in what they tell you about your heritage, which makes the imported stuff just about worthless.

If you're serious about buying antiques,

Carter's Price Guide to Antiques in Australia is an excellent price reference which is updated annually.

Opals

The opal is Australia's national gemstone, and opals and opal jewellery are popular souvenirs. They are beautiful stones, but buy wisely and shop around – quality and prices can vary widely from place to place.

Australiana

The term 'Australiana' is a euphemism for souvenirs. These are the things you buy as gifts for the folks back home or to remember your visit by, and are supposedly representative of Australia and Aussie culture. Some of the more popular items are:

Stuffed toys, especially koalas and kangaroos;
wool products such as hand-knitted jumpers;
sheepskin products;
Akubra bush hats and straw sunhats;
T-shirts, windcheaters and towels printed with Australian symbols or typical slogans like 'No flies on me, mate!';
Australia-shaped egg-flippers;
koala key-rings;
jewellery made from opals and pewter, often in the shape of native animals or flora;
boomerangs (most of which are decorative rather than of the returning variety);
painted didgeridoos;
local glassware and ceramics;
and high-kitsch items like ceramic flying pigs or koalas.

The seeds of many of Australia's native plants are on sale all over the place. Try growing kangaroo paws back home, if your own country will allow them in. For those last-minute gifts, drop into a deli. Australian wines are well known overseas, but why not try honey (leatherwood honey is one of a number of powerful local varieties) or macadamia nuts? We have also heard rumours of tinned witchetty grubs, honey ants and other bush tucker.

Aussie Clothing

While you're here, fit yourself out in some local clothes – made in Australia for Australian conditions. Start off with some Bonds undies and a singlet, a pair of Holeproof Explorer socks and Blundstone or Rossi boots. Then there's anything from the R M Williams line (boots, moleskin trousers, shirts), some Yakka or King Gee workwear, a shearer's top or bush shirt, a greasy-wool jumper, a Bluey (a coarse woollen worker's coat), a Driza-bone (an oilskin riding coat) – and top it off with an Akubra hat.

Or there are all sorts of sheepskin products. A high-quality sheepskin to put in a child's pushchair – or to sit on yourself! – can cost as little as $50.

Australia also produces some of the world's best surfing equipment and clothing, and clothing companies like 100% Mambo produce some mind-boggling off-the-wall designs.

Outdoor Gear
With Australians among the world's keenest travellers, Queensland's outdoor and adventure shops carry an excellent range of both Australian-made and imported gear. In many cases, the locally made products are of equivalent quality to (and cheaper than) the imports. Paddy Pallin, Mountain Designs, Kathmandu and the Scout Outdoor Centres are among the local firms.

Getting There & Away

Basically getting to Australia means flying, although it is sometimes possible to hitch a ride on a yacht or take a cargo ship to or from Australia. If you're already in Australia and heading for Queensland, you have a choice of flying, taking a bus or train, driving a car or motorcycle, or again, hitching a ride on a yacht.

AIR

The main problem with getting to Australia is that it's a long way from anywhere. Coming from Asia, Europe or North America there are lots of competing airlines and a wide variety of air fares, but there's no way you can avoid those great distances. Australia's current international popularity adds another problem – flights are often heavily booked. If you want to fly to Australia at a particularly popular time of year (the middle of summer, ie Christmas time, is notoriously difficult) or on a particularly popular route (like Hong Kong-Cairns) then you need to plan well ahead.

While Sydney and Melbourne are the busiest international gateways, Queensland has its own international airports in Brisbane and Cairns. Brisbane has direct international flights to and from Europe, as well as most major destinations in Asia and the South Pacific, including New Zealand and Papua New Guinea. Cairns has direct flights to and from Asia, Papua New Guinea and North America. Although Townsville also has an international airport, none of the international airlines currently fly there, so the airport operates strictly as a domestic terminal.

If you can't get a direct flight into Queensland, chances are you'll arrive via Sydney. Sydney's airport is stretched way beyond its capacity and flights are frequently delayed on arrival and departure. Furthermore, the Customs and Immigration facilities are cramped, crowded and too small for the current visitor flow, so even after you've finally landed you may face further long delays. If you can organise your flights to avoid Sydney, it's a wise idea.

Discount Tickets

Buying international airline tickets these days is like shopping for a car or a camera – five different travel agents will quote you five different prices. Rule number one if you're looking for a cheap ticket is to go to an agent, not directly to the airline. The airline can usually only quote you the regular fare, but an agent can offer all sorts of special deals, particularly on competitive routes.

Ideally, an airline would like to fly all its flights with every seat in use and every passenger paying the highest fare possible. Fortunately, life usually isn't like that and airlines would rather have a half-price passenger than an empty seat. When faced with too many seats, they will either let agents sell them at cut prices, or occasionally make one-off special offers on particular routes – watch the travel ads in the press.

What's available and what it costs depends on what time of year it is, what route you're flying and the airline. If you're flying on a popular route (like from Hong Kong) or one where the choice of flights is very limited (like from South America or Africa), the fare is likely to be higher or there may be nothing available but the official fare.

Similarly, the dirt-cheap fares are likely to be less conveniently scheduled, and to go by less convenient routes or with less popular airlines.

Things to consider when choosing a ticket are its validity (you don't want to buy a return ticket that's only valid for two weeks) and the number of stopovers you want. As a rule of thumb, the cheaper the ticket the fewer stopovers you'll be allowed. Also think about how much of a hassle it will be if you have to change planes on the way to Australia. Sometimes it's worth paying a bit more for a ticket to avoid sitting around a foreign departure lounge for hours on end.

Round-the-World Tickets

Round-the-World tickets have become very popular and many will take you through Australia. The airline RTW tickets are often real bargains and, since Australia is pretty much at the other side of the world from Europe or North America, it can work out no more expensive, or even cheaper, to keep going in the same direction right round the world rather than U-turn when you return.

The official airline RTW tickets are usually put together by a combination of two airlines and permit you to fly anywhere you want on their route systems so long as you do not backtrack. Other restrictions are that you (usually) must book the first sector in advance, and cancellation penalties then apply. There may be restrictions on how many stops you are permitted, and usually the tickets are valid from 90 days up to a year. Typical prices for these South Pacific RTW tickets are around £816 or US$1900.

An alternative type of RTW ticket is one put together by a travel agent using a combination of discounted tickets from a number of airlines. A UK agent like Trailfinders can put together interesting London-to-London RTW combinations including Australia for £750 to £930.

Circle Pacific Tickets

Circle Pacific fares are a similar idea to RTW tickets, using a combination of airlines to circle the Pacific – combining Australia, New Zealand, North America and Asia. Examples would be Qantas-Northwest, Canadian Airlines International-Cathay Pacific, and so on. As with RTW tickets, there are advance purchase restrictions and limits to how many stopovers you can take. Typically, fares range between US$1750 and US$2180. A possible Circle Pacific route is Los Angeles-Hawaii-Auckland-Sydney-Singapore-Bangkok-Hong Kong-Tokyo-Los Angeles.

To/From the UK

The cheapest tickets in London are from the numerous 'bucket shops' (discount ticket agencies) which advertise in magazines and papers like *Time Out, Southern Cross* and *TNT*. The magazine *Business Traveller* also has a great deal of good advice on airfare bargains, and the *Evening Standard's* travel section is also worth perusing. Most bucket shops are trustworthy and reliable, but the occasional sharp operator appears – *Time Out* and *Business Traveller* give some useful advice on precautions to take.

Trailfinders (☎ (0171) 938 3366), at 46 Earls Court Rd, London W8 and STA Travel (☎ (0171) 581 4132), at 74 Old Brompton Rd, London SW7 and 117 Euston Rd, London NW1 (☎ (0171) 465 0484) are good, reliable agents for cheap tickets.

The cheapest London to Brisbane or Cairns bucket-shop tickets are about £408 one way or £599 return. Such prices are usually only available if you leave London in the low season – March to June. In September and mid-December fares go up about 30%, while for the rest of the year they are somewhere in between.

From Australia you can expect to pay around $1200 one way and $1800 return to London and other European capitals, with stops in Asia on the way.

To/From North America

There are a variety of connections across the Pacific from Los Angeles, San Francisco and Vancouver to Australia, including direct flights, flights via New Zealand, island-hopping routes or more circuitous Pacific rim routes via nations in Asia. Qantas, Air New Zealand and United all fly USA-Australia, while Qantas, Air New Zealand and Canadian Airlines International all fly Canada-Australia.

If flying via Hawaii, it might pay to fly with Qantas or Air New Zealand. If you fly with a US airline, you might find that the west coast to Hawaii sector is treated as a domestic flight (this means that you have to pay for drinks and headsets, goodies that are free on international sectors).

To find good fares to Australia, check the travel ads in the Sunday travel sections of papers like the *Los Angeles Times, San Francisco Chronicle-Examiner, New York Times*

Air Travel Glossary

Apex Apex, or 'advance purchase excursion' is a discounted ticket which must be paid for in advance. There are penalties if you wish to change it.

Baggage Allowance This will be written on your ticket: usually one 20 kg item to go in the hold, plus one item of hand luggage.

Bucket Shop An unbonded travel agency specialising in discounted airline tickets.

Bumped Just because you have a confirmed seat doesn't mean you're going to get on the plane – see Overbooking.

Cancellation Penalties If you have to cancel or change an Apex ticket there are often heavy penalties involved, insurance can sometimes be taken out against these penalties. Some airlines impose penalties on regular tickets as well, particularly against 'no show' passengers.

Check In Airlines ask you to check in a certain time ahead of the flight departure (usually 1½ hours on international flights). If you fail to check in on time and the flight is overbooked the airline can cancel your booking and give your seat to somebody else.

Confirmation Having a ticket written out with the flight and date you want doesn't mean you have a seat until the agent has checked with the airline that your status is 'OK' or confirmed. Meanwhile you could just be 'on request'.

Discounted Tickets There are two types of discounted fares – officially discounted (see Promotional Fares) and unofficially discounted. The lowest prices often impose drawbacks like flying with unpopular airlines, inconvenient schedules, or unpleasant routes and connections. A discounted ticket can save you other things than money – you may be able to pay Apex prices without the associated Apex advance booking and other requirements. Discounted tickets only exist where there is fierce competition.

Full Fares Airlines traditionally offer first class (coded F), business class (coded J) and economy-class (coded Y) tickets. These days there are so many promotional and discounted fares available from the regular economy class that few passengers pay full economy fare.

Lost Tickets If you lose your airline ticket an airline will usually treat it like a travellers' cheque and, after enquiries, issue you with another one. Legally, however, an airline is entitled to treat it like cash and if you lose it then it's gone forever. Take good care of your tickets.

No Shows No shows are passengers who fail to show up for their flight, sometimes due to unexpected delays or disasters, sometimes due to simply forgetting, sometimes because they made more than one booking and didn't bother to cancel the one they didn't want. Full fare passengers who fail to turn up are sometimes entitled to travel on a later flight. The rest of us are penalised (see Cancellation Penalties).

On Request An unconfirmed booking for a flight, see Confirmation.

Open Jaws A return ticket where you fly out to one place but return from another. If available this can save you backtracking to your arrival point.

or *Toronto Globe & Mail*. The straightforward return excursion fare from the USA west coast is around US$1090, depending on the season, but plenty of deals are available. Return fares from the USA east coast range from US$1185 to US$2100. You can typically get a one-way ticket from US$800 (west coast) or US$1050 (east coast).

In the USA, good agents for discounted tickets are the two student travel operators, Council Travel and STA Travel, both of which have lots of offices around the country. Canadian west-coast fares out of

Vancouver will be similar to the US west coast. From Toronto, fares go from around C$1650 return.

If Pacific island-hopping is your aim, check out the airlines of Pacific island nations, some of which have good deals on indirect routes. Qantas can give you Fiji or Tahiti along the way, Air New Zealand can offer both and the Cook Islands as well. See the Circle Pacific section for more details.

Sample return fares from Australia include: Cairns-Los Angeles $1500, Cairns-New York (via Japan) $1950, Cairns-Vancouver $1630,

Overbooking Airlines hate to fly empty seats and since every flight has some passengers who fail to show up (see No Shows) airlines often book more passengers than they have seats. Usually the excess passengers balance those who fail to show up but occasionally somebody gets bumped. If this happens guess who it is most likely to be? The passengers who check in late.

Promotional Fares Officially discounted fares like Apex fares which are available from travel agents or direct from the airline.

Reconfirmation At least 72 hours prior to departure time of an onward or return flight you must contact the airline and 'reconfirm' that you intend to be on the flight. If you don't do this the airline can delete your name from the passenger list and you could lose your seat. You don't have to reconfirm the first flight on your itinerary or if your stopover is less than 72 hours. It doesn't hurt to reconfirm more than once.

Restrictions Discounted tickets often have various restrictions on them – advance purchase is the most usual one (see Apex). Others are restrictions on the minimum and maximum period you must be away, such as a minimum of 14 days or a maximum of one year. See Cancellation Penalties.

Stand by A discounted ticket where you only fly if there is a seat free at the last moment. Stand-by fares are usually only available on domestic routes.

Tickets Out An entry requirement for many countries is that you have an onward or return ticket, in other words, a ticket out of the country. If you're not sure what you intend to do next, the easiest solution is to buy the cheapest onward ticket to a neighbouring country or a ticket from a reliable airline which can later be refunded if you do not use it.

Transferred Tickets Airline tickets cannot be transferred from one person to another. Travellers sometimes try to sell the return half of their ticket, but officials can ask you to prove that you are the person named on the ticket. This is unlikely to happen on domestic flights. On an international flight tickets may be compared with passports.

Travel Agencies Travel agencies vary widely and you should ensure you use one that suits your needs. Some simply handle tours while full-service agencies handle everything from tours and tickets to car rental and hotel bookings. A good one will do all these things and can save you a lot of money but if all you want is a ticket at the lowest possible price, then you really need an agency specialising in discounted tickets. A discounted ticket agency, however, may not be useful for other things, like hotel bookings.

Travel Periods Some officially discounted fares, Apex fares in particular, vary with the time of year. There is often a low (off-peak) season and a high (peak) season. Sometimes there's an intermediate or shoulder season as well. At peak times, when everyone wants to fly, not only will the officially discounted fares be higher but so will unofficially discounted fares or there may simply be no discounted tickets available. Usually the fare depends on your outward flight – if you depart in the high season and return in the low season, you pay the high-season fare. ■

Cairns-Toronto $1950, Brisbane-Los Angeles $1650, Brisbane-New York (via Auckland) $2100 and Brisbane-Toronto $2090. Note that these are low-season fares, and that while many of these flights go via Sydney or Auckland, in most cases the cost of your connecting flight is partially or even fully absorbed in the ticket price.

To/From New Zealand

Air New Zealand and Qantas operate a network of trans-Tasman flights linking Auckland, Wellington and Christchurch in New Zealand with most major Australian gateway cities. You can fly directly between a lot of places in New Zealand and a lot of places in Australia.

From Auckland to Brisbane with Qantas or Air New Zealand you're looking at around NZ$580 one way and around NZ$720 return. The same fares are slightly cheaper with Malaysian airlines. From Auckland to Cairns you're looking at around NZ$960 return.

Another option is a relatively new charter group, Kiwi Charters, who have a once-weekly flight between Hamilton (on the north island) and Brisbane costing around NZ$580 return.

To/From Asia

Ticket discounting is widespread in Asia, particularly in Singapore, Hong Kong, Bangkok and Penang. There are a lot of fly-by-nights in the Asian ticketing scene, so a little care is required. Also, the Asian routes fill up fast. Flights between Hong Kong and Australia are notoriously heavily booked, while flights to or from Bangkok and Singapore are often part of the longer Europe to Australia route, so they are also sometimes very full. Plan ahead. For much more information on South-East Asian travel and on to Australia see Lonely Planet's *South-East Asia on a shoestring*.

Typical one-way fares to Australia from Asia include from Hong Kong for around HK$4400 or from Singapore for around S$540. These fares are to Sydney or Melbourne; fares to Cairns or Brisbane are sometimes a bit cheaper.

You can also pick up some interesting tickets in Asia to include Australia on the way across the Pacific. Air France were first in this market, but Qantas and Air New Zealand are also offering discounted trans-Pacific tickets.

From Cairns, return fares start from around $950 to Hong Kong and Singapore, and from around $1000 to Kuala Lumpur and Bangkok. Fares to Asia are slightly more expensive from Brisbane; for example, return fares to Hong Kong start from around $1100.

To/From Africa & South America

The flight possibilities from these continents are not so varied and you're much more likely to have to pay the full fare. There is only a handful of direct flights each week between Africa and Australia, and then only between Perth and Harare (Zimbabwe) or Johannesburg (South Africa). In many cases, the cost of your connecting flight to/from Queensland will be partially or even fully absorbed in the ticket price. Return fares

from Brisbane or Cairns to Harare or Johannesburg range anywhere from $1770 to $2100. A cheaper alternative from East Africa may be to fly from Nairobi to India or Pakistan and on to South-East Asia, and then to connect from there to Australia.

Two routes now operate between South America and Australia. The long-running Chile connection involves a Lan Chile flight Santiago-Easter Island/Tahiti, from where you fly Qantas or another airline to Australia. Alternatively, there is a route which skirts the Antarctic circle, flying Buenos Aires-Auckland-Sydney; this is operated by Aerolineas Argentinas.

Sydney to Santiago or Buenos Aires costs about $2100 return; again, the cost of your connecting flight to/from Queensland will be partially or fully absorbed.

Arriving & Departing

Australia's dramatic increase in visitor arrivals has caused some severe bottlenecks at the entry points, particularly at Sydney where the airport is often operating at more than full capacity and delays on arrival or departure are frequent. Even when you're on the ground it can take ages to get through Immigration and Customs.

First-time travellers to Australia may be alarmed to find themselves being sprayed with insecticide by the airline stewards. It happens to everyone.

A departure tax of $27 is payable by everyone leaving Australia. Before July 1995, you had to pay this tax separately at either a post office or at the airport, but under a revised system the tax is now added to the price of your air ticket.

Domestic Flights

Australia's major domestic carriers are Ansett, which also flies a few international routes, and Qantas, which is also the international flag-carrier. Both have flights from all the Australian capital cities to all the major towns and cities in Queensland.

You don't have to reconfirm domestic flights on Ansett and Qantas, but you should phone on the day of your flight to check the details. For Ansett, call ☎ 13 1515; for Qantas, call ☎ 13 1223.

Because Qantas flies both international and domestic routes, flights leave from both the international and domestic terminals. Flights with flight numbers from QF001 to QF399 operate from international terminals; flight numbers QF400 and above from domestic terminals.

Several smaller regional airlines fly into Queensland: Eastern Australia flies to Brisbane and Coolangatta from northern New South Wales, and Augusta Airways flies to Birdsville, Boulia and Bedourie from Port Augusta in South Australia.

All airports and domestic flights are non-smoking.

Fares Ticket prices on all domestic flights within Australia are determined by the airlines, which means that travel agents will quote you exactly the same fare as the airlines themselves. Given this, the quickest and easiest approach is to book directly through the airlines, then pay for and collect your ticket from your nearest travel agent. Alternatively, if you have a credit card and you book more than three days in advance, the airline can forward your ticket to you by express post. Both of the major domestic carriers have toll-free reservations numbers: For Ansett, call ☎ 13 1300; for Qantas, call ☎ 13 1313.

Discounted Fares Although full economy fares are quoted throughout this book, in practice very few people pay full fare on domestic travel, as the airlines offer a wide range of discounts. Discounted fares depend on various factors including your age, whether you're studying, where you're going, and how far in advance you book your ticket. It's worth noting that you only get one bite at the discount cherry – you can't qualify for an advance purchase discount *and* a student discount off the same fare, you only get one or the other.

Full-time university or other higher education students get 25% off the regular economy fare on production of student ID or an ISIC card, but you can usually find fares discounted by more than that. Children (between the ages of three and 14) and secondary students qualify for a 50% discount, and 'seniors' (travellers over the age of 60) qualify for discounts of up to 70% off the regular fares.

Note that there are no longer stand-by fares, but there are discount fares which allow same-day travel on certain flights, usually those which are uncomfortably early or late.

The airlines also offer substantial random discounts on selected routes (mainly the heavy-volume routes, but not always) and at quiet times of the year.

International travellers (Australians and foreigners) can get a 25% to 40% discount on Qantas or Ansett domestic flights simply by presenting their international ticket (any airline, one-way or return) when booking. It seems there is no limit to the number of domestic flights you can take, but there might be time limits, say 60 days after you arrive in Australia. Note that the discount applies only to the full economy fare, and so in many cases it will be cheaper to take advantage of other discounts offered.

Another thing to keep your eyes open for is special deals at certain times of the year. When the Melbourne Cup horse race is on in early November and when the football Grand Final happens (also in Melbourne) at the end of September lots of extra flights are put on. These flights would normally be going in the opposite direction nearly empty, so special fares are offered to people wanting to leave Melbourne when everybody else wants to go there. The IndyCar racing carnival in Surfers Paradise on the Gold Coast in mid-March is a similar one-way-traffic event.

Many of the smaller regional airlines in Queensland offer cheap deals on lesser routes and at certain times of the year, often undercutting Qantas and Ansett – see the individual chapters for more details.

Advance Purchase Fares In many cases, the cheapest fares available are advance purchase deals, which offer up to 33% off full one-way fares and up to 60% off full return fares. The basic rule with advance purchase fares is that the further ahead you book, the cheaper the fare, but certain conditions apply. There are restrictions on changing flights – you can reschedule your flight at any time (subject to availability) but you can't change your route, and you usually have to stay away at least one Saturday night. The other major disadvantage is that advance purchase tickets are nonrefundable so you lose 100% of the ticket price if you cancel, although you can buy health-related cancellation insurance.

As an example of how advance purchase fares work, the full economy return fare from Cairns to Brisbane costs $774. If you book the same ticket seven days in advance, the fare drops to $409; if you book 14 days in advance, it's $369; and if you book 21 days in advance it's $309. The full one-way Cairns to Brisbane fare is $387, whereas if you book seven days in advance it's $259.

Air Passes With so much discounting these days, air passes do not represent the value they once did, although pre-buying a pass does save you the hassle of hunting around for special deals. Both Ansett and Qantas offer two types of passes, one which you have to buy before you arrive in Australia and one which you can buy after you arrive. The passes which are sold overseas are supposed to be for non-Australians only, but it might be possible to get around this. You'll probably save more money if you buy a pass overseas, with the downside being a lack of flexibility in your itinerary.

Rules and prices for air passes change fairly frequently, so you should talk to a knowledgeable travel agent to find out what's currently available. You might have to be persistent, as it isn't unusual for airline booking staff to be unfamiliar with the passes on offer.

Qantas has two versions of the Australia Explorer Pass, available overseas only. One is for travel between major towns and cities, and the other is for longer-haul domestic destinations. Coupons for travel between major towns and cities (for example, from Cairns to Brisbane or Melbourne) cost $170 each; coupons for longer-haul destinations (for example, Cairns to Perth or Alice Springs) cost $220 each. While the initial purchase must be made before you arrive, you can also buy additional flight coupons once you are here. Contact a Qantas office or representative for more information.

The Qantas pass which is sold within Australia is called the Backpackers Pass. You have to be a member of one of the hostel organisations (YHA, VIP, ITC and perhaps others) or have a Greyhound Pioneer Australia bus pass. This pass can only be used for travelling in one direction (no backtracking), you have to buy at least three segments, and you have to stay a minimum of two nights in each destination. A sample fare using this pass would be Cairns-Brisbane ($209), Brisbane-Sydney ($129) and Sydney-Melbourne ($109).

Ansett's Kangaroo Airpass can be bought in Australia and it gives you two options – 6000 km with two or three stopovers for $949 ($729 for children), or 10,000 km with three to seven stopovers for $1499 ($1149 for children). Restrictions include a minimum travel time (10 nights) and a maximum (45 nights). One of the stops must be at a noncapital-city destination and be for at least four nights. All sectors must be booked when you purchase the ticket, although these can be changed without penalty unless the ticket needs rewriting, in which case there's a $50 charge. Refunds are available before travel commences but not after you start using the ticket.

In practice, these set-distance air passes are rarely sold nowadays. Unless you leave your booking until the last minute, advance purchase fares will usually work out much cheaper than a set-distance air pass. For example, on a 6000-km air pass you could fly Cairns-Alice Springs-Sydney-Brisbane-Cairns. The air pass will cost you $949, whereas the same flights booked 21 days in advance will cost only $643.

Ansett also has passes available only to foreign visitors. Currently, the Visit Australia

Pass must be bought and booked overseas, but you can alter your bookings and buy extra coupons after arrival. Four coupons (each giving a day's travel in the one direction) cost about $650, or $750 if you include Perth, and each additional coupon costs about $170, $220 if it includes Perth.

Warning

Prices for international travel are volatile: routes are introduced and cancelled, schedules change, rules are amended, special deals come and go, borders open and close. Airlines and governments seem to take a perverse pleasure in making price structures and regulations as complicated as possible, and you should check directly with the airline or travel agent to make sure you understand how a fare (and ticket you may buy) works.

In addition, the travel industry is highly competitive and there are many lurks and perks. The upshot of this is that you should get opinions, quotes and advice from as many airlines and travel agents as possible before you part with your hard-earned cash. The details given in this chapter should be regarded only as pointers and cannot be any substitute for your own careful, up-to-date research.

Flying Yourself

If you are a pilot, flying yourself can be an interesting option and a fairly efficient way to cover large distances.

Many flying schools and clubs hire out planes for private use, and are the best places to meet other pilots and find out about local flying conditions. They are listed in the *Yellow Pages* phone book or you can just go out to the local airport and ask around.

Most capital cities have a separate suburban airport for general aviation, such as Archerfield in Brisbane, Bankstown in Sydney or Moorabbin in Melbourne.

Typical single-engine hire charges start at around $85 an hour for a Cessna 152, or $95 for a Cessna 172 or a Piper Warrior. From this point on prices increase roughly in proportion to cruising speed. If you want a twin,

a Seminole is about $180 an hour. Rates at the lower end are usually 'wet VDO', ie engine hours inclusive of fuel and oil. You get a credit for any fuel you buy along the way, but only at the operator's local price, not what you paid for it. If you want to take the aircraft away overnight the operator will probably expect a minimum average usage.

Flying Conditions Anyone planning to fly in Australia will need more information than can be covered in these general comments, and any flying school or hire company will have instructors who are qualified to explain everything you need to know about local conditions and current regulations. They will also brief you on current airspace classifications which are in the process of being reviewed to bring them into line with international standards.

Australia has a fairly low level of air traffic, especially compared with North America and Europe, and it is mainly concentrated around a few cities and a couple of tourist areas. Elsewhere the sky is pretty empty but unfortunately navigation facilities are equally sparse. Radar coverage is limited to regions around the major cities and much of the country is outside the range of VOR transmitters so you have to rely on dead reckoning and the ADF for cross-country flying, especially in the outback. The use of GPS equipment is increasingly common but is not yet approved as a primary means of navigation.

Much of central Australia is classified as a 'Designated Remote Area' because of its inaccessibility or being beyond the range of VHF communications, and flights here must carry a higher level of on-board equipment, such as HF radio or an ELB.

Australia generally uses metric measurements but some imperial units are used in aviation for consistency with other countries. The result is a mixture, with altitudes in feet, winds and airspeeds in knots, long distances in nautical miles, short distances like runway lengths in metres and fuel in litres. Don't worry, it's not as confusing as it sounds.

Flight Planning Charts and other planning documents can be obtained from the Air Services Australia (ASA) Publications Centre in Melbourne (☎ (03) 9342 2000 or toll-free ☎ 1800 33 1676) or from aviation supply shops at the larger general aviation airports.

Most large country towns have a local airport with sufficient facilities for regional commuter airlines. Many smaller towns offer a licensed airfield, even if it's only a gravel strip, a windsock and (with luck) a public phone. The ASA's *En Route Supplement – Australia* (commonly known as *ERSA)* has details of all licensed airfields, including runway diagrams, navaids and fuel availability.

There are also a number of private and unlicensed airfields (some of them mentioned in *ERSA)*, and further down the scale numerous private strips and landing areas. Prior permission to land at these is usually required from the owner of the plane and also from the landowner if it is private property.

Avgas is widely available but prior notice may be required in some places. The price varies from around 75 cents a litre in the cities, increasing with distance to almost double in remote outback towns. Expect to pay a call-out fee (typically $20) to refuel outside normal hours.

Licences Licensing and all other regulations are controlled by the Civil Aviation Safety Authority (CASA), which has regional offices at airports in most capital cities and larger regional centres. The head office (☎ (06) 268 4393; fax 268 4729) can be contacted at GPO Box 367, Canberra, ACT 2601.

If you have a current foreign licence, the CASA will issue a Certificate of Validation which allows you to fly for up to three months. This costs $55 plus $20 per rating and is available over the counter from any regional office. No medical or flying test is required for visual flying but you must be able to speak English. For longer periods a Special Pilot Licence is available for private operations for a fee of $50. Again there is no

theory exam or flight test for VFR operations but you do need a current overseas medical certificate and to have had a flight check within the previous two years. You can apply at any CASA regional office, and the licence is then mailed to you from Canberra.

With either method, if you have an instrument rating you will generally need to pass a written exam and a flight test before flying IFR in Australia.

In addition to the CASA's legal requirements, any company hiring you an aircraft will require a check flight with an instructor to get you familiar with local conditions. Instructor rates are usually around $55 an hour on top of the normal hire cost.

LAND

Travelling overland from elsewhere in Australia to Queensland can mean a major journey. The nearest state capital to Brisbane is Sydney, 1030 km away by the shortest route. To Melbourne it's at least 1735 km, to Adelaide it's at least 2130 km, Perth is a mere 4390 km away and the shortest road to Darwin is 3495 km long.

Bus

Travelling by bus is usually the cheapest way to get around Australia, but you'll need to do a little shopping around to find the best and most suitable deal. You can book directly with the bus companies, although it's often worth checking with travel agents and fare-brokers such as Dial-a-Coach in Brisbane (☎ (07) 3221 2225) to find out about special deals.

There are basically two types of fares for bus travel – express fares and bus passes. Students, backpackers (YHA and VIP card holders) and pensioners get discounts of at least 10% off most express fares and bus passes.

There is only one truly *national* bus network – Greyhound Pioneer Australia (☎ 13 2030), which consists of the former Greyhound/Pioneer and Bus Australia companies. All were once separate companies, and in fact the buses are still done out in their original paint-jobs.

The Queensland-based McCafferty's (☎ (07) 3236 3033) is Australia's next biggest operator, with services all along the east coast as well as the loop through the Centre to Adelaide, Alice Springs and Darwin to Townsville. There are quite a few smaller companies running less extensive routes.

A great many travellers see Australia by bus because it's one of the best ways to come to grips with the country's size and variety of terrain, and because the bus companies have such comprehensive route networks – far more comprehensive than the railway system. The buses all look pretty similar and are similarly equipped with air-conditioning, toilets and videos. Big city bus terminals are generally well equipped – they usually have toilets, showers and facilities.

There are also a few interesting alternatives to straightforward bus travel – see the Tours section of the Getting Around chapter for details.

Express Fares Express fares are for straight point-to-point travel. On these tickets stopover conditions vary from company to company – some give you one free stopover or allow you to stopover wherever they have a terminal, and others charge a fee of perhaps $10 for each stopover. If you want to make multiple stopovers, you'll end up paying full fares on each separate segment – in these cases a bus pass may work out to be better value.

Quite a few companies ply the busy Brisbane to Sydney route, including Greyhound Pioneer Australia, McCafferty's, Kirklands (☎ (07) 3236 444) and Border Coaches (☎ (07) 3236 4189). The Pacific Hwy run along the coast takes around 14 hours; the inland New England Hwy takes a couple of hours' less. Fares for both routes are around $70, although these are competitive routes and you'll usually find discounted fares and special backpacker deals if you shop around.

Greyhound Pioneer Australia is the only company with a service between Brisbane and Perth, via Sydney. The trips takes around three and a half days and costs $323.

For direct buses to the other capital cities, you have a choice between Greyhound Pioneer Australia and McCafferty's. The Newell Hwy is the most direct route between Brisbane and Melbourne. This trip takes around 25 hours and costs around $125.

To Adelaide, the shortest route (via Dubbo) takes around 31 hours and costs around $155.

It's a 48-hour trip from Brisbane to Darwin (via Longreach), and the fare is around $240.

Bus Passes Greyhound Pioneer Australia and McCafferty's both have a wide variety of passes available, so it's a matter of deciding which best suits your needs. Their networks are fairly similar throughout eastern and central Australia, but at this stage only Greyhound Pioneer Australia has services throughout Western Australia.

Broadly, there are two different types of bus passes: set-route versions and set-duration versions.

Both companies have a range of set-route passes, which basically give you six or 12 months to cover a set route. For example, Greyhound Pioneer Australia's Aussie Highlights pass and McCafferty's Visit Australia Pass both allow you to loop around the eastern half of Australia and take in Cairns, Brisbane, Sydney, Melbourne, Adelaide, Alice Springs, Darwin and back across to Townsville. Both these passes are valid for 12 months and cost around $700 (or $630 if you qualify for concessions). Or you could choose a pass that will take you up the east coast, say from Melbourne to Cairns. This would be valid for six months and would cost around $240 ($215 concession). The main limitations with these passes are that you can only travel in one direction and you can't backtrack, except on 'dead-end' sectors like Townsville to Cairns, Darwin to Kakadu and Uluru (Ayers Rock) to the Stuart Hwy.

Greyhound Pioneer Australia also has set-duration passes, which allow travel on a set number of days during a specified period. There are no restrictions on where you can travel, so you can travel in any direction and backtrack if necessary. These passes range from $450 for seven days of travel in one month up to 90 days of travel in six months (what a nightmare!) for $2225.

Train

To a degree, rail travel in Australia today is more of a luxury than a convenience. Australia's railway system is less comprehensive than the bus networks, and train services are less frequent and more expensive.

Having said that, the trains are much more comfortable than buses, and you certainly see Australia at ground level in a way no other means of travel permits. Interstate trains are now as fast or faster than buses and in recent years the railways have cut their prices in an attempt to be more competitive with both bus fares and reduced airfares.

Somewhat confusingly, the individual states run their own railway services – Queensland has Queensland Rail, NSW has Countrylink, Victoria has V/Line and Western Australia has Westrail – and these combine to provide the interstate services. Australian National Railways is an association of the government-owned systems in Queensland, New South Wales, Victoria and Western Australia, and this body goes some way to co-ordinating the major services.

As the interstate railway booking system is computerised, any station (other than those on metropolitan lines) can make a booking for any journey throughout the country. For reservations telephone ☎ 13 2232 from anywhere in Australia; this will connect you to the nearest booking agent. The hours of this service vary slightly from state to state: in Queensland, the service is open from 6 am to 8.30 pm daily; in NSW, from 6.30 am to 10 pm; and in Victoria from 7 am to 9 pm.

Fares & Conditions There are three standard fare levels for interstate rail travel – economy, 1st class and sleeping berths, although sleeping berths aren't available on all trains. Depending on availability, a limited number of discounted fares are offered on all trains. These cut 10% to 40%

off the standard fares, and if you book early or travel at off-peak times, you'll usually qualify for one of these cheaper fares. There are also half-price concession fares available to children under the age of 16, secondary students and Australian tertiary students, but unfortunately there are no discounts for backpackers.

On interstate journeys you can make free stopovers – you have two months to complete your trip on a one-way ticket and six months on a return ticket.

There are no discounts for return travel – a return ticket is just double the price of a one-way ticket.

Interstate Services & Fares Interstate railway services basically operate between the capital cities. That means that while there are direct services from Brisbane to Sydney, if you want to go from Brisbane to either Melbourne or Adelaide, you have to go via Sydney, and if you want to go from Brisbane to Perth, you have to go via Sydney *and* Adelaide. Fares are also calculated on each sector; for example, to go from Brisbane to Melbourne you'll pay the Brisbane to Sydney fare *plus* the Sydney to Melbourne fare.

Countrylink has a daily XTP service between Brisbane and Sydney. The northbound service runs overnight, the southbound service runs during the day. The trip takes 13½ hours and costs $98/142 in economy/1st class, and $224.50 in a sleeper.

There are two daily XTP services between Sydney and Melbourne; one during the day, one overnight. The trip takes about 10 hours and costs $93/130 in economy/1st class, and $212.50 in a sleeper.

The *Overlander* is an overnight train which runs between Melbourne and Adelaide. It takes 12 hours and costs $50/104 in economy/1st class, and $170 in a sleeper.

The popular *Indian Pacific* covers 4350 km on its twice-weekly transcontinental journey from Sydney to Perth via Adelaide. It's about 26 hours from Sydney to Adelaide, and fares are $120 for an economy seat, $216 in an economy sleeper and $338 in a 1st-class sleeper. The Adelaide to Perth leg takes another 44 hours and costs $200 for an economy seat, $396 in an economy sleeper and $605 in a 1st-class sleeper. On both legs, all meals are included in the 1st-class sleeper fares.

Motorail services are also available on some interstate trains. On top of the individual passenger fares, it costs $175 to take your car with you from Sydney to Adelaide, $290 from Adelaide to Perth and $80 from Melbourne to Adelaide.

Rail Passes There are a number of passes available which allow unlimited rail travel either across the country or just in one state, but with the exception of Queensland's Sunshine Rail Pass (see the Getting Around chapter), these passes are now only available to international visitors.

With the Austrail Pass you can travel anywhere on the Australian rail network for a set number of days, in either 1st class or economy. The cost is $725/435 in 1st/economy class for 14 days, $895/565 for 21 days, $1100/685 for 30 days, $1535/980 for 60 days and $1765/1125 for 90 days.

The Austrail Flexipass differs in that it allows a set number of travelling days within a six-month period. The cost is $560/340 in 1st class/economy for eight days of travel, $790/500 for 15 days, $1100/700 for 22 days and $1400/900 for 29 days. (An eight-day Flexipass cannot be used for travel between Adelaide and Perth or Alice Springs.)

Also worth considering is the East Coast Discovery Pass, which allows you one-way travel along the east coast with unlimited stopovers in a six-month period. The pass is only available in economy class and costs $199 from Sydney to Cairns, or $123 from Brisbane to Cairns.

Surcharges are payable on sleeping berths in both classes, and on certain trains, such as the Ghan (Adelaide to Alice Springs) and the Indian Pacific (Sydney to Perth), there are compulsory meal charges as well.

The passes can be purchased at major railway stations and from travel agents. For details of passes and conditions contact Rail Australia on ☎ (08) 217 4479.

Car & Motorcycle
See the Getting Around chapter for details of road rules, driving conditions and information on buying and renting vehicles.

The main road route into Queensland from the west is the Barkly Hwy, which leaves the Stuart Hwy at Threeways (midway between Darwin and Alice Springs) and cuts across to Mt Isa. From Mt Isa, you can continue eastward along the Flinders Hwy to Townsville on the coast, or head south-east along the Matilda Hwy towards Brisbane.

There are a couple of major routes into Queensland from the south. The Pacific Hwy is the main coastal route between Sydney and Brisbane – it passes through a string of coastal resort towns, but can be slow going and isn't a particularly fun road to drive.

The New England Hwy is a longer inland route from Sydney to Brisbane, but it's a less stressful drive and can end up taking about the same number of driving hours as the slog up the coast.

The Newell Hwy is the most direct route from Brisbane to Melbourne – it's a good road through the heartland of rural NSW. The major route from Adelaide to Brisbane is the Barrier Hwy which takes you across to Dubbo via Broken Hill; from Dubbo, the Newell Hwy takes you up to Brisbane.

The other major route into southern Queensland is the Mitchell Hwy, which links Bourke in outback NSW with Charleville and Barcaldine in outback Queensland.

SEA
Crewing on Yachts
It is quite possible to make your way round the Australian coast to Queensland, or even to/from other countries like New Zealand, Papua New Guinea or Indonesia, by hitching rides or crewing on yachts. Ask around at harbours, marinas or yacht clubs. It's often worth contacting the secretaries of sailing clubs and asking whether they have a notice board where people advertise for crews – some of the major Australian clubs even run

waiting lists for people wanting to crew on yachts. Look under 'Clubs – Yacht' in the *Yellow Pages* telephone directory. It obviously helps if you're an experienced sailor, but some people are taken on as cooks (not very pleasant on a rolling yacht). Usually you have to chip in something for food, and the skipper may demand a financial bond as security. A lot of yachties head north for Queensland from south-east Australia to escape the winter, so April is a good time to look for a berth in the southern harbours.

Cargo Ships

If you like the idea of travelling the high seas as a paying passenger on a cargo ship, a Sydney-based company called Freighter Travel (☎ (02) 484 6100) can book you on a slow boat between Australia and New Zealand, Europe or the USA. The accommodation provided for passengers on cargo ships is often surprisingly comfortable – cabins are usually air-conditioned, and you get to dine in the officers' mess. Sounds great, doesn't it? But there are a few catches. Services are irregular and only leave once or twice a month; the fares cost an arm, a leg *and* a nose; and you'll have to provide your own entertainment program. But if you have plenty of time and money and enjoy reading, playing solitaire and navel (naval?) contem-

plation as hobbies, and don't get seasick, then I can't think of a better way to travel. From Brisbane, you'll be up for about $4500 for the 27-day trip to the USA east coast, and about $750 for the four-day trip to Dunedin in New Zealand. Ships between Europe and Australia only go via Melbourne; the 45-day trip costs around $6000.

WARNING

The information in this chapter is particularly vulnerable to change: prices for international travel are volatile, routes are introduced and cancelled, schedules change, special deals come and go, and rules and visa requirements are amended. Airlines and governments seem to take a perverse pleasure in making price structures and regulations as complicated as possible.

You should check directly with the airline or a travel agent to make sure you understand how a fare (and ticket you may buy) works. In addition, the travel industry is highly competitive and there are many lurks and perks. The upshot of this is that you should get opinions, quotes and advice from as many airlines and travel agents as possible before you part with your hard-earned cash. The details given in this chapter should be regarded as pointers and are not a substitute for your own careful, up-to-date research.

Getting Around

AIR

Ansett (☎ 13 1300) and Qantas (☎ 13 1313) have interstate flights connecting Brisbane with the other capital cities, as well as flights to many of the major cities within Queensland.

Queensland's major regional airlines are Sunstate (a subsidiary of Qantas; bookings handled by Qantas); and Flight West Airlines (☎ 13 2392 within Queensland or toll-free 1800 777 879 from elsewhere in Australia). Flight West is independently owned, although it is associated with Ansett and Ansett can also handle its bookings.

Sunstate and Flight West fly smaller planes on the shorter intra-state routes, working in with their larger associates. For example, if you wanted to get from Melbourne to Birdsville, you'd fly Melbourne-Brisbane with Ansett and Brisbane-Birdsville with Flight West. Similarly, if you were heading from Sydney to the Sunshine Coast you could fly Sydney-Brisbane with Qantas and with Sunstate from Brisbane-Maroochydore. There is quite a bit of overlap in the four airlines' networks, although their prices are identical on shared routes.

The Queensland Air Fares chart in this chapter quotes full one-way economy fares within the state – see the Domestic Flights section in the Getting There & Away chapter for details of discounted air fares.

There's also a multitude of smaller airlines operating up and down the coast, across the Cape York Peninsula and into the outback. During the wet season, such flights are often the only means of getting around the Gulf Savannah or the Cape York Peninsula. See the Getting There & Away sections in the individual chapters for details of these.

BUS

Greyhound Pioneer Australia (☎ 13 2030) and McCafferty's (☎ (07) 3236 3033) have the most comprehensive bus networks throughout Queensland. Their networks cover all of the major towns and destinations,

linking up with their interstate services into the Northern Territory and New South Wales. They also service many of Queensland's smaller towns on their express runs. The Queensland-based McCafferty's also has services to quite a few smaller centres which aren't covered by Greyhound Pioneer Australia.

They both offer either express bus fares or bus passes – see the Getting There & Away chapter for details of their passes, fares and conditions. Their prices are fairly similar, although McCafferty's express fares tend to be a dollar or two cheaper.

A company called Oz Experience offers an interesting alternative to buying a bus pass – see the Tours section later in this chapter.

There are also numerous smaller bus companies with more specialised local services – see the Getting There & Away headings under individual towns for details of these.

Express Fares & Major Routes

Express fares are for straight point-to-point travel, and if you don't have a bus pass and want to make stopovers between point A and point B, you'll either have to pay separate fares for each sector or pay a stopover fee of perhaps $10.

The busiest bus route is the coastal run up the Bruce Hwy from Brisbane to Cairns. Individual sector fares and travel times to the major destinations along the coast are: Brisbane-Hervey Bay ($34, 5½ hours); Hervey Bay-Rockhampton ($53, seven hours); Rockhampton-Mackay ($39, 4½ hours); Mackay-Airlie Beach ($26, about two hours); Airlie Beach-Townsville ($37, four hours); Townsville-Cairns ($38, six hours). The express Brisbane-Cairns fare would be $137, whereas the individual sector fares add up to $227. Both companies have passes which cover the coastal run: Greyhound Pioneer Australia's Sunseeker pass and McCafferty's Follow the Sun (ex Brisbane) pass both give you six months to travel along

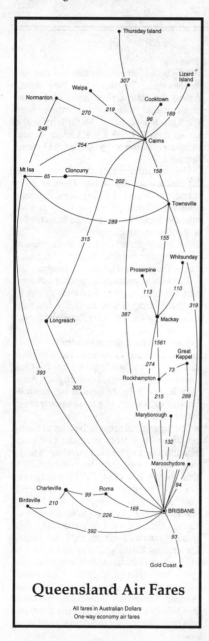

Queensland Air Fares

All fares in Australian Dollars
One-way economy air fares

the coast between Brisbane and Cairns, with unlimited stopovers. Both passes cost around $155 ($140 concession).

The other major bus route out of Brisbane is the inland service to Mt Isa, from where you can continue to either Darwin or Alice Springs in the Northern Territory. The express fare for the 22-hour trip is around $105. The individual sector fares include Brisbane-Roma ($37, five hours); Roma-Longreach ($42, 8½ hours); Longreach-Mt Isa ($53, 8½ hours).

The other major bus services are from Townsville to Mt Isa via Charters Towers (around $80, 11½ hours) and from Rockhampton to Longreach via Emerald and Barcaldine (McCafferty's only, $51, 9½ hours). McCafferty's also has a hinterland service which runs inland from and parallel with the coast from Brisbane to Toowoomba, Miles, Springsure, Emerald, Clermont and Charters Towers.

TRAIN

Rail services within Queensland are operated by Queensland Rail. There are five Queensland Rail Travel Centres throughout the state – these are basically booking offices which can advise you on all rail travel, sell you tickets and put together rail holiday packages which include transport and accommodation. There are Travel Centres based in the following cities:

Brisbane
    Ground floor, 305 Edward St (☎ (07) 3235 1323)
Cairns
    Cairns railway station, McLeod St (☎ (070) 52 6267)
Townsville
    Townsville railway station, Flinders St (☎ (077) 72 8546)
Rockhampton
    Rockhampton railway station, Murray St (☎ (079) 32 0234)
Surfers Paradise
    Cavill Park Building, corner of Beach Rd and Gold Coast Hwy (☎ (07) 5539 9088)

You can also buy train tickets through travel agents. Telephone reservations can be made through one of the Travel Centres or through

Queensland Rail's centralised booking service, which you reach by phoning ☎ 13 2232 from anywhere in Australia; in Queensland, this service operates daily from 6 am to 8.30 pm.

Rail travel within Queensland is slower and more expensive than bus travel, although some of the economy fares are now comparable with bus fares. Depending on your itinerary, a rail pass might also be worth looking into (see below). The trains are almost all air-con and you can get sleeping berths on most trains for $30 extra a night in economy, $50 in 1st class. You can break your journey on most services for no extra cost provided you complete the trip within 14 days (single ticket) or two months (return ticket).

Half-price concession fares are available to children under 16 years of age, Australian students, and seniors and pensioners from Queensland.

Rail Services

There are seven major rail services throughout Queensland, as well as three minor services in north Queensland which operate primarily as tourist routes:

Queenslander Promoted as a 'luxurious hotel on wheels', the *Queenslander* travels along the coast between Brisbane and Cairns once a week, leaving Brisbane on Sunday mornings and returning from Cairns on Tuesday mornings. All passengers on the *Queenslander* travel 1st class, with sleeping berths and all meals included in the fares. Brisbane to Mackay takes 16½ hours and costs $377; Brisbane to Townsville takes about 23 hours and costs $433; and Brisbane to Cairns takes about 32 hours and costs $489. The *Queenslander* is also a motorail service; for another $270 you can take you car with you from Brisbane to Cairns.

Spirit of the Outback This train travels the 1326 km between Brisbane and Longreach via Rockhampton twice a week, leaving Brisbane on Tuesday and Friday evenings and returning from Longreach on Thursday and Sunday mornings. Brisbane to Rockhampton takes 11 hours and costs $67 for an economy seat, $97 for an economy sleeper and $158 for a 1st-class sleeper. Brisbane to Longreach takes 24 hours and costs $118/148/226. A connecting bus service operates between Longreach and Winton.

Spirit of Capricorn This all-economy train does the Brisbane to Rockhampton trip in just under ten hours, leaving Brisbane every morning as well as on Wednesday and Sunday evenings, and returning from Rocky every morning and on Wednesday evenings. The one-way fare is $67.

Sunlander The *Sunlander* travels between Brisbane and Cairns three times a week and the trip takes 32 hours, leaving Brisbane on Tuesday, Thursday and Saturday mornings and Cairns on Monday, Thursday and Saturday mornings. Fares are $129 for an economy seat, $159 for an economy sleeper and $243 for a 1st-class sleeper.

Spirit of the Tropics The all-economy *Spirit of the Tropics* is a rather unique concept in train travel – a 'party train' with its own disco/bar called Club Loco. It runs from Brisbane to Proserpine on Thursday afternoons, from Brisbane to Cairns on Sunday mornings, from Cairns to Brisbane on Tuesday mornings and from Proserpine to Brisbane on Friday afternoons. Brisbane to Proserpine costs $105; Brisbane to Cairns costs $129. Boy oh boy, doing 'the locomotion' could take on a whole new meaning...

Westlander The *Westlander* heads inland from Brisbane to Charleville every Tuesday and Thursday evening, returning from Charleville to Brisbane on Wednesday and Friday afternoons. It takes 15½ hours and costs $77 for an economy seat, $107 for an economy sleeper and $172 for a 1st-class sleeper. From Charleville, there are connecting bus services to Cunnamulla and Quilpie.

Inlander The *Inlander* does what its name suggests from Townsville to Mt Isa twice weekly, leaving Townsville on Sunday and Wednesday afternoons and Mt Isa on Monday and Friday afternoons. Fares are $95 for an economy seat, $125 for an economy sleeper and $192 for a 1st-class sleeper. The trip takes 19 hours.

Kuranda Scenic Railway This is one of the most popular tourist trips out of Cairns – a spectacular 1½ hour trip on historic steam trains to Kuranda, a market town in the mountainous rainforests west of Cairns. See the Far North Queensland chapter for details.

Gulflander The *Gulflander* is a strange, snub-nosed little train that travels once a week between the remote Gulf towns of Normanton and Croydon – it's a unique and memorable journey. See the Gulf Savannah chapter for details.

Savannahlander Queensland's newest rail service is an abbreviated version of the 'Last Great Train Ride', the old Cairns to Forsayth service which was somewhat controversially discontinued in 1995. The new service runs between Mt Surprise and Forsayth in the Gulf Savannah, leaving Mt Surprise at lunch time on Mondays and Thursdays and returning from Forsayth on Tuesday and Friday mornings. The trip takes a leisurely five hours and costs $35. There are connecting bus services to/from Cairns, and in conjunction with your trip on the *Savannahlander* you can take tours to the Undara Lava Tubes and the Tallaroo Hot Springs. See the Gulf Savannah chapter for details.

Rail Passes

At the time of writing, Queensland was the only state with a rail pass available to both international and domestic visitors. The Sunshine Rail Pass gives you unlimited travel on all rail services in Queensland for 14, 21 or 30 days. Fares in economy/1st class are 14 days for $267/388, 21 days for $309/477 and 30 days for $388/582. A surcharge is payable if you want to travel on the Queenslander (to cover sleeping berths and meals); the surcharge is $260 from Brisbane to Townsville or $293 from Brisbane to Cairns.

CAR

Queensland is a big, sprawling state where public transport is not always very comprehensive or convenient – the car is the accepted means of getting from A to B. More and more travellers are also finding it the best way to see the country – with three or four of you the costs are reasonable and the benefits many, provided of course you don't have a major mechanical problem.

In fact, if you want to get off the beaten track – and in parts of Queensland, it's a *very* beaten track – then having your own transport is the only way to go. Many of the destinations covered in this book aren't accessible by public transport, so if you want to discover the undiscovered side of Australia's most popular holiday destination, you'll need your own car or motorcycle.

For hints on safe driving in the outback, see the Outback Survival section in the Facts for the Visitor chapter.

Road Rules

Driving in Queensland holds few real surprises. Australians drive on the left-hand side of the road just like in the UK, Japan and most countries in south and east Asia and the Pacific.

There are a few local variations from the rules of the road as applied elsewhere in the West. The main one is the 'give way to the right' rule. This means that if you're driving along a main road and somebody appears on a minor road on your right, you must give way to them – unless they are facing a give-way or stop sign. This rule caused so much confusion over the years – with cars zooming out of tiny tracks onto main highways and expecting everything to screech to a stop for them – that most intersections are now signposted to indicate which is the priority road.

It's wise to be careful because while almost every intersection is signposted in southern capitals, when you get up to towns in the north of Queensland, stop signs are few and far between and the old give-way rules still apply. With so many southerners and overseas visitors driving around in Queensland, it can be extremely confusing when half the drivers are looking for stop signs and the other half are expecting the give way rule to be applied – after my first few harrowing weeks driving around Cairns, I decided it might be safer to give way to everyone at intersections.

The general speed limit in towns and built-up areas is 60 km/h, sometimes rising to 80 km/h on the outskirts and dropping to 40 km/h in residential areas and school zones. Out on the open highway it's usually 100 or 110 km/h depending on where you are, (when you get to the Northern Territory there is no speed limit outside of built-up areas).

The police have radar speed traps and speed cameras and are very fond of using them in carefully hidden locations in order to raise easy revenue – don't exceed the speed limit; the boys and girls in blue may be waiting for you. When you're far from the cities and traffic is light, you'll see a lot of vehicles moving a lot faster than 100 km/h.

Oncoming drivers who flash their lights at you may be giving you a friendly indication of a speed trap ahead.

Australia was one of the first countries in the world to make the wearing of seat belts compulsory. All new cars in Australia are required to have seat belts back and front and if your seat has a belt then you're required to wear it. You're liable to be fined if you don't. Small children must be belted into an approved safety seat.

Driving standards in Australia aren't exactly the highest in the world and drink-driving is a real problem, especially in country areas. Serious attempts have been made in recent years to reduce the road toll – random breath tests are not uncommon in built-up areas. If you're caught with a blood-alcohol level of more than 0.05 then be prepared for a hefty fine, a court appearance and the loss of your licence.

Although overseas licences are acceptable in Australia for genuine overseas visitors, an International Driving Permit is preferred.

Road Conditions
Australia is not crisscrossed by multilane highways. There simply is not enough traffic and the distances are too great to justify them. You'll certainly find stretches of divided road, particularly on busy roads out of the major cites – the Surfers Paradise-Brisbane road, for example. Elsewhere Queensland's main roads are only two lanes and well-surfaced (though a long way from the billiard-table surfaces the Poms are used to driving on) on all the main routes.

You don't have to get very far off the beaten track, however, to find yourself on dirt roads, and anybody who sets out to see Queensland in reasonable detail will have to expect to do some dirt-road travelling. A few useful spare parts are worth carrying – a broken fan belt can be a damn nuisance if the next service station is 200 km away.

Between cities, signposting on the main highways is generally quite OK, but once you hit the backroads, you'll need a good map – see Maps in the Facts for the Visitor chapter for suggestions.

Cows, sheep and kangaroos are common hazards on country roads, and a collision is likely to kill the animal and seriously damage your vehicle. Kangaroos are most active around dawn and dusk, and they travel in groups. If you see one hopping across the road in front of you, slow right down – its friends are probably just behind it. Many Australians try to avoid travelling altogether between 5 pm and 8 am, because of the hazards posed by animals. Finally, if one hops out right in front of you, hit the brakes and only swerve to avoid the animal if it is safe to do so. Many people have been killed in accidents caused by swerving to miss an animal – better to damage your car and probably kill the animal than kill yourself and others with you.

Fuel Service stations generally stock diesel, super and unleaded fuel, although some of the more remote places may not stock unleaded. Liquid petroleum gas (LPG, Autogas) is often unavailable, even at larger service stations along the main highways.

Fuel is generally cheaper in Queensland than in the southern states, although prices vary from place to place and from price war to price war. Expect to pay anywhere between 62c and 75c a litre for unleaded fuel in the larger towns and along major highways (super and diesel cost a couple of cents more, LPG significantly less). Some of the service stations in the more remote outback are not above exploiting their monopoly positions and the prices can soar to between 75c and 95c a litre. Distances between fill-ups can be long in the outback and in some remote areas deliveries can be haphazard – it's not unknown to finally arrive at that 'nearest station for a few hundred km' only to find there's no fuel until next week's delivery!

Outback Travel
Although you can now drive all the way round Australia on Hwy 1 or through the middle all the way from Adelaide in the south to Darwin in the north without ever leaving sealed road, that hasn't always been so. The

Eyre Hwy across the Nullarbor Plain in the south was only surfaced in the 1970s, the final stretch of Hwy 1 in the Kimberley region of Western Australia was done in the mid-1980s and the final section of the Stuart Hwy from Port Augusta up to Alice Springs was finished in 1987.

If you really want to see outback Australia there are still lots of roads where the official recommendation is that you report to the police before you leave one end, and again when you arrive at the other. That way if you fail to turn up at the other end they can send out search parties. Nevertheless many of these tracks are now much better kept than in years past and you don't need 4WD or fancy expedition equipment to tackle them. You do need to be carefully prepared and to carry important spare parts, however. Backtracking 500 km to pick up a replacement for some minor malfunctioning component or, much worse, to arrange a tow, is unlikely to be easy or cheap.

When travelling to really remote areas it is advisable to travel with a high frequency outpost radio transmitter which is equipped to pick up the Royal Flying Doctor Service bases in the area.

You will of course need to carry a fair amount of water in case of disaster – around 20 litres a person is sensible – stored in more than one container. Food is less important – the space might be better allocated to an extra spare tyre.

The RACQ (Queensland's automobile association) can advise on preparation and supply maps and track notes. See the section on Travel Guides in the Facts for the Visitor chapter for some recommendations of books covering preparation for outback travel.

Most tracks have an ideal time of year – in central Australia it's not wise to attempt the tough tracks during the heat of summer (November-March) when the dust can be severe, the chances of mechanical trouble are much greater and when water will be scarce and hence a breakdown more dangerous. Similarly in the north travelling in the wet season may be impossible due to flooding and mud. You should always seek advice on

road conditions when you're travelling into unfamiliar territory. The local police will be able to advise you whether roads are open and whether your vehicle is suitable for a particular track. The RACQ has a telephone service with a pre-recorded report on road conditions throughout the state – dial ☎ 11655, 24 hours a day. For more specific local info, you can call into the nearest

4WD or 2WD?

You can cover most of Queensland in a standard 2WD vehicle, but there are quite a few places you *won't* be able to visit in your old Ford or Holden station wagon – places where the only access is by 4WD. The advantages of 4WDs are their high clearance, which helps cope with river crossings, minor floods and deep wheel ruts that would rip the guts out of an ordinary car; and their ability to handle different terrains like the sandy tracks of Fraser Island or the slippery bull dust-covered hills of the Bloomfield Track. Modern 4WDs also handle the endless bumps and corrugations of unsealed roads much better than conventional cars.

The following are some of the places in Queensland only accessible by 4WD vehicle: Moreton Island and the northern parts of Bribie Island (Moreton Bay), Fraser Island and the Woodgate National Park (Fraser Coast Area), Deepwater National Park (south of Agnes Water), Byfield National Park (north of Yeppoon), Cape Palmerston National Park (south of Sarina), Sundown National Park (the Darling Downs), and the Bloomfield Track (the coastal route between Cape Tribulation and Cooktown). Most of the Cape York Peninsula is also only accessible by 4WD – you *could* drive a conventional vehicle up the main route as far as Weipa, and every year a few crazies try and get all the way to the top in normal cars, but not too many make it back again. You'll also miss most of the Cape's highlights if you stick to the main road. During the Dry, you could also tackle most of the Gulf Savannah's roads in a conventional vehicle, but again, it ain't recommended. The unsealed outback roads to Birdsville in the south-west corner fall into the same category – your Toyota Corolla might make it to Birdsville, but it will never be the same afterwards. ∎

RACQ office – they're listed in the information sections throughout this book.

If you do run into trouble in the back of beyond, stay with your car. It's easier to spot a car than a human being from the air, and you wouldn't be able to carry your 20 litres of water very far anyway.

Buying a Car

Australian cars are not cheap – another consequence of the small population. Locally manufactured cars are made in small, uneconomic numbers and imported cars are heavily taxed so they won't undercut the local products. If you're buying a second-hand vehicle, reliability is all important. Mechanical breakdowns way out in the outback can be very inconvenient (not to mention dangerous) – the nearest mechanic can be a hell of a long way down the road.

Shopping around for a used car involves much the same rules as anywhere in the Western world but with a few local variations. First of all, some used-car dealers in Australia are just like other used-car dealers from Los Angeles to London – they'd sell their mother into slavery if it turned a dollar. You'll probably get any car cheaper by buying privately through newspaper classified ads rather than through a car dealer. Buying through a dealer does give the advantage of some sort of guarantee, but a guarantee is not much use if you're buying a car in Sydney and intend setting off for Cairns next week. Used-car guarantee requirements vary from state to state – check with the local automobile organisation.

It's worth remembering that the further you get from civilisation, the better it is to be in a Holden or a Ford. New cars can be a whole different ball game of course, but if you're in an older vehicle, life is much simpler when you can get spare parts anywhere from Miles to Mt Isa – every scrap yard in Australia is full of good ol' Holdens and Fords.

Note that in Australia third-party personal injury insurance is always included in the vehicle registration cost. This ensures that every vehicle (as long as it's currently registered) carries at least minimum insurance. You're wise to extend that minimum to at least third-party property insurance as well – minor collisions with Rolls-Royces can be amazingly expensive.

When you come to buy or sell a car there are usually some local regulations to be complied with. In Queensland, for example, a car has to have a compulsory safety check (Road Worthiness Certificate – RWC) before it can be registered in the new owner's name – usually the seller will indicate if the car already has an RWC. In New South Wales and the Northern Territory, on the other hand, safety checks are compulsory every year when you come to renew the registration. Stamp duty has to be paid when you buy a car and, as this is based on the purchase price, it's not unknown for buyer and seller to agree privately to understate the price! It's much easier to sell a car in the same state that it's registered in, otherwise it has to be re-registered in the new state. It may be possible to sell a car without re-registering it, but you're likely to get a lower price.

One way of getting around the hassles of buying and selling a vehicle privately is to enter into a buy-back arrangement with a car or motorcycle dealer. However, dealers will often find ways of knocking down the price when you return the vehicle, even if a price has been agreed in writing – often by pointing out expensive repairs that allegedly will be required to gain the dreaded RWC needed to transfer the registration. The cars on offer have often been driven around Australia a number of times, often with haphazard or minimal servicing, and are generally pretty tired. The main advantage of these schemes is that you don't have to worry about being able to sell the vehicle quickly at the end of your trip, and can usually arrange insurance, which short-term visitors may find hard to get.

A company that specialises in buy-back arrangements on cars and motorcycles, with fixed rates and no hidden extras, is Car Connection Australia. Also known as Bike Tours Australia, it has been organising adventure holidays and expeditions covering the entire continent for over 10 years, and has recently branched into this sideline. Its programme is basically a glorified long-term rental arrangement where you put down a deposit to the value of the vehicle and in the end you get your money back, minus the fixed 'usage' fee.

The bottom line is that a second-hand Ford station wagon or Yamaha XT600 trail bike will set you back a fixed sum of $1950 for any period up to six months; a Toyota Landcruiser, suitable for serious outback exploration, is $3500, also for up to six months. Prices include pick-up at Melbourne Airport and a night's accommodation in Castlemaine to help you acclimatise, and you'll be sent on your way with touring maps and advice. You can also rent camping equipment (but not sleeping bags). Car Connection Australia (☎ (054) 73 4469; fax (054) 73 4520) is at RSD Lot 8, Vaughan Springs Rd, Glenluce (near Castlemaine), Vic 3451. Information and bookings are handled by its European agent: Travel Action GmbH (☎ (0276) 4 78 24; fax (0276) 479 38), Einsiedeleiweg 16, 57399 Kirch-hundem, Germany.

Finally, make use of the RACQ – see the Facts for the Visitor chapter for more details about them. They can advise you on any local regulations you should be aware of, give general guidelines about buying a car and, most importantly, for a fee (around $90) will check over a used car and report on its condition before you agree to purchase it. They also offer car insurance to their members. Most mechanics will also check out a car for you – they are often a bit cheaper than the RACQ, but may do a less comprehensive check.

Car Rental

If you've got the cash there are plenty of car-rental companies ready and willing to put you behind the wheel. Competition in the Australian car-rental business is pretty fierce, so rates tend to be variable and lots of special deals pop up and disappear again. Whatever your mode of travel on the long stretches, it can be very useful to have a car for some local travel. Between a group it can even be reasonably economical. There are some places where if you haven't got your own wheels you really have to choose between a tour and a rented vehicle since there is no public transport and the distances are too great for walking or even bicycles.

The three major companies are Budget, Hertz and Avis, with offices in all major cities, and agents in most other reasonably sizeable towns. Thrifty and National are second-string companies which also have fairly wide networks. Then there is a vast number of local firms or firms with outlets in a limited number of locations. You can take it as read that the big operators will generally have higher rates than the local firms but it ain't necessarily so, so don't jump to conclusions.

The big firms have a number of big advantages, however. First of all they're the ones at the airports – Avis, Budget, Hertz and, quite often, Thrifty, are represented at most airports. If you want to pick up a car or leave a car at the airport then they're the best ones to deal with. Other companies will also arrange to pick up or leave their cars at some airports. It tends to depend on how convenient the airport is.

The second advantage of the big companies is if you want to do a one-way rental – pick up a car in Cairns and leave it in Sydney, for example. There are, however, a variety of restrictions on these. Usually it's a minimum-hire period rather than repositioning charges. Only certain cars may be eligible for one-ways. Check the small print on one-way charges before deciding on one company rather than another. The major companies all offer unlimited km rates in the city, but in country and 'remote' areas it's a flat charge plus so many cents per km. On straightforward off-the-card city rentals they're all pretty much the same price. It's on special deals, odd rentals or longer periods that you find the differences. Weekend specials – usually three days for the price of two – are usually good value.

Rates are typically about $70 a day for a

small car (Ford Laser, Toyota Corolla, Nissan Pulsar), about $90 a day for a medium car (Holden Camira, Toyota Camry, Nissan Pintara) or about $100 to $110 a day for a big car (Holden Commodore, Ford Falcon), all including insurance. These rates are just for one day's hire – obviously, the longer the hire period, the cheaper the daily rate.

Be aware that the insurance usually has an excess – if you have a prang, the excess is the amount you have to pay before the insurance company takes over. With some of the smaller companies the excess figure can be very high. Most companies prefer to rent to people over 21, and some require you to be over 25, although there are a few who will rent to 18-year-olds (often with higher insurance premiums or a greater excess).

And don't forget the 'rent-a-wreck' companies. They specialise in renting older cars, typically from around $35 a day. If you just want to travel around the city, or not too far out, they can be worth considering.

Moke Rental In lots of popular holiday areas – like on the Gold Coast, around Cairns and on Magnetic Island – right at the bottom of the rent-a-car rates will be the ubiquitous Moke. To those not in the know, a Moke is a totally open vehicle looking rather like a miniature Jeep. They're based on the Mini so they're FWD (front-wheel drive) not 4WD and they are not suitable for getting way off the beaten track. For general good fun in places with a sunny climate, however, they simply can't be beaten. No vehicle has more air-conditioning than a Moke, and as the stickers say 'Moking is not a wealth hazard' – they cover lots of km on a litre of petrol.

If you do hire a Moke there are a few points to watch. Don't have an accident in one; they offer little more protection than a motorcycle. There is absolutely no place to lock things up so don't leave your valuables inside, and the fuel tanks are equally accessible so if you're leaving it somewhere at night beware of petrol thieves – not that there are a great number in Australia, but it does happen.

4WD Rental Having 4WD enables you to get right off the beaten track and out to some of the great wilderness and outback places, to see some of the Australian natural wonders that most travellers don't see.

Renting a 4WD vehicle is within the budget range if a few people get together. Something small like a Suzuki costs around $100 per day; for a Toyota Landcruiser you're looking at around $150, which should include insurance and some free km (typically 100 km). Again, these daily rates start to drop when you rent for more than a few days. Check the insurance conditions, especially the excess, as they can be onerous.

Hertz has 4WD rentals, with one-way rentals possible between the eastern states and the Northern Territory. Budget also rents 4WD vehicles from Darwin and Alice Springs. Brits Australia (☎ (1800) 331 454) is a company which hires fully equipped 4WD vehicles fitted out as campervans. These have proved extremely popular in recent years, although they are not cheap at $155 per day for unlimited km, plus collision damage waiver ($12 per day). They have offices in Brisbane and the other mainland capitals, as well as in Cairns and Alice Springs, so one-way rentals are also possible.

In Brisbane, Four Wheel Drive Hire Service (☎ (07) 3357 9077) and Allterrain Rentals (☎ (07) 3257 1101) are both reputable local companies which rent vehicles for trips up to Fraser Island and various other places. You can also hire 4WDs from Noosa Heads and Hervey Bay for Fraser Island trips – see those sections for details. There are several companies in Cairns that will rent you a 4WD for a Cape York expedition – see Cairns' Getting There & Away section for details.

Renting Other Vehicles
There are lots of other vehicles you can rent apart from cars. In many places you can rent campervans. Motorscooters are also available in a number of locations – they are popular on Magnetic Island and in Cairns for example – and you only need a car licence to

ride one. Best of all, in many places you can rent bicycles.

MOTORCYCLE

Motorcycles are a very popular way of getting around. Between April and November, the climate is just about ideal for biking around Queensland, and the many small trails from the road into the bush often lead to perfect spots to spend the night in the world's largest camping ground.

The long, open roads are really made for large-capacity machines above 750 cc, which Australians prefer once they outgrow their 250 cc learner restrictions. But that doesn't stop enterprising individuals – many of them Japanese – from tackling the length and breadth of the continent on 250 cc trail bikes. Doing it on a small bike is not impossible, just tedious at times.

If you want to bring your own motorcycle into Australia you'll need a *carnet de passage*, and when you try to sell it you'll get less than the market price because of restrictive registration requirements. Shipping from just about anywhere is expensive.

However, with a little bit of time up your sleeve, getting mobile on two wheels in Australia is quite feasible, thanks largely to the chronically depressed motorcycle market. The beginning of the southern winter is a good time to strike. Australian newspapers and the lively local bike press have extensive classified advertisement sections where $2500 gets you something that will easily take you around the country if you know a bit about bikes. The main drawback is that you'll have to try and sell it again afterwards.

An easier option is a buy-back arrangement with a large motorcycle dealer in a major city. They're keen to do business, and basic negotiating skills allied with a wad of cash (say, $4000) should secure an excellent second-hand bike with a written guarantee that they'll buy it back in good condition minus $1500 or $2000 after your four-month, round-Australia trip. Popular brands for this sort of thing are BMWs, large-capacity, shaft-driven Japanese bikes and possibly

Harley-Davidsons (very popular in Australia). The percentage drop on a trail bike will be much greater (though the actual amount you lose should be similar), but very few dealers are interested in buy-back schemes on trail bikes.

You'll need a rider's licence and a helmet. A fuel range of 350 km will cover most fuel stops. Beware of dehydration in the dry, hot air – force yourself to drink plenty of water, even if you don't feel thirsty. The 'roo bars' (outsize bumpers) on interstate trucks and many outback cars tell you never to ride at night, or in the early morning and evening. Marsupials are nocturnal, sleeping in the shade during the day and feeding at night, and road ditches often provide lush grass for them to eat. Cows and sheep also stray onto the roads at night. It's wise to stop riding by around 5 pm.

Many roadhouses offer showers free of charge or for a nominal fee. They're meant for truck drivers, but other people often use them too.

It's worth carrying some spares and tools even if you don't know how to use them, because someone else often does. If you do know, you'll probably have a fair idea of what to take. The basics include: a spare tyre tube (front wheel size, which will fit on the rear but usually not vice versa); puncture repair kit with levers and a pump (or tubeless tyre repair kit with at least three carbon dioxide cartridges); a spare tyre valve, and a valve cap that can unscrew same; the bike's standard tool kit for what it's worth; spare throttle, clutch and brake cables; tie wire, cloth tape ('gaffer' tape) and nylon 'zip-ties'; a handful of bolts and nuts in the usual emergency sizes (M6 and M8), along with a few self-tapping screws; one or two fuses in your bike's ratings; a bar of soap for fixing tank leaks (knead to a putty with water and squeeze into the leak); and, most important of all, a workshop manual for your bike (even if you can't make sense of it, the local motorcycle mechanic can). You'll never have enough elastic straps (octopus or 'ocky' straps) to tie down your gear.

Make sure you carry water – at least two

litres on major roads in central Australia, more off the beaten track. And finally, if something does go hopelessly wrong in the back of beyond, park your bike where it's clearly visible and observe the cardinal rule: *don't leave your vehicle.*

BICYCLE

Queensland is a great place for cycling. There are bike tracks in most cities, and in the country you'll find thousands of km of good roads which carry so little traffic that the biggest hassle is waving back to the drivers. Especially appealing is that in many areas you'll ride a very long way without encountering a hill.

Bicycle helmets are compulsory, as are front and rear lights for night riding.

Cycling has always been popular in Australia, and not only as a sport: some shearers would ride for huge distances between jobs, rather than use less reliable horses. It's rare to find a reasonably sized town that doesn't have a shop stocking at least basic bike parts.

If you're coming specifically to cycle, it makes sense to bring your own bike. Check your airline for costs and the degree of dismantling/packing required. Within Australia you can load your bike onto a bus or train to skip the boring bits. Note that bus companies require you to dismantle your bike, and some don't guarantee that it will travel on the same bus as you. Trains are easier, but supervise the loading and if possible tie your bike upright, otherwise you may find that the guard has stacked crates of Holden spares on your fragile alloy wheels.

You can buy a good steel-framed touring bike in Australia for about $400 (plus panniers). It may be possible to rent touring bikes and equipment from a few of the commercial touring organisations. You can also rent mountain bikes from bike shops in many cities, although these are usually for short-term hire (around $20 a day).

Much of eastern Australia seems to have been settled on the principle of not having more than a day's horse ride between pubs, so it's possible to plan even ultralong routes and still get a shower at the end of the day.

Most people do carry camping equipment, but, on the east coast at least, it's feasible to travel from town to town staying in hotels or on-site vans.

You can get by with standard road maps, but as you'll probably want to avoid both the highways and the low-grade unsealed roads, the government series is best. The 1:250,000 scale is the most suitable but you'll need a lot of maps if you're covering much territory. The next scale up, 1:1,000,000, is adequate. They are available in capital cities and elsewhere.

Until you get fit you should be careful to eat enough to keep you going – remember that exercise is an appetite suppressant. It's surprisingly easy to be so depleted of energy that you end up camping under a gum tree just 10 km short of a shower and a steak.

No matter how fit you are, water is still vital. Dehydration is no joke and can be life-threatening. One Lonely Planet author rode his first 200-km-in-a-day on a bowl of cornflakes and a round of sandwiches, but the Queensland sun forced him to drink nearly five litres. Having been involved in a drinking contest with stockmen the night before may have had something to do with it, though.

Summer in Queensland isn't a great time for cycling – it can get very hot and incredibly humid, and it's no fun at all trying to ride through the torrential downpours which are commonplace during the Wet. At any time of year, you should wear plenty of sunscreen and drink *lots* of water.

Of course, you don't have to follow the larger roads and visit towns. It's possible to fill your mountain bike's panniers with muesli, head out into the mulga, and not see anyone for weeks: or ever again – outback travel is very risky if not properly planned. Water is the main problem in the outback, and you can't rely on it where there aren't settlements. That tank marked on your map may be dry or the water from it unfit for humans, and those station buildings probably blew away years ago. That little creek marked with a dotted blue line? Forget it – the only time it has water is when the country's flooded for hundreds of km around.

Always check with locals if you're heading into remote areas, and notify the police if you're about to do something particularly adventurous. That said, you can't rely too much on local knowledge of road conditions – most people have no idea of what a heavily loaded touring bike needs. What they think of as a great road may be pedal-deep in sand or bull dust, and cyclists have happily ridden along roads that were officially flooded out.

The Bicycle Institute of Queensland (☎ (07) 3844 1144), at 493 Stanley St, Mater Hill, Brisbane (or write C/-PO Box 8321, Woolloongabba, Brisbane, Qld 4101), is worth contacting for more information on cycling in Queensland. Some of the better bike shops can also be good sources of info on routes, suggested rides, tours and cycling events.

HITCHING

Hitching is never entirely safe in any country in the world, and we don't recommend it. Travellers who decide to hitch should understand that they are taking a small but potentially serious risk. Queensland is not exempt from danger, and even people hitching in pairs are not entirely safe. Before deciding to hitch, talk to local people about the dangers, and it is a good idea to let someone know where you are planning to hitch to before you set off. If you do choose to hitch, the advice that follows should help to make your journey as fast and safe as possible.

Successful hitching depends on several factors, all of them just plain good sense. Factor one is for safety and speed is numbers. More than two people hitching together will make things very difficult, and solo hitching is unwise for men as well as women. Two women hitching together may be vulnerable, and two men hitching together can expect long waits. The best option is for a woman and a man to hitch together.

Factor two is position – look for a place where vehicles will be going slowly and where

they can stop easily. A junction or freeway slip road is a good place if there is stopping room. Position goes beyond just where you stand. The ideal location is on the outskirts of a town – hitching from way out in the country is as hopeless as from the centre of a city. Take a bus out to the edge of town.

Factor three is appearance. The ideal appearance for hitching is a sort of genteel poverty – threadbare but clean. Looking too good can be as much of a bummer as looking too bad! Don't carry too much gear – if it looks like it's going to take half an hour to pack your bags aboard you'll be left on the roadside.

Factor four is knowing when to say no. Saying no to a car-load of drunks is pretty obvious, but you should also be prepared to abandon a ride if you begin to feel uneasy for any reason. Don't sit there hoping for the best: make an excuse and get out at the first opportunity.

It can be time-saving to say no to a short ride that might take you from a good hitching point to a lousy one. Wait for the right, long ride to come along. On a long haul, it's pointless to start walking as it's not likely to increase the likelihood of your getting a lift and it's often an awfully long way to the next town.

Trucks are often the best lifts but they will only stop if they are going slowly and can get started easily. Thus, the ideal place is at the top of a hill where they have a downhill run. Truckies often say they are going to the next town and if they don't like you, will drop you anywhere. As they often pick up hitchers for company, the quickest way to create a bad impression is to jump in and fall asleep. It's also worth remembering that while you're in someone else's vehicle, you are their guest and should act accordingly – many drivers no longer pick up people because they have suffered from thoughtless hikers in the past. It's the hitcher's duty to provide entertainment!

Of course people do get stuck in outlandish places but that is the name of the game. If you're visiting from abroad a nice prominent flag on your pack will help, and a sign announcing your destination can also be useful. Uni and hostel notice boards are good places to look for hitching partners. The main law against hitching is 'thou shalt not stand in the road' – so when you see the law coming, step back.

Just as hitchers should be wary when accepting lifts, drivers who pick up fellow travellers to share the costs should also be aware of the possible risks involved.

BOAT

At any time of the year, there are thousands of yachts and boats travelling up and down the Queensland coast. From time to time the owners of these vessels need to take on extra crew, and if you ask around at marinas and yacht clubs, it's quite possible to make your way along the coast by hitching rides or crewing on yachts. Moreton Bay near Brisbane, Rainbow Beach and Tin Can Bay, Hervey Bay, Gladstone, Airlie Beach, Bowen, Townsville, Cairns and Port Douglas are all good places to try. See the Sea section in the Getting There & Away chapter for more information.

LOCAL TRANSPORT

Brisbane has a comprehensive public transport system with buses, trains and river ferries. The larger cities like Surfers Paradise, Toowoomba, Mt Isa, Bundaberg, Rockhampton, Mackay, Townsville and Cairns all have their own local bus services. At the major tourist centres, most of the backpackers' hostels and some of the resorts and hotels have courtesy coaches which will pick you up from train or bus stations or the airport. Most tour operators will include courtesy coach transport to/from your accommodation in their prices. Elsewhere, all of the larger towns and cities have at least one taxi service.

TOURS

There are all sorts of tours around Queensland, although few that cover much of the state. Most are connected with a particular activity (eg bushwalking or horse riding tours) or area (eg 4WD tours to Cape York).

See the Activities section of the Facts for the Visitor chapter and the various chapters of this book for some suggestions.

If you're on the lookout for tours, the YHA or hostel notice boards can be good sources of information.

Up in the Far North, there are plenty of operators offering 4WD tours of the Cape York Peninsula, often with the option of driving one way and flying or boating the other. See Organised Tours in the Cape York Peninsula chapter for details.

There are all sorts of trips from the mainland out to the Great Barrier Reef. You can fly in a seaplane out to a deserted coral cay, take a fast catamaran to the outer reef and spend the day snorkelling, join a dive boat and scuba dive in a coral garden, or take a day trip to one of the many islands.

There are hundreds of tours operating out of Cairns and Port Douglas – as well as trips to the reef and islands, you can take the Kuranda Scenic Railway up to the Kuranda markets, tour the Atherton Tablelands, visit Cape Tribulation on a 4WD tour, cruise along the Daintree River, go white-water rafting, visit Aboriginal rock-art galleries in Cape York...

Tours to Fraser Island, organised by the backpackers' hostels in Noosa Heads and Hervey Bay, are convenient ways of seeing one of Queensland's natural wonders for those who don't have their own 4WD.

In the Whitsundays, there are dozens of operators offering cruises around the islands, or if you want to do your own thing, you could get a group together and charter your own yacht.

From the Gold Coast, there are tours to Lamington and Springbrook national parks in the hinterland and to South Stradbroke island.

Oz Experience (☎ (02) 9977 2688) offers an interesting alternative to travelling up the coast with one of the national bus companies. It's the new Australian operation of Kiwi Experience, a company which has been successfully transporting and entertaining backpackers around New Zealand for years. Oz Experience is basically a backpackers' bus line. They have frequent bus services up and down the east coast of Australia to all the major destinations, with off-the-beaten-track detours to outback cattle stations and national parks. You buy one of their eight passes, which range from $99 to $450 depending on the distance and are valid for up to six months. Their buses travel set routes, but your pass entitles you to unlimited stopovers, which means you can get on

and off the bus whenever and wherever you want. The drivers act as your guides, providing commentaries and advice, and they can also pre-book your hostels, stop at supermarkets so you can do the shopping, and arrange discounts on most tours and activities. Their buses are smaller and not necessarily as comfortable as those of the big bus companies, but it's a much more interesting way to travel.

Brisbane

Brisbane's origins date back to 1824, when a penal colony was established at Redcliffe Point on Moreton Bay to house Sydney's more recalcitrant convicts. After a difficult first couple of months, the colony was relocated south and inland to the banks of the Brisbane River - the site of the city centre today. As a penal colony, Brisbane was never the success it was intended to be – it only ever accommodated about 1100 convicts, and was abandoned in 1839. The Moreton Bay area was thrown open to free settlers in 1842, and by the time of Queensland's separation in 1859 Brisbane had a population of around 6000 residents. As Queensland's huge agricultural potential and then its mineral riches were developed, Brisbane grew to be a city, and today it is the third-largest in Australia with a population rapidly approaching 1.5 million.

While the pace of life is certainly more relaxed here than in the bigger southern capitals, Brisbane is no longer the slow-moving provincial centre of verandah-fronted timber houses on stilts so evocatively portrayed in the novels of David Malouf. Since hosting several major international events in the 1980s, including the 1982 Commonwealth Games and Expo '88, Brisbane has come of age and developed into a modern and cosmopolitan city.

Queensland's growing tourism industry has brought an influx of visitors to the capital, and with its near-perfect, year-round climate, Brisbane comes as a pleasant surprise to most visitors. The majority of places of interest to travellers are within the city centre and inner suburbs, and these areas have been revitalised and rejuvenated in recent years by a number of major developments, including the opening of the Queensland Cultural Centre (which includes the Performing Arts Complex, the Queensland Museum, the Queensland Art Gallery, and the State Library), the transformation of the former Expo site into the South Bank

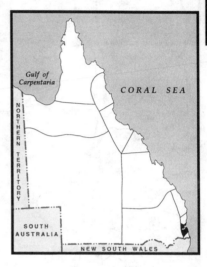

Parklands, and most recently, the opening of a new casino.

If you're prepared to do a little exploring, you'll find central Brisbane to be a lively and interesting place. Each of the suburbs that ring the city has its own distinct flavour, largely shaped by the multicultural influences of their past.

Brisbane is also surrounded by some of Queensland's major tourism destinations, and there are plenty of options for day trips within an hour or two's drive of the capital. The Gold and Sunshine coasts and their mountainous hinterlands are easy drives from the city, and you can also visit the islands of Moreton Bay or head inland towards the Great Dividing Range and the Darling Downs.

ORIENTATION

Looking at a map of Queensland or Australia, most travellers see Brisbane's location on the coast and assume it to be a beach city,

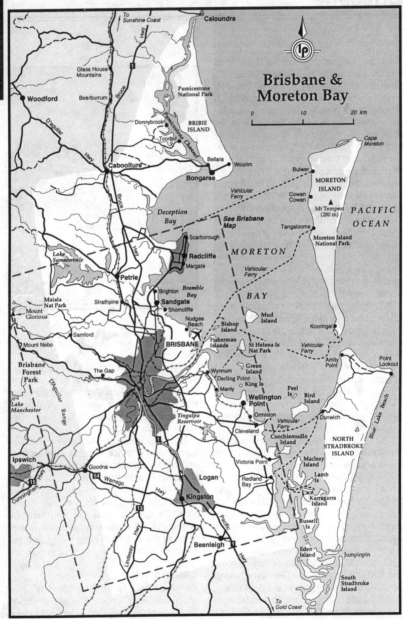

Brisbane & Moreton Bay

0   10   20 km

which it isn't really. The Brisbane River plays a much stronger defining role in Brisbane's persona than Moreton Bay and the bayside suburbs.

City Centre

Brisbane's city centre is built on the north side of a U-shaped loop in the Brisbane River. The city is a fairly compact area, with an orderly grid of streets set with a north-east to south-west orientation and measuring a little over one km by one km.

The Brisbane Transit Centre, where you'll arrive if you're coming by bus or train, is on Roma St about half a km west of the city centre. Head left as you leave the centre's main entrance and you'll find King George Square, the large open area in front of City Hall; it's a popular place to sit and watch the world pass by. One block further east is the Queen St Mall, the shopping heart of the city. On the Brisbane River, north-east of the city centre, are the Riverside Centre and Eagle St Pier complexes, which house bars, cafes and restaurants; the wharves for the river ferries are also here. The City Botanic Gardens occupy the south-eastern corner of the centre.

Inner Suburbs

You'll find most of the accommodation and eating options clustered in the suburbs surrounding the city. Immediately north of the city is Spring Hill, which blends residential with commercial buildings and has a good range of accommodation. Just west of the centre is Paddington, an attractive residential suburb with good cafes and restaurants.

Head south from Queen St across the Victoria Bridge and you'll come to South Brisbane, with the Queensland Cultural Centre and the South Bank Parklands. Further south again are the suburbs of Highgate Hill and the arty West End.

Heading north-east along Ann St from the city will take you to bohemian Fortitude Valley, one of the more cosmopolitan suburbs with lots of nightclubs, restaurants and a large ethnic population. To the east of the Valley is New Farm, which also has quite a few eating and accommodation options. East across the river from the city is Kangaroo Point.

Greater Brisbane

The Brisbane River meanders its way through the centre of the city, dividing it into north and south.

Most of the places of interest to travellers are within the inner suburban area. Along Moreton Bay are the bayside suburbs, including Scarborough, Redcliffe, Sandgate, Manly and Cleveland, and Moreton Bay itself is sprinkled with dozens of islands. (See the Moreton Bay section later in this chapter for details of the bayside suburbs).

The suburbs sprawl north and south for more than 25 km – the southern urban sprawl is one of the fastest growing areas in Australia, and threatens to link up with the similarly spreading Gold Coast suburbs before too long.

Less than 15 minutes drive west from the city is the Mt Coot-tha Park. Further out to the north-west are the mountainous forests and parklands of the Brisbane Forest Park.

INFORMATION
Tourist Offices

The Queen St Mall Information Centre (☎ 3229 5918), which is in the heart of the mall on the corner of Queen and Albert Sts, is open Monday to Thursday from 9 am to 5.30 pm, Friday from 9 am to 9 pm, Saturday from 9 am to 4 pm and Sunday from 10 am to 4 pm. There is a small police station within the centre which is staffed 24 hours a day.

At the Transit Centre, the Greater Brisbane Tourist Association runs a helpful information office (☎ 3236 2020) on level 2 which is open weekdays from 8 am to 6 pm and weekends from 9 am to 1 pm; they also have a free accommodation booking office on level 3 (see the Places to Stay section for details).

The Tourism Brisbane information desk (☎ 3221 8411), in the City Hall on King George Square, is open weekdays from 9 am to 4.30 pm and Saturday from 10 am to 1 pm.

The Queensland Government Travel

Centre (☎ 3221 6111), on the corner of Adelaide and Edward Sts, is more a booking office than an information centre but they may be able to answer some queries. The centre is open Monday to Friday, 8.30 am to 5 pm and Saturday, 9.30 am to 12.30 pm.

The Brisbane City Council also has a number of InfoBrisbane information booths around town. These touch-screen terminals have information on various categories, including transport, employment, events, things to do and places to go, and a gig guide. The terminals are easy and fun to use and have quite a bit of useful info – they were also reasonably up to date last time I checked one out.

At the Brisbane airport, the Brisbane Visitors & Conventions Bureau (☎ 3860 4688) has an information booth in the international terminal which is staffed by volunteers and opens to meet most incoming flights between 6 am and 8 pm. The new terminal complex, due to open early in 1996, includes plans for a 24-hours-a-day information desk and several touch-screen info terminals.

Interstate Tourist Offices

If you're moving on from Queensland soon and looking for information, Tasmania and New South Wales both have Travel Centres on the corner of Queen and George Sts.

Free Publications

There are a number of free information guides circulated in Brisbane, most of which are available at the information centres. The most useful of these is the monthly *Tourism Brisbane* newspaper, which has an events calendar and a useful information directory at the back that includes a list of foreign consulates in the city.

This Week in Brisbane is a small glossy booklet with lots of ads, information and What's On sections, and a useful map of the Citytrain network. It's worth picking up a copy of the Queensland edition of *For Backpackers, By Backpackers*, which has brief listings of budget places to stay and eat, what to see, etc. It appears bimonthly and is available from hostels and information centres.

The front pages of the A-K volume of the *Yellow Pages* telephone directory has useful info on Brisbane including an events calendar, a fast facts page, maps and transport information. *Brother Sister* is a fortnightly news and entertainment paper for gays and lesbians. There are also several free entertainment guides, including *Time Off*, *Rave* and *The Scene*.

Money

Westpac has two *bureau de change* booths at the Brisbane airport which open on weekdays from 8.15 am to 4 pm, and for all arriving flights. There's also a Travelex foreign exchange booth in the domestic terminal, beside gate 39, which is open daily from 6.30 am to 6.30 pm. (Both of these services will be moving into the new terminal early in 1996.)

Thomas Cook has three foreign exchange offices in the city. Their main branch is on Level E of the Myer Centre, on the corner of Elizabeth and Albert Sts (just beside the top of the escalators); it is open weekdays from 8.45 am to 5.15 pm and on Saturday from 9.30 am to 1 pm. The other branches are at 276 Edward St, and on the 1st floor at 241 Adelaide St (opposite Qantas' international office).

American Express (☎ 3229 2022) has its office at 131 Elizabeth St, near the Albert St corner.

Left Luggage

In the Brisbane airport, there are left-luggage lockers downstairs in the domestic terminal which cost $4 for 24 hours.

In the Transit Centre on Roma St, there are plenty of deep, backpack-sized lockers up on the 3rd level which cost $2 for 24 hours. If you need to leave luggage for longer, there is also a cloak room on the 3rd level, beside bays 24-26, which can store most items – backpacks, surfboards, golf clubs, etc are $2 a day, bikes are $3 day. It's open daily from 7.30 am to 6 pm.

Luggage can also be left in the cloakroom

at City Hall, and there are also lockers on Level E of the Myer Centre on Queen St.

Post & Telecommunications

Brisbane's major post office, the GPO, is in an imposing Victorian-era building on Queen St, between Edward and Creek Sts. The poste restante section is just inside the front door on the left-hand side. The post office is open on weekdays from 7 am to 6 pm.

There's another post office on level 2 of the Myer Centre in the Queen St Mall which opens on weekends.

If you have an American Express card or travellers' cheques, you can have mail sent to you care of American Express Client Mail at 131 Elizabeth St, Brisbane, Qld 4000. The office will hold standard mail for up to one month before returning it to the sender (unless they have received prior notification of a forwarding address).

The STD telephone area code for Brisbane is 07. There are public telephones throughout the city centre, including in the GPO arcade beside the post office and in the Queen St Mall.

Foreign Embassies

All foreign embassies are in Canberra, but quite a few countries have consulates in Brisbane. They include:

Austria
20 Argyle St, Breakfast Creek (☎ 3262 8955)
Denmark
180 Queen St (☎ 3221 8641)
France
10 Market St (☎ 3229 8201)
Germany
10 Eagle St (☎ 3221 7819)
Greece
215 Adelaide St (☎ 3228 5677)
Italy
133 Leichhardt St, Spring Hill (☎ 3832 0099)
Japan
12 Creek St (☎ 3221 5188)
Netherlands
101 Wickham Tce (☎ 3839 9644)
New Zealand
288 Edward St (☎ 3221 9933)
Norway
301 Wickham Tce, Fortitude Valley (☎ 3854 1855)

Spain
131 Elizabeth St (☎ 3221 8571)
Sweden
60 Edward St (☎ 3221 9797)
Thailand
101 Wickham Tce, Spring Hill (☎ 3832 1999)
UK
BP House, 193 North Quay (☎ 3236 2575)
USA
383 Wickham Tce, Spring Hill (☎ 831 3330)

Cultural Centres

Cultural organisations in Brisbane include the following:

Alliance Française
191 George St (☎ 3221 7957)
British Council
203 New South Head Rd, Edgecliff (☎ 3326 2365)
Japanese Cultural Centre
23 Ruskin St, Taringa (☎ 3371 8242)

Useful Organisations

Queensland's motoring association, the Royal Automobile Club of Queensland (RACQ) (☎ 3361 2444), has an office beside the GPO at 261 Queen St. They have good maps on Queensland and an accommodation-booking service, plus a while-you-wait passport photo service.

Queensland's Department of Environment & Heritage runs an excellent information centre called Naturally Queensland (☎ 3227 8186), at 160 Anne St, which is open on weekdays from 8.30 am to 5 pm. You can get maps, brochures and books on all of Queensland's national parks and state forests here, and they also stock a good range of posters, maps, books and souvenirs relating to conservation and the environment.

The Queensland Conservation Council Environment Centre (☎ 3221 0188), with a library and information desk open to the public on weekdays from 9 am to 5 pm, is on the 2nd floor of the School of Arts building at 166 Ann St.

Women's Organisations

Women's Infolink (☎ 3229 1264 or 1800 177 577 toll free), on the 2nd floor of the Pavilion Building on the corner of Albert and

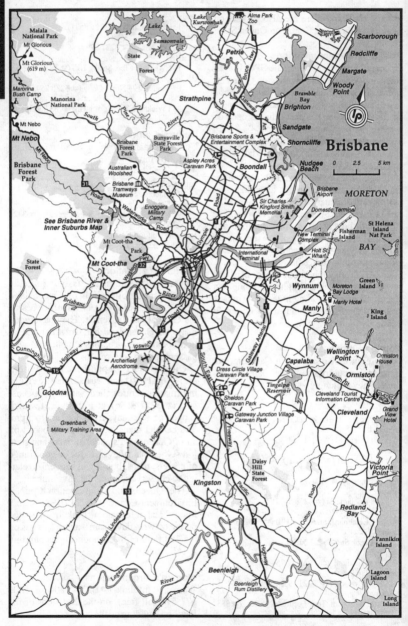

Queen Sts, is an information and referral service for women. They also have a counselling service, a library and a drop-in centre.

At 165 Gregory Tce in Spring Hill is the Women's Health Centre (☎ 3839 9988 or 1800 017 676 toll free).

Disabled Travellers

The Brisbane City Council runs an information service for disabled people – phone ☎ 3224 8031.

Access Brisbane (☎ 3225 4416) has info on access to buildings, attractions, banks and other facilities.

See the section for Disabled Travellers in the Facts for the Visitor chapter for more details.

Bookshops

Brisbane – Portrait of a City, published by Robert Brown & Associates in 1994, is a large-format paperback with good colour photos and descriptive text on Brisbane. It is widely available and costs around $10.

Brisbane has several large book chains including Dymocks, with several city shops including one at 235 Albert St; and Angus & Robertson Bookworld, with three city shops including one in Post Office Square in Adelaide St which has an excellent range of travel guides.

There are also many independent booksellers that specialise in particular types of books. The American Bookstore, at 173 Elizabeth St, has the city's best range of language books and courses; they also stock a wide range of books on business and computers, science, history and creative writing, particularly works by Australian Aboriginal and American Indian writers.

Nearby at 201 Elizabeth St, McGills Technical Books has extensive travel and language sections and a good range of architecture, design and photography books. Folio Books, at 80 Albert St, stocks an interesting range of books on architecture and design, art, film, photography, music and literature, and works by Australian and Aboriginal writers.

The University Bookshop, inside the old Customs House at 399 Queen St, also has an excellent range. At 40-42 Charlotte St, Archives Fine Books has a huge range of second-hand books spread over three different shops. They specialise in hard to get and out of print books.

At 350A Brunswick St in Fortitude Valley, Red Books is a tiny, narrow bookshop (not much wider than *War and Peace*) that specialises in design, art, architecture, gay and lesbian fiction and general fiction. It stays open until 10 pm from Tuesday to Saturday, and there's a coffee machine in the corner if you need a fix.

Travel Books, at 66 Boundary St in the West End, has an excellent range of travel guidebooks, maps and atlases and phrasebooks.

The Women's Bookshop , at 15 Gladstone Rd in Highgate Hill, specialises in books for, by and about women. It also has a separate section on non-sexist children's books.

Emma's Bookshop, at 82A Vulture St in the West End, is crammed to the ceiling with second-hand books – classics, popular fiction, travel, art and photography, film, poetry; long may you browse.

Maps

The tourist offices hand out simple maps of central Brisbane. If you're staying a while and need more detail than that provided by the maps in this book, Travelog, Sunmap and UBD all publish Brisbane city and suburban maps which are available from most bookshops and newsagencies for around $5.

The definitive guide to Brisbane's streets is UBDs *Brisbane Street Directory*, available in either small paperback (around $15) or a larger format ($24).

World Wide Maps & Guides (☎ 3221 4330) (formerly Hema Maps), at 239 George St (between Queen and Adelaide Sts), has the city's most comprehensive range of travel maps and atlases; both national and international. They also stock a wide assortment of travel guidebooks and language guides.

Newspapers & Magazines

Brisbane's daily newspaper is the *Courier Mail*. For a broader (but conservative)

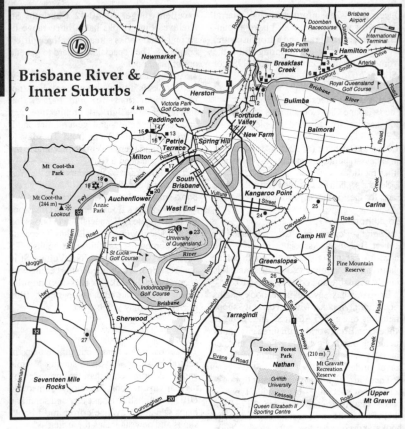

Brisbane River & Inner Suburbs

national view, *The Australian* is also widely available from newsagents.

TV

Brisbane has four major TV stations – the government-funded ABC (channel 2) and the three national commercial networks (channels 7, 9 and 10).

There's also a UHF channel, SBS, which is devoted to multicultural programmes and has excellent international news services, foreign movies and plenty of other great programmes.

Radio

The ABC's Brisbane stable of radio stations includes 4RN (Radio National, 792 AM), 4QR (Regional Radio, 612 AM), Classic FM (106.1 FM), and JJJ, their youth network which plays alternative and independent music (107.7 FM).

Brisbane also has an excellent alternative music station of its own, 4ZZZ (102.1 FM).

Laundry

Most places of accommodation will provide laundry facilities. Self-service laundrettes close to the centre include the New Farm

PLACES TO STAY

1   Ascot Budget Motel
2   Airport 85 Motel
3   Admiralty Motel
4   Airport Motel
5   Airport Heritage Motel
6   Airport International Motel
7   Kingsford Hall Private Hotel
8   Powerhouse Boutique Hotel
13 Waverley B & B
17 Coronation Motel
20 Inn on the Park
21 Forest Lodge Units
26 Amaroo Gardens Caravan Park

PLACES TO EAT

9   Breakfast Creek Hotel
14 Gavin's Studio Cafe
16 The Rest

OTHER

10 Breakfast Creek Wharf
11 Newstead House & Gardens
12 Miegunyah Folk Museum
15 Paddington Antique Centre
18 Planetarium
19 Botanic Gardens
22 University Information Office
23 The Great Court
24 Classic Cinema
25 Earlystreet Historical Village
27 Lone Pine Koala Sanctuary

Laundromat on the corner of Brunswick and Harcourt Sts in New Farm, and the East Brisbane Laundromat at 87 Lytton Rd in East Brisbane.

Film & Photography

There are two good camera repair outfits in the city centre. Anderson Camera Repair Service (☎ 3221 3133), in the centre of the Brisbane Arcade between Queen and Adelaide Sts, specialises in repairs to Bronica, Canon, Mamiya, Nikon and Olympus. Most repairs can be handled in two to three days, depending on what parts are needed.

Camera Tech (☎ 3229 5406), at 270 Adelaide St, is a repair agent for Canon and Konica, and can also handle repairs for all other brands.

Medical Services

The Travellers' Medical & Vaccination Centre (☎ 3221 9066), on the 6th floor at 247 Adelaide St, can handle all vaccinations and medical advice for travellers. The consultation fees depend on the length of your visit, ranging from $15 for 4 minutes to $89 for over 45 minutes; vaccines and medication are extra. The centre is open on weekdays from 8.30 am to 5 pm (Wednesday until 6 pm) and on Saturday from 8.30 am to 1.30 pm.

There are a number of other medical clinics in the city, including the Traveller's Medical Service (☎ 3221 8083), on the 5th floor of the Coles building at 210 Queen St in the mall.

The Brisbane Sexual Health Clinic (☎ 3227 7091) is at 484 Adelaide St; it is open on Monday, Tuesday, Thursday and Friday from 9 am to 5 pm and on Wednesday from 9 am to noon.

The Gay and Lesbian Health Service (☎ 3844 6806) is at 38 Gladstone Rd in Highgate Hill; it is open Monday to Thursday from 8 am to 8 pm, Friday from 8 am to 6 pm and Saturday from 9 am to noon.

Chemists which stay open late include the T&G Corner Pharmacy, at 141 Queen St in the mall, (Monday to Saturday from 8 am to 9 pm, Sunday 10 am to 5 pm) and the Transit Centre Pharmacy in Roma St (open weekdays 7 am to 6 pm and Saturday from 7 am to 1.30 pm).

Emergency

Dial ☎ 000 for emergency help from the police, ambulance or fire brigade. There's a police station in the centre of the city in the Queen St Mall Information centre which is staffed 24 hours a day – call ☎ 3220 0752 for emergency assistance.

Some other useful emergency numbers include:

Rape
    Rape/Incest Crisis Centre (☎ 3844 4008)
Life Crisis
    Life-Line Counselling Service (24 hours a day, ☎ 3252 1111)
    Women's Infolink counselling service (☎ 3229 1580 or 1800 177 577)

Youth Emergency Services Inc (☎ 3357 7655)
Salvo Careline (Salvation Army) (☎ 3221 1233)
Interpreter Service
Translating and Interpreting Service (24 hours a
day, ☎ 13 1450), 100 Edward St, Brisbane

BRISBANE WALKS

You can easily walk around the city centre,
and most of the inner suburbs can also be
covered on foot quite easily.

An exploration of the city centre could
start with a visit to the **lookout tower** in the
City Hall on King George Square (see the
following Views section). After you've taken
in a bird's eye view of the city, turn right out
of the City Hall and cross Adelaide St into
Albert St, which takes you into the busy
Queen St Mall. Turn left into the mall and
head north, past some of the city's major
department stores and shopping centres. On
your right is the historic **Hoyts Regent
Theatre**, an impressively restored cinema
complex. At Edward St, turn left and stroll
up to the **Shingle Inn**, a quaintly old-fashioned cafe. Enjoy a pot of tea and a slice of
pavlova here, to sustain you for the rest of the
walk and give you an insight into the Brisbane
of yore (see Places to Eat). Head back down
Edward St to Queen St and turn left – you'll
pass the **General Post Office** on your right and
Post Office Square on your left.

At the corner of Queen and Wharf St, turn
right and cross to the Brisbane River. After
visiting the historic **Customs House**, head
south along the riverfront, past the **Riverside Centre** and the **Eagle St Pier**, where
you'll find plenty of bars and eateries. Continue down to the corner of Edward and Alice
Sts, where you'll find the main entrance to
the **City Botanic Gardens**. There are plenty
of walking trails though the gardens, and
there's a cafe at the southern end. At the
south-west corner of the gardens is
Queensland's **Parliament House**. From
here, head straight up George St, passing
The Mansions on the corner of Margaret St
corner, the **Sciencentre** museum one block
further on, and the **Queensland Aboriginal
Creations** gallery in the block after Charlotte St. On the corner of George and Queen St

is the new **Treasury Casino** in the historic
former Treasury buildings. Turn right into
Queen St, which brings you back into the mall.

Alternatively you could turn left at Queen
St and stroll across the Victoria Bridge to the
Queensland Cultural Centre, with the
Queensland Art Gallery and the **Queens-
land Museum** on the right-hand side of
Melbourne St and the **Performing Arts
Centre** on the left-hand side. Beyond the
Performing Arts Centre are the **South Bank
Parklands**, where you can stroll along the
riverfront and visit the park's many attrac-
tions. At the southern end of the gardens is
the **Maritime Museum**, and if you continue
around the river towards the Captain Cook
Bridge you'll come to **The Cliffs** rock-
climbing area, which is floodlit by night.
Back at South Bank beside the **Boardwalk
Cafes**, you can take one of the river ferries
across to the city.

Another good walk is to head north out of
the city and explore Fortitude Valley,
Brisbane's most exotic inner suburb. From
Centenary Place, a wedge-shaped park at
the top end of Ann St, head north up
Wickham St, passing the cluster of **outdoor
adventure shops** between Gotha and Gipps
Sts. Cross Gipps St and continue past the
numerous **Asian restaurants** and take a
right into Duncan St, the **Chinatown Mall**.
At the end of the mall, turn right into Ann St
and visit the **Institute of Modern Art**, then
turn back and head north up Ann St and take
a left into Brunswick St. This section of
Brunswick St is closed off as a pedestrian
mall, and has numerous **bars and cafes**, and
a **market** on Saturday mornings. Head down
the **Brunswick St Mall** to the corner of
Wickham St, where you'll find **McWhirter's
Market**, with plenty of interesting shops and
stalls. Turn right up Wickam St and a futher
150 metres up on the left is the **Wickham
Hotel**, one of the Valley's more popular pubs
(see the Entertainment section). After you've
visited the pub, take Ballow St back to Ann
St and turn right, passing some of the
Valley's weirder shops and nightclubs. Turn
left into Brunswick St – the next block is
lined with groovy cafes and restaurants, with

the tiny **Red Books** shop tucked in amongst them. Continue down to the McLachlan St corner, where you'll see the big green **Dooley's Hotel**. After all that strolling you've earned a glass of Guinness in the downstairs Irish Bar, and, if you've timed your walk well there should be a band starting up before too much longer.

For longer bushwalks, head out to the Brisbane Forest Park north-west of the centre – see Brisbane Forest Park later in this chapter. See the Organised Tours section later for details of guided walks and bushwalking clubs.

VIEWS

There are good views of the city centre from the bell tower of the Brisbane City Hall on King William Square – a free lift operates up to the lookout platform. See the City Centre section for details.

The best views in Brisbane are from the One Tree Hill Lookout up on Mt Coot-tha, about eight km west of the city. You can see most of Brisbane laid out below like a giant urban carpet, with the Glass House Mountains to the north, the Gold Coast and its hinterland mountains to the south, and the river twisting its way out to Moreton Bay and the bay islands. If you want to linger over the views, there's a good restaurant and a cafe.

You get a unique perspective of Brisbane from the ferries which ply the Brisbane River. There are short services which shuttle passengers across the river and around the city (see the Getting Around section), or you could take a longer cruise (see the Organised Tours section).

MUSEUMS

Brisbane's major museum, the Queensland Museum, is just south of the city centre – see the section on the Queensland Cultural Centre for details.

At 110 George St in the city, there's the **Sciencentre**, a hands-on science museum with interactive displays, optical illusions, a perception tunnel and a regular 20-minute show in the theatre. This is a great place to visit, especially for families, but try not to come before 2 pm on school days as it is usually very crowded with school groups until then. Daily opening hours are 10 am to 5 pm, except for Christmas Day and Good Friday. Entry costs $7 for adults, $5 for children and students and $24 for a family ticket – tickets are valid all day.

The **Queensland Maritime Museum**, on Sidon St in South Brisbane (just south of South Bank), has a wide range of displays which include an 1881 dry dock, an impressive collection of model ships, relics from old shipwrecks, ships engines and machinery, and numerous boats including the WW II frigate HMAS *Diamantina*. It's open from 9.30 am to 5 pm daily; admission is $4 for adults, $3 for students and $2 for children.

Brisbane's trams no longer operate, but you can ride some early examples at the **Tramway Museum** at 2 McGinn Rd, Ferny Grove. The museum is 11 km north-west of the city centre, and is open from 1.30 to 4 pm Sunday and most public holidays; admission is $4.

Beside the airport freeway, opposite the new terminal complex, is the **Sir Charles Kingsford Smith Memorial**, featuring the famous *Southern Cross* plane in which he made the first Trans-Pacific flight in 1928. The plane is housed in a giant glassed-in hangar, and set around the old Fokker are commemorative plaques, model planes, photos, charts and log entries from the historic flight: well worth a visit, if you're not running late for your flight.

Postal enthusiasts could try the **GPO Museum** at 261-285 Queen St. It's open Tuesday to Friday from 9.30 am to 3.30 pm and admission is free. Out in St Lucia on Sir Fred Schonell Dve, the **University of Queensland** has anthropology, antiquities and art museums – see the section on the university for details.

The **Archerfield Warbirds Museum** at Archerfield Airport, about 12 km south-west of the centre, has a collection of fighter planes including a Russian Mig 15 jet, a Tiger Moth, a Trojan T28 and a Bird Dog, all in flying order. It's open daily from 10 am to 4 pm. While you're here, you can take a joy flight in an old Tiger Moth with Hempel's Aviation (☎ 3275 3391).

GALLERIES

See the section on the Queensland Cultural Centre for details of the excellent **Queensland Art Gallery**. Brisbane has a number of smaller art galleries and exhibition spaces, including the following:

Brisbane City Hall Art Gallery & Museum
  Small permanent collection and regular exhibitions – see the City Centre section.
Metro Arts Centre
  Various art and photography exhibition spaces and studios – see the City Centre section.
Museum of Contemporary Art
  See the Petrie Tce and Paddington section.
Queensland Aboriginal Creations
  A commercial gallery displaying and selling arts, crafts and souvenirs. See Aboriginal Art in the Things to Buy section.
Institute of Modern Art
  Warehouse with changing art exhibitions of modern art – see the Fortitude Valley section.
McWhirter's Artspace
  Three exhibition galleries with regular exhibits – see the Fortitude Valley section.
Customs House Gallery
  See the City Centre section.

See Galleries & Antiques in the Things to Buy section later for info on some of the commercial art galleries in Brisbane.

CITY CENTRE

Surrounded on three sides by the Brisbane River, the city centre is a pleasant and orderly precinct that combines a scattering of historic Victorian-era buildings with modern high-rise offices and hotels, shopping malls and department stores, some pleasant parks and squares, and the lovely City Botanic Gardens. Most of the hotels in the centre are in the four and five-star league, but there are plenty of affordable cafes and restaurants, as well as galleries, museums, theatres and cinemas, plus a few other worthwhile attractions to explore.

Historic Buildings

There are dozens of interesting old buildings

around the city centre. Quite a few of them are mentioned in this section, but for more in-depth info pick up a copy of the Brisbane City Council's *Heritage Trail Brisbane Centre* brochure, which details the history of 39 buildings in the city centre. It's available from the information centre in the City Hall. You could also visit the National Trust, which has its headquarters in **Old Government House** (1862), the former state governor's residence at the southern end of George St.

City Hall

Brisbane's City Hall, on **King George Square** between Adelaide and Ann Sts, has gradually been surrounded by skyscrapers but the **observation platform** up in the bell tower still provides one of the best views across the city.

There's a free lift (actually, two lifts) up to the observation deck, which run Monday to

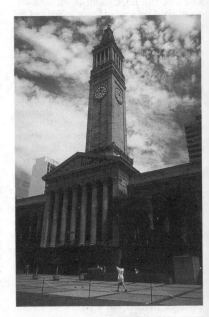

City Hall – beware the bells

Friday from 8.30 am to 3.30 pm and on Saturday from 10.30 am to 1.30 pm. The views up here are great, but a word of warning – beware the bells. It's truly a terrifying, deafening experience if you are up here and the bells start tolling unexpectedly. Don't say I didn't warn you.

The **City Hall Art Gallery & Museum** has a small, permanent museum collection and regularly exhibits local art; it's open daily from 10 am to 5 pm, except on public holidays, and admission is free.

One-hour **guided tours** of City Hall are conducted on weekdays at 10 am and 2 pm and on Saturday at 10 am. The cost is $6 for adults and $4.50 for children (free if they're 13 years or younger), which includes a souvenir tour kit.

Queen St & the Mall

Running two blocks from Edward St to George St, the attractive **Queen St Mall** is the shopping hub of the city. In addition to the hundreds of shops, there's an underground bus interchange, a Hilton Hotel, a tourist information office, eight cinemas and even an indoor funfair in the Myer Centre.

The mall is just about always busy and bustling with people – herds of shoppers, tourists and buskers by day, and people on their way to or from restaurants and nightclubs at night.

It's worth popping into the **Hoyts Regent Cinemas**, between Albert and Edward Sts. The original theatre was built here in 1928 in an extravagant blend of Spanish Perpendicular and Gothic Rococo styles – the complex has recently been redeveloped and divided up into five cinemas, with a couple of bars and eateries. Much of the original grandeur has been restored, particularly in the main cinema – well worth a look.

One block north, across Edward St, the **General Post Office** is an impressive neoclassical edifice dating from the 1870s; the **GPO Museum** is housed in the same building. **Post Office Square** is a very pleasant little park opposite the GPO – just the place to catch up on your mail from home. If you

get hungry reading, there are numerous food outlets in the arcade underneath the square. Up on the corner of Queen and Creek Sts, the **National Bank** building (1885) is reckoned to be one of the finest examples of the Italian Renaissance style in Australia. Its front doors were made from a single Queensland cedar log.

Treasury Casino

Brisbane's magnificent old Treasury Buildings, overlooking the Brisbane River from the block bordered by Queen, George, Elizabeth and William Sts, has been redeveloped to house the stylish Treasury Casino.

The block south-east of the casino has been transformed into a landscaped parkland, **Queen's Park**, with the new five-star *Hotel Conrad* (see Places to Stay) on the opposite side of the park to the casino. The complex opened in mid-1995.

The casino's main gaming room has over 100 gaming tables, with blackjack, roulette, craps, two-up and mini baccarat. There are also cafes, bars and restaurants in the complex, including a 24-hour restaurant, as well as a VIP gaming room for those with lots to lose. The casino is open 24 hours a day and has a smart-casual dress code. Shorts, T-shirts or singlets, sandals and work boots aren't allowed. You also have to be over 18 years of age to enter.

The Riverfront

The north-east corner of the city, fronting onto the Brisbane River, is one of the most attractive and lively areas in the centre, with cafes and restaurants, bars and nightclubs, docks for the river ferries, and a few other points of interest. Some of Brisbane's oldest buildings are in this area – pick up a copy of the Brisbane City Council's *Heritage Trail Brisbane Riverfront*, which maps out a good walking tour around 20 different buildings and points of interest.

The historic **Customs House** building, beside the Brisbane River at 399 Queen St, is owned and has been restored by the University of Queensland. There's an excellent brasserie (see Places to Eat) and a bookshop

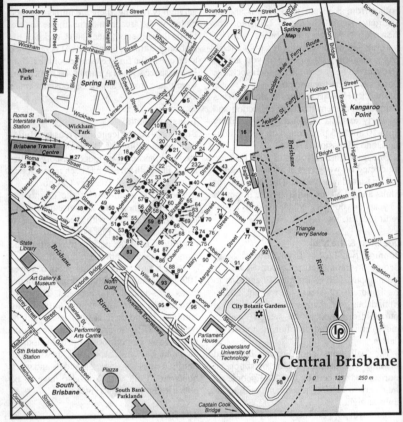

Central Brisbane

inside, as well as the small **Customs House Gallery** which houses the private collection of Dr Norman Behan. The collection mainly features early Australian paintings, including works by Charles Conder, Rupert Bunny and Arthur Streeton, plus a particularly impressive collection of ancient Chinese pottery dating back as far as the Zau Dynasty (1028-771 BC).

Further south, the **Riverside Centre** and the **Eagle St Pier** complexes both have plenty of good eateries, bars and nightclubs (see the Places to Eat and Entertainment sections), plus a market on Sunday (see Things to Buy).

See the Organised Tours section for details of the river cruises which leave from the docks here.

Ann St

The historic **School of Arts** building at 166 Ann St houses the Queensland Conservation Council – a good place for people interested in the environment to source information and make contacts. Just next door is **Naturally Queensland** is an information centre for national and state parks and the environment.

The block between Edward and Creek Sts is dominated by **Central Station**, built in impressive late-Victorian style in 1901.

PLACES TO STAY

7   Sheraton Brisbane Hotel
25 All Seasons Abbey Hotel
27 Brisbane City Travelodge and Jazz
    & Blues Club
39 Brisbane Hilton
40 Hotel Embassy
47 Mercure Hotel
55 Lennon's Hotel
79 The Beaufort Heritage Hotel
88 Bellevue Hotel
91 Parkroyal Brisbane
94 Hotel Conrad

PLACES TO EAT

2   The Orient Hotel
22 Shingle Inn
35 Jimmy's on the Mall
38 Jimmy's Downtown
42 Planet Energy
45 Crash & Burn
46 Eagle St Pier & Restaurants
56 Jo Jo's Food Centre
67 Govinda's
69 Cafe Mondial
78 Siggis at the Port Office
82 Jimmy's Uptown
84 Sennari
85 Parrots

OTHER

1   Brisbane Sexual Health Clinic
3   St John's Cathedral
4   Brisbane Tavern
5   Masonic Memorial Temple
6   Customs House Gallery &
    Brasserie
8   Central Station
9   Someplace Else Nightclub
10 Shrine of Memories & Cenotaph
11 Anzac Square
12 Angus & Robertson Bookworld
13 Travellers Medical & Vaccination
    Centre
14 Qantas Airlines
15 Post Office Square
16 Riverside Centre
17 Suncorp Theatre
18 School of Arts Building
19 Naturally Queensland (QNP&WS)
20 Queensland Government Travel
    Centre
21 Eastwest Airlines
23 RACQ Office

24 Post Office
26 YHA Travel Centre
28 Brisbane City Hall
29 King George Square
30 Rocking Horse Records
31 STA Travel
32 Dymock's Booksellers
33 Brisbane Arcade
34 Broadway on the Mall
36 Hoyts Regent Cinemas
37 Wintergarden Shopping Complex
41 McGills Technical Books
43 St Stephen's Cathedral
44 Metro Arts Theatre & Zane's Caffe
48 Dendy Cinema
49 Billabong Bookshop
50 Central City Library
51 Worldwide Maps & Guides
52 CES Job Centre
53 Ansett Airlines
54 Angus & Robertson Bookworld
57 Nightworks Nightclub
58 Queen St Mall Information Centre
59 Myer Centre
60 Greater Union Cinemas
61 Thomas Cook Foreign Exchange
    Office
62 American Express Office
63 Babble On
64 Queensland Irish Association
65 American Bookstore & Caffe Libri
66 Greater Union Cinemas
68 Elizabeth Arcade
70 Hogie's Pool Bar & Nightclub
71 Mary St Nightclub & Cafe Sports
72 Festival Hall
73 Mountain Designs
74 Wilderness Society Shop
75 Brisbane Bicycle Sales & Hire
76 Skate Biz
77 Port Office Hotel
80 Tasmanian & New South Wales
    Travel Centres
81 Info Brisbane Touch-screen
    Terminal
83 Treasury Casino
86 Queensland Aboriginal Creations
87 Archives Fine Books
89 Lands Office Hotel/Mass
    Nightclub
90 Folio Books
92 Botanic Gardens Main Entrance
93 Sciencentre
95 Commissariat Stores
96 The Mansions
97 Old Government House
98 River Stage Amphitheatre

Opposite the station, **Anzac Square** is a large park attractively planted with palm and bottle trees, with a couple of interesting bronze statues and war memorials. An eternal flame burns in a Greek Revivalist **Cenotaph** at the Ann St entrance to the park, in remembrance of Australian soldiers who died in WW I; beneath the Cenotaph is the **Shrine of Memories**, a sombre underground war memorial with wall plaques and artistic tributes to the war dead. It is open on weekdays from 10 am to 2.30 pm.

Up near the top end of Ann St, between Creek and Wharf St, is the **Masonic Memorial Temple**. Built by the Grand Lodge of the Freemason's between 1928 and 1930, it has an imposing, sheer Greek Revival facade of sandstone which incorporates six Corinthian columns.

Further north, across Wharf St, the French Gothic-styled **St John's Cathedral** is still under construction – work started in 1901, and continues at a cost of $1 million a year. You can watch the stonemasons at work and trace a century of construction work – the old and new sections are clearly definable. Guided tours are conducted at 10 am from Monday to Saturday. Queensland's first **Government House**, built in 1853, is now the deanery for the cathedral. The declaration of Queensland's separation from the colony of New South Wales was read here in 1859.

Adelaide St

If you're after somewhere quiet to read and/or write, the **Central City Library** is in the basement of the City Plaza complex, on Adelaide St near the George St corner. It's open to the general public on weekdays from 10 am to 8 pm and weekends from 10 am to 3 pm and has a good range of newspapers and magazines.

Up on the Albert St corner is **King George Square** – see the City Hall section.

Elizabeth St

The **Elizabeth Arcade** in the arcade between George and Albert Sts houses a fascinating range of shops and businesses – see the Things to Buy section later.

Up in the block between Edward and Charlotte St is the small and simple **Old St Stephen's Church** (1850), the oldest church in Brisbane. Next to it is the more impressive English Gothic-style **St Stephen's Cathedral**, which was built with gold-rush money and completed in 1874.

Edward St

The **Metro Arts Building** (☎ 3221 1527), at 109 Edward St, houses the Metro Arts Theatre (live stage productions) on the ground floor and a good cafe (see Places to Eat) in the basement. The upper floors house a variety of businesses linked to the arts – art exhibition spaces, artists' studios, dance and theatre studios, a vocal academy, and an art school.

George St

Some of Brisbane's finest old buildings line the southern half of George St, including the **Land Administration Building** and the former **Treasury Building**, both of which are now part of the casino complex – see the earlier Treasury Casino section.

Between Charlotte and Mary Sts is the **Sciencentre** – see the Museums section for details. **The Mansions**, on the corner of George and Margaret Sts, is a row of three-storey terrace houses built in 1890. Their design is distinctive and quite unusual, with red brickwork contrasting with lighter sandstone, and an elongated facade of small column-supported arches topped by a parapet. The buildings now house a number of private tenants including the elegant *Augustine's Restaurant*, a gift shop run by the National Trust, and a rare-books bookshop. The restored **Harris Terrace**, on the opposite corner, is also notable.

Parliament House, overlooking the Botanic Gardens from the corner of Alice and George Sts, dates from 1868, and was built in French Renaissance style; the roof is made from Mt Isa copper. On weekdays when parliament isn't sitting, free 20-minute tours are given at 10.30 and 11.15 am and 2.30 and 3.15 pm; when Parliament is sitting, you can sit in on the public gallery and watch the wheels of democracy turning. Ring ☎ 3226 7316 to find out when Parliament is in session.

William St

The 1828 **Commissariat Stores** building, at 115 William St, was used as a government store right up until 1962. Today it houses the Royal Historical Society of Queensland's library and museum, and can be visited for $1, Tuesday to Friday from 11 am to 2 pm, and Sunday from 11 am to 4 pm.

CITY BOTANIC GARDENS

Brisbane's 18-hectare City Botanic Gardens were established in 1855 inside a loop of the Brisbane River at the southern end of the city. Visiting these lovely gardens is a great way to escape the surrounding urban jungle. You can stroll around the walking paths and enjoy the shaded lawns and flower beds. there are hundreds of great old trees including Moreton Bay figs, bunya pines and macadamias, and there are lily ponds with ducks and geese feeding on scraps of bread.

There's also an interesting **mangrove boardwalk** which allows you to walk out over the Brisbane River amongst the mangroves – insect repellent is advisable. At the southern end of the gardens, beside the river, the **River Stage Amphitheatre** is a wonderful open-air venue with grassy slopes leading down to a large concert stage.

The gardens are open 24 hours a day (and lit at night) and are a great spot for strolling, in-line skating and bike riding – there's also a very pleasant cafe inside the former curator's cottage at the southern end (see Places to Eat). There are free guided tours of the gardens leaving from the information booth inside the Albert St entrance every day except Monday at 11 am and 1 pm; ring ☎ 3221 4528 for enquiries.

Other Gardens

There are good views from **Wickham Park** and **Albert Park** in Spring Hill, just north of the city centre. **New Farm Park**, by the river at the southern end of Brunswick St, is noted for its rose displays, jacaranda trees and

Devonshire teas. **Captain John Burke Park** is a nice little place underneath the towering Story Bridge at the top of Kangaroo Point.

HISTORIC HOUSES

There are a number of interesting old houses and period re-creations around Brisbane. **Newstead House**, four km north-east of the centre on Breakfast Creek Rd in Newstead, is the oldest surviving home in Brisbane. Built in 1846, overlooking the river, it is a stately mansion beautifully fitted out with Victorian furnishings and antiques, clothing and period displays. The house and its gardens are open from 10 am to 4 pm on weekdays and from 2 to 5 pm on Sunday and public holidays; entry costs $3 for adults, $2 for concessions and $1 for children; family tickets are $7. You can get there on bus No 160, 171 or 190 from the yellow stop on Edward St between Adelaide and Queen Sts.

Four km east of the centre, on McIlwraith Ave, and off Bennetts Rd in Norman Park is the **Earlystreet Historical Village**. It is a re-creation of Queensland colonial life with genuine old buildings including a slab timber hut, two homesteads and a pub, in a garden setting. Devonshire teas are available. Entry is $6 for adults, $4 for children and $16 for a family ticket, and it's open daily from 9 am to 4.30 pm. You can get there on bus No 125, 145, 155 or 255 from Ann St near King George Square, or by train to Norman Park.

The **Miegunyah Folk Museum**, just north of Fortitude Valley at 35 Jordan Tce in Bowen Hills, is housed in an 1884 building, a fine example of early Brisbane architecture. It's been furnished and decorated in period style as a memorial to the pioneer women of Queensland and is open from 10.30 am to 3 pm on Wednesday and 10.30 am to 4 pm on weekends. To get there, take an airport bus No 160 or Toombul bus No 170, 171 or 190.

QUEENSLAND CULTURAL CENTRE

This superb complex (☎ 3840 7200) spans two blocks, either side of Melbourne St in South Brisbane, just across Victoria Bridge from the city centre. It houses the Queensland Art Gallery, the Queensland Museum and the State Library, all on the northern side of Melbourne St, and, to the south, the Performing Arts Complex and the new Exhibition and Convention centres.

Within the **Performing Arts Complex** are the 2000-seat Lyric Theatre, the Concert Hall with its magnificent organ, and and the Cremorne Theatre, a small studio theatre; there are also several restaurants and cafes. You can take a guided tour of the complex with Behind the Scenes Theatre Tours – ring ☎ 3844 8800 for bookings. Their tours last two hours, with visits to the costume design and set construction departments, backstage areas and rehearsal rooms.

The **Queensland Museum** is well worth a visit. Its large collection features a dinosaur garden, exhibitions on whales, the history of photography, natural history, and an extensive collection of Melanesian artefacts. The aviation section includes the *Avian Cirrus*, in which Queensland's Bert Hinkler made the first England to Australia solo flight in 1928, as well as the wreck of Bill Lancaster's plane and the script of his poignant final message to his family. The museum is open daily from 9 am to 5 pm, except on Good Friday and Christmas Day. On Anzac Day it is open from 2 to 5 pm. Admission is free.

The **Queensland Art Gallery** has an impressive permanent collection and also features visiting exhibitions. Australian artists in the collection include Sir Sidney Nolan, William Dobell, Charles Blackman, Margaret Preston and Fred Williams. There's also a small but impressive collection of European art, including paintings by Peter Paul Rubens, Tintoretto, Camille Pissarro and Edgar Degas. The gallery is open daily from 10 am to 5 pm, again except for Good Friday and Christmas. Admission is free. During special exhibitions, the gallery is open daily from 9 am to 5 pm and on Wednesday until 8 pm, and an admission fee is charged. There are free guided tours on during the week at 11 am and 1 and 2 pm, and on weekends at 11 am and 2 and 3 pm. The gallery's courtyard cafe is a good spot for lunch or a snack, and is reasonably priced.

The **State Library's** excellent facilities include newspaper and magazine sections, audiovisual programmes, videos, music and of course plenty of books, as well as a good cafe (see Places to Eat). The library is open Monday to Thursday from 10 am to 8 pm and Friday to Sunday from 10 am to 5 pm.

SOUTH BANK PARKLANDS

Brisbane's South Bank, formerly the site of Expo '88, has been extensively redeveloped and is now one of the city's liveliest and most interesting areas. Covering 16 hectares, its attractions include restaurants and cafes, parklands and bike paths, a rainforest sanctuary and butterfly house, weekend market stalls and even a sandy swimming beach.

The South Bank Visitor Information Centre (☎ 3867 2051) is located in the main entrance court and is open daily from 8 am to 8 pm; you can also phone ☎ 3867 2020 for South Bank's recorded message with details about the current week's entertainment programme and gig guide.

The **Gondwana Rainforest Sanctuary**, just behind the main entrance court, is a quite amazing re-creation of a rainforest environment. Set inside and around a massive synthetic rock, it's populated by native birds, mammals and reptiles including crocodiles, koalas, possums, lorikeets and snakes. An elevated boardwalk winds through the sanctuary. Wildlife presentations are held in a theatre on weekdays at 11 am and 2 pm and on weekends at 11 am and 1 and 3 pm. These are good photo opportunities – you can have your snap taken while you're patting a koala or with a snake wrapped around your neck. Gondwana is open daily from 8 am to 5 pm; entry costs $9 for adults, $7.50 for students, $6 for children and $26 for a family of four.

In the Plaza in the centre of the parkland, the **Butterfly & Insect House** is a glass-enclosed tropical conservatorium that is home to hundreds of Australian butterflies, as well as a large collection of exotic insects and spiders. It's open daily from 10 am to 4 pm and entry costs $6.50 for adults, $5 for students, $3.50 for children, and $20 for a family.

At the southern end of South Bank behind the Boardwalk Cafes, **Our World Environment** has a collection of displays loosely relating to the environment. The displays are a bit of a mixed bag, ranging from the banal to the fascinating. Worth a visit, if just for the contrasting experience of visiting the sub-zero Antarctic base camp and then popping into the heat of the Birdsville pub display. Tickets are $6 for adults, $5 for students and children and $20 for a family.

If you're planning to visit these attractions, you can buy a Discovery Ticket which admits you to Gondwana, the Butterfly & Insect House and Our World Environment, and includes one ride along the waterway ferries. These cost $18 for adults, $15 for concessions, $10 for children and $50 for families.

A network of narrow canals runs through the parklands. You can take a ride along these on the **Southship Waterway Ferries**, although tickets are overpriced at $5 for adults, $2 for children and $10 for a family.

Don't forget to bring your swimming gear to South Bank. There's even a large **artificial beach and swimming lagoon**, complete with white sand, deckchairs for hire and bronzed lifesavers on duty. It's a great spot for a swim – there's something kind of surreal about lying on the beach here and looking across the river to the city skyline in the background.

Between late October and the end of March, a mobile **alfresco cinema** screens free latest release movies at various places in the parkland on Wednesday and Saturday nights at 7.30 pm (more frequently during the school holidays). The **Suncorp Piazza**, an outdoor entertainment venue, has regular concerts and performances, many of which are free. Check the entertainment programme (☎ 3867 2020) to see what's on.

South Bank also includes a beautiful **Nepalese Pagoda** that took 160 craftspeople two years to make; some great **restaurants and cafes** (see Places to Eat); a large **craft and clothing market** at the

Stanley St Plaza (see Markets); and plenty of good **picnic areas** with free gas barbecues.

BEACHES
Brisbane doesn't really have any beaches, apart from the artificial one in the South Bank Parklands. Moreton Bay is a shallow, muddy, mangrove-lined bay, sheltered from the ocean by a cluster of islands – some of its 'beaches' are OK for sunbaking if you're desperate, but that's about all. On the plus side, there are plenty of great beaches within an hour's drive of the city – head for North Stradbroke Island, the Gold Coast or the Sunshine Coast.

MT COOT-THA PARK
This large park has a lookout and an excellent botanic garden, and is just eight km west of the city centre. The views from the top are superb. On a clear day you can see the distant line of Moreton and Stradbroke islands, the Glass House Mountains to the north, the mountains behind the Gold Coast to the south and Brisbane, with the river winding through, at your feet. There are two eateries up here, both with sensational views – see Places to Eat for details.

There are some good walks around Mt Coot-tha and its foothills, like the one to J C Slaughter Falls on Simpsons Rd. There's also an **Aboriginal Art Trail**, a 1.5-km walking trail which takes you past eight art sites with work by local Aboriginal artists including tree carvings, rock paintings and a dance pit.

The **Mt Coot-tha Botanic Gardens**, at the foot of the mountain, are open daily from 8.30 am to 5 pm. The gardens include an enclosed tropical dome, an arid zone, rainforests and a Japanese garden, plus a library and a teahouse. There are free guided walks through the gardens at 11 am and 1 pm daily except Monday.

You'll also find the **Sir Thomas Brisbane Planetarium** here; also known as the 'Cosmic Skydome', it's the largest planetarium in Australia. Admission is $7.50 for adults, $6 for concessions and $3.50 for children, and there are 45-minute shows at 3.30

and 7.30 pm Wednesday to Friday; 1.30, 3.30 and 7.30 pm on Saturday; and 1.30 and 3.30 pm on Sunday.

There are buses to the lookout and botanic gardens at Mt Coot-Tha. Bus No 37A to the gardens leaves from Ann St at King George Square.

BRISBANE FOREST PARK

The Brisbane Forest Park is a 28,500-hectare natural bushland reserve in the D'Aguilar Range. The park starts on the outskirts of Brisbane and stretches for more than 50 km to the north-west. It's a great area for bushwalks, cycling, horse riding, camping and scenic drives.

At the entrance to the park there's an information centre, a freshwater wildlife sanctuary and restaurant, and further on are the mountain villages of Mt Nebo and Mt Glorious, both of which offer a range of accommodation options and eateries.

There are a number of good walking trails throughout the park, including the six-km Morelia Track at the Manorina Bush Camp and the five-km Greene's Falls Track at the Maiala National Park. Bushwalkers can also bush camp overnight in the park, although you need a permit to do so. These cost $2 per person per night and are available through the information centre. Unfortunately, only one short walking trail starts from the information centre, so bushwalkers will need their own transport.

Brisbane Forest Park Information Centre

The Brisbane Forest Park Information Centre (☎ 3300 4855) is at 60 Mt Nebo Rd, The Gap, at the start of the park. This is a good place to find out about the facilities in the park, including walking trails and picnic areas. It's open on weekdays from 8.30 am to 4.30 pm and on weekends from 10 am to 5 pm. The rangers also run regular guided bushwalks and tours – ring for details.

Walk-About Creek

Beside the information centre is Walk-About Creek, a freshwater study centre where you

can see fish, lizards, pythons and turtles at close quarters. It's open daily from 9 am to 4.30 pm (weekends from 10 am); entry costs $3.50 for adults, $2 for children and $9 for a family. Upstairs, there's the excellent open-sided *Walk-About Creek Restaurant* (☎ (07) 3300 2558) which serves snacks, lunches and dinners.

Mt Nebo

Mt Nebo Rd continues into the park from The Gap, winding its way through the mountains. It's an attractive and popular scenic drive with a number of good lookout points signposted along the way. Twenty-one km further on is Mt Nebo, a small hilltop village with a scattered handful of houses.

Places to Stay & Eat Mt Nebo has an unusual B&B. The *Railway Carriage* (☎ (07) 3289 8120) is a beautifully restored railway carriage in a landscaped garden setting with a bedroom, tiny bathroom and a kitchen. It is good value at $70 a double including breakfast ($80 on weekends). On the same property is a small self-contained cottage which has the same rates.

The *Mt Nebo Cafe* is a general store which has good meals including burgers, sandwiches and pies and a pleasant open-air decking area out the back.

Manorina Bush Camp

This camping ground beside the Mt Nebo Rd, midway between Mt Nebo and Mt Glorious, has a lovely forest setting with water and toilets. Several walking trails start from here. Camping permits cost $5 per site for up to six people, and can be booked through the Brisbane Forest Park Information Centre (☎ (07) 3300 4855).

Mt Glorious

This small and serene mountain village has a great setting atop a heavily forested mountain, with views back down to Brisbane and Moreton Bay. For motorcyclists, the ride from Samford up to Mt Glorious and down the other side to Lake Wivenhoe is rated as one of the top 10 rides in Australia – it isn't quite as much fun in a car, but still rates pretty highly as a scenic drive.

Mt Glorious has a couple of eateries and craft shops. It's quite a popular little place on weekends, although during the week it's still sleepy and laid-back.

About one km north of the town is the entrance to the **Maiala National Park**, which has some very pleasant picnic areas with barbecues, and several good walking trails.

Six km past Mt Glorious you come to the **Wivenhoe Outlook**, with a spectacular lookout platform with panoramic views down to Lake Wivenhoe. There's also a good picnic area here.

Places to Stay *Camp Constable* (☎ (07) 3300 2285), a holiday camp owned by the Uniting Church, is mainly used by school and church groups but also opens to the general public. Nightly costs are $7 per person in the cabins (minimum of 30 people), $4.50 per person in permanent tents, and $3 per person in the camp site. You need to ring and book in advance.

Mt Glorious Getaways (☎ (07) 3289 0172), signposted down Browns Rd just past the village, is an attractive bush property with three stylish timber cottages, each with its own kitchen, bathroom and one bedroom. The cottages sleep up to four people and cost $90 a night ($100 on weekends).

Places to Eat *Maiala Rainforest Teahouse* in the centre of town is a good, earthy cafe serving up Devonshire teas, home-made cakes, muffins, burgers and sandwiches. Their tofu burgers ($7) are particularly good. The teahouse has a pleasant outdoor decking which is visited by an assortment of birds, and you can get local information here including maps on walks in the area. It is open daily from 10 am to 5 pm.

Near the entrance to town, *Clover Cottage*, set on the side of the mountain, enjoys spectacular views from an open deck at the front of the cottage. It's menu is fairly diverse, with offerings including cooked breakfasts ($7.50), Devonshire teas ($5), burgers ($4 to $6) and pastas (around $10).

Getting There & Away
To get to the park from the city, follow Musgrave, Waterworks and Mt Nebo Rds. By public transport, you can take a No 506 express bus from the corner of Albert and Adelaide Sts in the city to The Gap – this service runs every day, and it's about a 700-metre walk from the bus stop to the info centre and Walk-About Creek.

WILDLIFE SANCTUARIES
Alma Park Zoo
Brisbane's best wildlife sanctuary is the Alma Park Zoo (☎ 3204 6566) at Kallangur, 28 km north of the city centre, off the Bruce Hwy. It's an excellent zoo set in eight hectares of subtropical gardens, with palm trees, ferns and native flora, and naturalistic enclosures. It has a large collection of Australian native birds and animals including koalas, kangaroos, emus and dingoes, and exotic wildlife including Malaysian sun bears, camels, leopards and lots of cute South American monkeys. You can touch and feed many of the animals – feeding times are: rabbits and agoutis, 11.30 am; monkeys and baboons, noon and 2.45 pm; and koalas, 12.30 and 3 pm.

There's a cafe, or if you want to cater for yourself there are good picnic areas with barbecues. The zoo is open every day (with the exception of Christmas Day) from 9 am to 5 pm, with last entries at 4 pm; admission costs $14 for adults and $7 for children.

A special 'zoo train' runs to the zoo every day on the Caboolture line, departing from the Transit Centre at 9.05 am and from Central Station at 9.09 am. If you get off at Dakabin Station, the zoo's courtesy bus will meet you and take you to the zoo.

Lone Pine Koala Sanctuary
The Lone Pine Koala Sanctuary at Fig Tree Pocket, 11 km south-west of the centre, receives much more publicity than Alma Park, but it's a disappointment in comparison. It promotes itself heavily to an overseas market as the 'World's Largest Koala Sanctuary', and thrives by exploiting the fascination foreign tourists have for koalas.

The sanctuary is set in spacious parklands but the enclosures are small and the animal facilities are less than state of the art.

Lone Pine has more than 100 koalas plus a variety of other Australian fauna including kangaroos, possums, emus, lyrebirds and wombats. Visitors can feed and touch many of the animals and pay to have their photos taken doing so.

Lone Pine is open from 8 am to 5 pm daily and entry costs $10.50 for adults, $6 for children and $24 for a family ticket. You can get to the sanctuary by bus, river cruise or bus tour. Cityxpress bus No 518 leaves from the Koala platform at the Queen St underground bus station hourly between 8.35 am and 3.35 pm, every day. Mirimar runs a daily river cruise here – see Organised Tours.

AUSTRALIAN WOOLSHED

The Australian Woolshed (☎ 3351 5366) is at 148 Stamford Rd in Ferny Hills, 15 km north-west of the centre. It's an impressively set up attraction which is very popular with bus tour groups. At the entrance there's a large souvenir shop specialising in Australiana. Beyond here is a spacious and attractive park with free picnic and barbecue facilities, a small fauna park with koalas and kangaroos, and a water slide ($4.50 an hour).

The one-hour Ram Show, which stars eight trained rams and several sheep dogs, includes shearing, wool-spinning demonstrations and other activities. Shows are held daily at 10 and 11 am and 2 pm; entry costs $11 for adults, $8 for concessions and $5 for children.

There are also two restaurants in the complex. Dinner dances with bush dancing and sing-alongs are held here every Friday ($28 per person) and Saturday ($30 per person) night.

If you don't have a car, you can get here by train – it's an 800-metre walk from Ferny Grove Station to the Woolshed. Three of the commercial bus tour operators also have day trips here – see Organised Tours.

SPRING HILL

Spring Hill, rising gently to the north of the city, is part residential and part commercial, with old timber Queenslander buildings nestling alongside clusters of modern office blocks and high-rise buildings. There is plenty of good accommodation here, placing you right on the city fringe – see Places to Stay for details.

The **Old Windmill & Observatory** on Wickham Tce, just north-east of the Transit Centre, is one of Brisbane's earliest buildings, dating from 1828. It was intended to grind grain for the early convict colony but, due to a fundamental design error, it did not work properly. In 1837 it was made to work as originally intended but the building was then converted to a signal post and later a meteorological observatory.

Beside the Old Windmill is **Wickham Park** and, further uphill and west, **Albert Park**. Spring Hill is bordered to the north by Victoria Park, a large open parkland with playing ovals, the **Centenary Swimming Pool** and a **golf course** (see Activities).

FORTITUDE VALLEY, NEW FARM & KANGAROO POINT

Fortitude Valley was named after the good ship *Fortitude*, which sailed up the Brisbane River in 1849 with more than 250 immigrants on board. These immigrants settled in the low, swampy valley north-west of the city centre, and the area gradually developed to become the commercial trading centre of Brisbane. Many of the area's most impressive buildings were built in the 1880s and 1890s at the height of the Victorian era.

The Valley's role as Brisbane's trading centre didn't last, and as this century progressed the area's fortunes declined. For many years the Valley was one of Brisbane's seediest, roughest areas, but in recent years it has undergone a transformation. Nowadays the revitalised Valley is the considered the bohemian centre of Brisbane, and one of the city's liveliest areas with a diverse range of restaurants, cafes and nightclubs. It attracts all sorts of people – punks and drunks, yuppies and ferals, backpackers and tourists, restaurant-goers and nightclubbers. The Valley is usually just waking up when the rest of Brisbane is going to bed. See the Entertainment and Places to Eat sections for details of some of the area's main attractions.

The **Brunswick St Mall** is the true heart of the Valley; an interesting market is held here on Saturday. At the west end of the mall is **McWhirter's Markets**, which was built in stages between 1912 and 1930 as McWhirter's Emporium. The impressive art deco corner facade was the last feature to be added. In 1989, the building was converted into an indoor market, and has a great produce market, a food court, and lots of clothing boutiques and gift shops. There are also several good art and craft outlets here selling works by local artists.

Across from the east end of the mall on the corner of Ann and Brunswick Sts is the **Empire Hotel**, a massive pub built in 1888 in ornate Victorian-Italianate style. The Empire is something of a local landmark, although its bars are still pretty rough around the edges – the best view is from the outside.

One block south of Brunswick St is the **Chinatown Mall** in Duncan St, with lots of Asian restaurants. Another block south on the corner of Ann and Gipps St is the **Institute of Modern Art**, a warehouse-type art space with constantly changing exhibitions of modern art. It's well worth a visit, and is open Tuesday to Friday from 11 am to 5 pm and Saturday from 11 am to 4 pm. It is also often used as a venue for performance art and live music.

Dooley's Hotel, on the corner of Brunswick and McLachlan Sts, is another vital part of the Valley's essence – see the Entertainment section for details.

If you want to make a more in-depth study of the Valley's architectural heritage, pick up a copy of the city council's brochure *Heritage Trail – Fortitude Valley*, which maps out a good walking tour around 20 different sights.

New Farm, the next suburb to the east of Fortitude Valley, also has some good restaurants and accommodation, including several of the backpackers' hostels. At the eastern end of Brunswick St, **New Farm Park** is a large open parkland with playgrounds, picnic areas with gas barbecues, playing ovals, jacaranda trees, beautiful rose gardens and a kiosk (see Places to Eat). The east side of the park slopes down to the Brisbane River.

Kangaroo Point, is a narrow finger of land east of the city, dominated by the **Story Bridge**, which links Fortitude Valley with East Brisbane. Built back in 1940, it's the largest steel cantilever bridge in Australia. It was named after J D Story, the former Public Service Commissioner.

Beneath the bridge is **Captain John Burke Park**, named after the owner of a 19th-century shipping company. There are a number of historic buildings along Main St, which runs parallel to and below the bridge. They include a former **police lockup** (1910) on the Thorton St corner; **Silverwells** at No 261, a private residence built during the 1860s; **Yungaba** at No 120, built in 1885 to house immigrants; and the **Story Bridge Hotel** (see the Places to Eat and Entertainment sections).

The Cliffs, a rock-climbing area which is floodlit by night, is at the southern end of Kangaroo Point opposite the City Botanic Gardens – see Rock Climbing in the Activities section.

The impressive **Dockside Complex**, on the east side of the point, includes residential apartments, a marina, an apartment hotel, several bars and eateries, and Brisbane's best comedy venue.

There are two ferry services linking Kangaroo Point to the city; at the end of Holman St, and at the end of Thornton St.

PETRIE TERRACE & PADDINGTON

One of Brisbane's oldest suburbs, Paddington is a hilly, leafy residential area with lots of renovated Queenslander houses and plenty of good restaurants, cafes, art galleries and antique shops. It's a gentrified suburb with fashionable, well-off residents with well-tended haircuts and designer clothes.

The main route into and through Paddington starts out as Caxton St, which becomes Given Tce, which then becomes Latrobe Tce. These three continuous boulevards wind

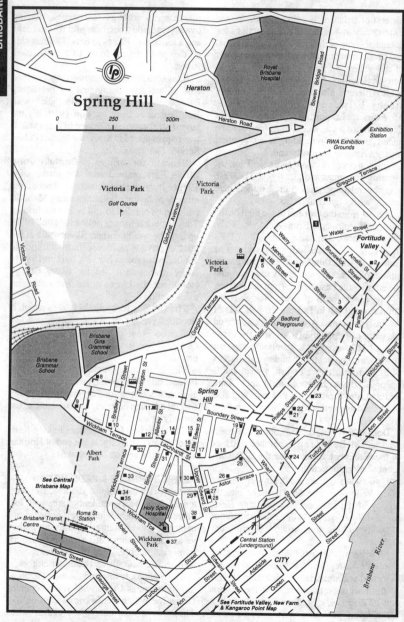

Spring Hill

0   250   500m

Royal Brisbane Hospital

Herston

Herston Road

Exhibition Station

RWA Exhibition Grounds

Victoria Park

Golf Course

Victoria Park

Victoria Park

Gilchrist Avenue

Victoria Park Road

Gregory Terrace

Water Street

Fortitude Valley

Gregory Terrace

Warry Street

Kennigo Street

Hill Street

Brunswick Street

Amelia St

1

1

6

5

3

Water Street

Bedford Playground

St Pauls Terrace

Barry Parade

Wickham Street

Brisbane Girls Grammar School

Brisbane Grammar School

Torrington St

Bradley Street

Spring Hill

Boundary Street

Phillips Street

Thornbury St

23

8

7

Allenby St

11

12

13

14

15

16

17

18

19

20

21

22

24

9

10

Leichhardt St

Little Edward St

Wharf Street

Wickham Terrace

Albert Park

32

31

30

33

34

35

Birley Street

Upper Edward St

Edward St

25

26

27

28

29

Astor Terrace

See Central Brisbane Map

Brisbane Transit Centre

Roma St Station

Holy Spirit Hospital

36

38

37

Wickham Park

Wickham Tce

Albert Street

Roma Street

George Street

Turbot Street

Ann Street

Edward Street

Central Station (underground)

CITY

Adelaide Street

Queen Street

Brisbane River

See Fortitude Valley, New Farm & Kangaroo Point Map

PLACES TO STAY

1   Tourist Private Hotel
2   Balmoral House
4   Spring Hill Terraces
5   Gregory Terrace Motor Inn
8   QCWA Ruth Fairfax House
9   Albert Park Inn Hotel
10 Wickham Terrace Motel
12 Summit Apartment Hotel
14 SDK Apartment Hotel
17 Metropolitan Motor Inn
21 Kookaburra Inn
22 Dahrl Court Apartments
23 Thornbury House B&B
25 Ridge Hotel
26 Camelot Inn
27 Yale Inner-City Inn
28 Annie's Shandon Inn
30 Dorchester Self-contained Units
31 Centrepoint Apartment Hotel
32 Chancellor on the Park Hotel
33 Marrs Townhouse Motel
34 Gazebo Hotel
35 Soho Club Motel
36 Tower Mill Motor Inn
38 The Astor Motel

PLACES TO EAT

11 Harold's Cafe
13 Papa Mio
24 Little Tokyo
29 Oriental Bangkok

OTHER

3   RACQ Head Office
6   Centenary Swimming Pool
7   Spring Hill Baths
15 Options Nightclub
16 Spring Hill Hotel
18 Sportsman's Hotel
19 The Actress & the Bishop Tavern
20 St Paul's Tavern
37 Old Windmill

built as a cinema in 1930. The Brisbane City Council's *Heritage Trail – Latrobe and Given Tces, Paddington* brochure describes the building: 'Its rather plain exterior belied the cinema's highly ornate interior. The Plaza's original owners went to great lengths to create atmosphere – stars and clouds were painted on its vaulted ceiling to add to the illusion of a night sky; wooden clouds were suspended from the ceiling and backlit to give the effect of the moon behind them...' The Plaza now houses an antiques gallery.

Back at No 292 Given Tce is the **Paddington Post Office**, built in 1900. Further down at No 265, **Faces Restaurant** occupies the former Urban Lane Bakery building (1888), which has a shop at the front and stables and ovens out the back. See the Places to Eat section for details.

Back on Petrie Tce near the intersection of Upper Roma St and Milton St is the **Museum of Contemporary Art**, in a converted grain silo. It's open Monday to Saturday from noon to 6 pm; admission is by $2 donation.

UNIVERSITY OF QUEENSLAND

The University of Queensland is on a 110-hectare site on a bend of the Brisbane River, seven km south of the city. You could easily spend a few hours or even a day here – it's an attractive and interesting place to visit, with some good museums, good sporting facilities, an excellent bookshop and a cinema. If you have a bike, you can ride all the way here from the city along the Bicentennial Bikeway, which follows the west bank of the Brisbane River out of the centre.

There's a helpful **information office** in a small building beside the main entrance to the uni, and you can get a map of the grounds and information about the facilities from here.

The university is centred around the lovely Great Court, a spacious area of lawns and trees surrounded by an impressive semi-circle of cloistered sandstone buildings.

The University Bookshop, on Staff House Rd, stocks a wide range of interesting reading matter, and if you get hungry while

their way through the heart of Paddington, with a different cluster of cafes and restaurants around each corner – see the Places to Eat and Entertainment sections. Latrobe Tce, on the western side of Paddington, has quite a few antique shops and galleries – see the Things to Buy section. The **Paddington Plaza** building at No 153-171 was originally

BRISBANE

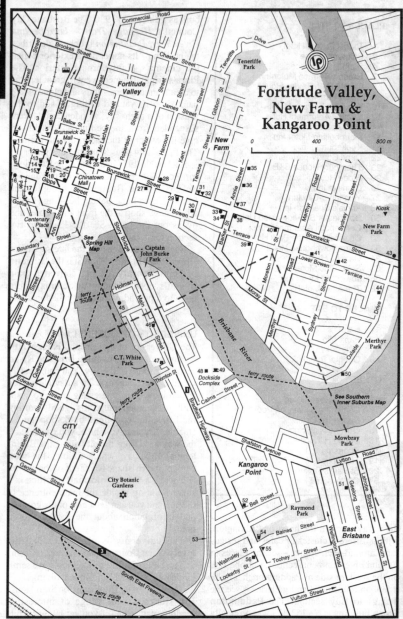

Fortitude Valley, New Farm & Kangaroo Point

Fortitude Valley

New Farm

Teneriffe Park

0   400   800 m

Kiosk

New Farm Park

See Spring Hill Map

Captain John Burke Park

ferry route

Holman

Brisbane River

C.T. White Park

Dockside Complex

ferry route

See Southern Inner Suburbs Map

Merthyr Park

City Botanic Gardens

CITY

Mowbray Park

Kangaroo Point

Raymond Park

East Brisbane

South East Freeway

ferry route

Centenary Place

Chinatown Mall

Brunswick Mall

PLACES TO STAY

27 Pete's Palace
30 Globe Trekkers Hostel
35 Atoa House Travellers Hostel
36 The Homestead
39 South Pacific Motel
40 Allender Apartments
41 Terrace Units
42 Edward Lodge
44 Boronia Lodge B&B
47 Ryan Lodge Motel
48 Dockside Apartment Hotel
50 Kirribilli Apartments
51 Courtney Place Backpackers
52 Kangaroo Motel
56 Southern Cross Motel

PLACES TO EAT

 5 Sala Thai
 7 Lucky's Trattoria
 9 Mellino's Restaurant &
    Cosmopolitan Cafe
14 Vietnamese Restaurant
15 Seoul Restaurant
18 Universal Noodle Restaurant
19 Enjoy Inn
22 The Eiffel Tower Cafe
24 Cafe Europe
25 Giardinetto's
31 Baan Thai
32 Famish
34 Continental Cafe
37 Le Bronx

49 Snug Harbour Dockside Comedy
    Cafe
55 Somewhere to Eat

OTHER

 1 Valley Swimming Pool
 2 Wickham Hotel
 3 Brunswick Railway Station
 4 The Roxy Nightclub
 6 The Zoo Nightclub
 8 The Beat Nightclub
10 McWhirter's Market
11 Signal Nightclub
12 Terminus Nightclub
13 The Tube Nightclub
16 Rocksports
17 Outdoor, Camping & Adventure
    Sports Shops
20 Institute of Modern Art
21 Ric's Cafe-Bar, Rhumba Reeba
    Cafe & The Deck Bar
23 Red Books
26 Dooley's Hotel
28 New Farm Laundromat
29 Brunswick Hotel
33 New Farm Mountain Bikes
38 Village Twin Cinerna
43 Main Entrance, New Farm Park
45 Brisbane Jazz Club
46 Story Bridge Hotel &
    The Bomb Shelter
53 The Cliffs Rockclimbing
    Area
54 Pineapple Hotel

browsing or want somewhere to read your new purchase, head for the nearby *Wordsmith's Writers Cafe*. There's an open-air courtyard and the cafe has surprisingly good gourmet food at very reasonable prices.

There are also several museums in the university which are open (and free) to the general public. With a collection of over 20,000 artefacts from Australia, Papua New Guinea and the Pacific islands, the **Anthropology Museum**, opens during semesters on Monday and Wednesday from 10 am to noon and from 1 to 4 pm.

The **Antiquities Museum**, in the Department of Classics & Ancient History, has a small collection of pottery, coins and glass from Rome, Greece, Persia and other ancient civilisations. It is open by appointment (☎ 3365 2643) weekdays from 9 am to 1 pm and from 2 to 5 pm.

The university's **Geology Museum** (☎ 3365 2668) and **Zoology Museum** (☎ 3365 2474) are also open by appointment.

The **Schonell Cinema** (☎ 3371 1879) screens discounted movies most nights and is open to the general public (see Cinemas in the Entertainment section). There are also tennis courts for hire, a swimming pool and other sporting facilities here.

ACTIVITIES
Rockclimbing It comes as a surprise to most people when they find out that there's an

BRISBANE

excellent rock-climbing venue in the heart of Brisbane. The Cliffs, on the south banks of the Brisbane River in Kangaroo Point (across the river from the City Botanic Gardens), is a long stretch of rock face with climbs from 10 to 18 metres, ranging from beginners climbs up to grade 26. The Cliffs are floodlit nightly until midnight or 2 am, and there are usually crowds of climbers and spectators along here.

Several local operators offer climbing and abseiling instruction here. They include Jane Clarkson's Outdoor Adventures (☎ 3830 5044 or 015 113 462). Jane is an experienced instructor and offers abseiling sessions ($30), top-roping courses ($120 for four sessions or $35 a session), and runs a social rock-climbing group on Wednesday nights ($10 per person); she also organises climbing trips out of Brisbane. For a list of other operators offering climbing and abseiling courses, look under 'Outdoor Adventure Activities & Supplies' in the *Yellow Pages* phone directory.

Abseiling in the heart of the city

Rocksports (☎ 3216 0462), at 224 Barry Pde in Fortitude Valley, is an indoor climbing factory with a variety of textured climbing walls and a weights gym. It is open on weekdays from 8.30 am to 9.30 pm and on weekends from 9 am to 6 pm. It's a good place to learn to climb or to improve your techniques. For $9 (plus another $3 for harness hire) you can climb for as long as you like. They also have technique courses on Monday nights ($25), yoga classes on Wednesday nights ($8) and competition nights on Tuesday and Thursday.

Cycling See the Getting Around section at the end of this chapter.

Golf There are a couple of good public golf courses close to the centre.

The most central is the Victoria Park Golf Course (☎ 3854 1406), on Herston Rd in Herston, immediately north of Spring Hill; 18 holes costs $15 during the week and $18 on weekends, and club hire is another $16.

The St Lucia Golf Course is an attractive, hilly course about eight km south of the centre; a round costs $15 during the week and $18 on weekends; club hire is available for another $15. Just south of here, the Indooroopilly Golf Club has two courses, one for members and one open to the public every day except Saturday. Eighteen holes costs $20 on weekdays and $28 on Sunday; club hire is another $16.

Horse Riding There are a few horse-riding schools on the outskirts of Brisbane, including Silverado (☎ 3890 2280), about 10 km east of the city in Hemmant, and the Samford Valley Riding Centre (☎ 3289 1046) in Samford about 14 km north-west of the city. Both charge around $15 an hour for trail rides.

In-Line Skating Skatebiz (☎ 3220 0157), in Mary St near the Albert St corner, hires out in-line skates and the necessary protective equipment for $10 for two hours ($15 on Sunday). Some of the best skating areas are

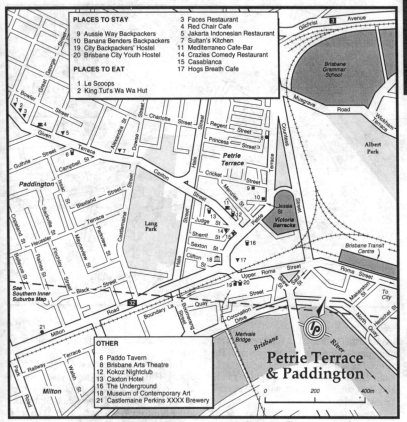

PLACES TO STAY
9 Aussie Way Backpackers
10 Banana Benders Backpackers
19 City Backpackers' Hostel
20 Brisbane City Youth Hostel

PLACES TO EAT
1 Le Scoops
2 King Tut's Wa Wa Hut

3 Faces Restaurant
4 Red Chair Cafe
5 Jakarta Indonesian Restaurant
7 Sultan's Kitchen
11 Mediterraneo Cafe-Bar
14 Crazies Comedy Restaurant
15 Casablanca
17 Hogs Breath Cafe

OTHER
6 Paddo Tavern
8 Brisbane Arts Theatre
12 Kokoz Nightclub
13 Caxton Hotel
16 The Underground
18 Museum of Contemporary Art
21 Castlemaine Perkins XXXX Brewery

Petrie Terrace & Paddington

0   200   400m

the City Botanic Gardens nearby, and the bike paths which follow the Brisbane River.

Running The walkways and bike paths around the Brisbane River attract lots of runners, as do the city's many parks including the Brisbane Botanic Gardens, New Farm Park and Victoria Park. South Bank is another popular spot with pavement pounders.

Walking For information about bushwalking near Brisbane, contact the Brisbane Bushwalkers Club on ☎ 33856 4050. *Family Walks In Brisbane*, by Julia Thorn ($10) has details of 20 walks in Brisbane; more than half of which are along and around the Brisbane River. Other suggested walks are along the coastal areas and in Brisbane's parks and gardens.

Camping Gear If you need to hire camping gear, Global Extremes (☎ 3391 5135) at 55 Shafston Ave in Kangaroo Point specialises in hiring outdoor adventure gear including tents, backpacks, wet weather gear, boots, cooking gear and sleeping bags.

BRISBANE

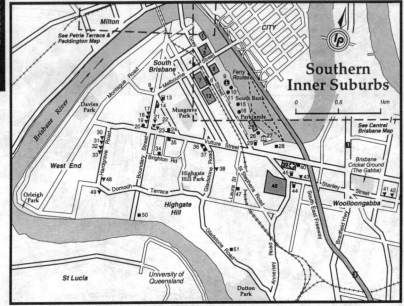

Swimming There are a several good swimming pools close to the city centre. The artificial beach and swimming lagoon at the South Bank Parklands are popular swimming and sunbaking spots with travellers – see that section for details.

The Valley Pool, on the corner of Wickham and East Sts in Fortitude Valley, is home to some world-champion swimmers including Samantha Riley, Suzie O'Neil, Glen Houseman and Ellie Overton. It is heated and open all year round; weekdays from 5.30 am to 8 pm, and on Saturday from 5.30 am to 6 pm and Sunday from 7.30 am to 6 pm.

The Spring Hill Baths in Torrington St, Spring Hill are amongst the oldest in the southern hemisphere. The 23-metre swimming pool is surrounded by colourful, painted, old-style changing cubicles, and is open from 5.30 am to 7 pm on weekdays and from 8 am to 7 pm on weekends. (It is currently closed during winter, but has recently applied for a license to open all year.)

The Centenary Pool, on Gregory Tce in Spring Hill, has an Olympic-sized pool, a kid's pool and a diving pool with a high tower. It's open daily between September and April from 6 am, and closes at either 6 or 8.30 pm.

Tennis Tennis Queensland (☎ 3369 5288), at 315 Milton Rd in Milton, about two km west of the city centre, is one of the closest places to the city. They have 25 day and night courts costing from $9 to $14 an hour. Other places include Masons East Brisbane Tennis Club (☎ 3391 0500) in Hilton St, East Brisbane; the University of Queensland Tennis Centre (☎ 3371 7906) in St Lucia; and the Action Tennis Centre (☎ 3395 1066) at 21 Boongall St in Camp Hill.

Sailing See the Moreton Bay section in this chapter for details of sailing clubs.

PLACES TO STAY

4   Sly Fox Hotel
24 Swagman's Rest Backpackers (New)
28 River Plaza Apartment Hotel
34 Somewhere to Stay
35 Swagman's Rest Backpackers (Old)
40 Hillcrest Apartment Hotel
47 Durham Villa
50 Riviera Apartments
51 Ambassador Brisbane Motel

PLACES TO EAT

8   Three Monkeys Coffee House
17 Qan Heng's Restaurant
18 Wholly Munchies & The Sitting Duck Cafe & Gallery
19 Caffe Tempo
21 Cafe Babylon
22 The Green Grocer
23 King Ahiram's
25 Boardwalk Cafes
30 Chutney Mary's
31 Cafe Bohemia
32 Khan's Kitchen
33 Kim Thanh
36 Genji Japanese Kitchen
38 Thai on High
41 Cloak & Dagger
42 Yianni's Greek Cafe

43 Hotel Morrison & Fiascos Restaurant
48 The Soup Kitchen
49 Caravanserai

OTHER

1   State Library
2   Queensland Art Gallery
3   Queensland Museum
5   Performing Arts Complex
6   South Brisbane Railway Station
7   Exhibition Centre
9   South Bank Visitor Information Centre
10 Gondwana Rainforest Sanctuary
11 Suncorp Piazza
12 Convention Centre
13 Melbourne Hotel
14 Travel Books
15 Stanley St Plaza & Crafts Village Markets
16 Butterfly & Insect House
20 Emma's Bookshop
26 Our World Environment
27 Maritime Museum
29 The Ship Inn
37 The Women's Bookshop
39 Mater Private Hospital
44 Clarence Corner Hotel
45 Van Gogh's Earlobe
46 Mater Misericordiae Hospital

Surfing Moreton Bay doesn't get any surf. The closest surf beaches are at North Stradbroke Island and on the Gold and Sunshine coasts.

Orienteering The Queensland Orienteering Association (☎ 3268 3338 or write to PO Box 114, Spring Hill, Qld 4000) holds regular events on Sunday mornings between March and October. Nonmembers are welcome to compete on a casual basis, with entry fees at around $8. Contact the association and they'll send you their programme of events.

Kayaking Kayak Escapes (☎ 13 1801) runs kayaking trips up the Upper Brisbane River. Their one-day discovery trip is a 22-km paddle that departs from the Transit Centre every Thursday and costs $75 per person, and they have two-day expeditions with camping gear and meals supplied, leaving from the Transit Centre every Tuesday ($175 per person) and every Saturday ($225 per person).

ORGANISED TOURS

There are all sorts of organised tours of Brisbane and the surrounding areas on offer – ask at any of the information centres for brochures and details.

Bus Tours Large bus-tour operators like Australian Pacific (☎ 13 1304), Coachtrans (☎ 3236 1000) and Boomerang Baxways (☎ 3236 3614) have a wide range of tours, including city sights tours, visits to wildlife sanctuaries, and trips to theme parks like Sea World and Movie World, and to the Sunshine and Gold coasts. The full range of tours and prices are detailed in their respective brochures.

The Brisbane City Council runs City Sights Trambus Tours, an open-sided bus which runs a shuttle service around the city's major sights and attractions. The bus operates every day except Tuesday from 9 am to 4 pm, passing each of the 18 stops every half hour; you can get on or off when you feel like it. Tickets cost $12 for adults, $8 for children and $25 for a family, which includes a souvenir booklet and discounts off some of the attractions. Stops include Post Office Square, City Hall, the City Botanic Gardens, the Sciencentre, South Bank and Chinatown in the Valley.

Far Horizons (☎ 3284 5475 or 015 151 631) runs small-group tours to some of the best natural attractions around Brisbane, including the Lamington National Park, O'Reilly's Guesthouse and the Springbrook National Park. The day trips cost $58 per person, which includes morning tea and lunch; backpackers and YHA members pay $52.

Allstate Scenic Tours (☎ 3285 1777) has day trips from Brisbane to O'Reilly's Guesthouse and the Lamington National Park, leaving every day (except Saturday) at 9.30 am. The return fare is $35.

For a day trip to the Gold Coast, the High Roller bus (☎ 3222 4067) to Jupiters Casino is good value. It leaves from the Transit Centre daily at 9 am and costs $10 return, which includes a $5 meal voucher and a $5 gaming voucher.

Brewery Tour From Monday to Wednesday there are free tours of the Castlemaine XXXX (pronounced four-ex) brewery (☎ 3361 7597) on Milton Rd, Milton, about 1.5 km west of the centre. Most hostels will organise trips to the brewery. The tour lasts about an hour, and is followed by about 40 minutes worth of free beer.

River Cruises The *Kookaburra Queens I* and *II* (☎ 3221 1300) are restored wooden paddle-steamers that cruises the Brisbane River. There are four different cruises: a 1½-hour morning tea cruise departs at 10 am ($14.90); a 1½-hour lunch cruise departs at 12.45 pm ($19.95); an afternoon tea cruise departs at 3.30 pm on Sunday only ($14.90); and the dinner cruises depart Monday to Saturday at 7.30 pm and Sunday at 6.30 pm (prices range from $19.90 with a hot roast to $49.90 with a seafood feast). The cruises depart from the Eagle St Pier, next to the Riverside Centre.

The *Brisbane Star* (☎ 018 190 604) does a four-hour cruise from the city to the mouth of the Brisbane River, departing every Sunday at 1 pm from the Edward St pier and at 1.15 pm from Mowbray Park. The fare is $10 for adults, $5 for children and $20 for a family.

Mirimar (☎ 3221 0300) runs a cruise around the Brisbane River to the Lone Pine Koala Sanctuary, costing $15 for adults and $8 for children. It departs daily at 11.30 pm from next to Victoria Bridge, at the end of the Queen St Mall.

Walking Tours Australian Heritage and Cultural Tours (☎ 3843 1035) takes guided walking tours through the city. Their one-hour tour costs $10 for adults, $5 for children; their two-hour tour costs $15/7.

Bicycle Tours Bicycle Bill's Tours (☎ 3203 2266) offers a variety of cycling tours out of Brisbane to places such as North Stradbroke Island and the Glass House Mountains. Their two-day tour destinations include Stanthorpe and the Granite Mountains ($175), the Cooloola Coast ($150) and the Glass House Mountains ($150). Meals are included in the price, and you can ride your own bike or they can arrange to hire one for you. You need to supply your own sleeping bag and tent.

Motorcycle Tours Brisbane Motorcycle Tours (☎ 018 073 496) takes people cruising on the back of Harley-Davidson bikes. They have short jaunts from $15 for 10 minutes or $40 for half an hour, one-hour rides up to the lookout at Mt Coot-tha for $60, or longer trips to places like Lake Wivenhoe (2½ hours, $135) and Maleny and Montville on the Sunshine Coast (four hours, $210).

FESTIVALS

Summer The week before Christmas is celebrated with a Christmas Festival at South Bank Parklands.

As with the rest of the country, Brisbane celebrates Australia Day each 26 January – the cockroach races at the Story Bridge Hotel in Kangaroo Point are one of the more unusual (and popular) events.

The Chinese New Year celebrations run for five days, starting 1 February, and feature fireworks, banquets and a temple dragon – it's a great time to visit Chinatown in Fortitude Valley.

The cricket season kicks off over summer, and regular interstate and international matches are played at the Brisbane Cricket Ground ('the Gabba') in Woolloongabba.

Car enthusiasts flood into the RNA Exhibition Grounds in Fortitude Valley in mid-February for Brisbane's International Motor Show.

Autumn If you're in Brisbane for St Patrick's Day (11 March), head for Dooley's Hotel in the Valley and/or the Queensland Irish Association's club in Elizabeth St in the city – guaranteed to be great fun. There's also a parade through the city.

The National Trust runs the Heritage Week Festival for two weeks in early April, celebrating Brisbane's architectural heritage. There's also an international comedy festival each April.

The Brisbane Marathon and the Brissie to the Bay Bike Tour are held at the end of May. Also in late May, the Paniyiri Festival is a Greek cultural festival with dancing, food and music.

The Brisbane Biennial, an international music festival held every second year (odd numbers), is an outstanding celebration of the world of music. Kicking off with a fire-

works display over the South Bank Parklands, the Biennial lasts for 10 days from late May to early June, featuring everything from classical, opera, military bands, world music, jazz and blues to rock. A food and wine festival is held in conjunction with the Biennial.

Winter The Winter Racing Carnival stretches from 1 May to 30 June, with major horse-race meetings each weekend at both Doomben and Eagle Farm racetracks, including the Brisbane Cup in mid-May.

Winter is also the football season in Brisbane – see the Spectator Sports section for details of rugby and Aussie Rules matches. A Festival of Winter is held at the South Bank Parklands over two weeks in mid-July. Fortitude Valley holds its own festival, the Valley Fiesta, over a weekend in mid-July.

Brisbane's annual agricultural show, the Royal National Exhibition (known as the Ekka) is held at the RNA Exhibition Grounds in Fortitude Valley for a week in the middle of August. The Ekka features agricultural and industrial displays, a carnival, and various ring events.

The Brisbane International Film Festival runs for 12 days every August, with a diverse range of Australian and foreign films. Special features include films from the South Pacific region and by indigenous film makers. It is based at the Hoyts Regent Theatres complex in the Queen St Mall.

Spring The arrival of spring is celebrated with a number of festivals. Held over two weeks from mid-September, the outdoor Warana Festival is Brisbane's major festival of the arts; buskers fill the streets and there are concerts and performances every day.

In early September, the Redland Strawberry Festival at the Cleveland Showground in Redland attracts thousands of strawberry lovers.

WORK

If you have a working holiday visa, you are entitled to work in Australia for up to three months. Without a visa, you're chances of finding work are slim, apart from perhaps the odd casual labouring job. See the Work section in the Facts for the Visitor chapter for more details.

Many of the backpackers hostels in Brisbane can find work for travellers – talk to the staff or check the notice boards. Telemarketing, door to door sales, au pair work and labouring in factories or on building sites are the most common jobs, although some of the hostels employ travellers to drive buses, work on the desk etc. Quite a few travellers seem to find work during the Ekka, Brisbane's agricultural show held in mid-August, erecting displays and stands or working on carnival stalls.

It's worth visiting the Department of Employment, Education and Training's CES Job Centre (☎ 3231 9999), who are at 15-23 Adelaide St in the city, or the CES Casual Employment Office (☎ 3250 3111) on the corner of Wickham and Gotha Sts in Fortitude Valley. These places have notice boards advertising positions vacant and the staff can advise you on what type of work might be available and how to go about a job search.

There are also numerous temp agencies in the city – check the *Yellow Pages* telephone directory under 'Employment Agencies' – and the *Courier Mail* has a daily 'Situations Vacant' listing. Wednesday and Saturday are the best days to look.

Programme 2000 (☎ 3221 6522), at 40 Queen St in the city, employs travellers with 'outgoing personalities' to sell educational programmes door to door. A couple of travellers have written to LP with good reports of this organisation.

PLACES TO STAY

Brisbane's accommodation options cover the full spectrum, with everything from backpackers' hostels to five-star hotels. Most of the places listed here are in the inner suburban area, generally within a couple of km of the city centre. The main accommodation clusters are the city centre itself (which mainly has the more expensive options); Spring Hill, immediately north of the city;

Petrie Terrace and Paddington, on the west side of the city; Fortitude Valley and New Farm, north-east of the city; Kangaroo Point, across the Brisbane River east of the city; and the southern inner suburbs, which include South Brisbane, the West End and Highgate Hill.

All of these areas have their own particular character, and whichever area you decide to stay in will have a significant impact on your impressions of Brisbane.

The accommodation listed here is divided into the following categories: caravan and camping parks (none of which are closer than 10 km from the city centre); backpackers' hostels, where you can get a dorm bed for $10 to $15, a single room for around $25 and a double room for $30 to $35; pubs, which have basic pub-style rooms from $12 to $20 and motel-style rooms for $50 to $60; B&Bs – there are only a handful of these in the inner suburbs, but they are all good value, costing from $60 to $80 a double; budget hotels, guesthouses and apartments, which vary enormously in quality and price and range from around $40 to $80 a double; motels, which also vary substantially and range from $50 to $130 for a double room; mid-range hotels, which are mostly in the city centre or Spring Hill and range from $100 to $150 a double; apartment hotels and serviced apartments, up-market self-contained places costing anywhere from $80 to $200 a night; and top-end hotels, which start from $180 a double and soar to over $1000 for a luxury suite.

There are several accommodation booking services in Brisbane, including the RACQ's Accommodation Booking Service (☎ 3361 2802), Central City Accommodation (☎ 3358 2366) and Accom Solutions (☎ 3221 2922). The Brisbane Visitors Service in the Transit Centre can also book accommodation for you – see the Hostels section for more details.

If you decide to stay longer, there are places advertised under the 'Share Accommodation' and 'Flats, Houses Let/Wanted' sections in the *Courier Mail* – Wednesday and Saturday are the best days to look. It's also worth checking the notice boards in the hostels, where travellers often place ads looking for other travellers to share accommodation, or, if you want to share with students, try the notice boards at the universities. Many places like cafes and bookshops in the inner suburbs also have notice boards advertising rooms to rent – a possible advantage with these notice boards is that you can often get a feel for the people you'll be sharing with by the type of place they advertise in.

Caravan Parks

There are no caravan parks or camping grounds close to the city centre, and in any case many of the caravan parks are full with permanent residents. The following places are all worth trying, and are amongst the closest to the city.

The *Aspley Acres Caravan Park* (☎ 3263 2668), at 1420 Gympie Rd (the Bruce Hwy) in Aspley, is a good camping and caravan park 13 km north of the centre. Tent sites start from $12 a double, there are on-site tents at $12/20 for singles/doubles, on-site vans are from $25 a double and self-contained cabins start from $35.

The *Amaroo Gardens Caravan Park* (☎ 3397 1774), about nine km south of the city at 771 Logan Rd in Holland Park, is a fairly basic van park with lots of permanent residents and no tent sites. Powered sites start from $12.50 a night.

The *Dress Circle Village Caravan Park* (☎ 3341 6133), 14 km south at 10 Holmead Rd, Eight Mile Plain, is a better option. It's a modern park with a kiosk, swimming pool and landscaped garden setting, and tent sites from $10, powered sites from $17 and on-site cabins and villas from $50 a double. Across the road is the *Sheldon Caravan Park* (☎ 3341 6166), which has tent and van sites from $12, on-site vans from $28 and cabins and units from $40. Holmead Rd can be a little tricky to get to – take the Logan Rd exit off the South Eastern Freeway, and it's off Logan Rd near the freeway overpass.

One of Brisbane's best caravan and camping parks is the *Gateway Junction*

(☎ 3341 6333), 19 km south of the centre at 200 School Rd in Rochedale. It's a large, modern park with landscaped grounds, a good pool, a tennis court and recreation room, and a bus service into the city from the front of the park. Powered sites are $18 a night, and there are good self-contained villas and cottages from $50 to $70 a night.

Alternatively, there are a couple of backpackers' hostels near the city that will allow travellers to camp in their backyards – see the following hostels section.

Hostels

Brisbane has a wide range of backpackers' hostels, with everything from large modern places to small intimate ones, and from quiet, relaxed hostels to full-on party places. The standards vary substantially, although the hostel scene here has been cleaned up in recent years with the introduction of new regulations aimed at raising standards, and a few of the dodgier places have closed or been renovated. In addition, a new hostel rating system being sponsored by the federal Department of Tourism looks like having a positive impact on the standard of hostels – many owners were talking about upgrading their facilities to attract a higher rating.

If you're travelling by train or bus, you'll arrive at the Brisbane Transit Centre in Roma St. The Brisbane Visitors Accommodation Service (☎ 3236 2020), on the third level of the Transit Centre, is a free accommodation booking service which is open on weekdays from 7 am to 6 pm and weekends from 8 am to 5 pm. This place has brochures and information on all the hostels and other budget options, and once you have decided where to stay they'll ring the hostel for you and arrange for someone to pick you up, usually within 10 or 15 minutes. Most of the hostels have their own courtesy buses for pick-ups, and some of those that don't will deduct the cost of a taxi from your bill. The YHA hostels don't have pick-up services.

Some hostels require a passport or photo ID when you book in, and a few no longer accept Australian travellers, mainly because of bad experiences with non-travellers using their hostels as dosshouses. Most places have cheaper weekly rates, it might be worth ringing around to negotiate the best rate.

Brisbane's hostels are concentrated in three main areas: Petrie Terrace and Paddington, just west of the city centre; Fortitude Valley and New Farm, north-east of the city; and south of the city in South Brisbane and West End. There are also hostels in East Brisbane and Spring Hill.

Fortitude Valley & New Farm The YHA-associated *Balmoral House* (☎ 3252 1397), at 33 Amelia St in Fortitude Valley, is a short walk from the Brunswick St railway station. The building has recently been renovated and the facilities are excellent. This place is clean, modern and quiet, but it's not the place to stay if you're planning to party, as it's not really a backpackers' place. It's popular with families and day patients from the nearby hospital. A bed in a three or four-bed dorm is $13, singles/doubles with shared bathrooms cost $28/32, and rooms with private bathrooms cost $45, or $48 for four.

Moving east into New Farm, you'll find four more hostels in and around Brunswick St. *Pete's Palace* (☎ 3254 1984), at 515 Brunswick St, is a rambling old three-storey timber house with a somewhat chequered history. It's a very relaxed, old-style hostel with adequate facilities; most of the interior has been painted with a variety of weird artwork by past residents, adding a touch of colour. Pete charges $12 for a dorm bed and $30 for a double. If the front gate is locked, there's a side entrance around the corner in Harcourt St.

A bit further along is the *Globe Trekkers Hostel* (☎ 3358 1251), at 35 Balfour St. This is a friendly and quiet hostel in a renovated old timber house, and the good atmosphere and small size make it quite popular. A bed in a five-bunk dorm costs $12, twins are $28 and doubles are $30 – one of the doubles has its own waterbed, if you're interested. This place also allows travellers with mobile homes to sleep in their vans or wagons out the back and use the hostel facilities for $5 a night.

The *Homestead* (☎ 3358 3538), at 57 Annie St, has recently had a new section built at the rear. It's a large, lively and modern place with good facilities including a small pool and various games. A bed in a six or eight-bed dorm costs $12; doubles and twins cost $30, or $39 with a private bathroom. This hostel has a free pick-up service from the airport.

Further along Annie St, at No 95, is the long-running *Atoa House Travellers' Hostel* (☎ 3358 4507). This quiet and relaxed hostel occupies three adjacent Queenslander-style houses, and has several TV lounges and living areas and various different types of rooms. Dorm beds cost $14 a night, singles/doubles are $25/30, and there are self-contained flats which cost $42 for up to three people or $56 for up to five people. The hostel has a spacious backyard with plenty of grass and shady trees, and if you have your own tent you can camp out the back for $7 a night.

Petrie Terrace & Paddington There are quite a few hostels on the west side of the city in and around Petrie Terrace, all within five to 10 minutes walk of the Transit Centre. The Petrie Terrace area isn't particularly appealing although its convenience to the centre is an advantage; Paddington, the adjacent residential suburb, is an attractive area with lots of good cafes, restaurants and bars.

The new *City Backpackers' Hostel* (☎ 3211 3221), at 380 Upper Roma St, is a new two-storey 76-bed hostel with good facilities. It's a fully air-conditioned, non-smoking hostel, and while Upper Roma St carries a lot of traffic, it's reasonably quiet inside. A bed in a four to six-bunk dorm costs $13, twins and doubles cost $32. The *Roma St Hostel*, right next door to this place, is not recommended – there are plenty of better options in town.

At 392 Upper Roma St is the *Brisbane City Youth Hostel* (☎ 3236 1004). The facilities are excellent, although it's still very much a youth hostel. The cost for YHA members is $14 per person in a four to six-bed dorm, or $32 for a twin room. The hostel has a new section with twins, doubles and triples with air-con and city views. Twins and doubles cost $40, or $48 with an ensuite: triples cost $48. Nonmembers pay an additional $2. The hostel has a restaurant which serves good breakfasts ranging from $1.50 to $5, and dinner costs $6.50.

Banana Benders Backpackers (☎ 3367 1157) is a short walk north, on the corner of Petrie Tce and Jessie St. The outside is painted bright yellow and blue, so you can't miss it. This is a small place in two sections with the usual facilities, and it has good views over to the west. The dorms are mostly four-share and cost $13 a night; doubles are $30. The only hassle here is that Petrie Tce can get noisy during peak hours.

Down the side street past Banana Benders is the small *Aussie Way Backpackers* (☎ 3369 0711) at 34 Cricket St. It's a 36-bed hostel in a recently renovated two-storey timber house with a front balcony. This place is clean and well set up, although the kitchen is quite small and gets crowded at meal times. A bed in one of the three to five-bunk dorms costs $13 for the first night, then $12 a night; there are also two single rooms at $25 and one double at $30.

South Brisbane & West End The *Sly Fox* (☎ 3844 0022), on the corner of Melbourne and Hope Sts in South Brisbane, is a popular place that occupies the top three storeys of an old pub. It's a lively, party-style place with plenty of action and regular nights out, although it's a little shabby and the kitchen is tiny and barely adequate – probably to encourage travellers to eat in the pub downstairs. The location is a bonus – it's a short walk from South Bank, the Cultural Centre and the city. If you're driving there's a car park behind the pub. The pub downstairs has live music, so it tends to be noisy. Dorm beds cost $12, twin rooms $28, and a double with a brass bed and ensuite $35.

The *Somewhere to Stay* hostel (☎ 3846 2858), at 45 Brighton Rd in the West End, is the biggest and one of the best in the city. It has two sections and a wide range of accommodation, although because of its size it can

seem a bit impersonal. There's a small pool, a cafe serving evening meals for $5, a garden and an outdoor area. The rooms in the newer section are the best, but also more expensive than the older ones. Dorm beds range from $11 to $15, with the newer ones having a TV, fridge, private bathroom and balcony. Single rooms cost $20 to $25, doubles and twins $28 to $35, and doubles/twins with TV, fridge and private bathroom $45. The hostel runs a regular bus service to the Transit Centre, or you can get there on bus No 178 from Adelaide St, opposite Anzac Square.

A short distance away is the family-run *Durham Villa* (☎ 3844 6853), on a hilltop at 17 Laura St. It's a small and laid-back hostel and also has a good pool and spacious gardens; dorm beds are $12, and singles/doubles cost $24/28.

The *Swagman's Rest* (☎ 3844 9956), at 145 Vulture St, is another West End option. It's on a busy road but has reasonably good facilities including access to a pool and regular barbecues. Dorm beds cost $10, twins/doubles $25. The owners of this hostel are planning to build a new place across the road at No 110, due to open early in 1996. The new hostel will be more up-market, with dorm beds from $14 and doubles at around $28 with shared bathrooms or $35 with ensuites.

East Brisbane Further from the centre in a quiet suburban street is *Courtney Place Backpackers* (☎ 3891 5166), at 50 Geelong St. This clean and quiet family-run place is in a two-storey house built many years ago by a dentist with 18 children! A bed in a four or eight-bed dorm costs $12, singles are $25 and doubles are $30, and each bed has its own security locker. This place has an in-house travel agent and is close to the bus and ferry services into the city. It also has a couple of good self-contained two-bedroom flats down the road, which cost $45 a double or $55 a triple.

Spring Hill The *Kookaburra Inn* (☎ 3832 1303), at 41 Phillips St, is an old Queenslander house converted into a backpackers' hostel, with communal kitchen, bathroom and laundry facilities. It's well located in a quiet, leafy street, and is especially popular with Japanese travellers. There are no dorms; singles/doubles cost $25/35.

Colleges

A number of the colleges at the University of Queensland in St Lucia offer accommodation during the university's vacation periods. St Lucia is about seven km south of the city centre. *International House* (☎ 3870 9593) is the only college that stays open throughout the year. It offers B&B at $32/54 for singles/twins, or full board (three meals a day) at $42/72 – travellers need to ask for the student rate when they book.

Pubs

There are a number of old pubs offering a varying range of accommodation in inner Brisbane.

City The 95-year-old *Hotel Embassy* (☎ 3221 7616), on the corner of Edward and Elizabeth Sts, has 19 old-fashioned but quite clean motel units upstairs starting from $50/60 for singles/doubles. You couldn't ask for a more central location, although this pub is a live band venue so if you're planning on early nights and sleep is a priority you might be better off looking elsewhere.

Spring Hill The *Spring Hill Hotel* (☎ 3831 0102), on the corner of Leichhardt and Little Edward Sts, is a relaxed inner city pub with clean and simple rooms upstairs, with shared bathrooms, from $25/35 for singles/doubles. Breakfasts start from $2.95, and the pub also has cheap lunch deals available – see Places to Eat.

Also in Spring Hill, the *Sportsman's Hotel* has accommodation for gay men – see the following section on Gay & Lesbian Accommodation for details.

New Farm The *Brunswick Hotel* (☎ 3358 1181), at 569 Brunswick St in New Farm, has basic backpacker-style accommodation upstairs in old pub rooms at $12 per person.

This pub also puts on various party nights for backpackers – see the Entertainment section.

South Brisbane The *Melbourne Hotel* (☎ 3844 1571), at 2 Browning St, a modern brick pub with motel-style rooms is upstairs at $50/60 for singles/doubles.

Across the road from the Mater Hospital on the corner of Stanley St and Annerley Rd, the *Clarence Corner Hotel* (☎ 3891 1011) has basic pub-style rooms with singles/doubles from $25/40.

Gay & Lesbian Accommodation

There are a couple of good places to stay in Brisbane catering for gay and lesbian travellers, and *Brother Sister*, the fortnightly gay and lesbian entertainment paper, also has an accommodation listing on its back pages.

The *Sportsman's Hotel* (☎ 3831 2892), at 130 Leichhardt St in Spring Hill, has simple pub-style rooms upstairs exclusively for gay men, costing $25/40 for singles/doubles, including a continental breakfast.

At 75 Sydney St in New Farm, *Edward Lodge* (☎ 3254 1078), is an excellent two-storey guesthouse catering exclusively for gays and lesbians, with eight immaculate double rooms each with their own ensuite. There's an attractive breakfast courtyard and a spa pool, and the tariff is $50/60 for singles/doubles, including breakfast.

B&Bs

Spring Hill The friendly *Thornbury House B&B* (☎ 3832 5985), at 1 Thornbury St, is located in a residential area on the city's edge. It's a charming two-storey timber Queenslander built in 1886 and attractively renovated in heritage style. There are four excellent double rooms and five smaller, attic-style single rooms, all with pale lemon-coloured walls, polished floorboards and shared bathrooms, and there's a very pleasant breakfast courtyard. Singles/doubles cost $45/80 including breakfast.

Paddington Another good B&B is the *Waverley B&B* (☎ 3369 8973), at 5 Latrobe Tce in Paddington, about two km west of the city centre. This place is also a renovated two-storey Queenslander, built on a sloping block with a family home upstairs and two excellent guest units downstairs. The units have a separate entrance, and each has its own ensuite and a modern, well-equipped kitchen. There are plenty of cafes and restaurants around here, and the owners are helpful with suggestions for good places to eat. Waverley is excellent value at $35/65 for singles/doubles – and if you're staying longer the weekly tariffs range from $200 to $230.

New Farm The *Boronia Lodge B&B* (☎ 3254 1371), at 37 Oxlade Dve in New Farm, is a solid family home from the 1930s. It has been renovated into a comfortable and modern B&B with a few original features, and has five guestrooms upstairs, all with shared bathrooms. Nightly tariffs are $40 for singles, $60 for doubles and $70 for the family room. The house is well presented, and is close to the river ferry into the city centre.

Nearby in New Farm is *Edward Lodge*, a guesthouse for gays and lesbians – see the earlier Gay & Lesbian Accommodation section for details.

Budget Hotels, Guesthouses & Apartments

Moving up a level from the backpackers' hostels, there are some good budget options around the city centre including small hotels, guesthouses, and self-contained units and apartments.

Spring Hill On the fringe of the city, Spring Hill has a good range of budget options, including three places in Upper Edward St which are only a 10-minute (uphill) walk from the Transit Centre.

Annie's Shandon Inn (☎ 3831 8684), at 405 Upper Edward St, is a charming and friendly guesthouse of 19 rooms, renovated in cute heritage-style with pinks and blues. Singles/doubles are $40/50 including a light breakfast and free tea and coffee throughout the day – there are also four rooms with

private bathroom for $50/60. The hotel has laundry facilities, a TV room and a small car park at the rear.

The *Yale Inner-City Inn* (☎ 3832 1663), next to Annie's, at 413 Upper Edward St, has singles/doubles at $30/42 and a few rooms with private bathrooms at $52. The tariff includes a light breakfast. Rooms are small and the facilities are quite old, but it's clean and has a laundry, TV room and car park.

The *Dorchester Self-contained Units* (☎ 3831 2967), at 484 Upper Edward St, is a two-storey block of renovated one-bedroom units, each with a kitchenette, air-con, phone and TV, and laundry facilities. There is also off-street parking here. These modern units are good value, costing from $60/70/80 for singles/doubles/triples.

About 500 metres further north-east, the *Dahrl Court Apartments* (☎ 3832 3458), at 45 Phillips St, have been recommended to LP by several travellers, and with good reason. It's a block of renovated 1930s apartments in a quiet, leafy residential street. The one-bedroom apartments have a separate kitchen, a small breakfast room, an ensuite with a full-sized bath, phones and TVs – one apartment even has its own piano! There's also a pool and a small gym. The apartments cost $60/70 for singles/doubles and $100 for four people, and there's also a large basement apartment that sleeps groups of up to 12 people at $25 a head.

Another good option if you're looking for somewhere self-contained is the *Spring Hill Terraces* (☎ 3854 1048), at 260 Water St, in Spring Hill, about 1.5 km north of the city centre. It's an attractive, modern place and offers split-level two-bedroom apartments with all the mod-cons for $69 a double plus $8 for each additional person. There's a small pool, a communal laundry and off-street parking. This place also has good budget rooms with shared bathrooms at $40 a single/double and motel-style units at $54/56.

The *QCWA's Ruth Fairfax House* (☎ 3831 8188), at 89 Gregory Tce, is a neat, 1950s-style guesthouse run by the Country Women's Association. For $44 a night you get a simple room with shared bathrooms and three meals a day – it's proximity to the hospitals makes this place popular with day patients.

Just over one km further north at 555 Gregory Tce, the *Tourist Private Hotel* (☎ 3252 4171) is a fairly dated guesthouse with singles/doubles from $33/46, with shared bathrooms. This isn't really a travellers' place – lots of patients from the nearby hospitals stay here too.

New Farm There are also a couple of affordable self-contained options in New Farm, north-east of the city centre.

On the corner of Brunswick St and Moreton St, the *Allender Apartments* (☎ 3358 5832) is a two-storey block of old cream-brick flats that have recently been refurbished. The studio units cost $50 a night; the one-bedroom units sleep up to five people and cost $50 a double plus $10 for each extra person.

The *Terrace Units* (☎ 3254 1161), at 542 Lower Bowen Tce, is a fairly uninspiring block of simple one-bedroom units which go for $55 a night.

Hamilton Just past Breakfast Creek on the way to the airport, the *Kingsford Hall Private Hotel* (☎ 3862 1317) is at 144 Kingsford Smith Dve (on the corner of Cooksley St). It's an old block of red-brick units with neat and clean rooms, and charges $34/37 for singles/doubles with shared bathroom. It has a guest kitchen.

Highgate Hill A good self-contained place south of the centre is the *Riviera Apartments* (☎ 3844 4407), on the corner of Boundary and Dudley Sts in Highgate Hill. It's a block of 14 older-style units on the banks of the Brisbane River, and the back units look out across the river to the University of Queensland. The units are quite straightforward but clean and comfortable, and this is an excellent location in a leafy suburban street. There are 10 two-bedroom units and four one-bedroom units, and the tariff is $55 a double plus $8 for each extra person. City bus No

29 stops at out the front of the apartments, and the ferry stop across to St Lucia is nearby.

Indooroopilly *Forest Lodge* (☎ 371 6600), at 140 Central Ave, is a complex of reasonable mid-range two-bedroom apartments in a small bushland setting. The apartments sleep up to six people and cost $69 a double, plus $10 for extra adults and $5 for children. You will need your own transport to get to this place – it's about a 15-minute drive south-west of the city. The lodge is smack bang in the middle of suburbia – it's conveniently close to the University of Queensland and a couple of good golf courses, but not much else.

Motels
City *Lennon's Hotel* (☎ 3222 3222), in the heart of the city at 66 Queen St, is a four-star motel and part of the nationwide Country Comfort motel chain. The 150 rooms have recently been refurbished, and facilities include several bars and restaurants, pool, spa and sauna, and undercover parking. Standard rooms are $134 a night, suites are $195 and spa rooms are $223.

Spring Hill There are plenty of motels in Spring Hill, just north of the centre. These places vary enormously, but as a rule you get what you pay for.

Opposite Victoria Park at 397 Gregory Tce, the *Gregory Terrace Motor Inn* (☎ 3832 1769), is a good four-star motel with a restaurant and pool (and the Centenary Olympic pool is just a short stroll away). The rooms have views of either the city or the park; motel units cost $88 a double, and there are two two-bedroom apartments that sleep up to eight people and cost $120 a double plus $10 for each extra person.

At 106 Leichhardt St, the *Metropolitan Motor Inn* (☎ 3831 6000) is a well-run, modern motel with units from $89, and a piano bar and restaurant downstairs.

There's a string of motels along the curvy and busy Wickham Tce, most of which overlook Albert Park or Wickham Park. The

Astor Motel (☎ 3831 9522) at No 193 is one of the best budget options, with recently renovated units from $59/65 for singles/doubles, and larger units from $79/85. *Marrs Townhouse Motel* (☎ 3831 5388) at 391 Wickham Tce is a budget motel with singles/doubles with shared bathrooms for $40/55, or from $55/65 with private bathrooms. The management is helpful and there are good views, but the rooms facing the road can be noisy. Back at No 333, the budget *Soho Club Motel* (☎ 3831 7722) charges $46/49 for fairly basic singles/doubles.

The circular design of the *Tower Mill Motor Inn* (☎ 3832 1421), at 239 Wickham Tce, mimics the design of the historic Old Windmill opposite. These wedge-shaped motel units are looking a little dated, and at $97 a double (including breakfast) there is better value around. The *Wickham Terrace Motel* (☎ 3839 9611), at 491 Wickham Tce, has singles/doubles starting from $66/72.

At 40 Astor Tce, *Camelot Inn* (☎ 3832 5115) is a 10-storey motel built in the 1970s. All rooms have kitchenettes and balconies, plus the usual mod-cons, and start from $85 a night.

New Farm The *South Pacific Motel* (☎ 3358 2366) on the corner of Bowen Tce and Langshaw St has good motel units with cooking facilities at $59/69 for singles/doubles.

Kangaroo Point There's a string of motels in Kangaroo Point along Main St (the Bradfield Hwy). One of the best is the *Ryan Lodge Motel* (☎ 3391 1011), at 269 Main St, a modern low-rise motel with good motel units from $75.

Further south are a couple of cheaper options: the *Kangaroo Motel* (☎ 3391 1145), at 624 Main St, and the *Southern Cross Motel* (☎ 33912881), at 721 Main St, have reasonably good budget rooms for $40/45.

Ascot & Hamilton There's a cluster of motels in the suburbs of Ascot and Hamilton, midway between the city centre and the airport. These places are conveniently placed

for the airport – several of them offer free pick-ups from the airport – and they're also close to Brisbane's racecourses, but unless you're about to catch a plane or back a winner there isn't much to recommend in this area.

Most of these places have been imaginatively named to emphasise their proximity to the airport. The *Airport International Motel* (☎ 3268 6388), at 528 Kingsford Smith Dve in Hamilton, is the pick of the motels in this area. It has good modern units from $79/84 for singles/doubles, one-bedroom apartments from $89 and two-bedroom apartments from $94. A bonus of staying here is that the motel houses the excellent *Hinkler's Restaurant*, which is licensed, opens nightly for dinner and specialises in Cajun and Creole cooking.

The *Airport Motel* (☎ 3868 2399), at 638 Kingsford Smith Dve, has basic singles/doubles from $59/64. Nearby at 620 Kingsford Smith Dve, the *Airport Heritage Motel* (☎ 3268 5899) has a better standard of rooms with prices starting at $72/77.

At 95 Nudgee Rd the *Admiralty Motel* (☎ 3268 7899) has good modern motel units at $70/74, and a courtesy bus doing pick-ups and drop-offs to the airport. A reasonable budget option in this area is the *Ascot Budget Inn* (☎ 3268 2823), at 143 Nudgee Rd. It's a plain but modern place with communal bathrooms, lounges and cooking facilities, and singles/doubles from $32/35. The *Airport 85 Motel* (☎ 3268 4966), across the road from the Doomben railway station at 40 Lamington Ave, has good motel units from $66/71.

Other Areas The *Coronation Motel* (☎ 369 9955), at 205 Coronation Dve in Milton, is a good modern motel with a restaurant, undercover parking and rooms from $69. Coronation Dve, a busy riverside boulevard which runs south-west out of the city, is predominantly a commercial business district and lined with offices.

In Highgate Hill, about two km south of the city centre, the *Ambassador Brisbane*

Motel (☎ 3844 5661) at 180 Gladstone Rd has oldish, unexciting rooms at $49/55.

Hotels – mid-range

Most of the hotels in this range cater predominantly for corporate clients, and on weekends they usually find themselves with lots of empty beds. You'll find that most of them have good weekend deals on offer which can cut the cost of accommodation dramatically, and offer incentives like champagne or breakfast.

City The *Brisbane City Travelodge* (☎ 3238 2222), right beside the Transit Centre in Roma St, is a four-star hotel with 191 rooms starting from $180 and suites from $340. On the weekend you can get a double room here for $105, or $120 with breakfast.

The *Parkroyal Brisbane* (☎ 3221 3411), opposite the City Botanic Gardens on the corner of Alice and Albert Sts, is another four-star hotel built in the early 1970s, with 150 rooms, a pool, spa, gym, parking and two restaurants. Rooms range from $195 to $255, and weekend packages start from $105 for room only or $140 with breakfast included.

At 103 George St, the *Bellevue Hotel* (☎ 3221 6044) is a 30-year-old 3½-star hotel with 100 rooms, a pool, spa, restaurant and underground parking. The rooms are smallish but have been pleasantly refurbished, starting at $120 for a standard room and $180 for a suite. Weekend deals are good value – standard rooms are $85 on a Friday, Saturday or Sunday night – and the casino is just a coin toss away.

The *Mercure Hotel* (☎ 3236 3300) at 85-87 North Quay is an average mid-range hotel on a busy street, with 175 rooms ranging from $105 a night for a standard room to $185 a night for an executive suite.

Spring Hill On the corner of Leichhardt St and Wickham Tce, the *Chancellor on the Park* (☎ 3831 4055) is an excellent four-star hotel with a roof-top pool, a piano bar and restaurant. It is particularly popular with corporate clients. Studio units start from $122,

and spacious suites with a separate living area and kitchenette start from $160. There are also VIP and family suites.

The *Gazebo Hotel* (☎ 3831 6177), at 345 Wickham Tce, is another good mid-range hotel with motel-style units with city and park views; the nightly tariff is $99 a night, including breakfast. The hotel has two restaurants – the street front *Terrace Bistro* with an open-air char-grill kitchen, and an à la carte restaurant upstairs.

The four-star *Albert Park Inn Hotel* (☎ 3831 3111), overlooking Albert Park from 551 Wickham Tce, has refurbished standard rooms from $110 and new executive rooms with spas from $125.

On the corner of Leichhardt and Henry Sts, the *Ridge Hotel* (☎ 3831 5000) is another mid-level hotel with motel-style units from $91 a night and self-contained suites with kitchenettes from $120 a night.

Apartment Hotels & Serviced Apartments

Brisbane has a wide range of up-market hotels and apartments with self-contained facilities. These places can work out to be better value than an equivalently priced hotel, especially for people travelling in a group. They are often more spacious than hotels, and if you don't want to eat out every night you have your own cooking facilities.

City Across the road from the Transit Centre at 160 Roma St, the *All Seasons Abbey Hotel* (☎ 3236 1444) is a good, modern hotel with spacious one-bedroom apartments. Each has a separate sitting room, kitchenette and a full-size bath in the bathroom. Facilities include the usual pool, spa and gym, and nightly tariffs start from $158.

Spring Hill The 10-storey *Summit Apartment Hotel* (☎ 3839 7000), on the corner of Leichhardt and Allenby Sts, is a good option if you're looking for a self-contained apartment. Studio units are $105, one-bedroom units are $125 for up to four people and two-bedroom units are $175 for up to five people.

The *Centrepoint Apartment Hotel* (☎ 3832 3000), on the corner of Leichhardt and Sedgebrook Sts, is a seven-storey block of refurbished apartments, each with a separate kitchen, lounge and laundry, and there's a pool, spa and sauna in the complex. Apartments start from $112 a night for one bedroom, $135 for two bedrooms and $170 for three bedrooms.

The same company owns the *SDK Apartment Hotel* (☎ 3832 3000), nearby at 28 Fortescue St. It's a smaller, older block of 12 units above a set of offices. This place is good value, with studio units from $68 for up to three people and one-bedroom units with private balconies with city views from $86 for up to four people. Guests here have use of the pool, spa and sauna at the Centrepoint Apartment Hotel.

New Farm The *Kirribilli Apartments* (☎ 3358 5622), fronting onto the Brisbane River at 150 Oxlade Dve, is a 10-storey block of modern one, two and three-bedroom apartments. The apartments are well equipped although the décor is fairly bland and uninspired, but the riverfront location is good and you're only 200 metres from the ferry into the city. Units range from $125 to $175 a night, with a minimum stay of two nights.

South Brisbane The *River Plaza Apartment Hotel* (☎ 3844 4455) at 21 Dock St is well placed beside the South Bank Parklands. It is another modern high-rise apartment hotel with hotel rooms from $106 to $123 (depending on the views) and one, two and three-bedroom apartments ranging from $150 to $280 a night. The facilities here are very good and include a pool, tennis courts and a restaurant.

Nearby at 311 Vulture St is the *Hillcrest Apartment Hotel* (☎ 3846 3000), on a busy road beside the Mater Private Hotel. These modern studio-style units start from $85 a night.

Kangaroo Point The *Dockside Apartment Hotel* (☎ 3891 6644), at 44 Ferry St, is in the centre of the new and impressive Dockside development, which includes residential apartments, a marina, and numerous cafes and restaurants. It's an excellent modern high-rise hotel with one and two-bedroom apartments ranging from $200 to $260 a night, with the usual facilities including a pool, spa, gym and tennis courts.

Auchenflower The *Inn on the Park* (☎ 3870 9222), three km south-west of the city at 507 Coronation Dve in Auchenflower, is an elegant and up-market inn with motel-style units from $110, one-bedroom loft-style apartments from $130 and two-bedroom apartments from $150. This place is in the centre of a business district and is very popular with corporate clients. It's next to a spacious park and has its own pool and restaurant.

Hotels – top end

Brisbane only has a handful of five-star hotels, and they generally quote prices of over $200 a night for rooms. In practice, you'll find these prices are fairly negotiable – you can often get better package deals through travel agents which might combine airfares with accommodation. Like the mid-range hotels, most of the five-stars have good weekend deals on offer. These vary from time to time – ring around to see who's offering what.

The *Beaufort Heritage Hotel* (☎ 3221 1999), on the corner of Edward and Margaret Sts, is perhaps the most elegant and sophisticated of Brisbane's five-stars. The hotel successfully manages to combine a feeling of understated luxury with excellent facilities including a pool, spa and sauna, gymnasium, several bars and good eateries including one of the city's best Japanese restaurants. Rooms overlook the Brisbane River, with standard rooms starting from $185 and suites ranging from $290 to $1500.

Built in 1984, the 21-storey *Sheraton Brisbane Hotel* (☎ 3835 3535), at 249 Turbot St, dominates the north side of the city. There are 420 rooms, starting at $250 a night for a standard room and ranging from $405 to $1200 for a suite.

The *Brisbane Hilton* (☎ 3231 3131), another large five-star hotel in the heart of the city at 190 Elizabeth St, has standard rooms from $215/245 for singles/doubles and suites ranging from $680 to $925. The Hilton also has a good range of weekend packages, including a double room, champagne, breakfast and tickets to the movies for $190, or two nights for $260.

The newest addition to Brisbane's top-end hotel scene is the *Hotel Conrad* (☎ 3306 8888). The hotel is part of the Conrad Treasury Casino complex, and is housed in Brisbane's former Land Administration Building (1901-5) on the corner of George and Charlotte Sts. The casino is just a short stroll across Queens Park. The hotel has 97 rooms and suites, with rooms from $280 to $400 a night and suites from $675 to $975 a night.

A couple of km north of the city, on the corner of Kingsford Smith Dve and Hunt St in Hamilton, is the *Powerhouse Hotel* (☎ 3862 1800), a top-class boutique hotel on the banks of the Brisbane River. It is modern, friendly and stylishly appointed, with 90 tastefully decorated rooms, 50 of which have river views. Double rooms start from $210 for a standard room, rising to $250 for a room with river views and $280 for a spa room, and suites range from $360 to $500. The hotel also has special weekend packages – for $160 you get a double room, breakfast, champagne and tickets to the races.

PLACES TO EAT

Brisbane's restaurant and cafe scene has blossomed in recent years, and you'll find that there's no shortage of good eateries in the city and surrounding areas. This section covers the full spectrum from bargain eateries to some of Brisbane's finest restaurants, and should have something to suit everyone.

The major clusters of eateries are in the city centre, Fortitude Valley, Paddington, the West End and South Bank. There are some great areas where you can wander and check

out a whole lot of different places before deciding where to eat – places like the Riverside Centre and Eagle St Pier on the riverfront north of the city; Chinatown and around Brunswick St in Fortitude Valley; the South Bank Parklands; Caxton St, Given and Latrobe Tces in Paddington; and Boundary St and Hardgrave Rd in the West End.

Brisbane's perfect climate makes a significant contribution to the pleasures of eating out, and many places take advantage of the weather with open-air courtyards, or tables out on the street.

Local chefs and cooks have ready access to a wealth of wonderful local produce. Beef and lamb from the state's rich pastoral areas, exotic tropical fruits from north Queensland, stone fruits and fresh vegetables from the state's cooler regions, and sensational seafood from the abundant waters around Queensland – wonderful fish like barramundi and coral trout, prawns direct from the Gulf of Carpentaria, and delicacies like mud crabs and Moreton Bay bugs from the mangrove-lined bays and estuaries.

Brisbane has a wide diversity of restaurants – great little Italian bistros, dirt-cheap Vietnamese places, Chinese restaurants with classical Cantonese cuisine and yum cha lunches, Greek taverns, elegant French brasseries, an abundance of Asian eateries including Thai, Japanese, Korean and Malaysian places, Mexican cantinas, Indian tandoori houses – there's even a Scottish restaurant here.

While Australia doesn't have its own distinct cuisine like France or China, it has something even better – food fusion. Free from the restrictions of culinary tradition, Australian chefs have taken some of the best features and techniques of the world's various cuisines, blended them with fresh local ingredients, and come up with original and innovative styles – collectively, these are currently being labelled 'modern Australian cuisine'.

Most of Brisbane's, indeed, Queensland's restaurants and cafes are either licensed to sell alcohol on the premises or BYO (meaning you can 'Bring Your Own' booze)

– and some places have it both ways. If you're not sure, check by phone when you book. Note that most BYO restaurants charge a small fee for 'corkage'.

If you're staying for a while and want to make an in-depth study of Brisbane's restaurant and cafe scene, the *Courier Mail* newspaper publishes the annual *Good Food Guide*, which covers most of the best eateries in Brisbane, the Gold Coast and the Sunshine Coast. It's available from most bookshops and newsagents and costs $12.95.

City

You'll find all sort of eateries around the central area, including plenty of cafes and fast-food places, and a few good restaurants, especially in the Riverside Centre and Eagle St Pier complexes.

Queen St Mall teems with possibilities. *Jo Jo's*, a very popular food centre upstairs at 130 Queen St, has Greek/Mediterranean, Thai, European and Middle Eastern counters, and a bar. Tables are scattered about and prices range from $8 to $13. It's open daily until midnight. There are more possibilities in the ritzy *Myer Centre* at the southern end of the mall. The lower level has a number of cafes and restaurants, and a couple of food courts with fast-food outlets and sandwich bars.

Jimmy's on the Mall has three excellent open-air, licensed cafes in the centre of the mall – one at the Edward St end (open 24 hours a day), one in the middle and the other near the Albert St corner (both are open from 7 am to midnight). They are very popular if not particularly cheap – meals like spanakopita or lasagna are $7.90, main courses like pastas, steaks and seafood dishes range from $14 to $19, and they also do sandwiches, bagels and croissants, and cakes and coffee.

Also on the mall, the Wintergarden shopping complex has a couple of food courts. On the first level, the straightforward *Tastes on the Go* has a sandwich bar, a bakery, a salad bar and Thai, Chinese and Italian food stalls, with most meals under $6. It opens during regular shopping hours. Up on the third level

is the more up-market *New Orleans Restaurant*, which has a licensed bar and Italian, Mexican, Thai, Japanese, steak and seafood stalls. This place is lively and popular and has live music on most nights. Meals generally range from $10 to $16, and the opening hours are Sunday to Thursday from 11 am to 11 pm and Friday and Saturday from 11 am to 1 am.

Across on the other side of the mall, Broadway on the Mall is another shopping complex with a small food court down in the basement. Eateries here include the excellent *Sumo*, a tiny Japanese takeaway with a good range of dishes at excellent prices. The chicken teriyaki with rice and salad, and the Shoyu ramen chicken soup are both good value at $6.50. Up on the second level of the same complex is *Food on Q*, a larger food court with a couple of bars and eight different eateries, including steaks and burgers, a Mexican/Creole stall and a salad and sangers bar.

A Kabab, just around the corner from the mall at 227 Albert St, makes very good kebabs – beef, lamb, chicken, felafel or salad – from $3.30 to $4.30.

L's Fine Foods is an elegant little coffee shop at the Adelaide St end of the Brisbane Arcade, just near STA Travel. It's a great spot for coffee and cakes; they also do an excellent tropical fruit platter with bread and cottage cheese ($6.50), as well as focaccias and bagels.

For a good, cheap vegetarian feed, *Govinda's Restaurant*, upstairs at 99 Elizabeth St, offers filling all-you-can-eat meals for $5. It's run by the Hare Krishnas, and opens weekdays for lunch and Friday and Sunday for dinner. The Sunday feast, with accompanying chanting and dancing, starts at 5 pm. Nearby at No 93 is *Parrots*, a stylish, licensed gourmet burger restaurant, open daily from 11.30 am to 10 pm. McDonald's certainly wouldn't recognise the fare that's dished up in this popular place. The various burgers cost from $8 to $10.50, and they also have soups, salads, lasagnas and sandwiches. *Sennari*, upstairs at 85 Elizabeth St, serves good Japanese food with mains from

$12 to $18, set menus from $25 and a four-course lunch for $17.

Cafe Mondial, in Albert St near the Elizabeth St corner, is a stylish street front cafe and a great spot for cakes and coffee. Breakfasts here range from $5 to $7, and their gourmet sandwiches are good but fairly pricey, costing from $4 to $8.

The *Queensland Irish Association*, upstairs at 175 Elizabeth St, is a lively Irish club which is open to visitors. The bistro here is good value, serving traditional favourites like Irish stew or beef and Guinness pie, with most meals in the $5 to $7 range. There's also a bar with Guinness on tap, and they have live Irish music on Friday and Saturday nights.

Next door at 173 Elizabeth St is *Caffe Libri*, a great little cafe in the middle of the American Bookstore. What a great idea – you can choose a book, then sit down and start reading over a meal or a coffee. You can get a huge bowl of home-made soup with bread for $4.50, the coffee is good, and they also have home-made cakes, focaccias, salads, and bagels.

Time has all but stood still since the *Shingle Inn*, at 254 Edward St, opened back in 1934. With its Tudor-style timber panelling, booth seating, cheap chandeliers, revolving cake cabinet and silver tea sets, the Shingle Inn is delightfully quaint and old-fashioned. The menu matches the décor, with old faves like cold roast lamb salad ($12.95), chicken Maryland ($13.95), scones with jam and cream ($4.20) and grilled cheese on toast ($3). They also make the definitive pavlova dessert here – not to be missed.

Planet Energy, at 171 Edward St, is an interesting new concept in healthy, energy-enhancing drinks made from a combo of fresh fruits, honey, yoghurt, vanilla and other ingredients, with the optional addition of one of their herbal formulas which battle anything from fatigue to chronic hangovers. As they say, these drinks are virtually a meal in a glass. Prices range from $3.20 to $4.

Zane's Caffe, in the Metro Arts building at 109 Edward St, is a hip basement cafe specialising in modern Italian food, with pastas, calamari, and salads mostly in the $7 to $8 range. It's open daily for breakfast, lunch and dinner.

On the corner of Mary and Edward Sts, *Crash & Burn* is a fairly funky restaurant by day and bar/nightclub by night. It opens on weekdays for lunch, mainly catering for younger corporate types. The menu is modern Mediterranean style, with pastas, chicken, fish and salad dishes in the $7 to $11 range.

One block further along Edward St on the Margaret St corner, the *Port Office Hotel* is an old pub with a rustic sand-blasted brick interior and a small beer garden. It's a popular place at lunch times, with meals like T-bone or fish with chips and salad for $4.95. The *Orient Hotel*, at the top end of Ann and Queen Sts, also has a restaurant with good lunches and opens between noon and 3 pm on weekdays. (Both of these pubs are also live music venues – see the Entertainment section for more details).

On the opposite side of Edward St is *Siggi's at the Port Office* (☎ 3221 4555). This is one of Brisbane's best and most elegant restaurants, set in the beautifully restored former Port Office building, complete with polished timber floors and antique furnishings. Siggi's specialises in simple, traditional French cuisine and is reasonably expensive, but highly recommended. They offer a 'window cuisine' menu which allows you to try five of their most popular dishes for $59 per person.

Around the corner in Margaret St is *Kabuki* (☎ 3221 2383), inside the Beaufort Heritage Hotel. It's an expensive, formal and up-market Japanese restaurant with a very good reputation for its food. Main meals range from $13 to $25, or there's a Kabuki banquet menu at $58 per person. Their businessperson's lunch time tepanyaki special is good value at $20 a head.

The *City Gardens Cafe*, at the southern end of the City Botanic Gardens, is a lovely old timber cottage with an outdoor courtyard. It isn't particularly cheap, but the setting is great. The cafe is open daily from 8 am to 5 pm. Breakfast will set you back $5

MARK ARMSTRONG

MARK ARMSTRONG

MARK ARMSTRONG

MARK ARMSTRONG

A	
B	C
D	

A: Brisbane skyline from South Bank Parklands
B: McWhirters markets, Fortitude Valley, Brisbane
C: The Greek revivalist cenotaph, Anzac Square, Brisbane
D: 1995 Sheffield Shield final, Queensland vs South Australia, at the 'Gabba'

MARK ARMSTRONG

MARK ARMSTRONG

MARK ARMSTRONG

Left: Boarding the paddlesteamer, South Bank, Brisbane
Right: City Hall, Brisbane
Bottom: Juice van, King George Square, Brisbane

to $8, a light lunch or Devonshire tea is $8 to $10, and main courses range from $12 to $14.

Riverfront

Two of Brisbane best and most popular food complexes, the Eagle St Pier and the Riverside Centre, are beneath the two modern, monolithic glass towers that front onto the Brisbane River in the north-east corner of the city. Further north, the historic Customs House has been converted into an art gallery, bookshop and brasserie.

Eagle St Pier The Eagle St Pier, between Eagle St and the Brisbane River, has everything from fast fried-chicken outlets to up-market Italian restaurants.

The award-winning *Pier Nine* (☎ 3229 2194) is a stylish and sophisticated oyster bar and seafood restaurant with a great outlook over the river and a hip, modern ambience. You can have oysters in about a dozen different ways, at $19.90 a dozen, and innovative and interesting seafood dishes range from $20 to $25 for main courses. There's also a supper menu which is available nightly until 11 pm.

Fuddruckers is a groovy, ultra-modern burger joint with beef, chicken and fish burgers from $5.50 to $8.50. There's also a bar here, so you can wash your burger down with a beer. Nearby, the *Coffee Club* specialises in coffee and deliciously fattening cakes.

Upstairs on the 1st level, the *City Rowers Club* is a popular bar and nightclub (see the Entertainment section for details). At the front of the club, overlooking the river, is the *Fish Cafe*, a pleasant open-air eatery with main courses in the $15 to $17 range.

Also up on the 1st level is *Compadre's Bar & Grill*. It's a lively licensed Mexican restaurant with a fun atmosphere and good food, with mains from $13 to $18. Compadre's opens every day for lunch and dinner, and has live entertainment on Friday and Saturday nights.

Back at ground level, *Il Centro* (☎ 3221 6090) is probably Brisbane's best and most impressive Italian restaurant. The stylish dining area is set around a large open kitchen, with a covered courtyard at the front. The food here is wonderful, with pastas in the $15 to $18 range and other main courses from $18 to $21. Highly recommended, if you can afford a splurge.

Riverside Centre The Riverside Centre, a hundred metres north at the north-eastern end of Elizabeth St, has several restaurants that enjoy terrific river views, including the award-winning *Michael's* (☎ 3832 5522), one of Brisbane's best restaurants. Michael's is licensed and specialises in classical cuisine with an emphasis on seafood – the seafood collation and barramundi dishes are particularly good. Main courses here are in the $21 to $26 range. Michael's opens for weekday lunches and dinner from Monday to Saturday – bookings are advised. Run by the same people, the adjoining *Marco's* is a classy Italian bistro with most mains from $15 to $18, and an excellent selection of seafood barbecued on a char-grill ($21.50).

For an inexpensive lunch try *On the Deck*, an excellent international food hall with a good range of choices. It's in the next building to the south of Michael's and Marco's.

Customs House North of the Riverside Centre is Brisbane's old Customs House building which houses the *Customs House Brasserie*, a stylish cafe with a small bar, a dining room of ochre and rust coloured walls, and an outdoor courtyard where you can dine under giant umbrellas and enjoy the riverside outlook. The food here is fresh and imaginative – main such as sage tagliatelle with duck liver and juniper berry cream, and wok-seared squid and baby octopus with Asian greens are around $14 to $15. The onion damper and carrot and sunflower-seed loaf are wonderful!

South Bank

There are about a dozen restaurants and cafes in the South Bank Parklands, as well as the usual fast-food outlets. There are also numerous excellent picnic settings throughout the gardens, with tables and free gas barbecues, which are especially popular on balmy nights and weekends.

Captain Snapper, a very large seafood and steak restaurant just south of the Stanley St Plaza, has a good selection of meals at around $5 to $6, and for another $2.95 you can attack the all-you-can-eat salad and fresh-fruit bar. Other main meals start from around $10, and there's a good takeaway section with tables by the canal.

The Riverside Restaurants building, on the riverfront near the Gondwana Rainforest Sanctuary, houses three places. *Cafe San Marco* is a fairly stylish open-fronted cafe overlooking the river. The setting is good, but you have to pay for it – they'll slug you $2.90 for a coffee, while gourmet sangers and toasted fingers are $6 and main meals range from $10 to $15. At least the scones with jam and cream ($2.50) are affordable. Next door, the licensed *Wang Dynasty* restaurant serves Asian food – Thai, Japanese, Malaysian, Vietnamese and Chinese dishes, including a range of kangaroo and crocodile meat dishes. Mains range from $9 to $16; their evening banquet menu is good value at $16 per person (not available Friday or Saturday); and they have a $7.80 lunch special. Upstairs, *Io Ti Amo* is a stylish Italian restaurant with main meals in the $18 to $35 range.

Sirocco, in the Waterway Cafes complex, is a large Mediterranean cafe/restaurant with Spanish, Italian and Greek food, with main meals around $15.

There are several other eateries in the Stanley St Plaza, just south of the 'beach'. The *Plough Inn*, a mock-maritime pub, has cheap meal and drink deals and is popular with backpackers. *Between The Flags* is a casual cafe with good wood-fired-oven pizzas for $11, and they have country rock bands and line dancing here on Friday nights.

Further south, the Boardwalk Cafes section of South Bank also has a couple of good eateries. *Ned Kelly's Bush Tucker Restaurant* is a modern yet rustic tavern which specialises in Aussie tucker. This is one of the few places I know of where you can try grilled witchetty grubs ($12.90) – ah, no, I didn't try them myself, but I'm assured they're very interesting... They also serve emu fillets, buffalo steaks, crocodile satays and a wide range of seafood, with mains in the $17 to $25 range. The tavern fronts onto the timber-decked boardwalks and has plenty of outdoor tables, and features live Irish-Australian folk and pop music every Friday and Saturday night and Saturday and Sunday arvo.

Next door, *Chez Laila* is a large Lebanese cafe/restaurant with a fascinating range of desserts and pastries and coffee that packs a punch. They also have things like kebabs, Lebanese pizzas and stuffed vine leaves, all costing from $6 to $9.

On the southern edge of South Bank is the *Ship Inn*, which has reasonably priced bistro meals like fettucine carbonara ($7), ploughman's platters ($8) and T-bone steaks ($9.90).

One of the best value eateries on the riverfront is the simple *Riverfront Cafe* at the State Library. It has great rolls and sandwiches, coffee and snacks, and the tables on the outdoor courtyard overlook the river.

Spring Hill

The *Spring Hill Hotel*, on the corner of Upper Edward and Leichhardt Sts, has good, cheap pub food ($2.50 lunches!) and a backyard barbecue.

At 48 Leichhardt St, *Papa Mio* (☎ 3831 1363) is an Italian bistro set in a wonderfully converted chapel. It's bright and spacious and has good food with mains ranging from $12 to $16.

Harold's Cafe, at 466 Boundary St, is a casual and friendly Italian bistro with a garden courtyard and a good gourmet takeaway section. Pastas are under $11 and other mains under $14. Harold's opens on weekdays from 10 am to 10 pm and Saturday from 6 to 10 pm.

Spring Hill has one of Brisbane's best Thai restaurants. The *Oriental Bangkok* (☎ 3832 6010), at 454 Upper Edward St, has authentic Thai food, all made without MSG or preservatives. The chilli factor is toned down, but if you like it hot let them know when you order. Vegetarian dishes are all $10.80 and other mains range from $12 to $16. This place is licensed.

Tucked away in narrow Bowen St, on the north edge of the city, *Little Tokyo* is an atmospheric Japanese restaurant which opens nightly for dinner. It is licensed and very reasonably priced, and they have good banquet menus at $30 per person. Don't let the brick facade 'and yellow flashing lights put you off – the interior is a lot more attractive.

Petrie Terrace & Paddington

Petrie Terrace and Paddington also have plenty of interesting cafes, restaurants, pubs and bars, mostly scattered along the two-km-long winding route of the adjoining Caxton St and Given and Latrobe Tces. This is a good area to go exploring – the following places are but a few suggestions.

At 5 Petrie Tce, near the Upper Roma St corner, the *Hog's Breath Cafe* is part of a nationwide chain of saloon-style bar and grills. This place is very popular with travellers, and has a wide range of imported beers as well as burgers, sangers, salads and grills which range from $7 to $17.

On the corner of Petrie Tce and Caxton St, *Casablanca* is a good Latin American restaurant, bar and eatery with live music – see the Entertainment section for details. Down the road at 28 Caxton St, the *Mediterraneo Cafe-Bar* is a trendy and modern place specialising in gourmet-style pizzas cooked in a wood-fired oven. The pizzas, as well as a variety of salads and pastas, range from $10 to $14. There's a bar, a large garden courtyard out the back, and tables spilling out of the dining room onto the footpath. The cafe's walls are hung with local artwork, and if you like what you see, most pieces are for sale.

The *Sultan's Kitchen* (☎ 3368 2194), at 163 Given Tce, is an excellent BYO Indian restaurant with great curries. It's open for lunch and dinner daily (except Saturday lunch), but it's pretty popular so book on weekends. The lunch time smorgasbord is $12.95, and at dinner mains are around $14.

At 215 Given Tce, the *Jakarta Indonesian*

Restaurant is a reasonably priced Indonesian restaurant with an evocative all-bamboo décor. Rice, noodle and vegetarian dishes are $6 to $10 and seafood and meat dishes are from $10 to $13.

Further west along Given Tce, at No 235, the *Red Chair Cafe* has a good atmosphere. It does excellent gourmet burgers ($9 to $12), plus pies, pastries, pastas, salads and sandwiches. It also opens for breakfasts.

Faces (☎ 3368 2413), at 267 Given Tce, is a tiny, up-market BYO restaurant with intimate upstairs/downstairs dining areas and a small garden courtyard. The food here is consistently wonderful. At lunch time, main courses like a coriander and ginger gnocchi or a calamari salad range from $7 to $13; at dinner main courses are around $18.

A little further on is the very popular *King Tut's Wa Wa Hut*. This outdoor cafe is a great spot for breakfast, lunch or dinner, and has good salads, pastas, burgers, juices and sandwiches, all reasonably priced.

Just up from King Tut's at 283 Given Tce, *Le Scoops* is another popular eatery with a large open-air courtyard. It opens for breakfast, lunch and dinner. I can recommend their club sandwich on rye bread ($6.50), and there's an outdoor crêperie serving up sweet and savoury crêpes and pancakes. Le Scoops is also a very popular spot for a late-night coffee or hot chocolate.

A couple of twists in the road further west is *The Rest*, at 20 Latrobe Tce. It's a funky, folky street front cottage with a rustic assortment of chairs and tables spilling onto the footpath – just the spot for a long, lingering brunch with the weekend papers. Try the interesting 'The Rest Breakfast' for something different – eggs, vegemite, tomato and pepper on toast ($5.50). They also have good pastas, risottos and salads, mostly under $9. This place sometimes has live music at night.

A couple of hundred metres further on is *Gavin's Studio Cafe*, a slick and up-market cafe with glass-topped tables, black cane chairs and a cathedralesque ceiling. The menu has Greek and Italian leanings; you could try a platter of mixed dips ($6.90) or a filled focaccia, and main courses are all

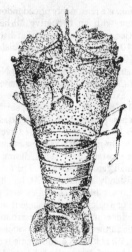

Moreton Bay Bug: great taste, shame about the name

around $17. There's a good range of wines available by the glass.

Fortitude Valley

The Valley is perhaps Brisbane's most exotic and cosmopolitan eating area, with a great range of restaurants, bars and cafes. The Valley's revitalisation is relatively recent, and new places are opening up here all the time.

Brisbane's Chinatown is centred around the Chinatown Mall in Duncan St, and there are good Chinese, Vietnamese, Korean, Thai and other Asian restaurants in the surrounding area, which include some of the best value places in town. Many of the Chinese places serve good yum cha lunches during the day. Other cafes and restaurants are clustered around Brunswick, Ann and Wickham Sts.

The excellent *Enjoy Inn* (☎ 3252 3838), on the corner of Wickham and Duncan Sts, is a little more up-market than most and specialises in Cantonese cuisine. It's a popular and lively place, with main courses in the $8 to $16 range and banquet menus which are very good value at either $18.80 or $22.80 per person (with a minimum of four people). It's licensed and open every day for lunch and dinner.

A good cheaper option is the *Universal Noodle Restaurant*, a block south at 145 Wickham St. It's an unpretentious cafeteria-style eatery with a huge range of dishes in the $5 to $8 range – this place opens daily from 11 am and stays open later than most other places.

Opposite the Enjoy Inn at 194 Wickham St, the *Vietnamese Restaurant* is also pretty straightforward but very popular, with most main dishes between $6 and $8 and banquet menus from $12 to $18. If you've never tried Korean food before, head down to the *Seoul Restaurant*, at 178 Wickham St. It is licensed and serves interesting, tasty and fairly authentic Korean dishes ranging from $6 to $10. Set menus range from $12 to $16, and there are lunch time specials from $6.

Sala Thai, one block north at 262 Wickham St, is a good, reasonably priced Thai restaurant with main meals from $10 to $16.

If you're self-catering, there's a good produce market inside *McWhirter's Markets* on the corner of Brunswick and Wickham Sts, with fruit and vegetable, seafood, poultry and meat sections. There's also a good food court on the ground floor with a bakery, fresh-squeezed juices, a salad bar, Japanese, Asian, Thai and vegetarian stalls, and fish & chips and pasta outlets.

There's a cluster of eateries up the east end of the Brunswick St Mall, most of which have open-air eating areas out on the mall. These include *Mellino's* at No 330, a casual bistro that opens 24 hours a day. It's not particularly flash, but it's much more reasonably priced than most of the more fashionable eateries in this area. You can get a cooked breakfast for $4, they do sandwiches and focaccias, pastas and pizzas are under $8, and other Italian main dishes are all $9.80. Nearby, the *Cosmopolitan Cafe* has inexpensive pastas, sandwiches, snacks and coffee.

The next block of Brunswick St, between

Ann and McLachlan Sts, has some of the Valley's best local eateries, and if you don't mind dining to an accompanying concerto of passing traffic most of the places along here have tables spilling out onto the footpath. The *Eiffel Tower Cafe & Patisserie*, at 346 Brunswick St, is a groovy French cafe with great pastries, some unusual and interesting pasta dishes, and a good selection of brunches on weekends.

At 360 Brunswick St, the hip and arty *Cafe Europe* (☎ 3252 2424) is a busy BYO street front cafe. As the name suggests, it has a very European feel, with timber booths topped with butcher's paper inside and a row of tables out on the footpath. The chef here is French, but Italian and Asian influences are also combined in the cooking. The home-made pastas ($10.90) are great, and mains such as Thai green curries and North African rack of lamb range from $14 to $16. The popular *Giardinetto's*, next door at No 366, is a small, traditional Italian bistro which is also a BYO. It also has very good pastas for under $10 as well as pizzas and Italian main courses around $15.

Around the corner at 683 Ann St is the long-running *Lucky's Trattoria*. It's a busy, no-frills Italian eatery with a bustling atmosphere, old-fashioned, hearty food and some weird local artwork on the walls. Pastas and pizzas range from $8 to $11, meat, chicken, seafood and game dishes are $14 to $16, and there's a separate vegetarian menu with main courses around $8.

Dooley's Hotel, the big green Irish pub on the corner of Brunswick St and McLachlan St, has a couple of eating options. You can get snacks like burgers, hot dogs and fish & chips up in the pool bar, or *Tom's Place* is an atmospheric bistro with main courses in the $6 to $10 range.

New Farm

A bit further down Brunswick St at No 630, *Baan Thai* is a reasonably priced BYO Thai restaurant, with mains between $8 and $12. At *Famish*, at No 640, you can get a very substantial hot roast meal – pork, chicken, lamb or beef with vegies – for around $10.

On the corner of Brunswick and Ann Sts, *Le Bronx* (☎ 3358 2088) is consistently rated as one of Brisbane's best restaurants. It's a sophisticated, intimate BYO serving 'innovative modern Australian cuisine' – a blend of various different influences including French, Thai and Cajun. It's reasonably expensive, with mains in the $17 to $25 range, but it's well worth the splurge.

The *Continental Cafe*, just off Brunswick St at 21 Baker St, is a friendly little gem of a place and very popular with locals in the know. Pastas and risottos are around $10, gourmet pizzas are $6 to $9, and open sandwiches are $5.50. Main meals range from $10 to $16. Last time I ate there I had a wonderful meal of veal shanks with roast garlic and mashed potatoes ($10.50) and sticky date pudding ($5.50). If you want to combine dinner with the movies, the Village Twin Cinema is just around the corner from here – the perfect double.

Further down in New Farm Park, the *New Farm Kiosk* is a little timber teahouse which is open daily from 10 am to 4 pm (to 5 pm on weekends). They serve affordable breakfasts, sandwiches and salads, Devonshire teas, cakes and gourmet burgers. It's a very pleasant spot, with outdoor tables overlooking a croquet lawn on one side and a rose garden on the other. The kiosk is also the venue for local poetry readings on the third Wednesday of each month.

Kangaroo Point

The *Story Bridge Hotel*, a classic old three-storey pub beneath the Story Bridge on the corner of Main and Baildon Sts, has been stylishly renovated in elegant heritage style. There's an up-market bistro here serving some of the best pub food in town – the theme is 'innovative contemporary cuisine' – worth checking out under any name. A slightly more down-market section of the same pub, known as the *Bomb Shelter*, has simple bistro-style food with burgers and schnitzels and the like at around $6 to $7.

There are some good eateries over in the Dockside Complex. *Snug Harbour Dockside Comedy Cafe* is a popular stand-up comedy and live music venue (see the Entertainment section), which also has good meals and snacks including pastas ($8), wood-fired-oven pizzas ($12), cakes and focaccias.

A little further south on the corner of Main and Baines Sts, the *Pineapple Hotel* is a great old pub with a long history. It has recently been renovated and has two eating areas – downstairs you can get cheap bar meals like fisherman's basket, roast and vegies or beef stroganoff for around $5 to $6. Upstairs is an elegant bistro restaurant with good pub food in the $10 to $12 range.

On the opposite corner is *Somewhere to Eat*, a popular eatery which specialises in roast dinners and vegetarian dishes. Meals like vegetarian lasagnas, Thai curries and tempeh and potato curries are all under $5, and roast lamb or pork with vegies, beef stroganoff and casseroles are all under $10. They also have good salads and cakes, and you can eat in or take away.

West End

Like the Valley, the West End has a fairly exotic and cosmopolitan range of cafes and restaurants, including quite a few bargain-priced places. There are two main clusters of eateries – in Boundary St, around the Vulture St corner; and in Hardgrave Rd, south of Vulture St.

Boundary St, from the Melbourne St roundabout down to Vulture St, is an interesting little shopping centre with good delis, fruit shops, cafes, a health-food shop, and a couple of good second-hand bookshops.

The *Three Monkeys Coffee House*, at 58 Mollison St just back from the roundabout, is a great place – if you can get in! It's relaxed and casual and has good coffee, amazing cakes and a wide range of tasty meals in the $4 to $7 range. It is open daily from 10.30 am until midnight.

The very down-to-earth *Qan Heng's* at 151 Boundary St is popular and inexpensive, with good Chinese and Vietnamese meals from $5.50 to $9. The *Sitting Duck Cafe*, upstairs at No 165, is an arty and fun cafe which puts on a great range of live entertainment – everything from play readings to

gospel singers. This place is one of Brisbane's centres for alternative culture – see the Entertainment section for more details. Most main courses – meals like spanikopita, Moroccan beef and olives, fettucine and pesto sauce – are $7.50. Meals are served tapas-style into the centre of the table to facilitate the sharing experience. There's also a market here on Saturday mornings, when breakfasts are served.

Further down at No 171, *Wholly Munchies* is a great wholefoods cafe and takeaway, with healthy sandwiches, juices and home-cooked goodies. It's open during the day only.

Caffe Tempo, a hip little street front eatery at No 181, is my favourite Brisbane cafe. They do great cooked breakfasts for about $6, croissants and raisin toast for $2, freshly squeezed OJ... (there's no breakfast menu, just ask what's available). Lunch and dinner offerings include bruschetta and focaccias ($6), gourmet pizzas (around $9), and pastas and other mains for $10 to $11. If it's still on the menu, try the wonderful fettucine with smoked salmon and scallops ($10.50). You can also get a Caesar or avocado salad for $6.

Across the road at No 142, *Cafe Babylon* has three separate sections – a coffee shop downstairs, a garden courtyard out back and a restaurant upstairs. This place is intriguingly decorated with an exotic mixture of relics from South-East Asia and the Middle East – Indian fountains, Turkish carpets and cushions, Indonesian madhuban beds etc. The menu is half-vegetarian, half-carnivorous – with soups, salads, pastas and pies, curries and casseroles, and great cakes and desserts. Main courses are in the $8 to $11 range, and the cafe is open daily for lunch and dinner.

At No 146, the *Green Grocer* is a good health-food shop with a wide range of organic fruit and vegies, juices, wheat and gluten-free breads etc. (This place also has a notice board with lots of accommodation ads.)

Around the corner at 88 Vulture St is *King Ahiram's*, a Lebanese place with good cheap takeaways like doner kebabs and chicken or felafel rolls from $2.50 to $3. There's also an eat-in section, with mains from $7.50 to $10 and a banquet menu for $15.

The other main restaurant cluster in West End is in Hardgrave Rd. There's a fascinating group of restaurants here, all within 100 metres of each other, and the competition has produced good food at very reasonable prices. If you're having trouble deciding where to eat, you can stroll along here and check them all out before making a choice.

Kim Thanh, at No 93, is a large and noisy Chinese and Vietnamese BYO with main courses from $5 to $7 and a Vietnamese banquet menu for $15 per person (minimum of four people). At No 75, the small *Khan's Kitchen* serves traditional Pakistani dishes at amazing prices. The most expensive dish here is $6.50, and there's a feast menu for $10 per person (again, a minimum of four people). At lunch time, there's a choice of lentil, lamb or vegetable curry for $4.95.

Cafe Bohemia, at No 69, is a dim and casual music-oriented cafe which has lasagnas, nachos, soups and curries. They sometimes have live jazz, blues and Latin music, and often have jam sessions, depending on who drops in. If you have you're own instrument you're welcome to turn up and play.

Chutney Mary's, at No 65, is the most stylish of these eateries, with powder-blue washed walls and wicker and iron chairs. It calls itself a 'modern Anglo-Indian restaurant', with dishes ranging from Bangalore bangers and mash to the more traditional tandoori chicken. Mains are from $13 to $17, and there's a slightly cheaper takeaway section next door.

A couple of blocks further south at 166 Hardgrave Rd is *The Soup Kitchen,* a very popular eatery fronted by an open-air courtyard. It's a cafe by day and a restaurant by night, and attracts a diverse and interesting local clientele. It specialises in soups ($6 to $7), pastas ($8 to $10), vegetarian dishes and exotic mains like Moroccan fish or Bombay beef curry ($10 to $13).

Around the corner in Dornoch Tce is *Caravanserai*, a former pawnbroker's shop converted into a spacious and attractive Turkish restaurant with an open kitchen in the centre. Entrées range from $5 to $7 and mains from $9 to $10 – the owners suggest ordering a few different dishes and sharing. This place features belly dancing on Saturday nights.

Highgate Hill

At 9 Gladstone Rd, near the Vulture St corner, the *Genji Japanese Kitchen* is a casual and very popular BYO Japanese restaurant. This place is excellent value – they have a good range of vegetarian dishes from $8 to $12, other mains range from $13 to $17, and there are banquet menus at $20, $26 and $30. It's open Tuesday to Saturday nights for dinner and only on Friday for lunch – they have a good lunch box special for $15.

At 36 Gladstone Rd, *Thai on High* is a tiny and simple Thai eatery with half a dozen tables and a roaring takeaway trade. They offer a huge range of vegetarian dishes, curry pots, stir-fries and rice and noodle dishes which are mostly $8. Their budget dinners are great value – for $10.50 you get entrées, mains, rice and a drink.

South Brisbane

The *Hotel Morrison*, at 640 Stanley St, houses one of Brisbane's best pub restaurants – *Fiasco's* (☎ 3391 4047). It's a groovy, up-market eatery that blends the old with the new, with a wood-fired oven that exudes tantalising aromas. Fiasco's specialises in gourmet pizzas ($11 to $13), and also has a good selection of salads and pastas ($10 to $12) – it's particularly popular, and you'll probably need to book. The pub features live bands on Thursday, Friday and Saturday nights.

East Brisbane

The *Cloak & Dagger*, at 888 Stanley St, is a warm and cosy BYO that specialises in modern Scottish cuisine – definitely the only Scottish restaurant in town. Mains like chicken 'och 'th'noo and Highland lavender lamb are around $18, and if you're game you could try haggis with stovies ($9.50) for entrée. The Cloak & Dagger opens from Tuesday to Saturday nights.

Down the road at 898 Stanley St is *Yianni's Greek Cafe*, a surprisingly modern cafe decorated in bright, bold colours, with iron chairs and polished timber floors. The food here is excellent – you can order off the menu and try a variety of dishes which range from $3 to $10, or there are banquet menus at $25 and $30 per person.

Breakfast Creek

On a northern bend of the Brisbane River, the Breakfast Creek Wharf is a riverfront development with shops, cafes and restaurants facing onto a riverfront boardwalk. These include the popular *Breakfast Creek Wharf Seafood Restaurant*, where you can dine out on the timber decking or in the maritime-style dining room. The seafood here is very good, with main meals around $15 to $19. There's also a *Taco Bill* Mexican restaurant, with main courses from $10 to $14 and various banquet menus from $16 to $22 per person.

Across the river, the famous *Breakfast Creek Hotel*, a great rambling building dating from 1889, is a real Brisbane institution. It's long been a Labor Party and trade-union hang-out. In the public bar, the beer is still drawn from a wooden keg. There are a couple of eateries in the open-air courtyard behind the hotel. There's a snack bar with hot roast sandwiches and other sandwiches from $1.40 to $3.20, as well as home-made pies and sausage rolls. The *Spanish Garden Steak House* is renowned for its barbecued steaks and spare ribs – a huge feed will set you back between $12 and $18. They also have daily specials like fish & chips or oriental chicken and rice for around $6.

Mt Coot-tha

There are two eateries up on the top of the One Tree Hill Lookout in Mt Coot-tha Park. The park is surprisingly close to the city and well worth a visit, especially for the great views.

The *Summit Restaurant* (☎ 3369 9922) opens every day for lunch and dinner, as well as morning and afternoon teas. Set in an attractively restored timber teahouse that was built here in the 1920s, it has spectacular views of Brisbane and Moreton Bay – its worth booking ahead and asking for a table with a view. The menu offers traditional but interesting international cuisine, and the Summit is licensed. At lunch time, mains are around $13 or there's a three-course menu for $24.50. The three-course dinner menu costs $37.50, with individual mains in the $17 to $24 range.

Nearby, the new *Kuta Cafe* is a modern, casual teahouse serving Devonshire teas, buffet-style lunches and dinners in the $5 to $10 range, sandwiches and filled croissants, cakes and coffee. It has similar views and an outdoor courtyard.

ENTERTAINMENT

The *Courier Mail* newspaper has daily arts and entertainment listings, and a 'What's On In Town' section each Thursday with listings of classical music concerts, jazz, pop and rock music gigs, comedy shows, theatre, art exhibitions and film festivals for the coming week.

There are also several free entertainment papers – *Time Off*, *Rave* and *The Scene* – which are widely available from cafes, pubs and venues. All of these have fairly comprehensive info on bands, pubs and clubs, theatre and concerts, as well as movie listings and reviews etc.

Ticketworld (☎ 13 1931; fax 13 2932) is a centralised phone booking agency which handles bookings for many major events, sports and performances, including those at the Brisbane Sports & Entertainment Complex. The Queensland Cultural Centre also has its own phone booking service called Dial 'N' Charge which handles bookings for the Performing Arts Complex theatres; call ☎ 3846 4646 for bookings and ☎ 3846 4444 for enquiries. You can book directly with most of the other venues.

Pubs, Bars & Live Music Venues

For the bigger local and international acts,

the major venues include Festival Hall (☎ 3229 7788), in the city on Albert St just down from Charlotte St, one of the biggest and oldest venues for big-name touring bands; and the Brisbane Sports & Entertainment Complex (☎ 13 1931 for bookings or ☎ 0055 39277 for information), a big modern multi-purpose venue on Melaleuca Dve in Boondall, about 15 km north-east of the city.

Brisbane has a good live music scene with plenty of pubs, bars and clubs featuring live bands, particularly later in the week. In general, pubs stay open until around midnight, or 1 am on the weekends; cover charges for local bands are around $5 and for touring bands you can pay up to $20 or more.

Lots of Brisbane's nightclubs and alternative venues also feature live bands – see the following sections.

City At the top of Ann and Queen Sts, the *Orient Hotel* (☎ 3839 4625) is one of Brisbane's oldest pubs and a long-running live music venue. Built in 1875, the pub still has plenty of character with original features like old wood panelling and leadlight windows. There are a couple of different sections with regular features including alternative bands, early 1980s UK pop music, jazz and blues, acoustic guitarists and jazz students from the local conservatorium of music.

Homebass, in the *Brisbane Tavern* on the corner of Wharf and Ann Sts has a funk and soul night on Friday and a reggae dance party on Saturday; the cover charge is $3 to $6 and it's open to 3 am. Another city music pub is the *Port Office Hotel*, on the corner of Edward and Margaret Sts, with bands on Friday and Saturday nights and Sunday afternoons. The *City Gardens Point Campus Club* at the Queensland University of Technology in George St is an occasional live band venue.

Spring Hill *St Paul's Tavern*, on the corner of Leichhardt and Wharf Sts in Spring Hill, has cover bands on most Friday and Saturday

nights, with a $7 cover charge and cheap drinks deals.

Fortitude Valley *Dooley's Hotel*, on the corner of Brunswick and McLachlan Sts, has live music in its downstairs Irish Bar every Wednesday to Sunday night. It's a small, atmospheric bar and features someone different every night – local musos jamming, solo guitarists, Irish and Australian folk music, and cover bands. Entry is free but the Guinness costs.

There are three good bar/cafes side by side in the Brunswick St Mall in the Valley, near the Ann St corner. They all have open-air tables out on the mall. *Ric's Cafe-Bar*, a small bar and snackery, has live folk, jazz, blues or rock music on Wednesday and Thursday nights and DJ music on Tuesday, Friday and Sunday. Next door are the *Deck Bar* and the *Rhumba Reeba Cafe*, which also has live music.

Petrie Terrace & Paddington The *Barracks Hotel*, on the corner of Petrie Tce and Caxton St, is a popular live band venue which is currently undergoing major renovations.

The *Caxton Hotel*, further east along Caxton St, is a big modern pub with attitude and a dress code. It's always crowded on weekends and has a piano bar and a bistro garden out back.

The *Paddo Tavern*, about one km further east on Given Tce, is a huge western-style saloon pub with four different bars and a beer garden, lots of urban cowboys and girls, and live music from Wednesday to Sunday. Cover charges are $7 on Friday and Saturday, and $5 Sunday – free entry during the week.

South Bank South Bank is another good live music venue. There are often concerts and live bands in the *Suncorp Piazza*, and live Australian and Irish folk and pop music at the open-air Boardwalk Cafes every Friday night, Saturday arvo and night and Sunday arvo. For details of who's playing when at South Bank, ring their recorded entertainment programme on ☎ 3867 2020.

The *Plough Inn*, a pub in the Stanley St

Plaza section of South Bank, has live bands from Wednesday to Saturday nights in its outside beer garden and karaoke in the inside bar. There's also a sports bar upstairs in the pub with lots of European and American sports channels on satellite. The *Ship Inn*, at the southern end of South Bank, has live bands on Friday and Saturday nights and pool competitions on Wednesday nights.

Kangaroo Point The *Bomb Shelter*, a section of the *Story Bridge Hotel* in Kangaroo Point, has bands in its beer garden from Tuesday to Saturday nights, as well as cheap meals and a backpacker night on Monday. *Snug Harbour Dockside Comedy Cafe*, in Ferry St in Kangaroo Point, is a comedy venue by night but has live jazz bands every Sunday afternoon.

South Brisbane *Hotel Morrison* at 640 Stanley St is a good pub with something for everyone. There's a small corner bar with three pool tables and music videos (Wednesday features a dangerous double of cheap cocktails and a pool competition), live bands in the back bar from Thursday to Saturday, and an excellent restaurant called Fiascos (see Places to Eat).

The *Sly Fox Hotel* in Melbourne St also has live reggae, soul and rock bands.

Nightclubs
Brisbane has a lively nightclub scene, especially if you know where to look. The mainstream clubs are mostly based in the city and around Petrie Terrace, and the alternative scene is centred in Fortitude Valley. Most clubs stay open until 3 am, some until 5 am; cover charges vary from around $4 to $8.

City At 127 Charlotte St in the city, *Hogie's Pool Bar & Nightclub* is a warehouse-sized club with a large pool hall upstairs, a quiet bistro and cocktail bar, and a nightclub section with DJs playing mainstream and alternative music. It opens every night until late, and there's a $5 cover charge. The cafe

and pool sections are also open during the day.

The *Hotel Embassy*, a feisty old pub on the corner of Edward and Elizabeth Sts in the city, houses various independent nightclubs on various different nights, including the *Byzantine Bar*, *Planet Earth*, *The Pit* and *Labyrinth* – names and themes change fairly often, so check out the entertainment papers for the latest. This pub also has live bands and musicians quite often – again, check with the gig guides.

Crash & Burn, in the basement on the corner of Mary and Edward Sts, is open Wednesday to Sunday nights until 3 am, and features good alternative music. It's a casual club with a couple of pool tables, and a munchies menu is available until midnight. When they have live bands, there's a cover charge of around $5.

Babble On is a dim, semi-alternative basement bar and club on Elizabeth St which opens Wednesday to Sunday and has live bands on Thursday and Saturday.

In Mary St, just south of the Edward St corner, are the *Mary St Nightclub & Cafe Sports*. The nightclub section opens Thursday to Saturday nights until 5 am, and is popular with uni students. There's a cover charge of around $6 – less if you have student ID. Upstairs is *Cafe Sports*, a stylish bar with pool tables and music videos that stays open until 1 am.

Mass, in the *Lands Office Hotel* on the corner of George and Mary Sts, is a good semi-alternative club that operates on Friday and Saturday nights till 5 am. The downstairs section features contemporary dance music, upstairs features '70s and '80s music or bands. Mass attracts a mostly 18 to 22-year-old crowd.

Someplace Else, on the first floor of the Sheraton Hotel complex (with an entrance next to Central Station on Ann St), is an up-market mainstream nightclub which attracts an older, more 'sophisticated' crowd. There are strict dress regulations here – you won't get in wearing jeans or T-shirts, but you'll feel very at home if you're wearing a jacket and tie or a cocktail dress.

Her Majesty's Bar, in the basement of the Hilton Hotel in the Queen St Mall, is mainly a live band venue which is popular with a young crowd. It's open every night except Sunday until 3 am; there's no cover charge. *Nightworx Nightclub*, in Albert St near the Queen St corner, is a big, glitzy and very mainstream, with 'ladies nights' (free cocktails) on Wednesday, live bands on Thursday and drinks deals on most other nights. The cover charge is around $6 and it opens every night until 5 am.

In the Eagle St Pier complex, the *City Rowers Club* is a big, trendy venue which is very popular with Brisbane's yuppie types, particularly on Friday nights. There's a nightclub upstairs (Wednesday to Sunday nights until 5 am, $6 cover charge), and a courtyard bar overlooking the river with giant video screens, DJ music and a snack bar. Dress up.

Further north in the Riverside Centre, *Fridays* is another fairly up-market place which attracts a similar crowd of uni students and young professionals. There's a large open-air beer garden, two smaller bars and a nightclub which is open until 5 am and has a $4 to $6 cover charge. Live bands play in Fridays' beer garden from Thursday to Saturday nights; their Sunday arvo session with a calypso band and cheap drinks is popular.

Petrie Terrace & Paddington The *Underground*, in the impressively converted former police barracks on Petrie Tce in Paddington, is Brisbane's most popular mainstream nightclub. It's a big, glitzy place with several sections featuring live bands and DJs. It opens until 1 am on Wednesday and Thursday (no cover charge), 5 am on Friday and Saturday ($7) and 3 am on Sunday ($5).

Casablanca, on the corner of Petrie Tce and Caxton St, is a Latin-American-style bar, restaurant and club that opens Monday to Thursday until 2 am and Friday and Saturday until 5 am. There are several sections including a dance club featuring lambada and flamenco dancing, a bar, and a restaurant that serves late meals (mains in the $12 to $16

range). There's no cover charge, but dress standards are fairly strict.

Down the road at 17 Caxton St, *Kokoz Nightclub* is a slick, up-market dance-music club with strict dress regulations. It opens Wednesday to Sunday nights and entry costs $7.

Alternative Clubs & Venues
Brisbane's alternative scene has blossomed in recent years and there are some great clubs and venues featuring a diversity of unusual and interesting entertainment, from performance art and poetry readings to live music. If you thought Brisbane was stuck in its conservative past, check out some of the following places and have your mind well and truly changed.

Fortitude Valley The Valley is the centre of Brisbane's alternative scene. Some would call it the darker side of town, but if you like your nightlife spicy, this is definitely the area to head for, with everything from techno dance clubs and strip joints to gay clubs and alternative-band venues. The Valley can still be a little rough around the edges, especially late at night, so don't go wandering off down darkened side streets on your lonesome.

The Beat, at 677 Ann St, is the Valley's best known alternative nightclub. It's a small, crowded, high-energy sweatbox with laser lights and lots of people dancing in singlets. It caters for a mixture of gay and straight people, and there's a gay cocktail bar upstairs that opens until 5 am. The cover charge for downstairs ranges from $2 to $6 after 9 pm.

Further up Ann St at No 711, *The Zoo* (☎ 3854 1381) is a fascinating alternative venue which is well worth a visit. It's a weird, arty space with painted walls, bare timber floors and trestle tables, and a constantly changing programme which features everything from DJs, dance shows, and live bands to performance art. (The first time I walked in there were two naked people on stage wielding Roman swords, watched over by a hippie policeman, while two blindfolded people dressed in black swayed to a raving, poetic chant. I'm still not sure what it meant, but it definitely wasn't Shakespearean.) The Zoo opens Wednesday to Sunday nights and the cover charge varies from $5 to $10, depending what's on.

The Tube, a dance club at 210 Wickham St, cultivates the grungy warehouse look – lots of dry ice and corrugated iron, DJs in cages playing techno, pool tables... It is open until late on Wednesday, Friday, Saturday and Sunday, and costs from $6 to get in (more for dance parties).

The Roxy, at the top (west) end of Brunswick St, is a grungy but good live band venue with an elevated stage and several bars. It often features alternative, blues and hardcore bands but also has dance parties, performance art and poetry readings. Cover charges range from $7 to $10 for local bands and up to $25 for big-name bands.

The Valley also has plenty of clubs of a seedier nature, with reasonably self-explanatory names like the *Red Garter*, *Girlworld* and the *Honey Pot*.

South Brisbane *Van Gogh's Earlobe* (☎ 3217 2111), at 588 Stanley St in South Brisbane, is another good alternative venue that always seems to have something interesting on. The downstairs area features live music (with an emphasis on 'original' bands), performance art and theatre, and there's an art exhibitions space upstairs. Cover charges are $12 for theatre shows, around $5 for local bands and around $25 for international bands; the Earlobe is open seven nights a week until 3 am.

West End The *Sitting Duck Cafe* (☎ 3844 8327), upstairs at 165 Boundary St in the West End, is an arty live entertainment venue which has everything from old movies, buskers, live documentaries, gospel singers and play readings to jazz and blues concerts. There is also an art exhibition space here, and craft markets on Saturday mornings. See the Places to Eat section for details of the cafe bit.

Backpackers' Pubs

Quite a few pubs now put on special nights for backpackers, with drinking competitions, giveaways, cheap drinks and music.

The *Bomb Shelter*, a separate section of the *Story Bridge Hotel* in Main St, Kangaroo Point, is the venue for the infamous Monday Madness – a wild, crazy and crowded backpackers' night of party games and beer-sculling competitions. Great fun, if you're into that sort of thing. Most of the hostels run buses to/from the pub on Monday. On other nights the Bomb Shelter is a live band venue.

The *Brunswick Hotel*, in Brunswick St in New Farm, has similarly styled backpacker nights on Friday.

The *Plough Inn*, in the South Bank Parklands, has a students' and backpackers' night on Wednesday with $5 jugs of beer, cheap meals and discounted drinks; the *Ship Inn*, at the southern end of South Bank, is also popular and offers discounted drinks.

Gay & Lesbian Venues

Brisbane's gay and lesbian scene is centred in Spring Hill and Fortitude Valley, and there are plenty of good venues to choose from. The fortnightly gay and lesbian news and entertainment paper, *Brother Sister*, lists a wide range of films, theatre, gigs, nightclubs and events.

The *Sportsman's Hotel*, at 130 Leichhardt St in Spring Hill, is open nightly until 1 am. The pub has a different theme or show for each night of the week: gay bingo on Monday; Tuesday is party night; there's a pool competition on Wednesday; the Super Quiz on Thursday; drag shows on Friday and Saturday; and an open-to-all-comers talent quest on Sunday.

The Actress & the Bishop, another converted old pub at 300 Boundary St in Spring Hill, has an interesting range of dinner-and-show nights from Tuesday to Saturday.

Options Nightclub, at 18 Little Edward St in Spring Hill, is a popular gay and lesbian club which attracts lots of males and females – straight and gay. There's a cafe and dance-room downstairs and a live show every night upstairs, with a $5 cover charge on week-ends. Options opens until around 5 am.

The *Wickham Hotel*, on the corner of Wickham and Allen Sts in Fortitude Valley, is an incredibly popular pub which is largely gay-oriented but attracts a fairly diverse crowd. In fact, the crowd usually spills out of the pub onto the adjacent footpath. It's an attractively renovated Victorian-era pub and has good dance music, drag shows, male dancers and Mardi Gras parties. There are also two restaurants here and a food and wine bar upstairs.

At 185 Brunswick St in the Valley, *Signal* is a dimly lit club exclusively for gay men. It has various sections including saunas, video and dark rooms, pool tables and bars. It opens until 4 am and there's a cover charge of $5 to $10. Nearby in the basement of 249 Brunswick St, *Terminus* is another gay venue and dance club with drag shows on Friday and Saturday nights.

There's also a gay cocktail bar upstairs at *The Beat* in Ann St in the Valley – see the earlier section on Alternative Clubs & Venues.

Jazz & Blues

The *Jazz & Blues Club*, on the ground floor of the Travelodge in Roma St in the city, is the city's major jazz and soul venue. It's a classy, modern venue and features good local and international acts from Tuesday to Saturday nights. The cover charge is $4 on weekends; more for big international acts.

The *Brisbane Jazz Club* is a simple old timber building down by the riverside in Annie St, Kangaroo Point. This is where the jazz purists head – there's a big wooden dance floor, a bar and a courtyard overlooking the river and city. It's open on Saturday nights (old-fashioned jazz and small combos) and Sunday nights (big band dance nights); entry costs around $8 for nonmembers. Ring ☎ 3391 2006 to find out who and what's on.

There are a number of places that have regular jazz sessions on Sunday afternoons, including the *Brunswick St Mall*, the *Story Bridge Hotel* and *Snug Harbour Dockside* –

check the gig guides to see who's playing where.

The *Orient Hotel*, at the top end of Ann St in the city, has a long rock & roll history but is also a jazz and blues venue, and students from the local conservatorium play here. (See Pubs & Live Music earlier.)

The *Gabba Hotel* in Woolloongabba has three blues bands on Sunday afternoons for $2, which includes lunch.

Theatre

The *Performing Arts Complex*, in the Queensland Cultural Centre in South Brisbane, has a constant flow of events in its three venues, including concerts, plays, dance performances and film screenings. Call the complex booking office (☎ 3845 4444 for enquiries or their Dial 'N' Charge bookings service on ☎ 3846 4646) Monday to Saturday between 9 am and 8.30 pm.

The *Suncorp Piazza* at South Bank features regular concerts and performances, many of them free – ring the South Bank entertainment programme on ☎ 3867 2020 to find out what's on.

The *Metro Art Theatre* (☎ 3221 1527), at 109 Edward St, is a community arts theatre. This building also houses art exhibition spaces, artists' studios and galleries, an art school, dance and theatre studios and a cafe.

The *Suncorp Theatre* (☎ 3221 5177 for bookings or 3221 5371 for enquiries), at 179 Turbot St in the city, is another of Brisbane's major theatres and hosts regular performances by the Queensland Ballet and the Queensland Theatre companies, amongst others.

The *Brisbane Arts Theatre* (☎ 3369 2344), at 210 Petrie Tce, is a smaller theatre venue that hosts amateur theatre productions.

Brisbane's main professional theatre companies are *La Boite*, based at 57 Hale St in the city, and the *Queensland Theatre Company*, based at the Cultural Centre.

Cinema

Movie tickets at the mainstream cinemas are normally $11, although most places have discounted tickets ($7.50) on one or more nights, usually Tuesday and perhaps Sunday or Monday; some cinemas also have cheap daytime tickets.

There are plenty of mainstream cinemas in the city centre. The historic Hoyts Regent Theatres complex (☎ 3229 5544), at 107 Queen St in the heart of the mall, has several bars and cafes and five cinemas showing both mainstream and art-house movies. The complex's original Showcase cinema has been beautifully restored to its former mock-medieval glory. Greater Union Cinemas (☎ 11659) has a three-cinema complex at 183 Albert St and a twin-cinema complex on the corner of Elizabeth and Albert Sts. The Hoyts 8 Cinema Complex (☎ 3229 2133) is inside the Myer Centre at the southern end of Queen St.

Brisbane also has a handful of independent cinemas screening art-house, foreign and other more unusual films. In the city, the Dendy Cinema (☎ 3211 3244) at 346 George St is an art-house cinema showing first-release and classic movies. The Classic Cinema (☎ 3393 1066) on the corner of Stanley and Withington Sts in East Brisbane, screens art-house and foreign films; tickets cost $6 on Tuesday and $9 on other nights. The Village Twin Cinemas, on the corner of Brunswick and Barker Sts in New Farm, screen a combination of art-house and mainstream releases. Tickets here are a bargain at $5 on Tuesday, Wednesday and Thursday nights, $9 the rest of the week. At the University of Queensland in St Lucia (seven km south of the city), the Schonell Cinema (☎ 3371 1879) screens mainly art-house movies every night (with a two-week break over Christmas). Tickets cost $8 to $10 for adults and $4 to $6 for students.

The Chinatown Twin Cinemas (☎ 3852 1464), near the Chinatown Mall at 175 Wickham St in Fortitude Valley, screens mainly Chinese films.

If you have a car, there are still a couple of drive-in theatres in Brisbane. The closest ones to the centre are the Starlight Twin (☎ 3263 1555) in Aspley and the Keperra Twin (☎ 3351 1555) in Keperra (both about 10 km north of the centre) and the Capalaba Twin (☎ 3390 1368) in Capalaba to the south-east.

There are also free open-air movies screened several nights each week in the South Bank Parklands from late October until the end of March – see the South Bank Parklands section for more details.

Comedy

Snug Harbour Dockside Comedy Cafe (☎ 3891 6644), in the Dockside Hotel complex in Ferry St, Kangaroo Point, is Brisbane's best stand-up comedy venue. It's a stylish cabaret-style place which is open nightly from Wednesday to Saturday – the cover charge ranges from $10 to $14, and meals and drinks are available (see Places to Eat).

Crazies Comedy Restaurant (☎ 3369 0555), on the corner of Caxton St and Judge St in Petrie Terrace, is one of the better examples of the theatre restaurant genre. It's a great night out and particularly popular with a youngish crowd – the evening features wacky character waiters, stand-up comedy, dancing, singing and acrobatics. Crazies opens Tuesday to Saturday nights, with dinner and show tickets costing $36 per person during the week, $40 on Friday and $45 on Saturday; bookings are essential.

Famous Bob's Comedy Cafe (☎ 3852 2585), at the Breakfast Creek Wharf complex, is another comedy venue with live shows every Friday and Saturday night.

Gambling

The pokies (poker machines) are everywhere in Brisbane's pubs and clubs. The new Treasury Casino also has plenty of pokies, and lots of other betting games – see the section on the casino earlier.

Brisbane's two major horse-racing venues are the Doomben and Eagle Farm racecourses, which are adjacent to each other and north-east of the city, two-thirds of the way to the airport.

The main venue for trotting (harness racing) is the Albion Park Raceway, just north of Breakfast Creek.

Spectator Sports

Like the rest of Australia, Brisbane is sports-mad. And as the old saying goes, those who can, play, while those who can't, watch. There's usually something in town worth watching.

Football Rugby league is Queensland's premier winter spectator sport, and the Winfield Cup, which now includes sides from Queensland, New South Wales, Western Australia and New Zealand, is the main competition. The all-conquering Brisbane Broncos play their home games at the ANZ/Queen Elizabeth II Stadium in Upper Mt Gravatt. (However, all of this may change in the next year or two, depending on the outcome of the current battle between the Australian Rugby League and Rupert Murdoch's News Corp, who recently bought the cream of the ARL's players including the entire Brisbane Broncos team with a view to setting up an international super league in 1996 or 1997.)

A major event on the rugby league calender is the best-of-three State of Origin series played between Queensland and New South Wales. These matches are some of the fiercest and best games you'll ever see, pitting the best players from each state against each other in a last-man-standing contest. The three games are usually played in May-June, with one game each in Sydney, Melbourne and Brisbane.

Australian Rules Football is mainly played in the southern states, but the Brisbane Bears were established in Queensland in the mid-1980s when the former Victorian footy league decided to go national. The Bears have struggled ever since and are yet to make a finals series. They play their home games at the Brisbane Cricket Ground (universally known as the Gabba) in Woolloongabba, south-east of the city, and attract a smallish but passionate following. If you've never seen a game of Aussie Rules, it's definitely worth checking out.

Cricket Each summer, you can also see inter-state Sheffield Shield cricket matches and international Test and one-day cricket matches at the Brisbane Cricket Ground (the Gabba) in Woolloongabba.

Yachting All of the yacht clubs in Moreton Bay have weekend and mid-week races, and numerous major races such as the Brisbane to Gladstone race (every April) depart from the bay – see the Moreton Bay section for details.

Basketball Australia has a National Basketball League, which is based on American pro basketball. It's the fastest growing spectator sport in the country, and the NBL games are of a high standard and draw large crowds. Brisbane's NBL side, the Brisbane Bullets, is based at the Sports & Entertainment Complex in Boondall, about 15 km north-east of the city.

THINGS TO BUY

The Queen St Mall is the city's major shopping precinct, and you'll find various large shopping complexes along its length. The biggest of these is the Myer Centre, which takes up most of the block bordered by Queen, Elizabeth and Albert Sts. As well as the large Myer department store, it houses dozens of fashion, footwear, gift and souvenir shops, a couple of eating sections and a cinema complex.

Another major department store is David Jones, which is also on the mall between Edward and Albert Sts and extends from Queen St through to Adelaide St.

Across the mall from David Jones is the Wintergarden Shopping Complex, with three levels of specialty shops and boutiques including a large range of men's and women's clothing boutiques, jewellery and shoe shops, and several food courts. In the same block, Broadway on the Mall also has plenty of fashion boutiques and shoe shops.

The historic Brisbane Arcade, which runs from the Queen St Mall through to Adelaide St, is one of Brisbane's most exclusive shopping arcades. It's worth wandering through to check out the old world opulence of marble, leadlights and timber, even if you can't afford to shop in any of the up-market jewellery, fashion and footwear boutiques in here.

The Elizabeth Arcade, which runs between Elizabeth and Charlotte Sts, is an alternative shopping arcade with some of the hippest and most interesting shops in the city. They include young designer boutiques, batik clothing, record and book shops, craft shops, a body-piercing specialist, a barber, naturopaths, health-food shops and a small sushi bar.

Aboriginal Art
There are several outlets for Aboriginal art in Brisbane city. Queensland Aboriginal Creations, at 135 George St, is a retail shop run by the Department of Aboriginal and Torres Strait Islander Affairs. It stocks a good range of art, crafts and souvenirs including woollen jumpers, paintings and prints, socks and ties, didgeridoos, boomerangs, jewellery, clapsticks, bullroarers, woomeras and clothing.

The Geerbaugh Cultural Centre, at 466 Ann St, is an Aboriginal and Islander meeting place with a range of items including Aboriginal artefacts and paintings, T-shirts and jewellery on sale.

The Fire Works Gallery, on level one at 336 George St, is an art gallery that promotes, displays and sells the work of Queensland Aboriginal and Torres Strait Islander artists.

Australiana
Arts and crafts, T-shirts, souvenirs, bush gear and the like are sold in dozens of places in the centre, and there are plenty of specialised souvenir shops in town.

The Wilderness Society Shop, at 99 Albert St, has environmentally relevant and friendly gear including books, clothing, toys, posters, mugs and wind chimes. Profits from these shops help protect Australia's wilderness areas.

There are several good Australiana souvenir shops in the Brisbane Arcade, off the Queen St Mall, including Arunga Gifts. Currans are one of the biggest souvenir outlets in the city, with shops at 66 Queen St, 136 Queen St and on the corner of Adelaide and Edward Sts.

A good place to try for last minute gifts is Airport Fine Foods, out at the Brisbane airport, who stock a wide range of Australian food products and wines.

If you're heading out to the Australian Woolshed in Ferny Hills, the excellent Woolshed Supply Store there has one of the best ranges of Aussie gear and souvenirs.

Many of the market stalls also sell a range of Australiana products – see the following Markets section.

Aussie Clothing
R M Williams has a shop in the Wintergarden complex in Queen St. They are one of the best known makers of Aussie gear, and stock an excellent range of boots, oilskins, moleskins, belts, jumpers and flannelette shirts.

Greg Grant Country Clothing, at shop 133 in the Myer Centre on Queen St, also stocks a wide range of bush gear including Akubra hats, Driza-bone oilskin coats and R M Williams boots. Hats by the Hundred, a specialty hat shop in the Wintergarden complex, also stocks Akubra hats.

Outdoor Gear
The best area in Brisbane for outdoor gear is along Wickham St in Fortitude Valley, just south of the intersection with Gipps Sts. There are four specialist outdoor shops side by side: the Scout Outdoor Centre, at 132 Wickham St, Jim the Backpacker, at No 138, K2 Base Camp, at No 142, and Kathmandu, at No 144. They all have different specialties, and stock a wide range of travel gear and books, clothing, boots, camping and climbing gear – if you can't find what you're looking for at one of these places, it probably doesn't exist.

There are also some good shops in the city. Mountain Designs, at 105 Albert St, is a specialist outdoor shop with gear for skiers, rock climbers and bushwalkers. They stock clothing, books and maps, boots and more. Direct Camping & Outdoors, at 142 Albert St, stocks a wide range of camping, outdoor and backpacking gear including tents and sleeping bags, boots, Akubra hats and oilskin coats. At 33 Adelaide St, Sherry's Disposals is a discount camping and outdoor shop with a reasonably extensive range of gear.

Galleries & Antiques

Fortitude Valley is Brisbane's major centre for contemporary art, and has a number of good commercial galleries. They include the Phillip Bacon Galleries, at 2 Arthur St; the Artspace Gallery Shop in McWhirter's Markets, on the corner of Brunswick and Ann Sts; Fusions Gallery, on the corner of Brunswick and Malt Sts; and David Pestorius Gallery, at 26 Church St. Pick up a copy of the *Valley Art Guide* brochure, available at info centres.

In the city, the Verlie Just Town Gallery & Japan Room, on the 6th floor of the McArthur Chambers on the corner of Queen and Edward Sts, has works by contemporary Australian artists and Japanese printmakers. The Cordelia Street Antiques & Art Centre, in an old church on the corner of Glenelg and Cordelia Sts in South Brisbane, is also worth checking out. The Asian Connections gallery, at 6 Edmonstone St in South Brisbane, has a large collection of tribal art and Asian antiques. ArTerra, at 31 Kennedy Tce in Paddington, sells an interesting range of locally made arts and crafts.

Paddington has a small cluster of antique shops along Latrobe Tce, near where it intersects with Prince St. Inside the Paddington Plaza at 167 Latrobe Tce is the huge Paddington Antique Centre, a warehouse crammed with antiques and collectibles, bric-a-brac and furniture. There are another half a dozen antique shops in the immediate area.

Fashion & Clothing

The city's major shopping centres have the best range of fashion boutiques and clothing stores – try the Wintergarden Shopping Complex, the David Jones and Myer department stores, and for designer fashion, the Elizabeth arcade on Elizabeth St. There are also some good designers based in the Valley – try McWhirter's Markets on the corner of Brunswick and Ann Sts.

Crafts

Brisbane's markets carry a great range of craft products – see the following Markets section.

Duty Free

Duty-free shops abound in the city centre, the Valley and at the airport. Remember that a duty-free item might not have much duty on it in the first place and could be available cheaper in an ordinary shop – shop around.

Music

There are plenty of music stores in the city selling the latest CDs and tapes. Tragically, vinyl LPs are getting harder and harder to find. Brashs, in the Myer Centre in the Queen St Mall, has one of the biggest ranges of mainstream music.

There are also numerous independent shops. Rocking Horse Records, at 101 Adelaide St, is an import specialist with a great range of alternative music – world, dance, hard-core, garage, punk and others. They have another shop at 83 Elizabeth St, which specialises in rare music and collectibles, T-shirts, posters etc. Central Station Records, on the 2nd level at 121 Queen St, stocks dance, hip-hop, R&B, techno, funk & soul, and lots of imports.

Galaxy Music, at 45 Adelaide St, has a good range of new and used tapes, CDs and LPs – a weird assortment, with everything from Herman's Hermits to Juliana Hatfield. Country music devotees should get on down to The County Music Store, at 68 Charlotte St.

Markets

The popular Crafts Village markets at South Bank have a great range of clothing, crafts, arts, handmade goods and interesting souvenirs. Stalls are set up in the Stanley St Plaza in rows of colourful tents which are erected every weekend. Opening hours for the markets are Friday nights from 5 to 10.30 pm (known as the Lantern Markets), Saturday from 10 am to 6 pm and Sunday from 9 am to 5 pm.

Every Sunday, the carnival-style Riverside Centre and Eagle St Pier Markets have over 150 stalls, including glass blowing, weaving, leather work and children's activities. On Saturday, the Fortitude Valley Market, with a diverse collection of crafts, clothes and junk, is held in the Brunswick St Mall.

Popular permanent markets include McWhirter's, on the corner of Brunswick and Wickham Sts in Fortitude Valley, which has art and craft galleries, clothing boutiques, a food court and a produce market; and the West End Market, on the corner of Melbourne and Boundary Sts in the West End, which is predominantly a produce market.

GETTING THERE & AWAY

For bus and train travellers, arriving in and leaving Brisbane has been simplified by the Transit Centre on Roma St, about half a km west of the central King George Square. The Transit Centre is the main terminus and booking point for all long-distance buses and trains, as well as the airport bus. The centre has shops, banks, a post office, and plenty of places to eat and drink. There's also a tourist information office on level 2 and an accommodation booking service on level 3.

Air

Brisbane's main airport, Eagle Farm Airport, is north-east of the city; the international terminal is 13 km from the city centre and the domestic terminal is a further four km away. A new terminal complex which will service both international and domestic flights is being constructed midway between these two terminals, and is due to open early in 1996.

Brisbane is a busy international arrival and departure point with frequent flights to Asia, Europe, the Pacific islands, North America, New Zealand and Papua New Guinea.

There are frequent Ansett and Qantas flights from the southern capitals and north to the main Queensland centres like Rockhampton, Mackay, Townsville and Cairns. Eastwest also flies from Sydney and Cairns. Air NSW flies daily from Sydney.

Standard one-way fares from Brisbane include Sydney ($254), Melbourne ($371), Adelaide ($470), Darwin ($595) and Perth ($620). Within Queensland, one-way fares include Townsville ($319), Rockhampton ($215), Mackay ($274), Cairns ($387) and Mt Isa (Ansett only, $393).

There are numerous connections to smaller centres by smaller airlines. Flight West (☎ 13 2392) goes to Roma ($93 one way), Charleville ($125), Quilpie and Barcaldine ($154), Blackall ($147), Longreach ($167), Winton and Windorah ($187) and Birdsville ($216).

Qantas have their domestic travel office (☎ 13 1313) on the ground floor at 247 Adelaide St. Their international office (☎ 3234 3747) is next door at No 241, up on the first level. Ansett (☎ 13 1300) has an office on the corner of Queen and George Sts. Both airlines also have several other offices in Brisbane.

See the Getting There & Away and the Getting Around chapters for more details of flying to and from Brisbane and around Queensland.

Bus

Long-distance bus services operate from the Transit Centre on Roma St, and most of the bus companies have booking desks or agents on the 3rd level of the centre.

The two major bus companies, Greyhound Pioneer Australia (☎ 13 2030) and McCafferty's (☎ 3236 3033) both have booking desks open daily from 6 am to 8.30 pm. See the Getting There & Away chapter for details of their major routes, fares and passes. For advice on bus services and fare deals, try calling Dial-a-Coach (☎ 3221 2225), a bus-fare broker. From Brisbane, approximate fares and journey times to places along the coast are as follows:

Destination	Time	Cost
Noosa Heads	3 hours	$14
Hervey Bay	4 hours	$33
Rockhampton	9 hours	$60
Mackay	13 hours	$87
Townsville	19 hours	$115
Cairns	24 hours	$133

McCafferty's and Greyhound Pioneer also run daily services to the Northern Territory via Longreach (17 hours, $80) and Mt Isa (24 hours, $120).

There are numerous smaller bus companies offering more specialised services and routes – these operators often undercut the big companies on shared routes. They include the following:

Coachtrans (☎ 3236 1000) has over 20 services a day between Brisbane and the Gold Coast; the first departure is at 6.40 am and the last at 9.45 pm. One-way fares are $12 for adults, $9.50 for students and $6 for kids; return fares are double, except for same-day returns which cost $20/16.50/10. Most of the buses stop en route at the Gold Coast's major theme parks, but you have to pay full fare. Alternatively, there's a 'Theme Park Special' service which departs daily at 9 am; the return fare is $15 for adults, $12.50 for students and $8 for children.

Kirklands (☎ 3236 4444) operates bus services from Brisbane to the north coast of New South Wales, including Byron Bay, Lismore, Ballina and Tenterfield. They have four services each weekday and two a day on weekends. Kirklands is also the agent for Crisps Coaches, who has two services a day to Ipswich, Warwick, Toowoomba, Inglewood, Goondiwindi and Moree.

Border Coaches (☎ 3236 4189) has daily services (except Saturday) from Brisbane along the New England Hwy as far as Tamworth in New South Wales, via Toowoomba, Warwick and Tenterfield.

Baxway Coaches (☎ 3844 0666) has daily buses from the Brisbane airport and the Transit centre to Ballina and Byron Bay, via Coolangatta.

Brisbane Bus Lines (☎ 3355 0034) has two services a day (one on Saturday) north from Brisbane to Murgon, via Caboolture and Kingaroy. On Tuesday, Thursday, Friday and Saturday, these services continue up the Burnett Hwy onto Gayndah and Biloela.

Allstate Scenic Tours (☎ 3285 1777) has day trips from Brisbane to O'Reilly's Guesthouse and the Lamington National Park; they leave every day (except Saturday) at 9.30 am. The return fare is $35, or you can use it as a camping drop-off service for $20.

Train
Brisbane's main station for long-distance trains is the Transit Centre. For reservations and information, telephone ☎ 13 2232 or call into the Railway Travel Centre at Central Station, on the corner of Ann and Edward Sts in the city.

For details of interstate and intrastate train services to/from Brisbane, see the Getting There & Away and the Getting Around chapters.

Car & Motorcycle
There are five major routes into and out of the Brisbane metropolitan area – these routes are numbered from M1 to M5.

The major north-south route is the M1, which starts from the Pacific Hwy in the Gold Coast. The Pacific Hwy leads into the South Eastern Freeway and then the Gateway Motorway, which bypasses the city centre to the east and crosses the Brisbane River at the Gateway Bridge (toll payable). There's a turn off to the Brisbane Airport, then the Gateway leads into the Gympie Arterial Rd, which continues north to Pine Rivers. At Pine Rivers, the Bruce Hwy starts – this is the major coastal route from Brisbane to Cairns.

Confused yet? To put all that in simpler terms, if you're passing through Brisbane from south to north or vice versa just follow the M1.

Route M2, the Ipswich Motorway starts south of the centre at the Gateway Motorway, heading westwards to Ipswich and the Darling Downs. Route M3 is an alternative to the M1 city bypass – the South Eastern Freeway takes you into the heart of the city. Route M4, the Logan Motorway, is a tollway which links the Pacific Hwy to the Ipswich Motorway. Route M5 bypasses the city on its west, linking the M2 with the M3.

4WD & Car Rental
All of the major companies – Hertz (☎ 13 1918), Budget (☎ 3860 4466) and Avis

(☎ 3860 4200) – have offices at the Brisbane airport terminals and throughout the city. Thrifty (☎ 3860 4588), a smaller national operator, also has offices at the airport. Their deals are competitive and well worth checking out.

There are also several local firms which advertise cars from around $30 a day, with free airport pick-ups included. These include Ace Car Rentals (☎ 3252 1088), Shoe String Rentals (☎ 3268 3334) and Roadway Rent-a-Car (☎ 3868 1500).

Other smaller local operators include Cut Rate Rentals (☎ 3854 1809), Crown Rent a Car (☎ 3854 1848), Dollar (☎ 3854 1848), Low Price Hire Cars (☎ 3891 1799), Penny Wise (☎ 3252 3333), Dam Cheap (☎ 3252 1177) and National (☎ 3854 1499). Some companies do one-way rentals to Cairns and southern capitals, depending on availability, the season, and the hire period – it's best to ring around and haggle.

There are a number of places hiring 4WDs, starting from around $90 a day for a Suzuki Sierra and around $110 a day for a Toyota Land Cruiser. There's a three-day minimum hire period if you're heading to Fraser Island. Two of the most reputable operators are Four Wheel Drive Hire Service (☎ 3357 9077 or 1800 077 353 toll free) and Allterrain Rentals (☎ 3257 1101). Both of these places also hire out camping gear.

Motorcycle Rental

Australian Motorcycle Adventure (☎ 3865 3176 or 1800 811 876) have off and on-road bikes for hire starting from $95 a day and $180 for a weekend. Weekly rates are from $570 to $660, and they also do motorcycle tours and have buy-back deals.

Harley Hire (☎ 018 981 158) will hire you a 1994-model Harley-Davidson for $200 a day or $400 for three days, including insurance and 200 km a day free. You need to be over 25 years of age.

Both of these companies require a $1000 credit card bond.

Travel Agents

STA Travel have several branches in Bris-

bane. Their city office (☎ 3221 9388) is at 111-117 Adelaide St, and is open on weekdays from 9 am to 5 pm and Saturday from 9 am to 3 pm. Other branches include the University of Queensland (☎ 3371 2433) and the Queensland University of Technology (☎ 3229 0655).

There are a number of other agents worth trying if you're looking for discounted fares, including Flight Centres (☎ 3229 6600) and Brisbane Discount Travel (☎ 3221 9211).

There's an American Express Travel Office (☎ 3229 2022) in the city at 131 Elizabeth St.

The YHA's travel and membership office (☎ 3236 1680) is at 154 Roma St, opposite the Transit Centre; it opens weekdays from 8 am to 4.45 pm. *Courtney Place Backpackers* in East Brisbane has its own in-house travel agent.

GETTING AROUND

Queensland Rail runs Brisbane's Citytrain services, and Brisbane Transport runs local bus and ferry services. For bus, train and ferry transport information, ring the Trans-Info Service on ☎ 13 1230; it operates daily from 6 am to 10 pm. The operators can tell you the shortest, cheapest and easiest way to get to wherever you're going.

There's also a train information office at Central Station, and bus and ferry information is available at the Queen St Information Centre and in the Queen St Bus Station Information Centre, beneath the mall.

To/From the Airport

Coachtrans (☎ 3236 1000) runs the Skytrans bus service between the Transit Centre and the airport. Services depart from the Transit Centre daily at 5 am and 6 am, then every half hour until 8.30 pm; from the airport, departures are daily at 5.30 am and 6.30 am, then every half hour until 9 pm. There are other services to cover any departures and arrivals after 9 pm. Buses will also stop at most hotels and various points in the city centre and Fortitude Valley. The fares are $5.40 from the Transit Centre or $6.50 for hotel pick-ups – children pay half-price. A taxi into the centre from either terminal will cost around $18.

Airport to the Gold Coast & Beyond

Coachtrans also runs the Airporter transfers service between the Brisbane airport and the Gold Coast. Services leave the airport daily at 6 am, 6.45 am and 7.15 am, then every 45 minutes until 8 pm, after which time all flights are met. The buses will drop you anywhere on the Gold Coast between Sanctuary Cove and Palm Beach. The first service from the Gold Coast to the airport departs at 3.15 am, then every 45 minutes until 10 pm. Fares are $26 for adults, $13 for children.

Baxway Coaches (☎ 3844 0666) has daily buses from the Brisbane airport and the Transit centre to Ballina and Byron Bay, via Coolangatta.

Airport to the Sunshine Coast

Two companies have bus services from Brisbane airport to the Sunshine Coast. Suncoast Pacific (☎ 3236 1901) have 10 scheduled services a day from the Transit Centre to the Sunshine Coast, six of which go via the airport. Sunair (☎ (074) 78 2811) also has an airport-to-your-door bus service.

Public Transport Fare Deals

There are various fare deals available that can cut the cost of public transport around Brisbane. A Rover Ticket allows unlimited travel on bus and ferry services for the day, and costs $5.50. The Off-peak Saver allows unlimited bus and ferry travel between 9 am and 3.30 pm and after 7 pm on weekdays, and all day on weekends, and costs $3.

Roverlink tickets allow unlimited travel on buses, ferries and trains, and cost $8. There's also an off-peak version which costs $6. There are also weekly and monthly ticket deals.

You can buy tickets from various places, including the city council's Customer Service Centre at 69 Ann St. There are also several hundred ticket agencies around town – look for the small 'Bus Tickets Sold Here' flag. Most newsagencies are ticket sales agents.

Bus

There's a bus information centre in the underground Queen St Bus Station, under the Myer Centre and the Queen St Mall. It's open weekdays from 8.30 am to 5 pm; the Queen St Mall Information Centre is also helpful with transport info.

The red City Circle bus No 333 does a clockwise loop round the area along George, Adelaide, Wharf, Eagle, Mary, Albert and Alice Sts every five minutes between 8 am and 5.30 pm Monday to Friday; rides are 60c. The open-sided City Sights tour bus also does a loop around the city centre and some of the major attractions – see the Organised Tours section for details.

In addition to the normal city buses, there are Cityxpress services, which run between the suburbs and the centre, and Rockets, which are fast peak-hour commuter buses. From the Transit Centre, you need to walk into the city centre to pick up some buses. Most above-ground bus stops in the city are colour coded to help you find the right one. The underground bus station beneath the Myer Centre is used mainly by Cityxpresses and buses to and from the south of the city. There is a map of the station, above ground in the mall on the corner of Queen and Albert Sts.

Useful buses from the city centre include No 177 and 178 to Fortitude Valley and New Farm (from the brown stops on Adelaide St between King George Square and Edward St). Bardon bus No 144 to Paddington leaves from the red stops opposite the transit centre or from outside the Coles store on Adelaide St.

Buses to Fortitude Valley (Nos 160, 180, 190), Newstead House and Breakfast Creek leave from the yellow stops on Edward St between Adelaide and Queen Sts. Bus No 177 to West End leaves from the brown stop on Edward St, opposite Anzac Square.

Buses run every 10 to 20 minutes Monday to Friday till about 6 pm, and on Saturday mornings. Services are less frequent on weekday evenings, Saturday afternoons and evenings, and Sunday. Bus services stop at 7 pm on Sunday, around midnight on Friday and Saturday and on other days at 11 pm.

In the city centre buses cost just 60c a trip. Other fares are on a zone system costing $1.20, $1.80, $2.40 or $2.80 for zones 1, 2, 3 or 4, respectively. On Sunday all bus trips are a flat $1.20. See the Fare Deals section for other special deals.

Bayside Buslines (☎ 3245 3333) runs between Brisbane and the southern Bayside (Capalaba Park, Wellington Point, Cleveland, Koala Park and Redland Bay). Hornibrook Bus Lines (☎ 3284 1622) runs between Brisbane and the northern Bayside (Sandgate, Clontarf, Redcliffe and Scarborough).

Train

The fast Citytrain network has seven lines, out to Ipswich, Beenleigh and Cleveland in the south and Pinkenba, Shorncliffe, Caboolture and Ferny Grove in the north. All trains go through the Roma St Transit Centre and Central Station in the city, and Brunswick St Station in Fortitude Valley.

There are different fare zones, with ticket prices increasing as you go further from the centre. A journey in the city zone is the cheapest at $1.20, a journey to Caboolture the most expensive at $4. You get 30% off return fares if you travel after 9 am, and all fares are half price on weekends.

There are various train passes available. You can buy Day Rover tickets ($8.50) a day ahead, from any station, which give you unlimited train travel for one day (after 9 am on weekdays). A Weekly Ticket ($9.60) is good value, giving you one week's use of all trains in the city zone. If you have bought a long-distance Sunshine Rail Pass, it also entitles you to free travel on the city train network.

All trains run from around 4.30 am until midnight, with the last train to each line leaving Central Station between 11.30 pm and midnight. On Sunday the last trains run at around 10 pm.

The frequency of trains varies substantially – basically, you can expect a train every 10 minutes on weekdays from 7 to 9.30 am and from 3 to 6 pm; once an hour on weekends and after 10 pm during the week; and half-hourly at other times.

Bicycles can be taken on city trains, except during peak hours.

Taxi

There are usually plenty of taxis around the city centre, and there are taxi ranks at the Transit Centre, Central Station, the Cultural Centre and numerous other places.

You can also book a taxi by phone. The major taxi companies are Yellow Cabs (☎ 3391 0191), Brisbane Cabs (☎ 3360 0000), Black & White (☎ 3238 1000) and Q Cabs (☎ 3213 1222).

Taxi fares are as follows: flagfall is $2.90 between 8 pm and 6 am on weekdays and between 1 pm on Saturday and 6 am on Monday, and $1.80 at all other times; on top of that, there's a rate of 79c per km; and the phone-booking fee is 60c.

Car

Compared to Sydney or Melbourne, getting around in Brisbane is quick and easy – once you know your way around. Until then, all those bridges, overpasses, underpasses and ringroads around the city can be a nightmare, and as with the rest of Queensland the signposting leaves a lot to be desired. A good map or street directory will help – see the earlier Maps section.

Parking spaces in the city centre are extremely limited, but there are plenty of commercial car parks around. Quite a few accommodation places have off-street parking facilities, many of which are mentioned in the Places to Stay section. Drivers need to beware of the two-hour parking limit in the city and inner suburbs – there are no signs, and the parking inspectors are merciless!

See the earlier Getting There & Away section for details of car rental companies.

Ferry

Brisbane has a fast, efficient ferry service along and across the Brisbane River. Cross-river ferries cost $1.20 one way and generally run every 10 to 15 minutes from around dawn until after 11 pm Monday to Saturday; there are shorter hours on Sunday. You can take a bicycle on the ferry for free.

The most central ferry stops are the Riverside Centre/Eagle St Pier; Edward St (on the corner of the Botanic Gardens); Thornton St, Holman St and Dockside, all on Kangaroo Point; the South Bank Parklands; the River Plaza Hotel in South Brisbane; the QUT Gardens Point; and New Farm. Maps of the ferry routes are available at all the stops, as well as from information centres.

Bicycle

Brisbane is a good city for cycling, with some excellent bike tracks in the city and suburbs, particularly around the Brisbane River. The Brisbane City Council's Bikeways programme has more than 300 km of bike paths in and around the city centre. Pick up a copy of their *Safe Bikeways* brochure from information centres, which includes nine good maps of the city's bike routes.

A good way to spend a day is to ride the riverside bicycle track from the city Botanic Gardens out to the University of Queensland. It's about seven km one way and you can stop for a beer at the Regatta pub in Toowong, use the cheap swimming pool or hire a tennis court at the university, and have a meal in one of the reasonably priced eateries in Toowong on the way back.

Remember that the wearing of helmets is compulsory here – you're up for a $30 fine if you're caught without one – and lights are required at night.

There are several places that hire out bikes. At 87 Albert St in the city, Brisbane Bicycle Sales (☎ 3229 2433) hires out mountain bikes for $9 an hour or $20 a day; they are open every day. New Farm Mountain Bikes (☎ 3254 0544), at 697 Brunswick St in New Farm, also hires out good quality mountain bikes for $7 an hour, $25 a day or $70 a week, with helmets included. Quite a few of the backpackers' hostels also have bikes available for guests, often free.

Bicycles are allowed on city trains, except on weekdays during peak hours (7 to 9 am and 3 to 6.30 pm). Bikes must go into the first carriage of the train. You can also take bikes on ferries for free.

Moreton Bay

Moreton Bay, at the mouth of the Brisbane River, is said to have 365 islands. Sheltering a large stretch of coast are the larger islands: South Stradbroke Island, just north of the Gold Coast; Bribie Island, just south of the Sunshine Coast; and in between, North Stradbroke and Moreton islands.

THE BAYSIDE

Brisbane's bayside suburbs are predominantly residential areas, with only a handful of attractions of interest for travellers. Sadly, the Moreton Bay 'beaches' are mostly shallow and often muddy, and while some are OK for sunbaking or beach cricket, if you're looking for real beaches you'll have to head across to one of the islands, or to the Gold or Sunshine coasts.

Situated 35 km north of Brisbane is the **Redcliffe Peninsula**, the site of the first White settlement in Queensland. The Aborigines called the place Humpybong or 'Dead Houses' and the name is still applied to the peninsula. The peninsula is linked to Brisbane by a long bridge across Bramble Bay. **Scarborough**, **Redcliffe**, **Margate** and **Woody Point** are now outer suburbs of Brisbane and popular retirement places.

South of Redcliffe, **Brighton** and **Sandgate** are long-established seaside resorts which are now more like outer suburbs.

Wynnum & Manly

South of the Brisbane River mouth are two of the more attractive bayside suburbs, Wynnum and Manly. These are popular fishing and boating areas, with several large marinas and boat harbours along the waterfront. There are also quite a few good restaurants in the area including numerous seafood cafes and fish & chips shops along the foreshore.

Yacht & Boat Clubs The Royal Queensland Yacht Squadron (☎ (07) 3396 8666) has yacht races every Wednesday and Saturday afternoon. People wanting to crew on a yacht should contact the secretary, David Kemp, a few days before the races. The Wednesday races are social events and open to all comers, whereas experienced sailors are preferred for the more competitive Saturday races.

This is also a good place to look for yacht rides along the coast. The club has a notice board where people advertise for crew, and if you contact the secretary they may be able to place you onto their crew list. It might also be worth contacting the Wynnum-Manly Yacht Club (☎ (07) 3393 5708) or the Moreton Bay Trailer Boat Club (☎ (07) 3396 8161).

Places to Stay & Eat The *Moreton Bay Lodge* (☎ (07) 3396 3020), in the heart of Manly Village on Cambridge Pde, is a new backpackers' hostel with a wide range of accommodation starting from $12 per person. The hostel is close to the waterfront, has its own cafe and organises various tours and day trips for guests.

The *Manly Hotel* (☎ (07) 3396 8188), on the corner of Cambridge Pde and Stratton Tce, has pub-style rooms at $25/35 for singles/doubles, or $35/45 with their own bathrooms. This pub also has karaoke nights on Wednesday and various other entertainment ranging from trivia nights, palm readings, karaoke and pianists to jazz bands on Sunday afternoons.

Cleveland

Cleveland is the main access point for North Stradbroke Island. The Redland Bay area is a fertile market garden for Brisbane and a Strawberry Festival is held on the first weekend in September.

Ormiston House in Wellington St, Ormiston, is a very fine home built in 1862 and open for inspection and Devonshire teas on Sunday afternoons from 1.30 to 4.30 pm between March and November. The first commercially grown sugar cane in Queensland came from this site.

Whepstead on Main Rd, Wellington Point, is another early home, built in 1874; it's now a restaurant and reception centre. **Cleveland Point**, a narrow peninsula jutting into Moreton Bay, is one of Brisbane's most historic sites with numerous old buildings surviving from the colonial days.

There's an 1864 simple white timber lighthouse at Cleveland Point and the 1853 Cleveland Courthouse is now a restaurant.

Places to Stay & Eat The *Grand View Hotel* (☎ (07) 3286 1002), in North St on Cleveland Point, is a great big old pub that has been impressively renovated in 'modern heritage' style. The pub has two very pleasant guestrooms upstairs that share the one bathroom and cost $60 a double. There is also a stylish à la carte restaurant upstairs and a courtyard bar/bistro and coffee shop downstairs. The pub has live music on Friday and Saturday nights and Saturday and Sunday afternoons.

NORTH STRADBROKE ISLAND
(pop 2290)

Until 1896 the two Stradbroke islands were one but in that year a storm cut the sand spit joining the two at Jumpinpin. Today, South Stradbroke is virtually uninhabited but it's a popular day trip from the Gold Coast.

North Stradbroke is the larger island and it has a permanent population. Although it's a popular escape from Brisbane it's still relatively unspoilt (although the Christmas and Easter holidays can get pretty hectic). 'Straddie' is a sand island, and despite the sand-mining operations in the south, there's plenty of vegetation and beautiful scenery in the north.

In 1828 Dunwich was established on the west coast of the island as a quarantine station for immigrants but in 1850 a ship brought cholera and the cemetery tells the sad story of the 28 victims of the outbreak that followed. Dunwich, Amity Point and Point Lookout, the three small centres on the island, are all in the north and connected by paved roads. Most of the southern part of the island is closed to visitors due to ongoing sand mining; the only road into this swampy, more remote area is a private mining-company road.

Information
The Stradbroke Island Visitors Centre (☎ (07) 3409 9555), near the ferry terminal in Dunwich, is open on weekdays from 8.30 am to 5 pm and weekends from 9 am to 4 pm. There's a small art gallery upstairs in the same building.

There are post offices in Dunwich and Point Lookout.

There's an ANZ bank in Dunwich which opens on weekdays from 10 am to 2.30 pm, but there are no banks in Point Lookout apart from the Commonwealth Bank agency at the post office in Endeavour St. The BP Road-house and the Bowls Club have EFTPOS facilities.

Things to See
Straddie's best beaches are around Point Lookout, where there's a series of points and bays around the headland, and then the endless white sand stretch of Main Beach. There are some excellent surfing breaks here, and you can hire surfboards and boogie boards from various places. A surf life-saving club overlooks Main Beach.

On the ocean side you may even spot a humpback whale or two on their northward migration to the Great Barrier Reef where they breed during the winter months. Dolphins and porpoises are common.

Apart from beach activities, there's the island to explore. A sealed road runs across from Dunwich to **Blue Lake** in the centre of the island; a 2.7-km walking track leads from the road to the lake. You can swim in the freshwater lake or nearby **Tortoise Lagoon**, or walk along the track and watch for snakes, goannas, wallabies and birds. **Brown Lake**, about three km along the

Blue Lake road from Dunwich, also offers deep freshwater swimming, and is more easilyaccessible.

If you want to hike the 20 km across the island from Dunwich to Point Lookout, a number of dirt-track loops break the monotony of the bitumen road. A pleasant diversion is to **Myora Springs**, surrounded by lush vegetation and walking tracks, near the coast about four km north of Dunwich.

The **North Stradbroke Island Historical Museum**, at 17 Welsby St, in Dunwich has a collection of displays and old photos relating to the island's history. It is open on Wednesday from 1 to 4 pm, or by appointment. The brochure *Take a walk around Historical Dunwich*, available from the tourist office, guides you around the town's various historical sites including the museum, the quarantine station and the Catholic Mission.

Activities
Diving The Stradbroke Island Scuba Centre (☎ (07) 3409 8715), beneath the Stradbroke Island Guesthouse in Point Lookout, runs five-day diving courses costing $395. They also hire out a complete range of diving gear and run diving and snorkelling trips.

Tennis The Point Lookout Tennis Club has two good floodlit courts and is open to the general public. Courts cost $6 an hour during the day and $8 at night; bookings are handled by the BP Roadhouse nearby, who also have racquets and balls for hire.

Horse Riding The Sandy Trails (☎ 018 888 896) horse-riding centre offers a range of trail rides around the island. They can pick you up if you ring in advance.

Gym The Island Fitness Gym at the *Pandanus Palms Holiday Resort* (see Places to Stay) is open to the public.

Organised Tours
Stradbroke Island Tours (☎ (07) 3409 8051) runs good 4WD tours of the island. Prices range from $25 for a fishing trip or half-day

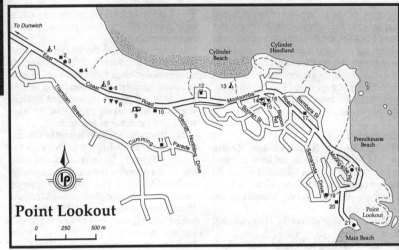

Point Lookout

0   250   500 m

PLACES TO STAY

1   Adder Rock Camping Ground
2   Stradbroke Island Guesthouse &
    Stradbroke Island Scuba Centre
4   Anchorage Village Beach Resort
5   Thankful Rest Caravan &
    Camping Ground
9   Stradbroke Island Carapark
10 The Islander Holiday Apartments
11 Pandanus Palms Holiday Resort
13 Cylinder Beach Caravan &
    Camping Ground
17 Straddie Hostel
19 Headland Chalet
20 Samarinda Holiday Village

PLACES TO EAT

7   Point Lookout Masonic Club
8   Point Lookout Bowls Club
12 Stradbroke Hotel
15 Pasta Fino
16 La Foccacia

OTHER

3   BP Roadhouse & General Store
6   Point Lookout Tennis Club
14 Post Office
18 Point Lookout Local Store
21 Surf Life-Saving Club

tour, $12 for a night tour, to $50 for a full day.

Straddie Experience Canoe Trips (☎ (07) 3409 8279) offers a half-day canoeing trip to the island's mangrove creeks and freshwater lakes. The $35 cost includes transport and a picnic lunch.

Festivals

The Straddie Pro is a major competition on the surfing calendar, and is held at Point Lookout every year in early March. The island is also famous for its fishing, and the annual Straddie Classic, held in August, is one of Australia's richest and best known competitions.

Places to Stay

Dunwich, Amity Point and Point Lookout all have caravan and camping parks, although Dunwich and Amity Point are mainly residential towns. Point Lookout is the main town and has the best beaches and facilities plus a wide range of accommodation, ranging from camping grounds and backpackers' hostels to apartments and resorts.

Camping There are seven council-run camping grounds on the island. Those in Point Lookout include the *Adder Rock Camping Ground*, a good camp site amongst shady eucalypts just back from the pleasant Rocky Point Beach; the *Cylinder Beach Caravan & Camping Ground*, close to a rocky headland and a good surf beach with picnic tables and barbecues on the foreshore; and the *Thankful Rest Caravan & Camping Park*, off East Coast Rd. Rates for all the council-run camping grounds are $10 for a tent site and $13 for a powered site, and sites can be booked through the council's office on ☎ (07) 3409 9025.

The *Stradbroke Island Carapark* (☎ (07) 3409 8127), on East Coast Rd, has tent sites ranging from $8 to $13, backpacker cabins at $15 per person, and fully self-contained cabins from $43 to $50 a double.

Hostels & Cabins The *Stradbroke Island Guesthouse* (☎ (07) 3409 8888), at 1 East Coast Rd, is the first place on the left as you come into Point Lookout. This is an impressive new guesthouse with excellent, modern facilities. It costs $15 for a bed in a four-bed dorm, singles/doubles $35, and tariffs include the use of a surf ski and sand sailer (wind and tide permitting). The guesthouse runs a pick-up bus from Brisbane, which leaves from opposite the Transit Centre every Monday, Wednesday and Friday at 2.30 pm, and also stops at hostels; you need to book, and it costs $5.

Also on the main road, on the left just after the Stradbroke Hotel, the *Straddie Hostel* (☎ (07) 3409 8679) (formerly Point Lookout Backpackers) is in a two-storey beach-house. It has recently been renovated and has good facilities. The large dorms each have their own kitchen and bathroom; bunks cost $12 a night, doubles $28 a night.

A little further up the road on the right-hand side, the *Headland Chalet* (☎ (07) 3409 8252) is an old-style holiday village,

with a collection of cabins scattered across a hillside overlooking beautiful Main Beach. It doesn't look much from the outside, but it's an interesting, arty place. The rooms have a fridge, tea and coffee-making gear, great views and a maximum of four beds and cost $20 per person for the first night then $15 per person for subsequent nights. There's a pool, a games and TV room, free washing machines and a small kitchen.

The Pub On a headland above Cylinder Beach, the *Stradbroke Hotel* (☎ (07) 3409 8188) (the only pub on the island) has motel-style rooms with singles/doubles ranging from $35/58 in the low season to $50/70 in the high season.

Holiday Units & Resorts If you're thinking of staying awhile, a holiday flat or house can be good value, especially outside the holiday seasons. There are several real estate agents, including the Accommodation Centre (☎ (07) 3409 8255), which is below the Stradbroke Island Guesthouse.

The *Islander Holiday Apartments* (☎ (07) 3409 8388), on the inland side of East Coast Rd, are quite good value, with studio units from $50 a night and one and two-bedroom units starting from $60 a double. The complex has its own pool and tennis court, and a minimum two-night stay applies during the holiday season.

The *Anchorage Village Beach Resort* (☎ (07) 3409 8266), on East Coast Rd, is a three-storey mid-range resort with a pool, laundry and restaurant. Prices change with the seasons – motel-style units range from $80 to $95 a night; one-bedroom units range from $90 to $120; and two-bedroom units range from $100 to $135.

Point Lookout's most up-market accommodation is the *Pandanus Palms Holiday Resort* (☎ (07) 3409 8106), set up on the hillside at 21 Cumming Pde. The resort has modern townhouses with good views, a gym, tennis courts and a Chinese restaurant. The nightly rate starts at $100, although weekly rates apply in the holiday seasons – these range from $320 to $620 for the two-bedroom units and from $410 to $710 for the three-bedroom units.

Places to Eat

There are several general stores in Point Lookout that have some supplies and do takeaway food. If you're fixing your own meals bring basic supplies as the mark-up on the island is significant. The *Point Lookout Local Store* is a general store with a good range of groceries, fruit and vegies and fresh seafood.

The *Stradbroke Hotel* in Point Lookout has meal specials for $4 to $6 and a carvery with main courses from $9 to $12. It also has a great beer garden with an ocean outlook, and live music on most Saturday nights and Sunday afternoons.

There's a small cluster of eateries in the Point Lookout Shopping Village in Endeavour St. *Pasta Fino* is a modern, beachy cafe with pastas and pizzas from $9, a Mexican menu on Friday nights, and a Thai menu on Sunday. Most main courses are under $11. *La Focaccia* is your basic pizza and pasta joint fronted by a small courtyard with a couple of tables.

The *Point Lookout Masonic Club,* on East Coast Rd, has good meals from $3.50 to $9; it's open for lunch and dinner Wednesday to Sunday. The *Point Lookout Bowls Club* next door also does meals, including a $4 roast night on Tuesday.

Dela's Quarterdeck Restaurant, at the Anchorage Village Beach Resort, is a pleasant, formal restaurant and cocktail bar which opens daily for lunches and dinner. Lunches range from $7 for a T-bone and salad to $12 for a coconut chicken curry, and at night main courses are in the $14 to $19 range.

Getting There & Away

Cleveland, on the southern Bayside, is the departure point for ferries to the mainland. There are numerous ways of getting from central Brisbane to the island. The cheapest way for backpackers to get here is on the Stradbroke Island Guesthouse's bus – see Places to Stay earlier.

Water Taxi/Bus North Stradbroke Coach Service (☎ (07) 3807 4299) runs daily services between Brisbane and the island, combining a bus to Cleveland, a water taxi to the island and another bus to Point Lookout. Buses depart from Brisbane from stop 1, outside the Transit Centre, at 9.30 am and 4 pm on weekdays and 7.45 am on weekends; the trip takes about two hours all up, and the return fare is $24. Returning from the island to Brisbane, buses depart Point Lookout at 6.50 am and 1.20 and 4 pm on weekdays, 2.30 pm on Saturday and 3 pm on Sunday.

Train/Bus Trains leave Brisbane for Cleveland about every half hour from 5 am. The journey takes about an hour.

Bayside Buslines (☎ (07) 3245 3333) runs a weekday 40-minute service between Brisbane and Cleveland on the Bayside Bullet, and a regular service (Nos 621 and 622) which takes about an hour. Both cost $3.50 and depart about every half hour (less frequently at weekends) from Elizabeth St in central Brisbane. In Cleveland, the buses stop at the railway station. A free bus service covers the one km or so from the station to the ferry terminals, leaving about 15 minutes before the water taxis are due to depart for Straddie.

Water Taxi Two water-taxi companies operate between Cleveland and Dunwich. Stradbroke Ferries (☎ (07) 3286 2666) has three boats – the *Spirit*, the *Pride* and the *Gateway* – and charge $9 return. There's also the *Stradbroke Flyer* (☎ (07) 3286 1964), which costs between $7.50 and $10, depending on the season.

The trip takes 20 minutes and the boats depart hourly from 6 am to 6 pm weekdays, to 6.30 am to 6 pm Saturday and 7.30 am to 6.30 pm Sunday.

Car Ferry Stradbroke Ferries (☎ 3286 2666) also runs the vehicle ferry from Cleveland to Dunwich about 12 times a day. It costs $63 return for a vehicle plus passengers, and $7 return for pedestrians. The first ferries depart

Cleveland at 5.30 am, with last departures at 6 pm, excepting Friday when there are late ferries at 7.30, 8 and 10 pm.

Getting Around

Stradbroke Island Coaches (☎ (07) 3807 4299) runs 10 services a day between the three main centres; Dunwich to Point Lookout costs $3.50, and short trips around Point Lookout cost 50c to $1. The Stradbroke Island Taxi Service (☎ (07) 3409 9124) charges about $25 from Dunwich to Point Lookout.

You can rent a 4WD for $100 a day ($60 a half day) from Point Lookout Hire (☎ (07) 3409 8353). The Stradbroke Island Guesthouse rents out motor scooters for $15 an hour or $70 a day (less for guests).

MORETON ISLAND (pop 200)

North of Stradbroke, Moreton Island is less visited and still almost a wilderness. Apart from a few rocky headlands, it's all sand, with **Mt Tempest**, towering to 280 metres, the highest coastal sandhill in the world. It's a strange landscape, alternating between bare sand, forest, lakes and swamps, with a 30-km surf beach along the eastern side. The island's birdlife is prolific, and at its northern tip is a **lighthouse**, built in 1857. Sandmining leases on the island have been cancelled and 96% of the island is now a national park. There are several shipwrecks off the west coast.

Moreton Island has no paved roads but 4WD vehicles can travel along beaches and a few cross-island tracks – seek local advice about tides and creek crossings. The QNP&WS publishes a map of the island, which you can get on the ferry or from the QNP&WS office at False Patch Wrecks. The Sunmap Tourist Map, also available on the ferries, is very good. Vehicle permits for the island cost $15 and are available through the barge operators or QNP&WS offices.

Tangalooma, halfway down the western side of the island, is a popular tourist resort and site of an old whaling station. The only other settlements, all on the west coast, are **Bulwer** near the north-western tip, **Cowan Cowan** between Bulwer and Tangalooma, and **Kooringal** near the southern tip. The shops at Kooringal and Bulwer are expensive, so bring what you can from the mainland. For a bit of shark spotting, go to the Tangalooma Resort at 5 pm, when resort staff dump garbage off the end of the jetty.

Without your own vehicle, walking is the only way to get around the island, and you'll need several days to explore it. There are some trails around the resort area, and there are quite a few decommissioned 4WD roads with good walks. It's about 14 km from Tangalooma or the Ben-Ewa camping ground on the western side to Eagers Creek camping ground on the east, then seven km up the beach to Blue Lagoon and a further six to Cape Moreton at the north-eastern tip. There's a strenuous track to the summit of Mt Tempest, about three km inland from Eagers Creek; the views from the top are worth the effort.

About three km south and inland from Tangalooma is an area of bare sand known as the **Desert**, while the **Big Sandhills** and the **Little Sandhills** are towards the narrow southern end of the island. The biggest lakes and some swamps are in the north-east, and the west coast from Cowan Cowan past Bulwer is also swampy.

Organised Tours

Several companies offer 4WD tours of the island. Sunrover Expeditions (☎ (07) 3203 4241) has good day trips departing from the Transit Centre in Brisbane on Saturday, Sunday and Monday. The cost is $80 per person which includes lunch. Sunday and Monday are the best days to do this trip, as you get about six hours on the island – the Saturday trip is much shorter. The same company also has three-day camping trips costing $250 per person with everything supplied.

On Friday nights, the *Tangalooma Resort* (☎ (07) 3268 6333) runs night cruises costing $75 for adults and $45 for children. You get to feed dolphins and enjoy a three-course dinner before returning to Brisbane.

The cruises leave from the Holt St Wharf in Pinkenba at 5.30 pm on Friday, returning around 11.15 pm.

Moreton Island Tourist Services (☎ (07) 3203 6399) runs tours on the *Combie Trader* (see Getting There & Away) every Monday, Friday and Sunday; the cost is $55 for adults and $35 for children, which includes a barbecue lunch, an island tour and the ferry trip across.

Places to Stay

Camping National Parks camping grounds, with water, toilets and cold showers, are at Ben-Ewa and False Patch Wrecks, both between Cowan Cowan and Tangalooma, and at Eagers Creek and Blue Lagoon on the northern half of the ocean coast. Camping permits cost $3 per person per night and are available from the barge operators or through the QNP&WS offices at 160 Ann St in Brisbane (☎ (07) 3227 8185), or at False Patch Wrecks on the island (☎ (07) 3408 2710).

Resort The *Tangalooma Resort* (☎ (07) 3268 6333), on the west side of the island, has four different styles of accommodation ranging from $145 a double in the hillside units to $245 a double in a villa. The resort has its own restaurant and a more casual beach cafe, and runs 4WD tours of the island. Every evening, dolphins from Moreton Bay come into the shallows in front of the resort to be fed.

There are a few holiday flats or houses for rent at Kooringal, Cowan Cowan and Bulwer.

Getting There & Away

The *Tangalooma Flyer* (☎ (07) 3268 6333), a fast catamaran operated by the resort, leaves from Brisbane every day except Monday. You can use it for a day trip to the island or as a ferry if you're going to camp; A day trip from Brisbane costs $25 return; for any trip, it's advisable to book a day in advance. In Brisbane, the dock is at Holt St, off Kingsford Smith Dve in Pinkenba.

The *Moreton Venture* (☎ (07) 3895 1000) is a vehicle ferry which runs every day except Tuesday to Tangalooma or to Short Point. The ferry leaves from Whyte Island, which is joined to the mainland by road, at the southern side of the Brisbane River mouth. You can take your own 4WD across for $85 return (including passengers); pedestrians are charged $18 return.

Another ferry to the island is the *Combie Trader* (☎ (07) 3203 6399), with several services between Scarborough and Bulwer every day except Tuesday. Fares are $50 one way and $90 return for a 4WD and four people, and $13 one way and $20 return for pedestrians. The ferry also does day trips on Monday, Wednesday, Saturday and Sunday for $20 for adults, $17 for students and $10 for children.

ST HELENA ISLAND

Just six km from the mouth of the Brisbane River, little St Helena Island was used as a high-security prison from 1867 to 1932. The island is now a national park. There are remains of several prison buildings on the island, plus the first passenger tramway in Brisbane which, when built in 1884, had horse-drawn cars. Sandy beaches and mangroves alternate around the island's coast.

Organised Tours

Several outfits run day trips to St Helena. St Helena Island Guided Tours (☎ (07) 3260 7944) has day trips leaving from the BP Marina on Kingsford Smith Dve, Breakfast Creek, at 9 am every Sunday and two or three other days each week, returning at 5 pm. The price is $29 for adults and $15 for children with lunch included, or $23/13 without lunch. St Helena Ferries (☎ (07) 3393 3726) runs two to three trips a week on their *Cato' Nine Tails* catamaran, leaving from Manly Harbour, opposite Cardigan Pde, on the southern Bayside. The day trip costs $23 for adults, $13 for children and $55 for a family, which includes a tour of the island and prison, a horse-drawn wagon ride and entry to the national park. You can reach Manly from central Brisbane in about 35 minutes by train.

COOCHIEMUDLO ISLAND

Coochiemudlo (or Coochie) Island is a 10-minute ferry ride from Victoria Point on the southern Bayside. It's a popular outing from the mainland, with good beaches, although it's more built-up than most other Moreton Bay islands you can visit. You can rent bicycles, boats, catamarans and surf skis on the island.

Places to Stay

The *Coochie Ville Holiday Units* (☎ (07) 3207 7521) has one and two-bedroom units starting from $45 a night.

Getting There & Around

Combined Ferry Services (☎ (07) 3207 8960) has ferry services to the island from the Victoria Point jetty, running every 20 minutes between 6.30 am and 6.20 pm daily. The one-way fare is $1.50. The same company runs the MV *Island Link*, a vehicle ferry which costs $30 per vehicle. Bookings are essential. The Coochie Bus Service (☎ (07) 3207 7046) runs bus services around the island and island tours.

BAY ISLES

The Bay Isles, made up of **Russell**, **Lamb**, **Karragarra** and **Macleay** islands, are between the southern end of North Stradbroke and the mainland. At about seven km long, Russell is the largest; it features the interesting Green Dragon Museum in the north-west of the island. Bay Islands Ferries (☎ (07) 3286 2666), operating from the Banana St ramp in Redland Bay, does a loop around the islands three or four times a day; fares are $32 return for a car and passengers, or $2 each way for pedestrians.

BRIBIE ISLAND

Bribie Island, at the northern end of Moreton Bay, is 31 km long but apart from the southern end, where there are a couple of small towns, the island is largely untouched. The island is separated from the mainland by the narrow Pumicestone Channel, with a bridge across to Bellara on the south-west coast.

There are three main towns at the southern end of the island – Bellara and Bongaree on the west coast and Woorim on the east coast. Woorim is probably the best of these from the travellers' point of view. It's an old-fashioned holiday township with good, sandy ocean beaches and a range of accommodation. Bellara and Bongaree are much more residential.

The north-west coast of the island is protected as the Pumicestone National Park, which is only accessible for 4WD vehicles. Much of Bribie Island was devastated by the bushfires of 1994, but the island has been quick to regenerate.

Tourist Information

As you cross the bridge onto the island, you'll see the Bribie Island Tourist Information Centre (☎ (07) 3408 9026) in the middle of the Benabraw Ave medium strip. It is open Monday to Saturday from 9 am to 4 pm and Sunday from 9 am to 12.30 pm.

Places to Stay & Eat

Woorim The *Bribie Island Caravan Park* (☎ (07) 3408 1134), in Jacana Ave one block back from the beach, is an impressive caravan park with a pool, landscaped grounds, and a shop. Tent sites are $11, powered sites $15, on-site vans $25 and cabins $30, or $45 with their own bathroom.

The *Koolamara Beach Resort* (☎ (07) 3408 1277), on the beachfront in Woorim, is a good modern resort built around a swimming pool in a landscaped garden setting. The resort has motel-style units from $68 a double, and its own licensed restaurant.

The *Blue Pacific Hotel-Motel* ,on North St, has bistro meals and budget motel-style units. Across the road from the pub on the beachfront are the *Ocean Beach General Store* and *Rosanna Coffee Bar*, both of which have a range of meals and snacks. The small shopping centre on Jacana Ave has a good bakery, a couple of takeaway places and a pizza shop.

Bongaree Bongaree, the oldest settlement on the island, also has several motels and caravan parks, as well as numerous restaurants and cafes. The *Bongaree Caravan Park* (☎ (074) 408 1054), on Welsby Pde, has tent sites ranging from $10 to $14 and powered sites from $12.50 to $16. This large park is popular with boat owners, as it's right across the road from the boat ramps into Bribie Passage.

Getting There & Away

There are frequent train services between Brisbane and Caboolture, and Bribie Island Bus & Coaches (☎ (07) 3408 2562) runs bus services from the Caboolture railway station to Bribie Island; the one-way fare is $3.80.

Aerial view of Surfers Paradise

TONY WHEELER

MARK ARMSTRONG

MARK ARMSTRONG

Top: Fraser Island from Rainbow Beach
Middle: Coloured sands, Fraser Island
Bottom: Sunshine Coast surfer

Gold Coast

The Gold Coast (population 330,000 and growing) is a 35-km strip of beaches running north from the New South Wales/Queensland border. It's the most thoroughly commercialised resort area in Australia and is virtually one continuous development culminating in the high-rise splendour of Surfers Paradise.

This coast has been a holiday spot since the 1880s, but only after WW II did developers start taking serious notice of Surfers, as it's called. More than two million visitors a year come to the Gold Coast. Accommodation on the Gold Coast ranges from backpackers' hostels to resort hotels, and there's quite a range of things to do – good surf beaches, excellent eating and entertainment possibilities and a hinterland with some fine natural features. There's also a huge variety of artificial 'attractions' and theme parks, although most are very commercial and fairly expensive.

Orientation

The whole coast from Tweed Heads in New South Wales up to Main Beach, north of Surfers Paradise, is developed, but most of the real action is around Surfers itself. Tweed Heads and Coolangatta, at the southern end, are older, quieter and cheaper resorts. Moving north from there, you pass through Kirra, Bilinga, Tugun, Currumbin, Palm Beach, Burleigh Heads, Miami, Nobby Beach, Mermaid Beach and Broadbeach – all lower key resorts.

Southport, the oldest town in the area, is north and just inland from Surfers, behind the sheltered expanse of the Broadwater which is fed by the Nerang and Coomera rivers. The Gold Coast Hwy runs right along the coastal strip, leaving the Pacific Hwy just north of Tugun and rejoining it inland from Southport.

The Coolangatta airport services the Gold Coast and is at Bilinga, about two km north of Coolangatta and 20 km south of Surfers

Paradise. Most buses to the Gold Coast travel the full length of the strip.

Information

Tourist Information There are tourist information centres in Surfers Paradise and Coolangatta, and at Canungra and Tamborine Mountain in the hinterland – see those sections for details.

There are plenty of free glossy booklets available, including *Wot's On*, *Destination Surfers Paradise* and *Point Out* – these have street plans of the whole strip, as well as entertainment and eating details, although it must be said that they are mostly full of ads.

Money There's a Travelex Currency Exchange booth at the Coolangatta Airport which is open from 5.30 am to 5.30 pm daily (6.15 am to 6.15 pm on Sundays).

Activities

Water Sports & Surfing Numerous places rent all sorts of water-sports equipment.

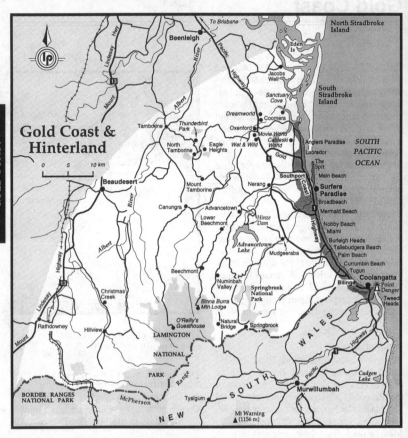

Gold Coast & Hinterland

0   5   10 km

Aussie Bob's (☎ (07) 5591 7577), at the Marina Mirage in Main Beach, and Budd's Beach Water Sportz (☎ (07) 5592 0644), on River Dve at Surfers, rent a wide range of gear including jet skis, fishing boats and sailboards, and can take you paragliding, water-skiing and more.

You can hire small motorboats from Popeye Marine & Boat Hire (☎ (07) 5532 5822) at Mariner's Cove on The Spit, amongst other places. Jet skis can be rented from a number of places, including Gold Coast Jet Ski Hire (☎ (07) 5592 2415), on Thomas Dve, Chevron Island.

Kirra Surf (☎ (07) 5536 3922), on the corner of Coolangatta Rd and the Pacific Hwy, South Kirra, rents surfboards and boogie boards, as does Surfers Blades (☎ (07) 5538 3483), at 10 Hanlan St.

The Australian Surfriders Association runs a School of Surfing (☎ (07) 5535 6978), on Surfers Paradise Beach. A 1½-hour lesson costs $12 per person.

Horse Riding Numinbah Valley Adventure Trails (☎ (07) 5533 4137) has three-hour horse-riding treks through beautiful rainforest and river scenery in the Numinbah Valley near Nerang, costing $35 per person or $40 with pick-ups from the coast.

The Gold Coast Riding Ranch (☎ (07) 5594 4255), on Nerang-Broadbeach Rd next to the Surfers Raceway, does trail rides from $20 an hour, and at Gum Nuts Horse Riding Resort (☎ (07) 5543 0191) also on Nerang-Broadbeach Rd, in Carrara, half a day costs $35 and a full day $60.

Joy Flights Vintage Flights (☎ (07) 5538 9083) has joy flights in an open-cockpit Tiger Moth from the Carrara airport, six km inland from Broadbeach. Ken Keane's Air Adventures (☎ (07) 5598 2643) also has joy fights in a two-passenger seaplane from $45 per person, departing from Fisherman's Wharf.

Adventure Activities Off the Edge (☎ (07) 5530 7699) has two to three-hour mountain bike rides from $25. They also have a range of adventure tour 'challenges' – you can combine a mountain bike ride with a speed-boat ride and a meal for $79, or $149 with a bungy jump or helicopter ride, or do all four for $179. They have discounted deals for backpackers – check with your hostel.

The Clifftop Adventures Co (☎ 018 752 510) offers forward abseiling from $40, and the Indoor Rock Climbing Centre (☎ (07) 5593 6919), at 38 Hutchinson St, West Burleigh, offers unlimited climbing for $10. They also have training courses, are open daily from 10 am to 10 pm, and do pick-ups from some of the hostels on Thursdays.

Bungy jumpers are catered for at Bungee Down Under, on The Spit by Sea World. First-time jumpers pay $69, while for experienced jumpers it's $50. Backpackers pay $49 on Mondays. There's another bunge jump at Cableski World in Runaway Bay; see the Theme Parks section later in this chapter.

You can also go tandem skydiving (☎ (07) 5599 1920) if you have a spare $250, or go for an early morning balloon ride with Balloon Down Under (☎ (07) 5530 3631).

Organised Tours & Cruises
Hinterland Trips Plenty of tour operators offering bus trips into the hinterland. You can

also take a bus trip to the mountains with one of the local bus services – see the Gold Coast Hinterland section for details of these.

Doug Robbins, a keen bushwalker and owner of the Springbrook Mountain Lodge, runs Off The Beaten Track (☎ (07) 5533 5366), offering overnight trips from the Gold Coast to the Springbrook Plateau. These trips are great value: Doug takes two to six people, and the cost, at $40 per person, includes return transport from anywhere on the coast, overnight accommodation, one meal, and a half to full-day bushwalk (depending on the weather and your fitness level). Doug will pick you up in the morning and drop you back on the coast the following morning.

There are several operators offering 4WD trips to the hinterland, including Backtrack 4WD Tours (☎ (07) 5573 5693), Southern Cross 4WD Tours (☎ 1800 067 367 toll free) and Mountain Trek Adventures (☎ (07) 5536 1700). They all have day trips for around $100 for adults and $50 for children, including lunch.

Motorcycle Tours Eagle Harley Tours (☎ (07) 5592 3722) offers tours on the back of a Harley-Davidson. They include a half-hour jaunt ($35), a two-hour ride to Tamborine Mountain ($100) and half-day trips to Springbrook or Byron Bay ($200). They also do the same trips for two people (one on the back and one in a sidecar) these cost 50% more.

Cruises There's a wide variety of cruises on offer at Surfers, including river or canal trips, cruises to South Stradbroke Island and evening dinner cruises. Most cruises depart from the Marina Mirage or Fisherman's Wharf on The Spit in Main Beach, or from the Tiki Village Wharf at the river end of Cavill Ave. Most of the cruise operators offer pick-ups from your accommodation.

Tall Ship Sailing Cruises (☎ (07) 5596 5480) has cruises aboard the *Sir Henry Morgan*, a modern square-rigger, to Sanctuary Cove and South Stradbroke Island. The cruise costs $49 with a steak and seafood lunch or $75 with paragliding as well, and they have discounts for backpackers at $45/69.

Top Cruises (☎ (07) 5543 6354) runs a similar trip on the MV *Rani*, costing $45 for adults, $23 for children and $120 for a family, with lunch included.

Shangri-La Cruises (☎ 07) 5591 1800) has a wide range of cruises on offer including two-hour harbour and canal trips ($24 for adults, $18 for children), a South Stradbroke Island day cruise ($50/28 with lunch), a cruise to Sanctuary Cove with a bus trip to Movie World or Dreamworld ($24/18), and a seafood buffet and cabaret dinner cruise ($55/33).

There are lots of other operators – check with the tourist offices for other cruises.

Festivals

There are a number of major events on the coast. The Magic Millions Summer Carnival, held at the Gold Coast Turf Club on Racecourse Dve in Bundall, three km west from Surfers, in early January, is a 10-day carnival of horse-racing, glamorous social events and thoroughbred sales. In March, the three-day IndyCarnival focuses around the international Indy Car Race and draws huge crowds. Various life-saving carnivals and ironman and ironwoman events are held on the coast during summer; the Surfers Paradise International Triathalon in April is another major sports event.

June sees the Gold Coast International Jazz and Blues Festival held over two days at the Gold Coast International Hotel, and the Gold Coast International Marathon is run in July. Each October, the Tropicarnival Festival is a week-long festival with street parades, concerts, sporting events and other activities.

Places to Stay

Hostels and backpackers' places apart, accommodation prices are extremely variable according to the season. They rise severely during the school holidays and some motels push prices higher over Christ-

mas than at other holiday peaks, although they may not rise at all if there's a cold snap.

All types of accommodation are cheaper outside Surfers.

There are backpackers' hostels in Surfers, Southport, Broadbeach and Coolangatta, and camping and caravan parks all along the coast. You'll find a selection of cheap motels at the southern end of the coast, at places like Mermaid Beach, Palm Beach and Coolangatta.

The holiday flats which are found all along the coast can be better bargains than motels, especially for a group of three or four. In peak seasons especially, flats will be rented on a weekly rather than overnight basis, but don't let that frighten you off. Even if they won't negotiate a daily rate, a decent $225-a-week, two-bedroom flat is still cheaper than two $30-a-night motel rooms, even for just four days.

The tourist information offices can provide you with lists of accommodation in every price bracket, including backpackers' places, but they can't hope to be comprehensive given there are a huge number of possibilities – an estimated 3000 in all.

If you have a vehicle, one of the easiest ways to find a place to stay is simply to cruise along the Gold Coast Hwy or the Esplanade and try a few places that have 'vacancy' signs out.

Getting There & Away

Air The Gold Coast is only a couple of hours by road from the centre of Brisbane but has its own busy airport at Bilinga, just north of Coolangatta.

Ansett and Qantas fly direct from the southern capitals. Standard fares are: Sydney $260, Melbourne $380, Adelaide $422 and Perth $655. Eastwest also flies daily from Albury, Brisbane, Cairns, Hobart and Sydney, while Eastern Australia flies daily from Brisbane ($93) and several New South Wales coastal towns.

Booking numbers for the airlines include Ansett and Eastwest (☎ 13 1300), Qantas (☎ 13 1313) and Eastern Australia (☎ (07) 5538 1188).

Impulse Airlines (bookings through

Gold Coast
Locator Map

0   2   4 km

See Main Beach &
Southport Map

Main Beach

See Surfers Paradise Map

Surfers
Paradise

SOUTH
PACIFIC
OCEAN

Broadbeach

See Broadbeach &
Mermaid Beach Map

Mermaid Beach

Miami

See Burleigh
Heads Map

Burleigh Heads

Palm Beach

Currumbin

See Coolangatta &
Tweed Heads Map

Bilinga

Coolangatta

Tweed
Heads

Fingal Head

NEW SOUTH WALES

Kingscliff

Lake
Coombabah

Gold Coast Hwy

The Broadwater

Nerang River

Pacific Hwy

Tallebudgera Creek

GOLD COAST

Coast to Brisbane ($12), Byron Bay ($18) and Sydney ($65). Greyhound Pioneer Australia has services to Sydney ($73), Byron Bay ($16), Brisbane ($12), and one service a day to Noosa ($25).

Kirklands (☎ (07) 5531 7145) undercuts the bigger operators on some of the main routes into the Gold Coast. They offer discounted services to students, backpackers and YHA members, costing $8.40 to Brisbane and $14.25 to Byron Bay. They also offer fares between Brisbane and Sydney for $64 with unlimited stopovers. For YHA members, they offer a Brisbane-Gold Coast-Byron Bay-Sydney fare for $44.80, with unlimited stopovers in these four places.

The Bus Stop (☎ (07) 5592 5800) at the Surfers Paradise Bus Station acts as the booking agent for Baxways ($20 to Ballina) and Lindsays ($64 to Sydney).

Between Brisbane, Surfers and Coolangatta, Coachtrans (☎ (07) 5538 9944) operates buses almost every half-hour from around 6.40 am to 8.15 pm. The trip from Brisbane to Surfers takes about 1½ hours and just over two hours to Coolangatta, and costs $12 for adults, $9.50 for students and $6 for children. Coachtrans has frequent services from the Brisbane airport to the Gold Coast; the fare is $26/22/13. They also run a shuttle service up the coast to Sanctuary Cove ($3/1.50, adults/children).

Train There's no railway station on the Gold Coast but there are connecting bus services once daily to Murwillumbah (one hour) and Casino (three hours) in northern New South Wales; from there you can take a train to Sydney. There's a Queensland Rail booking office (☎ (07) 5539 9088) in the Cavill Park building on the corner of Beach Rd and the Gold Coast Hwy in Surfers Paradise.

Getting Around

To/From the Airport Coolangatta Airport is the seventh busiest in Australia. Several bus companies run airport shuttle buses. Gold Coast Airport Transit (☎ (07) 5536 6841) from Surfers Paradise meets every Qantas arrival and departure. It costs $8 between the

Ansett) flies from Brisbane to Coolangatta ($97).

Bus Long-distance buses stop at the bus transit centres in Surfers Paradise and Coolangatta – see those sections for details.

The main bus companies and their booking numbers are: McCafferty's (☎ (07) 5538 2700), Kirklands (☎ (07) 5531 7145) and Greyhound Pioneer Australia (☎ 13 2030). Most companies will allow you a free stopover on the Gold Coast if you have a through ticket.

McCafferty's has services from the Gold

airport and Surfers and $4 to Coolangatta, and they will do pick-ups or drop-offs from your accommodation. Airport & Charter Services (☎ (07) 5576 4000) meets all Ansett and Eastwest arrivals and departures, leaving Surfers 75 minutes before takeoff. They do accommodation pick-ups and drop-offs and the one-way fare is $8.

A taxi from the airport will cost around $6 to Coolangatta and around $20 to Surfers Paradise.

Avis, Thrifty, Hertz and Budget all have desks at the airport.

Bus Surfside Buslines (☎ (07) 5536 7666) runs a frequent 24-hour service up and down the Gold Coast Hwy between Southport and Tweed Heads and beyond. You can buy individual fares, get a Day Rover ticket for $8, or buy a weekly one for $26.

Car & Moped Rental There are stacks of car-rental firms along the Gold Coast, particularly in Surfers – pick up any of the free Gold Coast guides or scan the *Yellow Pages*, and see Getting There & Around in the Surfers section for details. All the big companies are represented, plus a host of local operators in the small car and rent-a-wreck categories.

Taxi Ring Regent Taxis (☎ (07) 5588 1234) to book a taxi.

THEME PARKS

There are several major theme parks on the Gold Coast. While they are generally quite expensive, the ticket prices usually cover all rides and shows, so for a full day's entertainment they can be worthwhile and good fun.

Note that the theme parks define 'children' as anyone between four and 13 years of age. Anyone three or younger gets in for free, but anyone 14 or older pays the adult price.

If you don't have your own transport, there are plenty of tour operators and bus companies offering combined or individual trips to the theme parks.

Sea World

On The Spit in Main Beach, Sea World is one of the longest running and most popular theme parks in the country. It started out in 1958 as a water-ski show on the Nerang River, and has grown into a major tourist attraction. It's live 'performances' include dolphin and sea lion shows, a penguin parade, shark-feeding and a water-ski extravaganza, and there are also some great rides here like the corkscrew rollercoaster, a monorail, a locomotive train, a swinging pirate ship, waterslides and toboggan rides, and the latest addition, the Bermuda Triangle.

There are plenty of snack bars, cafes and restaurants here, and souvenir shops galore. Bring lots of spendoolies – Sea World might be great fun, but bargain city it ain't.

The Sea World Helicopters offer four different tours, ranging from a seven-km flight over South Stradbroke Island ($30 per person) to a 60-km flight to the Springbrook Plateau in the hinterland ($150 per person). There is also a water-sports section at Sea World where you can go paragliding, hire jet skis, ride the 'blue banana', and learn to water-ski. Water-sports activities cost extra.

Sea World is open every day from 10 am to 5 pm and admission is $34 for adults and $22 for children.

Movie World

Otherwise known as 'Hollywood on the Gold Coast' Movie World is next to the Warner-Roadshow film production studios on the Pacific Hwy at Oxenford, about 16 km north-west of Surfers. It's a re-creation of the Warner Brothers film studio in Hollywood, and one of the most popular attractions on the coast. You can start the day at 9.30 at 'Breakfast with the Stars', and the rides and attractions start up at 10 am. There are characters from Warner Brothers movies and cartoons wandering around including Bugs Bunny, Yosemite Sam and Tweetie Pie, familiar places like the Daily Planet building, and theme eateries like Willy Wonka's Chocolate Factory & Candy Store and the

Gotham City Cafe, plus the usual array of souvenir shops.

Shows throughout the day include stunt shows, western shoot-outs and performances by trained animals and their trainers, and you can watch classic cartoons, tour the studios and see special effects demos.

Movie World is open daily from 9.30 am to 5 pm. Entry costs $34 for adults and $22 for children and includes 'Batman Adventure – The Ride'.

Dreamworld

Dreamworld, at Coomera on the Pacific Hwy 17 km north of Surfers, is a Disneyland-style creation of 10 areas with different themes including a wildlife sanctuary of Australian animals and birds, the Blue Lagoon aquatic playground, a re-creation of a gold-rush-era town, and a Bavarian village.

Rides include the Thunderbolt (a double-loop rollercoaster), a Gravitron, a raft ride through rapids, roller coasters, water slides, a three-km-long railway, and the latest addition, Wipeout (likened to windsurfing in a washing machine). There's also a giant-screen Imax Theatre which screens films throughout the day.

Dreamworld is open daily from 10 am to 5 pm and costs $34 for adults and $21 for children.

Wet 'n' Wild

Beside the Pacific Hwy at Oxenford, just south of Movie World, Wet 'n' Wild is a fun water-sports park with good swimming pools and great water slides, a one-metre-wave pool, twisters, beach volleyball and other games, and a water-sports stunt team.

Entry costs $17 for adults and $13 for children – kids under three are free. Opening hours vary with the seasons: 10 am to 4 pm in winter; 10 am to 5 pm in summer; 10 am to 9 pm during January.

Wet 'n' Wild also screens 'Dive-In Movies' every Saturday night from September to April (and every night during January) – you get to watch a film while floating on a rubber tube in the wave pool. Ring their info line (☎ (07) 5573 2255) to see what's on.

Cableski World

At Cableski World, 12 km north of Surfers on Pine Ridge Rd in Runaway Bay, near Sanctuary Cove, you can water-ski without a speedboat by being towed around a large network of lakes by overhead cables.

Water-skiing costs $30 for a full-day pass or $17 for a night pass (from 5 to 10 pm), and wetsuit hire is another $8. They also have wind surfers, jet skis and paddle boats for hire. You can also bungy jump here from a crane suspended over the lakes for $68, or $49 for backpackers.

It's open on weekdays from 11 am to 5 pm (till 9 pm Fridays) and weekends from 10 am to 5 pm. From November to April, they stay open till 10 pm most nights.

You can get here on the Sanctuary Cove Shuttle Bus (☎ (07) 5573 3777) which does pick-ups from various places along the coast, or with Baxway Day Tours (☎ (07) 5576 4696) or Coachtrans (☎ (07) 3236 1000).

MAIN BEACH & SOUTHPORT

Sheltered from the ocean by The Spit, Southport was the original town on the Gold Coast but it's now modern, residential and rather nondescript. The built-up area continues north of Southport through Labrador, Anglers Paradise and Runaway Bay to Paradise Point. **Sanctuary Cove**, about 10 km north of Southport on Hope Island, is an up-market resort with a Hyatt hotel, two golf courses, a marina, flats and houses.

Between Southport and Surfers is Main Beach, and beyond that The Spit – a narrow, three-km-long tongue of sand dividing the ocean from the Broadwater. On the Broadwater side of The Spit, **Fisherman's Wharf** is the departure point for most pleasure cruises, and has a pub, restaurant, swimming pool and shops. Across the road on the ocean side is the Sheraton Mirage Gold Coast Resort, while up from Fisherman's Wharf is **Sea World**, a huge aquatic amusement centre (see the Theme Parks section earlier). The beach at the northern end of The Spit is not developed and is good for relatively secluded sunbathing.

GOLD COAST

GOLD COAST

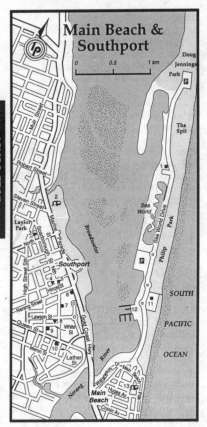

Main Beach & Southport

PLACES TO STAY

1   Sea World Nara Resort
2   Broadwater Tourist Park
9   Trekkers Guest House
10 Gold Coast Backpackers Resort
11 Sheraton Mirage Gold Coast
    Resort
13 Main Beach Caravan Park

PLACES TO EAT

4   The Ecology Shop
5   The Tandoori Place
8   Southport RSL Club

OTHER

3   Southport Transit Centre
6   Skate Biz
7   Southport 6 Cinema Centre
12 Mariners Cove, Marina Mirage &
    Fishermans Wharf

5581 7722), on Main Beach Pde, Main Beach, is a council-run camping park opposite the beach and surrounded by high-rises, with tent sites at $12 and a few powered sites from $14 to $18.

Hostels Southport has one of the nicest hostels on the south coast – the *Trekkers Guest House* (☎ (07) 5591 5616) at 22 White St, about four km north of Surfers. It's in an old house which has been well renovated and furnished, and has all the usual facilities – laundry, kitchens, pool, TV lounge, courtesy bus – and accommodation is in three or four-bed rooms, most with bathroom. The atmosphere is very appealing and the staff organise trips to nightclubs and other events most evenings. The twice-weekly $5 barbecues are also popular. The nightly cost is $14 and doubles are $30.

The *Gold Coast Backpackers Resort* (☎ (07) 5531 2004) is nearby at 44 Queen St. It's a modern, purpose-built hostel but it lacks atmosphere; dorm beds are $12.

Resorts & Hotels There always seems to be a steady stream of stretch limos pulling into the *Sheraton Mirage Gold Coast Resort*, on

Activities

Skate Biz (☎ (07) 5527 0066), in the Southport Mall near the corner of Marine Pde hires out in-line skates with pads and all the gear for $10 for two hours or $20 for 24 hours.

Places to Stay

Camping The *Broadwater Tourist Park* (☎ (07) 5581 7733), off the Gold Coast Hwy in Southport, is a very neat council-run park with good facilities on the banks of the Broadwater River, with tent sites from $14 to $16 and powered sites from $16 to $23.

The *Main Beach Caravan Park* (☎ (07)

Sea World Dve on The Spit in Main Beach. It's probably the best of the Gold Coast's five-star hotels, with over 300 rooms and suites overlooking either the surf beach or the Broadwater River. Standard rooms start from $420 a night, suites from $800 and the penthouses and villas range from $800 to $1000. There's a huge boat marina across on the other side of The Spit.

Further up The Spit, the *Sea World Nara Resort* (☎ (07) 5591 1000 or toll-free 1800 074 448) is very popular with families and has 400 rooms ranging from $195 to $225 a double, which includes entry to Sea World. The resort is linked to Sea World by monorail.

Places to Eat
Southport The *RSL Club*, near the Trekkers Guest House on the corner of Scarborough and White Sts, has good-value roasts and casseroles for $4 to $5. One km north, *The Ecology Shop*, at 116 Scarborough St, is a good health-food shop with salads, sandwiches and juices. Across the road at No 119, *The Tandoori Place* is a popular BYO Indian restaurant with set-menu lunches for $9.95, mains around $10 and evening banquet menus from $17 to $27.

Main Beach There are three adjacent waterside complexes on The Spit – Mariner's Cove, the Marina Mirage and Fisherman's Wharf. Between them they have a huge range of eateries offering something for just about everyone. There are also a couple of good live music venues out here – see the Entertainment section for details.

At Mariner's Cove, *Friday's* is a tavern/bar with a pleasant waterside deck, bistro meals in the $10 to $15 range and specials like T-bone and salad ($9.95) and chicken schnitzel burgers ($6.95). On Sunday nights they have an all-you-can-eat barbecue at $13.95 per person. *Zorba's Greek Tavern* has banquet menus from $30 per person and main courses in the $17 to $23 range, and live music and belly dancing from Thursday to Sunday nights. You can also break plates on the dance floor here – they cost $12 a dozen. The *British Arms* is an English-style

tavern with Guinness, Newcastle Brown and Bass beer on tap, and classic meals like pork pies and salad, bangers and mash, or rabbit & bacon pie. Wednesday is 'soup and pie night' ($10), Sundays you can get a good old roast with Yorkshire pudd ($12.50). The *Barefoot Bar & Grill* is a casual seafood bistro where you can have fish & chips for $6; *Grumpy's Wharf* upstairs is a seafood restaurant with lunch deals at $15 for two courses or $19.90 for three courses.

The Marina Mirage has more up-market eateries. *La Mex* is a Tex/Mex seafood and steak restaurant with an identity crisis and all-you-can-eat lunch buffets for $5.95, and dinner mains in the $17 range. The award-winning *Omero Brothers Seafood Restaurant* has good seafood with mains from $15. They also offer two courses with coffee at $18.90 for lunch or $26.90 for dinner. The *Eat Street Food Hall* is an excellent up-market food hall with a wide range of choices.

The Fisherman's Wharf complex is more casual and downmarket, with a family-style bistro, a schooner bar, a pub and a seafood restaurant.

Entertainment
Live Music There's usually something happening at Mariner's Cove or Fisherman's Wharf on The Spit. *Friday's* is a popular spot for a drink and has DJ music from Thursday to Sunday nights till 1 am and live music on Sunday arvos, and the *British Arms* has live musos on Friday, Saturday and Sunday nights. Fisherman's Wharf is also popular on a Sunday afternoon, with live bands in the outdoor area.

Cinemas The Southport 6 Cinema Centre (☎ (07) 5531 2200) in Scarborough St has six cinemas screening latest releases.

Getting There & Away
Long-distance buses stop at the Southport Transit Centre in Scarborough St.

SOUTH STRADBROKE ISLAND
This narrow, 20-km-long sandy island is

GOLD COAST

GOLD COAST

The charming Surfers Paradise skyline

separated from the northern end of The Spit by a 200-metre-wide channel. The island is an undeveloped environmental park, with a handful of holiday houses, a yacht club, four council-run camping grounds and several low-key resorts. There are no developed walking trails, but you can explore the island on foot and there are some great beaches which are particularly popular with surfers. It has good breaks all the way up the east coast, picks up a bit more swell than the southern breaks and is much less crowded. Experienced surfers can paddle across to the island from the northern end of The Spit, but there's a signboard here warning of the dangers of doing so. The rip is strong, and it's often hard for passing boats to see or avoid paddlers – never try this alone and make sure you allow for the rip. If you haven't done the paddle before, it's worth waiting until someone who has comes along. Watch what they do, or better still, paddle across with them.

Contact the Department of Environment & Heritage (☎ (07) 5577 3555) if you want more information on the island.

Places to Stay

Two-thirds of the way up the island on the west coast, the *South Stradbroke Island Resort* (☎ (07) 5577 3311) has two restaurants, tennis courts, a pool and spa and 40 Polynesian-style cabins starting from $70 a double.

Getting There & Away

The South Stradbroke Island Express ferry service leaves from the Runaway Bay Marina at the north end of the Gold Coast every day at 10.30 am and 4.30 pm; the return fare is $20.

Several tour operators also offer cruises up the Broadwater to the island.

SURFERS PARADISE

The centre of the Gold Coast is a real high-rise jungle; in fact there is such a skyscraper conglomeration that in the afternoon, much of the beach is in shadow! Still, people pack in for the lights, activities, nightlife, shopping, restaurants, attractions and that strip of ocean sand.

Surfers has come a long way since 1936 when there was just the brand-new Surfers Paradise Hotel, a little hideaway nine km from Southport. The hotel has now been swallowed up by a shopping/eating complex called the Paradise Centre. Yet, despite all the changes and growth, at most times of the year you may not have to go very far north or south to find a relatively open, quiet, sunny beach.

Cavill Ave, with a pedestrian mall at its beach end, is the heart of Surfers. **Ripley's Believe It or Not**, just off the mall, is an odditorium with hundreds of fairly bizarre exhibits; it's open daily and costs $9.

The Gold Coast Hwy runs right through Surfers, only one block back from the beach. It takes the southbound traffic, while Remembrance Dve and Ferny Ave, a further block back from the beach, take the north-bound traffic. Another block back is the looping Nerang River. The Surfers Paradise rich and famous live around the surrounding canals.

Information

Tourist Information The Gold Coast Tourism Bureau (☎ (07) 5538 4419), on Cavill Ave Mall in the heart of Surfers Paradise, is open from 8 am to 5 pm Monday to Friday, 9 am to 5 pm Saturday and 9 am to 3.30 pm Sunday.

The Surfers Paradise Bus Station, on the corner of Beach and Cambridge Rds, is where you'll arrive if you're coming by bus. Inside the terminal are the bus companies' booking desks, a cafeteria, and an accommo-dation-booking desk.

In Transit (☎ (07) 5592 2911) can book you into one of the five hostels it represents, or, if you don't want to stay in a hostel, Jane can recommend a good range of alternatives. There are also left-luggage lockers in the station, costing $3 a day.

See the start of this chapter for details of bus services to/from here.

Post The new Surfers Paradise post office is in the Paradise Centre, off the Cavill Ave Mall. It's open on weekdays from 9 am to 5.30 pm and Saturdays from 9 am to 1 pm.

Money American Express (☎ (07) 5538 7588) has an office at 21 Cavill Ave which is open on weekdays from 8.30 am to 5.30 pm and on Saturdays from 9 am to noon. Thomas Cook (☎ (07) 5531 7770) has a foreign currency exchange office nearby in Cavill Ave near the Gold Coast Hwy corner, which is open weekdays from 8.30 am to 9 pm and weekends from 9 am to 9 pm.

Books Hooked on Books, in the Paradise Centre, has a good range.

Organised Tours & Activities
See the start of this chapter for details of some of the tours, cruises and activities on offer here.

Places to Stay
Hostels The most impressive of the hostels here is the *Surfers Paradise Backpackers Resort* (☎ (07) 5592 4677), at 2835 Gold Coast Hwy, about one km south of the centre. It's clean and modern and has good facilities including a pool, a small gym and basement parking. There are two sections, one with four-bed dorms, and the other with excellent self-contained apartments, mostly accom-modating four or five people in two bedrooms. A dorm or unit bed costs $14, doubles are $32. The hostel also runs tours to various places.

A block south of the bus stop, at 40 Whelan St, is the friendly and relaxed *Surfers Central Backpackers* (☎ (07) 5538 4344) which has bunk rooms and a few doubles. There are two sections: one has 18 units (with private bathrooms) taking up to four people, the other has larger dorms. The communal kitchen is small, but there's a good pool with plenty of space for sunbath-ing and outdoor eating. Dorm beds cost $14, doubles $30.

At 18 Whelan St, *Couple O' Days Accom-modation* (☎ (07) 5592 4200) is a converted old apartment block, and looks a bit worn around the edges these days. Dorm beds here are $10.

North of the town centre, at 3323 Gold Coast Hwy, *Surf & Sun Backpackers* (☎ (07) 5592 2363) is a converted motel with four-bed units with private bathroom, TV and fridge. It's a good place if you're in party mode. There's a pool, and this is the closest hostel to the beach. Dorm beds are $14.

Surfers' latest addition to the hostel scene is the 100-bed *Cheers Backpackers* (☎ (07) 5531 6539) at 8 Pine Ave. It's well set up with a good pool, a garden and large barbecue courtyard. Four to six-bed dorms cost $12 to $14, doubles and twins $28. Cheers is fairly party-oriented, with video nights and vouchers for the nightclubs, many of which are within staggering distance of here.

Motels If you're after a motel, the *Silver Sands Motel* (☎ (07) 5538 6041), at 2985 Gold Coast Hwy, is a good option. The rooms have been attractively refurbished and there's a small pool, a barbecue and parking. Singles/doubles range from $40/50 to $50/60, peaking at $90 during Christmas. Close by at No 2965, the *Admiral Motor Inn* (☎ (07) 5539 8759) has rooms from $50.

The *Delilah Motel* (☎ (07) 5538 1722), on the corner of Ferny and Cypress Aves, has rooms from $40/45 for singles/doubles.

Holiday Apartments There are hundreds upon hundreds of holiday apartments and flats to choose from here. The following places should give you an idea of the range and type of places available. Many of these places have a two-night minimum stay, and a seven-night minimum in the peak holiday seasons.

At 24-30 Trickett St, the *Trickett Gardens Holiday Inn* (☎ (07) 5539 0988) is a pleasant place to stay. It's a small low-rise block of 33 refurbished apartments with a good pool, and is well located in a (relatively) quiet street but still close to the action. One-bedroom apartments range from $80 to $108 a night, two-bedroom apartments from $88 to $136.

The *Anchor Inn Holiday Apartments* (☎ (07) 5592 0914), at 27 Whelan St, are another good option. It's a pleasant block of two-bedroom apartments set around a leafy courtyard with a pool, in a quiet street. The units sleep up to four people and range from $60 to $90 a night. In the next block at 22-24 Leonard Ave, the *Candle Light Apartments*

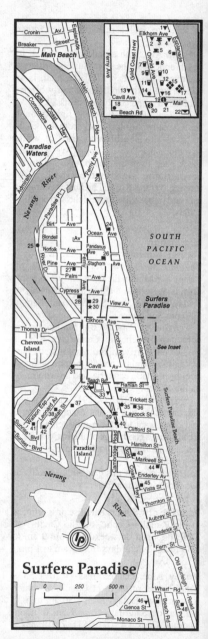

Surfers Paradise

SOUTH PACIFIC OCEAN

PLACES TO STAY

6 The Sands
8 Diamonds Resort & Santa Fe Gold Nightclub
23 Pacific Point Apartments
24 Surf & Sun Backpackers
26 Gold Coast International Hotel
27 Cheers Backpackers
28 Delilah Motel
29 Quarterdeck Apartments
36 Trickett Gardens Holiday Inn
37 Anchor Inn Holiday Apartments
38 Surfers Central Backpackers
41 Candle Light Apartments
42 Couple O' Days Accommodation
43 Silver Sands Motel
44 Villas De La Mar
45 Admiral Motor Inn
47 Surfers Paradise Backpackers Resort
48 Warringa Surf Units

PLACES TO EAT

1 The Chateau
2 The Latin Quarter
3 Beachside Cafe
4 Montmartre French Patisserie
5 The Artist's Cafe
13 Bavarian Steakhouse
16 Shell Bar
21 Charlie's, Tamari & Juke Malone
33 Bunga Raya, La Rustica, La Paella, Maharani & C'Est Paris
39 Global Cafe
46 New Mexico

OTHER

7 The Tunnel Nightclub
9 Fever Nightclub
10 Cocktails & Dreams & The Party Nightclubs
11 The Avenue & The Penthouse Nightclubs
12 Crazy Horse Nightclub
14 American Express Office
15 The Mark
17 Raptis Plaza
18 Ansett Airlines
19 Gold Coast Tourism Bureau
20 Thomas Cook Foreign Exchange Office
22 Paradise Centre & Post Office
25 Budd's Beach Water Sportz
30 Police
31 Tiki Village Wharf
32 Surfers Paradise Bus Station
34 Surfers Blades
35 Qantas Airlines
40 Hoyts Cinema Centre Surfers Paradise

GOLD COAST

(☎ (07) 5538 1277) is a neat block of simple units that sleep four to six people and start from $50 a night.

Diamonds Resort (☎ (07) 5570 1011) is a small, refurbished budget resort in the heart of Surfers at 19 Orchid Ave, with motel-style units from $55 to $85, one-bedroom apartments from $75 to $120, and one three-bedroom penthouse from $180 to $350.

An excellent mid-range option is *Villas De La Mar* (☎ (07) 5592 6644), on the corner of Northcliffe Tce and Markwell Ave. It's a new three-storey complex of up-market Mediterranean-styled villas. Two-bedroom units are $120 a night for up to four people, three-bedroom units are $145 for up to six.

The Sands (☎ (07) 5539 8433), a large and long-established waterfront complex, at 40 The Esplanade, has one-bedroom flats from $60 to $100 a night (from $100 to $115 with ocean views), and two-bedroom flats from $120 to $165 a night.

The *Quarterdeck Apartments* (☎ (07) 5592 2200 or toll-free 1800 635 235), at 3263 Gold Coast Hwy, is a high-rise that was built in 1980 and has comfortable one-bedroom apartments from $70 to $100 a night, plus an indoor pool and sauna and a larger outdoor pool.

Pacific Point Apartments (☎ (07) 5531 7120) is a nine-storey beachfront block at 3468 Main Beach Pde, with one-bedroom apartments from $70 to $110 and two-bedroom apartments from $85 to $130.

South of the centre, *Warringa Surf* (☎ (07) 5570 2466), at 219 Surf Pde, has self-contained units from $55 for one bedroom or from $70 for two bedroom.

Hotels The *Gold Coast International Hotel* (☎ (07) 5592 1200) on the corner of the Gold Coast Hwy and Staghorn Ave has standard rooms from $185 a night, or $205 with ocean views. Suites start from $350.

Places to Eat

There are plenty of choices in and around the Cavill Ave Mall. In the centre of the mall, *Charlie's* is open 24 hours a day and has breakfasts from $2.50 for a Danish pastry to $5.90 for pancakes, maple syrup, bacon & eggs; burgers from $5 to $10; sandwiches from $3; and other mains from $9 to $12. Next door, *Tamari* is a traditional Italian bistro with pizzas and pastas from $9.50 and other mains from $14 to $17. On the other side of Charlie's, *Juke Malone's* is an American-style burger joint with a shiny chrome and red vinyl décor and individual jukeboxes – very glitzy, very Surfers. They do good burgers, pancakes, open sandwiches, and mains like seafood gumbo ($7.95) and chilli con carne ($10.95).

Upstairs in the Paradise Centre just off the mall, *The Picnic Place* is a food court with pizzas and pastas, salads and juices, burgers and sangers, Chinese and Japanese, French pastries and Thai tucker. Most meals are in the $4 to $7 region.

On the corner of Cavill and Orchid Aves, the busy *Shell Bar* offers good-value snacks and meals. Breakfasts for $6 include juice, one of five hot dishes, toast and tea or coffee.

With a much-photographed replica of Michelangelo's David in the centre, the L-shaped Raptis Plaza Arcade off Cavill Ave has a good cross-section of budget eateries. *Muffin Break* has huge and delicious muffins and good coffee. *Sumo* is a tiny Japanese takeaway with dishes from $4.50 to $6.50. *Mr Wong* and the *Saigon* both have all-you-can-eat Chinese and Vietnamese food deals from $3, *Boonchu* has cheap Thai food, and *Pure & Natural* does fresh salads and juices.

On the corner of Cavill Ave and the inland side of the Gold Coast Hwy, the very popular *Bavarian Steakhouse* has straightforward dishes such as steak & chips, and also a soup, pasta and salad buffet bar for $10 at lunch time and $13 at night.

Orchid Ave also has some good eateries. In The Mark shopping complex, at shop 38, *Sukho Thai* is a small place with good Thai food; mains range from $10 to $14. Two shops south is the excellent and popular *Sweetheart's*, which offers healthy rolls, burgers, salads and juices. It's open daily from 8.30 am to 8 pm. Near the north end of Orchid Ave, *The Artists Cafe* is a casual place with outdoor tables; it serves breakfasts, sandwiches and snacks.

Around the corner in Elkhorn Ave, *The Latin Quarter* is a great little BYO Italian bistro with a good atmosphere, pastas from $10 to $14 and main courses like roast duckling au grappa or scaloppine al funghi from $15 to $18. Recommended for a splurge.

Further along Elkhorn Ave, the *Beachside Cafe* has a good breakfast deal – for $5.50 you get OJ, cereal, bacon & eggs, and tea or coffee. It is open 24 hours and serves the usual fast foods, including burgers, sandwiches and kebabs. On the corner of Elkhorn Ave and the Esplanade, the *Montmartre French Patisserie* is good for breakfasts and lunches. On the adjacent corner, *The Chateau* has an all-you-can-eat breakfast buffet for $8.

On the Gold Coast Hwy, in the block south of Beach Rd, there are six restaurants side-by-side, and you can choose from Malaysian, French, Spanish, Italian and Indian food. At No 3118, *La Rustica* is a small and popular Italian bistro with pastas and pizzas from $9 to $12 and veal and beef dishes at $16.50. *C'est Paris* is a stylish French restaurant with main meals in the $16 to $19 range. At No 3114, *La Paella* is a new Spanish restaurant where you can have tapas (six different dishes, for $10.50), paella or zarzuela ($16.50 per person), or other mains in the $14 to $18 range. *Maharani*, at No 3120, has Indian food with mains from $10 to $14, set-menu banquets from $12 per person and $9.95 lunches. And on the Trickett St corner is *Bunga Raya* with Malaysian dishes in the $10 to $14 range.

A block further south, the *Global Cafe* at

No 3070 is a tiny, hip, European-style cafe with great coffee, cakes and pastries.

Further south again is *New Mexico*, on the corner of the highway and Genoa St opposite the Surfers Paradise Backpackers Resort. It opens nightly for dinner with an all-you-can-eat buffet for $9.90, steaks also at $9.90, and margaritas and sangria. This place is popular with backpackers.

Entertainment

Entertainment is what it's all about on the Gold Coast. There are more than 30 night-clubs around Surfers alone, as well as the Conrad Jupiter's Casino at Broadbeach, live-music venues, plenty of cinemas, and even a cultural centre.

Nightclubs & Live Music Orchid Ave is the main nightclub strip in Surfers, and a stroll down here will reveal an abundance of flashing lights, club touts, and beckoning darkened doorways. Fun on tap.

Some places have reasonably strict dress codes. Lots of the nightclubs give away free entry passes, both at their doors and on the streets, and most of the backpackers' hostels organise nights out at clubs, with cheap drink nights and free entry.

One of the most popular backpackers' nightclubs is *Cocktails & Dreams*, in The Mark shopping complex off Orchid Ave. They have different themes here most week nights; party games on Mondays, flares, funksters and 1970s music on Tuesdays, toga parties and slave auctions on Wednesdays, and 'man-o-man' contests on Thursdays. Fridays to Sundays are theme-free, party-hard nights. Entry costs $5, although free admission cards are available through most of the hostels. Downstairs here, *The Party* is another fairly wild place with live bands, drinks deals and lots of backpackers.

The Penthouse, near the Cavill Ave corner, has four floors of nightlife with a piano bar, a pool hall, a showroom and a disco. It is open nightly till 5 am; entry costs $7 on Fridays and Saturdays. Nearby, *The Avenue* is a restaurant by day and a saloon bar by night – it stays open until 2 am during the

week and 5 am on weekends. At 18 Orchid Ave, *Fever Nightclub* is a fairly sophisticated 'over-25s' club with dress regulations. It is open Wednesday to Sunday nights till 5 am; entry costs $5. Moving on up the street, *The Tunnel* is a funky and popular basement club with hip hop and funk on Tuesdays, reggae on Wednesdays, club hits from the 1970s and '80s on Thursdays and techno dance music on Friday, Saturday and Sunday nights. It is open till 5 am; entry costs $5 to $7.

There are a couple of clubs of a more dubious nature across the road. *Santa Fe Gold* at 19 Orchid Ave has scantily clad women dancing on table tops and a separate sports bar that screens everything from golf tips to female mud wrestling – well, that's what the bloke on the door told me, anyway. Further south, *Crazy Horse* features a 'nude catwalk revue' with male and female strippers – an up-market strip joint, if there is such a thing.

The waterside complexes on The Spit at Main Beach also include some good live music venues – see that section earlier. The long-running *Playroom*, on the Gold Coast Hwy in Tallebudgera, often has big-name bands.

Bars The *Shooters Bar* upstairs in The Mark complex off Orchid Ave is a popular American-style saloon with pool tables, big-screen videos and occasional live entertainment. It is open until 3 am, and has bar meals and snacks in the $4 to $8 range.

Cinemas The Hoyts Cinema Centre Surfers Paradise (☎ (07) 5570 3355), on the corner of Gold Coast Hwy and Gifford St, has three cinemas showing mainstream movies. Tickets are $7.50. In the cinema complex, *Pancakes in Paradise* has a movie and meal deal which is good value at $9.90 for adults or $7.90 for students and kids.

Cabaret A popular cabaret restaurant is *Dracula's* (☎ (07) 5575 1000), on Hooker Blvd in Broadbeach. Dracula's offers a three-course meal served by waiters and waitresses who throw themselves into the

GOLD COAST

GOLD COAST

Dracula theme. The night climaxes in a disco. The dinner-and-show costs $35 per person from Tuesday to Friday and $45 on Saturdays.

Cultural Centre After all this, it may be a relief to know that there is the *Gold Coast Arts Centre* (☎ (07) 5581 6500), beside the Nerang River at 135 Bundall Rd. The centre has a 1200-seat theatre which hosts live productions and screens art-house movies, a restaurant and bar, and incorporates the Gold Coast Art Gallery which is open on weekdays from 10 am to 5 pm and weekends from 1 to 5 pm. Ring the box office to see what's on while you're in town.

Things to Buy
Surfers Paradise could appropriately be renamed Shoppers Paradise. There are shops galore here, and you'll probably see more people walking around clutching shopping bags than surfboards or towels.

The Gold Coast Hwy between Cavill Ave and Elkhorn Ave is literally wall to wall with shops (and a few eateries), and if you're in the market for opals, duty-free goods, tacky souvenirs, Australiana, clothing, travel goods or jewellery, this is the area to head for. Just don't expect any bargains.

Getting Around
Car, Bicycle & Moped Rental Red Back Rentals (☎ (07) 5592 1655), at 3 Beach Rd opposite the Bus Station, hires out mountain bikes ($20 a day), mopeds (from $35 to $55 a day) and a range of cars starting from $35 a day for a Suzuki Squirt, $60 a day for a Suzuki Sierra, and $95 a day for a Ford Capri convertible. Other cheapies include Rent-a-Bomb (☎ (07) 5538 8222), at 8 Beach Rd, and Costless (☎ (07) 5592 4499) and Airport Rent-a-Car (☎ (07) 5538 0700), both of which have agents inside the Bus Station.

Green Bicycle Rentals (☎ 018 766 880) has good mountain bikes from $18 a day and will deliver a bike to wherever you're staying. Surfers Blades (☎ (07) 5538 3483) at Shop 1, 40 Hanlan St, has mountain bikes from $15 a day; they also rent out in-line

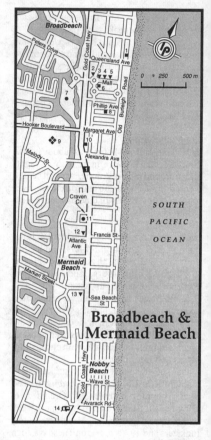

skates ($20 a day), surfboards, boogie boards, fishing gear and lots of other stuff.

BROADBEACH & MERMAID BEACH
Broadbeach has become a popular alternative to the hustle and bustle of Surfers, and is probably a bit less hectic and more relaxed. The beaches here are just as good and less crowded, there are some good restaurants and cafes, and of course you're within striking distance of the casino.

Between the Gold Coast Hwy and the canals, the **Cascade Gardens** is a lovely slice of nature in the midst of this concrete

PLACES TO STAY

1 King Tide Beachfront Apartments
6 Pan Pacific Hotel
8 Broadbeach Central Apartments
10 Big Backpackers
14 Miami Caravan Park

PLACES TO EAT

2 Cha Cha & Double Eight Chinese Restaurant
3 Thana Thai & Da Carlo
4 House of India
5 Kokoz Nightclub & Cafe Affair
12 Lebanese Palace & The Great Khan
13 Mandarin Court & Thai Siam

OTHER

7 Conrad Jupiter's Casino & Hotel
9 Pacific Fair Shopping Centre
11 Mermaid 5 Cinemas

jungle. Shady lawns, palm trees, eucalypts, a kid's playground, picnic tables and barbecues – you could almost forget you're on the Gold Coast.

Conrad Jupiter's Casino

On the inland side of the Gold Coast Hwy at Broadbeach, the Conrad Jupiter's Casino is a Gold Coast landmark, it was Queensland's first legal casino.

The casino is open 24 hours a day and has more than 100 gaming tables, including blackjack, roulette, two-up and craps, as well as hundreds of poker machines.

Admission is free but you have to be over 18 years of age, and dress codes of 'neat casual' before 6 pm and 'smart casual' after 6 pm apply – basically, long socks if you're wearing shorts, no T-shirts, no ripped or torn jeans. In other words, try to look like you've got lots of money to lose.

The complex also includes a five-star hotel (see Places to Stay), the Showroom with live floor shows, and the up-market Fortunes nightclub.

Places to Stay

Camping To the south, the *Miami Caravan Park* (☎ (07) 5572 7533), at 2200 Gold Coast Hwy, charges $13.50 for tent sites and $25 for on-site units.

Hostels At 2623 Gold Coast Hwy, the *Big Backpackers* (☎ (07) 5538 4633) certainly lives up to its name – it's so big even the staff get lost. This converted nursing home is clean and spacious but it feels a bit clinical. Dorm beds are around $14, doubles with showers are from $28. There are cheaper rates for longer stays.

Motels & Holiday Units The *King Tide Beachfront Apartments* (☎ (07) 5531 7124) are in a great spot at 136 Old Burleigh Rd. I stayed in these apartments with my family when I was about 13 (which was a long time ago) and they haven't changed much since then. It's a U-shaped, three-storey block of clean and comfortable self-contained units with a pool; the shops and casino are nearby, and the beach is right across the road. One-bedroom units start from $70 a night, two-bedroom units from $100, and the three-bedroom units are rented weekly and range from $560 to $900 a week.

Also worthwhile is *Broadbeach Central Apartments* (☎ (07) 5592 6322), at 18 Phillip Ave, a small and cheerful block of self-contained apartments with a good pool. One-bedroom units range from $60 to $95, two-bedroom units from $80 to $125 and three-bedroom units from $100 to $150.

There are quite a few good cheap motels along the Gold Coast Hwy at Mermaid Beach. The *Red Emu Motel* (☎ (07) 5575 2748), at No 2583, has doubles from $28 in the low season. The *Mermaid Beach Motel* (☎ (07) 5575 1577), at No 2395, is good value with clean units from $25, and, at No 2267, the small *Van Diemen Motel* (☎ (07) 5572 7611) has units from $28 a night.

Hotels If you want to stay at the casino, *Conrad Jupiter's Hotel* (☎ (07) 5592 8130 or toll-free 1800 074 344) is a 600-room hotel operated by Hilton Hotels, offering

GOLD COAST

standard rooms from $210 and suites from $400 to $925. The hotel's facilities are an abbreviated version of the twelve days of Christmas – six restaurants, four tennis courts, three pools, two spas, and a gym. No mention of partridges in a pear tree.

Broadbeach's other big five-star is the *Pan Pacific Hotel* (☎ (07) 5592 2250), on the other side of the highway at 81 Surf Pde. A monorail runs from the third floor of the hotel across to the casino. Standard rooms start from $200, suites from $500.

Places to Eat

Broadbeach Broadbeach has a good selection of eateries along Victoria Ave and the adjoining mall. *Cha Cha*, on the corner of Surf Ave and Victoria Ave, is a simple little Japanese tepanyaki eatery run by a young Japanese couple. It's great value – most dishes, like my grilled chicken teriyaki with rice, are $6 to $7. Next door, the very straightforward *Double Eight Chinese Restaurant* specialises in Sichuan cuisine, with main courses around $8.

There are more restaurants, cafes and bars further east along the mall. On the opposite corner, *Thana Thai* is a BYO Thai restaurant with outdoor tables, mains from $10 to $14 and banquets at $18, $22 and $27 per person. Next door, the up-market *Da Carlo* is a pricey Italian bistro. Further along the mall at the front of the Niecon Plaza arcade, *Cafe Affair* is a stylish Mediterranean cafe and bar which is open from 7 am till late. Try their raspberry pancakes and cream ($5.80) for a breakfast with a difference. They also have wood-fired-oven pizzas ($12) and stir-fries, pastas, focaccias and open sandwiches ranging from $9 to $17. Also in the mall, the *House of India* has mains from $10 to $14.

Mermaid Beach There are more eateries south along the highway at Mermaid Beach. At 2484 Gold Coast Hwy, the *Lebanese Palace* is an up-market Lebanese restaurant with belly dancing on Friday and Saturday nights. They have a 12-dish set menu at $25 per person, or you can order off the menu with mains in the $11 to $17 range. *The*

Great Khan, at No 2488, is a Mongolian barbecue restaurant with banquet menus at $16 for lunch or $18 for dinner. You get to fill a bowl with your choice of ingredients, which are then cooked for you on a circular hotplate that looks like a Mongolian warrior's shield. The trick is not to get carried away and squeeze everything into one bowl – less is more, as they say, and you can go back as many times as you like. You also get soups, appetisers, desserts and fruit.

A couple of blocks south at No 2374, *Mandarin Court* is a plush licensed Chinese restaurant with most mains around $8 – seafood dishes are more expensive. They also open for yum cha every day at 9 am. Next door, *Thai Siam* has good MSG-free Thai food with most mains under $10.

Entertainment

At 2514 Gold Coast Hwy, the Mermaid 5 Cinemas (☎ 11 621) has five cinemas screening mainstream releases.

BURLEIGH HEADS

In the centre of the Gold Coast coastal strip, Burleigh Heads is perhaps best known as the home of one of Australia's legendary surfing breaks. Burleigh is a classic right-hand point break, famous for its fast and deep barrel rides. This definitely isn't a break for beginners – the shore is lined with vicious black rocks and there is often a strong rip, and if you make it out the back you'll find out that most of the locals have a definite attitude problem. If you're just starting out, you'll have much more fun around at one of the hundreds of beach breaks that stretch along the coast.

The **Burleigh Heads National Park**, on the northern side of the mouth of Tallebudgera Creek, is a small but diverse forest reserve with walking trails around the rocky headland, a lookout and picnic area. On the Gold Coast Hwy at the entrance to the park, there's a Queensland National Parks & Wildlife Service (QNP&WS) information centre (☎ (07) 5535 3032), a useful place to call in if you're planning to visit some of the area's national parks. It's open daily.

There are three excellent wildlife sanctuaries in this area. **Fleay's Wildlife Park**, just two km back along the Tallebudgera Creek in West Burleigh, has an excellent collection of native wildlife and four km of walking tracks through mangroves and rainforest. The platypus was first bred in captivity here. The centre is open daily from 9 am to 5 pm and costs $9 for adults, $4 for children and $25 for a family of up to six.

Back towards the coast, flocks of technicoloured lorikeets and other birds flutter in for morning and afternoon feeds at the **Currumbin Sanctuary**. Within the large bushland park there are also tree kangaroos, koalas, emus and lots more Australian fauna, plus a two-km miniature railway, an Australian botanical garden and wildlife presentations. The extremely popular lorikeet-feeding sessions are held between 8 and 9.30 am and 4 and 5 pm, and there are various other activities throughout the day. The sanctuary is half a km south of

Currumbin Creek, on both sides of the Gold Coast Hwy; open daily from 8 am to 5 pm, and entry costs $14 for adults, $8 for children and $38 for a family. If you're travelling by the Surfside bus, get off at stop No 20.

See the following Currumbin Valley section for details of Olson's Bird Gardens.

Currumbin Valley
About four km south of Burleigh Heads, the Currumbin Creek Rd runs inland along the southern side of the Currumbin Creek into the Currumbin Valley, a green pocket of hinterland area with fruit orchards, farmlets, nurseries and gardens.

About eight km inland from the coast, **Olson's Bird Gardens** is an attractive subtropical garden with a collection of exotic birds in enclosures, although the gardens are somewhat more impressive than the aviaries. The gardens are open every day from 9 am to 5 pm and cost $9.

Further along, the **Currumbin Rockpool** is a popular swimming hole with picnic tables and barbecues and a kiosk and Devonshire tea rooms opposite.

At the end of the road, about 17 km inland, is the tropical landscape of the **Mt Cougal National Park**, adjoining the Springbrook Plateau. From the car park at the base of the mountain, walking trails lead to Cougal Cascades (250 metres), the Mountain Pool (400 metres) and a disused sawmill (800 metres).

Places to Stay
Camping The well-located *Burleigh Beach Tourist Park* (☎ (07) 5581 7755), set back from Goodwin Tce, is a good council-run park with tent sites from $12 to $14 and powered sites from $14 to $18.

One km south the *Tallebudgera Creek Caravan Park* (☎ (07) 5581 7700), on the southern banks of the creek and the inland side of the Gold Coast Hwy, is another council-run park with the same prices and good facilities, although not much shade.

Motels In Burleigh Heads, the *Casino Motel* (☎ (07) 5535 7133), at 1761 Gold Coast Hwy, has rooms from $35 a double.

Rainbow lorikeets are a feature of the Currumbin Sanctuary

GOLD COAST

GOLD COAST

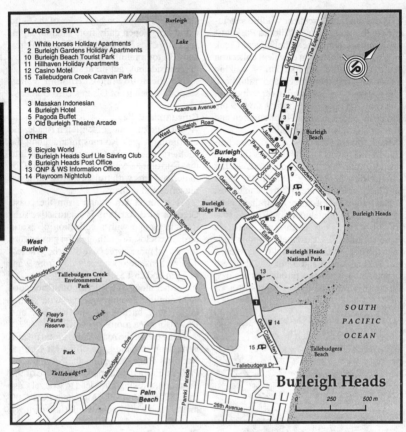

PLACES TO STAY
1 White Horses Holiday Apartments
2 Burleigh Gardens Holiday Apartments
10 Burleigh Beach Tourist Park
11 Hillhaven Holiday Apartments
12 Casino Motel
15 Tallebudgera Creek Caravan Park

PLACES TO EAT
3 Masakan Indonesian
4 Burleigh Hotel
5 Pagoda Buffet
9 Old Burleigh Theatre Arcade

OTHER
6 Bicycle World
7 Burleigh Heads Surf Life Saving Club
8 Burleigh Heads Post Office
13 QNP & WS Information Office
14 Playroom Nightclub

Burleigh Heads

SOUTH PACIFIC OCEAN

0   250   500 m

Further south in Palm Beach, there are dozens more budget motels along the highway. They include the *Cheshire Cat Motel* (☎ (07) 5534 2017), at 1005 Gold Coast Hwy, with units from $20/30 for singles/doubles, and the *Motel Moana* (☎ (07) 5535 1131), at 1461 Gold Coast Hwy, with units from $30. Both are close to the beach, and both adjust their tariffs according to demand, which means prices go up in winter and during Christmas.

Holiday Units The *Hillhaven Holiday Apartments* (☎ (07) 5535 1055,) at 2 Goodwin Tce, have the prime position in Burleigh, high on the headland with great views along the coast all the way to Surfers. It's a 10-storey apartment building that was built in the mid-1960s, and has oldish but comfortable two-bedroom units starting from $80 a night and three-bedroom units from $115 a night. Rates are cheaper by the week.

The *Burleigh Gardens Holiday Apartments* (☎ (07) 5576 3955), at 1849 Gold Coast Hwy, is a well-kept two-storey block of units. One-bedroom units range from $70 to $110 a night, and two-bedroom units cost from $105 to $145 a night.

The *White Horses Holiday Apartments* (☎ (07) 5535 1626), at 50-60 The Esplanade, is a three-storey block of two-bedroom holiday units. They're a bit tatty, but comfortable enough and cheap at $50 a night, although they're usually let out weekly from $200 a week.

Places to Eat

The *Masakan Indonesia*, at 1837 Gold Coast Hwy, has good Indonesian dishes with mains from $8 to $12. Across the road, the *Pagoda Buffet* has all-you-can-eat Asian buffets at $5.50 for lunch and $8.50 for dinner.

Around the corner, facing the beach, the Burleigh Hotel has the *Four Seasons Bistro*, with good pub fare and mains in the $10 to $15 range.

A block south of the pub, the Old Burleigh Theatre Arcade on Goodwin Tce has several good restaurants. *Tim's Malaysian Hut*, in the upstairs section, has good hawker-style noodles, vegetables, seafood and meat dishes in the $7 to $12 range, is BYO, and opens nightly for dinner and for yum-cha-style lunches from Friday to Sunday. *Montezuma's* is a licensed Mexican eatery with mains from $8 to $11 and combo dishes from $9 to $13. *Arlett* is a small BYO French bistro with classic French cuisine and mains from $15 to $17. At the front of the arcade, the *Bluff Cafe* is a good place for breakfast. For $7.50 you get OJ, coffee and a cooked breakfast – they also have croissants, omelettes, pancakes etc. For lunch and dinner the cafe has modern Australian cuisine with pastas from $9 to $15, good salads from $8 to $12 and other mains from $15 to $19.

Getting Around

Bicycle World (☎ (07) 5576 4503), opposite the post office at 7 James St, hires non-geared mountain bikes with helmets and locks at $15 a day.

COOLANGATTA

The 'twin towns' of Coolangatta and Tweed Heads mark the southern end of the Gold Coast. Tweed Heads is in New South Wales but the two places merge into each other. At **Point Danger**, the headland at the end of the

state line, there are good views from the Captain Cook memorial. Coolangatta is a bit more laid-back than the northern reaches of the Gold Coast, and has a backpackers' hostel and some other good budget accommodation. The beaches here are fine, with good surf at Kirra, Point Danger and Greenmount.

Information

Tourist Information The Beach House Plaza Information Booth (☎ (07) 5536 7765), on the corner of Marine Pde and McLean St, is open on weekdays from 8 am to 2 pm and 3 to 4 pm, and Saturdays from 8 am to 3 pm.

The Tweed Heads Visitors Centre (☎ (07) 5536 4244) on the corner of Wharf and Bay Sts in Tweed Heads is open daily from 9 am to 5 pm.

Books If you're looking for some reading matter, The Bookshop, at 133 Boundary St opposite the McCafferty's bus terminal, has a huge range of second-hand books. They specialise in pulp fiction – thrillers, westerns, romance etc – just the stuff for a bus trip.

Places to Stay

Camping On Boundary St on the New South Wales side of the border, the *Border Caravan Park* (☎ (07) 5536 3134) has tent sites ranging from $11 to $18, powered sites from $13 to $21, and on-site vans from $27 to $60. Tent sites aren't available here during winter or at Christmas time.

Hostels *Linnie's Bunk House* (☎ (07) 5538 3717), at 203 Boundary St, is a newly established backpackers' hostel with bunk beds at $14 per person, and free use of bikes and boogie boards for guests.

The *Gold Coast Youth Hostel* (☎ (07) 5536 7644) is on Coolangatta Rd, Bilinga, just north of the airport and about three km from central Coolangatta. For members, a bed in a six or eight-bed dorm costs $12 and doubles are $32; nonmembers pay an extra $2. It's a newish building, with good facilities including a pool, but it's not really in a

GOLD COAST

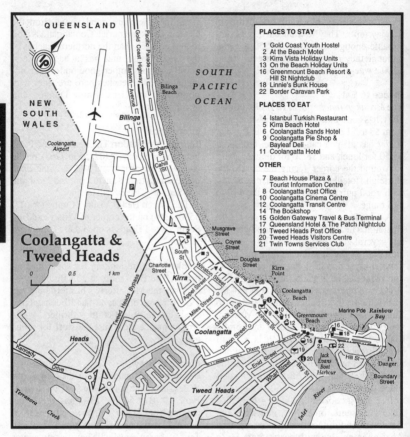

convenient location for anything except the
airport.

Pubs The *Coolangatta Sands Hotel* (☎ (07)
5536 3066), on the corner of Griffith and
McLean Sts, has reasonably good pub rooms
from $25/35. On the corner of Hill and
Boundary St, the *Queensland Hotel* (☎ (07)
5536 2600) also has rooms at $20 per person,
or $25 with breakfast.

Motels & Holiday Units *On the Beach
Holiday Units* (☎ (07) 5536 3624), at 118
Marine Pde, is a complex of older-style units

on the foreshore. These are simple, roomy
flats with basic cooking facilities – a toaster,
frypan etc – and are good value, ranging
from $45 to $65 a double, plus $10 for extras.

In Kirra, the *Kirra Vista Holiday Units*
(☎ (07) 5536 7375), at 12-14 Musgrave St,
is a block of budget holiday units, with one-
bedroom units from $65 and two-bedroom
units from $85, plus $10 for extras. They are
quite comfortable, and the beachfront position
is good. Further north, the straightforward *At
the Beach Motel* (☎ (07) 5536 3599), on the
corner of Musgrave St and Winston St, has
motel units ranging from $50 to $80 a night,

as well as self-contained one-bedroom units from $60 to $120 and two-bedroom units from $100.

Resorts The *Greenmount Beach Resort* (☎ (07) 5536 1222), well located on a headland on the corner of Marine Pde and Hill St, is a high-rise resort with a pool, restaurant, bar and nightclub. Standard motel-style units range from $120 to $145 a night, but they often have discounted package deals.

On the corner of Marine Pde and McLean St, the *Beach House Resort* (☎ (07) 5536 5566) towers 16 storeys over Coolangatta Beach. It's a fairly typical Gold Coast high-rise with 132 modern two-bedroom apartments ranging from $125 to $145 a night.

Places to Eat

The huge *Twin Towns Services Club* has a Snack Bar on the 2nd floor, which has good meals for $4 to $6 and $2.50 lunches on weekdays. On the corner of McLean St and Marine Pde, the Beach House Plaza shopping complex has a number of eateries: *Farley's Coffee Lounge* has good breakfast specials – for $6.95 you get cereal, juice, tea or coffee, and a choice of cooked meals. Nearby, the *Aussie Eatery* also has reasonably priced breakfasts and lunches. *The Jungle Mexican Cantina* is a small and casual BYO with mains in the $10 to $14 range and open-air tables. *Casa Mia Piccola* is an Italian bistro with pastas, veal and chicken dishes in the $7 to $12 range. On the McLean St side of the plaza, *Little Malaya* is a pleasant BYO with Malaysian and Chinese dishes, including a good range of vegetarian dishes around $8 and other mains from $9 to $14.

The famous *Coolangatta Pie Shop*, at 50 Griffith St, has good pies, pastries and fresh bread. It is open 24 hours a day on weekends and from 5 am to 10.30 pm on other days. The nearby *Bayleaf Deli* is a good spot for lunch with gourmet sandwiches, pies, hot roast meals and a good salad bar.

The *Coolangatta Hotel* on the corner of Marine Pde and Warner St has a bistro with all-you-can-eat soup, salad and pasta deals for $6.50, and main courses around $10. In the snack bar next door, you can get a meal and a beer for $3.50 on weekdays for lunch and dinner. Further north on the corner of

GOLD COAST

Surfin' the line

Marine Pde and Miles St, the *Kirra Beach Hotel* also has cheap meals with $2.50 counter lunches every day and $2.50 dinners from Wednesday to Friday night.

At 32-34 Musgrave St in Kirra, the *Istanbul Turkish Restaurant* is very popular and has good Turkish tucker, with set menus for $10, $15 and $20 and most dishes in the $3 to $6 range. They also do takeaways, are BYO, and have belly dancing on Saturday nights.

Entertainment
Nightclubs & Live Music *The Patch* in the Queensland Hotel on Hill St is a popular live music venue, with cheap meals, discounted drinks and live bands on Thursday and Friday nights and Sunday afternoons. They also have cane toad races here. Nearby, *The Hill St Nightclub* inside the Greenmount Resort on Hill St is a fairly up-market disco-style club that opens most nights. The *Coolangatta Sands Hotel* also has live bands. Much of the entertainment on the southern Gold Coast revolves around the clubs and pokies in Tweed Heads.

Cinema The Coolangatta Cinema Centre (☎ (07) 5536 8900), on level two in the Beach Shopping Centre on Griffith St, has four cinemas screening latest release movies.

Getting There & Away
Bus Golden Gateway Travel (☎ (07) 5536 1700), on Boundary St, just south of the border, is the terminal for McCafferty's, Kirklands and Coachtrans buses. McCafferty's has regular buses from here to Brisbane ($12), Byron Bay ($18) and Sydney ($65). Kirklands also runs to Sydney ($62) and Byron Bay ($12.80), as well as Ballina, Lismore, Murwillumbah and other towns on the north coast of NSW. Coachtrans has services to Brisbane ($12) and Brisbane airport ($26).

A block north on the corner of Griffith and Warner Sts, the Coolangatta Transit Centre (☎ (07) 5536 6600) is the terminal for Greyhound Pioneer Australia ($15 to Brisbane, $73 to Sydney) and Lindsay Coaches ($64 to Sydney). Coachtrans' buses also stop here.

Gold Coast Hinterland

The mountains of the **McPherson Range**, about 20 km inland from Coolangatta and stretching about 60 km back along the New South Wales border to meet the Great Dividing Range, are a paradise for walkers. The great views and beautiful natural features are easily accessible by car, and there are plenty of wonderfully scenic drives. Otherwise, there are several places offering tours and day trips from the coast. Expect a lot of rain in the mountains from December to March, and in winter the nights can be cold.

TAMBORINE MOUNTAIN
Just 45 km north-west of the Gold Coast, this 600-metre-high plateau is on a northern spur of the McPherson Range. Patches of the area's original forests remain in nine small national parks. There are gorges, spectacular waterfalls like Witches Falls and Cedar Creek Falls, great views inland or over the coast, and walking tracks, although because of its proximity to the coast this area is more developed and quite commercialised compared to the ranges further south. The main access roads to this area are from Oxenford on the Pacific Hwy or via Nerang from the coast.

The adjoining townships of North Tamborine and Eagle Heights are popular destinations for daytrippers and bus tours from the coast, and both have a collection of art and craft galleries, Devonshire teahouses, cafes and restaurants. There's a visitor information centre (☎ (07) 5545 1171) at Doughty Park, North Tamborine.

Some of the best lookouts are in **Witches Falls National Park**, south-west of North Tamborine, and at **Cameron Falls**, north-west of North Tamborine. **Macrozamia Grove National Park**, near the Tamborine Mountain township, has some extremely old macrozamia palms.

The *Tall Trees Motel* (☎ (07) 5545 1242) in Tamborine Mountain is a small and friendly motel with five units from $42. In

Tamborine (confusingly 13 km north of North Tamborine) *St Bernards Hotel* (☎ (07) 5545 1177), at 101 Alpine Tce, is a rustic old mountain pub (1911) with a bar, bistro and restaurant. They have cosy pub-style rooms with shared bathrooms at $35/50 for singles/doubles including breakfast, and newer motel units next door at $45/70.

Four km north of North Tamborine, **Thunderbird Park** (☎ (07) 5545 1468) is a small theme park in a bush setting. The park has its own tavern restaurant, mini-golf, a bird-feeding area, a small paint-ball course, tennis courts, and you can ride horses or fossick for thunder eggs. Thunder eggs are spherical rocks of volcanic origin which contain quartz crystals or semi-precious gems. They range in size from a cm in diameter to about the size of a cricket or baseball, and were formed when gas cavities in hardened lava filled with mineral deposits or crystal. Thunderbird Park also has a decent range of accommodation with camp sites at $5 per person per night, good motel units from $52/65 for singles/doubles, and self-contained two-bedroom cabins from $85 a night.

Beside Thunderbird Park is the entrance to the **Cedar Creek National Park**, with a pleasant picnic area and a circuit walk to the Cedar Creek Falls.

SPRINGBROOK PLATEAU

This forested 900-metre-high plateau, like the rest of the McPherson Range, is a remnant of the huge volcano which used to be centred on Mt Warning in New South Wales. It's a lovely drive from the Gold Coast and can be reached by paved road via Mudgeeraba.

Springbrook National Park has three sections: Springbrook, Mt Cougal and Natural Bridge. The vegetation is temperate rainforest and eucalypt forest, with gorges, cliffs, forests, waterfalls, an extensive network of walking tracks, and several picnic areas.

There are rangers' offices and information centres at Natural Bridge and Springbrook. Pick up a copy of the National Parks walking tracks leaflet.

Springbrook

This mountain village is on the edge of the plateau, at the end of the road 26 km south of Mudgeeraba. It has a general store, tea rooms and craft shops, and accommodation, as well as some great picnic areas and a camping ground. Actually, it's not so much a village as a scattering of guesthouses, farmlets and teahouses stretched along the plateau.

At the **Gwongorella picnic area**, just off the Springbrook road, the lovely Purling Brook Falls drop 109 metres into rainforest. Beside the car park there's a grassy area with picnic tables and barbecues, and walking trails, including a short stroll to the falls lookout, a four-km circuit walk to the falls, and a six-km-return walk to the Waringa Pool, a beautiful summer swimming hole. There's a good camping ground beside the picnic area.

Two good walking trails start from the **Canyon Lookout**: A four-km circuit walk to **Twin Falls**, and the 17-km **Warrie Circuit**.

At the end of the road, the **Goomoolahra Picnic Area** is another pleasant picnic area with barbecues beside a small creek. A little further on there's a great lookout point beside the falls with views across the plateau and all the way back to the coast, with Surfers and its high-rises dotting the coastline like Lego blocks.

The **Best of All Lookout** isn't quite, but is still fairly spectacular with views from the southern edge of the plateau to the flatlands below. There's a 350-metre trail from the car park to the lookout which takes you past a clump of unusual Antarctic Beech trees.

Places to Stay & Eat You can camp at the national park *Gwongorella Camp Ground*. There's a self-registration booth at the site, and camping permits can be booked through the ranger at Springbrook (☎ (07) 5533 5147, between 3 and 4 pm weekdays only).

There are a number of guesthouses here, generally along, or signposted off, the Springbrook Rd. The first place you come to, just before you reach Springbrook, is the *Springbrook Mountain Chalets* (☎ (07) 5533

5205). These stylish and unusual cathedral-like chalets are in a lovely bush setting, are self-contained, and range from $85 a double to $110 a double for the deluxe chalet with a spa.

The *Mouses House* (☎ (07) 5533 5192) consists of 10 impressive Alpine-style timber chalets, all self-contained with a loft bedroom and wood stove. Facilities here include half-court tennis, a spa and sauna, and bikes. The tariffs are $230 a double for two nights, with a minimum two-night stay.

The *Springbrook Mountain Lodge* (☎ (07) 5533 5366), three km off the Springbrook Rd on the Best of All Lookouts road, has a lodge and cabins. The lodge is a large, timber-lined building reminiscent of a ski lodge, and has five bedrooms with ensuites, a large communal kitchen and lounge, a recreation room and great views. It's popular with groups but also welcomes individuals, and costs $80 a double plus $20 for each extra person. There are also three good self-contained cabins at $100 a double. The owner of this place takes guests on bushwalking tours, and also runs good overnight tours from the Gold Coast – see Getting There & Away.

The *Canyon Lookout Guesthouse* (☎ (07) 5533 5120), beside the lookout of the same name, is an attractive timber restaurant which opens for lunch from Wednesday to Sunday and dinners from Tuesday to Sunday. A three-course dinner will cost around $25 per person. Downstairs behind the restaurant are two simple, comfortable guest rooms with ensuites that cost $76 a double.

The *Tulip Cottage Guesthouse* (☎ (07) 5533 5125) is a straightforward timber guesthouse with five rooms, with B&B costing $39 per person or $59 on weekends. The *Springbrook Mountain Manor* (☎ (07) 5533 5344) is a charmless and modern mock-Tudor guesthouse with double rooms from $90 and dinner, B&B packages from $170 a double.

The *Springbrook Homestead Bar & Eatery* is a modern pub-like tavern which opens for lunch and dinner from Wednesday to Sunday. For lunch they do things like

ploughman's lunches or gourmet pies and salads ($6 to $10) and the dinner menu has an assortment of main courses at $10.90.

The only general store here is the *Purlingbrook Store* on the road to the Gwongorella picnic area. It sells fuel, takeaway meals and a limited range of groceries.

Natural Bridge

The Natural Bridge section of the national park is just a couple of km west of Springbrook as the crow flies. By road, you have to drive back up to Numinbah and then down the Murwillumbah road to Natural Bridge – a total trip of about 35 km. There are picnic areas beside the car park, and a steep one-km walking circuit leads to a rock arch spanning a water-formed cave which is home to a huge colony of glow-worms, with a small waterfall tumbling into a swimming hole.

One km north of the turn off to Natural Bridge, the *Two Pines Cafe* sells fuel and has takeaway meals and Devonshire teas.

Getting There & Away

The only bus service is the Springbrook Bus Service (☎ (07) 5533 5133), a school bus which runs up and down the mountain on school days. At the time of going to print there was a chance that this service may change hands. For current details check with the rangers at the QNP&WS office or the tourist office in Surfers.

Off The Beaten Track (☎ (07) 5533 5366) offers good-value overnight trips from the Gold Coast to Springbrook for backpackers and bushwalkers. For $40 you get return transport, overnight accommodation and a half to full-day guided bushwalk. See Organised Tours at the start of the chapter for more details.

CANUNGRA (pop 460)

This small town 25 km west of Nerang is at the junction of the northern approach roads to the Green Mountains and Binna Burra sections of the Lamington National Park. It has a few eateries and accommodation options, as well as a couple of shops where you can buy groceries and supplies.

There's a tourist information office (☎ (07) 5543 5156), on the corner of Kidston St and Lawton Lne, which is open Sunday to Friday from 10 am to 4 pm and Saturdays from 10 am to 12.30 pm.

Near Canungra, the Gold Coast Riding Ranch (☎ (07) 5543 0191) has horse-trail rides from $35 for a 1½-hour morning ride, $40 for a 2½-hour afternoon ride and $65 for a full-day ride with lunch.

Places to Stay & Eat
The *Canungra Hotel* (☎ (07) 5543 5233), a popular white timber pub on Kidston St, has rooms upstairs at $30/35 for singles/doubles, and one room with its own bathroom at $45. The *Canungra Motel* (☎ (07) 5543 5155), on Kidston St has budget units at $35/45.

In the centre of town, *The Outpost Cafe* has breakfasts, sandwiches, burgers and the like, and the *Canungra Seafood & Italian Bistro* next door serves lunch and dinner daily with pastas under $9 and main meals from $10 to $14. They also have good takeaway fish & chips ($3.70).

LAMINGTON NATIONAL PARK
West of Springbrook, this 200-sq-km park covers much of the McPherson Range and adjoins the Border Ranges National Park in New South Wales. It includes thickly wooded valleys, 1100-metre-high ranges, plus most of the Lamington Plateau. Much of the vegetation is subtropical rainforest. There are beautiful gorges, caves, superb views, a great many waterfalls and pools, and lots of wildlife. Bower birds are quite common and pademelons, a type of small wallaby, can be seen on the grassy forest verges in late afternoon.

The two most popular and accessible sections of the park are **Binna Burra** and **Green Mountains**, both reached via paved roads from Canungra. The 24-km Border Trail walk links the two.

The park has 160 km of walking tracks ranging from a 'senses trail' for the blind at Binna Burra to a tree-top canopy walk along a series of suspension bridges at Green Mountains. Walking trail guides are available from QNP&WS offices. There are rangers stations at both Binna Burra (☎ (07) 5533 3584, open daily from 8 am to 4 pm) and Green Mountains (☎ (07) 5544 0634, open weekdays from 1 to 3.30 pm).

Places to Stay & Eat
Binna Burra The *Binna Burra Mountain Lodge* (☎ (07) 5533 3622) is a good mountain retreat with three types of rustic log cabins which cost from $99 to $149 per person per night, which includes all meals, free hiking and climbing gear, and activities like guided walks, bus trips and abseiling. The lodge has an attractive restaurant with good views and very good smorgasbord-style meals.

The *Binna Burra Camp Ground* (☎ (07) 5533 3758) has a great setting with a laundry, hot showers, cooking shelters and coin-operated barbecues and hotplates. Tent sites and van sites cost $7 per person, plus another $3 per site for power. On-site tents with lights and mattressed beds cost $36 a night for two people or $52 for four people. The camping ground is very popular, and you'll need to book on weekends and during holidays.

The *Binna Burra Kiosk*, next to the camping ground, is open daily from 8 am to 7.30 pm. They have good breakfasts (BLTs or scrambled eggs $5, cooked breakfast with the works $7), as well as sandwiches, rolls, hot dogs, burgers and Devonshire teas. There are great views from the outdoor tables out on the patio.

Green Mountains The famous *O'Reilly's Guesthouse* (☎ (07) 5544 0644), at Green Mountains, has three levels of accommodation. The original guesthouse units, that were built back in the 1930s, have twin single beds and communal bathrooms and cost $105 per person per night; motel-style units cost $140 per person per night; and larger balcony units cost $150 per person per night. Tariffs include all meals and activities including bushwalks, spotlighting walks and 4WD bus

GOLD COAST

The Crash of the Stinson
On 19 February 1937, a Stinson airliner carrying seven people crashed in the thick, impenetrable forests of the McPherson mountain range. Four passengers were killed instantly, and another died after falling over a cliff when he went for help. The plane had been missing for nine days and search parties had almost given up when Bernard O'Reilly, owner of the Lamington Guesthouse, found the wreck and its two survivors. O'Reilly later said that one of the first questions the two men asked was 'What's the cricket score?'. Apparently, they were considerably cheered to hear that Don Bradman was 165 not out.

Parts of the wrecked plane, and photographs of the rescue, are on display at O'Reilly's Guesthouse. ■

trips. The restaurant here is also open to the public ($20 for lunch, $25 for dinner), but you'll need to book during holiday seasons.

There's also a kiosk, and a National Parks camping ground about 600 metres away with sites for $3 per person per night.

You can bush camp in Lamington, but only a limited number of permits are issued. You can get information from the QNP&WS offices at Burleigh Heads or Brisbane, but camping permits must be obtained from the ranger at Green Mountains.

Getting There & Away
The Binna Burra bus service (☎ (07) 5533 3622) operates daily between Surfers and Binna Burra. The trip takes one hour and costs $16. The bus departs from Surfers from

the Coachtrans terminal at the bus station at 1.15 pm; departures from Binna Burra are at 10.30 am daily. Bookings are essential.

Allstate Scenic Tours (☎ (07) 3285 1777) runs a bus service six times a week between Brisbane and Green Mountains (O'Reilly's). Trips depart from the Brisbane Transit Centre at 9.30 am, Sunday to Friday, take about three hours and cost $20 one way or $35 return for a day trip.

Mountain Coach Company (☎ (07) 5524 4249) has a daily service from the Gold Coast to Green Mountains via Tamborine Mountain, costing $30 return or $16 one way. They do pick-ups from your accommodation.

MT LINDESAY HIGHWAY
This road runs south from Brisbane, across the Great Dividing Range west of Lamington, and into New South Wales at Woodenbong. **Beaudesert**, in cattle country 66 km from Brisbane, is just 20 km southwest of Tamborine Mountain. It's a busy commercial centre with several motels and hotels, a pioneer museum and tourist information centre on Jane St.

West of Beaudesert is the stretch of the Great Dividing Range known as the **Scenic Rim** (see the Darling Downs section). Further south, **Mt Barney National Park** is undeveloped but popular with bushwalkers and climbers. It's in the Great Dividing Range just north of the state border. You reach it from the Rathdowney to Boonah road. There's a tourist information office (☎ (07) 5544 1222) on the highway at Rathdowney.

Sunshine Coast

The stretch of coast from the top of Bribie Island to just north of Noosa is known as the Sunshine Coast. It's a popular holiday area, renowned for fine beaches, good surfing and fishing. Although it doesn't have the high-rise jungle and neon-lit strips of the Gold Coast, the coast is still quite commercial and has been heavily developed, especially in the last decade.

Noosa Heads is the most fashionable and exclusive town on the coast, and it has a good range of accommodation and restaurants, an excellent national park and great beaches. Maroochydore is also quite popular. North of Noosa is the Cooloola National Park and Rainbow Beach, an access point for Fraser Island.

Activities

Climbing & Walking The Glass House Mountains have some good bushwalks and are very popular with rock climbers. There are several small national parks in the hinterland with good bushwalks, and the Noosa National Park also has some great short walking tracks. North of Noosa, the Cooloola National Park is another good walking area, and the 46-km Cooloola Wilderness Trail takes you through the park all the way up to Rainbow Beach, with camp sites along the route.

Swimming & Surfing The Sunshine Coast is renowned for its great beaches. There are surf beaches all along the coast, ranging from endless stretches of sandy beach breaks to the rocky point-breaks at Alexandra Headland. The most famous (and unfortunately, most popular) breaks are the series of classic right-hand points around the Noosa National Park.

Golf Golf is another popular activity, and there are public golf courses at most of the towns along the coast. The two best known

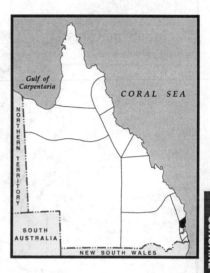

courses are the resort courses at the Hyatt Regency Coolum and the Novatel Twin Waters Resort.

Getting There & Away

Air The Sunshine Coast Airport is on the coast road at Mudjimba, 10 km north of Maroochydore and 26 km south of Noosa.

Sunstate has daily flights between Brisbane and the Sunshine Coast ($94 one way). Ansett and Qantas also fly to the Sunshine Coast from all major capitals – some flights are direct, others go via Brisbane. The one-way fare from Melbourne is $390; from Sydney it's $269.

Bus Both Greyhound Pioneer Australia and McCafferty's travel along the Bruce Hwy, but not across to the coast, although Greyhound Pioneer Australia now has one service a day that detours across to Maroochydore and Noosa.

Suncoast Pacific (☎ (074) 43 1011) is the

237

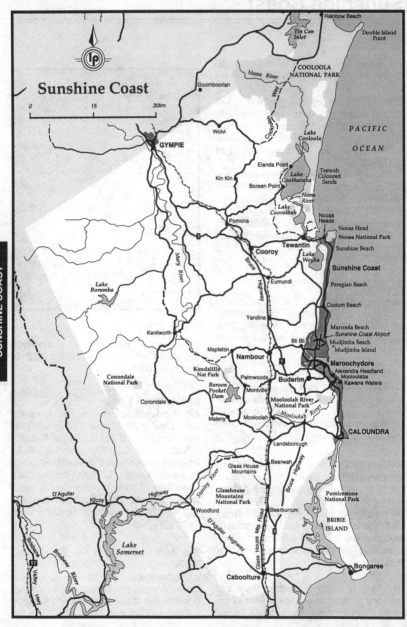

Sunshine Coast

0   15   30km

SUNSHINE COAST

GYMPIE

Wolvi

Goomboorian

Noosa River

COOLOOLA NATIONAL PARK

Tin Can Inlet

Rainbow Beach

Double Island Point

Cooloola Way

Lake Cooloola

PACIFIC OCEAN

Elanda Point

Lake Cootharaba

Teewah Coloured Sands

Kin Kin

Boreen Point

Noosa River

Lake Cooroibah

Pomona

Noosa Heads

Noosa Head

Noosa National Park

Sunshine Beach

Cooroy

Tewantin

Lake Weyba

Sunshine Coast

Mary River

Eumundi

Peregian Beach

Bruce Highway

Coolum Beach

Yandina

Kenilworth

Marcoola Beach

Sunshine Coast Airport

Mapleton

Bli Bli

Mudjimba Beach

Nambour

Mudjimba Island

Kondalilla Nat Park

Palmwoods

Buderim

Maroochydore

Alexandra Headland

Mooloolaba

Conondale National Park

Baroon Pocket Dam

Montville

Kawana Waters

Conondale

Lake Borumba

Maleny

Mooloolah

Mooloolah River National Park

Mooloolah River

CALOUNDRA

Landsborough

Beerwah

Stanley River

Glass House Mountains

Glasshouse Mountains National Park

Bruce Highway

Pumicestone National Park

D'Aguilar

Kilcoy

Highway

Woodford

D'Aguilar Highway

Beerburrum

Glass House Mtns Road

BRIBIE ISLAND

Lake Somerset

Brisbane Valley Hwy

Brisbane River

Bongaree

Caboolture

major company servicing the coast from Brisbane, with nine to 10 services a day between Brisbane and Noosa via Caloundra and Maroochydore. Six of these run via the Brisbane Airport. Their one-way fares from Brisbane include Maroochydore $14 and Noosa $17.

There are a couple of other companies offering local services: Tewantin Bus Services (☎ (074) 49 7422) has 10 services a day (six on Sundays) up and down the coast between Maroochydore, Noosa and Tewantin. They also have services linking Noosa with Cooroy and Nambour on the Bruce Hwy.

Sunshine Coast Coaches (☎ (074) 43 4555) has about 15 services on weekdays and nine on weekends south from Maroochydore to Caloundra and inland across to Landsborough. They also go north from Maroochydore as far as Mt Coolum, and across to Nambour on the Bruce Hwy. See the following Getting Around section for details of bus services to/from the airport.

Train The main coastal railway line runs roughly alongside the Bruce Hwy inland from the coast, and there are daily services along here on the Brisbane to Rockhampton run. The most convenient stations for the Sunshine Coast are Nambour and Cooroy – there are bus services linking both of these places with the coast.

Car & Motorcycle The Bruce Hwy runs parallel with the coast, 20 to 30 km inland. There are half a dozen roads linking the highway with the coast.

The major coastal road between Maroochydore and Noosa is David Low Way, which is scenic but can be slow going. If you're in a hurry, the new Sunshine Motorway will whiz you north from Maroochydore. A toll is payable, and the northern section of the motorway is still under construction.

The Sunshine Coast hinterland offers some outstanding scenic drives – see that section for details.

Getting Around
To/From the Airport If you want to rent a car, Avis, Hertz, Budget and Thrifty all have desks at the Sunshine Coast Airport.

There are two local bus services that meet every flight into the airport. Henry's (☎ (074) 49 1440) has buses going north from the airport and will drop you at the door of wherever you're staying. One-way fares are $4 to Coolum and $8 to Noosa. Airport Bus Service (☎ (074) 44 7288) has airport-to-your-door bus services to the towns south of the airport, including Maroochydore ($4 one way), Mooloolabah ($5), Caloundra ($8) and Golden Beach ($9).

CABOOLTURE (pop 12,700)
This region, 49 km north of Brisbane, once had a large Aboriginal population. Nowadays, it's a prosperous dairy centre famous for its yoghurt. The Community Information Centre (☎ (074) 95 3122), in the centre of town at 43 King St, is staffed by helpful volunteers and has information on the surrounding area.

The **Caboolture Historical Village**, on Beerburrum Rd, two km north of the town, has about 30 early Australian buildings in a bush setting and a huge range of memorabilia ranging from the fascinating to the kitsch. There's an impressive maritime museum with model ships depicting the First Fleet, a car museum, typewriter and radio displays, slab huts, an old pub and lots more. It is open daily from 9.30 am to 3.30 pm. Entry costs $5 for adults, $3 for children and is free for people under 14 years if they're accompanied by adults.

Seven km east of Caboolture, the **Abbey Museum** is a world social history museum with a small but well-presented collection of ancient artefacts, weaponry, pottery and costumes. This collection had previously been housed in London, Cyprus, Egypt and Sri Lanka before finding its home in Australia. It's open on Tuesdays, Thursdays, Fridays and Saturdays from 10 am to 4 pm, and entry is $4. The Abbey is on Old Toorbul Point Rd, signposted off the road to Bribie Island.

SUNSHINE COAST

GLASS HOUSE MOUNTAINS

About 20 km north of Caboolture, the Glass House Mountains are a dramatic visual starting point for the Sunshine Coast. They're a bizarre series of volcanic crags rising abruptly out of the plain to 300 metres or more. They were named by Captain Cook and, depending on whose story you believe, he either noted the reflections on the glass-smooth sides of the rocky mountains, or thought they looked like the glass furnaces in his native Yorkshire.

This is a great area for scenic drives, bushwalking and rock climbing, with four small national parks around Mts Coonowrin, Ngungun, Beerwah and Tibrogargan. There are various picnic grounds, walking trails, climbs and lookouts within the parks, but no camping grounds. The main access is via Forest Dve, a 22-km-long series of sealed and unsealed roads which runs off the Glass House Mountains Rd (also known as the Old Bruce Hwy) and winds through the ranges from Beerburrum to the Glass House Mountains township, with several spectacular lookout points en route.

The mountains are particularly popular with rock climbers. A good reference book is *A Guidebook to Rockclimbing on the Glass House Mountains* by Col Smithies – it's available locally and at climbing shops in Brisbane and costs $9.95.

Mt Coonowrin is a tall and pointy shaft of rock which is only suitable for experienced rock climbers, with climbs up to grade 21. The mountain's vegetation was devastated by the 1994 bushfires and it is currently closed to visitors until it has had a chance to revegetate – check with the rangers for the latest.

Mt Ngungun (pronounced *Gun-gun*) has an easy one to two-hour return walk to the summit as well as several rock face climbs. The trails to the summits of **Mts Beerwah** and **Tibrogargan** are steep and difficult three-hour return climbs.

The QNP&WS has a rangers' office at Beerwah. Contact them on ☎ (074) 94 6630 for more information.

Wildhorse Mountain Lookout

There are great views from this lookout tower on Wildhorse Mountain, which is about 15 km north of Caboolture beside the (new) Bruce Hwy. You can drive to the car park and walk up to the lookout – it's a steep 700-metre walk – but don't leave any valuables in your car, as people are quite often ripped off from here. A safer and less strenuous way of getting to the lookout is to park at one of the Mobil roadhouses on either side of the highway and take their free courtesy bus up to the summit. The bus runs every hour on the hour between 9 am and 2 pm on weekdays and 9 am and 4 pm on weekends. It's about a 35-minute round trip, and you get

The Glass House Mountains

a commentary on the legend of the mountains on the way up.

Places to Stay & Eat
There are a few accommodation options along the Glass House Mountains Rd near the towns of Glass House Mountains and Beerburrum.

Mt Tibrogargan Relaxapark (☎ (074) 96 0151), 1.5 km north of Beerburrum, is the best caravan and camping park in the area, with a shop and pool, walking trails, information on the area's walks and wildlife, and a neat landscaped setting with lots of trees and mountain views. Tent sites are $10, powered sites $13, on-site vans $21 and self-contained units that sleep up to six cost $31 a double plus $4 for extras (BYO linen).

One km north of Beerburrum, the *Beerburrum Motel* (☎ (074) 96 0126) has six budget units for $30/35.

The *Log Cabin Caravan Park* (☎ (074) 96 9338), one km south of Glass House Mountains, has a rambling setting amongst big old trees and a noteworthy absence of log cabins. Tent sites are $10, on-site vans $20.

One km north of Glass House Mountains, the *Glass House Mountains Motel* (☎ (074) 96 9900) has units from $40.

CALOUNDRA (pop 22,100)
At the southern end of the Sunshine Coast strip, Caloundra has some decent beaches and excellent fishing but compared with places further north, it's a bit faded these days. It's still a popular holiday town with families and has a wide range of accommodation, although there isn't a backpackers' hostel here.

Orientation & Information
Caloundra is located on a low headland opposite the northern end of Bribie Island, and at the northern entrance to the Pumicestone Passage. The town centre is along Bulcock St, which is where you'll find the post office and major banks.

The Caloundra Tourist Information Centre (☎ (074) 91 0202) is on Caloundra Rd, just west of the town centre. It is open on weekdays from 8.15 am to 4.45 pm and on weekends from 9 am to 5 pm.

Things to See & Do
Caloundra's **beaches** are its major attraction, and they range from long, sandy surf beaches to small rocky coves and sheltered bays. Spread along the headland and separated by a series of rocky coves and points, most of the beaches are backed by bunya pine trees and attractive foreshore parks. Bulcock Beach, good for windsurfing, is just down from the main street, overlooking the northern end of Bribie Island.

Points of interest include the **Queensland Air Museum** at Caloundra Aerodrome, which is open Wednesday, Saturday and Sunday from 10 am to 4 pm and costs $3, and the **Ettamogah Pub** on the Bruce Hwy, just north of the Caloundra turn off. You can also take cruises around the channels and to Bribie Island from Caloundra.

Places to Stay
Caloundra has about eight caravan parks. The *Caloundra Holiday Resort* (☎ (074) 91 3342), at Dicky Beach, is a good camping park with tent sites from $14 to $18, powered sites from $16 to $25 and self-contained units that sleep four and range from $35 to $60 a night. They also have a bunk-style lodge that sleeps eight people and costs $70 to $80 a night.

The *Hibiscus Holiday Park* (☎ (074) 91 1564), on the corner of Bowman Rd and Landsborough Park Rd, is close to both the waterfront and the city centre. Tent sites start from $10, powered sites from $13, on-site vans from $25 and cabins from $35.

There are plenty of motels and holiday units. The *Dolphins Motel* (☎ (074) 91 2511), opposite the bus terminal at 6 Cooma Tce, has good units ranging seasonally from $40/45 to $65/75 for singles/doubles. The *Caloundra Motel* (☎ (074) 91 1411), which is at 30 Bowman Rd, is one of the cheapest,

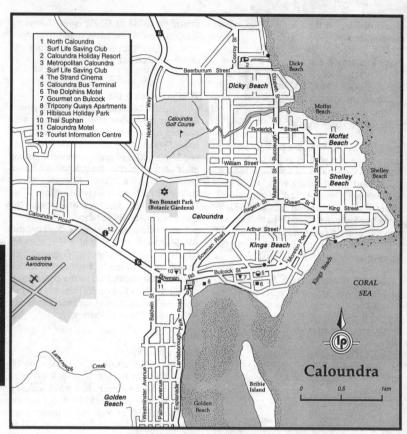

Caloundra

1 North Caloundra
  Surf Life Saving Club
2 Caloundra Holiday Resort
3 Metropolitan Caloundra
  Surf Life Saving Club
4 The Strand Cinema
5 Caloundra Bus Terminal
6 The Dolphins Motel
7 Gourmet on Bulcock
8 Tripcony Quays Apartments
9 Hibiscus Holiday Park
10 Thai Suphan
11 Caloundra Motel
12 Tourist Information Centre

with basic units ranging from $35/40 to $45/50.

On the waterfront, the *Tripcony Quays Apartments* (☎ (074) 91 1166), at 42 Maloja Ave, is a stylish, three-storey apartment block with well-equipped two and three-bedroom apartments from $100 a night. The weekly rates are better value, ranging from $340 to $490 for two bedrooms and $400 to $600 for three bedrooms.

Places to Eat

The *Metropolitan Caloundra Surf Life-Saving Club*, at the north end of Kings Beach, has a casual upstairs bistro where you can have breakfast overlooking the beach. It's $6 for a continental breakfast or $8 for the hot buffet. They also serve bistro meals for lunch and dinner, ranging from $8 to $10.

At lunch time, head for *Gourmet on Bulcock*, a small deli and cafe with good burgers, sangers and meals such as chicken & chips for $3.90. And at night, *Thai Suphan*, on the corner of Bowman Rd and First Ave, has good MSG-free Thai food with vegetarian, seafood, beef and lamb dishes in the $9 to $14 range. It is open for dinner every night except Mondays.

Entertainment
The Strand Cinema (☎ (074) 91 1165) is on Bulcock St near the Knox Ave corner.

Getting There & Away
Long-distance buses stop at the Caloundra Bus Terminal (☎ (074) 91 2555), on Cooma Tce. See the Getting There & Away section at the start of this chapter for details of bus services.

MAROOCHYDORE, ALEXANDRA HEADLAND & MOOLOOLABA (pop 28,500)
Not so very long ago, in a place that seems far, far away, Maroochydore, Alexandra Headland and Mooloolaba were idyllic little coastal centres with fine beaches, backed by the waterways and rivers of the Maroochy and Mooloolah rivers. The beaches and waterways haven't changed much, but nowadays these three centres are adjoining 'suburbs' in the Sunshine Coast's biggest and most heavily developed urban conglomeration.

Maroochydore, the main town, is a busy commercial centre and popular tourist spot, with both an ocean beach and the Maroochy River, which has lots of pelicans and a few islands. Nearby, Alexandra Headland has a pleasant beach and good surfing off a rocky point.

Mooloolaba has the brightest atmosphere, with a long, sandy beach and a strip of shops (including cafes, restaurants and the odd nightspot) along the beachfront.

Orientation & Information
The Maroochy Tourist Information Centre (☎ (074) 79 1566) is near the corner of Aerodrome Rd and Sixth Ave.

The Maroochydore post office is in the centre of the main shopping area on Ocean Ave. The Mooloolaba post office is on Mooloolaba Esplanade.

Things to See & Do
Like Caloundra, the main attractions here are the excellent beaches.

At Mooloolaba, **The Wharf** is an impressive riverfront development with shops, eateries, a tavern, and a marina from where you can take cruises along the Mooloolah River. The excellent **Underwater World**, the largest oceanarium in the southern hemisphere is also here. A transparent tunnel takes you underneath the oceanarium, and there are performing seal shows five times a day. It's open daily from 9 am to 6 pm; entry costs $15.50 for adults, $10 for students, $8 for children and $42 for a family of five.

If you're into themed tourist attractions, the Sunshine Coast has plenty to offer. At Bli Bli, about 10 km north-west of Maroochydore along the Maroochy River, **Bli Bli Castle** is a concrete-block castle with a doll museum, a kiosk and souvenir shop, torture chamber and fairy tales told in dioramas. It is open daily from 9 am to 5 pm; entry costs $6 for adults, $3.50 for kids.

Nostalgia Town, two km south of the airport on the north side of the Maroochy River, has various rides and attractions and a large souvenir shop. You can experience Albert's Incredible Time Trip ($4 for adults, $3 for kids), the Enchanted Railway ($4/3) and play Graveyard Mini-Golf ($4/3). Then again, you could go to the beach (free/free).

Activities
There are about half a dozen surf shops along the coast that hire out surfboards and boogie boards, and a couple of the hostels also have them. Dan's Bike 'n' Surf Hire (☎ (074) 43 2245) at 110 Sixth Ave, opposite the tourist office, hires out good malibus, short boards and wave skis for $8 an hour or $24 a day.

Maroochy Skate Biz (☎ (074) 43 6111), on Alexandra Pde, Alexandra Headland, hires out in-line skates with all the gear for $7 an hour or $20 a day. They also have mountain bikes for the same rates. There are good **walking & cycling trails** all along the Maroochy River and the beachfront.

The **Cotton Tree Olympic Swimming Centre**, on the Esplanade in Maroochydore,

SUNSHINE COAST

SUNSHINE COAST

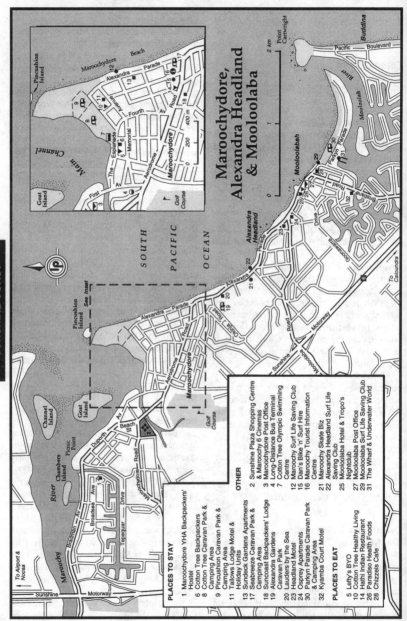

Maroochydore, Alexandra Headland & Mooloolaba

PLACES TO STAY

1 Maroochydore YHA Backpackers'
  Hostel
6 Cotton Tree Backpackers
8 Cotton Tree Caravan Park &
  Camping Area
9 Pincushion Caravan Park &
  Camping Area
11 Tallows Lodge Motel &
  Holiday Units
13 Sundeck Gardens Apartments
17 Seabreeze Caravan Park &
  Camping Area
18 Suncoast Backpackers' Lodge
19 Alexandra Gardens
  Caravan Park
20 Lauders by the Sea
23 Headland Motel
24 Osprey Apartments
30 Parkyn Parade Caravan Park
  & Camping Area
32 Kyamba Court Motel

PLACES TO EAT

5 Lefty's BYO
10 Cotton Tree Healthy Living
14 Hathi Indian Restaurant
26 Paradiso Health Foods
28 Chizzels Cafe

OTHER

2 Sunshine Plaza Shopping Centre
  & Maroochy 6 Cinemas
3 Maroochydore Post Office
4 Long-Distance Bus Terminal
7 Cotton Tree Olympic Swimming
  Centre
12 Maroochy Surf Life Saving Club
15 Dan's Bike 'n' Surf Hire
16 Maroochy Tourist Information
  Centre
21 Maroochy Skate Biz
22 Alexandra Headland Surf Life
  Saving Club
25 Mooloolaba Hotel & Tropo's
  Nightclub
27 Mooloolaba Post Office
29 Mooloolaba Surf Life Saving Club
31 The Wharf & Underwater World

is a great pool which is open all year round from 6 am on weekdays and 9 am on weekends.

Organised Tours

There are a number of operators offering tours of the Cooloola National Park, north of Noosa, and to Fraser Island. Check with the tourist office, and see Organised Tours in the Noosa section for more details.

Goldline Motorcycle Tours (☎ (074) 92 3220) offer a range of motorcycle tours on the back of a Honda Gold Wing, including a 1½-hour trip to the Glass House Mountains ($60) and a three-hour cruise of the Blackall Ranges and hinterland ($120) (see the Hinterland section).

Places to Stay

Camping Some of the best camping and caravan parks here are the foreshore parks run by the local council. They include the *Cotton Tree Caravan Park & Camping Area* (☎ (074) 43 1253) and the *Pincushion Caravan Park & Camping Area* (☎ (074) 43 7917), both on Cotton Tree Pde beside the river in Maroochydore; the *Seabreeze Caravan Park & Camping Area* (☎ (074) 43 1167), behind the Maroochydore tourist office (powered sites only); and the *Parkyn Parade Caravan Park & Camping Area* (☎ (074) 44 1201), opposite the Wharf Complex in Mooloolaba. These places have tent sites from $10 and powered sites from $12, but no van or cabins.

The *Alexandra Gardens Caravan Park* (☎ (074) 43 2356), on Okinja Rd, Alexandra Headland, is 200 metres back from the beach and has powered sites from $14 to $17 and on-site cabins and villas ranging from $30 to $67.

Hostels There are three backpackers' hostels in Maroochydore: the friendly *Maroochydore YHA Backpackers' Hostel* (☎ (074) 43 3151), which is in a residential area at 24 Schirrmann Dve, is a neat, 48-bed brick hostel with a pool, gardens, and six to eight-bed dorms from $12 a night and twins and doubles for $30 a night; nonmembers

pay $1 extra. The managers organise nights out to various pubs and clubs, and there are bikes, canoes, boogie boards and surfboards for hire. They have a courtesy bus and will pick you up from the bus station if you ring.

Cotton Tree Backpackers (☎ (074) 43 1755), at 15 The Esplanade, is a friendly hostel in an old timber guesthouse overlooking the river. Dorm beds cost $12 and doubles $26. At 50 Parker St, the *Suncoast Backpackers' Lodge* (☎ (074) 43 7544) is a modern, purpose-built hostel with two 10-bed dorms costing $12 a night and singles/doubles for $22/30. They have free surfboards and boogie boards, and will pick you up from the bus terminal if you ring.

Motels & Holiday Apartments There are plenty of motels and hundreds of holiday apartments available for rent here. Most of the apartments have a two-night minimum stay, and a seven-night minimum in the peak holiday seasons. The best (and most expensive) place to stay is along the beachfront.

Tallows Lodge Motel & Holiday Units (☎ (074) 43 2981), one block back from the beach at 10 Memorial Dve, Maroochydore, has plain and simple old one and two-bedroom units ranging from $40 to $70 a double plus $10 for each extra person. At the other end of the scale, the impressive *Sundeck Gardens Apartments* (☎ (074) 43 2797), on Alexandra Pde, Maroochydore, has two pools, a spa and sauna, and two-bedroom apartments ranging from $80 to $120 a night for up to four people.

Lauders by the Sea (☎ (074) 43 1800), at 120 Alexandra Pde, Alexandra Headland, is a good mid-range option with oldish two-bedroom holiday units built around a central pool, ranging from $60 to $130 a night.

On the corner of Alexandra Pde and Buderim Ave, the *Headland Motel* (☎ (074) 44 1600) has motel units high on the headland which range from $45 to $130 a night, depending on your view and the time of year. Nearby on Alexandra Pde, the *Osprey Apartments* (☎ (074) 44 6966) is a large complex of luxury apartments with great views and a pool and spa, starting from $100 a night in the low season.

The small *Kyamba Court Motel* (☎ (074) 44 0202), at 94 Brisbane Rd, Mooloolaba, is one of the cheapest of the motels and has doubles from $40.

Places to Eat

Maroochydore At 24 The Esplanade, *Lefty's BYO* (☎ (074) 43 7891) is one of the best eateries here. It's an intimate little BYO that specialises in Greek, Italian and Mexican food, with main meals in the $14 to $18 range and a kid's menu with meals for $5. Lefty's opens Tuesday to Saturday for dinner, and bookings are advised.

Hathi Indian Restaurant, at 25 Aerodrome Rd, has all-you-can-eat Indian smorgasbords for $14 a head and main courses in the $8 to $10 range. In King St, *Cotton Tree Healthy Living* is a good little health food shop with fresh and interesting mega-rolls, flatbreads, home-made pies, smoothies and juices.

Mooloolaba There's a good range of eateries in The Wharf complex, between Parkyn Pde and the Mooloolah River. *Murphy's* is a large family restaurant with an all-you-can-eat buffet costing $8.50 for lunch and $10.50 for dinner. They also have good steaks from $10 to $16 and other dishes from $9 to $12, with lunch specials around $7. There's a small *food court* in the centre of the complex where you can choose from sandwiches, kebabs, hot dogs and freshly squeezed juices. Nearby, *Spud Mulligan's* has roast potatoes stuffed with everything from baked beans to prawns, costing from $3.50 to $5.50. *Friday's* is a popular tavern/bar, nightclub and eatery with a decking area overlooking the water and live music (see Entertainment). They have a great deal on T-bone steaks ($4.95 for lunch, $6.95 for dinner) and have seafood, chicken and rib fillet mains from $10 to $17. On Wednesdays they have all-you-can-eat seafood nights for $14.95.

Paradiso Health Foods, at 105 Mooloolaba Esplanade, has good rolls and sandwiches, pies and pastries, juices etc. Further along the Esplanade on the corner of

Burnett St, *Chizzels Cafe* is a good gourmet eatery with pastas, salads, focaccias and other goodies in the $6 to $9 range.

Entertainment

At The Wharf in Mooloolaba, *Friday's* has live bands on Friday and Saturday nights and Sunday afternoons, and a nightclub upstairs that opens from Wednesday to Sunday.

The *Mooloolaba Hotel*, on the corner of Mooloolaba Esplanade and Venning St, has live bands in the small *Canoe Bar* downstairs on Tuesday, Friday and Saturday nights and karaoke on Sundays. Upstairs in the pub is *Tropo's* Nightclub, which opens till 3 am Wednesdays to Sundays and has live bands on weekends. The Maroochydore 6 Cinemas (☎ (074) 79 2799) in the huge Sunshine Plaza shopping centre on Aerodrome Rd screens mainstream films.

Getting There & Away

Long-distance buses stop at the Suncoast Pacific Bus Terminal (☎ (074) 43 1011), on First Ave in Maroochydore, just off Aerodrome Rd (near KFC). See the start of this chapter for details of bus services to and from Maroochydore.

Getting Around

Bugs Convertible (☎ (074) 43 7555) on Aerodrome Rd, near the tourist office, has convertible Volkswagens and beetles from $45 a day, as well as mopeds from $40 a day. Can Do Rentals (☎ (074) 43 8101) at 71 Aerodrome Rd also hires cars.

Dan's Bike 'n' Surf Hire (☎ (074) 43 2245), at 110 Sixth Ave opposite the tourist office, hires out good mountain bikes and tandems for $14 a day.

PEREGIAN BEACH & COOLUM BEACH

Peregian Beach and Coolum Beach are much less developed than most other parts of the coast. Both are laid-back, low-rise residential areas, with long stretches of sandy beaches.

Stretching along the foreshore between Coolum and Peregian, the **Peregian Beach Environmental Park** is a large reserve of

Peregian Beach & Coolum Beach

PACIFIC OCEAN

0   0.5   1km

Mt Peregian (Emu Mt) 71m ▲

Peregian Beach South

Peregian Beach Environmental Park

David Low Way

To Noosa

Noosa/Lake Weyba National Park

Peregian Beach

Coolum Environmental Park

Coolum Beach

Cinnamon Ave

Yandina-Coolum Rd

To Maroochydore

Point Perry

PLACES TO STAY

2   Peregian Motor Inn
4   Peregian Beach Caravan Park
5   Sails Lifestyle Resort
7   Coolum Sands Holiday
    Apartments
8   Coolum Motel Lodges
9   Stewart's Coolum Beach Hotel
10 Coolum Gardens Caravan Park
11 Coolseas Caravan Park &
    Camping Area

PLACES TO EAT

1   Cheers Bar & Ristorante
13 Coolum Natural Foods
14 Coolum Gourmet Deli

OTHER

3   Peregian Beach Surf Life-Saving
    Club
6   Coolum Aquatic Centre
12 Coolum Beach Surf Life-Saving
    Club

SUNSHINE COAST

coastal heathland with several walking trails leading through to the beach.

Peregian Beach has a foreshore reserve along the beachfront and is backed by the **Noosa/Lake Weyba National Park** on the other. It's mainly a residential area but has several accommodation options.

Places to Stay

Camping On the foreshore at Coolum Beach, the *Coolseas Caravan Park & Camping Area* (☎ (074) 46 1474) is a good council-run park with tent sites for $10.50 and powered sites for $12.50. Across the road, the *Coolum Gardens Caravan Park*

(☎ (074) 46 1177) has caravan sites for $12, on-site vans from $22 and cabins from $25.

Further north, the *Peregian Beach Caravan Park* (☎ (074) 48 1223), on David Low Way, has an attractive bushland setting with tent sites from $12, powered sites from $14, on-site vans from $25 and self-contained cabins from $38.

B&Bs *Coolum Dreams B&B* (☎ (074) 46 3868), opposite the Hyatt Regency at 28 Warran Rd, Yaroomba (two km south of Coolum Beach) is a modern timber house with four very pleasant guest rooms costing $45/70 for singles/doubles and one self-contained unit upstairs for $90 a night.

Motels & Units At 1822 David Low Way, *Stewart's Coolum Beach Hotel* (☎ (074) 46 1899) is a big modern pub with motel units starting from $35/45.

Set on a hillside at 297 The Esplanade, *Coolum Motel Lodges* (☎ (074) 46 1155) has two strips of old-fashioned one and two-bedroom holiday units which range from $45 to $55 a double, plus $10 for each extra person. These units have a great position but the site has been earmarked for development, so they may not be here for too much longer...

Next door, the *Coolum Sands Holiday Apartments* (☎ (074) 46 4523), at 34 First Ave, is a complex of up-market Mediterranean-style apartments with a pool and spa, games room and underground parking. One-bedroom units range from $85 to $130 a night, two-bedroom units from $95 to $140.

In Peregian Beach, the *Peregian Motor Inn* (☎ (074) 48 1110), at 224 David Low Way, has motel units ranging from $35 in the low season to $90 in the high season.

Resorts The *Hyatt Regency Coolum* (☎ (074) 46 1234) is another impressive resort hotel in the shadow of Mt Coolum, two km south of Coolum Beach. The Hyatt has a similar setup to the Novatel Twin Waters Resort, with attractively landscaped grounds, an excellent golf course, and several swimming pools, bars and restaurants etc. The resort has a wide range of activities on offer, including tennis, aerobics, swimming in a 25-metre lap pool and golf. It also has good conference facilities and is popular with business execs. Packages start from $200 a night for a double room with breakfast, or $220 with a round of golf thrown in, although you can usually find cheaper packages that combine airfares with accommodation – check with your travel agent.

Sails Lifestyle Resort (☎ (074) 48 1011), at 43 Oriole Ave in Peregian Beach, is a stylish new complex of 21 two and three-bedroom timber houses in a residential area two blocks back from the beach. The houses are all self-contained and cost from $70 a double or $80 for four people.

About nine km north of Maroochydore on the northern side of the Maroochy River, the *Novatel Twin Waters Resort* (☎ (074) 48 8000 or toll-free 1800 642 244) is a very impressive resort hotel in an appealing and isolated setting. Surrounded by a melaleuca forest, the resort is built around a large central lagoon with landscaped tropical gardens. It is close to the beachfront and has

an excellent golf course nearby. Standard rooms start from $195 a night, one-bedroom suites from $235, and two-bedroom apartments from $390 a night. They usually have package deals available for longer stays, and you may find package deals combining airfares and accommodation – check with your travel agent.

Places to Eat

Coolum Beach On the corner of David Low Way and Beach Rd, the *Coolum Gourmet Deli* is a glass-fronted cafe with good ocean views and a wide range of gourmet tucker, including sandwiches, salads, muffins, cakes, and good coffees. A couple of shops north, *Coolum Natural Foods* is a small health-food shop with tasty filled sandwiches, pita bread roll-ups, salads, juices and smoothies.

Peregian Beach *Cheers Bar & Ristorante*, at 124 David Low Way, is a modern colonial-style bar and eatery with a garden courtyard and live music from Thursday to Saturday nights. The menu blends Italian, Asian and Mediterranean cuisines, with most main courses from $10 to $12. Cheers is licensed and opens nightly for dinner.

NOOSA HEADS (pop 9800)

A surfers' Mecca since the early 1960s, Noosa has become a resort for the fashionable – with beaches, good restaurants, the fine coastal Noosa National Park and, just to the north, the walks, waterways and beaches of the Cooloola National Park. Noosa remains a far cry from the hype of the Gold Coast, and has more character than the rest of the Sunshine Coast.

Orientation

Noosa is actually a string of small, linked centres – with confusingly similar names – stretching back from the mouth of the Noosa River and along its maze of tributary creeks and lakes. The slickest resort area is Noosa Heads, on the coast between the river mouth and rocky Noosa Head. From Noosa Heads

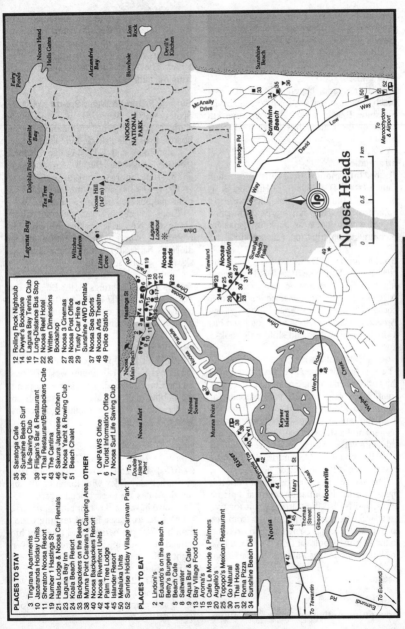

SUNSHINE COAST

PLACES TO STAY

3 Tingirana Apartments
10 Jacaranda Holiday Units
11 Sheraton Noosa Resort
19 Number 1 Hastings St
21 Halse Lodge & Noosa Car Rentals
23 Laguna Bay Inn
24 Koala Beach Resort
33 Backpackers on the Beach
38 Munna Point Caravan & Camping Area
40 Noosa Backpackers Resort
42 Noosa Riverfront Units
44 Palm Tree Lodge
45 Islander Resort
50 Melaluka Units
52 Sunrise Holiday Village Caravan Park

PLACES TO EAT

1 Lindoni's
4 Eduardo's on the Beach &
    Betty's Burgers
5 Beach Cafe
8 Saltwater
9 Aqua Bar & Cafe
13 Bay Village Food Court
15 Aroma's
18 Cafe Le Monde & Palmers
20 Augello's
25 Topopo's Mexican Restaurant
30 Go Natural
31 Thai House
32 Roma Pizza
34 Sunshine Beach Deli

35 Saratoga Cafe
36 Sunshine Beach Surf
    Life-Saving Club
39 Filligan's Bar & Restaurant
41 Thai Restaurant/Bratpackers Cafe
43 The Cantina
46 Sakura Japanese Kitchen
47 Noosa Yacht & Rowing Club
51 Beach Chalet

OTHER

1 QNP&WS Office
6 Tourist Information Office
7 Noosa Surf Life Saving Club
12 Rolling Rock Nightclub
14 Dwyer's Bookstore
16 Laguna Bay Tennis Club
17 Long-Distance Bus Stop
22 Noosa Reef Hotel
26 Written Dimensions
    Bookshop
27 Noosa 3 Cinemas
28 Noosa Post Office
29 Trusty Car Hire &
    Sunshine 4WD Rentals
37 Noosa Sea Sports
48 Noosa Arts Theatre
49 Police Station

Noosa Heads

two roads lead back to Noosaville, about three km away. One goes across an island known as Noosa Sound, the other circles round to the south through Noosa Junction. Noosaville is the departure point for most river cruises.

Further inland, beyond Noosaville, you reach Tewantin, six km from Noosa Heads. Sunshine Beach, which is about three km south of the centre, has long, sandy surf beaches.

Information
Tourist Information The Tourist Information Centre (☎ (074) 47 4988), in Hastings St, is open daily from 9 am to 5 pm. There are also a number of privately run tourist information offices which double as booking agents for accommodation, trips, tours and so on.

Books Written Dimensions, near the cinemas on Sunshine Beach Rd in Noosa Junction, has an extensive travel section, an ABC shop and a good selection of other books. Dwyer's Bookstore, in the Laguna Arcade in Hastings St, is also good and has a small travel section and children's books.

Noosa National Park
The spectacular cape at Noosa Head marks the northern end of the Sunshine Coast. This small but lovely national park extends for about two km in each direction from the headland, and has fine walks, great coastal scenery and a string of bays on the northern side with waves which draw surfers from all over the country. Alexandria Bay on the eastern side is the best sandy beach.

The main entrance, at the end of Park Rd, has a car park, information centre and picnic areas, and is also the starting point for five great walking tracks, which range from one to four km in length. You can also drive up to the **Laguna Lookout** from Viewland Dve in Noosa Junction, or walk into the park from McAnally Dve or Parkedge Rd in Sunshine Beach.

Activities
Adventure Activities Total Adventures

(☎ (074) 49 0943 or 018 148 609) runs a good range of adventure activities including abseiling and rock-climbing trips, mountain bike tours and canoeing trips up the Noosa River. They also offer sea-kayaking trips from September to June.

Surfing, Fishing & Water Sports Noosa Sea Sports (☎ (074) 47 3426), in Noosa Sound shopping centre, rents surfboards, boogie boards, fishing and snorkelling gear.

Catamarans and surf skis can be hired from the Noosa Main Beach. Most of the surf shops rent boards, including Ozmosis (☎ (074) 47 3300) in Hastings St, which has mini-malibus for hire for $30 a day.

There are about seven different places along the Noosa River in Gympie Tce, Noosaville, where you can rent out fishing dinghies, barbecue pontoons, catamarans, jet skis, canoes and surf skis.

Tennis Just off Hastings St, the Laguna Bay Tennis Club (☎ (074) 47 4020) has good mod-grass courts costing around $20 an hour; it is open daily from 7 am to 10 pm.

Golf The Noosa Valley Country Club (☎ (074) 49 1411) is a good golf course in the Noosa Valley, 15 minutes west of Noosa on the Eumundi road. The course is open to the public, and they also have squash and tennis courts. There's another golf course west of Noosa at Tewantin.

Horse Riding & Camel Safaris South of Noosa at Lake Weyba, Clip Clop Treks (☎ (074) 49 1254) offers two-hour rides ($30), half-day rides with lunch ($60), and full-day rides for experienced riders ($95). They also have six-day camping and horse-riding trips to Fraser Island leaving once a month ($780 per person) and five-day hinterland treks, staying in a different pub every night ($900 per person).

The Lake Cooroibah Holiday Park (☎ (074) 47 1225), about 10 km north-west of Noosa on Lake Cooroibah, offers horse riding and camel safaris – see the Cooloola Coast section for details.

Other Activities Other activities on offer include paraflying (☎ (074) 49 9630), joy flights in the Red Baron bi-plane (☎ (074) 74 1200) and hot-air ballooning (☎ (074) 95 6714).

Organised Tours & Cruises

Fraser Island There are a number of operators offering trips from Noosa up to Fraser Island via the Cooloola National Park and the Coloured Sands.

Adventure Tours (☎ (074) 47 2411) has good day trips to Fraser Island every day, costing $110 for adults and $75 for children. You get five to six hours on the island and the cost includes morning and afternoon tea and a good barbecue lunch. They do pick-ups from anywhere on the coast. Ranger Personalised Tours (☎ (074) 49 9999) also has day trips out of Noosa costing $95 for adults and $65 for children with lunch, morning and afternoon tea included.

Adventure Tours (☎ (074) 47 2411) also has good three-day camping safaris to Fraser Island departing twice a week. The trips cost $148 per person, which covers everything including your driver and guide, all meals and camping gear. You can book direct or though most of the hostels here.

Other Tours & Cruises You can do all sorts of boat cruises from Noosa, including trips up the Noosa River to the Cooloola National Park and dolphin-spotting ocean trips. There are also 4WD tours up the coast to the Tewah Coloured Sands and the Cooloola National Park. Check with the tourist office to see what's available. Brochures and booking agents are everywhere.

Places to Stay

Although it has a reputation as a resort for the rich and fashionable, Noosa has a huge range of accommodation covering everything from caravan parks and backpackers' hostels to resort hotels and apartments.

With the exception of the backpackers' hostels, accommodation prices can rise by 50% in busy times and by 100% in the December to January peak season. If you're going to stay a few days, it's worth asking at information offices and estate agents about holiday flats or units. These can be economical, especially for a group. In the off season, some estate agents rent private holiday homes at bargain rates, or advertise for caretakers – look on Sunshine Beach Rd in Noosa Junction or Hastings St in Noosa Heads for estate agents.

There are quite a few accommodation booking agents in Noosa, including Accom Noosa (☎ (074) 47 3444) and Holiday Noosa (☎ (074) 47 4011).

Camping One of the best caravan parks here is the *Sunrise Holiday Village* (☎ (074) 47 3294), on David Low Way in Sunshine Beach, three km south of Noosa. The park is on a hillside overlooking the beach, and has tent sites ranging seasonally from $10 to $15, powered sites from $12.50 to $20, on-site vans from $25 to $45, and good self-contained cabins that sleep up to five people and cost from $30 to $55 a double, plus $3 to $5 for extra people. In the off season only, they also have a backpackers' section with a bed in an on-site van costing $16.

Another good option is the *Munna Point Caravan & Camping Area* (☎ (074) 49 7050), in Russell St, Noosaville. It has a good setting beside the river with lots of grass and shady trees, with tent sites from $11 and powered sites from $13.

Hostels All of Noosa's hostels have courtesy buses and do pick-ups from the bus stop.

The *Noosa Backpackers Resort* (☎ (074) 49 8151), at 9 William St, Munna Point, Noosaville, is a popular hostel fronted by a Thai restaurant (see Places to Eat) with good cooking and sitting areas and a pool. The owners can also organise river cruises or trips to the Cooloola area or Fraser Island. Dorm beds are $13, doubles $28 and they have good breakfasts from $2.

In Sunshine Beach, *Backpackers on the Beach* (☎ (074) 47 4739), at 26 Stevens St, is close to the beach and has good two-bedroom self-contained units. Beds cost $14 a night, and bikes, surfboards, boogie boards and laundry are free. This place also runs a complex of one-bedroom units next door that sleeps up to eight people.

Another good option in Sunshine Beach is the *Melaluka Units* (☎ (074) 47 3663), at 7 Selene St. It's also close to the beach, and has two and three-bedroom holiday units spread across three separate blocks, with beds costing $15 per person. It has a pool, sauna and free laundry.

The large *Koala Beach Resort* (☎ (074) 47 3355), at 44 Noosa Dve in Noosa Junction, is a converted motel with good facilities including a pool, cafe, bikes and surfboards. A bed in a six-bed unit costs $13 and doubles are $30. You can also have a motel unit to yourself; these range from $45 to $65, depending on the season and the type of room. Koala is a party-oriented place with a cafe with evening meals from $5 to $7, as well as a bar, barbecues and nightly entertainment.

Guesthouses In Noosa Heads itself, *Halse Lodge* (☎ (074) 47 3254) is a comfortable guesthouse owned by the Anglican Church. It's a beautiful 100-year-old building, complete with polished wooden floors and great views over the town and sea. The staff are friendly, the position is great and it's excellent value, with simple two to six-bed rooms with shared bathrooms costing $20 per person per night, including a continental breakfast. You supply your own linen, or it can be hired for a fee.

Motels & Units The prime location in Noosa would have to be on the Main Beach side of Hastings St. You can literally step out of your unit onto the beach, and there are dozens of restaurants, cafes and bars just the toss of a credit card away. You have to pay for the privileges, of course, although there are still a couple of places around Hastings St that are surprisingly affordable.

Tingirana (☎ (074) 47 3274), on the beachfront at 25 Hastings St, is excellent value considering the location with good budget accommodation ranging from $65 to $85 for motel-style units, $85 to $115 for

one-bedroom units and $130 to $230 for three-bedroom penthouses.

The *Jacaranda Holiday Units* (☎ (074) 47 4011), on the south side of Hastings St, is another complex of well-presented budget units. The motel-style units sleep up to three people and range from $60 to $90 a night, and the self-contained one-bedroom units sleep up to five people and range from $80 to $120. The back units have river views, and there's a pool.

Moving up a notch to the next price bracket, other beachfront options include *Netanya Noosa* (☎ (074) 47 4722), at 75 Hastings St, a hotel with garden rooms from $160 to $210 a night and beachfront units from $230 to $280 a night; and *The Breakers* (☎ (074) 47 5399), in Hastings St, with self-contained one-bedroom units from $130 to $170 a night in the low season and from $200 to $250 a night in the high season.

Just under one km back from Hastings St, the *Laguna Bay Inn* (☎ (074) 49 2873), at 2 Viewland Dve in Noosa Junction, has four excellent self-contained units in an attractive and shady garden setting, with a good pool and barbecue area. These comfortable one and two-bedroom units sleep up to six people and range from $60 to $100 a night.

One of the best areas for cheaper accommodation is along Gympie Tce, the main road through Noosaville. The *Noosa Riverfront Units* (☎ (074) 49 7595), at 277 Gympie Tce, is a small two-storey block of good budget holiday units starting from $40 for a studio unit or $80 for a two-bedroom unit. At No 281, *Noosa River Beach* (☎ (074) 49 7873) has four small, old-fashioned budget units which range from $40 to $100 a night.

Further along at No 233, the *Palm Tree Lodge* (☎ (074) 49 7311) has eight motel style units and eight self-contained units that range from $35/40 to $60/70 for singles/doubles in the low/high season.

At No 187-193, the *Islander Resort* (☎ (074) 49 7022) is a tropical-style mid-range resort with self-contained units. The two-bedroom units sleep up to four people and range from $100 to $140; the three-bedroom units sleep six people and range from $130 to $180.

Resorts & Hotels The *Sheraton Noosa Resort* (☎ (074) 49 4888), between Hastings St and the Noosa Sound, is Noosa's only five-star hotel. It's an impressive but relaxed low-rise hotel with 140 rooms and 30 suites, four bars, three restaurants, a gym, pool, sauna, spa etc. Rooms start from $320 a night, suites range from $370 to $750.

Terraced into the hillside at the east end of Hastings St, *Number 1 in Hastings St* (☎ (074) 49 2211) is an exclusive complex of 20 apartments and four penthouses, all with great views over Laguna Bay, with a gym, pool, spa and barbecue area. Nightly tariffs for the apartments start from $150 for one bedroom, $185 for two bedrooms, and $220 for the penthouses and three bedroom apartments.

Places to Eat

Noosa is one of Queensland's epicurean capitals, and there are some outstanding restaurants in town, many of which are in the Hastings St area. Hastings St is glamorous, mega-trendy and generally expensive, but those ample of wallet can dine very well here in stylish surrounds.

There are clusters of more affordable restaurants and cafes on Gympie Tce in Noosaville, on Sunshine Beach Rd in Noosa Junction, and in Sunshine Beach.

Hastings St Hastings St is lined with restaurants and cafes, many with candle-lit outdoor tables under umbrellas or canopies.

Eduardo's on the Beach (☎ (074) 47 5875), at the end of an arcade at 25 Hastings St, is about the best setting in town. It's a relaxed BYO with a beachy décor and a small beachfront deck, and opens every day for breakfast, lunch and dinner. Brekkies range from $2.50 for raisin toast to $9.90 for eggs Benedict; for lunch, meals such as pastas, seafood curries or reef fish with lime and ginger sauce range from $12 to $14. The dinner menu mains are around $18. Eduardo's is very popular and it's a good idea to book ahead – ask for a table on the deck.

In the arcade leading to Eduardo's is *Betty's Burgers*, a small takeaway with a wide range of cheap burgers from $1 to $4.50.

At 8 Hastings St, *Saltwater* (☎ (074) 47 2234) is a stylish all-white building that evokes memories of the Greek Isles. Upstairs is an open-air rooftop restaurant with great seafood and salads in the $12 to $20 range; downstairs is a gourmet-style takeaway with fish & chips, prawns, calamari, tempura etc. Next door, the Mediterranean-styled *Aqua Bar & Cafe* has good pastas, salads, meat and seafood dishes, with main courses ranging from $10 to $15 at lunch time and from $15 to $23 at night.

Across the road, *Lindoni's* is a seriously sophisticated licensed Italian restaurant with candle-lit tables, Italian-speaking waiters in black-and-whites, and main courses in the $18 to $22 range.

Back on the southern side of the street and set back from Hastings St, the *Bay Village Food Court* has a great selection of eateries, including a gourmet deli, a carvery, a fish & chippery, a pizza & pasta bar and a bakery. They all open daily for lunch, and also for dinner during the tourist season.

Further along, *Aromas* is a good place for coffee and cakes after you've done the obligatory Hastings St stroll; they also have salads, breakfasts and sandwiches.

The *Beach Cafe*, on the beachfront just down from the tourist office, is a good spot for breakfast with a menu including muesli with fresh fruit ($4) or bacon & eggs ($5.90). They also do pastas, salads and sandwiches.

Just past the roundabout, the ever-popular *Cafe Le Monde* is fronted by a large covered courtyard and has a huge menu that covers everything from breakfasts ($4 to $8), open sandwiches and salads ($8 to $11), pastas and vegetarian meals ($7 to $14) and meat and seafood dishes. It's also a good place for coffee and cake, or you could just order a drink and stare at everyone else – most people come here to be seen, so you'll be doing them a favour. They also have live music here, usually acoustic and usually on Tuesday and Thursday nights and Friday and Sunday afternoons. Upstairs, *Palmers* is one of Noosa's most up-market restaurants.

Augello's, on Noosa Dve near the Hastings St roundabout, is a small BYO Italian bistro with good pastas from $8 to $12, salads from $7 to $10, gourmet pizzas and calzone for around $11 and focaccias for around $6.

Noosa Junction On Sunshine Beach Rd, *Roma Pizza*, at the southern end, is a casual Italian bistro with red vinyl booths and fish nets and chianti bottles hanging from the roof – very cosy. Pastas and pizzas are around $10 and other main dishes are from $12 to $15. On Monday, Tuesday and Wednesday nights they have an all-you-can-eat pasta or pizza special for $6. *Thai House*, upstairs at the Sunshine Centre opposite the cinemas, is a simple little BYO with main courses from $12.50 to $14.50. *Go Natural*, a health-food shop on the corner of Arcadia St, is a good spot for lunches with burgers, pies, rolls and sangers, jaffles and salads.

Around the corner at 73 Noosa Dve, *Topopo's Mexican Restaurant* is a colourful cantina with main courses for around $10 and combo dishes for around $13, as well as margaritas and sangria by the glass or by the jug.

Noosaville *Filligan's Bar & Restaurant*, at 9 Russell St, is a stylish eatery in a small aqua-coloured cottage. It serves up innovative modern food that blends Cajun, Creole, Asian, South American, Jamaican and probably a few other styles that I forgot to write down. Filligan's is licensed, and opens daily for lunch and dinner. Main courses range from $8 to $17. They also make their own maize and corn bread – wonderful.

In front of the Noosa Backpackers' Resort in William St, the *Thai Restaurant* (formerly the Bratpackers Cafe) is a small and popular Thai eatery with a good range of stir-fries, curries and salads, with mains in the $8 to $13 range. It's BYO and opens nightly for dinner.

At 247 Gympie Tce, *The Cantina* is a BYO Mexican restaurant that opens nightly for dinner, with main courses in the $10 to $14 range.

Next to the Islander Resort on Gympie Tce, *Sakura Japanese Kitchen* is a small and casual BYO eatery with half a dozen tables. At lunch time they offer three-course meals for $10 or a choice of six main dishes ranging from $7 to $8, all with miso soup or salad. At night, they have a good range of combination dishes from $14 to $22 and sushi for $6 to $8 a piece. Sakura opens daily for lunch (except Tuesday and Saturday) and dinner (except Tuesday).

Further along Gympie Tce, just before you cross the river, the *Noosa Yacht & Rowing Club* is a new two-storey riverfront building which opens every day for lunch and dinner and on Sundays for breakfast. The food here is cheap and hearty, with roasts ($6.50), seafood platters ($8.50), lasagna ($6), and kid's meals under $5.

Sunshine Beach If you're staying in Sunshine Beach, there's a general store, a fruit and vegie shop, and a couple of eateries in the small shopping centre in Duke St. The *Saratoga Cafe* is a stylish little place with pastas from $8 to $13 as well as pizzas, salads and good coffee. The *Sunshine Beach Deli* is a good gourmet deli with vegetarian dishes, home-made pastries and cakes, rolls and sandwiches. It's also a good place for breakfast. Down at the beach, the *Sunshine Beach Surf Life-Saving Club* serves bistro meals and has a courtyard overlooking the ocean.

Further south at 1 Tingira Cres, the *Beach Chalet* (☎ (074) 47 3944) is a fun and funky cafe above a general store, with an open-air balcony overlooking the ocean, a bar/eatery and a small fernery room that seats about 20 people. The chalet is a popular live music venue that opens on Mondays, Fridays and Saturdays. On Mondays they have a set menu that costs $14, which includes food and music, and on weekends they have an à la carte menu with pastas, salads, seafoods and good vegetarian meals. Main courses range from $10 to $17. See the Entertainment section for more details.

Entertainment

Nightclubs & Live Music At 1 Tingira Cres in Sunshine Beach, the *Beach Chalet* is a good live music venue, bar and eatery that features everything from world music, reggae and African soul music to jazz and rock 'n' roll. It currently opens on Mondays, Fridays and Saturdays. Ring to see who's playing while you're in town, and see the Places to Eat section for details of their meals.

Cafe Le Monde in Hastings St is another live music venue – see the Places to Eat section for details.

Noosa's main nightclub is the *Rolling Rock*, upstairs in the Bay Village Plaza off Hastings St. It's open every night until around 3 am, with a 'smart casual' dress code and cover charges between $5 and $7. Nearby and run by the same operator, the *New York Bar* is a quieter, more sophisticated cocktail bar with an outdoor courtyard.

Downstairs at the Noosa Reef Hotel on Noosa Dve, the *Reef Nightclub* opens from Thursday to Sunday nights till late. The pub also has occasional live bands and Sunday afternoon sessions.

Theatre & Cinema The *Noosa Art Theatre* has theatre productions throughout the year. Check with the tourist office to see what's on.

The *Noosa 3 Cinemas* (☎ (074) 47 5300) on Sunshine Beach Rd, Noosa Junction, shows latest release movies. If you get a chance, don't miss the wonderful Majestic Theatre in Pomona and its screenings of Valentino's cult classic *The Son of the Sheik* – see the Pomona section for details.

Getting There & Around

Bus Long-distance buses stop at the bus terminal near the corner of Noosa Dve and Noosa Pde, just back from Hastings St. McCafferty's doesn't have services to Noosa, and Greyhound Pioneer Australia only has one service a day. Suncoast Pacific is the main company linking Brisbane with

Noosa. See Getting There & Away at the start of this chapter for more info on bus services.

Tewantin Bus Services (☎ (074) 49 7422) runs frequent daily services up and down the coast between Noosa and Maroochydore, and has local services linking Noosa Heads, Noosaville, Noosa Junction, etc. They also run a special service on Saturdays to the Eumundi Markets.

Car Rental Noosa Car Rentals (☎ (074) 47 3777), right opposite the bus terminal in Noosa Heads, has mini-mokes from $35 a day, Mazda 121s from $55 and Mazda 323s from $65. There are a number of other local operators, plus national firms like Avis and Thrifty.

If you want to drive up the Cooloola Coast beach to the Teewah Coloured Sands, Double Island Point, Rainbow Beach or Fraser Island, Sunshine 4WD Rentals (☎ (074) 47 3702), beside the Noosa Junction post office, rents Suzuki 4WDs for $100 a day and Toyota Landcruisers for $150 a day. They have a two-day minimum hire for trips to Fraser Island. In the same office, Trusty Car Hire (☎ (074) 47 4777) has mokes from $35 a day, Charades from $40 and Toyota Corollas from $45 a day.

Bicycle Hire Bikes can be hired from a number of places, including Noosa Sea Sports (☎ (074) 47 3426) and Koala Bike Hire (☎ (074) 48 0599), who has mountain bikes and helmets from $10 a day and will deliver to wherever you're staying.

TEWANTIN (pop 5500)

Seven km west of Noosa along the Noosa River, Tewantin is now almost joined to Noosaville by urban sprawl. It's more of a residential town than a tourism hotspot, but it does have a couple of minor points of interest.

The **Noosa Regional Gallery**, below the council chambers in Pelican St, has a permanent collection of digital art and features regular exhibitions. It is open Tuesday to Saturday from 10 am to 5 pm.

The **Tewantin/Noosa Golf Club** is on the western outskirts of town, on the road to Cooroy. Tourist attractions in town include the **House of Bottles** in Myles St, with a large bottle collection in a house made out of thousands of bottles, and **The Big Shell** in Gympie St featuring a collection of sea shells and hats.

In the centre of town on the corner of Poinciana and Diyan Sts, the *Royal Mail Hotel* (☎ (074) 47 1644) has budget accommodation and good meals. They have rooms with shared bathrooms for $25/35 for singles/doubles. You can have a casual bite in the bar where meals range from $5 to $8, or there's a very pleasant bistro, *Moreton's Restaurant*, overlooking the river with meals from $7 to $20. They have live bands on Friday nights and pool competitions on Saturday nights.

Signposted off the main road 2.5 km south of town, the **Noosa River Ferry** runs across the river continuously every day from 6 am to 10 pm (until midnight on Fridays and Saturdays). Cars cost $4, motorcycles and horses $3.

COOLOOLA COAST

Stretching for 50 km between Noosa and Rainbow Beach, the Cooloola Coast is a remote strip of long sandy beaches backed by the Cooloola National Park. Although this stretch is undeveloped it is so popular with campers at times that you may be excused for thinking otherwise. The Noosa River runs through the centre of the park, with a series of lakes at its southern end.

The Cooloola Way, a gravel road which runs from Tewantin (via Boreen Point and Kin Kin) through the western catchment area of the national park all the way up to Rainbow Beach, is open to conventional vehicles unless there has been heavy rain. If you have a 4WD, you can drive right up the beach to Rainbow Bay, and from there cross to Fraser Island. On the way you'll pass the Teewah coloured sand cliffs and the rusting *Cherry Venture*, a 3000-tonne freighter swept ashore by a cyclone in 1973.

See the previous Tewantin section for details of the vehicle ferry across the Noosa River.

Lake Cooroibah

A couple of km north of Tewantin, the Noosa River widens out into Lake Cooroibah. If you take the ferry across the Noosa River, you can drive across to this secluded stretch of coast in a conventional vehicle, and there are a couple of good camping grounds between the east side of the lake and the coast. With a 4WD, you can continue up the coast all the way to Rainbow Beach.

The *Lake Cooroibah Holiday Park* (☎ (074) 47 1225) is a low-key resort on 20 hectares with a wide range of accommodation, a pub and restaurant, general store, tennis and squash courts, and horse riding. Camp sites cost $3 to $4 per person per night plus another $2 a night for a powered site, on-site tents that sleep four people cost $20 a night, and four to six-berth cabins start from $35 a night. There's also a resort section with cottages, units and apartments from $80 to $140 a night. The park offers various horse rides including one-hour rides ($16), two-hour bush and beach rides ($30), day rides with lunch ($70) and 1½-hour moonlight rides with dinner ($40).

Operating from the park, *Camel Company Australia* offers camel rides and safaris ranging from one-hour ($20) and half-day beach rides ($45) to overnight safaris ($125 with meals, BYO sleeping bag) and six-day safaris to Fraser Island ($720 adults, $475 children, with all meals and camping gear supplied, BYO sleeping bag). See the Fraser Coast chapter for further details.

Boreen Point (pop 230)

On the western shores of Lake Cootharaba and at the southern edge of the Cooloola National Park, Boreen Point is a relaxed, laid-back little town with a couple of places to stay, a pub and a good lakeside restaurant.

There are two roads up to Boreen Point, both accessible in a conventional vehicle. It's 21 km north from Tewantin by mostly unsealed road, or 19 km by sealed road north-west from Pomona. From Boreen Point, an unsealed road leads another five km up to Elanda Point where there's a rangers' station for the Cooloola National Park.

Places to Stay & Eat You can pitch a tent at the *Boreen Point Camp Grounds* on the foreshore of the lake for $8 a night, or the *Everglades Caravan Park* (☎ (074) 85 3213) on Boreen Pde has caravan sites from $12, on-site vans from $20 and cabins from $30. The *Lake Cootharaba Holiday Units* (☎ (074) 85 3153) at 64 Laguna St sleep up to four people and start from $40 a double.

The historic *Apollonian Hotel* (☎ (074) 85 3100), which was built in Gympie in the 1870s and later transported here, is a charming timber pub in a garden setting with broad, shady verandahs and good country cooking. Lunch and dinner are served daily, and Sunday lunches feature a spit roast and live entertainment. Beside the pub is an accommodation building with 10 double rooms with shared bathrooms from $30 a double.

The Jetty (☎ (074) 85 3167), with a lovely setting on the edge of Lake Cootharaba, is a stylish licensed restaurant with an excellent reputation for its food. It is open every day for lunch and on Friday and Saturday for dinner, and has a six-course set menu for $36 per person. You can drive up or come by boat up the Noosa River, or the restaurant runs a free courtesy bus from Noosa every day if you book in advance.

Cooloola National Park

North of Noosa, the Cooloola National Park covers over 54,000 hectares and stretches around 50 km north to Rainbow Beach. A couple of km upstream from Noosaville, the Noosa River takes a northward bend and widens out into Lake Cooroibah then Lake Cootharaba, which is at the southern end of the national park. It's a varied wilderness area with long sandy beaches, mangrove-lined waterways, forest, heath and lakes, all of it featuring plentiful birdlife and lots of wildflowers in spring.

You can drive into and through the park, although the best way to see Cooloola is from

a boat up the Noosa River. Boats can be hired from Tewantin and Noosa and various operators offer cruises into the area.

Five km north of Boreen Point at Elanda Point there's a lakeside camping ground and a ranger's office (☎ (074) 85 3245). Several walking trails start from here including the 46-km Cooloola Wilderness Trail and a seven-km trail to the National Parks visitors centre (☎ (074) 49 7364) at Kinaba Island.

There are around 10 camping grounds in the park, many of them alongside the river. The main ones are Fig Tree Point at the north of Lake Cootharaba and Harry's Hut about four km upstream. Freshwater is the main camp on the coast; it's about six km south of Double Island Point. For site bookings and info, contact one of the ranger's offices.

The camping grounds in the northern section of the park are accessible from Rainbow Beach. Northern Cooloola has camping grounds between Freshwater Lake and the eastern beach, and near Double Island Point on the north-facing beach (both 4WD or foot access only). There are several walking tracks, and the main vehicle access is from the Gympie to Rainbow Beach road, four km south of Rainbow Beach. You can get information and camping permits for northern Cooloola from the National Parks information centre in Rainbow Beach (☎ (074) 86 3160).

POMONA (pop 880)

Pomona is a small rural centre in the shadows of Mt Cooroora (440 metres), 30 km west of Noosa. A King of the Mountain footrace to the top of the mountain is held every year in July.

The town has a small **historical museum**, and the *Pomona Hotel* (☎ (074) 85 1187) has budget accommodation.

Pomona is also home to the wonderful Majestic Theatre (☎ (074) 85 2330), at 3 Factory St.

EUMUNDI (pop 400)

Just off the east side of the Bruce Hwy, Eumundi is a charming little rural township

Son of Sheik

Built in 1921, Pomona's Majestic is the oldest continuously running cinema in the country. As it has done every week since 1987, the Majestic screens Rudolph Valentino's last film *The Son of the Sheik* every Thursday night at 8.30 pm. Ron West, the theatre's owner, accompanies the film live on his Wurlitzer pipe organ, and the $7 admission price includes wine, nibbles and supper. A unique evening's entertainment from another era – highly recommended. Ron also has an extensive collection of other great old films and comedy shorts from the 1920s, which he screens five or six times a week. Give him a call and find out what's on, or check with one of the tourist offices. ■

that is famous for its beer and its Saturday markets.

The local boutique beer, **Eumundi Lager**, is a great drop. It was originally brewed in the Imperial Hotel, but nowadays it's made down at Yatala on the Gold Coast. Oh well, you can still sample it on tap in the Imperial Hotel, and the former brewery is now an art gallery with glass-blowing displays.

On Memorial Dve, the **Eumundi Historical Museum** (☎ (074) 42 8762) opens on Wednesday and Saturday mornings, or at other times by arrangement.

There are a number of interesting **craft shops, pottery galleries** and **antique shops** along Memorial Dve, the main street. West of Eumundi, you can fossick for thunder eggs at **Thunder Egg Farm**.

Markets

Every Saturday morning, thousands of people flock to Eumundi for the famous **Eumundi Village Markets**. There are more than 200 stalls along the main street and in front of the old railway station, selling everything from art and handicrafts, clothing, woodwork, pottery and furniture to fruit and vegies. The markets run from 6.30 am to 12.30 pm.

Places to Stay & Eat

The *Imperial Hotel* (☎ (074) 42 8303) is a charismatic old pub in the centre of town. It has basic budget accommodation upstairs for $25 a room, a pleasant beer garden and good bistro meals. On Saturday mornings they serve up cooked brekkies on the balcony for $4, or $7 with all the trimmings. They have live bands here on Friday and Saturday nights.

The *Eumundi Motel* (☎ (074) 42 8215), about two km south of town, has units from $35.

Bartu Jimba, at 101 Memorial Dve, is a groovy little BYO cafe in a renovated timber building with an open-air courtyard next door. It does breakfasts on weekends (from $3 to $8) and opens for lunch and dinner from Tuesday to Saturday. The menu is fairly exotic with Korean, Moroccan, Asian and Mediterranean influences: main courses range from $14 to $18.

YANDINA (pop 700)

On the Bruce Hwy 10 km south of Eumundi, Yandina's biggest attraction is **The Ginger Factory** on Pioneer Rd. This place is very popular with tourists and has train rides, tours of the factory and plantations, a wildlife park, audio-visual shows, a car museum, a cafe and a huge range of ginger products and souvenirs on sale. The factory opens daily from 9 am to 5 pm. Entry is free, train rides cost $3 for big kids and $2 for little kids.

In the centre of the town, the *Blue Moon Cafe* is a blue timber cottage with tasty tucker including sangers and rolls, good vegetarian meals, burgers, steaks and seafood dishes. It is open daily from 8 am to 8 pm – eat in or takeaway.

On the highway 600 metres south of the centre, the riverside *Yandina Caravan Park* (☎ (074) 46 7332) has tent sites for $11 and powered sites for $13.

Sunshine Coast Hinterland

The Blackall Range rises just in from the coast, and this scenic hinterland area has mountain villages, guesthouses and B&Bs, national parks with rainforests and waterfalls, and some great restaurants. There are also numerous art, craft, pottery and antique shops and galleries to visit, as well as a few other interesting tourist attractions. It's a great area for scenic drives, bushwalks or leisurely exploring, and it's worth considering hiring a car for a day or two if you don't have your own.

The short drive from Maleny to Mapleton is one of southern Queensland's outstanding scenic routes. The road follows a ridge across the Blackall Mountains that runs parallel with the coast, with great views across the Sunshine Coast lowlands to the ocean beyond.

NAMBOUR (pop 10,350)

Nambour is the main commercial centre for the hinterland. Set amongst hills and surrounded by cane farms and pineapple plantations, it's an attractive town with a wide range of services and facilities, but holds little of interest for travellers unless you need a bank or shops or some such thing.

The **Big Pineapple**, one of Queensland's superbly kitsch 'big' creations, is just off the Bruce Hwy about six km south of Nambour. This place has become a major tourist attraction. You can climb up inside a 15-metre fibreglass pineapple, and there are various rides. A combined tour of the plantations, visit to the animal nursery and a cane-train ride costs $10.50 for adults, $8 for kids and $29.50 for a family. The main building has all sorts of souvenirs and products on sale including macadamia nuts, pineapples and other fruit.

MALENY (pop 800)

In the heart of the hinterland, Maleny is a laid-back rural township with an attractive mountain setting. It's something of an alternative centre, with lots of artists and craftspeople living in the area, and has a couple of good restaurants and cafes as well as craft and antique shops and several interesting accommodation options.

There's a small information centre (☎ (074) 99 9033) at the Maleny Community Centre, which is open every day from 9 am to 3 pm. The Community Centre, a yellow timber building in the centre of town, screens art-house movies on Saturday nights.

Lake Baroon, signposted nine km north of Maleny, is the main water supply for the coast as well as a popular swimming, boating, fishing and picnicking venue. You can hire boats at the lake.

Festivals

The famous Maleny Folk Festival, which moved south in 1995 and is now held on a

The mega kitsch Big Pineapple

property near the town of Woodford, runs annually over the five days leading up to New Year's Day. The festival programme features a huge diversity of music including folk, traditional Irish, indigenous and world music, as well as buskers, belly dancers, craft markets, visual arts performances and lots more. If you want to settle in for the festival, camping grounds are set up on the property with toilets, showers etc. It's the closest thing Australia has to Woodstock, to run out an old cliché.

You can buy tickets at the gate or in advance through the festival office (☎ (074) 76 0600). Season tickets cost $125, and day or night passes cost $30 – they're slightly cheaper if you buy in advance.

Places to Stay

Maleny Palms (☎ (074) 94 2933), at 23 Macadamia Dve, 500 metres north of the centre, is an up-market caravan park with on-site vans from $23, self-contained cabins from $38 and villas from $60. They also have tent sites, but these aren't always available due to the often wet weather.

The *Hotel Maleny* (☎ (074) 94 2013), on Bunya St in the centre of town, is a stylishly restored old timber pub with renovated pub rooms for $30/34 for singles/doubles, plus another $6 for a continental breakfast.

The *Maleny Lodge* (☎ (074) 94 2370), right in the centre of town at 58 Maple St, is a beautifully restored 1894 timber guesthouse furnished in period style with antiques. B&B costs $76/100 for singles/doubles; they also have dinner and weekend packages. Highly recommended.

South of Maleny at Mt Mellum, *Rowan House* (☎ (074) 94 1042) is a grand old timber mountain home with spectacular views across to the coast and Brisbane. There are four comfortable guest rooms, two with ensuites, with doubles ranging from $100 to $160 a night for B&B. There's also a tennis court and pool, and a small self-contained cottage beside the main house for rent. Rowan House is signposted off the Maleny-Landsborough road.

Places to Eat

On Maple St in the centre, the *Up Front Club* is a licensed club and co-op that has vegetarian and meat meals in the $6 to $9 range, as well as herbal teas, smoothies and juices. It's a casual, earthy place with healthy and wholesome food. It is open every day for lunch and dinner and on Sundays for breakfast. Nearby, the *Food Gallery* is an up-market gourmet deli and cafe with good, if somewhat pricey, food.

Malcolm's (☎ (074) 94 2825), two km south of town, is set on a hillside with magnificent views of the bizarre Glass House Mountains. It's an attractive licensed restaurant which opens from Wednesday to Sunday for lunch and on Friday and Saturday for dinner. Main courses range from $15 to $23. Come for lunch, the views are inspirational.

MONTVILLE (pop 400)

On a ridge midway between Mapleton and Maleny, Montville is a historic mountain village that has developed into a major tourist attraction. Sadly, somewhere in the transformation Montville lost much of its original charm and character and became a commercialised version of the quaint 'Olde English' village – many of the 'historic' buildings are relatively new. Still, the setting is beautiful and there are some lovely original cottages and houses that have been restored.

There are half a dozen up-market guesthouses and resorts on the mountain, and the village has quite a few restaurants, tea rooms, art and craft and pottery galleries, herb gardens, gift and souvenir shops. A heritage trail guides you around the village.

Three km north of Montville is the turn off to the lovely **Kondilla Falls National Park**, where the falls drop 80 metres into a rainforest valley. There are picnic areas and good walking trails.

Places to Stay

In the centre of the village, the *Montville Mountain Inn* (☎ (074) 42 9499) has modern motel-style rooms from $65 during the week, and dinner and B&B packages on weekends from $130 a double.

On Western Ave, about four km west of Montville, the *Genfield Boutique Guesthouse* (☎ (074) 42 9366) is an elegant and luxurious guesthouse on an eight hectare property overlooking Lake Baroon, with landscaped gardens, a pool and tennis court. B&B costs $175 a double.

MAPLETON (pop 400)

Mapleton is a laid-back little township eight km north of Montville, with a good pub, a couple of caravan parks, an excellent guesthouse and a couple of craft and pottery galleries.

Continuing westwards from Mapleton, the unsealed **Obi Obi Rd** is a rough but very scenic drive through state forests to the small town of **Kenilworth** (20 km). Along the route is the **Mapleton Falls National Park** where the Pencil Creek plunges 120 metres. This is a great park for exploring, with lots of birdlife and several walking tracks.

Places to Stay & Eat

The best of the two caravan parks here is the *Lilyponds Caravan Park* (☎ (074) 45 7238) in Warruga St, about 400 metres north of the pub. It has a good setting overlooking the Mapleton Lily Ponds, with tent sites from $10 and self-contained cabins that sleep up to six people and cost from $30 a double.

The *Mapleton Tavern* is a relaxed old timber pub with great views from its front balcony – a good place for a counter meal or a cold beer. Meals range from $8 to $13 for roasts, calamari, veal schnitzel, seafood baskets and steaks.

St Isidore's Guesthouse (☎ (074) 45 7288) was built as an agricultural college in 1897, and is named after the patron saint of farmers. It has been transformed into an up-market guesthouse, set amidst lovely gardens, with four ensuite rooms ranging from $165 to $200 a double, which includes a four-course gourmet brunch and afternoon tea. St Isidore is about 200 metres north of the pub.

PALMWOODS (pop 1200)

Palmwoods is another small township eight km south of Nambour and 10 km east of Montville. A couple of km west of town is the **Forest Glen Deer Sanctuary**, with hundreds of deer as well as kangaroos, koalas, emus and geese, plus a restaurant. It is open daily from 9 am to 5 pm.

Places to Stay & Eat

On the western outskirts, just off the Montville road, the pleasant *Palmwoods Caravan Park* (☎ (074) 45 9450) has tent sites for $9, on-site vans for $25 and good cabins from $25.

In Main St, the *Palmwoods Hotel* (☎ (074) 45 9003) has clean pub rooms upstairs for $15/25 (singles/doubles) and bar meals ranging from $5 to $7. There's also a bistro here.

Also in Main St, *Clio's* (☎ (074) 45 9844) is a BYO restaurant in a simple two-room cottage which opens from Tuesday to Saturday for dinner. It has a good reputation, with traditional international cuisine and mains for around $16.

Darling Downs

West of the mountains of the Great Dividing Range stretch the rolling plains of the Darling Downs, some of the most fertile and productive agricultural land in Australia. This area was the first part of Queensland to be settled after the establishment of the Moreton Bay penal colony, and towns like Warwick and Toowoomba are amongst the most historic in the state. There are also some interesting attractions scattered through the region, including the scenic Granite Belt region (near Stanthorpe) with Queensland's only wine-growing district and some fine national parks, the historic Jondaryan Woolshed complex west of Toowoomba, and Miles' excellent Historical Village.

To the north and west of Brisbane is the South Burnett region, with the popular Bunya Mountains National Park and a string of small rural centres along Hwy 17.

History

English botanist Allan Cunningham first visited Moreton Bay in 1823. Four years later he led an expedition from Sydney to explore the area inland from the Great Dividing Range, and after six weeks his party arrived in a large valley which he described as the best piece of country he had ever seen. He named the valley the Darling Downs after the then governor of New South Wales, and later discovered Spicer's Gap, a path through the mountains to Brisbane. The following year he discovered Cunningham's Gap, which is now the main route into the Downs from Brisbane.

In 1840 brothers Patrick and George Leslie became the first Europeans to settle in the region when they established a sheep station at Toolburra, near Warwick. The success of their venture attracted an influx of other settlers, and within a few years the entire region had been taken up. The Darling Downs lived up to Allan Cunningham's earlier claims, and soon became the colony's richest pastoral region and major producer of wool.

In 1872 deposits of tin were discovered near Stanthorpe, and thousands of diggers rushed to join a tin boom that lasted some 15 years.

Getting There & Away

Air Sabair have flights from Brisbane to Toowoomba, and from Toowoomba to St George, Cunnamulla and Thargomindah.

Flight West have daily flights between Brisbane and Roma.

Bus Greyhound Pioneer Australia have two major bus services that pass through the Darling Downs. Their Brisbane-Longreach service runs along the Warrego Hwy via Toowoomba, Dalby, Miles and Roma, while their inland Brisbane-Melbourne service along the Newell Hwy goes via Toowoomba and Goondiwindi.

McCafferty's, who originated in Toowoomba

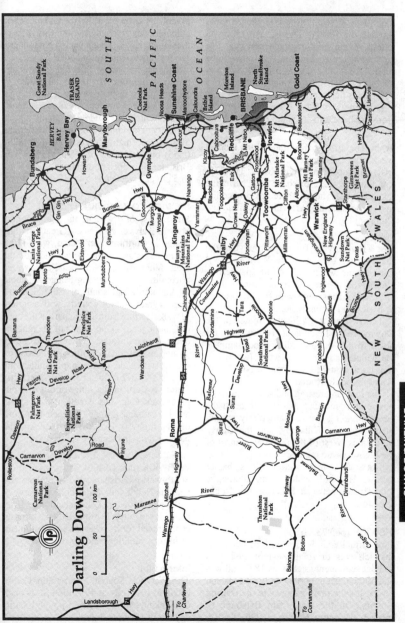

DARLING DOWNS

more than 50 years ago, has similar services through the Darling Downs, as well as an extensive range of regional services. See Getting There & Away in the Toowoomba section for more details of McCafferty's services, as well as those of smaller regional bus companies that service this region.

Brisbane Bus Lines have daily services from Brisbane into the South Burnett region.

Train The air-con *Westlander* runs twice a week from Brisbane to Charleville, through Ipswich, Toowoomba and Roma. The 777-km journey from Brisbane to Charleville takes about 17 hours; there are connecting bus services from Charleville to Quilpie and Cunnamulla.

Car & Motorcycle The major route through the Darling Downs is the Warrego Hwy, which runs westwards from Ipswich to Charleville. There's also the Cunningham Hwy, which runs south-west from Ipswich to Warwick and Goondiwindi.

The two main north-south routes in the Downs are the Leichhardt Hwy, which runs north from Goondiwindi to Rockhampton via Miles, and the Carnarvon Hwy which runs north from Mungindi on the New South Wales border to Roma.

The most interesting and scenic drives in this region are those that pass through the Great Dividing Range, particularly around Stanthorpe and Killarney, and the Bunya Mountains. West of the mountains, most of the highways are pretty dull going.

The South Burnett section of this chapter follows Hwy 17, which is an alternative inland route between Brisbane and Rockhampton.

IPSWICH (pop 73,310)

Now virtually an outer suburb of Brisbane, Ipswich was originally established as a convict settlement as early as 1827 and was one of the most important early Queensland towns. It's the main gateway to the Darling Downs. On the way from Brisbane to Ipswich, **Wolston House**, at Grindle Rd,

Wacol, 18 km west of Brisbane, is an early colonial country residence, built in 1852 of local materials. It's open from 9 am to 5 pm, Wednesday to Sunday and costs $3.

Ipswich has many fine old houses and public buildings: if you're interested in Queensland's distinctive architecture, pick up the excellent *Ipswich City Heritage Trails* leaflets which will guide you around a great diversity of buildings. The Ipswich Regional Tourist Information Centre (☎ (07) 3281 0555) on the corner of D'Arcy Place and Brisbane St is open on weekdays from 9 am to 5 pm and weekends from 10 am to 4 pm.

IPSWICH TO WARWICK (120 km)

South-west of Ipswich, the Cunningham Hwy to Warwick crosses the Great Dividing Range at **Cunningham's Gap**, with 1100-metre mountains rising either side of the road. **Main Range National Park**, which covers the Great Dividing Range for about 20 km north and south of Cunningham's Gap, is great walking country, with a variety of walks starting from the car park at the crest of Cunningham's Gap. Much of the range is covered in rainforest. There's a camping ground and information office by the road on the western side of the gap: contact the ranger (☎ (076) 66 1133) for permits. **Spicer's Gap**, in the range south of Cunningham's Gap, has excellent views and another camping ground. To reach it you turn off the highway five km west of Aratula, back towards Ipswich.

WARWICK (pop 10,400)

South-west of Brisbane, 162 km inland and near the New South Wales border, Warwick is the oldest town in Queensland after Brisbane. It's a busy Darling Downs farming centre noted for its roses, its dairy produce, its historic buildings and for its rodeo.

Information

The Warwick Tourist Information Centre (☎ (076) 61 3122) ,at 49 Albion St, is open on weekdays from 9 am to 5 pm and Saturdays from 10 am to 3 pm.

Darling Downs – home of the 'Jackie Howes'

Things to See & Do

Warwick's major attraction is the **Pringle Cottage & Museum** on Dragon St. The cottage dates from 1863, and the collection of old telephones, costumes, photos and machinery includes a Kalliope, a fascinating musical instrument made in Germany in 1885. This not-so-compact disc is still in working order. The museum is open every day (except Tuesdays) from 10 am to noon and 2 to 4 pm; entry costs $3.50 for adults, 50c for children.

On the corner of the Cunningham Hwy and Glengallan Rd, the **Jackie Howe Rest Area** is fronted by a giant pair of blade shears atop a block of stone. This monument commemorates the 'gun shearer' Jackie Howe, who was born on Canning Downs Station near Warwick back in 1861. Jackie went on to become the greatest shearer the country has ever seen, and still holds the amazing record of having shorn 321 sheep in one day (by hand!) at Alice Downs Station in 1892. Jackie had a habit of ripping the sleeves off his singlets when he was working, and nowadays the sleeveless blue singlets favoured by many Australian workers are known as 'Jackie Howes'.

Warwick has plenty of impressive old buildings, many built from locally quarried sandstone. They include the **post office** on the corner of Palmerin and Grafton Sts, a solid structure with unusual Moorish-style arches and topped with a copper-domed tower; **St Mary's Catholic Church** on the corner of Palmerin and Wood Sts; the **Masonic Temple** on Guy St; and the magnificent **Warwick Convent** (1891) on Locke St. There are plans afoot to 'convert' the convent into a guesthouse – ask at the tourist office.

Next to the tourist office, the **Warwick Regional Art Gallery** houses regular exhibitions and is open Tuesday to Saturday from 10 am to 4 pm and Sunday from 1 to 4 pm. Warwick's famed roses are on display in **Leslie Park**, the **Queen Elizabeth Jubilee Rose Gardens**, and in plantations down the centre of Palmerin St.

If you're deeply interested in Warwick's heritage, the tourist office's *Heritage Trail* brochure guides you around the Warwick General Cemetery, explaining the symbolism used by the Victorian-era stonemasons and giving brief biographies for many of the cemetery's residents. There are good **tennis courts** for hire on the corner of Fitzroy and Lyons St, and swimmers can head for the **E J Portley Olympic Pool** on the corner of Palmerin and Albert Sts.

Festivals

Warwick's major annual event is the Warwick Rodeo & Campdraft. The rodeo and its accompanying festival and street parade are held on the last weekend in October.

Other festivals and events include the Warwick Show, held in March; the Warwick Country & Western Singers Competition in September; and the Facetors' Guild Meeting, said to be the country's biggest swap-meet for collectors of precious and semi-precious

DARLING DOWNS

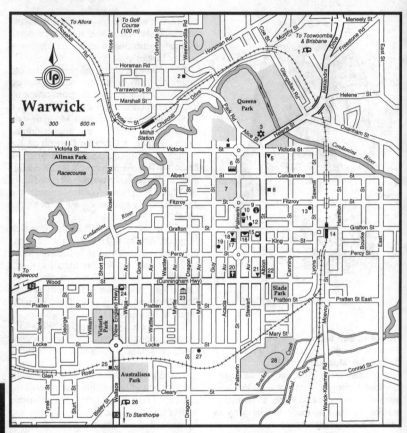

Warwick

stones. The meet is held at the Warwick Showgrounds every year over Easter, although in 1996 it will be held in January.

Places to Stay

Camping The *Warwick Caravan Park* (☎ (076) 61 8335) is on Palmer Ave, off the New England Hwy on the northern outskirts of town. The *Oasis Caravan Park* (☎ (076) 61 2874) is on the New England Hwy one km south of the centre. Both have tent sites at around $10, powered sites at $12, on-site vans at $25 and cabins ranging from $25 to $40.

Pubs The *Criterion Hotel* (☎ (076) 61 1042), at 84 Palmerin St, is a huge old country pub with clean and simple rooms opening up onto a broad front verandah costing $20 per person, including a cooked breakfast.

B&Bs *Aberfoyle B&B* (☎ (076) 61 8334), on the corner of Wood and Albion Sts, is a lovely old Federation-style (1910) timber homestead which is in the process of being restored. There are two attractive guest rooms, furnished and decorated in period

PLACES TO STAY

1 Warwick Caravan Park
2 Hillside B&B
4 Jackie Howe Motel
8 Centre Point Mid City Motor Inn
22 Aberfoyle B&B
25 McNevin's Gunyah Motel
26 Oasis Caravan Park

PLACES TO EAT

5 Dome Deli
11 Criterion Hotel
17 Belle Vue Cafe
18 Ettore – House of Coffee
21 The Elms

OTHER

3 Jubillee Rose Gardens
6 EJ Portley Olympic Pool
7 Leslie Park
9 Tourist Information Centre, Warwick
   Regional Art Gallery & Warwick Library
10 Warwick Town Hall, Cinema & Theatre
12 Warwick Twin Cinema
13 Tennis Courts
14 Railway Station
15 Crisp's Coaches
16 Post Office
19 Masonic Temple
20 St Mary's Catholic Church
23 Pringle Cottage & Museum
24 Bub's Roadhouse & Bus Terminal
27 Warwick Convent
28 Warwick Showgrounds

style, that cost $45/70 for singles/doubles including breakfast.

Hillside B&B (☎ (076) 61 2671), at 25 Weewondilla Rd, is an elegant sandstone former rectory on a hill overlooking Warwick. It's now a private house with a separate guest wing with two simple, family-style rooms sharing a bathroom and sitting room. B&B here costs $35 per person.

Motels The *Centre Point Mid City Motor Inn* (☎ (076) 61 3488), at 32 Albion St, has units from $46/56, some with baths and one with a spa. *McNevin's Gunyah Motel* (☎ (076) 61 5588) on the corner of the New England Hwy and Glen Rd is the most up-market of the motels here, and has a restaurant, pool and spa, and singles/doubles ranging from $54/63 to $75/85. The *Jackie Howe Motel* (☎ (076) 61 2111) on the corner of Palmerin and Victoria Sts has budget units from $38/48.

Places to Eat

At 119 Palmerin Ave, the *Belle Vue Cafe* is a classic country town cafe/milk bar with a Laminex and vinyl décor straight out of the 1950s. The walls are decorated with painted panels of farming scenes alternating with mirrors – brilliantly kitsch. They serve up a good range of meals and snacks, including great milk shakes in the old aluminium containers. Around the corner at 19 Grafton St, *Ettore – House of Coffee* has good Italian coffee and great cakes and pastries, as well as filled croissants and sandwiches and a range of cooked meals.

Under a multi-coloured geodesic dome on the corner of Albion and Victoria Sts, the *Dome Deli* is a good gourmet deli with cooked breakfasts, burgers, sandwiches, cakes and pastries. *The Elms*, on the corner of Albion and Wood Sts, is a family-style pizza and pasta restaurant.

For a pub meal, head to the *Criterion Hotel* at 84 Palmerin St. They have daily specials like beef stroganoff at $4.50 and other dishes from $5 to $9, and desserts like plum pudding and custard at $3.

Entertainment

The lovely old Warwick Town Hall on Palmerin St, fronted by a classical sandstone facade, has been converted into a live music and theatre venue. The **Warwick Twin Cinema** (☎ (076) 61 9685), at 81 Grafton St, screens latest release movies.

Getting There & Away

Bus Greyhound Pioneer Australia and Border Coaches both stop at Bub's Roadhouse (☎ (076) 61 7539), which is the Caltex service station on the corner of Wallace and

Wood Sts (the New England and Cunningham Hwys).

Crisp's Coaches (☎ (076) 61 2566), at 72 Grafton St, near the Albion St corner, has daily services to Ipswich, Inglewood, Stanthorpe, Allora, Tenterfield, Toowoomba and Brisbane. Crisp's are also the agents for McCafferty's, whose buses stop at their office.

ALLORA (pop 900)

This peaceful little township is 26 km north of Warwick, just off the road to Toowoomba. Herbert St, the main drag, is lined with old Victorian-era shopfronts with gently sloping verandahs, and has three old timber pubs with typically unimaginative names – the Commercial, the Railway and the Royal.

The small **Allora Historical Museum** in Drayton St is open on Sunday from 1.30 to 4 pm.

South of Allora, on the road to Warwick, is the historic **Glengallan Homestead**. Built in 1867, this was one of the district's earliest homesteads. It had fallen into disrepair but is gradually being restored as part of a National Trust project. It isn't open to the public at this stage.

Places to Stay & Eat

The *Railway Hotel* (☎ (076) 66 3402), on the corner of Warwick and Herbert Sts, has pub-style rooms at $15 per person, or $20 with a cooked breakfast. Bistro meals here range from $5 to $8.50.

Eight km west of Allora is one of Queensland's most impressive farmstays. *Talgai Homestead* (☎ (076) 66 3444), set on a large cattle-stud farm, is a magnificent sandstone homestead of palatial proportions that has been classified by the National Trust. Superbly transformed into an elegant restaurant and guesthouse, it still manages to retain a lived-in, comfortable feel. Recline in an armchair on one of the broad verandahs and watch peacocks dance around the gardens to a soundtrack provided by birds and cows. The enormous honeymoon suite, with a bathroom bigger than most bedrooms, costs

$260 a night, and there are five smaller suites with their own bathrooms that cost $220 a double. Breakfast is included in the tariffs, as is a tour of the farm in a horse-drawn carriage. Lunch and dinner are also available, and if you just want a brief sample of Talgai, the restaurant is open to the general public. You need to book ahead.

KILLARNEY (pop 830)

Killarney, 35 km south-east of Warwick near the New South Wales border, is a pretty little town in an area of fine mountain scenery. Among the many lovely waterfalls nearby is Queen Mary Falls, tumbling 40 metres into a rainforested gorge 10 km east of Killarney.

Places to Stay

The *Queen Mary Falls Caravan Park* (☎ (076) 64 7151), on the road near the falls, has tent sites for $8 and on-site vans from $20.

There are also a couple of good resorts near Killarney. *Adjinbilly* (☎ (076) 64 1599), a forested property 12 km north in the Condamine River Gorge, has three secluded, self-contained cabins (with pot belly stoves) that sleep up to five people; the tariffs are $110 a double plus $30 for each extra person, with a minimum two-night stay. Adjinbilly is signposted from opposite the Westpac bank in Killarney.

Cherrabah Homestead Resort (☎ (076) 67 9177) is a modern, hilltop homestead on a 2000-hectare property. The resort has its own restaurant, tennis courts, a nine-hole golf course and horse riding, as well as conference facilities. Accommodation is in motel-style units and costs $95 per person per night, which includes all meals and activities. Cherrabah is off the Warwick to Killarney road, and is well signposted from Warwick.

WARWICK TO STANTHORPE (59 km)
Vecchio's Fruit Barn

The area around Stanthorpe is known as Brisbane's fruit orchard, and as you drive around here you'll see numerous roadside stalls selling fruit and vegies straight off the farms. So how come this one gets its own heading? Well, apart from having a great selection of lovingly presented fruit and vegies, it's the only fruit barn I've ever been into that has its own cappuccino machine. I pulled up here early one frosty morning planning to buy a mixed bag of fruit for breakfast. Next thing I knew I was enjoying an authentic Italian coffee with almond macaroons – what a great start to the day.

The Vecchio family have been farming in this area for 25 years, and they always have a warm welcome for visitors. Their fruit barn is beside the New England Hwy, 17 km north of Stanthorpe. Call in and say hi, but be warned – Mrs Vecchio is a ferocious (but very likeable) saleswoman. I should know – I left with enough fruit to open up my own roadside stall.

STANTHORPE (pop 4500)

At 915 metres, Stanthorpe is the coolest town in the state. This is one of the few places in Queensland where you might need a jumper – and in winter, a coat, a beanie and gloves might also come in handy.

Stanthorpe celebrates its winters with its Brass Monkey Festival, and the region's four seasons climate provides the basis for a flourishing fruit and vegetable industry. The town is also at the centre of Queensland's only wine-making region, with more than 20 boutique wineries which open to the public. Stanthorpe is a popular base for people visiting the wineries and has a good range of accommodation.

Information

There's a tourist office (☎ (076) 81 2057), in the Civic Centre on the corner of Marsh and Lock Sts, which is open on weekdays from 8.45 am to 5 pm.

Things to See & Do

The **Stanthorpe Historical Museum**, on the northern outskirts on High St, has a slab-timber jail (1876), an old shire council building (1914) a former school residence (1891), plus a meticulously presented collection of local memorabilia. It is open Tuesday to Friday from 11 am to 4 pm and Sundays from 2 to 4 pm.

The **Stanthorpe Art Gallery**, in Lock St, has exhibitions of works by local artists. It is open on weekdays from 10 am to 4 pm and weekends from 1 to 4 pm.

Red Gum Ridge Trail Rides (☎ (076) 83 7169) offers various horse rides ranging from a one-hour trot to a tour of the wineries or overnight pub rides – ring them for details.

Festivals

Stanthorpe's major festivals and events include the Stanthorpe Agricultural Show (February), the Stanthorpe Rodeo (early March), and the Brass Monkey Festival (July). Every second year (even-numbered years) the Apple and Grape Harvest Festival runs for 10 days from late February to early March.

Places to Stay

Caravan Parks The *Top of the Town Caravan Village* (☎ (076) 81 2030), at 10 High St, on the northern edge of town, is a good caravan park with tent sites for $10, powered sites for $13, on-site vans from $26 and cabins and units from $34.

Hostels *Summit Lodge Backpackers* (☎ (076) 83 2599), on the New England Hwy, 12 km north of Stanthorpe at Thulimbah, specialises in finding fruit and vegetable-picking work for travellers. It ain't exactly the Hilton, but you can make good money here picking apples, tomatoes, pears, capsicums, cabbages etc. The hostel often has a waiting list for work, so you need to ring ahead rather than just turn up. The main harvesting season starts in October and runs through to mid-June, although work is sometimes available in the winter months. Dorm beds costs $12.50 a night or $80 a week. Buses running between Brisbane and Stanthorpe can drop you at the door – otherwise the owners will pick you up from Stanthorpe.

DARLING DOWNS

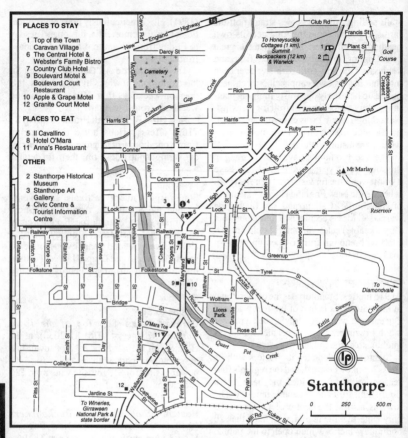

PLACES TO STAY
1 Top of the Town Caravan Village
6 The Central Hotel & Webster's Family Bistro
7 Country Club Hotel
8 Boulevard Motel & Boulevard Court Restaurant
10 Apple & Grape Motel
12 Granite Court Motel

PLACES TO EAT
5 Il Cavallino
8 Hotel O'Mara
11 Anna's Restaurant

OTHER
2 Stanthorpe Historical Museum
3 Stanthorpe Art Gallery
4 Civic Centre & Tourist Information Centre

Stanthorpe

DARLING DOWNS

Pubs On the corner of High and Victoria Sts, the *Central Hotel* (☎ (076) 81 2044) is a good pub to stay in. It's run by friendly young people and has good meals and accommodation, with clean pub-style rooms upstairs costing $25/40/45 for singles/doubles/triples, including a continental breakfast.

The *Country Club Hotel* (☎ (076) 81 1033), at 26 Maryland St, has pub rooms at $15/25 or motel-style units for $35/48.

Motels There are half a dozen motels in town to choose from. One of the best and most

central is the *Apple & Grape Motel* (☎ (076) 81 1288), at 63 Maryland St, with units from $50/57. Across the road, the *Boulevard Motel* (☎ (076) 81 1777) has budget rooms overlooking a small park from $38/42. Half a km south of the centre, the *Granite Court Motel* (☎ (076) 81 1811), at 34 Wallangarra Rd, has tidy units at $47/55.

B&Bs *Diamondvale* (☎ (076) 81 3367) is an attractive 12-hectare property beside Quart Pot Creek two km east of the centre. The owners offer B&B accommodation in their beautifully restored homestead – the guest room has its own ensuite and costs $110 a double. They also have two stylish self-contained cottages which cost between $80 and $110 a double plus $25 for each extra person.

Cabins & Cottages *Honeysuckle Cottages* (☎ (076) 81 1510), on Mayfair Lane (beside the BP service station one km north of the centre), is a set of three modern brick cottages in a bush setting. There are two one-bedroom cottages and one two-bedroom cottage, each fully self-contained with a wood heater, kitchen and laundry, and a colonial-style décor. The tariff is $110 a double plus $30 for each extra adult, which includes a breakfast basket.

Four km west of Stanthorpe (signposted off the Texas road), the *Happy Valley Homestead* (☎ (076) 81 3250) is an impressive resort complex on a bush property studded with granite outcrops, with a good range of cabins and units, a tennis court and a restaurant. Accommodation-wise, you have a choice between the modern homestead units or more secluded timber cabins, all with their own bathrooms and wood fires. Tariffs include breakfast and dinner and range from $79 per person per night in the two to five-bedroom cabins to $99 per person per night in the homestead units or smaller cabins. The restaurant specialises in good old country-style meals served buffet-style – you definitely won't go hungry. The resort also runs daily winery tours in their mini-buses.

Places to Eat
Il Cavallino, at 136 High St, is a straightforward little Italian eatery which, despite appearances, has better than average Italian food, including good pizzas and pastas for around $10 – try the spaghetti marinara, it's a winner. Il Cavallino opens for lunch and dinner every day except Monday. A few doors along is the popular and attractive *Webster's Family Bistro* inside the Central Hotel, with lunches from $5 to $9 and dinners from $9 to $12. Another pub with good meals is the *Hotel O'Mara*, in Maryland St.

Anna's Restaurant, on the corner of

Wallangarra Rd and O'Mara Tce, is a family-run BYO Italian restaurant set in a cosy old Queenslander. They serve good, hearty tucker, with pastas from $9 to $13 and other main courses from $10 to $15. On Friday and Saturday nights they have a popular smorgasbord for $20 a head.

Next to the Boulevard Motel, at 76 Maryland St, is the *Boulevard Court Restaurant*, a Chinese restaurant with mains from $7 to $10 and a Friday night smorgasbord at $11 per person.

The restaurant at the Happy Valley Homestead (see Places to Stay) is also open to the public, with dinner costing $25 per person or $30 on weekends.

GRANITE BELT WINERIES
Set amidst the spectacular scenery of the Granite Belt, these wineries constitute Queensland's only true winery district – this is the only part of the Sunshine State with a climate suitable for viticulture. The Granite Belt is an elevated plateau of the Great Dividing Range and ranges from 800 to 950 metres above sea level.

Grapes were first grown in the district in the mid-19th century and an influx of Italian immigrants after WW I led to the establishment of the region as a producer of bulk wine. In recent years the number of small wineries has blossomed and there are now some 20 wineries to visit.

None of these are large producers, all are boutique wineries selling the majority of their wines through their 'cellar doors', which range from small tin sheds draped in vines to impressive stone chalets. The region produces everything from sparkling wines and vermouth to the more traditional styles using riesling, savignon blanc, cabernet savignon and shiraz grapes.

All of the wineries are open on weekends for cellar-door sales, and most also open during the week. Finding these places isn't hard – most are spread along either side of the 17-km stretch of the New England Hwy between Stanthorpe and Ballandean to the south.

Wineries south of Stanthorpe include

Kominos Winery at Severnlea, with its famous grape-eating dog; **Granite Cellars** at Glen Aplin; **Felsberg Winery**, an impressive stone building high on a hill on the east side of the highway; **Rumbalara Vineyards**, with a wide variety of styles including a sweet vermouth and a cider; and the scenic **Bald Mountain Winery** near Wallangarra.

There are also a couple of wineries north of Stanthorpe, including **Heritage Wines** (☎ (076) 85 2197), at Cottonvale, 16 km north, which has a craft shop and gallery and accommodation in a small heritage-style timber cottage; **Mt Magnus Winery**, seven km west of the highway at Pozieres (turn off at Thulimbah, 13 km north of Stanthorpe); and the **Old Caves Winery**, one km north of Stanthorpe.

Festivals
The wineries hold a Spring Wine Festival every year, and the Australian Small Winemaker's Show is held here in October.

Places to Stay & Eat
Stanthorpe is a popular base for visits to the wineries, and has a good range of accommodation and eateries. See that section earlier.

Whatever else you do, don't miss visiting *The Picnic Basket* at Glen Aplin, 10 km south of Stanthorpe. It's a small, plain-looking cottage tucked behind the Granite Cellars winery, but the owner/chef Una produces an outstanding range of home-made gourmet goodies using fresh local produce. The Picnic Basket is open every Friday, Saturday and Sunday from 8 am to 5 pm. Breakfasts range from $4.50 up to $10.50 for a huge country-style feed, and Una's famous Sunday brunches cost $15 per person. You can also get soups, sandwiches, home-made pies, cakes and scones, or meals like Rumbalara sausages with salad ($8.50). As the name suggests, this is also a great place to get a picnic basket made up for your visits to the wineries, many of which have outdoor picnic areas for visitors.

On the northern outskirts of Ballandean, 17 km south of Stanthorpe, the *Vineyard Cottages & Restaurant* (☎ (076) 84 1270)

has four comfortable and attractive heritage-style brick cottages with their own ensuites and spas costing from $130 to $145 a double or $220 for up to four people. The restaurant here is a tiny cream-coloured church which has been converted into a cute BYO restaurant with a garden courtyard; it is open for lunch from Friday to Sunday and for dinner on Saturday night.

GIRRAWEEN NATIONAL PARK
From the New England Hwy 26 km south of Stanthorpe, a paved road leads nine km east to **Girraween National Park**, an area of 1000-metre-high hills, valleys and huge granite outcrops. The park has a visitor centre (☎ (076) 84 5157) which (usually) is open Monday to Saturday between 8 am and 4 pm, two good camping grounds with hot showers, and several walking tracks.

Girraween adjoins Bald Rock National Park over the border in New South Wales. It can fall below freezing on winter nights here, but summer days are warm. Call the park's visitor centre to book camp sites.

Places to Stay
Apart from the two camping grounds in the national park, there are a couple of accommodation options close to the park.

Two km west of the visitors' centre, *Wisteria Cottages* (☎ (076) 84 5121) is a modern two-bedroom timber cottage on a cleared property behind a craft and pottery gallery. The cottage is fully self-contained and costs $50 per person per night, including breakfast. The owners of this place are planning to build five more cottages on the property in the not-too-distant future.

The *Girraween Inn* (☎ (076) 83 7109), on the northern edge of the park, is a brand new two-storey chalet-style guesthouse with nine ensuite rooms upstairs and a restaurant downstairs. Dinner, B&B costs $90 per person per night. The inn also has conference facilities. To get there, turn off the New England Hwy at Ballandean and follow the Eukey Rd for nine km.

SUNDOWN NATIONAL PARK
On the Queensland/New South Wales border, about 80 km south-west of Stanthorpe, the Sundown National Park is a rugged and rocky landscape dominated by the steep, spectacular gorges of the Severn River. The park is largely undeveloped and offers good fishing and swimming, with an abundance of birdlife. The Broadwater camping ground can be reached in a conventional vehicle along a four-km gravel road. The northern section of the park is only accessible by 4WD vehicles from Ballandean south of Stanthorpe.

For information and to book camping permits, contact the park rangers on ☎ (067) 37 5235.

INGLEWOOD (pop 1000)
On the Cunningham Hwy, midway between Warwick and Goondiwindi, Inglewood has two motels and a caravan park. The *Motel Olympic* (☎ (076) 52 1333), in the centre of town on Albert St, has good budget rooms at $32/40.

TEXAS (pop 800)
Texas, Queensland. Great name for a movie sequel, perhaps, but sadly this sleepy border town 55 km south of Inglewood doesn't live up to the romantic images conjured up by its name. The name is derived from the nearby Texas Station, which in turn was named after an ownership battle that coincided with the war of independence between Mexico and Texas. Apparently, two brothers who had settled the property left to try their luck on a goldfield, and by the time they returned someone else had claimed their land. The ensuing fight was likened to a small-scale version of the war taking place at the same time.

The town has a small **historical society museum** which is open on Saturdays from 1 to 3 pm; entry costs $2. The **Glenlyon Dam** east of Texas is a popular boating and camping destination.

The *Yellow Rose Guesthouse* (☎ (076) 53 1592), behind the Chinese restaurant at 52 High St, is a simple, somewhat eccentric guesthouse in a private home. B&B costs $35/50 for singles/doubles. Also on High St, the *Texas Motel* (☎ (076) 53 1300) has ordinary motel units at $35/45.

Twenty three km north-east of Texas on the Stanthorpe road, *Arcot Homestead* (☎ (076) 53 1360) is a large property with guest accommodation in an old homestead that dates back to 1910. The daily tariff is $80 with all meals provided, or $99 with farm activities thrown in – kid's pay half price. They also have budget accommodation at $20 per vehicle in the shearers' quarters or $10 per vehicle at the camp site. Ring for directions.

GOONDIWINDI (pop 4300)
West of Warwick, Goondiwindi is on the New South Wales border and the MacIntyre River. It's a popular stop for travellers on the Newell Hwy between Melbourne and Brisbane.

Perhaps Goondiwindi's greatest claim to fame is as the home of the great *Gunsynd* – 'The Goondiwindi Grey'. There's a memorial statue of the racehorse in MacIntyre St, beside the bridge across the MacIntyre River, with a brass plaque listing *Gunsynd's* amazing race record from 1969 to 1973.

Near the Gunsynd monument, the **Customs House Museum** houses an interesting collection put together by the local historical society. It is open daily (except Tuesday) from 10 am to 4 pm. There's also a wildlife sanctuary at the Boobera Lagoon.

Information
There's a tourist information office (☎ (076) 71 2653) in the base of a concrete water tower on McLean St, near the town centre.

Places to Stay
Goondiwindi has seven motels, two caravan parks and quite a few pubs with accommodation. Most of the pubs and motels are spread along Marshall St in the centre of town.

The two caravan parks are between the town centre and the river. The *Goondiwindi*

DARLING DOWNS

Mobile Village (☎ (076) 71 2566) on Hunger ford St has tent sites at $8, powered sites at $12 and on-site vans and cabins from $28 a double.

The *Victoria Hotel* (☎ (076) 71 1007) on the corner of Marshall and Herbert Sts is a solid old country pub (1888) topped with a tower and renovated in strange mock-Tudor style. There are simple pub rooms upstairs at $20 per person, plus another $5 for a cooked breakfast.

The *MacIntyre Motor Inn* (☎ (076) 71 2477), opposite the tourist office near the corner of McLean and Callandoon Sts, is a good modern motel with singles/doubles from $66/73 and triples/quads from $88/96. The *Pioneer Motor Inn* (☎ (076) 71 2888) at 145 Marshall St also has good units from $74.

WEST OF GOONDIWINDI

At the junction of the Carnarvon, Moonie and Balonne highways, **St George** (population 2500), is 200 km west of Goondiwindi. It's at the centre of a major cotton-growing district, and has two motels and a caravan park. From here it's another long and lonely 290 km westwards to Cunnamulla, which is well and truly in the outback. See the Outback Queensland chapter for details of this area.

TOOWOOMBA (pop 76,000)

On the edge of the Great Dividing Range and the Darling Downs and 138 km inland from Brisbane, Toowoomba is the largest city in the region. It's a gracious city with parks, tree-lined streets, several art galleries and many early buildings.

Information

Tourist Information The Toowoomba Tourist Information Centre (☎ (076) 39 3797) is in the City Hall at 541 Ruthven St, and is open weekdays from 8.30 am to 5 pm and weekends from 9.30 am to 3 pm.

The Queensland National Parks & Wildlife Service (QNP&WS) (☎ (076) 39 4599) has an office in James St which is open weekdays from 8.30 am to 5 pm and Saturday from 8.30 to 11.30 am.

Books The Mary Ryan Bookshop, at 55 Russell St, is an excellent bookshop with a cafe upstairs.

Marie's Book Exchange, at 69 Russell St, has a good range of second-hand (mostly pulp) fiction. Mack Campbell's Bookstore, at 356 Ruthven St, also has lots of second-hand books and mags.

The Toowoomba City Library in Victoria St is open weekdays from 10 am to 8 pm and Saturdays from 9.30 am to 2 pm.

Things to See & Do

On Lindsay St, Toowoomba's **Botanic Gardens** occupy the northern section of Queens Park. The gardens have a tranquil and serene setting, with lawns, rose gardens and flower beds shaded by old bunya pines and other trees.

Immediately north of the gardens there is the **Cobb & Co Museum** which has a great collection of old horse-drawn carriages and buggies, Cobb & Co mail coaches, bullock wagons and sulkies. It is open on weekdays from 9 am to 4 pm and every weekend and public holiday from 1 to 4 pm. Entry costs $3 for adults and $2 for children, and if you are lucky enough to be here at the right time, it's free on the first Monday of each month.

The **Toowoomba Regional Art Gallery,** on Ruthven St, is open Tuesday to Saturday from 10 am to 4 pm and on Sunday from 1 to 4 pm. It houses three permanent collections: the Lindsay Collection (colonial Australian paintings), the City Collection (contemporary Australian paintings, photography and ceramics), and the Gould Collection (European and Asian paintings, porcelain, furniture, gold and silverware). Entry is free.

Ju Raku En (The Toowoomba Japanese Garden) at the University of Southern Queensland in West St, south of the centre, is a large-scale Japanese garden with three km of walking trails, a lake, waterfalls, and streams. The garden is open daily from 7 am to 7 pm.

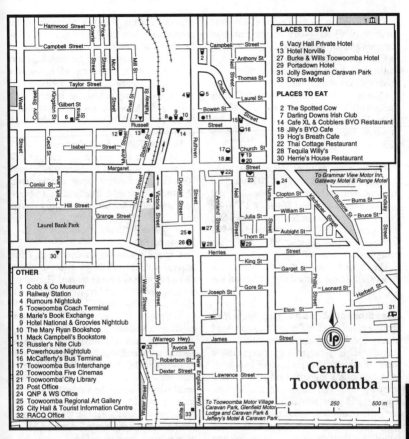

Central Toowoomba

PLACES TO STAY
6 Vacy Hall Private Hotel
13 Hotel Norville
27 Burke & Wills Toowoomba Hotel
29 Portadown Hotel
31 Jolly Swagman Caravan Park
33 Downs Motel

PLACES TO EAT
2 The Spotted Cow
7 Darling Downs Irish Club
14 Cafe XL & Cobblers BYO Restaurant
18 Jilly's BYO Cafe
19 Hog's Breath Cafe
22 Thai Cottage Restaurant
28 Tequila Willy's
30 Herrie's House Restaurant

OTHER
1 Cobb & Co Museum
3 Railway Station
4 Rumours Nightclub
5 Toowoomba Coach Terminal
8 Marie's Book Exchange
9 Hotel National & Groovies Nightclub
10 The Mary Ryan Bookshop
11 Mack Campbell's Bookstore
12 Russler's Nite Club
15 Powerhouse Nightclub
16 McCafferty's Bus Terminal
17 Toowoomba Bus Interchange
20 Toowoomba Five Cinemas
21 Toowoomba City Library
23 Post Office
24 QNP & WS Office
25 Toowoomba Regional Art Gallery
26 City Hall & Tourist Information Centre
32 RACQ Office

DARLING DOWNS

Other parks and gardens include **Laurel Bank Park** on the corner of Hill and West Sts and **Picnic Point** off Tobruk Memorial Dve, on the edge of the ranges on the eastern outskirts.

The old **Royal Bull's Head Inn** on Brisbane St, Drayton, seven km west, dates from 1859 and you can visit it from 10 am to 4 pm, Thursday to Monday, for $2.50.

About 40 km south of Toowoomba, you can also visit the historic **Rudd's Pub** in the township of Nobby, where Steele Rudd wrote a number of his Dad and Dave stories. The pub's resident storyteller does readings from Rudd's *On Our Selection* series.

Festivals

Toowoomba's Carnival of Flowers is a colourful celebration of spring that is held over the last week in September, and includes floral displays, a grand parade and exhibition gardens. In early September, the Ag Show is a three-day agricultural festival.

Places to Stay

Caravan Parks The modern *Toowoomba Motor Village Caravan Park* (☎ (076) 35 8186), at 821 Ruthven St, is the best of the caravan parks here, with tent sites at $10, powered sites at $14, on-site vans at $24 and cabins and units from $27 to $53.

The *Glenfield Motor Lodge & Caravan Park* (☎ (076) 35 4466), on the corner of Ruthven and Stenner Sts, and *Jeffrey's Motel & Caravan Park* (☎ (076) 35 5999), at 864 Ruthven St, have camping and caravan sites as well as motel units on offer.

Closer to the centre, the small *Jolly Swagman Caravan Park* (☎ (076) 32 8735), at 47 Kitchener St, has tent sites for $9, powered sites at $13 and on-site vans for $23.

Pubs Near the railway station, the *Hotel Norville* (☎ (076) 39 2954), at 70 Russell St, has clean upstairs rooms from $20 per person. The *Portadown Hotel* (☎ (076) 32 2611), on the corner of Neil and Herries Sts, has rooms at $25/35 for singles/twins or $40 for doubles, plus another $6 if you want breakfast.

The *Hotel National* (☎ (076) 39 2706), at 59 Russell St, has fairly dodgy pub rooms at $10 per person.

Guesthouses & B&Bs The *Vacy Hall Private Hotel* (☎ (076) 39 2055), a couple of blocks uphill from the town centre at 135 Russell St, is a rather magnificent 1880s mansion which offers heritage-style accommodation of the highest standard – it's like stepping back 100 years into another era. There are 12 guest rooms. Those in the side wing share bathrooms and range from $74 to $94 a double, while the rooms in the main house have their own ensuite, open fires and open onto the verandah, and range from $110 to $140 a night. Breakfast is served in the mornings and dinners are available on Friday nights only. Highly recommended.

Argyle Homestead (☎ 076) 96 6301), which is 20 km north on the New England Hwy, is an excellent B&B in a historic homestead on a 20-hectare property, with five guest rooms costing $45 per person.

Motels & Hotels The *Range Motel* (☎ (076) 32 3133), at the eastern entrance to town on the corner of the Warrego Hwy and Tourist Rd, has oldish but good budget rooms at $35/40 for singles/doubles. There's a string of motels along Ruthven St south of the centre, including the *Downs Motel* (☎ (076) 39 3811) with budget units from $36/42.

Opposite Toowoomba Grammar School on the eastern outskirts of town, the *Grammar View Motor Inn* (☎ (076) 38 3366), at 39 Margaret St, has modern units from $75/85, while the *Gateway Motel* (☎ (076) 32 2088) next door has budget units from $42/48.

Burke & Wills Toowoomba Hotel (☎ (076) 32 2433), in the centre of town at 554 Ruthven St, is a good five-storey hotel with 90 recently renovated rooms ranging from $85 to $130 a night. The hotel has several bars and an up-market conservatory restaurant.

Places to Eat

The friendly *Darling Downs Irish Club*, upstairs at 93 Russell St, has poker machines and a bar with Guinness on tap. They serve dinners from Thursday to Saturday and lunch on Sunday – roasts, stews etc in the $8 to $11 range. The club often has free folk bands, jazz sessions and the like.

On the corner of Ruthven and Campbell Sts, the popular *Spotted Cow* hotel has been renovated in the style of an English country pub. It's a relaxed, elegant place with three small bars including the Udder Bar (just the spot for an udder drink – sorry), a covered courtyard and a restaurant serving up-market pub food with light meals for around $8 and main courses from $9 to $15.

At 160 Margaret St, the BYO *Thai Cottage Restaurant* has vegetarian dishes from $6.50 to $9.50, seafood dishes from $16 to $19 and other mains around $10. Across the road, *Jilly's BYO Cafe* has gourmet-style burgers and sandwiches, home-made pastas around $10 and cooked breakfasts.

Cafe XL, at 24 Russell St, is a casual breakfast or lunch cafe, and next door the rustic *Cobblers BYO Restaurant* has good modern Australian cuisine with mains around $18, and opens for dinner from Tuesday to Saturday.

The *Hog's Breath Cafe,* on the corner of Neil and Bell Sts, is a popular American-style bar and grill, or there's *Tequila Willy's Bar & Grill* on the corner of Ruthven and Herries Sts with burgers, grills, pastas and salads.

Set in a resorted homestead, *Herrie's House Restaurant*, at 210 Herries St, is a somewhat formal licensed restaurant that combines bush tucker with Italian cuisine, with main courses in the $16 to $19 range.

Entertainment
The historic Empire Theatre in Neil St is currently undergoing major restoration works; until it is completed, the City Hall is the main venue for live theatre performances.

The Toowoomba Five Cinemas (☎ (076) 39 3400), on the corner of Margaret and Neil Sts, screens mainstream releases, as well as art-house films on Sunday and Monday nights.

Tequila Willy's, on the corner of Ruthven and Herries Sts, is a three-in-one entertainment centre with a sports saloon, a bar and grill, and a nightclub section which opens Thursday to Saturday nights till 2 am ($5 cover charge) and Sunday till midnight.

Other nightclubs here include *The Powerhouse*, a live band venue on Neil St beside the McCafferty's terminal, and *Rumours*, in the Centrepoint Shopping Centre on the corner of Ruthven and Piper Sts.

Russler's Nite Club, in the Canberra Hotel on the corner of Russell and Station Sts, has country & western bands on Friday and Saturday nights.

Getting There & Away
Air Sabair (☎ (076) 33 1533) has daily flights between Toowoomba and Brisbane; the one-way fare is $84. They also have twice-weekly services from Toowoomba to St George ($143), Cunnamulla ($225) and Thargomindah ($276).

Bus McCafferty's started in Toowoomba more than 50 years ago and has grown into one of the largest bus companies in Australia, has their bus terminal (☎ (076) 90 9888) at 28-30 Neil St. McCafferty's has about 20

services a day from Toowoomba to Brisbane ($15) and the Gold Coast ($20). They also have regular services west along the Warrego Hwy to Dalby ($10), Chinchilla ($14), Roma ($27) and Charleville ($38). McCafferty's also acts as the local agent for Polley's Coaches who have services to Gympie ($30) and Kingaroy ($18). Crisp's Coaches runs to Stanthorpe ($18.60), Warwick ($10.40) and Moree ($35). Graham's Coaches runs to St George ($47.50), Cunnamulla ($75) and Lightning Ridge. Suncoast Pacific runs to the Sunshine Coast ($21.70). All of these services leave from the McCafferty's terminal and tickets can be booked through them.

Greyhound Pioneer Australia's buses stop at the Toowoomba Coach Terminal on the corner of Ruthven and Hodgson Sts.

Train You can get here on the *Westlander*, which runs between Brisbane and Charleville twice-weekly. The railway station is close to the town centre, just off Russell St.

Getting Around
Local bus services depart from the Toowoomba Bus Interchange on Neil St. There's an information booth in the terminal where you can find out which bus will take you where.

TOOWOOMBA TO MILES (211 km)
Jondaryan Woolshed Complex
At Jondaryan, 45 km north-west of Toowoomba, is the *Jondaryan Woolshed* (☎ (076) 92 2229). Built in 1859, this enormous woolshed holds a significant place in Queensland's history books – it was here in 1890 that the first of the great shearers' strikes began, when maritime workers refused to handle Jondaryan wool because it had been shorn by non-union labour.

Today the woolshed is the centrepiece of a large tourist complex with an interesting collection of rustic old buildings, daily blacksmithing and shearing demonstrations, period displays, and antique farm machinery. The complex is open daily from 8.30 am to 5 pm. Entry costs $9 for adults and $4.50 for

DARLING DOWNS

children, which includes a tour with demonstrations. Tours are given every day at 1 pm, as well as at 10.30 am on weekends and during school holidays.

There's also a YHA-affiliated youth hostel and camping ground here. The hostel has been set up in authentically spartan shearers' quarters, with old mattresses on old iron beds in old tin sheds. There's an open-sided, sawdust-floored communal cooking and dining shelter, as well as hot showers and toilets. You need to bring your own linen. Beds cost $9 a night, tent sites cost $8 a double and caravan sites cost $10 a double.

Jondaryan hosts a number of annual events, including an Australian Heritage Festival over nine days in late August and early September, a New Year's Eve bushdance, an Australia Day celebration, and a Working Draft Horse Expo in June.

Dalby (pop 9400)

Dalby is a dusty rural town in the centre of Queensland's richest grain-growing region. It has a good range of services and facilities but is only really of passing interest to travellers.

There's a tourist office (☎ (076) 62 1066), in front of Thomas Jack Park on the corner of Drayton and Condamine Sts; it is open daily from 9.30 am to 4.30 pm (to 2.30 pm on Sunday).

The **Pioneer Park Museum**, signposted off the Warrego Hwy a couple of km west of the centre, has a collection of old buildings and farm machinery, and is open daily from 10 am to 3 pm; entry costs $4 for adults and $1 for children. The **Cactoblastis Cairn**, beside Myall Creek in Marble St, is possibly the only monument ever erected in honour of an insect. *Cactoblastis catrorum*, an Argentinean caterpillar/moth, saved much of rural Queensland when it was recruited into the country in 1925 to combat the dreaded prickly pear cactus which had overrun huge tracts of farming land.

The **Dalby Saleyards** are amongst the largest in Queensland – if you're interested in attending, sheep and lamb sales are held on Monday, cattle and pig sales on Wednesday.

About 30 km north of Dalby is the historic **Jimbour House**, where parts of the less-than-memorable TV series *Return to Eden* were filmed. Back in 1844, Ludwig Leichhardt's 13-month expedition to Port Essington in the Northern Territory started out from here. You can visit the property's gardens, but the house itself isn't open to the public.

Places to Stay If you decide to stop over, the *Pioneer Caravan Village* (☎ (076) 62 1811), on the western outskirts, has sites, cabins and on-site vans, and there are five motels to choose from. The *Dalby Motel* (☎ (076) 62 3222), on Drayton St opposite the tourist office, has budget units at $42/48, or there's the modern *Dalby Manor Motor Inn* (☎ (076) 62 1011), on the corner of Drayton and Pratten Sts, with units at $55/68.

Chinchilla (pop 3150)

Eighty-three km north-west of Dalby, Chinchilla is another rural centre with a wide range of services and facilities, including four motels and two caravan parks.

The **Chinchilla Folk Museum** is open daily from 8.30 am to 4.30 pm; entry costs $2. The **Barkula State Forest**, 40 km north of town, is the largest commercial forest plantation in the state.

MILES (pop 1260)

This small rural centre at the intersection of the Warrego and Leichhardt Hwys is known as 'The Crossroads of the Golden West'. Miles is on the banks of Dogwood Creek, named by the eccentric Prussian explorer Ludwig Leichhardt, who stopped here on his birthday on 23 October, 1844.

The town is at the centre of a district famous for its spring wildflowers, and also has the excellent **Miles Historical Village**, on the main road on the east side of town. This is one of the best historical villages in the state and is definitely worth a visit.

The main building houses a collection of glass cabinets crammed with all sorts of interesting bits and pieces, from rocks and gems to tie stretchers and silk-screen printers.

There are also numerous historic shop settings, including a bootmakers, a saddlery, a general store, a bakery and a bank, as well as a war museum and displays on the Artesian Basin and Aboriginal heritage. The village is open daily from 8 am to 5 pm and costs $8 for adults, $2 for children and $16 for a family ticket.

Festivals
Miles' Back to the Bush Weekend, which incorporates a wildflower festival, is held over four days in early September at the Miles Historical Village.

Places to Stay
The *Miles Caravan Park* (☎ (076) 27 1640), beside the Ampol service station on Murilla St, has tent sites at $8, powered sites at $10 and on-site vans at $22. There's also a good council-run caravan park, opposite the Miles Historical Village, with similar prices.

The *Hotel Australia* (☎ (076) 27 1106), in the centre of town at 55 Murilla St, has clean and comfortable rooms upstairs with shared bathrooms for $18/30 for singles/doubles.

The *Golden West Motor Inn* (☎ (076) 27 1688); at 50 Murilla St, is a neat beige-brick motel with singles/doubles from $54/64.

Possum Park, 20 km north of Miles, has excellent camping facilities and cabins – see the Capricorn Coast chapter for details.

Places to Eat
If you're passing through at breakfast time, the 24-hour Caltex Roadhouse on the west side of town has good truckie-sized cooked breakfasts. *Lorraine's Coffee Shop,* at 79 Murilla St, has home-made meals such as quiches, lasagnas, chicken salad, and Devonshire teas.

NORTH FROM MILES
The Leichhardt Hwy runs north from Miles all the way to Rockhampton. If you're heading this way, see the Banana to Miles –

the Leichhardt Highway section in the Capricorn Coast chapter.

ROMA (pop 5700)
An early Queensland settlement, and now the centre of a sheep and cattle-raising district, Roma also has some curious small industries. There's enough oil in the area to support a small refinery, which produces just enough petroleum for local use. Gas deposits are rather larger, and Roma supplies Brisbane through a 450-km pipeline.

Information
A new tourist information centre (☎(076) 22 1416) is currently being built on at the eastern entrance to town, in the shadows of the Historic Oil Rig.

There's a 24-hour BP Roadhouse on Bowen St, next to the Roma Central Accommodation Park in the centre of town. The Roma Automotive Service Centre (☎ (076) 22 4255), on the corner of Bowen and Quintin Sts, is the local RACQ depot.

Things to See & Do
The town centre has some wonderful turn-of-the-century pubs and buildings – the **School of Arts Hotel** and the **Hotel Royal**, on opposite corners of McDowall and Hawthorne Sts, are two of the best examples.

Roma's **Heroe's Avenue** is a plantation of bottle trees which stretches along Station, Wyndham and Bungil Sts. The trees were planted after WW I to honour the young men from the district who were killed in the war. Each of the 90-plus trees originally planted bore a brass plaque with the name of the soldier to whom it paid homage. Despite their similar appearances, there are distinct differences between bottle trees and boab trees, the latter related to African baobab trees.

Bassett's Romavilla Winery, one km north of town on the Carnarvon Developmental Rd, is open daily.

There are cattle sales at the **Roma Saleyards** on the eastern outskirts of town every Tuesday (from 11 am) and Thursday (from 8 am).

DARLING DOWNS

Festivals

Roma's major festival is Easter in the Country, which includes a rodeo, markets, horse races, bushdances and country music, a street parade and an art show.

Places to Stay

The *Big Rig Caravan Park* (☎ (076) 22 2538), on McDowall St, has tent sites from $9 and on-site vans from $25.

On the corner of McDowall and Hawthorne Sts, the *School of Arts Hotel* (☎ (076) 22 2122) has pub rooms at $10 a single or $25 a double with a private bathroom. Across the road, the *Hotel Royal* (☎ (076) 22 1324) has rooms at $12 per person. Both are very basic.

The *Roma Central Accommodation Park* (☎ (076) 22 1333), at 24 Bowen St, is a good budget option, with air-con motel-style units in transportable buildings from $35/39 for singles/doubles or $42 for twins.

The *Mandalay Motel* (☎ (076) 22 2711), on Quintin St, has good motel units starting from $50/60.

The best motel in town is the colonial-style *Overlander Homestead Motel* (☎ (076) 22 3555), on the highway on the eastern outskirts of town. Singles/doubles start from $65/75 plus $10 for each extra person, and the motel has its own licensed steak and seafood restaurant.

Places to Eat

The pleasant *Queens Arms Hotel,* on McDowall St, has good pub meals ranging from $4.50 for chicken in a basket to $9 for a mixed grill or a fisherman's basket. There's a baby grand piano in the dining room, and you can dine to musical accompaniment here on Friday and Saturday nights. For Chinese food, try the licensed *Golden Dragon Restaurant*, opposite the post office, with main courses in the $8 to $10 range. Next door, the

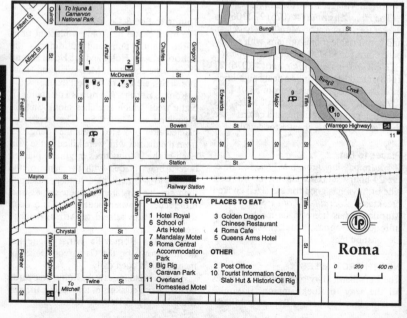

PLACES TO STAY
1 Hotel Royal
6 School of Arts Hotel
3 Mandalay Motel
8 Roma Central Accommodation Park
9 Big Rig Caravan Park
11 Overland Homestead Motel

PLACES TO EAT
3 Golden Dragon Chinese Restaurant
4 Roma Cafe
5 Queens Arms Hotel

OTHER
2 Post Office
10 Tourist Information Centre, Slab Hut & Historic Oil Rig

Roma

0   200   400 m

Roma Cafe has sandwiches, milk shakes, burgers, fish & chips and the like.

Getting There & Away

Flight West have regular flights between Roma and Brisbane.

McCafferty's have daily buses through Roma on the Brisbane to Mt Isa run.

The *Westlander* train passes through twice-weekly on the Brisbane-Charleville run.

ROMA TO CHARLEVILLE (265 km)
Muckadilla

Forty km past Roma, Muckadilla is just a pub, a service station, a railway station and a couple of houses.

If you're looking for a meal or a bed, or just want to wet your whistle, call in at the friendly *Muckadilla Hotel-Motel* (☎ (076) 26 8318). It's a modern colonial-style pub with rooms with their own bathrooms, TVs and fans at $15/25 for singles/doubles – great value, and there's a pool and barbecue area out the back. They also serve breakfast, lunch and dinner here, with bistro meals around $7 to $10.

Mitchell (pop 1100)

On the Maranoa River, Mitchell was named after the Surveyor-General of NSW, Major Thomas Mitchell, who passed this way in 1845. It's a relaxed commercial centre with a couple of pubs and supermarkets, a butcher, a baker and a newsagent. The local library, beside the huge windmill in the centre of town, has a small tourist information section with brochures on the local area.

A road heads north from Mitchell to the Mt Moffat section of the Carnarvon National Park. It's a remote 200-km trip, and the road is mostly unsealed after the first 50 km. See the section on the Carnarvon Gorge in the Capricorn Coast chapter for more details.

Places to Stay There's a straightforward council-run caravan park beside the river on the east side of town; the first two nights are free. Closer to the centre, the *Bridge Service Station & Caravan Park* (☎ (076) 23 1125) has tent sites at $8, powered sites at $10 and on-site vans at $25; the town's swimming pool is across the road.

The blue and white *Devonshire Arms Hotel* (☎ (076) 23 1321), on the corner of Cambridge and Alice Sts, has very basic pub rooms at $14/24, or the new *Berkeley Lodge Motel* (☎ (076) 23 1666), at 20 Cambridge St, has units at $50/60.

Morven (pop 210)

Continuing west from Mitchell, it's another 89 km to the small highway town of Morven. Originally called Saddler's Waterhole, nowadays Morven is something of a driver's water hole with two pubs, a cafe and a general store.

If you need a bed for the night, the *Royal Hotel* (☎ (076) 54 8106) has single rooms at $12 and one double at $22, or the *Morven Hotel-Motel* (☎ (076) 54 8101) has motel-style units out the back from $27/35.

Both pubs have bistro meals, and the *Duck Inn Cafe* has a good range of takeaway tucker and also sells fuel – it is open every day from 7 am to 8 pm. There's also a Mobil Roadhouse a couple of hundred metres east of town which is open daily from 7 am to 3 am.

The junction of the Warrego and Landsborough highways is three km west of Morven. From here, you can continue west to Charleville (90 km) or take the Landsborough Hwy north-west to Augathella (90 km) – see the Outback Queensland chapter for details of these places.

South Burnett Region

Stretching north-west from Brisbane, the South Burnett is centred around the Burnett River and its various tributaries. Highway 17, which is made up of sections of the Brisbane Valley, D'Aguilar and Burnett highways, starts near Ipswich and runs north for almost 600 km to Rockhampton. Highway 17 is a popular alternative inland

DARLING DOWNS

route for travellers between Brisbane and Rocky who want to avoid the much more hectic Bruce Hwy. It's a slower, more laid-back route which takes you through a string of small rural centres which service the surrounding cattle and dairy properties, peanut farms and citrus orchards.

There are several natural attractions in the region, including the popular Bunya Mountains National Park and the Cania Gorge National Park.

Getting There & Away
Bus Brisbane Bus Lines (☎ (07) 3355 0034 in Brisbane) have two services a day (one on Saturday) north from Brisbane to Murgon ($35 one way), via Caboolture ($7.50) and Kingaroy ($30.50). On Tuesday, Thursday, Friday and Saturday, these services continue up the Burnett Hwy onto Gayndah ($46.50) and Biloela ($68). They also have services from Brisbane to Bundaberg ($55) via the Burnett on Wednesdays only.

BUNYA MOUNTAINS NATIONAL PARK
The Bunya Mountains, outliers of the Great Dividing Range, rise abruptly to over 1000 metres from the country south-west of Kingaroy. This is the second-oldest national park in Queensland (first declared in 1908) and one of the most popular, with vegetation ranging from rainforest and eucalypt forest to heath, and an abundance of birdlife and wildlife. An extensive network of walking tracks leads to numerous waterfalls and lookouts; walks range from a 500-metre discovery walk to a 10-km trail to the Big Falls Lookout.

The park takes its name from the native bunya pine trees that grow here. Every three years or so these trees produce a crop of edible nuts, each of which grows to about the size of a football. Before the European settlers came and started logging these forests in the 1860s, local Aboriginal tribes used to gather for feasts and ceremonies whenever the bunya nuts were ripe.

The QNP&WS has an Information Centre (☎ (076) 68 3127), at Dandabah near the southern entrance to the park, which is open on weekdays from 7 am to 4 pm and weekends from 10 to 11 am and 2 to 4 pm. The centre is staffed by park rangers between 2 and 4 pm on weekdays. Also at Dandabah are a kiosk and the excellent *Rosella's Restaurant* (☎ (076) 68 3131), which opens nightly for dinner.

The main access route from the south is via Dalby or Jondaryan on the Warrego Hwy. The park is 65 km north of Jondaryan, with a short section of gravel road. If you're coming from the north, the park is 56 km south from Kingaroy by sealed road.

Places to Stay
Camping There are national park camping grounds at Dandabah, Westcott and Burton's Well. All have toilets, water and picnic areas; Dandabah also has hot showers. Sites cost $3 per person per night. Camping here is very popular and you'll need to book in advance through the QNP&WS office (☎ (076) 68 3127) at Dandabah, especially during holiday periods.

Other Accommodation *Rice's Bunya Mountain Retreat* (☎ (076) 68 3133) has five self-contained log cabins costing from $40 a double plus $8 for extra people. The *Dandabah Holiday Units* (☎ (076) 68 3131), on Bunya Ave, sleep up to five people and start from $48 a double plus $7 for extras.

On Bunya Mountains Park Rd, the *Bunya Mountain Lodge* (☎ (076) 68 3134) is a guesthouse with four ensuite rooms costing $110/160 for singles/doubles with all meals included.

KINGAROY (pop 6700)
Kingaroy, at the junction of the Bunya Mountains and D'Aguilar highways, is in the centre of Australia's most important peanut growing area. Kingaroy almost means 'peanuts' in Australia, not least because the well-known ex-premier of Queensland, Sir Joh Bjelke-Petersen, hails from here.

Kingaroy is the 'capital' of the South Burnett, and it's a prosperous commercial centre with a surprisingly wide range of facilities and services including modern shopping centres, big-name food chains and half a dozen motels. It has a couple of points of interest if you're passing by, but don't bust a gasket to get here.

Information
There's a tourist office (☎ 62 3199), at 128 Haly St just north of the centre, opposite a cluster of enormous white peanut silos. It is open on weekdays from 9 am to 4 pm and weekends from 10 am to 2 pm.

Things to See & Do
Next to the tourist office, the **Heritage Museum and Peanut Exhibition** has displays with photos and machinery associated with the early days of the peanut industry. Its opening hours are the same as for the tourist office.

If you want to sample the region's most famous products, visit the **Peanut Van** on Kingaroy St, which sells a range of peanuts, souvenirs and other local products.

The Kingaroy Soaring Club (☎ (071) 62 2191) offers **glider flights** on weekends – ring them for details.

Kingaroy is the northern access point for the Bunya Mountains National Park – see that section earlier.

Places to Stay
On the Brisbane Hwy, one km south of the centre, the *Fairfield Caravan Park* (☎ (071) 62 1808) has tent sites at $10, on-site vans at $25 and cabins at $35.

The *Carrollee Hotel* (☎ (071) 62 1055), on King St, just south of the tourist office, has rooms at $20 per person, or $25 with breakfast.

In the centre of town, the *Pioneer Lodge Motel* (☎ (071) 62 3999), at 100 Kingaroy St, has singles/doubles from $47/52, and across the road the *Burke & Wills Motor Inn* (☎ (071) 62 2933) has units from $55.

Places to Eat
The *Kingaroy Steakhouse,* at 198 Haly St, has all-you-can-eat meal deals at $13.90 per person, with a choice of steaks, pork chops, chicken, a salad bar and dessert. Kids pay half price. Across the road, *Elio's* is a casual-looking Italian bistro with very good food at reasonable prices. For a pub feed, try the *Kingaroy Hotel,* on the corner of Haly and Youngman Sts.

NANANGO (pop 2200)
Twenty-five km south-east of Kingaroy, at the intersection of the D'Aguilar and Burnett highways, Nanango is another peanut town but with an earlier history of gold mining. You can fossick for gold at Seven Mile Diggings, 11 km from Nanango.

The town has three motels and two caravan parks. The *Tarong Village Caravan Park* (☎ (071) 63 2322), three km south of town, has sites from $13 and on-site vans from $22. The *Fitzroy Motor Inn* (☎ (071) 63 1100) at 55 Fitzroy St has good units from $40/45.

MURGON (pop 2300)
Murgon is the main town of the region north of Kingaroy, and a centre for the surrounding cattle industry. On the northern outskirts, opposite the saleyards, the **Queensland Dairy Industry Museum** is open on weekdays from 1 to 4 pm or by appointment – contact the local council on ☎ (071) 68 1499.

Six km south of Murgon the Cherbourg Aboriginal community runs the **Barambah Emu Farm** (☎ (071) 68 2655). The farm is open to visitors daily from 8 am to 3 pm, and there are tours every day except Friday costing $3 for adults and $8 for families. The farm has a shop selling Aboriginal crafts and emu products such as decorated eggs, emu oil and leather.

Places to Stay & Eat
The council-run *Murgon Caravan Park* in Krebs St is a straightforward park with tent sites for $6 and caravan sites for $8.50.

The *Australian Hotel-Motel* (☎ (071) 68 1077), in the centre of town on the corner of Lamb and Gore Sts, is a solid two-storey pub with rooms upstairs at $16/24 for singles/ doubles or motel units which are next door

DARLING DOWNS

at $33.50/43. The pub has a lounge bar with counter meals and a steakhouse restaurant.

The *Murgon Motor Inn* (☎ (071) 68 1400), at 193 Lamb St (the Bunya Hwy) 500 metres north of the centre, has units from $40/48.

At 129 Lamb St, *Antoinnes* is a coffee shop by day (serving burgers, toasted sandwiches, pies etc) and a pizza and pasta restaurant by night. It is closed on Sunday.

GAYNDAH (pop 1750)

Officially gazetted back in 1852, Gayndah is an attractive little township that is famous for its oranges and mandarins. The town's Orange Festival, held every second year (odd-numbered years) on what is currently called the Queen's Birthday weekend in June, includes a parade, the crowning of the Orange Queen, and demonstrations of old machinery at the town's museum.

The **Gayndah & District Historical Museum** has an interesting local history collection spanning three buildings, including a one-teacher school display, war memorabilia and an 1864 slab-timber hut. The museum also maintains a large and impressive collection of old farming and timber milling equipment, most of which is in working order. The museum is open daily from 9 am to 4 pm; entry costs $2 for adults, 50c for kids. The museum is worth a visit.

Places to Stay

The *Riverview Caravan Park* (☎ (071) 61 1280), has an attractive setting by the river and good tent sites for $9, powered sites from $12 and on-site vans from $20.

The *Orange Hotel* (☎ (071) 61 1107), in Malty St, has cheap, run-down motel units across the road from the pub at $25/30, or better units behind the pub at $40/48.

The *Colonial Motel* (☎ (071) 61 1999), at 58 Capper St, is more up-market with good units from $48/55.

MUNDUBBERA (pop 1100)

Twenty-five km west of Gayndah, Mundubbera is on the banks of the Burnett River. It's at the centre of another citrus-growing area, and you can buy local crafts and products from the **Big Mandarin** inside the Citrus Country Caravan Village (see Places to Stay section).

Based at Mundubbera, BJ's Packhorse Tours (☎ (071) 65 4713) offers a good range of one to five-day guided tours on horse back. Tours cost $85 per person per day, and they provide tents and sleeping bags, fishing gear, all meals – and the horses.

Places to Stay

The best of the two motels in town is the *Billabong Motor Inn* (☎ (071) 65 4410), on Durong Rd, with a licensed restaurant, a pool and singles/doubles from $48/54. Across the road, the *Citrus Country Caravan Village* (☎ (071) 65 4549) has on-site vans from $25, cabins from $30 and tent sites at $10.

EIDSVOLD (pop 600)

The Eidsvold district was settled in 1848 by two brothers with Norwegian backgrounds – thus the name. Gold was discovered here in 1887, and in the ensuing rush a town sprang up from out of nowhere with some 15 pubs catering to several thousand hopeful diggers. The rush didn't last, and nowadays Eidsvold relies on the cattle industry for its existence.

The **Eidsvold Historical Complex** comprises seven heritage buildings housing an extensive and quirky range of displays, including the Schultz Duncan collection of several thousand bottles (no two the same!) and the George Schafer collection of rocks, gems, more bottles and other bits and pieces. The complex is open daily from 9.30 am to 3 pm.

The Eidsvold Motel & General Store (☎ (071) 65 1209), in the centre of town at 51 Morton St, is a general store, tourist information centre, cafe, service station and motel all rolled into one. It is open daily from 6 am to 9.30 pm and sells super, unleaded and diesel fuel.

Places to Stay

The *Eidsvold Caravan Park* (☎ (071) 65 1168), on the Esplanade one block back from the main road, has tent sites at $6 and powered sites at $8.50. The *Eidsvold Motel & General Store* (☎ (071) 65 1209) at 51 Morton St has six old and simple motel-style units with shared bathroom facilities costing $18/30 for singles/doubles. The pub also has a couple of motel units.

MONTO (pop 1300)
Monto is near the junction of the Burnett River and Three Moon Creek. According to local legend, the creek was named by a swagman who was boiling his billy on the banks of the creek one night when he saw three moons – one in the sky, one reflected in the creek and another reflected in his billy.

Monto is a small, pleasant and friendly country town, with a main street lined with charming old timber buildings. The town holds a Dairy Festival every second year (even-numbered years) on the Queen's Birthday weekend in early June.

Places to Stay & Eat
The *Albert Hotel* (☎ (071) 66 1380), an old timber pub on the corner of Newton and Rutherford Sts, has budget rooms with shared bathrooms at $12.50 per person, plus another $7 for a cooked breakfast. The pub serves bistro meals ranging from $2.50 to $9. It's a popular local meeting place, particularly on Friday nights.

The *Monto Three Moon Motel* (☎ (071) 66 1777), at 4 Flinders St, is a budget motel with singles/doubles at $38/45. At 6 Thomson St, the *Colonial Motor Inn & Restaurant* (☎ (071) 66 1377) has modern motel

units out the back costing $39/48. The motel is fronted by a 100-year-old timber building which houses an atmospheric, colonial-style restaurant and a great bar which is decorated with old photos, horse-riding gear and memorabilia from the town's timber-milling days. The restaurant is licensed and is open from Monday to Saturday for dinner. Main courses range from $12 to $20, and a piano player entertains diners on Friday and Saturday nights.

CANIA GORGE NATIONAL PARK
This small national park 26 km north of Monto features some spectacular scenery, with strange rock formations, rugged sandstone escarpments, rainforests and bushland. The park has an abundance of wildlife and birds, and walking trails starting from the main picnic area take you past many of the more interesting formations.

Nearby, the large Cania Dam is a popular recreational area with good fishing, boating facilities and picnic areas.

The *Cania Gorge Tourist Park* (☎ (071) 67 8188) is a good accommodation park with a shop, a pool, campers' kitchens and a playground, as well as hot showers, laundries etc. Tent sites are $10, a bed in the backpackers' bunkhouse costs $8.50, and cabins range from $32 to $54.

MONTO TO ROCKHAMPTON
The Burnett Hwy continues north from Monto to Rockhampton via Biloela and Mt Morgan. See the Capricorn Coast chapter for details of this area.

Fraser Coast

The focal point of the Fraser Coast is majestic Fraser Island, the world's largest sand island. Hervey Bay, the major access point for the island, has grown into a busy tourist town with a wide range of accommodation and facilities for those wanting to visit Fraser Island. The other access point for the island is Rainbow Beach, a sleepy and attractive seaside town near the southern tip of the island.

Bundaberg, the largest city in the area, is famous throughout Australia as the home of the distinctive Bundaberg Rum. For travellers, Bundy offers access to the Southern Reef Islands, turtle-watching at Mon Repos beach, and seasonal fruit-picking work.

Along the Bruce Hwy are the rural centres of Gympie, the turn off for Rainbow Beach, and Maryborough, the turn off for Hervey Bay.

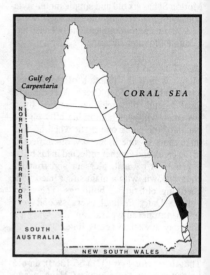

Activities

Fraser Island and Hervey Bay are amongst Queensland's most popular destinations for fishing and boating. Fraser Island offers great bushwalking and camping, and there are popular whale-watching trips out of Hervey Bay between late July and mid-October.

Getting There & Around

Air Flight West and Sunstate have daily flights to Hervey Bay and Bundaberg from all major centres. You can are also fly from Hervey Bay across to Fraser Island and from Bundaberg to Lady Elliot and Lady Musgrave islands.

Bus The major bus companies have regular services along the Bruce Hwy, with detours to Bundaberg and across to Hervey Bay on the coast. There are local bus services from Gympie to Rainbow Beach and Tin Can Bay.

Train Gympie, Maryborough and Bundaberg are all on the main coastal train route between Brisbane and Rockhampton.

Boat Ferry services from the mainland to Fraser Island operate from Rainbow Beach and near Hervey Bay.

GYMPIE (pop 10,800)

Gympie came into existence with a gold rush in 1867. Today it's a pleasant and historic town with many reminders of its glory days, including a town centre with dozens of old buildings, a gold-mining museum and a timber and forestry museum.

Gympie is also the turn off point for the towns of Rainbow Beach and Tin Can Bay and the northern section of the Cooloola National Park.

History

In the early 1860s, the Queensland government had borrowed heavily to finance the

Fraser Coast

0   25   50 km

construction of public buildings and the expansion of the state's much-needed railway network. In mid-1866, the collapse of several major European banks initiated a sudden economic crisis and caused mass unemployment in the fledgling colony. On the brink of bankruptcy and desperate for cash, the government offered rewards of £3000 – a huge sum in those days – to anyone who could find payable goldfields in Queensland.

In mid-October of 1867 James Nash was prospecting solo on the Mary River when he discovered gold in a small gully. Six days of panning the river yielded 2.7 kg of gold, and when Nash's discovery was announced in Brisbane and Maryborough, gold fever struck and more than 15,000 diggers rushed to the diggings. The town that sprung up was initially called Nashville, but was soon renamed Gympie after *gimpi gimpi*, the Aboriginal name for a local tree.

Gympie became one of Queensland's richest goldfields. In the field's first year more than 3000 kg of alluvial gold weres found, including the famed Curtis Nugget which was found in 1868 and weighed in at 37 kg – the largest single nugget ever found in the state. Within a couple of years the alluvial gold was all but exhausted, but by then the rich underground reefs has been found. Reef-mining continued here up until the 1920s, reaching its peak in 1903.

Information
Tourist Information The Cooloola Regional Information Centre (☎ (074) 82 5444), beside the Bruce Hwy on the southern outskirts of town, is open daily from 8.30 am to 3.30 pm. In the same building there's a QNP&WS office (☎ (074) 82 4189) where you can get permits and information for Fraser Island and the Cooloola National Parks and other parks in the area – it is open Monday to Friday from 8.30 am to 4 pm.

Things to See & Do
The **Gympie Gold Mining & Historical Museum**, just north of the tourist office on the southern outskirts of town, has a large and diverse collection of old buildings, artefacts and displays. Allow yourself at least an hour or two to visit this place – it's very extensive and there's lots to see, including mining exhibitions, the former house of Andrew Fisher (a Gympie train driver who went on to become the first Labor prime minister), a military museum, an old steam locomotive and assorted rolling stock, and an impressive collection of restored steam-driven equipment. It is open daily from 9 am to 4.30 pm; entry costs $6 for adults and $2 for children, or you can buy an annual pass for a family of five for $18.

A few km north of Gympie on Fraser Rd (which runs off the Bruce Hwy on the north side of the golf course) is a second museum devoted to another source of Queensland's early wealth – the timber industry. The **Woodworks Forestry & Timber Museum** is open Monday to Friday from 9 am to 4 pm; entry costs $2.50 for adults, $1.20 for students and is free on the first Monday of each month. You can get information on camping in nearby state forests here.

The *Discover Gympie* map and brochure, available from the tourist office, outlines a **heritage walk and a driving tour** which take you past many of the town's significant buildings.

The 50-metre **Gympie Memorial Pool**, in Nelson Park just south of the centre, is open from September to April. The excellent **Gympie Golf Course**, alongside the Bruce Hwy on the northern outskirts, is open to the public.

Festivals
Gympie's Country Music Muster is one of Australia's major country music festivals, held over a weekend every year in August. A week-long Gold Rush Festival is held in Gympie every October.

Places to Stay
At 1 Jane St, the small *Gympie Caravan Park* (☎ (074) 83 6800) has an attractive setting, with tent sites at $10, powered sites at $12, on-site vans from $22 and cabins from $25 to $35 a double. They also have a backpackers' section which costs $10 a night.

A couple of Gympie's old pubs have budget accommodation. The *Freemason Hotel* (☎ (074) 82 1377), on the corner of Channon and Duke Sts, and the *Commercial Hotel* (☎ (074) 82 1007), on the corner of Channon and Mary Sts, both have singles/doubles at $15/25.

The *Great Eastern Motor Inn* (☎ (074) 82 7288), across the highway from the tourist office, is a modern motel with singles/doubles from $55/60. The motel has its own licensed restaurant, *Geordie's*, and a swimming pool. Another good motel is the *Gympie Muster Inn Motel* (☎ (074) 82 8666), closer to the centre at 21 Wickham St, with singles/doubles from $58/63. The *Gympie Motel* (☎ (074) 82 2722), at 83 River Rd, is quite a good budget option with rooms from $36/42.

Places to Eat
Set in an old timber Queenslander with broad, verandahs, the *Kingston Tea Rooms* is a very pleasant spot for Devonshire tea ($3). They also have lunches such as sandwiches and rolls, vegetarian meals, lasagnas and

To Maryborough

Henry St
Mnall St
King St
Duke St
Clematis
Bruce Hwy
Mulcahy Tce
Poper Rd
Musgrave St
Horseshoe Bend Road
Stewart Tce
Tucker St
Rifle Range Road

Jane St
Alfred St
Barter Hwy
Channon St
Street St
Lawrence St
Gympie St
Tozer St
Tozer Park Road
To Rainbow Beach & Tin Can Bay Road

Queen St
Reef St
Monkland St
O'connell St
Nash St
Mary St
Mellor St
Alma St
Station Road
Coonaraba Road
Ashford Road

River Rd
Church St
Caldon Hill
Bligg St
Nelson St
Red Hill Rd
Road

Mary River
Bruce Hwy
Hall Lane
Hilton Rd
Excelsior Rd
Stanley St
Perseverance St
Hilton Rd
St
Mt Pleasant
John St
Brisbane Road
Wises Road

Power
River Road
Graham St
Nashville St
Deep Ck
East Deep Creek Rd
Noosa Rd

Gympie

0   250   500 m

Road

Gympie - Brooloo Road
Bruce Hwy
Smith St
Monkland
Jubilee
Brisbane Road

PLACES TO STAY
1 Gympie Caravan Park
2 Freemason Hotel
3 Gympie Muster Inn Motel
6 Commercial Hotel
11 Gympie Motel
13 Great Eastern Motor Inn

PLACES TO EAT
4 Kingston Tea Rooms
5 Mamma Rosa's Pizzas
10 Indulgence Cafe

OTHER
7 Bus Terminal
8 Post Office
9 Gympie Memorial Pool
12 Gympie Gold Mining Museum
14 Cooloola Regional Information Centre

Old Imbil Rd
12
13   14

To Cooroy & Nambour

FRASER COAST

quiches, salads etc, in the $4 to $6 range. It's on the corner of Channon Rd and Barter St, and opens every day.

One block down Channon St on the corner of Reef St, *Mamma Rosa's Pizzas* is a little BYO eatery with pastas and pizzas.

There are more eateries along Mary St. The *Brown Jug*, near the post office at No 79, is a straightforward coffee lounge with burgers, quiches and sandwiches etc. The *Indulgence Cafe*, at No 46, is a tiny gourmet cafe with a good range of sandwiches, salads and filled croissants; it also opens as a restaurant on Friday and Saturday nights with main courses under $10.

Entertainment
The *Commercial Hotel*, on the corner of Channon and Duke Sts, hosts a 'poets and musos' night every second Thursday as well as on the third Sunday of each month, and has country music bands on the first Sunday of each month.

Getting There & Away
Gympie is on the major train and bus routes between Brisbane and Rockhampton. Long-distance buses stop at the Polley's Coaches (☎ (074) 82 2700) terminal in the centre of town, on the corner of Channon and Mary St, while the main railway station is one km east of the post office on Tozer St.

See the Rainbow Beach section for details of bus services between here and there.

RAINBOW BEACH (pop 726)
This little town on Wide Bay, 70 km northeast of Gympie, is the southern access point for Fraser Island and the northern access point for the Cooloola National Park.

Orientation & Information
From Rainbow Beach it's a 13-km drive north along the beach to Inskip Point, where ferries leave for Fraser Island. South-east of the town, the beach curves away 13 km to Double Island Point at the top of the Cooloola coast. One km north is the 120-metre-high **Carlo Sandblow**, and beyond it

are the coloured sand cliffs which gave the town its name. You can walk behind or along the beach all the way from the town and up to the lighthouse on Double Island Point.

The privately run Rainbow Beach Tourist Information Centre (☎ (074) 86 3227), at 8 Rainbow Beach Rd, has a list of other walks in the area. In a 4WD it's possible to drive to Noosa, 70 km south, along the beach most of the way. See the Cooloola National Park section in the Sunshine Coast chapter for more details.

Obtain Fraser Island vehicle and camping permits and northern Cooloola National Park camping permits from the QNP&WS office situated beside the main road as you enter Rainbow Beach; it's open daily from 7 am to 4 pm (☎ (074) 86 3160).

Organised Tours
Sun Safari Tours offers day trips to Fraser Island costing $58 for adults and $30 for children, which includes morning tea and lunch. The tour follows the coastline north as far as Eurong, and then heads inland to explore the island and its lakes. Sun Safari Tours also offers a half-day tour south from Rainbow Beach to Double Island Point, the wreck of the *Cherry Venture*, and the Cooloola National Park; the cost is $30/20 and includes morning tea. Tours can be booked through the tourist information centre.

Places to Stay
The *Rainbow Beach Holiday Village* (☎ (074) 86 3222), on Rainbow Beach Rd, is a good foreshore camping and caravan park that has a backpackers' section with three-bed tents and basic cooking facilities for $7.50 per person. Tent sites start from $10, powered sites from $12, on-site vans from $25 and cabins from $45.

Rainbow Beach Backpackers (☎ (074) 86 3288), at 66 Rainbow Beach Rd (the first place on the left as you enter town), charges from $12 per person in a dorm or from $28 for doubles and twins. It's a small, clean

The *Cherry Venture* wreck

place with a kitchenette, pool and restaurant next door (but no laundry).

The *Rainbow Beach Hotel/Motel* (☎ (074) 86 3125), which is near the beachfront, has motel-style units $38/45.

The new *Rainbow Sands* (☎ (074) 86 3400), on Rainbow Beach Rd, has modern one and two-bedroom apartments with all the mod cons starting from $50 a double, as well as a swimming pool, a spa and a sauna.

The *Gazebo Gardens Motel* (☎ (074) 86 3255) on Spectrum Ave is a modern two-storey motel with a licensed restaurant, pool, and units ranging from $50 to $70 a double.

Places to Eat

You can get a bistro meal at the *Rainbow Beach Hotel/Motel*. There are a couple of cafes and takeaways in the main shopping arcade in the centre of town on Rainbow Beach Rd; *Papa's Cafe* has burgers, pizzas, salads and fish & chips, and does stir-fried Chinese tucker.

Lilly's, around the corner on Clarkson Dve, is a friendly little eatery with a small, interesting menu ranging from moussaka and mixed satays to seafood tempura and Italian chicken. Mains range from $10 to $14. Lilly's is BYO and opens from Tuesday to Sunday.

Getting There & Away

Polley's Coaches (☎ (074) 82 2700) in Gympie runs bus services between Gympie and Rainbow Beach every weekday. Buses leave Gympie at 6 am, 2 and 3 pm, and leave Rainbow Beach at 7.45 am and 4 pm. The one-way fare is $9.25. These services may change throughout the year – ring Polley's to confirm departure times.

Another way to Rainbow Beach is to hitch along the beaches up from Noosa or on to Fraser Island. If you have a 4WD vehicle you can drive this way too.

See the Fraser Island section for details of ferry services.

Getting Around

In Rainbow Beach, the tourist information centre and Jeep City (☎ (074) 86 3223), at 10 Karounda Court, rent 4WDs from around $90 a day with a two-day minimum hire.

TIN CAN BAY (pop 1500)

Tin Can Bay is a narrow inlet at the southern reaches of the Sandy Straits, the body of water separating Fraser Island from the mainland. The township has in recent years begun to change from a sleepy fishing village and retirement centre into a popular

FRASER COAST

destination as more people are attracted by the area's excellent boating and fishing.

Things to See & Do
The town has a golf club and an impressive boat marina, and fishing dinghies and houseboats are available for hire. The Tin Can Bay Yacht Club hosts the Bay to Bay race, between Hervey Bay and Tin Can Bay, every May.

The **Tin Can Bay Swimming Pool** at the end of the main road, near the boat harbour, is open on weekdays from 7 am and weekends from 10 am.

Two local companies, *Fraser Island Houseboats* (☎ (074) 86 4444) and *Luxury Afloat* (☎ (074) 86 4864), hire out **houseboats** for leisurely cruising holidays in the Sandy Straits.

Places to Stay
There are three caravan parks here. The *Golden Trevally Caravan Park* (☎ (074) 86 4411), on Trevally St, about one km south of the centre, has good facilities with tent sites from $8, on-site vans from $20 and cabins from $30. The *Kingfisher Caravan Park* (☎ (074) 86 4198), on the Esplanade, has a better location and is close to the boat harbour, and has tent sites from $10 and cabins from $25.

The *Tin Can Bay Motel* (☎ (074) 86 4269), in Mitchell St, has budget units from $32/40, some with limited cooking facilities. The modern *Sandcastle Motel* (☎ (074) 86 4555), on Tin Can Bay Rd, has good units from $40/48.

Places to Eat
Tin Can Bay has a couple of good eateries. At the marina on Oyster Pde, the *Marina Bistro* is a good BYO with a very pleasant open-air deck overlooking the harbour. It's also very affordable, with salads, steaks, chicken and seafood dishes all under $10 and kid's meals for $4, which means you can also afford a dessert – maybe the banana pie or profiteroles ($4)? The bistro opens nightly (except Tuesdays) for dinner and for Sunday lunches. They host good musical jam sessions here every full moon.

The *Cockatoo Restaurant*, in a small cottage at 4 Gympie Rd, is a front room BYO that specialises in seafood. It's open for lunch and dinner daily except Tuesdays – lunches such as fish & chips, garlic prawns etc, range from $3 to $7 and at night seafood and other mains are in the $12 to $17 range.

Getting There & Away
The Gympie-Rainbow Beach bus services runs via Tin Can Bay – see the earlier Rainbow Beach section for details.

MARYBOROUGH (pop 20,800)
Maryborough's early importance as an industrial centre and port on the Mary River led to the construction of a series of imposing Victorian buildings.

The greatest concentration of old buildings is on Wharf St. The **post office**, built in 1869, is just one of the many buildings which reflect Maryborough's early prosperity; some of the old hotels are also fine examples of Victorian architecture.

Today, Maryborough is predominantly a working town and service centre for the local timber and sugar industries. Its major claim to fame is as the turn off point for Hervey Bay, although it has a couple of points of interest if you're passing through.

Information
The Maryborough & District Tourist Information Centre (☎ (071) 23 2682), on the corner of Ferry and Queen Sts, is open weekdays from 8.30 am to 5 pm and weekends from 10 am to 4 pm; the centre has good info on the whole Fraser Coast region.

Things to See & Do
Maryborough's best attraction is the remarkable National Trust-classified **Brennan & Geraghty's Store**, at 64 Lennox St. This historic general store, which opened for business in 1871 and was run by the same family for 100 years, has been preserved intact as a museum with its original stock, shelving, trading records and other fascinating remnants. Definitely worth a visit. The shop is open daily from 10 am to 3 pm; entry costs

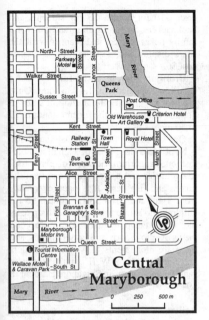

Central Maryborough

0   250   500 m

$3 for adults, $2 for kids and $7 for a family. **Queens Park**, immediately north of the centre between Lennox St and the Mary River, is an attractive open parkland with two ferneries, a band rotunda and a miniature railway which runs on the last Sunday of each month. Maryborough also has a **railway museum** in the old railway station on Lennox St.

The **Heritage City Markets** are held in Kent and Adelaide Sts every Thursday, with a wide range of craft, produce, clothing and other stalls.

Maryborough's *Walk and Drive Tours* brochure, available from the tourist office, outlines a walking tour around the town centre and a longer driving tour, and gives the historical background of various buildings en route.

Places to Stay & Eat
At 98 Wharf St, the old *Criterion Hotel* (☎ (071) 21 3043) has pub-style rooms at $15/30 for singles/doubles. They're not terribly

flash, but they are cheap and you get to enjoy the great views from the front balcony of the pub. It's worth noting that the pub has live bands on Friday and Saturday nights and Sunday arvos – great fun, but not if you're trying to sleep upstairs. Another old pub with budget rooms is the *Royal Hotel* (☎ (071) 21 2241) on the corner of Kent and Bazaar Sts, with simple rooms with shared bathrooms from $16/28 or motel-style units from $34/46.

Next to the tourist office in Ferry St, the *Wallace Motel & Caravan Park* (☎ (071) 21 3970) has motel-style units with limited cooking facilities from $32/42, tent sites at $10 and on-site cabins at $26 for a double or $38 with a bathroom and kitchenette. Nearby, on the corner of Ferry and Queen Sts, the *Maryborough Motor Inn* (☎ (071) 22 2777) has better units from $50/56, if you can afford a little more.

The *Parkway Motel* (☎ (071) 22 2888), at 188 John St, is an excellent modern motel with three types of units ranging from $50/58 to $68/78 for singles/doubles. The rooms have all the mod cons and there's a licensed restaurant, a pool, sauna and spa.

Getting There & Away
Maryborough's railway station is on Lennox St just west of the centre. Long-distance buses stop at the bus terminal beside the railway station.

Maryborough-Hervey Bay Coaches (☎ (071) 21 3719) has nine bus services every weekday and three services on Saturdays between Maryborough and Hervey Bay. Buses depart in Maryborough from outside the Town Hall in Kent St.

HERVEY BAY (pop 22,200)
The once sleepy settlement of Hervey Bay has grown at an astronomical rate in the last decade, and it's now one of the major destinations along the Queensland coast. The main attractions are Fraser Island, for which Hervey Bay is the main access point, and whale-watching trips in the bay.

The five small settlements which make up the town are popular family holiday spots with safe beaches and a huge number of caravan parks. There's no surf here, and the best beach is at Torquay.

Orientation

The five suburbs of Hervey Bay are strung along a 10-km-long, north-facing stretch of coast. From west to east they are Point Vernon, Pialba, Scarness, Torquay and Urangan. Pialba is the main business and shopping centre, although Torquay is where most of the action is. Fraser Island is 12 km across the Great Sandy Strait from Urangan, with Woody Island in between. River Heads, the departure point for the main Fraser Island ferries, is 15 km south of Urangan.

Information

Tourist Information There are numerous privately run information centres and tour booking offices, including the Hervey Bay Tourist & Visitors Centre (☎ (071) 24 4050), at 63 Old Maryborough Rd in Pialba. It is open daily from 7.30 am to 5 pm.

Laundry The Coin-Op Laundromat is in a small arcade near the corner of Charlton Esplanade and Frank St in Scarness.

Things to See

Situated near the corner of Maryborough Rd and Fairway Dve in Pialba, **Hervey Bay Natureworld** has native fauna including wedge-tailed eagles and koalas, as well as introduced species such as camels and water buffaloes. Crocodiles are fed at 11.30 am and lorikeets at 3.30 pm. Natureworld opens daily from 9 am; entry costs $7.

Vic Hislop's Shark Show, on the corner of Charlton Esplanade and Elizabeth St in Urangan, has a collection of photos, newspaper articles, jaw bones, a Great White shark (decaying in a glass tank), and continuously screens shark documentaries. Vic is a famous renegade shark catcher. The displays, facts and figures presented here are pretty gruesome and sensational, but Vic claims the main aim of the exhibition is to be educational – you decide for yourself. The centre is open daily from 8.30 am to 6 pm; entry

costs $10 for adults, $8 for students and backpackers, $4 for children and $24 for a family ticket. If you just want to visit the shark display and skip the movies, tickets cost $6.

Urangan Pier, a little further along Charlton Esplanade, is 1.4 km long. Once used for sugar and oil handling, it's now a popular fishing spot, the far end stands in 25 to 30 metres of water.

One km east of the pier, at Dayman Point, is **Neptune's Reef World**, a small and old-fashioned aquarium with coral displays, fish, seals, turtles and a croc. Kids can feed the turtles and fish here. It is open every day from 9 am and costs $8 for adults, $5 for children and is free for kids under four years old. From the point itself, there are good views over to Woody and Fraser islands, and there are monuments to Matthew Flinders and the Z Force WW II commandos who sank Japanese ships in Singapore Harbour in 1943.

Activities

There are a couple of places along the waterfront where you can hire water-sports gear. Torquay Beach Hire, a beach shed on the foreshore, has catamarans ($20 an hour), windsurfers ($15 an hour), fishing dinghies ($60 a day) and will take you water-skiing ($20 for 10 minutes); they also have canoes, deck chairs and other beach essentials. The Hervey High Flyer (☎ 018 366 897) operates paragliding flights, departing from the Urangan Harbour; they also do pick-ups from Torquay Beach Hire daily.

The Hervey Bay Golf & Country Club is open to the public every day; 9 holes costs $10, 18 holes costs $18 and club hire is $8.

You can go horse riding at the Susan River Homestead (☎ (071) 21 6846; they offer two-hour rides through a bushland property for $30, or $35 including picking you up and dropping you off from your accommodation.

Organised Tours

Fraser Island Day Trips Prices for day tours to Fraser Island are around $55 for adults and $28 for children with the larger operators like

Top Tours (☎ (071) 25 3933) or Fraser Venture Day Tours (☎ (071) 27 9122). Each outfit follows a different route but a typical tour might take in a trip up the east coast to the *Maheno* wreck and the Cathedrals, plus Central Station and a couple of the lakes in the centre of the island. Note that most day tours to Fraser Island allow you to split the trip and stay a few days on the island before coming back.

The Kingfisher Bay Resort (☎ (071) 25 5511) offers ranger-guided ecotours costing $63 for adults and $31.50 for children, including lunch.

Aboriginal Tours The Thoorgine Educational & Cultural Centre (☎ (071) 24 4100) runs three-day trips to Fraser Island for groups of eight to 10 people, costing $90 per person. Run by Aboriginal guides, the trips include visits to significant cultural sites, bush-tucker walks and camp-fire barbecues. You need to bring your own food and bedding.

Fraser Island Flying Tours Two local operators, Air Fraser Island (☎ (071) 25 3600) and Harry's Air Charter (☎ (071) 28 9056) offer flights and tours to the island, leaving from the Hervey Bay airport and landing on the beaches on the east coast. You can do a day trip for $35 per person, or around $80 per person with 4WD hire included; they also have two-day tours for around $150 per person which includes return flights, overnight accommodation and one day's 4WD hire.

Backpacker Tours Self-drive tours to Fraser Island organised by the backpackers' hostels are popular, and currently cost around $85 per person for a three-day trip. This doesn't include food or fuel but all the gear is organised for you. These trips are an affordable and (usually) fun way to see the island, but you'll probably be in a group of nine, and, like relatives, you can't choose who you go with.

There are plenty of alternative ways to see the island, but unfortunately some of the hostels tell travellers that the only way to get there is on one of their trips. If you'd rather do your own thing, you could quite easily get a group together yourself. 4WDs and camping gear can be hired from various places (see Getting Around), permits are readily available and you have a choice of catching a ferry or flying to the island.

Whale Watching Boat tours to watch the

Humpback whale breaching

PLACES TO STAY

2 Pialba Caravan & Camping Park
5 Midway Terraces
8 Mango Tourist Hostel
10 Scarness Caravan & Camping Park
11 Friendly Hostel
12 Olympus Backpackers Villas
14 Fraser Magic Backpackers
15 Beaches Hervey Bay Backpackers
16 Delfino's Bay Resort
17 Riviera Resort
18 Bay View Motel
19 Koala Backpackers
26 Torquay Caravan & Camping Park
29 The Charlton
31 Playa Concha Motor Inn
32 Silver Sands Apartments
36 Colonial Log Cabin &
    Backpackers Resort
38 Magnolia Caravan Park

PLACES TO EAT

3 Pialba Hotel
4 RSL Club
6 Red Parrot
7 Scarborough Hotel
9 Brollies Deli Cafe
20 Dolly's Restaurant
22 Torquay Hotel
24 Sail's Brasserie & Cafe
25 Toto's Restaurant
28 O'Riley's
30 Gringo's Mexican Cantina
41 Stockman's Bar & Grill

majestic humpback whales on their annual migration operate out of Hervey Bay most days between late July and mid-October. There are more than 20 boats offering these trips, including one owned by Mimi Macpherson, sister of supermodel Elle Macpherson. Half-day tours cost from $42 to $55, full-day tours from $40 to $65 including lunch. Book through your accommodation or one of the information centres.

Fishing Trips Various vessels such as MV *Snapper I* (☎ (071) 24 3788), MV *Princess II* (☎ (071) 28 9087) and MV *Reel Easy* (☎ (071) 24 1300) offers fishing tours into

Hervey Bay starting from around $25 for adults and $12 for kids for a half-day tour.

Festivals

The Hervey Bay Whale Festival, held over a fortnight each year in August, celebrates the return of these magnificent creatures. The Bay to Bay yacht race from Hervey Bay to Tin Can Bay is held every year in May.

Places to Stay

Camping There are at least a dozen caravan parks in Hervey Bay. Some of the best are the council-run parks along Charlton Esplanade – you'll need to book ahead during the

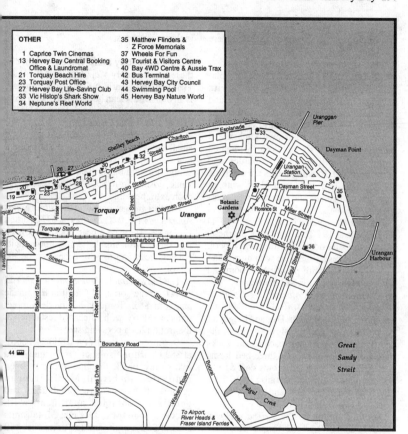

OTHER
1 Caprice Twin Cinemas
13 Hervey Bay Central Booking Office & Laundromat
21 Torquay Beach Hire
23 Torquay Post Office
27 Hervey Bay Life-Saving Club
33 Vic Hislop's Shark Show
34 Neptune's Reef World
35 Matthew Flinders & Z Force Memorials
37 Wheels For Fun
39 Tourist & Visitors Centre
40 Bay 4WD Centre & Aussie Trax
42 Bus Terminal
43 Hervey Bay City Council
44 Swimming Pool
45 Hervey Bay Nature World

holiday seasons. The *Pialba Caravan Park* (☎ (071) 28 1399) is the largest and perhaps the best of these, with plenty of grass and big old trees, a camper's kitchen and barbecues. The *Scarness Caravan & Camping Park* (☎ (071) 28 1274) occupies a narrower strip along the foreshore, as does the *Torquay Caravan & Camping Park* (☎ (071) 25 1578). All of these places charge the same rates, which go up in the holiday seasons – tent sites start from $11, powered sites from $13 ($14 on the waterfront), and on-site vans from $28 a double.

The closest camp ground to the bus terminal is the *Magnolia Caravan Park* (☎ (071) 28 1700), on the corner of Boatharbour Dve and Taylor St, which has tent sites from $13 and on-site cabins from $45.

Hostels Hervey Bay has a growing number of backpackers' hostels, spread between Scarness and Urangan. All do pick-ups from the main bus stop, and most organise trips to Fraser Island.

The friendly *Mango Tourist Hostel* (☎ (071) 24 2832), in a small timber house at 110 Torquay Rd, Scarness, has bunks at $12 and one double $35. It's a laid-back, alternative hostel run by people who are passionate about Fraser Island, and it's a

FRASER COAST

good place for getting info about the island and finding out about ways of getting there and seeing it.

The impressive *Koala Backpackers* (☎ (071) 25 3601) is at 408 Charlton Esplanade, Torquay. It's a large place with excellent facilities including a good pool and recreation room, and the beach is just across the road. Accommodation is in either two-bedroom units with their own kitchen and bathroom ($14) or six-bed dorms with good communal facilities ($13); doubles and twins cost $30. Evening meals are available for $5. This is a party-type place, with its own bar, and games and entertainment most nights.

Beaches Hervey Bay Backpackers (☎ (071) 24 1322) is at 195 Torquay Tce in Scarness. It has the usual hostel facilities and a pool. There are two sections, one with dorms and one with rooms with private bathroom and TV; the nightly cost is $13 per person.

At Urangan, the *Colonial Log Cabin & Backpackers Resort* (☎ (071) 25 1844), on the corner of Boatharbour Dve and Pulgul St, is very well set up. It's a few km out of the centre, but it's quiet and spacious and backs onto bushland. The two and three-bed dorms cost $13, self-contained cabins cost $13 to $15 per person, and doubles are $30. Visitors have free use of bicycles, and there's a good pool and two tennis courts.

Another option is the *Friendly Hostel* (☎ (071) 24 4107), at 182 Torquay Rd, Scarness. It's a small, quiet place with three separate units, each with three bedrooms (with two to three beds), a TV lounge, kitchen and bathroom. The cost here is $10 per person.

The new *Olympus Backpackers' Villas* (☎ (071) 24 5331), next door at 184 Torquay Rd, Scarness, is an impressive, purpose-built hostel with eight separate two-storey apartments, each with two bathrooms, a kitchen and a TV lounge. There's also a good swimming pool. There is no laundry, but a laundrette is nearby on Charlton Esplanade. Dorm beds cost $13, twins and doubles are $28.

The recently opened *Fraser Magic Backpackers* (☎ (071) 24 3488), at 369 Charlton Esplanade, Scarness, has dorms and doubles at $12 per person, which includes breakfast.

Motels & Holiday Flats There are plenty of these too. The *Bay View Motel* (☎ (071) 28 1134), at 399 Charlton Esplanade, Torquay, is an oldish but clean budget motel with units starting from $30/35 for singles/doubles.

The *Midway Terraces* (☎ (071) 28 4119), at 335 Charlton Esplanade, Scarness, is a small block of one and two-bedroom units that sleep up to five people. They are pretty straightforward but well equipped and good value, costing from $35 a double plus $5 for each extra person.

Another budget option is the *Silver Sands Apartments* (☎ (071) 25 2629) at 477 Charlton Esplanade, Torquay: a neat, brick block from the 1960s with simple two-bedroom units ranging from $55 to $80, depending on the season.

The *Playa Concha Motor Inn* (☎ (071) 25 1544), on the corner of Charlton Esplanade and Ann St in Torquay, has modern motel units at $58/68, with a licensed restaurant at the front, plus a pool and spa.

Delfino's Bay Resort (☎ (071) 24 1666), at 383 Charlton Esplanade in Torquay, is a two-storey block that has recently been renovated in bright Mediterranean colours. It has modern motel units and good self-contained apartments with kitchens, laundries, TVs etc. Motel units start at $50 a night and the units cost $60 for one bedroom, $80 for two bedrooms and $100 for three bedrooms. It's worth paying an extra $10 for one of the front units with ocean views. There's also a pool, a sauna and a licensed seafood restaurant.

The developers have recently moved into the Hervey Bay waterfront, and there are several new accommodation complexes along Charlton Esplanade (and several more going up as you read this). The six-storey *Riviera Resort* (☎ (071) 24 3344), at 385-387 Charlton Esplanade in Torquay, has one, two and three-bedroom apartments ranging from around $100 to $130 a night, with a pool, spa, sauna, floodlit tennis court and a licensed restaurant. The apartments are modern and spacious, if somewhat sterile. At 447 Charlton Esplanade, *The Charlton* (☎ (071) 25 3661) is another new up-market complex with two and three-bedroom apartments at similar prices.

Places to Eat

Despite being the 'business' centre, Pialba has few places to eat. The *Pialba Hotel* has excellent meals in the $9 to $13 range and an all-you-can-eat salad and dessert bar ($10 for lunch, $12 for dinner). Visitors are welcome at the *RSL Club*, on Torquay Rd, which offers an insight into Aussie club culture with its bars, pool tables, poker machines, and a small display of war memorabilia. Meals range from $5 to $11, and they have a 'theme smorgasbord' every Friday and Saturday night at $8.50 a head – sounds scary.

Charlton Esplanade in Torquay is the food focus in Hervey Bay. *Sails Brasserie & Cafe*, on the corner of Charlton Esplanade and Fraser St, is a chic Mediterranean-style eatery with main courses in the $14 to $16 range. Sails is licensed and is open Monday to Saturday nights and Thursday and Friday for lunch. For somewhere more casual and a bit cheaper, try *Toto's,* at 2 Fraser St. It's fronted by a takeaway section and has high-backed booths out the back, with good pizza and pasta as well as Italian, Malaysian and Thai dishes – something for everyone!

Gringo's Mexican Cantina, at 449 Charlton Esplanade, has good Mexican tucker with mains in the $10 to $14 range, steaks around $15 and kid's meals under $4. Most of the dishes are also available as vegetarian meals, with beans substituted for meat. Gringo's is BYO and opens nightly for dinner. Nearby at No 446, *O'Riley's* is a relaxed pizza and pasta joint with savoury crepes under $9 and a range of dessert pancakes from $4 to $6.

The *Torquay Hotel* has the *China Garden* restaurant and a beer garden, on the corner of Charlton Esplanade and Bideford St. You can sit outside to eat, often with musical accompaniment. They have all-you-can-eat deals at $8 for lunch and $9.50 for dinner.

Brollies Deli Cafe, at 353 Charlton Esplanade in Scarness, is a good place for breakfast or lunch and has real coffee and excellent sandwiches. Nearby at No 341, the *Red Parrot* is another good daytime cafe and gourmet sandwich bar with salads, rolls and sandwiches, smoothies, home-made cakes, good coffee and herbal teas.

The popular *Stockman's Bar & Grill*, near the bus terminal on Boatharbour Dve, is a verandah-fronted timber tavern specialising in steaks and seafood, with bistro meals in the $8 to $15 range and budget bar meals like roasts or pork chops with vegies from $5 to $7. This place also has live bands on weekends.

Entertainment

Quite a few pubs in town have live bands, especially on weekends, including the *Torquay Hotel,* on Charlton Esplanade, Torquay. The *Stockman's Bar & Grill,* on Boatharbour Dve, has live rock bands on Friday and Saturday nights; there's no cover charge, and it is open till midnight. There's a disco at the *Pialba Hotel* on Wednesdays (till 1 am) and Saturdays (till 3 am). *Dolly's Restaurant*, next to Koala Backpackers', has a bar with nightly entertainment.

The Caprice Twin Cinemas (☎ (071) 28 4211), in Watson St, Pialba, screens mainstream movies every night, and has discounted tickets ($6) on Tuesday and Thursday nights.

Getting There & Away

Air Sunstate and Flight West have daily flights between Brisbane and Hervey Bay. The one-way fare is $136. Hervey Bay Airport is off Booral Rd, Urangan.

Bus Hervey Bay is on the major bus route, and Greyhound Pioneer Australia and McCafferty's both have frequent services through here. It's about 4½ hours from Brisbane (around $30), and about 5½ hours from Rockhampton ($55).

Maryborough-Hervey Bay Coaches (☎ (071) 21 3719) runs a service between the

FRASER COAST

two centres, with nine trips every weekday and three on Saturdays.

Hervey Bay's main bus stop is Geldard's Coach Terminal (☎ (071) 24 4000), in Central Ave, off Boatharbour Dve in Pialba.

Getting Around

Air There are a couple of local operators offering affordable flights from Hervey Bay to Fraser Island – see Organised Tours for details.

Bus Maryborough-Hervey Bay Coaches (☎ (071) 21 3719) also runs local bus services linking the suburbs of Hervey Bay every weekday and on Saturday mornings.

4WD Rental There are several good 4WD hire places. The Bay 4WD Centre (☎ (071) 28 2981), at 54 Boatharbour Dve in Pialba, and Allterrain (☎ (07) 3257 1101 in Brisbane or book though Koala Backpackers) have good, reliable vehicles ranging from about $85 a day for a Suzuki Sierra to $125 for a Toyota Landcruiser, usually with a two-day minimum.

Aussie Trax (☎ (071) 24 4433), at 56 Boatharbour Dve, Pialba, has old ex-army jeeps from $77 a day. Wheels for Fun (see Trail Bike Hire below) also has Land Rover and Nissan soft-tops from $70 per day. All of these companies also have camping gear available for hire.

You can also hire 4WD from several places on the island – see the Fraser Island section for details.

Trail Bike Wheels for Fun (☎ (071) 25 4499) at 3 Florence St, Urangan, hire out trail bikes from $60 a day with helmets included.

Bicycle Some of the backpackers' hostels have bikes available for guests. Otherwise, you can hire bikes from the Hervey Bay Central Booking Office (☎ (071) 24 1300), at 363 Charlton Esplanade, Scarness, and Toyworld (☎ (071) 25 2540), at 402 Charlton Esplanade, Torquay.

FRASER ISLAND

Fraser Island, the world's largest sand island, was inscribed on the World Heritage List in 1993. The island is 120 km long by about 15 km wide and rises to 200 metres above sea level in places. Apart from three or four small rock outcrops, it's all sand – mostly covered in vegetation. Here and there the cover is broken by sandblows – dunes that grow, shrink or move as the wind pushes them. The island also has about 200 lakes, some of them superb for swimming. Almost half of the island forms the Great Sandy National Park.

Fraser Island is a delight for those who love fishing, walking, exploring by 4WD or trail bike, and for those who simply enjoy nature. There are superb beaches (though swimming in the ocean can be dangerous due to severe undertows and the odd shark or ten!), towering dunes, thick forests, walking tracks, interesting wildlife and clear freshwater lakes and streams for swimming. You can camp or stay in accommodation. The island is sparsely populated and although more than 20,000 vehicles a year pile on to it, it remains wild. A network of sandy tracks crisscrosses the island and you can drive along great stretches of beach – but it's 4WD or trail bike only; there are no paved roads.

History

The island takes its name from Eliza Fraser, the wife of the captain of a ship which was wrecked further north in 1836. Making their way south to look for help, a group from the ship fell among Aborigines on Fraser Island. Some of the group died during their two-month wait for rescue, but others, including Eliza Fraser, survived with Aboriginal help.

The Butchulla Aborigines, who used Fraser Island as a seasonal home, were driven out onto missions when timber cutters moved on to the island in the 1860s. The cutters were after satinay, a rainforest tree which is highly resistant to marine borer; this timber was used to line the Suez Canal. It was not until 1991 that logging on the island ceased.

In the mid-1970s, Fraser Island was the

subject of a bitter struggle between conservationists and industry – in this case a sand-mining company. The decision went to the conservationists.

Information

There's a visitor centre on the east coast of the island at Eurong (☎ (071) 27 9128), and ranger's offices at Dundubara and Waddy Point. These places all have plenty of leaflets detailing walking trails and the flora and fauna found on the island.

At Central Station (the old forestry depot) there's a small display on the history of exploration and logging on the island.

General supplies are available from stores at Eurong, Happy Valley and Cathedral Beach, but as you might expect, prices are high. There are also public telephones at these sites.

Permits You'll need a permit to take a vehicle onto the island, and to camp. The most convenient place to get permits is the River Heads general store, just half a km from the ferry to Wanggoolba Creek (also called Woongoolber Creek). Vehicles cost $15, and camping costs $7.50 per site per night. If you're staying in cabin accommodation, or camping in one of the island's private camping grounds, there's no need to pay the $7.50.

Permits can also be obtained from any of the QNP&WS offices in the area, or from the Hervey Bay City Council (☎ (071) 25 0222) in Tavistock St, Torquay.

Books & Maps The *Bushpeople's Visitor Guide to Fraser Island & Cooloola* ($16) is an excellent 250-page paperback guide to Fraser Island and the Cooloola National Park. It's worth investing in as both a guidebook and souvenir of the island, and includes colour photos, notes on natural history, tips on photography, and advice on camping and bushwalking, canoeing and whale watching.

An essential read for those interested in the background of Fraser Island and how it eventually became a World-Heritage-listed conservation area is *Fighting for Fraser Island*, the autobiography of John Sinclair (written with prolific crime-fiction writer Peter Corris).

The book tells the story of Maryborough-born Sinclair, whose passion for the island led him to form FIDO (Fraser Island Defence Organisation), and of his 25-year battle to stop sand mining and the logging of rainforest timbers on the island. It's an intriguing tale of passionate, extraordinary individuals and their fight against the Queensland government and multi-national corporations. In one episode, Sinclair tells of how, in 1975, he and friends flew over the island and took an aerial photo showing the cancerous spread of the sand-mining operations. They sent the photo to Malcolm Fraser, whose Liberal Party had recently formed a caretaker government, with this note: 'This photograph was taken on 13 December 1975. Every inch that is mined after this date is your responsibility'.

A good map is essential if you will be spending a few days exploring. The Sunmap 1:140,000 ($6) provides all the detail you need, and is widely available in Hervey Bay.

Driving on the Island The only thing stopping you taking a conventional (non-4WD) vehicle onto the island is the fact that you probably won't get more than half a km before you get bogged in sand. Small 4WD sedans are OK, but you may have ground-clearance problems on some of the inland tracks – a 'proper' 4WD gives maximum mobility.

Ask on the mainland about island driving conditions before renting a 4WD vehicle. Sometimes rain and storms can make beaches and tracks very heavy going, if not impassable. The best sources of such information are probably the offices issuing the vehicle permits.

Driving on the island requires a good deal of care, to protect not only yourself but the fragile environment. Apart from the beaches, where you are free to drive at will, all tracks are obvious and you should stick to them. Most major junctions are signposted, but only the two dedicated 'scenic routes' are signposted along their length. When driving, you should have 4WD engaged at all times, not so much because of the danger of getting stuck, but because your wheels are less likely to spin and damage the sandy tracks.

When driving on the beaches, keep an eye out for washouts at the many creek outlets, especially after heavy rain. An additional hazard is that the beach directly outside the resorts is used as a landing strip for small aircraft. Low tide is the best time to travel as large expanses of smooth, hard sand are exposed. Use your indicators to show oncoming vehicles which side you intend passing on. At high tide it is much more difficult, and quite slow going. The speed limit on the beaches is 80 km/h, and on the inland tracks it's 35 km/h, although there's little opportunity to reach that speed.

Drive slowly when passing walkers and people fishing, as they probably won't hear you coming above the roar of the surf!

Driving on the eastern beach is fairly straightforward; the western beach is more treacherous and has swamps and holes – avoid it.

Around the Island

Starting from the south at Hook Point, you cross a number of creeks and get to Dilli Village, the former sand-mining centre. After the settlements of Eurong and Happy Valley, you cross Eli Creek, the largest stream on the east coast. About 65 km from Hook Point are the remains of the *Maheno*, a former passenger liner which was wrecked here in 1935 as it was being towed to a Japanese scrap yard.

Four km beyond Eurong is a signposted walking trail to the beautiful **Lake Wabby**, which is being slowly filled by a massive sandblow that advances about three metres a year. It's a 45-minute walk (rewarded by a swim in the lake), or you can drive a further 2.6 km north along the beach to take a scenic route to a lookout on the inland side of the lake. *Don't* dive into the lake after running down the steep sand dunes – in the last few

years, five people have suffered spinal injuries doing just that.

A popular inland area for visitors is the south-central lake and rainforest country around Central Station and McKenzie, Jennings, Birrabeen and Boomanjin lakes. **Lake McKenzie** is unbelievably clear. Known as a 'window' lake, the water here is actually part of the water table, and so has not flowed anywhere over land.

Two signposted vehicle tracks lead inland from Happy Valley: one goes to **Lake Garawongera**, then south to the beach again at Poyungan Valley (15 km); the other heads to **Yidney Scrub** and a number of lakes before returning to the ocean beach north of the wreck of the *Maheno* (45 km). The latter route will take you to some fine lakes and good lookout points among the highest dunes on the island.

Not far north of Happy Valley you enter the national park and pass the *Maheno* and the **Cathedrals**, 25 km of coloured sand cliffs. Dundubara has a ranger's hut, and probably the best camping ground on the island. Then there's a 20-km stretch of beach before you come to the rock outcrops of Indian Head, Middle Rocks and Waddy Point. Just past here is **Orchid Beach**, and it's a further 30 km of beach up to **Sandy Cape**, the northern tip, with its lighthouse a few more km to the west.

Walking Tracks   There are a number of 'walkers-only' tracks, ranging from the one-km Wungul Sandblow track at Dundubara to the 13-km trail between Wabby and McKenzie lakes. The useful *Fraser Island Recreation Area* leaflet put out by the National Parks & Wildlife Service lists several more.

Organised Tours

A wide range of island tours operate out of Hervey Bay, Rainbow Beach and Noosa Heads – see those sections for details.

Places to Stay & Eat

Come well equipped since supplies on the island are limited and only available in a few

Fraser Island

0   10   20 km

places. And be prepared for mosquitoes and horseflies.

Camping This is the cheapest way to stay on the island and gives you the chance to get closer to Fraser Island's unique natural environment. The QNP&WS and Forestry Department operate 11 camping grounds on the island, some accessible only by boat or on foot. Those in the north at Dundubara, Waddy Point and Wathumba and in the south at Central Station, Lake Boomanjin and Lake McKenzie have toilets and showers. You can also camp on some stretches of beach. To camp in any of these public areas you need a permit.

A word of warning: backpackers' tours have a bad reputation amongst the rangers here, and they will quite happily throw you off the island and/or fine you if they find you drunk and disorderly or disturbing other campers.

There's also the privately run *Cathedral Beach Resort & Camping Park* (☎ (071) 27 9177), 34 km north of Eurong. Tent sites cost $14 and cabins cost $75 for up to four people – note that they don't take backpacker groups here.

Other Accommodation The *Dilli Village Recreation Camp* (☎ (071) 27 9130) is 200 metres from the east coast, 24 km from Hook Point and nine km from Eurong. A four-bed cabin with shower and kitchen costs $40 per night for up to four people ($45 in the holiday season), or there are cabins without kitchens or bathrooms at $10 per person. You can also camp here for $3 per person.

The *Eurong Beach Resort* (☎ (071) 27 9122), 35 km north of Hook Point on the east coast, has several sections ranging from motel rooms with kitchenettes for $70 a double to two-bedroom apartments for $160. The resort also has a general store, bar and bistro.

Just south of Happy Valley, the low-key *Yidney Rocks Cabins* (☎ (071) 27 9167) are right on the edge of the beach. They're old but comfortable; the nightly rate is $65 for up to six people or $80 for up to eight.

FRASER COAST

The *Happy Valley Resort* (☎ (071) 27 9144) has good self-contained timber lodges for $120/150 a night for doubles/triples, and larger lodges for $170 a night for up to four people. The resort also has a bar, bistro and shop.

The impressive and luxurious *Kingfisher Bay Resort* (☎ 1800 072 555) on the west coast has hotel rooms from $119 per person per night with breakfast and transfers included, two-bedroom villas from $690 for three nights and three-bedroom villas from $870 for three nights. The resort has restaurants, bars and shops, and, architecturally, it's worth a look even if you're not staying here. There's also a day-trippers' section near the jetty, with the *Sandbar* bar and brasserie.

Getting There & Away
Air Two operators offer flights across to the island from Hervey Bay – see Organised Tours in the Hervey Bay section for details.

Bus Also see Organised Tours in the Hervey Bay section – some bus tour operators allow you to split your trip.

Ferry Vehicle ferries (known locally as barges) operate to the southern end of Fraser Island from Inskip Point, and to the west coast of the island from River Heads, south of Urangan. The *Rainbow Venture* (☎ (074) 86 3154) operates the 10-minute crossing from Inskip Point (near Rainbow Beach) to Hook Point on Fraser Island. It makes this crossing regularly from about 7 am to 4.30 pm daily. The price is $45 return for a vehicle and passengers, and you can get tickets on board the ferry. Walk on passengers pay $5.

The *Fraser Venture* (☎ (071) 25 4444) makes the 30-minute crossing from River Heads to Wanggoolba Creek (also called Woongoolber Creek) on the west coast of Fraser Island. It departs daily from River Heads at 9 and 10.15 am and 3.30 pm, and returns from the island at 9.30 am, 2.30 and 4 pm. On Saturdays there is also a 7 am service from River Heads, which returns at 7.30 am from the island. The barge takes 27

vehicles but it's still advisable to book. The return fare for vehicle and driver is $55, plus $3 for each extra passenger. Walk-on passengers pay $10 return.

The Kingfisher Bay Resort (☎ (071) 25 5155) also operates two boats. The *Fraser II* does the 25-minute crossing from River Heads to Kingfisher Bay daily. Departures from River Heads are at 7 and 11 am and 2 pm, and from the island at 9.45 am, 12.45 and 4.30 pm. The return fare is $55 for a vehicle and driver, plus $3 for extras. The *Kingfisher 1* is a passenger catamaran that crosses from the Urangan Boat Harbour to Kingfisher Bay, leaving from Urangan at 8.30 am, noon and 4 pm and returning at 9.30 am, 2 and 5 pm. The return fare is $28 for adults and $14 for children, which includes lunch.

There's also a ferry, the *Fraser Dawn*, from Urangan to Moon Point on the island, but this is an inconvenient place to land as it's a long drive across to the other side.

Getting Around
It's quite possible to make your own way around the island, and hitching along the main tracks and beaches is pretty common practice. River Heads is probably the best place to try your luck, as this is where most of the island's traffic starts its journey.

Otherwise, you'll be needing a 4WD vehicle. On the island, vehicles are available through Kingfisher Bay 4WD Hire (☎ (071) 20 3366), with Lada Nivas from $120 a day and Landrover Defenders from $150 a day; Happy Valley 4WD Hire (☎ (071) 27 9260) with Suzuki Sierras from $100 a day and Toyota Landcruisers from $160 a day; and Shorty's Off Road Rentals (☎ (071) 27 9122) at Eurong with a couple of Suzukis for $90 per day. See the Hervey Bay and Rainbow Beach sections for details of 4WD hire from the mainland. On the island you can get fuel at Eurong, Happy Valley, Cathedral Beach and Kingfisher Bay.

CHILDERS (pop 1470)
On the Bruce Hwy 60 km north-west of Maryborough is the historic township of Childers. The town centre features numerous

turn-of-the-century buildings, and most of the main street has been classified as a heritage area by the National Trust.

Things to See & Do
A visit to the **Childers Pharmaceutical Museum**, opposite the post office at 90 Churchill St, is like a trip back in time. All of the old bottles, instruments, potions and prescription books that were used by the town's first pharmacist are on display – it is well worth a visit. The **Childers Regional Art Gallery** is upstairs in the same building, and the shop also acts as the tourist information centre. It's open weekdays from 8.45 am to 4.30 pm and Saturday from 8.30 am to noon.

Other interesting old buildings along the main street include the **Federal Hotel** on the corner of North St, which still has its original swinging doors leading into the corner bar; **Ye Olde Boutique** on the corner of Ashby Lane, which was built as the Queensland Bank; and the **Palace Hotel**, which is now a backpackers' hostel (see Places to Stay). There's a small **historical complex** in Taylor St, off the main road just south of the centre, but it's only open by appointment. Check with the information centre.

During the cane-crushing season (July to November) you can take a tour through the **Isis Sugar Mill** at 2 pm on weekdays; ring ☎ (071) 26 6166) to book.

Childers is also where you turn off the highway for the beach town of Woodgate and the Woodgate National Park.

Places to Stay
The *Sugarbowl Caravan Park* (☎ (071) 26 1521) is a neat and well-kept park on the north side of town with good valley views from a hillside. Tent sites cost $10, on-site vans $25 and there are cabins from $30 a double.

The *Palace Backpackers Hostel* (☎ (071) 26 2244) is right in the centre of Childers at 72 Churchill St. It's in a historic two-storey pub that has been impressively restored, and has excellent facilities and two to six-bed dorms for $12 per person. It's mainly a workers' hostel, and the owners can often find harvest work for travellers picking tomatoes, zucchini, snow peas and citrus fruits.

The *Federal Hotel* (☎ (071) 26 1438), on the corner of Churchill and North Sts, has basic rooms at $16/26 for singles/doubles.

The *Avocado Motor Inn* (☎ (071) 26 1608) on the highway one km north of the centre has budget units from $35.

Places to Eat
Try the *Federal Hotel*, on the corner of Churchill and North Sts, for a pub feed. It's a relaxed, big old pub with bistro meals in the $6 to $10 range and kid's meals for $3.50, and a good $8 smorgasbord on Friday nights.

Getting There & Away
Childers is on the main bus run up the Bruce Hwy; long-distance buses stop at the Shell service station just north of the town centre.

WOODGATE (pop 500)
Woodgate, 37 km east of Childers, is basically a string of holiday houses stretching for about four km along the coast. It's a very quiet and laid-back town with pleasant beaches, a pub, a bowling club and a general store. You can access the Woodgate National Park from here.

From the point where the road into Woodgate meets the coast, you can either head north or south along The Esplanade. Three km north you'll come to the broad estuary of Theodolite Creek, where there's a picnic area, a good calm-water swimming spot and a boat ramp. I'm told the creek offers excellent fishing and mud-crabbing.

Places to Stay
The *Barkala Caravan Park* (☎ (071) 26 8802), in the centre of The Esplanade, is a good park with a shop, tent sites at $10, on-site vans at $22 and self-contained cabins from $25 to $40 a double. You need to supply your own bedding for the cabins.

The *Beach Hotel-Motel* (☎ (071) 26 8988), on the Esplanade one km north of the main road into Woodgate, is a modern, brick beer barn with motel units next door at $50 a double in the low season and $60 in the high season.

There are quite a few holiday units along the beachfront. The *Hibiscus Holiday Units* (☎ (071) 26 8709), next to the general store at 139 The Esplanade, is a renovated block of oldish one and two-bedroom units that range from $40 to $60 a night.

At the other end of the scale, you could rent *Barcoo* (☎ (071) 26 8816), an ultra-modern split-level timber and iron beach-house designed by the architects responsible for the Kingfisher Bay Resort on Fraser Island. The house has four bedrooms and all the mod cons, and goes for $400 a week in the low season and $600 a week in the high season. It's at the southern end of The Esplanade – you can't miss it.

Places to Eat

The *Beach Hotel-Motel* has a large bistro with a pleasant courtyard area at the front, and the *Woodgate General Store* has pretty good burgers.

WOODGATE NATIONAL PARK

A couple of km south of Woodgate is the Woodgate National Park, at the mouth of the Burrum River. The park has good beaches and is popular with anglers, and you'll probably need to book camp sites during holiday periods. The road down to the park is sealed and you can drive part way into the park in a conventional vehicle, but to get to the camping ground and the Burrum River you'll need a 4WD.

A 400-metre boardwalk through a melaleuca swamp and a five-km circuit walk are in the northern corner of the park; both start from Acacia St, which runs parallel with The Esplanade one block back from the beachfront. There are several other walking tracks starting from near the camping ground. Contact the QNP&WS rangers at the park (☎ (071) 26 8810) to book camping permits or for more information.

GIN GIN (pop 900)

Back on the Bruce Hwy, Gin Gin is a small pastoral centre and the northern turn off for people heading for Bundaberg.

The town's old railway station has been converted into a **Historical Society Museum**, with a collection of memorabilia, old farming equipment and machinery, and a slab-timber hut. The museum is open every day from 9 am to 4 pm.

Information

Fuel & Services The Matilda Roadhouse, on the northern outskirts of Gin Gin, is open 24 hours a day.

Places to Stay

There are four motels in town. The cheapest option is the *Gin Gin Motel* (☎ (071) 57 2260) around 1½ km north of the centre, with singles/doubles from $35/38. At 44 Mulgrave St, the *Gin Gin Village Motor Inn* (☎ (071) 57 2599) has units from $38/45.

BUNDABERG (pop 38,000)

At the northern end of Hervey Bay and on the southern edge of the Capricorn Coast, Bundaberg is a major sugar-growing, processing and exporting centre. Some of the sugar ends up in the famous Bundaberg Rum. The town is 50 km off the Bruce Hwy and 15 km inland from the coast on the Burnett River. It's the southernmost access point for the Great Barrier Reef and the departure point for Lady Elliot and Lady Musgrave islands.

Bundaberg attracts a steady stream of travellers looking for harvest work picking everything from avocados to zucchinis, and the hostels here can often help you find work – but be wary of promises of work that doesn't exist. It's worth ringing a few of the hostel managers and enquiring before you come. The main harvest season runs from mid-March until Christmas.

Information

The Bundaberg Tourist Information Centre (☎ (071) 52 2333) is on the corner of the Isis

Hwy, the main road as you enter the town from the south, and Bourbong St. It's open daily from 9 am to 5 pm. The QNP&WS (☎ (071) 53 8620) has an office in Quay St.

The post office is on the corner of Bourbong and Barolin Sts. All the major banks have branches along Bourbong St.

There is a public telephone centre on Bourbong St beside the post office.

Things to See

Aficionados of Bundy rum can tour the **Bundaberg Rum Distillery** on Avenue St in East Bundaberg, about two km east from the centre of town. Tours start off with an introductory video before visiting the fermentation house, distillery, bottling plant and store.

At the end of the tour you visit Spring Hill House, with a museum, souvenir shop and a bar where you can do a taste test. Tours are run every day between 10 am and 3 pm and cost $4 for adults (which includes a sample of the product) and $1 for anyone under 18 years of age. While you're here it's worth visiting **Schmeider's Cooperage & Craft Centre** nearby on Alexandra St, where you can watch the coopers hand-making timber barrels and other craft products, all of which are for sale. Schmeider's is open on weekdays from 9 am to 5 pm and on weekends from 9 am to 3 pm, and entry is free.

Bundaberg's attractive **Botanic Gardens** are two km north of the centre on Gin Gin Rd. Within the gardens reserve are rose gardens, walking paths, a historical museum, and the **Hinkler House Museum**, dedicated to the life and times of the aviator Bert Hinkler, who was born in Bundaberg and in 1928 made the first solo flight between England and Australia. Hinkler's former home was transported here from Southampton, England, and rebuilt to house a collection of memorabilia and information on the aviation pioneer. Nearby is the **Bundaberg & District Historical Museum**. Both museums are open daily from 10 am to 4 pm, and both charge $2 for adults and 50c for children.

The **Bundaberg Art Gallery**, in the his-toric School of Arts building beside the Civic Centre in Bourbong St, is open on weekdays from 10 am to 3 pm and on Sundays from 12.30 to 3 pm; entry is free. The gallery houses a small permanent collection and features regular exhibitions.

The **Bundaberg Reptile Reserve** on the Isis Hwy four km south of the centre and 200 metres south of the airport, is open every day from 9 am to 5 pm, with crocodiles, snakes, lizards and, ah, giant cane toads. Entry costs $3/2. On Gin Gin Rd one km west of the Botanic Gardens, Bundaberg's **Tropical Winery** makes an interesting range of wines and soft drinks from tropical fruits. It opens daily for tastings and sales.

The strange **Mystery Craters** – 35 small craters, said to be at least 25 million years old – are 17 km along the Bundaberg road from Gin Gin. Entry to the craters costs $3 for adults and $1 for children.

Organised Tours

Island Trips Lady Musgrave Barrier Reef Cruises (☎ 1800 072 110), based on the riverfront at 1 Quay St, have day trips to Lady Musgrave Island every Tuesday, Thursday, Saturday and Sunday (more often during school holidays). The cruises depart from Port Bundaberg, 17 km north-east of Bundaberg, at 8.30 am. The cost is $92 for adults and $47 for children (plus another $6 for the return bus trip to Port Bundaberg), which includes lunch, snorkelling gear, and rides in a semi-submersible, glass-bottomed boat.

Alternatively, you can fly to Lady Musgrave Island with Bundaberg Seaplane Tours (☎ (071) 56 2068). A day trip costs $160 per person for between two and four people, including lunch and snorkelling gear. You get around five hours on the island.

You can fly to Lady Elliot Island with Whitaker Air Charters (☎ (071) 52 2322 or 1800 072 200 toll free). Daytrippers pay $99 for a return flight or $120 for a deluxe day trip which includes the return flight, lunch and snorkelling gear. Children pay only half price.

Bundaberg

Botanic Gardens

Hinkler Park

Gin Gin Road

Hinkler Avenue

Gavegan Street

Agnes Street

Rojan Street

Stewart Street

Gavin Street

Queen Street

Wolca Street

Burnett Bridge

Burnett River

River

Gargen Road

Princess Street

Eastgate Street

Scotland Street

Olsen Park

Steindl Road

Cran Street

Baldwin Swamp Environment Park

Baldwin Swamp

Lake Ellen

Kennedy Bridge

Playing Fields

Burrum River

Reserve

Wallis Street

Boundary Street

Boundary Street

South Bundaberg

Totten Street

Weir Street

Elliot Heads Road

Kroll Road

Pitt Street

Hunter Street

High Street

McCracken Street

Water Street

Targo Street

Barolin Street

Watson Street

Barber Park

Rudell Street

Cuttis Street

Crofton Street

Electra Street

Bourbong Street

George Street

Bolsover Street

Boundary Street

Coburg Street

Burnett Street

Quay Street

Toonburra Street

Woondooma Street

Targo Street

Barolin Street

Crofton Street

Maryborough Street

McLean Street

Burrum Street

Bingera Street

Branyan Street

Electra Street

Powers Street

Adams Street

George Street

Walker Street

Mulgrave Street

West Bundaberg

Woongarra Street

Bourbong Street

Woondooma Street

Crofton Street

Saltwater Creek

Showground

Barkam Street

O'Connel Creek

Scenic Drive

Queens Park

Garden St – Hope Street

Harriett Island

Alexandra Park

0   250   500 m

PLACES TO STAY

10	Royal Motel & Coffee House
13	Federal Guesthouse Backpackers
22	City Centre Backpackers
23	Sugar Country Motor Inn
25	Finemore Caravan Park
31	Bundaberg Backpackers & Travellers Lodge
33	Midtown Caravan Park

PLACES TO EAT

5	The Spinnaker Stonegrill & Bar
8	Grand Hotel
9	Charley Magee's
15	Numero Uno
19	Cafe Royal
20	The Healthy Lifestyle
21	Il Gambero
24	Sizzler
28	McDonald's Garden Centre & Cafe

OTHER

1	Hinkler House Museum
2	Bundaberg Historical Museum
3	Bundaberg Rum Distillery
4	Schmeider's Cooperage
6	Lady Musgrave Barrier Reef Cruises
7	Bundaberg Olympic Swimming Pool
11	QNP&WS Office
12	Police Station
14	Moncrieff Theatre
16	Telephones
17	Post Office
18	Bundaberg Art Gallery
26	Tourist Information Centre
27	Hospital
29	Railway Station
30	Casey's Cabaret
32	Bundaberg Bus Terminal

Whale Watching From mid-August to mid-October, Lady Musgrave Barrier Reef Cruises (☎ 1800 072 110) runs whale watching trips out of Port Bundaberg.

Activities

Diving Two local diving companies offer certified courses, with discounts to people staying at one of the workers' hostels (see Places to Stay). Anglo Diving Services (☎ (071) 51 6422) offers courses for $159 with dives off the local beaches, and Salty's (☎ (071) 53 4747) offers a course for $169 which includes a dive off Lady Musgrave Island. Check with the hostel managers for details.

The Bundaberg Dive Centre (☎ (071) 52 6707) offers dive trips for experienced and novice divers to various sites offshore from Bundaberg. Two dives will cost around $70 with equipment supplied.

Other Activities Swimmers can head for the **Bundaberg Olympic Swimming Pool** on Quay St.

If you're interested in other activities and events in Bundaberg, the tourist office has a community directory which lists local groups and societies including bushwalking, orienteering and sailing clubs.

Festivals

Bundy's major festivals include the Country Music Festival at Easter; Bundy in Bloom, a spring floral festival held in the first week of September and featuring fashion parades, garden competitions and garden parties; a week-long Arts Festival each October featuring film, music and theatre; and the Bundaberg Rum Rebellion, held over a weekend in October.

Places to Stay

Caravan Parks The *Finemore Caravan Park* (☎ (071) 51 3663), on the riverfront at the west end of Quay St, has powered caravan sites at $14 and two and four-bed 'Camp-o-tels' – permanent tents with beds and lighting – for $10 per person. There are no tent sites here though.

The *Midtown Caravan Park* (☎ (071) 52 2768), at 61 Takalvan St, is a good park about 2 km south-west of the post office, with a pool, shop and camper's kitchen. Tent sites are $9, powered sites are $12, cabins start at $30 and self-contained villas start at $40.

Hostels Bundaberg has a number of backpackers' hostels that specialise in finding harvesting work for travellers – some

FRASER COAST

more reputable than others. The following have received good reports from travellers.

The *Bundaberg Backpackers & Travellers Lodge* (☎ (071) 52 2080) is diagonally opposite the bus terminal, on the corner of Targo and Crofton Sts. It's a clean and modern workers' hostel with a friendly atmosphere; a bed in a four-bed dorms costs $13 a night, which includes transport to and from work.

The very well set up *City Centre Backpackers* (☎ (071) 51 3501), in the former Grosvenor Hotel at 216 Bourbong St, has two sections: two to eight-bed bunkrooms upstairs, and six-bed motel units out the back. Bunk beds cost $11, or $13 for workers which includes transport to and from work, or a bed in one of the motel units costs $12 ($15 with transport). They also have three doubles at $26.

Pubs The *Grand Hotel* (☎ (071) 51 2441), on the corner of Bourbong and Targo Sts, has basic rooms upstairs at $20/28. It also has cheap meals and is a live music venue – see Entertainment.

Motels The *Royal Motel* (☎ (071) 51 2201), on the corner of Barolin and Bourbong Sts, has good budget motel units from $28/35 for singles/doubles. The motel is upstairs with an entrance in Barolin St – if there's no-one at reception, the coffee shop downstairs handles bookings. Another cheap motel option is the *Lyelta Lodge & Motel* (☎ (071) 51 3344), at 8 Maryborough St, which has motel-style rooms at $30/34 for singles/doubles and a guesthouse section with rooms with shared bathrooms from $25/28. This place is quite old and fairly basic though.

The *Sugar Country Motor Inn* (☎ (071) 53 1166), at 220 Bourbong St, is much more impressive, with modern units starting from $56/60 plus a pool and a licensed restaurant. There are another 10 or so motels strung along Bourbong St between the tourist office and the town centre.

Places to Eat
For a cheap pub feed, head for the *Grand*

Hotel on the corner of Bourbong and Targo Sts. The public bar offers a choice of three dishes for $2.50, or you can get a steak or a roast with vegies for around $6. The bistro has a more extensive menu with mains ranging from $7 to $12.

Across the road at 88 Bourbong St, the *Cafe Royal* is a narrow and popular little place with a good range of cheap lunches. Lasagna, veal schnitzels, chicken fillets, roasts and crumbed fish are all $3.95. *The Healthy Lifestyle* at 21 Woongarra St is a small health food shop with tasty sandwiches, smoothies and juices, vegetarian pies and rolls, and organic fruits and vegies.

At 34 Quay St, the popular *Charley Magee's* is a casual bar and eatery that plays blues and 1960s music. The menu covers Thai, Cajun, Tex/Mex, Italian, Greek and a few other cuisines, with most main dishes from $10 to $17, or if you're on a budget they have nightly backpacker specials like Thai chicken curries for $5.50. They often have live music here on weekends.

Numero Uno, at 163 Bourbong St, is an attractive Italian bistro with good pastas under $12, pizzas under $10 and mains like calamari and veal parmagiana from $12 to $15, as well as pancakes, gelati, cappuccino etc. They open nightly for dinner and on weekdays for lunches, and are licensed. *Il Gambero*, at 57 Targo St, is run by an Italian family and has pastas, pizzas, seafood and steak dishes for between $12 and $18. This place is also licensed, and has a strangely comforting décor straight out of the 1970s – dim lighting, brick arches and all.

McDonald's Garden Centre & Cafe in Takalvan St is an unusual combo – a courtyard cafe in the midst of a plant nursery. They serve breakfast and lunch, including very tasty 'eggs Benedict' – there's no menu, just wander in and ask what's on.

If you're after fast food, most of the big chains have outlets along Bourbong St west of the town centre. The tragically popular *Sizzler*, on Bourbong St just south of the railway line, is a modern and soulless eating house with steaks, seafood and salads. Main courses range from $11 to $15.

Down at the riverfront off Quay St, *The Spinnaker Stonegrill & Bar* (☎ (071) 52 8033) specialises in meals cooked at your table on a white-hot volcanic stone. Their lunches range from $6 to $8 for open sandwiches to $12 for pastas and $18 for a steak; at dinner, mains are in the $14 to $18 range or they have a three-course menu at $24 per person. This place enjoys a great setting, and has an outdoor decking area overlooking the river. On weekends the downstairs bar becomes a jazz lounge – see the Entertainment section.

Entertainment

Live Music & Nightclubs The *Grand Hotel,* on the corner of Bourbong and Targo Sts, has live bands every Thursday, Friday and Saturday night.

The *Spinnaker Stonegrill & Bar* (☎ (071) 52 8033), on Quay St, has jazz bands downstairs on Friday and Saturday nights, and Sunday afternoon sessions with live music out on their riverfront decking area – well worth checking out.

There are a couple of discos spread around town, including *Casey's Cabaret* in Electra St.

The Moncrieff Theatre (☎ (071) 53 1985), at 177 Bourbong St, alternates between being a theatre, a cinema and a music venue. Check with the tourist office to see what's on while you're in town.

Bundaberg's new five-cinema complex is currently being built out towards the airport.

Getting There & Away

Travel Agents Stewart & Sons Travel (☎ (071) 52 9700), based at the coach terminal on Targo St, can handle bookings for planes, trains and buses.

Air Bundaberg's Hinkler Airport is about four km south-west of the centre on Takalvan Rd.

Air services are by Sunstate (from Brisbane, Gladstone, Rockhampton, Mackay and Townsville daily) and Flight West (daily from Brisbane and Gladstone). One-way fares include Brisbane $165, Rockhampton $163 and Gladstone $90.

Bus All the main bus companies serve Bundaberg on the main north-south route. The main stop is Stewart's Coach Terminal, at 66 Targo St. One-way bus fares from Bundaberg include Brisbane ($42), Hervey Bay ($20), Rockhampton ($42), Noosa Heads (Greyhound Pioneer Australia only, $42), Maryborough ($21) and Gladstone ($33).

Local buses services are handled by Duffy's Coaches (☎ (071) 51 4226). They have four services every weekday to the local beaches and Port Bundaberg; buses depart from the Shire Office bus stop in Barolin St, and one-way fares are around $2.

Train Bundaberg is also a stop for trains between Brisbane and Rockhampton or Cairns. There are daily trains heading both north and south. The one-way fare to Brisbane is $43 for an economy seat or $73 for an economy sleeper.

BUNDABERG BEACHES

The beaches of **Moore Park**, 20 km north, and **Bargara**, 13 km east, are popular with families. Local buses go to Bargara and Moore Park a few times on weekdays from Bundaberg post office.

Australia's most accessible mainland **turtle rookery** is at Mon Repos Beach, 15 km north-east of Bundaberg. Four types of turtle – loggerhead, green, flatback and leatherback – have been known to nest here from late November to January, but it's predominantly the loggerhead which lays its eggs here. The rookery is unusual, since turtles generally prefer sandy islands off the coast. The young emerge and quickly make their way to the sea from mid-January to March. You're most likely to see the turtles laying their eggs around midnight when the tide is high.

Observation of the turtles is controlled by staff from the QNP&WS Information Centre (☎ (071) 59 2628). The centre is open between 7 pm and 6 am every day during the

FRASER COAST

turtle season, with informative displays, lighting and boardwalk access to the beach. Entry costs $4 for adults, $2 for children and $1 for students. The centre is also open to visitors during the day, when entry is free.

Places to Stay

At Bargara Beach, the *Linksview Motel* (☎ (071) 59 2295), at 13 See St, has backpackers' units at $11 per person or $26 a double.

The *Turtle Sands Caravan Park* (☎ (071) 79 2340), on the beachfront at Mon Repos Beach, has tent sites from $13, powered site from $14, on-site vans from $20 and cabins from $35. The park also has catamarans, windsurfers and surfboards available for hire.

Capricorn Coast

This central coastal area of Queensland takes its name from its position straddling the Tropic of Capricorn. Rockhampton is the major population centre in the area, and just off the coast lies the popular Great Keppel Island and the other islands of the Keppel Bay group.

South of Rockhampton is the city of Gladstone, one of Queensland's major industrial and shipping centres. Off shore from Gladstone is the Capricornia Marine Park and the Southern Reef Islands, the southernmost part of the Great Barrier Reef. Lady Elliot Island and Heron Island both have resorts that are popular with divers, and you can take day trips to and camp on Lady Musgrave Island and several other islands in the group.

On the coast south of Gladstone are the laid-back holiday towns of Seventeen Seventy and Agnes Water.

Inland, the Capricorn Hinterland has the fascinating Gemfields region and the spectacular Carnarvon and Blackdown Tableland national parks.

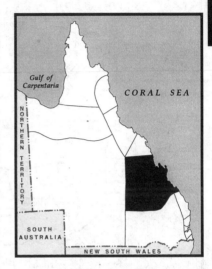

Geography

The Tropic of Capricorn passes through the centre of this region, just south of Rockhampton and just north of Emerald. Geographically, the Capricorn Hinterland is dominated by the broad, flattened plateaus of the Great Dividing Range, with numerous spectacular outcrops of sandstone escarpments, most notably around the Carnarvon and Blackdown Tableland national parks. This Central Highlands region is one of Queensland's richest natural resources, with the fertile soils supporting major pastoral and agricultural industries and the area's vast coal deposits supplying the majority of the state's coal exports.

Between the mountains and the coast are the flatter coastal plains. The off-shore islands in this region vary from the coral cays of the Southern Reef Islands to the continental islands around Keppel Bay, which are closer to the mainland.

Activities

The Southern Reef Islands offer some of the best diving and snorkelling on the entire Barrier Reef. The Gemfields region in the Capricorn Hinterland is the best area in Queensland to go fossicking for gemstones, particularly sapphires. And for bushwalkers, the Carnarvon and Blackdown Tableland national parks offer a wide range of walking trails and climbs.

Getting There & Around

Air Rockhampton and Gladstone both have major regional airports, and you can also fly out to Lady Elliot, Heron and Great Keppel islands – see those sections for details.

Sunstate and Flight West both have flights linking Brisbane with Emerald.

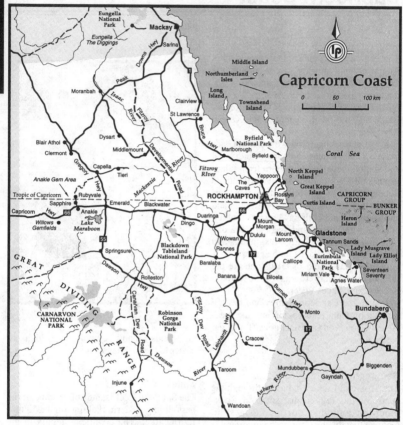

Bus Greyhound Pioneer Australia and McCafferty's both have frequent services up and down the Bruce Hwy, and from Rockhampton inland to Emerald, Longreach and Mt Isa.

McCafferty's also has a number of regional runs, including a daily inland service from Rockhampton to Mackay via Emerald and Clermont; a daily inland service from Rockhampton to Brisbane via Mt Morgan and the Burnett Hwy; and a weekly service from Emerald up to Charters Towers.

Train The major coastal railway line follows the Bruce Hwy up the coast. Twice weekly, the *Spirit of the Outback* train does the inland run from Rockhampton to Longreach.

Car & Motorcycle The Bruce Hwy runs all the way up the Capricorn Coast, although it runs a long way inland and only touches the coast briefly at the township of Clairview. The major inland route is the Capricorn Hwy, which takes you west from Rockhampton through Emerald and the Gemfields. From Gladstone, the Dawson Hwy takes you west towards the Carnarvon National Park and the town of Springsure.

The Burnett Hwy (Hwy 17), which starts

at Rockhampton and heads south through the old gold-mining town of Mt Morgan, is an interesting and popular alternative route to Brisbane – see the Darling Downs chapter for details of the Burnett Hwy south of Biloela.

Gladstone Area

MIRIAM VALE (pop 450)
Miriam Vale, on the Bruce Hwy 70 km south of Gladstone, has one of Queensland's less convincing Big Things – a sickly-looking giant red crab atop the roof of the Shell Roadhouse in the centre of town. For $4.80, you can try one of the roadhouse's mudcrab sandwiches.

Miriam Vale is the administration centre of the surrounding shire, and the main turn off point for the coastal towns of Agnes Water and Seventeen Seventy.

Information
The Discovery Coast Information Centre (☎ 079) 74 5428), across the highway from the Shell Roadhouse, is open on weekdays from 8.30 am to 5 pm and on weekends from 9 am to 5 pm; this is the main information centre for the Discovery Coast region, which includes Rules Beach, Agnes Water and Seventeen Seventy.

Places to Stay
The *Caltex Roadhouse Caravan Park* (☎ (079) 74 5249), on the highway on the north side of town, has tent sites from $6, powered sites from $10, on-site vans from $15 and self-contained cabins from $35.

The *Miriam Vale Motel* (☎ (079) 74 5233), on the highway in the centre of town, has budget motel rooms starting from $30.

AGNES WATER & SEVENTEEN SEVENTY
These two coastal towns are amongst the less commercialised destinations on the Queensland coast. It's 57 km of mostly unsealed roads from the Bruce Hwy across to Agnes Water, then another six km along the coast up to Seventeen Seventy. There are several small national parks in the surrounding area.

Seventeen Seventy, on a narrow and hilly peninsula on the south side of the estuary of Round Hill Creek, was named in 1970 in honour of Captain Cook's landing here on 24 May 1770 – the second place he landed in Australia, and the first in Queensland. It's a relaxed, low-key holiday town with an attractive bush setting and houses discreetly built up into the headland. With a flotilla of yachts and cruisers moored in the inlet of Round Hill Creek, it's clearly a popular spot with the fishing and boating fraternities – the creek provides a calm anchorage for boats, there's good fishing and mudcrabbing upstream, and the southern end of the Great Barrier Reef is easily accessible from here with Lady Musgrave Island about two hours off shore.

Things get fairly hectic around here at Christmas and Easter time – you'll need to book ahead to secure accommodation at these times – but for the rest of the year this area is a peaceful and unhurried getaway.

Facilities
There are no banks here, and only a couple of shops and one pub. Agnes Water Autos (the Shell service station) is open daily from 7 am to 6 pm; it sells super, unleaded and diesel fuel, has EFTPOS facilities and takes all major credit cards. *1770 Foods & Liquors* (see Places to Eat) also has EFTPOS facilities, and sells super and unleaded fuel.

Things to See & Do
Most activities here are related to **fishing, boating** and the **beaches**. Agnes Water is Queensland's northernmost surf beach. A surf life-saving club patrols the main beach, and there often good beach breaks along the coast. The surf beaches south of Agnes Water are only accessible by 4WD.

The **Agnes Water Historical Museum** has a small collection of artefacts, rocks and minerals, and assorted flotsam and jetsam, as well as extracts from Cook's journal. It is open on weekends from 10 am to noon.

See the following National Parks section for details of parks in the area.

Boating & Water-sports Hire You can hire paddle boats, catamarans and powered dinghies from beside the boat ramp at Seventeen Seventy.

1770 Marine Services (☎ (079) 74 9227) hires out 12-foot dinghies for exploring Round Hill Creek at $25 for two hours or $60 a day.

Charter Boats There are a number of charter boats available for fishing trips, including the MV *Jetty II* (see the following Organised Tours section) and the MV *Flamingo* (☎ (079) 74 9174) which sleeps up to 10 people, and the MV *James Cook* (☎ (079) 74 9241) which sleeps up to nine people.

Organised Tours
The LARC *Sir Joseph Banks* (☎ (079) 74 9422), a large amphibious vehicle, does environmental tours of Round Hill Creek, Bustard Head and Eurimbula National Park. Tours operate on Wednesday and Saturday (more often during the peak season), and cost $50 which includes morning tea and lunch.

The MV *Jetty II* (☎ (079) 74 9077) has day trips to Lady Musgrave Island costing $80 for adults and $40 for children, with lunch, snorkelling and fishing gear included. Cruises depart from Seventeen Seventy most weekends – more often during holiday periods. They also have a camping drop-off service – they'll take campers to Lady Musgrave or Masthead Island for $80 per person each way or to North-West Island for $100 per person each way; camping gear and dinghies are available for hire. The boat is also available for fishing trips and private charters.

Places to Stay
Agnes Water The *Agnes Water Caravan Park* (☎ (079) 74 9193), on the foreshore in Jeffery Crt, has tent sites from $8 and cabins from $30. Nearby, the *Mango Tree Motel* (☎ (079) 74 9132) is a good budget motel with singles/doubles from $45/54.

Four km west (inland) from Agnes Water,

Hoban's Hideaway (☎ (079) 74 9144) is a friendly, well-run B&B in an attractive, colonial-style timber homestead on an 18-hectare property, with bushwalking tracks and a small practice golf area. There's a separate guests' section with three immaculately presented double bedrooms with ensuites, a lounge room and dining room, an outdoor patio and a barbecue area. The tariff for singles/doubles is $70/86 including breakfast. (Children aren't catered for here.)

About seven km west of Agnes Water, the *1770 Holiday Cabin Retreat* (☎ (079) 749 270) is a 15-hectare bushland property with six timber cabins that sleep from four to 10 people. The cabins are simple, clean and well equipped with cooking facilities, bathroom, linen etc. Tariffs are $40/50 for singles/doubles plus $10 for additional adults and $5 for additional kids.

Seventeen Seventy The *Seventeen Seventy Camping Ground* (☎ (079) 74 9286) is a spacious camping ground right beside the mouth of Round Hill Creek, with plenty of grass and shady trees, a small shop and hot showers. Tent sites cost $10, powered sites are $12, and there are four on-site vans at $30 a double.

One km south, the *Captain Cook Holiday Village* (☎ (079) 74 9219) is an excellent camping and caravan park in a great bush setting, with genial owners, a bar/bistro (see Places to Eat), a general store and a 300-metre walking trail to the beach. Nightly costs are $10 for tent sites, $12 for powered sites, $15 for a bed in a backpackers' bungalow and $20 for an on-site van. There are also self-contained timber bungalows and cabins that sleep up to seven people; the bungalows cost $45 a double plus $5 for extras (BYO linen), the cabins cost $60 a double plus $10 for extras (linen supplied).

Places to Eat
Agnes Water Next to the Shell service station, the *Hard Rock Cafe* sells takeaway meals and a limited range of groceries. They also do evening meals such as calamari, lasagna or crumbed fish for under $10. You

can get a bistro meal at the *Agnes Water Tavern*, a modern timber pub on the outskirts of town.

Seventeen Seventy *1770 Foods & Liquors*, on Captain Cook Dve just south of the camping ground, is a great little general store with a bottleshop and an outdoor courtyard with good home-made meals. Breakfasts range from $2.50 for muesli to $6 for eggs Benedict; lunch offerings such as focaccias, flat-bread rolls, Greek salads and calamari are all from $4 to $6; and for dinner meals such as Thai curries, reef fish or steak and salads, ranging from $7 to $10. They also do good pizzas and cappuccinos.

At the Captain Cook Holiday Village, *The Deck* is a very pleasant licensed bistro with great views from an outdoor decking area. Light lunches like burgers, chicken pie or reef fish and salad range from $6 to $11, and at dinner mains range from $12 to $14. Downstairs, there's a garden patio with a self-serve char-grill where for $6 you can cook yourself fish, chicken or steak.

Getting There & Away
There are no bus or train services into the area, so you'll need your own transport. From Miriam Vale, on the Bruce Hwy, it's 57 km westwards across to Agnes Water, and after the first 12 km it's mostly over unsealed roads. Alternatively, it's 123 km north from Bundaberg to Agnes Water via Rosedale, with the last half of the trip over unsealed roads. These dirt roads are in reasonably good condition, although less so after heavy rains.

LOCAL NATIONAL PARKS
There are several coastal national parks around Agnes Water and Seventeen Seventy. For information or to book camping permits, contact the QNP&WS in Gladstone on ☎ (079) 72 6055.

The 5000-hectare **Eurimbula National Park** is on the north side of Round Hill Creek, and has a varied landscape of coastal dunes, mangroves, salt marshes and eucalypt forest. There's a basic camping ground with

toilets, but no drinking water, at Bustard Beach. The main access road to the park is about 11 km south-west of Agnes Water. From the entrance, it's another 11 km along a sandy bush track to the camping ground – conventional vehicles can make it with care, although you'll need a 4WD after rain. Alternatively you could hire a dinghy from Seventeen Seventy and cross Round Hill Creek to the park.

South of Agnes Water, **Deepwater National Park** is only accessible by 4WD vehicles. The park has an unspoilt coastal landscape with long sandy beaches, freshwater creeks, good fishing spots and a camping ground. It's also a major breeding ground for **loggerhead turtles** which build their nests and lay eggs on the beaches here between November and February. Visitors to the park can watch the turtles laying eggs and see hatchlings emerging at night, but you need to observe various precautions to protect the turtles and their environment. The QNP&WS brochure on the park outlines these precautions, which include not driving onto the beaches and minimising noise and light on the beaches in summer. You can use torches to watch the turtles lay their eggs, but once the nest is covered and the turtle is returning to the sea, all lights should be turned off or they could become disoriented. The hatchlings emerge at night between January and April, and shouldn't be handled. You also need to avoid standing on the nests, which could collapse.

The park entrance is about eight km south of Agnes Water, then it's another seven km from the entrance to the camping and picnic areas.

GLADSTONE (pop 23,500)
Twenty km off the Bruce Hwy, Gladstone is one of the busiest ports in Australia. It handles agricultural, mineral and coal exports from central Queensland, plus the alumina which is processed in Gladstone from bauxite ore shipped from Weipa on the Cape York Peninsula. The huge smelter here produces more than a quarter of Australia's aluminium.

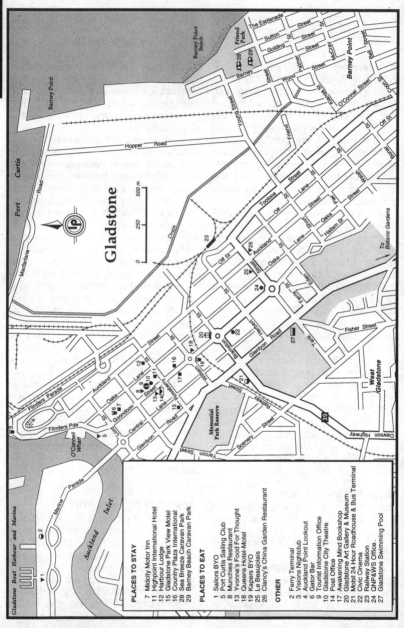

Gladstone

0   250   500 m

PLACES TO STAY
7   Midcity Motor Inn
11   Highpoint International Hotel
12   Harbour Lodge
15   Gladstone Park View Motel
16   Country Plaza International
28   Sea Breeze Caravan Park
29   Barney Beach Caravan Park

PLACES TO EAT
1   Sailors BYO
5   Port Curtis Sailing Club
8   Munchies Restaurant
13   Yvonne's Food For Thought
18   Queens Hotel-Motel
19   Kapers BYO
25   Le Beaujolais
26   Clancy's China Garden Restaurant

OTHER
2   Ferry Terminal
3   Visions Nightclub
4   Auckland Point Lookout
6   Gator Bar
9   Tourist Information Office
10   Gladstone City Theatre
14   Post Office
17   Awakening Mind Bookshop
20   Gladstone Art Gallery & Museum
21   Mobil 24 Hour Roadhouse & Bus Terminal
22   Civic Cinema
23   Railway Station
24   QNP&WS Office
27   Gladstone Swimming Pool

Despite being a major industrial and shipping city, the town centre is surprisingly attractive, particularly the central area and the marina.

Gladstone's impressive new marina is the main departure point for boats to Heron, Masthead and Wilson islands on the Barrier Reef. Gladstone's own harbour, Port Curtis, has many islands.

Information
The Gladstone Regional Information Office (☎ (079) 72 4000), at 56 Goondoon St, is open on weekdays from 8.30 am to 5 pm and on weekends from 9 am to 5 pm.

The QNP&WS (☎ (079) 72 6055) has an office in Tank St, near the Goondoon St corner, which is open on weekdays from 9 am to 5 pm. You can get info on all the Southern Reef Islands here, as well as the mainland parks in the area.

The Awakening Mind Bookshop at 115 Goondoon St, has a good selection of travel, fiction, and children's books, plus plenty of books of a more esoteric nature.

Things to See & Do
Housed in the old town hall, on the corner of Goondoon and Bramston Sts, the **Gladstone Art Gallery & Museum** has a small permanent collection of contemporary Australian paintings and ceramics, and regularly features theme exhibitions of art and craft. It is open on weekdays from 10 am to 5 pm and Saturday and public holidays from 10 am to 4 pm.

Barney Point Beach, two km east of the centre, is a small rocky cove which doesn't have much of a beach, although it's backed by a good foreshore reserve with lawns and shady trees.

The **Auckland Point Lookout** has good views over the harbour, port facilities and shipping terminals. A brass tablet on the lookout maps the harbour and its many islands.

The **Tondoon Botanic Gardens**, on Glenlyon Rd about seven km south of the town centre, is a 55-hectare garden specialising in rainforest and Australian native plants,

with walking trails including a three-km circuit, barbecue and picnic facilities and a kiosk.

Gladstone is a popular **sailing centre**, and the yacht clubs are often looking for people to crew on yachts during races – particularly experienced sailors. Ask at the information centre or call the secretary of the Gladstone Sailing Club on ☎ (079) 72 2294.

Organised Tours
You can tour around Gladstone on the back of a Harley-Davidson motorcycle with Port Curtis Harley Tours (☎ (079) 79 2037) to various places including the Round Hill Lookout and the marina (half hour, $30), Awoonga Dam (one hour, $60) and north to Mt Larcom (half day, $120).

There are also day trips to Lady Elliot Island from Thursday to Sunday, costing $130 for adults and $65 for children, which includes a return flight, use of the resort facilities, snorkelling gear and lunch. Trips can be booked through the information centre or any travel agent, including Gladstone Traveland (☎ (079) 72 2288).

Festivals
The Gladstone Harbour Festival is held every year from the Monday before Easter until Easter Monday. The festival coincides with the Brisbane to Gladstone yacht race, and features different activities each day including street parties, an Easter Pde, a birdman rally, mudcrab races and a prawn-peeling competition.

Places to Stay
Caravan Parks There are two good caravan parks down at Barney Point Beach, about two km east of the centre. Take your pick of the *Sea Breeze Caravan Park* (☎ (079) 72 1736) or the *Barney Beach Caravan Park* (☎ (079) 72 1366); both are well-established parks near the foreshore with tent sites from $10, powered sites from $12 and on-site vans from $25. The Barney Beach Caravan Park also has on-site cabins from $35, or $40 with an ensuite.

See Getting Around for details of bus services from the centre.

Hostel The *Harbour Lodge* (☎ (079) 72 6463), at 16 Roseberry St, is an excellent travellers' hostel close to the city centre. The facilities are good, it's clean as a whistle and good value at $10 for a dorm bed and $15/25 for singles/doubles; air-con is available for another $2. There's off-street parking in front of the hostel.

Hotels & Motels The *Queens Hotel-Motel* (☎ (079) 72 6615), on the corner of Goondoon and William Sts, has budget motel units from $27/37.

The *Midcity Motor Inn* (☎ (079) 72 3000), at 26 Goondoon St, is a good mid-range motel with singles/doubles from $45/50. At 42 Roseberry St, the white and pink-trimmed *Gladstone Park View Motel* (☎ (079) 72 3344) has similar rooms at similar prices.

Gladstone's best motel is the *Country Plaza International* (☎ (079) 72 4499), at 100 Goondoon St; singles/doubles start at $79/89. The 12-year-old *Highpoint International Hotel* (☎ (079) 72 4711), which is at 22 Roseberry St, has singles/doubles from $100/115.

Places to Eat

Don't miss the *Bellowing Bull Char Grill Steak House* at the *Queens Hotel*, on the corner of Goondoon and William Sts – it's one of the best-value eateries you'll come across. A huge T-bone, rump or fillet steak with salad or vegies costs $4.50 at lunch or $6 at dinner. Other meals such as lasagna, pork chops, reef fish and chicken kebabs all range from $5 to $6.

Kapers BYO (☎ (079) 72 7902), nearby at 124 Goondoon St, is a bright, beachy, quirky cafe with sky-blue walls and hand-painted tables. The food is interesting, with good seafood, vegetarian and other dishes, all moderately priced. Kapers is open for dinner from Wednesday to Saturday and lunches on Thursday and Friday. (If you're coming for dinner, Irene will be *much* nicer to you if you ring and book.)

The popular *Yachties Bistro*, upstairs at the Port Curtis Sailing Club at the north end of Goondoon St, serves lunch and dinner every day, with good bistro meals in the $8 to $10 range, desserts like apple crumble from $2.50, and kid's meals for $4.50. You can dine out on the balcony overlooking the harbour – this is a popular spot for Sunday breakfasts.

At the marina, *Sailors BYO* is a casual and modern seafood restaurant with three-course lunches for $10.50 and three-course dinners (between 5.30 and 7 pm) for $15.50.

Munchies Restaurant, at 42 Goondoon St, has 'Mexican munchouts' on Tuesday nights costing $8 for all-you-can-eat, and $5 all-you-can-eat lunches from Tuesday to Friday. Their regular menu specialises in steaks and seafood with mains in the $13 to $18 range. Across the road from the information centre, *Yvonne's Food for Thought* is a good daytime cafe with breakfasts including tropical fruit platters and bacon & eggs, sandwiches and burgers, and more substantial meals.

Clancy's China Garden Restaurant, at 19 Tank St, has good Chinese food with main courses in the $7 to $12 range; they also have good takeaway deals, with two meals, two spring rolls and fried rice for $12.90. Also in Tank St is *Le Beaujolais* (☎ (079) 72 1647), a popular licensed French restaurant which also has a good 'early-bird' menu – if you eat before 8 pm, you get three courses for $17.90.

Entertainment

Visions Nightclub, in an unusually renovated waterfront building up on Flinders Pde, is a spacious club with a good atmosphere, DJ music and, occasionally, live bands. It is open from Wednesday to Sunday until around 3 am; on weekends a courtesy bus ferries punters between the club and the centre of town. The cover charge ranges from $1 to $6, depending on when you go.

The Gator Bar, on Goondoon St near the Lord St corner, is a groovy bar with pool tables and an eatery section which sells burgers and chips. It is open every night except Monday until around 3 am; on weekends there's a $3 cover charge.

The *Civic Cinema*, at 165 Goondoon St, screens latest-release movies. The *Gladstone City Theatre* (☎ (079) 72 2822), in an arcade off Goondoon St beside the information centre, is the main venue for live theatre, concerts and performances – ring to find out what's on.

Getting There & Away

Air Sunstate and Flight West have daily flights between Brisbane and Gladstone, a couple of them via Bundaberg. Sunstate also flies north to Cairns every day, via Rockhampton, Mackay and Townsville.

Lloyd Helicopters (☎ (079) 78 1177) has daily flights out to Heron Island, and the resort on Lady Elliot Island has its own plane – see Organised Tours for details of day trips to that island.

Bus Most of Greyhound Pioneer Australia's and McCafferty's coastal services stop at Gladstone; the terminal for long-distance buses is at the Mobil 24-hour Roadhouse, on the Dawson Hwy a couple of hundred metres south-west of the centre.

Train Gladstone is on the main Brisbane-Rockhampton rail route. The *Spirit of Capricorn*, the *Spirit of the Outback*, the *Queenslander* and the *Sunlander* all stop in Gladstone.

Getting Around

Gladstone Bus & Coach (☎ (079) 72 1670) runs local bus services on weekdays only, including a service along Goondoon St to Barney Point and the beach which stops out the front of the two caravan parks there.

Avis (☎ (079) 78 2633) and Hertz (☎ (079) 78 1687) both have desks at the Gladstone airport. Other car rental agencies in town include Thrifty (☎ (079) 72 5999), Network (☎ (079) 72 3066) and Gladstone Car Rentals (☎ (079) 72 3755).

To book a taxi, call Blue & White Taxis on ☎ (079) 72 1800.

GLADSTONE HARBOUR ISLANDS

There are numerous islands scattered throughout Gladstone Harbour. The largest of these, the 40-km-long **Curtis Island**, is predominantly used for grazing cattle but there's a small settlement at the southern end with a general store, camping ground and lodge. The long and narrow **Facing Island** also has picnic and camping grounds.

The Calypso Ferry Service (☎ (079) 72 1261) operates services around several of the harbour islands on weekends and several days during the week, departing from O'Connell Wharf at the north end of Oaka Lane in Gladstone.

In the inner harbour, the small **Quoin Island** has the Quoin Island Resort (☎ (079) 72 2255), with self-contained cabin-style accommodation and facilities that include tennis courts, a swimming pool and spa, a bar and restaurant, and a miniature train ride. The resort has its own ferry, and daytrippers are welcome to use the facilities. The resort was closed at the time of writing, but should be open by the time you read this.

AROUND GLADSTONE

Calliope, on the Calliope River 26 km south of Gladstone, has the **Calliope Historical Village**, with 10 restored, heritage-style buildings including an old pub, a railway station and a slab hut. The village is open daily from 8 am to 4 pm. A good craft and food market is held here about six times a year.

Lake Awoonga, created by the construction of the Awoonga Dam in 1984, is a popular recreational area south of Gladstone, with good swimming, fishing, sailing and water-skiing facilities. The main access road to the lake is from Benaraby, on the Bruce Hwy about 22 km south of Gladstone; it's another eight km to the lake from the turn off. Backed by the rugged Mt Castletower National Park, the lake has a scenic setting with landscaped picnic areas, barbecues, walking trails, and an abundance of birdlife. There's also a caravan park and a hilltop restaurant here.

On the coast south-east of Gladstone are

Tannum Sands and **Boyne Island**, two attractive residential centres with reasonably good beaches. Lots of people live here and commute to Gladstone to work, but there isn't much of interest here for travellers, apart from the beaches. There are several motels and caravan parks along the foreshore at Tannum Sands.

SOUTHERN REEF ISLANDS

The Capricornia section of the Great Barrier Reef, which includes the Southern Reef Islands, begins 80 km north-east of Bundaberg around Lady Elliot Island. The coral reefs and cays in this group dot the ocean for about 140 km up to Tryon Island east of Rockhampton.

Several cays in this part of the reef are excellent for snorkelling, diving and just getting back to nature – though reaching them is generally more expensive than reaching islands nearer the coast. Access is from Bundaberg, Gladstone or Rosslyn Bay near Yeppoon. A few of the islands are important breeding grounds for turtles and sea birds, and visitors to the islands should be aware of the precautionary measures necessary to ensure the protection of the turtles and sea birds – precautions are outlined in the QNP&WS brochures on the islands.

Camping is allowed on the Lady Musgrave, Masthead, Tryon and North West national park islands, and campers must be totally self-sufficient. Numbers of campers are limited so it's advisable to apply well ahead for a camping permit. You can book up to 12 months ahead for these islands instead of the usual six to 12 weeks for other Queensland national parks. Contact the QNP&WS (☎ (079) 72 6055), on the corner of Goondoon and Tank Sts in Gladstone. If you get a permit you'll also receive information on any rules, such as restrictions on the use of generators, and on how to avoid harming the wildlife.

Lady Elliot Island

Eighty km north-east of Bundaberg, Lady Elliot is a 0.4-sq-km vegetated coral cay at the southern end of the Great Barrier Reef.

The island has a simple, no frills resort and its own airstrip. It is very popular with divers and snorkellers, and has the advantages of superb diving straight off the beach, as well as numerous shipwrecks, coral gardens, bommies and blowholes to explore.

Lady Elliot Island is not a national park, and camping is not allowed.

Places to Stay The *Lady Elliot Island Resort* (☎ (071) 56 4444) was updated in 1985, but it's still a very straightforward place with a couple of different styles of accommodation. There are tent-cabins and timber lodges which cost $115 per person per night, and motel-style units which cost $140 per person per night for a garden view room, $10 more in a beachfront unit, or $30 more in a suite. Costs include breakfast and dinner, and children pay half the adult rate.

The resort has good diving facilities and you can take certificate courses there. The six-day courses operate once a month and cost $440.

Bookings for the resort are handled by the Sunstate Travel Centre (☎ (079) 51 6077 or 1800 072 200 toll free).

Getting There & Away Lady Elliot is the only cay on the Great Barrier Reef with its own airstrip. You can fly there from Bundaberg, Hervey Bay or Gladstone with Whitaker Air Charters – phone the Sunstate Travel Centre (☎ (071) 51 6077 or 1800 072 200 toll free) for bookings. Resort guests pay $120 for return transfers. From Bundaberg or Hervey Bay, daytrippers pay $99 for the basic return flight or $120 for the deluxe daytrip, which includes the flight, lunch, snorkelling gear etc. See Organised Tours in the Gladstone section for details of day trips from there.

Lady Musgrave Island

This 0.15-sq-km cay in the Bunker Group is an uninhabited national park about 100 km north-east of Bundaberg. The island sits at the western end of a huge lagoon which is one of the few places along the entire Barrier

The Great Barrier Reef is formed by a marine polyp of the family *Coelenterata*

Reef where ships can safely enter, and is a popular stopover for passing yachties.

Lady Musgrave offers some excellent diving opportunities, and the day-trip boats can supply you with snorkelling and diving gear. The lagoon offers excellent snorkelling and some good shallower dives for beginners, and there are good reef dives of up to 20 metres off the northern side of the lagoon.

The island itself is covered with a dense canopy of pisonia forest. You can walk right around the island in half an hour and there is a trail across the centre of the island from the usual landing place to the camping ground. Shearwaters, terns and white-capped noddies nest here from October to April, and green turtles nest here from November to February.

Places to Stay There's a national park camping ground on the western side of the island, but there are no facilities apart from bush toilets. Campers – a maximum of 50 at any one time – must be totally self-sufficient. You'll need to bring your own drinking water and a gas or fuel stove – open fires are not permitted, and the island's timber and driftwood cannot be burned.

Getting There & Away The MV *Lady Musgrave* (☎ (071) 52 9011) operates day trips from Bundaberg, leaving from Port Bundaberg on Tuesday, Thursday, Saturday and Sunday at 8.30 am. The cost is $96 which includes lunch, snorkelling gear and a glass-bottomed boat ride. The trip take 2½ hours and you have about four hours on the island. The connecting bus service from Bundaberg to the port costs another $7. You can use this service for camping drop-offs for $190 return.

There are also day trips to Lady Musgrave

GREAT BARRIER REEF

Facts & Figures

The Great Barrier Reef is 2000 km in length. It starts slightly south of the Tropic of Capricorn, somewhere out from Bundaberg or Gladstone, and ends in the Torres Strait, just south of Papua New Guinea. This huge length makes it not only the most extensive reef system in the world, but also the biggest structure made by living organisms. At its southern end, the reef is up to 300 km from the mainland, while at the northern end it runs nearer to the coast, is much less broken and can be up to 80 km wide. In the 'lagoon' between the outer reef and the coast, the waters are dotted with smaller reefs, cays and islands. Drilling on the reef has indicated that the coral can be more than 500 metres thick. Most of the reef is around two million years old, but there are sections dating back 18 million years.

What is It?

Coral is formed by a small, primitive animal, a marine polyp of the family *Coelenterata*. Some polyps, known as hard corals, form a hard surface by excreting lime. When they die, the hard 'skeletons' remain and these gradually build up the reef. New polyps grow on their dead predecessors and continually add to the reef. The skeletons of hard corals are white and the colours of reefs come from living polyps.

Coral needs a number of preconditions for healthy growth. First the water temperature must not drop below 17.5°C – thus the Barrier Reef does not continue further south into cooler waters. The water must be clear to allow sunlight to penetrate, and it must be salty. Coral will not grow below depths of 30 metres because the sunlight does not penetrate sufficiently, nor does it grow around river mouths. The Barrier Reef ends near Papua New Guinea because the Fly River's enormous water flow is both fresh and muddy.

One of the most spectacular sights of the Barrier Reef occurs for a few nights after a full moon in late spring or early summer each year, when vast numbers of corals spawn at the same time. The tiny bundles of sperm and eggs are visible to the naked eye and the event has been likened to a gigantic underwater snowstorm.

Reef Types

What's known as the Great Barrier Reef is not one reef but about 2600 separate ones. Basically, reefs are either fringing or barrier. You will find fringing reefs off sloping sides of islands or the mainland coast. Barrier reefs are further out to sea: the 'real' Great Barrier Reef, or outer reef, is at the edge of the Australian continental shelf, and the channel between the reef and the coast can be 60 metres deep. In places, the reef rises straight up from that depth. This raises the question of how the reef built up from that depth when coral cannot survive below 30 metres? One theory is that the reef gradually grew as the sea bed subsided, implying that the reef was able to keep pace with the rate of subsidence. Another theory is that the sea level gradually rose, and again the coral growth was able to keep pace.

Reef Inhabitants

There are about 400 different types of coral on the Great Barrier Reef. Equally colourful are the many clams which appear to be embedded in the coral. Other reef inhabitants include about 1500 species of fish, 4000 types of mollusc (clams, snails, etc), 350 echinoderms (sea urchins, starfish, sea cucumbers and so on, all with a five-arm body plan), and countless thousands of species of crustaceans (crabs, shrimps and their relatives), sponges and worms.

Reef waters are also home to dugong (the sea cows which gave rise to the mermaid myth) and breeding grounds for humpback whales, which migrate every winter from Antarctica. The reef's islands form important nesting colonies for many types of sea bird, and six of the world's seven species of sea turtle lay eggs on the islands' sandy beaches in spring or summer.

Crown-of-Thorns Starfish One reef inhabitant which has enjoyed enormous publicity is the crown-of-thorns starfish – notorious because it appeared to be chewing through large areas of the Great Barrier Reef. It's thought that the crown-of-thorns develops a taste for coral when the reef ecology is upset – as, for example, when the supply of bivalves (oysters, clams), which comprise its normal diet, is diminished.

Dangerous Creatures Hungry sharks are the usual idea of an aquatic nasty but the Barrier Reef's most unpleasant creatures are generally less dramatic. For a start, there are scorpion fish with highly venomous spines. The butterfly cod is a very beautiful scorpion fish and relies on its colourful, slow-moving appearance to warn off possible enemies. In contrast, the stonefish lies hidden on the bottom, looking just like a rock, and is very dangerous to step on. Although they're rather rare, it's a good idea to wear shoes when walking on the reef – this is sensible anyway to protect yourself against sharp coral and rocks.

Stinging jellyfish are a danger only in coastal waters and only in certain seasons. The deadly 'sea wasp' is in fact a box jellyfish (see Dangers & Annoyances in the Facts for the Visitor chapter). As for sharks, there has been no recorded case of a visitor to the reef islands meeting a hungry one.

Viewing the Reef
The best way of seeing the reef is by diving or snorkelling in it. Otherwise you can walk on it, view it through the floor of glass-bottom boats or the windows of semisubmersibles, or descend below the ocean surface inside 'underwater observatories'. You can also see a living coral reef and its accompanying life forms without leaving dry land, at the Great Barrier Reef Wonderland aquarium in Townsville.

Innumerable tour operators run day trips to the outer reef and to coral-fringed islands from towns on the Queensland coast. The cost depends on how much reef-viewing paraphernalia is used, how far the reef is from the coast, how luxurious the vessel that takes you there is, and whether lunch is included. Usually, free use of snorkelling gear is part of the package. Some islands have good reefs too: they're usually cheaper to reach and you can stay on quite a few of them.

The Great Barrier Reef Marine Park Authority (GBRMPA) is the body looking after the welfare of most of the reef. Its address is PO Box 1379, Townsville, Queensland 4810 (☎ (077) 81 8811). It also has an office in Great Barrier Reef Wonderland in Townsville.

Islands
There are three types of island off the Queensland coast. In the south, before you reach the Barrier Reef, are several large vegetated sand islands like North Stradbroke, Moreton and Fraser islands. These are interesting to visit for a variety of reasons but not for coral. Strung along the whole coast, mostly close inshore, are continental islands like Great Keppel, most of the Whitsundays, Hinchinbrook and Dunk. At one time, these would have been the peaks of coastal ranges, but rising sea levels submerged the mountains. The islands' vegetation is similar to that of the adjacent mainland.

The true coral islands, or cays, may be on the outer reef, or may be isolated between it and the mainland. Green Island near Cairns, the Low Isles near Port Douglas and Heron Island off Gladstone are all cays. Cays are formed when a reef is above sea level, even at high tide. Dead coral is ground down by water action to form sand and, in some cases, eventually vegetation takes root. Coral cays are low-lying, unlike the often hilly islands closer to the coast. There are about 300 cays on the reef, 69 of them vegetated.

The Queensland islands are extremely variable so don't let the catchword 'reef island' suck you in. Most of the popular resort islands are actually continental islands and some are well south of the Great Barrier Reef. Being a reef island is not necessarily important, since many continental islands will still have fringing reefs as well as other attractions that a tiny dot-on-the-map coral cay is simply too small for – like hills to climb, bushwalks, and secluded beaches where you can get away from other island lovers.

The islands also vary considerably in their accessibility – Lady Elliot for instance is a $100 return flight, others are just a few dollars by ferry. If you want to stay on an island rather than make a day trip from the mainland, this too can vary widely in cost. Accommodation is generally in the form of expensive resorts, where most visitors will be on an all-inclusive package holiday. But there are a few exceptions to this rule, plus on some islands it's possible to camp. A few islands have proper camping areas with toilets and fresh water on tap while, at the other extreme, on some you'll even have to bring drinking water with you.

For more information on individual islands, see the Whitsunday Coast, North Coast and Far North Queensland chapters of this book. Also good is Lonely Planet's *Islands of Australia's Great Barrier Reef.* ∎

from Seventeen Seventy – see Things to See & Do in the earlier Agnes Water & Seventeen Seventy section for details.

Heron Island

Only one km long and 0.17 sq km in area, Heron Island is 72 km east of Gladstone. This fascinating island is a true coral cay, densely vegetated with pisonia trees and surrounded by 24 sq km of reef. There's a resort and research station on the north-eastern third of the island – the rest is national park.

Heron, famed for superb scuba diving, is something of a Mecca for divers. There's good snorkelling over the shallow reef, and the resort's dive boat runs excursions to the many good diving sites. The dive shop has a full range of diving equipment available for hire – you can do a day trip for $35 including diving equipment and one dive – and six-day certificate courses are available for $350.

The resort also arranges guided reef walks, nature walks and fishing trips for guests.

Places to Stay Owned by P&O Resorts, the *Heron Island Resort* (☎ (079) 78 1488) covers the north-eastern third of the island; the rest is national park, but you can't camp there. The resort has room for more than 250 people, and facilities include a bar, disco and tennis courts.

The cheapest accommodation here is the Lodge rooms, simple three to four-bed bunk-rooms with shared bathroom facilities, which cost $140 per person per night. There are also modern motel-style suites with all the mod-cons (except phones and TVs); Reef Suites cost $198 per person, Heron Suites cost $215 per person and Point Suites cost $260 per person. Tariffs include all meals.

For bookings and information, contact P&O Resorts in Sydney on ☎ 13 2469.

Stand-by rates are often available from travel agents in Gladstone – contact the tourist information office there on ☎ (079) 72 4000 for details.

Getting There & Away Lloyd's Helicopters (☎ (079) 78 1177) can fly guests to the resort

from Gladstone in half an hour for $218 one way or $364 return. Alternatively, the high-speed catamaran *Reef Adventurer* does the trip from Gladstone in two hours, costing $136 return.

Transfers are only for resort guests – there are no day trips to Heron.

Masthead & Erskine Islands

Masthead Island is an uninhabited coral cay slightly south-west of Heron Island. The entire island is protected as a national park, and is an important nesting ground for log-gerhead turtles, as well as for shearwaters, black noddies and other birds. The main turtle-nesting season is from November to January; for seabirds, nesting season is from October to April.

Camping is permitted, with limits of 30 people in the summer birdwatching season and 60 people at other times, but there are no facilities and campers have to be totally self-sufficient.

Erskine Island is just north of Masthead and only day visits are permitted.

Getting There & Away The MV *Jetty II* (☎ (079) 74 9077) operates a camping drop-off service from Seventeen Seventy to Masthead Island for $80 per person one way; they also have camping gear and dinghies available for hire.

Wilson Island

North of Heron, Wilson Island is a national park and a popular day trip for Heron guests looking for a break from diving. The resort operates day trips to the island which cost $28 for adults and $16 for children, which includes a barbecue lunch. You can swim at the island's excellent beaches and there's superb snorkelling around the island.

However, not everyone enjoys the visitors. Apparently 300 nesting pairs of endangered roseate terns temporarily abandoned the island when regular visitors began turning up – it's important to avoid disturbing them.

North West Island
At 0.9 sq km, North West Island is the second biggest cay on the Barrier Reef. Guano was mined on the island from 1894 to 1900, and a turtle-soup factory operated here up until 1928. Nowadays the entire island is a national park, and it's one of the major nesting sites for green turtles, with nesting occurring between November and February.

North West Island is a popular destination for campers and daytrippers. There's a limit of 150 campers – again, you need to be fully self-sufficient, with facilities limited to pit toilets.

Getting There & Away There are no regular services to the island, but several tour operators offer camping drop-off services. Operating out of Seventeen Seventy, the MV *Jetty II* (☎ (079) 74 9077) will drop off campers for $100 per person each way; they also have camping gear and dinghies available for hire.

The *Robert Poulsen* also operates to North West Island, costing $1300 for a return trip for 14 people or more. Ring P&O Marine Division (☎ (079) 72 5166) for details.

Tryon Island
Immediately north of North West Island, this tiny, beautiful, six-hectare national park cay is another important nesting area for sea birds and green turtles. There is a camping ground on the island, but at the time of writing, the island was closed to visitors to allow for revegetation, and there were no regular boat services from the mainland. Check with the QNP&WS office in Gladstone (☎ (079) 72 6055) to find out whether the island has been re-opened yet.

Rockhampton Area

ROCKHAMPTON (pop 65,900)
Rockhampton, which sits astride the Tropic of Capricorn, is the administrative and commercial centre of central Queensland. Its fortunes are closely linked to the cattle industry, and the city proclaims itself the 'beef capital' of Australia. It's said that there are more than two million cattle within a 250-km radius of the city, and it could be said that Rocky has something of an obsession with beef – large statues of Brahman, Braford and Santa Gertrudis bulls mark the northern and southern approaches to the city. Not surprisingly, this is a great place to tuck into a steak.

Queensland's largest river, the Fitzroy, flows through the heart of the city. The city centre, on the southern side of the river, has numerous historic buildings, many of which are classified by the National Trust. This compact centre is surrounded by a progressive city of attractive gardens, huge shopping plazas and modern housing estates.

Rocky has a few tourist attractions of its own, including a good art gallery, an Aboriginal cultural centre and some excellent gardens and parklands. It's also the access point for Great Keppel and other islands, with boats leaving from Rosslyn Bay, on the coast about 40 km away near Yeppoon. Other popular day-trip destinations include the spectacular limestone caves in the Berserker Range north of Rocky; Mt Morgan, a historic mining town 38 km south-west; and the Koorana Crocodile Farm near Emu Park. (These places are all covered in following sections.)

History
Rockhampton was established as a river trading port in 1853 by the Archer brothers, the first white settlers to establish a property in the area. The port's growth was boosted by a minor gold rush at Canoona in 1858, but the real development began with the discovery of the rich gold and copper deposits at Mt Morgan in 1882. Rockhampton quickly developed into the major trading centre for the surrounding region, and its turn-of-the-century prosperity is evident in the many fine Victorian-era buildings around the older parts of the city.

This century, mining was gradually replaced by sheep, and later cattle-farming, as the region's major source of income.

Orientation

Rockhampton is about 40 km inland from the coast. The Fitzroy River flows through the heart of the city, with the small city centre, the oldest part of Rocky, on the southern banks of the river. Quay St, along the riverfront, has many historic buildings, whilst East St is a pedestrian mall between Fitzroy and William Sts. The post office, on the corner of the mall and Denham St, is pretty much the centre of town. The long Fitzroy Bridge connects the city centre with the newer suburbs to the north.

Driving in from the south, the Bruce Hwy skirts the town centre and crosses the river via the Neville Hewitt Bridge. To get to the city centre, turn right up Fitzroy St off George St. You can rejoin the highway from the centre by going north over the Fitzroy Bridge then on up Queen Elizabeth Dve and Musgrave St.

Information

Tourist Information The Capricorn Information Centre (☎ (079) 27 2055), on the highway as you enter Rocky from the south, is beside the Tropic of Capricorn marker and three km from the town centre. It is open daily from 9 am to 5 pm.

The more central Riverside Information Centre (☎ (079) 22 5339) is in a riverfront rotunda, on Quay St, and is open on weekdays from 8.30 am to 4.30 pm and on weekends from 9 am to 4 pm. This centre is particularly helpful for backpackers, and the staff here can suggest various tours and ways of getting to attractions in the surrounding area even if you don't have your own transport.

Post & Telecommunications Rockhampton's post office, in the centre of the East St Mall and on the corner of Denham St, is certainly one of the city's most impressive historic buildings. It is open on weekdays from 8.30 am to 5 pm.

Useful Organisations The RACQ (☎ (079) 272 255) has an office at 134 William St. The QNP&WS district office (☎ (079) 36 0511) is on Yeppoon Rd, about seven km north-west

Cattle farming and sales are the region's major source of income

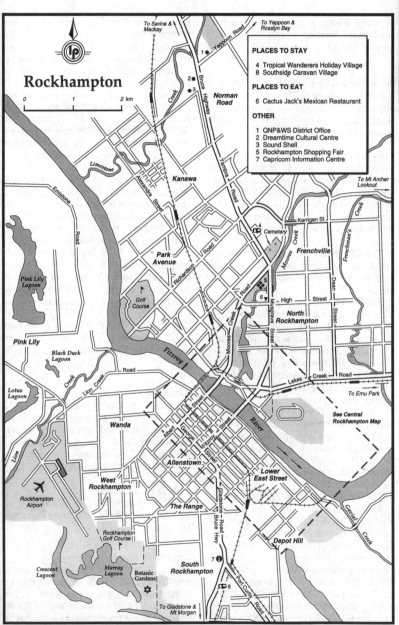

Rockhampton

0   1   2 km

PLACES TO STAY

4 Tropical Wanderers Holiday Village
8 Southside Caravan Village

PLACES TO EAT

6 Cactus Jack's Mexican Restaurant

OTHER

1 QNP&WS District Office
2 Dreamtime Cultural Centre
3 Sound Shell
5 Rockhampton Shopping Fair
7 Capricorn Information Centre

of central Rocky. Head out the Bruce Hwy and take the Yeppoon turn off – you'll see it on your left, about 200 metres after the turn off.

Bookshops The national chain Angus & Robertson Bookworld has a large outlet inside the City Centre Plaza shopping centre (locally known as the Target centre), on the corner of Fitzroy and Bolsover Sts.

Things to See

There are many fine old buildings in the town, particularly on **Quay St**, which has a number of grand Victorian-era buildings which date back to the gold-rush days. You can pick up tourist leaflets and magazines which map out walking trails around the town.

The **City Heart Markets**, with arts and crafts, plants, clothing and food on sale, are held in the East St Mall every Saturday morning.

The **Rockhampton City Art Gallery**, on Victoria Pde, is open on weekdays and public holidays from 10 am to 4 pm, and on weekends from 1.30 to 4.30 pm; admission is free. The gallery houses a small but impressive collection of Australian paintings, with works by John Brack, Arthur Boyd, Norman Lindsay, Rupert Bunny, Lloyd Rees and Jeffrey Smart.

On the Bruce Hwy, seven km north of the centre, is the **Dreamtime Cultural Centre**, an Aboriginal and Torres Straits Islander heritage display centre. It's open daily from 10 am to 5.30 pm, and tours are run daily at 11 am and 2 pm; admission is $11 for adults and $5 for children.

The **Botanic Gardens**, situated at the end of Spencer St in the south of the city, were established in 1869. If you have a car, you can drive right into these large and very beautiful gardens, which include a children's playground, a lovely picnic area, a formal Japanese garden, a wetlands area with prolific birdlife, a walk-through aviary and a kiosk which serves Devonshire teas. There's also a grove of pine trees grown from seeds from the Gallipoli Peninsula, which were a gift from the Turkish government to commemorate the Australian troops who fought and died there in WW I, and a German Howitzer which was captured by the Australian Light Horse Regiment in Palestine in WW I.

North of the city centre, just across the Fitzroy River, the **Cliff Kershaw Gardens** is an excellent botanical park devoted to Australian native plants. Within the park are numerous walking trails, a slab timber cottage which serves Devonshire teas, picnic and barbecue areas, a monorail and a children's playground, and an impressive artificial waterfall. To get to the gardens, cross the Fitzroy Bridge and take a left into Charles St, which runs off Musgrave St.

Mt Archer, on the city's northern outskirts, is an environmental park with lots of walking trails, wildlife and several swimming holes. The landscape is mostly eucalypt forest, with a couple of small patches of rainforest. An 11-km trail leads from the summit to the lower entrance, and there are also shorter walks to several lookout points. The QNP&WS publishes a brochure to the park which is available from the information centres. There is no public transport to the park.

Activities

Rockhampton Golf Course (☎ (079) 22 4098), beside the Botanic Gardens, is an excellent course and opens to the general public every day. A round costs $12 on weekdays and $15 on weekends; you can hire clubs for another $11 and a motorised buggy for $20.

Rocky has several public swimming pools; the Southside Swimming Pool is on the southern banks of the Fitzroy River one km west of the centre.

Organised Tours

Fitzroy River Historic Cruises offers a two-hour river cruise with an accompanying commentary on Rockhampton's history. The tour costs $19.90 for adults and $8.50 for children. Departure times vary according to

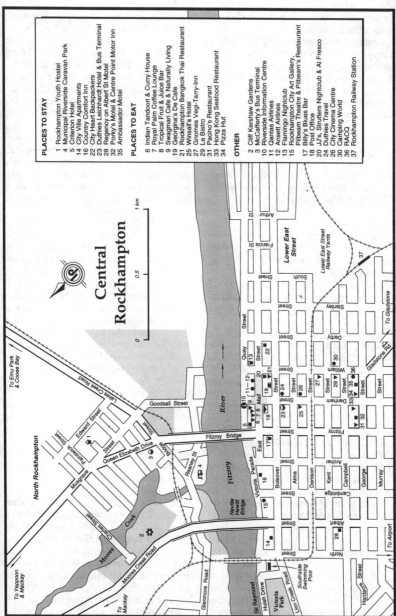

Central Rockhampton

PLACES TO STAY

1 Rockhampton Youth Hostel
4 Municipal Riverside Caravan Park
5 Criterion Hotel
14 City Ville Apartments
16 Country Comfort Inn
22 City Heart Backpackers
23 Duthies Leichhardt Hotel & Bus Terminal
28 Regency on Albert St Motel
32 Porky's Motel & Centre Point Motor Inn
35 Ambassador Motel

PLACES TO EAT

6 Indian Tandoori & Curry House
7 Royal Palm Coffee Lounge
8 Tropical Fruit & Juice Bar
9 Swagman Cafe & Naturally Living
19 Georgina's De Cafe
21 Rockhampton Bangkok Thai Restaurant
25 Winsall's Hotel
27 Gnomes Vegi-Tarry-Inn
29 Le Bistro
31 Pacino's Restaurant
33 Hong Kong Seafood Restaurant
34 Pizza Hut

OTHER

2 Cliff Kershaw Gardens
3 McCafferty's Bus Terminal
10 Riverside Information Centre
11 Ansett Airlines
12 Qantas Airlines
13 Flamingo Nightclub
15 Rockhampton City Art Gallery,
   Pilbeam Theatre & Pilbeam's Restaurant
17 Billy's Blues Bar
18 Post Office
20 JJ's, Strutts Nightclub & Al Fresco
24 Duthies Travel
26 City Cinema Centre
30 Camping World
36 RACQ
37 Rockhampton Railway Station

the seasons – check with the Riverside Information Centre for times.

Rothery's Coaches (☎ (079) 22 4320) has a range of tours to various attractions in and around Rocky. They have day tours to the Koorana Crocodile Farm (Monday only, $48 adults, $24 children) and the Capricorn Coast (Thursday only, $48/24), and half-day tours to Olsen's Caves (Monday, Wednesday and Friday mornings, $24/12), the Dreamtime Cultural Centre (Monday, Wednesday and Friday afternoons, $18/9) and around the city sights (Wednesday and Friday mornings, $18/9). Tours depart from Duthies Leichhardt Hotel, or they'll pick you up from wherever you're staying.

Festivals

Rocky's main annual festival is the Capricana Festival, held over 10 days in early September. It features a street parade, a carnival and daily activities. The Bauhinia Arts Festival, held in early August, features a range of stage productions, art exhibitions and musical performances.

Places to Stay

Camping There are half a dozen caravan parks in Rocky. The most central place is the pleasantly situated *Municipal Riverside Caravan Park* (☎ (079) 22 3779), in Reaney St, just across the bridge to the north of the city centre. It has tent sites for $9 and powered sites for $12, but no on-site vans or cabins.

The *Southside Caravan Village* (☎ (079) 27 3013) is on the Bruce Hwy three km south of the centre, near the Capricorn Information Centre. It's a well set up park with a shop, swimming pool, half-court tennis court and a courtesy coach that runs into the centre three times a day (except Sunday). Prices vary seasonally: there's a backpackers' section from $11 to $14 per person in on-site vans; tent sites from $10 to $13; and self-contained cabins from $38.

On the Bruce Hwy, about three km north of the centre, the *Tropical Wanderers Holiday Village* (☎ (079) 26 3822) is another good camping and caravan park with similar

facilities; tent sites start from $12 and on-site cabins and villas from $33.

Hostels The *Rockhampton Youth Hostel* (☎ (079) 27 5288), over the river at 60 MacFarlane St, has dorms at $12 ($14 for nonmembers) and twin rooms at $28/32. It's a spacious hostel with good facilities, and evening meals are available here for $3 to $4. The hostel is five minutes walk from McCafferty's terminal and a 20-minute walk north of the centre. Greyhound Pioneer Australia will drop you nearby on request, or if you ring the hostel they can pick you up. This is a good place to organise trips to Great Keppel Island, and to make bookings for the popular YHA hostel there.

Duthies Leichhardt Hotel (☎ (079) 27 6733), on the corner of Denham and Bolsover Sts (where the Greyhound Pioneer Australia buses stop), has backpackers' accommodation with three beds in a motel unit at $15 per person. These rates are available unless the motel is booked out, which it sometimes is on weekends. This place is clean and conveniently central, although when I visited the staff tended to have an attitude problem when it came to backpackers – they seemed to be proportionally nicer to people who were paying $50-plus for a room.

City Heart Backpackers (☎ (079) 22 2414), at 170 East St, is quite central and has all the usual facilities, although the sleeping areas are huge and lack privacy. Dorms are $12 a night. This building was up for sale when I visited, so if you're thinking of staying here it might be worth ringing to check that it's still operating first.

Pubs On Quay St, overlooking the river from beside the Fitzroy Bridge, the *Criterion Hotel* (☎ (079) 22 1225) is one of Rockhampton's most magnificent old buildings. It's a good place to stay, with the feel of a friendly country pub. The hotel has recently been renovated, the meals are good, and the small Newsroom Bar has live music most nights. Upstairs, there are budget rooms with shared bathrooms which can be had for

$20/30 (singles/twins), and a few rooms with their own shower for $25/30. There are also motel-style units and attractive hotel suites renovated in period-style, which are good value from $40/45 including air-con.

Motels *Duthies Leichhardt Hotel* (☎ (079) 27 6733), on the corner of Denham and Bolsover Sts, is a six-storey hotel with 120 motel-style rooms, a bistro, shops, a bar and restaurant. It's fairly old-fashioned, but still one of the most popular places to stay. Older motel units are $40/48 for singles/doubles, units in the north wing are $50/60 and tower rooms start from $70/75. They also have backpackers' accommodation (see Hostels).

Porky's Motel (☎ (079) 27 8100), at 141 George St, is quite central and affordable, and despite the dodgy name has respectable rooms at $38/42 for singles/doubles and $46/49 for triples/quads. Next door at No 131 the *Centre Point Motor Inn* (☎ (079) 27 8844) is a little more up-market and has a licensed restaurant, a pool and rooms from $60/66.

The *Ambassador Motel Inn* (☎ (079) 27 5855), at 161-167 George St, is a modern six-storey motel with a pool, restaurant, and units from $79/85. You'll find lots of other motels on the Bruce Hwy as you come into Rockhampton from both the north and south.

One of Rocky's newest accommodation complexes is the impressive *Regency on Albert St Motel* (☎ (079) 22 6222), on the corner of Albert and Campbell Sts, which has a pool, a cocktail bar and an up-market restaurant. Motel units range from $72/76 for a standard room to $92/96 for an executive room with a spa. This place also has selfcontained apartments (see the following section).

The *Country Comfort Inn* (☎ (079) 27 9933), at 86 Victoria Pde, is an up-market high-rise motel on the riverfront. Standard rooms start at $94, family rooms sleep up to four and cost $103, and there are five luxury penthouses at $163.

Self-contained Apartments If you're looking for somewhere self-contained, the *City Ville Apartments* (☎ (079) 22 8322), at

21 Bolsover St, can be highly recommended. These new apartments are stylish and well equipped, and there's a small pool. Costs start from $65 for a studio-style unit; from $120 for a two-bedroom unit; and from $160 for a three-bedroom unit. The larger units have a separate lounge, laundry and full kitchen, and upstairs bedrooms.

The previously mentioned *Regency on Albert St Motel* (☎ (079) 22 6222), on the corner of Albert and Campbell Sts, has apartments with separate kitchens and laundries costing $110 for a one-bedroom unit, $150 for two bedrooms and $210 for three bedrooms.

Places to Eat
Cafes & Takeaways The *Swagman Cafe*, at 8 Denham St, has cooked breakfasts at $5 to $7 as well as the usual burgers, sangers and pies. Two shops north, *Natural Living* is a good health-food shop with delicious filled pita bread and tortillas, rolls and sangers, smoothies, fresh juices, salads and cakes. The *Tropical Fruit & Juice Bar*, on the mall across from the post office, has good fruit salads and smoothies.

Also in the mall at 61 East St the *Royal Palm Coffee Lounge* is a pleasant sit-down coffee lounge with cooked breakfasts, cappuccinos, toasted sangers, burgers, quiche and lasagna. At the other end of the mall, on the corner of William St, *Al Fresco* is a small international food court where you can choose from Chinese food, pasta, seafood, and steaks. There's a courtyard dining area on the mall.

Georgina's De Cafe, at 171 Bolsover St, is a trendy new cafe-eatery which is open daily from 10 am till midnight. Pastas are all $10.50, salads $7.50, and they have sangers, focaccias, filled croissants, great coffee and a sensational array of cakes and pastries. Patrons who wear their pyjamas to the cafe on a Sunday qualify for a 10% discount!

Pubs The *Criterion Hotel*, on Quay St, has excellent public bar meals with the likes of veal schnitzels, fish fillets, steaks, chicken Kiev and calamari & chips ranging from

$6.50 to $7.50. The pub also has a restaurant which does a carvery smorgasbord for $7 every night, or you can order from the menu which specialises in steaks and seafood.

Winsall's Hotel, on the corner of Denham and Alma Sts, has a reasonably priced bistro.

Restaurants On the corner of William St and Denison Lane, *Gnomes Vegi-Tarry-Inn* is an excellent vegetarian restaurant and coffee shop. Housed in a charmingly renovated Victorian-era building, it has an open-sided courtyard and garden section. Interesting mains such as pumpkin pie, mushroom and avocado quiche and spinach cheesecake are all $8 with salad, and they also have great desserts and cakes, smoothies, juices and a huge range of herbal teas. You place your orders at the kitchen window out the back. Gnomes is open from Tuesday to Saturday for lunch and dinner.

The *Indian Tandoori & Curry House*, at 39 East St, has good-value Indian food. On weekdays it has smorgasbord-style lunches from $5.50 to $10, and at night its main courses are all around $10. This place is BYO, and closes on Monday.

The *Rockhampton Bangkok Thai Restaurant*, on the corner of Bolsover and William Sts, is a large and popular Thai restaurant with main meals from $9 to $13 and vegetarian dishes from $6 to $7. It is closed on Monday.

Pacino's, on the corner of Fitzroy and George Sts, about a km south of the Fitzroy Bridge, is a good Italian restaurant if you're in the mood for a minor splash-out. It is open nightly for dinner and has pastas from $12 to $14, pizzas for $12.50 and main courses from $17 to $19. For French food, try *Le Bistro*, an intimate little BYO at 120 William St with main courses for around $18.

The *Pizza Hut*, in Denham St near the George St corner, has all-you-can-eat pizza and pasta special for $5.95 every Tuesday and Wednesday night. Across the road, the *Hong Kong Seafood Restaurant* has Chinese food with main meals around $10. *Cactus Jack's Mexican Restaurant*, a couple of km north of the centre, on the corner of

Musgrave and High Sts, is a popular licensed Mexican restaurant.

Pilbeam's, between the Pilbeam Theatre and City Art Gallery, on Victoria Pde, is a stylish cafe-bar-bistro which combines crisp white linen with casual directors' chairs. It is open for lunch on weekdays and for dinners from Monday to Saturday, and caters to theatre-goers with early dinners and late suppers. The food is fresh and interesting, with entrées, light meals and lunch specials ranging from $8 to $11, and main courses from $13 to $16.

Entertainment

Pubs & Live Music The Criterion Hotel has a busy but relaxed scene in its small *Newsroom Bar* where local musicians and groups play from Wednesday to Saturday nights. Jazz, blues, folk, pop and rock all feature, and they also have an open-to-all-comers jam session on Monday nights. There is no cover charge.

Billy's Blues Bar, on the corner of Fitzroy and Bolsover Sts, has two sections – a large poolhall with eight tables, and a music bar with a small stage dwarfed by giant video screens. It is open nightly until around 3 am, and has live music with everything from solo pianists to hard-core rock bands.

Nightclubs Rockhampton has several nightclubs. The largest and most popular place is the *Flamingo*, on Quay St between William and Derby Sts, which is open from Wednesday to Sunday until around late. It has a large dance floor and DJ music, a section with live bands on weekends, and a poolroom. The cover charge is $3 on Wednesday and Thursday and $5 on Friday and Saturday. The club also has a popular Sunday session which starts at 5 pm, with $1 spirits until 9 pm.

Strutters Nightclub, upstairs in JJ's, on the corner of William and East Sts, is also worth checking out. It has a similar set-up to the Flamingo, and its opening hours and cover charges are about the same.

Theatre & Cinema The *Pilbeam Theatre* (☎ (079) 27 7129), on Victoria Pde, is the main venue for theatrical and musical productions. There's also a huge open-air *Sound Shell*, off the Bruce Hwy about seven km north-west of the centre, which is the venue for large rock concerts and the annual carols by candlelight.

The *City Cinema Centre* (☎ (079) 22 1511) is on Denham St.

Things to Buy
Camping World, on the corner of Kent and William Sts, has a wide range of camping and outdoor gear.

Getting There & Away
Air You can fly to Rocky from all the major centres along the coast with Ansett or Qantas. Sunstate does a daily coastal hop from Brisbane to Rockhampton ($215), Rockhampton to Mackay ($161), and back. Other one-way fares include Cairns $293, Proserpine $217, Townsville $249 and Gladstone $101.

Qantas and Sunstate are on the mall at 107 East St and Ansett is nearby at 137 East St.

Bus McCafferty's and Greyhound Pioneer Australia's buses all pass through Rockhampton on the coastal route. From Rockhampton to Cairns is 13 hours ($90); to Mackay, four hours ($38); and to Brisbane, 10 hours ($60). McCafferty's also has daily services inland as far as Emerald, and continues on to Longreach ($51) on Tuesday, Thursday and Sunday.

McCafferty's terminal (☎ (079) 27 2844) is just north of the Fitzroy River, off Queen Elizabeth Dve. Greyhound Pioneer Australia buses all stop outside Duthies Leichhardt Hotel, on the corner of Bolsover and Denham Sts.

Duthies Travel (☎ (079) 27 6288), on Denham St opposite the hotel, handles tickets for all destinations.

Train The Rockhampton railway station is about one km south-east of the centre. The *Sunlander* (three times a week), the *Queenslander* (once a week) and the *Spirit of the Tropics* (twice a week) all travel between Brisbane and Cairns, stopping at Rockhampton. The *Spirit of Capricorn* travels between Rockhampton and Brisbane daily. Twice weekly, the *Spirit of the Outback* runs between Brisbane, Rockhampton, Emerald and Longreach. For more information, contact the Queensland Rail Travel Centre at the station (☎ (079) 32 0242).

Getting Around
Rockhampton Airport is about five km south of the centre. There are no bus services from the airport into the centre – a taxi will cost you about $7. To book a taxi, call Rocky Cabs on ☎ (079) 22 7111.

There's a reasonably comprehensive city bus network which operates from Monday to Friday.

Young's Bus Service (☎ (079) 22 3813) has services from Rockhampton to Mt Morgan every day except Sunday. The one-way fare is $6. Young's also has frequent daily services to the Capricorn Coast, doing a loop from Rocky to Yeppoon, Rosslyn Bay, Emu Park and back. Rothery's Coaches (☎ (079) 22 4320) also has services from Rocky to Yeppoon and Rosslyn Bay which connect with the ferries to Great Keppel Island. Both companies charge $6 one way or $10 return, and both depart from outside Duthies Hotel. Rothery's will also do pick-ups from accommodation places.

AROUND ROCKHAMPTON
The Caves
The rugged Berserker Range, to the north of Rockhampton, is noted for its spectacular limestone caves and passages. There are a couple of places where you can take tours through the caves region, both of which are within a couple of km of The Caves township, 23 km north of Rocky. In the town itself, *The Country Pub* is a friendly corner pub which has bistro meals in the $8 to $10 range and a cook-your-own barbecue on Sunday nights.

Olsen's Capricorn Caves (☎ (079) 34 2883) is the most impressive of the two operations here. The main entrance to these caves is via a collapsed cave framed by a canopy of remnant vegetation, with enormous fig tree roots which seem to have carved their way through the rock face. Tours include a visit to the impressive Cathedral cave, complete with church pews, where songs. Amazing Grace are played to demonstrate the cave's great acoustics. The caves are open daily from 8.30 am, with the first tour at 9 am and the last at 4 pm. There are six different tours you can take, including a one-hour cathedral tour ($9), an adventure tour where you don overalls and helmets ($22) and a night tour ($12). You need to book in advance for the adventure and night tours. Children pay half price.

There are barbecue areas, a swimming pool and walking trails on the property, as well as a good self-contained *holiday cabin* which sleeps up to eight people and costs $60 a night for up to four, plus $5 for extras. The owners are also planning to build more cabins and a camping ground. For tours to Olsen's Caves see Organised Tours under Rockhampton.

The **Camoo Caves** is a smaller, family-run operation. Tours here are self-guided, with six audio stations providing commentary on the various formations. A tour will take around half an hour if you listen to all the audios. These caves are open daily from 8.30 am to 4.30 pm. There are no set tour times, and entry costs $7 for adults, $6 for students and $3 for children. There is also a 1½ hour guided adventure tour to the Flogged Horse cave which costs $10 – you'll need a torch and good walking shoes or boots.

Nearby, the **Mt Etna National Park** is the habitat of the endangered ghost bat. There are no facilities here and access to the park is restricted, but the park rangers run tours of the bat caves from early December until mid-February. Tours depart from The Caves township, and cost $6 for adults and $3 for children; bookings are essential, ring (☎ (079) 36 0511).

BOULDERCOMBE

If you're looking for somewhere to get away from it all, *Belgamba Cottage* (☎ (079) 38 1818) is a three-bedroom cottage on a 500-hectare property between Rocky and Mt Morgan. The property is a nature reserve for Australian native plants. The landscape is predominantly dry but quite interesting, and there are plenty of walking trails to explore. Cathy and Ian, the owners, are passionate about the local flora and fauna and will take guests on free guided walks through the property and the adjacent Bouldercombe Gorge Reserve.

The timber cottage is bright, spacious and sleeps up to six people, and nightly costs are $55 a double or $80 for up to six people (cheaper rates for longer stays), with everything supplied except food. Belgamba is 22 km south-west of Rockhampton and 16 km north-east of Mt Morgan – ring for driving directions, or if you're coming by bus Cathy and Ian can pick you up from the turn off.

MT MORGAN (pop 2800)

The historic gold and copper-mining town of Mt Morgan is 38 km south-west of Rockhampton on the Burnett Hwy. Gold was first discovered here in 1880 by William Mackinlay, a stockman.

Two years later the Morgan brothers, Thomas, Frederick and Edwin, arrived and commenced mining operations here, and within a couple of years they had made their fortunes.

Thinking the mine's future prospects were limited, the Morgan brothers then sold out to a mining syndicate for £90,000 – a huge sum of money at the time, but nothing compared to what would later come out of the ground. In its first 10 years of operations from 1886, the Mt Morgan Gold Mining Company returned massive dividends on the initial capital, making its major investors into some of the richest and most powerful men in Australia. Gold yields fell dramatically by the turn of the century, but in 1903 the company began extracting the rich copper deposits that were found deeper in the mine. Open-cut operations continued until 1981.

Mt Morgan has a well-preserved collection of turn-of-the-century buildings, and is registered as a heritage town. There's an

Left: Local character, Mt Morgan
Right: Mt Morgan Railway station
Bottom: Mt Morgan

MARK ARMSTRONG

TONY WHEELER

MARK ARMSTRONG

Top: Fisherman's Beach, Great Keppel Island
Middle: Wreck, Lady Elliot Island
Bottom: Great Keppel Island ferry

interesting historic museum, and you can take a tour of the former mine site.

Information
The Golden Mount Tourist Information Centre (☎ (079) 38 2312), in the old railway station, is open daily from 9 am to 4 pm.

Things to See & Do
The **Mt Morgan Historical Museum**, on the corner of Morgan and East Sts, is very well set up with displays including an old kitchen, a 1921 black Buick hearse, and collections of sewing machines, cameras, musical instruments, riding and farming gear, as well as old photos tracing the history of the mine. The museum is open Monday to Saturday from 10 am to 1 pm and Sunday from 10 am to 4 pm; admission costs $2 for adults, 50c for children.

Silver Wattle Tours (☎ (079) 38 1081), with an office next to the Golden Nugget Hotel at 38 Central St runs 2½-hour tours that take in the town's sights, the open-cut mine, and a large cave which has dinosaur footprints on the roof and is home to a colony of bats. Tours depart from their office and the museum every day at 9.30 am and 1 pm and cost $18.50 for adults, $10 for children and $45 for a family; afternoon tea is included in the cost.

Mt Morgan's lovely old **railway station** is something of a focal point for the town. It houses the tourist office, and a **market** is held at the station on the first Saturday of each month from 2 pm. On Saturday afternoons from 2 pm, you can take a historic 3.5 km **train tour** which costs $5 for adults, $2.50 for children and $15 for families. Rides on one of the old fettler trolleys are also available here on request; they also cost $5/2.50/15.

The **Running the Cutter** monument, opposite the post office, on the corner of Morgan and Central Sts, commemorates the old custom of serving 'cutters' (two-quart billy cans) of beer to the mine workers in Cutter Lane behind the hotels.

Festivals
Mt Morgan's major festival is the Golden

Mount Festival held every May. It features a 'Running the Cutter' event.

Places to Stay
The *Silver Wattle Caravan & Tourist Park* (☎ (079) 38 1550), on the southern outskirts of town, is a good camping ground with an attractive bush setting and tent sites from $10, powered sites from $12, on-site vans from $18 and cabins from $30.

The old two-storey *Leichhardt Hotel* (☎ (079) 38 1851), opposite the museum, on the corner of Morgan and East Sts, has basic but clean timber-lined pub rooms upstairs at $10/15 for singles/doubles.

The *Miners' Rest Motel Units* (☎ (079) 38 2350), one km south of the centre on the outskirts of town, is a set of three small Victorian-style cottages, each with its own ensuite, kitchenette, spa, TV and air-con. Tariffs range from $40 to $50 a double, which includes breakfast. Cooked meals and picnic lunches are also available here.

Places to Eat
The *Mt Morgan Hot Bread Shop*, on Morgan St near the museum has good rolls and sandwiches and home-made pies, pastries and cakes. At 65-67 Morgan St the *Rainbow Cafe* is a simple country-style cafe with burgers, sandwiches, fish & chips, roast chicken etc. The adjoining *Meredith's Restaurant* is an old-fashioned dining room which is open for dinner from Wednesday to Saturday nights; the menu always has fish, chicken and meat dishes, ranging from $7 to $14.

Getting There & Away
Young's Bus Service (☎ (079) 22 3813) operates a regular bus from Rockhampton to Mt Morgan three times daily on weekdays, twice on Saturday. The one-way fare is $6, and buses leave from outside Duthies Hotel, on the corner of East and William Sts in Rocky.

You can also get to Mt Morgan every day with McCafferty's (☎ (079) 27 2844) – their buses pass through several times a day on the inland route between Rocky and Brisbane. The one-way fare from Rocky is $5.

ROCKHAMPTON TO BARALABA

Myella Farm Stay (☎ (079) 98 1290) is a 1050-hectare Brahman-cross cattle property 125 km south-west of Rockhampton and about 22 km east of Baralaba, the nearest town. Myella is owned by a very friendly and hospitable family who take in travellers who are looking for that 'City Slickers' experience of life on a working property. Guests stay in a simple and breezy old timber farmhouse which has three bedrooms, nine beds, a central living area and a broad, shady verandah. You join the family for home-cooked meals in their house nearby. You can do whatever you want during your stay – join in the cattle mustering or fence building, ride horses, climb the local mountain, or just lounge around on the verandah. Costs for a single/double/triple are $70/60/55 per person per day, which includes all meals and activities; children pay $30 a day, and all rates are cheaper for longer stays. Myella has received some very good reports from travellers.

Getting There & Away

If you're driving, take the Leichhardt Hwy and turn off towards Baralaba, midway between Wowan and Banana. The farm is signposted off the Baralaba Rd, 18 km west of the Leichhardt Hwy.

If you're travelling by bus, take a McCafferty's bus to Dululu at the junction of the Burnett and Leichhardt Hwys – if you ring in advance, the owners will pick you up from there.

YEPPOON (pop 7000)

Yeppoon is a relaxed seaside township 43 km north-east of Rockhampton. It's the main centre on the coast, and although Great Keppel Island is the area's main attraction, Yeppoon has quite good beaches and is a reasonably popular holiday town with a pleasant hinterland (see the following Yeppoon to Byfield section). Boats to Great Keppel leave from Rosslyn Bay, seven km south.

Orientation

The Rockhampton to Yeppoon road finishes at the large Ross Creek Roundabout. If you're driving, turn right at the roundabout to continue on to Rosslyn Bay and Emu Park; if you turn left, an exaggerated S-bend brings you to Anzac Pde, which runs along the Yeppoon waterfront. Yeppoon's town centre is wedged between two small hills. Normanby St, which runs inland from the end of Anzac Pde, is Yeppoon's main street and is lined with shops and eateries. After one block it becomes James St at the end of which is the large and modern Keppel Bay Plaza shopping complex.

South across the Ross Creek are the towns of Cooee Bay and Lammermoor Beach, which are virtually southern suburbs of Yeppoon.

Information

The Capricorn Coast Information Centre (☎ (079) 39 4888), beside the Ross Creek Roundabout, has a good range of info on the Capricorn Coast and Great Keppel Island, and is open daily from 9 am to 5 pm.

Places to Stay

One km north from the centre of town, the *Beachside Caravan Park* (☎ (079) 39 3798) is a neat beachfront caravan park with tent sites from $8 and powered sites from $12.

Up on the hill behind the town, *Barrier Reef Backpackers* (☎ (079) 39 4702), at 30 Queen St, is a relaxed place in a comfortable old timber house. It has all the usual facilities, a large backyard and good views of the town. Four-bed dorms cost $14, doubles $28, and they offer a free pick-up service from Rocky and will drop you at the Rosslyn Bay harbour if you're going to Great Keppel.

There's a string of motels and holiday units along Anzac Pde, opposite the beachfront. The *Surfside Motel* (☎ (079) 39 1272), at No 30, has budget units with kitchenettes from $35/40. At No 32 the *Como Holiday Units* (☎ (079) 39 1213) is a two-storey block of good one and two-bedroom self-contained units which start from $45 a double, plus $10 for each extra person.

Further along the beachfront, on the corner of Normanby and Adelaide Sts, is the *Bayview Towers International* (☎ (079) 39 4500), a tall, modern high-rise motel. All the rooms have good ocean views, and prices range from $68 a double on the second floor to $96 a double on the eighth floor – the higher you go, the more you pay.

On the coast eight km north of Yeppoon, the *Capricorn International Resort* (☎ (079) 39 511 or toll-free 1800 075 902) is a large four-star resort hotel, owned by the Japanese corporation Iwasaki Sangyo Australia. This hotel is very 1980s with its pasty pink colour scheme; it has a huge swimming pool, tennis courts, a gym, and several cafes and eateries including an authentic Japanese restaurant. This place has several different types of accommodation, with rates from $145 to $160 a night for a hotel room and around $200 a night for a suite or self-contained apartment.

The resort also has a great golf course, which is open to the public. The $50-a-round fee includes lunch and a motorised buggy – it's another $20 if you need to hire clubs.

Places to Eat

Most of Yeppoon's eateries are along the adjoining Normanby and James Sts. At 10 Normanby St, *Simply Health* is a small health food store, and straight across the road is *El Dino's*, a coffee lounge by day and a BYO Mexican restaurant by night, with main courses for around $11.

For a counter meal, try the Tide Inn bistro in the *Strand Hotel*, on the corner of Anzac Pde and Normanby Sts.

Across the road from the pub, above KFC, *Thai Ayutthaya* is an up-market Thai restaurant with sea views, a bar and main meals in the $10 to $12 price range.

The *Happy Sun,* at 34 James St, serves up MSG-free Chinese food.

Entertainment

The *Strand Hotel*, on the corner of Anzac Pde and Normanby St, is a popular pub with live bands on Friday, Saturday and Sunday nights. Back on Hill St is the flashier *Bonkers*

disco/nightspot, which is open from Wednesday to Saturday until around 5 am. It usually has DJ music, but also has karaoke sessions and sometimes has live bands on weekends.

The *Yeppoon Cinema* (☎ (079) 39 5411) is upstairs, on the corner of Normanby and Hill Sts.

Getting There & Away

If you're heading for Great Keppel or the reef, some of the ferry operators will transport you between your accommodation and Rosslyn Bay Harbour. Otherwise, Young's Bus Service (☎ (079) 22 3813) and Rothery's (☎ (079) 22 4320) both run buses from Rockhampton to Yeppoon ($10 return) and the rest of the Capricorn Coast, departing from Duthies Hotel, on the corner of Denham and Bolsover Sts in Rocky.

If you're driving to Rosslyn Bay there's a free day car park at the harbour, and the Kempsea lock-up car park (on the main road just north of the harbour turn off) charges $6 a day ($2 for motorcycles) and runs a free bus to and from the harbour.

YEPPOON TO BYFIELD

The coastal hinterland north of Yeppoon is largely undeveloped, and there are a number of state forest parks and one national park in the area. You can't get across to the coast without a 4WD, but there are some good picnic and camping grounds in the state forests, and you can visit a pottery and a historic homestead near the small township of Byfield, 40 km from Yeppoon. There is also an excellent bush retreat and restaurant nearby.

Heading out of Yeppoon, the road follows the coast for a short way before heading inland, with a turn off after four km to the Capricorn International Resort (see Places to Stay in the Yeppoon section). The drive north takes you through the pine plantations of the Byfield State Forest, with turn offs along the way to various other state forest parks and the Upper Stoney Dam. After about 30 km the sealed road ends, and the last section alternates between sealed and unsealed (but well maintained) roads.

Just south of Byfield, there are turn offs to the **Nob Creek Pottery** (two km west), where you can visit the workshop and gallery, and to the **Waterpark Creek Forest Park**. It's two km east from the main road to the creek crossing, beyond which are an attractive picnic area with tables and gas barbecues and a self-registration camping ground. From here, a red dirt road continues through the pine plantations to the **Byfield National Park**, which is an undeveloped area of mostly low coastal scrub. If you have a 4WD, you can continue through the park to the coast – the beach along here is very popular with anglers.

The town of **Byfield** consists of a general store (which sells delicious fruit and coconut slices), a school and a handful of houses. One km north of the town is the historic **Rasberry Creek Homestead**, which was moved here from Shoalwater Bay in 1988. It houses the local library and has a small collection of local history items, documents and photos. The homestead is open on Sunday from 1 to 4 pm, on Tuesday from 3 to 5.30 pm and on Friday from 9.30 to 11.30 am. At other times, if you ring Mary on ☎ (079) 35 1169 she'll come down and show you through.

Places to Stay & Eat

There are camping grounds in several of the state parks in the area.

Signposted off the road a couple of km north of Byfield is the *Ferns Hideaway* (☎ (079) 35 1235), a wonderful bush retreat on a 40-hectare property beside the Waterpark Creek. There are five self-contained cabins and a three-bedroom house here, all in secluded settings, and all quite different – from a two-storey timber cottage to a colonial-style log cabin, with a dash of modern styling. The cabins sleep up to six people and cost from $80 to $100 a night; the house costs $25 for each adult and $12 for each child. There are also some good camp sites down near the creek, which cost $8 per person; firewood and hot showers are provided. This place is very well set up – there are marked walking trails through the property, and you can play tennis, swim in the

pool, paddle canoes down the creek and go horse riding here. There's also a licensed restaurant which is open for lunches on Saturday and Sunday and dinner on Saturday night. Main courses are from $8 to $12 at lunch time and around $15 at dinner, and a solo guitarist keeps diners entertained. You'll need to book.

YEPPOON TO EMU PARK

There are beaches dotted all along the 19-km coast running south from Yeppoon to Emu Park. At **Cooee Bay**, a couple of km from Yeppoon, the annual Australian 'Cooee' Championships are held each August.

Reached by a short side road about seven km south of Yeppoon, **Rosslyn Bay Harbour** is the departure point for trips to Great Keppel and other Keppel Bay islands.

South of Rosslyn Bay are three fine headlands with good views – **Double Head**, **Bluff Point** and **Pinnacle Point**. After Pinnacle Point the road crosses **Causeway Lake**, a saltwater inlet where you can rent canoes and sailboards. Further south at **Emu Park** there are more good views and the 'Singing Ship' memorial to Captain Cook – a series of drilled tubes and pipes which emit whistling or moaning sounds when there's a breeze blowing. Emu Park also has a museum which doubles as a tourist information centre.

The **Koorana Crocodile Farm** is five km off the Emu Park to Rockhampton road. The turn off is 15 km from Emu Park. The farm has hundreds of crocs, and is open daily from 11.30 am, and has 1½-hour tours every day at 1 pm. Entry costs $9 for adults and $4.50 for children.

Places to Stay

There are many possibilities along this stretch of coast, including several caravan parks. Two km south of Yeppoon at Cooee Bay the *Poinciana Tourist Park* (☎ (079) 39 1601) has tent sites from $8, powered sites from $13 and cabins from $28. Further along at Lammermoor Beach just before the turn off to Rosslyn Bay Harbour, *Golden Sands* (☎ (079) 33 6193) has two-bedroom holiday flats opposite the beach from $45.

The *Rosslyn Bay Inn Resort* (☎ (079) 33 6333), a large multi-level accommodation complex at the harbour, has good units starting from $65 a double and from $130 for a family unit, although it's hard to figure out why you would stay here instead of out on Great Keppel.

A couple of km south of the Rosslyn Bay turn off at Mulambin Beach, *Capricorn Palms Holiday Village* (☎ (079) 33 6144) is a modern, well-kept place with tent sites for $12, powered sites for $15 and on-site cabins from $30. Further south, the *Coolwaters Holiday Village* (☎ (079) 39 6102), at Kinka Beach, has tent sites for $11, powered sites at $13, on-site vans from $22, and cabins from $34.

At Emu Park, the *Endeavour Inn Motel* (☎ (079) 39 6777), at 18 Hill St, in the centre of town, has singles/doubles from $38/44, and the *Bell Park Caravan Park* (☎ (079) 39 6202) has tent sites from $6 and powered sites from $12.

GREAT KEPPEL ISLAND
Although it's not actually on the reef, Great Keppel is the equal of most islands up the coast. It's 13 km off shore, and big enough to take a few days to explore. It covers 14 sq km and boasts 18 km of very fine beaches.

The Great Keppel Island Resort, owned by Qantas Airlines, was given a $14 million facelift in 1991 and is now a very popular resort, especially among young families and couples. Keppel is promoted as the 'active island', with a wide range of activities and entertainment to keep guests busy – 'Forget the Rest', as they say.

The good news about Great Keppel is that, unlike many of the resort islands, there are some good budget accommodation alternatives, and it's also one of the cheapest and easiest Queensland islands to reach. Great Keppel is a popular destination for day trips; the resort has a separate section for daytrippers with a small pool, a bar, outdoor tables and umbrellas, a restaurant and a cafe, and there is all sorts of water-sports gear available for hire.

Things to See & Do
Great Keppel's beaches are amongst the best on any of the resort islands. It only takes a short stroll from the main resort area to find your own deserted stretch of white, sandy beach. The water is clear, warm and beautiful, and there is good coral at many points around the island, especially between Great Keppel and Humpy Island to the south. A 30-minute walk around the headland south of the resort brings you to **Monkey Beach** where there's good snorkelling. Another walking trail from the southern end of the airfield takes you to **Long Beach**, perhaps the best of the island's beaches.

There are a number of bushwalking tracks from **Fishermans Beach**, the main beach. The longest, and one of the more difficult, goes across to the lighthouse near **Bald Rock Point** on the far side of the island (2½ hours one way). Some beaches, like **Red Beach** near the lighthouse, are only accessible by boat.

There's a fine **underwater observatory** by Middle Island, close to Great Keppel. A confiscated Taiwanese fishing junk was sunk next to the observatory to provide a haven for fish.

There are two places where you can hire water-sports equipment – use of all non-powered water-sports gear is free for resort guests. The Beach Shed on Putney Beach and Keppel Watersports on Fisherman's Beach both have sailboards, catamarans, motorboats, fishing tackle and snorkelling gear, and they can also take you paragliding or water-skiing. Keppel Reef Scuba Adventures (☎ (079) 39 5022) on Putney Beach offers introductory dives for $60, or, if you're qualified, two dives with all gear supplied for $50. You can also do a five-day diving course for $385.

Organised Cruises
Keppel Tourist Services (☎ (079) 33 6744) runs various cruises aboard the *Reefseeker*. Their island cruise departs daily from Rosslyn Bay at 9.15 am and from Fisherman's Beach at 10 am, and continues on a three-hour cruise around the island,

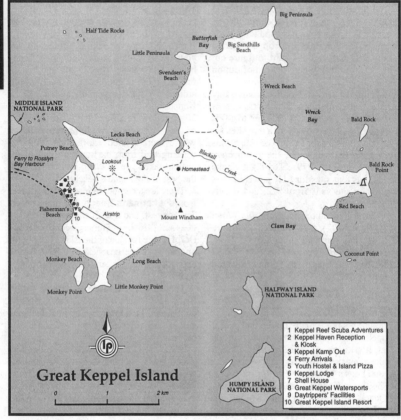

Great Keppel Island

0   1   2 km

1 Keppel Reef Scuba Adventures
2 Keppel Haven Reception
  & Kiosk
3 Keppel Kamp Out
4 Ferry Arrivals
5 Youth Hostel & Island Pizza
6 Keppel Lodge
7 Shell House
8 Great Keppel Watersports
9 Daytrippers' Facilities
10 Great Keppel Island Resort

which includes boom netting, snorkelling and an optional visit to the underwater observatory ($10 extra). You then have the afternoon on the island before returning at 4.30 pm; the cruise costs $35 from Rosslyn Bay or $10 if you're already on the island.

The *Reefseeker* also does inner reef trips on Tuesday and Thursday to Barren Island, departing from Rosslyn Bay at 9.15 am. The cost of $90 ($47 for children) includes lunch, snorkelling gear and a glass-bottomed boat ride; scuba dives are an optional extra.

Every Wednesday, Friday and Sunday, the *Capricat*, a sailing catamaran, does a three-

hour sailing and snorkelling cruise for $20 (departing at either 9.30 am or 12.30 pm, depending on the tides), and a sunset 'booze cruise' for $30 from 5 to 7 pm.

Places to Stay

Camping, Hostels & Motels *Keppel Haven* (☎ (079) 39 1907) (formerly Wapparaburra Haven) has semi-permanent safari tents that sleep up to four people and cost $15 per person. The tents come complete with mattresses, and communal facilities in the tent village include fridges, barbecues and basic kitchen equipment. There are also cabins at

$75 for two people plus $15 for each extra person; the cabins sleep up to six people, have bedding, kitchen and laundry facilities and shared bathrooms. Note that the resort is planning to build new cabins and add en-suites to the existing cabins in the near future – prices will increase accordingly. Ring to find out the latest.

Next door to Keppel Haven is *Keppel Kamp Out* (☎ (079) 39 2131), which is geared to the 18 to 35 age bracket, and has organised activities. The cost of $69 per person per day includes twin-share tents, three meals and activities such as water sports, parties and video nights. A stand-by rate of $49 is sometimes available.

There are some excellent alternatives on the island for the budget traveller, although unfortunately camping beside the beaches is no longer permitted.

The *Great Keppel YHA Hostel* (☎ (079) 39 4341) is quite old and very straightforward, but it's still very popular and is often booked out well in advance. There are two 16-bed dorms at $13, and two eight-bed cabins with their own bathrooms at $15; nonmembers pay $2 extra. The hostel rents snorkelling gear and organises bushwalks and other activities. You can book through either the Rockhampton Youth Hostel (☎ (079) 27 5288) or the YHA office in Brisbane (☎ (07) 3236 1680). The YHA offers members a special deal – for $66 you get one night's accommodation in Rocky, two nights on the island, bus and boat transfers from Rocky to the island, and the three-hour island cruise.

Keppel Lodge (☎ (079) 39 4251) is a pleasant and modern little place with four spacious motel-style units, a large communal lounge and kitchen, and an outdoor barbecue area. Each room sleeps up to five people, and the nightly costs are $80 a double plus $25 for each adult or $12.50 for each child under 12 years old.

Resort The popular Qantas-owned *Great Keppel Island Resort* (☎ (079) 39 5044) is quite stylish and comfortable without being sophisticated. The facilities include squash courts, tennis courts, a couple of swimming pools, a six-hole golf course, and water-sports gear including catamarans and windsurfers; use of these, plus a range of activities including volleyball, archery and aerobics, are included in the tariffs.

There are over 190 units, ranging from the older motel-style Garden and Beachfront Units to the impressively up-market Ocean View Villas. Daily costs are $148/248 for a single/double in the Garden Units, $174/290 in the Beachfront Units, and $206/344 in the Ocean View Villas.

You have the option of taking a three-meals-a-day package for another $55, or paying for meals separately.

Stand-by rates are available if you book three days or less before you arrive – they are roughly half the price of normal rates. Qantas also has a variety of package deals available which include return airfare and accommodation – contact Australian Resorts (☎ 1800 812 525) for details.

Places to Eat
If you want to cook it's best to bring a few basic supplies. Fruit, vegetables, groceries and dairy foods are sold at the reasonably pricey kiosk at *Keppel Haven*, which also does breakfasts and takeaways. Next door, the *Wappa Bar & Bistro* does lunches and evening meals ranging from $10 to $15. In front of the YHA hostel, the friendly *Island Pizza* makes good pizzas, pastas and submarines, eat in or takeaway.

There are several possibilities in the resort area. The *Keppel Cafe* has burgers from $3.50, meat pies, sandwiches etc, and nearby the *Anchorage Char Grill* serves lunches and dinners with grilled steak or fish with salad and chips for $10.50. Daytrippers can also have a buffet lunch in the resort's *Admiral Keppel Restaurant* for $15.

Halfway along Fisherman's Beach, the *Shell House* not only has a shell or two, but also does excellent Devonshire teas. The friendly owner has lived on Keppel for many years. His tropical garden offers a pleasant break from the sun.

Entertainment

The *Anchorage Bar* at the resort is open to all comers every night until 2 am, with live bands from Monday to Saturday and on Sunday afternoon from 1 to 4 pm. The *Wappa Bar & Bistro* is currently undergoing renovations; when it reopens, it will have live entertainment and karaoke nightly until midnight.

Getting There & Away

Air Qantas flies at least twice daily between Rockhampton and Great Keppel; the one-way fare is $73.

Boat Ferries for Great Keppel leave from Rosslyn Bay Harbour on the Capricorn Coast. You can book the ferries through your accommodation or agents in Rockhampton and on the Capricorn Coast. If you're staying at the YHA hostel in Rocky, they have a special deal of $35 for the bus trip, the ferry across and a three-hour island cruise.

Keppel Tourist Services (☎ (079) 33 6744) operates two boats, the *Reefseeker* and the *Spirit of Keppel*. The *Reefseeker* leaves Rosslyn Bay at 9.15 am and returns from Great Keppel at 4.30 pm, and the return fare is $35 with an island cruise included (see Organised Cruises earlier) or $25 without the cruise. The *Spirit of Keppel* leaves Rosslyn Bay at 11.30 am and 3.30 pm, and returns from Great Keppel at 2 and 4.30 pm; it costs $25 return.

Another boat, the *Australis* (☎ (079) 33 6865), leaves Rosslyn Bay at 9 and 11 am and returns from Great Keppel at 9.45 am and 4 pm, and costs $20 return.

OTHER KEPPEL BAY ISLANDS

Great Keppel is only the biggest of the 18 continental islands which are dotted around Keppel Bay, all within 20 km of the coast. It's possible to visit **Middle Island**, with its underwater observatory, or **Halfway** and **Humpy** islands if you're staying on Great Keppel.

Some of the islands are national parks where you can maroon yourself for a few days of self-sufficient camping, while Pumpkin Island is privately owned and has a few cabins. Most of the islands have clean, white beaches and several, notably Halfway, have good fringing coral reefs which are excellent for snorkelling or diving.

Places to Stay

To camp on a national park island, you need to take all your own supplies including water. Numbers of campers allowed on each island are restricted – for example, eight on Middle and six on Miall. You can get information and permits from the QNP&WS office near Rockhampton (☎ (079) 36 0511) or the ranger's office at Rosslyn Bay Harbour (☎ (079) 33 6608).

The second largest of the group and one of the most northerly is **North Keppel Island**. It covers six sq km and is a national park. The most popular camping spot is Considine Beach on the north-west coast, which has well water for washing, and toilets. Take insect repellent.

Other islands with camping grounds include Humpy, Halfway, Miall and Middle.

Just south of North Keppel, tiny **Pumpkin Island** has five cabins (☎ (079) 39 2431) which accommodate five or six people at a cost of $100 to $110 per night per cabin. There's water and solar electricity, and each cabin has a gas stove and fridge, a barbecue and a bathroom with shower. All you need to bring is food and linen. You can also camp on the island for $10 per person – the camping ground has tank water, a shower and toilet, and a fireplace.

Getting There & Away

Keppel Tourist Services (☎ (079) 33 6744), who operates the ferry services from Rosslyn Bay Harbour to Great Keppel Island, also have camping drop-off services on request to the Keppel Bay islands, including Pumpkin, North Keppel, Middle and Humpy islands. You need to book a couple of days in advance; prices start from $120 per person return. Keppel Tourist Services also has day trips to Barren Island on Tuesday and Thursday – see Organised Tours in the Great Keppel Island section for details.

Also operating out of Rosslyn Bay, the

Billfisher does regular charter trips around Keppel Bay on Wednesday and Saturday, and is also available for group charters. They take up to eight people at a cost of $145 per person, which includes lunch, bait and tackle, and snorkelling gear. The same boat also does camping drop-offs to Pumpkin and Humpy and other Keppel Bay islands – contact Bill or Dianne on ☎ 015 760 813 or ☎ (079) 28 0044 for more information.

ROCKHAMPTON TO SARINA

It's almost 300 km from Rockhampton to Sarina, with only a handful of small towns and roadhouses, and a couple of points of interest, between the two. This stretch of highway passes through cattle country and low hills covered with eucalypt forests, and after a while the monotony of the landscape makes it hard to resist the temptation to tread a little more firmly on the accelerator. Every time I've driven along here, the police have had radar patrols at different points along the route, so don't say I didn't warn you.

Near The Caves, a small township 23 km north of Rocky, daily tours are offered through limestone caves – see the Around Rockhampton section for details.

Stanage Bay

50 km north of The Caves, there's a turn off to Stanage Bay. It's 100 km of rough dirt road from here to the tip of the Torilla Peninsula. There are no facilities up here, but this area is popular with anglers.

Marlborough

Marlborough, 102 km north-west of Rockhampton, is a quiet little one-pub town just east of the highway. It has a railway station, lots of cattle yards, a takeaway food shop, a garage and a small public pool, as well as the interesting **Marlborough Historical Museum**. This neat little museum has several sections, featuring pottery, personal effects, a bottle collection, old sulkies and carriages and a shed full of antiquated farming equipment. According to records in the museum, the famous bushranger Frank

Gardiner spent a night in Marlborough when he was captured in 1864, before being taken to Rockhampton and tried. The museum is open most days, but doesn't advertise set hours.

Places to Stay & Eat The 100-year-old *Marlborough Hotel* (☎ (079) 35 6103) is a straightforward little yellow timber pub. Back in 1907, if you wanted a drink here you had a choice of rum, or rum and milk, and the menu offered a selection of roast goat or roast goat. Nowadays the selection is a little more varied – you can get the usual bistro meals such as burgers, steak and crumbed fish. Meals range from $7 to $10 and lunch and dinner are served every day except Sunday. The pub also has a couple of clean and simple rooms which open out onto the front verandah – singles/twins cost $19/30.

On the west side of the highway, the *Marlborough Motel & Van Park* (☎ (079) 35 6112) is a big, modern accommodation complex with tent sites for $5 per person, on-site vans for $25 a double and motel units with good views at $42/48 for singles/ doubles.

Marlborough to Sarina

At **Clairview**, about 100 km north of Marlborough, the highway meets the coast and you get a tantalising but brief glimpse of the blue ocean waters. Clairview itself is just a string of old houses along the foreshore, but the beach is quite nice, and, outside the stinger season, you can swim here and bask on the beach while enjoying the views across to numerous off-shore islands. There's also a boat ramp here, so if you happen to have a tinnie hitched to the rear of your car, you could even head across for a visit. The *Golden Mermaid Caravan Park* is pretty run down, but has a good setting right on the foreshore.

Twenty-eight km north of Clairview is **Carmila**, which has a roadhouse with a caravan park attached. There's also a 24-hour Ampol roadhouse on the highway, midway between Carmila and Sarina.

The **Cape Palmerston National Park**, a

small coastal park, is off the Bruce Hwy about 32 km south of Sarina. There doesn't seem to be a signpost marking the turn off, although maybe I blinked and missed it. The park is only accessible to 4WD vehicles. There are basic camping facilities only, and the park features long sandy beaches, inland lagoons and Melaleuca forests. See the Whitsunday Coast chapter for details of the area north of here.

Capricorn Hinterland

The Capricorn Hwy runs inland from Rockhampton, virtually along the Tropic and across the central Queensland highlands to Barcaldine, from where you can continue west and north-west along the Landsborough Hwy to meet the Townsville to Mt Isa road.

The area was first opened up by miners chasing gold and copper around Emerald, and sapphires around Anakie, but cattle, grain crops and coal provide its main living today. Carnarvon, south of Emerald, and the Blackdown Tableland, south-east of Blackwater, are two of Queensland's most spectacular and interesting national parks.

The Gemfields region, around the towns of Sapphine and Rubyvale, is a fascinating area to visit and explore, and you can fossick for valuable gemstones here.

Several of the massive open-cut coal mines in the area give free tours lasting about 1½ hours; you generally need to book ahead.

ROCKHAMPTON TO EMERALD
It's 270 km from Rockhampton to Emerald. On the way, you can take an interesting detour to the spectacular Blackdown Tableland National Park, and visit the coal-mining centre of Blackwater.

Blackdown Tableland National Park
The Blackdown Tableland is a spectacular sandstone plateau which rises suddenly out of the flat plains of central Queensland to a height of 600 metres. The Tableland is a

northern extension of the escarpment country that includes the more famous Carnarvon Gorge. Blackdown is definitely worth a visit, and features stunning panoramas, great bushwalks to waterfalls and lookout points, Aboriginal rock art, eucalypt forests, creeks and waterfalls, and several unique species of flora including the Blackdown stringybark and Blackdown macrozamia. If you have time, there's also a good camping ground here.

The turn off to the park is signposted from the Capricorn Hwy, 11 km west of Dingo and 40 km east of Blackwater. A reasonably good dirt and gravel road takes you south for about 15 km to the base of the tableland. For the next seven km the road is a very steep, winding climb, and the red gravel surface can be incredibly slippery – so take it slowly! The access road can be unsafe in wet weather, and is not suitable for caravans at any time.

At the top of the climb you come to the spectacular **Horseshoe Lookout**, with picnic tables, barbecues and toilets beside the car park. Walking trails also start from here to **Two Mile Falls** (2.2 km), **Sunset Lookout** (500 metres) and **Peregrine Lookout** (1.3 km).

Further on is the spacious camping ground at **Mimosa Creek**, with toilets, water and fireplaces. Bring a gas stove for cooking and to boil drinking water. The camping ground is sometimes booked out during school holidays – sites can be booked up to 12 months in advance through the QNP&WS rangers at Dingo (☎ (079) 86 1964).

Several other walking trails start from the camping ground. Eight km south of the camping ground is the beginning of the steep 1.3 km trail to **Rainbow Falls**, which has a lovely rock gorge and good swimming holes. There's also a 4WD-only loop road which takes you to the **Charlevue Lookout** and the start of the walking trail to **Stony Creek Falls**.

Blackwater (pop 6700)
Blackwater is one of Queensland's major

coal-mining centres, with half a dozen large mines in the vicinity of the town. Rail yards and coal-shipping facilities line the southern side of the highway, while motels, road-houses and eateries line its northern side.

The **Frank Tutungi Memorial Park**, on the highway west of the centre, flies a collection of 37 flags representing the different nationalities of people who have worked in local mines. The park is dominated by a huge Olympic-torch-shaped water tower, and has picnic facilities. Beside the park, the **Black-water Community Pool** is a good place for a refreshing dip.

You can take a guided tour of the huge **Blackwater Open-cut Mine** (☎ (079) 82 5166), 20 km south of the town, on Wednesday at 10 am. Tours leave from the mine site, and you need to ring in advance to book.

Facilities The Shell Roadhouse on the highway is open 24 hours a day. If you turn down Arthur St beside the Ampol service station, and turn left at the end, you'll come to The Town Centre, a large modern shopping plaza with banks, supermarkets and shops.

Places to Stay The *Bottle Tree Motel & Caravan Park* (☎ (079) 82 5611), on the highway on the western outskirts, has motel units from $39/49 for singles/doubles, tent sites from $8, powered sites from $10 and on-site vans from $22.

The *Black Diamond Motel* (☎ (079) 82 5944), on the highway in the centre of town, is a good motel with a pool and singles/doubles from $50/65.

Places to Eat There are a couple of cafes and roadhouses along the highway dishing up typically bleak fast food. There's also a *Red Rooster* where you can get fast chicken. Next door, *Mama Rosa's Pizzas* is a small pizza and pasta joint with good eat-in or takeaway meals and four small tables at the front. The Black Diamond Motel has a licensed restaurant plus an open-air char-grill beside the pool.

EMERALD (pop 6500)
At the junction of the Gregory and Capricorn Hwys, Emerald is the gateway town of the Capricorn Hinterland region. Established back in 1879 as a railway siding, Emerald has grown into a major centre for the surrounding mining and agricultural industries.

Most of the town's older buildings were destroyed in a series of disastrous fires in 1936, 1940, 1954 and 1968. One notable exception is the fine old **Emerald Railway Station**, on Clermont St in the centre of town, built in 1900 and restored in 1987. The rest of the town has a modern, progressive appearance, with several large shopping centres and clusters of new housing estates.

Information & Facilities
The Central Highlands Tourist Information Centre (☎ (079) 82 4142), at the western end of Clermont St, is open daily from 10 am to noon and from 3 to 5 pm.

The Shell Roadhouse, on Clermont St, is open 24 hours a day. Oates Engineering (☎ (079) 82 2200), in Hicks St, is the local RACQ depot.

Orientation
The Capricorn Hwy (Clermont St) runs east-west along the southern side of the town centre. Egerton St, which runs parallel with Clermont St one block north, is the main shopping centre.

The Gregory Hwy (Hospital Rd) intersects with Clermont St in the centre of town, and heads north out of town towards Clermont.

Things to See & Do
The **Emerald Pioneer Cottage & Museum**, in Centenary Dve, has a collection of historic buildings including the town's first church and gaol. During summer it is open on Sunday, Tuesday and Friday from 3 to 4 pm; for the rest of the year it is open Saturday from 9 am to noon and other days from 2 to 4 pm. Entry costs $2 for adults and is free for children.

The very pleasant **Botanic Gardens** are

on Clermont St, beside the Nogoa River, and have walking trails and picnic and barbecue facilities.

Places to Stay

On the corner of Clermont and Opal Sts, the *Karinya Caravan Park* (☎ (079) 82 2268) has tent sites at $10 and park cabins starting from $32. Almost opposite the old railway station, the *Emerald Hotel* (☎ (079) 82 1810) has pub rooms at $20/30 for singles/doubles. Breakfast will cost another $4.50 for continental or $8 for cooked.

The *Emerald Hostel* (☎ (079) 82 4188), opposite the racecourse, on Hospital Rd, has air-con single rooms for backpackers and workers costing $12 a night.

If you're after a budget motel, the *A & A Lodge Motel* (☎ (079) 82 2355), on Clermont St in the centre of town, has units from $45/52.

One block north of Clermont St, on the corner of Opal and Egerton Sts, the *Emerald Meteor Motel* (☎ (079) 82 1166) has good modern units from $65/75, and a licensed steak restaurant.

Places to Eat

The *Steakhouse Restaurant*, on the corner of Opal and Egerton Sts, has good steaks, while the *Emerald Memorial Club* across Opal St has excellent bistro-style meals.

There are three cafes along Clermont St, as well as three pubs serving counter meals and a *Red Rooster*. Beside the *Emerald Star Hotel*, *Pantha Pizza & Kebabs* does takeaway pizzas and kebabs.

There are more eateries heading north along Hospital Rd, including a *KFC* and the huge *Maraboon Tavern*, with several bars and restaurants.

Getting There & Away

McCafferty's (☎ (079) 82 2755) has a terminal at 115 Clermont St. Their buses pass through daily on the Rockhampton to Longreach run. You can also get here on the twice-weekly *Spirit of the Outback* train, which runs from Rocky to Longreach.

AROUND EMERALD

There are free tours of the **Gregory Coal Mine** (☎ (079) 82 8200), 50 km north-east of Emerald, every Tuesday and Thursday at 1 pm.

Queensland's second-largest artificial lake, **Lake Maraboon**, is 18 km south-west of Emerald. Created by the construction of the Fairbairn Dam in 1972, the lake provides irrigation for surrounding farms and mines, as well as recreational facilities for the town. There's a boat ramp and attractive picnic areas at the lake, and the *Sunrover Resort Caravan Park* (☎ (079) 82 3677) has tent sites from $10, on-site vans from $16, and cabins from $40, as well as a kiosk and restaurant. The MV *Beachlander* offers sunset cruises on the lake.

CAPELLA (pop 870)

Midway between Emerald and Clermont, the township of Capella has the **Capella Pioneer Village**, set in a historic 1869 homestead building with an interesting collection of memorabilia and machinery. The village is open on Tuesday and Sunday from 10 am to 4 pm or by appointment (ring ☎ (079) 84 9311); entry costs $1.

Based in Capella, Leichhardt Tours (☎ (079) 84 9224) offers trail rides and overnight horse-riding tours to the Peak Range area for groups of four to 10 people. Their overnight tours cost from $70 per person for one day, or $100 per day for two or more days, and include all meals and camping gear. They also do 4WD tours of the Central Highlands for four to six people costing $70 per person per day.

CLERMONT (pop 2700)

Just over 100 km north of Emerald is Clermont and the huge Blair Athol open-cut coal mine, Australia's largest exporter of steaming coal with a production level of 11 million tonnes a year. Clermont is Queensland's oldest tropical inland town, founded on wealth from copper, gold, sheep and cattle. It was the scene of goldfield race riots in the 1880s, and a military takeover of the town occurred in 1891 after a confrontation between striking sheep shearers and non-union labour.

In December 1916 a flood virtually destroyed the town and claimed 65 lives. The **Flood Memorial**, a concrete 'tree stump' in Drummond St, has an indicator showing the high water mark during the flood.

The **Clermont Museum**, near the junction of the Gregory and the Peak Downs highways about three km north of the centre, has an interesting collection of relics and memorabilia, a historic slab timber hut and old machinery.

Free tours of the **Blair Athol Mine** (☎ (079) 83 1866) depart from the mine office at 38 Jellico St every Tuesday at 9 am. You need to ring in advance to book.

Places to Stay
At 1 Haig St the *Clermont Caravan Park* (☎ (079) 83 1927) has tent sites from $8, powered sites from $12 and on-site vans from $25. The *Clermont Motor Inn* (☎ (079) 83 3133), on the corner of Box and Capella Sts, has singles/doubles from $55/60.

CLERMONT TO MACKAY
The 274-km-long Peak Downs Hwy runs north-east from Clermont to Mackay. There isn't much of interest for travellers along this route – most people will be using it to cut across to/from the coast.

The only towns along this route with shops and fuel are **Coppabella**, 133 km north-east of Clermont, and **Nebo**, 92 km south-west of Mackay. Nebo also has an RACQ depot, the B&S Service Centre (☎ (079) 50 5150).

The landscape along the first section of the route, from Clermont to Moranbah, is dominated by the rugged volcanic outcrops of the **Peak Range Mountains**.

Purpose-built as a coal-mining centre in 1971, **Moranbah** (pop 6500) services three large coal mines – Peak Downs, Goonyella and Riverside. Bus tours of the Goonyella (☎ (079) 41 3333) and Peak Downs (☎ (079) 41 6233) mines depart from Moranbah's town square at 10 am on Tuesday and Thursday. There are a couple of caravan parks in town, and the *Black Nugget Hotel* (☎ (079) 41 7185), in Griffin St, has motel-style units with singles/doubles from $60/75. Moranbah is 13 km north-west of the highway; the turn off is 97 km north-east of Clermont.

GEMFIELDS
West of Emerald, about 270 km inland from Rockhampton, the gemfields around Anakie, Sapphire, Rubyvale and Willows Gemfield are known for their sapphires, zircons, amethysts, rubies, topaz, jasper, and even diamonds and gold.

The gemfields are the world's richest sapphire deposits, and it is still possible to find valuable gems in the area. In 1993 a couple from Mt Isa found a sapphire worth $300,000, and back in 1979 a 14-year-old boy found the 2000-carat Centenary Sapphire here, which is currently worth more than $1 million.

If you're just passing through, there are a couple of fossicking parks in the area which sell buckets of dirt which you can wash and sieve by hand – 'doing a bucket' is great fun and a good way to learn how to identify raw sapphires.

Every bucket of dirt contains at least a few sapphire chips, and you might even find something worthwhile. There are also several tourist mines that will take you on underground or surface tours.

If you catch the bug and decide to go fossicking, you need a 'fossicking licence', sold from the Emerald Courthouse or from one of the general stores and post offices on the gemfields. Licenses are valid for one, six or twelve months – the one-month version costs $5 for one person or $7 for a family. You can buy permits for bush camping from the same places – these cost $2 per night, and allow you to pitch a tent anywhere in the fields. Basic fossicking equipment includes sieves, a pick and shovel, water and a container. You can bring this with you, or hire it when you arrive.

The gemfields attract a fascinating diversity of characters – adventurers, alternative lifestylers, battlers and travellers, all hoping to strike it lucky. The collection of dwellings scattered around the area is equally diverse – stone and timber cottages, ancient caravans and tumble-down shacks, even a few substantial houses belonging to the more prosperous prospectors. The most popular times to visit are the drier, cooler months from April to September, but you can come here at any time of year.

Festivals

Two major annual festivals are held in the area – the Gemfields Ironman Wheelbarrow Derby every June and the Gemfest Festival held in August, which features exhibitions of gems, jewellery, mining and fossicking equipment, art and craft markets, and a variety of entertainment.

Getting There & Away

You can get to Anakie on a McCafferty's bus or on the *Spirit of the Outback* train. From there you'd need to get a lift up to Sapphire or Rubyvale, although a couple of the accommodation places might pick you up if you ring and book in advance.

Rubyvale (pop 720)

Rubyvale is the main centre for the gemfields, but don't expect any bright lights or hustle and bustle. It's a small, ramshackle place with a scattered collection of dwellings and a few gem shops and galleries.

The town centre is basically the intersection of Goanna Flat Rd and Keilambete Rd. On one side of the intersection is the Rubyvale post office, which has a Commonwealth Bank agency. Across the road is **Capricornia Gems & Crafts**, a general store and coffee shops that sells groceries, takeaway meals and fossicking licenses, and has mining gear available for hire. Rubyvale is 18 km north of Anakie. From here, it's another 62 km of often slippery dirt road to Capella on the Gregory Hwy.

Mine Tours & Gem Galleries There are a couple of commercial mines and galleries around Rubyvale which open up to tourists. One of the best of these is the **Silk 'n' Sapphire Mine**, on Heritage Rd, 1.5 km north of town.

Run by Dave and Fran Dougall, former West Australian gold miners, this place offers hands-on adventure tours down a 17-metre vertical shaft to a working mine. You get to work the mine face with an electric jackhammer, shovel and barrow before taking your diggings up to the surface for a mechanical wash.

This tour isn't for the faint-hearted and the work can be strenuous stuff, but it's great fun and a realistic experience of life underground. Tours cost $30 for two hours, $60 for a half day and $90 for a full day. Half and full-day tours both start daily at 8 am. There's

---

Darkie Garnet

Gemfields Ironman Wheelbarrow Derby is held every year in June. This gruelling race, which was first held in 1980, requires contestants to push a wheelbarrow containing a pick, a shovel and a 10 kg rock from Anakie to Sapphire, where they throw out the boulder and replace it with sand before continuing on to Rubyvale – a total distance of over 18 km. The winner pockets $1000 cash and collects two trophies and $1000 worth of sapphire jewellery.

The Derby was conceived in remembrance of local character Darkie Garnet. Legend has it that Darkie arrived in the gemfields on foot early this century, pushing a wheelbarrow containing all of his worldly possessions. Before long he struck it rich with sapphires, but after over-indulging in the good life he soon found he was broke again. Over the next few years, Darkie made and lost his fortune several times over, before eventually leaving the gemfields on foot, pushing a wheelbarrow containing all his worldly possessions... ■

also a small shopfront here selling gems, jewellery and Fran's hand-painted silks.

Also on Heritage Rd is the **Miners' Heritage Walk-in Mine**. Half-hour tours of the tunnels of the underground mine here cost $5 for adults and $2 for children. There's also an underground showroom with gems and jewellery on sale and gem-cutting services. Up on the surface, you can buy a bucket of wash for $4. The mine is open every day from 9 am to 5 pm.

The **Miners Cottage** is owned by Margaret and Sheila, two former Melburnians who came here on holidays in 1994 and decided to ditch the rat race and stay. Their small timber cottage has a collection of crafts, jewellery and gems on sale, and you can do a two-hour surface tour which involves filling a barrow with dirt from the creek bed and learning how to sieve, wash and sort it. Tours cost $25 per barrow, and up to three people can work one barrow. The cottage is signposted off Goanna Flat Rd a couple of hundred metres from the centre.

The **Bobby Dazzler Mine**, just south of the centre, with 20-minute underground mine tours costing $3 for adults and $1.50 for children, is also open daily from 9 am to 5 pm. There's also a jumbled little museum and jewellery shop here.

Places to Stay & Eat The not-terribly-impressive *Rubyvale Caravan Park* (☎ (079) 85 4118), on Goanna Flat Rd, has tent sites from $8 and on-site vans from $20.

The *Gemfields Motel* (☎ (079) 85 4150), in Keilambete Rd just up from the post office, has accommodation in transportable cabins at $28/38 for singles/doubles, which includes a light breakfast. The cabins are tiny and cramped, but at least they have air-con – otherwise I'd be tempted to call them cell-like. There's also an old-fashioned, low-ceilinged dining room and bar here serving breakfast, lunch and dinner daily – not much charm, lots of character. You can get a sandwich for $3.50 or a steak or a roast for $10 to $12.

Bedford Gardens Caravan Park & Holiday Units (☎ (079) 85 4175), in Vane Tempest Rd one block back from the post

office, has five good self-contained units which sleep up to eight people and cost $45/50 for singles/doubles plus $5 for each extra person. You can also camp here at $9 for a tent site or $10 for a powered site – there are showers, a barbecue area and a campers' kitchen with a fridge and stove.

Sapphire (pop 710)
Ten km north of Anakie, Sapphire has a petrol station, a post office, and a few houses scattered around the hillside. It also has one of the best accommodation places in the area, and a couple of fossicking parks.

Fossicking Parks At **Pat's Gems**, one km north of Sapphire, buckets of dirt cost $4 each or you can have six for $20. You can hand-sieve and sort the dirt outside, and if you find anything worthwhile they offer a gem-cutting and setting service. They also have fossicking gear available for hire.

The **Ransom Mine**, on the northern outskirts of Sapphire, has a kiosk, a cutting room and jewellery on sale. You can buy a bucket of dirt for $4 and wash it by hand, or a tractor-scoop of dirt for $30 and put it through the mechanical pulsator before hand washing it.

Places to Stay About a km out of Sapphire, on the road to Rubyvale, *Sunrise Cabins & Camping* (☎ (079) 85 4281) has simple timber and stone cabins that sleep from one to six people, with communal toilets, shower blocks, and a cooking and dining cabin. The nightly cost of the cabins is $12/25 for singles/doubles, $30 for up to four people or $38 for six people, and there are a couple of self-contained cabins at $32 a double. You need to bring your own linen. If you have a tent, camp sites cost $9. You can get information, licences and maps, and hire fossicking gear here.

Anakie (pop 400)
One km south of the highway, Anakie consists of not much more than a pub, a railway station and a caravan park.

Between the town and the highway is the

Gemfields Information Centre (☎ (079) 85 4525), which sells fossicking licences and has mud maps of the gemfields.

The *Anakie Hotel* (☎ (079) 85 4100) has motel-style units at $20/40 for singles/doubles, some with air-con, and serves bistro meals at nights. Steaks, chicken and seafood dishes are in the $7 to $10 range. They also sell pizzas and snacks during the day.

The *Anakie Gemfields Caravan Park* (☎ (079) 85 4142) has tent sites for $10 and on-site vans for $22.

Willows Gemfields (pop 290)
This gemfield has limited facilities and is more of a place for the hard-core fossicker. To get there, turn off the Capricorn Hwy 27 km west of Anakie, and it's another 11 km south to the township.

There are two caravan parks here, both with similar facilities. The *Willows Gemfields Caravan Park* (☎ (079) 85 5128) and the *Gem Air Village Caravan Park* (☎ (079) 85 5124) both have sites for around $10 and on-site vans for around $25.

SPRINGSURE (pop 730)
Springsure, 66 km south of Emerald, has an attractive setting with a backdrop of granite mountains and surrounding sunflower fields (the sunflowers are used to produce oil and seed). There's a small **historical museum** by the windmill as you enter town from the south. The **Virgin Rock**, an outcrop of Mt Zamia on the northern outskirts, was named after early settlers claimed to have seen the image of the Virgin Mary in the rock face.

Ten km south-west at Burnside is the **Old Rainworth Fort**, built following the Wills Massacre of 1861 when Aborigines killed 19 Whites on Cullin-La-Ringo Station northwest of Springsure.

Places to Stay
The *Springsure Roadhouse & Caravan Park* (☎ (079) 84 1418), on the south side of town, has tent sites for $6 and on-site vans for $25. The *Springsure Zamia Motel* (☎ (079) 84 1455), on Charles St, has units from $40/48 for singles/doubles.

ROLLESTON
Rolleston, on the Dawson Hwy 70 km southeast of Springsure, is the northern turn off for Carnarvon National Park. The town has a couple of service stations, and Rolleston Motors (☎ (079) 84 3102) is the local RACQ depot. There's a basic caravan park, and the *Rolleston Hotel* (☎ (079) 84 3288) has motel-style units at $40/48.

CARNARVON NATIONAL PARK
Rugged Carnarvon National Park, in the middle of the Great Dividing Range, features dramatic gorge scenery and many Aboriginal rock paintings and carvings. The national park has several sections, but the impressive Carnarvon Gorge is the one that most people see as the others are pretty inaccessible.

Carnarvon Gorge is stunning, partly because it's an oasis surrounded by drier plains and partly due to its scenic variety, which includes sandstone cliffs, moss gardens, deep pools, and rare palms and ferns. There's also lots of fauna. Aboriginal art can be viewed at three main sites – **Balloon Cave**, the **Art Gallery**, and **Cathedral Cave**.

From Rolleston to Carnarvon Gorge, the road is bitumen for 20 km and unsealed for 75 km. From Roma via Injune and Wyseby, the road is good bitumen for about 200 km then unsealed and fairly rough for the last 45 km. After rain, both roads become impassable.

Three km into the Carnarvon Gorge section, there's an information centre and a scenic camping ground. The main walking track starts beside the information centre and follows the Carnarvon Creek through the gorge, with detours to various points of interest such as the Moss Garden (3.6 km from the camping ground), Ward's Canyon (4.8 km), the Art Gallery (5.6 km) and Cathedral Cave (9.3 km). You should allow *at least* half a day for a visit here, and you must bring lunch and water with you as there are no shops!

To get into the more westerly and rugged **Mt Moffatt** section of Carnarvon National Park, there are two unsealed roads from Injune: one through Womblebank Station, the other via Westgrove Station. There are no through roads from Mt Moffatt to Carnarvon Gorge or to the other remote sections of the park – Salvator Rosa and Ka Ka Mundi. Mt Moffatt has some beautiful scenery, diverse vegetation and fauna, and **Kenniff Cave**, an important Aboriginal archaeological site. It's believed Aborigines lived here as long as 19,000 years ago.

Places to Stay
Camping You need a permit to camp at the main National Parks camping ground, and it's advisable to book by phoning the Carnarvon Gorge rangers (☎ (079) 84 4505). Camping permits cost $3 per person per night. Wood for cooking is scarce, so bring your own gas cooking equipment.

You can also camp at Big Ben camping area, 500 metres upstream from Cathedral Cave – a 10-km walk up the gorge – and walkers can bush camp anywhere in the park beyond Big Ben. Again, permits are required.

In the Mt Moffatt section, camping with a permit is allowed at six sites but you need to be completely self-sufficient, and a 4WD is advisable; phone the Mt Moffatt rangers for details (☎ (076) 26 3581).

Self-Contained Cabins A couple of properties near the park have self-contained cabins available. *Early Storms* (☎ (079) 84 4564), a cattle station which is off the main approach road 14 km before the Carnarvon Gorge section, has a large open-plan cabin that sleeps up to eight people. The nightly cost is $50 for up to five people, plus $10 for each extra person; all you need to bring is linen and food.

Lodge The *Oasis Lodge* (☎ (079) 84 4503), near the entrance to the Carnarvon Gorge section of the park, offers safari cabins from $150 a night per person, including all meals

and organised activities. From December to March, the cost is $96 per person, not including activities. There's a general store with fuel.

INJUNE (pop 400)
Injune is the southern gateway to the Carnarvon National Park. You can continue along the Carnarvon Developmental Rd to the turn off to the Carnarvon Gorge section of the park, 110 km north, or turn off here and take the unsealed road which leads 140-km north-west into the Mt Moffat section of the park.

The town has a pub, a motel and a caravan park. The Carnarvon Gateway Service Station (☎ (076) 26 1279), which is the local RACQ depot, is open every day from around 7 am to 7 pm (from 8 am on Sunday). The *Injune Caravan Park* (☎ (076) 26 1222) has tent sites for $8, and the friendly *Injune Motel* (☎ (076) 26 1328) has motel units from $40/45.

ROLLESTON TO BANANA – THE DAWSON HIGHWAY
Thirty km east of Rolleston, the *Planet Downs Station* (☎ (079) 84 3167) is a working cattle station with luxurious accommodation at $460/720 for singles/doubles, including all meals, tours and activities. About 150 km east of Rolleston is the coal-mining centre of **Moura**. The town holds an infamous place in Queensland's mining history, having been the site of three of Queensland's most tragic mining disasters. In September 1975, 13 miners were killed; in July 1986, 12 miners were killed; and in the most recent accident in August 1994, 11 miners were killed.

A simple brass memorial, with a statue of a mine worker, stands on the main road opposite the post office. Moura has a couple of motels, a pub and a caravan park. The *Burradoo Motel* (☎ (079) 97 1588), which is on the Dawson Hwy on the east side of town, has singles/doubles from $42/50. It's another 19 km from Moura to Banana.

BANANA TO MILES – THE LEICHHARDT HIGHWAY

It's a fairly uneventful 280 km south along the Leichhardt Hwy from Banana to Miles.

Banana has a caravan park and a service station. The *Cooper Downs Cattle Station* (☎ (079) 96 5276), 37 km north-east of Banana, is a working cattle property that has up-market accommodation at $180/300 for singles/doubles, which includes all meals and activities such as horse riding and 4WD tours. For similar accommodation see Myella Farm Stay under Baralaba earlier in this chapter.

It's 59 km from Banana down to **Theodore**, a neat and unexceptional town one km east of the highway. It was built during the 1930s to house workers from the local irrigation projects and has the appearance of being a planned town, with its wide streets and central plantations. The **Dawson Folk Museum** in Second Ave has an impressive collection of memorabilia and local history items. It opens by appointment – ring ☎ (079) 93 1686 or enquire at the nearby pub. The *Hotel Theodore* (☎ (079) 93 1244), a simple two-storey white pub on The Boulevard, has rooms upstairs with shared bathrooms costing $22/34 for singles/doubles, budget motel units at $30/42 and newer units at $40/55. You can also stay in the former workers' barracks across the road – a bunk bed costs $15. There's also a caravan park beside the town's small swimming pool.

Forty km south of Theodore is the **Isla Gorge National Park**; a 1.5-km gravel road leads off the highway to the **Isla Gorge Lookout** where there is a small self-registration camping ground and a picnic area. The lookout has 180° views over a somewhat eerie landscape of eroded gorges and escarpments, and a rough walking track leads from the car park across a narrow saddle of rock for about 500 metres, with gorges dropping away on either side of the track.

Taroom is 95 km south of Theodore, on the banks of the Dawson River. Ludwig Leichhardt passed this way on his expedition of 1844, carving his initials into a coolibah tree which still stands in the centre of town. There's a stone memorial to Leichhardt in the small park opposite the Ford dealer on the main street, with brass plaques giving details about the man and his expeditions. The town's small **historical society museum** is in Kelman St, and there's a very pleasant public golf course on the outskirts of town. The *Cattle Camp Motel* (☎ (076) 27 3412), on Taroom St, has units from $40/50 for singles/doubles. The *Leichhardt Hotel-Motel* (☎ (076) 27 3137) is a modern timber pub with motel units from $36/42 and counter meals ranging from $5 to $12 – they serve lunch and dinner daily (no meals Sunday nights). There's also a small caravan park one km north of the centre.

Wandoan, a small township just off the highway 59 km north of Miles, is dominated by a cluster of huge concrete grain silos. The town has a cafe, a caravan park and a pub. See the Darling Downs chapter for details of Miles and surrounds.

About 45 km south of Wandoan (and 20 km north of Miles) and off the Leichhardt Hwy, is *Possum Park* (☎ (076) 27 1651), a 280-hectare bushland property that was a RAAF base and ammunition store during WWII. About 10 years ago, David and Julie Hinds converted the old underground bunkers and admin buildings into a unique accommodation complex. It's a friendly and peaceful place to stay, with a good range of accommodation, walking trails, games rooms, a campers' kitchen, amenities blocks, laundry facilities etc. The bunkers are now simple, self-contained guest units which cost $40 a double and $10 for extras, or there are three former troop-train carriages which also cost $40 a double. Tent sites cost $4 per person per night and caravan sites are $10 a double.

BILOELA (pop 5000)

Biloela at the junction of the Dawson and Burnett highways is a modern commercial centre for the surrounding agricultural, pastoral and coal-mining industries.

The town has a couple of points of interest.

Greycliffe Homestead, built from slab timber around 1870, was relocated to the corner of Gladstone Rd and Lawrence St from Greycliffe Station north of Biloela. It is listed by the National Trust and is open by appointment – ring ☎ (079) 92 1121. You can also take a tour of the huge **Callide B Power Station** 18 km east of town – check with the information centre.

Orientation & Information
The town centre is on the north side of Gladstone Rd (the Dawson Hwy). You'll find most of the banks, shops and the post office along Kariboe and Callide Sts, on the east side of the railway line.

The small Tourist Information Centre (☎ (079) 92 2405), beside the Shell service station, on the corner of Gladstone Rd and Callide St in the centre of town, is open on weekdays from 9 am to 5 pm and most Saturday from 9 am to noon.

Places to Stay
Biloela's accommodation options include half a dozen motels and two caravan parks. The *Boomerang Caravan Park* (☎ (079) 92 1815) is on Dunn St, just across the railway line from the town centre, and has tent sites from $10 and five on-site cabins from $25 a double. The *Apollo Motor Inn* (☎ (079) 92 1122), on the corner of Gladstone Rd and Rainbow St, is a good modern motel with a pool, bar and restaurant, and singles/doubles from $48/54. It's the one with the cute little windmill out front.

Whitsunday Coast

This chapter covers the coastal strip from Sarina to Bowen, as well as the corresponding inland areas. Mackay is the major town in the region, while the Whitsunday Islands are the major point of interest for travellers.

Accordingly, the chapter is split into two sections: the area around Mackay, which includes the wonderful Eungella National Park and numerous off-shore islands such as Brampton, Carlisle, Newry and Rabbit; and the Whitsunday area, which includes the islands themselves as well as the mainland towns and access points for the Whitsundays.

Activities

There are trips to the outer Barrier Reef from Mackay, as well as a huge range of boat trips on offer in the Whitsundays. For bushwalkers, the Eungella National Park is a highlight; Cape Hillsborough National Park and Brampton Island also have some excellent walks.

There are a few good golf courses in this area, including those at Mackay and the Laguna

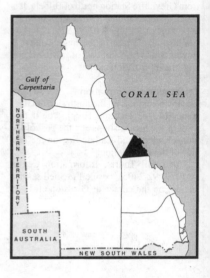

The Whitsundays are a Mecca for sailors

Quays Resort. Lindeman Island, South Molle Island, and Brampton Island also have courses.

See the Whitsunday section for info on more activities in the region.

Getting There & Away

Air Mackay has a major domestic airport, and Ansett and Qantas both have regular flights to all the major centres. Brampton Island also has its own airport, and Qantas flies between Mackay and Brampton.

If you're heading for the Whitsundays, Ansett has frequent flights to Hamilton Island, from where there are transfers to all the other islands. Qantas flies into Proserpine on the mainland – from there, you can take a charter flight to the islands or a bus to Airlie Beach or Shute Harbour, just south of Airlie Beach.

There's also the Whitsunday Airport, a small airfield near Airlie Beach with regular services to the islands. Lindeman Island also has its own airstrip.

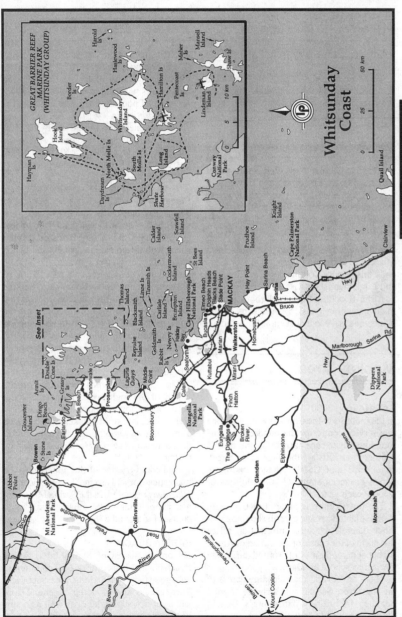

WHITSUNDAY COAST

Whitsunday Coast

Bus The major bus companies have regular services along the Bruce Hwy with stops at all the major towns. They also make the detour off the highway from Proserpine to Airlie Beach.

There are no bus services from Mackay to Eungella National Park, although one of the local tour operators has a drop-off service if you want to stay overnight.

Train The only passenger-carrying railway line in the region is the main coastal line from Brisbane to Cairns; trains on this run stop at Sarina, Mackay, Proserpine and Bowen.

There's another rail service from Bowen to the coal-mining centre of Collinsville, but it no longer carries passengers.

Sea There are regular ferry services from Mackay to Brampton Island, and on weekends this service continues on to Hamilton and Lindeman islands.

Airlie Beach and Shute Harbour are the main launching pads for boat trips to the Whitsundays – see that section for details.

Mackay Area

SARINA (pop 3000)

In the foothills of the Connors Range, Sarina is a service centre for the hundreds of surrounding sugar cane farms. On the town's southern outskirts are the huge Plane Creek sugar mill and CSR's ethanol distillery, which produces about 43,000 kilolitres of alcohol each year.

The town centre is quite attractive, with central plantations and a small shopping precinct. There's a tourist information office just north of the centre on the corner of Anzac St, but apparently it's only staffed during the Christmas school holidays.

There are several roads leading across to the coast from Sarina, with a choice of good beaches including Armstrong's Beach, Sarina Beach and Campwin Beach.

Places to Stay

The *Sarina Caravan Park* (☎ (079) 56 1480) on the outskirts of town along Clermont Rd, has tent sites and on-site vans.

The *Tramway Motel* (☎ (079) 56 2244) on the highway north of the centre has good motel units with singles/doubles at $40/48, and a small pool. In the centre of town, the *Sarina Motor Inn* (☎ (079) 43 1431) has singles/doubles from $47/50 and twin rooms for $55, and a licensed restaurant. Across the road, the *Tandara Hotel* (☎ (079) 56 1323) has basic motel-style units with air-con at $27/37.

Places to Eat

Sarina has one of the quaintest and most enduring eateries in Queensland. Known just as *The Diner*, it's a tiny roadside, timber shack with tilt-up wooden panels and bench seats. It is open on weekdays from 4 am to 6 pm and on Saturday from 4 am to 10 am, so if you're driving through you can stop and have an early breakfast with the truckies and cane farmers who've been frequenting the place for the last 70 years. Burgers, sangers, pies and kebabs are all available. To find it, take the turn off to Clermont and Moranbah in the centre of town – you'll see it on your left, just before the railway crossing.

The *Colonial Corner Takeaway*, on the corner of the highway and Anzac St, just north of the town centre, has sandwiches, pies, drinks and roast chicken. There's also a small but very good fruit and vegie market next door, and *Alcorn's Hot Bread Shop* next to that.

You could try one of the pubs along the main street for a bistro meal, or the licensed *Hideaway* restaurant in the Sarina Motor Inn has international-style cuisine with main courses for around $16.

SARINA BEACH

Set on the shores of Sarina Inlet, Sarina Beach is a laid-back little coastal community with good fishing and a long, pleasant beach. There are a couple of motels, a general store and a service station here, as well as a surf life-saving club on the beachfront and a boat ramp at the inlet. The town is 13 km east of the Bruce Hwy.

At the north end of The Esplanade, the friendly *Sarina Beach Motel* (☎ (079) 56 6266) is a two-storey red-brick motel on the beachfront, with a tennis court, a licensed restaurant and a good swimming pool surrounded by grass and palm trees. There are motel units for $48 and self-contained units from $55 to $65; across the road there are more self-contained units at $44.

At the south end of The Esplanade, the *Sandpiper Motel* (☎ (079) 56 6130) has units from $40 a double and family units from $50 a double plus $7 for each extra person. This place also manages the adjacent *Sarina Beach Caravan Park* – which is basically a grassy field with a row of pine trees and an amenities block. Tent sites cost $11 and powered sites $14.

SARINA TO MACKAY

It's 36 km from Sarina to Mackay via the Bruce Hwy, but if you have a little time a longer alternative route takes you past a few local points of interest. The brochure *Discover the Homebush Connection*, available from the Mackay and Sarina information centres, is a guide to the route. There are five different attractions covered by the brochure, but you'll have to do a bit of doubling back if you want to visit them all.

Heading along the Bruce Hwy, take the turn off to Homebush two km north of Sarina. This section of the road is quite narrow, and takes you through the cane fields with regular cane-train crossing points – so drive carefully.

The first stop, **Orchidways**, is an attractively landscaped orchid garden with a kiosk and Devonshire teas; entry costs $5 for adults and $3 for children. Farther on is the **Homebush Store**, a craft and pottery gallery. The **General Gordon Hotel** is an old country pub surrounded by sugar cane farms. It's a friendly place and a good spot for a cold drink, or you can get a counter meal. Burgers, steak sandwiches, steaks and mixed grills range from $5 to $8.50.

Three km south of the town of Walkerston is **Greenmount Homestead**, a house built

by the Cook family in 1915 on the property where Mackay's founder, John Mackay, first settled in 1862. It houses a collection of memorabilia, personal effects and old farm equipment. It's open to the public on weekdays from 9.30 am to 12.30 pm and on Sunday from 10 am to 3.30 pm; entry costs $3 for adults and $1 for children.

If you've always wanted to visit a working sugar cane farm, Merv Harris offers good tours of his **Polstone Sugar Cane Farm**. The 2½-hour tours start at 1.30 pm every weekday between May and November, and also at 1.30 pm on Sunday during July and August. The cost is $12.50 for adults, $6.25 for children and $32 for a family, which includes an educational video, a wagon ride and afternoon tea.

MACKAY (pop 40,250)

Mackay is surrounded by sugar cane – a crop which has been farmed here since 1865. One-third of Australia's sugar crop is processed here and loaded onto bulk carriers at one of the world's biggest sugar-loading terminals at Port Mackay.

Mackay is nothing special, although its town centre is quite attractive and has a number of historic buildings, and there are some good beaches a bus ride away. It's also an access point for the national parks at Cape Hillsborough and Eungella, and for the Great Barrier Reef; there are some interesting islands just an hour or two away, including the popular resort at Brampton Island.

Orientation

Mackay is split into two halves by the broad Pioneer River. The city centre is a compact area, with the main streets laid out in a simple grid on the southern side of the river. Victoria St, the main street, is an attractive thoroughfare with a central plantation, lots of trees and other greenery, paved and decorated footpaths and quite a few historic buildings. The bus terminal is a few hundred metres west of the centre on Milton St. Heading east from the centre, Gordon St, which runs parallel to

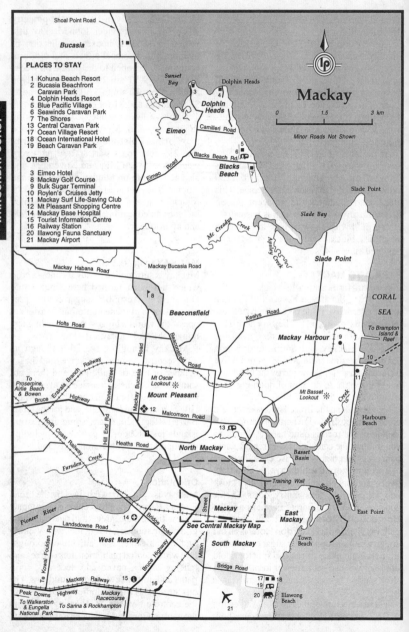

Mackay

PLACES TO STAY

1 Kohuna Beach Resort
2 Bucasia Beachfront
   Caravan Park
4 Dolphin Heads Resort
5 Blue Pacific Village
6 Seawinds Caravan Park
7 The Shores
13 Central Caravan Park
17 Ocean Village Resort
18 Ocean International Hotel
19 Beach Caravan Park

OTHER

3 Eimeo Hotel
8 Mackay Golf Course
9 Bulk Sugar Terminal
10 Roylen's Cruises Jetty
11 Mackay Surf Life-Saving Club
12 Mt Pleasant Shopping Centre
14 Mackay Base Hospital
15 Tourist Information Centre
16 Railway Station
20 Illawong Fauna Sanctuary
21 Mackay Airport

Victoria St, takes you past Queens Park to Town Beach.

The railway station, the airport and the tourist information centre are all about three km south of the city centre.

Sydney St takes you across Forgan Bridge to North Mackay and the city's newer suburbs. The Mackay Harbour, six km north of the centre, is predominantly an industrial area, dominated by a massive bulk sugar terminal which is one of the largest of its kind in the world. The jetty here is the departure point for Roylen's Cruises to the islands and the reef. There's a good beach just south of the harbour.

Mackay's best swimming spots are at the Northern Beaches, about 15 km north of the centre.

Information

Tourist Information Mackay's tourist information centre (☎ (079) 52 2677) is about three km south of the centre on Nebo Rd (the Bruce Hwy). It is open from 8.30 am to 5 pm Monday to Friday, and from 9 am to 4 pm on Saturday and Sunday. The building is a replica of the old Richmond Sugar Mill, and there's a kiosk and souvenir shop inside. While you're here, pick up a copy of the very handy *Things to See & Do in Mackay* brochure.

Post Mackay's post office is in Sydney St, near the corner with Gordon St and next to Billy Baxter's Cafe.

Useful Organisations The RACQ (☎ (079) 57 2918) is at 214 Victoria St. The QNP&WS district office (☎ (079) 51 8788) is on the corner of Wood and River Sts, and is open on weekdays from 8.30 am to 4.30 pm.

Bookshops Next to the newsagency at 35-37 Wood St White's Book Worm is a long and narrow bookshop with a reasonably wide range of reading matter.

Things to See & Do

Despite the effects of several severe cyclones, particularly one that devastated the city in January 1918, Mackay still has a number of historic buildings around the city centre. The most impressive of these include the neo-Georgian **Court House** (1938), on the corner of Victoria and Brisbane Sts, and the **Commonwealth Bank** (1880) next door, the impressive **Masonic Lodge** (1925) in Wood St, and the **Old Courthouse** (1885) in Brisbane St, which is now the police station. The brochure *A Heritage Walk in Mackay*, available from the tourist centre, guides you around 21 of the town's historic sites.

There are botanic gardens and an orchid house in the attractive **Queen's Park**, along Gordon St about one km east of the centre. The orchid house is open on weekdays from 10.30 to 11 am and from 2 to 2.30 pm and on weekends from 2 to 5 pm. There are good views over the harbour from **Mt Basset**, and at **Rotary Lookout** on Mt Oscar in North Mackay.

The **Illawong Fauna Sanctuary** is two km south of the centre, at Illawong Beach. It's a small private fauna park with a collection of birds, kangaroos and crocodiles – the crocs are fed at 3.30 pm every day. There's also a swimming pool and trampolines here. The park is open daily from 9.30 am until dark; entry costs $3 for adults and $1 for kids.

In the cane-crushing season (July to mid-November), you can visit the **Farleigh Sugar Mill** (☎ (079) 57 4727), 12 km north-west of Mackay, at 1 pm on weekdays for a two-hour tour; costs are $10 for adults, $5 for children or $25 for a family. You can also visit the Polstone Sugar Farm and historic Greenmount Homestead, south of Mackay. See the earlier Sarina to Mackay section for details.

If you feel like going to the dogs, there are **greyhound races** at the Mackay Showgrounds on Milton St every Thursday night.

The Mackay Golf Course (☎ (079) 42 1362) on the Northern Beaches road about six km north of the centre, is an attractive course and open to the general public. Eighteen holes costs $15, and you can hire clubs here if you need to.

Beaches & Swimming Mackay has plenty of beaches, although not all of them are particularly idyllic or great for swimming.

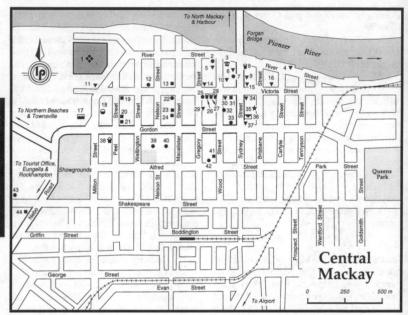

Town Beach is the closest to the city centre – to get there, follow Gordon St all the way east from the centre. You'll come to a sweeping, shallow bay, which is backed by a foreshore reserve. There is a sandy strip, but the water is very shallow and subsides a long way out at low tides, leaving a long stretch of sand and mud flats – in fact, at low tide you can almost walk across to the islands four km off shore. The situation is similar at **Illawong Beach**, a couple of km farther south, although the beach here is probably the more attractive of the two.

A better option is **Harbour Beach**, six km north of the centre and just south of the Mackay Boat Harbour. There's a long stretch of sandy beach, which is patrolled by the Mackay Surf Life-Saving Club. The beach is backed by a large foreshore reserve, with picnic tables and wood barbecues among tall stands of pine and palm trees.

But the best beaches are about 16 km north of Mackay at Blacks Beach, Eimeo and

Bucasia. See the following section on the Northern Beaches for details.

Back in town, the **Memorial Swimming Pool** on Milton St is an excellent Olympic-sized swimming pool which opens at 5 am and closes at 8.45 pm on Monday, Tuesday, Thursday and Friday, and closes at 6 pm on Wednesday, Saturday and Sunday. It closes for about a month in mid-winter; entry costs $1.

Organised Tours

Cruises Roylen's Cruises (☎ (079) 55 3066) runs fast catamaran day trips from Mackay Harbour to Brampton Island, Credlin Reef on the Barrier Reef, and Lindeman and Hamilton islands in the Whitsundays.

The day trip to Credlin Reef, which departs on Monday, Wednesday and Friday at 9 am, takes you to a pontoon on the outer reef with an underwater observatory and costs $90. It includes a semisubmersible ride and lunch, and you can hire snorkelling or diving gear. Roylen's catamarans cruise out to Brampton

PLACES TO STAY

13	Hotel Whitsunday
19	Austral Hotel
20	Paradise Lodge Motel
21	Backpackers Retreat
23	International Lodge
24	Coral Sands Motel
31	Mackay Townhouse
38	Larrikin Lodge
41	Taylor's Hotel
44	Cool Palms Motel

PLACES TO EAT

4	Waterfront Restaurant & Espresso Bar
5	Woody's Bakehouse
6	Toong Tong
9	Akbar
10	Gourmet Sandwich Bar & Mackay Kebab House
11	Pizza Hut
14	Wilkinson's Hotel and The Blue Moose& The Balcony Restarant
15	Tropical Salad Bar
16	Mariners
29	Creperie
30	Hog's Breath Cafe
34	The Meeting House
37	Billy Baxter's Cafe

OTHER

1	Caneland Shopping Centre
2	QNP&WS Office
3	Telephones
7	P Comino & Sons
8	Prince of Wales Hotel
12	RACQ Office
17	Memorial Swimming Pool
18	Mackay Bus Terminal
22	Ansett Airlines
25	Qantas Airlines
26	Huckleberrys Nightclub
27	Paro's Nightclub
28	Australian Hotel & The Loaded Dog
32	White's Book Worm
33	Mackay Five Cinemas
35	Police Station
36	Post Office
39	Mackay Library
40	Mackay Entertainment Centre
42	Camping World
43	Queensland Conservatorium of Music

Island every day – see the later Brampton & Carlisle Islands section for details. They also continue on from Brampton Island to Lindeman and Hamilton islands in the Whitsundays on Saturday and Sunday. The cruise to Lindeman takes about two hours from Mackay and costs $40 one way or $90 return, which includes a buffet lunch at the Club Med resort. It's about 2½ hours to Hamilton Island, and the cost is $36 one way or $40 return.

Flights A couple of local operators, Fredrickson's (☎ (079) 42 3161) and Air Pioneer (☎ (079) 57 6661), offer seaplane flights from Mackay out to Bushy Atoll on the Barrier Reef for around $150 per person. Both are also available for charter flights if you want to go somewhere in particular.

Helijet (☎ (079) 57 3574) offers a range of flights from Mackay to the Whitsundays by either seaplane or helicopter, including scenic flights, island transfers and day trips to the reef and islands.

Motorcycle Tours Ivan from Mackay Harley-Davidson Tours (☎ (079) 59 8734) has an Electra Glide, and can take you on one of seven different tours, including a one-hour mystery tour ($45), a 2½-hour zip to the Northern Beaches ($100) and a three-hour tour to Cape Hillsborough National Park ($120).

Eungella National Park Reeforest Tours (☎ (079) 53 1000) has a day trip from Mackay to Eungella National Park costing $45 for adults and $10 to $20 for children (depending on their age).

Outback Tours Reef-Gem Adventures (☎ (079) 57 7591) has extended outback tours from Mackay to the gemfields around Sapphire, 300 km south-west of Mackay. The tours are for groups of up to 12 people, and costs include all meals, accommodation and prospecting equipment. The three-day tour costs $250 per person; the four-day tour costs $400 per person.

Places to Stay

Camping The *Beach Caravan Park*
(☎ (079) 57 4021), on Petrie St at Illawong
Beach, about three km south of the centre, is
a large and modern beachfront caravan park
with a shop, a good pool, a campers' kitchen
and a barbecue area. Tent sites are $12,
powered sites are $15, camp-o-tels are $16 a
double, cabins range from $28 to $38, and
self-contained villas and flats range from
$45 to $48.

Across the river and about two km north of
the centre, the *Central Caravan Park* (☎ (079)
57 6141), at 15 Malcomson St in North
Mackay, is another good camping option. It
also has a shop and a pool. Tent sites cost $8
a double and self-contained cabins cost $30
a double, or $32 with air-con. This place also
has a strip of clean and simple units which
cost $20 a double plus $5 for extra adults and
$2 for extra kids – the units have a communal
amenities block, and you need to supply your
own linen.

There are other caravan parks along the
Bruce Hwy south of the centre, and at the
Northern Beaches – see that section later.

Hostels *Larrikin Lodge* (☎ (079) 51 3728),
at 32 Peel St, is a small YHA-associate hostel
in an airy timber house. The hostel itself is
pretty straightforward, but it's well run and
has a friendly atmosphere – it's one of those
places where you always seem to meet
everyone else. There's a small pool in the
backyard. A dorm bed here costs $12 a night.

Behind the bus terminal, at 21 Peel St, the
Backpackers Retreat (☎ (079) 51 1115) is an
attractive-looking two-storey hostel, with
accommodation in six-bunk units, each with
its own kitchen and bathroom. A bunk costs
$12, and spacious double rooms cost $30.
This place is neat and clean, has a small pool,
a security-coded front door, and home-
cooked meals are available at night for $3 to
$5. They also have a barbecue on Friday
nights.

Pubs *Taylor's Hotel* (☎ (079) 57 2500), on
the corner of Wood and Alfred Sts, has clean
single rooms upstairs for $15. The *Austral

Hotel* (☎ (079) 51 3288), on the corner of
Victoria and Peel Sts, has singles/doubles
with shared bathrooms for $20/30 (although
a couple of the doubles have their own bathrooms) and family rooms for $35.

On the corner of Victoria and Macalister
Sts, the *Hotel Whitsunday* (☎ (079) 57 2811)
is sort of a cross between a pub and a motel.
It's an oldish, three-storey building with a
bar and nightclub downstairs, budget rooms
from $39/49 and renovated rooms from
$49/59; all rooms have their own bathroom.

Motels The friendly *International Lodge*
(☎ (079) 51 1022), at 40 Macalister St, is quite
central, and has good, clean motel rooms from
$38/40 for singles/doubles. Next door, at No
44, the *Coral Sands Motel* (☎ (079) 51 1244)
is a little more modern and up-market, and has
a swimming pool and restaurant. Rooms here
start from $58/68. The *Paradise Lodge Motel*
(☎ (079) 51 3644), close to the bus terminal
and next to the Backpackers Retreat, at 19 Peel
St, has singles/doubles from $44/48. Right in
the centre of town, down an arcade at 73 Victoria St, is the *Mackay Townhouse* (☎ (079) 57
6985), an oldish motel, with singles/doubles
from $30/35 and family units from $35
upwards. The rooms are quite clean and cosy,
although most are internal and don't see much
daylight.

There are about a thousand motels strung
along the Bruce Hwy between the tourist
information centre and the town centre – if
you drive in at night, this is one long strip of
motel signs and neon lights. Most of these
places have their prices posted out the front.
The closest of these to the centre is the *Cool
Palms Motel* (☎ (079) 57 5477), which is at
4 Nebo Rd. It has simple budget rooms from
$40.

Hotels & Resorts Mackay's most up-
market accommodation is at the four-star
Ocean International Hotel (☎ (079) 57 2044
or toll-free 1800 635 104), which is about
two km south of the centre, at 1 Bridge Rd
Illawong Beach. It's an impressive four-
storey complex overlooking Sandringham
Bay, with a restaurant and cocktail bar, a pool

and a spa. Tariffs are $130 a night for a double, $150 for a family room or $205 for a luxury suite.

Right next door, at 5 Bridge Rd, the *Ocean Village Resort* (☎ (079) 51 3200 or toll-free 008 075 144) is a good mid-range resort with a pool, a barbecue area and half-court tennis courts. There are 34 self-contained apartments in the complex, ranging from $65 a night for a studio unit to $120 for a two-bedroom apartment that sleeps up to six people.

Places to Eat

Cafes, Delis & Takeaways The *Tropical Salad Bar*, on the corner of Victoria and Sydney Sts, is run by a very friendly Scottish couple, and has freshly crushed fruit and vegie juices, smoothies, and good sandwiches and salads.

At 23 Wood St, the narrow and popular *Gourmet Sandwich Bar* is a lunch time bargain, with fresh rolls and sandwiches for $1.95, and cheap salads and cakes. Nearby, the *Mackay Kebab House* has chicken and lamb kebabs and felafels. *Woody's Bakehouse*, in an arcade off Wood St, has home-made pies, cakes and breads.

Billy Baxter's Cafe, on the corner of Sydney and Gordon Sts, is a stylish new cafe which serves breakfast, lunch and dinner. Part of a small national chain, it has a diverse menu with things like grilled open sandwiches, salads, sandwiches and rolls, pizzas and focaccias, all from $4 to $8. Their bacon & eggs on pancakes ($6.95) is a pretty good start to the day, and their coffee is great.

The *Waterfront Restaurant* has great takeaway fish & chips – see the restaurant section.

There's a *Pizza Hut*, on the corner of Milton and Victoria Sts, with all-you-can-eat pizza, pasta, salad and dessert deals costing $4.95 for weekday lunches and $6.95 for dinner and weekend lunches.

Pubs Mackay seems to have a pub on every corner in the city centre, so finding a counter meal is not a problem. *Wilkinson's Hotel*, on the corner of Victoria and Gregory Sts, has

the up-market *Balcony Restaurant* upstairs, with lunch and dinner mains for around $10; bar meals are available downstairs from $3 to $5.

At the friendly *Austral Hotel*, on the corner of Victoria and Peel Sts, *Coco's* is a tropical-style eatery with slate floors, cane furniture and lots of palm trees. It has up-market pub food like seafood crêpes or carpetbag steaks from $14 to $18, and features live music on Friday and Saturday nights. *Taylor's Hotel*, on the corner of Wood and Alfred Sts, is another pub with good food. It has a small bistro with a courtyard area, burgers for $4.50 and main courses in the $9 to $15 range.

Restaurants Mackay's most fashionable restaurant, by a country mile, is the *Waterfront Restaurant and Espresso Bar* (☎ (079) 57 8131), at 8 River St, in the midst of the warehouses along the riverfront. The minimalist dining room has a fun seaside mural along one wall, but if the weather is good, sit out on the covered decking area overlooking the river. The restaurant is licensed and is open every day from 10 am until late. The menu has light meals like Greek octopus salad, seafood antipasto and gourmet-style focaccias for $8.50, or main courses like fish & chips, baked whole barramundi and roast lamb cutlets for $12.50. Side orders – salad, vegies or potato wedges – are $3.50 to $4.50. There's also an excellent takeaway fish & chips section at the front of the restaurant.

At 10 Sydney St, *Toong Tong* is a cosy wood-panelled Thai restaurant with great Tom Kah Gai soup for $4.50, a wide range of curries and other mains from $9.50 to $13.50 and a small selection of vegetarian mains for $8.50. For Indian food, try *Akbar* across the road, at No 27. It has seafood dishes from $11 to $13, other mains around $9.50, and vegetable dishes from $5 to $7.50. It also has a small lunch menu with mains from $6 to $7. Both of these places are BYO.

The *Creperie* on Gregory St serves excellent savoury pancakes for around $10, and dessert crêpes with strawberries, apples, blueberries and liqueurs. The *Hog's Breath*

Cafe on Wood St, just south of Victoria St, is a saloon-style bar and grill with burgers and snacks around $8 and steaks and grills around $16.

The Meeting House on Sydney St, near the Victoria St corner, has a lunch menu with soups, crêpes, quiches and curries from $5 to $7, and interesting dinner mains like Thai chicken salad, home-made pastas and fish of the day from $12 to $15. It's a warm and friendly little BYO. *Mariners*, at 44 Victoria St, is a licensed seafood buffet with a wide selection of hot and cold seafood dishes, salads and desserts. You can eat as much as you like for $35.

Entertainment

Pubs & Live Music The *Austral Hotel* has live entertainment every Friday and Saturday night, and a great jazz night on the first Thursday of each month. A few other pubs have live bands on the weekends, including the *Prince of Wales* on River St, although most of the bands play in the nightclubs.

The Mackay campus of the Queensland Conservatorium of Music, at 418 Shakespeare St, has regular jazz and classical performances throughout the year, at lunch time and in the evenings. Call ☎ (079) 57 3727 for details.

Nightclubs Mackay has a small cluster of nightclubs along Victoria St in the heart of the city. The *Blue Moose* nightclub, upstairs at Wilkinson's Hotel, is pretty groovy and apparently the best club in town. It has good DJ music and occasional live bands, and is open Tuesday to Sunday until about 5 am, with a $5 cover charge from Wednesday to Saturday. In the same pub, the *Balcony Restaurant* becomes a nightclub after dinner on Friday and Saturday nights, and is popular with a slightly older crowd.

The *Loaded Dog*, upstairs in the Australian Hotel on the corner of Wood and Victoria Sts, is a bit more laid-back – more of a meeting place – with pool tables, a couple of balconies looking over Wood St, and live bands on weekends. In between these clubs are *Huckleberrys*, upstairs at 99 Victoria St,

and *Paro's*, upstairs in Toucan's Arcade at 85 Victoria St. Both of these are big, disco-style clubs with dance floors and pool tables and DJs and flashing lights – all your usual meat-market trimmings. Both have a $5 cover charge on weekends and when bands play, and Paro's has a popular Sunday session which starts at 5 pm.

Theatre & Cinema The *Mackay Entertainment Centre* on Gordon St is the city's main venue for theatre, ballet, musicals and other live productions. Phone the box office on ☎ (079) 57 2255 or toll-free on 1800 646 574 to find out what's on during your visit.

The *Mackay Five Cinemas* (☎ (079) 57 3515) are at 30 Gordon St, and screen all the latest release flicks.

Things to Buy

Camping World, in Alfred St next to Taylor's Hotel, is well stocked with just about everything for the happy camper. Eskies, tents, sleeping bags, stoves, boots, torches – all that sort of stuff. They also have a selection of bushwalking and hiking maps.

At 14 Sydney St, P Comino & Sons is crammed with classic Aussie clothing – work wear, Akubra hats, oilskin coats, boots for riding, walking or working, moleskins etc. They also stock a range of camping gear and accessories.

Getting There & Away

Air Ansett and Qantas have direct flights most days between Mackay and Brisbane ($274), Cairns ($245), Rockhampton ($161) and Sydney ($379), and you can get to most other cities along the coast with Flight West and Sunstate. Ansett also flies from here to Hamilton Island; Qantas flies to Brampton Island and Proserpine.

In Mackay, Ansett's offices are on the corner of Victoria and Macalister Sts; Qantas, Sunstate and Queensland Regional (☎ (079) 57 1411) are at 105 Victoria St.

Helijet Air Services (☎ (079) 46 8249) has helicopter and seaplane flights from here to the Whitsunday Islands and Airlie Beach.

Bus Greyhound Pioneer Australia and McCafferty's buses doing the coastal run all stop at the Mackay Bus Terminal (☎ (079) 51 3088) on Milton St, about a 10-minute walk west of the town centre. The terminal is open 24 hours, but the booking office's hours are from 7.30 am to 8.30 pm every day.

Average journey times and typical fares are: Cairns, 10½ hours ($70); Townsville, four hours ($48); Airlie Beach, two hours ($26); and Brisbane, 14 hours ($90).

Train The *Sunlander* and *Queenslander* (both from Brisbane to Cairns) stop at Mackay. The *Sunlander* costs $100 for an economy seat and $199 for a 1st-class sleeper from Brisbane, while the *Queenslander* only has 1st-class sleepers at $379. All trains now stop at the new railway station at Paget, about three km south of the centre.

Train bookings are handled by any travel agent, including the Mackay Bus Terminal (☎ (079) 51 3088).

Sea If you're heading for the Whitsundays, you can get to Hamilton and Lindeman islands from Mackay with Roylen's Cruises – see the earlier Organised Tours section for details.

Getting Around

For a taxi, call Mackay Taxis on ☎ (079) 51 4999). Count on about $8 for a taxi from either the railway station or the airport to the city centre. Thrifty, Avis, Budget and Hertz have counters at the airport. For a cheaper, slightly older car, try Cut Rate Rentals (☎ (079) 53 1616).

Local bus services are operated by Transit Coaches (☎ (079) 57 3330) and Mackay City Buses (☎ (079) 57 8416).

MACKAY'S NORTHERN BEACHES

The coastline north of Mackay is made up of a series of headlands and bays. The small residential communities strung along here are virtually outer suburbs of Mackay, although they are all about 15 km from the centre of town. If you're prepared to do a bit of exploring, there are some reasonably good

beaches at these places. There are also a few beachfront caravan parks, holiday flats and resorts in the various centres.

About five km north of the Mackay Harbour, **Slade Point** is mainly a residential suburb, but Lambert's Beach is quite a good swimming spot.

To get to the other northern beaches, you turn right at the 'Northern Beaches' sign four km north of town on the Bruce Hwy.

Black's Beach

At Black's Beach the *Seawinds Caravan Park* (☎ (079) 54 9334), on Bourke St, is a rambling beachfront park with lots of shade and plenty of grass. It has tent sites and on-site vans. In the same street, the *Blue Pacific Village* (☎ (079) 54 9090) is a well-kept, family-run set of holiday units, with a restaurant, swimming pool and tennis court. Tariffs range from $48 for a studio unit to $90 for a beachfront unit. *The Shores* (☎ (079) 54 8322), at 9 Pacific Dve , is a set of modern two-bedroom apartments which start from $50 a double plus $5 for each extra person.

Dolphin Heads

At Dolphin Heads, the *Dolphin Heads Resort* (☎ (079) 54 9666 or toll-free 1800 075 088) is the most impressive of the northern beaches resorts. It's a modern resort in a garden setting, overlooking an attractive (but rocky) bay. The beach isn't much but the pool and spa more than make up for it, and there's a poolside cocktail bar and restaurant, so you don't have to move too far. Tariffs vary seasonally, with studio units ranging from $70 to $96, one-bedroom units from $75 to $110 and two-bedroom condos from $120 to $130. The pool here is open to day visitors and costs $5 per person for the day. The restaurant serves light lunches like quiche or lasagna and salad or seafood baskets, costing from $5.50 to $9.50. The dinner menu is more elaborate, with pastas, seafood, salads and meat dishes in the $13 to $18 range. The resort has a courtesy coach for guests.

WHITSUNDAY COAST

Eimeo

Beside Dolphin Heads is Eimeo. The *Eimeo Hotel* is a fairly straightforward old pub, but its wonderful location atop a headland makes it a great spot to come to for a meal or just a drink. There's a concreted beer garden where you can sit and gaze out across the ocean to numerous off-shore islands, and to the resort at Dolphin Heads. The food here is your basic pub grub, with seafood, and steak and chicken dishes in the $10 to $14 range. There are also rooms here, but when I visited they said they weren't renting them out – they might have changed their minds by the time you get there. Ask at the bar.

Bucasia

Bucasia is just across Sunset Bay from Eimeo and Dolphin Heads, but you have to head all the way back to the main road to get up there. The *Bucasia Beachfront Caravan Park* (☎ (079) 54 6375) doesn't have much going for it apart from being on the beachfront. Seemingly in the midst of a residential development, the *Kohuna Beach Resort* (☎ (079) 54 8555 or toll-free 1800 075 128), on Griffin Ave, is actually a very pleasant eight-year-old resort with a cluster of timber cabins in a tropical garden setting. The resort has catamarans for hire, an excellent swimming pool, a bar, a casual bistro and an à la carte restaurant. There are 60 self-contained cabins, with costs ranging from $80 a double to $100 for a family unit. The resort has a courtesy coach which does pick-ups and drop-offs from Mackay.

BRAMPTON ISLAND

About 32 km north-east of Mackay, Brampton Island has a popular mid-range resort which was taken over and upgraded by Qantas Airlines in 1985. Brampton is also the access point for adjacent Carlisle Island, which has a couple of national park camp sites.

This is an excellent island to visit if you're considering making a day trip, with quick access from Mackay, good beaches and walking trails and a range of water sports equipment available for hire. The Brampton resort also has live jazz sessions every Sunday afternoon.

Mountainous Brampton Island is part of the Cumberland Islands group which, together with the Sir James Smith Group further north, is sometimes referred to as the southern Whitsundays. These forested continental islands are essentially very similar in appearance to those of the Whitsundays.

Brampton is a national park and wildlife sanctuary with lush forests surrounded by coral reefs. It is connected to nearby Carlisle Island by a sand bar which you can walk across at low tide. Last century, the island was used by the Queensland government as a nursery for palm trees, and there are still plenty of these fine trees on the island. The Busuttin family, who moved to the island in 1916 to raise goats and horses, established the first resort here in 1933.

Activities

The resort has two swimming pools, tennis courts, a small golf course and a games room. There's a water sports shed on the main beach where daytrippers can hire snorkelling gear, catamarans, windsurfers and paddle skis – this equipment is free for resort guests.

The **main beach** at Sandy Point is very pleasant. There's good snorkelling over the coral in the channel between Brampton and Carlisle islands, and at low tide you can wade from one to the other.

There are two excellent **walking trails** on the island. The seven-km walk circumnavigates the central section of the island, with a spur track leading down to Echo Point on the east coast. The two-km steady climb to the top of 219-metre Brampton Peak takes about two hours, and is rewarded with fine views along the way and from several lookout points.

Organised Tours

Roylen's Cruises (☎ (079) 55 3066) has day trips from Brampton to Credlin Reef on the outer Barrier Reef on Monday, Wednesday and Friday ($80), and on Saturday and Sunday to Lindeman Island ($90 return including lunch) or Hamilton Island ($40 return).

MARK ARMSTRONG

MARK ARMSTRONG

Top: South Molle Island Jetty, Whitsundays
Bottom: Island Ferry, Whitsundays

MARK ARMSTRONG

MARK ARMSTRONG

MARK ARMSTRONG

Top: Pleasure sloop, Whitsundays
Left: Canefields, near Mackay
Right: Masonic Lodge, Mackay

WHITSUNDAY COAST

Coral Reef – Snorklers' delight

Places to Stay

The *Brampton Island Resort* (☎ (079) 51 4499), run by Qantas, is a very pleasant mid-range resort which is popular with couples, families and honeymooners – in fact, just about everyone except the 'young singles' crowd – it's definitely not a party island.

The resort is at Sandy Point in the north of the island, and consists of a cluster of attractive two-storey motel-style units, with their own balcony or verandah. Daily costs are $125/200 for singles/doubles in the older and smaller Carlisle Units. Costs in the newer Blue Lagoon Units are $147/244 for a garden-view room, and $160/272 for an ocean-view room. Rates don't include meals but do include use of all non-powered equipment for activities including golf, tennis, windsurfing and catamarans.

Qantas also has a variety of package deals available from the capital cities – ring Australian Resorts on ☎ 1800 812 525 for details.

Places to Eat

Resort guests have the option of paying an additional $65 a day for a full meals package, or paying for meals separately. Daytrippers can also eat at the resort.

The main dining room, the *Carlisle Restaurant*, serves buffet-style breakfasts (from $9.50 to $17.50) and buffet-style lunches

($20). Dinner is from a menu, and ranges from $30 to $35. There's also the *Saltwater Rocks* cafe, where you can get good sandwiches, salads and light meals.

Getting There & Away

Air Qantas/Sunstate does the 10-minute flight from Mackay to Brampton for $71 one way.

Sea Roylen's Cruises (☎ (079) 55 3066) has two fast cats, the *Sunbird* and the *Spirit of Roylen*, which take turns to make the 40-minute run to Brampton. They leave Mackay Harbour every day at 9 am, and the fares are $25 one way or $45 return (including lunch). A bone-shaking mini-railway transports visitors from the wharf to the resort.

CARLISLE ISLAND

Carlisle Island is connected to Brampton Island by a narrow sand bar, and at low tide you can walk or wade from one island to the other. Carlisle is covered in dense eucalypt forests, and there are no walking trails. The wreck of the iron steamship SS *Geelong* lies just off the north-west coast. It ran ashore during a storm in 1888, and two crew members were drowned.

There's a national park camping ground at Southern Bay, which is directly across from the Brampton resort, and another site which is further north at Maryport Bay. Both sites are undeveloped and have no facilities, so you need to be totally self-sufficient – although you could always pop across to the resort at low tide for a meal or a cold beer.

The Southern Bay camp site has a limit of 15 people. Nightly site fees are $3 per person. Bookings and permits are handled by the QNP&WS office in Mackay (☎ (079) 51 8788).

The Brampton resort will ferry campers across to Carlisle Island at high tide if you ring and ask them before you come.

OTHER CUMBERLAND ISLANDS

If you fancy a spot of Robinson Crusoeing and have your own boat, or can afford to charter a boat or seaplane, most other islands in the Cumberland Group and the Sir James Smith Group to the north are also national parks.

Scawfell Island, 12 km east of Brampton, is the largest island in the group. Refuge Bay on its northern side has a safe anchorage, a beach and a basic camping ground, but no facilities or water.

About three km east of Brampton, **Cockermouth Island** also has a good anchorage and beach on its west side, and a basic camping ground.

In the Sir James Smith group of islands north-west of Brampton, **Goldsmith Island** has a safe anchorage on its north-western side, good beaches and a camp site with toilets, tables and fireplaces.

Contact the National Parks offices in Mackay (☎ (079) 51 8788) or Seaforth (☎ (079) 59 0410) for all camping permits and information.

CAPE HILLSBOROUGH NATIONAL PARK

This small coastal park, 54 km north of Mackay, takes in the rocky, 300-metre-high Cape Hillsborough and nearby Andrews Point and Wedge Island, which are joined by a causeway at low tide. The scenery ranges from cliffs, a rocky coastline, sand dunes and scrub, to rainforest and woodland. Kangaroos, wallabies, sugar gliders and turtles are quite common in the park.

There's a ranger's office and visitors

information centre (☎ (079) 59 0410) on the foreshore here, and a good picnic and barbecue area nearby.

There are also some good short walking trails through the park. From near the Cape Hillsborough resort, a trail leads via several lookout points to Andrews Point, and at low tide you can walk across the causeway to Wedge Island. South of the resort is the Hidden Valley rainforest walk, a 1.4-km circuit. And from the western end of the foreshore reserve, there's a 1.6-km trail to Beachcombers Cove.

Places to Stay

Situated at the end of Cape Hillsborough Rd, the *Cape Hillsborough Resort* (☎ (079) 59 0152) has tent sites for $6 a double, on-site vans and cabins from $20, villas from $30 a double and two-bedroom units from $50. Facilities include a swimming pool, a laundry, bar and restaurant.

There's a small National Parks camping ground at Smalleys Beach, in the western part of the park; you'll need a permit, which can be booked through the ranger's office.

At Halliday Bay (the next bay heading west from Cape Hillsborough), the *Halliday Bay Resort* (☎ (079) 59 0121) is a large, isolated and slightly dishevelled mid-range resort with a pool, tennis courts and a shop. The older beachfront units sleep up to four and cost $55 a night, and the newer villas are set back from the beach, sleep up to six and cost $85 a night. There's a bar and restaurant, with bistro-style meals in the $10 to $12 range.

Getting There & Away

A school bus, which anyone can take, leaves Mackay post office at 2.45 pm Monday to Friday during the school term. It only goes to Seaforth, but if you're staying at Cape Hillsborough Resort, the driver might drop you there.

NEWRY ISLAND GROUP

The Newry Island Group is a cluster of small, little-known islands just off the coast from the town of Seaforth, about 40 km north-west of Mackay. They are rocky, wild-looking continental islands with grassy open forests and small patches of rainforest. Five of the islands are national parks.

Newry Island

In the centre of the group, one-km-long Newry Island, has a small and very low-key resort (☎ (079) 59 0214) which accommodates up to 30 people. Camping is $7 per site, a bunk is $12, and cabins which sleep up to five and have their own bathrooms and cooking facilities cost $20 per person, with a maximum charge of $60. The resort has a bar and a restaurant with breakfasts around $5 and dinners around $12.

Most of the visitors to Newry are locals, here for the good fishing and oystering. The beaches aren't great, but there's a good short walk from the resort to a picnic site at Fish Point on the other side of the island.

Getting There & Away The resort picks up guests from Victor Creek, four km west of Seaforth, for $15 return. There is no public transport to Victor Creek, but you could catch the same school bus mentioned earlier in the Cape Hillsborough section. Ring the resort for details.

Other Newry Group Islands

Rabbit Island, the largest of the group at 4.5 sq km, has a national parks camping ground with toilets and a rainwater tank which can be empty in dry times. It also has the only sandy beaches in the group along its eastern side, although due to its proximity to the mainland, box jellyfish could be present in the summer months. From November to January green turtles nest on the beaches here.

There's also a camping ground with toilets and picnic tables on **Outer Newry Island**. Contact the QNP&WS offices at Mackay (☎ (079) 51 8788) or Seaforth (☎ (079) 59 0410) for permits and information.

EUNGELLA NATIONAL PARK

Most days of the year you can be pretty sure of seeing platypuses in the pools near the Broken River bridge and camping ground in this large national park, 84 km west of Mackay. The best times to see the creatures are the hours immediately after dawn and before dark; you must remain patiently silent and still.

Eungella (pronounced *Young*-gulla, meaning Land of Clouds) covers nearly 500 sq km of the Clarke Range, climbing to 1280 metres at Mt Dalrymple. The area has been cut off from other rainforest areas for probably 30,000 years and has at least six life forms which exist nowhere else: the Eungella honeyeater (a bird), the orange-sided skink (a lizard), the Mackay tulip oak (a tall, buttressed rainforest tree) and three species of frog, one of which – the Eungella gastric brooding frog – has a highly unusual habit of incubating its eggs in its stomach and then giving birth by spitting out the tadpoles!

Mackay to Finch Hatton

The main access road to the park takes you through the centre of the long and narrow **Pioneer Valley**, which is framed by low mountains on three sides. The first sugar cane was planted here in 1867, and today almost the entire valley is planted with the stuff.

The road takes you through a string of small townships: **Marian** is mainly notable for its enormous sugar mill. At **Mirani**, there's a local history museum in Victoria St behind the library. There's an interesting collection of local history relics, including a tribute to Dame Nellie Melba, whose husband used to manage the Marian sugar mill. The museum is open from Sunday to Friday from 10 am to 4 pm; entry costs $3.

Finch Hatton

Twenty-seven km west of Mirani, just before the town of Finch Hatton, is the turn off for the **Finch Hatton Gorge** section of the park. The last two or three km of the 12-km drive from the main road are quite rough and involve several creek crossings. At the car park, there's a good picnic area with push-button gas barbecues, and a couple of small swimming holes where the creek tumbles over huge boulders. A 1.6-km walking trail leads from the picnic area to Araluen Falls, with its spectacular waterfalls and swimming holes. There's a kiosk one km south of the gorge, and a bush retreat two km south (see Places to Stay).

In the township of Finch Hatton, the Cedar Gallery houses an amazing collection of timber sculptures, carvings and furniture by Jack Wilms – it's open every day except Monday.

Places to Stay Just a couple of km from the Finch Hatton Gorge is the *Platypus Bush Camp* (☎ (079) 58 3204). It's a bush retreat in a beautiful forest setting beside a creek. You can camp here for $5 per person, or there are three slab-timber huts which are basically roofed-over sleeping platforms, sleeping up to three people and costing $45 a night. There are communal cooking shelters, hot showers and toilets, and you need to bring your own food and linen. If you phone from Finch Hatton township, someone will pick you up.

In Finch Hatton township, the *Finch Hatton Caravan Park* (☎ (079) 583222) is a well-established park with a swimming pool; tent sites cost $9, on-site vans are $25.

Eungella

From Finch Hatton, it's another 28 km to the township of Eungella. The last section of this road climbs suddenly and steeply, with several incredibly sharp corners – trying to tow a caravan up here is not recommended. At the top of the climb, Eungella is a quiet and old-fashioned mountain village with a general store, a chalet and a couple of tea room/galleries.

Places to Stay & Eat In Eungella township there's the *Eungella Chalet* (☎ (079) 58 4509), an old-fashioned guesthouse perched on the edge of the mountain, with views all the way back down the Pioneer Valley; on a clear day you can see forever – well, all the way back to the coast, anyway. There are clean and simple guest rooms upstairs with shared bathrooms, costing $25/39 for singles/

doubles or $15 per person for backpackers. Motel-style units are $50 a double. Up on the hill behind the chalet are modern one and two-bedroom timber cabins which cost $70 a double or $90 for a family. The chalet has a cosy bar and a dining room which serves breakfast, lunch and dinner. The food is straightforward, country-style cooking with steaks, chicken, seafood and pasta dishes from $13 to $16. There's a swimming pool and a hang-gliding platform at the front of the chalet, and you'll often see hang-gliders launch themselves from here. Competitions are held each year in September and November.

There are also several tea rooms in Eungella. The *Rainforest Cafe-Gallery* is a simple little place with a balcony and lovely valley views. The resident German artist serves Devonshire teas, apple strudels and light lunches, and his fascinating timber sculptures are well worth a look. Nearby is the *Coach House Gallery*, a stylish Queenslander with broad verandahs, Devonshire teas, lunches and a collection of local arts and crafts.

Broken River

There's a ranger's office, camping ground, picnic area and kiosk near the bridge over **Broken River**, five km south of the Eungella township. There's a platypus viewing platform near the bridge, and a short walk downstream there's a good swimming hole. Near the bridge colourful birds are prolific, while at night the rufous bettong, a small kangaroo, is quite common. You might also see two types of brush-tailed possum and two species of glider. Park rangers sometimes lead wildlife-watching sessions, or night spotlighting trips to pick out nocturnal animals.

There are some excellent walking tracks which start from either the Broken River picnic ground, or along the road between Broken River and Eungella. They include a rainforest discovery circuit (2.1 km), the Sky Window circuit (2.5 km) and the Palm Walk (8 km). The people at the ranger's office are friendly and helpful, and can advise you on the various walks and provide you with maps. The office, which has displays on the park's wildlife, is staffed daily between 7 and 8 am, 11 am and noon, and 3 and 3.30 pm.

Places to Stay & Eat The national park camping ground is beside Broken River, about 500 metres past the information centre and kiosk. You'll need to get camping permits ($3 per person per night) from the ranger at Broken River (☎ (079) 58 4552). During school holiday periods it's advisable to book.

On the other side of Broken River, the *Broken River Mountain Retreat* (☎ (079) 58 4528) has modern timber cabins set in landscaped grounds. Motel-style rooms are from $48 and one and two-bedroom self-contained cabins sleep up to six people and range from $62 to $72 a double, plus $10 for extras. The retreat has its own restaurant and organises various tours for its guests.

Getting There & Away There are no buses to Eungella, but hitching is quite possible. Reeforest Adventure Tours (☎ (079) 53 1000) runs day trips from Mackay costing $45 for adults and $10 to $20 for children (depending on their age).

Reeforest also do a camping drop-off service from Mackay, which costs $20 up and $10 back to Finch Hatton, and $30 up and $10 back to Broken River. If you're going to Broken River, you have to join the first section of the tour, which means you get to visit Finch Hatton first.

Whitsunday Area

The 74 Whitsunday Islands are probably the best-known Queensland islands. The group was named by Captain Cook, who sailed through here on 3 July 1770. They're scattered on both sides of the Whitsunday Passage and are all within 50 km of Shute Harbour. The Whitsundays are mostly continental islands, the tips of underwater mountains, but many of them have fringing

coral reefs. The actual Barrier Reef is at least 60 km out from Shute Harbour; Hook Reef is the nearest part of it.

The islands – mostly hilly and wooded – and the passages between them, are simply beautiful, and while seven of the islands are developed with tourist resorts, most are uninhabited and several offer the chance of some back-to-nature beach camping and bushwalking. All but four of the Whitsundays are predominantly or completely national park. The exceptions are Dent Island, and the resort islands of Hamilton, Daydream and Hayman. The other main resorts are on South Molle, Lindeman, Long and Hook islands.

Information
Airlie Beach is the mainland centre for the Whitsundays and there are plenty of travel agents and tour operators based here. The tourist information offices at Mackay, Proserpine and Airlie Beach can also provide you with all sorts of brochures on the Whitsundays, as well as book tours and accommodation.

The Whitsunday District office of the QNP&WS (☎ (079) 46 7022) is two km past Airlie Beach on the road to Shute Harbour. This office deals with camping permits for the islands, and the rangers here are generally very helpful and good sources of information on a wide range of topics. This is a good place to visit when you first arrive, particularly for travellers who are interested in exploring the islands independently rather than joining a packaged tour.

Books & Maps *100 Magic Miles of the Great Barrier Reef – The Whitsunday Islands* by David Colfelt is commonly referred to as the bible to the Whitsundays. Now in its fourth edition, this large format paperback guide has some great colour photos, articles on the islands and resorts, features on diving, sailing, fishing, camping and natural history, and an exhaustive collection of charts with descriptions of all boat anchorages around the islands. The book costs around $45 and is widely available.

Two of the best maps to this area are the Travelog *Great Barrier Reef* map, which has a *Whitsunday Passage* map on the back, and Sunmap's *Australia's Whitsundays*.

Zoning The Great Barrier Reef Marine Park Authority's zoning system divides the waters around the Whitsundays into five different zones, each with certain restrictions on what you can and can't do in each particular area. The widely-available brochure *Boating in the Whitsundays* contains a colour-coded map which clearly shows the different zones, with an accompanying chart explaining the restrictions which apply to each zone.

Briefly, most of the waters around the Whitsundays are zoned General Use A and B with some important exceptions around the islands. In those areas Marine National Park A and B zoning applies. The main difference for the visitor is that although both zones are 'look but don't take', Zone A permits limited fishing whereas Zone B permits no fishing at all.

Zone A applies to the waters around Long Island, the Molle islands, Lindeman Island, Hamilton Island, Cid Harbour, Henning Island, between Whitsunday and Haslewood islands, Nara Inlet and Saba Bay on Hook Island and the area around Hayman Island, Black and Langford islands and across from there to Hook Island.

The more restrictive Zone B applies to Butterfly Bay and the other bays at the north of Hook Island, to Border Island and to Lupton Island and the east side of Haslewood Island.

The outer reef off from the Whitsundays is also a mix of zones. The main reefs visited from the islands are Marine National Park A (Bait and Hook reefs) and B (Hardy Reef).

Activities
Diving & Snorkelling There are at least five companies offering learn-to-dive courses in Airlie Beach, and most of the island resorts also have their own dive schools.

For certified divers, there's a huge range of boats offering diving trips to the islands, or further out to the outer reef areas.

Fishing Trips Numerous charter boats offer fishing trips out of Shute Harbour. They include the following:

MV *Jane II* (☎ (079) 46 6224) is a 50-ft timber fishing trawler which has all inclusive day trips for $55 for adults and $27.50 for children, and is also available for charter trips to the reef for up to eight people.

The GFV *Invader* (☎ 46 6848 or 018 186 900) is a 32-ft cruiser which has reef and gamefishing trips to the outer reef for $155 per person, all inclusive.

The MV *Moruya* (☎ (079) 46 6665 or 018 185 653) has day trips leaving from Shute Harbour at noon, returning at 8 pm, for $59 per person. It's a 54-ft timber fishing boat; lunch, dinner, bait and tackle are included in the price.

You could also hire your own boat. There are quite a few operators hiring boats with fishing gear, including the Shell Garage (☎ 018 182 584) at Shute Harbour. They have cruisers for $98 a day and dinghies for $65 a day, including fuel.

Sail Yourself/Bareboat Charters Sailing through the Whitsunday Passage in 1770, Cook wrote that 'the whole passage is one continued safe harbour'. In actual fact stiff breezes and fast flowing tides can produce some tricky conditions for small craft but, with a little care, the Whitsundays offer superb sailing and bareboat charters have become enormously popular. 'Bareboat' doesn't refer to what you wear on board, it simply means you rent the boat without skipper, crew or provisions.

The operators usually require a $500 bond, payable on arrival and refunded after the boat is returned undamaged. Bedding is usually supplied and provisions can also be provided if you wish. Most companies have a minimum hire period of five days, although during the low season of January to March a few companies offer three-day hires at standby rates.

Most operators have a wide range of yachts and cruisers available. You'll pay around $220 a day for a Holland 25 yacht which sleeps two people, around $380 a day for a Robertson 950 yacht which sleeps up to four people, around $400 a day for a Spacesailor 36 which sleeps up to six people, and around $375 a day for a Clipper 34 motor cruiser which sleeps up to six people.

There are quite a number of bareboat charter companies at Airlie Beach. If you contact any (or all) of the following operators, they'll send you one of their brochures detailing their boats, rates and conditions:

Mandalay Boat Charters
    PO Box 273, Airlie Beach, Whitsunday Qld 4802
    (☎ (079) 46 6298 or toll-free 1800 075 123)
Whitsunday Rent-a-Yacht
    PMB 25 Mackay, Qld 4741 (☎ (079) 46 9232 or toll-free 1800 075 111)
Cumberland Charter Yachts
    PO Box 49, Airlie Beach, Qld 4802 (☎ (079) 46 7500 or toll-free 008 075 101)
Sail Whitsunday
    PO Box 929, Airlie Beach, Qld 4802 (☎ (079) 46 7070 or toll-free 008 075 045)
Queensland Yacht Charters
    PO Box 293, Airlie Beach, Qld 4802 (☎ (079) 46 7400 or toll-free 008 075 013)
Australian Bareboat Charters
    PO Box 357, Airlie Beach, Whitsunday Qld 4802
    (☎ (079) 46 9381 or toll-free 1800 075 000)

Organised Tours
Island & Reef Cruises All boat trips to the Whitsundays depart from either Shute Harbour or the Abel Point Marina near Airlie Beach. There's a bamboozling array of trips on offer, and all the accommodation places and agencies have dozens of brochures. Most of the cruise operators do coach pick-ups from Airlie Beach and Cannonvale. You can take a bus to Shute Harbour, or you can leave your car in the Shute Harbour car park for $7 for 24 hours. There's a lock-up car park a few hundred metres back along the road by the Shell service station, costing $5 from 8 am to 5 pm or $8 for 24 hours.

All of the boats and trips are different, so it's worth speaking to a couple of booking agents to find out what trip will suit you. There are leisurely sailing cruises to uninhabited islands, high-speed diving trips to the outer reefs, and cruises that take in several different destinations. Most day trips include activities like snorkelling and boom netting, with scuba diving as an optional extra. Children generally pay half fare.

The following are some of the day trips on offer:

Nari (☎ (079) 46 5755)
    The twin-keeled *Nari* operates sailing cruises to the Hook Island reefs or Blue Pearl Bay on Hayman Island, costing $45 including lunch.
On the Edge (☎ (079) 46 5433)
    A large sailing catamaran with cruises to Whitehaven Beach or to Mantaray Bay on Hook Island, costing from $49 with lunch.
Gretel (☎ (079) 46 6224)
    This maxi-yacht, a former challenger for the America's Cup, sails out to the lovely Langford Reef. The day trip costs $55 including lunch.
Reef Express (☎ (079) 46 6177)
    A fast motor cruiser which takes you out to Mantaray Bay on Hook Island and to Whitehaven Beach, costing $45. Lunch can be bought on board.
Maxi Ragamuffin (☎ (079) 46 7777)
    Another maxi-yacht which alternates between reef trips and Whitehaven Beach, costing $55 for the day including lunch.
Whitsunday Diver (☎ (079) 46 5366)
    A specialised dive boat which cruises out to Bait Reef on the outer reef. The day trip costs $70 for snorkellers and $115 for certified divers, with two dives and all gear supplied. Lunch is included.
Pro Diver (☎ (079) 46 6996)
    Another dive boat, operated by Pro Dive, which also cruises out to the outer reefs, costing $75 for snorkellers and $120 for certified divers, with two dives and all gear supplied. Again, lunch is included.

There are also dozens of overnight or longer trips around the islands on offer. Meals and snorkelling gear are usually included, and you either sleep on board or in tents on an island. The following are just a few of the trips on offer:

Anaconda II (☎ (079) 46 6032 or toll-free 1800 075 035)
    This nine-cabin maxi-yacht has three-day three-night cruises to Bait, Black and/or Fairey Reefs for up to 20 passengers. Cruises cost $295 for snorkellers, $325 for divers with their own gear or $370 for divers with gear supplied.

WHITSUNDAY COAST

Coral Trekker (☎ (079) 46 7197 or toll-free 008 075 042)

A refitted 75-ft Norwegian square rigger with two four-share cabins and one six-share cabin, the *Coral Trekker* has four-day three-night cruises for $485 and seven-day six-night cruises for $825. Scuba diving is available at an additional cost.

Southern Cross (☎ (079) 46 7619 or 018 776 631)

An America's Cup challenger designed by Ben Lexon in the 1970s, *Southern Cross* is a refitted maxi-yacht which has three-day two-night snorkelling cruises from $230.

Prosail (☎ (079) 46 5433)

Prosail runs adventure sailing cruises for the 18-to-35s market on a range of modern sailing yachts, costing from $245 per person.

SV *Basilea* (☎ (079) 46 7173)

This luxury yacht offers chartered cruises around the Whitsundays for up to six guests. There are three double cabins with ensuites; all meals, snorkelling gear and other water sports gear are included. Diving and fishing are available at an additional cost. The charter cost is $1400 a day for up to four people and $1500 a day for six people.

Flights Coral Air Whitsundays, based at the Whitsunday Airport, has the only day trip to exclusive Hayman Island. For $120 per person, they'll fly in one of their seaplanes from the mainland to the island, where you have use of all the resort facilities for the day. You can also combine this trip with their flight from Hayman out to the beautiful Blue Lagoon at Hardy Reef – the combo deal costs $265 per person.

Also based at the Whitsunday Airport, Heli Reef (☎ (079) 46 9102) has helicopter flights out to Fantasea's huge Reef World pontoon on the outer reef. The fare is $195, which includes snorkelling gear, rides in the glass-bottomed boat and semisubmersible, and lunch.

Places to Stay
Camping Although accommodation at the island resorts is mostly expensive, it's possible to camp on several islands. Hook Island has a privately run camping ground, and on North Molle, Whitsunday, Henning, Border, Haslewood, Shaw, Thomas, Repulse and Hook islands you can camp cheaply at

National Parks sites. Self-sufficiency is the key to camping in National Parks sites; some have toilets, but only a few have drinking water, and then not always year round. You're advised to take five litres of water per person per day, plus three days extra supply in case you get stuck. You should also have a fuel stove – wood fires are banned on some islands and unwelcome on the others. There's a National Parks leaflet which describes the various sites, and provides detailed information on what to take and do. The National Parks district office (☎ (079) 46 7022) is two km east of Airlie Beach on Shute Harbour Rd.

For information on boat transport to and from the islands, contact one of the many booking agencies in Airlie Beach. For $40 to $65 return per person, a number of the regular day trip boats will drop you off at the end of a cruise and pick you up again on an agreed date. Some boat operators will rent you water containers or help you organise other gear.

Contact the National Parks office to arrange a camping permit ($3 per person per night); sites take up to six people and numbers are limited for each camping ground.

The possibilities for camping in national parks in the Whitsundays are summarised in the table.

Resorts There are resorts on seven of the Whitsunday Islands. Most were built or revamped during the tourism boom of the 1980s, and with the exception of the Hook Island resort they are reasonably expensive. All the resorts are quite different, ranging from the five-star luxury of the Hayman Island resort to the simple little beachfront huts of the Long Island Palm Bay resort, and from the high-rise development of Hamilton Island to the simple cabins of Hook Island.

The rates quoted in this chapter are the standard rates, but hardly anyone will be paying these. Most travel agents can put together a range of discounted package deals which combine air fares and/or transfers to the resort with accommodation, and in some cases, meals.

It's also worth noting that, unless they're full, all of the resorts offer heavily discounted stand-by rates. The amount of discount depends on the time of year. As an example, in January/February of 1995 (traditionally the quietest time), the following per-person stand-by rates were on offer from travel agents in Airlie Beach: Hayman Island $100, Hamilton Island $60, Daydream Island $79, South Molle Island $90 (meals included), Whitsunday Long Island Resort $39 and Long Island Palm Bay Resort $45.

Getting There & Around
Air The two main airports for the Whitsundays are Hamilton Island and Proserpine. Only Ansett flies into Hamilton Island, whereas both Ansett and Qantas fly into Proserpine. See those sections for more details.

The Whitsunday Airport also has regular flights from the mainland to the island – light planes, seaplanes and helicopters. See Getting There & Away in the Airlie Beach section for details. Lindeman Island also has its own airstrip.

Bus Greyhound Pioneer Australia and McCafferty's both have bus services that detour off the Bruce Hwy to Airlie Beach. Local bus services also operate between Proserpine, Airlie Beach and Shute Harbour.

Train Proserpine is the closest town on the main railway line to the Whitsundays; connecting bus services operate to Airlie Beach and Shute Harbour from there.

Sea Roylen's Cruises has weekend trips from Mackay to Hamilton and Lindeman islands – see the Mackay section for details.

The other services to the islands all operate out of Shute Harbour or the Abel Point Marina near Airlie Beach. Fantasea Cruises and Whitsunday Allover are the two major operators for transfers to the islands – see the Getting There & Away sections for the individual islands for details of water taxis and ferries. There are also dozens of different cruise operators heading out to the islands – see the previous section on Organised Tours.

WHITSUNDAY COAST

Whitsunday Islands Camping Grounds			
Island	**Location**	**Sites**	**Drinking Water**
Shute	Northern End	2	no
North Molle	Cockatoo Beach	5	seasonal
Whitsunday	Whitehaven Beach	10	no
	Scrub Hen Beach	3	no
	Dugong Beach	7	seasonal
	Sawmill Beach	5	seasonal
	Joe's Beach	4	no
Hook	Curlew Beach	4	no
Thomas	Sea Eagle Beach	3	no
Shaw	Neck Bay Beach	3	no
South Repulse	Western Beach	3	no
Gloucester*	Bona Bay	7	no
Armit*	Western Beach	5	no
Saddleback*	Western Side	3	no
Grassy	South-West Point	2	no

* Northern islands like Armit, Gloucester and Saddleback are harder to reach since the water taxi and cruises from Shute Harbour don't usually go there. Gloucester and Saddleback are best reached from Earlando, Dingo Beach or Bowen. ∎

LAGUNA QUAYS

Two-thirds of the way from Mackay to Proserpine, there are two turn offs from the Bruce Hwy leading to Midge Point and Laguna Quays on the coast. Midge Point is a small and undeveloped settlement with two caravan parks.

A couple of km north, Laguna Quays is an elaborate and up-market tourism resort and residential development, centred around a boat marina and a golf course. The resort's **Turtle Point golf course** is one of the best resort courses in Australia, and features a couple of sensational ocean holes. It's the home of the rich Australian Skins Tournament, held every year in February, and is open to the general public on Tuesday and Friday. A round costs $70 and you can hire clubs here for another $20.

The *Laguna Quays Resort* (☎ (079) 47 7777) is very impressive – as their brochure says, it's somewhere between a five-star hotel and a country club. There are several restaurants and cocktail bars, a 'beach club' with a lagoon and a range of water sports equipment, a huge swimming pool, tennis courts, a 'kid's club' which organises all sorts of games and activities for children, and the great golf course. Daily tariffs are around $240 for a lodge room, from $200 to $360 for the one, two and three-bedroom villas and condos, and around $620 for the presidential suite (named, presumably, in anticipation of an Australian republic).

Despite all this, it's hard to figure out why you would stay here unless you're an absolute golf fanatic or a yachtie. It's a scenic and isolated setting, but the beaches aren't great and if you want to take a boat to the Whitsundays, you have to drive to Airlie Beach or Shute Harbour first. For these prices, you could be out on one of the island resorts.

PROSERPINE (pop 3000)

The turn off point for Airlie Beach and the Whitsundays, Proserpine is pretty typical of the numerous sugar-mill towns that are strung along the Bruce Hwy in north Queensland. A tourist information centre (☎ (079) 453 711) on the highway, next to the BP service station, provides information about the Whitsundays and the surrounding region. They are open on weekdays from 8.30 am to 5 pm.

Proserpine's main street is a busy little shopping precinct, with four pubs, a few eateries, a post office, and Westpac, ANZ and National banks. The **Proserpine Cultural Hall** is a theatre complex which also acts as the local cinema, screening a different movie each week. At the end of Main St, before the railway crossing, the **Proserpine Historical Museum** is open on Tuesday and Thursday from 9.30 am to 4 pm.

During the processing season, from June to November, there are tours of the **Proserpine Sugar Mill** every weekday at 10 am and 2 pm. The tour costs $7 for adults and $3 for kids, and you need to wear enclosed shoes. Bookings can be made through the information centre.

Places to Stay

There are three or four motels along the Bruce Hwy south of Proserpine. The first place you come to, the small *Whitsunday Palms Motel* (☎ (079) 45 1868), is good value with clean budget units from $36/38 for singles/doubles. Further on at 156 Main St the *A&A Motel* (☎ (079) 45 1888) also has good budget rooms from $42, and a small pool.

Getting There & Away

Air Ansett and Qantas both have direct flights between Proserpine and Brisbane ($290), Mackay ($113), Townsville ($149) and Cairns ($212). The airport is 14 km south of town.

Island Air Taxis (☎ (079) 46 9933) has flights from Proserpine airport to Hamilton Island or Lindeman Island for $60 one way.

Bus Sampson's (☎ (079) 45 2377) runs bus services from Proserpine to Airlie Beach ($11 one way) and Shute Harbour ($13). As well as their regular services, which run frequently every day between 6 am and around

7 pm, they also meet all scheduled planes and trains.

Train Proserpine is on the main Brisbane-Cairns railway line; the *Sunlander*, *Spirit of the Tropics* and *Queenslander* trains all stop here.

AIRLIE BEACH (pop 2700)

Airlie Beach, 25 km north-west of Proserpine, is the gateway to the Whitsunday Islands. It's a small but lively centre which has grown phenomenally over the past 10 years or so, a pattern which seems set to continue for some years to come. The whole town now revolves around tourism and pleasure boating, and it attracts a diverse bunch of boaties, backpackers, tourists, and divers, all of whom are here for a good time. Apart from being the main access point for the Whitsundays, Airlie's attributes include a good range of accommodation – from backpackers' hostels to resorts – plenty of good eateries and restaurants, a broad range of activities on offer, and a lively nightlife.

Airlie Beach also has a reputation as a centre for learning to scuba dive. Whale-watching boat trips, between July and September, are another attraction. Despite all the recent development, it's still a small place which has managed to retain its relaxed air.

Orientation

Airlie Beach itself stretches for less than one km from end to end. Shute Harbour Rd runs through the centre of town, and you'll find just about everything of importance along here, including the post office, the banks and most of the shops and restaurants.

The town is backed by low hills and set back from Airlie Bay, which has two small crescent-shaped beaches, separated by a creek. There's plenty of sand for sunbakers, but these aren't great beaches for swimming, especially at low tide when the water subsides to leave a shallow and muddy strip.

Long-distance buses stop in the car park in the centre, between Shute Harbour Rd and

the bay. Boats to the Whitsundays leave from either Shute Harbour, eight km east of Airlie Beach, or from the Abel Point Marina, one km west.

Before you arrive in Airlie Beach, you pass through Cannonvale, which is virtually a newer (and bigger) satellite suburb of Airlie Beach. There's a gap of about one km between the two. Cannonvale sprawls along the Proserpine-Shute Harbour road for about four km, and is growing quickly with several housing and industrial developments on its outskirts. Cannonvale has a good golf course, several shopping centres, a handful of resorts and restaurants and a beach with a stinger enclosure.

Information

Tourist Information The Whitsunday Visitors Bureau (☎ (079) 46 6673), upstairs in the Beach Plaza shopping arcade, is mainly a marketing body but has a good collection of brochures and can answer most enquiries.

While every second shopfront in Airlie Beach claims to be a 'tourist information centre', these places are all privately run tour-booking and ticket agencies. They include the Airlie Beach Tourist Information Centre (☎ (079) 46 6665) on Shute Harbour Rd, near the bus stop, and Destination Whitsundays (☎ (079) 46 6846), upstairs on the corner of Shute Harbour Rd and Airlie Esplanade.

All of the accommodation places can also give advice and book tours, boat trips and transport to the islands.

Money The ANZ, National and Westpac banks all have branches along Shute Harbour Rd. There is a Thomas Cook Foreign Exchange booth, at 287 Shute Harbour Rd, which is open Monday to Saturday from 8 am to 6 pm (Friday from 8.30 am) and on Sunday from 1 to 6 pm.

Post Airlie Beach's post office, on the corner of Shute Harbour Rd and Broadwater Ave, is open on weekdays from 9 am to 5 pm and Saturday from 9 am to noon.

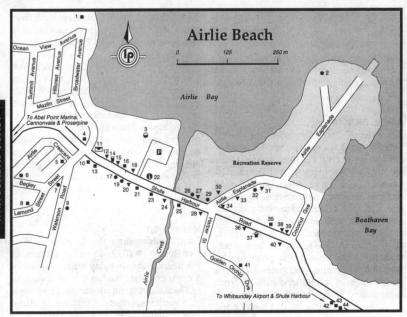

Useful Organisations There's a combined QNP&WS and Great Barrier Reef Marine Park Authority office (☎ (079) 46 7022), on the corner of Shute Harbour Rd and Mandalay Rd, about two km past Airlie Beach towards Shute Harbour. It is open from 8 am to 5 pm Monday to Friday and at varying weekend hours, and deals with camping bookings and permits for Conway and the Whitsunday Islands national parks. The rangers here are very helpful and can advise you on which islands to camp on, how to get there, what to take etc.

Bookshops The newsagency on Shute Harbour Rd has a large selection of holiday reading and beach literature, as well as a small travel section with a range of books on the Whitsundays. It also stocks a wide range of interstate and overseas newspapers.

Airlie Stationery & Bookshop, in the Beach Plaza shopping arcade, has a small, diverse and rather esoteric selection of books. In the same

arcade, The Sanctuary has a range of books for disciples of the New Age.

Laundry The Airlie Beach Coin Laundromat is in the Beach Plaza shopping arcade, and is open daily from 7 am to 9 pm.

Notice Board A notice board outside the newsagency on the main street has notices for work, lifts offered, things for sale, rooms to rent and boat crews needed.

Things to See & Do
Wildlife Park The Wildlife Park has a large collection of Australian mammals, birds and reptiles, with various shows each day such as crocodile-feeding, koala-feeding and snake handling. The park is open daily from 8.30 am to 5 pm and entry costs $14 for adults, $6 for children. It's eight km west of Airlie Beach, and a courtesy bus does pickups and drop-offs from wherever you're staying.

PLACES TO STAY

1 Coral Sea Resort
4 Colonial Court Motel
5 Club 13 Begley Street
6 Sunlit Waters Holiday
  Flats
8 Airlie Beach Motor Lodge
10 Whitsunday Wanderers
   Resort
13 Blue Waters Lodge
16 Whitsunday on the Beach
21 Beaches Backpackers
23 True Blue Backpackers
25 Whitsunday Village Resort
35 Airlie Beach Hotel
37 Club Habitat YHA
41 Whitsunday Terraces Resort
42 Boathaven Lodge
43 Backpackers by the Bay
44 Colonial Palms Motor Inn

PLACES TO EAT

12 Hog's Breath Cafe
15 Happy Gourmet
18 Cafe Le Mignon
20 Beaches Bar & Bistro
24 Magnums Bar & Grill
27 Cafe Gourmet
28 KC's Char Grill
30 Pinky's
31 Airlie's Own
33 Sidewalk Cafe
34 Figaro's
36 Chatz Bar & Brasserie
38 Da Marino's
39 Charlie's Round the Bend
40 Grasshoppers Cafe

OTHER

2 Whitsunday Sailing Club
3 Long-distance Bus Stop
7 Airlie Beach Rentals
9 Whitsunday Fitness & Leisure
  Centre
11 Post Office
14 Main Street Nightclub
17 Tricks Nightclub
19 Newsagent & Notice Board
22 Airlie Beach Tourist Information
   Centre
26 Thomas Cook Foreign Exchange
29 Destination Whitsundays
32 Beach Plaza Arcade

Diving This is one of the best and most popular places to learn to dive, and at least five outfits in and around Airlie Beach offer five to seven-day scuba-diving certificate courses. Costs for open-water courses vary from $250 to $500, but note that with the cheaper courses you spend most of your time in the pool and classroom and you might only do four or five dives. For another couple of hundred dollars, you get to enjoy what you've learned and, more importantly, build up invaluable experience with 10 or more dives. Generally, courses involve two or three days tuition on the mainland with the rest of the time diving on the Great Barrier Reef – ask whether meals and accommodation are included in the price. Book where you are staying, or at one of the agencies on the main road in Airlie Beach.

The companies include: Oceania Dive (☎ (079) 46 6032), Reef Enterprise Dive Services (☎ (079) 46 7228) and Pro-Dive (☎ (079) 46 6508), all on Shute Harbour Rd; Barrier Reef Diving Services (☎ (079) 46 6204) on Airlie Esplanade; and Kelly Dive (☎ (079) 46 6122), based at the Reef Oceania Village resort in Cannonvale.

The same companies also offer a good range of diving trips for certified divers, from day trips to overnighters which combine the reef with the islands.

Swimming & Water Sports There are reasonable beaches at Airlie Beach and Cannonvale, although at low tide you'll have a long walk before you get more than your knees wet, and the presence of marine stingers means that swimming isn't advisable between October and May. There is a swimming enclosure at the Cannonvale beach.

There are two operators down at Airlie Bay who hire out a range of water sports equipment, including jet skis, catamarans, windsurfers and paddle skis.

As an alternative to the beaches, there's an excellent 25-metre freshwater pool at the Coral Sea Resort, on Ocean View Ave, open to the public daily from 7 am to 6.30 pm, and costs $3 per person. There's a poolside bar and restaurant, and good grassy areas with sun-lounges overlooking the ocean. The pool at the Cannonvale State School is also open to the public.

Horse Riding You can take horseback trail rides with Brandy Creek Trail Rides (☎ (079) 46 6665), 12 km from Airlie Beach back towards Proserpine. They can pick you up from your accommodation. The three-hour rides cost $35 and depart every day at 9 am, and at 3 pm from October to April and at 2 pm from May to September.

Adventure Activities Airlie Beach has developed into something of a centre for adrenaline junkies. You can go bungy jumping with Total Extreme for $65, or do a tandem skydive from 10,000 feet for $239.

Other possibilities include a joy flight in an ultralight plane ($50), spending a day learning to abseil at Cedar Creek Falls ($45, including lunch), and land-sailing at low tide along the foreshore at Conway Beach ($35). For the combat-minded, there's also a skirmish (paintball) course near the Bowen turn off, 12 km west of Airlie Beach. It costs $49 per person to 'play'. You can book any of these activities through your accommodation or one of the agents in Airlie Beach.

Organised Tours
Cruises and Fishing Trips A huge range of cruisers, yachts and boats offer trips out to the Whitsundays from the Abel Point Marina and Shute Harbour. See the introduction to this section for details of some of these.

Rainforest Tours There are a couple of operators offering tours of the rainforest areas of the Conway National Park. Whitsunday Attractions have a half-day tour which leaves at 9 am daily and costs $35/15 for adults/children, including a stop in billy tea and damper. Fawlty's 4WD Tropical Rainforest Tour leaves at 10.45 am daily and costs $35/17, including a barbecue lunch.

Both of these can be booked through your accommodation or one of the agencies in Airlie Beach.

Festivals
Airlie Beach is the centre of activities during the annual Whitsunday Fun Race Festival (for cruising yachts) each September. The festivities include a Miss Figurehead competition where the contestants traditionally compete topless.

Places to Stay
Camping There are no caravan parks in Airlie Beach itself, but there are plenty of choices within a couple of km of the centre. Most of these places tend to be busy during the school holidays, but at other times you won't have any trouble finding somewhere to pitch your tent or park your van.

There are four good caravan parks along the road between Airlie Beach and Shute Harbour. The closest of these, the *Island Gateway Caravan Village* (☎ (079) 46 6228), is about 1.5 km east of Airlie Beach. It has good facilities including a campers' kitchen, a pool, a shop and half-court tennis. Tent sites cost $12 a double, camp-o-tels (semi-permanent tents) $18 a double, on-site vans $25 a double and on-site units and cabins start at $35. Farther along are the *Shute Harbour Gardens Caravan Park* (☎ (079) 46 6483), two km east; the *Airlie Cove Resort Van Park* (☎ (079) 46 6727), 2.5 km east; and the *Flame Tree Tourist Village* (☎ (079) 46 9388), six km east. All of these have comparably good facilities, and tent sites for around $10, on-site vans around $25 and on-site cabins around $35.

Also just off the road to Shute Harbour, there's a good camping ground in the Conway National Park, seven km east of Airlie Beach. There are 16 shady tent sites, with showers, toilets, picnic tables and barbecues. It's a self-registration site, and the fee here is $3 per person, with a maximum stay of two weeks. For camping permits and bookings, contact the QNP&WS office (☎ (079) 46 7022), on Shute Harbour Rd, three km east from Airlie Beach.

In Cannonvale, 1.5 km west of Airlie Beach, the *Seabreeze Tourist Park* (☎ (079) 46 6379), has tent sites from $10 a double and on-site vans from $25.

Hostels Airlie Beach has become one of the main stopovers on the backpackers' circuit and has a good range of hostels, so there should be something to suit most tastes, whether you're after a big party place or somewhere small and quiet.

There is fierce competition to get bodies on beds, with a couple of places offering bunks for $6 in the quiet times, but as with most things, you generally get what you pay for. The standard price for a dorm bed is usually around $12. At the main bus stop there's a row of booths where the hostel reps tout for trade when the buses arrive. All the places out of the centre run courtesy buses to and from Airlie Beach.

Right in the centre, the *Whitsunday Village Resort* (☎ (079) 46 6266) is a huge place, set out in a very pleasant tropical garden with two pools. The emphasis here is on partying, with a restaurant and bar next door which has activities each night. The standard of accommodation varies: bunks in the basic six-share units near the bar, which tend to be noisy and have limited cooking facilities, range from $6 to $10. For $12 you get a bed in a four-share timber cabin back in the gardens. Doubles range from $30 to $50.

Also in the centre is *Beaches Backpackers* (☎ (079) 46 6244), another big place with a party attitude and its own bar and restaurant. The rooms and facilities in this converted motel are good, with five-bed (not bunk) units with their own bathroom and balcony, TV and air-con, a pool and a good kitchen. Beds cost $12.

Sandwiched between these two places is *True Blue Backpackers* (☎ (079) 46 6662), another converted old motel. One of the dive companies operates out of here, and they were in the process of renovating the place when I last visited. The six and eight-bunk units upstairs have bathrooms and basic cooking facilities and cost $10 to $12, and the twins and doubles downstairs are $30.

A little further along Shute Harbour Rd is *Club Habitat YHA* (☎ (079) 46 6312), yet another motel converted to backpackers' accommodation. A night in a four to six-bed unit with bathroom costs $13, and twin rooms cost $32; nonmembers pay an extra $2. There's a pool, good communal kitchen and lounge, and the atmosphere is friendly.

Up the other end of Shute Harbour Rd, at No 348, *Blue Waters Lodge* (☎ (079) 46 6182) is a small block of backpackers' units with four to five-bed units at $12 and double rooms at $29. The units and the doubles share a bathroom and kitchen with basic cooking facilities.

Club 13 Begley St (☎ (079) 46 7376) overlooks the bay from the hill just above the centre. This is a multilevel complex of five three-bedroom apartments, with each apartment sharing two bathrooms (some with spa), a kitchen and laundry. There's a pool and spa, undercover parking and great views from the balconies. A bed in a four or six-share room costs $12, including breakfast.

A couple of hundred metres out of town towards Shute Harbour is *Backpackers by the Bay* (☎ (079) 46 7267), at Lot 5, Hermitage Dve. It's a small, relaxed hostel with a good atmosphere, and is probably quieter than those in the centre. The nightly cost in a small four-bed dorm is $12 and doubles are $29.

Back the other way from the centre is the *Beach House* (☎ (079) 46 6306), overlooking Shingley Beach. It's about 1.5 km from Airlie Beach – take the Abel Point Marina turn off and turn left. This is a two-storey block of units, with a pool and a backpackers' section downstairs. Each unit has a double bed and two bunks, its own bathroom and a kitchenette, and costs $25 a night for a double, $30 for a triple or $35 for four people, plus another $5 if you want air-con.

Further along towards Cannonvale, about 1.5 km west from Airlie Beach, is the *Bush Village Backpackers Resort* (☎ (079) 46 6177) in St Martin's Lane (just off Shute Harbour Rd). Run by a friendly and helpful family, this place has clean and simple four-bed cabins in a pleasant garden setting. Dorms range from $10 to $14, twins are $30 and doubles are $32; prices include breakfast. Each cabin has cooking facilities, fridge, bathroom and TV. There's also a pool and a spa, bikes and mopeds for hire, and a courtesy bus which makes frequent runs into the centre.

The *Reef Oceania Village* (☎ (079) 46 6137), at 141 Shute Harbour Rd in Cannonvale, is about three km west of Airlie Beach. This is a good resort complex (see the resort section for details) and has a small section for backpackers, with a bed in the basic two or four-bunk room costing from $5 or in a four to six-share cabin for $12.

Hotels The *Airlie Beach Hotel* (☎ (079) 46 6233), which occupies a large site stretching from Shute Harbour Rd through to Airlie Esplanade, currently has standard motel-style units from $49 a double. There are plans to redevelop this hotel into an up-market four-star resort, in which case prices will rise substantially. Ring them for the latest.

Motels There are a couple of budget motels in central Airlie Beach. The *Airlie Beach Motor Lodge* (☎ (079) 46 6418), up on Lamond St, has motel rooms from $46/50 for singles/doubles and two-bedroom self-contained units from $60. Opposite the post office, on the corner of Shute Harbour Rd and Broadwater Ave, the *Colonial Court Motel* (☎ (079) 46 6180), has motel units with kitchenettes from $40/50.

The *Colonial Palms Motor Inn* (☎ (079) 46 7522), a couple of hundred metres out of Airlie Beach on the road to Shute Harbour, is a modern two-storey motel on a hillside overlooking Boathaven Bay. There's a pool and a pleasant licensed restaurant, and singles/doubles start from $65/72.

Holiday Flats & Apartments There are quite a few blocks of older-style holiday flats and apartments in and around Airlie Beach which can be good value, especially for a group of friends travelling together or a family. Generally, these places have cooking facilities and supply bed linen.

Right in the centre of town, at 26 Shute Harbour Rd, *Whitsunday on the Beach* (☎ (079) 46 6359) is a two-storey block of modest studio units. They have air-con and TVs, but the cooking facilities are limited to a fridge and a toaster, although the new owners are planning to renovate and upgrade the facilities. Tariffs range from $55 to $65 for doubles and from $10 to $15 for extras, depending on the season.

In the hills above Airlie Beach, *Sunlit Waters* (☎ (079) 46 6352), on the corner of Begley St and Airlie Cres, has five small and basic studio-style flats with great views, and a pool. The flats can sleep up to four people (at a squeeze) and cost around $38 a double plus $8 for each extra person.

Boathaven Lodge (☎ (079) 46 6421), a couple of hundred metres east of the town centre, at 440 Shute Harbour Rd, is a small strip of neat, renovated studio units on a hill overlooking Boathhaven Bay. The units sleep two or three people and cost $40, or $50 with a carport. The lodge has a small pool.

On the beachfront in Cannonvale, the *Whitsunday Apartments* (☎ (079) 46 6860), at 48 Coral Esplanade, has one and two-bedroom self-contained units starting from $55 for a double.

Resorts Most of the resorts here have package deals and stand-by rates which are much cheaper than their regular rates.

In Cannonvale, *Club Crocodile* (☎ (079) 46 7155), 1.5 km west of Airlie Beach on Shute Harbour Rd, is a popular and modern mid-range resort with 160 motel-style units built around an attractive central courtyard with landscaped gardens, fountains, a pool, spa, tennis court, and a courtyard bar. There's a casual bistro with pub-style meals in the $10 to $12 range, or a more expensive restaurant. The normal tariffs are $99 for a standard double room or $120 for a deluxe room – stand-by rates for the same rooms are $65/85.

The *Coral Sea Resort* (☎ (079) 46 6458), at 25 Ocean View Ave, sits at the end of a low headland overlooking the ocean and the Abel Point Marina. The resort has a large and excellent pool, a poolside cocktail bar and a good restaurant. Standard motel units range from $99 a double to $125 for a room with ocean views, and two-bedroom units are $165 for up to four people. Stand-by rates are about $20 cheaper.

Set on eight hectares in central Airlie Beach, *Whitsunday Wanderers* (☎ (079) 46 6446) on Shute Harbour Rd is another large resort. There are four pools, tennis courts, landscaped gardens, a bar, restaurant and nightly live entertainment, plus 124 modern Melanesian-style units. Normal rates are around $100 a double, stand-by rates around $65. The *Reef Oceania Village* (☎ (079) 46 6137), mentioned earlier in the hostels section, is in Cannonvale about three km east of Airlie Beach. It has a pleasant garden setting, a large pool, a bar with a covered courtyard, a restaurant and communal cooking and laundry facilities. Modern timber cabins cost $49 for a double or $69 for a family – their stand-by rates are good value at $36/49. A courtesy bus runs a shuttle service into Airlie Beach.

The large *Whitsunday Terraces Resort* (☎ (079) 46 6788), up on Golden Orchid Dve overlooking Airlie Beach and the ocean, has modern studio-style and one-bedroom apartments with cooking facilities and all the mod cons from $125 a night.

Eight km east at Shute Harbour on Harbour Ave, *Coral Point Lodge* (☎ (079) 46 9500) is a small, quiet, low-key resort with 10 motel-style units, five of which have kitchenettes. All the rooms have been renovated and have private balconies with good views over the harbour, and there's a small pool and restaurant. Singles/doubles cost $76/82, or $84/90 for the kitchenette rooms.

Places to Eat

If you're preparing your own food, there's a small supermarket on the main street (near the car park entrance) which has a good range of groceries, fruit and vegies.

Cafes, Delis & Takeaways Airlie Beach may be small, but it has some great eateries, including a good selection of delis, cafes and sandwich bars.

The *Happy Gourmet*, at 263 Shute Harbour Rd, is a great place for lunch, and you can eat in or takeaway. They make delicious filled rolls and sandwiches for $3 to $4.50, and I can tell you that both the carrot and chocolate cakes are wonderful. By night this place sells takeaway pizzas. Further along Shute Harbour Rd, beside the main car park, is the small and popular *Cafe Le Mignon*. They do good breakfasts, including croissants, muesli with fresh fruit and continentals from $4 to $6, or if you haven't eaten for about a week, tuck into their Bavarian Breakfast ($12). They also have good coffee, filled croissants and sandwiches, pancakes and omelettes.

At another good gourmet sandwich bar, *Cafe Gourmet*, at 289 Shute Harbour Rd, you can invent your own or order from their suggestion menus. Filled focaccias, bagels, French sticks and sandwiches range from $2.50 to $5.50. This place also has fresh fruit and vegie juices, smoothies and shakes.

If you're after a good cooked breakfast, head for the *Sidewalk Cafe*, on Airlie Esplanade. This friendly place looks like a basic takeaway, but has good food with everything from toasted sandwiches to cooked meals. It's open for breakfast, lunch and early dinners. Further along Airlie Esplanade, *Airlie's Own* is a budget-priced eatery serving hamburgers, pies, dogs and other snacks. *Pinky's*, near the corner of Shute Harbour Rd and Airlie Esplanade, is a casual coffee shop with cooked breakfasts from $4 to $6, crêpes, omelettes, pancakes, burgers, and a range of cooked meals from $7 to $9. *Grasshoppers* on Shute Harbour Rd, opposite the pub, is yet another gourmet deli with fresh, natural and healthy tucker – sandwiches, salads and juices.

Bars & Bistros *Beaches Bar & Bistro*, in the Beaches Backpackers complex, is popular with both travellers and locals and serves lunches and dinners. The dining area, a large covered courtyard with long timber tables, always seems to be pretty crowded, and the bar has various happy hours and plays good music. Meals range from salads, pastas and burgers from $5 to $6; roasts, chicken, calamari and fish dishes from $6 to $8; and steaks from $10 to $12. They have nightly specials and a Mexican buffet on Tuesday.

At the Whitsunday Village Resort, *Magnums Bar & Grill* is equally popular and equally lively, but mainly attracts the backpackers. It's only open for dinner, and you get a free beer with your meal. You can attack the salad bar for $3.50; vegetarian dishes, burritos, Thai curries and pastas range from $4 to $6; and chicken, steak and seafood dishes are all $6.

Restaurants At 261 Shute Harbour Rd is the *Hog's Breath Cafe*, one of a chain of bar & grill places. It has burgers, salads, sandwiches, steaks, seafood and prime ribs, with lunches from $6 to $10 and dinners from $13 to $17. On the corner of Shute Harbour Rd and Airlie Esplanade, *Figaro's* is a popular BYO pasta and pizza place with a cluster of tables out on the footpath. Pastas, including some interesting vegetarian choices, range from $7 to $9; small pizza from $9 to $10; and other Italian mains from $10 to $14.

Across the road, *KC's Char Grill* is a bit more up-market, and good for a splurge. It has a rustic, lively atmosphere and excellent food, with char-grilled steaks and seafood in the $16 to $22 range. It's licensed, is open for lunch and dinner and has live music most nights.

Further along Shute Harbour Rd is *Chatz Bar & Brasserie*. At the front is a lively little bar, with an eatery out the back offering burgers, salads, vegetarian meals, seafood and Italian-style main courses, all in the $8 to $14 range.

On the corner of Shute Harbour Rd and Coconut Grove, *Charlie's Round the Bend* is a fairly trendy bar/eatery with a small courtyard on the streetfront. This place has an interesting and diverse menu, with gourmet pizzas around $13, burgers and focaccias around $10, and main courses from $14 to $18. The bar here features live acoustic music every night. Next to Charlie's is *Da Marino's*, a casual and friendly little BYO bistro with excellent pastas for $9.50, and mains like pepper steak, saltimbocca or

grilled fish for $14. It also opens for lunches, with pastas, salads and Italian rolls from $3.50 to $9.50.

Airlie Beach's most up-market restaurant is *The Brasserie*, a sophisticated licensed restaurant upstairs in the Beach Plaza shopping arcade. The dining room is quite romantic, or there are tables out on the balcony. Main meals, which include some interesting seafood dishes, stir-fried Thai beef, rack of lamb and pork fillets, range from $16 to $20.

There are a couple of other restaurants in Cannonvale, including two in the main shopping centre on Shute Harbour Rd. The *Whitsunday Palace* is a modern and licensed Chinese restaurant which has the usual huge range of mains from $10 to $14. The *Post & Rail Steakhouse & Bar* is a western-style steakhouse with a wagon out front and outdoor tables. They specialise in steaks, but also throw lamb, chicken and fish on the barbie, with all mains around $13. This place has live music on Friday nights.

Entertainment

Airlie Beach has a reputation for partying hard, and has a small but lively nightlife scene. The bars at *Magnums* and *Beaches*, the two big backpackers' resorts in the centre of town, are usually pretty crowded, and good places to meet other travellers. Drinks also tend to be cheaper here than elsewhere.

At the time of writing, the *Airlie Beach Hotel* was the place to go for live rock music (and a bout of uninhibited slam-dancing), but once the proposed renovations are completed the pub may be upgrading its image somewhat – ask around when you arrive. Several of the bar/restaurants along Shute Harbour Rd also have regular live music. *Charlie's Round the Bend* has live acoustic music every night and stays open until 2 am; *KC's Char Grill* also has live music most nights.

There are a couple of nightclubs on Shute Harbour Rd: *Tricks*, upstairs next to the newsagent, and *Main Street*, upstairs in an arcade near the post office. Both stay open until 5 am. Tricks seems to be popular with the locals and the boaties, whereas Main Street seems to attract the backpackers.

You can also try night party cruises to a couple of resort islands.

There isn't a cinema in Airlie Beach, but the Whitsunday Fitness & Leisure Centre (☎ (079) 46 6928), at 13 Waterson Rd, has a big screen with movies at 8.15 pm on Tuesday, Saturday and Sunday. Entry costs $8.50 for adults and $5 for kids.

Getting There & Away
Air The Whitsunday Airport, a small airfield midway between Airlie Beach and Shute Harbour, is six km west of Airlie Beach. There are half a dozen different operators based here, and you can take a helicopter, a light plane or a seaplane out to the islands or the reef.

Island Air Taxis (☎ (079) 46 9933) has regular flights from here to Hamilton Island ($40 one way) and Lindeman Island ($50 one way). They also do charters and scenic flights. Island Air Taxis and Eagle Air (☎ (079) 46 9176) are both available for charter flights to wherever you may want to go.

Heli Reef (☎ (079) 46 9102) has a range of helicopter tours on offer – see the earlier Organised Tours section for details.

Bus About half of McCafferty's and Greyhound Pioneer Australia's bus services along the Bruce Hwy make the detour to Airlie Beach. (If you happen to be reading this while sitting on a bus that doesn't make the detour, you'll have to get off in Proserpine and catch a local bus from there.)

There are buses between Airlie Beach and all the major centres along the coast, including Brisbane (18 hours, $100), Mackay (two hours, $26) and Townsville (four hours, $36).

Long-distance buses all stop in the car park behind the shops, about halfway along Shute Harbour Rd. Any of the booking agencies along Shute Harbour Rd can make reservations or sell bus tickets.

Sampson's (☎ (079) 45 2377) runs regular bus services between Proserpine and Shute Harbour, via Airlie Beach and Cannonvale.

Their services operate seven days a week, from around 6 am till around 7 pm. The one-way fare from Proserpine to Airlie Beach is $11; from Proserpine to Shute Harbour is $13; and from Airlie Beach to Shute Harbour costs $3.

Sea The sailing club is at the end of Airlie Esplanade. There are notice boards at the newsagent in Airlie Beach and at Abel Point Marina showing when rides or crewing are available. Ask around Airlie Beach or Shute Harbour.

Getting Around
Airlie Beach is small enough to cover by foot, and all of the cruise boats have courtesy buses that will pick you up from wherever you're staying and take you to either Shute Harbour or the Abel Point Marina.

Several car-rental agencies operate locally; Avis, Hertz, Thrifty and National all have agencies on Shute Harbour Rd. Airlie Beach Rentals (☎ (079) 46 6110) one block back from the main street, on the corner of Begley St and Waterson Rd, has cars from $45 a day and scooters from $30 a day.

There's a taxi rank in Shute Harbour Rd, opposite Magnums. To book a taxi, call Whitsunday Taxis on ☎ 008 811 388.

CONWAY NATIONAL PARK
This national park is the mainland equivalent of the Whitsunday Islands. These mountains and the islands were once part of the same coastal mountain range, but rising sea levels after the last Ice age flooded the lower valleys and cut off the coastal peaks from the mainland.

Most of the park is composed of rugged ranges and valleys covered in rainforest, although there are also areas of mangroves and open forest. Only a small area of the park is accessible by road.

The road from Airlie Beach-Shute Harbour road passes through the northern section of the park. Several walking trails start from near the national park camping ground (see Camping in the section on Airlie Beach), including a one-km circuit track to a mangrove creek. About a km past the camping ground and on the north side of the road, there's a 2.4-km walk up to the Mt Roper lookout, which provides good views of the Whitsunday Passage and islands.

CEDAR CREEK FALLS & CONWAY BEACH

To reach the beautiful **Cedar Creek Falls**, turn off the Proserpine to Airlie Beach road on to Conway Rd, eight km north of Proserpine. It's then about 15 km to the falls – the roads are well signposted. It's a short walk from the small car park to a large swimming hole at the base of the falls. This is a popular picnic spot, and several tour operators run day trips into this area – see Organised Tours in the Airlie Beach section.

At the end of Conway Rd, 20 km from the turn off, is **Conway Beach**. A small coastal community on the shores of Repulse Bay and at the southern end of the Conway National Park, it consists of a few old houses and pleasant picnic areas along the foreshore. The *Black Stump Caravan Park* (☎ (079) 47 3147) has a bar and a pool, and tent sites from $6.50 a double and on-site vans from $18.

LONG ISLAND

The closest of the resort islands to the coast, Long Island has two active resorts and is nearly all national park. The island is about 11 km long but no more than 1.5 km wide anywhere, and a channel only 0.5 km wide separates it from the mainland. The 16.5-sq-km island has lots of rainforest, 13 km of walking tracks and some fine lookouts. Daytrippers to the island have use of the facilities at the Happy Bay resort, which is where the boats arrive.

Activities

The beaches on Long Island are quite attractive and tropical-looking, although severe tidal variations mean that low tide at Happy Bay is time to head for the swimming pool. The walking trails include a two-km trail between the two resorts, a three-km loop from Happy Bay to the north of the island,

and a four-km walk from Palm Bay south to Sandy Bay.

Both resorts have a range of water sports equipment. The *Whitsunday Long Island Resort* has a wider range, and hires out dinghies ($80 a day) and jet skis ($40 a half hour), and you can go water-skiing ($20) or paragliding ($45). Daytrippers and guests at Palm Bay can also avail themselves of these facilities.

Places to Stay

At Happy Bay in the north of the island, the *Whitsunday Long Island Resort* (☎ (079) 46 9400 or toll-free 008 075 125) is operated by Club Crocodile Holdings, which runs a similarly styled resort in Airlie Beach. It's a modern mid-range resort with three levels of affordable accommodation, and is popular with families and couples, with plenty of activities to keep children and adults busy.

The Beachfront Units, modern motel-style units overlooking Happy Bay, cost $170 a double. The Garden Rooms, which are of a similar standard but look out on the garden, are $140 a double. The Lodge Units are more basic rooms with shared bathrooms and no air-con, and go for $70 a double (including transfers). The resort has two swimming pools, tennis courts, a gym, a games room, windsurfers and catamarans, and use of all of these is included in the tariffs.

Two km south, the *Long Island Palm Bay Resort* (☎ (079) 46 9233 or toll-free 1800 334 009) is a low-key, old-fashioned retreat with just 14 individual cabins and bures (Melanesian-style bungalows) set around the sandy sweep of Palm Bay. They all have a double bed and four bunks, a kitchenette, a bathroom and their own little verandah, complete with a hammock for lazing the days away. There are no TVs or telephones. In the centre of the resort is a large island-style building which serves as the main dining area, bar, lounge and meeting place.

This is a good place to visit if you want to see what the island resorts used to be like before all the developers and hoteliers moved into the Whitsundays. The only catch is that the prices are certainly no reminder of days gone by – you're paying a premium for the individuality and smallness of the resort. The simple cabins cost $120/198 for singles/doubles; the newer and cuter bures are $168/234. Extra adults cost another $29, extra children another $15.

Places to Eat
At the *Whitsunday Long Island Resort*, guests have the option of buying a meals package for $40 (breakfast and dinner) or $50 (breakfast, lunch and dinner) or paying separately for meals. *Cafe Paradiso* is a pleasant indoor/outdoor cafe with rolls and sandwiches, chicken burgers, salads, pizzas, reef fish and the like, in the $5 to $10 range. The more formal *Palms* restaurant serves continental and buffet-style breakfasts, while for dinner you have a choice of buffet-style ($26) or ordering à la carte, with mains ranging from $14 to $20.

The *Long Island Palm Bay Resort* has a similar setup. A full meals package costs $53 for adults, $36 for children. There are straightforward home-style meals available or you can prepare your own meals in your room. The resort shop sells a small range of groceries.

Entertainment
The *Whitsunday Long Island Resort* has two bars, the Pool Bar and the Sand Bar. The latter becomes a disco as the night progresses, staying open until 2 am.

Getting There & Away
Whitsunday Allover (☎ (079) 46 6900) has three or four services a day from Shute Harbour to Long Island, including a day trip that leaves at 9.15 am. The return fare is $22 for adults and $12 for children. They also do airport runs to Hamilton Island, meeting all outgoing and incoming flights. The trip takes about 20 minutes from either place.

HOOK ISLAND
Second largest of the Whitsundays, Hook Island is 53 sq km and rises to 450 metres at Hook Peak. There are a number of good beaches dotted around the island, and Hook has some of the best diving and snorkelling locations in the Whitsundays, mostly at the northern end of the island.

The southern end of the island is indented by two very long and narrow fjord-like bays. Beautiful Nara Inlet is a very popular deep-water anchorage for visiting yachts, and Aboriginal wall paintings have been found in the inlet.

There's an **underwater observatory** at the southern tip of the island, although its coral displays aren't particularly impressive and it isn't worth the $8.50 entry fee.

Hook also has a small and low-key resort and camping ground. The resort facilities include a new swimming pool, a volleyball net and a couple of paddle skis. There's also a dive shop based here, offering a five-day certificate course for $277 including accommodation and transfers – one of the cheapest deals around.

Places to Stay
Camping There's a national park camping ground with 10 sites at Curlew Beach in Macona Inlet, at the southern end of the island.

Resort The *Hook Island Wilderness Lodge* is the only true budget resort in the Whitsundays. Its long accommodation block has 12 adjoining units, each with either eight bunks or a double bed and four bunks. The lodge is fairly old and basic, but it's clean, comfortable and cheap at $17 per person per night. Two people can have a unit to themselves for $46 a night. There are also good camping areas at both ends of the resort and the cost is $8.50 per person. Toilets and showers are shared by cabins and campers, but there are no laundry facilities.

The resort has a radio telephone (☎ 018 775 142), although all bookings and transfers are handled by the South Molle Island resort (☎ (079) 46 9433).

Places to Eat
The resort has a very casual restaurant with lunches like sandwiches, burgers and fish &

chips from $2.50 to $6. Dinner costs $10 for something simple like pasta, chicken, baked fish or a barbie. You can also use the barbecues or kitchen area to prepare your own food.

Getting There & Away

There's only one boat a day to Hook Island. It departs from Shute Harbour at 9 am, stopping at Daydream Island on the way to Hook. The return trip departs from Hook Island at 2 pm, and stops at South Molle Island for an hour before getting back to Shute Harbour at 5 pm. The return fare is $15, and bookings are handled by the resort or through South Molle Island (☎ (079) 46 9433).

DAYDREAM ISLAND

Daydream, the closest of the resort islands to Shute Harbour, is just over one km long and only a couple of hundred metres across at its widest point. The island has a large and modern resort with a mini-marina at its northern end, and a daytrippers' facility at its southern end.

Daydream is a popular island for day trips. Boats drop you at the Beach Club, which has a good sandy beach, an excellent kidney-shaped pool, a bar, several shops and a cafe. Catamarans, windsurfers, paddle boards, dinghies, jet skis and snorkelling equipment are available for hire (free for resort guests), and you can also go water-skiing here.

A nature walk links the Beach Club with the resort. It's a steep and rocky path which climbs over the centre of the island, and takes about 20 minutes. Just before the resort, a short path branches off to the tiny but lovely Sunlovers Beach. There's also a concrete path around the east side of the island. And once you've done these three walks, you've just about covered this little island from head to foot.

Places to Stay

The *Daydream Island Travelodge Resort* (☎ (079) 48 8488 or toll-free 008 075 040) is a stylish and modern family resort. Built in 1990, it's a three-storey complex with over 300 rooms, surrounded by impressively landscaped tropical gardens. The resort caters for children particularly well and offers plenty of activities, but with such a large resort on such a small island it's not the place to come to if you're looking for isolation. You certainly won't be lost or lonely on Daydream.

The rooms are comfortable motel-style units which sleep up to four people. There are three types of rooms, with daily tariffs at $90 per adult in a Garden View room, $105 per adult in an Ocean View room and $130 per adult in the deluxe Sunlover units. Children are charged $15 a night.

Included in the room rates are the use of tennis courts, a gym, sauna and spa, two swimming pools, aerobics classes, snorkelling gear, catamarans, windsurfers and more. The free Kids Only club keeps children entertained day and night with a diverse range of activities.

Places to Eat

The resort has half a dozen different eateries. The *Waterfall Cafe* specialises in buffet-style breakfasts, lunches and dinners. *Langford's Lounge* in the centre of the atrium area serves light snacks and sandwiches, and the *North Pool Bar* has various snacks and meals if you want to eat poolside. *Sunlovers*, a more formal à la carte restaurant, opens for dinners with main courses around $20.

Down at the Beach Club, *Skip's Cafe & Bakery* has a great selection of pies, sandwiches, rolls and cakes, and the *South Pool Bar* sells hot dogs.

Getting There & Away

Whitsunday Allover (☎ (079) 46 6900) has eight services a day from Shute Harbour and Hamilton Island to Daydream Island, including a day trip which departs daily from Shute Harbour at 9 am. The return fare is $22 for adults and $12 for children. They also have evening cruises from Shute Harbour nightly, departing at 6 pm and returning at 11.30 pm and costing $22/12.

Fantasea Cruises (☎ (079) 46 5111) also has day trips to Daydream on Monday, Wednesday, Friday, Saturday and Sunday.

They depart from Abel Point Marina at 9 am; return fares are $16/8.

SOUTH MOLLE ISLAND

Largest of the Molle group of islands at four sq km, South Molle is virtually joined to Mid Molle and North Molle islands – you can actually walk across a causeway to Mid Molle island. Apart from the resort area and golf course at Bauer Bay in the north, the island is all national park. There is some forest cover around the resort area, but due to overgrazing in the years before it was declared a national park, the rest of the island is mainly rolling grasslands. The island is crisscrossed by numerous walking tracks, and has some superb lookout points. The highest point is 198-metre Mt Jeffreys, but the climb up Spion Kop is also worthwhile.

The island is known for its prolific birdlife. The most noticeable birds are the dozens of tame, colourful lorikeets that will eat out of your hand at feeding time (3 pm). Currawongs and the endangered stone curlews are also common.

The island's beaches are reasonably good at high tide, but due to the severe tidal shifts in the Whitsundays, low tides tend to reveal unattractive mud flats. The resort has a big pool, a nine-hole golf course, a gym, and tennis and squash courts. There is also a wide range of water sports gear available for daytrippers to hire (non-powered water sports equipment is free for resort guests).

Places to Stay

The *South Molle Island Resort* (☎ (079) 46 9433 or toll-free 008 075 040) is one of the older resorts in the Whitsundays. It's not particularly sophisticated, but it's a good family resort as children are well catered for here. Most activities and all meals are included in the tariffs, which makes it a little more affordable than most other resorts.

Accommodation is in straightforward motel-style units. There are six different accommodation blocks, some looking out over Bauer Bay, some overlooking the golf course. Daily costs are $140 per person in the Golf and Family units, $160 per person in the Polynesian, Beachcomber and Reef units, and $175 per person in the Whitsunday units.

Places to Eat

The resort's main restaurant, the *Island Restaurant*, serves plain buffet-style breakfasts and lunches. The dinner menu offers bistro-style mains – steak, chicken and seafood dishes. Most nights there is the alternative of a barbecue beside the pool, and Friday are Island Feast Nights, with an extensive spread and live entertainment.

There's also the smaller *Coral Room* restaurant, although the food here is more up-market and you have to pay a little extra on top of your room rate. You get a $10 credit against the price of meals here; starters are $8 to $13, mains $12 to $20 and desserts from the trolley $3.

Getting There & Away

The resort has its own boat, *Seatrek*, which departs daily from Shute Harbour at 9 am, 12.30 and 5 pm, leaving the island at 7.45 and 10.30 am and 4.15 pm. The fare is $15 each way.

Whitsunday Allover (☎ (079) 46 6900) also has day trips every day, departing Shute Harbour at 9 am and costing $25 for adults and $13 for children.

HAMILTON ISLAND

The most heavily developed resort island in the Whitsundays, Hamilton is more like a town than a resort, with its own airport, a 200-boat marina, shops, restaurants and bars, and accommodation for more than 2000, including three high-rise tower blocks.

Hamilton was originally the creation of Gold Coast entrepreneur Keith Williams, who somehow managed to convince the Bjelke-Petersen state government to convert his 'deer farming' lease into a tourism one in the early 1980s. Williams' bulldozer-driven transformation of the island was not only ambitious but somewhat controversial, but by the end of 1986 the resort was up and running.

However, after the success of the early years various adverse circumstances led to

WHITSUNDAY COAST

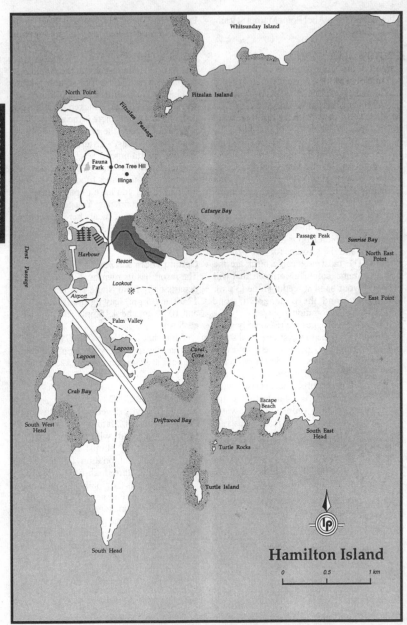

Hamilton Island

Hamilton Island being placed in receivership in 1992. Keith Williams returned to live on the Gold Coast, only to reappear as the star player in a another controversial development proposal in 1994 (see the Cardwell section for details). In 1994 Hamilton Island was successfully floated on the Australian Stock Exchange, and the international hotel chain Holiday Inns took over the management.

Hamilton Island still attracts plenty of tourists. It isn't everyone's cup of tea, but it does have an extensive range of accommodation, restaurants, bars and shops, plus plenty of entertainment possibilities including helicopter joy rides, gamefishing, paragliding, cruising, scuba diving and a hill-top fauna reserve. It can make an interesting day trip from Shute Harbour, and you can use all of the resort facilities.

Things to See & Do
The **fauna park**, at the northern end of the island, has koalas, kangaroos, deer and other wildlife. Crocodile-feeding at 10.15 am and cockatoo capers at 10.30 am are the most popular shows; entry costs $10 for adults, $5 for kids.

The resort has tennis courts, squash courts, a gym, a golf-driving range and a mini-golf course. From Catseye Beach, in front of the resort, you can hire windsurfers, catamarans, jet skis and other equipment, and go paragliding or water-skiing.

You can also go tandem skydiving, although at $480 a jump it's much more expensive here than elsewhere. The Wire Flyer, a cross between a hang-glider and a flying fox, costs $25 a ride.

There's a dive shop by the harbour which organises dive trips and offers open-water certificate courses, and you can take a variety of cruises to other islands and the outer reef. Dinghies are available for hire at $55 a half day or $80 a full day, with fishing gear supplied.

There are a few walking trails on the island, the best being the walk from Catseye Bay up to 230-metre Passage Peak on the north-east corner of the island.

A variety of cruises operate from the island, including trips to Whitehaven Beach ($28) and to the outer Barrier Reef ($105).

Hamilton also has a Day Care centre and a free Fun Club, with activities for kids from 5 to 18 years old.

Places to Stay
Hamilton has a huge range of accommodation, with hotel rooms, self-contained apartments, penthouses and private villas. All of the accommodation is modern and of a good standard, and all rates are room only.

Flanking the main resort complex and reception area, the *Bougainvillea Lodge* has 60 hotel rooms for $295 a night while the *Allamanda Lodge* has 60 hotel rooms for $195 a night.

The 19-storey *Hamilton Towers* has 368 rooms ranging from $195 to $295 a night and 18 suites ranging from $660 to $1595 a night.

Then there are the two 14-storey *Whitsunday Towers*, each with 84 self-contained one-bedroom apartments, which sleep up to five people, at $335 a night. The *Hibiscus, Frangipani* and *Lagoon* lodges have 60 two-bedroom apartments, which sleep up to six people, and cost $445 a night.

If you really need room and cost is no obstacle, then the *Yacht Harbour Towers* has penthouses that sleep up to eight people and cost a cool $1980 a night. Or you could rent *Illalangi*, a private villa costing around $1450 a night.

Places to Eat
Hamilton Island has a wide range of places to eat. If you're just here for a day trip, the *Beach Bar & Grill* beside the swimming pool and beach has rolls, hot dogs and other snacks.

In the main resort complex, the *Coffee Shop* is open from 10 am till 10 pm and serves light meals and drinks, and the *Dolphin Room* serves breakfasts and dinners beside the pool. The *Outrigger Restaurant* is more up-market and expensive, specialising in seafood.

Cascades Brasserie, in the Hamilton Towers, is open for buffet-style breakfasts, lunches and seafood-buffet dinners every day.

Down at the village around the harbour, there's a good *bakery*, and *Harpoon Harry's* has a variety of seafood including excellent fish & chips for $6. Also at the harbour are the self-explanatory *Pink Pizza Parlour* and *Romeo's*, an Italian bistro with pastas from $12 to $16 and other mains from $18 to $24.

Entertainment
The *James Cook Bar* in the main resort complex has a pianist play in the evening, or you can head to *Nellie's Nightclub* at the harbour with a bar and disco from 10 pm until late. The *Compass Bar* also has live entertainment, and the *Barefoot Bar* features a guitarist on Friday nights.

Getting There & Away
Air Hamilton Island's airport is one of the main arrival centres for the Whitsundays and takes both domestic flights and international charters. Ansett flies here from all capital cities, with direct flights from Brisbane ($289 one way), Cairns ($230), Melbourne ($485) and Sydney ($407). Qantas doesn't fly here at all.

Island Air Taxis (☎ (079) 46 9933) flies here from Whitsunday Airport ($40 one way) and Proserpine ($60 one way).

Helijet (☎ (079) 46 8249), based at Hamilton Island, has helicopter and seaplane transfers to the mainland and all islands, as well as a range of air tours and reef trips. One-way fares include Mackay $95, Shute Harbour $45, Lindeman Island $45, or you can do a day trip to Lindeman Island for $95 including lunch.

Sea Fantasea Cruises (☎ (079) 46 5111) has fast cats departing from Shute Harbour daily at 8.30 am and 5.15 pm and returning from the island at 7.30 am and 4.30 pm. The trip takes 35 minutes and costs $22 one way or $34 return (children pay half fare). You can also combine a visit to Hamilton with a cruise to Whitehaven Beach and/or Daydream Island.

Whitsunday Allover (☎ (079) 46 6900)

meet all incoming and outgoing flights from Hamilton Airport, with transfers to South Molle, Daydream and Long Islands, all costing $37. Transfers to Hayman and Lindeman islands are usually included in the tariffs.

You can also get here from Mackay on the weekends with Roylen's Cruises – see the Mackay section for details.

Getting Around
A bus shuttle takes incoming passengers from the airport or the marina to the resort area for $2.50 per person. There's also an island taxi service, or you could hire a golf buggy for $20 an hour or $55 a day.

HAYMAN ISLAND
The most northern of the Whitsunday Group, Hayman has an area of four sq km, and rises to 250 metres above sea level. It has forested hills, valleys and beaches. It also has one of the most luxurious resorts on the Barrier Reef, owned by Ansett Airlines. The resort is fronted by a wide, shallow reef which emerges from the water at low tide.

Hayman is closer to the outer reef than the other islands, and there is good diving around its northern end and at nearby Hook Island. There are several small, uninhabited islands close to Hayman. You can walk out to Arkhurst Island at low tide. Langford Island, a couple of km south-west, has some good coral around it, as do Black and Bird islands nearby.

Activities
Resort guests have free use of catamarans, windsurfers and paddle skis, but you have to pay for just about everything else, including paragliding, water-skiing, tennis and squash. There's also a golf-driving range, putting green and a well-equipped gymnasium.

Hayman has a free Kidz Club which keeps children entertained, and a creche. The resort has its own dive shop, and the *Reef Goddess* does a range of diving and snorkelling trips to the Barrier Reef. Dinghies can be hired for $60 a day, including fishing and snorkelling gear.

Bushwalks include an eight-km island circuit, a 4.5-km walk to Dolphin Point at the northern tip of the island, and a 1.5-km climb up to the Whitsunday Lookout.

Organised Tours

Coral Air Whitsundays (☎ (079) 46 9130) offers a variety of seaplane tours for resort guests. They'll fly you to Whitehaven Beach for 1½ hours for $120; to Blue Lagoon at Hardy Reef for 2½ hours of snorkelling for $190; or to Laguna Quays for $245, which includes lunch at the resort and a round of golf on the great Turtle Cove course.

Places to Stay

Hayman Island Resort (☎ (079) 46 9100 or toll-free 008 075 175) recently became a member of the exclusive 'Leading Hotels of the World' group. It's the most luxurious big resort on the Great Barrier Reef, and if you're looking for a big five-star hotel dripping with style and sophistication, look no further.

An avenue of stately nine-metre-high date palms leads to the main entrance, and with its 214 rooms, six restaurants, five bars, a hectare of swimming pools, landscaped gardens and grounds, an impressive collection of antiques and arts, and exclusive boutiques, Hayman is certainly impressive. And, in keeping with the island setting, it manages to combine all this style with a reasonably laid-back atmosphere and friendly, *almost* informal staff.

The rooms have all the usual five-star facilities, and tariffs include breakfast. Nightly costs start from $375 for the Palm Garden rooms, climb to $550 to $650 for the newer Beachfront, West and East Wing rooms, and the West and East Wing suites go for a bit over $1000 a night. There are also 11 individually styled penthouses if you really feel the need to spend up big.

Places to Eat

Breakfast is served buffet-style in the *Coffee House*, a relaxed indoor/outdoor cafe with a great outlook over the beach. At lunch time, head down to the *Beach Pavilion*, a casual open-air eatery where you have a choice of grills, salads, sandwiches and desserts for $25.

La Fontaine is the most formal of the restaurants, with a Louis XIV-style dining room and French cuisine. It is open in the evenings, and 'a jacket is preferred'.

The other restaurants are the *Oriental Seafood Restaurant*, with Japanese food in a formal Japanese garden setting; *La Trattoria*, a casual Italian bistro with an al fresco dining area; and *Planters Restaurant*, which has an Australiana theme and crocodile, emu and barramundi dishes.

Dining at Hayman's restaurants is something of an exercise in culinary extravagance – expect to pay between $100 and $200 for a three-course meal for two.

Getting There & Away

Air Helijet (☎ (079) 46 8249) has seaplane transfers to Hayman from Hamilton Island and the mainland.

Coral Air Whitsundays has the only day trip to Hayman Island, by seaplane from the mainland – see the earlier Organised Tours section for details.

Sea The resort's luxury cruisers, *Sun Goddess* and *Sun Paradise*, transfer guests to the resort from Hamilton Island or Shute Harbour.

LINDEMAN ISLAND

One of the most southerly of the Whitsundays, Lindeman covers eight sq km, most of which is national park. In 1992, Lindeman Island became the home of Australia's first Club Med resort.

The island has 20 km of walking trails and the highest point is 210-metre Mt Oldfield. With plenty of little beaches and secluded bays on Lindeman it's no hassle at all to find one to yourself. There are also a lot of small islands dotted around, some of which are easy to get across to.

Activities

The resort's daily activities sheet lists a mind-boggling array of things to do, although nothing is compulsory or too regimented. There's a good golf course here, as well as tennis courts, an archery range, a gym, beach volleyball, bingo, basketball etc...

The usual range of water sports equipment is available, and a diving school offers various dive courses and snorkelling trips. Children are also kept busy with all sorts of organised activities.

Walking trails include a four-km climb to the top of Mt Oldfield, with a trail branching off to Gap Beach; a six-km loop walk from the airstrip down to Boat Port and Coconut Beach; and a trail around the south-eastern side of the island to Plantation Beach, via Hempel's Lookout.

Places to Stay
The *Club Med Resort* (☎ (079) 46 9333 or toll-free 008 807 973) opened in 1992. The internationally famous Club Med style is very evident here, with a heavy emphasis on fun, fun, fun. There are plenty of activities, nightly entertainment and young, friendly staff to help you enjoy yourself.

The main resort complex, with its pool, dining and entertainment areas, is flanked by three-storey accommodation blocks looking out over the water, and all the motel-style rooms have their own balcony.

Nightly rates range from $195 to $250, depending on the time of year you visit. Rates include all meals and most activities. There are also five-day four-night packages available from major cities, which include airfares and transfers, and one and two-night deals from Mackay and Airlie Beach – ring the resort for details.

Places to Eat
All meals and beer, wine and juices are included in the tariffs. The *Main Restaurant* serves buffet-style breakfasts, lunches and dinners. The casual *Top Restaurant*, by the pool and tennis courts, has barbecued steaks and chicken, salads and fruit; *Nicholson's*, a smaller à la carte restaurant, opens nightly for dinner.

Entertainment
Every night at 9.30 pm, there's a live show in the main theatre, and you're just as likely to find yourself up on stage at some time. Later in the evening *Silhouettes* nightclub opens up.

Getting There & Away
Air Island Air Taxis (☎ (079) 46 9933) has flights to Lindeman from Proserpine ($60 one way) and Whitsunday Island ($50 one way).

Sea Whitsunday Allover (☎ (079) 46 6900) has an early morning day trip from Shute Harbour to Lindeman, which costs $100 including lunch and use of all of the resort's facilities – golf, tennis, windsurfers etc. Ring for departure times. They also have regular services to collect resort guests from the airport at Hamilton Island and from Shute Harbour.

You can also get here from Mackay on weekends with Roylen's Cruises – see the Mackay section for details.

WHITSUNDAY ISLAND
The largest of the Whitsunday Group, this island covers 109 sq km and rises to 438 metres at Whitsunday Peak. There's no resort, but six-km-long **Whitehaven Beach** on the south-east coast is the longest and finest beach in the group (some say in the country!), with good snorkelling off its southern end. Many of the day-trip boats visit Whitehaven Beach, and if you want to camp on the island you can easily get one of these operators to drop you off.

There are national parks camping grounds with toilets and picnic areas at the southern end of Whitehaven Beach, Scrub Hen Beach in the north-west, Dugong and Sawmill beaches on the west, and Joe's Beach.

OTHER WHITSUNDAY ISLANDS
North Molle Island has a camping ground at Cockatoo Beach on its southern end with tables, toilets and water. **Henning Island**, just off the west side of Whitsunday Island,

also has a camping ground at Geographers Beach on its western side.

Between Cid and Whitsunday islands, **Cid Harbour** was the anchorage for part of the US Navy before the Battle of the Coral Sea, the turning point in the Pacific theatre of WW II. Today, visiting ocean cruise liners anchor here.

NORTHERN WHITSUNDAY ISLANDS
The northern islands of the Whitsundays group are undeveloped and seldom visited by cruise boats or water taxis. Several of these – Gloucester, Saddleback, Grassy and Armit islands – have national park camping grounds, and the QNP&WS office in Airlie Beach (☎ (079) 46 7022) can issue camping permits and advise you on which islands to visit and how to get there. The northern islands are best reached from Dingo Beach or Earlando on the mainland.

Dingo Beach
This secluded coastal township is north of Proserpine and Airlie Beach. To get there, you turn off the Bruce Hwy 12 km north of Proserpine – the road is sealed for the first eight km, then unsealed for the next 22 km. You can also cut across to this road from the Proserpine-Airlie Beach road.

Dingo Beach is a quiet, sleepy little place set on a long sandy bay backed by low, forested mountains. Nothing much happens here, but it's a popular spot with the fishing fraternity and there's a pleasant foreshore reserve with shady trees, picnic tables and barbecues.

The only facilities are at the Dingo Beach General Store on the foreshore, which sells fuel, booze, takeaway meals, a small range of groceries and bait. Adjoining the store is the *Dingo Beach Resort* (☎ (079) 45 7153), a two-storey block of holiday flats. These are straightforward, comfortable enough two-bedroom flats, with one double bed and four bunks, a kitchen and lounge area. Costs are $55 a night for up to four people, and $5 for each additional person.

There are a couple of islands a little way off shore from either end of the bay.

Gloucester Island, to the north-west, and **Saddleback Island**, to the north-east, both have small national park camping grounds. If you don't have your own boat, you could hire a dinghy from Dingo Beach Watersports (☎ (079) 45 7215) for around $50 a day.

Five km north of Dingo Beach (by road) is **Hideaway Bay**, a residential development that never really took off. Only about 30 houses have been built here. There are no shops or facilities, apart from the kiosk at the *Hideaway Bay Caravan Park* with its rather bleak setting.

Earlando
Fifteen km south of Dingo Beach, there's a turn off to the *Earlando Tourist Resort* (☎ (079) 45 7133), a budget resort set on an attractive bay. The signs are a little faded and the resort is a little past its prime, but if you're looking for somewhere quiet and secluded this could fit the bill. The resort is fronted by well-tended lawns and palm trees, and has good views across to **Grassy Island** (which also has a national park camping ground). There's a bar with a shady beer garden, and a casual restaurant that serves things like burgers, sandwiches, steaks, seafood baskets and fish & chips.

The resort has camp sites for $11 a double and on-site vans from $30 a double. There are also four old fibro cabins along the beachfront, which are clean, simple and self-contained. These cost $50 a double, or $55 with air-con.

There's a small jetty and boat ramp near the resort, and you can hire dinghies here for fishing or getting to the islands for $45 a day.

BOWEN (pop 8300)
Bowen, founded in 1861, was the first coastal settlement to be established north of Rockhampton. Although soon overshadowed by Mackay to the south and Townsville to the north, Bowen survived, and today it's a thriving fruit and vegetable-growing centre which attracts hundreds of people for seasonal picking work. The main picking season stretches from April to November, with the

WHITSUNDAY COAST

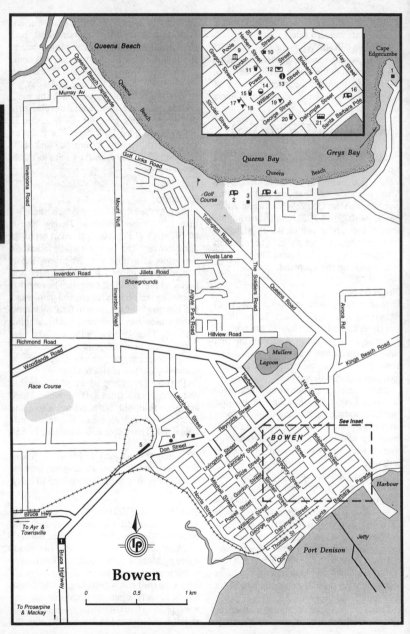

Bowen

0   0.5   1 km

PLACES TO STAY

1   Whitsunday Sands Resort
2   Tropical Beach Caravan Park
3   Palm View Holiday Units
4   Coral Coast Caravan Park
7   Castle Motor Lodge
8   Barnacles Backpackers
10 Bowen Backpackers
16 Harbour Lights Caravan Park

PLACES TO EAT

11 Club Hotel
15 Denison Hotel
17 Hot Wok
18 Fellow's Fish Bar
19 Good Times Restaurant
20 Grandview Hotel

OTHER

5   Railway Station
6   Brazil's Auto Service
9   Bowen Historical Museum
12 Post Office
13 Tourist Information Centre
14 Long Distance Bus Stop & Blue Bird Cafe
21 Bowen Swimming Pool

major crops being tomatoes, beans, corn, rockmelons and pumpkin. There's also a short mango-picking season in December.

Although it's fairly laid-back and has some pleasant beaches a couple of km north of the centre, Bowen is much more a working and fishing town than a scenic seaside resort.

Bowen's Gem of the Coral Coast festival is held each October.

History

On his 1770 voyage up the Australian coast, Captain Cook named Cape Gloucester east of Bowen, which he thought was part of the mainland. It was actually the island now known as Gloucester Island which forms the eastern flank of Edgecumbe Bay.

In 1859 Captain Henry Sinclair sailed into Edgecumbe Bay, returning two years later with George Elphinstone Dalrymple. Dalrymple was a dynamic Scot who also pioneered a route inland from near present-day Cardwell to the Valley of Lagoons in the upper Burdekin Valley.

Together, Sinclair and Dalrymple founded Bowen, naming it after the first governor of the new colony of Queensland which had just separated from New South Wales. Bowen became the base from which white settlers struck west and north to set up pastoral stations in the Burdekin valley.

Information

There's a tourist information centre (☎ (077) 86 2175) between the post office and the court house on Herbert St.

The local RACQ depot is Brazil's Auto Service (☎ (077) 86 1412), at 28 Don St.

Things to See & Do

The **Bowen Historical Museum**, at 22 Gordon St, has displays relating to the town's early history. It's open on weekdays from 10.30 am to 4 pm and Sunday mornings during the tourist season; entry costs $2.

Bowen has an interesting collection of **murals** painted on various buildings around the centre. There are 11 of these large murals, which depict different phases in the town's history, on buildings in Powell, Herbert, Williams and George Sts.

Herbert St, the main street, leads down to Port Denison. It's worth a visit to the harbour to see all the fishing boats and yachts down here, and there's a seafood co-op where you can buy fresh seafood.

A couple of km north from the centre of town are Bowen's **beaches**. Queens Beach is a long crescent-shaped stretch of sandy beach. Driving west around Queens Bay, you come to a series of secluded coves and bays. Greys Bay and Horseshoe Bay, on either side of Cape Edgecumbe, are popular swimming and snorkelling spots.

Places to Stay

Central Bowen The *Harbour Lights Caravan Park* (☎ (077) 86 1565) is close to the centre of town, opposite the harbour at 40 Santa Barbara Pde. It has tent sites from $10 a double and on-site vans from $25.

Barnacles Backpackers (☎ (077) 86 1245), at 16 Gordon St, is a workers' hostel with a relaxed atmosphere and good facilities. The owner can often find seasonal work for travellers. They'll pick you up from the bus stop if you ring, and their courtesy bus also runs people to and from wherever they're working. Dorm beds are $10, doubles $24.

Bowen Backpackers (☎ (077) 86 3433) is nearby at 56 Herbert St (the main road). It's a long-running workers' hostel with a good reputation for finding fruit-picking work, although the hostel itself is fairly basic. The owners will also get very annoyed if they find you work and you subsequently move somewhere else, like the (cheaper) caravan park. The nightly cost is $12 in four to eight-bed dorms or $12 in a twin or double room.

On the main road into town from the highway, the *Castle Motor Lodge* (☎ (077) 86 1322), at 6 Don St, is one of the better motels here, with good units from $55/60 a single/double, a pool and a licensed restaurant.

Catering for the more transient traffic, there is also a string of motels and caravan parks along the Bruce Hwy south of Bowen.

Beach Suburbs There are also quite a few accommodation possibilities in the beach suburbs to the north of Bowen.

Out on the headland of Cape Edgecumbe, the *Whitsunday Sands Resort* (☎ (077) 86 3333) is quite a good mid-range resort in a pleasant setting, with gardens and palm trees and access to several coves and beaches. The complex has a bar, a kiosk and a restaurant. There are motel units from $47/55 for singles/doubles, and self-contained units from $45/55 for one bedroom or from $65 for two bedrooms.

There is also a caravan park and another budget resort out on the cape, overlooking Horseshoe Bay.

Around at Queens Beach, there are several caravan parks along the foreshore including the *Coral Coast Caravan Park* (☎ (077) 85 1262), on Horseshoe Bay Rd, which has tent sites from $12 a double and on-site vans from $25, and the *Tropical Beach Caravan Park* (☎ (077) 85 1490), in Argyle St, which has

tent sites from $12, on-site vans from $25 and cabins from $28.

Between these two caravan parks, the *Palm View Holiday Units* (☎ (077) 85 1415), on the corner of Soldiers Rd and Howard St, is a set of four basic holiday units which start from $40 a night.

Places to Eat
The *Club Hotel*, on the corner of Herbert and Powell Sts, is close to both the hostels and is the most popular watering hole for pickers, packers and backpackers. It also has reasonably good bistro meals. The *Grandview Hotel*, farther down Herbert St, on the corner of Dalrymple Sts, also does decent counter meals and has a good beer garden out the back. The *Denison Hotel* on Powell St is also good, and has a nightclub of sorts.

On Gregory St, parallel to Herbert St, *Fellows Fish Bar* is a popular little takeaway fish & chip place, and nearby the *Hot Wok* has cheap Chinese takeaways. There's also the *Blue Bird Cafe* in William St, next to the long-distance bus stop, which is a typical country town cafe with a range of cooked breakfasts, burgers, pies and sandwiches.

At 37 Herbert St, *Good Times* is a bright and interesting licensed restaurant in a restored old building with pressed-metal ceilings. The food is 'international cuisine', with mains like grilled coral trout, Bowen pork medallions, spaghetti marinara and eye fillet steak priced from $14 to $17.

Getting There & Away
Bus Long-distance buses stop outside the Traveland travel agency (☎ (077) 86 2835), in Williams St, between Herbert and Gregory Sts.

Greyhound Pioneer Australia and McCafferty's both have frequent bus services to and from Rockhampton (6½ hours, $68), Airlie Beach (two hours, $20) and Townsville (2½ hours, $28).

Train The *Sunlander* and *Queenslander* trains both stop here, but note that they stop at Bootooloo Siding three km south of the centre, *not* at the Bowen Railway Station.

The fares from Brisbane are $109 for an economy seat, $139 for an economy sleeper and $214 for a 1st-class sleeper.

Getting Around

Bowen Bus Services (☎ (077) 86 1529) runs local buses on weekdays from near the post office to Queens Beach and Horseshoe Bay. They also have a service out to the coal-mining centre of Collinsville.

COLLINSVILLE (pop 2500)

It's 85 km south-west from Bowen to the coal-mining town of Collinsville. Coal was first discovered here in the 1860s, but the coalfield wasn't fully developed until the rail link to Bowen was completed in 1917.

Coal is sent from here to Abbott Point north of Bowen, where it is loaded onto container ships and transported to locations around the world. The town itself offers little in the way of tourist attractions, although the surrounding area is popular with fossickers looking for gemstones such as agate and amethyst.

For advice on where to hunt for which gems, you can contact the Bowen Lapidary Club on ☎ (077) 86 1346.

North Coast

This chapter covers Queensland's North Coast – an area that stretches from the Cape Upstart National Park up to the Mission Beach area, and inland as far as the Gregory Developmental Rd.

At the centre of the North Coast is Townsville, the largest city in north Queensland. Townsville has a fine aquarium, good dive courses and trips to the outer Barrier Reef, and Magnetic Island is just a short boat ride off shore.

Inland from Townsville you can visit the former gold-mining centres of Charters Towers and Ravenswood; Charters Towers is still a busy provincial city, whereas Ravenswood was all but a ghost town until its relatively recent revival. From Charters Towers, the Flinders Hwy continues its run clear across outback Queensland.

There are some wonderful national parks along this stretch of the coast. The majestic Hinchinbrook Island is one of Queensland's great natural wonders; there's an up-market resort on the island's north coast, or you can pack your tent and walking boots and tackle the 32-km Thorsborne Trail. South of Hinchinbrook is Orpheus Island, with an exclusive resort and excellent diving off its fringing reefs.

Further north is Mission Beach, a cluster of settlements scattered along a scenic strip of coastline. This area is an increasingly popular destination, with rainforests running right down to the coast, good beaches, and the Family Islands (including the resort islands of Dunk and Bedarra) just off shore.

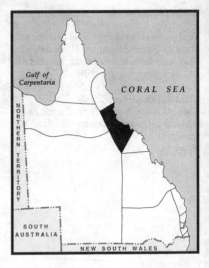

Geography & Climate

The south-west corner of this region is dominated by the valleys of the Burdekin River and the massive Burdekin Falls Dam. The Burdekin areas are some of the richest farmlands in the state, with sugar cane and rice being the major crops. The mountain ranges of the Great Dividing Range form the catchment areas for the river systems.

These ranges run parallel with the coast, and become higher and move closer to the coast the further north you go. Largely covered in thick rainforests, these mountains are part of the Wet Tropics World Heritage Area, which starts just north of Townsville and stretches along the Queensland coast almost as far as Cooktown.

The off-shore islands along here are mostly continental islands – extensions of the coastal mountain ranges that were separated from the mainland as the sea levels rose at the end of the last Ice age.

Like the rest of the north, this region has a tropical climate. Summer (December to March) is hot, wet and humid; the rest of the year you can expect predominantly warm, sunny weather with no great extremes. The northern section of this coast, from Ingham to Innisfail, is the wettest part of Queensland – and Tully is the wettest place in Australia, receiving over 4000 mm of rain annually.

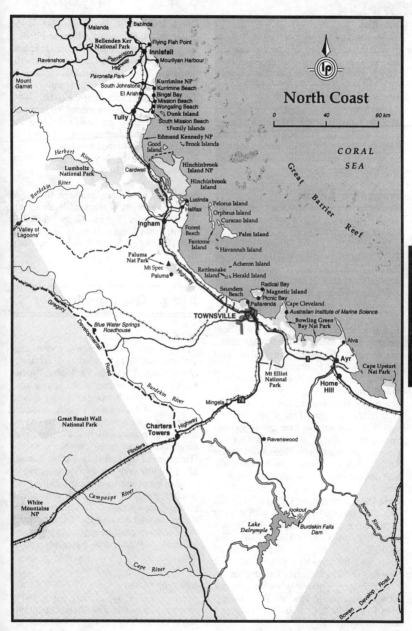

North Coast

0   40   80 km

CORAL SEA

Great Barrier Reef

Activities

White-water rafting trips on the Tully River operate out of Mission Beach. You can also take trips to the outer Barrier Reef from Mission Beach, Magnetic Island and Townsville, and dive courses are offered at the same three places.

Highlights for bushwalkers in this area include Hinchinbrook Island, Magnetic Island, the Mission Beach area, the Jourama Falls and Mt Spec national parks (south of Ingham), and the Mt Elliot National Park (south of Townsville).

Getting There & Away

Air Townsville is the major airport for the North Coast, with flights to/from all major centres and capital cities.

Dunk Island has its own airport, with regular flights to/from Townsville and Cairns, and the Orpheus Island resort has its own seaplane for transfers from the mainland.

Charters Towers has an airfield, but it doesn't receive any scheduled flights.

Bus Bus services in this area are almost identical to the routes covered by the trains. Greyhound Pioneer Australia and McCafferty's both have frequent services up the Bruce Hwy on the Brisbane-Cairns run, with detours off the highway to the Mission Beach area. Brisbane to Townsville takes 18 to 21 hours and costs $116.

Both companies also have inland services from Townsville to Mt Isa, via Charters Towers, continuing onto Three Ways in the Northern Territory (from where you can either head north to Darwin or south to the Alice).

Train The main Brisbane-Cairns railway line runs alongside the Bruce Hwy, with stops at all the major centres including Ayr, Townsville, Ingham, Cardwell and Tully. The Brisbane-Townsville trip takes around 25 hours and the one-way fare is $118 in economy or $226 for a 1st-class sleeper.

The *Inlander* operates twice a week between Townsville and Mt Isa. The trip from Townsville to Charters Towers takes 3 hours and costs $20.

Car & Motorcycle The Bruce Hwy is the major route up the coast, while the Flinders Hwy from Townsville is the major inland route. If you have a little time, the detour off the Bruce Hwy to the mountain village of Paluma is one of the most spectacular scenic drives along this section of the coast.

The Gregory Developmental Rd runs parallel with the coast, on the inland side of the Great Dividing Range, passing through Charters Towers to the Lynd Junction. From here, the Kennedy Hwy continues north to the Atherton Tableland.

Sea If you're heading off shore, the major ferry services out to the islands along this coast are from Townsville to Magnetic Island, from Cardwell to Hinchinbrook Island, and from Mission Beach to Dunk and Bedarra islands.

Ayr to Townsville

HOME HILL (pop 3190)

At Home Hill, a small highway town nine km south of Ayr, a faded sign modestly announces **Ashworth's Fantastic Tourist Attraction**. This is one of the largest souvenir shops you'll ever see, with a wild collection of tea-towels, T-shirts, watches, place mats, jewellery and teaspoons. There's also a large pottery gallery at the front, and, down a couple of stairs from the shop, the 'Treasures of the Earth' exhibition. It costs $2 to see this very impressive collection of fossils, gemstones and rocks. Ashworth's brochure sums things up with a masterful piece of copy-writing: 'Recommended for the person who has imagination, is mentally alert, admires great beauty and appreciates wonders...'. What could I possibly add to that?

AYR (pop 8630)

Ayr is a fairly busy country town, but it seems to pop up out of nowhere: one minute you're driving along through cane fields, the next you're surrounded by car dealers, fast food outlets and a bustling shopping centre...and a couple of minutes later you're back in the cane fields.

Ayr is on the delta of one of the biggest rivers in Queensland, the Burdekin, and is the major commercial centre for the rich farmlands of the Burdekin Valley. Sugar cane and rice are the major crops grown in the area.

There's a community information centre (☎ (077) 83 2888) in the Burdekin Cultural Complex, on Queen St, which also acts as a tourist information centre. The town's cultural centre is an impressive complex which includes the **Burdekin Theatre** (☎ (077) 83 3455), a modern theatre which alternates as a venue for live performances and cinema. At the front of the complex is an interesting fountain and rockpool, featuring brass sculptures of birds, turtles and snakes.

The **Ayr Nature Display**, in a section of a private house in Wilmington St (signposted off the main roads), has a collection of thousands of butterflies preserved under glass, as well as moths, beetles and sea shells. The display is open daily from 8 am to 5 pm and entry costs $2.50 for adults, $1 for children.

Ayr also has a good **swimming pool** on the main road south of the centre and the **Burdekin Bowl** opposite the cultural centre, where you can break your drive with a game of ten-pin bowling. It's open every day and night, and a game costs $5.10 with shoes.

Places to Stay

The *Ayr Caravan Park* (☎ (077) 83 1429) is next to the swimming pool on Queen St, just south of the centre. Across the road is the *Ayr Country Motel* (☎ (077) 83 1700), at 197 Queen St, which has modern motel units from $50/58 for singles/doubles.

The *Parkside Motel* (☎ (077) 83 1244), just off the highway on the west side of the centre at 74 Graham St, is another good motel with renovated units from $49/52 or old budget units from $39. This place also has a good restaurant (see Places to Eat).

All those butterflies on poles you saw as you drove into Ayr were advertising the *Butterfly Units* (☎ (077) 83 3433), behind the Ayr Nature Display at 118 Cameron St. These simple self-contained units have air-con and start at $34 a night for up to four people.

Places to Eat

There are quite a few eateries along Queen St in the centre of town. The best of these is the *Wich Bar*, just north of the main intersection at 95 Queen St. It has a takeaway section at the front which makes great sandwiches and rolls for $2.50 to $3.50, as well as salads, burgers and home-made cakes. There's a comfortable air-con coffee lounge out the back where you can get toasted or open sandwiches, salads, lasagna, crumbed whiting and other dishes.

The *Country Kettle*, at 148 Queen St, is a typical country-town coffee shop, where you can get quiches, salads, burgers and lasagna. For a counter meal, you could try the *Queens Hotel* in the centre of town.

Ivories Restaurant at the Parkside Motel in Graham St is a very stylish licensed restaurant with an all-white décor and black iron-and-glass tables. The small menu offers steaks, reef fish, chicken dishes and Thai curries in the $14 to $16 range.

ALVA BEACH

It may look promising on a map, but it isn't really worth the 16-km drive from Ayr out to this rather sad, forgotten beachside township. The drive is uninteresting, the beach isn't terribly attractive, and most of the old fibro and timber houses have faded 'for sale' signs tacked to the outsides. There is a kiosk and a caravan park here.

AUSTRALIAN INSTITUTE OF MARINE SCIENCES (AIMS)

If you're interested in marine biology, you can visit the Australian Institute of Marine Sciences (☎ (077) 78 9211), a marine research facility at Cape Ferguson between

NORTH COAST

Ayr and Townsville. It's open to the public every weekday between 9 am and 3 pm, although visitors are restricted to the 'blue carpet' area which means you only get to see the reference library and a collection of photo display boards. The best time to visit is on a Friday between March and November, when free two-hour guided tours are conducted at 10 am. A slide show and a visit to the wharves are included, and you can have lunch in the canteen afterwards.

The turn off to AIMS is on the Bruce Hwy about 53 km north-west of Ayr or 35 km south-east of Townsville.

MT ELLIOT NATIONAL PARK

At Alligator Creek, 28 km south of Townsville or 72 km north-west of Ayr, there's a turn off from the Bruce Hwy to the **Mt Elliot National Park**. Alligator Creek tumbles down between two rugged ranges which rise steeply from the coastal plains. The taller range peaks with Mt Elliot (1234 metres), whose higher slopes harbour some of Queensland's most southerly tropical rainforest.

A sealed road heads six km inland from the highway to the park entrance, from where a good gravel road leads to some pleasant picnic areas with tables and barbecues. Further on there's a good camping ground with lawns, shady trees, toilets, showers and barbecues. There are 20 self-registration sites, which can be booked through the QNP&WS ranger (☎ (077) 78 8203).

About 300 metres beyond the camping ground, there are good swimming holes in Alligator Creek. Two walking trails start from the camping ground. One follows Alligator Creek through a forest to Hidden Valley and the Alligator Falls – it's a 17-km, five-hour return walk. The other trail follows Cockatoo Creek south, taking about six hours return.

The park gates are closed from 6.30 pm to 6.30 am, so if you're planning to arrive or leave at night, you'll need to make arrangements with the ranger. There's no public transport to the park.

TOWNSVILLE (pop 101,000)

The third largest centre in Queensland and the main centre in the north of the state, Townsville is the port city for the agricultural and mining production of the vast inland region of northern Queensland.

Townsville is a working city, a major armed forces base, and the site of James Cook University. It's also the start of the main route from Queensland to the Northern Territory. It's the only departure point for Magnetic Island (20 minutes away by ferry), while the Barrier Reef is about 1¾ hours away by fast catamaran.

In recent years, millions of dollars have been spent in an effort to encourage more visitors to stop in Townsville, rather than going straight through to Cairns. A Sheraton hotel/casino and a marina have been built on Townsville's oceanfront, and the Flinders St East and Palmer St areas on opposite sides of Ross Creek have been redeveloped. Along with these big-money efforts, there's been a boom in budget accommodation and in the eating and entertainment scene; yet the visitors are still staying away in droves. Apart from a few attractions, such as the excellent Great Barrier Reef Wonderland, and its role as an access point for Magnetic Island and the reef itself, Townsville still hasn't really got a lot going for it from a traveller's point of view.

History

Townsville was founded in 1864 by the work of a Scot, John Melton Black, and the money of Robert Towns, a Sydney-based sea captain and financier. Together these two owned pastoral lands in the high country inland which had already been pioneered. Their sheep and cattle farms couldn't survive without a boiling-down works on the coast for animal carcasses. Towns aimed to build this at Bowen, but Bowen residents objected and instead the pair set up the works on Cleveland Bay to the north of Bowen. Towns wanted it to be a private depot for his stations but Black saw the chance to make his fortune by founding a settlement and persuaded Towns to part with £10,000 for the project.

NORTH COAST

Townsville

To Pallarenda
To Magnetic Island

Rowes Bay
Cleveland Bay
Townsville Harbour
South Townsville

Railway Estate

To Charters Towers (Flinders Hwy) & Ayr (Bruce Hwy)

See Central Townsville Map

Jezzine Military Museum
Kissing Point
Coral Sea Memorial Rockpool & The Beach Club
Stinger Enclosure
Motel Shorestrive
Townsville Seaside Apartments
Aquarius on the Beach Hotel
Tropical Hideaway House
The Banksia Guest Motel
Townsville Reef International
Harold's Seafood
Seaview Hotel
Rasa Prang, El Charro & Norma's

Townsville General Hospital
Queens Park
Queens Gardens

Castle Hill
Quarry

Reid Park

Townsville West
Showgrounds
Hyde Park
Showgrounds Caravan Park

West End

Belgian Gardens
Hasley's Pile
Rowes Bay Caravan Park

Townsville Airport

To Ingham & Cairns

To Ingham & Cairns

Cape Pallarenda Rd
The Strand
Warburton
Bundock
Castle Hill Road
Gregory
Stanley St
Fryer St
Stokes St
Blackwood St
Stanley St
Denham St
Wills St
Stanton
Sturt
Flinders
Ross Creek
Ross Street
Palmer St
Dean St
Morey St
Plume St
Railway Street
Boundary
Queens Road
Stuart
Surrey
Ingham Hwy
Francis
Staboode
Crawford St
Percy
Bundock Street
Halifax Street
Dearness Street
Garbutt Siding
Meenan
Bruce Hwy
Woolcock
Hugh
Bayswater
Currajong

North Ward
Jezzine Army Barracks

Strand Park

Marina
Sheraton Breakwater Hotel & Casino
Townsville Breakwater Entertainment Centre

TOWNSVILLE

0   0.5   1 km

Despite a cyclone in 1867, Black persisted and was elected Townsville's first mayor the same year. The town developed mainly due to Chinese and Kanaka labour. European attitudes at the time were such that there was more alarm when a horse rather than a Kanaka was snatched from the banks of the creek by a crocodile. The horse was considered to be of more value! Eventually a road was forged up to Towns' stations inland, contributing to both their survival and Townsville's.

By the start of WW II, Townsville was a busy port town with a population of around 30,000, but with the outbreak of the war Townsville became one of the major bases for the Australian and US armed forces, boosting the population overnight to more than 100,000.

Orientation

Townsville's sprawl is extensive, but the centre, which is the only real area of interest to travellers, is a fairly compact area that you can easily get around on foot. The Bruce Hwy bypasses the city centre, but there are roads leading into the centre from the south and the west.

The city centre is flanked by Ross Creek to the south-east and Cleveland Bay to the north-east, with 290-metre Castle Hill towering over the centre to the west. Flinders St, which runs parallel to Ross Creek, is a pedestrian mall between Denham and Stanley Sts. The Great Barrier Reef Wonderland is at the north-east end of Flinders St East, and beyond this a breakwater stretches out into Cleveland Bay. The Sheraton Breakwater Hotel/Casino and the Entertainment Centre are out at the end of the breakwater, and there's a boat marina on the west side. There are two terminals on Ross Creek for the ferries to Magnetic Island; one at the Great Barrier Reef Wonderland and one on the breakwater.

The transit centre, the arrival and departure point for long-distance buses, is on the corner of Palmer and Plume Sts South Townsville, on the south side of Ross Creek.

The railway station is south of the centre near the corner of Flinders and Blackwood Sts.

Information

Tourist Information Townsville Enterprises' main tourist information office (☎ (077) 78 3555) is on the Bruce Hwy, eight km south of the city centre. It is open every day from 9 am to 5 pm. There's also a more convenient information centre (☎ (077) 21 3660) in the middle of Flinders St Mall, between Stokes and Denham Sts. It's open Monday to Friday from 9 am to 5 pm, and Saturday and Sunday from 9 am to noon.

Post The main post office is on the corner of the Flinders St Mall and Denham St. It is open on weekdays from 9 am to 5 pm. The poste restante section is a small window around the back. You ring a bell and wait for service – sometimes you'll be waiting a while. There's also a post office branch in the Barrier Reef Wonderland which is open weekends as well as weekdays.

Useful Organisations The QNP&WS has an information office (☎ (077) 21 2399) at the Great Barrier Reef Wonderland, open from Monday to Saturday between 9 am and 5 pm.

The RACQ (☎ (077) 75 3999) is at 202 Ross River Rd, in the suburb of Aitkenvale, about seven km south of the centre.

Bookshops The Mary Who Bookshop at 155 Stanley St is a small bookshop with a good range of literature, travel and environmental books, children's books and classical music. QBD's Bumble Bee Bookshop on the Flinders St Mall is a larger mainstream bookshop which includes a large travel section.

The Ancient Wisdom Bookshop, in Shaw's Arcade off the Flinders St Mall, has a more esoteric collection of new-age books, covering subjects like natural medicine, astrology, prophecy and self-help. (There's also a notice board here where you can find out about things like reiki, yoga and astrology workshops and Tarot readings, and there's an acupuncture and Chinese herbal clinic upstairs.) Also in Shaw's Arcade is Jim's Book Exchange, which has a pretty wide selection of second-hand books.

Library The Townsville Municipal Library is next to the post office in the Flinders St Mall. It's open Monday to Thursday from 9.30 am to 5 pm, Friday from 9.30 am to 9 pm and Saturday from 9.30 am to noon.

Film & Photography There are two camera shops in the Flinders St Mall between Stokes and Stanley Sts. Both places can arrange camera repairs, although they have to send them south and you're looking at a minimum five-day turnaround.

There are plenty of film-developing and printing shops in the mall.

Great Barrier Reef Wonderland

Townsville's top attraction is at the end of Flinders St East beside Ross Creek. While its impressive aquarium is the highlight, there are several other sections including a theatre, a museum, shops, a good National Parks information office, the Great Barrier Reef Marine Park Authority office and a terminal for ferries to Magnetic Island.

A combined ticket to the aquarium, theatre and museum costs $24 for adults, $20.50 for students, $12 for children or $60 for a family. Otherwise, you can pay for each individually.

Aquarium This is said to be the largest coral reef aquarium in the world. The huge main tank has a living coral reef and hundreds of reef fish, sharks, rays and other life, and you can walk beneath the tank through a transparent tunnel. To maintain the natural conditions needed to keep this community alive, a wave machine simulates the ebb and flow of the ocean, circular currents keep the water in motion and marine algae are used in the purification system. The aquarium also has several smaller tanks, extensive displays on the history and life of the reef, and a theatrette where slide shows on the reef are shown. There are guided tours every day at 11.20 am and 2.30 pm, as well as daily diver shows, turtle-feeding and various other activities. It is open every day from 9.30 am to 5 pm and admission is $14 for adults, $12 for students, $7 for children or $35 for a family.

Omnimax Theatre This cinema has angled seating and a dome-shaped screen to create a 3-D effect. Hour-long films on the reef and various other topics, such as outer space, alternate through the day from 9.30 am till 5.30 pm. Omnimax film is a unique large-format film which is projected through a fish-eye lens four times faster than normal 35 mm film. You can read these and other fascinating facts here, or, perhaps more interestingly, you can see the huge film reels in operation in a small glass room beside the entrance. Admission to one film is $10 for adults, $8.50 for students, $5 for children and $25 for a family.

Museum of Tropical Queensland This small museum has two sections: one display focusing on the Age of Reptiles, with a collection of fossils found throughout Queensland and several reconstructions of dinosaurs, and the other devoted to the natural history of north Queensland, including wetland birds and other fauna, rainforests, ocean wrecks and Aboriginal artefacts. The museum is open every day from 9 am to 5 pm and admission is $3.50 for adults, $3 for students, $1.75 for children and $9 for a family.

Other Museums & Galleries

The **Townsville Museum** on the corner of Sturt and Stokes Sts has a permanent display on early Townsville and the north Queensland independence campaigns, as well as temporary exhibitions. It's open daily from 10 am to 3 pm (to 1 pm on weekends); entry costs $2 for adults and $1 for children.

The **Jezzine Military Museum** is in an 1890s fort and command post atop Kissing Point, in the grounds of the Jezzine Army Barracks beyond the northern end of The Strand. The museum has a collection of military paraphernalia dating back to the 1880s, and is open on Monday, Wednesday and Friday from 9 am to 12.30 pm.

There's also a **Maritime Museum** on Palmer St, beside Ross Creek in South Townsville. Housed in two heritage-style buildings, one section has an exhibition which focuses on north Queensland's maritime history, while the Gallery section exhibits old B&W photos of Port Townsville's golden olden days. The museum opens up on weekdays from 10 am to 4 pm and on weekends from 1 to 4 pm; entry costs $3 for adults, $2 for children.

The Perc Tucker Regional Gallery at the Denham St end of the Flinders St Mall is a good regional art gallery and admission is free. It is open Tuesday, Wednesday, Thursday and Saturday from 10 am to 5 pm, Friday from 2 to 9 pm, and Sunday from 10 am to 1 pm.

Parks & Gardens

The **Queens Gardens** on Gregory St, one km north-west from the town centre, contain sports playing fields, tennis courts and Townsville's original **Botanic Gardens**, dating from 1878. The entrance to these lovely gardens is on Paxton St. The new botanic gardens, **Anderson Park**, were established in 1932. These gardens cover a 27-hectare site and feature mostly rainforest plants and palms from north Queensland and the Cape York Peninsula. A conservatory houses almost 500 species of tropical plants. The gardens are six km south-west of the centre on Gulliver St, Mundingburra. The **Kokoda Swimming Pool** is in the south-west corner of the gardens.

The **Palmetum**, about 15 km south-west of the centre, off University Rd, is a 25-hectare botanic garden devoted to native palms in their natural environments, ranging from desert to rainforest species.

For a chance to see some birdlife, make your way out to the **Town Common Environmental Park**, five km north of the centre, just off Cape Pallarenda Rd. A seven-km road leads through this 32-sq-km area, which ranges from mangrove swamps and salt marsh to dry grassland and pockets of woodland and forest. It's not a terribly attractive

park, but the common is known for water birds such as magpie geese, which herald the start of the wet season, and stately brolgas, which gather in the Dry. There's an observation tower overlooking the wetlands area – early morning is the best time to see the birds.

Pallarenda is a fairly quiet little residential area on the waterfront about eight km north from the centre of Townsville. There isn't much incentive to drive out this way unless you live here, but if you do, you'll find the **Cape Pallarenda Environmental Park** on the headland at the end of the road. There are picnic tables and walking tracks in the park, which is centred around a historic quarantine station.

Wildlife Sanctuary

The **Billabong Sanctuary**, 17 km south on the Bruce Hwy, is a 10-hectare wildlife park of Australian native animals and birds. There are barbecue areas, a swimming pool and a kiosk in the park, and various shows throughout the day including koala-feeding (10.30 am and 3 pm), a python show (11.30 am and 3.30 pm), and, last but not least, crocodile-feeding (noon and 2.30 pm). It's open daily from 9 am to 5 pm, and admission costs $13 for adults, $11 for students, $7 for children and $35 for a family.

There is no public transport to the sanctuary, although two companies run daily tours here – see the Organised Tours section later.

Other Attractions

The **Flinders St Mall** is the retail heart of the city. It's bright, breezy and full of interest, with fountains, plantations and crowds of shoppers. Every Sunday morning, the busy **Cotters Market** is held in the mall, with a wide range of crafts and local produce on offer. A block back from the mall is **Fisherman's Wharf**, a collection of riverfront eateries with open-air tables and live music most nights.

East of the mall you can stroll along **Flinders St East** beside the creek. Many of the best 19th-century buildings are in this part of town, while further out on a breakwater at the mouth of Ross Creek, the casino, entertainment centre and a couple of up-market seafood restaurants are located on the waterfront. A more pleasant walk is north along **The Strand**, a long beachfront drive with a marina, gardens, some awesome banyan trees, the Tobruk Memorial Baths swimming pool and a big artificial waterfall.

The road up to the top of **Castle Hill** is very popular with joggers and power-walkers, especially at dawn and sunset. If you're feeling more adventurous, there's also a steeper but shorter walking track to the top from the end of Hillside Cres on the city side of the hill. If you're feeling lazy, you can drive up like I did. Regardless of how you do it, it's worth coming up here as there are great 360° views from several lookout points, and you can see the whole town, the harbour and Magnetic Island.

The **Tobruk Memorial Baths** on The Strand is an Olympic-sized swimming pool with good grassed areas and umbrella-shaded tables on either side of the pool. The opening hours change with each season, but generally it is open from around 6 am on weekdays and between 8 am and 10 am on weekends, and closes between 5 and 8 pm.

Up the top end of The Strand is the **Coral Sea Memorial Rockpool**, a huge artificial swimming pool on the edge of the ocean. There's a pontoon out in the middle, and lawns and sandy beaches around the shore, and a huge filtration system keeps it clean and stinger-free. There is no admission fee. During the summer months when stingers are a problem on the beaches, there's a **Stinger Enclosure** on the beach at the north end of The Strand, about 100 metres south of the rockpool.

The **Townsville Showgrounds Markets** are held in the showgrounds on Ingham Rd every Sunday from 6.30 am to 1 pm. It's a large flea market with all sorts of stalls, including clothes, fruit and vegies and plenty of recycled gear.

Activities
Dive Courses Townsville has four or five diving schools, including one of Australia's best – Mike Ball Dive Expeditions (☎ (077)

72 3022), at 252 Walker St. They have two versions of their five-day certificate course, both of which include free accommodation. The basic course starts every Saturday and costs $359, with three days training in Townsville and two day trips out to the reef. The more expensive course is better value – it starts every Wednesday and costs $445, with three days training in Townsville and two days/three nights spent out on the reef, staying on board their boat *Watersport*. You have to take a $50 medical before you start the course.

Pro-Dive, another well-regarded diving school, also runs courses in Townsville. Its office (☎ (077) 21 1760) is in the Great Barrier Reef Wonderland. Pro-Dive's five-day certificate course costs $400, starts twice a week, and includes two nights and three days on the reef, with a total of eight dives.

Diving Trips For experienced divers, there are diving trips from Townsville out to the wreck of the *Yongala*, one of the best dives in Australia.

The *Yongala* was a passenger liner which sank off Cape Bowling Green during a cyclone in 1911. She went down with all 122 of her crew and passengers and for years her disappearance was a complete mystery.

During WW II the ship's location was discovered and the first diver went down to the *Yongala* in 1947. The 90-metre-long wreck lies intact on the sea bottom in 30 metres of water and has become a haven for a huge variety of marine life.

Pro-Dive (☎ (077) 21 1760) has three-day trips out to the wreck, departing on Monday and Friday. The cost is $355 which includes all meals and equipment.

Mike Ball Dive Expeditions (☎ (077) 72 3022) has day trips to the wreck on Tuesday, Thursday and Sunday. These cost $165, plus $35 if you need to hire equipment, and you do two dives. They also have three-day trips departing every Tuesday, and a weekend trip once a month, which cost from $360 to $500 per person, depending on the time of year and the type of accommodation you choose. Prices include all meals. You do six dives,

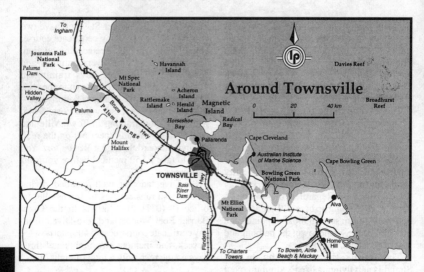

and equipment can be hired for another $20 a day.

The wreck of the *Yongala* is more of an attraction than the John Brewer Reef, the destination for many day trips. John Brewer Reef has been damaged by cyclones and the crown-of-thorns starfish, and parts of the reef have little live coral.

Fishing Charters A number of charter boats operate fishing trips out of Townsville. Operators include MV *Reef Magic* (☎ 018 782 286), MV *True Blue* (☎ (077) 71 5474) and Hyperspace Sportsfishing Tours (☎ (077) 79 6370).

The tourist information centre has a full list of fishing and yacht charter operators.

Massage If you've got backpacker's back or some other bodily ailment, Roz at NQ Relaxation Resources (☎ (077) 72 2563), 13 Palmer St, has a great pair of hands. A half-hour therapeutic massage costs $20, a full hour is $35.

Other Activities Parasail Magnetic (☎ (077) 78 5884) operates from The Quarterdeck at the Sheraton Breakwater Hotel/Casino every

day between 1 and 5 pm. A ten-minute tandem flight costs $35, a solo flight $45.

Risky Business (☎ (077) 25 4571) has experienced abseiling teachers and offers lessons for $55 for two hours.

Organised Tours

Reef Trips Pure Pleasure Cruises (☎ (077) 21 3555) has day trips on their 30-metre Wavepiercer catamaran to Kelso Reef, east of the Palm Island group, where they have a large floating pontoon. The cost is $110 for adults and $55 for children, which includes lunch, viewing from a glass-bottomed boat and snorkelling equipment. You can also do scuba dives as an optional extra. Certified divers get two dives for $70, and beginners can try a resort dive for the same price.

Cruises The *Coral Princess* does a four-day cruise between Townsville and Cairns every week – see Cruises in the Cairns section of the Far North Queensland chapter for more details.

Day Tours Detour Coaches (☎ (077) 21 5977) offers a variety of tours in and around Townsville, including a city sights tour ($14 adults, $7 kids), bus trips to the Billabong Sanctuary ($23/10 including entry fee), and an outback tour to Charters Towers ($48/24). Detour also has day trips to Mt Spec from Townsville, with visits to a butterfly farm, Paluma, a rainforest walk and more (see the later Mt Spec section for details on this national park). The cost is $48 for adults or $24 for children.

Pure Pleasure Tours & Cruises (☎ (077) 21 3555) has a very similar range of tours and trips which are slightly more expensive.

Cycling Tours The Tour de Townsville (☎ (077) 21 2026) is a cycling tour around the sights of the city, including the marina, the rockpool, the botanic gardens and Rowes Bay. The 3½-hour tour costs $20 per person which includes lunch or dinner and a bike.

Tours to Cairns If you're heading for Cairns, Ringtail Tours (☎ (077) 75 5719) has a three-day bus tour between Townsville and Cairns with overnight stops at Mission Beach and the Atherton Tablelands and visits to Jourama Falls, Cardwell, the Palmerston National Park and Kuranda. The trip departs from Townsville every Wednesday and from Cairns every Saturday and costs $475 per person, which includes accommodation, breakfasts and lunches.

Pop Sullivan's Side Track Tours (☎ 1800 648 036) does a two-day trip to Cairns via the inland route, with stops at Mt Fox (an extinct volcano), the Burdekin River, the Undara lava tubes (where you stay overnight) and the Atherton Tableland. The trip costs $230 which includes accommodation and a tour at Undara and all your meals.

Festivals
Townsville's major annual event is the Festival of Townsville (formerly the Pacific Festival). Held each August, it features 10 days of carnivals, parades and a Mardi-Gras.

Places to Stay
Camping There are two caravan parks which are only about three km from the centre of town. The best option would be the

Rowes Bay Caravan Park (☎ (077) 71 3576), which is opposite the beach on Heatley's Pde in Rowes Bay. It has good facilities including a pool and a shop. Tent sites are $12 a double, and their on-site cabins start from $34 a double, rising to $38 with air-con and $46 with ensuites. They also have self-contained villas from $49 a double.

The *Showground Caravan Park* (☎ (077) 72 1487), at 16 Kings Rd, West End, has tent sites for $10 and on-site vans for $25.

If you don't need to be close to the centre, there are quite a few caravan parks strung along the Bruce Hwy to the north and south of Townsville. These include the following: *Coonambelah Caravan Park* (☎ (077) 74 5205), seven km north of the centre at 547 Ingham Rd (the Bruce Hwy); and the *Magnetic Gateway Holiday Village* (☎ (077) 78 2422), eight km south of the centre across the highway from the tourist information centre.

Hostels Townsville's hostel scene is probably the best example of large operators jumping on the budget accommodation bandwagon. Two huge backpackers hostels in Townsville (both of which opened a few years ago when the backpacking scene was much busier) is *at least* one too many. As a result, Townsville has more budget accommodation than it will ever need. The general standard of hostels here is not as good as in many other towns along the coast.

There are four hostels in or near Palmer St, on the southern side of Ross Creek. These places are close to the bus transit centre and convenient if you're just passing through, although this area can feel a little isolated and you'll find that most of Townsville's eateries, attractions and nightclubs are on the other side of the river. The *Adventurers Resort YHA* (☎ (077) 21 1522), at 79 Palmer St, is a modern multilevel complex with over 300 beds, a shop, a car parking area and a swimming pool. The facilities are quite good, although the kitchen badly needs to be stocked with some decent equipment, and because the place is so large it can feel a bit anonymous. Their courtesy bus does regular runs to the city centre and the ferry terminals.

NORTH COAST

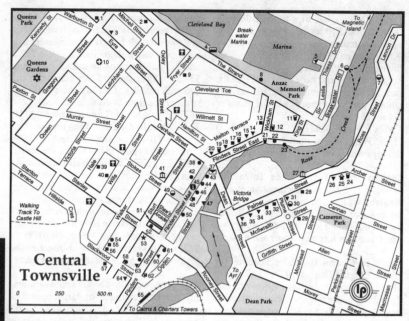

Central
Townsville

0   250   500 m

NORTH COAST

Accommodation in a four-bunk dorm costs $13 for YHA members, $15 for nonmembers; singles cost $22/24 and doubles $30/34.

Townsville's other huge offering is *Andy's Backpackers* (☎ (077) 21 2322), which is upstairs on top of the transit centre. Although convenient for bus departures, the place lacks atmosphere. Dorm beds are $12, twins are $28 and doubles are $30. Included in the price is a sunset tour of the city, and they also have a courtesy bus which runs to the ferry terminals and the beach.

Between these two places is the smaller *Globetrotters Hostel* (☎ (077) 71 3242), behind a house at 45 Palmer St. This relaxed hostel has all the usual facilities – kitchen area, lounge, pool, laundry – and it's clean and well run. Six-bed dorms cost $12 per night, singles cost $24, and a twin room is $30.

South-east of the transit centre and across McIlwraith St is the *Southbank Village Backpackers* (☎ (077) 71 5849), at 33 Plume St. It's an old, rambling hostel spread over

several buildings and, although it's pretty run-down and disorganised, it's cheap at $10 a bed.

Townsville's other hostels are on the north side of Ross Creek, in and around the city centre. The pick of this bunch is probably *Civic House Backpackers Inn* (☎ (077) 71 5381), at 262 Walker St. This clean and easy-going hostel has three or four-bed dorms for $13 or six-bed dorms with bathroom and air-con for $14. It also has very pleasant singles from $28, twin and double rooms from $30, and doubles with a private bathroom from $35. Their courtesy bus does pick-ups and drop-offs to the transit centre, and on Friday nights there's a free barbecue for guests.

Next up is *Backpackers International* (☎ (077) 72 4340), which occupies the two levels above a cafe at 205 Flinders St East. There are two dorms on the 2nd floor and a kitchen and lounge on the 1st floor. This place is central and has two broad balconies

PLACES TO STAY

1 Hotel Allen
2 The Strand Motel
9 Yongala Lodge Motel & Restaurant
13 Reef Lodge
17 Backpackers
   International & Luvits Cafe
25 YHA Adventurers Resort
28 Globetrotters Hostel
29 Southbank Village Backpackers
32 Shamrock Hotel
33 Southbank Motor Inn
39 Coral Reef Lodge
40 Rex Inn the City
48 Townsville Travelodge
55 Civic House Backpackers Inn
56 Central City Garden Apartments
57 Sunseeker Private Hotel
62 Great Northern Hotel

PLACES TO EAT

3 C'est Si Bon
5 Spinnakers on the Breakwater
14 The Magnet
15 Exchange Hotel
18 Thai International & Zouí Cafe-Deli
20 Hog's Breath Cafe
24 Metropole Hotel
26 Crown Tavern
31 Andy's Budget Bistro
34 Cactus Jack's Bar & Grill
35 Australian Hotel
36 L'Escargotiére & Michel's Cafe &
   Bar
47 Fisherman's Wharf
60 Jun Japanese Restaurant
63 The Reef Thai Restaurant
64 Cafe Nova

OTHER

4 Tobruk Memorial Baths
6 Magnetic Island Ferry Terminal
7 Car Ferry Terminal
8 Centenary Fountain
10 Townsville General Hospital
11 Criterion Tavern
12 Tattersall's Hotel
16 Bank Nightclub
19 Hard Blues Bar
21 Bullwinkle's Cabaret & Bar
22 Great Barrier Reef Wonderland
23 Magnetic Island Ferry Terminal
27 Maritime Museum
30 Bus Transit Centre &
   Andy's Backpackers
37 Post Office
38 Perc Tucker Regional Gallery
41 Townsville Museum
42 QBD's Bumble Bee Bookshop
43 Townsville Municipal Library
44 Northtown on the Mall
45 Tourist Information Centre
46 Qantas Airlines
49 Transit Mall (Local Bus Depot)
50 Ansett Airlines
51 The Cat & Fiddle Centre
52 Mary Who Bookshop
53 Police Station
54 Mike Ball Dive Expeditions
58 Townsville Five Cinema Centre
59 John Mellick & Co
61 STA Travel
65 Railway Station

NORTH COAST

looking out over the river, although the dorms are quite large and it's a bit run-down. Dorm beds are $12, and there's one double room at $28. The price includes a continental breakfast.

The *Reef Lodge* (☎ (077) 21 1112), at 4 Wickham St, is close to the Great Barrier Reef Wonderland and the ferry terminals. It's another small, old-fashioned but fairly clean place with various types of rooms spread over several buildings. There seem to be different prices for every room, but dorm beds are around $10, singles/doubles start at $26/32, and twin rooms are from $26. Most rooms have coin-in-the-slot air-con ($1), and the stoves in the kitchen also require coins (20c). This place also has a courtesy bus.

Guesthouses At 32 Hale St, the *Coral Reef Lodge* (☎ (077) 71 5512) is a recently renovated Queenslander which has two self-contained units upstairs and eight guest rooms with shared bathroom and cooking facilities downstairs. The guesthouse rooms cost $35/40 for singles/doubles; the self-contained units start at $50. Breakfast is included in the tariffs.

Pubs & Private Hotels A number of Townsville's traditional old pubs offer accommodation. Generally, these pub rooms are fairly basic, with shared bathroom facilities but no cooking facilities.

The *Great Northern Hotel* (☎ (077) 71 6191), across the road from the railway station at 500 Flinders St, is a good old-fashioned pub with clean, simple rooms, most of which open out onto a broad verandah. Nightly costs are $18/30; some doubles have private bathrooms for an extra $5. The food downstairs is good.

On the corner of Palmer and Plume Sts, opposite the transit centre, the *Shamrock Hotel* (☎ (077) 71 4351) has 10 single and four double rooms upstairs at $20/35.

The *Sunseeker Private Hotel* (☎ (077) 71 3409), situated at 10 Blackwood St, has small singles/doubles with shared bathrooms at $25/28 and triples at $33, but it's a pretty gloomy and cheerless place. There's a communal kitchen downstairs.

The *Hotel Allen* (☎ (077) 71 5656), on the corner of Eyre and Gregory Sts, has motel-style rooms with air-con which start from $35/45 for singles/doubles.

Motels There are plenty of motels in Townsville. One of the better areas to stay is along The Strand, which runs along the waterfront from the centre to the north.

The *Beach House Motel* (☎ (077) 21 13330), at 66 The Strand, is a neat, recently renovated budget motel with good units from $50/55 for singles/doubles. The Regatta restaurant at the front of the motel is quite good, and overlooks a small pool. The *Tropical Hideaway Motel* (☎ (077) 71 4355), at 74 The Strand, has budget rooms starting from $45 a double, and the *Strand Motel* (☎ (077) 72 1977), at 51 The Strand, has rooms from $46/50. Farther up The Strand, at No 117, *Motel Shoredrive* (☎ (077) 71 6048) is across the road from the Coral Sea Memorial Rockpool and the swimming enclosure. Units here start from $50/55.

If you can afford a little more, the *Historic Yongala Lodge Motel* (☎ (070) 72 4633), at 11 Fryer St, has modern motel units and self-contained rooms starting from $65 a double, and period-style units from $79. At the front of the motel is a lovely 19th-century building which houses a Greek restaurant (see Places to Eat).

Closer to the centre of town, *Rex Inn the City* (☎ (077) 71 6048), at 143 Wills St, is a bright, renovated motel with a good pool, a barbecue area and a guest laundry. Standard units start from $59, there are units with kitchenettes from $60 and family units which sleep up to six people cost from $100.

The *Southbank Motor Inn* (☎ (077) 21 1474) on the south side of Ross Creek at 23 Palmer St is a modern eight-storey motel with 100 air-con rooms with good views, as well as a pool, a bar and a licensed restaurant. Singles/doubles cost $85 during the week, but on Friday and Saturday nights they have a weekend special of $65, which is good value.

The *Townsville Reef International* (☎ (077) 21 1777), overlooking the waterfront from 63-64 The Strand, is a modern four-star, three-storey motel with a restaurant and a pool. Rooms here start from $98, suites from $125.

If you're passing through Townsville, you'll find plenty of other motels strung along the Bruce Hwy on either side of Townsville.

Holiday Flats The *Townsville Seaside Apartments* (☎ (077) 21 3155), at 105 The Strand, is a long, two-storey strip of 1960s apartments which have recently been renovated. The units don't win any interior design prizes, but they're comfortable enough and fully equipped with good kitchens and air-con. Prices vary according to the season and the number of people, but the one-bedroom units start from $55 and the two-bedroom units from $72.

If you want to be closer to the centre, the *Central City Garden Apartments* (☎ (077) 72 2655), at 270-286 Walker St, is a four-storey complex of reasonably modern apartments with a good pool area and underground parking. All the units have a separate kitchen and lounge. One-bedroom units are from $75 a double, two-bedroom units from $100 for up to four people, and three-bedroom units are from $130 for up to six people.

Hotels & Apartment Hotels *Aquarius on the Beach* (☎ (077) 72 4255), at 75 The Strand, is an excellent all-suite hotel. At 14 storeys this is the tallest building on the waterfront, with more than 130 self-contained units, all of which have great views, air-con, kitchenettes and all the other modcons. There's a pool and a restaurant on the 14th floor. Rooms here range from $90 a double and from $115 for four people.

You can't miss the *Townsville Travelodge* (☎ (077) 72 2477) – it's the prominent 16-storey circular building in the centre of the Flinders St Mall. The Travelodge is a four-star hotel and has 186 rooms, two gyms, a rooftop pool, a piano bar and a restaurant. Rooms start from around $90 a night.

Townsville's only five-star hotel is the *Sheraton Breakwater Casino/Hotel* (☎ (077) 22 2333), perched on the breakwater at the end of Sir Leslie Thiess Dve. Rooms here range from $210 to $235, depending on your views. For the high-rollers, suites range from $300 to $850.

Places to Eat

Cafes, Delis & Takeaways *Luvits Cafe*, below the Backpacker International Hostel, at 205 Flinders St East, is a great place for breakfast. It's one of the few places in Townsville with real, strong coffee, and they have toasted sandwiches, filled croissants, muesli with yoghurt and fruit, bacon & eggs with pancakes and maple syrup, and best of all, sensational blueberry pancakes. Breakfast dishes range from $4 to $7. They also open for lunch, with quiches, lasagna, salads and sweet or savoury pancakes. Dinner offerings include pastas, salads and a range of Indian dishes. It's a casual, relaxed and friendly place, and a BYO.

C'est Si Bon, about a km north of the centre on Eyre St near the Gregory St corner, is an excellent little gourmet deli and takeaway which has good salads, sandwiches, marinated chicken pieces, pork pies, home-made cakes and other goodies.

Back in town, there are quite a few cafes and other eateries along the Flinders St Mall, although most of them are hidden in arcades and shopping centres off the mall. Northtown on the Mall, an arcade opposite the tourist information centre, has a couple of good places including *Le Cafe de France*, a sit-down cafe which serves sandwiches and cakes, and the *Danish Cone Co*, a tiny takeaway which makes good fresh sandwiches and rolls, and great mango and/or banana smoothies. *Strollers Cafe*, in Shaw's Arcade up near the Stanley St end, is another popular sit-down lunch place with sandwiches, burgers, filled croissants and quiches.

If you're looking for a health food store, try *Townsville City Health Foods*, which is in the Cat & Fiddle Centre off the mall close to Stanley St.

Over on The Strand, almost opposite the Tobruk Memorial Baths swimming pool, the *Ozone Cafe* is a small takeaway with outdoor tables which has the usual sandwiches and burgers, plus a few Chinese dishes for around $7 to $8.

There's also a cluster of eateries farther up The Strand around the Gregory St corner. On the corner itself, *Harold's Seafood* is a takeaway fish & chippery with good burgers and fish & chips. The coral trout is especially good – you can have it crumbed, battered or grilled, but I reckon grilled is best by a mile. There's a kebab place next door on The Strand. Heading up Gregory St there are three restaurants, two of which do takeaways: *Rasa Pinang* has takeaway Malaysian dishes for around $5, and *Norma's* BYO has a small takeaway section around the back where you can get great felafel or chicken rolls and other Lebanese goodies. You might even be able to have a dance here while you're waiting for your food – see the Restaurants section later for more details.

If you're waiting for a bus, the *cafeteria* in the transit centre on Palmer St serves quite substantial meals and is open from 5 am to 11.30 pm. *Andy's Budget Bistro*, at the front of the transit centre, has a range of cooked evening meals from $4 to $8, and you get a free beer with your meal if you're staying upstairs.

Pubs Many of the pubs do decent counter meals. The *Great Northern Hotel*, on the corner of Flinders and Blackwood Sts, has an excellent bistro with mains from $10 to $12 and good bar meals from $4 to $7. The *Exchange Hotel*, at 151 Flinders St East, has a bistro downstairs with meals from $8 to $12 and the more expensive *Melton Black's* restaurant upstairs with a pleasant balcony and live music on weekends.

There are a few good pubs over the creek along Palmer St. The *Metropole Hotel*, next to the YHA Adventurers Resort, has a covered garden bistro out the back with pastas, seafood and steaks from $10 to $15, and a good range of 'chef's specials' such as fish & chips, lamb chops and pastas from $5 to $8. Also in the pub is a good little à la carte restaurant, *La Met*, with main meals around $18. On the other side of the YHA, the *Crown Tavern* has a beer garden and bistro meals from $6 to $10. Farther down, the *Shamrock Hotel* has bistro meals from $8, and the nearby *Australian Hotel* is a little more up-market, with a covered courtyard bistro out the back and live music on Sunday.

The *Seaview Hotel*, on The Strand, and the *Hotel Allen*, around the corner on Gregory St, are also popular places to eat, and both have pleasant beer gardens.

Behind the Coral Sea Memorial Rockpool at the northern end of The Strand is the *Beach Club*, which is a pleasant alternative to the pubs. This place has a bar, poker machines and tables overlooking the rockpool and the ocean. Bistro meals are mostly $8.50. This is a licensed club – nonmembers are welcome but they have to sign in first.

Restaurants Flinders St East is one of the main areas for eateries, and offers plenty of choices. The *Hog's Breath Cafe*, one of a chain of saloon-style bar & grills, is near the Denham St corner. It has burgers (including a pretty tasty chicken burger) from $8 to $9, salads from $9 to $12, and steak, chicken and

fish grills for around $14. Their specialty is the prime ribs, which cost around $17.

Moving along the street, the *Thai International Restaurant*, upstairs at No 235, has fine soups for $6, a good range of vegetarian dishes from $5 to $9, and imaginative main courses for $10 to $14. Downstairs, *Zouí Cafe-Deli* is a busy and modern Mediterranean-style eatery with Greek/Italian cuisine such as char-grilled sardines, marinated lamb and grilled chicken with rosemary, with mains in the $14 to $16 range. Both of these places are BYO.

At No 179, the licensed *Capitol* Chinese restaurant has two sections: a seafood smorgasbord at $31 a head, or an à la carte restaurant with mains from $9 to $12. Farther along, next to the Exchange Hotel, is *The Magnet*. With its all-white décor and candle lit tables, this small and elegant BYO is about as romantic as things get in Townsville. The menu offers pastas for around $10 and dishes such as flamed apricot chicken, a seafood garden plate or scallopine marsala ranging from $14 to $17.

Fisherman's Wharf, overlooking Ross Creek from near the western end of Victoria Bridge, has an inviting collection of food stalls and open-air tables. Cuisines featured include Italian, seafood, Mexican, health food and more, all at reasonable prices, and there's also a bar and live entertainment from Wednesday to Sunday nights.

Back on Flinders St, past the southern end of the mall, is the small *Jun Japanese Restaurant*, which is nothing special but has main courses from $13 to $17 and a range of set five-course menus from $24 to $28 per person. The *Reef Thai Restaurant* on Flinders St, near Blackwood St, is a spacious Thai restaurant which is open on weekdays for lunch and every night for dinner. Main courses are in the $9 to $13 range.

Cafe Nova, on Blackwood St, near the Flinders St corner, is an interesting little BYO cafe which is open from 6 pm till late. It has good coffee, milk shakes and a great range of cakes and desserts, as well as toasted sandwiches from $3 to $4, open sandwiches with salad from $7 to $8, and a few mains like lasagna, home-made curries or grilled felafels with salad from $7 to $10. On the corner of Blackwood and Sturt Sts, *Admiral's Seafood Restaurant* serves seafood in a nautical-style setting.

Spinnakers on the Breakwater (☎ (077) 21 2567) is an up-market seafood restaurant perched out on the breakwater on Sir Leslie Thiess Dve, surrounded by water on three sides. It's a cosy, stylish restaurant with a vaguely nautical feel. It's licensed, and as well as a wide range of seafood, the menu offers turkey, steak and chicken dishes. At lunch time, main courses range from $13 to $18 or they have a two-course deal for $15. The dinner menu has mains in the $18 to $28 range.

Just off The Strand in Gregory St are three restaurants. *El Charro* is another lively and popular Mexican 'cantina' with mains in the $9 to $16 range, and next door the small *Rasa Pinang* has Malaysian dishes for around $10. Next to this is *Norma's BYO* (☎ (077) 21 4555), a small Lebanese BYO. It may not look much, but this place is great fun. Norma is an excellent host who always has a big smile on her face, and as the evening progresses she plays loud Lebanese music and encourages her daughter, and everyone else in the place, to dance. The food is fresh, healthy and good value – you usually get to try a bit of everything. Norma's is open for dinner from Tuesday to Sunday.

The *Historic Yongala Lodge*, at 11 Fryer St, has a Greek restaurant in a lovely old building, with displays of period furniture, memorabilia, and finds from the *Yongala* wreck. Main meals are in the $16 to $20 range, or there's a banquet menu at $30 a head. There's live Greek music here on Friday and Saturday nights.

Palmer St also has a handful of good restaurants. At No 21, *Cactus Jack's Bar & Grill* (☎ (077) 21 1478) is a lively Tex/Mex place with burgers from $8 to $9 and enchiladas, vegetarian burritos, tostadas, fajitas and other mains in the $9 to $13 range. It's pretty popular, and the sangria and margaritas tend to flow thick and fast; you'll need to book on weekends.

At 7 Palmer St, *Michel's Cafe & Bar* is one of Townsville's most stylish eateries. The dining room is set around an open kitchen and bar. At lunch time you can choose from sandwiches, grilled focaccias and salads, and at dinner meals such as char-grilled lamb cutlets or a Cajun steak range from $13 to $16.

At 3 Palmer St, *L'Escargotiére* is a simple BYO French restaurant with a small courtyard out the back. Main courses are around $18, or you can have three courses for $30.

Entertainment
Townsville's nightlife is almost as lively as Cairns' and ranges from pub bands to flashy clubs and, of course, the casino. The main nightlife area is along Flinders St East, with a couple of other places along The Strand.

Pubs & Live Music The *Hard Blues Bar*, in the James Cook Tavern at 237 Flinders St East, is one of the main venues for live music in Townsville. They have a different theme each night; Monday is muso's night, with jam sessions and try-outs; Tuesday is acoustic and blues night; Wednesday features alternative music; Thursday is jazz night; and Friday and Saturday feature rock & roll bands and blues bands. There's a cover charge on the weekend, which ranges from $5 for local bands to $30 or more for major international acts.

Most of the other pubs along Flinders St East have live bands or DJs on weekends. The Exchange Hotel, in the centre of the action at 151 Flinders St East, has *Melton Black's* upstairs, which features live bands on Friday and Saturday nights and stays open until 3 am (no cover charge); and *Portraits Wine Bar* downstairs, which attracts a more sophisticated (older) crowd.

The *Tattersalls Hotel*, on the corner of Flinders St East and Wickham St, also has a nightclub which is open from Wednesday to Sunday nights until 3 or 4 am. There's no cover charge, and they usually have drinks specials here to lure in thirsty punters.

The big and colourful *Criterion Tavern*, on the corner of The Strand and King St, is quite popular, and has a big beer garden, nightclub, restaurant and several bars. Moving along The Strand, the Seaview Hotel, on the corner of Gregory St, also has a large beer garden and several sections. The downstairs *Arizona Bar* has a 'rock & roll with a dash of country' theme and a $3 cover charge on weekends; they have a Sunday afternoon session with live bands in the beer garden; and *Breezes* upstairs is an over-25's nightclub.

The *Australian Hotel*, south of the creek on Palmer St, is a relaxed, old-fashioned pub with live music sessions on Sunday afternoons.

Nightclubs *The Bank*, in a former bank building at 169 Flinders St East, is the city's most up-market nightclub. It's open nightly until around 5 am, with a $3 to $5 cover charge and dress regulations. *Bullwinkle's Cabaret & Bar*, on the corner of Flinders St East and Wickham St, has a nightclub section which stays open nightly until 3 am, and a coffee shop and eatery area upstairs.

Casino Townsville's *Sheraton Breakwater Casino* is at the end of Sir Leslie Thiess Dve in the Sheraton Hotel complex. You can try your luck at roulette, blackjack, two-up, keno or various other games from 9 am to 3 am every day (until 4 am on Friday and Saturday). There's no admission fee, although dress regulations specify neat casual wear, which means no T-shirts, runners, thongs or bare feet.

Theatre & Cinema The *Townsville Five Cinema Centre* (☎ (077) 71 4101), on the corner of Sturt and Blackwood Sts, has five cinemas showing mainstream current releases.

The impressive new 5000 seat *Townsville Breakwater Entertainment Centre* (☎ (077) 71 4000) is now the main venue for concerts, the performing arts and other major events.

The *Civic Theatre* (☎ (077) 72 2677), on Boundary St South Townsville, is a smaller venue for performing arts and other varied cultural pursuits.

Things to Buy

At 481 Flinders St, John Melick & Co sells a good range of camping and bushwalking gear, Driza-bone oilskins, Akubra hats, work boots and walking boots, tents, sleeping bags and work wear. Another place to try for this type of stuff is Askern's Army Disposals, farther down at 531-525 Flinders St, which sells tarps, jerry cans, stoves and various camping and walking gear.

Getting There & Away

Travel Agents STA Travel (☎ (077) 72 7055) has an office at 100 Stanley St, just off the Flinders St Mall.

Air Ansett and Qantas have regular flights between Townsville and the major destinations in Australia. Regular one-way fares include Cairns $158, Brisbane $319, Sydney $440, Melbourne $504, Darwin $446, Perth $600, Hobart $571 and Adelaide $530. Both airlines have offices in the mall, with Qantas at 320 Flinders St and Ansett at 350 Flinders St.

Sunstate Airlines has services between Townsville and Cairns ($158), Dunk Island ($108), Mackay ($166), Proserpine ($149), Rockhampton ($239), Gladstone ($293) and Bundaberg ($355).

Flight West has flights to Mt Isa ($280) at least once a day, often with stops at smaller places on the way. It also flies direct to Cairns ($158), Mackay ($166) and Rockhampton ($239).

Bus Townsville is on the main Brisbane to Cairns coastal run, and both Greyhound Pioneer Australia (☎ 13 2030) and McCafferty's (☎ (077) 72 5100) have frequent daily services to and from here. All the long-distance buses operate from the Townsville transit centre on Palmer St. Average fares and times from Townsville include Brisbane (18 to 21 hours, $116), Rockhampton (11 hours, $72), Mackay (six hours, $48), Airlie Beach (3½ hours, $36), Mission Beach (three hours, $35) and Cairns (4½ hours, $37).

Townsville is also the start of the main inland route from Queensland across to Darwin and Alice Springs. If you're heading west, the trip to Charters Towers takes 1¾ hours and costs $16; to Mt Isa the trip takes 11 hours and costs around $80.

Train The Brisbane-Cairns *Sunlander* travels through Townsville three times a week. The trip from Brisbane to Townsville takes 25 hours ($118 for an economy seat, $148 for an economy sleeper and $226 for a 1st-class sleeper). From Townsville, Proserpine is a five-hour journey, Rockhampton is 14½ hours and Cairns seven hours. The *Queenslander* does the same Brisbane-Cairns run once a week (leaving Brisbane on Sunday mornings and Cairns on Tuesday mornings). It's a bit faster than the *Sunlander*, as well as being a lot more luxurious and much more expensive – the fare from Brisbane to Townsville is $433 which includes all meals and a sleeping compartment.

The *Inlander* operates twice weekly from Townsville to Mt Isa (18 hours; $95 for an economy seat, $125 for an economy sleeper and $192 for a 1st-class sleeper). Townsville to Charters Towers takes three hours ($20 in economy only).

Getting Around
To/From the Airport Townsville Airport is five km west of the city centre at Garbutt; a taxi to the centre costs $9. Acacia Luxury Transport runs the Airport Shuttle (☎ (077) 75 5544), servicing all main arrivals and departures. It costs $5 one way or $8 for two people travelling together, and they will drop off or pick up almost anywhere fairly central.

Bus There are two companies that run local bus services around Townsville. Hermit Park Bus Service (☎ (077) 79 1658) runs from the centre to the southern suburbs, terminating at the Plaza City Shopping Centre. Campbell's Coaches (☎ (077) 74 5099) has services from the centre to the western and northern suburbs, including the beaches as far as Pallaranda. All local buses operate from the Transit Mall on Stokes St, near the Flinders St Mall. Routes and timetables are posted on notice boards in the mall.

Taxi There's a taxi rank at the Transit Mall on the corner of Stokes St and the Flinders St Mall. To book a taxi, call Standard White Cabs (☎ (077) 72 1555).

Car Rental The larger car-rental agencies are all represented in Townsville. Thrifty (☎ (077) 72 4600), Avis (☎ (077) 21 2688), Budget (☎ (077) 13 2727), and Hertz (☎ (077) 71 6003) all have rental desks at the airport. Smaller operators include Rent-a-Rocket (☎ (077) 72 7444), at 14 Dean St, South Townsville; Sunrunner Moke Hire (☎ (077) 21 5038), at 11 Anthony St, South Townsville; and Townsville Car Rentals (☎ (077) 72 1093), at 12 Palmer St, South Townsville. All of these places are close to the bus transit centre.

Four Wheel Drive Hire Service (☎ (077) 21 2404), at 711 Flinders St, has a wide range of 4WDs available for rent.

MAGNETIC ISLAND (pop 2500)
Magnetic Island is one of Queensland's oldest resort islands, with the first tourists arriving from the mainland more than 100 years ago. It's a large (52 sq km) and scenic continental island, and today it remains a popular if somewhat old-fashioned resort island, with the main attractions being its fine beaches, excellent bushwalks, an abundance of wildlife and its laid-back nature.

Only eight km off shore, the island is almost an outer suburb of Townsville, with many of the 2500 residents commuting to the mainland by ferry every day. Ferries across are frequent, affordable and fast (15 minutes).

There are four small townships spread around the east coast, with a wide range of budget to mid-range accommodation and a good range of restaurants and cafes. About 70% of the island is national park, with the

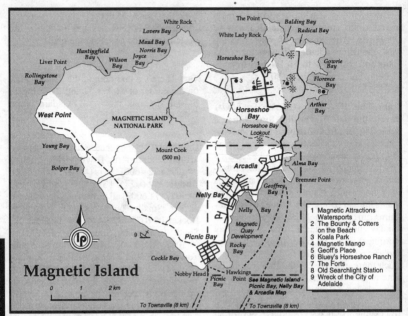

Magnetic Island

1 Magnetic Attractions
   Watersports
2 The Bounty & Cotters
   on the Beach
3 Koala Park
4 Magnetic Mango
5 Geoff's Place
6 Bluey's Horseshoe Ranch
7 The Forts
8 Old Searchlight Station
9 Wreck of the City of
   Adelaide

500-metre Mt Cook in the centre of the island being the dominant point.

History

The island was named by Captain Cook, who thought his ship's compass went funny when he sailed by in 1770.

Aborigines were frequent visitors to the island, which they could easily reach from the mainland, but the first European settlement was established by timber cutters in the early 1870s. In 1887 Harry Butler and his family settled at Picnic Bay and started putting up visitors from the mainland in thatched huts, and thus the Magnetic Island tourist business was born. In 1899, Robert Hayles saw the potential of the island as a holiday destination for the booming gold-mining centre of Charters Towers. The Hayles family built a hotel and dance hall and started up the first ferry service, and they remained involved in the Magnetic Island tourist industry for the next 90 years.

Orientation & Information

Magnetic Island is roughly triangular in shape, with Picnic Bay, the main town and ferry destination, at the southern corner. The main road runs up the eastern side of the island through a string of small towns to Horseshoe Bay, with a turn off to Radical Bay. There's also a rough track along the uninteresting west coast. Along the north coast it's walking only.

The Island Travel Centre (☎ (077) 78 5155) has an information centre and booking office between the end of the pier and the Picnic Bay Mall. You can book local tours and accommodation here, and they can also handle domestic and international travel arrangements.

The QNP&WS (☎ (077) 78 5378) has an office in Picnic Bay.

There's a National Bank in the Picnic Bay Mall, as well as a post office with a Commonwealth Bank agency. There are no ATMs on the island, although most of the supermarkets on the island have EFTPOS facilities.

Zoning

Geoffrey Bay, Arcadia and Five Beach Bay on the north coast of the island are all zoned Marine Park B and fishing is not permitted.

Warning

Box jellyfish are found in the waters around Magnetic Island between October and April. There is a netted swimming enclosure at Picnic Bay, and Alma Bay is usually safe for swimming, but in other areas swimming is not recommended during the danger months.

Things to See

Picnic Bay The main settlement on the island, and the first stop for the ferries is Picnic Bay. The new mall along the waterfront has a good selection of shops and eateries, and you can hire bikes, mokes and scooters here. Picnic Bay also has quite a few places to stay, and the main beach has a stinger-free enclosure and is patrolled by a life-saving club.

There's a lookout above the town and just to the west of Picnic Bay is **Cockle Bay** with the wreck of the *City of Adelaide*. Heading around the coast in the other direction is **Rocky Bay** where there's a short, steep walk down to a beautiful beach.

Nelly Bay Next around the coast is Nelly Bay, which has a good beach with shade, and a reef at low tide. At the far end of the bay there are some pioneer graves.

The north end of Nelly Bay is enclosed by a half-finished rocky marina. The developers of this project went broke and disappeared a few years ago, and the future of the project is unknown.

Arcadia Round the next headland you come to **Geoffrey Bay**, a marine park area which has an interesting 400-metre low-tide reef walk over the fringing coral reef from the southern end of the beach; a board indicates the start of the trail. Some of the ferries also stop at the jetty on Geoffrey Bay.

Overlooking the bay is the town of Arcadia, with shops, more places to stay and the Arcadia Hotel Resort (where there are live bands at weekends. Just around the next headland is the very pleasant **Alma Bay beach**.

Radical Bay & The Forts The main road runs back from the coast between Arcadia and Horseshoe Bay, with a turn off mid-way to Radical Bay. This narrow, winding and hilly road is private, and if you're in a rental vehicle your insurance doesn't cover you on this section. On the way to Radical Bay, there are tracks leading off to the old **Searchlight Station** on a headland between **Arthur and Florence bays**. There are fine views from up here, and the bays are also pleasantly secluded.

Radical Bay has a very attractive beach, although a resort that closed down here is now private property and there is limited access to the beach. From the car park here a walking trail leads across the headland to Horseshoe Bay, with a turn off halfway to the beautiful and secluded **Balding Bay**, which is an unofficial nude-bathing beach.

Back at the junction of the road to Radical Bay, there's also a walking track leading to **The Forts**, an old WW II command post and signal station with gun sites and an ammunition store.

Horseshoe Bay Horseshoe Bay, on the north coast of the island, is the longest and most sheltered, although not necessarily the best, beach on the island. This quiet town has a few shops and a couple of fairly dated tourist attractions. **Magnetic Mango**, a working mango plantation, has an outdoor eatery which serves Devonshire teas and lunches, although a 'Closing Down Sale' when I was last there suggested it might not be operating by now... There's also a fairly desolate **Koala Park**, although there are so many koalas on the island that you'll be better off skipping this place and just looking up a tree.

At the beach there are boats, sailboards and canoes for hire and you can also paraglide. From the beach you can walk to Maud Bay, around to the west, or back east to Radical Bay.

Activities

Bushwalking The National Parks service produces a leaflet for Magnetic Island's excellent bushwalking tracks. Possible walks, with distances and one-way travel times, include:

Walk	Distance		Time
Nelly Bay to Arcadia	6	km	2 hours
Picnic Bay to West Point	8	km	2½ hours
Horseshoe Bay road to Arthur Bay	2	km	½ hour
Horseshoe Bay to Florence Bay	2.5	km	1 hour
Horseshoe Bay to the Forts	2	km	¾ hour
Horseshoe Bay to Balding Bay	3	km	¾ hour
Horseshoe Bay to Radical Bay	3	km	⅓ hour
Mt Cook ascent	8	km	all day

Diving Several of the Townsville-based dive companies, including Mike Ball Dive Expeditions, run dive courses on Magnetic. See the Townsville Diving section for details.

There is also a dive company on the island. Magnetic Island Pleasure Divers (☎ (077) 78 5788) offers a basic five-day course for $249, or a course that includes one day's diving on the reef for $295. They also offer introductory dives for $59, and a range of certified dives.

Water Sports On the beach at Horseshoe Bay, Magnetic Attractions has a range of water-sports gear for hire, including jet skis ($25 for 15 minutes), dinghies ($70 a day), aquabikes, canoes and surf skis (all $7 a half hour). You can also go water-skiing ($20 for 15 minutes) or paragliding ($35 for 15 minutes) here.

Based at the southern end of Nelly Bay, Island Watersports also has jet skis, catamarans, surf skis and dinghies for hire at similar rates.

Horse Riding Bluey's Horseshoe Ranch (☎ (077) 78 5109), at Horseshoe Bay, offers horse rides at $18 an hour, $30 for two hours or $45 for a half-day.

Organised Tours

Reef Trips Pure Pleasure Cruises (☎ (077) 21 3555) does a day trip out to Kelso Reef on the outer Barrier Reef, usually stopping at Magnetic on their way out from Townsville. See Townsville's Organised Tours section for details.

Cruises & Fishing Trips Barnacle Bill (☎ (077) 58 1237) takes up to three people out on fishing expeditions, with all gear and bait supplied. Two hours costs $35, four hours $60.

The *Worripa* (☎ (077) 78 5937) is a sailing catamaran that runs day trips around the island for $50, including lunch, boom netting and snorkelling gear, although the cruises weren't operating last time I visited the island. Check locally to see if they've started back up.

Motorcycle Tours You can also take a tour of the island on the back of a Harley-Davidson. Based at the end of the jetty in Picnic Bay, the tours cost $35 for an hour or $25 for half an hour.

Places to Stay

Camping Camping facilities on the island are somewhat limited, and camping isn't allowed anywhere in the national park. Two of the backpackers' hostels, *Geoff's Place* and the *Beachfront Resort*, have areas set aside for campers – Geoff's Place probably has the better setup out of the two. See the Hostels section below for more details.

Hostels There's a good selection of backpackers' hostels on the island and it's a competitive scene, with several hostels sending vehicles to meet the ferries at Picnic Bay. Most places have cheaper rates during the quiet times and for longer stays, and there are also package deals on accommodation and transport (see Getting There & Away).

Picnic Bay Only a minute's walk from the Picnic Bay ferry pier, the small *Hideaway Budget Resort* (☎ (077) 78 5110), at 32

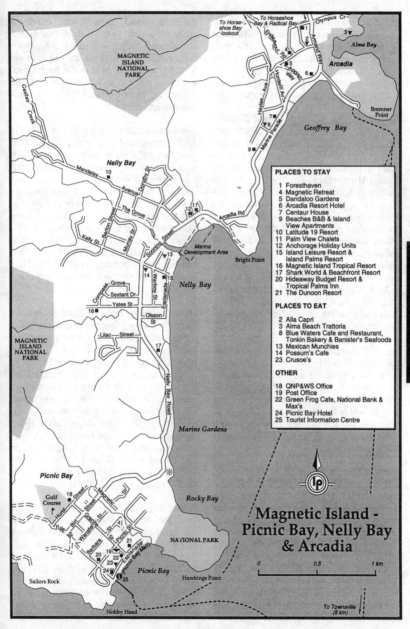

PLACES TO STAY
1 Foresthaven
4 Magnetic Retreat
5 Dandaloo Gardens
6 Arcadia Resort Hotel
7 Centaur House
9 Beaches B&B & Island
  View Apartments
10 Latitude 19 Resort
11 Palm View Chalets
12 Anchorage Holiday Units
15 Island Leisure Resort &
   Island Palms Resort
16 Magnetic Island Tropical Resort
17 Shark World & Beachfront Resort
20 Hideaway Budget Resort &
   Tropical Palms Inn
21 The Dunoon Resort

PLACES TO EAT
2 Alla Capri
3 Alma Beach Trattoria
8 Blue Waters Cafe and Restaurant,
  Tonkin Bakery & Banister's Seafoods
13 Mexican Munchies
14 Possum's Cafe
23 Crusoe's

OTHER
18 QNP&WS Office
19 Post Office
22 Green Frog Cafe, National Bank &
   Max's
24 Picnic Bay Hotel
25 Tourist Information Centre

NORTH COAST

Magnetic Island –
Picnic Bay, Nelly Bay
& Arcadia

0   0.5   1 km

Picnic St, is a clean, renovated place with a kitchen, a good pool, a TV room with a video library and laundry facilities. It's well located and good value, with a bed in a twin or double room (no dorms) costing $14, and singles/doubles costing $25/28. The owners of this place speak Swiss and German.

Nelly Bay The *Magnetic Island Tropical Resort* (☎ (077) 78 5955), on Yates St, just off the main road, is a very good budget resort with a good swimming pool, an inexpensive restaurant and a pleasant garden setting. Backpackers can stay in a four to six-bed A-frame cabin with its own bathroom for $14. Alternatively, you can rent a whole cabin, which costs $40 a double for the standard model, $60 a double for the deluxe model with TV, fridge and tea and coffee-making facilities, or $75 a double with self-contained facilities and air-con. It's another $10 for each extra adult, or $5 per child. This place is good if you're after somewhere quiet.

At the southern end of Nelly Bay is the *Beachfront Resort* (☎ (077) 78 5777), which is attached to the Shark World 'aquarium'. Lonely Planet has received letters from travellers who refused to stay here once they saw the conditions of the aquarium, but if that doesn't worry you, it costs $7 per person to camp in your own tent, $12 per head in a four or eight-bed A-frame cabin, and $14 per head in the camp-o-tels (a cross between a cabin and a tent, which apparently get unbearably hot in summer).

Arcadia *Centaur House* (☎ (077) 78 5668), at 27 Marine Pde, is a small, rambling, old-style hostel opposite the beach. The atmosphere is relaxed, and there's a pleasant garden out the back with hammocks and a barbecue. A bed in the large downstairs dorm costs $14; double rooms upstairs range from $30 to $34. This place is quiet and friendly.

Also in Arcadia, at 11 Cook Rd, is *Foresthaven* (☎ (077) 78 5153). This hostel has seen better days, and the buildings and facilities are pretty old and basic, although the peaceful bush setting is nice. Accommo-

dation is spread across several buildings, with units with two or three-bed rooms sharing one kitchen and eating area. Dorm beds cost $14, and twins and doubles are $34. Barbecues are held in the large courtyard, and you can rent mountain bikes for $10 a day. The owners of this place speak German and French.

Horseshoe Bay *Geoff's Place* (☎ (077) 78 5577), on Horseshoe Bay Rd, is one of the island's most popular places for travellers, with its party atmosphere and nightly activities. There are extensive grounds, and you can camp for $6 per person, take a bunk in a marquee for $8 or share a four or eight-bed A-frame cedar cabin for $12. (The eight-bed cabins have their own bathroom.) There's a communal kitchen, a popular pool, a bar and a restaurant with meals from $4 to $7. You can hire mountain bikes for $10 a day. Their courtesy bus shuttles between here and Picnic Bay to meet the ferries.

Hotels, Motels, Holiday Flats & Resorts

There are lots of other accommodation options on the island. There are a couple of pubs and motels, and a few fairly new resorts, but by far the most common type of accommodation is in self-contained holiday flats. Many of these are quite old-fashioned, some are downright ancient, although there are a handful of newer places on the island.

Rates for all of these places vary with the seasons and demand, and most have cheaper 'stand-by' rates. They're also cheaper if you rent by the week. When you book, check whether linen, towels, etc are included in the tariff – you may have to BYO.

Picnic Bay The *Picnic Bay Hotel* (☎ (077) 78 5166), on the Esplanade in Picnic Bay, has motel rooms from $40 to $50 for twin rooms. In Picnic St next to the Hideaway hostel, the *Tropical Palms Inn* (☎ (077) 78 5076) has good motel units from $58, and self-contained cottages from $325 a week.

The *Dunoon Resort* (☎ (077) 78 5161), on the corner of Granite St and the Esplanade, is an older place that has been renovated and is set in good landscaped gardens, with two pools and laundry facilities. The one and two-bedroom self-contained units sleep four to six people and cost from $72 a double, plus $10 for extra adults and $6 for extra children.

Nelly Bay The *Island Leisure Resort* (☎ (077) 78 5511), close to the waterfront at 4 Kelly St, is an impressive resort with good facilities including a pool in a garden setting, a floodlit tennis court, a gym and a games room. All the units have a double bed and three bunks and cost $89 a double – children are free. Around the corner at 13 the Esplanade, the *Island Palms Resort* (☎ (077) 78 5571) is also good and has 12 self-contained two-bedroom units that cost from $89 a double.

The *Palm View Chalets* (☎ (077) 78 5596), at 114 Sooning St, is a collection of stylish A-frame timber chalets which sleep up to six people, and are self-contained. These places are excellent value from $50 a double. Also on Sooning St, the *Anchorage Holiday Flats* (☎ (077) 78 5596) is a good complex of two-bedroom units that start from $75 a night. Unfortunately, the waterfront position of both these places is rather spoilt by the unfinished Magnetic Quay Development.

The *Magnetic Island Tropical Resort* also has a good range of cabins – see the Hostels section earlier.

The *Latitude 19 Resort* (☎ (077) 78 5200), a couple of hundred metres back from the beach on Mandalay Ave, is the biggest resort on the island and has a pool, a tennis court, and 66 units ranging from $65 to $90.

Arcadia The *Arcadia Hotel Resort* (☎ (077) 78 5177) has motel-style units which range from $55 to $75, depending on the time of year and how close to the pool you want to be.

There are a number of budget holiday flats along Hayles Ave. Starting from the Alma Bay end of the street, *Magnetic Retreat* (☎ (077) 78 5357), with its entrance a little way up Rheuben Tce, has one and two-bedroom units from $65 to $75. The *Magnetic North*

Holiday Units (☎ (077) 78 5647), on the corner of Hayles Ave and Endeavour Rd, have two-bedroom units for up to six people from $50 a night, and a three-night special for $130.

The *Dandaloo Gardens* (☎ (077) 78 5174), at 40 Hayles Ave, has eight one-bedroom units that sleep up to five and range from $50 to $80 a night.

The *Island View Apartments* (☎ (077) 78 5387), at 40 Marine Pde, have two-bedroom units ranging from $55 to $75.

B&Bs There are also a couple of B&Bs on the island. *Marshall's B&B* (☎ (077) 78 5112), at 3 Endeavour Rd in Arcadia, is a simple little fibro house with B&B from $35/45 for singles/doubles. It has received good reports.

On the Arcadian waterfront, *Beaches B&B* (☎ (077) 78 5303), at 39 Marine Pde, is a very stylish new timber cottage which has a separate B&B section with two bedrooms, each with iron-framed beds and slate floors, air-con and a central bathroom. There's a good pool out the back and a front verandah overlooking the bay, and the rates here are good value at $55 a double, including breakfast.

Places to Eat

Picnic Bay The Picnic Bay Mall, along the waterfront, has a good selection of eating places. The *Picnic Bay Hotel* has counter meals from $6 to $12, and there are cheaper snacks. Further along the mall heading north-east, *Crusoe's* is a casual little BYO restaurant with a takeaway section and a few outdoor tables. For breakfast, they serve pancakes, muesli and yoghurt, ham and cheese croissants; lunch offerings include sandwiches, home-made pies or cooked meals; and at dinner main courses range from $8 to $12. Further along, the *Green Frog Cafe* is good for breakfasts, Devonshire teas or lunches.

At the far end of the mall is *Max's*, a very stylish bar and restaurant which is open nightly for dinner and has steaks, Thai and Malaysian meals with main courses from $10 to $17.

Nelly Bay *Mexican Munchies,* at 31 Warboy St, runs the gamut from enchiladas to tacos, and is open daily from 6 pm. Main courses are in the $10 to $12 range. There's a blackboard outside where you can chalk up your reservation during the day. Nearby, in the small shopping centre on the main road, is *Possum's Cafe,* good for snacks and takeaways. There's also a large supermarket in this centre.

Arcadia The *Arcadia Hotel Resort* has a number of eating possibilities; bistro meals range from $10 to $12, and you can eat outdoors by the pool. *Gatsby's* has more expensive meals.

Alla Capri, on Hayles Ave, is a licensed place with a pleasant outdoor eating area. They specialise in steaks and Italian food. The *Alma Beach Trattoria,* with a great setting overlooking this pretty little bay, does the pizza, pasta and seafood thing for lunches and dinner.

In the small Arcadia shopping centre on the corner of Hayles Ave and Bright St, the *Blue Waters Cafe & Restaurant* (☎ (077) 78 5645), which looks deceptively like a basic takeaway joint, actually has some of the best food on the island. There's a pleasant courtyard out the back, and they have an interesting selection of mains ranging from $8 to $14, or a three-course set menu for $12.95. They open for dinner from Monday to Saturday. Nearby, the *Bakehouse* is open early and is a good place for a coffee and croissant breakfast. Next door is *Banister's Seafood,* which is a basically a fish & chips place with an open-air BYO dining area. They have fish & chips from $2.70, burgers from $3.50 and fishermen's baskets for $10.

Horseshoe Bay On the waterfront at the bay, *Cotters on the Beach* is a relaxed little licensed restaurant with sandwiches, bagels and other lunches from $5 to $7, and steak, chicken and seafood mains from $10 to $17 at night. Next door, the *Bounty Snack Bar* has takeaways. There's also a small general store if you're preparing your own food.

Getting There & Away

Magnetic Island Ferries has two terminals in Townsville; one at the Great Barrier Reef Wonderland (☎ (077) 21 1913), and one at the breakwater on Sir Leslie Thiess Dve near the casino (☎ (077) 72 7122).

They run a virtual shuttle service to the island, with about 20 ferries a day making the 15-minute trip. The first ferry leaves Townsville at 6.05 am every day; the last service from Townsville to the island is at 6.45 pm on Sunday, Monday and Wednesday, at 10.40 pm on Tuesday, at 9.30 pm on Thursday and at 12.10 am on Friday and Saturday nights. The return fares are $19 adults, $14 Students, $9 children or $44 for a family (2 adults and 2 children). All ferries go to Picnic Bay and some continue on to Arcadia.

You can also buy package deals which include return ferry tickets and accommodation; one-night packages start at $29.

You can also take you're own vehicle across to the island, which works out cheaper than renting a car if there's more than three of you. The Capricorn Barge Company (☎ (077) 72 5422) runs a vehicle ferry to Arcadia from the southern side of Ross Creek four times a day during the week and twice a day on weekends. It's $89 return for a car and up to six passengers.

Getting Around

Bus The Magnetic Island Bus Service (☎ (077) 78 5130) operates between Picnic Bay and Horseshoe Bay 12 to 18 times a day, meeting all ferries and dropping off at all accommodation places. Some bus trips include Radical Bay, others the Koala Park. You can either get individual tickets ($1.20 to $3) or a full-day pass ($7 adults, $3.50 children).

Taxi For a taxi, ring (☎ (077) 78 5946) or (☎ (077) 78 5484).

Car & Moke Rental There are two companies renting out mini-mokes, which are the most popular way of getting around the island. The biggest operator is Moke Magnetic (☎ (077) 78 5377), in an arcade just off the Picnic Bay Mall. They charge $31 a day if you're aged between 21 and 25 years, $28 a day if you're over 25. Petrol and insurance is included, but there's also a 30c-per-km distance charge, which will add on about another $12 if you just drive from one end of the island to the other (and back).

The other company, Holiday Moke Hire (☎ (077) 78 5703) has similar vehicles and prices; its office is in the Jetty Cafe in the Picnic Bay Mall. Both companies also have Suzuki Sierras, Mazda 121s and other vehicles available.

It's worth noting that the road to Radical Bay is a private road, so your rental insurance won't cover any accidents along here. It's also the most dangerous road on the island – narrow, hilly and winding – so if you do drive along here, take it easy!

Moped Rental Roadrunner Scooter Hire (☎ (077) 78 5222) has an office in an arcade just off the Picnic Bay Mall. You don't need a motorcycle license for these 50cc scooters, just a valid car driver's licence. Day hire is $25, half-day hire $20, and 24-hour hire $35.

Bicycle Magnetic Island is ideal for cycling, and there are mountain bikes available for rent at various places including the Esplanade in Picnic Bay and Geoff's Place in Horseshoe Bay. Bikes cost $10 for a day, $6 for half a day.

Townsville to Charters Towers

The Flinders Hwy heads inland from Townsville and runs virtually due west for its entire length – almost 800 km from Townsville to Cloncurry. The first section of the highway takes you 135 km south-west from Townsville to the gold-mining town of Charters Towers, with a turn off at the halfway mark to Ravenswood, another gold-mining centre.

Refer to the Charters Towers to Camooweal section in the Outback chapter for details of the Flinders Hwy west of Charters Towers.

RAVENSWOOD
At Mingela, 88 km from Townsville, a paved road leads 40 km south to Ravenswood, a former ghost town from the gold rush days which has returned to life in recent years. The town is spread across a series of hills of rough red earth, and although most of the buildings were demolished or fell down years ago, two pubs, a church, a school and a couple of hundred people linger on amid the old mines.

The **old post office** (1878) is a lovely timber building which now houses a general store. The **old court house, police station and cell block**, up on the hill between the two pubs, are being restored and will become a mining and historical museum. There are also a couple of antique and craft shops along the main street.

A series of **old photos** mounted in steel boxes along the main street show Ravenswood in its boom years. A visit to the town **cemetery**, which is signposted from Macrossan St, is somewhat sobering. Graves date back to the 1880s, and it soon becomes evident that they died young around here.

Ravenswood is one of the friendliest mining towns I've been to. Everyone says g'day in the pubs, and there seems to be a good spirit about the place. There's an appreciation of the town's history, and a sense of optimism about the future. Then again, maybe it's just that I visited late on a Friday afternoon. It's amazing how a few beers can cheer you up at the end of a hard week down the mines...

History
Gold was first discovered in this area in 1868. In October 1869 a rich deposit of alluvial gold was found at Top Camp, north of Ravenswood, and the first rush was on. In 1870 W O Hodgkinson visited the field and later agreed to set up an ore-crushing plant. The first crushings in 1870 were incredibly

rich, and the field prospered for two years, but by 1872 the 'brownstone' (surface ore that had been oxidised and was easily crushed) was exhausted. The deeper ore proved almost impossible to work, and the field suffered a steady decline over the next 20 years.

In 1893 mine manager Laurence Wilson travelled to London and convinced a number of British investors to invest in the mines. Using new crushing and processing techniques, the mines again proved to be viable and people began to return to the area.

During Ravenswood's boom years, from 1900 to 1912, the area produced an incredible 12,500 kg of gold, and the population peaked at around 4000. But by 1912 the ore bodies appeared exhausted, and operations ceased in 1917.

Ravenswood became a virtual ghost town. Then in 1987 the Carpentaria Gold company established a new open-cut mine here which successfully extracted gold using the heap leaching process. In 1994 another new mine opened, bringing another couple of hundred people back to the area and breathing new life into Ravenswood.

Places to Stay & Eat

The *Imperial Hotel* (☎ (077) 70 2131) is an absolute gem of a pub. This Victorian-era hotel is virtually unchanged from 100 years ago. The public bar features a magnificent old red cedar bar with leadlight inserts; the dining room is set with lace tablecloths, with antique timber sideboards and balloon-backed chairs; and the facade is a solid red-brick structure, with a verandah trimmed with iron lace. The old pool room, complete with a full-sized slate-topped table, is currently being restored. There are 18 timber-lined bedrooms upstairs, some with old brass beds and opening out onto the verandah. They are clean and well presented, and B&B costs $23/36 for singles/doubles.

The dining room serves simple, hearty tucker. Lunches range from $3 to $9, and during the week you get something like toasted sandwiches or spaghetti carbonara. A full menu is offered at weekends. Dinners are a set menu, costing $8 for a main course only or $10 for soup, main course and dessert.

The *Railway Hotel* (☎ (077) 70 2144) is another solid old red-brick pub that was built in 1902. It also has pub rooms upstairs, although they are often booked out by miners during the week. When they're available, they cost $22/35 with a continental breakfast or $26/43 with a cooked breakfast. The dining room here serves a set-menu meal for $12, and Friday night is fish & chip night.

The *Top Camp Resort* (☎ (077) 70 2188), two km north of town, has a caravan park with sites from $14 and motel units from $38.

CHARTERS TOWERS (pop 9000)

This busy town, 130 km inland from Townsville, was Queensland's fabulously rich second city in the gold-rush days. Many old houses, with classic verandahs and lace work, and imposing public buildings and mining structures remain. It's possible to make a day trip here from Townsville and get a glimpse of outback Queensland on the way.

At 336 metres above sea level, the dry air of Charters Towers makes a welcome change from the humid coast.

History

The gleam of gold was first spotted in 1871, in a creek bed at the foot of Towers Hill, by an Aboriginal boy called Jupiter Mosman. Within a few years, the surrounding area was peppered with diggings and a large town had grown. In its heyday (around the turn of the century) Charters Towers had a population of 30,000, nearly 100 mines, and even its own stock exchange. It attracted wealth seekers from far and wide and came to be known as 'the World'. Mosman St, the main street in those days, had 25 pubs.

When the gold ran out in the 1920s, the city shrank, but survived as a centre for the beef industry. Since the mid-1980s, Charters Towers has seen a bit of a gold revival as modern processes have enabled companies to work deposits in previously uneconomical areas. It is now a prosperous, lively country town with a growing population. There are now three gold mines being worked in the area, and another company is re-exploring *underneath* the town. Local legend has it that you can literally walk under the town through the old tunnels and mines.

Orientation & Information
Gill St, which runs from the railway station to Mosman St, is Charters Towers' main street. It's a busy shopping centre lined with shops, pubs, banks and eateries and the tourist information office. Mosman St is at the western end of Gill St. Towers Hill stands over the town to the south. Lissner Park, a couple of blocks north of the centre, is the town's best park and the swimming pool is at its north end.

Buses arrive at and depart from the Goldfield Star Caltex service station on the corner of Gill and Church Sts. The railway station (☎ (077) 87 3521) is on Enterprise Rd, about 2.5 km east along Gill St from the centre.

The National Trust of Queensland (☎ (077) 87 2374) has an office in the Stock Exchange Arcade on Mosman St which doubles as a tourist information office. The office is open on weekdays from 8.30 am to 1 pm and from 2 to 4.30 pm and on Saturday from 9 am to 3 pm. Pick up the free *Guide to Charters Towers* booklet and a copy of the National Trust's walking tour leaflet.

The post office at 17 Gill St is open on weekdays from 9 am to 5 pm.

Things to See & Do
On Mosman St a few metres up the hill from the corner of Gill St is the picturesque **Stock Exchange Arcade**, built in 1887 and restored in 1972. Today it houses the National Trust office and several shops, and there are two art galleries upstairs. At the end of the arcade, opposite the information office, the **Assay Room & Mining Museum** is a former metallurgical laboratory for smelting gold and silver and determining the content of ore and minerals. Inside is a model of a mine in a glass case, a collection of rocks, and tools and equipment that were used in the lab. It's open the same hours as the tourist informa-

tion office and entry costs $1 for adults and 50c for children.

At 62 Mosman St, the **Zara Clark Museum** is well worth a visit, with an interesting collection which includes old photos of Charters Towers, farming equipment, a great collection of Royal Doulton toby jugs, and period costumes. It also includes the **Charles Wallis military museum**, dedicated to a local hero who was killed in WW I. It has a fascinating collection of medals, weaponry, uniforms, documents and photos. The museum is open everyday from 10 am to 3 pm; entry costs $3 for adults, $1 for children.

The former **ABC Bank Building** (1891) on Mosman St, just up from the Stock Exchange, is currently undergoing an $8 million restoration and will become the Charters Towers Theatre Complex, due to open in 1996. The facade is a magnificent mixture of Doric and Corinthian styles. (The ABC Bank collapsed in 1893 – probably because of all the money they lavished on this building – and was taken over by the Australian Bank of Commerce.)

Probably the finest of the town's old houses is Frederick Pfeiffer's on Paull St. It's now a Mormon chapel, but you can walk around the outside. Pfeiffer was a gold-miner who became Queensland's first millionaire.

Five km from town is the **Venus Gold Battery**, where gold-bearing ore was crushed and processed from 1872 until as recently as 1972. The battery has been restored to working order and is open from 9 am to 3 pm every day, with guided tours at 10 am and 2 pm; entry is $3 for adults and $1 for children.

The **Miner's Cottage** at 26 Deane St is a typical timber miner's cottage which has been restored and now houses an antique shop.

Organised Tours
Gold Nugget Scenic Tours (☎ (077) 87 1568) runs a half-day city tour at 10 am and 3 pm every Monday, Tuesday, Thursday and Friday. The cost is $15.

Gold City Bush Safaris (☎ (077) 87 4145)

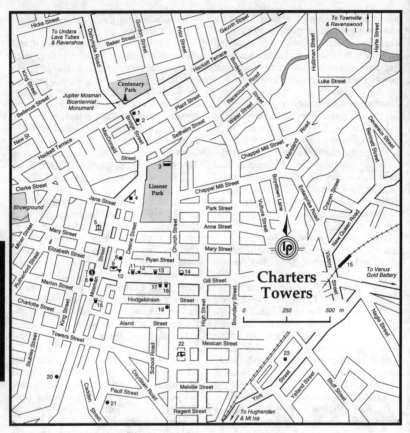

will take you to an old goldfield 40 km east of town, and demonstrate gold panning, whip cracking and trick shooting. The tour runs daily (on demand) and costs $25 for adults and $15 for children.

Festivals

During the Australia Day weekend in late January, more than 100 cricket teams and their supporters converge on Charters Towers for a competition known as the Goldfield Ashes.

Charters Towers holds a major rodeo every Easter. The town also hosts one of Australia's biggest annual country music festivals on the May Day weekend each year.

Places to Stay

Camping There are three caravan parks in town. The most central is the *Mexican Caravan Park* (☎ (077) 87 1161), at 75 Church St. It has tent sites at $9 and on-site vans for $25, plus a swimming pool and store.

Pubs The next cheapest beds in town are in the old *Court House Hotel* (☎ (077) 87 1187), at 120 Gill St, which has very basic pub rooms at $15/25 a single/double.

PLACES TO STAY

1 Charters Towers Motel
2 Cattlemen's Rest Motel
4 Park Motel
17 Court House Hotel
22 Mexican Caravan Park
23 Scotty's Outback Inn Backpackers

PLACES TO EAT

10 Naturally Good Cafe
18 Crown Hotel

OTHER

3 Swimming Pool
5 Zara Clark Museum
6 Miner's Cottage
7 Stock Exchange Arcade, Tourist
  Information Office, Ye Olde
  Coffee
  Shop, Assay Room & Mining
  Museum
8 ABC Bank Building
9 Post Office
11 Whitehorse Tavern
12 Police Station
13 Regent's Club 69 Bar
14 Long-distance Bus Stop
15 Railway Station
16 Excelsior Hotel
19 Court House & School of Mines
20 St Paul's Playhouse
21 Frederick Pfeiffer's House

Hostel The excellent *Scotty's Outback Inn Backpackers* (☎ (077) 87 1028) is at 58 York St, 1.4 km south of the town centre. The owner will pick you up from the bus stop if you ring. It's a renovated timber house built in the 1880s, with pleasant breezy verandahs and sitting areas. The cost is $12 a night and you can rent bedding for $1. There are bikes for rent and you can get a cheap combined ticket for some of the town's museums and the Venus Battery. Canoe trips are also organised through cattle stations along the Burdekin River – when the river's flowing.

Motels The *Park Motel* (☎ (077) 87 1022), at 1 Mosman St, has pleasant grounds, a pool and a good restaurant. Standard motel units

go for $55/63 a single/double, and they have two excellent heritage-style 'honeymoon suites' upstairs which go for $68/75, or $73/80 with champagne.

The *Charters Towers Motel* (☎ (077) 87 1366), on the corner of Bridge and Hackett Sts, is about the cheapest motel with units for $36/42 a single/double. The *Cattleman's Rest Motel* (☎ (077) 87 3555), on the corner of Bridge and Plant Sts, has good modern motel units from $60/66.

Places to Eat

There are plenty of pubs in town serving counter meals. The *Crown Hotel* in Mosman St has an all-you-can-eat Chinese smorgasbord for lunch or dinner which is great value at $5.90. For atmosphere, try the *Court House Hotel* on Gill St.

Ye Olde Coffee Shop, at the Stock Exchange Arcade, has delicious chicken burgers as well as kebabs, sandwiches and cakes. The *Naturally Good Cafe*, on Gill St, opposite the library, is a good gourmet cafe with great sandwiches, smoothies, burgers and other snacks. It has a pleasant heritage-style dining room with fresh flowers on the tables.

The front section of the *Park Motel* is an old pub (1888), and houses two good restaurants. *Lissner's* is a formal à la carte restaurant with international cuisine and mains from $17 to $20, and the great *Courtyard Bistro* has meals ranging from $14 to $16.

Entertainment

There are a couple of nightclubs in town. The *Regent's Club 69 Bar*, on Gill St, is open from Wednesday to Saturday (and some Sundays) until 3 am. It's a saloon-style country bar at the front, and a modern disco out the back, and has DJs and live bands. *Pegasus*, the nightclub at the Whitehorse Tavern, on the corner of Gill and Deane Sts, also opens until 3 am on Friday, Saturday and Sunday nights.

There's no cinema here, but the Tors Drive-In (☎ (077) 87 1086) on the west side of town screens latest releases.

The Charters Players stage regular plays

NORTH COAST

throughout the year. They are based at the St Pauls Playhouse, a restored timber church at the south end of Mosman St.

Getting There & Around
McCafferty's and Greyhound Pioneer Australia both have buses from Townsville to Charters Towers (1¾ hours, $16) and from Charters Towers on to Mt Isa (nine hours, $74).

The twice-weekly *Inlander* service takes three hours from Charters Towers to Townsville and costs $20, economy only. The *Inlander* continues on to Mt Isa, taking another 16 hours and costing $85 in economy or $115 for an economy sleeper.

You can make transport bookings and enquiries at Harvey World Travel (☎ (077) 87 1546), at 92 Gill St, or at Traveland (☎ (077) 87 2622), at 13 Gill St.

Scotty's Backpackers hires bikes.

Townsville to Mission Beach

MT SPEC NATIONAL PARK
About 60 km north-west of Townsville is the Mt Spec National Park (7200 hectares), which straddles the 1000-metre-plus high Paluma Range on the inland side of the Bruce Hwy. There are quite a few creeks running throughout this national park, and the landscape varies from open eucalypt forests on the lower slopes to the rainforests of the upper, wetter areas. Bower birds are relatively common here.

There are two main access roads into the park, which both lead off a bypassed section of the Bruce Hwy. To get to these, turn off the new highway either 61 km north of Townsville or 40 km south of Ingham.

The southern access route, known as the Mt Spec Rd, was built by relief labour during the depression years from 1931 to 1935. It's a narrow and spectacular road which twists its way up the mountains to the village of Paluma. After seven km you come to **Little**

Crystal Creek, where a pretty stone bridge arches across the creek. (Although it looks surprisingly like a Roman relic, the bridge was actually built by the road crew in 1932.) This is a great swimming spot with waterfalls and a couple of deep rockpools, and there's a small picnic area opposite the car park. From here it's another eleven km up to Paluma (see the following section).

The northern access route is a four-km dirt road into **Big Crystal Creek**, which has a good self-registration camping ground with toilets, hot showers, firewood and water. Sites cost $3 per person per night – to book, contact the park ranger (☎ (077) 70 8526). Beyond the camping ground is **Paradise Waterhole**, a good swimming and picnic area. (See the Townsville, Organised Tours section for details on tours to Mt Spec National Park.)

PALUMA
The Mt Spec Rd, which follows the southern boundary of the Mt Spec National Park up to the mountain village of Paluma, leaves the Bruce Hwy 61 km north of Townsville. It's a scenic and winding 18-km drive, with panoramic views down to the floodplains of the Big Crystal Creek and the ocean beyond. Just before Paluma is **McClelland's Lookout**, which is the start of walking trails to **Benham's Lookout** (600 metres), **Witt's Lookout** (1.5 km) and last but not least **Cloudy Creek** (two km).

Paluma is a sleepy little top-of-the-mountain place with a handful of old holiday shacks, a couple of craft shops and a tea room. The town was founded in 1875 when tin was discovered in the area. If you decide to stay here overnight, the old *Misthaven Units* (☎ (077) 70 8620) have self-contained holiday flats which sleep up to six people and cost $45 a double plus $5 per extra person; or there's the *Mt Spec Cottage* (☎ (077) 70 8520), a tiny and simple timber shack. The *Ivy Cottage Tearooms*, where you'll enjoy Devonshire teas, sandwiches or home-made pies, is open from Tuesday to Thursday from 10 am to 4 pm and on weekends from 10 am to 5 pm. An environmental walking track starts beside the cottage.

Four km beyond Paluma is the turn off to **Paluma Dam**, a popular boating and water-skiing spot. Another 20 km past this turn off you come to Hidden Valley. The *Hidden Valley Cabins* (☎ (077) 70 8088) are a group of six log cabins which sleep up to four people each and cost $60 a night for the cabin. The cabins complex includes a licensed restaurant with home-cooked meals, a pool and spa.

JOURAMA FALLS NATIONAL PARK

Jourama Falls National Park is six unpaved km off the highway, 91 km north of Townsville. Centred around Waterview Creek, this small but beautiful park has good swimming holes, several lookouts, a picnic area and a camping ground with toilets and barbecues. Sites cost $3 per person per night, and you can self-register or book a site through the QNP&WS office in Ingham (☎ (077) 76 1700). One km past the camping ground is the start of a walking trail to the waterfalls (600 metres) and the falls lookout (1.2 km).

INGHAM (pop 5100)

Ingham is the centre of a large sugar-producing district. The first sugar cane farms were established in this area in the 1880s, and from early in its history the region attracted a large number of Italian immigrants. The town's Italian heritage is celebrated with the Australian-Italian Festival, held each year for a week in May.

Ingham is a busy commercial centre and a pleasant enough town with all the usual services, although it has few pretensions to being a tourism hotspot. The **Memorial Gardens**, signposted off the main highway from the centre of town, are the town's botanical gardens and a good place for a stroll or a picnic lunch.

Orientation & Information

Lannercost St is Ingham's main street. It's a busy shopping precinct with all the major banks, as well as pubs, shops, eateries and supermarkets. The post office and tourist office are both on Lannercost St, near the intersection with Townsville Rd (the Bruce Hwy).

There's a good tourist information centre (☎ (077) 76 5211), on the corner of Lannercost St and Townsville Rd. It's well stocked with info on all the surrounding area's attractions, and is open on weekdays from 8 am to 5 pm and on weekends from 9 am to 2 pm.

The QNP&WS office (☎ (077) 76 1700), at the end of an arcade at 11 Lannercost St, deals with information for Mt Spec, Wallaman Falls and Jourama Falls national parks and Hinchinbrook and Orpheus islands. It is open on weekdays from 9 am to 5 pm.

Places to Stay & Eat

The cheapest place to stay is the *Royal Hotel* (☎ (077) 76 2024) on Lannercost St, across from the intersection with Townsville Rd. The upstairs rooms are about as spartan as they come, and a bed costs $10. The *Hinchinbrook Hotel* (☎ (077) 76 2227), down the road at 83 Lannercost St, is a much nicer pub and has backpacker beds for $12. This is also a good place to eat, with meals in the *Garden Court* bistro from $6 to $9 and a restaurant with mains around $16.

If you're after a motel, the *Herbert Valley Motel* (☎ (077) 76 1777), on the Bruce Hwy just south of the centre, has singles/doubles from $40/48.

Getting There & Away

McCafferty's and Greyhound Pioneer Australia both stop in Ingham on the main coastal run. Long-distance buses stop in the centre of town on Townsville Rd, close to the corner of Lannercost St (and the information centre). Ingham is on the main Brisbane to Cairns railway line.

AROUND INGHAM

There are a number of places to visit around Ingham including **Wallaman Falls National Park**, 48 km inland, where a tributary of the Herbert River cascades for 305 metres, creating the longest permanent single-drop falls in Australia. The falls are much more spectacular in the wet season. You can normally reach them by conventional vehicle along an unpaved road; there's a National Parks camping ground with a swimming hole nearby.

Only seven km east of Ingham is the **Victoria Mill** (☎ (077) 76 1722), the largest sugar mill in the southern hemisphere. Free tours are given in the crushing season.

27 km north-east of Ingham is **Lucinda**, a port town at the southern entrance to the Hinchinbrook Channel. Most visitors to Lucinda come for the fishing, or to have a look at the town's amazing six-km-long jetty which is used for shipping the huge amount of sugar produced in the area. Lucinda is also the access point for the southern end of Hinchinbrook Island. The *Wanderer's Holiday Village* (☎ (077) 77 8213) has tent sites, a bunkhouse and on-site units, or the *Lucinda Point Hotel-Motel* (☎ (077) 77 8103) has air-con motel units from $33/38 for singles/doubles.

Forrest Beach, a laid-back seaside community 17 km east of Ingham, also has a few accommodation options: the *Forrest Beach Caravan Park* (☎ (077) 77 8806), with tent and caravan sites; the *Forrest Beach Hotel* (☎ (077) 77 8700), with motel units from $30/40; and the *Wilbry Holiday Units* (☎ (077) 77 8755), with self-contained one-bedroom units from $40 a double.

ORPHEUS ISLAND

Lying about 20 km off the coast east of Ingham, Orpheus is a long (about 11 km from end to end) and narrow (less than a km wide) continental island, with some fine beaches and some of the best fringing reef to be found on any of the Great Barrier Reef islands. The second largest of the Palm Islands Group, it's a quiet, secluded island which is good for camping, snorkelling and diving. Orpheus is mostly national park and is heavily forested, with lots of birdlife; turtles also nest here.

There is a fairly expensive resort on the island, as well as three national park camping grounds and a giant clam research station.

During the 1800s goats were released on

the island as part of a madcap scheme to provide food for possible shipwreck survivors. There obviously weren't enough Robinson Crusoes washed ashore here – the goats thrived to the extent that at one stage they numbered over 4000. A 'control programme' initiated by the QNP&WS in 1991 has proved largely successful in culling the goats, and nowadays there are only about 100 left on the island.

Zoning
Most of the water around the island is zoned Marine Park B – 'look but don't touch'. From the top of Hazard Bay to the southern tip is zoned 'A' which allows limited line fishing. Collecting shells or coral is not permitted.

Things to See & Do
With its fine fringing reefs, Orpheus is a great island for snorkelling. It also has some pleasant sandy beaches, including those at Mangrove Bay and Yankee Bay, south of the resort, and at Pioneer Bay north of the resort. Some of the beaches are quite shallow, which rules out swimming at low tide.

The island also has a great reputation as a diving resort. The dive centre caters exclusively to resort guests, and conducts dive courses and a range of diving and snorkelling trips.

At Little Pioneer Bay, north of the resort, the James Cook University **Marine Research Station** specialises in breeding and raising giant clams and other Barrier Reef clams. Clams raised here are being transplanted to Pacific island reefs where overgathering has wiped them out. In the station you can see the clams in the large water tanks (including the 'stud clams' used for breeding) while other clams are raised out in the shallow waters of the bay. Phone ☎ (077) 77 7336 to enquire about visiting the station.

While you're at the station, ask about the **Aboriginal shell midden** nearby.

Places to Stay
Camping There are national park camp sites at Yankee Bay and Pioneer Bay. Both sites

have toilet facilities and a picnic area but there is no regular fresh water supply and a fuel stove should be used as open fires are not allowed. Yankee Bay offers better low-tide swimming and snorkelling.

Camping permits are available from the QNP&WS offices at Ingham (☎ (077) 76 1700) and Townsville (☎ (077) 21 2399).

Resort The *Orpheus Island Resort* (☎ (077) 77 7377) was established here in the 1940s. In 1981 it was completely rebuilt as an up-market Mediterranean-style resort. There are 23 studio units along the beach and two larger bungalows. The rooms are quite stylish and very comfortable, with ensuites, air-con and ceiling fans, but there are no TVs or telephones in the rooms. The studios cost $480/770 for singles/doubles, and the bungalows cost $910 a double. There are also the beachfront terraces, which cost $390/670. Rates are cheaper for stays of five or more nights. Tariffs include all meals and use of all the resort's facilities, which include a tennis court, swimming pool, catamarans, windsurfers and dinghies. A snorkelling trip is organised each afternoon.

Up the hill from the resort there are also six very impressive two-bedroom villas, which cost from $1030 a double or $1300 for up to four people.

The resort doesn't cater for anyone under 15 years of age. For reservations phone ☎ (008) 077 167 or write to Orpheus Island Resort, Private Mail Bag 15, Townsville, Qld 4810. Children aged under 15 years are not permitted.

Places to Eat
The resort's restaurant is only open to house guests, so if you're camping you'll have to be totally self-sufficient.

If you're staying at the resort, all meals are included in the tariffs. Orpheus has quite a good reputation for its food – breakfasts are buffet-style and lunch and dinner are à la carte. The restaurant is licensed and there's a small bar. The resort will also pack picnic hampers for guests who are taking a dinghy out for the day.

Getting There & Away
Air Most resort guests fly into either Cairns or Townsville; the resort has a seaplane which handles transfers from these airports to Orpheus. One-way fares are $130 from Townsville or $200 from Cairns.

Occasionally the resort does day trips to Zoe Bay on Hinchinbrook Island.

Sea There are no regular boat services to Orpheus, but if you want to camp you can get out to the island from Dungeness, near Lucinda, by water taxi. Count on about $120 per person return – contact the MV *Scuba Doo* (☎ (077) 77 8220) for details.

OTHER PALM ISLANDS
Orpheus is part of the Palm Island group, which consists of 10 main islands. Apart from Orpheus, which is predominantly national park, and nearby Pelorus, which is crown land, all of the islands are Aboriginal reserves and permission must be obtained from the chairman of the Palm Island Council (☎ (077) 70 1177) before you can land on them. You'll need to declare the purpose of your visit, and when and how long you're planning to stay.

The main islands of the group (and their Aboriginal names) are Orpheus (Goolboddi), Pelorus (Yanooa), Brisk (Culgarool), Curacao (Inoogoo), Eclipse (Garoogubbee), Esk (Soopun), Falcon (Carbooroo), Fantome (Eumilli), Havannah and Great Palm (Bukaman) islands.

CARDWELL (pop 1300)
South of Cardwell, the Bruce Hwy climbs high above the coast with tremendous views down across the winding, mangrove-lined waterways known as the Mangroves, which separate Hinchinbrook Island from the coast.

Cardwell's main claim to tourism fame is as the access point for Hinchinbrook Island, but it is also a popular fishing spot and there are quite a few interesting sights in the immediate area. Cardwell itself is a fairly old-fashioned holiday town, sprawled along a three-km length of the Bruce Hwy between the mountains and the ocean. It's the only town on the highway between Brisbane and Cairns which is actually right on the coast.

History
Cardwell is one of north Queensland's very earliest towns, dating from 1864, though there's little evidence of its origins now. It predates Townsville and was intended as a port and supply centre for pioneer cattle stations inland in the Valley of Lagoons on the upper Burdekin River – but it had a shaky start since finding a decent route over the forested ranges proved very difficult and the early settlement suffered from constant Aboriginal harassment. It was the determination of Cardwell's founder George Elphinstone Dalrymple, who had also got Bowen going, that saw the establishment of a rough track, after many attempts even in the rainy season, through to the Valley of the Lagoons.

Dalrymple was rewarded for his work by being elected to the Queensland Legislative Assembly in 1865 as representative for the district. Unfortunately for Cardwell, it was out-developed by Townsville from where an easier route was found to the high country.

Orientation & Information
The Bruce Hwy passes through the centre of Cardwell and is the town's main street, and almost all of the facilities and services are found along the highway.

Cardwell has a QNP&WS office (☎ (070) 66 8601), at the end of an arcade off the highway in the middle of town – it's signposted as the Rainforest & Reef Centre. The office handles camping permits and bookings for Hinchinbrook Island and the other national parks in the area, and is open Monday to Friday from 8 am to noon and also on Friday afternoons from 1 to 4 pm.

The Seaview Cafe (☎ (070) 66 8690), next

Development vs Conservation – the Oyster Point Experience
In 1994, a proposal by well-known Queensland developer Keith Williams to built a 500-bed tourist resort at Oyster Point, just south of Cardwell, sparked a major controversy.

On one side were the environmental activists and protesters, who claimed the development would destroy mangrove areas that were vital to the coastal ecosystem and bring unsustainable numbers of tourists to Hinchinbrook Island. Keith Williams' previous record also worked against him from the conservationists' point of view – after starting the Sea World theme park and playing a major role in developing the Gold Coast, in the 1980s he transformed Hamilton Island from an untouched continental island into a concrete jungle of high-rise hotels and apartments. Pro-development lobbyists argued that the resort would be the economic life-blood that would save a dying town, create employment and finance badly needed development in Cardwell.

The controversy divided the town – not quite to the extent of verging on a civil war, although that was the way the popular media portrayed it. Most people I spoke to could see both sides – they were concerned about the environmental impact, but excited by the potential economic impact it would have on the local economy. There was a definite backlash against the greenies from some quarters – one local Kombi driver had painted the back of his vehicle with the proclamation 'I am not a Greenie' to let people know he wasn't 'one of them'.

The Cardwell dispute typifies the dilemmas that Queensland faces as its tourism industry grows and provides an increasing proportion of the state's income. The questions that are being asked – such as whether the Gold-Coast-style develop-at-all-costs mentality should be allowed to spread along the coast, and to what extent Queensland's natural resources should be exploited to take advantage of the current boom in ecotourism – are as relevant in the rest of Queensland as they are in Cardwell.

At the time of writing, the Oyster Point development was still on hold. Whether it goes ahead or not remains to be seen, but in terms of the ongoing 'development versus conservation' debate its future has taken on a significant symbolism. ■

to the BP service station in the centre of town, has a small information section and a travel agency where you can buy bus or train tickets. Long-distance buses stop out the front of the cafe. This place *may* also be able to issue permits for Hinchinbrook when the QNP&WS office is closed.

Cardwell has a post office, Westpac and National banks and two supermarkets.

Things to See & Do
In the town centre, there's a small **stone cairn** beside the pub which commemorates the landing of Edmund Kennedy's ill-fated exploration party in 1848. Cardwell's **swimming pool** is up from and opposite the main boat jetty. It is open from August to May, usually from 6 am to 6 pm.

The **Cardwell Forest Drive** starts from the centre of town and is a 26-km round trip, taking you to some excellent lookouts, swimming holes, walking tracks and picnic areas. Turn off the highway beside the BP service station in the centre of town – the drive is signposted from the other side of the railway station.

Most of the coastal forest north of Cardwell is protected as the **Edmund Kennedy National Park**, named after the ill-fated explorer who was killed by Aborigines at Cape York. At the southern end of the park, there's a camp site close to the beach and some walking tracks – turn off the highway four km north of Cardwell to reach them. Don't swim or cross any of the creeks in the park – the mangroves here are home to estuarine crocodiles.

The **Murray Falls** have fine rockpools for swimming, a walking track, camping ground and a barbecue area. They're 22 km west of the highway – turn off at the 'Murray Upper Road' sign about 27 km north of Cardwell. Take care when swimming, as the rocks are incredibly slippery – there have been several drownings here.

Just off the Bruce Hwy, seven km south of Cardwell, the **Five Mile Swimming Hole** is another good swimming spot with picnic facilities.

The **Dalrymple Gap Walking Track**, orig-inally an Aboriginal trail which was upgraded by George Dalrymple in the 1860s as a stock route to the Valley of Lagoons, passes through the **Lumholtz National Park**. The track is nine km long and takes eight hours return, although you have the option of a two-hour three-km walk to an old stone bridge which is registered by the National Trust. The turn off to the track is off the highway 15 km south of Cardwell.

Boating & Fishing
A number of operators have boats available for hire. U-Drive Cardwell (☎ (070) 66 8064) has fishing dinghies for $50 a day or $30 a half-day – plus fuel costs. Hinchinbrook Rent-A-Yacht (☎ (070) 66 8007) has yachts, motor cruisers and houseboats for cruising around Hinchinbrook, Dunk and Brook islands.

Cardwell Fishing Safaris (☎ (070) 66 8176) takes small groups (up to four people) on fishing trips and supply all tackle and bait. They depart daily at 7.45 am and cost $45 per person.

Organised Tours
Hinchinbrook Adventures (☎ (070) 66 8270), at 131 Bruce Hwy, who currently operate one of the ferry services to Hinchinbrook Island, are planning to start offering tours in a 13-seat minibus from Cardwell to several of the places mentioned above, and further afield to places like the Undara lava tubes. Ring them to find out the latest.

See Getting There & Away in the Hinchinbrook Island section for details of tours and trips to the island itself.

Places to Stay
Camping & Caravan Parks The *Kooka-burra Holiday Park* (☎ (070) 66 8648), 800 metres north of the centre at 175 Bruce Hwy, is the best set-up of the three caravan parks here. They have tent sites from $10 for two, on-site vans from $26, on-site cabins from $35 and self-contained units and cabins from $45 a double. There's also a youth hostel within the park (see below).

Across the highway at 186 Bruce Hwy, the *Pacific Palms Caravan Park* (☎ (070) 66

8671) has tent sites from $10 and on-site vans and cabins from $25. Further north at 43 Marine Pde is the *Sunrise Village & Leisure Park* (☎ (077) 66 8550), a large accommodation complex with a motel and restaurant, as well as tent sites from $11 and on-site cabins and self-contained cottages from $45 a double.

Hostels The YHA *Hinchinbrook Hostel* (☎ (070) 66 8648), within the grounds of the *Kookaburra Holiday Park*, at 175 Bruce Hwy, is about a 10-minute walk north from the town centre and the bus stop. The small hostel has dorm beds at $11 and doubles at $25; nonmembers pay another $1. Backpackers can also camp beside the hostel, and use the facilities, for $6 each. This place has good facilities including a pool and free use of mountain bikes, fishing gear, tennis racquets and golf clubs. It's also a good source of info about Hinchinbrook Island and other attractions in the area. There's a small kiosk with supplies for people heading to Hinchinbrook, and they have camping gear – tents, stoves, water bottles etc – for hire. They can also store your luggage while you're on the island.

The *Cardwell Backpackers Hostel* (☎ (070) 66 8014) is at 178 Bowen St – just over a km north of the centre, in the street behind the 'big crab'. It's a new 30-bed hostel in a clean, renovated house, with a good kitchen and free use of mountain bikes. There's a large dorm in the centre of the house, as well as a few two-bed cubicles. Bunks are $10 a night and there are two doubles at $25. Quite a few travellers find fruit-picking work through this hostel, and because the workers stay for more than the usual night or two the atmosphere is often quite lively. They have camping gear for hire if you're going to Hinchinbrook, and a courtesy bus does pickups from the bus stop and takes people to work.

Motels & Holiday Units The previously mentioned *Sunrise Village & Leisure Park* (☎ (070) 66 8550), 43 Marine Pde, has motel units from $45/55 for singles/doubles. The *Lyndoch Motor Inn* (☎ (070) 66 8500) on the highway at the north end of town has oldish motel units from $35/45 or self-contained units from $50.

Cardwell Beachfront Holiday Units (☎ (070) 66 8776), opposite the waterfront at 1 Scott St, is a small 1960s-style complex of two-bedroom holiday units. The units are fairly basic, costing around $50 a double or $65 for up to five people.

Places to Eat
Cardwell has about half a dozen cafes and eateries. If you're after a quick snack, there are usually two pie vans parked on the foreshore beside the highway at the southern end of town. There's also a good bakery in the arcade next to the QNP&WS office – great vegie pasties!

The *Seaview Cafe*, next to the BP service station, has sandwiches, salads, hot snacks and meals, and you can eat in or takeaway. The *Cardwell Diner* does pizzas and other fast foods, and the *Marine Hotel* has reasonably good pub meals. There's a casual bistro out the back or the concrete beer garden. The menu offers snacks like burgers or sausages and onion for $4 to $5, and steaks, schnitzels and fish dishes from $8 to $10.

Cardwell Muddies is a licensed seafood cafe with excellent food at reasonable prices. Main meals like barramundi and prawns, seafood gumbo, pepper steak or fisherman's basket all range from $11 to $16, and they also have sandwiches, salads, bagels and omelettes for lunch. You can eat inside or out on the balcony, and they also do great takeaway fish & chips. Muddies is on the highway about a km north of the centre – you can't miss it, it's the place with a giant crab-on-a-stick out the front.

The *Edmund Kennedy Restaurant*, at the Sunrise Village Leisure Park, also has a good reputation.

Getting There & Away
All Greyhound Pioneer Australia and McCafferty's buses between Townsville and

Cairns stop at Cardwell. The fare is around $20 from either place. Cardwell is also on the main Brisbane to Cairns railway.

Buses stop outside the Seaview Cafe, which has a travel agency – see Orientation & Information for details.

HINCHINBROOK ISLAND

Hinchinbrook Island is a spectacular and unspoiled wilderness area, with granite mountains rising dramatically from the sea and a varied terrain – lush tropical forest on the mainland side, thick mangroves lining the shores, towering mountains in the middle and long sandy beaches and secluded bays on the eastern side. All 635 sq km of the island is a national park and rugged Mt Bowen, at 1121 metres, is the highest peak. There's plenty of wildlife, especially pretty-face wallabies and the iridescent blue Ulysses butterfly.

Hinchinbrook Island is very popular with bushwalkers and naturalists and has some excellent walking tracks. The highlight is the **Thorsborne Trail** (also known as the East Coast Trail), a 32-km walking track from Ramsay Bay to Zoe Bay and on to George Point at the southern tip. You need to allow three to five days for the whole walk, although individual sections can be walked if you don't have that much time. There is a limit of 40 people allowed on the trail at any one time, so it's worth booking, especially if you're planning to visit during the school holidays. Zoe Bay, with its beautiful water-fall, is one of the most scenic spots on the island. Walkers are warned to take plenty of insect repellent – the sandflies and mosqui-toes on Hinchinbrook can be a real pest – and if you react badly, some sort of treatment like antihistamine tablets. You'll also have to learn how to protect your food from the native bush rats, and there are estuarine croc-odiles in the mangroves!

Apart from the national park camping grounds spread across the island, the only accommodation is at an excellent and unob-trusive resort at Cape Richards, the northernmost tip of the island.

Information & Permits

The QNP&WS has two useful leaflets on Hinchinbrook and the islands to the north. Those planning to walk the coastal track from Ramsay Bay to George Point on Hinchinbrook should get a copy of the *Thorsborne Trail* leaflet. The *Hinchinbrook to Dunk Island* park guide is a small brochure full of fascinating information about Hinchinbrook Island, Goold Island, the Brook Islands, the Family Islands and Dunk Island.

You can make bookings for camping permits and the Thorsborne Trail through the QNP&WS offices at either Cardwell or Ingham (see those sections for details). Note that the Ingham office handles all telephone bookings, whereas if you're already in Card-well you can call at that office in person. Don't leave arranging your permit until the last minute – the Cardwell office often gets people rushing in five minutes before their ferry leaves, expecting a permit at the drop of a hat, and people have been known to miss their ferry because of this. Try and ring in advance to make sure there is a vacancy, and arrive at the office well before the ferry's departure time.

The *Seaview Cafe* and the *Hinchinbrook Hostel* in Cardwell are other useful sources of information for Hinchinbrook – see the Cardwell section for details on these.

Hinchinbrook Island with text by Arthur and Margaret Thorsborne and photos by Cliff and Dawn Frith is a coffee-table book on the wonders of Hinchinbrook with some superb photos and an engrossing text reveal-ing a real love for the island.

Things to See & Do

There are some fine beaches on Hinchin-brook Island. The resort's main beach, **Orchid Beach**, is an idyllic little stretch of sand framed by granite boulders at either end. Also near the resort is **Turtle Bay**, a rocky inlet further west.

It's worth noting that Hinchinbrook is close enough to the mainland for you to be cautious about box jellyfish during the November to March summer season.

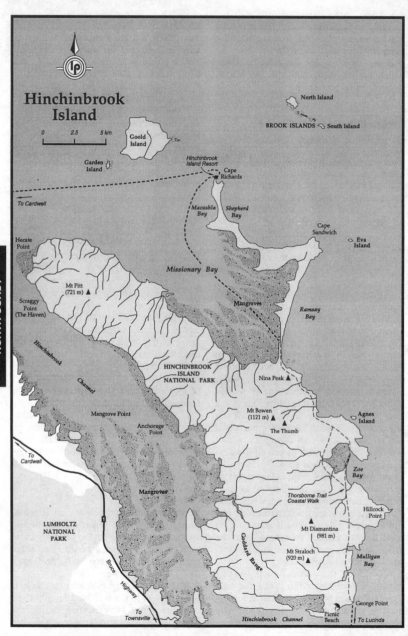

There are several **walking trails** starting from the resort, including short strolls to the top of Cape Richards or to Turtle Bay, and a two-km walking trail through the rainforest to North Shepherd Beach, with a continuation on to South Shepherd Beach.

The Thorsborne Trail

Previously known as the East Coast Trail, this 32-km coastal track from Ramsay Bay to Zoe Bay and on to George Point is the finest island walk along the Great Barrier Reef. The walk *can* be completed in two hard days but allowing at least three nights camping on the island is a much better idea.

The southern part of the walk between Zoe Bay and George Point was only opened in 1988 and many walkers still do just the northern part as a Ramsay Bay-Zoe Bay-Ramsay Bay return trip.

The walk includes long sandy beaches, mountain streams, humid rainforests and magnificent mountain scenery. The trail is ungraded and includes some often challenging creek crossings. The maximum elevation along the trail is 260 metres, reached on Stage 8 between Upper South Zoe Creek and Sweetwater Creek.

The *Thorsborne Trail* brochure, published by and available from the QNP&WS offices, is an essential guide for those intending to walk the trail. It gives you advice on how to plan your trip, book permits and how to conserve the delicate island environment. It divides the walk into stages giving pertinent advice for each section.

The trail is recommended for moderately experienced bushwalkers who should be adequately prepared and carry a map, compass and drinking water. Water is reliably available year-round only at **Nina Bay**, **Little Ramsay Bay** and at the southern end of Zoe Bay. During the dry season, from July to December, water may be very scarce and adequate supplies should be carried. If you find a dry creek or the water is salty it's often possible to find freshwater further upstream. During the wet season, from December to March, too much water can pose problems at the opposite extreme. The trail may be very

slippery, creek crossings can be difficult and you should be prepared for heavy rainfall. In tropical conditions walking in a raincoat or poncho is likely to be very uncomfortable – better to simply get wet and have dry clothes to change into later.

At any time of the year it can be hot and humid during the daytime but from May to September the nights can be cold enough to require a sleeping bag. A good tent is necessary if there is heavy rain at night.

Insects like mosquitoes, sandflies and march flies can be a nuisance so bring a good insect repellent. As anywhere along the Great Barrier Reef, a good sunscreen and a shady hat are also vitally important.

Protecting your food supplies from melomys (native bush rats) is another of Hinchinbrook's challenges. These ever-hungry critters will eat anything and can chew their way through just about any type of food container, including metal ones. Check with the national park rangers for advice on ways of protecting your food.

One of the most effective methods is to hang your food container from a metal wire strung between two trees, with a plastic bottle on either side of the container – the rats can walk along the wire, but when they get to the bottles they (hopefully) spin off.

See Getting There & Away at the end of this section for information on drop-offs at the beginning and end of the coastal walk.

Places to Stay

Camping There are seven national parks camping grounds along the Thorsborne Trail, plus ones at Macushla and Scraggy Point in the north. The Thorsborne Trail camping grounds include Nina Bay, Little Ramsay Bay, Zoe Bay, Mulligan Bay and George Point. Numbers for each camping ground are limited and depend on the total number of walkers on the island. For camping permits and detailed trail information, contact one of the QNP&WS offices mentioned earlier. Permits should be applied for at least six but no more than 12 weeks in advance.

Bush camping is permitted almost anywhere on the island except near the Cape

Richards resort, but you are requested to use the recommended sites wherever possible in order to minimise damage.

Resort The Hinchinbrook Island Resort (☎ (070) 66 8585) was established in 1975 when 15 simple cabins were built at Cape Richards. In 1989 the resort received a major upgrade when another 15 architect-designed 'treehouses' were built. These impressive timber cottages are built into the steep hillside behind Orchid Beach and linked by a series of timber boardwalks. Each cottage is timber-lined and has its own bathroom and separate lounge area, ceiling fans, fridges and tea and coffee-making facilities. There are no radios, TVs or phones in the rooms. The one-bedroom treehouses cost from $260/480 for singles/doubles; the two-bedroom prices are $290/530, plus $90 for children.

Seven of the older cabins are still in use. These are fairly basic and straightforward, but comfortable enough with two bedrooms, a bathroom and ceiling fans. These cabins cost $200/380 for singles/doubles, plus $65 for children. These rates include all meals and use of most equipment.

The resort's facilities include a bar, restaurant, an excellent swimming pool, canoes, snorkelling gear, surf skis and fishing equipment.

You can book by phoning the resort or writing to PO Box 3, Cardwell, Qld 4816.

Places to Eat

The resort's restaurant is in a very pleasant open-sided building beside the pool, and has a small bar. Breakfast is buffet-style, lunch can be in the restaurant or a packed lunch if you're heading out for the day, and dinner is a more elaborate four-course affair. Hinchinbrook has an excellent reputation for its food. The restaurant is only open to resort guests.

Getting There & Away

Ferry Services There are ferry services and day trips from Cardwell, at the northern end of the island, and from Lucinda at the southern end. The ferry operators work together,

so you can easily arrange to be picked up and dropped off from either end of the island, and your surplus gear can be stored or transported as well.

Cardwell is the main access point for the resort and the northern end of the island. There are two ferry services from Cardwell to the northern end of the island:

Hinchinbrook Travel & Booking Office (☎ (070) 66 8539), at 131 Bruce Hwy, Cardwell, operates the *Hinchinbrook Explorer*, departing daily at 9 am and returning at 4 pm. Hinchinbrook Adventures (☎ (070) 66 8270), at 135 Bruce Hwy, operates the *Reef Cat*, departing daily at 9 am and returning around 4.30 pm.

Both of these companies combine day trips to the island with drop-offs at the resort and at the start of the Thorsborne Trail, camping drop-offs to Goold Island and snorkelling trips to the Brook Islands. Their routes and schedules vary significantly, so depending on where you want to get to when, one of the services will probably suit you better than the other.

It's worth ringing or visiting their offices to ask a few pertinent questions, like where the boat goes first and how quickly it gets to wherever you're going, before you book. Both operators charge about $45 for a day trip, and about $25 one way or $45 return for camping or Thorsborne Trail drop-offs. Children's fares are half-price. Services operate daily for most of the year, but are less frequent during the wet season (January to March).

Hinchinbrook Wilderness Safaris (☎ (070) 77 8307) operates a transfer service between Lucinda and the southern end of the island. The boat departs at different times each day depending on the tides – ring to find out – and the cost is around $20 each way. Pick-ups from Ingham and Cardwell can also be arranged.

Trips & Tours An excellent way of seeing the island is by boat. Hinchinbrook Sail Safaris (☎ (070) 66 8143) has day trips for $48 including lunch and snorkelling, or two and three-day safaris for around $100 a day including all meals. R'n'R (☎ (070) 51 7777 or toll-free 1800 079 039) also operates four-day sea-kayaking expeditions along the east coast of Hinchinbrook from Lucinda every two weeks. The $480 cost includes all meals and equipment.

Raging Thunder (☎ (070) 31 1466) operates a seven-day sea-kayaking trip around Hinchinbrook every two weeks or so. The cost is $790 per person, which includes all meals, camping gear and equipment.

House Boats Cardwell Love Boats (☎ (077) 76 3466), which rather confusingly operates out of Lucinda at the southern entrance to the Hinchinbrook Channel, has three houseboats for hire for cruising in the Hinchinbrook Channel between Lucinda and Cardwell. They sleep four to eight people, have their own shower and toilet, fridge and cooking facilities, plus an aluminium dinghy. You need to BYO linen and towels. There's a minimum hire of two-nights-three-days, which costs from $385 to $435 per boat.

ISLANDS NEAR HINCHINBROOK

There are two small island groups just north of Hinchinbrook Island. Both are national parks, and both are accessible by ferry from Cardwell. **Goold Island** is just 4.5 km north-west of Cape Richards and 17 km north-east of Cardwell. The whole 8.3-sq-km island is a national park. The granite island is covered in eucalyptus forest with smaller patches of rainforest in the gullies, and there is a wide arc of sandy beach on the western side with a national park camp site nearby. There are toilets, picnic tables and barbecues at the camping ground, but you'll need to bring your own drinking water. There is a limit of 60 campers, and permits are available from the QNP&WS office in Cardwell.

Just south of Goold Island is tiny **Garden Island** with a recreation reserve controlled by the local council. Unlike the national park restrictions which apply to Goold there are no restrictions on camping here and the island has a good sandy beach but, as usual, no freshwater is available.

Both Cardwell ferry operators can drop campers at Goold Island on request.

About eight km north-east of Cape Richards are the four small islands of the **Brook Islands group**. South Island has a Commonwealth lighthouse but the other three islands – Middle Island, Tween Island and North Island – are all national parks and covered in thick vegetation. Both ferry operators run

NORTH COAST

Torresian Imperial Pigeons
The Brook Islands are a nesting place for thousands of Torresian Imperial Pigeons, which fly from Papua New Guinea to Australia to breed over the summer months. The birds arrive each September and establish large nesting colonies on the islands, flying to the mainland each day to feed on fruit trees before returning to the islands each afternoon, and they depart with their offspring in February. Farmers on the mainland used to consider the birds pests, and regularly shot them on the islands in their thousands.

Margaret and Arthur Thorsborne (authors of the book *Hinchinbrook Island*) first saw the pigeons arriving here in 1964. The following year they decided to return and try to count the birds, and in December 1965 they sat back-to-back on North Island and counted 3342 birds arriving. They returned in 1967 only to find that thousands of birds had been shot by farmers. Outraged by the slaughter, they made moves to stop the shooting and protect the birds. Their efforts were gradually successful, and by 1975 the bird count had been formalised by the QNP&WS.

Since then, the number of pigeons arriving on the islands has continued to rise dramatically each year, and by 1994 the count was in excess of 30,000.

The Brook Islands are also a breeding place for black-naped terns over summer. If you're visiting the islands over the summer months, you should be extremely careful not to disturb the birds or their nests. Nesting areas are indicated by signs on the beach. ∎

half-day snorkelling trips to the Brook Islands, which cost $35 to $45. The fringing reef around the three northern islands offers fine snorkelling and North Island's beach is a good picnic spot, but there are no facilities on the island and camping is not permitted.

TULLY (pop 2700)

Tully, a small township wedged between the Bruce Hwy and Mt Tyson (678 metres), is the wettest place in Australia with a drenching average of over 4000 mm of rain a year. The town is almost completely ringed by mountains and, as you would expect, the surrounding areas are green and fertile.

Tully is the cheapest place to start from if you're doing a white-water rafting trip on the Tully River, although nearby Mission Beach is a much more appealing place to stay, and the rafting operators will pick you up from there.

The Tully Information Centre (☎ (070) 68 2288) on the highway just south of the Tully turn off is open on weekdays from 8.45 am to 5 pm and during the tourist season on weekends from 9 am to 1 pm. Eight km north of Tully is **Alligator's Nest**, a great swimming spot with picnic tables, barbecues and lawns. To get there, follow Murray St north from the town centre.

Places to Stay

Tully has a caravan park and a couple of pubs with cheap accommodation. There's also the *Tully Backpackers Hostel* (☎ (070) 68 2820), at 19 Richardson St, one block north of the main street. It's a small and fairly basic worker's hostel – most people staying here are picking bananas, watermelons or lychees or working on the sugar cane harvest. Dorm beds cost $11 a night or $60 a week.

On the highway, the *Mons Mari Motel* (☎ (070) 68 2233) has singles/doubles from $42/50.

Getting There & Away

Tully is on the main Brisbane to Cairns train line. Greyhound Pioneer Australia and McCafferty's buses also stop here on demand.

MISSION BEACH AREA (pop 1000)

This small stretch of coast has become an increasingly popular tourist destination in recent years. The name Mission Beach actually covers a string of small settlements along a 14-km coastal strip east of Tully. Mission Beach, where the long-distance buses stop, is in the centre; Wongaling Beach and South Mission Beach are to the south, and Bingil Bay Beach and Garners Beach are to the north.

The coastal strip is surrounded by large areas of dense rainforest, which comes right down to the beach in places. The area has a wide (and growing) range of accommodation, from beachfront camping grounds and backpackers' hostels to exclusive and expensive resorts. These places are spread up and down the coast between Bingil Bay and South Mission Beach, with most of the developments being fairly low-key and low-rise. There are also some great restaurants along here.

The area is a good base for a number of activities, including visits to Dunk Island and boat trips out to the reef, white-water rafting trips on the Tully River, and walks through the rainforest.

It's a great drive north from Mission Beach to **Bingil Bay**. Beyond the Clump Point jetty, the road hugs the coastline and winds past a series of bays and beaches. Bingil Bay, five km north of Mission Beach, is one of the best beaches in the area, backed by a cluster of shady trees. North from here, a dirt and gravel road loops back to join the main road to Mission Beach. This is a pretty drive through farmlands, although there's nothing in particular to look out for.

History

On 21 May 1848 the barque *Rattlesnake* landed on the southern side of Tam O'Shanter Point, south of South Mission Beach, dropping the 30-year-old explorer Edmund Kennedy and his companions at the start of their ill-fated overland expedition towards Cape York. All but three of the party's 13 members died, and Kennedy himself was speared to death by Aborigines a little way south of Cape York. There's a memorial to the expedition at Tam O'Shanter Point.

The first White settlement in the area was by a group of pioneers who gradually established a series of crops, planting mangoes, bananas, coconuts and tea and coffee. A timber mill was also built to process the locally cut cedar.

In 1914 the Queensland government established an Aboriginal mission to house the remainder of the local Aboriginal population. The site of the old mission, from which the area takes its name, can still be seen at South Mission Beach.

One of Queensland's worst-ever cyclones struck this stretch of coast in 1918, with winds of over 150 km/h, floods and tidal waves destroying the mission and many other buildings and claiming a number of lives.

Information

Tourist Information The Mission Beach Tourist Information Centre (☎ (070) 68 7099) is on Porters Promenade at the north end of Mission Beach. It's well set up with good displays and a small library with books on the environment and local history. It's open from 9 am to 5 pm from Monday to Saturday and from 9 am to 4 pm on Sunday.

Right next door is the Wet Tropics Visitors Centre (☎ (070) 68 7179), an environmental interpretative centre which focuses on the cassowary conservation, and has videos and displays plus a range of environmental-style gifts on sale.

Shops & Banks Mission Beach proper is a compact little holiday village with a good selection of restaurants and cafes, a butcher, a supermarket, a chemist and an ANZ Bank. Wongaling Beach to the south has its own shopping centre, with a supermarket, an Ampol service station and a National Bank.

Activities

Walks & Walking Tours The rainforest around Mission Beach is a haunt of cassowaries but unfortunately the population has been depleted by road accidents and the destruction of rainforest by logging and cyclones. There are some impressive walks including the **Licuala Walking Track** (two hours), **Laceys Creek Walk** (half hour), the **Bicton Hill Lookout** (1½ hours) and the **Edmund Kennedy Walking Track** (three hours). The local tourist information centre produces an excellent *Walking Track Guide*, a brochure and map which details these and other walks. The guide is available for 20c.

Mission Beach Rainforest Treks (☎ (070) 68 7152) takes guided walks through the forests – the morning walk costs $24 and the night walk is $14. They also have a three-day camping trek which costs $230 per person.

The Girramay Walkabout (☎ (070) 68 8676) combines a walking trek guided by people from the local Girramay tribe with a barbecue lunch, a rainforest tour, boomerang and spear-throwing demonstrations and bush tucker. The trek costs $45 per person, and you can book by phone or through Scotty's Mission Beach House.

White-Water Rafting Raging Thunder (☎ (070) 31 1466) and R'n'R (☎ (070) 51 7777 or toll-free 1800 079 039) charge around $112 from Mission Beach for trips on the Tully River. These are the same as the trips on offer in Cairns, but you'll save about $10 and several hours travel by doing them from here. See the Cairns section for more details on white-water rafting trips.

Raging Thunder also offers three-day sea-kayaking expeditions to Dunk Island and the Family Islands for $375 including meals and equipment (but not sleeping bags). R'n'R runs three-day sea-kayaking trips from Kurrimine Beach, 10 km north of Mission Beach, to the Barnard Islands for $360.

Other Activities The Jumbun Horseride Adventure (☎ (070) 68 8676) is a day's ride through the rainforest to a swimming hole, guided by locals from the Girramay tribe.

NORTH COAST

The $65 includes lunch and morning and afternoon tea.

Equitreks (☎ (070) 68 7501) offers 1½-hour dawn and dusk horse rides along the beach and through the bush at Bingil Bay for $25 a head.

With Parachuting Down Under (☎ 1800 638 005), you can do a tandem parachute jump from 8000 feet onto Mission Beach for $198.

Mission Beach Scuba School (☎ (070) 68 8288), based at the Mission Beach Resort in Wongaling Beach, has a five-day dive course for $299.

Organised Cruises

There are three cruise companies based at the Clump Point jetty just north of Mission Beach. Friendship Cruises (☎ (070) 68 7262) takes day trips out to the reef, with snorkelling and a ride in a glass-bottomed boat, for $55, and you can do a resort dive for another $50. Certified divers can do one dive for $35 or two dives for $45.

The *Quick Cat* (☎ (070) 68 7289) is a fast catamaran which does the trip to Dunk Island in 20 minutes for $22 ($11 for children). You can also combine their trip to Dunk with a cruise to the outer Barrier Reef for $110 ($55 for children), which includes lunch and snorkelling gear.

Dunk Island Ferry & Cruises (☎ (070) 68 7211) operates the MV *Lawrence Kavanagh*, an old passenger ferry that does a day trip to Dunk for $22. For another $18 you can also do their cruise around Bedarra and the Family Islands, and a barbecue lunch is available for $8.

See the Dunk Island section later for details of the water taxi services from Mission Beach to Dunk Island.

River Rat Wildlife Cruises (☎ (070) 68 7250) runs evening cruises with mud-crabbing, fishing and crocodile-watching along the Hull River from South Mission Beach. This trip departs daily at 4.30 pm and returns at 8 pm, and costs $28 for adults and $14 for kids.

The *Spirit of Dunk* (☎ (070) 68 7250) offers fishing trips out to Forty Foot Reef, and they supply all fishing gear, bait and snorkelling gear. Trips depart on Monday, Wednesday and Friday and cost $55 per person.

The *Hooker* (☎ (070) 68 8550) is a fishing charter boat that is available for gamefishing and reef trips.

Places to Stay

Camping The *Hideaway Caravan Park* (☎ (070) 68 7104), in the centre of Mission Beach, is an excellent camping village with tent sites from $11 and on-site cabins from $36. Right across the road on the beachfront is the council-run *Mission Beach Caravan Park*, with good grassy areas and tent sites for $6.

There's also a very good council-run camping ground set among trees on the foreshore, just north of the Clump Point jetty. Sites here cost $6 a night.

At South Mission Beach, the *Beachcomber Coconut Village* (☎ (070) 68 8129) is another good camping ground with tent sites from $12, camp-o-tels from $9 per person and a range of on-site cabins from $33.

Hostels There are three very good hostels in the area, all of which have courtesy buses and do pick-ups from the bus stop in Mission Beach proper.

Two of the hostels are at Wongaling Beach, five km south of the bus stop. *Mission Beach Backpackers Lodge* (☎ (070) 68 8317), at 28 Wongaling Beach Rd, is a modern, well-equipped place with a pool and garden. There are two buildings, one with spacious dorms at $13 a bed, the other with very good double rooms priced from $30 to $36. This easy-going hostel is a five-minute walk from the beach.

Scotty's Mission Beach House (☎ (070) 68 8676) is at 167 Reid Rd, also at Wongaling Beach. This friendly and fun-oriented place is right opposite the beach. Dorm beds range from $13 to $15 and twins are from $30 to $45, with the more expensive rooms having their own bathrooms and air-con. There's a pool, evening meals from $5 to $7.50, and barbecues every Wednesday and Saturday night and roast dinners on Sunday and Monday.

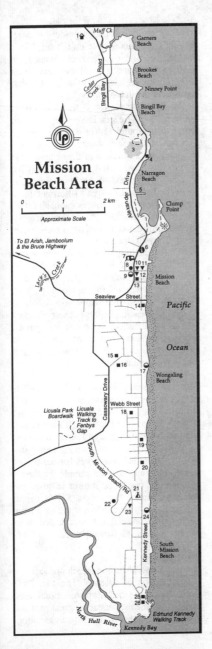

PLACES TO STAY

1   The Treehouse
2   Bingil Bay Resort Motel
4   Clump Point Ecovillage
7   Hideaway Caravan Park
13 Ceud Mile Failte
14 Castaways
15 Mission Beach Backpacker's
    Lodge
16 Mission Beach Resort Hotel
18 Scotty's Mission Beach House
19 The Wongalinga
20 Beachside
21 Beachcomber Coconut Village
25 Lugger Bay Rainforest Apartments
26 The Point Resort

PLACES TO EAT

10 Friends Restaurant
11 Piccolo Paradiso
12 Butterflies/Lamas
23 Blarney's

OTHER

3   Clump Mountain National Park
5   Clump Point Jetty
6   Tourist Information Centre & Wet
    Tropics Visitors Centre
8   Hubb Arcade
9   PC's Cafe & Long-distance Bus
    Stop
17 Dowd's Water Taxi
22 Old Mission Site
24 Mission Beach-Dunk Island Water
    Taxi

The *Treehouse* (☎ (070) 68 7137), an
YHA-associate hostel, is at Bingil Bay, six
km north of Mission Beach. It's a quiet,
relaxed place in an impressive timber stilt
house with a pool and good views over the
surrounding rainforest and the coast. This
secluded and earthy place is one of the most
popular along the coast. A bed in a six-bed
dorm costs $14, doubles cost $35, or you can
camp here for $9. There are bikes for hire for
$12 a day. See the following Farmstays
section for details of another good budget
option.

Motels The *Bingil Bay Resort Motel*
(☎ (070) 68 7208), overlooking Bingil Bay

from high on a hillside, is a good mid-range motel with rooms ranging from $55 to $85 for a double. The upstairs front rooms are the most expensive, but it's worth paying a bit extra for these great views. The motel has lovely gardens and a good swimming pool, plus its own Italian restaurant (see Places to Eat).

The *Mission Beach Village Motel* (☎ (070) 68 7212), at 7 Porter Promenade in Mission Beach, has rooms from $50.

Holiday Units Just south of the bus stop in Mission Beach, *Ceud Mile Failte* (☎ (070) 68 7444) is a bright yellow block of 1960s holiday flats. They're pretty basic and light on for glam, but reasonably cheap at $55 a double plus $10 for extra people.

Beachside (☎ (070) 68 8890), at 32 Reid Rd Wongaling Beach, has good, oldish, self-contained holiday units on the waterfront. There's also a small pool. The one-bedroom flats sleep up to six and cost from $39/45 for singles/doubles, plus $6 for each extra person; the two-bedroom flats sleep up to eight and start at $55 a double.

There are plenty of other holiday units scattered along the length of Reid Rd. If you're after somewhere a little more up-market, *The Wongalinga* (☎ (070) 68 8221), at 64 Reid Rd, Wongaling Beach, is a waterfront complex of nine luxurious self-contained apartments. The one-bedroom units start at $140 a night, two-bedrooms at $180 and three-bedrooms from $220.

Resorts The *Clump Point Ecovillage* (☎ (070) 68 7534), which is on the foreshore at Clump Point, is a brand-new mid-range resort with good, modern self-contained timber bungalows. The units sleep up to five people and cost $80 a night or $85 for a unit with a spa. During school holiday periods the prices go up to $100 and $110. The resort is close to the beach and has a great pool and pleasant gardens.

With 54 units, two bars, two restaurants and a great pool, *Castaways* (☎ (070) 68 7444) is an impressive big resort on the beachfront in central Mission Beach. There

are four styles of accommodation here, ranging from motel-style units from $98 a double, one and two-bedroom units from $140 to $160 and a penthouse unit from $200. The resort has a good range of watersports gear available for its guests.

The *Point Resort* (☎ (070) 68 8154), at South Mission Beach, is very stylish with rooms from around $140 a double.

If you're after somewhere self-contained, secluded and a little out of the ordinary, the *Lugger Bay Rainforest Apartments* (☎ (070) 68 8400), right next to the Point Resort, is about the best of this area's offerings. It's a set of nine wonderful timber cabins built on timber poles on the side of a rainforest-covered hillside, and most have great ocean views. They all sleep up to six people and are brilliantly designed in fairly minimalist style. They start at $225 a double plus $30 for extra people, but are cheaper by the week.

The *Mission Beach Resort Hotel* (☎ (070) 68 8288 or toll-free 1800 079 024), in Wongaling Beach, is a large resort complex with a pub attached. There are four pools, spacious grounds and tennis courts, and motel-style units start at $85 a double, or $95 for a self-contained unit.

Farmstay *Jamboolum* (☎ (070) 68 5240) is an excellent guesthouse set on a tropical fruit farm, 15 km inland from Mission Beach and close to the town of El Arish. It's a modern, comfortable and quite stylish three-bedroom home with 12 bunks, its own kitchen, bathroom, air-con and free bikes for the use of guests, and you can even sample the farm's products for free! The setting is quiet and peaceful, and a bed costs $12 a night. Jamboolum is a short way off the road from El Arish to Mission Beach, signposted about one km west of the Bruce Hwy.

Places to Eat
Mission Beach Mission Beach proper has a good selection of eateries. The tiny *PC's Cafe*, beside the bus stop, has breakfasts, home-made meals, pancakes, great pies and good coffee. In the arcade just across Campbell St is *On the Bite*, a casual seafood cafe

with excellent takeaway fish & chips, burgers, pizzas and sandwiches.

Across the road is *Butterflies*, a friendly and laid-back little Mexican place with vegetarian and seafood main courses from $9 to $13, and a few other dishes with an exotic twist. By day, this place becomes *Lama's*, a breakfast and lunch bar run by an earthy Swiss guy who makes sensational crêpes and muesli fresh to order. He grinds his own flour and buckwheat, and makes freshly squeezed juices – a great start to the day. Lama's closes on Thursday.

Nearby is *Friends*, a popular and stylish open-air BYO restaurant with meals like barramundi, Moreton Bay bugs, chicken hot-pots and roast lamb shanks for around $17. Further down David St is a casual Italian bistro called *Piccolo Paradiso*, with open-air dining at candle lit courtyard tables. Pizzas and pastas are around $8, other Italian mains are $12 to $14, and they have a selection of great-looking deserts including gelati and a Gran Marnier torte. This place is BYO but should be licensed by the time you read this.

Other Areas The *Mission Beach Resort Hotel*, in Wongaling Beach, has a vast bistro with a giant video screen, poker machines and main meals in the $8 to $16 range, or meals in the public bar from $4 to $6. It also has the more up-market *Rainforest Restaurant* for intimate wining and dining, with main meals from $17 to $20. If you're preparing your own food, there are supermarkets at Mission Beach and Wongaling Beach.

At South Mission Beach there's *Blarney's* (☎ (070) 68 8472), a popular little BYO with a great open-sided dining area upstairs. It's a soft-lights-and-music type of place, with mains like grilled coral trout and roast rack of lamb from $13 to $17.

Filippo's, the licensed Italian restaurant at the Bingil Bay Resort Motel, has pastas from $10 and other Italian mains for around $16.

Getting There & Around
To/From the Airport Mission Beach Con-

nections (☎ (070) 68 8266) do pick-ups from Cairns airport at 1 pm every day (by request), and leave Mission Beach daily at 8.30 am for the Cairns airport. The fare is $30 one way.

Bus Around four buses a day make the detour here off the Bruce Hwy, stopping outside Harvey World Travel (☎ (070) 68 7187) in central Mission Beach. The average fare is $13 from Cairns and $35 from Townsville.

Most of the tour and cruise companies and accommodation houses have courtesy buses. Bazz's Bus Service (☎ (070) 68 8707) operates regular daily services along the coastal strip.

Car Rental Car rental companies include Island Coast Moke Hire (☎ (070) 68 8668) and Sugarland Car Rentals (☎ (070) 68 8668).

Bike Hire You can hire good bikes for $12 a day from Mission Beach Bike Hire (☎ (070) 68 7220) in the Hubb Arcade in Mission Beach.

Taxi Call ☎ (070) 68 8266 if you need a taxi.

DUNK ISLAND
The Family Group of islands, a little way off shore from Mission Beach, consist of Dunk Island and seven smaller islands. The islands of the group (and their Aboriginal names) are Dunk (Coonanglebah), Thorpe (Timana), Richards (Bedarra), Wheeler (Toolghar), Coombe (Coomboo), Smith (Kurrumbah), Bowden (Budjoo) and Hudson (Coolah). Dunk is about three-quarters national park, and of the other islands five – Wheeler, Coombe, Smith, Bowden and Hudson islands – are national parks while two – Timana and Bedarra – are privately owned. The privately owned islands are now known by their Aboriginal names.

There is a large resort and an area with daytrippers' facilities on Dunk, two small and very exclusive resorts on Bedarra, and you can camp on Dunk, Wheeler or Coombe islands. Due to the heavy rainfall in this area all of the islands are cloaked in dense rainforest, and most have excellent beaches.

The islands were named by Captain Cook, who sailed through the group on 8 June 1770. Lord Montague Dunk was at that time the First Lord of the Admiralty.

Just 4.5 km off the coast, Dunk is a lush rainforest island with steep hills, some fine walking trails and good sandy beaches. The island has a large resort, owned by Qantas Airlines, a good camping ground and a separate daytrippers' section with a kiosk, showers, toilets, and a water-sports shop with windsurfers, catamarans, paddle skis and snorkelling gear for hire.

From 1897 to 1923 E J Banfield lived on Dunk and wrote *The Confessions of a Beachcomber* and several other books describing life on Dunk; the island is remarkably little changed from his early descriptions. Dunk is noted for its prolific birdlife (nearly 150 species) and many butterflies. There are superb views over the entrances to the Hinchinbrook Channel from the top of 271-metre Mt Kootaloo. Thirteen km of **walking tracks** lead from the camping ground area to headlands and beaches, including a 10-km circuit walk around the north and western half of the island.

There is a small **artists' colony** at the southern end of the circuit walk, centred around Bruce Arthur, a tapestry maker and former Olympic wrestler. The colony is open to visitors on Tuesday and Friday mornings – they charge $4 and give you a brief introduction to the island and their activities and an opportunity to purchase their work, which includes pottery, ceramics, jewellery and Bruce Arthur's tapestries.

Dunk is an easy and affordable day trip from the mainland, with regular water taxis and cruise boats running between Mission Beach and the island.

Places to Stay

Camping There's also a national parks camping ground next to the daytrippers' area. There are toilets, showers, fireplaces and picnic tables, and drinking water is available. There is a limit of 30 campers and a maximum stay of three days here. Camping permits are booked through the resort's water-sports office (☎ (070) 68 8199). You can rent camping gear from Outpack Rentals (☎ (070) 68 7220), in the Hubb Arcade in Mission Beach.

Resort The Dunk Island Resort (☎ (070) 68 8199), at Brammo Bay, on the northern end of the island, has accommodation for up to 400 guests, although it has managed to avoid being too 'mass market'. Architecturally the rooms are straight out of the 1960s bland-box school, but inside they are quite comfortable and the lush Dunk greenery certainly helps to hide them.

The resort has 141 rooms in four different styles. The older Banfield and Garden Cabana rooms are mostly set back from the bayfront while the Beachfront units face the water. The new Bayview Villas, with their ultra-modern white and blue décor, also have impressive views over Brammo Bay. All the rooms have ensuites, air-con and ceiling fans, a verandah, TV and telephones, a fridge and tea and coffee-making facilities.

Daily rates for singles/doubles are $193/322 in the Banfield units; $222/370 in the Garden Cabanas; $285/472 in the Beachfront units; and $297/496 in the Bayview Villas. The tariff is room-only, but includes most activities. Cheaper package deals are usually available through Qantas.

The resort's facilities include squash and tennis courts, a small golf course, two swimming pools, and laundry facilities, and the activities desk can also arrange things like tandem skydiving, horse riding, clay-target shooting and diving and snorkelling trips to the Barrier Reef.

Places to Eat

Resort guests have the choice of taking a meal package which includes three meals a day for $70 per person, or the dinner and breakfast package for $54.

The main restaurant is the large, tropical-style *Beachcomber* restaurant. Breakfast and lunch are fairly elaborate buffets, with a good range of fresh fruit, cereals, hot foods, salads, cold meat and seafood. Dinner is served from a menu, and Friday night is seafood smorgasbord night.

The resort also has the smaller *Rainforest Brasserie*, which is open for dinner with more exotic and inspired food, and main courses ranging from $21 to $23.

Even if you're not staying in the resort, you can eat in the Beachcomber restaurant by buying a resort pass. Breakfast costs $18, lunch is $23 and dinner is $35 (or $45 on the Friday seafood night).

The *Jetty Bar*, in the daytrippers' area, is a fast-food cafe with burgers, sandwiches, salads and fish & chips.

Getting There & Away

Air Qantas has regular flights to and from Townsville (45 minutes, $107) or Cairns (40 minutes, $97).

Sea It's a 10-minute trip from the mainland to the island. Dowd's Water Taxis (☎ (070) 68 8310) has seven daily services from Wongaling Beach to Dunk and back, with the first departure at 8 am and the last boat back from the island at 5 pm.

Mission Beach-Dunk Island Water Taxis (☎ (070) 68 8333) has six similar services from South Mission Beach, with the first departure at 9 am and the last boat returning at 5 pm. Both companies charge $22 return, although the backpackers' hostels can usually get you across for less.

There are also several boats offering cruises from the mainland to Dunk Island and the Barrier Reef – see Organised Cruises in the earlier Mission Beach Area section for details of these.

BEDARRA ISLAND
Bedarra Island is just six km south of Dunk and about five km off shore. The island is rocky, hilly and cloaked in rainforest, and fringed with some fine, sandy beaches, a short stretch of mangroves and wildly tumbled collections of giant boulders.

The island is home to one of Australia's best island resorts, which is operated by Qantas Airlines. The resort is in two sections,

(although only one is currently operating), and is very exclusive and expensive, with a maximum number of 32 people and costs starting at over $500 a day per person. If you can afford that sort of money, Bedarra is about the best resort island on the Great Barrier Reef, perhaps only matched by Lizard Island.

Places to Stay & Eat
For bookings, phone (☎ (070) 68 8233) or write to Bedarra Bay Resort, Bedarra Island, via Townsville, Qld 4810.

The accommodation here is stylish without being over the top or at all glitzy. The resort has 16 architect-designed timber cottages, each with a two-level room with a sleeping area above and a lounge area below. The cottages are almost hidden from each other by the rainforest, and have their own private verandah.

There is a central restaurant, bar and lounge area, as well as swimming pools, spas, tennis courts, catamarans, windsurfers, paddle skis and dinghies for the guests.

The daily costs are from $532 per person for one to two days, or $479 for three days or longer. These costs are twin-share and include all meals, drinks, activities and equipment – in fact just about everything your heart may desire. The resort hangs its hat on its reputation for great food. You can order from the menu, or just eat oysters and lobster and drink champagne all day if that's what you feel like. It's up to you.

Getting There & Away
Bedarra is reached from Dunk, a 20-minute boat ride away. The resort's boat connects with Dunk flights or the water taxis between the mainland and Dunk.

OTHER FAMILY ISLANDS
The other five small national park islands of the Family group are Wheeler, Coombe, Smith, Bowden and Hudson islands. With a permit from the Cardwell or Ingham QNP&WS office, you can camp on Wheeler or Combe islands. There are tables and fireplaces at the camp sites, but no toilet

facilities. Wheeler Island has fresh water during the cooler months.

Charter boats operate from the Clump Point jetty at Mission Beach to the islands.

MISSION BEACH TO INNISFAIL

The small township of, El Arish, just off the highway 17 km north of Tully, is the main turn off point to Mission Beach. In the town is the El Arish Tavern, a historic timber pub draped in hanging baskets and assorted greenery – it's a popular watering hole. The town also has a very pleasant if somewhat flat public golf course. A round costs $10 and for another $10 you can hire a set of clubs.

Eight km north of El Arish there's a turn off to **Kurrimine Beach**, another quiet little beachfront community. From the beach here you can sometimes wade through knee deep water all the way out to **King Reef**, which is about one km off shore. The walk takes about 45 minutes and can *only* be done on minus tides during winter – check local advice before attempting the walk, as people have been stranded out here in the past.

The *Kurramine Beach Camping Area*, a council-run camping ground right on the foreshore, has good, shady tent sites for $6, or $7 with hot showers. The *King Reef Hotel* (☎ (070) 65 6144) is a pleasant spot, with lawns and palm trees leading down to the beach. There's a camping ground here with sites for $11, and a few holiday units costing $55 a double, or $65 for a beachfront unit.

At **Mourilyan**, seven km south of Innisfail, there's the Australian Sugar Industry Museum, with an impressive collection of old tractors, harvesters, steam-driven crushing engine and backlit displays depicting the sugar production process. The museum is open from 9 am to 4.30 pm daily. An export terminal on the coast east of Mourilyan handles the sugar produced in Innisfail, Tully and Mourilyan.

Old Bruce Highway

An interesting alternative route to Innisfail is to turn off the Bruce Hwy and take the Old Bruce Hwy north through Silkwood, Mena Creek and South Johnstone. This route leaves

Cane Cutting – imagine doing this by hand

the highway eight km north of El Arish, meeting up with the main highway again at the southern outskirts of Innisfail. It's a slower but much more scenic drive, taking you through banana plantations and cane fields surrounded by densely forested mountains on either side. It also takes you to the fascinating Paronella Park, one of the weirdest and most interesting attractions in this area.

After turning off, you drive through the small and old-fashioned sugar cane township of Silkwood. The *Silkwood Hotel* has budget accommodation. From here the road follows and frequently crosses the cane railways, so take care if you're here during the harvesting season (June to December).

It's 22 km to Mena Creek, where the very pleasant *Mena Creek Hotel* (☎ (070) 65 3201) has good pub-style rooms at $18/25 for singles/doubles. The pub also has a shady verandah and a good beer garden out the back, and bistro meals here range from $7 to $9.

Paronella Park This unusual place was the dream-child of José Paronella, a Spaniard who came to Australia from Catalonia in 1913. After working as a cane cutter and farmer for 10 years, he returned to Spain, married his wife, Margarita, and brought her back to Australia. Together, they bought a block of land and started building a house in 1929. Next they built a castle, the Grand Staircase down to the river, a Lovers' Tunnel and a hall, all out of poured concrete reinforced with old railway tracks. They also planted thousands of trees and commissioned a hydroelectric plant to supply power to the park.

Paronella Park was opened to the public

in 1935, and was an instant success. There was a refreshments room, a swimming pool, tea gardens, a theatre which screened movies on Saturday nights, and dances and parties were held in the hall, which was also a popular wedding venue. For the next 10 years, Paronella Park was one of the most popular tourist attractions in north Queensland.

During the wet season of 1946, floods broke the railway bridge near the castle and washed through the park, causing massive destruction. Most of the park and its buildings were repaired and rebuilt over the next few years, but José died in 1948. His family continued running the park until 1977, when it was sold. Then, in 1979, a fire destroyed the hall and cafe and damaged many of the other buildings.

Today its still a fascinating and quite bizarre place to visit. Many of the buildings are in ruins, but large parts remain and you can walk through the remains of the castle, down the grand staircase to the river and stroll through Lovers' Tunnel. You can swim in the river or feed the ducks, walk the suspension bridge across the falls, and walking trails lead through several hectares of lovely tropical gardens, which include an avenue of Kauris, a fernery, a bamboo forest and a palm grove. The park is open every day from 9 am to 5 pm; entry costs $6 for adults, $4 for students and $2 for children. There's a Devonshire tea room in the old cottage.

There is also a camping and caravan park with tent sites for $10, powered sites for $12 and on-site cabins for $25 a double. Campers also pay the entry fee for the park, but you then have 24-hour access for the duration of your stay.

Far North Queensland

Although the region covered by this chapter is geographically small, it's an area packed with a wealth of natural assets. The strength of the region's tourist industry is based on this unique combination – as the brochures say, the reef, the rainforest and the outback can all be easily accessed from here.

Cairns and Port Douglas are the main tourist centres, and both have a huge range of accommodation possibilities. A virtual armada of boats operate out of both places, offering trips to the numerous islands, reefs and coral cays of the Great Barrier Reef.

Inland from Cairns is the high plateau of the Atherton Tableland, which offers a cool respite from the heat of the coast. There are some interesting places to visit and things to do – waterfalls and lakes, old mountain villages, bushwalks through the forests – and great places like old pubs, guesthouses and farms to stay in.

North of Port Douglas is the majestic Daintree River. A cruise along this river is a wonderful experience – there's an abundance of birdlife on the river, you might even spot a croc, or you can just relax and absorb the beauty of your surrounds. North of the Daintree River are the rainforested mountains of Cape Tribulation National Park, the place where the rainforest meets the reef.

Further north is the remote town of Cooktown, which is refreshingly unaffected by the hype of tourism – just getting there is an adventure in itself.

An hour or two's drive inland from the coast the great Australian outback begins, stretching clear across to the other side of the continent. You can get a taste of the outback by visiting Chillagoe, an interesting former mining centre 2½-hours drive west of Cairns.

History

The gold discoveries of the 1870s were primarily responsible for opening up this area

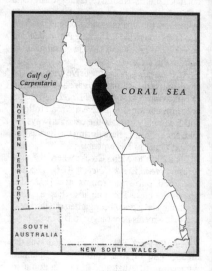

to European settlers. Cooktown was established as a port town for the fabulously rich Palmer River goldfield in 1873, and became the first major township in the Far North, virtually overnight. Cairns (in 1876) and Port Douglas (in 1877) were both established as ports for the Hodgkinson River goldfields; Cairns gained the upper hand when it was later chosen as the terminal for the railway line from the rich tin-mining township of Herberton, in the Atherton Tableland.

Many of the area's mines had short life spans, and the diggers lived transient lives, drifting from one rush to the next. The port towns, on the other hand, prospered and grew into permanent fixtures and soon became the main centres for life in the Far North.

As the initial flurry of mining activity gradually waned, agriculture and pastoral activities became the mainstays of the region, with the sugar industry quickly becoming the major source of income.

Far North Queensland

0   30   60km

Geography & Climate

Geographically, the Far North is a microcosm of the entire state of Queensland. The mountains of the Great Dividing Range run parallel with the coast, dividing the region into two distinct zones: a green and fertile coastal strip which runs between the mountains and the oceans; and a harsher, outback-type region which stretches from the western side of the mountains out towards the Gulf and Cape York.

The coastal mountain ranges are densely forested, and large areas of these rainforests are protected as national parks and included in the Wet Tropics World Heritage Area. Inland from Cairns is the Atherton Tableland, a high plateau of rich, fertile farming land.

Climatically, the Far North has two distinct seasons – summer, and the rest of the year. This is something of a simplification, of course, but the summer months (December to March) are characterised by high temperatures and humidity, and tropical downpours are a regular feature – wet weather gear may be a good idea if you're visiting during summer. The rest of the year tends to be what summer is like elsewhere – plenty of sunshine and warm weather. It seldom gets cold here – with the exception of the Atherton Tableland, which is one of the few areas where you may require a jumper or a jacket.

Activities

There are many activities on offer in the Far North, and they are detailed in the Activities sections throughout this chapter. There are diving courses in Cairns and Port Douglas, and if you want to go snorkelling or diving there are dozens of boat trips out to the reef and islands.

There are some spectacular national parks in the area, and bushwalking is a popular activity here. South of Cairns is the Bartle Frere National Park, and the Daintree and Cape Tribulation national parks north of Mossman also have some great walks.

White-water rafting trips on the Tully and North Johnstone rivers are among the most popular activities, or if you'd rather move a little slower you can try canoeing or sea-kayaking. Paragliding, bungy jumping and hang-gliding are other popular adventure activities. There are also quite a few horse riding ranches in this area.

Getting There & Away

Air Cairns is the major airport for the Far North, with international flights and domestic flights to all the major cities in Australia. See the Cairns section later in this chapter for details.

There are also various small airfields and airstrips in the region, at places like Cooktown, Cow Bay (Cape Tribulation) and Chillagoe.

Bus The two major bus companies, McCafferty's and Greyhound Pioneer Australia, ply the coastal route up the Bruce Hwy as far as Cairns. The trip from Brisbane takes 23 to 27 hours and costs around $135.

Coral Coaches continues the run up the coast from Cairns, with services to Port Douglas, Mossman, Daintree, Cape Tribulation and Cooktown; see the Port Douglas and Cooktown sections for details. There are also local bus services from Cairns to the Northern Beaches, up to the Atherton Tableland, and across to the Gulf Savannah; again, see the Cairns section for details.

Train Cairns is the end of the main coastal railway link from Brisbane. Three trains (the *Queenslander*, the *Sunlander* and the *Spirit of the Tropics*) run up and down the coast; see the Cairns section for details. From Cairns, the popular Kuranda Scenic Railway climbs spectacularly through the mountains to the market town of Kuranda.

Sea *Quicksilver's* daily fast catamaran service connects Cairns with Port Douglas. There are also a huge number of boat trips from Cairns and Port Douglas (and a couple from Cape Tribulation) out to the Great Barrier Reef and islands.

Several cruise ships operate along this stretch of the coast – see Cruises under Organised Tours in the Cairns section for details of these.

Car & Motorcycle The Bruce Hwy, which runs all the way up the Queensland coastline from Brisbane, finishes in Cairns. From Cairns, the Captain Cook Hwy continues along the coast as far as the town of Daintree – the Cairns-Port Douglas stretch is one of the most scenic coastal drives in Queensland.

Just south of Daintree is the turn off to the ferry across the Daintree River. The Cape Tribulation road which starts on the other side was once notoriously rough, but it is now mostly sealed and well maintained, making Cape Trib an easily accessed and popular day trip destination. Beyond Cape Trib, the unsealed Bloomfield Track is 4WD territory all the way to Cooktown. There's also an inland route from Cairns to Cooktown, via Mareeba and Mt Molloy. This road can be tackled by conventional vehicles, although the second half is over unsealed, rough and bumpy roads.

There are two major routes heading inland to the Atherton Tableland from Cairns. Leaving the Captain Cook Hwy at Smithfield, north of Cairns, the Kennedy Hwy climbs up to Kuranda and across to Mareeba. From Mareeba you can head north up the inland route to Cooktown and beyond, you can continue west out to the old mining township of Chillagoe, or you can head south and into the heart of the Atherton Tableland. The second route, the Gillies Hwy, leaves the Bruce Hwy at Gordonvale, south of Cairns, and climbs up to the Tableland via Yungaburra and Atherton.

Apart from these major routes, there are plenty of smaller roads leading to interesting, out-of-the-way places. Far North Queensland is a beautiful and diverse area – don't be afraid to explore the backroads, you never know what you might find.

Innisfail to Cairns

INNISFAIL (pop 8500)

Innisfail is a solid and prosperous country town at the junction of the North and South Johnstone rivers. The North Johnstone, flowing down from the Atherton Tableland, is popular for white-water rafting and canoeing.

Innisfail has been a sugar city for over a century. It's a busy place, with a large Italian population. The Italians first arrived early this century to work the cane fields – some became plantation owners themselves and in the 1930s there was even a local branch of the Mafia, called the Black Hand!

Despite being in the centre of a popular tourism area, Innisfail is a largely unaffected working town. Perhaps more than anything else, it offers a chance to get a feel for what life was like in the Far North pre-tourism.

Orientation & Information

Innisfail sprawls around the banks of the Johnstone River, with the town centre just west of where the North and South Johnstone rivers meet. The Bruce Hwy passes through the centre of town, with a couple of name changes along the way. The main streets are Edith St (the central section of the highway), Grace St and Rankin St.

The Cassowary Coast Information Centre (☎ (070) 61 6448), one km south of the centre on the Bruce Hwy, is open daily from 9 am to 5 pm.

The QNP&WS has an office (☎ (070) 61 4291) in the Rising Sun shopping complex on Owen St.

The Shell Johnstone Driveway (☎ (070) 61 1941), on the corner of Ernest and Lily Sts, is the local RACQ depot and does 24-hour towing.

Things to See & Do

Innisfail is something of a fishing centre, and from the town centre you can wander down to the banks of the Johnstone River and have a look at the colourful fishing trawlers

FAR NTH QUEENSLAND

moored alongside. There's a fish depot on Fitzgerald Esplanade, near the bottom end of Grace St, where you can buy seafood fresh off the boats.

On Owen St you can find a **Chinese Joss House**, a small temple that was built in the 1940s. The original Joss House, built in 1900, was destroyed in a cyclone. The temple's opening hours vary – check with the information centre. **Warrina Lakes**, at the north end of Charles St, is a pleasant park with gardens, walking paths, a lake, a kid's playground, barbecues and picnic areas and a pool with a large spa. The gardens are open weekdays from 9 am to 6.30 pm and weekends from 10 am to 6.30 pm.

The town's **Historical Society Museum** is upstairs in the old School of Arts building, at 11 Edith St. It is open on Monday from 1 to 3 pm and Tuesday to Friday from 10 am to noon and from 1 to 3 pm; entry costs $1.

Places to Stay

There are three caravan parks here. The best, and closest to the centre, is the *River Drive Caravan Park* (☎ (070) 61 2515), on the Bruce Hwy one km south of the centre, on the banks of the South Johnstone. Tent sites cost $12 and on-site cabins start at $32.

Backpackers Innisfail (☎ (070) 61 2284), at 73 Rankin St, is an old timber house with the usual hostel facilities, plus free bikes and canoes for paddles along the Johnstone River. Quite a few workers stay here – picking bananas is the most common job. Dorm beds cost $10, although they could be cheaper soon due to the competition in the town.

Speaking of competition, *The Endeavour* (☎ (070) 61 6610), at 31 Gladys St, is another workers' hostel in a more comfortable two-storey timber Queenslander. Dorm beds here cost $10, a bed in a twin room costs $15 and singles/doubles cost $20/30.

Another budget option is the *Queen's Hotel* (☎ (070) 61 1399), at 74 Rankin St, which has basic pub-style rooms upstairs for $10 a bed.

The *Moondarra Motel* (☎ (070) 61 7077), at 21 Ernest St, is a friendly little budget motel with singles/doubles from $35/40 – they'll even wash your windscreen for you before you leave in the morning! The *Barrier Reef Motel* (☎ (070) 61 4988), on the Bruce Hwy near the information centre, has rooms from $52/60.

Places to Eat

There are plenty of cafes and takeaways in town and along the highway, including all the big-name chains.

Susie's Salads & Sangars, at 49 Edith St, is a little sandwich bar with better-than-average takeaway tucker. If you need a decent coffee, try *Magg's Coffee Bar*, at 88 Edith St.

The *Queen's Hotel*, at 74 Rankin St, has budget bistro meals from $4. The *Chinese Garden Restaurant*, on Ernest St, is a modern Chinese place with $5 lunch specials and $16.50 smorgasbord deals on Friday, Saturday and Sunday nights.

Entertainment

Some of the nightclubs in Innisfail have a reputation for being more than a bit rowdy, so don't just wander into any old place with flashing lights. The *Outback Club* in the previously mentioned Queens Hotel is more respectable than most, and is open on Friday and Saturday nights until 3 am.

Getting There & Away

Innisfail is on the main north-south railway line. Long-distance buses stop opposite King George V Park on Edith St.

Panorama Buses (☎ (070) 61 1146) has regular bus services south from Innisfail to Mourilyan and Silkwood.

AROUND INNISFAIL

The residential community of **Flying Fish Point**, seven km east of Innisfail on the northern side of the Johnstone River mouth, is reported to be a good camping spot.

Halfway along the road to Flying Fish Point is the **Johnstone River Crocodile Farm**, which has a large collection of breeding crocs and is open daily from 9 am to 5 pm; entry costs $8 for adults and $4 for children.

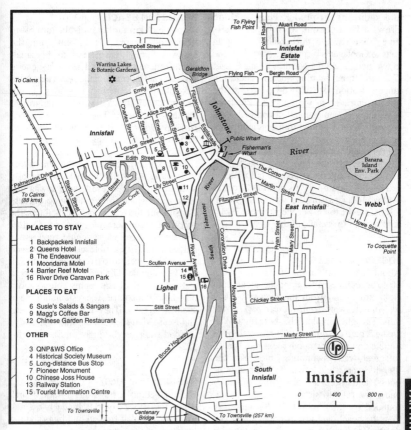

PLACES TO STAY

1 Backpackers Innisfail
2 Queens Hotel
8 The Endeavour
11 Moondarra Motel
14 Barrier Reef Motel
16 River Drive Caravan Park

PLACES TO EAT

6 Susie's Salads & Sangars
9 Magg's Coffee Bar
12 Chinese Garden Restaurant

OTHER

3 QNP&WS Office
4 Historical Society Museum
5 Long-distance Bus Stop
7 Pioneer Monument
10 Chinese Joss House
13 Railway Station
15 Tourist Information Centre

Innisfail

Heading north along the Bruce Hwy from Innisfail, there's a turn off after about one km to the *Garadung Hotel*, a rambling 1888 pub sitting alone in the midst of the cane fields. The pub has rooms for $20 per person, and apparently the counter meals here are excellent.

WEST FROM INNISFAIL

The Palmerston Hwy, which leaves the Bruce Hwy five km north of Innisfail and winds westwards up to the Atherton Tableland, follows the original route taken by the famous bushman Christie Palmerston. In 1882, Palmerston and his Aboriginal companions set out from the tin-mining town of Herberton, walking about 100 km through thick jungle in search of a useable route to the coast, finally arriving at Innisfail after 12 days.

Twenty-eight km west of Innisfail is the **Nerada Tea Plantation & Factory** (☎ (070) 64 5177), which is open to visitors daily from 9 am to 4.30 pm. After Nerada, the highway passes through the rainforests of the **Palmerston National Park.** There are some great walking trails through the park, leading to waterfalls and creeks and linking the picnic and camping grounds. They include Crawford's Lookout to Tchupala Falls (five_20km, two to three hours), Tchupala Falls to Goolagan's picnic area (three km, one to two hours) and the Nandroya Falls Circuit (7.2 km, three to four hours). There's a rangers station (☎ (070) 64 5115), at the eastern entrance to the park, 33 km from Innisfail, and you can call in and pick up a copy of the self-guided trail brochure from here. There are also picnic areas throughout the park, and a camping ground at Henrietta Creek just off the highway with toilets, picnic tables and coin-operated barbecues.

The Palmerston Hwy continues on to Millaa Millaa, passing the 'waterfalls circuit' just before the town. See the Atherton Tableland section for details of this area.

JOSEPHINE FALLS

About 22 km north of Innisfail there's a turn off to Josephine Falls, a popular picnic spot eight km inland from the highway. It's a five-minute walk from the car park to the falls. This place couldn't be more fun if Walt Disney had designed it. Huge waterfalls tumble down over smooth rocks into beautiful green-water swimming holes. You can literally waterslide down the rocks into the pools, and there are also little spa-holes under the falls to sit in. All of this is surrounded by thick rainforest. It's more fun than the beach and just as popular, but you do need to take care, especially after the rains when the falls become heavy – people have drowned here in the past.

The falls are at the foot of the Bellenden Ker Range which includes Queensland's highest peak, **Mt Bartle Frere** (1657 metres). The **Mt Bartle Frere Hiking Track** leads from the falls car park to the Bartle Frere summit. The ascent is for fit and experienced walkers only – it's a 15-km, two-day return trip, and rain and cloud can close in suddenly. There's an alternative 10-km return walk to Broken Nose. You need a camping permit from the QNP&WS office in Innisfail (☎ (070) 61 4291) for either of these walks.

BRAMSTON BEACH (pop 320)

A couple of km further on is the turn off to Bramston Beach. It's 17 km from the highway through cane fields to this small beachfront community. There's a general store and a stinger net on the beach here, plus a couple of accommodation options.

The council runs a basic camping ground on the foreshore. The *Bramston Beach Holiday Motel* (☎ (070) 67 4139) has your basic motel units, costing $40/48 for singles/doubles.

One km further south, the *Plantation Village Resort* (☎ (070) 67 4133) is a really well set up budget resort, with lawns and palm trees which front onto a good beach. Considering the setting and the facilities, the accommodation here represents good value, with tent sites from $9 a double, motel-style lodges from $29 a double and self-contained units which sleep up to five ranging from $39 to $49 a double. The resort has two bars, a restaurant, a pool and tennis courts, and a nine-hole golf course. The restaurant's menu changes nightly. They have chicken, beef and seafood dishes for around $9, and a seafood smorgasbord night on Saturday for $22.

BABINDA (pop 1260)

Hidden behind a huge sugar mill, which fronts the Bruce Hwy, Babinda is a small town of verandah-fronted buildings and old timber pubs. You can take a trip back in time with a visit to the **Munro Theatre** (☎ (070) 67 1566), a quaint cinema that dates back to the 1940s and still has those old hessian-slung seats and a hessian-covered ceiling. The cinema screens latest releases and tickets are just $4.50.

Across the road on the corner of School and Munro Sts, the **Oolana Gallery** is run by the Deeral and Torres Strait Islander community, and sells indigenous arts and crafts including hand-made didgeridoos and boomerangs.

The *Babinda Hotel* (☎ (070) 67 1202) is a huge old two-storey timber pub. It's bars were once regularly flooded with cane cutters at the end of their shifts, and locals can remember it being so crowded that drinkers would spill out onto the streets. Back in those days the pub was owned by the state government, the license having been granted by a special act of parliament. The pub has simple but clean and freshly painted rooms upstairs which go for $15/30 singles/doubles, and backpacker bunks for $8. The bistro serves Thai/Australian cuisine, whatever that may be, with mains ranging from $9 to $14.

BABINDA BOULDERS

Babinda Boulders, where a creek rushes between enormous rocks, is seven km inland from Babinda. This is truly a lovely (and accordingly popular) spot, with lawns and gardens and great picnic areas with push-button barbecues, and walking trails leading to Devil's Lookout (470 metres) and the Boulders Gorge Lookout (600 metres). There's a huge swimming hole, with water so clear I could count the fresh water prawns on the sandy bottom.

A suspension bridge takes you across the river to an 850-metre circuit walk through the rainforest.

There's also a small, basic camping ground 100 metres back from the main car park. The ranger comes around to collect the $3 per person site fee.

Just before the entrance to the Boulders' car park is *Bowenia Lodge* (☎ (070) 67 1631), a modern, timber homestead which offers B&B accommodation. There are two guest bedrooms with their own ensuites, a guest kitchen and a lounge area, and it's a relaxed place and great value at $15 per person. Meals are available if you don't want to cook for yourself. The owners of this place also have a two-bedroom cottage on their property, set in the hills behind the main house. It's simple and fully self-contained, but the setting is wonderful, in the heart of the rainforest and close to a lovely creek with swimming holes. The cost here is also $15 per person.

From the Boulders you can walk the **Goldfield Track** – first opened up in the 1930s when there was a minor gold rush. It leads

10 km to the Goldsborough Valley, across a saddle in the Bellenden Ker Range. The track ends at a causeway on the Mulgrave River, from where a forestry road leads eight km to a camping ground in the **Goldsborough Valley State Forest Park**. From there it's 15 km on to the Gillies Hwy between Gordonvale and Atherton.

GORDONVALE (pop 2660)

Back on the Bruce Hwy, Gordonvale is another town with a huge sugar mill. The town sits at the base of **Walsh's Pyramid** (922 metres), which is at the northern tip of the Bellenden Ker National Park. On the highway north of the town are two Sikh gurdwaras (places of worship).

Also at Gordonvale is the **Mulgrave Rambler**, a steam-train which runs through sugar-cane country along the course of the Little Mulgrave River. Unfortunately the train no longer runs regularly – it's only available on a charter basis. During the cutting season (June to November), you can take a tour of the **Mulgrave Sugar Mill** (☎ (070) 56 3300). Tours depart each weekday during the season at 10 am, 1.30 and 3 pm; the tour lasts 1½ hours and costs $5 for adults, $2.50 for children and students.

GORDONVALE TO YUNGABURRA

The winding Gillies Hwy leads from here up onto the Atherton Tableland. It's 43 km from here to Yungaburra. The first section twists and climbs steeply as you head up into the mountains, and you can feel the temperature drop as you climb higher.

Thirteen km from Gordonvale is the turn off to **Orchid Valley**, a lovely orchid garden in the Little Mulgrave Valley. It's open daily with tours every half hour, costing $10 for adults and $5 for kids.

Just near this turn off is the *Mountain View Hotel*, which is a great spot for a meal or a cool drink.

YARRABAH ABORIGINAL COMMUNITY
(pop 1800)
Midway between Gordonvale and Edmon-

ton is a turn off to the Yarrabah Aboriginal community. It's a scenic 37-km drive from here through the cane fields and mountains to Yarrabah. Unlike many Aboriginal communities, you don't need permission to visit here.

Three km after you leave the highway there's another turn off to the **Edward River Crocodile Farm**. It's another five km from the turn off to the farm, which is owned and run by the Pormpuraaw Aboriginal Community from Cape York. This place is very different to most croc farms – it's not here to entertain tourists, it's a commercial breeding and hatching farm with over 3000 crocs housed in spacious, natural enclosures. This means it might be hard to see them sometimes, but you can buy croc meat and leather products from the shop here. The farm is open daily from 8.30 am to 4.30 pm. There's a tour at 11 am, but feeding time at 2 pm is the best time to come. Entry costs $10 for adults, $5 for children. A couple of companies run cruises to here from Cairns, including the *Terri-Too* (☎ (070) 31 4007), which has a half-day cruise for $39.

The road to Yarrabah runs parallel with the Bruce Hwy almost as far as Cairns, before turning east and running alongside Trinity Bay. There are good views across the bay to Cairns and some good-looking beaches along here, but swimming isn't advised unless you want to become croc bait.

The road then climbs through the mountains and across to Yarrabah. The community is set on Mission Bay, a pretty cove backed by palm trees and decorated with the rusting hulls of two large ships, which were dumped here a few years ago. In the town you can visit the **Menmuny Museum**, which has a collection of Aboriginal artefacts and cultural exhibits from a number of different communities. There is also a commercial section with locally made T-shirts, spears, pottery and crafts on sale. Traditional dances are also performed at various times. Behind the museum there's a boardwalk through the rainforest, with signboards pointing out the traditional uses of various native plants. The museum is open on weekdays from 8.30 am to 4.30 pm; entry costs $6 for adults and $3 for students and children.

Another way of visiting Yarrabah is to paddle across – Foaming Fury runs a paddletrek across Trinity Bay to here from Cairns. See Activities in the Cairns section for details.

Cairns (pop 70,000)

The 'capital' of the Far North and perhaps the best known city on the Queensland coast, Cairns is now firmly established as one of Australia's top travellers' destinations.

Not so long ago, Cairns was a laid-back country town, all but languishing in the tropics. Today, it's a modern, vivacious and somewhat precocious city that literally lives and breathes tourism. Cairns' airport is the fourth busiest in Australia, and international arrivals are growing at a rate of over 20% a year.

On the debit side, Cairns' rapid tourist growth has destroyed much of its laid-back tropical atmosphere. It also comes as a surprise to many travellers that Cairns doesn't have a beach, although there are some good ones not far north. And you can always head out to the islands.

Cairns is primarily a base for getting to the many attractions that surround it. Top of the list is the Great Barrier Reef, and there are dozens of operators running trips out to the reef and islands from Cairns. The Atherton Tableland, Port Douglas, Chillagoe and Mission Beach are all within a couple of hour's drive from Cairns.

Cairns is also a centre for a whole host of activities – not just scuba diving but also white-water rafting, canoeing, horse riding and, of course, the latest lunatic crazes like bungy jumping and sky diving. It also has some excellent restaurants and a more than lively nightlife. Lots of international travellers start or finish their Australian odyssey in Cairns, and either way, wild celebrations seem to be in order.

TONY WHEELER

TONY WHEELER

MARK ARMSTRONG

MARK ARMSTRONG

MARK ARMSTRONG

TONY WHEELER

MARK NORMAN

A	B
	C
D	E
F	G

A: Wild mushrooms, Hinchinbrook Island
B: Rainforest, Hinchinbrook Island
C: The Inlander, North Coast
D: Imperial Hotel, Ravenswood
E: Abandoned mining equipment, Ravenswood
F: Yankee Bay, Orpheus Island
G: Seastar on coral shelf, Heron Island

DAVID SHERMAN

Mossman Gorge, Far North Queensland

HISTORY

Trinity Bay was named by Captain Cook, who sighted the bay on Trinity Sunday in 1770.

The town came into existence in 1876, a beachhead in the mangroves intended as a port for the Hodgkinson River goldfield which was 100 km inland. Initially, it struggled under rivalry from Smithfield 12 km north, a rowdy frontier town that was washed away by a flood in 1879 (it's now an outer Cairns suburb), then from Port Douglas, founded in 1877 after the famous bushman Christie Palmerston discovered an easier route from there to the goldfield. What saved Cairns was the Atherton Tableland 'tin rush' from 1880. Cairns became the starting point of the railway to the Tableland, built a few years later in 1886, and its supremacy was consolidated as the Tableland was opened up for agriculture and timber, and sugargrowing started in the lowlands.

Despite being the regional capital, Cairns settled into its role as a sleepy and remote northern outpost, with progress and life both moving along in the slow lane. Most of the mining activity in the surrounding regions had dried up by the end of WW I, and the rail iink with Brisbane wasn't completed until 1924. Economically, the town was mainly dependent on the sugar industry, with some support coming from pastoral activities, the timber industry and the Tableland's agriculture.

By 1947, Cairns had a population of just 16,000, but fuelled by a booming sugar industry, it grew rapidly through the 1950s and '60s. The first tourists started arriving around this time, and a trickle of visitors throughout the 1970s suddenly became a flood with the opening of Cairns International Airport in 1984.

ORIENTATION

Cairns is ringed on three sides by green and forested hills – probably the most noticeable feature when you first arrive. On the fourth side is the V-shaped Trinity Bay. At the southern end of the bay Trinity Inlet and Smith's Creek form a loop around Admiralty Island; north of the bay is the Barron River estuary.

The urban area is predominantly flat, and sprawls back from the bay to the foot of the hills. Development had threatened to extend up into the hills, but because of their significant environmental value the hillslope areas have recently been protected.

The Bruce Hwy leads into Cairns from the south. After it enters the city it becomes Mulgrave Rd, which takes you west towards the city centre, before turning north and heading out of town, with another change of name – to the Captain Cook Hwy.

The city centre is a relatively compact area, roughly bordered by the Esplanade, Wharf St, McLeod St and Aplin St. Off Wharf St (the southern continuation of the Esplanade), you'll find Marlin Jetty, the Great Adventures Wharf and the Pier – the main departure points for reef trips. Further round is Trinity Wharf (a cruise-liner dock with shops and cafes) and the Transit Centre, where long-distance buses arrive and depart. The airport is about six km north of the city centre, just south of the Barron River estuary.

Back from the waterfront is City Place, a pedestrian mall at the meeting of Shields and Lake Sts.

Cairns is surrounded to the south and north by mangroves, and the sea in front of the town is shallow and at low tide becomes a long sweep of mud, although there are lots of interesting water birds. The closest swimming beaches to Cairns are at Yorkeys Knob and Trinity Beach, about 20 km to the north.

INFORMATION
Tourist Information

There's no shortage of tourist information in Cairns. The Far North Queensland Promotion Bureau (☎ (070) 51 3588) is on the corner of Grafton and Hartley Sts; it's open on weekdays from 9 am to 5 pm and on Saturday and public holidays from 9 am to 1 pm.

There are dozens of privately run 'information centres' in Cairns. These include the Cairns Tourist Information Centre (☎ (070) 31 1751), at 99 the Esplanade (this office may be closing soon due to redevelopment);

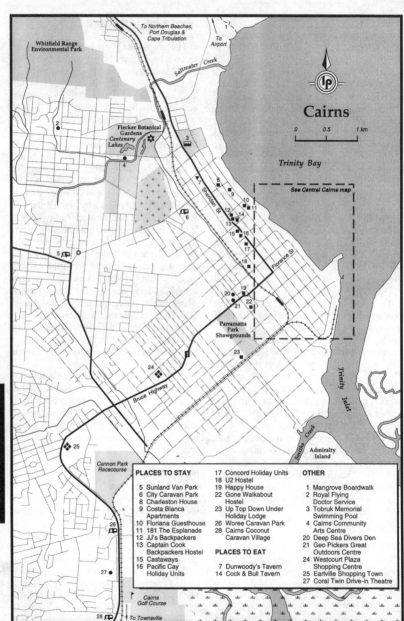

Cairns

Whitfield Range
Environmental Park

To Northern Beaches,
Port Douglas &
Cape Tribulation

To
Airport

Saltwater Creek

Flecker Botanical
Gardens
Centenary
Lakes

Trinity Bay

See Central Cairns map

Sheridan St

Florence St

Parramatta
Park
Showgrounds

Bruce Highway

Trinity Inlet

Smiths Creek

Admiralty
Island

Cannon Park
Racecourse

Cairns
Golf Course

To Townsville

PLACES TO STAY

5   Sunland Van Park
6   City Caravan Park
8   Charleston House
9   Costa Blanca
    Apartments
10 Floriana Guesthouse
11 181 The Esplanade
12 JJ's Backpackers
13 Captain Cook
    Backpackers Hostel
15 Castaways
16 Pacific Cay
    Holiday Units

17 Concord Holiday Units
18 U2 Hostel
19 Happy House
22 Gone Walkabout
    Hostel
23 Up Top Down Under
    Holiday Lodge
26 Woree Caravan Park
28 Cairns Coconut
    Caravan Village

PLACES TO EAT

7   Dunwoody's Tavern
14 Cock & Bull Tavern

OTHER

1   Mangrove Boardwalk
2   Royal Flying
    Doctor Service
3   Tobruk Memorial
    Swimming Pool
4   Cairns Community
    Arts Centre
20 Deep Sea Divers Den
21 Geo Pickers Great
    Outdoors Centre
24 Westcourt Plaza
    Shopping Centre
25 Earlville Shopping Town
27 Coral Twin Drive-in Theatre

Cairns Eco Tours (☎ (070) 51 1500), next to McDonald's on the corner of the Esplanade and Shields St; Tropical Paradise Travel (☎ (070) 51 9533), on the corner of Spence and Lake Sts; and Going Places (☎ (070) 51 4055), on the corner of Sheridan and Aplin Sts. These places are basically tour-booking offices. Also good for information are the various backpackers' hostels, as most have a separate tour-booking service. The only problem with all of these places is that each booking agent and hostel will be selling different tours, depending on the commission deal they have with the tour companies – so shop around.

The Community Information Service (☎ (070) 51 4953) in Tropical Arcade off Shields St, half a block back from the Esplanade, is good for some tourist information plus more offbeat things like where you can play croquet or do t'ai chi. It also has details on foreign consulates in Cairns and health services.

Money
All of the major banks have branches throughout central Cairns, and most of these have foreign exchange sections. Thomas Cook has a Bureau de Change on the Esplanade, near the Shields St corner, and there's another currency exchange booth in the Pier Marketplace.

Post
The main post office, on the corner of Grafton and Hartley Sts, is open on weekdays from 8.30 am to 5 pm. The poste restante service prints a daily alphabetical list of all mail that has arrived, so you can check in the window first to see whether it's worth queuing. For general business (stamps, etc), there's also an Australia Post shop in the Orchid Plaza on Lake St.

The American Express agency in Cairns is the Northern Australian Travel Agency (☎ (070) 51 6472), at 91 Grafton St.

Useful Organisations
The RACQ office (☎ (070) 51 4788), at 112 Sheridan St, is a good place to get maps and information on road conditions, especially if you're driving up to Cooktown or the Cape York Peninsula, or across to the Gulf of Carpentaria. It is open on weekdays from 8.30 am to 5 pm.

The QNP&WS office (☎ (070) 52 3096), at 10 McLeod St, is open on weekdays from 8.30 am to 4.30 pm and deals with camping permits for Davies Creek, the Frankland Islands, Lizard Island and Jardine River.

Medical & Emergencies
If you need the police, an ambulance or the fire brigade, dial 000.

The Cairns Base Hospital (☎ (070) 50 6205) is on the Esplanade just north of the centre, and has a casualty ward and a free STD (sexually transmitted diseases) clinic.

Bookshops
Proudmans, in the Pier complex, and Walkers Bookshop, at 96 Lake St, both have a good range of travel books, local history, literature and children's books. Becker's Books, at the gallery level in the Orchid Plaza, is another good bookshop and has an ABC shop.

The Cairns Book and Ecology Centre, at 27 Shields St, has a range of books on ecology, the new age, crystals, happiness, bush medicine and astronomy, amongst other subjects. The Green Possum Environmental Bookshop, in an arcade off Grafton St right by Rusty's Bazaar, is also interesting. For maps, check out Sunmap, at 15 Lake St.

The Bookshelf, at 65 Grafton St, has a pretty wide range of second-hand books and magazines.

Laundry
Most of the accommodation places have laundry facilities, but if you need a laundrette, try the Central Laundromat, at 145 Lake St, or the Cairns City Laundromat, at 49 Grafton St.

Camera Repairs
There are three or four large camera stores in Cairns, including the Sunbird Camera House

FAR NTH QUEENSLAND

on the corner of Grafton and Shields St, which can arrange repairs to most models.

THINGS TO SEE

Cairns' main attraction for tourists is as a base for heading to the places that surround it – the Barrier Reef, the Atherton Tableland, Cape Trib and beyond. The town itself has a relatively small number of actual tourist attractions, and if you're stuck in town for too long you may soon run out of things to see and do.

A walk around the town centre turns up a few points of historical interest, although with the spate of recent development, the older buildings are now few and far between. The oldest part of town is the **Trinity Wharf** area, but even this has been redeveloped. There are still some imposing neoclassical buildings from the 1920s on Abbott St, and the frontages around the corner of Spence and Lake Sts date from 1909 to 1926.

The **Esplanade Walking Trail**, which follows the foreshore for almost three km north from the centre of town, can make for an agreeable stroll with views over to rainforested mountains across the estuary and cool evening breezes.

The **Pier Marketplace** is an up-market shopping plaza with a good range of specialty shops and boutiques selling books, music, clothes, art, jewellery, gifts, souvenirs and lots more. There are also some good eateries here (see Places to Eat), plus a collection of stalls selling local crafts and art (see the Things to Buy section); a large **aquarium** is being built and should also be open by the time you read this. The Pier complex is open daily from 9 am to 9 pm.

Right in the centre of town, on the corner of Lake and Shields Sts, the **Cairns Museum** is housed in the 1907 School of Arts building, an excellent example of early Cairns architecture. It has Aboriginal artefacts, a display on the construction of the Cairns to Kuranda railway, the contents of a now demolished Grafton St joss house, exhibits on the old Palmer River and Hodgkinson goldfields, and material on the early timber industry. It is open Monday to Saturday from 10 am to 3 pm and entry costs $2 for adults and 50c for children.

The **Cairns Regional Gallery**, on the corner of Abbott and Shields Sts, is another of the city's few remaining historic buildings. It is currently undergoing restoration and will house an art collection that features the work of local artists.

A colourful part of town on weekends is the **Rusty's Bazaar** area bounded by Grafton, Spence, Sheridan and Shields Sts. The bustling weekend markets held here are great for people-watching and for browsing among the dozens of stalls, which sell produce, arts and crafts, clothes and lots of food. The markets are held on Friday nights and Saturday and Sunday mornings; Saturday is the busiest and best. This part of Grafton St used to be the Cairns Chinatown and also a red-light district.

The **Flecker Botanic Gardens** are bordered by Collins Ave and Greenslopes St, in Edge Hill, three km north-west from the centre of Cairns. The gardens are quite lovely, with their flower beds, lawns, lakes and lily ponds, and there are walking trails and plenty of birdlife here.

The gardens have various sections including an Aboriginal plant use area, a palmetum, bamboos, tropical fruits and a formal botanic gardens. There is a small restaurant in the centre of the gardens where you can get a meal or a snack, and the administration office nearby supplies visitors with tapes (in English, German, French or Japanese) for the self-guided walks through the rainforest. The tapes cost $4.50 an hour plus a $20 deposit for the walkman. The gardens are open from 7.30 am on weekdays and 8.30 am on weekends, but unfortunately they close at 5.30 pm. There are free guided walks through the gardens every weekday at 1 pm.

Over the road from the gardens, a boardwalk leads through a patch of rainforest to **Saltwater Creek** and **Centenary Lakes.**

Near the gardens is the entrance to the **Whitfield Range Environmental Park**, the last remnant of rainforest environment around Cairns. There are two walking tracks, a one-hour walk (marked in red) and a 3½-hour walk (marked in blue) which give good views over the city and coast. You can get to the gardens or the park with Cairns Trans Buses or the Red Explorer from the Lake St Transit Centre.

The **Tank Arts Centre**, which is at 46 Collins Ave, Edge Hill, just north of the Botanic Gardens, is one of Cairns' most interesting art spaces. These circular cement and iron WW II naval supply tanks were recently transformed into an exhibition and function centre, and they now host a variety of art exhibitions throughout the year. Ring the centre on ☎ (070) 32 2349 to see what's currently on. Future plans for the centre include artists' workshops, a dance studio and a recording studio.

Also in Edge Hill, the **Royal Flying Doctor Service** regional office, at 1 Junction St, is open to visitors daily from 9 am to 4.30 pm; entry is $5. You'll find out all about the service and its origins, and there are pedal radios and other items on display.

The **Cairns Library**, at 117 Lake St, has a good range of books, magazines, local and overseas newspapers, and music tapes and CDs. It is open on weekdays from 10 am to 7 pm (6 pm Monday) and on Saturday from 10 am to 4 pm.

Heading out of Cairns, towards the airport, you'll find an interesting and informative elevated **mangrove boardwalk** off Airport Ave, a couple of hundred metres before you reach the airport. There are explanatory signs at regular intervals, and these give some insight into the surprising ecological complexities of swamp vegetation. There's also a small observation platform.

Kamerunga Rd, off the Cook Hwy just north of the airport turn off, leads inland to **Freshwater Connection**, which is a railway museum complex where you can also catch the Kuranda Scenic Railway. It's 10 km from the centre of town. Just beyond Freshwater is the turn off south along Redlynch Intake Rd to **Crystal Cascades**, a popular outing with waterfalls and swimming holes 22 km from Cairns.

ACTIVITIES

There is a huge range of activities on offer in Cairns. Bookings can be made through your accommodation or one of the booking agencies here – see the Information section earlier.

Dive Courses

Cairns is the scuba-diving capital of the Barrier Reef and the reef is closer to the coast here than it is further south. The competition is cutthroat – and the company offering the cheapest deal one week may be old news the next.

Most people look for a course which takes them to the outer Barrier Reef rather than the reefs around Green or Fitzroy islands. Some places give you more time on the reef than others – but you may prefer an extra day in the pool and classroom before venturing out. A chat with people who have already done a course can tell you some of the pros and cons. A good teacher can make all the difference to your confidence and the amount of fun you have. Another factor is how big the groups are – the smaller the better if you want personal attention.

Two schools with good reputations are Deep Sea Divers Den (☎ (070) 31 2223), at 319 Draper St, and Pro-Dive (☎ (070) 31 5255), with shops at 116 Spence St and at Marlin Jetty. But that's not to dismiss the others, which include: Down Under Dive (☎ (070) 31 1288), at 155 Sheridan St; Peter Tibbs Dive Shop (☎ (070) 51 2604), at 370 Sheridan St; and Cairns Dive Centre (☎ (070) 51 0294), at 135 Abbott St. Most of these places can be booked through the hostels.

If you want to learn about the reef before you dive, an entertaining and educational lecture is given at the Cairns Library, at 117 Lake St, every night (except Sunday) from 6.15 to 8.30 pm. The cost is $10 – for more details ring Reef Teach (☎ (070) 51 6882).

Prices differ quite a bit between schools but usually one or other of them has a discount going. Expect to pay from $350 to $450 for the standard five-day course, with two days in the pool and classroom, one day

White-water rafting on the Tully River – take a ticket and join the queue

trip to the reef and back, and two more days on the reef with an overnight stay on board. There are cheaper short courses, but the longer courses give you more pleasure dives and a chance to reward yourself for all the work it takes to get certified, which makes sense if you have the time.

White-Water Rafting & Canoeing

Three of the rivers flowing down from the Atherton Tableland make for excellent white-water rafting. Most popular is a day in the rainforested gorges of the Tully River, 150 km south of Cairns. So many people do this trip that there can be 20 or more craft on the river at once, meaning you may have to queue up to shoot each section of rapids – yet despite this, most people are exhilarated at the end of the day. The Tully day trips leave daily year-round. Two companies running them from Cairns are Raging Thunder (☎ (070) 31 1466), at 111 Spence St, and R 'n' R (☎ (070) 51 7777 or ☎ 1800 079 039 toll free), at 74 Abbott St. Day trips on the

Tully cost around $120 from Cairns. There are cheaper half-day trips on the Barron River ($65), not far inland from Cairns, or you can make two-day ($360) or five-day ($750) expeditions on the remote North Johnstone River which rises near Malanda and enters the sea at Innisfail.

Foaming Fury (☎ (070) 32 1460), at 13 Moody St, offers white-water rafting for $99 on the Russell River, south of Bellenden Ker National Park, half-day trips on the Barron River for $64 and two-day trips on the North Johnstone River for $220.

Peregrine Adventures (☎ (07) 3854 1021), in Brisbane, offers more sedate and pleasant canoe trips along the Mulgrave River, costing $80 for a day trip.

Sea-Kayaking

Raging Thunder and R 'n' R also offer a range of sea-kayaking expeditions from Cairns. R 'n' R runs a day trip from Palm Cove, just north of Cairns to Double Island for $85.

Foaming Fury (☎ (070) 32 1460) has a

unique sea-kayak trip from Cairns across Trinity Bay and around the coast to the Aboriginal community at Yarrabah, where you can visit their heritage museum and buy local crafts. The day trip costs $85.

Beaches & Swimming
Cairns doesn't have a beach of its own – Trinity Bay is quite shallow and muddy. If you want to go swimming you'll have to head out to the islands, or up to the Northern Beaches – see the later Cairns to Port Douglas section.

Alternatively, you could head for one of the swimming pools in town. The Tobruk Memorial Swimming Pool, on Sheridan St, is an excellent 50-metre swimming pool and is open at 5.30 am on weekdays and 6 am on weekends. From Easter to October it closes every night at 6 pm; over summer it closes at 9 pm from Monday to Thursday and on Saturday, at 7 pm on Friday and 6 pm on Sunday.

Horse Riding
There are plenty of options if you want to go horse riding around Cairns. Check with the information centres for full details.

Some of the possibilities include Brumby Bob's (☎ (070) 59 1730), at Palm Cove, north of Cairns, who has two-hour beach rides for $50, half-day rides for $80 and full-day rides for $100. Mulgrave River Horse Adventures (☎ (070) 56 3000) has half-day trail rides in the mountains about 30 km south of Cairns for $55. And Springmount Station (☎ (070) 93 4493), 110 km south-west of Cairns on the edge of the Tableland, has a half-day ride for $50 or a full-day ride for $70. All of these prices include pick-ups from Cairns.

Scenic Flights & Helicopters
The following flights all operate from the general aviation section of the Cairns Airport: Reef Air Tours (☎ (070) 35 9530) has good joy flights and tours of the Barrier Reef, ranging from $45 for a half-hour buzz to $175 for a three-hour tour. Air Cairns (☎ (070) 35 9003) will fly you along the coast to Palm Cove and out over the reef to Upolo Cay for $90.

The self-explanatory Cairns Tiger Moth Flights (☎ (070) 35 9400) has four different flight options in a WW II-veteran plane, ranging from $70 to $350.

Helijet (☎ (070) 35 9300) and Jayrow (☎ (070) 31 4214) both do helicopter flights ranging from $80 for a short spin to $300 for a day trip out to the reef.

Other Activities
There are two A J Hackett (☎ (070) 31 1119) bungy jumping sites near Cairns. The closest is 15 km north on the Cook Hwy, just past the Kuranda turn off, where for $89 you can take the plunge from a steel tower with sensational views. A courtesy bus does pick-ups from hostels. There's another within the markets at Kuranda – see the Atherton Tableland section.

Airplay (☎ (070) 51 1340) is a hang-gliding school and you can do a four-day course for $395 or try a one-day sample for $65 ($89 with transport provided). Airplay operates from Ellis Beach, north of Cairns, or in the Tableland – depending on wind conditions.

There's an indoor go-kart track on the Captain Cook Hwy near the airport. It costs $7 to get your licence, then $15 for 10 minutes on the fast track.

The Cairns Tennis Club, on the corner of the Esplanade and Upward St, has four floodlit courts for hire to the public. They can supply balls and racquets.

ORGANISED TOURS
As you'd expect, there are hundreds of tours available from Cairns. Some are specially aimed at backpackers and many of these are pretty good value. You can make bookings through your accommodation or at travel agencies which specialise in this type of trip – see the Information section earlier.

Cairns
Half-day trips around the city sights, or two-hour cruises from Marlin Jetty up along

FAR NTH QUEENSLAND

Trinity Inlet and around Admiralty Island, cost from $20.

Atherton Tableland

Day trips to the Atherton Tableland with the 'conventional' tour companies, which usually include the waterfalls and lakes circuit and a trip on the Kuranda Scenic Railway to the Kuranda markets, will cost anywhere from $60 to $80. The smaller companies which specialise in tours for backpackers, such as Jungle Tours (☎ (070) 32 2111) and KTC Connections (☎ (070) 50 0663), offer similar but much more enjoyable trips for $45 to $50. Again, tours can be booked through your accommodation or one of the booking agencies.

The *On the Wallaby* hostel in Yungaburra offers an overnight trip to the Tableland for $35 including meals and activities – see Yungaburra in the Atherton Tableland section later in this chapter for details.

Daintree & Cape Tribulation

Cape Trib is one of the most popular day-trip destinations from Cairns, and there are literally dozens of different companies offering trips up here. Don't be fooled by those '4WD adventure' brochures – the tour companies do all use 4WD vehicles, but almost the whole of the route to Cape Trib is now over sealed roads, and with the daily flood of tourists making this trip, the adventure has gone out of it a little. Most day trips range from $75 to $100.

Cape Trib is still a beautiful area to visit, and while the day trips can be worthwhile, you'd be better off taking one of the overnight or longer packages. Two of the most popular companies with backpackers are Jungle Tours (☎ (070) 32 2111) and KTC Connections (☎ (070) 50 0663), and you'll pay around $74 for two days, $86 for three days or $110 for five days, which includes visits to Mossman Gorge and the Daintree River, and accommodation at Crocodylus Village and/or PK's Jungle Village.

Jungle Tours also has a popular two-day rainforest trek, where you camp out in the rainforest overnight. The trek costs $158, which includes all meals, camping and sleeping gear and your own guide.

Mountain Bike Adventures (☎ (070) 51 8311) has mountain bike tours around Port Douglas, Daintree and Cape Trib. Half-day trips cost $49, full-days $85.

Cooktown

Strikie's Safaris (☎ (070) 99 5599) runs a good 4WD day trip to Cooktown from Cairns & Port Douglas, visiting places like Black Mountain and the Lion's Den Hotel along the way. Day trips depart from Cairns every Monday, Wednesday and Friday; costs are $74 for adults, $45 for kids. Strikie's also runs a two-day trip every Wednesday, Friday and Sunday which costs $199 (not including meals or accommodation).

Wet Tropics Safaris (☎ (070) 50 0673) also has a two-day trip to Cooktown, going up via the coast road and back via the inland route. Their trip departs every Friday and costs $175, which includes a Daintree River cruise (but not meals or accommodation).

Wild Trek Adventure Safaris (☎ (070) 55 2247) offers a similar two-day trip for $199. They also have one-day trips where you fly up and drive back, or vice versa, which cost $229 via the coastal road or $179 via the inland road.

If you'd rather fly both ways, Hinterland Aviation (☎ (070) 35 9323) and Aussie Airways (☎ (070) 53 3980) both offer a one-day Cooktown Heritage Tour from Cairns which costs $185 – you need a minimum of four people.

Barrier Reef & Islands

There are dozens of options available for day trips to the reef. It's worth asking a few questions before you book, such as how many passengers the boat takes, what's included in the price and how much the 'extras' (such as wetsuit hire and introductory dives) cost, and exactly where the boat is going. Some companies have a dubious definition of 'outer reef'; as a general rule, the further out you go, the better the diving.

Great Adventures (☎ (070) 51 0455) is the major operator. They have the biggest boats and a wide range of trips, and it's worth picking up one of their brochures to see what's on offer. Apart from their trips to Green and Fitzroy islands (see the Islands off Cairns section for details), they have various combination trips including a nine-hour, $120 outer reef trip which includes a two-hour stop on Green Island. You get three hours on the reef itself, lunch, snorkelling gear, and a semisubmersible and glass bottomed boat ride thrown in. Great Adventures also does a nine-hour cruise to Fitzroy Island and Moore Reef for $85 with free use of snorkelling gear. Great Adventures has its own wharf on Trinity Inlet near the Transit Centre.

The MV *Seastar. II* (☎ (070) 31 2336), *Compass* (☎ (070) 32 0888) and Noah's Ark Cruises (☎ (070) 35 4054) all offer day trips to Hastings Reef and Michaelmas Cay for $40 to $45, including boom netting, snorkelling gear and lunch. Certified divers can take two dives for an extra $40.

Ocean Free (☎ (070) 31 6601), *Falla* (☎ (070) 31 3488), the *Golden Plover* (☎ (070) 31 3513) and *Passions of Paradise* (☎ (070) 31 6465) are all ocean-going yachts which 'sail' out to Upolo Cay, Green Island and Paradise Reef daily for around $45, which again includes lunch and snorkelling gear.

The majority of cruise boats depart from Trinity Wharf, Marlin Jetty or the Pier Marina in Trinity Inlet – check with the agent when you book.

There are many, many other boats and operators, so shop around. See the Islands off Cairns section for details of trips to Green, Fitzroy and the Frankland islands.

Diving Trips
Apart from the popular day trips to Hastings, Moore and Norman reefs and Michaelmas Cay, there are also quite a few operators offering longer trips for certified divers who want to dive on the outer Barrier Reef. They include the following: *Nimrod III* (☎ (070) 31 5566), which has trips to Ribbon Reef and the famous Cod Hole from $800 per person for four days and $1550 per person for seven days; the *Rum Runner* (☎ (070) 32 1699),

with seven-day trips out to Holmes and Flinders Reefs, with a dive to the *SS Yongala* wreck near Townsville, from $1600; and *Taka II* (☎ (070) 51 8722), which has four-day trips to the Coral Sea *or* the Cod Hole from $650 and seven-day trips to the Coral Sea *and* the Cod Hole from $1300.

Cruises
There are several cruise ships which run trips out of Cairns. The *Reef Escape* (☎ (070) 31 4433) does two different trips: their four-night James Cook Cruise follows Cook's route north of Cairns to Cooktown and Lizard Island; and their three-night Joseph Banks Cruise heads south to Hinchinbrook and Dunk islands, then back up to Cairns via Fitzroy Island. Three nights aboard starts from $875, the four-night cruise starts from $1165, or you can combine the two and do seven nights from $1835.

The *Coral Princess* (☎ (070) 31 1041) does four-day cruises between Cairns and Townsville, via Hinchinbrook, Dunk, Pelorus and Orpheus islands and Sudbury Reef. You can board at either end, and the four days starts from $922 per person, including all meals and activities except diving.

There are also several cruise ships which leave from Cairns for the Cape York Peninsula – see the Organised Tours section at the start of that chapter for details.

Tours to Townsville
There are a couple of companies that run two and three-day tours between Cairns and Townsville, with stops at various places of interest along the way. See Organised Tours in the Townsville section of the North Coast chapter.

Chillagoe & Mt Mulligan
Chillagoe is a fascinating place to get to and to visit, and there are a couple of companies offering tours out of Cairns, or you can make your own way there.

New Look Adventures (☎ (070) 31 7622) has day trips from Cairns to Chillagoe every day except Sunday. The cost is $89 for adults and $45 for children, which includes lunch, museum entry and a national parks tour.

Jungle Tours (☎ (070) 32 2111) has six-day guided walking expeditions to the Chillagoe area, following the path of the 1848 Edmund Kennedy expedition through the Walsh River gorges. Trips leave from Cairns on Monday and cost $588 per person, which includes meals and camping equipment. Ring them to find out when the next trip departs. There are also several off-the-beaten-track tours to a couple of cattle stations around Mt Mulligan – see Mareeba to Chillagoe in the Atherton Tableland section for details of these.

Gulf Savannah & Undara Lava Tubes

Several companies run tours to various places in the Gulf Savannah, including the Undara Lava Tubes, the Tallaroo Hot Springs, and Karumba. You can also link up with the *Gulflander* and the *Savannah-lander*.

Australian Pacific (☎ 13 1304) has day trips from Cairns to Undara on Tuesday, Thursday and Saturday costing $92 per person; and Ventry's Coaches (☎ (070) 320 300) has similar tours on Monday, Wednesday, Friday and Sunday costing $105.

Undara Experience (☎ (070) 31 7933) has two-day bus tours from Cairns to Undara. The cost is $28 per person staying in the lodge, or $188 per person staying in the semi-permanent tents, and includes transport, all meals and tours of the lava tubes. For an additional fee, you can fly one leg of the trip – ring for details.

Cape York

For something completely different, Cape York Air Services (☎ (070) 35 9399), the local mail contractor, does mail runs to remote outback stations on weekdays. Space permitting, you can go along on these runs, but it's not cheap at $140 to $275, depending on the length of the trip. Flights depart from the Cairns Airport.

See the Cape York chapter for details of other organised tours from Cairns to Cape York.

FESTIVALS

Cairns' major annual festival is Fun in the Sun, held for a week in the second week of October. The festival includes live entertainment, an amusement park, a Mardi Gras and parade.

Jazz in June is a two-day jazz festival which attracts jazz musos from around the country, and includes jam sessions, open-air concerts and a gala ball.

Cairns Amateur Race Weekend, dubbed the Melbourne Cup of the Far North, is held in early September.

PLACES TO STAY

As you would expect, Cairns has a wide range of tourist accommodation catering for everybody from budget-conscious backpackers to deep-pocketed package tourists. The city still attracts huge numbers of backpackers, and there are plenty of hostels and guesthouses to choose between. There are also a couple of caravan parks in town, although none very close to the centre. The next level up are the motels and holiday apartments, and at the top of the price scale there are a few five-star hotels and resorts for those with cash to splash.

The accommodation business is extremely competitive here and prices go up and down with the seasons. Lower weekly rates are par for the course. Prices given here for the more expensive places can rise 30% or 40% in the peak season, and some of the hostels will charge $1 or $2 less in the quiet times.

Camping

There are about a dozen caravan parks in and around Cairns, though none really central. Almost without exception they take campers as well as caravans. The closest to the centre is the *City Caravan Park* (☎ (070) 51 1467), about two km north-west of the city centre on the corner of Little & James Sts. It's quite well set up, with plenty of shady trees, a sheltered barbecue area and tent sites from $12 a double, and on-site vans for $30.

The *Sunland Van Park* (☎ (070) 53 2901) is the next closest option, two km farther

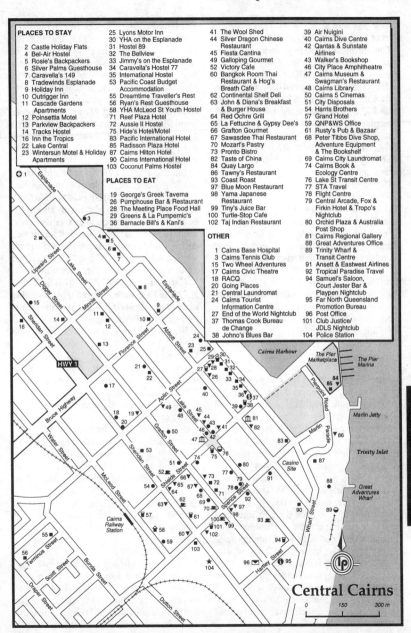

PLACES TO STAY

2 Castle Holiday Flats
4 Bel-Air Hostel
5 Rosie's Backpackers
6 Silver Palms Guesthouse
7 Caravella's 149
8 Tradewinds Esplanade
9 Holiday Inn
10 Outrigger Inn
11 Cascade Gardens Apartments
12 Poinsettia Motel
13 Parkview Backpackers
14 Tracks Hostel
16 Inn the Tropics
22 Lake Central
23 Wintersun Motel & Holiday Apartments
25 Lyons Motor Inn
30 YHA on the Esplanade
31 Hostel 89
32 The Bellview
33 Jimmy's on the Esplanade
34 Caravella's Hostel 77
35 International Hostel
53 Pacific Coast Budget Accommodation
55 Dreamtime Traveller's Rest
57 Ryan's Rest Guesthouse
58 YHA McLeod St Youth Hostel
71 Reef Plaza Hotel
72 Aussie II Hostel
85 Hide's Hotel/Motel
83 Pacific International Hotel
85 Radisson Plaza Hotel
87 Cairns Hilton Hotel
90 Cairns International Hotel
103 Coconut Palms Hostel

PLACES TO EAT

19 George's Greek Taverna
26 Pumphouse Bar & Restaurant
28 The Meeting Place Food Hall
29 Greens & La Pumpernic's
36 Barnacle Bill's & Kani's
41 The Wool Shed
44 Silver Dragon Chinese Restaurant
45 Fiesta Cantina
49 Galloping Gourmet
52 Victory Cafe
60 Bangkok Room Thai Restaurant & Hog's Breath Cafe
62 Continental Shelf Deli
63 John & Diana's Breakfast & Burger House
64 Red Ochre Grill
65 La Fettucine & Gypsy Dee's
66 Grafton Gourmet
67 Sawasdee Thai Restaurant
72 Mozart's Pastry
73 Pronto Bistro
82 Taste of China
84 Quay Largo
86 Tawny's Restaurant
93 Coast Roast
97 Blue Moon Restaurant
98 Yama Japanese Restaurant
99 Tiny's Juice Bar
100 Turtle-Stop Cafe
102 Taj Indian Restaurant

OTHER

1 Cairns Base Hospital
3 Cairns Tennis Club
15 Two Wheel Adventures
17 Cairns Civic Theatre
18 RACQ
20 Going Places
21 Central Laundromat
24 Cairns Tourist Information Centre
27 End of the World Nightclub
37 Thomas Cook Bureau de Change
38 Johno's Blues Bar
39 Air Nuigini
40 Cairns Dive Centre
42 Qantas & Sunstate Airlines
43 Walker's Bookshop
46 City Place Amphitheatre
47 Cairns Museum & Swagman's Restaurant
48 Cairns Library
50 Cairns 5 Cinemas
54 City Disposals
54 Harris Brothers
57 Grand Hotel
59 QNP&WS Office
61 Rusty's Pub & Bazaar
68 Peter Tibbs Dive Shop, Adventure Equipment & The Bookshelf
69 Cairns City Laundromat
74 Cairns Book & Ecology Centre
76 Lake St Transit Centre
77 STA Travel
78 Flight Centre
79 Central Arcade, Fox & Firkin Hotel & Tropo's Nightclub
80 Orchid Plaza & Australia Post Shop
81 Cairns Regional Gallery
88 Great Adventures Office
89 Trinity Wharf & Transit Centre
91 Ansett & Eastwest Airlines
92 Tropical Paradise Travel
94 Samuel's Saloon, Court Jester Bar & Playpen Nightclub
95 Far North Queensland Promotion Bureau
96 Post Office
101 Club Justice/ JDLS Nightclub
104 Police Station

Central Cairns

0   150   300 m

FAR NTH QUEENSLAND

west at 49 Pease St, Manoora. They have tent sites at $12 and on-site cabins from $28.

Out on the Bruce Hwy, about eight km south of the centre, is the *Cairns Coconut Caravan Village* (☎ (070) 54 6644), a huge and modern caravaning and camping village with camp sites from $14, on-site cabins from $32 and self-contained units from $45. This place is almost as big as Cairns itself! Also on the Bruce Hwy is the more low-key *Woree Caravan Park* (☎ (070) 54 1305), at No 664, with tent sites from $10 and on-site cabins and units from $30.

If you want to camp by the beach, the nearest option is at Yorkeys Knob, about 20 km north from the centre of Cairns. A little farther north, Ellis Beach and Palm Cove also have very good beachfront camping grounds – see the Cairns to Port Douglas section for details of all of these.

Hostels

The Cairns hostel scene is constantly changing as new places open up, old ones change hands and others rise and fall in quality and popularity. The type of accommodation is pretty standard – fan-cooled bunk rooms with shared kitchen and bathroom, and usually sitting areas, laundry facilities and a swimming pool. Cairns has had a reputation for fairly dodgy accommodation, but recent changes in council regulations and increased competition has forced many places to decrease the number of beds in dorms and upgrade their facilities. Unfortunately, you still have to beware of theft in some places – use lock-up rooms and safes if they're available.

The Esplanade has the greatest concentration of hostels, and is a lively place. The hostels here tend to pack them in, and have very little outside space – any outdoor area is usually cramped with a swimming pool. On the plus side, these hostels are ideally located. The hostels away from the centre offer much more breathing space and are generally quieter, and the inconvenience of being out of the centre is minimal as there are courtesy buses which make regular runs into town.

Esplanade When I was researching this book, I heard plenty of 'rumours' that this section of the Esplanade was about to be redeveloped in a big way, meaning demolition of some buildings to make way for high-rises. Actually, I heard the same rumours the previous year and nothing had changed in the ensuing 12 months, but it does seem likely that by the time you read this a couple of the places mentioned here will have disappeared, or at least changed substantially.

Starting from the corner of Shields St and heading along the Esplanade, the *International Hostel* (☎ (070) 31 1424), at No 67, is a big old multi-level place with about 200 beds. The accommodation is fairly basic, with fan-cooled four, six and eight-bed dorms for $12 or twin rooms for $28. There are also doubles from $28 to $32, with either air-con and TV or a private bathroom.

Caravella's Hostel 77 (☎ (070) 51 2159), at 77 The Esplanade, is another big rambling place with about 160 beds. It's one of the longest established Cairns hostels and has old-fashioned but clean rooms, most with air-con. The cost in the dorms ranges from $11 to $14, depending on the size of the rooms and whether you have your own bathroom, and doubles range from $28 to $30, or $36 with private bathroom.

Jimmy's on the Esplanade (☎ (070) 31 6884), at No 83, is a recently renovated place with 46 beds. The dorms have two bedrooms, each with four beds, plus their own bathroom and a fridge, and there's a new pool and kitchen. There are also double rooms with shared bathrooms for $32 to $36, or with ensuites for $45. The front rooms have sea views and are popular, and all rooms have air-con. This place has the same owners as Hostel 89, and seems to be very popular with young Japanese travellers.

The *Bellview* (☎ (070) 31 4377), at No 85, is a good, quiet hostel with clean and comfortable four-bed dorms at $14 per person, singles at $27 and twin rooms at $32, and all rooms are air-conditioned. There are also motel-style units from $45 to $55, depending on the size of the room. The kitchen facilities are good, and there's a small pool, a laundry and an excellent breakfast cafe with continental breakfasts for $5.50. This place has good security, but as one LP staff member found out the hard way, they won't let you stay here without photo ID.

Hostel 89 (☎ (070) 31 7477 or ☎ 008 061 712 toll free), at No 89, is one of the best kept hostels on the Esplanade. It's a smallish and helpful place, with twin and double rooms and a few three or four-bed dorms, all air-conditioned. Nightly costs are from $15 per person, with singles/doubles at $25/32. Security is good, with a locked grille at the street entrance.

At No 93 is *YHA on the Esplanade* (☎ (070) 31 1919). There are two blocks, one with spacious, airy five-bed dorms with their own bathroom, the other with small twins and doubles. All the dorms have air-con. Dorm beds cost $14 and doubles $32, and non-members pay an extra $2.

Three blocks further along the Esplanade there's another cluster of backpackers' hostels. At No 149 is another bigger hostel, the 150-bed *Caravella's 149* (☎ (070) 31 5680). Its popularity means that even the big cooking/sitting/TV/pool/games area at the back can get pretty busy. You pay $12 in a 14-bunk dorm, $13 in a four-bunk room, and $14 in a six-bunk dorm with air-con and a bathroom. Doubles and twins cost $26, or $28 with air-con.

Rosie's Backpackers (☎ (070) 51 0235), at No 155, has several buildings with either spacious dorms in the main building or eight-bunk flats out the back at $12 per person. There are also three doubles at $30. This place is helpful, well-run and has a small pool, and they have a barbecue every second Wednesday.

Next door, at No 157, the YHA-associate *Bel-Air Hostel* (☎ (070) 31 4790) is a recently renovated two-storey Queenslander, with doubles and twins downstairs for $30, four-bunk dorms for $15 and seven-bunk dorms for $14. There's also a huge 'honeymoon suite' for $35. All rooms have air-con, and there's a spa, kiosk and pool table here.

Around Town Close to the centre, *Parkview Backpackers* (☎ (070) 51 3700) is at 174 Grafton St, three blocks back from the Esplanade. This is a very laid-back place where you can relax by the pool and listen to reggae music. It's one of the friendliest and most sociable hostels in town. It's in a rambling old timber building with a large tropical garden. Four to eight-bed dorms cost $12 per person, and twin rooms cost $26.

Tracks Hostel (☎ (070) 31 1474), on the corner of Grafton and Minnie Sts, spans three old timber houses and has a number of kitchens and plenty of other facilities. Costs are $10 per person in four-bed dorms or twin rooms, or $24 a double, and you get a voucher for a free evening meal at one of the nightclubs.

At 72 Grafton St, the *Aussie II Hostel* (☎ (070) 51 7620) is a bit of a crash pad, with space for about 60 people. It's cheap, though – dorm beds are $10 and doubles are $25. The hostel has two kitchens and a TV room. There's no pool but you can use the pools at the two Caravella hostels.

Opposite the railway station, the YHA *McLeod St Youth Hostel* (☎ (070) 51 0772), at 20-24 McLeod St, has dorm beds for $13 and singles/doubles for $22/32. Nonmembers pay $2 extra. The facilities are good and the hostel has car parking spaces.

On the corner of Spence and Sheridan Sts, the *Coconut Palms Hostel* (☎ (070) 51 6946) has dorm beds for $10, twin rooms at $22 and doubles at $24. It's a clean, simple place in an old timber house, with a nice garden and a pool.

Two blocks west of the railway station, at 274 Draper St, *Gone Walkabout Hostel* (☎ (070) 51 6160) is one of the best in Cairns. It's small, simple and well-run with a friendly atmosphere. Rooms are mostly twins and doubles, with a few four-bed dorms, and there's a tiny pool. You pay $10 in a dorm, $22 for a twin room and $24 for a double. It's not a place for late partying however.

The *Up-Top Down Under Holiday Lodge* (☎ (070) 51 3636), at 164-170 Spence St, is a spacious backpackers' complex 1.5 km from the town centre. Facilities include a well-equipped kitchen, two TV lounges and a pool. Cooked meals are available, and there is entertainment most nights including a free barbecue every Sunday night when the guitar-playing, singing Englishman who owns the place hits the stage. Dorm beds are $12 and there are good single/double rooms for $25/30, all with shared bathrooms.

A recent addition to Cairns' backpacker scene is the *U2 Hostel* (☎ (070) 31 4077), at 77 McLeod St. It's a two-storey Queenslander divided into five flats, with a pool and a communal kitchen and lounge. It's clean and basic, although most of the rooms are internal and windowless. Dorm beds cost $12, singles/doubles are $26/28.

JJ's Backpackers (☎ (070) 51 7642), at 11 Charles St, is a small block of apartments converted into a hostel. There are dorm beds for $10 and doubles for $28, and there's a small pool, a pool table and a TV room here.

Captain Cook Backpackers Hostel (☎ (070) 51 6811), at 204 Sheridan St, is a huge and somewhat shabby place with over 300 beds in two sections. It's a converted old motel, with dorm beds for $10 and doubles for $28 in the backpackers' section, and motel units for $30 unserviced or $35 serviced in the motel section. The facilities include two pools, a bar, and a restaurant with free evening meals for those in the backpackers' section. You can't miss this place – there's a giant statue of Captain Cook out the front.

At 207 Sheridan St is *Castaways* (☎ (070) 51 1238), a quiet and smallish place with mostly double and twin rooms costing $30 or $34 with air-con. There are also five singles at $20, plus a few three-bed dorms at $13 per bed. All rooms are fan-cooled and have a fridge, and there's a communal kitchen, a pool, bikes for hire ($10 a day) and a courtesy bus. This place also has its own in-house travel agent.

Guesthouses

A couple of places in this bracket are in the hostel price range, the difference being that their emphasis is on rooms rather than dorms. There are also a couple of places that cater for people staying on a weekly basis, and these can work out to be very good value.

Dreamtime Travellers Rest (☎ (070) 31 6753), at 4 Terminus St, is a small guesthouse run by a friendly and enthusiastic young Irish/English couple. It's in a brightly renovated timber Queenslander and has a good pool, double rooms at $28 to $30 and three or four-bed (no bunks) rooms at $12 per person. Another good guesthouse with a similar set-up is *Ryan's Rest* (☎ (070) 51 4734), down the road at 18 Terminus St. It's a cosy and quiet family-run place with three very cosy double rooms upstairs at $30, and two self-contained flats downstairs with twins/doubles at $25 and a four-bed dorm at $12.50 per person. Cooked and tropical breakfasts are available for $4 and $5.

The *Floriana Guesthouse* (☎ (070) 51 7886), at 183 the Esplanade, is a 1920s-era guesthouse with two sections. The reception foyer reminds me of my grandmother's house, with its dark plywood, deco furniture and memorabilia. There are four self-contained units above the reception area, all clean and simple, with polished timber floors, ceiling fans, TVs, ensuites and kitchenettes. These sleep up to four and cost $50 to $60 a night. There is also one double room with an ensuite for $45. In the old building next door, there are 24 simple rooms, with a communal laundry, kitchen, pool and TV lounge. The upstairs rooms with ocean views are great value at $45, and the rest of the rooms go for $28 a single or from $35 for doubles.

At 8 McKenzie St, *Charleston House* (☎ (070) 51 6317) is an old Queenslander renovated in deco style. It's generally for people staying weekly, although they also take overnighters. There are eight rooms with two or three beds in each, with singles/doubles/triples costing $125/150/225 a week; two self-contained flats which sleep four and cost $225 per flat per week; and a unit out the back with two doubles for $110 per week. The communal lounge and living areas are very comfortable, and there's a spa, kitchens and laundry, and a decking area out the back where a country music band practises and country dancing is taught on Tuesday nights.

The *Happy House* (☎ (070) 31 5898), at 25 Maranoa St in Parramatta Park, is an old Queenslander that has been restored with tender loving care, and a bit of artistic flair. It's a bright, cheerful place divided up into seven one to three-bedroom flats, each with its own kitchen, bathroom and living area. There's a spa, laundry and barbecue area out the back. The weekly rate is $65 per person downstairs or $70 upstairs, there's a two-week minimum stay and you *must* be working or studying to stay here.

At 153 the Esplanade, the *Silver Palms Guesthouse* (☎ (070) 31 6099) is a clean, quiet little place with singles/doubles from $29.50/34.50 with shared bathrooms, or $39.50 with an ensuite. There's also a self-contained six-bed flat here with a kitchen and lounge room, which costs $55 a double or $85 for four people. Guests here have use of a kitchen, laundry, pool and TV room.

At 100 Sheridan St is *Pacific Coast Budget Accommodation* (☎ (070) 51 1264), an old guesthouse with basic rooms with shared bathrooms from $29/39 for singles/doubles.

Motels

The popular *Inn The Tropics* (☎ (070) 31 1088), at 141 Sheridan St, is a relatively new place with a good pool, a small guests' kitchen and an open-air courtyard with tables. Clean and modern motel-style rooms with shared bathrooms cost $32/38 for singles/doubles, or $45/48 with an ensuite. The air-conditioning is coin-operated.

The *Poinsettia Motel* (☎ (070) 51 2144), at 169 Lake St, is one of the cheapest central motels, and has clean budget rooms at $42/46.

The *Wintersun Motel & Holiday Apartments* (☎ (070) 51 2933) are centrally located at 84 Abbott St, and you have a choice of standard motel units with immaculate '60s décor or rooms with a kitchenette. The rooms have air-con and TVs and cost $45/50 plus $5 for extra people.

The high-rise *Lyons Motor Inn* (☎ (070) 51 2311), on the corner of the Esplanade and Aplin Sts, is also in the thick of things, and has budget rooms from $50/60 or rooms with a view from $82/97.

Hides Hotel/Motel (☎ (070) 51 1266), a big pub in the heart of town on the corner of Lake and Shields Sts, has old pub-style rooms with shared bathrooms from $45 and motel-style units from $80.

Top of the motel range would have to be the *Outrigger Inn* (☎ (070) 51 6188), on the corner of Abbott and Florence Sts, where rooms go for $118/136 for singles/doubles.

Holiday Flats & Apartments

Holiday flats are well worth considering, especially for a group of three or four people who are staying a few days or more. Expect pools, air-con, cooking and laundry facilities in this category. Holiday flats generally supply all bedding, cooking utensils, etc.

At 209 Lake St, the *Castle Holiday Flats* (☎ (070) 31 2229) is an oldish red-brick place with clean, well-kept flats and units. There are one-bedroom flats from $45, two-bedroom flats that sleep up to four and cost $60, and singles/doubles with shared bathroom and kitchen facilities for $25/30. There's a small pool.

The *Costa Blanca Apartments* (☎ (070) 51 3114), at 241 the Esplanade, is one of the few affordable places along the waterfront. There are seven one-bedroom units, plus one two-bedroom unit, and rates range from $45 to $80 a double plus $5 per extra person. They aren't flashy, but they're all clean and comfortable and sleep four people, and have kitchens and ceiling fans. The upstairs units have good views, and there's a guest laundry and a big old pool here.

Lake Central (☎ (070) 51 4933), at 137 Lake St, is a modern complex of motel-style units around a central courtyard. All the rooms have air-con, ensuites and kitchenettes, and doubles range from $80 to $92 depending on the season. The family units sleep up to five and cost from $95 to $130 a night.

At 175 Lake St, the *Cascade Gardens*

FAR NTH QUEENSLAND

Apartments (☎ (070) 51 8000) has a similar setup, with modern self-contained apartments with full kitchens. The studio apartments here range from $89 to $112; the one-bedroom apartments sleep up to four and range from $99 to $124 a double plus $10 for extra adults.

There's a string of motels and holiday units along Sheridan St, including the *Pacific Cay* (☎ (070) 51 0151), at No 193, with one-bedroom holiday units from $65 and two-bedrooms units from $85, and the *Concord Holiday Units* (☎ (070) 31 4522), at No 183, with one-bedroom units from $50 to $75.

181 The Esplanade (☎ (070) 52 6888), obviously at 181 the Esplanade, is a 10-storey complex of modern, up-market one, two and three-bedroom apartments which range from $165 to $220 a night – they're cheaper by the week.

Hotels

The *Pacific International Hotel* (☎ (070) 51 7888), on the corner of the Esplanade and Spence St, is one of Cairns' original hotels. It's a bit smaller and more laid-back than some of the newer places, and has 176 rooms starting from $195.

The *Holiday Inn* (☎ (070) 31 3757), on the corner of the Esplanade and Florence Sts, is a modern four-star hotel with rooms from $175, although it's worth paying another $20 for a room with ocean views. Nearby and similar is the *Tradewinds Esplanade* (☎ (070) 52 1111), at 157 the Esplanade, with rooms from $170 to $190 and suites from $230.

The *Reef Plaza Hotel* (☎ (070) 41 1022), on the corner of Grafton and Spence Sts, is a modern 3½-star hotel with 100 rooms from $145.

The most impressive of Cairns' five-star hotels is the *Cairns International Hotel* (☎ (070) 31 1300), at 17 Abbott St. It has a cavernous marble foyer and the rooms are tastefully furnished in tropical-style décor. Rooms range from $225 to $275, and suites from $420 to $1400.

The *Radisson Plaza Hotel* (☎ (070) 31 1411), in the Pier Marketplace complex, is another good five-star hotel with an interesting rainforest recreation in the foyer and 218 rooms ranging from $220 to $280, depending on the view. Suites range from $345 to $475.

The *Cairns Hilton Hotel* (☎ (070) 52 1599), beside Trinity Inlet, is another five-star with 265 rooms from $200 to $260 and suites from $750 to $1050.

PLACES TO EAT

Cairns is certainly well stocked with eateries of all types, and you shouldn't have too much trouble finding something to satisfy your particular gastronomic cravings. A lot of backpackers end up eating in bars and night-clubs, lured by free, or heavily discounted, meal vouchers which are handed out by the hostels.

The Esplanade, between Shields and Aplin Sts, is virtually wall-to-wall eateries, and you'll find Italian and Chinese food, seafood restaurants, burgers, kebabs, pizzas, seafood and ice cream – at all hours. Quite a few places take advantage of the climate by providing open-air dining.

The division of the places mentioned below into cafes, restaurants and whatever is fairly loose, and there are plenty of places that could have gone under several different headings. Most of the breakfast places also do lunches, some of the cafes and delis do breakfast, lunch and dinner etc, but after you've had a read through the next couple of pages, you'll at least have a pretty good idea of what's around.

Breakfast

Mozarts Pastry, on the corner of Grafton and Spence Sts, is a popular spot to browse through the morning papers over coffee and a pastry. The coffee is good, there are outdoor tables and they serve a range of pastries, cakes and sandwiches. The staff are friendly and most of them speak German, if that helps.

The *Galloping Gourmet*, a casual little place, on Aplin St near the Lake St corner, offers a cooked breakfast deal for $5. Over at 35 Sheridan St, *John & Diana's Breakfast & Burger House* is fairly down market, but offers virtually every combination of cooked breakfast imaginable for $5 or less.

Also on Sheridan St, near the Shields St corner, the *Continental Shelf* is an excellent gourmet deli which has a breakfast special of juice, coffee and a filled croissant for $5. They also have a great range of sandwiches, as well as pastas, pancakes and pastries.

Cafes & Delis

Greens, on Aplin St near the Esplanade corner, is a vegetarian and health-food takeaway, with salads, smoothies, juices and good tofu or lentil burgers for $3.95.

Tiny's Juice Bar, on Grafton St near the Spence St corner, is my favourite lunch spot in Cairns. They have a great range of freshly squeezed fruit and vegetable juices, milk and tofu smoothies as well as healthy filled rolls and lentil and tofu burgers at good prices. The *Turtle-Stop Cafe*, right next door on the corner of Grafton and Spence Sts, is a groovy if somewhat chaotic cafe which has filled focaccias, salads, sandwiches, juices and good coffee.

Speaking of good coffee, caffeine fiends should search out *Coast Roast*, a coffee house at the east end of Lake St. This place sells a wide range of coffee beans (smells great in there!), huge cups of coffee, sensational hand-made chocolates, and a selection of cakes, rolls, focaccias and filled croissants. It is open from 7 am until 11 pm; midnight on weekends.

At 105 Grafton St, *Grafton Gourmet* is a friendly little deli which makes great sandwiches, cakes and other delicacies. The coffee here is also good.

The *Victory Cafe*, at 62 Shields St, is a narrow and atmospheric BYO cafe with timber booths and decorated with pictures, drawings and nick-nacks from the 1920s to the 1950s. They play blues, jazz and soul music and serve food with vegetarian, seafood, Thai and Indian influences. Cooked breakfasts are around $6; lunches range from $8 to $14; and dinners range from $14 to $20.

Nightclubs, Bars & Pubs

Most of the hostels will supply you with vouchers for cheap meals at various nightclubs, pubs and bars around town, often with free or discounted drinks thrown in. *Samuel's Saloon*, near the corner of Hartley and Lake Sts, is one of the most popular places, with burgers, roasts, pastas and chillis from $4 to $6 – a voucher gets you a $2 discount and a free beer. They even have a bus that picks hungry travellers up from the hostels!

End of the World, a nightclub on the corner of Abbott and Aplin Sts, has very basic food, but it's cheap and a lot of people seem to eat here, again with hostel meal vouchers. Next door at 70 Abbott St, *The Pumphouse* is a popular backpackers' bar/restaurant with a good range of evening meals in the $4 to $7 range – steaks, pastas, chicken parmagiana etc. It is open from 5 pm to 2 am.

The *Wool Shed*, on Shields St in the mall, is another very popular backpackers' bar and restaurant. Their meals include pastas, stews, steaks, and schnitzels, and range from $5 to $15. On Sunday they have a $1 barbecue. It is open daily from 5 pm until 2 am.

The *Pier Tavern*, on the north-west side of the Pier Marketplace, is a popular pub with several bars and an outdoor decking area overlooking Trinity Bay and the Esplanade. Bistro meals in the Boatbar range from $6 to $10. The *Fox & Firkin Hotel*, an English-style tavern on the corner of Spence and Lake Sts, also has good bistro meals.

The *Cock & Bull*, on the corner of Digger and Grove Sts, is an excellent and *very* popular English-style tavern. The atmosphere at this place is lots of fun, and they have a good range of beer, a darts bar, friendly staff and even a snorkelling boar on the wall! The meals are of the hearty, stodgy English variety – roasts, curries, shepherd's pie, veal steaks – and all cost from $7 to $10. It's so authentically English that by the time you leave, you'll be wondering where you left your umbrella...

Restaurants & Food Halls

If you're doing a spot of shopping at the Pier Marketplace, there are plenty of eateries up on the 1st level. The *Food Court* offers a good choice, including Thai or Mongolian food, Chinese noodles, sushi, pizzas, gourmet sandwiches, seafood and fresh juices, to name but a few. Nearby is the *Beach Hut*, a seafood and Aussie-style buffet with all-you-can-eat deals – $6.45 for breakfast, $11.45 for lunch and $19.95 for dinner. Then there's *Johnny Rocket's*, a 1950s-American burger joint complete with red vinyl booths and personal juke boxes. Burgers start at $3.85, sandwiches at $2.95, and yep, you can finish off with a slice of good ol' apple pie ($1.95).

Also on the first level is *Donnini's* (☎ (070) 347 3128), which is a smart but casual licensed restaurant with some of the best Italian food in town; gourmet pizzas from $9 to $16, pastas from $12 to $16, salads and antipasto from $8.50 to $11.50 and Italian mains around $17. It is open daily for lunch and dinner.

Over on the east side of the Pier complex, next to the Radisson Hotel, *Quay Largo* is a trendy bar and eatery with a good outdoor decking area overlooking Trinity Inlet and the boat marina. It serves breakfasts, lunches and dinners, from burgers, salads, focaccias and pancakes to lamb fillet and pumpkin and ricotta ravioli. On Friday and Saturday nights the bar here is a popular watering hole, and stays open until 2 am.

Also overlooking Trinity Inlet, from between the Pier and the Hilton Hotel, is *Tawny's* (☎ (070) 51 1722), which has a reputation as Cairns' best seafood restaurant. It has an elegant dining area with full-length windows, is licensed and is open nightly and on Friday for lunch. Main courses like steamed mudcrab, barramundi and Cajun-style salmon range from $23 to $30.

There are two seafood restaurants side-by-side on the Esplanade, both open-fronted with tables spilling out onto the footpath: *Barnacle Bill's* is the more casual of the two, with most mains in the $20 to $24 range and kid's meals for $9. *Kanis* is a little more up-market, with mains from $23. Both places are licensed and open nightly for dinner. *La Pizza*, a tiny shopfront pizza joint near the Aplin St corner, has tasty pizzas and

is a great spot for a cappuccino – you can sit and watch the passing parade.

La Pumpernic's, on Aplin St, is a popular tourist restaurant with main meals in the $12 to $22 range, although they have an 'early-bird' special with three courses for $16.50 if you finish your meal by 7.30 pm.

The Meeting Place, on Aplin St near the Abbott St corner, is a good international foodhall with nine different stalls, and you can choose between Japanese, Thai, Chinese, Italian, and steak and seafood meals in the $7.50 to $14 range. My favourite place here is *Ichi-Ban Ramen*, which serves huge bowls of Japanese broth for under $10 – try the *gyoza* dumplings for an entrée. There's also a small bar in the complex.

Sawasdee (☎ (070) 31 7993), at 89 Grafton St, is a BYO Thai restaurant with lunch specials for $7.50 and dinner mains ranging from $11 to $16. It's a very friendly place with wonderfully fresh food – they only have half a dozen tables, so it's a good idea to book.

Across the road at 74 Grafton St is *Pronto* (☎ (070) 51 2407), a groovy little Italian bistro with hip music and friendly staff. Their pastas range from $10 to $12, other classic Italian mains are around $15 – and the coffee's great. Fellow Melburnians will feel very at home here – this place could easily have been transported straight out of Brunswick St or Chapel St. As the motto on the back of their card says, 'Life's a bistro, and then you dine'.

There are quite a few Japanese restaurants in Cairns. One of the best is *Yama*, on the corner of Spence and Grafton Sts. It's a fairly casual place and has a good range of lunch specials from $4 to $8. The dinner menu has mains for around $15, although when I ate there we ordered all entrées ($4 to $9) so we could try a bit of everything! Yama is licensed.

The *Blue Moon Restaurant*, at 45 Spence St, is a friendly little MSG-free Chinese and vegetarian restaurant, with main courses around $10 and seafood mains from $10 to $15. It's BYO and is open nightly for dinner.

Another popular Chinese restaurant is the more stylish *Taste of China*, at 36 Abbott St, which serves 'fresh, light and healthy' yum chas and dinners, with mains from $13 to $20. The *Silver Dragon*, a straightforward Chinese restaurant at 102 Lake St, has a great lunch deal whereby you get three courses for $4.90 – soup, a main and ice cream. It also opens nightly for dinner, with mains in the $10 to $14 range.

The *Bangkok Room Thai Restaurant*, at 62 Spence St, has a pleasant setting and friendly service, with tasty Thai dishes for around $12. Next door is the popular *Hog's Breath Cafe*, a saloon-style bar and grill. Lunch time offerings like burgers, sandwiches and salads will set you back $6 to $8, and in the evening main courses like prime ribs, grilled fish and steaks are in the $15 to $18 range. They also have a kid's menu at $6.

Across the road at 61 Spence St, the *Taj* serves pretty good Indian food with main meals around $13.

If you've always wanted to try emu pate or eucalyptus salmon, head for the *Red Ochre Grill*, at 43 Shields St. It's a bush-tucker restaurant which uses indigenous seeds, plants, leaves, flowers and animals in the cooking. The décor is very smart – ochre colours with raw timber and Aboriginal artwork. Main meals range from $15 to $20, (less at lunch time), and they have good mixed platters so you can try a bit of everything. They also have some great Australian wines available by the glass.

La Fettucine (☎ (070) 31 5959), at 43 Shields St, is a narrow and atmospheric little BYO place with excellent home-made pastas for $10.90 and Italian mains around $16. It is open nightly for dinner. Next door at No 41 is *Gypsy Dee's* (☎ (070) 51 5530), a dim and rather exotic place with a bar, a stage and live acoustic music every night. The menu is also fairly exotic – yellowfin tuna, sashimi, Thai curries, polenta lasagna – and mains range from $11 to $17. You'll probably need to book.

George's Greek Taverna, on the corner of Grafton and Aplin Sts, is a fairly up-market place with Greek and seafood mains around

$16. For Mexican food, try the *Fiesta Cantina*, in an arcade at 96-98 Lake St; it's a bright little place with a bar, and beef, chicken and vegetarian main meals ranging from $7 to $15.

All of Cairns' big hotels have their own restaurants, and quite a few of these are very popular with locals as they often offer good meal deals in stylish surrounds. *Mangrove Jack's*, the seafood restaurant at the Reef Plaza Hotel on the corner of Grafton and Spence Sts, has a three-course set menu for $19.50, and on Friday they have $10 lunch specials. *Cafe Coco*, at the Cairns International Hotel, has an excellent buffet selection (which includes plenty of seafood) for $24 at lunch time or $27 at night.

Another place popular with locals is *Dunwoody's Tavern*, about two km north of the centre on the corner of Sheridan and Smith Sts. It's a huge, modern, barn-sized tavern which is open for lunch and dinner daily, and has a bar, lounge area and a restaurant. You can get just about anything here – pastas, salads, sandwiches, gourmet pizzas, seafood, steaks – with lunches in the $7 to $12 range and dinners from $8.50 to $16.

ENTERTAINMENT

The best guide to what's on is the free entertainment rag, *Son of Barfly*, which covers music gigs and reviews, movies, pubs and clubs, restaurants etc. It appears weekly and is available all over town in cafes and shops, and is usually pretty entertaining reading in itself.

Pubs & Live Music

Free lunch time concerts are held every day at the City Place Amphitheatre, in the mall on the corner of Lake and Shields Sts.

The *Pier Tavern*, at the Pier Marketplace complex, has live bands from Wednesday to Sunday. It's a popular pub at anytime, and *the* place to be on a Sunday afternoon – a blues band usually kicks off the Sunday sessions at around 2.30 pm. It has a good outdoor decking area which overlooks Trinity Bay. *Gypsy Dee's*, an exotic bar and restaurant at 41 Shields St, has live acoustic music. There's no cover charge, and you can dine here cabaret-style (see Places to Eat) or just have a drink and a listen at the bar. It is open every night until 2 am. *Dunwoody's Tavern* (see Places to Eat) also has live acoustic music.

Johno's Blues Bar, above McDonald's on the corner of Shields St and the Esplanade, is a big, lively place with blues, rock and R&B bands every night until at least 4 am. There's a cover charge of $5 to $10, depending on the night and who's playing.

Quite a few pubs in Cairns have regular live bands, including the *Fox & Firkin*, on the corner of Spence and Lake Sts, *Rusty's Pub* on the corner of Spence and Sheridan Sts, the *Crown Hotel* on the corner of Shields and Grafton Sts, and *The Big O* on Wharf St opposite the Transit Centre. Check with *Son of Barfly* to see who's on where.

Bars

At 70 Abbott St, the *Pumphouse* is a backpackers' favourite, with a rowdy bar atmosphere, pool tables, a beer garden and cheap meals. It's a good pre-nightclub option, and stays open until 2 am. The *Wool Shed* on Shields St in the mall has a similar setup and is even more popular. They have pool tables, a quiet cocktail bar downstairs, meals and regular party games – toga parties, drinking competitions, bare-it-all events – it's usually pretty lively.

Palm Court, the cocktail bar at the Hilton Hotel, is a hell of a lot quieter, and a good spot for pensively looking for the bottom of your glass. There is often someone tickling the ivories in the lobby, and the bar stays open until midnight, or 1 am on weekends.

Nightclubs

Cairns' nightclub scene is notoriously wild, especially in the early hours of the morning. The huge complex on the corner of Lake and Hartley Sts houses three places; *Samuels Saloon*, a backpacker bar and eatery; the *Playpen International*, a huge nightclub which often has big-name bands, stays open until sunrise and charges from $5 entry; and the more up-market *Court Jester* bar.

The *End of the World* nightclub, on the corner of Abbott and Aplin Sts, is another popular place for a drink and a bop, with huge video screens, a party-sized dance floor, pool tables, loud music and cheap drinks deals. They run various 'theme' nights – free kegs, karaoke, Mr Backpacker competitions – and have a cover charge of around $5, although backpackers with hostel vouchers get in free. End of the World closes around 5 am.

Tropos, upstairs in Central Arcade near the Fox & Firkin, is a lively dance club with good music, pool tables, a wide outdoor balcony area and a $5 cover charge on weekends. It closes at 5 am.

Casino

Cairns' Reef Casino is currently being built on the site bordered by the Esplanade, and Wharf and Spence Sts, and will open in 1996. I'm assured it will be very big and very impressive, and will include a botanical conservatory, a nightclub, a convention centre and a five-star hotel. Oh, and a whole bunch of different ways to lose your money.

Gay Venues

Rusty's Pub, on the corner of Spence and Sheridan Sts, has a gay night with a floor show every Saturday night. Across the road from Rusty's, at 53 Spence St, is Club Justice – also known as JDL's. It's a gay-oriented dance club and entertainment venue: open Wednesday to Saturday nights until 5 am.

Theatre, Cinema & Drive-In

If you want to catch a movie, there's the Cairns 5 Cinemas (☎ (070) 31 1077), at 108 Grafton St, or the Coral Twin Drive-in, on the Bruce Hwy on the southern edge of town.

The Cairns Civic Theatre (☎ (070) 51 3211), a large modern theatre complex, near the corner of Florence and Grafton Sts, is the city's main theatre venue and hosts regular performances throughout the year.

THINGS TO BUY

Many artists live in the Cairns region, so there's a wide range of local handicrafts available – pottery, clothing, stained glass, jewellery, leather work and so on. Aboriginal art is also for sale in a few places, as are crafts from Papua New Guinea and places further afield in the Pacific.

Apart from the many souvenir shops dotted around the town centre, there are a couple of good markets in town. The previously mentioned Rusty's Bazaar is mainly a food market, but also has a few craft stalls. The long-running Night Markets, in the centre of the Esplanade between Shields and Aplin Sts, has always had a good collection of stalls, but by the time you read this they will have been 'redeveloped' (read demolished) and replaced by the Esplanade Market Place, a 'boutique shopping complex'.

The Mud Markets, held in the Pier Marketplace every Saturday and Sunday, feature the best collection of stalls selling everything from souvenirs, clothes, beachwear, jewellery, leatherwork, hats, boomerangs, hand-painted T-shirts and woodwork. Quite a lot of the Kuranda people also have stalls here, which makes it a convenient alternative to going up to Kuranda. The Mud Markets are always busy, and with live musicians to keep shoppers entertained, they're well worth a visit.

If you're in the market for opals, duty-free goods or souvenirs, you've come to the right place. There are dozens of these shops in the centre of town, especially along Abbott and Lake Sts, which if nothing else at least gives you a chance to shop around and compare.

Sounds Aboriginal, a small shop at 83 the Esplanade, is owned and run by the Aboriginal and Torres Strait Islander community, and sells hand-made boomerangs and didgeridoos as well as a selection of music tapes and CDs. They quite often have live music and jam sessions out the front of the shop.

Camping & Outdoor Gear

At 71 Grafton St, Adventure Equipment is a great outdoor adventure shop which sells walking, camping, climbing and canoeing gear, tents, jackets, boots, rucksacks and backpacks, and travel guidebooks (it's the place with all the LP book covers in the window!).

City Place Disposals, on the corner of Grafton and Shields Sts, is one of several disposal-type shops in town, and sells a range of cheaper camping and outdoor gear.

Another good place for camping gear is the huge Geo Pickers Great Outdoors Centre, at 108 Mulgrave Rd. It sells camping gear, tents, backpacks, tarps, outdoor cooking gear and yacht chandlery. They also rent out camping gear, which is handy if you're heading to Cape York or the islands. Tents cost $37.50 a week, and a 'camp box' with a billy, toaster, frypan, camp oven, gas lamp and stove, costs $42 a week. They also have tables, chairs, eskies etc.

If you're in the market for an Akubra hat, Harris Bros, a 'gentlemen's outfitter' on the corner of Shields and Sheridan Sts, has the best selection in town. They also have a good range of travel goods, workwear and boots.

GETTING THERE & AWAY
Travel Agents

There are plenty of travel agencies in town, and a couple of the larger international agencies are represented here: STA Travel (☎ (070) 31 4199) has an office at 43 Lake St, next to the Central Arcade. Trailfinders (☎ (070) 41 1199) has an office in Shields St, next to Hides Hotel.

Air

In Cairns, Qantas and Sunstate Airlines (☎ (070) 50 4000) are on the corner of Shields and Lake Sts, and Ansett and East West (☎ (070) 50 2211) are at 13 Shields St.

Domestic Flights Airlines serving Cairns include Ansett, Qantas, Flight-West and East-West. Regular one-way economy fares to the major destinations are Melbourne $576, Sydney $509, Brisbane $387, Townsville $158, Darwin $404, Alice Springs $377, Perth $621, Hobart $583 and Adelaide $579. You can get cheaper advance-purchase fares by booking your ticket three, seven, 14 or 21 days in advance – the further ahead you book, the cheaper the fare. See the Getting There & Away chapter for more details.

Flights inland and up the Cape York Peninsula from Cairns are shared amongst a number of airlines. Sunstate flies to Bamaga ($279), Lizard Island ($144) and Thursday Island ($307). Ansett flies to Weipa ($219) and Mt Isa ($254). Flight West (☎ (070) 35 9511 or through Ansett) operates a service through the Gulf, the Cape York Peninsula and to Bamaga and the Torres Strait Islands.

International Flights At the time of writing, Qantas, JAL, Cathay Pacific, Garuda and Air Nuigini were the only airlines with direct flights into Cairns.

Cairns International Airport has regular flights to and from North America, Papua New Guinea and Asia. Air Niugini (☎ (070) 51 4177) is at 4 Shields St; the Port Moresby flight costs $378 one way and goes daily except Sunday. Qantas (☎ (070) 50 4000), on the corner of Lake and Shields Sts, also flies to Port Moresby (daily except Wednesday and Sunday), as well as direct to the US west coast (daily except Tuesday) and to Hong Kong every Thursday.

Bus
All the bus companies operate from the Transit Centre at Trinity Wharf. Most of the backpackers' hostels have courtesy buses which meet the arriving buses to ferry you off to your waiting bed.

Greyhound Pioneer Australia (☎ 13 2030) and McCafferty's (☎ (070) 51 5899) both run at least five buses a day up the coast from Brisbane and Townsville to Cairns. Journey times and average fares are: from Brisbane, 23 to 27 hours ($135); from Rockhampton, 14 to 16 hours ($90); Mackay, 10 to 12 hours ($70) and Townsville, 4½ hours ($37).

Coral Coaches (☎ (070) 31 7577), also based at the Transit Centre, runs regular daily services from Cairns to Port Douglas ($14.20 one way), Mossman ($15.70), and on to Cape Tribulation and Cooktown via either the inland or the coast road. See those sections later in this chapter for more details.

Coral Coaches also has a regular tour to the Atherton Tableland.

White Car Coaches (☎ (070) 91 1855) has bus services from Cairns to Kuranda and around the Atherton Tableland, with connections on to Chillagoe. See the Atherton Tableland section later in this chapter for details.

Cairns-Karumba Coachline (☎ (070) 35 1853) has a service three times a week between Cairns and Karumba, on the Gulf of Carpentaria. See the Gulf Savannah chapter for details.

Train
There are three trains which run between Brisbane and Cairns; the *Queenslander*, which runs weekly and has a motorail service; the *Sunlander*, which runs three times a week; and the *Spirit of the Tropics*, a party train which also runs weekly.

The 1681-km trip from Brisbane takes about 32 hours. The 1st-class Brisbane-Cairns fare on the *Queenslander* costs $489 (including sleeping berth and all meals); the economy fare from Brisbane is $129 on the other trains, while 1st class costs $243 on the *Sunlander*. Call Queensland Rail in Cairns for bookings (☎ 13 2232) or information (☎ (070) 52 6249). See the Getting Around chapter for more details.

Car & Motorcycle Rental
It's well worth considering renting a car. There's plenty to see and do on land around Cairns, whether it's making the beach crawl up to Port Douglas or exploring the Atherton Tableland. Mokes are about the cheapest cars to rent and ideal for relaxed, open-air sightseeing. Most of the car-rental firms in Cairns have Mokes. While the major firms are along Lake St, local firms have mushroomed all over Cairns and some of them offer good deals, particularly for weekly rental. However, don't be taken in by cut-rates advertising – once you add in all the hidden costs, prices are fairly similar everywhere. Shop around and find the deal that suits. Generally, Mokes are around $45 per day, VW convertibles $55, and regular cars from

$50 up. It's also possible to rent 4WDs from around $110 and motor scooters from $30 a day.

Note that most Cairns rental firms specifically prohibit you from taking most of their cars up the Cape Tribulation road, on the road to Cooktown, or on the Chillagoe Caves road. A sign in the car will usually announce this prohibition and the contract will threaten dire unhappiness if you do so. Of course, lots of people ignore these prohibitions, but there have been letters from travellers (which have been confirmed by some car-rental agencies) which suggest that some rental companies pay people a 'spotter's fee' to report anyone who goes across the river in a rental car, and as this is the only way to get to Cape Trib you'll lose your bond or be up for a hefty fine when you return. Be warned that these roads can be fairly rough and sometimes impassable in conventional vehicles. Also note that a sizeable deposit is generally required for car rental, anything from $100 to $250 in Cairns, although this is waived if you're paying with a credit card.

Two Wheel Adventures (☎ (070) 31 5707), at 148 Sheridan St, rents out motorcycles from 250cc to 600cc. Prices range from $60 to $75 a day, although there are restrictions on where you can take their bikes. You generally have to stick to sealed highways, although they allow you to go as far as Cape Trib or Chillagoe.

Boat
The daily *Quicksilver* (☎ (070) 99 5500) fast catamaran service links Cairns with Port Douglas. The trip takes 1½ hours, departing from the pier Marina in Cairns at 8 am and from Port Douglas at 5.30 pm. Adult fares are $20 one way, $30 return, children's fares are $10/15.

GETTING AROUND
To/From the Airport
The airport in Cairns has two sections, both off the Captain Cook Hwy north of the town. The main domestic and international airlines use the new section, officially called Cairns International Airport. This is reached by an approach road that turns off the highway about 3.5 km from central Cairns. The other part of the airport, which some people still call Cairns Airport, is reached from a second turning off the highway, 1.5 km north of the main one.

The Australia Coach shuttle bus (☎ (070) 35 9555) runs a regular pick-up and drop-off service between the airport and wherever you're staying in Cairns. They meet all incoming flights, and will pick you up from your accommodation and take you to the airport. The one-way fare is $4; book in advance. A taxi is about $9. Avis, Budget, Hertz and Thrifty have desks at the international terminal.

Bus
There are a number of local bus services in and around Cairns. Schedules for most of them are posted at the main city stop (known as the Lake St Transit Centre) in City Place. Buses on most routes leave hourly from around 7 am to 6 pm, Monday to Friday, and less frequently on Saturday mornings. Most routes close down from Saturday lunch time to Monday morning.

The Beach Bus, (No 208), run by Marlin Coast Buslines (☎ (070) 57 7411), goes up to Trinity and Clifton beaches, Wild World, Palm Cove and Ellis Beach. The last buses back to Cairns leave Ellis Beach at 4.40 pm Monday to Friday and at 4 pm on weekends.

Cairns Trans (☎ (070) 35 2600) operates the local bus services including buses to Yorkeys Knob and Holloways Beach, with the last buses leaving Yorkeys Knob at 6.15 pm Monday to Friday and 1.10 pm on Saturday. From Holloways Beach, last buses are at 5.55 pm on weekdays, 12.50 pm on Saturday. There are no services on Sunday. Southern Cross Bus Services (☎ (070) 55 1240), which runs to Machans Beach, has last buses to Cairns leaving at 4.50 pm Monday to Friday and 10 am Saturday; there's no service on Sunday.

The Cairns Red Explorer (☎ (070) 55 1240) is an air-con service which plies a circular route around the city, and you can get on or off at any of the nine stops. It departs every hour from 9 am to 4 pm from Monday to Saturday (and on Sunday from May to October) from the Lake St Transit Mall, and a day ticket costs a hefty $20 for adults or $10 for kids. The main stops of interest are No 4 (Freshwater Creek swimming hole), No 5 (Freshwater Connection), No 6 (Mangrove Boardwalk near the airport), No 7 (Botanic Gardens) and No 8 (Royal Flying Doctor Complex).

Bicycle
Most of the hostels and car-rental firms, plus quite a few other places, have bikes for hire so you'll have no trouble tracking one down. Expect to pay around $10 a day.

Islands off Cairns

Off the coast from Cairns are Green Island, a coral cay, and Fitzroy Island, a continental island. Both of these very pretty islands attract hordes of day trippers (some say too many), and both have resorts operated by the cruise company Great Adventures, which in turn is owned by the Japanese corporation Daikyo. In true Disneyland style, you can exchange your dollars for 'cruise currency' which entitles you to a small discount off anything you buy on the islands or even on the boats across. This practice is optional though – they still accept real Australian currency.

South of Cairns, the Frankland Islands group is a cluster of undeveloped national park islands. You can do day trips to these islands or camp overnight or longer.

There are also numerous off-shore reefs which are popular destinations for day trips out of Cairns – see Organised Tours in the earlier Cairns section for details of some of these.

GREEN ISLAND
Green Island, 27 km north-east of Cairns, is a true coral cay, 660 metres long by 260 metres wide. The beautiful island and its surrounding reef are all national park,

although the luxurious new five-star resort which opened in 1994 takes up a substantial proportion of the island. The resort has good daytrippers' facilities, which were extensively upgraded as part of the same development.

Green is a tiny island which you can walk around in about 15 minutes. A stroll from the resort area to the far end of the island will remind you that the beach is beautiful, the water fine, the snorkelling good and the fish prolific.

Green Island was named by Captain Cook after the chief astronomer on the *Endeavour*. The island was home to a bêche-de-mere boom, and from the 1870s most of the island's trees were cut down for fires to boil the bêche-de-mere.

Things to See & Do
The island's most interesting attraction is the long-running **Marineland Melanesia**. It houses a gallery, museum and aquarium, with a bizarre collection of Melanesian artefacts and crafts, plus a wide variety of fish, turtles, stingrays and crocodiles in ponds and tanks. Admission costs $7 for adults, $3 for children.

Glass bottomed boats operate trips from the pier, costing $13.

The new daytrippers' facilities are very impressive, and include a swimming pool, a bar and several eateries. There's a dive shop which rents out snorkelling and diving gear, and offers introductory dives.

Places to Stay & Eat
The new five-star *Green Island Reef Resort* (☎ (070) 31 3300) has luxury accommodation for up to 92 guests. There are two types of units, all very impressive and linked by timber boardwalks. The Island Rooms cost $390 per person and the Reef Suites $400 per person, with rates including breakfast, dinner and use of all water-sports equipment.

Getting There & Away
Aquaflight Airways (☎ (070) 31 4307) will fly you in a seaplane from the Pier Marina in Cairns to the island and back for $80.

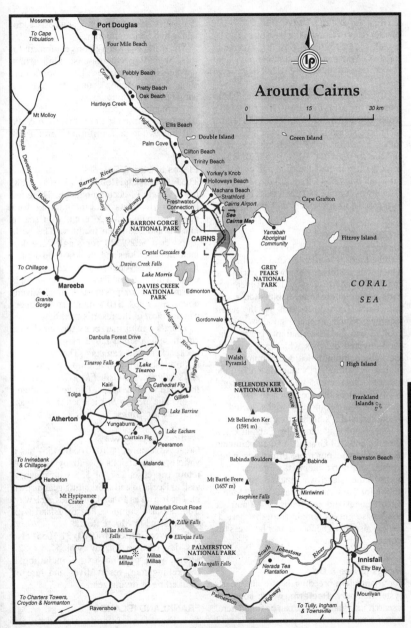

Around Cairns

0   15   30 km

Mossman
To Cape
Tribulation
Port Douglas
Four Mile Beach
Cook
Pebbly Beach
Pretty Beach
Oak Beach
Hartleys Creek
Highway
Mt Molloy
Ellis Beach
Double Island
Green Island
Palm Cove
Clifton Beach
Trinity Beach
Peninsula Developmental Road
Barron River
Clohesy River
Kuranda
Yorkey's Knob
Holloways Beach
Machans Beach
Strathford
Cairns Airport
Cape Grafton
Kennedy
Highway
Freshwater
Connection
See
Cairns Map
BARRON GORGE
NATIONAL PARK
CAIRNS
Yarrabah
Aboriginal
Community
Fitzroy Island
To Chillagoe
Crystal Cascades
Davies Creek Falls
Lake Morris
DAVIES CREEK
NATIONAL PARK
Edmonton
GREY
PEAKS
NATIONAL
PARK
CORAL
SEA
Mareeba
Granite
Gorge
Gordonvale
Mulgrave River
Danbulla Forest Drive
Tinaroo Falls
Lake
Tinaroo
Cathedral Fig
Gillies
Lake Barrine
Kairi
Tolga
Walsh
Pyramid
High Island
BELLENDEN KER
NATIONAL PARK
Highway
Atherton
Yungaburra
Curtain Fig
Peeramon
Lake Eacham
Mt Bellenden Ker
(1591 m)
Frankland
Islands
To Irvinebank
& Chillagoe
Malanda
Babinda Boulders
Babinda
Bramston Beach
Herberton
Mt Hypipamee
Crater
Mt Bartle Frere
(1657 m)
Josephine Falls
Mirriwinni
Waterfall Circuit Road
Zillie Falls
Millaa Millaa
Falls
Ellinjaa Falls
PALMERSTON
NATIONAL PARK
Mungalli Falls
South Johnstone River
Nerada Tea
Plantation
Innisfail
Etty Bay
Millaa
Millaa
Millaa
Millaa
To Charters Towers,
Croydon & Normanton
Ravenshoe
Palmerston
Highway
To Tully, Ingham
& Townsville
Mourilyan

Bruce Highway

FAR NTH QUEENSLAND

Great Adventures (☎ (070) 51 0455) has two services to Green Island – you can go by launch for $29 return or by fast catamaran for $48. You can also combine a visit to Green Island with Fitzroy Island or Norman Reef.

Other operators with trips to Green Island include the *Big Cat* (☎ (070) 51 0444), which takes 80 minutes and costs $32 return, including snorkelling gear or a glass bottomed boat trip, or $39 with lunch as well; and the *Reef Jet* (☎ (070) 31 5559), which does the trip in half the time and costs $32 for a half day or $37 for a full day – you can also pay a bit more and get a glass bottomed boat trip, snorkelling gear and lunch.

FITZROY ISLAND

Six km off the coast and 26 km south-east of Cairns, Fitzroy is a large continental island which is incredibly popular with daytrippers, and also has a resort run by Great Adventures with camping grounds, a bunkhouse and villa units. Daytrippers can use the resort facilities, which include a good swimming pool, a bar and a restaurant. Fitzroy has coral-covered beaches which are good for snorkelling, but not ideal for swimming and sunbaking, although Nudey Beach is quite pleasant. Snorkellers will find good coral only 50 metres off the beach in the resort area. There are some fine walks, including one to the island's highest point.

The island was named by Captain Cook after the Duke of Grafton, a noted politician of the era who put more effort into wine, women and horse racing than government. In 1877 the island was made a quarantine station for Chinese immigrants bound for the north Queensland goldfields, and a number of Chinese graves remain from that period. Fitzroy also had a bêche-de-mer business for a time.

Things to See & Do

The giant clam-breeding centre and pearl-oyster hatchery, **Reefarm**, which conducts research into giant clams, can be found here. A half-hour educational programme is held daily at 10.45 am and 1 pm, and costs $6 for adults and $3 for children.

The resort has water-sports equipment for hire, including catamarans, windsurfers, paddle-skis and canoes. The resort's dive shop conducts diving courses and hires out snorkelling and diving gear.

There are two good walking trails on the island: the 20-minute **Secret Garden Walk**, and the two-hour **Lighthouse and Peak Circuit**.

Places to Stay & Eat

The Fitzroy Island Resort (☎ (070) 51 9588) has a variety of accommodation. There are hostel-style units accommodating four people in bunks at $26 each, with shared kitchen and bathroom facilities. The 'villa units' cost $229/320 for singles/doubles, including activities and breakfast and dinner. If all that's beyond your budget, you can camp at the National Parks camping grounds (permits and bookings through Great Adventures). Sites cost $10 a night, and campers can use *most* of the resort's facilities.

There's a mini-market by the bunkhouse which sells a small range of groceries for backpackers and campers. The resort also has a kiosk with fish & chips, pizzas, pies and sandwiches, and the *Flare Grill* does pub food like steak & chips, fish and salad and so on. The *Mango Bar* is open from 10 am until late for drinks.

Getting There & Away

Great Adventures (☎ (070) 51 0455) has a variety of excursions to Fitzroy Island. A return trip costs $27, or $55 with lunch, a visit to Reefarm and snorkelling gear thrown in. The trip takes about 45 minutes each way. You can also combine Fitzroy Island with Green Island or Moore Reef.

Sunlover Cruises (☎ (070) 31 1055) also has day trips to Fitzroy, which cost $22 return, with optional extras including a snorkelling tour, resort dives and hire of snorkelling or diving gear.

FRANKLAND ISLANDS

The Frankland Islands are relatively

untouched national park islands south of Fitzroy Island and about 12 km off the coast. They were named by Captain Cook after Admiral Sir Thomas Frankland. The islands consist of High Island to the north and four smaller islands – Normanby, Mabel, Round and Russell islands – to the south. They're continental islands with good beaches and some fine snorkelling. On the day trips from Cairns the island time is usually spent on Normanby Island while divers go to Round Island.

Places to Stay
If you like the idea of camping overnight on your own deserted island, Frankland Islands Cruise & Dive (☎ (070) 31 6300 or 008 079 039 toll free) offers a drop-off service to Russell Island for $100 return ($80 for children). There are no facilities on the islands so you must come totally equipped – camping gear can be supplied on request. Usually campers go to Russell Island; High Island drop-offs are only made at peak periods (like Christmas) when Russell is full. A maximum of 15 campers is allowed on each island and permits are available from the QNP&WS in Cairns.

Getting There & Away
Frankland Islands Cruise & Dive (☎ (070) 31 6300 or 008 079 039 toll free) operates regular day trips to the Frankland Islands. You're taken by bus from Cairns to Deeral on the Mulgrave River from where you go out through the mangroves to the islands. The day trip costs $98 for adults and $49 for kids, which includes a barbecue lunch, morning and afternoon tea, transport from wherever you're staying and snorkelling gear. Certified divers pay another $50 for one dive, or you can do an introductory dive for $60.

Atherton Tableland

Inland from the coast between Innisfail and Cairns, the land rises sharply then rolls gently across the lush Atherton Tableland towards the Great Dividing Range. The Tableland's altitude, more than 900 metres in places, tempers the tropical heat, and the abundant rainfall and rich volcanic soil combine to make this one of the greenest places in Queensland. In the south are Queensland's two highest mountains – Bartle Frere (1657 metres) and Bellenden Ker (1591 metres).

Little more than a century ago, this peaceful, pastoral region was still wild jungle. The first pioneers came in the 1870s, looking for a repeat of the Palmer River gold rush, further north. As elsewhere in Queensland, the Aboriginal population was violently opposed to this intrusion but was soon overrun. Some gold was found and rather more tin, but although mining spurred the development of roads and railways through the rugged, difficult land of the plateau, farming and timber soon became the chief activities.

The Tableland is a great contrast to the hustle and bustle down on the coast. It's a region of beautiful scenery, with its lakes and waterfalls, national parks and state forests, small villages and several busy rural centres. There are some excellent accommodation options, including old pubs, timber guesthouses, farmstays and B&Bs, and you can visit some of the farms, go bushwalking, check out the Kuranda markets or just relax.

West of the Tableland are some fascinating old mining areas, including the historic tin-mining centre of Herberton and edge-of-the-outback Chillagoe with its limestone caves and mining relics.

Getting There & Around
The Kuranda Scenic Railway train ride from Cairns to Kuranda is a major Tableland attraction, and the new Skyrail Rainforest Cableway will probably become one – but without a car the rest of the Tableland can be hard to reach. From south to north, the three major roads from the coast are the Palmerston Hwy from Innisfail to Millaa Millaa and Ravenshoe; the Gillies Hwy from Gordonvale past Lakes Tinaroo, Barrine and

Eacham to Yungaburra and Atherton; and the Kennedy Hwy from Cairns to Kuranda and Mareeba. Heading north from Mareeba, the Peninsula Developmental Road runs through Mt Molloy to Mossman.

White Car Coaches (☎ (070) 91 1855) has regular bus services connecting Cairns with the main towns on the Tableland. They have two or three services on weekdays, and one on weekends, leaving from outside Tropical Paradise Travel, at 25 Spence St in Cairns. The buses travel one way from Cairns to Mareeba ($12), Atherton ($16), Yungaburra ($20.10), Malanda ($22.30), Herberton ($19) and Ravenshoe ($23), as well as Kuranda and Chillagoe. See the Kuranda and Chillagoe sections for more details.

Organised Tours

There are plenty of companies offering day trips and tours from Cairns. The *On the Wallaby* backpackers' hostel runs overnight trips to the Tableland from Cairns every Monday, Wednesday and Friday for $35, which includes accommodation, transport, all meals, and activities such as rainforest walks, canoeing and platypus spotting.

There are also some interesting tours on offer to Chillagoe and Mt Mulligan – see the Mareeba to Chillagoe and Chillagoe sections for details.

KURANDA (pop 620)

Famed for its markets, this beautiful mountain village is surrounded by spectacular tropical scenery. Unfortunately, Kuranda's charms have long been discovered by the masses, and the place is flooded with busloads and train-loads of tourists on market days.

Kuranda can still be a pleasant place to stay overnight. While it's no longer the sleepy, old-fashioned hippy village it once was, in the afternoons and evenings, and on non-market days, it reverts to the laid-back atmosphere it was once renowned for.

Seventh Day Adventists founded the Mona Mona mission near Kuranda around the turn of the century. At the time the government's policy was to collect north Queensland Aborigines into missions and reserves. Mona Mona was one of the more successful missions, almost self-sufficient and with about 350 people at its peak. It was closed in 1962 and many of the people and their descendants now live in or near Kuranda.

Things to See & Do

The **Kuranda markets** are held every Wednesday, Thursday, Friday and Sunday, although things quieten after about 2 pm. There's a huge range of stalls here, and if you can ignore the tea-towels, plastic boomer-angs and 'I'm with stupid' T-shirts, there are some excellent hand-made arts and crafts on sale – leather belts, wooden puzzles, painted T-shirts, bush saxophones, jewellery, essential oil burners, sarongs, hats, pottery and didgeridoos.

Within the market area is **Kuranda Bungy**, and for $56 you can fling yourself from a cage suspended by an old crane. For $100 you also get a video and T-shirt.

Near the market area, the **Australian Butterfly Sanctuary** ($9.50, adults, $5 children) is open daily from 10 am to 3 pm and has regular guided tours. On Coondoo St, the **Kuranda Wildlife Noctarium** ($8 adults, $4 children), where you can see nocturnal rainforest animals like gliders, fruit bats and echidnas, is open from 10 am to 3 pm daily. Feeding times, which are the best times to visit, are at 10.30 and 11.30 am, and 1.15 and 2.30 pm.

Also on Coondoo St, the award-winning **Tjapukai Dance Theatre**, a local Aboriginal dance troupe, goes through its paces daily at 11 am and 1.30 pm, and at 12.15 pm on market days ($16). The hour-long perfor-mance tells you a few basic things about Aboriginal culture with song, dance and humour and features didgeridoo playing and dancing. Almost across the road is the **Jilli Binna Aboriginal Crafts & Museum**; there's a small display (admission free) on Aboriginal culture and the old Mona Mona mission.

Based over the footbridge behind the railway station is **Kuranda Rainforest**

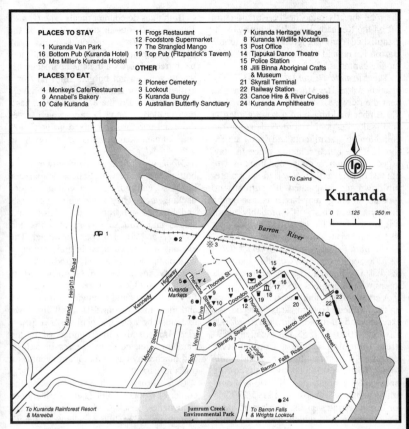

PLACES TO STAY
1 Kuranda Van Park
16 Bottom Pub (Kuranda Hotel)
20 Mrs Miller's Kuranda Hostel

PLACES TO EAT
4 Monkeys Cafe/Restaurant
9 Annabel's Bakery
10 Cafe Kuranda

11 Frogs Restaurant
12 Foodstore Supermarket
17 The Strangled Mango
19 Top Pub (Fitzpatrick's Tavern)

OTHER
2 Pioneer Cemetery
3 Lookout
5 Kuranda Bungy
6 Australian Butterfly Sanctuary

7 Kuranda Heritage Village
8 Kuranda Wildlife Noctarium
13 Post Office
14 Tjapukai Dance Theatre
15 Police Station
18 Jilli Binna Aboriginal Crafts & Museum
21 Skyrail Terminal
22 Railway Station
23 Canoe Hire & River Cruises
24 Kuranda Amphitheatre

FAR NTH QUEENSLAND

Tours. You can hire a canoe from them to paddle along the Barron River. They also run four 45-minute riverboat cruises each day which cost $9 for adults or $4.50 for children, and they have a guided one-hour walk through the rainforest every day at 10.30 am which costs $10/5.

On Therwine St, **Kuranda Bad Hog Harley Tours** (☎ (018) 187 909) takes passengers for short cruises, and you might also be able to get a ride all the way back to Cairns (for $40).

There are several picturesque walks starting with short, signed tracks down through

the market. **Jumrum Creek Environmental Park**, off Barron Falls Rd, 700 metres from the bottom of Thongon St, has a short walking track and a big population of fruit bats. Further down, Barron Falls Rd divides: the left fork takes you to a lookout over the falls, while a further one km along the right fork brings you to Wrights Lookout where you can see back down the Barron Gorge to Cairns.

Places to Stay

The *Kuranda Van Park* (☎ (070) 93 7316) is in a quiet setting a few km out of town, up the road directly opposite the Kuranda turn off on the Kennedy Hwy. It's a bushy, well-established camping ground close to the Barron River, and has camp sites for $12 or on-site cabins at $33.

The *Kuranda Hostel* (☎ (070) 93 7355), also known as *Mrs Miller's*, is at 6 Arara St, near the railway station. It's a big, rambling old timber building with a huge garden, a small saltwater pool, a sitting/video room, an enlightening graffiti room and a separate TV room. It's a quiet, relaxing place to stay, especially if you've got a good book or two, but last time I was there it was looking pretty run down and dilapidated. It's currently up for sale, so things may have changed by the time you read this – it's probably worth ringing to check the latest. Dorm beds cost $13 and there are double rooms for $32.

The *Bottom Pub/Kuranda Hotel* (☎ (070) 93 7206), on the corner of Coondoo and Arara Sts, has a pool and 12 very basic motel-style rooms with ceiling fans at $35/45.

A couple of km south-west of town, back on the Kennedy Hwy towards Mareeba, the excellent and up-market *Kuranda Rainforest Resort* (☎ (070) 93 7555) has excellent facilities, including a bar, a tropical-style restaurant, a great swimming pool and tennis courts. There are 40 motel-style units costing from $118 a night, and 30 two-bedroom timber cabins which cost from $195/220/245 for doubles/triples/quads. The resort has a free courtesy bus which makes pick-ups three times daily from Trinity Wharf in Cairns and also does airport transfers. (This place used to have a backpackers' section, but it went exclusively up-market in 1994.)

Places to Eat

Some of the best eats are found in the food stalls scattered around the markets – you can get a freshly squeezed juice, a sandwich, satays, a Thai stir-fry, an Indian curry – just follow your nose! There are also quite a few cafes, bakeries and coffee shops in the village. If you're staying at the hostel, the *Foodstore Supermarket* on the corner of Coondoo and Thongon Sts has a good range of groceries, fruit and vegies.

Both pubs do counter meals. The *Garden Bar & Grill*, out in the backyard of the Bottom Pub, is a surprisingly pretty spot, with a swimming pool, shady lawns and palm trees. There's a thatched barbecue bar where you can get burgers for $4.50 or a grilled steak for around $8.50 – and have a swim while you're there! The *Top Pub* has a bistro called *Troppo's Lounge*, which serves the usual pub fare like mixed grills, fish & chips or ham steak and pineapple from $7 to $9.

Monkey's Cafe/Restaurant, down at the bottom end of Therwine St near the markets, is a good, earthy BYO cafe with an outdoor decking area. They serve good breakfasts and lunches – bacon & eggs, croissants, salads and fruit salads, sandwiches and bagels – and are also open for dinner. The evening menu specialises in grain-fed beef, with main courses from $16 to $18.

Frogs Restaurant on Coondoo St is another good local. It serves full breakfasts for $7, burgers and sandwiches around $6 and main meals from $10. They also have live music here on Sunday nights. *The Strangled Mango*, also in Coondoo St in the Faraway Tree complex, serves breakfasts and lunches by day and at night becomes a pizza restaurant.

Cafe Kuranda, with two sections on the corner of Coondoo and Therwine Sts, does sandwiches, snacks and takeaways. Just a few doors along, the excellent *Annabel's Bakery* has a large range of pastries, and the *Bakehaus Cafe* over in the new Kuranda Village complex is also good.

Getting There & Away

Bus White Car Coaches (☎ (070) 91 1855) has five buses from Cairns to Kuranda on weekdays and two to three on weekends, leaving from outside Tropical Paradise Travel (☎ (070) 51 9533), at 25 Spence St in Cairns. The fare is $7 one way, $14 return.

Train The most popular way of getting to Kuranda is on the appropriately named Kuranda Scenic Railway that winds 34 km from Cairns to Kuranda. This line, which took five years to build, was opened in 1891 and goes through 15 tunnels, climbing more than 300 metres in the last 21 km. Kuranda's railway station, decked out in tropical flowers and ferns, is justly famous.

The historic steam-trains operate daily and the trip takes 1½ hours. The one-way/return fares are $23/39 for adults, $12/20 for children and $60/85 for a family of two adults and three kids. There are uni-formed hostesses, free orange juice, and a commentary. You also get a booklet on the line's history and a photo stop at the 260-metre Barron Falls. The train has its own ticket office at Cairns railway station (☎ (070) 52 6249) – or you can board at Freshwater Connection (☎ (070) 55 2222), 10 km out of Cairns.

Cable Car Kuranda's somewhat controversial Skyrail Rainforest Cableway (☎ (070) 38 1555), vigorously opposed by conservationists, should be open for business by the time you read this. The last protester was lured down from his tree and arrested early in 1995.

The 7.5-km gondola cableway will run from Smithfield, a northern suburb of Cairns, to Kuranda in about 30 minutes. There will be two stops along the route, at Red Peak and at Barron Falls, and both will have rainforest interpretive centres. The cableway will run daily from 8 am to 5 pm. One-way/return fares will be $23/39 for adults and $11.50/19.50 for children; accommodation transfers are available at an extra cost.

KURANDA TO MAREEBA

It's 37 km from Kuranda to the town of Mareeba, along the Kennedy Hwy. The first section of the drive continues to twist and climb through the green mountains, but the road soon levels out as you enter the flatter, drier farmlands to the west of the Tableland.

There's a rather intriguing accommodation possibility along this route. Fourteen km from Kuranda is the turn off to the *Cedar Park Rainforest Resort* (☎ (070) 93 7077) – it's another six km of dirt road from the turn

off to the resort. This place is in the middle of nowhere, on 240 hectares. The resort building can only be described as different – a quirky blend of raw timber poles, medieval brick arches, second-hand materials and tacky 1970s architecture. There are eight spacious and comfortable suites that sleep up to four, a bar and a restaurant, but the best parts are the forest environment, the lovely gardens and the small stream running through the property. Rooms go for $130 a double plus $30 for each extra person, and they can do airport pick-ups for $40 (or helicopter transfers if you've got cash to splash). They'll also do free pick-ups from Kuranda.

Twenty-three km south-west of Kuranda is the turn off to the **Davies Creek National Park**. It's another seven km of gravel road to this small and pretty park of eucalypt forest. This is a great spot for short bushwalks, picnics or camping. There's a self-registration camping ground with toilets, fireplaces and picnic tables, and several walking tracks lead to the creek, a waterfall and a lookout point.

MAREEBA (pop 6800)

Mareeba is in the far corner of the Tableland, in the centre of a rich farming area. The main crops are tobacco, macadamia nuts, coffee, sugar and cattle. The cattle saleyards, on the northern outskirts of town, are an interesting place to visit when the auctions are on – you'll see more Akubra hats and bowed legs than I've had hot steaks.

Regular cattle sales are held every Tuesday morning, and the more prestigious bull sales are held at various times throughout the year.

Mareeba itself is a busy commercial centre, and the Mareeba Rodeo held each July is one of Australia's biggest rodeos, but most tourists will just be passing through here on their way to somewhere else. The Peninsula Developmental Road heads north to Mt Molloy, and you can continue all the way to Cooktown or the Cape York Peninsula from here. Alternatively, you can head west from Mareeba along the Burke Developmental Rd to Chillagoe.

Granite Gorge, 10 km south-west of Mareeba, is famous for its large population of rock wallabies. It's a very scenic spot and a popular day-trip destination, with walking trails, huge granite formations and waterfalls. There is also a camping ground here.

Places to Stay

The *Riverside Caravan Park* (☎ (070) 92 2309), on Egan St, has tent sites for $8.50 and on-site vans for $25. There are two motels in town. The *Golden Leaf Motel* (☎ (070) 92 2266), on the main highway just south of the centre, is a friendly little budget motel with singles/doubles at $44/50.

The recently renovated *Ant Hill Hotel* (☎ (070) 92 1011), in the centre of town at 79 Byrnes St, has classic pub-style rooms upstairs at $19/28 for singles/doubles.

Places to Eat

There are plenty of cafes and takeaways along the main street, and there's even a KFC and a Red Rooster if you're that way inclined. The previously mentioned *Ant Hill Hotel* is a good place for a counter meal and continental breakfasts are $7, cooked breakfasts $10. It has a pleasant, high-ceilinged courtyard restaurant with great steaks, seafood dishes, and Asian-style chicken in the $14 to $16 range, or there are simpler bistro meals – roasts, steaks and chicken – for $4 to $10.

MAREEBA TO CHILLAGOE

The Burke Developmental Rd leaves the Kennedy Hwy at Mareeba and heads west all the way across to Karumba and Normanton on the Gulf of Carpentaria. The majority of the route is unsealed and passes through some of the most remote and inhospitable parts of the state, and as such is only suitable for serious, well-equipped and experienced 4WD adventurers, preferably travelling in a convoy.

However, the first section of the route, the road to Chillagoe, has improved dramatically in the last few years and is well within the reach of your average daytripper. It's less than 150 km from Mareeba to Chillagoe, a fascinating old mining town where you can get a brief taste of life in the outback, visit impressive limestone caves and rock pinnacles, Aboriginal rock-art galleries, ruins of smelters from early this century, a working mine and a museum. All but the last 34 km of the route is along sealed roads, and while these last 34 km are pretty bumpy, they won't present a problem for conventional vehicles during the dry season.

Dimbulah

The tobacco-growing centre of Dimbulah, 47 km west of Mareeba, is a quiet, neat little one-pub town with a petrol station and a couple of takeaway food places. The *Dimbulah Caravan Park* (☎ (070) 93 5242) is an immaculately kept camping ground next to the town swimming pool. Tent sites are $12, on-site vans are $20 and cabins cost $28.

Dimbulah is also the turn off for the former coal-mining town of Mt Mulligan.

Mt Mulligan & Kondaparinga Station

Mt Mulligan is known as the site of Queensland's worst mining disaster. Mt Mulligan itself is an eerie and spectacular formation, and has been nicknamed Queensland's Ayers Rock. There isn't much left of the old mining township but it's an interesting area if you have time to explore, and the town's former hospital, a big old timber Queenslander, is now used as the homestead for *Mt Mulligan Station* (☎ (070) 94 8360). The owner of this large cattle station runs good 'bush experience' tours from Cairns, costing $120 per person for two nights and three days here. The price includes return transport, all meals and horse riding, and there are some fine bushwalking areas around the homestead. If you have your own vehicle, you can stay here overnight for around $40 per person, which includes breakfast and dinner. Mt Mulligan is 50 km north from Dimbulah. The unsealed road is rough in patches; 4WDs are recommended,

Top: Low tide, Cape Tribulation
Middle: Daintree River basin
Bottom: Marina Mirage, Port Douglas

MARK ARMSTRONG

RICHARD I'ANSON

MARK ARMSTRONG

MARK ARMSTRONG

A	B
C	
D	

A: Camel rides, Palm Cove
B: Palm Cove
C: Daintree River estuary
D: Herberton Post Office

although you *can* make it in a conventional vehicle during the Dry.

The Ku Ku Djungun Aboriginal Corporation (☎ 1800 627 454) offers tours from Cairns to the large Kondaparinga cattle station north of Mt Mulligan. Mt Mulligan is known to the Aborigines as 'Ngarrabullgan', and during the tour tales and stories relating to the mountain's Dreamtime significance are told. Meals and horse riding are also included in the tours. The day trip from

---

The Mt Mulligan Mining Disaster

Mt Mulligan won an infamous place in Queensland's history in 1921 when it became the site of the state's worst mining disaster. Rich coal deposits were discovered here in 1910, and a town was established and named after James Venture Mulligan, the famous prospector who discovered the Palmer River goldfields and opened up much of Cape York in the 1870s. By 1914 a train line had been constructed to link Mt Mulligan to Dimbulah, and the mine became one of Queensland's most productive coal mines.

On the morning of September 19, 1921, 75 men went to work down the mine. At 9.25 am an explosion ripped through the mine and a ball of fire flashed out of the tunnel entrance. Reports at the time claim the explosion was heard 60 km away. Rescue teams and medical staff rushed from Mareeba to help, but to no avail. Everyone who was down the mine that morning was killed in the blast. The last casualty was Thomas Evans, the mine's underground manager, who was found barely alive with a piece of timber speared through his throat. He died a few days later in the Mareeba hospital.

A Royal Commission into the disaster that opened 10 days later vaguely attributed the explosion to the fact that the mine had been poorly ventilated, dusty and that explosives were '...stored underground in a careless manner, without regard to the regulations'. The actual explosion was suspected to have been triggered by the accidental firing of explosives.

The mine was reopened for work five months later, and operations continued until it was finally closed in 1957. ■

Cairns costs $105 by 4WD or $195 by light plane, or there's a three-day two-night trip which costs $280 by 4WD or $350 by light plane. There's a bush camp near the homestead, and all meals are included.

Irvinebank

At Petford, 33 km west of Dimbulah, there's a turn off which leads south and then west across to Herberton, via the old mining township of Irvinebank. This road is unsealed dirt all the way, but it's reasonable and you can easily attempt it in a conventional vehicle if it hasn't been raining.

There are still a few people living out at Irvinebank, in an interesting collection of restored old houses and cottages. Tin, copper and silver were the main targets here, and the old privately run mill still crushes tin a few days a week.

The **Loudoun House Museum** is set in the former home of John Moffat, one of Queensland's most successful mining pioneers. Built in 1884, it's said to be the oldest erect two-storey timber and iron building in north Queensland. The museum is run by Tony Derksen, and you can take a guided tour through the relics from the mining era – old photos and mining records, Moffat's personal effects, railway equipment etc. The museum is open daily except Thursday from 10 am to noon and from 1 to 4 pm; entry is free, although donations are accepted gratefully.

If you decide to stop overnight, you can camp in the backyard of the *Irvinebank Tavern* (☎ (070) 96 4176), or they have single beds in dongas at $15 a pop. The pub sells fuel, is a post office agency and does counter meals in the $4.50 to $8 range. There's also a barbecue for the use of guests. Apparently the *Old Post Office*, which is now a private house, also offers B&B accommodation, although no-one was around when I called in.

Petford to Chillagoe

Back on the road to Chillagoe, it's another seven km west from Petford to the **Lappa**

Junction Hotel, a ramshackle cluster of tin and timber buildings that are gradually being restored (at least, being prevented from falling down) by a bloke called Tim, known to some as the Yapper from Lappa. Tim has established a small museum here from the various bits and pieces he found while he was cleaning the place up. There's an old pub that was built in 1901, and a railway station. Tim's an interesting bloke and a bit of bush poet, and it's well worth calling in if you're not in a hurry. There's no entry fee, but a contribution to the donation box on the bar would help with the renovations.

Twenty-five km on is **Almaden**, a nondescript little place with an interesting old pub and a very general store.

Beyond Almaden the gravel sections of the road begins, and the landscape really starts to take on the feel of the outback, with its distinctive red earth scattered with trees, jagged outcrops and rocky hills.

CHILLAGOE (pop 450)

A visit to the old mining village of Chillagoe offers a fascinating glimpse into life in the outback. There are plenty of relics from the not-so-good old days when gold, silver, copper, lead, and wolfram were mined in the area around Chillagoe. Although Chillagoe's ore deposits were extensively explored by a number of major companies, the Red Dome gold mine which started here as recently as the 1980s has been one of the area's few profitable ventures. Marble is also still being mined in the area.

Apart from the mining relics and the old town itself, Chillagoe is famous for its spectacular limestone caves, and there are a number of significant Aboriginal rock-art sites around the town.

It may only be a couple of hour's drive from the coast, but it's a long, long way from the commercialisation of Cairns or the glamour of Port Douglas. If you're feeling a little jaded by bright lights and tourist traps, Chillagoe is definitely worth a day trip, and if you feel like staying longer there are some rather unusual accommodation possibilities.

Information

The *Chillagoe Tourist Village* (the BP service station in Queen St) is the only fuel outlet in town. It has EFTPOS facilities and takes all major credit cards.

The QNP&WS office (☎ (070) 94 7163) and the post office, which has a Commonwealth Bank agency, are both on the corner of Queen and Cathedral Sts. The QNP&WS office is open daily from 8 am to 5 pm; the post office is only open Monday to Friday from 8 am to 1 pm and from 2 to 5 pm.

Things to See & Do

There are extensive cave systems within the limestone pinnacles that surround Chillagoe. The **Chillagoe-Mungana Caves National Park** which protects the cave areas is in nine separate sections. The main caves are the Donna, Royal Arch and Trezkinn, and QNP&WS rangers run daily guided tours of the Donna Cave at 9 am (one hour, $4 adults, $2 children), the Trezkinn Cave at 11.30 am (half hour, $2/1) and the Royal Cave at 1.30 pm ($4/2). The Donna and Trezkinn Caves are both electrically lit, with steep steps taking you through their delicate formations. The Royal Cave is a larger, more open cave system with daylight chambers.

It's worth visiting the QNP&WS office when you first arrive in town, as the tours can be booked out, especially in the tourist season, and times can vary at other times of year. The rangers are also very helpful and can also tell you about other caves with self-guiding trails, for which you'll need a torch.

A 3.5 km walking trail links the Royal Arch Cave section with the Donna and Trezkinn caves car park, taking you through a harsh, craggy landscape via the interesting **Balancing Rock** formation. It's a great walk, but make sure you wear a hat and bring drinking water.

The Chillagoe Museum, otherwise known as the **Chillagoe Historical Centre**, is an interesting place on Hill St, with a diverse collection of odds and sods that includes rocks and minerals, gemstones, bottled snakes, old mining leases, photos, pinned

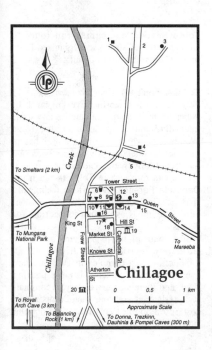

PLACES TO STAY

1 Chillagoe Creek Homestead
4 Chillagoe Bush Camp & Ecolodge
15 Chillagoe Tourist Village & BP Service Station
16 Chillagoe Caves Lodge Motel

PLACES TO EAT

7 Butcher
8 General Store
10 Queen St Takeaway

OTHER

2 Airstrip
3 Cemetery
5 Railway Station
6 Black Cockatoo Hotel
9 Post Office Hotel
11 Old Post Office
12 Old Bank Vault
13 Laundromat, Bakery & Souvenirs
14 QNP&WS Office & Post Office
17 Police Station
18 School
19 Chillagoe Museum
20 Chillagoe Station Homestead

butterflies, old cinema projectors and Papua New Guinean artefacts. It is open daily from 8.30 am to 4.30 pm and entry costs $2.50 for adults and $1 for children.

Two km north-west of town are the ruins of the **Chillagoe Smelters**, which were built at the turn of the century and operated until 1943. This was obviously once a major operation, but all that remains now are some crumbling stone and brick walls, three massive brick chimneys and a jumble of rusting tanks and machinery. The QNP&WS office has a brochure which details the background of the smelters – grab a copy before you head out there.

Places to Stay

There's a small QNP&WS camping ground at the Royal Arch Cave section of the national park.

In Queen St, the *Chillagoe Tourist Village* (☎ (070) 94 7177) behind the BP service

station has tent sites for $5 per person, on-site vans at $25 a double and on-site cabins at $40. There is also a pool, as well as four surprisingly modern and comfortable units here, with kitchens, air-con, TVs and en-suites, costing $50 a double and $5 for extra people.

The *Post Office Hotel* (☎ (070) 94 7119), at 37 Queen St, is a classic old country pub with quaint but simple rooms upstairs costing $15/30 – these iron beds are about the narrowest thing I've slept in, at least in this lifetime. The *Black Cockatoo Hotel* (☎ (070) 94 7168), in Tower St, has basic motel-style rooms at $30/40.

At the *Chillagoe Caves Lodge Motel* (☎ (070) 94 7106), at 7 King St, you can camp in the yard at $4 for adults and $2 for kids; there are budget rooms with shared bathrooms at $20/25; or the motel-style units (which sleep up to six) cost $40/45 plus $5 for extras. The motel has a pool and a restaurant.

FAR NTH QUEENSLAND

One km from the centre of town, near the railway station, the *Chillagoe Bush Camp & Ecolodge* (☎ (070) 94 7155) is a former miners' village with accommodation in dongas and transportables. There are backpacker beds for $12, doubles for $35 or family units (up to four people) for $45. It's a friendly place to stay, and attracts a blend of tourists, workers and geologists. Home-cooked meals are available. Breakfast and lunch will cost $5 to $10, dinner is $12.50 and the Saturday smorgasbord costs $15.

About a km farther out of town is the *Chillagoe Creek Homestead* (☎ (070) 94 7160), which has three guest rooms which cost $50 a double for B&B. One of the rooms sleeps up to four and has its own bathroom, the other two are smaller and share a bathroom.

You can also camp in the yard here for $10 a site, and Mary, the owner, can supply camping gear and barbecue facilities. She also does walking tours around the town and the local area, depending on what people are interested in seeing. To get to the homestead, follow the signs to the airstrip, then turn left. You'll see two houses – it's the one on the right.

Places to Eat

The cafe at the *Chillagoe Tourist Village*/BP service station is the best bet for roadhouse-style meals and takeaway food. The *general store* also does takeaways.

The *Black Cockatoo Hotel* has basic pub grub, with lunches from $3 to $5 and dinner mains around $8. The *Chillagoe Caves Lodge* has its own restaurant, and you can also eat out at the *Chillagoe Bush Camp & Ecolodge* even if you're not staying there – see Places to Stay earlier.

Getting There & Away

Bus There's a bus service from Cairns to Chillagoe every Monday, Wednesday and Friday. White Car Coaches (☎ (070) 91 1855) takes you from Cairns to Mareeba, from where a connecting local service continues on to Chillagoe. The full trip takes about 3½ hours and costs $39.05 each way.

Tours Several companies run tours to Chillagoe from Cairns – see Organised Tours in the Cairns section for details.

TOLGA (pop 840)

Tolga, a small township five km north of Atherton, has a couple of eateries and some interesting craft shops including the Tolga Woodworks, which is worth a visit. It has an impressive collection of wood crafts on sale – all beautifully made, with prices to match.

You can turn east at Tolga to reach the **Danbulla Forest Drive**, which technically starts at Tinaroo Falls 13 km north-east of here (see the Lake Tinaroo section for details).

Just south of town is a turn off to the *Homestead Tourist Park* (☎ (070) 95 4266), a modern tourist complex in an 80-hectare avocado farm. You can visit the packing shed, and there's an art gallery, a colonial-style restaurant and four motel units which cost $60 a double. This place is a popular stop for the tourist buses.

ATHERTON (pop 5200)

Atherton is the major township in the Tableland. While it's a busy commercial centre and a pleasant, prosperous town, Atherton has little of interest to tourists in its own right.

Information

The Atherton Tableland Promotion Bureau (☎ (070) 91 4222), on the corner of Mable and Vernon Sts, has good general information on the Tableland, especially if you're looking for local farmstays, guesthouses and B&Bs. The Old Post Office Gallery, at the south end of town on the road to Herberton, is a small art gallery and museum and also has general information, and is open daily from 10 am to 4 pm.

The Department of Primary Industries (Forest Services) (☎ (070) 91 1844) has an office in Main St. This is the place to come for camping permits and information on the state forests in the Tableland.

Things to See & Do

At the south end of town on the Herberton road is **Platypus Park**, which has a few picnic tables beside the creek plus a collection of old railway carriages on display. The park is also the starting point for the **Herberton Range Historic Railway**, which runs from Atherton to Herberton via the Herberton Ranges. The railway line passes through the Herberton Ranges, passing through two long tunnels and climbing a grade of one in 33 over seven km, making it the steepest railway in Queensland. Check with the information centre for fares, running times etc.

Places to Stay

The *Woodlands Tourist Park* (☎ (070) 91 1407), on the Herberton road at the southern entrance to town, is a pleasant little camping ground with tent sites for $5.50 per person and on-site cabins from $40 a double.

Atherton Backpackers (☎ (070) 91 3552), at 37 Alice St near the town centre, is a very comfortable, quiet and friendly family-run hostel with dorm beds from $11 to $13 and singles/doubles for $16/28. It's signposted off the main road into town from Yungaburra, just before it meets the Kennedy Hwy. They have bikes for hire, and also do pickups from Cairns if you're planning to stay more than a night or two.

There are three motels in town, all of a fairly similar standard. The most central option is the *Motel Hinterland* (☎ (070) 91 1885), at 44 Cook St, which has rooms at $45/50 for singles/doubles.

LAKE TINAROO

From Atherton, Tolga or Yungaburra it's a short drive to this large lake created for the Barron River hydroelectric power scheme. The Queensland Forest Service publishes a good map/brochure called the *Danbulla Forest Drive*, which highlights the main camping grounds and sights on the circuit drive around the lake.

The drive starts at **Tinaroo Falls**, a sleepy village at the north-western corner of the lake. Beside the boat ramp here you can usually hire sailboards, catamarans and paddle skis. The *Tinaroo Pines Caravan Park* (☎ (070) 95 8232) is a good place to camp, with tent sites from $10 and on-site cabins from $34. There's also the *Tinaroo Lakes Motel* (☎ (070) 95 8200), which has budget motel units from $48/52.

Just out of town there's a lookout point over the huge **Tinaroo Falls Dam**. At the lookout, *Cafe Pensini's Deckbar & Bistro* is a fairly mod bar and bistro with great views. You can eat indoors or out on the decking, and they open for lunch daily, with snacks and burgers as well as a $10 all-you-can-eat smorgasbord. They also do dinners on Friday and Saturday nights, with mains ranging from $7 to $17.

Once you're past the dam, the road turns to dirt and the Danbulla Forest Drive officially starts. The drive is a 31-km circuit around the lake, finally emerging on the Gillies Hwy at Boar Pocket Rd, four km north of Lake Barrine. It passes several free lakeside camping grounds, run by the Department of Primary Industries (☎ (070) 91 1844) (there are showers and toilets). One of the most pleasant places is **Platypus Rocks Lookout**, which is the first place you come to. There's a great camping ground with grass and shady pine trees and a boat ramp. Further on, just after the **Kauri Creek camping area**, you pass a 4WD track which leads north through the hills all the way to Mareeba. There's no signpost, just a 'Restricted Access' sign. It's a spectacular drive with some great views along the way, but you need a permit from the Department of Primary Industries (Forest Services) (☎ (070) 91 1844) in Atherton to do the drive.

Lake Euramoo, about halfway around the circuit, is in a double volcanic crater; there's a short botanical walk around the lake. There is another crater at **Mobo Creek**, a short walk off the drive. Then, 25 km from the dam, it's a short walk to the **Cathedral Fig**, a truly gigantic strangler fig tree.

YUNGABURRA (pop 807)

This pretty village is 13 km east of Atherton

along the Gillies Hwy. It's right in the centre of the Tableland, and if you have transport it's a good base from which to explore the lakes, waterfalls and national parks nearby. There are a couple of craft shops and galleries here, some good restaurants, and the central streets of the town have been classified by the National Trust and are quite atmospheric.

Three km south of Yungaburra is the **Curtain Fig**, a strangler fig named for its aerial roots which form a 15-metre-high hanging screen.

Places to Stay

The excellent *On the Wallaby* (☎ (070) 51 0889), at 37 Eacham Rd, is a small backpackers' hostel sleeping 15, with double and twin rooms upstairs and good living areas downstairs. There's a free pick-up bus from Cairns and the nightly cost is $10 per person including breakfast, or you can camp in the backyard for $5 per tent. This hostel also offers an overnight Tableland trip (see the earlier Cairns and Atherton Tableland Organised Tours sections).

The *Lake Eacham Hotel* (☎ (070) 95 3515), is a fine old village pub with a magnificent old timber dining room and comfy pub-style rooms upstairs at $40/45 – breakfast costs $7 to $10. The *Kookaburra Lodge* (☎ (070) 95 3222), on the corner of Oak St and Eacham Rd, is a small, friendly and peaceful place with bright modern units from $45 a double. They have a no-smoking, no-kids policy. There's a pool and tiny dining room with three-course meals for $17.

The *Yungaburra Park Motel* (☎ (070) 95 3211), on the Atherton road, has modern motel units with air-con and TVs from $52.

Places to Eat

There are three good restaurants in Yungaburra, which just about certifies the town as the eating capital of the Tableland. The *Lake Eacham Hotel* also has a dining room that does buffet meals or you can eat in the public bar.

The *Burra Inn* is a charming little BYO gourmet restaurant opposite the pub. The country-style food is excellent, with main meals for around $18.

On the Gillies Hwy (the road to Yungaburra), *Nick's Swiss-Italian Restaurant* is a modern chalet-style building with a yodelling, accordion-playing chef/owner who comes out to entertain the guests once he's finished cooking. The lunch menu here covers sandwiches, salads and pastas, with mains mostly from $9 to $12, and at night the pastas range from $11 to $12 and other mains like a Matterhorn-platter of pork, sauerkraut and sausage, or medallions of venison are $15 to $19.

Also on the Gillies Hwy is *Snibbles BYO*. It's set in a restored old Queenslander, and you can eat inside or out on the verandah. They serve light lunches like sandwiches, crêpes and filled croissants from $6 to $8, and at night main courses are in the $15 to $18 range. On Tuesday they do a three-course family roast special for $12 for adults and $7 for children. This place also has a takeaway section that sells pre-prepared restaurant-quality meals for under $8 – you just choose from the menu, take it home and heat it up!

LAKES EACHAM & BARRINE

These two lovely crater lakes are off the Gillies Hwy just east of Yungaburra. Both are reached by paved roads, and are great swimming spots. There are rainforest walking tracks around their perimeters – six km around Lake Barrine, four km around Lake Eacham.

At Lake Barrine the *Lake Barrine Tea House* serves Devonshire teas, snacks and light lunches daily from 9 am to 5 pm. From the teahouse, you can take a 45-minute cruise (at 10.15 am or 3.15 pm) which costs $7 for adults or $4.50 for kids. Lake Eacham is quieter and more beautiful – an excellent place for a picnic or a swim, and there's a small kids' pool.

Both lakes are national parks and camping is not allowed. However, there are camp sites at *Lake Eacham Tourist Park* (☎ (070) 95 3730), two km down the Malanda road from Lake Eacham. The secluded *Chambers*

Wildlife Rainforest Apartments (☎ (070 95 3754) has self-contained one-bedroom apartments sleeping one to four people at $240 for three nights, usually with a three-night minimum stay. There's also one three-bedroom unit sleeping up to five at $300 for three nights. They supply binoculars and bird books here.

PEERAMON

This tiny village is tucked into the hills midway between Malanda and Yungaburra. The *Peeramon Hotel* (☎ (070) 96 5873) is a wonderful old country pub with a great atmosphere. They have old-fashioned accommodation upstairs, in timber-lined rooms which open out onto a broad verandah. The beds are comfortable and the rooms are well presented. There's a bunk room with five beds at $10 per person, or you can have a double room for $30. Breakfast is included. The pub also has a restaurant and beer garden, and the food is good pub tucker with an exotic twist. Main courses range from $10 to $12.

MALANDA (pop 900)

About 15 km south of Lake Eacham, Malanda is one of the most pleasant spots to stay on the Tableland – a small town with some old buildings in its centre, a couple of pubs and some good places to eat and stay. Malanda also has a huge dairy and claims to have the longest milk run in Australia since it supplies milk all the way to Darwin and the north of Western Australia.

Things to See & Do

On the outskirts of town, beside the Johnstone River crossing, the **Malanda Falls** drop into a big old pool which is surrounded by lawns and forest. It's a popular swimming spot, and there are picnic tables and a one-km walking trail through the forest nearby.

If you're staying in town, the **Majestic Theatre** (☎ (070) 96 5726), on Eacham Place, is a great old-fashioned cinema which screens the latest releases.

A couple of km west of Malanda is the

Broomfield Swamp, where a viewing platform beside the road overlooks an eroded volcanic crater. This swampy wetlands is an important sanctuary for waterbirds, although you can't see a whole lot from the lookout without binoculars. Sunset is the best time to come.

Places to Stay

Next to the Malanda Falls, the *Malanda Falls Caravan Park* (☎ (070) 96 5314), at 38 Park Ave, has tent sites at $10 and on-site cabins from $32.

The *Malanda Hotel* (☎ (070) 96 5101), in the centre of town on the corner of James and English Sts, has pub-style rooms at $15/30 or basic motel-style units next door at $24/ 34.

The *Malanda Lodge Motel* (☎ (070) 96 5555), on the edge of town on the Millaa Millaa road, has good modern units from $55.

There are also a couple of good places to stay in the hills around Malanda – see the following Around Malanda section.

Places to Eat

The *Malanda Hotel* is renowned for its food. It's a huge old timber pub with a great dining room. The menu includes steaks ($9), Thai curry prawns ($13) and barramundi and salad ($12.50), and on Friday and Saturday nights they have an incredibly popular smorgasbord meal. *Muppee's BYO*, at 22 James St, is a casual pizza and pasta joint.

AROUND MALANDA
Places to Stay & Eat

The *Honeyflow Country Guesthouse* (☎ (070) 96 8173), signposted off the road heading north to Lake Eacham, is an old heritage homestead set in lovely gardens. There are four guest suites, each with its own bathroom and living area, TV, ceiling fan and heater, and tea and coffee-making facilities. Dinner, and B&B costs $145 a double, and all the guests dine together so it's like a little dinner party.

Platypus Forest Resort (☎ (070) 96 5926) is also off the Lake Eacham road at 12 Topaz Road, about six km north of Malanda. This friendly and relaxed place has received very good reports from travellers. It's a rustic lodge in a small cluster of rainforest, with lots of wildlife including platypus in a creek and Lumholtz tree-climbing kangaroos. The accommodation is backpacker-style, with bunk beds at $15 a night and one double room at $34. There's a swimming hole in the creek, a hot tub and sauna, and you can get a home-cooked evening meal for $5, and vegetarians are catered for. You can get here from Cairns with the tour company KTC Connections (☎ (070) 50 0663). (See Organised Tours in the Cairns section for details.)

Fairdale Farm (☎ (070) 96 6599) is on Hillcrest Rd, three km south of Malanda – take the turn off near the Malanda Lodge Motel on the Millaa Millaa road, it's signposted from there. This is a 120-hectare dairy farm in a scenic setting, with a charming Federation-style cottage that sleeps up to six and has great valley views. The cottage costs $100 a night for a family of four, plus $20 for each extra person. There is also a renovated farmhouse with B&B rooms at $60/85 for singles/doubles, or full board is available for $100 per person. Guests can get involved in the farm activities, or just relax and enjoy the setting. The *Roundhouse Tavern* at Tarzali, nine km south of Malanda, has a very good reputation for its food and rustic setting.

MILLAA MILLAA (pop 330)
Set in the heart of dairying country 24 km south of Malanda, the tiny township of Millaa Millaa has a caravan park with tent sites and cabins, and the *Millaa Millaa Hotel* has accommodation and meals. The **Eacham Historical Society Museum** (☎ (070) 97 2147), on the main street, has a collection of tools, equipment and local history items relating to the area's timber and dairy industries. It is open on Thursday from 9 am to noon and Friday from 10 am to noon, or by appointment. A few km west of Millaa Millaa, the East Evelyn road passes the **Millaa Millaa Lookout** with its superb panoramic view.

Waterfalls Circuit
The start of this 16-km 'waterfall circuit' road is a little way east of Millaa Millaa, and passes some of the most picturesque falls on the Tableland. You enter the circuit by taking Theresa Creek Rd, one km east of Millaa Millaa on the Palmerston Hwy. **Millaa Millaa Falls**, the first you reach, are the most spectacular, and have the best swimming hole and a grassy area in front of the falls where you can have a picnic.

Continuing around the circuit, you reach **Zillie Falls**, where a short walking trail leads to a lookout point beside the falls. Farther on you come to **Ellinjaa Falls**, with a 200-metre walking trail down to a swimming hole at the base of the falls, before returning to the Palmerston Hwy just 2.5 km out of Millaa Millaa. A further 5.5 km down the Palmerston Hwy there's a turn off to **Mungalli Falls**, five km off the highway, where the *Mugalli Falls Outpost* (☎ (070) 31 1144) has a teahouse/restaurant and offers horse-trail rides for $65 a half day, $85 a full day. There are also 10 modern self-contained cabins here with communal cooking facilities, which go for $40 a double plus $5 for extra bodies.

The Palmerston Hwy continues through Palmerston National Park to Innisfail.

MT HYPIPAMEE NATIONAL PARK
The Kennedy Hwy between Atherton and Ravenshoe passes the eerie Mt Hypipamee crater. It's a scenic 800-metre looped walk from the car park, past **Dinner Falls**, to this narrow, 138-metre-deep crater with its spooky, evil-looking lake far below. The lake's surface is covered in a green crust of duckweed. Back at Dinner Falls, there's a good swimming area and there is a picnic area beside the car park, but you can no longer camp here.

HERBERTON (pop 950)
On a slightly longer alternative route between Atherton and Ravenshoe, this old tin-mining town holds a colourful Tin Festival each September. The town is basically a collection of old timber buildings scattered

across a cluster of hills, and there are three pubs and a couple of cafes on the main street. On Holdcroft Dve is the **Herberton Historical Village**, made up of about 30 old buildings which have been transported here from around the Tableland.

Herberton is also one of the departure points for the **Herberton Range Historic Railway** – see the Atherton section for details.

If you're feeling adventurous, you can also head west from Herberton through the old mining township of **Irvinebank**, eventually linking up with the road to Chillagoe – see the Mareeba to Chillagoe section for details.

Places to Stay
Herberton has a caravan park with tent sites and cabins, and the *Royal Hotel* (☎ (070) 96 2231), on Grace St in the centre of town, has average pub-style rooms at $15/25.

Signposted off the highway nine km south of Herberton, *Banyula Homestay* (☎ (070) 96 2668) is a modern, comfortable home in a peaceful bush setting, run by a friendly couple. They have two guest rooms costing $60 a double for B&B, and for another $20 you can enjoy a three-course home-cooked dinner. It's another four km from the turn off to the house.

RAVENSHOE (pop 880)
At an altitude of 915 metres, Ravenshoe is a forestry centre on the western edge of the Tableland. It was once a thriving timber town, and while there are still a couple of mills operating here, most of the logging has stopped and things are pretty quiet around here nowadays.

From Ravenshoe you can take a ride on the **Millstream Express**, an historic steam-train which runs north along a seven-km track to Tumoulin. The train runs every Saturday and Sunday at 2.30 pm, as well as on public holidays except Christmas and Good Friday, and it doesn't run during February or March. The cost is $10 for adults and $5 for children, and light refreshments are available.

Little Millstream Falls are two km south

of Ravenshoe on the Tully Gorge road, and the **Tully Falls** are 24 km south.

Six km past Ravenshoe and one km off the road are the **Millstream Falls**, the widest in Australia although only 13 metres high. There are some great swimming areas here, but camping is no longer permitted.

Places to Stay
The *Tall Timbers Caravan Park* (☎ (070) 97 6325), on the Kennedy Hwy, has tent sites at $12 and four cabins at $30. The *Club Hotel/Motel* (☎ (070) 97 6109), at 47 Grigg St, has pub rooms at $15/25 for singles/twins, and motel units at $30/40.

The *Kool Moon Motel* (☎ (070) 97 6325), at 6 Moore St, has units for $30/40.

Places to Eat
The *Club Hotel* does reasonably good counter meals with mains from $7 to $9. Alternatively, the *Popular Cafe*, across the road at 66 Grigg St, is a pleasant little cafe with booths and tables, and a good selection of cooked meals from $6 to $10. They also do pizzas and have live music here some Saturday nights.

RAVENSHOE TO UNDARA OR CHARTERS TOWERS
The Kennedy Hwy continues south-west from Ravenshoe for 114 km, from where you can head south to Charters Towers by paved road all the way, or west by the Gulf Developmental Road to Croydon and Normanton via the Undara Lava Tubes.

The small mining town of **Mt Garnet**, 47 km west of Ravenshoe, comes alive one weekend every May when it hosts one of Queensland's top outback race meetings. The *Norwestgate Travellers Rest* (☎ (070) 97 9249), at the BP service station in the centre of town, has tent sites and budget motel units and does takeaway meals.

Fifteen km east of Mt Garnet are the **Innot Hot Springs**, where you can lie in one of the sandy bath-like springs beside the highway and watch the traffic go by – kind of a bizarre experience, really.

About 60 km past Mt Garnet, the road

passes through **Forty Mile Scrub National Park**, where the semi-evergreen vine thicket is a descendant of the vegetation that covered much of the Gondwanaland supercontinent 300 million years ago – before Australia, South America, India, Africa and Antarctica drifted apart.

A little farther on is the turn off to Undara Lava Tubes and the Gulf country – see the Gulf Savannah chapter for details.

Cairns to Port Douglas

The Bruce Hwy, which runs nearly 2000 km north from Brisbane, ends in Cairns, but the surfaced coastal road continues for another 110 km north to Mossman and Daintree, with a turn off to Port Douglas. This final stretch, the Captain Cook Hwy, is one of Queensland's most scenic coastal drives, along what is known as the Marlin Coast. The middle section, from Ellis Beach to Port Douglas, runs right along the coastline past a string of pretty coves and superb beaches.

NORTHERN BEACHES
North along the Captain Cook Hwy are Cairns' Northern Beaches, which are really a string of coastal suburbs. In order, these are Machans Beach, Holloways Beach, Yorkeys Knob, Trinity Beach, Kewarra Beach, Clifton Beach and Palm Cove. Holloways, Trinity and Palm Cove are the best for a short beach trip from Cairns. See Getting Around in the Cairns section for details of buses to these places.

Machans Beach & Holloway's Beach
Machans Beach is a quiet little residential community. It doesn't really have much of a beach – the sandy strip starts a little further north at Holloway's Beach, which has a life-saving club and a netted swimming enclosure. There's a beachfront kiosk here, as well as *Green's Restaurant* (☎ (070) 55 9200), which has a great setting overlooking the beach. The restaurant takes advantage of the views with full length windows, and has

an outdoor decking area and the small *Beach Bar*. The menu specialises in seafood and has good vegetarian dishes, with main courses from \$17 to \$19, or there's a three-course special for \$19.95. Green's is open nightly for dinner and is licensed, and on Sunday they put on an all-you-can-eat barbecue lunch at \$10 a head.

Yorkeys Knob
Yorkeys Knob also has sandy beaches, and the *Yorkeys Knob Beachfront Van Park* (☎ (070) 55 7201) has the closest beachfront camping to Cairns. It's a well-established park with plenty of trees, and tent sites from \$12 and on-site vans from \$24 a double.

Trinity Beach
Trinity is one of the best of Cairns' northern beach suburbs. It has a long stretch of sand sheltered by a high headland at the southern end, and there's a life-saving club and a stinger net here over summer.

Places to Stay The *Sundowner Motor Inn* (☎ (070) 55 6194), on the corner of the main road in and the Esplanade, has six motel-style units. They don't look much from the outside, but they are clean and neat and good value. Backpackers can share a four-bed room for \$15 per person, or you can have your own unit for \$45 to \$55, depending on the season.

At 47 Vasey Esplanade, the rather unique *Casablanca Domes* (☎ (070) 55 6339) is a set of ten white concrete domes which each house a fully self-contained and very comfortable holiday unit, each with air-con and a full kitchen. The one-bedroom domes sleep up to four and cost around \$60 a double; the two-bedroom models sleep up to six and cost around \$70 a double; each extra person costs another \$5. The complex has its own pool and restaurant.

Trinity Beach is being developed at a fierce pace. There are a couple of big, up-market apartment complexes along the beachfront – including the *Roydon Apartments* (☎ (070) 57 6512), at 85 Vasey

Esplanade, with two and three-bedroom apartments from $100 to $220 a night.

Places to Eat Trinity Beach has a couple of good eateries on the beachfront, too. *Trinity Pizza* is a tiny place which serves a great range of salads at lunch time, as well as pastas and mini-pizzas. At night they serve gourmet pizzas, pastas and salads. There's a covered courtyard or tables out on the footpath. Also opposite the beach, and across on the other side of the main road, is the new *Beaches on Trinity* (☎ (070) 57 8855), a very impressive Mediterranean-style restaurant with a stylish décor in whites and aquagreens. It opens for lunch and dinner daily, and has home-made pastas for $10, wood-fired oven pizzas for $10 to $13, and mains like calamari, char-grilled sirloin and seafood casserole for around $18. The home-made olive bread is delicious.

High up on the hill overlooking the waterfront is the old *Trinity Beach Hotel*. It's a popular spot for a cool drink, and has a covered beer garden with a bistro section serving the usual steaks, schnitzels and seafood for around $9.

Clifton Beach

Another three km north of the Trinity Beach turn off is Clifton Beach, a laid-back residential community which is a lot less developed than its neighbours Palm Cove and Trinity Beach.

Places to Stay There are two caravan parks at Clifton Beach. The *Paradise Gardens Caravan Resort* (☎ (070) 55 3712), on the corner of the highway and Clifton Rd, has tent sites from $12 and on-site vans.

There are a couple of holiday apartments along the beachfront: *Agincourt Holiday Apartments* (☎ (070) 55 3500), 69 Arlington Esplanade, has one-bedroom units from $65, and *Argosy* (☎ (070) 55 3333), 119 Arlington Esplanade, has units starting at $110.

Dolce Vita B&B (☎ (070) 55 3889), at 133 Arlington Esplanade, is one of the few B&Bs in this area. It's a modern and comfortable home run by a friendly young couple, and

they have two guest rooms which cost $35/60 for singles/doubles, including a tropical breakfast.

Wild World

Wild World, on the highway between Clifton Beach and Palm Cove and 22 km north of Cairns, is a fauna theme park with kangaroos, wombats, snakes and crocodiles. It's pretty tacky, with regular 'shows' throughout the day, including a koala photo session and an Aboriginal cultural performance. It is open daily from 8.15 am to 5 pm; entry costs $15 for adults, $8 for children.

Palm Cove

Since the mid-1980s, Palm Cove has developed from a sleepy little beach community into an exclusive resort town. It's still quite small and a very pretty spot despite all the development, and has a good beach, some excellent restaurants and a collection of expensive shops and boutiques. Most of the accommodation is of the up-market resort/hotel variety, and you'll see as many Rolex watches and gold-embossed T-shirts around here as you would in Port Douglas.

Palm Cove has its own jetty, and many of the cruise boats call in for pick-ups on their way out to the reef and islands. There are no banks here, but the shopping village in the centre of Williams Esplanade has a post office, clothes boutiques, a tour-booking desk and several cafes and restaurants.

The **golf course** at the Novatel Palm Cove Resort is open to the public. A round costs $15 for nine holes, $30 for 18 holes and club hire costs $15.

Places to Stay The *Palm Cove Camping Area* (☎ (070) 55 3824), at 149 Williams Esplanade, is a beautifully kept beachfront camping ground run by the local council. Sites cost $7 a night or $45 a week; dogs aren't allowed, and the showers are cold water only.

The *Palm Cove Retreat* (☎ (070) 55 3636) is a horse-riding ranch with bunkhouse accommodation in log cabins for $12 per person. There are 24 beds in four-bed rooms, with communal kitchen and laundry facilities. This place is on the inland side of the highway, opposite the Palm Cove turn off. The *Silvester Palms Holiday Apartments* (☎ (070) 55 3831), at 32 Vievers Rd, has old but pleasant units starting from $60.

The *Coconut Lodge Motel* (☎ (070) 55 3734), at 95-97 Williams Esplanade, has modern motel units with kitchenettes which go for $69, or $89 with air-con. The *Reef Retreat* (☎ (070) 59 1744), 100 metres back from the beachfront at 10-14 Harpa St, is an attractive complex of 10 self-contained one-bedroom units which start at $80 a night. There's a great pool here, surrounded by towering melaleuca trees, and fourteen new one and two-bedroom units are currently being built and should be open by the time you read this.

Marlin Waters (☎ (070) 55 3933), at 131 Williams Esplanade, is a four-storey complex of modern serviced apartments. There are 21 one-bedroom units, a pool and spa, and rooms start at $100 a night. The jointly managed *Paradise Village Resort* (☎ (070) 55 3300) and *Villa Paradiso* (☎ (070) 59 1818), on either side of the Paradise Village shopping complex, have motel-style units from $120, one-bedroom units from $160 and two and three-bedroom apartments from around $200 to $300.

The *Allamanda* (☎ (070) 55 3000), at 1 Vievers Rd, is an impressive four-star resort hotel on the beachfront, with three pools, a spa and a good bar/restaurant. The units are all self-contained and range from $225 to $450. The *Novatel Palm Cove Resort* (☎ (070) 59 1234), on Coral Coast Dve a couple of hundred metres back from the beach, is a huge four-star resort with a golf course,10 pools, squash and tennis courts and much more. Rooms range from $170 to $315 a night.

Places to Eat & Drink There are several eateries in the Paradise Village shopping complex in the centre of Williams Esplanade: *Cocky's at the Cove* is a casual eatery fronted by umbrella-shaded tables, and a good spot for a cappuccino, a sandwich or a muffin. *Il Forno Pizza* is a small and stylish BYO pizza joint with pizzas from $10 to $12 and a few pasta dishes. *Hannah's* is a more up-market licensed restaurant with mains in the $16 to $20 range.

The *Palm Cove Tavern Bar* on Vievers Ave is the local pub. The bistro serves counter meals, and on weekends they do barbecue lunches for $10.50 a head, and on Sunday night they have a three-course meal deal for $14.

On the corner of the Captain Cook Hwy and Vievers Rd, the *Coach House* is a popular and cosy licensed restaurant. It has a good reputation for its food, and specialises in seafood and steaks with mains in the $16 to $22 range.

The *Beach Bar* is a colourful little cocktail shack next to the shopping village. It's a popular spot for a drink and is open from 2 pm until around midnight most nights, and has live entertainment most Wednesday to Sunday nights.

Double Island

This small tropical island is just a couple of hundred metres off shore from Palm Cove. There's an exclusive resort on the island, the *Double Island Retreat* (☎ (070) 57 7222), which is the former home of the businesswoman Janet Holmes a Court. The resort building is a beautiful timber roundhouse; the room tariff is $380 a night, plus $80 per person for meals, with a minimum three-night stay. When there's room, the resort's BYO restaurant is open to the public on Friday, Saturday and Sunday nights, with a set menu at $75 per person, and for Sunday lunches at $80 per person. The water taxi across to the island costs $7.

Ellis Beach

Round the headland past Palm Cove and Double Island, the highway meets the coast at **Ellis Beach**, which is a lovely spot. Its southern end is an unofficial nude-bathing beach and the central part of the beach has a good camping ground. The *Ellis Beach Resort* (☎ (070) 55 3538) has excellent beachfront camping grounds with tent sites at \$10, on-site vans from \$45 and motel units for \$55. The resort's kiosk and cafe serves sit-down meals and takeaways, and there is live music here most Sunday afternoons. There was talk of the resort undergoing a major redevelopment, so all this may have changed by the time you get there.

ELLIS BEACH TO PORT DOUGLAS

This section of the Captain Cook Hwy follows the coastline for much of its length. Soon after Ellis Beach and 40 km from Cairns, **Hartleys Creek Crocodile Farm** has a collection of Australian wildlife typical of the Far North. Most of the enclosures are a bit shoddy but showmanship makes it one of the most interesting 'animal places' in Australia. When they feed Charlie the crocodile you know for certain why it's not wise to get bitten by one! And you've never seen anything eat apples until you've seen a cassowary knock back a dozen of them. The park is open daily and there's a park tour at 11 am and a snake show at 2 pm, but make sure you're there at crocodile-feeding time which is at 3 pm; entry is \$12 for adults and \$6 for children.

Forty-five km north of Cairns is the *Turtle Cove Resort* (☎ (070) 59 1800), an exclusive beachfront resort for gays and lesbians. The resort has good motel-style units with aircon, TVs etc, its own restaurant, access to a private beach and a great swimming pool and spa. They run various tours for their guests and have a pick-up service from Cairns' airport. Rates in the garden units are \$84/98/117 for singles/ doubles/triples; the beachfront units are \$130/146/165.

Port Douglas to Cape Tribulation

PORT DOUGLAS (pop 3800)

In the early days of Far North Queensland's development, Port Douglas was a rival for Cairns, but when Cairns eventually got the upper hand, Port Douglas became a sleepy

Port Douglas

0   400   800 m

1 Port o' Call Lodge
2 Aussie Bike Hire
3 Going Bananas
4 The Mango Tree
5 Pandanus Caravan Park
6 Lazy Lizard Motor Inn
7 Rusty Pelican Motel
8 Sheraton Mirage Resort
9 Vacation Village
10 Radisson Royal Palms Resort
11 Reef Terraces Resort
12 Four Mile Beach Caravan Park
13 Nimrod Apartments
14 Rainforest Habitat

FAR NTH QUEENSLAND

little backwater. In the mid-1980s, however, entrepreneurs like Christopher Skase began to realise what a delightful place it was, and up went the multimillion dollar Sheraton Mirage and Radisson Royal Palms resorts. These were quickly followed by a golf course, a heliport, hovercraft services from Cairns, a marina and shopping complex, and an avenue of palms lining the road from the Captain Cook Hwy to Port Douglas – all the ingredients of a retreat for the rich and fashionable. Yet, despite all this development, 'Port' has managed to keep most of its original charm and there is still cheap accommodation.

The town still has relaxed village feel about it, with its open-air Sunday markets, a long stretch of beach backed by palm trees and a couple of good old pubs on Macrossan St with outdoor courtyards. Of course, it also has plenty to offer in the glitz and glamour stakes, like the marina with its own shopping complex, a golf course that has played host to some of the world's great golfers and an excellent range of restaurants that would do any inner-city suburb of Melbourne or Sydney proud.

Notwithstanding its own charms, part of Port's appeal lies in the fact that it's such a great base from which to explore the rest of Far North Queensland. You can take a cruise out to the Great Barrier Reef or the Low Isles, visit Mossman Gorge or Cape Tribulation, cruise the Daintree River, or even head west into the outback or north to the Cape York Peninsula.

History

Port Douglas was founded in 1877 as the port town for the Hodgkinson River goldfields, and went through several name changes – Island Point, Owensville and Salisbury – before it was named Port Douglas, in honour of the then Queensland premier John Douglas. The town flourished from the outset, and by 1879 had 14 hotels and a fleet of Cobb & Co coaches linking the town with the goldfields. All this prosperity came to a grinding halt in the mid-1880s when Cairns

Port Douglas' Prodigal Son

Port Douglas is one of the few places in Australia where people talk openly in admiration of the high-flying 1980s entrepreneur Christopher Skase. It was Skase's vision that transformed Port Douglas from a sleepy seaside village into one of Australia's most prestigious tourist destinations, and most people who live here now owe at least a part of their livelihood to the fact that Skase poured millions of dollars of his investors' money into the town during the 1980s. If Skase ever returned to Port Douglas, all would be forgiven and he would probably receive a ticker-tape parade along the length of the avenue of palms he had planted here.

The rest of Australia would also like to see Christopher come home some day, although his reception elsewhere would probably be closer to a lynching than a ticker-tape parade. When Skase's media and tourism empire, Quintex, collapsed in 1989 with debts of $1.6 billion, he fled the country and left his investors holding the burnt end of a very blackened stick.

Skase and his wife, Pixie, took refuge on the Spanish island of Mallorca, and although the Australian government persistently sought his extradition to face 32 company law charges over the Quintex collapse, Skase's lawyers and his convenient medical condition have so far combined to keep him in Spain. His team of doctors and lawyers claimed he was desperately ill with a terminal lung disease which prevented him from travelling, and every time he appeared in public he was in a wheelchair with an oxygen mask clamped to his mouth. Back in Australia, the cartoonists were having a field day.

In 1994, the Spanish courts finally agreed to extradite Skase back to Australia, but a last-minute appeal based on his illness overturned the decision and he was granted immunity from further prosecution. Soon after, Skase appeared in public for the first time without wheelchair or oxygen mask – a remarkable and timely recovery. It now seems unlikely that Skase will ever be seen in Australia again – not even in Port Douglas. ■

was chosen ahead of Port Douglas as the terminal for the new rail line from Kuranda and Mareeba. A disastrous cyclone in 1911 destroyed most of the town's buildings, and Port remained a sleepy Brigadoon-like coastal village until its recent emergence from the mists of obscurity into the glare of the tourism spotlight.

Orientation
Port Douglas is spread along a long, low spit of land, with the Coral Sea on the east side and Packers Creek on the west. It's six km from the highway along Port Douglas Rd, then Davidson St, into the town centre. About half-way in you'll pass the Sheraton Mirage resort, and its golf course. Davidson St ends in a T-intersection with Macrossan St; to the right is the start of Four Mile Beach, which stretches all the way south; to the left is the town centre with most of the shops and restaurants. There are fine views over the coastline and sea from Flagstaff Hill lookout.

The Marina Mirage, just west of the centre, is the departure point for most of the trips to the reef and the Low Isles. Buses arrive at and depart from the Coral Coaches terminal, which is off Wharf St just north of the marina.

Information
Tourist Information While there isn't an independent tourist information office in Port Douglas, there are quite a few private booking agencies which display the big 'i'. These places are generally very helpful with booking tours and general advice, although it may be worth checking with a couple of different ones to see how opinion and advice differs.

The Port Douglas Tourist Information Centre (☎ (070) 99 5599), at 23 Macrossan St, the Adventure Centre (☎ (070) 99 4650), at 8 Macrossan St, and the Port Douglas Visitors Bureau (☎ (070) 99 4644), at 28 Wharf St, are all good places to start out.

Money The ANZ, National and Westpac banks all have branches with ATMs along Macrossan St, and there's a Commonwealth

Bank agency inside the post office. There's also a Thomas Cook Foreign Exchange office, on Macrossan St opposite the Courthouse Hotel, which is open on weekdays from 9.30 am to 6 pm and on Saturday from 9.30 am to 5 pm. There's another foreign exchange booth in the Mirage Marina.

Post & Telecommunications Port's post office is in Owen St, just off Macrossan St, and is open on weekdays from 9 am to 5 pm and Saturday from 9 am to 11 am. There's a cluster of public telephone booths, including a credit-card phone, on Macrossan St between Grant and Owen Sts.

Bookshop & Newsagency The Jungle Bookshop, at 46 Macrossan St, has a good range of novels, travel guides, books on the environment and lots more. The Port Douglas Newsagency, also on Macrossan St, has a wide range of holiday reading material and stocks most major interstate newspapers and several international papers.

Things to See
On the pier off Anzac Park, Ben Cropp's **Shipwreck Museum** has an interesting collection of maritime relics and displays. There's a 'tomb' dedicated to the famous wreck of the *Yongala*, a luxury steamship which sank in the Whitsundays in 1911 with the loss of 120 people; there's also a *Titanic* display and you can watch continuous maritime films. The museum is open from 9 am to 5 pm daily; admission is $5 for adults and $2 for kids.

Port's **Sunday Markets**, held every Sunday in Anzac Park (at the north end of Macrossan St), are great fun to visit. There's always a good crowd wandering around amongst dozens of different stalls and tents, selling everything from hats, sarongs, wind chimes, wood carvings and painted T-shirts to fresh tropical fruit and vegies. Try a glass of freshly crushed sugar-cane juice with ice and lime – a taste sensation!

The **Old Courthouse** (1879), on Wharf St just north of the Macrossan St intersection, is the oldest building in Port, and the only public building to have survived the 1911 cyclone. The courthouse is currently being restored, and there are plans to turn it into a historical museum.

The **Rainforest Habitat**, near where the Port Douglas road meets the main highway, is a fairly new 'eco-attraction' – a huge enclosed canopy forms an artificial rainforest environment with elevated timber boardwalks, and this is home to a large number of birds and butterflies. It's an interesting concept, but disappointing in its execution and a bit pointless, especially when the real thing is so close. It's open daily from 8 am to 5 pm and entry costs $14 for adults and $7 for kids. There's a kiosk serving lunch and dinner, and they also have a brunch deal costing $28/14 for adults/children.

The **Marina Mirage** is a glamorous and up-market shopping complex full of exclusive specialty shops – fashion boutiques, gift and souvenir shops, jewellery shops and the like. There are also a couple of dive companies and several cafes, restaurants and nightclubs in the complex. The marina here is lined with dozens of boats of every size and shape, and this is where the trips out to the reef and the Low Isles depart from.

The Port Douglas Restoration Society has mapped out several walking trails through the town and along the waterfront. A series of brass plaques relate the history of various building sites, and maps and brochures for the walks are available from the information centres.

Activities

Diving Courses This is quite a popular place to learn to dive, although it's not particularly cheap when compared to places further south. It's worth shopping around as there is healthy competition between the (currently) three companies which offer PADI (Professional Association of Diving Instructors) open-water courses.

The cheapest option is Douglas Budget Dive (☎ 015 163 243), which has a four-day course for $349. Port Douglas Dive Centre (☎ (070) 99 5327), with a shop down near

the public wharf at the end of Anzac Park, has a four-day course for $450. Based at the marina, Quicksilver (☎ (070) 99 5050) is the biggest operator, and their five-day course costs $395.

Other Activities If you are after a long stretch of sandy beach, backed by palm trees, then try **Four Mile Beach**. At the north end is a life-saving club, and this section of the beach is patrolled all year round. The club also erects a netted enclosure to protect against box jellyfish from 1 November until mid-May. Windsurfers, paddle-skis, beach chairs and umbrellas can be hired from in front of the life-saving club.

The **Bally Hooley Railway** is a small steam-train that runs a daily shuttle service between the marina, the Radisson Hotel and St Crispins station (at the southern end of the golf course). It operates hourly between 9 am and 5 pm, and return tickets cost $6 for adults and $2 for kids. The **Lady Douglas Paddlewheeler** runs four cruises each day from the marina down Packers Creek to St Cripins station, and you can buy a combination ticket to take the steam-train one way and the paddlewheeler the other way for $20/10 for adults/kids.

You can go **paragliding** with Get High II (☎ 018 187 325), which departs from the marina hourly. Rides cost $48, or you can go along as a spectator for $25.

There are a couple of **horse-riding ranches** in the area. Mowbray Valley Trail Rides (☎ (070) 99 3268) is based south of Port Douglas on the Mowbray River. Their half-day rides depart at 8 am and 1.30 pm and cost $45, and their full-day rides depart at 8 am and cost $79, which includes lunch. Prices include transport to and from Port Douglas – transfers from Cairns can be arranged for another $15. Wonga Beach Trail Rides (☎ (070) 98 7583) and Mt Perseverance Station (☎ (070) 94 1438) also have good reputations – see the Mossman to Daintree and Mossman to Mt Molloy sections later for details of their rides.

Golfers will be thrilled to hear that the **Mirage Country Club** is open to the general public. The not-so-thrilling catch is that it costs $120 a round, although if you're staying at the Sheraton it's only $100. If you think that's a bit steep, the Mossman Golf Club is only a 15-minute drive away and a lot more reasonably priced – see the Mossman section for details.

Organised Tours

There's a huge range of tours operating out of Port Douglas. Options include trips to Cape Tribulation and the Daintree River, the Kuranda Markets and the Atherton Tableland, white-water rafting trips, and 4WD safaris to places like Chillagoe, Cooktown and the Cape York Peninsula. Almost all of the tours operating out of Cairns also do pick-ups from Port Douglas – check with one of the information centres or booking offices, and see Organised Tours in the Cairns section for more details.

Reef Trips There are various operators offering trips out to the Barrier Reef, with boats of all shapes, sizes and speeds. Before deciding which trip to take, it's worth checking on a few different points, such as how many passengers the boat takes, where it goes and how quickly it gets there. Everyone will have a preference for something different – for example, if you're just interested in diving, you'll prefer to be on something that gets you out to the reef quickly rather than on a leisurely yacht cruise.

Quicksilver's (☎ (070) 99 5500) 300-passenger fast cats depart daily from the marina at 10 am, travelling out to Agincourt Reef on the outer reef. The cruise costs $118 for adults, which includes snorkelling gear, a semisubmersible ride, underwater observatory viewing and lunch. Optional extras include a snorkelling expedition ($25), an introductory dive ($80) or two 40-minute dives for certified divers ($80), or a helicopter flight over the reef ($80). Children pay half fare.

If you'd rather go in a smaller group, there are quite a few boats which offer similar but much more personalised reef, snorkelling

and diving trips. These include the following:

Wavelength (☎ (070) 99 5031)
    Snorkelling cruise $80
Haba Queen (☎ (070) 99 5254)
    Snorkelling cruise $93, with resort dive $153, with two certified dives $163
MV Freestyle (☎ (070) 99 5327)
    Snorkelling cruise $90, with resort dive $155, with two certified dives $165
Impulse (☎ (070) 99 5967)
    Snorkelling cruise $95, with resort dive $150, with two certified dives $160
Phantom (☎ (070) 94 1220)
    Snorkelling cruise $120, with resort dive $185
MV Aristocat (☎ 1800 650 063)
    Fishing and snorkelling cruise $124
MV Outer Edge (☎ 1800 650 063)
    Snorkelling cruise $96, with two resort dives $172, with three certified dives $183
Poseidon (☎ 015 162 500)
    Snorkelling cruise $80, with resort dive $130, with two certified dives $155

These costs generally include lunch and transfers from your accommodation. You can book these trips through your accommodation or at one of the booking agencies.

Low Isles There are also cruises out to the Low Isles, a fine little coral cay surrounded by a lagoon and topped by an old lighthouse (1878). Several smaller boats offer good day trips: *Shaolin* (☎ (070) 99 4650), a refitted Chinese junk, has snorkelling cruises for $75; *Willow* (☎ 018 772 479), a stylish timber yacht, has luxury sailing cruises from around $100; *Sail Away* (☎ (070) 99 5070), a sailing catamaran, has a snorkelling cruises for $70; and *Wavelength* (☎ (070) 99 5031) has half-day snorkelling trips on Wednesday and Saturday for $45. Costs for the full-day trips include lunch, snorkelling gear and boom netting.

Quicksilver (☎ (070) 99 5500) also offers trips out to the Low Isles on their *Wavedancer*, a huge sailing catamaran. The cruise costs $82 for adults or $41 for children, which includes lunch, a trip in a glass bottomed boat, a guided beach walk and

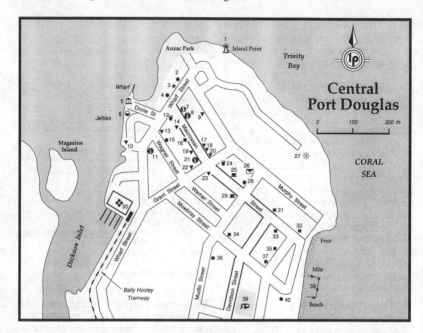

Central
Port Douglas

presentations by a marine biologist. A resort dive is also available for another $65.

Mossman Gorge Coral Coaches (☎ (070) 99 5351) has three services a day out to Mossman Gorge and back. The return fare is $13 and they'll pick you up from wherever you're staying. See the Mossman section for more information on the gorge.

River Cruises Amber Dahlberg's Eco Cruises (☎ (070) 99 5327) offers cruises and birdwatching tours of the mangroves and wetlands of Dickson Inlet. Cruises depart from the marina every day at 7 and 9 am and 3 pm. The cost is $25 per person, with a maximum of six passengers.

Places to Stay

Although it's sometimes perceived as an exclusive and expensive resort town, Port also has a pretty good range of more affordable accommodation, from caravan parks and backpackers' hostels to holiday apartments and motels. Even if you don't have a bulging wallet, you'll more than likely be able to find somewhere to match your budget.

Almost all of the accommodation places here vary their prices depending on the season. During the high season (June to October), not only are prices considerably higher but you'll probably need to make your reservations well in advance. It's also worth having a close look at our maps before you book your accommodation – Port may be small, but it's well spread out, and if you don't have your own transport you could be in for a long walk into the centre.

Caravan Parks Port Douglas has three caravan parks: the *Kulau Caravan Park* (☎ (070) 99 5449), at 28 Davidson St, is the closest to the centre and a short walk from the beach, and has shady tent sites for $13 and on-site cabins from $45. The facilities are good and include a pool and a sheltered cooking area. About a km further south, the

PLACES TO STAY

31 Coconut Grove Motel & Restaurant
32 Archipelago Motel &
   Holiday Apartments
33 Mantaray & Driftwood Apartments
34 Hibiscus Lodge
35 Garrick House
36 The Queenslander
37 The Beach Terraces
39 Kulau Caravan Park

PLACES TO EAT

9 Nautilus
10 Combined Services Club
12 Court House Hotel
13 Danny's
14 Iron Bar Restaurant
16 Central Hotel
17 Thai By Night
18 Ada's Gourmet
19 Jade Inn
20 Mango Jam Cafe
22 Mariposa Health Foods, EJ's
   Takeaway & Bakery

23 Portofino's
25 Cafe Macrossan
29 Namaste Cafe

OTHER

1 Lighthouse
2 Old Courthouse
3 Police Station
4 Sunday Markets
5 Ben Cropp's Shipwreck
   Museum
6 Port Douglas Transit Centre
7 Thomas Cook Foreign Exchange
8 Adventure Centre
11 Port Douglas Visitors Bureau
15 The Laundry
21 Port Douglas Tourist
   Information Centre
24 The Wave Nightclub
26 Post Office
27 Flagstaff Hill Lookout
28 Port Douglas Bike Hire
30 Marina Mirage & Shopping Centre
38 Swimming Enclosure
40 Life-Saving Club

Pandanus Caravan Park (☎ (070) 99 5944), at 111 Davidson St, has tent sites at $12, on-site units with air-con at $42 and self-contained cabins at $57. This place is also well set up and has a pleasant swimming pool. Almost four km south of the town centre is the *Four Mile Beach Caravan Park* (☎ (070) 98 5281). It has a nice setting with plenty of big old trees and beach frontage, and there are tent sites for $13, on-site vans for $35 and on-site units from $50.

Hostels The only backpackers' accommodation in Port is the excellent *Port o' Call Lodge* (☎ (070) 99 5422), in Port St about one km south from the centre – signposted off the main road (Davidson St) as the Port o' Call Motel. It's a YHA associate and has modern four-bed units with private bathrooms at $16 per person for YHA members or $17 for nonmembers. Private rooms are also available; rates vary seasonally. There's a pool, cooking facilities, a licensed restaurant and a free courtesy coach to and from Cairns. You can also hook up with a couple

of the tours which operate between Cairns and Cape Trib from here.

Motels Of the motels here, the *Coconut Grove Motel* (☎ (070) 99 5124), at 58 Macrossan St, is the cheapest and the most central. Their double rooms range from $50 to $75. The *Central Hotel* (☎ (070) 99 5271), at 9 Macrossan St, also has motel units out the back, with singles/doubles at $65/70. If you're after a more modern motel, try either the *Lazy Lizard Motor Inn* (☎ (070) 99 5900), at 121 Davidson St, or the *Rusty Pelican Motel* (☎ (070) 99 5266), next door at 123 Davidson St – both are very good and have rooms with all the mod-cons from around $75 to $95.

Holiday Flats and Apartments Moving up a level, Port has a huge range of apartments and holiday flats on offer. They all have a fairly similar range of features – full kitchen, laundry facilities, air-con, TV, phone and swimming pool, and some also have tennis courts. Rates for these places are generally cheaper by the week.

While most of these places are fairly expensive, there are a few affordable exceptions. *Hibiscus Lodge* (☎ (070) 99 5315), on the corner of Mowbray and Owen Sts, has three simple one-bedroom holiday units which range from $45 to $65 a double depending on the season. The well-located *Archipelago Motel & Holiday Units* (☎ (070) 99 5387), at 72 Macrossan St, has small self-contained studio apartments which range from $60 to $95 a double. The managers of this place speak German and Spanish. Another option is the *Vacation Village* (☎ (070) 99 5183), on Port Douglas Rd two km south of the centre. This place has 18 freestanding units spread out over a large, leafy property. The units are oldish but clean, comfortable and fully self-contained. One-bedroom units range from $65 to $75; two-bedroom units range from $85 to $95; and four-bedroom units range from $120 to $150. They have a minimum stay of three nights.

There are several good options in the area between the town centre and the beach – perhaps one of the best areas to stay in. *Garrick House* (☎ (070) 99 5322), at 11-13 Garrick St, has 18 cool and bright apartments which have been recently renovated. The studio apartments range from $85 to $105 a night; one-bedrooms apartments range from $95 to $125 a night; two-bedroom apartments range from $100 to $135 a double; and their two penthouses range from $125 to $160 a double. Additional adults cost another $15. The jointly managed *Mantaray Apartments* and *Driftwood Apartments* (☎ (070) 99 5119) are side by side at 65 Macrossan St. These apartments are slightly older, but they're cosy, comfortable and very good value. The standard two-bedroom units range from $85 to $105 a double; two-bedroom penthouses range from $110 to $130 a double; and three-bedroom units range from $130 to $150 for up to four people. Additional adults cost another $15.

The Mango Tree (☎ (070) 99 5677), at 91-93 Davidson St, is a friendly place with 20 bright and spacious apartments, and a tennis court. There are two types of units: the single-storey villas sleep up to four people, and range from $85 to $110 a double; and the two-storey townhouses sleep up to six, and range from $105 to $130 a double. Each extra adult costs another $10, and there's a minimum stay of three nights. *The Beach Terraces* (☎ (070) 99 5998), closer to the beach and the centre at 15 Garrick St, has 21 newly renovated apartments. One-bedroom units range from $95 to $125; two-bedroom units range from $130 to $165; and three-bedroom units range from $185 to $250. *The Queenslander* (☎ (070) 99 5199), at 8-10 Mudlo St, is another good option. They have studio units ranging from $75 to $100; one-bedroom units from $85 to $115; two- bedroom units from $95 to $130; and two-bedroom deluxe suites from $115 to $150.

The *Nimrod Apartments* (☎ (070) 99 3399), at 31 Nautilus St, in Four Mile Beach, is an impressive complex of 50 two and three-bedroom apartments. There is a tennis court for guests' use. Four Mile Beach is four km south of the centre – good if you're after a little peace and quiet, but it's a disadvantage if you don't have your own car. The two-bedroom apartments range from $139 to $200; the three-bedroom ones range from $188 to $245.

The *Reef Terraces Resort* (☎ (070) 99 3333), beside the Radisson on Port Douglas Rd, has 181 two-storey townhouse apartments, three swimming pools, tennis courts, a gymnasium, a kid's club and an hourly shuttle bus into town. There are one, two and three-bedroom apartments, and tariffs start from $160 a double plus $20 for each additional adult.

Resort Hotels At the top of the range, Port Douglas has two resort hotels. The *Radisson Royal Palms Resort* (☎ (070) 99 5577) has 301 rooms and 16 suites. Standard rooms range from $155 to $170 a double, and suites range from $300 to $550 a double. Christopher Skase's creation, the *Sheraton Mirage Resort* (☎ (070) 99 5888), is in a league of its own. It rates as one of the best resort hotels in Australia, somehow managing to be over the top without being too ostentatious. It's set among tropical gardens, and surrounded by its own 18-hole golf course and a truly amazing and enormous saltwater swimming lagoon, complete with private beaches. (If you'd rather the real thing, it's a short stroll from the hotel to Four Mile Beach.) There are also nine tennis courts, six restaurants, a gymnasium, a sauna and freshwater swimming pools. Rooms range from $400 to $520 a night; two, three and four-bedroom villas range from $650 to $850; or you can take the Presidential suite for $1800 or the Royal suite for a mere $2000. Even if you can't afford to stay here, at least pop in and have a drink or a (discrete) swim and a look around.

Places to Eat

Considering the size of the place, Port Douglas has a surprisingly good array of cafes and restaurants. Together with Noosa, the range and quality of food available here is probably better than what you'll find anywhere else in Queensland, although eating here isn't particularly cheap and there are few places catering to budget travellers. Most of the eateries are along or near Macrossan St.

Cafes & Takeaways For breakfast, try *Namaste Cafe*, at 43 Macrossan St. You can sit outside at an umbrella-shaded table, and choices include muesli with fruit, croissants or eggs on toast, all from $3 to $6. It's also a good place for lunch, with gourmet sandwiches, salads and burgers around $5. They also have fresh juices and good vegetarian dishes. Across the road at No 42, *Cafe Macrossan* also serves good breakfasts ranging from $4 to $7.50, as well as lunches like burgers and dogs, salads, pastas and focaccias from $5 to $9. They also open for dinner, with main courses ranging from $13 to $20. Further down the road, *Ada's Gourmet* also does good breakfasts and sandwiches, and specialises in ice creams and sundaes.

For takeaways, there's a good range of choices side-by-side in Grant St, near the corner of Macrossan St. The very friendly *Mariposa Health Foods* has great smoothies, juices and healthy sandwiches and rolls; *EJ's*

Takeaway does fish & chips and burgers; and the *Port Douglas Bakery* has pies, breads and pastries.

Pubs If you're after a pub meal, the *Court House Hotel* on the corner of Macrossan and Wharf Sts has an outdoor garden bistro with meals ranging from $9 to $13, or the *Central Hotel* further up Macrossan St has reasonably good bistro meals ranging from $7 to $10. An interesting alternative to the pubs is the *Combined Services Club* down on the waterfront near the marina. It's a great old tin and timber building with a balcony overlooking the water – very laid-back, and just the spot to watch the sun go down. Visitors are welcome, and their bistro meals range from $6.50 to $9.50. Kid's meals are around $3.50, and kids under 14 eat for free if they're with their parents.

Restaurants The restaurant at the *Coconut Grove Motel*, near the intersection of Davidson and Macrossan Sts, is popular with the locals and is said to be good value. They have a cheap-eats menu with burgers, satays and fish & chips for $5 to $6, or an à la carte menu with steaks, seafood, pasta, curries and chicken dishes from $7 to $13. At 25 Macrossan St, the *Jade Inn* is a popular and affordable Chinese seafood restaurant – they do good takeaways.

The *Mango Jam Cafe*, at 24 Macrossan St is a funky, lively and very popular bar/restaurant which features live bands on Friday and Saturday nights. The menu offers gourmet pizzas from their wood-fired oven ($12 to $15), a great range of salads ($5.50 to $14), pasta and noodle dishes ($10 to $12), and other mains like niçoise salad, Thai chicken curry and Indian vegetarian platters from $12 to $15. Nearby is *Thai By Night* (☎ (070) 99 5058), a small Thai place with excellent curries, salads and seafood dishes ranging from $12 to $18, and a takeaway menu with mains from $7 to $12. You'll probably need to book.

Portofinos, at 31 Macrossan St, is a casual and earthy licensed bistro with gourmet pizzas, pastas, chicken curries, fish of the day, and salads – all from around $10 to $15, plus a kid's menu with $5.50 meals. It's open for lunch and dinner. The *Iron Bar Restaurant*, wedged between the pubs at 5 Macrossan St, has been decked out like an outback wool shed, with slab-timber furniture, bush dunnies and corrugated iron walls – it's fairly impressive and worth a visit. They have live music in the back bar most nights, and specialise in pasta and Aussie tucker with main meals in the $12 to $22 range.

Danny's, at 26 Wharf St, is a popular seafood restaurant with a good reputation. It's a relaxed place with a pleasant open-air courtyard and a small bar. Main meals range from $20 to $23, and apart from seafood they offer things like crocodile ravioli, kangaroo fillet and vegetarian curries.

Port's best-known restaurant is the bizarre *Going Bananas* (☎ (070) 99 5400), at 87 Davidson St. The décor is almost beyond description – a sort of post-cyclone tropical forest look – and the service is often equally strange. The eclectic menu includes Afghani lamb shanks, Spanish-style rabbit, Polynesian seafood combo, 'well-hung' venison and local seafood dishes, with main courses ranging from $20 to $26. There's a small bar and a good wine list, and they open for dinner from Monday to Saturday – you'll need to book.

Nautilus (☎ (070) 99 5330), at 17 Murphy St (with another entrance on Macrossan St), is another local restaurant with a great reputation. It has a magical open-air setting under a canopy of tall palm trees and ferns, lit by huge wax-dripping candelabras with elegantly dressed waiters hovering nearby – the perfect place if you're feeling romantic. They specialise in fresh seafood – coral trout, mud crabs, seared yellowfin tuna – or you can have something else like King Island beef or spatchcock. Mains range from $25 to $29 and the wine list features good Australian wines. They open nightly for dinner.

Entertainment

On the corner of Macrossan and Wharf Sts, the *Court House Hotel* usually has live bands

appearing in their beer garden on Friday and Saturday nights and Sunday arvos (more often during the peak tourist season). Next to the pub is the *Iron Bar* restaurant, which often has acoustic music in its back bar, and further up Macrossan St, the *Mango Jam Cafe* also features live music on weekends and is usually still firing when most other places have wound down for the night.

The *Wave Bar & Nightclub*, upstairs on Macrossan St near the Grant St corner, is open Wednesday to Saturday from 10 pm to 5 am, and has pool competitions, happy hours and other wild and crazy stuff. Port's two other nightclubs are both upstairs in the Marina: *FJs Nightspot*, a disco/bar with a restored FJ Holden as its centrepiece, has a pool table, pinball machines and a balcony overlooking the marina. They serve meals and have regular happy hours for cocktail drinkers: open daily from 11 am until 3 am.

The *Tide Tavern* is open every day from 10 am to 3 am, and has three bars, a disco and dance floor, and features live bands three nights a week. They also serve lunch and dinner. The small bar out on the balcony, run by the very gregarious Michelle, is a good place to sit and watch the boats coming back from the reef.

The bar at *Going Bananas* is a popular watering hole, as is the *Combined Services Club* down on the waterfront. If you'd rather drink in more opulent surrounds, the bars at the *Sheraton Mirage Resort* seem to be open to non-guests. I once went to the Sheraton with a group from the backpackers' lodge, and despite our somewhat scruffy appearances we were made to feel very welcome – the fact that our drinks cost almost as much as our night's accommodation was somewhat sobering, but when you're living on the razor's edge you have to splash out now and then.

It's also worth asking at the Jungle Bookshop or one of the information centres about the Karnak Playhouse, an amphitheatre set in the Daintree rainforest north-west of Mossman. They stage regular productions and also have a new sound and light show. See the Mossman to Daintree section for details.

Getting There & Away

Air It comes as a surprise to some people that Port Douglas doesn't have its own airport, or even an airstrip. It's about an hour by road to Cairns' international airport. Many accommodation places provide pick-up services, and Coral Coaches (☎ (070) 98 2600) has 15 daily services (between 6 am and 9.15 pm) between the airport and Port Douglas. The one-way fare is $17.

Bus Coral Coaches (☎ (070) 98 2600) is a Mossman-based bus company which covers the Cairns to Cooktown coastal route via Port Douglas, Mossman, Daintree, Cape Tribulation and Bloomfield. Bookings and departures in Port Douglas are from the Port Douglas Transit Centre (☎ (070) 99 5351). Coral Coaches runs several buses daily between Cairns and Port Douglas (1½ hours, $14.20), Mossman ($15.70), and on to Daintree village ($18.40). Road conditions permitting, services from Cairns to Cape Tribulation go twice daily ($25.30). They also operate to Cooktown via the inland road every Wednesday, Friday and Sunday ($44.90) and via the Bloomfield Track on Tuesday, Thursday and Saturday ($49.60).

Coral Coaches usually lets you stop over as often as you like along the route, so they're as good as any tour. Owing to the ruggedness of some of the roads, the possibility of delays, and the frequent hopping in and out of the variety of vehicles which cover different sections of the route, riding with Coral Coaches is about as close as Australia comes to travelling in the Third World – and it's fun.

Boat Apart from the Coral Coaches buses, there's the daily *Quicksilver* fast catamaran service from Port Douglas to Cairns and back. The trip takes 1½ hours, departing from Cairns at 8 am and from Port Douglas at 5.30 pm. Adult fares are $20 one way, $30 return, children's fares are $10/15. The *Quicksilver* booking office (☎ (070) 99 5500) in Port Douglas is in the Marina Mirage complex.

Getting Around

Bus The Port Douglas Bus Service runs in a continuous loop from the Rainforest Habitat (near the Captain Cook Hwy turn off) to the town centre, stopping at all the major accommodation places. It operates daily from 7.30 am until midnight, and you can either wait at a designated stop or flag the driver down. One-way fares cost from $1.30 to $2, or you can buy a weekly ticket for $12.

Train The Bally Hooley railway is a small steam-train that runs a daily shuttle service between the marina, the Radisson Hotel and St Crispins station (at the southern end of the golf course). It operates hourly between 9 am and 5 pm, and return tickets cost $6 for adults and $2 for kids.

Car Rental Avis (☎ (070) 99 4331), National (☎ (070) 99 4652) and Budget (☎ (070) 99 4690) all have offices in Port Douglas, and all have a wide range of cars and 4WDs available. There are also a few smaller operators in town. Sunny Top (☎ (070) 99 5379) and Network (☎ (070) 99 5111) both have convertibles and other cars for rent, and Network also has scooters for $25 a day. Port Douglas Moke Hire (☎ (070) 99 5550) and Holiday Car Hire (☎ (070) 99 4999) both have Mini-mokes from $45 a day. Allcar Rentals (☎ (070) 99 4123) advertises one-way rentals between Cairns and Port Douglas.

Crocodile Car Rentals (☎ (070) 99 5555) specialises in 4WD hire. They have Suzuki Sierra soft-tops at $69 a day on sealed roads or $99 a day on unsealed roads, and Suzuki Vitara hard-tops at $79 a day on sealed roads or $109 a day on unsealed roads.

Bicycle Port is very compact, and the best way to get around is by bike. Port Douglas Bike Hire, at 40 Macrossan St, and Aussie Bike Hire, at 79 Davidson St, both hire good bikes for $10 a day or $45 a week, with helmets and locks provided. The Port o' Call Lodge also has good bikes for $10 a day.

Taxi To book a taxi call Port Douglas Taxis on ☎ (070) 99 5345.

MOSSMAN (pop 1800)

Mossman is at the centre of Queensland's most northerly sugar-growing district, and is also a centre for tropical fruit growing. It's an unpretentious working town, largely unaffected by the frenzied tourist activity which surrounds and passes through it. Although it's a fairly pleasant little country town, it is of little interest in its own right. The sugar mill, established back in 1894, is open for tours, but the main attraction here is the beautiful Mossman Gorge, five km west of the town centre.

Mossman Gorge

The Mossman Gorge is one of this area's most popular day trip destinations, and while it's a lovely spot, it can get pretty crowded here at the height of the tourist season.

From the main car park, there are walking trails leading to various points of interest. Bring your togs – there are some great swimming holes here, with crystal clear water tumbling over giant boulders, all shaded by the rainforest. Beyond the swimming spots, a suspension bridge takes you across the river to a 2.4-km circuit trail through the rainforests. Back at the car park, there are toilets and picnic facilities.

The Gorge is in the southern section of the Daintree National Park. The upper reaches of the park are also accessible, but this area is only suitable for fit and experienced bushwalkers, and you need to be self-sufficient if you want to camp overnight.

There's a QNP&WS ranger's office (☎ (070) 98 2188) in the Mt Demi plaza on the corner of Front and Johnston Sts in Mossman (near the main turn off to the gorge). They issue camping permits for the national park ($3 per person), and have a pamphlet and map to guide you through the park.

Coral Coaches (☎ (070) 98 2600) runs regular bus services from Mossman and Port Douglas out to the Gorge and back, and they can pick you up from wherever you're staying. The return fare is $5 from Mossman or $13 from Port Douglas.

Other Attractions

During the sugar-processing season (July to October), the **Mossman Sugar Mill** runs tours every weekday at 10 am and 1.30 pm. The two-hour walking tour includes an educational video, a wander through the mill, morning or afternoon tea and a ride through the cane fields on the Bally Hooley steam-train. Tours cost $20 for adults, $10 for kids or $58 for a family – and you must wear shoes (no thongs or sandals).

Mossman has a good **swimming pool** behind the caravan park, which is open from 6 am to 7.30 pm (7 am to 7 pm on Sunday). The **Mossman Golf Club**, alongside the turn off to Newell Beach four km north of town, is quite a good country course and welcomes visitors. Green fees are $18 and you can hire clubs at $10 for a half set or $20 a full set.

As you drive through Mossman, keep your eyes out for Ernie Lone's house on the southern approach to the town centre. His front fence is lined with a wonderfully colourful collection of hand-made wooden wind-toys; you can't miss it. The pieces aren't for sale, but they give plenty of people plenty of pleasure.

Places to Stay

There are no designated camping grounds out at the Gorge.

The *Mossman Bicentennial Caravan Park* (☎ (070) 98 1922), on Foxton Ave at the northern end of Mossman, has tent sites for $10 and on-site vans for $25 a double. The park has plenty of grass and the town swimming pool and the Mossman River are right beside it.

The old green and cream *Exchange Hotel* (☎ (070) 98 1410), at 2 Front St, in the centre of town, is a classic Aussie pub which features the usual cast of front-bar characters. You can stay upstairs at $15/30 for singles/ doubles. This is no-frills accommodation, but the rooms are clean, freshly painted and open up onto a broad verandah that overlooks the main street.

If you can afford a little more, the best place to stay is at the *White Cockatoo Cabins* (☎ (070) 98 2222), at 9 Alchera Dve (the main road), one km south of the centre. These free-standing timber cabins are in a garden setting, with a nice swimming pool. The cabins are straightforward but spacious, with their own bathroom, fully equipped kitchen, air-con, TVs and a phone. Prices vary seasonally – singles range from $55 to $65, doubles from $65 to $80, plus another $5 for each extra person.

Another option is the *Demi-View Motel* (☎ (070) 98 1277), at 41 Front St, an oldish budget motel with clean rooms at $50/60.

Places to Eat
Temptations, a coffee lounge and takeaway on Front St opposite the Royal Hotel, has a good range of sandwiches, hot dogs, cakes and ice-cream sundaes.

There are four pubs in town, although a couple of them are a little rough around the edges. The *Exchange Hotel* on the corner of Front and Mill Sts has a large bistro out the back where you can get a decent pub meal for around $9 to $12. The *Royal Hotel* also has reasonable meals.

The *Who's Who Coffee Lounge*, in Mill St opposite the Exchange Hotel, is a very casual-looking cafe with a rambling, eclectic décor, but the food is great. They do lunches from Monday to Friday – sandwiches, light meals and salads – and dinners from Tuesday to Saturday, with main meals ranging from $14 to $16.50.

About 1.5 km south of the centre is *Lynne's BYO*, a laid-back little pizza and pasta joint with a takeaway section on one side and a dining area with outside tables on the other. It's a friendly place and reasonably priced, and they open nightly for dinner.

Getting There & Away
Coral Coaches (☎ (070) 98 2600), based at 37 Front St, runs regular daily bus services to and from Port Douglas, Cairns, Newell Beach and Wonga Beach, Daintree, Cape

Tribulation and Cooktown, amongst other places. Ring them for departure times and fares, or check the Port Douglas and Cairns Getting There and Away sections for more information.

MOSSMAN TO MT MOLLOY
Just south of Mossman is the turn off to Mt Molloy, which links up with the inland route to Cooktown. For 33 km this road climbs and winds its way through some very pretty and productive farmlands (mainly tropical fruit and cattle farms). Along the early sections of the route are two sensational lookout points – on a clear day it's worth pulling over to take advantage of this panoramic photo opportunity of the Mossman valley, with the deep blue sea laid out in the distance. Further on are two interesting places, a horse-riding ranch and a birdwatcher's lodge:

Mt Perseverance Station (☎ (070) 94 1438), about 15 km from the turn off, has horse-trail rides from $10 an hour or $40 a half day. Their full-day tour costs $80, which includes a barbecue lunch, and transport from wherever you're staying.

About five km further on is *Kingfisher Park* (☎ (070) 94 1263), a birdwatcher's lodge and private sanctuary. The lodge has a very serene garden setting, and a good range of accommodation. There are modern self-contained units costing $80 a double plus $20 for each extra person; a bunkhouse (two beds per room) costing $20 per person; and camp sites at $8.50 per person. Campers and bunkers share communal kitchen facilities.

MOSSMAN TO DAINTREE
It's another 36 km north from Mossman to the tiny village of Daintree. The road ambles along through the cane fields and farms, with turn offs en route to Newell Beach, Wonga Beach and Cape Tribulation. If you have a little time, there are a few potentially interesting detours along here – exotic fruit farms, a spectacular open-air theatre and some interesting accommodation possibilities.

A couple of km north of Mossman you'll see the turn off to *Silky Oaks Lodge* (☎ (070)

98 1766), one of the area's most up-market nature retreats. Set in the thick of the rainforest, beside the Mossman River, the lodge has 60 individual timber chalets, its own restaurant and bar, a pool, a tennis court, a mini-boutique and full conference facilities. Their daily activities programme includes cruises along the Daintree River, guided walks along nature trails, canoe trips and slide shows, and they can arrange trips to the Great Barrier Reef, Cape Tribulation and the outback. The chalets are very comfortably set up, with timber floors, pale yellow walls and tropical soft furnishings. Each has its own bathroom, a mini-bar, aircon, ceiling fan and tea and coffee-making facilities. To help city slickers resist techno-temptation, there are no phones or TVs in the rooms. The chalets cost $350 a night, or there's a stand-by rate of $198 if you book within 48 hours of your stay.

The lodge's *Treehouse Restaurant*, an all-timber open-sided affair, has a great outlook over the Mossman River. The menu is fairly exotic, featuring local seafood and produce, with Thai and Italian influences. Main meals cost around $15 at lunch time and from $18 to $25 at dinner.

At Miallo, about eight km north-west of Mossman, is the **Karnak Playhouse** (☎ (070) 98 8144) (signposted off the main highway). This amphitheatre has a magical setting – the open-air seats look down onto a timber stage set beside a small lake, surrounded by a backdrop of rainforest-covered hills. Karnak is the creation of renowned actress Diane Cilento and playwright Anthony Shaffer. Various theatrical and musical productions are staged throughout the year (from June to December), and a high-tech sound-and-light show which will depict the history of Far North Queensland from the beginning of time should be operational by the time you read this. Ring and enquire about show times. The theatre also has its own restaurant and bar.

Newell Beach, a sleepy little beach community about six km north of Mossman, has the small *Newell Beach Caravan Park* (☎ (070) 98 1331), where two people can camp for $10, stay in an on-site van for $30 or in a self-contained unit for $40. The beach is right across the road.

The turn off to **Wonga Beach** is 22 km north of Mossman. One km after this road is the turn off to the *Pinnacle Village Holiday Park* (☎ (070) 98 7566), one of the best caravan and camping parks around. This place has a great setting – it's well-grassed with huge old trees providing plenty of shade, and has frontage onto a long, sandy beach. It has all the usual facilities including a kiosk, pool and a charming restaurant in converted old railway carriages. Tent sites cost $10, cabins are $38, ensuite units are $48 and self-contained villas with air-con are $55. All these prices are for two people; each extra adult costs $5.

Just north of the Wonga Beach turn off is **Wonga Beach Trail Rides** (☎ (070) 98 7583). Every day at 3 pm, they take 2½-hour horse rides through the surrounding cane fields, rainforest and beaches. They don't take more than eight people, so it's worth booking. Trail rides cost $35 per person, or $50 with return transport from Port Douglas.

The **Wonga-Belle Orchid Garden**, signposted off the highway 23 km north of Mossman, is a tropical orchid and fern garden which is open to visitors.

Further on is the turn off to the Daintree River ferry crossing and Cape Tribulation; continue straight on for another 11 km to get to Daintree village.

DAINTREE

Daintree, a small village on the banks of Daintree River, marks the end of the sealed highway to the north. Originally established as a logging town, with timber cutters concentrating on the prized red cedar trees that were so common to this area, it is now known as a centre for river cruises along the mighty Daintree River. It's a fairly quiet little backwater, although with a recent influx of tourists things have livened up somewhat, and several new B&Bs and a stylish resort have opened up in the last couple of years to cater for the added demand. The 'town' consists of a couple of shops and cafes, and several booking agencies for river cruises.

FAR NTH QUEENSLAND

Things to See & Do
In the centre of the village, the **Timber Museum, Gallery & Shop** is worth a visit. Out the back there's a timber workshop where you can watch local craftsmen at work; the museum houses a large collection of old woodworking tools; and if you're in buying mode, there's a gallery with some expensive but beautifully crafted clocks, bowls, Irish golf tees and mirrors on sale.

A couple of operators have recently started offering guided walking tours in this area – check with the booking offices in the village.

Fine Feather Tours (☎ 015 163 493) specialises in birdwatching and takes people out on birdbanding expeditions. They run birdwatching tours of the rainforests every day except Saturday, departing at 6.30 am and returning at 1 pm, costing $75 per person, which includes brunch and pick-up from your accommodation. They also have afternoon tours leaving at 2.30 pm from Sunday to Thursday, costing $35 per person.

Organised Tours
There are more than a dozen river tour operators spread along the Daintree between the village and the ferry crossing. You can book a cruise direct with the operators, or through booking agents everywhere – there are at least four agents in Daintree village. It's certainly a worthwhile activity. Birdlife is prolific, particularly early in the mornings, and in the colder months (April to September) croc sightings are common, especially on sunny days when the tide is low, as they love to sun themselves on the exposed banks.

There are a number of larger commercial operators, such as Daintree Rainforest River Trains (☎ (070) 90 7676) (based beside the ferry crossing to Cape Trib). The more low-key Daintree River Cruise Centre (☎ (070) 98 6115), four km north-west of the ferry turn off on the Mossman to Daintree road, has three boats taking from 30 to 52 passengers. Their trips take one hour, cost $10 and depart daily at 9.50 am, 1.10, 2.15 and 3.30 pm. A longer tour (1½ hours) departs daily at 11.10 am and costs $15.

There are several smaller operators that offer more personalised and specialised tours. Chris Dahlberg's Specialised River Tours (☎ (070) 98 6169), based at Daintree village, takes small groups of up to 12 people on early morning river trips, and Chris is an enthusiastic birdwatcher and knowledgeable guide. The two-hour trips depart at 6.30 am in winter and 6 am in summer and cost $25. Mangrove Adventures (☎ (070) 90 7017), based about 300 metres before the ferry crossing, also takes small groups of two to five people on fishing trips, night tours and cruises. Their two-hour tour costs $30, a half-day cruise is $50 and a two-hour night tour $30.

Far North River Safaris (☎ (070) 98 6119) takes up to four people on two-hour safaris ($25 per person) along the river. They are also based at Daintree Village.

Places to Stay
Caravan Park The *Daintree Riverview Caravan Park* (☎ (070) 98 6119) is well located in the heart of the village, and close to the river and jetty. Grassy tent sites are $12, although there isn't much shade around. On-site vans are $32 a double, or $34 with air-con.

B&Bs There are quite a few B&Bs in Daintree. The excellent *Red Mill House* (☎ (070) 98 6169) in the centre of town has three comfortable rooms – one single, one double and one triple – with shared bathroom facilities. The house is a breezy two-storey Queenslander, set in lovely gardens which are great for birdspotting. There is also a pool. The tariff is $25/60 for singles/doubles, and includes a delicious breakfast on the balcony. The owners of this place also run Chris Dahlberg's Specialised River Tours – see the earlier Daintree River Tours section for details.

Views of the Daintree (☎ (070) 98 6118), on Stewart Creek Rd, is a modern homestead with great views over the big river. There are two double rooms, one in the main house and one in a separate section. Both have ensuites, and there's a timber decking area where you can enjoy the sensational views. The cost is $75 a double, including breakfast.

Billirene B&B (☎ (070) 98 6199), in the centre of the village beside the information centre, is the home of a friendly retired couple. They have an attractive garden with a swimming pool, a huge fish pond and a variety of wildlife wandering round. It's a cosy family home with two guest rooms with private bathrooms, and guests become part of the household during their stay. The cost is $60 a double, including breakfast.

Weroona B&B (☎ (070) 98 6198), at 2 Douglas St, is a small cabin set behind the main house. The cabin has air-con, its own bathroom, a fridge and a microwave, and there's a small pool. Singles/doubles cost $35/55 with breakfast.

Resort Set in the thick of the rainforest three km south of the village is the impressive *Daintree Eco Lodge* (☎ (070) 98 6100). The resort has 15 very stylish timber cabins, all built on elevated stilts so they look out onto the rainforest canopy. Inside, the cabins have a bright, tropical feel with marble floors and cane furniture, and all the mod-cons like air-con, TV, phone and a minibar. The resort has a swimming pool, a bar and an excellent restaurant – see Places to Eat below. The tariff is $275/325/400 for singles/doubles/triples, which includes breakfast and transfers from Cairns or Port Douglas. They don't cater for kids under 10 years of age.

Places to Eat

There are a couple of eateries in the centre of the village. *Barney's Place*, a casual cafe and takeaway with an open-air section, serves sandwiches, burgers and snacks, and main meals such as seafood baskets, and steak or barramundi from $10 to $13. Nearby is the *Daintree Coffee Shop*, where you can get anything from open sandwiches at $7.90 to a prawn and avocado salad at $15. Across the road, the *Big Barramundi*, beside the Timber Museum, has an outdoor eating area and serves sandwiches, hot dogs and barra-burgers. Their barbecued barramundi with a tropical salad ($13) is delicious, or you can

have a rump steak ($12) or barbecued chilli prawns ($12).

The *Daintree Tea House*, at Barratt Creek, three km south of Daintree, is an old-fashioned timber tea room in a peaceful setting which serves open sandwiches, morning and afternoon teas, seafood dishes and salads. It is open from 10 am to 6.30 pm.

Baaru House (☎ (070) 98 6100), the restaurant at the Eco Lodge three km south of Daintree, is open to guests and the public for breakfast, lunch and dinner. They serve a full buffet breakfast for $15 (included in guests' tariff); lunches like barramundi or burgers from $5 to $11; and at night you have a choice of three entrées and three mains, with main meals such as coral trout in coconut milk, lime and coriander ranging from $17 to $19. Vegetarian meals are also available.

Getting There & Away

Coral Coaches (☎ (070) 98 2600) has a twice-daily bus service from Cairns to Cape Tribulation which will detour to Daintree on request. The one-way fare is $18.40 – ring them in advance to check times and make reservations.

Many of the river cruise operators can pick you up from your accommodation if you don't have your own transport.

DAINTREE TO COOKTOWN VIA THE CREB TRACK

The Creb Track is maintained by the state electricity authority and you need permission from the landowner at the southern end of the route to travel it. While it may be the shortest distance from here to Cooktown, it is also the hardest and the slowest and is only recommended for 4WD vehicles.

From the village of Daintree, follow the Upper Daintree Road for 17 km to near its end. Pass through a gate on your right and you will soon reach the headwaters of the Daintree River, which is easily forded in the Dry.

For the next 55 km the route is spectacular, taking you over high mountains and across many picturesque creeks. For most of the way, you pass through rich and varied

Queensland's Wet Tropics World Heritage Area

Nearly all of Australia was covered in rainforest 50 million years ago, but by the time Europeans arrived, only about 1% of the rainforest was left. Today, logging and clearing for farms have reduced that to less than 0.3% – about 20,000 sq km. More than half of this, and nearly all the tropical rainforest, is in Queensland.

The biggest area of surviving virgin rainforest covers the ranges from south of Mossman up to Cooktown. It's called the Greater Daintree.

Throughout the 1980s, a series of battles over the future of the forests was waged between conservationists, the timber industry and the Queensland government. The conservationists argued that apart from the normal reasons for saving rainforests – such as combating the greenhouse effect and preserving species' habitats – this forest region has special value because it's such a diverse genetic storehouse. The timber industry's case, aside from job losses, was that only a small percentage of the rainforest was used for timber – and then not destructively, since cutting is selective and time is left for the forest to regenerate before being logged again.

The 1983 fight over the controversial Bloomfield Track, from Cape Tribulation to the Bloomfield River, attracted international attention to the fight to save Queensland's rainforests. The greenies may have lost that battle but the exposure of the blockade indirectly led to the Federal government's moves in 1987 to nominate Queensland's wet tropical rainforests for World Heritage listing. Despite strenuous resistance by the Queensland timber industry and state government, the area was listed in 1988, with one of the key outcomes being a total ban on commercial logging in the area.

Stretching from Townsville to Cooktown, the Wet Tropics World Heritage Area covers 900,000 hectares of the coast and hinterland and includes the Atherton Tableland, Mission Beach, Mossman Gorge, Jourama Falls, Mt Spec and the Daintree-Cape Tribulation area. The scenery is diverse and spectacular, ranging from coastal mangroves and eucalypt forests to some of the oldest rainforests in the world.

Despite the recent discord, a 1993 survey found that 80% of north Queenslanders now support the wet tropics area. Part of the reason for the turnaround has been the buzzword of the 1990s – ecotourism – north Queensland's green gold mine. With reef and rainforest-related tourism now easily eclipsing sugar production to become the Far North's biggest industry, the rainforests have become a vital part of the area's livelihood. The challenge now is to learn how to manage and minimise the environmental impact of the enormous growth in tourism and population. ■

rainforest before coming out on the north side of the **Wujal Wujal Aboriginal Community**. From here it is 74 km via Helenvale and the Lion's Den Hotel to Cooktown. The track is treacherous and impassable after rain.

CAPE TRIBULATION AREA

Cape Tribulation is famed for its superb scenery, with long beaches stretching north and south and a backdrop of rugged, forest-covered mountains. It's an incredibly beautiful stretch of coast, and is one of the few places in Australia where tropical rainforest meets the sea.

It has long held a reputation as one of the Far North's best spots for those who want to get away from it all, although things have changed somewhat in the last decade. With the region's booming tourism industry and the continuing improvements to the access roads, Cape Trib has become one of the most popular day trips from Port Douglas and Cairns. Whereas once you'd pass the occasional 4WD or battered old station wagon, nowadays there's a steady stream of tour operators heading up to the area.

Most of this area is national park – there aren't any towns in the area, just a scattering of accommodation places, general stores, camping grounds and the like.

After crossing the Daintree River by ferry, it's another 34 km of alternating paved and unpaved road, with a few hills and creek crossings, to Cape Tribulation. More than

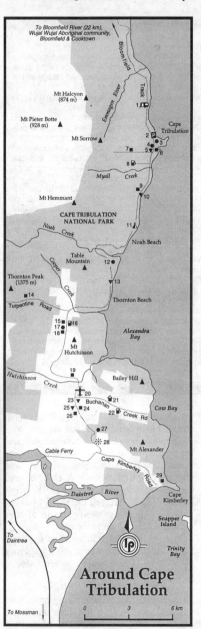

Around Cape Tribulation

PLACES TO STAY

1   Pilgrim Sands Holiday Park
6   PK's Jungle Village
7   Ferntree Rainforest Resort &
    Cape Tribulation Educational &
    Adventure Lodge
9   Coconut Beach Rainforest Resort
11 Noah Beach Camping Area
14 Heritage Lodge
15 Inn the Rainforest
18 Lync Haven
19 Daintree Wilderness Lodge
21 Crocodylus Village
24 Cow Bay Hotel
26 Rainforest Retreat
29 Club Daintree

PLACES TO EAT

5   Boardwalk Takeaway
10 The Long House
13 Thornton Beach Kiosk
23 Floravilla Tea Garden
25 Latitudes 16.12°

OTHER

2   Cape Tribulation Car Park
3   QNP&WS Ranger's Station
4   Bat House
8   Cape Trib Store
12 Marrdja Botanical Walk
16 The Rainforest Camp
17 Wundu Trailrides
20 Cow Bay Airstrip
22 Matt Lock's Service Station &
    General Store
27 Daintree Rainforest
    Environmental Centre
28 Alexandra Range Lookout

half of the road has been sealed in recent years and, unless there has been exceptionally heavy rain, conventional vehicles can easily make it, with care, to Cape Trib.

Remember, however, that this is rainforest – you'll need to take mosquito repellent with you, and wet weather gear may come in very handy. Approaching Cape Trib from the south, the last bank is at Mossman. You can get petrol at two or three places between Mossman and Cooktown by this coastal route.

History
Cape Tribulation was named by Captain Cook, since it was a little north of here that his troubles started when his barque, the *Endeavour*, struck an off-shore reef. Mt Sorrow was also named by Cook.

The first European to settle permanently in the area was Andrew Mason, father of the present-day owner of the Cape Trib Store. In 1928, Mason started building a house beside Myall Creek, and his family moved to join him in 1931. It was the middle of the Depression, and a couple of other families moved up to join him to grow fruit and vegies. Collectively, they started to send their crops to Cairns by boat.

During WW II, a number of land army women came to the area to work on properties and help grow food for the war effort. After the war, sawmilling and then cattle grazing became the area's main sources of income.

The first ferry service across the Daintree River began in 1956. By the 1970s, a trickle of visitors had started to arrive, and Cape Trib started to gain a reputation for its remote beauty. The area became something of a hippie outpost, with settlements like the alternative Cedar Bay community in the rainforests north of Cape Trib. By the 1980s the trickle had developed into a steady stream.

Climate
Because of the mountain ranges which hug the coast along here, Cape Trib is one of the wettest places in this area. As with the rest of Far North Queensland, the main wet season is from December to March, but heavy rains can arrive suddenly at anytime. The road condition deteriorates rapidly with heavy rain.

Cape Tribulation National Park
Due to its mountainous terrain, the area north of the Daintree is one of the few areas in Queensland that was never cleared for agriculture.

In 1981, recognition of the unique natural values of this area led to the declaration of the Cape Tribulation National Park. The park stretches from the Daintree River to the Bloomfield River, with the mountains of the McDowell Range providing the western boundary. As part of the Wet Tropics area, Cape Trib was also granted World Heritage listing in 1988.

Cape Trib's rainforests, dry woodlands and coastal mangroves are home to a wide variety of unique flora and fauna, including numerous rare and threatened species such as the Bennett's tree kangaroo.

Information
There isn't an official information centre here, although the Bat House and the Daintree Rainforest Environment Centre are both good sources of info on the rainforests – see the Things to See & Do section.

There's also a small QNP&WS ranger station (☎ (070) 98 0052), on the main road just before the turn off to Cape Trib beach. It's only staffed on weekdays between 12.30 and 2.30 pm. For info at other times, contact the main QNP&WS office at Mossman on ☎ (070) 98 2188.

Most of the accommodation places are also very helpful, and they can book tours and give general advice.

Facilities
Banking The Cow Bay Hotel has EFTPOS facilities, but apart from that there are no banking facilities here. The closest banks are in Mossman.

Fuel & Supplies Matt Lock's service station and general store (☎ (070) 98 9127) is halfway along Buchanan Creek Rd (the road to Cow Bay). It is open daily from 7.30 am to 6 pm, and sells fuel (diesel, super and unleaded), fishing tackle, bait and general groceries.

The *Rainforest Camp* (☎ (070) 98 9015), five km north of the Cow Bay turn off, sells fuel (diesel, unleaded, super and outboard) and has a small general store.

The *Cape Trib Store* (☎ (070) 98 0070), just off the main road about 1.5 km south of the Cape, is open every day from 8.30 am to

Cassowaries – the Vital Link

The cassowary, an enormous flightless bird, was once a common and vital feature of these rainforest areas. A 1993 CSIRO report revealed that there were only 54 adult cassowaries left in the area north of the Daintree River, and their numbers were rapidly declining, mainly due to land-clearing destroying their natural habitat. They are also being killed by feral pigs and dogs, and are frequently hit by cars – so drive slowly and keep your eyes peeled.

The CSIRO's report emphasised the vital role played by the cassowary in this rainforest environment. The bird is perhaps the *only* 'dispersal agent' for some 70 species of plants in the rainforest, as well as the *main* dispersal agent for another 30 species. They carry out their crucial role by swallowing fruits and berries whole – the seeds are later deposited in their dung elsewhere in the forest.

Mission Beach, south of Cairns, also has a dwindling population of cassowaries. Mission Beach is now the home of C4 (the Consultative Committee for Cassowary Conservation), which is dedicated to gathering information on the birds and proposing a management plan. They have an office beside the Mission Beach Information Centre – drop in and pay them a visit when you're in town.

If you happen to be 'lucky' enough to see a cassowary in the forest, take care – people are sometimes chased and attacked by these birds, which is probably fair enough when you consider what we've done to their homes. ■

5.30 pm. It sells a reasonably good range of groceries, takeaway meals, film and booze, and also sells fuel (diesel, unleaded and super). There are some interesting photos and tidbits of information up on the walls inside this place, and a swimming hole near the store is open to the general public during daylight hours.

Things to See

Three km past the Daintree River crossing, Cape Kimberley Rd turns off the main road and heads east down to **Cape Kimberley beach**, near the estuary of the Daintree River. There are boat trip and sea kayaking expeditions out to **Snapper Island**, which is just off shore from the Cape. The island has several national park camp sites.

Nine km from the ferry, just after you cross the spectacular **Heights of Alexandra Range**, is the **Alexandra Range Lookout**, with panoramic views out over the Daintree River estuary and the national park. The QNP&WS has plans to erect viewing platforms and information boards here soon.

Further on is the **Daintree Rainforest Environmental Centre**. This is a great place to learn more about rainforests. There's a self-guided boardwalk with informative signboards, an information centre with rainforest displays, and a small theatre that screens a choice of six videos. It's open daily from 9 am to 5 pm; entry is $8 for adults, $6 for concessions (pensioners, children or people staying at Crocodylus) and $17 for a family.

About 12 km from the ferry you reach Buchanan Creek Rd, which is the turn off for **Cow Bay** (5.5 km) and the Crocodylus Village hostel.

Further on, the road strikes the shore at **Thornton Beach**. The **Marrdja Botanical Walk**, at Noah Creek, is an interesting 800-metre boardwalk which follows the creek through the rainforest. There are information signboards along the way, and the final section is through mangroves. Don't forget your insect repellent – you might not be able to see those damn sandflies, but believe me, they're there! At the north end of Noah

Beach there's a very pleasant **picnic ground** with tables.

The **Bat House**, opposite PK's Jungle Village, is a small rainforest information and education centre, open daily from 10 am to 4 pm. This place is run by volunteers from AUSTROP, a local conservation organisation which operates a research station, and your $2 donation goes towards the running of the station. As the name suggests, it's also a nursery for fruit bats.

A little further north, you can visit **Memaleca Orchard**, an exotic fruit orchard which sells durian, rambutan, mangosteen and other fruits in season. If you see their sign up on the front fence, it means they're open.

The car park at **Cape Tribulation** is usually fairly crowded with tour buses and 4WDs. The beach on the north side of the cape is a beautiful stretch of white sand, although severe tidal changes mean it's a long walk out to the water at low tide. Near the car park is a **Wet Tropics information board** which describes many of the plants and animals in the area, and a 350-metre **walking trail** follows the Cape south to a timber boardwalk and lookout point. There's also a picnic area here with toilets and water.

The road heading north becomes progressively rougher after Cape Tribulation itself. With care, conventional vehicles can easily make it another five km to the Emmagen Creek crossing – despite a sign saying '4WD Vehicles Only Past This Point' about three km past the Cape. Just before you reach Emmagen Creek, the road passes a huge strangler fig. From beside the tree, a walking path leads down to a pretty crescent-shaped beach.

The creek crossing is 100 metres further on. If you feel like a swim, park here and follow the creek upstream for about 400 metres, and you'll come to two deep swimming holes and a sandy 'beach'. Don't go downstream; there may be crocs.

Activities

If you want to do more than relax on the beach, there's a good range of activities on offer up here including reef trips, fishing, horse riding and guided bushwalks.

Swimming If you are heading for the beach, remember that deadly box jellyfish are a hazard in these waters between October and April. Check with the locals before going swimming.

Saltwater crocodiles also inhabit the mangroves, creeks and estuaries here, so avoid swimming near river mouths or wading across creeks or rivers where they meet the sea.

Guided Walks Paul Mason's Cape Trib Guided Rainforest Walks (☎ (070) 98 0070), based at the Cape Trib Store, takes people on informative guided walks along private trails through the forest. Their day walk takes about four hours and covers four to five km, and the night walk takes 2½ hours and covers around two km. Either walk costs $17.80 per person, or you can do both for $32. Paul advises booking ahead if you want to do the night walk during the busy season (July to October). You can book at the store or wherever you're staying.

Reef Trips There are at least two boats offering trips out to the Great Barrier Reef – both depart from Cape Trib Beach.

Escape II (☎ (070) 98 9166), a high-speed catamaran, departs daily at 8.30 am, returning at 4.20 pm. The cost is $57 which includes lunch and snorkelling gear. Introductory scuba dives are available for $45, and certified divers can do one dive for $25 or two dives for $45.

The *Taipan Lady* (☎ (070) 98 0040) is a large sailing catamaran. It departs every day at 9 am, returning at 4 pm, and costs $69 for adults or $49 for kids. Again, lunch and snorkelling gear are included and introductory and certified dives are available at the same prices.

River Cruises Cooper Creek Wilderness Cruises (☎ (070) 98 9118), based at the Thornton Beach Kiosk, takes groups of up to 20 on a one-hour morning cruise up the

Cooper Creek, which meets the ocean a little way south of the kiosk. The cruise costs $10 for adults and $6 for children, or $20/12 with lunch thrown in. Departure times depend on the tides – ring the kiosk to check.

Horse Riding Wundu Trailrides (☎ (070) 98 9156), on the main road about five km north of the Cow Bay turn off, has three-hour horse-trail rides departing from here daily at 9 am and again at 2.30 pm. You ride through local plantations to a water hole, have a swim and finish up with a cuppa at Lync-Haven. The rides cost $35 per person.

You can also go horse riding with PK's Jungle Village – see Places to Stay later.

Joy Flights Hinterland Aviation (☎ (070) 98 9153), based at the airstrip just north of the Cow Bay turn off, offers joy flights in a light plane over Cape Trib and the reef from $38 per person. They also have regular flights to Cairns (see Getting There & Away), as well as flights to Bloomfield and day trips to Cooktown and the rock-art sites at Laura on the Cape York Peninsula.

Places to Stay – Daintree River to Cape Trib
Camping & Cabins At Cape Kimberley beach, *Club Daintree* (☎ (070) 90 7500) is a beachfront camping park with camp sites for $6 per person, tent-cabins for $8 per person and 10 four-share cabins for $90 a night. The resort has a casual and inexpensive restaurant, a small pool and a pool table, and offers boat trips to Snapper Island, day trips to Cooktown and guided walks. Cape Kimberley is on the lowlands of the Daintree River estuary, so mosquitoes are sometimes a problem here.

There are also four *QNP&WS camp sites* on Snapper Island, just off shore from Cape Kimberley. There are toilets, showers and water on the island, and wood fires are banned, so you'll need a fuel stove. Sites for up to six people are $3 per person per night. You can either get a permit from the QNP&WS office in Mossman (☎ (070) 98 2188) or self-register when you arrive.

About five km north of the Cow Bay turn off is *Lync-Haven* (☎ (070) 98 9155), a 16-hectare property with walking trails and plenty of wildlife. There are tent sites at $10 a double plus $4 for each extra person, on-site vans at $35 a double, and one self-contained seven-berth cabin which costs $65 à double plus $10 for each extra person. There is a kiosk and cafe here (see Places to Eat).

A little way north, on the opposite side of the road, is the *Rainforest Camp* (☎ (070) 98 9015), a budget camping ground on cleared land behind a general store and petrol station. There isn't much shade for campers and the facilities are fairly basic. Camping here costs $5 per person, and there are on-site vans for $40.

Further north at Noah Beach there's the QNP&WS *Noah Beach Camping Area*, with 16 good, shady sites set 100 metres back from the beach. There are toilets and water is available. It's a self-registration site, with sites costing $3 per person per night for up to six people. Permits can be booked through the QNP&WS rangers at Cape Trib (☎ (070) 98 0052).

Hostels *Crocodylus Village* (☎ (070) 98 9166) is a YHA-associate hostel 2.5 km off the main Cape Trib road, down Buchanan Creek Rd. It is set in the rainforest and has spacious, elevated canvas cabins. Nightly costs in the 16 to 20-bed dorms are $13 ($14 for nonmembers). There are also cabins with a double bed, six bunks and bathrooms – these cost $45 a double plus $10 for each extra person. There's a swimming pool, a bar and a small cafe that serves good breakfasts, lunches and dinners. The meals are cheap, healthy and hearty, and vegetarians are well catered for. You can hire bikes ($10 a day) and the hostel vehicle runs guests to and from Cow Bay beach. The hostel also organises quite a few activities, including informative guided walks through the forests each morning ($10) and evening ($14), three-hour horse rides ($35), a reef trip ($57), a three-hour sunrise paddletrek ($30), and a two-day sea-kayak trip to Snapper Island ($139 with everything supplied).

Hotels & Motels Back on the Cape Trib road, just south of the Cow Bay turn off, is the new *Cow Bay Hotel* (☎ (070) 98 9011), which has modern motel units with air-con at $55/60 for singles/doubles. Across the road is the *Rainforest Retreat* (☎ (070) 98 9101), with motel-style units with cooking facilities at $50/70 for singles/doubles or $90 for a family unit. They also have a 20-bed bunkhouse at $15 per person.

Self-contained Units About five km north of the Cow Bay turn off, *Inn the Rainforest* (☎ (070) 98 9162) has two motel-style units with kitchen facilities which can sleep up to four people (although they're better for two). The units cost $50 or $60 a night, depending on the season.

Lodges One km north of the Cow Bay turn off is the *Daintree Wilderness Lodge* (☎ (070) 98 9105), a small and quiet resort built in the heart of the rainforest. There are five timber bungalows (with another five planned for the end of 1995), all linked by timber boardwalks. The bungalows are bright and modern, with ceiling fans and their own bathroom, and the tariff is $150 a double plus $30 for each extra person, which includes breakfast.

Two km along Turpentine Rd, which runs inland along the left bank of the Cooper Creek near Thornton Beach, is the secluded *Heritage Lodge* (☎ (070) 98 9138). This is a small, low-key resort with comfortable timber cabins, a pool and a wonderful swimming hole down on Coopers Creek. The restaurant has a small but varied menu, with Thai curries, vegetarian dishes, fresh fish and steaks ranging from $15 to $19. The nightly tariff is $109 a double, plus $10 for a third person. Ask about the two-hour hike up to Alexandra Falls from here.

Places to Stay – Cape Trib
Camping & Cabins Two km north of Cape Trib is the *Pilgrim Sands Holiday Park* (☎ (070) 98 0030). This camping ground has a great setting in the thick of the forest, and a short path leads down to a lovely secluded beach. The emphasis here is on peace and quiet. The tent sites are well shaded and close to the beach, and cost $11.50 for two people. They also have four self-contained two-bedroom units that sleep up to five and cost $63 a double plus $10 for each extra adult; and a smaller cabin that sleeps up to four people and costs $46 a double plus $8 for extras (this cabin doesn't have its own bathroom). Bed linen is included in the price, and there is a minimum two-night stay in the units and cabin. Note that Pilgrim Sands closes for the Wet, from November until Easter.

Things That Go 'Munch' in the Night

Crocodylus Village is one of the most popular backpacker's hostels on the Queensland coast. Accommodation is in large, airy canvas cabins, and you really get the feeling that you're in the heart of the rainforest, complete with the sounds of birds in the trees and visits from insects and animals. Last time I stayed there a bandicoot spent most of the night in the dining area, hopping from table to table and feasting on the crumbs under them.

Melomies are also common visitors. They are small and friendly native bush rats. Unlike brown rats, melomys aren't disease-carrying, but due to their acute sense of smell and sharp teeth they can pose another type of threat to the unsuspecting backpacker. If you leave *any* food in your luggage, no matter how well wrapped up or sealed it is, chances are a melomy will pay you a visit and chew its way through whatever's between it and the food. This can be an expensive experience – one unlucky traveller wrote to tell how her new Gore-Tex jacket was ruined by hungry melomys – and can also make you unpopular with everyone else in the dorm, as these chewing machines aren't very discriminating once they sniff out a meal. The only answer is to stick to Crocodylus' golden rule – no food anywhere in the dorms. Unless, that is, you prefer your luggage ventilated. ■

Hostels *PK's Jungle Village* (☎ (070) 98 0040) is a very well set up backpackers' hostel, with comfortable log cabins, a pool, bar and a restaurant with breakfasts, lunches and dinners (see Places to Eat). The nightly cost in an eight-bed cabin is $15 per person. There are also four-share rooms which cost $44 for a double, or $54/74 for triples/quads, or you can camp in the grounds for $7 per person. PK's is fun-oriented with a strong party atmosphere, so if you're looking for peace and quiet you'll be better off down at Crocodylus Village.

PK's has a bar and restaurant – see Places to Eat. As well as the various activities mentioned at the start of this section, they have a half-day paddletrek (departing at 8.30 am or 2 pm) for $35; three-hour horse rides for $44; and a 4WD safari trip at $78 for the day. They also hire out mountain bikes ($20 a day) and 4WDs ($110 for a day including a full tank of petrol).

Resorts Three km south of the cape is Cape Trib's most up-market accommodation, the *Coconut Beach Rainforest Resort* (☎ (070) 98 0033). The resort has 27 hillside units and 40 new rainforest villas, built predominantly with black wattle and cypress pine respectively. All rooms have their own bathrooms, and there are no phones or TVs in the rooms. (There are phones in the 'business centre' and a TV/video lounge above one of the restaurants.) The resort has two pools, two restaurants and its own shop, and can arrange a wide range of activities – fishing, guided walks, 4WD expeditions, reef trips and scenic flights. The units cost $180 a night for one or two people, $225 for three and $270 for four. The villas, which are freestanding and offer a bit more privacy, cost $250 a night for one or two people or $296 for three people.

Closer to the Cape and just off the main road is the *Ferntree Rainforest Resort* (☎ (070) 98 0000), which has two sections. One section has four-star accommodation with 20 impressive timber cabins in a landscaped garden setting, plus eight suites overlooking the pool. The cabins are linked by timber boardwalks, and each has its own bathroom, a double bed downstairs and two single beds in a loft. Air-con, ceiling fans, ISD phones, a mini-bar and all the other mod cons are included. The nightly cost is $100 per person in the cabins and $120 per person in the suites; breakfast is included in the tariffs. The other section of the resort, on an adjacent property, has renovated three-star bungalow-style accommodation at $85 per person, including breakfast. (This section was formerly The Lodge backpackers' resort.) The resort also has its own bar and restaurant (see the Places to Eat section).

Educational Lodge On the same property as the Coconut Beach resort, the *Cape Tribulation Educational & Adventure Lodge* (☎ (070) 98 0033) is a group-style accommodation complex with 24 four-share rooms. The cost is $60 per night per room, and walks, eco-adventures and rainforest education tours can be arranged.

Places to Eat

There are no supermarkets or convenience stores up here, so if you're planning to do your own cooking it might be worth buying a few supplies before coming. Having said that, there are several general stores where you can get basic supplies like meat, fruit, vegies and booze. There are also a few good restaurants, cafes and kiosks along the coast.

Just south of the Cow Bay turn off, *Latitudes 16.12°* (☎ (070) 98 9133) is a relaxed open-sided restaurant with cane furniture, slow-spinning ceiling fans and open-flamed burners lighting the garden at night. It serves a great range of local seafood – coral trout, barramundi, prawns – as well as Thai chicken curries, calamari and burgers, with meals from $7.50 to $17.50. It's licensed, and is open for lunch and dinner daily.

The *Cow Bay Hotel* has a pleasant bistro which serves lunch and dinner seven days a week, with main meals in the $10 to $14 range. Nearby is the *Floravilla Tea Garden*, an open-air tea room that serves meals and snacks and has a shop and an art gallery.

Lync Haven, about five km north of the

Cow Bay turn off, is a kiosk and licensed cafe which is open from 8 am to 9 pm. You can get takeaway burgers, sandwiches and snacks. In the cafe, lunches range from $4 to $6 and dinners from $5 to $10; they have a barbecue on Saturday nights and a video night on Thursday.

At Thornton Beach, the *Thornton Beach Kiosk* is a laid-back beachfront cafe and takeaway. The takeaway section makes great sandwiches and rolls, and sells pies, drinks etc. The open-sided cafe has a small bar and serves vegetarian meals, focaccias, fish & chips, burgers, seafood and steaks, all in the $5 to $12 range, as well as good cappuccinos. The kiosk is open from 7.30 am until around 5 pm, except on Friday when it has a pizza-and-pasta night and stays open until around 11 pm.

Opposite PK's, the *Boardwalk Takeaway* is open from 8 am to 7 pm and serves good breakfasts, burgers and sandwiches at very reasonable prices. They also sell a limited range of groceries, film and a few other essentials.

PK's Jungle Village has a casual restaurant which serves simple meals, and you can eat here even if you're not staying here. Breakfasts range from $2 to $5, a smorgasbord lunch is around $6 and for dinner you usually have a choice of three or four dishes at $8 or $9.

The *Long House* (☎ (070) 98 0033) restaurant at the Coconut Beach resort is open to the public for lunch and dinner. The Long House is quite a spectacular Melanesian-style building with its own turtle pond and a bar overlooking the pool, and is well worth a visit.

The restaurant at the *Ferntree Rainforest Resort* is also open to the public for lunch and dinner. It's a breezy timber building with alfresco dining. The lunch menu is light and simple, with things like open sandwiches and seafood stir-fries ranging from $8 to $20. The dinner menu offers five entrées (around $12) and mains like coral trout, rack of lamb or eye fillet from $20 to $25.

Getting There & Away
Air Hinterland Aviation (☎ (070) 98 9153)

has daily flights between the Cow Bay airstrip and Cairns. At the moment they depart from Cow Bay at 10.20 am and from Cairns at 1.15 pm – ring to check the times. The one-way fare is $60.

Bus Coral Coaches (☎ (070) 98 2600) has a daily bus service from Cairns and Port Douglas to Cooktown, via Cape Trib. See Getting There & Away in the Port Douglas section for details, times and fares.

Tours There are dozens of operators offering tours up to Cape Trib from Port Douglas and Cairns, and some excellent deals can be found that combine tours and transport to Cape Tribulation with hostel accommodation – for instance $74 including one night's accommodation or $86 including two nights. See Organised Tours in the Cairns section for more details.

Resort Transfers Most of the resorts up here can arrange transfers from Cairns or Port Douglas (for a price) – ask for details when you're booking your accommodation.

Ferry The cable ferry across the Daintree River operates every few minutes from 6 am to midnight and costs $5 for a car, $3 for a motorcycle, $1 for a bicycle and $1 for a pedestrian.

Car & Motorcycle As mentioned, the roads to Cape Trib are now quite good and shouldn't present any problems for conventional vehicles or bikes.

Note that most car hire companies won't allow you to take a 2WD hire car to Cape Trib – they'd much rather hire you a (more expensive) 4WD. According to the bush telegraph, the car hire companies pay the bloke on the Daintree car ferry a commission to ring them with the rego numbers of any hire cars that go across, so you'll be up for a hefty fine if you break this condition.

Hitching It's reasonably easy to hitch, since beyond the Daintree ferry, all vehicles *have*

The Stinging Plant & Wait-a-While

As you're wandering through the rainforest, be aware that there are a couple of sinister plants laying in wait for you. The most dangerous of these, the Gympie-Gympie, also known as the 'Stinging Plant', can cause very severe and long-lasting pain if you so much as brush against it. The plant is a small shrub with green, hairy, heart-shaped leaves with serrated edges which can grow up to six metres high.

Another of nature's terrors are the Lawyer Vines, long thin strands of barbed creepers that trail from rainforest ferns. Appropriately enough, the plant has been nicknamed 'Wait-a-While' – when you're hooked by one, you have to wait patiently until you can unhook yourself. The charming name can be misleading though – the barbs can be very painful on bare skin, and they'll do a pretty good job of ruining your favourite T-shirt. ■

to head to Cape Trib, there's nowhere else to go!

Getting Around

Apart from Coral Coaches passing through, there are no public transport services here. Both of the backpackers' hostels, and a few of the other accommodation places, have mountain bikes for hire, and PK's also has 4WDs for hire.

North to Cooktown

FAR NTH QUEENSLAND

There are three possible routes to Cooktown from the south. The first two, the Bloomfield Track (known as the 'coast road') and the Peninsula Developmental Road (known as the 'inland route'), are covered in this section. The third, a rough 4WD-only route that starts from the Daintree village, is covered in the earlier Daintree to Cooktown via the Creb Track section.

CAPE TRIBULATION TO COOKTOWN –
THE COAST ROAD

The controversial Bloomfield Track, also known as the 'coast road', starts at Cape Tribulation and carves its way through mountains and rainforest for almost 80 km before linking up with the 'inland route' 28 km south of Cooktown.

The Track was built back in 1983, when the local Douglas Shire Council decided to

bulldoze a gravel road through the forest from just north of Cape Tribulation to the Bloomfield River. The proposal was vigorously opposed by local conservationists who were concerned about the impact the track would have on the local environment, and Cape Trib became the scene of a classic 'greenies vs bulldozers' blockade. Several months and numerous arrests later, the road builders won and the Bloomfield Track was opened, despite serious concerns that soil run off from the track would wash into the ocean and damage the Great Barrier Reef.

The scenery along this route is quite spectacular, although while the coast is never too far away, you don't get to see much of it because of the dense jungle that all but encloses the road in parts. The road is generally well maintained, although some sections are steep and perilously slippery with bull dust, and this road is only recommended for 4WD vehicles. While it is *possible* for a conventional 2WD vehicle to drive the track in the Dry, you do so at your own risk, and if you get stuck you'll probably have trouble finding help or sympathy. During the Wet this road can be closed – check with the RACQ in Cairns (☎ (070) 51 4788) before heading off.

Cape Tribulation to the Bloomfield River

It's five km from Cape Trib to the Emmagen Creek, which is the actual start of the Bloomfield Track. A little way beyond this crossing, the road begins to climb a series of hills. With a combination of very steep climbs and descents, sharp corners, and fine, slippery bull dust, this is the most challenging section of the drive – in fact, especially after rain, this climb can even be difficult for 4WD vehicles. There are some great views of the off-shore reefs and surrounding rainforest along here.

The road then follows alongside the broad expanse of the **Bloomfield River**, before crossing the river 30 km north of Cape Trib. This crossing used to be notoriously dangerous, but a new concrete causeway means it's a piece of cake nowadays. The **Wujal Wujal Aboriginal Community** is on the northern bank of the river. If you stick to the main road heading north to Ayton and Cooktown, (ie, turn right at the T-intersection), you won't need a permit.

About five km beyond Wujul Wujul is the *Bloomfield River Inn* (☎ (070) 60 8174), which sells fuel (super, unleaded and diesel) as well as takeaway food, drinks and limited grocery supplies. From here it's another five km to the tiny hamlet of **Ayton**, where the *Ayton Store* (☎ (070) 60 8125) sells a small range of groceries and takeaway meals; there's also an eatery called the *Boomerang Cafe*.

Just north of Ayton is *Bloomfield Beach Camping* (☎ (070) 60 8207). It has a great setting and is well grassed with plenty of tall, shady gum trees, and the beach is only 400 metres away. There's a bar and casual restaurant serving breakfast, lunch and dinner. Reef trips, river cruises, scenic flights and bushwalks can be arranged; they offer day flights to Lizard Island and take campers to Hope Island, by boat. Tent sites cost $6 per person per night, or if you don't have your own camping gear there are on-site tents here which cost $16 with bedding supplied or $10 per person if you don't need bedding. There are also plans to build cabins here in the near future.

The *Bloomfield Wilderness Lodge* (☎ (070) 35 9166), close to the mouth of the Bloomfield River, is set back from the beach on Weary Bay and is surrounded by the Cape Tribulation National Park. This remote resort is only accessible from the sea, and the tariff includes scenic air transfer, all meals, and accommodation in luxury suites. The lodge offers river cruises, guided rainforest walks, local fishing, reef trips and 4WD safaris. Packages start at $885/1500 a single/double for three nights up to $1785/2860 for seven nights.

Bloomfield River to Cooktown
North of Bloomfield, the road passes through the **Cedar Bay National Park**, which stretches inland a short distance. There are no facilities here, and access into the park is either by boat or by walking along the numerous small tracks through the bush.

The turn off to the *Home Rule Rainforest Lodge* (☎ (070) 60 3925) is signposted from Rossville, 33 km north of the Bloomfield River crossing. At the end of a very long and bumpy driveway, this place has a surprisingly lovely setting and is a great spot if you're after a little peace, quiet and relaxation. You can go horse riding, swim in the river and there's a two-hour return walk from the lodge to the Homerule Waterfalls. The lodge has good, simple budget accommodation in either bunkrooms or double or triple rooms at $12 per person, or you can camp here for $6 per person; children pay half price. The facilities include a laundry, a well-set up guest kitchen, a bar and a small general store, and cooked meals are available at reasonable prices. They also sell fuel (super, unleaded and diesel).

At Helenvale, nine km further north, the famous *Lion's Den Hotel* (☎ (070) 60 3911) is a colourful bush pub that dates back to 1875. With its corrugated, graffiti-covered tin walls and slab-timber bar, it attracts a steady stream of travellers and local characters. The pub is open daily from 8 am until 10 pm or later – usually until midnight on weekends – and serves lunch and dinner from Monday to Saturday. Lunches like burgers, sandwiches or fish & chips are $4 to $6; for dinner they have roasts, chicken, steaks or pizzas from around $8 to $10. You can camp out the back of the pub beside the Annan River for $2 per person, or they have basic rooms at $15/20 for singles/doubles.

A little further on is *Wilma's Country Kitchen*, which is sort of a cafe/kiosk in an open-sided shed. Wilma sells drinks, burgers and sandwiches, fruit and vegies, and a few other bits and pieces.

Across the road from Wilma's place is the entrance to *Mungumby Lodge* (☎ (070) 60 3972). Mungumby comes as a very pleasant surprise – after bouncing along a rough track through the property, you come to a verdant little oasis of lawns and mango trees, with 10 timber cabins scattered around. The cabins are straightforward and comfortable, with a bathroom, a double bed and a single bed. There's also a spacious, open-sided lodge overlooking the pool where breakfasts ($10 to $13), lunches ($14) and dinners ($27) are served. The nightly tariff is $119 a double – less for stays of three or more nights. Various guided tours are offered, such as walks to local waterfalls, day trips to Cape Trib and the Bloomfield River or tours of the Split Rock Aboriginal rock-art galleries at Laura.

Four km further on, the road meets the Cooktown Developmental Rd (the inland route) – from here, it's another 28 km to Cooktown.

CAIRNS TO COOKTOWN – THE INLAND ROUTE

The 'inland route', the main route between Cairns and Cooktown, is 332 km long; you need to allow 4½ to five hours for the trip. The road is open to conventional 2WD vehicles and shouldn't present any major problems, although the second half of the trip is over unsealed roads which tend to be rough, corrugated and mighty dusty – it can be slow going, but it's all part of the challenge of getting to Cooktown! The scenery is in dramatic contrast to the lush rainforests which surround the coastal road. This route is more like an outback trip, passing through dry open forests of stringybarks, ironbarks, bloodwoods and other species of eucalypt.

As with the coast road, this route may be closed during the Wet – check with the RACQ in Cairns (☎ (070) 51 4788) before heading off.

Cairns to the Palmer River Roadhouse
After heading north out of Cairns, take the turn off to Kuranda and climb up and over the Atherton Tableland. At Mareeba, you meet the Peninsula Developmental Road which takes you north, and about 40 km further on is the small township of **Mt Molloy**.

James Venture Mulligan, the man who started both the Palmer River and Hodgkinson River gold rushes, is buried in the Mt Molloy cemetery. *Mt Molloy Trail Rides* (☎ (070) 94 1382) offers trail rides to the ruins of an old copper smelter and to Rifle Creek. Costs are two hours for $30, three hours for $45 and a full day for $80. They can arrange pick-ups from Port Douglas and you can camp out or stay overnight at the pub in town. The *National Hotel* (☎ (070) 94 1133) has cheap accommodation and is a pleasant place for a cool refreshment, although don't drink if you're driving on – I once got breathalised halfway to Cooktown, late on a Friday night, by a 'mobile booze-busting squad'!

The former wolfram-mining town of **Mt Carbine**, 30 km north-west of Mt Molloy, consists of a pub, a roadhouse and a handful of houses. Just south of the town is the *Mt Carbine Village & Caravan Park* (☎ (070) 94 3160), a former mining village which has been transformed into a scenic, if somewhat secluded, holiday park. You can camp there for $5 per person or stay in one of their self-contained units for $30 a double. In town, the *Mt Carbine Roadhouse* (☎ (070) 94 3128) is open from 6 am to 10 pm, and has 24-hour emergency fuel supply, a towing and repair service and EFTPOS facilities. Accommodation is available for $12.50/25 for singles/doubles, or you can camp for $5 per person.

The **McLeod River** crossing, 14 km west of Mt Carbine, is one of the best spots to camp along this section of road and it is popular with travellers. Further north the road climbs through the DeSailly Range and there are panoramic views from **Bob's Lookout** that are worthy of a quick photo stop.

At the **Palmer River** crossing, 85 km

north-west of Mt Carbine, is the *Palmer River Roadhouse* (☎ (070) 60 2152), a solitary stone and timber building which sits on a rise. It has fuel, a bar, and a cafe/restaurant serving snacks like toasted sandwiches, burgers and pies, and main meals ranging from $7 to $13.50. There's an interesting collection of paintings inside, including James Baines' *River of Gold*, a huge mural which depicts the times and characters of the Palmer River gold rush. The roadhouse is open daily from 10 am to midnight, and they only accept BP fuel cards or cash. On Friday evenings during the tourist season there is a barbecue, sometimes with a live band or topless barmaids serving drinks. With miners from the local area, it can be a colourful night. There is a caravan and camping park behind the roadhouse. Camping costs $7 per person and on-site vans cost $25 a double, but you need to supply your own linen.

The bitumen finishes a couple of km beyond the roadhouse. There are a couple of sealed sections further on, but the majority of the trip from here to Cooktown is along unsealed roads of varying standards.

Palmerville & Maytown
The 1873 to 1883 gold rush, for which the Palmer River is famous, happened in very remote country about 70 km west of the Palmer River Roadhouse. Its main towns were Palmerville and Maytown, of which very little is left today, but the area is protected as a historic site and if you have a 4WD and a little time, a visit to the former goldfields can make for an interesting side trip.

The turn off from the Peninsula Developmental Rd is about 17 km south of the Palmer River Roadhouse, near the White's Creek crossing – it isn't signposted, but there's usually a tree with white plastic tied around it to mark the road. There are other roads leading into this area from the Burke Developmental Rd north of Chillagoe and from the Peninsula Developmental Rd north of Laura. These roads are all 4WD-only, and some of them pass through private property so you'll

need to ask the property owners' permission beforehand. Before heading west, bear in mind that this is wild, remote country – the roads are very rough and you are unlikely to encounter any other traffic. Good maps, a companion vehicle, local advice and proper preparation are essential.

Contact the QNP&WS ranger at Chillagoe (☎ (070) 94 7163) for information, a camping permit, maps and current track details. There are no facilities at Maytown or Palmerville. The road from Maytown to Laura is *not* recommended – if you want to continue north, cut across to Palmerville and then head north. This road meets the Peninsula Developmental Rd about 20 km north-west of Laura.

Lakeland to Cooktown
It's another 30 km from the Palmer River Roadhouse to **Lakeland**, a small hamlet at the junction of the Peninsula Developmental Rd and the Cooktown Developmental Rd. Turn left (west) and you're on your way to Laura and Cape York; continue straight on (north-east) and you've got another 82 unsealed and bumpy km to Cooktown. Lakeland has a roadhouse, a hotel/motel, a caravan park and a homestead with farm-style accommodation.

The *Lakeland Cash Store* (☎ (070) 60 2133) is a general store and service station, as well as the local RACQ Service Depot. They open seven days a week and accept major credit cards and cold hard cash. Attached is the *Gateway to the Peninsula Caravan Park*, which has tent sites at $4 per person and powered sites at $5 per person, and will store caravans for $10 a week. The owner of this place also runs Wobbly Bob's Wallaby Walk, a free 20-minute stroll along a 'nature trail' taking in local birdlife, roos and a few other things.

The *Lakeland Downs Hotel-Motel* (☎ (070) 60 2142) serves lunch and dinner seven days a week and has motel-style rooms available at $35/45 for singles/doubles.

The *Lakelands Roadhouse* (☎ (070) 60 2188) has fuel, tyres, batteries, camping gas etc, and can do mechanical repairs and provide emergency towing. They also have showers and a cafe/restaurant. It's open from 7 am to 10 pm, has EFTPOS facilities and accepts major credit cards.

The *Butcher Hill Homestead* (☎ (070) 60 2155), a 400,000-hectare cattle property which was established in 1874, has basic but comfortable accommodation in dongas beside the homestead. Dinner, B&B costs $40 per person, and meals are served in the old homestead. The entrance to the property is opposite the Lakeland Downs Hotel, and you'll find the homestead about three km down the driveway.

The next major point of interest to watch out for is the **Annan River Gorge**, which is about 52 km past Lakeland. It's well worth stopping here and walking downstream a little way – the river has carved an impressive gorge through solid rock, and you'll soon come to a waterfall which is equally impressive, especially during the rains.

A little further on is the turn off to **Helenvale** and the famous Lion's Den Hotel, which is just about an essential visit – see the previous section for details.

Continuing to Cooktown, the road soon passes **Black Mountain**, a pile of thousands of oddly stacked granite boulders. It's said there are ways between the huge rocks which will take you under the hill from one side to the other, but people have died trying to find them. Black Mountain is known to Aborigines as Kalcajagga – 'Place of the Spears'. The colour comes not from the rocks themselves, but from lichen which grow on them. From here, it's only another 28 km to Cooktown itself.

COOKTOWN (pop 1300)

Cooktown is just far enough away from Cairns, and just hard enough to get to, to have remained relatively untouched by mass tourism. It's a fascinating, no-frills place to visit, pretty rough around the edges but at least it's authentic. The fishing is great, the three pubs are full of interesting characters, and there's an excellent historical museum housed in an old convent.

Cooktown is something of a 'last-frontier' town – for 2WD travellers, anyway. Beyond the town stretches the wilds of the Cape York Peninsula. The task of getting here is rewarded not just by the relaxed atmosphere but by some fascinating reminders of the area's past. With a vehicle, you can use the town as a base for visiting the Quinkan rock art near Laura or even Lakefield National Park.

For details on the area north of Cooktown, including the Hope Vale Aboriginal Community, the Lakefield National Park, and Laura, see the relevant section in the Cape York Peninsula chapter.

History

On 17 June 1770, Cooktown became the site of Australia's first White settlement when Captain James Cook beached his barque, the *Endeavour*, on the banks of the river here. The *Endeavour* had earlier struck a reef off shore from Cape Tribulation, and Cook and his crew spent 48 days here while they patched up the damage. During this time, Joseph Banks, the chief naturalist, and botanist Daniel Solander took the chance to study Australian flora and fauna along the banks of the Endeavour River. Banks collected 186 plant species and wrote the first European description of a kangaroo. The north side of the river has scarcely changed since then.

The explorers had amicable contacts with the local Aborigines, but race relations in the area turned sour a century later when Cooktown was founded as the unruly port for the 1873 to 1883 Palmer River gold rush 140 km south-west. Hell's Gate, a narrow pass on the track between Cooktown and the Palmer River, was the scene of frequent ambushes as Aborigines tried to stop their lands being overrun. Battle Camp, about 60 km inland from Cooktown, was the site of a major battle between Whites and Cape York Aborigines.

In 1874, before Cairns was even thought of, Cooktown was the second biggest town in Queensland. At its peak there were no less than 94 pubs, almost as many brothels, and the population was over 30,000! As much as half of this population was Chinese, and their

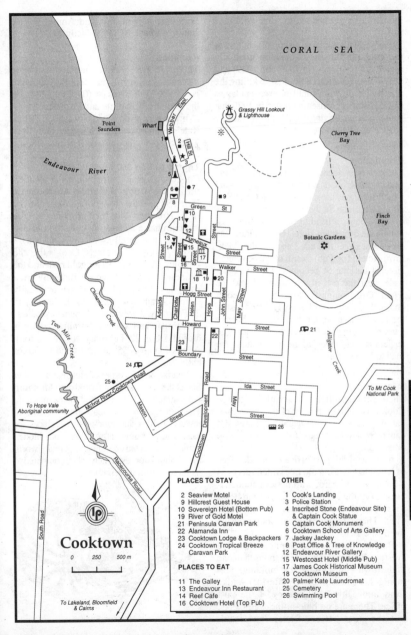

CORAL SEA

Point Saunders

Endeavour River

Wharf

Webber Esp.

Grassy Hill Lookout & Lighthouse

Cherry Tree Bay

Finch Bay

Botanic Gardens

Green St

Furneaux Street

Walker Street

Hogg Street

Howard Street

Boundary Street

Ida Street

Chinaman Creek

Two Mile Creek

Adelaide Street

Charlotte Street

Helen Street

Hope Street

John Street

May Street

Alligator Creek

McIvor River Cooktown Road

Mason Street

Racecourse Road

South Road

To Hope Vale Aboriginal community

To Mt Cook National Park

To Lakeland, Bloomfield & Cairns

Cooktown

0   250   500 m

PLACES TO STAY

2   Seaview Motel
9   Hillcrest Guest House
10 Sovereign Hotel (Bottom Pub)
19 River of Gold Motel
21 Peninsula Caravan Park
22 Alamanda Inn
23 Cooktown Lodge & Backpackers
24 Cooktown Tropical Breeze Caravan Park

PLACES TO EAT

11 The Galley
13 Endeavour Inn Restaurant
14 Reef Cafe
16 Cooktown Hotel (Top Pub)

OTHER

1   Cook's Landing
3   Police Station
4   Inscribed Stone (Endeavour Site) & Captain Cook Statue
5   Captain Cook Monument
6   Cooktown School of Arts Gallery
7   Jackey Jackey
8   Post Office & Tree of Knowledge
12 Endeavour River Gallery
15 Westcoast Hotel (Middle Pub)
17 James Cook Historical Museum
18 Cooktown Museum
20 Palmer Kate Laundromat
25 Cemetery
26 Swimming Pool

FAR NTH QUEENSLAND

industrious presence led to some wild race riots.

Cooktown's glory was short-lived, and as the gold ran out the population gradually dwindled. Cyclones (in 1907 and 1949) and a WW II evacuation came close to killing the place off, and it wasn't until the excellent James Cook Historical Museum opened in 1970 that visitors started arriving and Cooktown's steady decline was halted.

Orientation

Cooktown is located at the mouth of the Endeavour River, on a north-pointing headland which separates the river from the Coral Sea. Along Charlotte St, the main street, is the post office, a bank, a handful of shops, and three pubs – the Sovereign Hotel (Bottom Pub), the Westcoast Hotel (Middle Pub) and the Cooktown Hotel (Top Pub). North of the Sovereign Hotel, Charlotte St becomes Webber Esplanade, near the end of which you'll find the wharf. Overlooking the town from the north end of the headland is Grassy Hill, and east of the town centre are the beaches, the botanic gardens and the Mt Cook National Park. The airfield is 10 km west of the centre, along the road to Hope Vale.

Information

There isn't an official information office in Cooktown, although most of the accommodation places carry the usual brochures and can offer advice, book tours and tell you what's on.

In front of the post office stands the Tree of Knowledge, a big old tree which serves as a local notice board, with notices announcing everything from rooms to rent and items for sale to when the dentist is next coming to town. There are public phone booths beside the post office.

Banking facilities are limited: there's a Westpac Bank on Charlotte St (housed in one of the town's most impressive buildings, featuring a beautiful cedar interior) and a Commonwealth Bank agency at the post office. There are no hole-in-the-wall banks, but the post office, Sovereign Hotel,

Foodstore supermarket and Ampol service station all have EFTPOS facilities.

Facilities

There are two service stations and three mechanics in town. The local RACQ depot is at Cape York Tyres (☎ (070) 69 5274), on the corner of Charlotte and Furneaux Sts.

If you need to do a load of washing, Palmer Kate's Laundry on Hope St is open daily from 7 am to 9 pm – they also do service washes.

Things to See & Do

Cooktown's major attraction is the wonderful **James Cook Historical Museum** on Helen St, near the corner of Furneaux St. Set in a 106-year-old former convent, the museum has a fascinating collection of displays relating to all aspects of Cooktown's past – Aboriginal artefacts, Cook's life and voyages, the Palmer River gold rush and the Chinese community, and a particularly gruesome dental room. The museum is open daily from 9.30 am to 4 pm. (From 12 January to 21 February, it only opens Monday, Wednesday, Friday and Sunday mornings, and it is closed from 22 February to 21 March). Admission costs $5 for adults and $1.50 for children.

Nearby, on the corner of Helen and Walker Sts, is the rather strange **Cooktown Museum** – it's more of a souvenir shop than a museum. The front section has a weird array of shells, tea towels, T-shirts and croc-tooth necklaces for sale. The maritime museum section, hidden behind a veil of tatty curtains, isn't really worth the $5 admission, especially when compared to its more illustrious neighbour.

Nautilus Shell

A visit to the town's **wharf** is always entertaining. You'll find plenty of people fishing here, jigging for live bait and then hoping to hook a big one – barramundi, trevally and mackerel are often caught. There are also a couple of huge old groper fish that swim around the pylons – they've been here for years. If you don't have you're own fishing gear, you can buy a line from the Lure Shop in Charlotte St.

Charlotte St has a number of interesting **monuments** starting with one to the tragic Mary Watson (see the Lizard Island section) opposite the Sovereign Hotel. She is buried in the Cooktown cemetery. A little further towards the wharf are memorials to the explorer Edmund Kennedy and to Captain Cook. Behind these stands a cannon, which was sent from Brisbane in 1885 along with three cannonballs, two rifles and one officer in response to Cooktown's plea for defences against a feared Russian invasion! Further on there's an impressive and much-photographed bronze statue of Cook, and right by the waterside, a stone with an inscription marks the spot where the *Endeavour* was careened.

There are also a couple of interesting galleries along Charlotte St, including the **Endeavour River Gallery**, in the complex of shops beside the Sovereign Hotel. It houses the Vera Scarth-Johnston collection, a series of 106 beautifully detailed colour paintings of local flowering plants – well worth a visit. Opening hours vary seasonally – usually from 10 am to 2 pm – and admission costs $2. The **Gungarde Aboriginal Centre**, south of the Cooktown Hotel, has on sale a small selection of work by local Aboriginal artists. The **Cooktown School of Art Gallery** beside the post office houses a varied collection of local art works, and across the road is the **Jacky Jacky**, a small timber building with a window display of interesting historical photos.

The **Grassy Hill Lookout** has sensational 360° views of the town, river and ocean. Captain Cook climbed this hill looking for a passage out through the reefs – there's a signboard with extracts from his journal, as well as an old lighthouse. A **walking trail** leads from the summit down to the beach at Cherry Tree Bay. East of the town is the **Mt Cook National Park**, where there's another walking trail leading to the 430-metre summit of Mt Cook. It's a great half-day climb, although the views from the top are mostly obscured by trees.

The **Cooktown Cemetery** on McIvor Rd is worth a visit. There are many interesting graves dating back to the 1870s, including those of Mary Watson and the 'Normanby Woman' – thought to have been a north European who survived a shipwreck as a child and lived with Aborigines for years until 'rescued' by White people. She died soon after.

The very pleasant **Botanic Gardens**, off Walker St, were first planted in 1886 and restored in 1984. This is a great spot for a picnic, with shady lawns and colourful flower beds, and two walking trails lead from the gardens to the beaches at Cherry Tree Bay and Finch Bay.

Warning If you're visiting any of the local beaches, remember that deadly box jellyfish are present in these waters, particularly from around October to April – if in doubt, seek local advice *before* swimming. Saltwater crocodiles, another potential hazard, can be found in the open sea and in tidal creeks and rivers – don't even think about swimming or dangling your toes in the Endeavour River, and take care when walking along its banks.

Activities
River Cruises Cooktown Cruises (☎ (070) 69 5712) runs an interesting two-hour commentary cruise up to the head of the Endeavour River, then back down to a mangrove creek. The boat departs from the Cook's Landing jetty daily at 2 pm (and some days at 9 am); costs are $18 for adults, $8 for children.

Fishing Charters & Cruises MV *Trudena* is a 45-foot charter boat operated by Jim Fairbairn (☎ (070) 69 5546). Chartering the boat costs $800 a day for up to six people, with everything supplied (except drinks).

There are day cruises to the adjacent reefs for fishing and snorkelling, trips to Lizard Island and the nearby reef, or charters to Princess Charlotte Bay and surrounding coast and islands.

MV *Reef Safari* (☎ (070) 69 5605 in Cooktown, ☎ (070) 55 1100 in Cairns) runs seven-day fishing safaris aboard the 54-foot boat. The boat takes up to seven people and the cost for the week is $1400 per person, with everything supplied. It departs from Cooktown or Lizard Island for Princess Charlotte Bay and the Great Barrier Reef. Write to PO Box 2086, Cairns, Qld 4870.

The *Coral Vista*, an eight-metre fast cat, is available for fishing charters for groups of up to six people. A full day costs from $110 per person, which includes all fishing tackle, snorkelling gear and bait. Ring ☎ (070) 69 5519, or write to PO Box 465, Cooktown, for more info.

Flights Endeavour Air (☎ (070) 69 5860) offers various scenic flights and day trips from Cooktown airfield: local scenic flights cost $60 for 45 minutes; a day trip to the tip of Cape York costs $395; and a day on Lizard Island costs $130. All these prices are per person, and you need at least four people. They are also available for general charter flights, if you want to go somewhere in particular.

Organised Tours
Cooktown Tours (☎ (070) 69 5301) offers a two-hour around-the-town tour, departing at 9 am on Monday, Wednesday and Friday. The cost is $15, or $19 including entry to the museum.

Cooktown Destinations (☎ (070) 69 5166), operated by the backpackers' lodge, offers various day tours in a seven-seater 4WD, including trips to the Quinkan Aboriginal rock-art galleries and Split Rock ($75), a waterfalls tour ($50 including lunch), and a sightseeing tour that takes in Black Mountain, the Annan Gorge and Archer Point Roadhouse, with a lunch stop at the Lion's Den Hotel ($60). They can also arrange four

and seven-day tours up the Cape York Peninsula – ring for details.

There are various tours and day trips to Cooktown from Port Douglas and Cairns – see the Getting There & Away section for details.

Festivals
The Cooktown Discovery Festival, commemorating Captain Cook's landing in 1770, is held over the Queen's Birthday weekend every June. Highlights of the three-day event include a re-enactment of Cook's landing, a gala ball, a parade, various sporting events and a fishing competition.

The Cooktown Amateur Turf Club holds two-day race meetings twice a year – in June and August. These are popular events and the town is crowded with people from the stations as far away as Weipa for the sport and the socialising.

Places to Stay
Camping & Caravan Parks Cooktown has three camping and caravan parks. The *Cooktown Tropical Breeze Caravan Park* (☎ (070) 69 5417), on McIvor Rd, has good facilities including a small shop and two swimming pools. Tent sites cost $11, on-site vans are $29 a double, and motel-style cabins and self-contained units start from $49. On the outskirts of the town at the eastern end of Howard St, the *Peninsula Caravan Park* (☎ (070) 69 5107) has a lovely bush setting, with stands of big old paperbark and gum trees. Tent sites here cost $10, on-site vans are from $25 and self-contained units from $45.

Hostels *Cooktown Lodge & Backpackers* (☎ (070) 69 5166), on the corner of Charlotte and Boundary Sts, is a comfortable, well-equipped place. There's a good kitchen, dining area, pool, garden and TV lounge. A bunk is $13 the first night, then $12 a night, and singles/doubles cost $20/30. The owners also run various tours and day trips – see Organised Tours for details.

Guesthouses There are two old-fashioned guesthouses in town, both offering clean and simple private accommodation. The *Hillcrest Guest House* (☎ (070) 69 5305), in Hope St, is a friendly place with 12 guest rooms, all with shared bathroom facilities. There's a spacious lounge, a pool, a butterfly enclosure, and a two-room display of fish tanks and sea shells. Singles cost $20 to $25, doubles cost $40. The *Alamanda Inn* (☎ (070) 69 5203), also in Hope St, has 10 bright rooms all with air-con and TVs. Singles/doubles cost $24/32 with shared bathrooms or $32/40 with private bathrooms. There's a small kitchen for guests' use.

Hotels & Motels The impressive *Sovereign Hotel* (☎ (070) 69 5400) is in the middle of town on the corner of Charlotte and Green Sts. Also known as the Bottom Pub, it has a superb pool and a wide range of accommodation: standard motel-style units at $42/52, similar units with kitchenettes at $63/75, resort apartments at $103/114, and two-bedroom apartments at $132. It also has a pretty good restaurant – see the Places to Eat section.

The *Seaview Motel* (☎ (070) 69 5377), on Webber Esplanade, is a pleasant little motel overlooking the Endeavour River, with a small pool and guest barbecue area. Room costs range with the seasons from $52 to $60 a double. The more modern *River of Gold Motel* (☎ (070) 69 5222), on the corner of Hope and Walker Sts, has singles/doubles from $53/64.

Places to Eat

If you're planning to do your own cooking, you'll find several supermarkets in town, as well as a butcher and a bakery.

If you're after a decent takeaway meal, there are a few cafes and takeaways, although they're nothing to write home about. The *Reef Cafe* in Charlotte St makes good toasted sandwiches and also has a wide range of takeaway or eat-in meals like fish & chips, chicken and burgers. The *Cook's Landing Kiosk*, just south of the wharf, has outdoor tables overlooking the river and is a pleasant spot for a drink, a cuppa or a snack.

Next to the Sovereign Hotel is the *Galley*, which has pizzas and burgers.

The *Cooktown Hotel*, also known as the Top Pub, serves excellent bistro meals and also has a great beer garden. Main meals range from $6 to $12 and they serve lunch and dinner every day except Sunday. The *Sovereign Hotel* also has reasonably priced meals in the public bar downstairs.

If you're looking for something a little more up-market, there are two good restaurants to choose between. The *Endeavour Inn* (☎ (070) 69 5384), on the corner of Charlotte and Furneaux Sts, opens nightly for dinner and specialises in seafood and steaks. It's a relaxed, colonial-style place with a small bar and a courtyard dining area. The menu features barramundi, coral trout, kangaroo and buffalo fillets, and King Island steaks, with mains from $17 to $19.50; and they have a good selection of Australian wines. They also have live entertainment, including a pianist on Saturday and Sunday nights.

The *Sovereign Hotel* has a very good restaurant upstairs with tables on a broad verandah which overlooks the river and the main street. It's open daily for lunch and dinner, with an interesting selection of main meals for around $14 at lunch time and from $16 to $19 at dinner. On Sunday they serve a buffet barbecue.

Getting There & Away

Air Cooktown's airfield (☎ (070) 69 5360) is 10 km west of town, along McIvor Creek Rd.

Flight West Airlines (☎ (070) 13 2392) operates flights between Cairns and Cooktown twice daily (one flight only on Tuesday and Saturday), costing $96 each way, although a discount fare of $78 is often available. The booking agent in Cooktown is the Seaview Motel (☎ (070) 69 5377).

An alternative to the scheduled flights is chartering a light plane. Both Hinterland Aviation (☎ (070) 35 9323) and Endeavour Air (☎ (070) 69 5860) will fly groups of up to five people from Cairns or Port Douglas to Cooktown for around $420. Endeavour Air can also fly you from here to Lizard

Island – see Getting There & Away in the Lizard Island section for details.

Bus Coral Coaches (☎ (070) 98 2600) operates two regular services between Cairns and Cooktown, one via the coast road and the other via the inland route. The coast road service, via Port Douglas and Cape Tribulation, departs from Cairns at 7 am (and from Port Douglas at 8.20 am) every Tuesday, Thursday and Saturday, and returns from Cooktown at 11 am on the same days. The trip takes eight or nine hours and the one-way/return fare is $49.60/95. The inland route service departs from Cairns at 7 am every Wednesday, Friday and Sunday and returns from Cooktown at 2.30 pm on the same days. The trip takes almost six hours and the one-way/return fare is $44.90/86. Kids from four to 14 travel half-price.

For details and bookings, you can contact the agent in Cooktown, the Cooktown Motor Inn (☎ (070) 69 5357).

Car & Motorcycle If you're driving up here, there are two main roads from the south – the coastal road (4WD only) and the inland road. Both routes present something of a challenge, and they both offer great scenery and some fascinating places to stop along the way. If you have a 4WD, it's worth heading up one way and coming back the other. For more info, read the relevant sections earlier in this chapter.

Tours There are numerous operators offering tours to Cooktown from Cairns and Port Douglas – see Organised Tours in the Cairns section for details.

Getting Around

Cooktown is small enough to cover on foot, if you have the time and energy.

The Hire Shop (☎ (070) 69 5601), on Charlotte St just south of the Sovereign Hotel, rents out cars ($70 a day) and boats ($50 for a half day, $80 for a full day with fuel supplied). Endeavour Air (☎ (070) 69 5860), also on Charlotte St, has two 4WD Suzukis available for local sightseeing at $90 a day.

LIZARD ISLAND

Lizard Island, the furthest north of the Barrier Reef resort islands, is about 100 km from Cooktown and 240 km from Cairns. Lizard is a continental island with a dry, rocky and mountainous terrain – a far cry from the tropical paradise of swaying palm trees that some people seem to expect. Nevertheless, the island has superb beaches, probably the best on any of the Barrier Reef islands. It's a great island for swimming, snorkelling and diving, and has some good bushwalks and great views from Cook's Look – at 368 metres the highest point on the island.

The accommodation here covers both ends of the spectrum – with nothing in between. You can either stay in an exclusive (and expensive) resort frequented by millionaires and big-game fishers, or pitch a tent in the national park camping ground. Camper's aren't exactly welcomed or encouraged by the resort, so if you choose the latter you'll have to be totally self-sufficient for the period of your stay. Almost all of the island is national park, which means it's open to anyone who makes the effort to get here.

Lizard is quite readily accessible by air or boat from either Cairns or Cooktown, although due to the distances involved it's a pricey place to get to. However, the expense is more than justified, especially if you're staying a few days or more.

History

Captain Cook and his crew were the first Europeans to visit Lizard Island, in 1770. Having successfully patched up the *Endeavour* in Cooktown, they set sail north and stopped on Lizard Island, where Cook and the botanist Joseph Banks climbed to the top of Cook's Look to look for a way out through the Barrier Reef to the open sea. Banks named the island after the large lizards that were its only apparent occupants. Meanwhile, other crew members had found a safe route out to deeper water, and the *Endeavour* continued its journey.

During Cook's visit Banks had noticed that 'the Indians had been here in their poor embarkations' and later visits also noted that Aborigines had visited the island, visits that were to lead to a Queensland tragedy. In 1881 Robert and Mary Watson settled on the island in order to collect bêche-de-mer, or sea slugs, a noted Chinese delicacy. They built a small stone cottage overlooking what is now Watson's Bay. In September of that year, Robert Watson and his partner left the island to search for new fishing grounds, leaving Mary Watson with her baby, Ferrier, and their two Chinese servants Ah Sam and Ah Leong. On 29 September a party of Aborigines arrived on the island and attacked the group, killing Ah Leong and wounding Ah Sam. The next day Mary Watson decided to leave the island, and with a few supplies, her baby and her wounded houseboy, paddled away in an iron tank used for boiling up the bêche-de-mer. For 10 days they drifted from sandbank to island to reef to mangrove swamp, narrowly missing passing steamers or signalling unsuccessfully to them until eventually all died of thirst. Their bodies weren't found until January the next year. During this ordeal she kept a diary, which is now held by the Queensland Museum in Brisbane.

The ruined walls of the Watson's cottage can still be seen on the island today. Near the top of Cook's Look there are also traces of stones marking an Aboriginal ceremonial area and it's possible that Mary Watson's unhappy end may have come about because they had unwittingly strayed into an area sacred to Aborigines.

Zoning

The waters immediately around Lizard Island are all zoned as Marine National Park where shell and coral collecting and spear fishing are not permitted. Around the northern part of the island it's Zone A, which permits limited line fishing. The southern part, including all of Blue Lagoon and the waters around Palfrey and South islands and Seabird Islet, as well as Watson's Bay and Turtle Beach north of the resort, are all Zone B where all fishing is prohibited.

Things to See & Do

Lizard Island's **beaches** are nothing short of sensational, and range from long stretches of white sand to idyllic little rocky bays. The water is crystal clear, and the island is surrounded by magnificent coral. Snorkelling here is superb.

Immediately south of the resort are three postcard beaches – Sunset Beach, Pebbly Beach and Hibiscus Beach. Watson's Bay to the north of the resort is a wonderful stretch of sand with great snorkelling at both ends and a clam field in the middle, and there are plenty of other choices right around the island.

The island is noted for its **diving**. There are good dives right off the island, and the outer Barrier Reef is less than 20 km away, including what is probably Australia's best known dive, the Cod Hole. The resort offers a full range of diving facilities to its guests, although this isn't a particularly cheap place

Mary Watson

FAR NTH QUEENSLAND

to dive. For a day's diving on the outer reef you're looking at around $180.

Lizard is also famed for its fishing, particularly **heavy tackle fishing** for which the annual competition over Halloween night (31 October) is a big attraction. September through December is the heavy tackle season. The Marlin Centre, at the north end of the resort bay caters for the many game-fishing boats that use Lizard as a base at the height of the season. Its bar is renowned for extremely tall fishing tales. The resort's MV *Gamefisher* is available for charter during the marlin season, or if you'd rather tackle something a bit smaller you can take out one of their dinghies.

The climb to the top of **Cook's Look** is undoubtedly the most popular walk on the island. The trail, which starts from the northern end of the beach near the camp site, is clearly signposted and, although it can be steep and a bit of a clamber at times, is easy to follow all the way with regular white or blue painted arrows. The views from the top are sensational, and on a clear day you can see the opening in the reef where Cook made his thankful escape. The climb can take anywhere from 45 minutes to 1½ hours.

The privately funded **Lizard Island Research Station** (☎ (070) 60 3977) pursues research projects as diverse as examining marine organisms for cancer research, trying to explain the deaths of giant clams, coral reproductive processes, sea bird ecology, life patterns of reef fish during their larval stage and many other subjects. Tours of the station are conducted at 9.30 am each Monday and Friday. The station also has accommodation for visiting researchers.

Lizard has plenty of **wildlife**. There are 11 different species of lizards, including large sand goannas which are often up to a metre long. More than 40 species of birds have also been recorded on the island and a dozen or so actually nest there, including the beautiful little sunbirds with their long, hanging nests. They even build them inside the small, open airstrip terminal! Bar-shouldered doves, crested terns, Caspian terns and a variety of other terns, oystercatchers and the large sea

eagles are other resident species. Seabird Islet in the Blue Lagoon is a popular nesting site for terns and visitors should keep away from the islet during the summer months.

Places to Stay

Camping The national parks camp site is at the north end of the Watson's Bay beach. The site has toilets, barbecues, tables and benches, and freshwater is available from a pump about 250 metres from the site. Campers must be totally self sufficient. You also need take your garbage with you when you leave, and bring charcoal for the barbecues as all timber on the island (including driftwood) is protected, and fuel stoves aren't allowed on aircraft. Sites cost $3 per person per night, and permits are available from the QNP&WS office (☎ (070) 52 3096) in Cairns.

Resort The Lizard Island Resort (☎ (070) 60 3999), run by Qantas Airlines, is one of the most exclusive and expensive resorts on the Great Barrier Reef. The resort is modern and 1st class, but quite straightforward – you're paying for the isolation and the great location less than 20 km from the outer edge of the reef rather than for glossy five-star luxury.

There are 32 double rooms, each with air-con and ceiling fans, fridges, tea and coffee-making equipment, bathrobes and toiletries, and telephones. There are no TVs or radios in the rooms. The tariffs are $520/860 per night for singles/doubles. There are also two larger suites with a separate lounge and living area at $600/980 per night. These rates include all meals and general equipment use and activities. The resort's facilities, which are exclusively for the use of house guests, include a floodlit tennis court, swimming pool, windsurfers, catamarans, outboard dinghies and water-skiing.

Boating trips do cost extra and these are put on every day, either for fishing, diving and snorkelling, picnic and barbecue excursions to neighbouring islands, or various combinations of these activities.

Children between six and 14 pay half

price, and children under six are banned. For bookings, write to the Lizard Island Resort, Private Mail Bag 40, Cairns, Qld 4870.

Places to Eat

The restaurant at the resort is only open to house guests, so if you're camping here you'll have to bring all your supplies from the mainland.

The resort has an excellent reputation for its cuisine. The main dining area is an open-air sundeck with a great outlook across the lawns to the sea. For breakfast you can eat buffet-style or à la carte. A typical lunch menu will offer a choice between a cold soup and an entrée, three main courses and two desserts. The dinner menu is more extensive, or if you don't see what you want on the menu, you can order whatever you like. The resort will also pack picnic hampers if you're heading out for the day.

Getting There & Away

Air Sunstate Airlines (☎ 13 1313) has daily flights from Cairns and the hour-long flight by Twin Otter costs $144.

Aussie Airways (☎ (070) 53 3980) has a day trip from Cairns to Lizard Island several days a week, which costs $299 per person including lunch and snorkelling gear.

Endeavour Air (☎ (070) 69 5860), based in Cooktown, has day trips to the island for $130 per person (minimum of four). They can also do camping drop-offs from Cooktown, which cost $370 for up to five people – well worth considering, especially if you're planning to stay a few days or longer.

Sea There is no regular shipping or ferry service to Lizard Island, although several cruise ships call in here. The *Reef Escape*, the SV *Atlantic Clipper* and the *Kangaroo Explorer* all have stopovers at Lizard Island. See Cruises under Organised Tours in both the Cairns and Cape York Peninsula sections for details.

There are also several smaller charter boats based in Cooktown that operate trips to and around Lizard Island – see Fishing

Charters & Cruises in the Cooktown section for details of these.

Yachties can anchor in sheltered Watson's Bay or in the Blue Lagoon. Intrepid madmen have even come over to Lizard Island from the mainland in outboard powered 'tinnies'. It's about 30 km from Cape Flattery. The red carpet is not, however, rolled out to yachties by the resort.

ISLANDS AROUND LIZARD ISLAND

There are four other smaller islands in the Lizard group. **Osprey Island**, with its nesting birds, is right in front of the resort and can be waded to. Around the edge of Blue Lagoon, south of the main island, are **Seabird Islet**, **South Island** and **Palfrey Island** with its automatic lighthouse.

There are a number of continental islands and small cays dotted around Lizard Island and south towards Cooktown. Camping is permitted on a number of the islands with a QNP&WS permit. The sites are all very basic and the permits cost just $3 per person a night.

Immediately south of Lizard Island is **Rocky Islet**, wooded and with good beaches, and two adjoining islets, one covered in scrub, one bare rock. Day trips are sometimes made to the islets from Lizard Island and there is good snorkelling and diving there. Camping is permitted on the north side of the main island between February and September.

Just north of the Rocky Islets, **South Direction Island** is scrub-covered but without beaches. Yachts sometimes anchor here although it's not easy to get inside the reef. **North Direction Island** is another popular destination for day trips from Lizard Island. There's a good beach and sand spit and some fine coral for divers or snorkellers. Aboriginal rock paintings can be seen on the island.

Eagle Islet, a small cay at the northern end of Eyrie Reef, is only about eight km from Lizard. The islet is noted for its three eagle nests. From December to March it harbours a huge number of sea birds, particularly nesting sooty terns and white-crested terns.

About 25 km west of Lizard Island is **Nymph Island**, a good picnic spot with good snorkelling around the reef. Reportedly there have even been crocodiles in the island's inner lagoon. It's a good island for walking and camping is permitted. Slightly south-west of Nymph Island are the islands of the Turtle Group, small sand and vegetated cays. Camping is permitted on three of the islands in the group.

Cape York Peninsula

Cape York is one of the last great frontiers of Australia. It is a vast patchwork of tropical savannah cut by numerous rivers and streams, while along its eastern flank is the northern section of the Great Dividing Range.

In amongst the Range's rugged peaks and deep valleys are some of the best and most significant rainforests in Australia. Streams tumble down the rocky mountains to the sea, where just off shore the coral ramparts of the Great Barrier Reef stretch over thousands of sq km. The reef is protected in a marine park, and much of the land mass of the Cape is protected in a number of spectacular, rarely visited and wild national parks.

Giving access to that vast natural wonderland is the route to the Cape. Initially the corrugated road you follow is the Peninsula Developmental Road, but once that heads away to the mining town of Weipa, you follow the Telegraph Track to the 'Tip', and the real adventure begins.

North of the Weipa turn off the track definitely requires a 4WD vehicle, and as you head further north, the creek crossings become more common and more challenging. By the time you get back from a trip to the Tip, you'll be an expert in water crossings!

From Cairns to the top of Cape York it is 952 km via the shortest and most challenging route. Most travellers will want to visit Cooktown, Weipa and a few other places off the main route, and those diversions will add considerably to the total distance covered.

There are a number of alternative routes. Down south you can choose between the inland route, or the coastal route via Daintree and Cape Tribulation. From Lakeland you can travel straight up the heart of the Cape or go via Cooktown and Battle Camp to Laura or Musgrave.

From the Archer River you can head north via Weipa and Stones Crossing, or via the Telegraph Track. Further north you have the

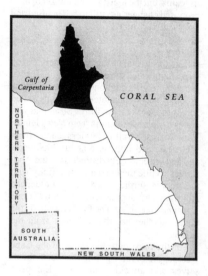

choice of continuing on the Telegraph Track or taking the newer bypass roads.

Vast areas of Cape York are also designated Aboriginal land, while the rest is mainly taken up with large pastoral holdings.

Covering an area totalling around 207,000 sq km, which is about the same size as the state of Victoria, Cape York has a population of around 15,000 people.

The largest towns in the region are Cooktown, on the south-east coast, and Weipa, a large mining community on the central-west coast. A handful of smaller towns make up the remainder of the communities throughout the Cape.

During the 1995 state government campaign, Premier Wayne Goss promised that if re-elected he would declare the entire Cape York Peninsula, from north of the Daintree River to the Tip, a 'Wilderness Zone'. The proposal was acclaimed by the Cape York Aboriginal Council and environmental groups, but greeted less than enthusiastically by many of the Cape's pastoralists and land owners. The Goss government was subsequently re-elected – by the proverbial skin of its teeth – but the logistics and impact of their proposed changes are still to be finalised and assessed. Stay tuned.

History

Before the arrival of Europeans there were a large number of different Aboriginal tribal groups spread throughout the Cape. A unique group of people inhabited the islands dotted across the reef-strewn Torres Strait that separates mainland Australia from New Guinea. The Torres Strait Islanders came from Melanesia and Polynesia about 2000 years ago and are culturally distinct from the Aborigines. While they had a close affinity with the people further north, they influenced Aboriginal tribal groups near the top of Cape York and vice versa. The further south on the mainland, the less the influence from the north.

For the most part, the tribes of the Cape were aggressive, fighting between themselves and attacking the early European explorers. In fact, there are few accounts of early explorers that do not relate attacks by Aborigines or Islanders.

The rich Aboriginal and Torres Strait heritage is alive and well today and travellers will see much of it on their way through the Cape. Of special importance is one of the world's most significant collections of prehistoric art in the escarpment country surrounding Laura.

European history in Australia can trace its beginnings back to the early Dutch navigators who from 1606 explored much of the coastline. Willem Jansz and Abel Tasman, were the first Europeans to report seeing the Great South Land. (It is unclear whether the Spanish navigator Torres, after whom the strait is named, actually sighted the land.) Their exploits are remembered in the names of bluffs and bays dotted down the Gulf side of the Cape.

James Cook mapped the east coast of Australia in 1770, and claimed the continent for England while on Possession Island, just off

the northerly tip that he named Cape York. Over the next 100 years, other great English navigators, including Bligh, Flinders and King, mapped sections of the coast and bestowed their names upon it.

Ludwig Leichhardt was the first explorer to journey over a section of the Cape during his 1845 expedition from Brisbane to Port Essington on the Cobourg Peninsula in the Northern Territory. South of the Mitchell River they were attacked and John Gilbert, the great collector of animals and birds for the naturalist John Gould, was killed.

Edmund Kennedy and his party had a horrific time in 1848 heading up the east coast along the Great Dividing Range. Continually splitting his party, Kennedy was fatally speared by Aborigines amongst the swamps and waterways of the Escape River, south-east of the Tip. Only Jacky Jacky, his Aboriginal guide, reached their destination just a few km north at Albany Passage. (For more information on Edmund Kennedy see the History section in the Facts about Queensland chapter.)

Frank Jardine and his brother led a group taking cattle from Rockhampton to the new government outpost at Somerset in 1863. This was to be the start of the Jardine legend on Cape York, with Frank Jardine dominating the top of the Cape until his death in 1919.

Other explorers followed, opening up the region. The discovery of gold on the Palmer River in 1873 was the great catalyst for the development of Cooktown, Laura and, later, Cairns.

In 1887 the Overland Telegraph Line from near Somerset to Palmerville and Cooktown was finally completed, linking the northernmost outpost with Brisbane. This is the route most travellers to Cape York follow today.

During WW II, Cape York was a major staging post for the battles going on in New Guinea and the Coral Sea. Some 10,000 troops were stationed on the Cape at such places as Iron Range and Portland Roads, on the mid-east coast; Horn Island, Mutee Heads and Jacky Jacky Airfield (then called Higgins Field) at the northern tip of Cape

Cape York Peninsula

0   75   150 km

Gulf Of Carpentaria

Thursday Island
Heron Island
Cape York
Prince of Wales Island
Somerset Ruins
Possession Island
Bamaga
Mottee Heads
Jacky Jack Airfield
Jardine River NP

CORAL SEA

Wenlock
Iron Range NP
Portland Roads
Lockhart River
Welpa
River

Great Barrier Reef

Archer Bend National Park
Archer River Roadhouse
Archer River
Rokeby NP
Coen
Kendall River
Holroyd River
Edward River

Cape Melville NP
Normanby River
Starke NP
Musgrave
Lakefield National Park

Mitchell & Alice Rivers National Park
Kowanyama
Alice River
Mitchell River
Laura
Cooktown
Lakeland
Cape Tribulation
Daintree
Mossman
Port Douglas
Staaten River
Staaten River National Park
CAIRNS
Mareeba
Burke Dev Road
Gilbert River
Karumba
Bullepinga National Park
Normanton
Ravenshoe
Innisfail

Peninsula Dev Road

York; as well as around Cooktown. Many relics of those days can still be seen, including wrecks of some of the 160-odd aircraft that were reported lost over the region.

During the 1950s bauxite was discovered along the coast near Weipa, and by the 1980s it had grown into the world's biggest bauxite mine. With reserves stockpiled well into the next century, Weipa will continue to be a major community and a place to visit for years to come.

When to Go & Road Conditions

The wet season greatly restricts vehicle movement on Cape York. For that reason the best time to go is as early in the Dry as possible, generally from the beginning of June. The country is greener, there is more water around, there are less travellers and generally the roads are better than later in the season. The peak period is between August and September, with the last travellers being out of the Cape by around mid-November.

If you plan to visit early or late in the season, it pays to check with the locals to see what is happening weather-wise and what the roads are like. Speaking to the police in Coen, Weipa or Cooktown wouldn't go astray, nor would a phone call to the friendly people at the Archer River Roadhouse. Alternatively, you can contact the Queensland Department of Transport (☎ 008 077 247) or the RACQ Road Reports (24 hours ☎ (070) 51 6711, or ☎ (07) 11 655).

Occasionally people get caught out by the early rains of the Wet when they're at the very top of Cape York. They'll be looking at either an extended stay or an expensive barge trip with their vehicle back to Cairns.

Information

Of course you need all the usual gear for travelling in a remote area, and you must carry water. Although you will cross a number of rivers south of the Archer River, water can be scarce along the main track north, especially late in the Dry.

It is possible to take a well-constructed off-road trailer all the way to the top, but be prepared to get bogged occasionally. Lesser built trailers will fall apart somewhere along the track. Caravans can make it to Cooktown, driven with care. They can even make it further north to Weipa, but the going is hard and we would not recommend it.

You are also entering crocodile country, so, while there are plenty of safe places to swim, be aware that any deep, dark, long stretch of water can hold a big hungry saltie.

The most common accident on the Cape is head-ons in the heath country south of the Jardine River. The track is narrow here with many blind corners, people travel too fast and sometimes they meet head-on. Nobody has been killed yet – more by good luck than good fortune. Drive slowly and keep your wits about you.

Tourist Information There are no official tourist information centres along the route, although travellers will find information readily available from the many helpful locals in the roadhouses and towns along the way, such as Cooktown, Coen, Weipa and Bamaga. The Seisia Camping Ground, at the very top of Australia, is also a mine of information.

The following places are also useful sources of information:

Far North Queensland Promotion Bureau
  Corner of Grafton and Hartley Sts, Cairns, Qld 4870 (☎ (070) 51 3588)
Queensland National Parks & Wildlife Service
  Far North Regional Centre, 10-12 McLeod St, PO Box 2066, Cairns, Qld 4870 (☎ (070) 52 3096)
Cook Shire Council
  Charlotte St, PO Box 3, Cooktown, Qld 4871 (☎ (070) 69 5444)
Croc Shop
  8 Charlotte St, Cooktown (☎ (070) 69 5880) This company has spent years exploring and working on Cape York. It also has a range of maps and books.
Ang-Gnarra Aboriginal Corporation
  Post Office, Laura, Qld 4871 (☎ (070) 60 3214). Information on Aboriginal rock-art sites around Laura. Brochures and maps are available of the sites open to the public.

Money Banking facilities are very limited on Cape York, and full banking facilities are only available at three places: Weipa, Cooktown and Thursday Island. Probably the best option is to have a passbook account with the Commonwealth Bank, which enables you to withdraw cash at any post office or agency.

Cheques are not normally accepted, but major credit cards, such as Bankcard, MasterCard and Visa, are accepted widely for most services. Australian travellers' cheques are also exchanged in some places along the way. However, in many places cash is still the only form of currency accepted.

Telephones STD phones are located at most roadhouses and certainly in the towns.

Police The police can provide information to travellers on road conditions etc. Contact the following police stations: Cooktown (☎ (070) 69 5320), on Charlotte St; Hopevale Aboriginal Community (☎ (070) 60 9224), 4 Flierl St; Laura (☎ (070) 60 3244); Coen (☎ (070) 60 1150); Weipa (☎ (070) 69 9119), Rocky Point; Lockhart River Aboriginal Community (☎ 070) 60 7120); and Bamaga (☎ 070) 69 3156), Sagauka St.

Medical Services Hospitals on Cape York include: Cooktown (☎ (070) 69 5433) on Hope St; Coen (☎ (070) 60 1141); Weipa (☎ (070) 69 9155) at Rocky Point; and Bamaga (☎ (070) 69 3166). There is also a dentist (☎ (070) 69 9411) at Rocky Point, Weipa, and a clinic (☎ (070) 60 3320) in Laura.

Permits Permits are not required for travelling to Cape York via the main route described. This situation may change as the effects of Mabo and land rights become more advanced. This may affect camping in national parks as well, as these areas may be claimed by Aboriginal groups.

Once you are north of the Jardine River, however, you will need a permit to camp on Aboriginal land, which in effect is nearly all the land north of the river. The Injinoo people are the traditional custodians of much of this land, along with other Aboriginal communities at Umagico and New Mapoon. Please respect the signs and bylaws of the community councils.

Designated camping grounds are provided in a number of areas, including Seisia, Pajinka and Punsand Bay. Camping elsewhere in the area requires a permit from the Injinoo Community Council (☎ (070) 69 3252) or Pajinka Wilderness Lodge. You can write to the Injinoo Community Council, PO Box 7757, Cairns, Qld 4870.

Alternatively, you can wait until you get to the Injinoo owned and operated ferry across the Jardine River. The $80 (return) fee includes the cost of camping at a number of pleasant, isolated sites, and the permit fees.

A plan of management is being developed for the area with a range of access fees, so things may change in the near future.

Travelling across Aboriginal land elsewhere on the Cape may require a permit. Some are easy to obtain while others are difficult – it all depends on the community concerned. It is best to write to the relevant community council stating the reason for your visit, dates etc. Allow plenty of time for an answer. There are more than a dozen different communities on the Cape – contact the Aboriginal Co-ordinating Council (☎ (070) 31 2623) in Cairns for contact numbers and addresses for the relevant community.

Books & Maps There is a wide range of books and maps on Cape York available in Cairns, Cooktown or Weipa and from good bookshops Australia-wide.

The Hema map *Cape York* and the RACQ maps *Cairns/Townsville* and *Cape York Peninsula* are the best. Ron & Viv Moon's *Cape York – an Adventurer's Guide* is the most comprehensive guidebook for the do-it-yourself camper and 4WD traveller.

The Last Frontier: Cape York Wilderness, by Glenville Pike, really covers the history of the region well. For those interested in the Palmer River goldfields, the book *River of Gold* by Hector Holthouse is by far the best. If you want to know a little about the flowers

CAPE YORK PENINSULA

of the region, a colourful, small book, *A Wilderness in Bloom*, written and published by B & B Hinton, is a good one to start with.

The best book on Cooktown is the *Queen of the North* by Glenville Pike; *Cape York* by Hector Holthouse also covers this area.

There are no modern books readily available that give a comprehensive look at the Aboriginal art of the area. Percy Trezise wrote *Quinkan Country* and *Last Days of a Wilderness*, as well as a report titled *Rock Art of South-East Cape York*, which was produced by the Australian Institute of Aboriginal Studies some years ago. They are difficult to get now.

Radio Frequencies Unless you are doing something way out of the ordinary, an HF radio, while nice to have, is not really necessary for the Cape.

The RFDS base in Cairns (call sign VJN) has a primary channel of 5145 and secondary channels of 2260, 4926, 6785 and 7465. The Mt Isa base (call sign VJI) has a primary channel frequency of 5110, with secondary frequencies of 4935, 6965, and 7392.

For those with a Telstra account, Sydney is the base to work through (call sign VIS). The OTC radphone channels available 24 hours a day at Sydney include 405, 607, 802, 1203 and 1602. All these channels are voice call, Selcall or Tonecall. Others are available for Tonecall and Selcall, while other frequencies are request only. Selcall for the beacon is 0899, while the operator is 0108.

Fuel The distances between fuel stops aren't great and the condition of the road is pretty fair at most times of the year. Diesel, unleaded and super are generally readily available along the route to the Cape, but there is no LPG after Cairns, except at Cooktown. Prices for fuel will vary between fuel stops and can be quite expensive in places. Weipa and Bamaga always seem to be cheaper.

Towing Should you need a tow to the nearest town, the following towing services will be extremely useful:

Mt Molloy Service Centre & RACQ Service Depot, Brown St, Mt Molloy (24 hours ☎ (070) 94 1260)
Lakeland Cash Store & RACQ Service Depot (24 hours ☎ (070) 60 2133)
Cooktown Towing & Transport, McIvor Rd, Cooktown (☎ (070) 69 5545)
Weipa Service Centre & RACQ Service Depot, Boundary Rd, Weipa (24 hours ☎ (070) 69 7277)
WRAFTEC Industries, 1 Iraci Ave, Weipa (☎ (070) 69 7877)

Camping Equipment Rental Geo Pickers Great Outdoors Centre (☎ (070) 51 1944), 108 Mulgrave Rd, Parramatta Park, Cairns, has a range of camping equipment and accessories for hire.

Some of the 4WD hire companies, such as Marlin Truck & 4WD Rentals, have camping gear available for people renting their vehicles. See the Getting There & Away section for details.

Organised Tours
For most people travelling to the Cape, Cairns is the stepping-off point, and has everything you need to organise a trip north: rental vehicles, camping equipment rentals, guiding services, as well as a host of tour operators who can organise part, or all, of your trip to the Cape.

Tour Operators A host of companies operate 4WD tours from Cairns to Cape York. The trips generally range from six to 16 days, and take in Laura, the Quinkan rock-art galleries, Lakefield National Park, Coen, Weipa, Indian Head Falls, Bamaga, Somerset and Cape York itself. Most trips also visit Thursday Island, as well as taking in Cape Tribulation, Cooktown and/or the Palmer River goldfields at the start or end of the odyssey.

For a comprehensive list of established and well-known tour operators, contact the Far North Queensland Coach & Off Road Association (☎ (070) 31 4565).

Travel on standard tours is in 4WDs with five to 12 passengers, accommodation is generally in tents and all food is supplied. Most of the companies offer a variety of alternatives, such as to fly or sail one way, and travel overland the other. Expect to pay around $1000 to $1300 for a seven-day fly/drive tour, around $1600 for a seven-day sail/drive tour, and anywhere from $1200 to $2000 for a 12 to 14-day safari. Prices vary depending on a range of factors: the time of year; whether you drive, fly and/or cruise; the type of accommodation; and the food and level of service provided.

The following are some of the better known 4WD tour companies:

New Look Adventures
   PO Box 7505, Cairns, Qld 4870, or 109 Draper St, Cairns (☎ (070) 31 7622)
Wild Track Adventure Safaris
   PO Box 2397, Cairns, Qld 4870 (☎ (070) 55 2247)
Australian Outback Travel
   42 Abbott St, Cairns, Qld (☎ (070) 31 5833)
Oz Tours Safaris
   PO Box 6464, Cairns, Qld 4871 (☎ (070) 55 9535)
Heritage 4WD Tours
   17 Pennine Close, Smithfield (☎ (070) 38 2186)
Kamp Out Safaris
   PO Box 1894, Cairns, Qld 4870 (☎ (070) 31 4862)

Another company, Trezise Bush Guides (☎ (070) 55 1865), based at Jowalbinna near Laura, offers more specialised one, three and four-day tours from Cairns to Cape York. Their Quinkan Country Day Tour costs $295 per person – they fly you into their private airstrip and take you on a hiking tour of the Aboriginal rock-art galleries. They also have three-day safaris to the Deighton River Valley ($395) or to Jowalbinna ($395), and a four-day safari that takes in the Daintree, Cooktown, Lakefield National Park and the Quinkan rock-art sites ($675). This company also offers local tours of rock-art galleries – see the Laura section for details.

Guide Services One of the most popular ways to see the Cape is in the company of a tag-along operator. Some companies supply a cook and all the food, while others only act as guides, supplying information, permits, HF radio facilities and recovery expertise. While they do not supply a vehicle, if you need to hire one they can organise it for you. Tag-along companies include the following:

Cape York Connections
   PO Box 371, Port Douglas, Qld 4871 (☎ (070) 98 4938 or (018) 770 569)
Guides to Adventure
   PO Box 908, Atherton, Qld 4883 (☎ (070) 91 1978)
Oz Tours
   PO Box 6464, Cairns, Qld 4870 (☎ (070) 55 9535)
Russell Guest 4X4 Safaris
   38 Station Street, Fairfield, Vic 3078 (☎ (03) 481 5440)

Motorcycle Tours There are also a couple of operators offering motorcycle tours of the Cape:

Cape York Motorcycle Adventures
   PO Box 525, Manunda, Cairns, Qld 4870 (☎ (070) 58 1148, mobile (018) 77 0399). They offer a five-day trip for $700 or a 10-day trip for $1450. Prices include all meals and equipment, and you can ride your own bike or hire one of theirs for another $85 a day.
Two Wheel Adventures
   PO Box 397, Manunda, Cairns, Qld 4870 (☎ (070) 31 5707). They have one to 12-day guided motorcycle tours, or you can hire your own bike – see the Cairns Getting There & Away section for details.

Mail Run Based in Cairns, Cape York Air Services (☎ (070) 35 9399) operates the Peninsula Mail Run, the world's longest. They fly a different route every weekday, delivering mail to remote cattle stations and towns including Laura. Space permitting, you can go along on these runs, but it's not cheap at $140 to $275, depending on the length of the trip.

Cruise Ships Even without your own yacht, visiting the islands north from Lizard to Torres Strait is certainly possible. Two cruise ships, the SV *Atlantic Clipper* and the *Kangaroo Explorer* operate regular trips from Cairns to Thursday Island and back, stopping at a number of islands along the way.

The *Atlantic Clipper* (☎ (070) 31 2516 or toll-free 008 079 099), operated by Clipper

CAPE YORK PENINSULA

Sailaway Cruises (PO Box 2377, Cairns, Qld 4870), is a modern square-rigged sailing ship which can accommodate up to 34 passengers in two and three-berth cabins. The cabins are air-conditioned, and there's a bar and an on-deck spa pool. Departures are on Saturday evening at 5 pm from Trinity Wharf in Cairns, arriving back on the following Saturday morning. Stops are usually made at Lizard Island, Cape York, Cooktown and Hope Island, with a few alternatives depending on anchorages and conditions. Fares for the week's cruise range from $1190 per person in the three-berth cabins up to $1490 in a twin-share cabin with an ensuite; fares include all meals, fishing and snorkelling gear, and entertainment.

The *Kangaroo Explorer* (☎ (070) 55 8188 or toll-free 008 079 141) offers a variety of cruises between Cairns and Cape York. These include four and seven-day return cruises, or seven-day one-way cruises (with a return flight). Launched in 1990, the ship is a 25-metre cruising catamaran with 15 twin cabins, each air-conditioned and with its own bathroom. Departures are on Saturday at 1 pm from Trinity Wharf in Cairns. Fares for the seven-day cruises range from $1655 per person for a twin cabin on the lower deck up to $2199 for a cabin on the main or upper deck. Costs include all meals and activities. Write to PO Box 7110, Cairns, Qld 4870 for more details.

Fishing Safaris & Charters With magnificent off-shore reefs and islands, the coast of Cape York is a popular destination for fishing enthusiasts and divers. Many charters and safaris operate from Cairns. Contact the Far North Queensland Promotion Bureau for details (see the Information section earlier).

There are also a number of local charter operators mentioned throughout this chapter.

Festivals
Cape York's major festivals include the Cape York Aboriginal Dance Festival, held near Laura on the banks of the Laura River; the Hopevale Show & Rodeo, staged in July or August each year; the Bamaga Annual

Show, normally run in August or September each year; and the Torres Strait Cultural Festival, held annually in May. See the Thursday Island & the Torres Strait, Jardine River to Cape York, and North of Cooktown sections respectively for full details.

Getting There & Away
Air Flight West Airlines (☎ (070) 13 2392) has flights from Cairns to Cooktown, Kowanyama, Pormpuraaw, Coen, Lockhart River, Bamaga, Horn Island and Thursday Island. Sunstate/Qantas (☎ 13 1313) have flights from Cairns to Lizard Island, Bamaga and Thursday Island. Ansett (☎ 13 1300) has a daily flight from Cairns to Weipa. Ring the respective airlines for current flight details and reservations.

Skytrans (☎ (070) 69 7248), based in Weipa, has flights from Weipa to Bamaga and Thursday Island, and several feeder airlines operate flights throughout the Torres Strait Islands. See those sections for details.

A wide range of charter aircraft operate all over Cape York. Each company usually has its own scheduled scenic flights and safari tours. Contact the Far North Queensland Promotion Bureau for full details (see Information earlier).

Airfields There are four public airfields on the Cape York Peninsula: at Cooktown, Coen, Iron Range and Laura, while throughout the Cape there are small, privately owned and maintained airstrips on station properties. Aviation fuel can be organised from most of the airstrips, but you need to give prior notice of your requirements.

Weipa has a major airport with aviation fuel available. Jacky Jacky Airfield, nine km south-east of Bamaga, is the main airfield for the Top.

Bus No bus company actually runs a service all the way to the top of Cape York, but Cape York Coaches has a twice-weekly service from Cairns to Weipa – see the Weipa section for details.

Sea A number of shipping companies cruise the coast of Cape York carrying a variety of cargo and stores. While many can transport vehicles, only a couple actually take passengers.

Jardine Shipping (☎ (070) 35 1900) operates a weekly service from Cairns to Thursday Island and Bamaga, taking vehicles, general cargo and passengers. They leave Cairns every Monday. It costs around $650 to take a vehicle from Cairns to Thursday Island; passenger fares are $250/400 one way/return.

Gulf Freight Services (☎ (070) 69 8619 in Weipa or ☎ (077) 45 9333 in Karumba) operates regular barge services between Karumba and Weipa carrying freight, passengers and vehicles. Their barge leaves Weipa every Monday and Karumba every Saturday, taking about two days to do the trip. The one-way fare is from $260 to $300 for a vehicle, plus $200 per passenger, which includes cabin accommodation and all meals. There are only three cabins and this service is very popular during the tourist season, so you should book as far in advance as possible.

4WD Rentals There are a number of rental companies based in Cairns and Port Douglas that hire 4WDs, but the majority will only let you take them as far as Cooktown and Laura. In Cooktown there are a couple of places where you can get a vehicle, but again you'll only be able to drive it in the surrounding area, or in some instances as far as Laura.

Only a few companies will allow you to take the vehicle beyond Laura; these include:

Marlin Truck & 4WD Rentals
35 McLeod St, Cairns (☎ (070) 31 2360) – 4WDs available for hire to drivers over 21 years of age. From $130 a day, minimum 14-day hire to go the Top, and they can supply all camping and cooking gear
Brits Rentals
411 Sheridan St, Cairns (☎ (070) 32 2611) – 4WDs and 4WD campervans available for hire to drivers over 23 years of age, minimum seven-day hire to go the Top, from $155 a day plus insurance

4WD, or not 4WD – that is the question!

Before I made my first trip up to the Top, I held the not uncommon perception that Cape York was only accessible for well-equipped and experienced 4WD adventurers. This idea was soon challenged by the not insubstantial number of 2WD vehicles I saw on the roads – at one stage, I was overtaken by an ancient and battered Toyota Corolla. I also heard plenty of tales of people making it to the Top in old Holdens and Fords, although not so many tales of them making it back again...

While the roads on the Cape are all unsealed – some sections are smooth dirt, others are soft sand, and others are rocky and corrugated – the majority of them are reasonably well maintained. The main route to Weipa is used by mining company vehicles and is virtually a dirt highway. It is certainly *possible* to drive as far as Weipa in a conventional vehicle – whether you attempt to or not depends as much as anything on how much (or how little) respect you have for your car. North of Weipa, the road conditions deteriorate rapidly and the numerous river crossings, from the Wenlock north, make it inadvisable to attempt going beyond Weipa in the family station wagon.

The other major drawback about not having a 4WD is that you'll have to stick to the main road, which means you'll miss out on the most spectacular parts of the Cape such as the national parks.

The conditions of the roads can also vary substantially depending on a number of factors, including how recently the roads have been graded, the time of year and how much water is about, the effects of recent rain, and the amount of traffic using the roads.

Whatever type of vehicle you take, the important thing with a Gulf trip is to be well prepared. Before heading off, seek expert advice on road conditions and routes (see the earlier Information section). It's also vital to make sure your vehicle is in good condition for the trip, and to carry plenty of water plus all the spares, tools and equipment that you might need. If you do break down or get stuck, it's a long way between mechanics, and even if you find one, repairs will probably be costly. ■

Cairns Leisure Wheels
  196A Sheridan St, Cairns (☎ (070) 51 8988) –
  4WDs available for hire to drivers over 26 years
  of age, minimum 14-day hire to go to the Top,
  from $165 a day
Crocodile Car Rentals
  50 Macrossan St, Port Douglas (☎ (070) 99
  5555) – 4WDs available for hire (to Cooktown,
  Laura and Chillagoe only) to drivers over 21
  years of age, from $99 a day

There are local car hire companies in Weipa
and Seisia, near Bamaga.

Motorcycle Rental It is very difficult to hire
a motorcycle to take up to the top of Cape
York, although there are a couple of motorcycle tour operators running trips up here –
see the Organised Tours section earlier.

The Route

CAPE YORK SAMPLER
For those who don't have time to travel to
the very top of Cape York, but still want to
sample the delights of this region away from
the glitz and glamour of Cairns and Port
Douglas, then an interesting loop to do is
from Cairns to Cooktown and on to
Musgrave via Battle Camp and Lakefield
National Park, returning to Cairns via Laura
and the Peninsula Developmental Road.
Even if you are travelling to the top, this is
an enjoyable alternative to the main route.
  The first sector of this route – from Cairns
to Cooktown – is covered in the earlier Far
North Queensland chapter. You have a
choice of two routes to Cooktown – the
inland route or the coast road. If you have a
4WD, it's worth considering taking the coast
road up to Cooktown, and coming back via
the inland road.
  The second sector – from Cooktown to
Musgrave via the Lakefield National Park,
then from Musgrave back to Lakeland via
Laura – is covered later in this chapter.
  North of Cooktown the route cuts across
the Great Dividing Range before descending
onto the vast flood plains that make up much

of Lakefield National Park. During the Wet
the rivers often coalesce to make a shallow
inland sea, which in turn is replaced during
the Dry by a sea of waving grass cut by
tree-lined billabongs and lagoons.
  At its northernmost point the route passes
very close to the shores of Princess Charlotte
Bay, before swinging westwards to the Peninsula Developmental Road at the small
enclave of Musgrave.
  Cooktown is just one of the highlights of
this trip, and the natural delights of Lakefield
National Park and the Aboriginal rock art in
the Laura area are a couple of others. You
could easily spend a couple of weeks just in
this region of Far North Queensland.

NORTH OF COOKTOWN
The McIvor River Rd heads west out of
Cooktown, taking you past the cemetery and
racecourse. The bitumen soon ends, and
10 km west of town you cross the **Endeavour River** before passing the Cooktown
airfield. The *Endeavour Falls Tourist Park*
(☎ (070) 69 5431) is 33 km north-west of
Cooktown and offers camping and a kiosk
for basic supplies.
  At the 36-km mark is the turn off for Battle
Camp and Lakefield (see the following
Cooktown to Musgrave section). Continue
straight on (north) to get to the **Hopevale
Aboriginal Community**. The community
has a number of shops including a hardware
shop, butcher and a general store selling a
variety of goods, including Aboriginal artefacts. Fuel (super, unleaded and diesel) is
available at the service station. The
Hopevale Show & Rodeo is staged in July or
August each year. For further information,
contact the Administration Clerk (☎ (070)
60 9185), Hopevale Community Council.
  Munbah Cultural Tours (☎ (070) 60
9173) or write C/-Post Office, Hopevale, Qld
4871, is operated by the local Aboriginal
community. The programme costs $80 per
person per day. Visitors are shown many
aspects of traditional life and enjoy a river
cruise or bushwalking. Accommodation is
provided in bush-timber huts which are on
the beachfront, and all meals are included in

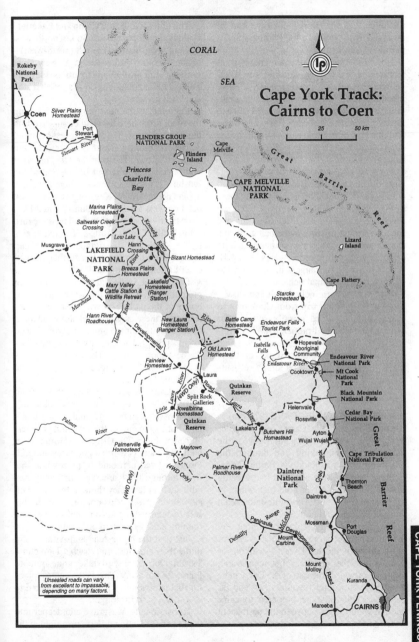

the tour. Pick-up from Cooktown can be arranged for another $40. Photography is permitted on the tour.

North of Hopevale this road quickly deteriorates, and is only suitable for 4WD vehicles. Points of interest north of here include **Cape Flattery**, where a huge sand-mining operation exports processed silica to Japan; the **Starke National Park**; and **Cape Melville National Park**, made famous by the controversial and ongoing fox-tail palms smuggling saga.

For several years, people have been illegally collecting the seeds of the rare fox-tail palms which grow here, and exporting them to the USA and Asia where they fetch big dollars. The practice has threatened this rare species – no palm seeds were being given a chance to germinate, and there has been little or no new growth in recent years. The park is now patrolled by rangers in an attempt to stamp out this criminal behaviour.

This road is extremely rough and slow – it's about a 12-hour trip from Cooktown to Cape Melville – and is only suitable for experienced and well-prepared 4WD travellers, preferably travelling in convoy. There are no facilities at either Starke or Cape Melville, so you have to be totally self-sufficient.

COOKTOWN TO MUSGRAVE (275 km)

As mentioned in the Cape York Sampler section, this route is a great alternative to the main road north, taking you through the Lakefield National Park via Battle Camp. Battle Camp was the site of a major battle during the Palmer River gold rush when, in 1873, a group of 500 Aborigines attacked a party of diggers and police.

This route is very isolated, without any facilities or fuel stops along the way. For those doing it the hard way – walking or pedalling – the distances between water, especially towards the end of the Dry, can be a fair way and other travellers few and far between. You must be prepared to carry enough water to get between the permanent water points.

The turn off to Battle Camp and Lakefield is along the Hopevale Rd, 36 km north-west of Cooktown. Turn to the left (north-west) – about five km further on is a stony river crossing and just downstream is **Isabella Falls**. This is a magic spot; it's worth a stop and even a swim!

Keep left at the next junction 2.5 km up the road. From here the road begins to climb the range and patches of rainforest begin.

The **Normanby River** is crossed 63 km from Cooktown. Early in the Dry this river will have water in it, but by the end of the season it is just a sandy bed. There are pools up and down stream. Keep on the main track heading west across flat country and 20 km from the river crossing you will pass the turn off to **Battle Camp Station**. The mountains to the south are the rugged Battle Camp Range. Less than three km further on you enter **Lakefield National Park**.

There is a large number of camping grounds spread along the rivers and billabongs of the park. You will often see tracks leading to these as you travel along the main track. If you want to camp here, you'll need to get a permit. The ranger will let you know the best spot to camp. The ranger station is at New Laura Homestead, 51 km from the park boundary.

The **Laura River** is crossed 25 km from the park boundary (112 km from Cooktown). This crossing can be a little hairy early in the Dry, but by the end of the season it is generally no problem. The **Old Laura Homestead** on the far bank is worth a good look around. Pioneers lived here and in places like this right through the Cape, and after they had built such a place they thought they were on easy street. Most of us couldn't handle this sort of luxury for too long before we'd be running back to modern civilisation!

Just past the homestead and within a km of the river crossing, you reach a T-junction. Turning left here will take you south to Laura, 28 km away. This is the nearest place for fuel and supplies if you have decided to stay in the park for longer.

To continue to Musgrave and deeper into the Lakefield National Park, turn right at the

MARK ARMSTRONG

MARK ARMSTRONG

MARK ARMSTRONG

MARK ARMSTRONG

A: James Cook Historical Museum, Cooktown
B: Aboriginal rock art, Jowalbinna Station, Cape York Peninsula
C: Dry creek crossing, Cape York Peninsula
D: Black Mountain, near Cooktown

TONY WHEELER

MARK ARMSTRONG

TONY WHEELER

Top: Ocean view from Cape York
Middle: Landscape, Jowalbinna Station, Cape York Peninsula
Bottom: Morris Islet, Cape York Peninsula

Lakefield National Park

Lakefield National Park is the second-largest national park in Queensland and covers over 537,000 hectares. It encompasses a wide variety of country around the flood plains of the Normanby, Kennedy, Bizant, Morehead and Hann rivers.

During the wet season these rivers flood the plains, at times forming a mini inland sea. Access during this time is limited or nonexistent. As the dry season begins, the rivers gradually retreat to form a chain of deep waterholes and billabongs. Along these rivers, rainforest patches are in stark contrast to the surrounding grass plains and eucalypt woodland.

Flora & Fauna In the north of the park, around Princess Charlotte Bay, mud flats and mangroves line the coast and the estuaries of the rivers. It might be an area that is full of sandflies, mosquitoes and crocodiles, but this area is the nursery for the rich fish and marine life for which the area is so well known.

As the Dry progresses, the bird life begins to congregate around the permanent waters, and at times thousands of ducks and geese create an unholy noise but a spectacular sight. Groups of brolgas dance on the open plain, and tall stately jabirus stalk their way through the grass. Birds of prey soar on the thermals looking for a meal, while in the deepest, darkest patches of the rainforest, pheasant coucals and Torres Strait pigeons can be found. In all, over 180 species of birds have been identified in the park. At times like these, a small pair of binoculars come in handy.

Agile wallabies are probably the most commonly seen mammal in the park, but feral pigs are prevalent and a problem for the park staff. Bats make up the largest group of mammals found here. The large flying foxes are an impressive sight as they burst from their roosting spots in their thousands on their evening search for nectar and fruit. You won't forget the sight, the smell, or the damage they can do to the trees in which they roost.

Crocodiles Both the freshwater and saltwater (estuarine) crocodile are found in this park. Lakefield National Park is one of five areas in the state designated as important for the ongoing conservation of the estuarine crocodile in Queensland, and for many people it offers the best chance of seeing one of these animals in the wild.

Fishing Lakefield National Park is one of the few parks in Queensland where you are allowed to fish, and the barramundi is the prize catch. A closed season applies between 1 November and 31 January, and at other times there's a bag limit of two fish per day, with no more than five fish to be taken out of the park. Line fishing is the only method allowed to catch these magnificent fish.

Canoeing & Boating Many of the big waterholes make for excellent canoeing or boating, and you can spend many enjoyable hours paddling a quiet stretch of water, watching birds or the animals as they come down to drink.

Camping Camping is allowed in a number of places, with a permit. A camping fee is payable for each night spent in the park, with a maximum of 21 nights allowed. Permits are available from the rangers at New Laura (☎ (070) 60 3260) or Lakefield (☎ (070) 60 3271). Bookings may be made six to 12 weeks in advance by writing to the ranger, Lakefield National Park, PMB 29, Cairns Mail Centre, Qld 4870. Say what you are interested in and the vehicle you have, and the ranger will let you know the best spots to camp. If you have the time, try a couple of different locations.

Ron & Viv Moon

T-junction where you turned left to go to Laura. The **ranger station** at New Laura Homestead is 25 km north of the junction.

Heading north from here, you pass across vast grass plains, bordered by trees that line the rivers. Termite hills tower above the gold of drying grass and occasionally you'll see a shy wallaby skip across the road, or the occasional mob of wild pigs. The track can be deep in dust, and walkers and cyclists will

CAPE YORK PENINSULA

find the sun unrelenting. After travelling 33 km, you pass the ranger station at **Lakefield Homestead**.

The turn off to **Bizant**, occasionally a ranger station, is 15 km past the Lakefield ranger station, with yet another turn off 10 km further on.

Just a few hundred metres past this track junction is the **Hann crossing** of the North Kennedy River. For travellers passing through the national park, this is by far the best place to stop.

Just downstream from the crossing there are a couple of waterfalls that drop into a large pool. The river is tidal to the base of the falls and I wouldn't advise swimming here. If you want to see how many crocodiles can inhabit a small stretch of water, take a spotlight down and check the pool one night. Count the eyes and divide by two!

There is some excellent camping upstream from the crossing. The sites are numbered and at times the place is booked out. It's safe to swim or paddle in the shallows here and the kids will love it. There are turtles in some of the pools that like a feed of bread.

The crossing itself demands a little care as it has potholes and is rough. Generally it doesn't cause any difficulty.

The **Morehead River** is crossed 13 km from the Hann crossing and is normally an easy crossing. The turn off to **Low Lake**, a spectacular bird habitat, especially at the end of the Dry, is found 15 km further on. Continue straight ahead, and in less than two km you will come to the **Saltwater Creek** crossing. The crossing is sandy, but is generally no problem in a 4WD. You can camp around here, but it isn't as good as the Hann crossing.

The road swings south-west as it begins to head towards Musgrave. Keep left at the next few track junctions, as the tracks on the right lead to Marina Plains Station. You leave the national park 16 km west of Saltwater Creek.

Stick to the main track heading westward and 34 km later you will hit the Peninsula Developmental Road, opposite Musgrave.

LAKELAND TO LAURA (64 km)
Lakeland

Lakeland, the 'inland road' to Cooktown, is at the junction of the Peninsula Developmental and the Cooktown Developmental Rds. See the Far North Queensland chapter for details of that route, and of Lakeland itself.

Unless you're heading to Cooktown, turn left (west) at Lakeland and you're on your way to Laura and Cape York on a formed dirt road and this is about as good as the run north to the top gets. The turn off to the **Split Rock galleries** is about 52 km futher north, and 12 km south of Laura.

These Aboriginal rock-art galleries are well worth a look as they are the most accessible of the 1200 galleries found in this area. Together they represent one of the biggest and most important collections of prehistoric art in the world. From the car park, there is a looped walking trail up onto the escarpment and across the plateau to the various galleries. Just a few km further on, north of the Laura River crossing, Laura is a well spread-out town with the 'centre' being around the pub.

Laura

Laura is a good little town in which to enjoy a beer at the pub, or to use as a base to explore the surrounding area. From here, you can easily visit the Lakefield National Park, the Aboriginal rock-art galleries at Split Rock, and the Jowalbinna Bush Camp, a wilderness reserve 40 km west of Laura.

Facilities The Laura Store (☎ (070) 60 3238), next to the pub, sells a good range of groceries including fresh fruit and vegies, gas refills for camping bottles and fuel (super, unleaded and diesel). They accept major credit cards, Ampol cards and Australian travellers' cheques. The store opens daily from 7 am to 6 pm. There is also a post office at the store, open weekdays from 9 am to 5 pm.

There is a small airfield just outside town. Aviation fuel can be organised through the Laura Store, but you'll need to give notice beforehand.

Quinkan Art

Quinkan art, as it is called, is one of the great art styles of northern Australia. Vastly different to the X-ray art of Arnhem Land in the Northern Territory, or the Wandjina art of the Kimberley in Western Australia, Quinkan art gets its name from the human-shaped, spirit figures with unusually shaped heads, called Quinkans.

Much study on the sites has been done since 1960 by Percy Trezise, an amateur archaeologist. Over 1200 galleries have been discovered. All of these are around the settlement of Laura, in the escarpment country that surrounds the lowlands along the great rivers of Lakefield National Park.

This great body of art is testimony to the Aborigines who once lived here. When the Palmer River gold rush began in 1873, the Aborigines fought to defend their land against the new invaders. Those who survived the bullets succumbed to disease, and the few remaining Aborigines became fringe dwellers on the outskirts of towns and missions.

The rock-art galleries contain many fine paintings of kangaroos, wallabies, emus, brolgas, jabirus, crocodiles, snakes and flying foxes - in fact, all the wildlife still seen along the rivers and plains.

Spiritual figures and ancestral beings also point to a lifestyle that was rich in culture and religious beliefs. Amongst the paintings there are 'good' and 'bad' spiritual figures, the 'good' being heroes of old and the figures depicting fertility and ritual increase, while the 'bad' were depicted by spirit figures such as Quinkans.

Other paintings depict tools such as boomerangs and axes, while in some galleries stencils of hands and implements can also be seen. Rock engravings are also found in small numbers, and in a couple of galleries there is evidence of the European invasion with images of horses.

Only the Split Rock and Guguyalangi galleries are open to the public. South of Laura and close to the main road, they are readily accessible, with a walking track joining the two.

There are a number of overhangs in the Split Rock group of galleries, and while Split Rock itself is the most visually stunning, within 100 metres there are smaller galleries containing flying foxes, tall Quinkans and hand stencils.

The Guguyalangi group consists of over a dozen overhangs that are adorned with a vast array of figures, animals and implements and are possibly the best of the lot.

A walking trail leads from the car park at Split Rock, past the galleries in this group and then up onto the plateau and to a lookout at Turtle Rock. The view from here is stunning. From this point the trail wanders through the open forest of the plateau for one km to the Guguyalangi group of galleries. The views here are, once again, spectacular. If you are going to do this walk, save it for the late afternoon or early morning as it can get quite warm wandering across the plateau at midday. Take some water and food and enjoy the art and solitude of this place.

The Giant Horse galleries, across the road from the Split Rock and Guguyalangi sites, are a little harder to see and consist of five shelters depicting many animals, including a number of horses. These galleries can only be visited with a guide from the local community, and pre-arrangement with the ranger is essential.

Percy Trezise and his sons, Steve and Matt, have established a wilderness reserve at Jowalbinna. The Jowalbinna Bush Camp is open to travellers and Steve runs the Trezise Bush Guide Service, specialising in guided walking trips to the many magnificent galleries in the nearby area.

The Magnificent Gallery, deep in the ranges behind Jowalbinna Bush Camp, stands out from the rest. Along a rock shelter, 50 metres or more in length, there is a profusion of colour, life and movement. Animals of all descriptions and sizes, along with spirit figures and Quinkans, adorn each and every available spot.

For more information on the Quinkan art around Laura, contact the Ang-Gnarra Aboriginal Corporation on ☎ (070) 60 3214 or fax 60 3231. Maps, brochures and information for self-guided walks around the art sites are obtainable from the ranger station, which is beside the caravan park.

It may also be possible to organise a tour of the art sites with a ranger, providing one is available. There is a ranger station, which is usually staffed, at the Split Rock Gallery car park. Although there is no fee to visit the art sites, visitors are requested to make a donation of $3 per adult.

If you want to join Steve Trezise at Jowalbinna, ring ☎ (070) 60 3236. Alternatively, contact the Trezise Bush Guide Service (see the Organised Tours section).

Ron & Viv Moon

Organised Tours The Ang-Gnarra Aboriginal Corporation (see the Information section at the start of this chapter) has a ranger service based beside the caravan park on the main north-south road. If the ranger is available, a guided tour of the rock-art galleries may be arranged.

Trezise Bush Guides (☎ (070) 55 1865), based at Jowalbinna, 40 km west of Laura, offers excellent guided trips to some of the magnificent rock-art sites in the area. The cost of the guide service is $50 per adult per day, or $100 per family. A 4WD is essential to reach Jowalbinna and maps are available in Laura. Visitors can also fly into Jowalbinna airstrip and stay for a day or overnight.

Trezise Bush Guides also offers various one to four-day tours from Cairns – see Organised Tours at the start of this chapter for details.

If you're using their guide service, you can stay overnight at the Jowalbinna Bush Camp beside the peaceful headwaters of the Little Laura River. There are comfortable tent-cabins costing $20 a night, or if you have your own gear you can camp here ($5 per adult, kids free). The bush camp has its own showers, toilets and cooking facilities, and meals can also be organised.

Festivals The Cape York Aboriginal Dance Festival is held near Laura, on the banks of the Laura River. It brings together Aborigines from all over Cape York for three excellent days. The festival is usually held every year during the Queensland September school holidays, although timing does vary from year to year. Currently, festival times are irregular, but from 1995 it may be held every two years. Contact the Ang-Gnarra Aboriginal Corporation (☎ (070) 60 3214) for up-to-date information on festival dates and activities.

The Laura horse races and rodeo are held from Friday to Sunday on the first weekend in July. It is a great weekend where the locals from the surrounding stations show their skills and let down their hair. It has become a tradition on the Cape with people coming from far afield.

Places to Stay & Eat Apart from camping near the Laura River, you have a choice of staying at the pub or in the caravan park. There is also accommodation at Jowalbinna (see Organised Tours earlier).

The *Quinkan Hotel* (☎ (070) 60 3255), in the main street, is a great old pub clad in green corrugated iron and shaded by three giant mango trees. They have clean and simple rooms with shared bathrooms. A bed costs $20 per person, $30 with breakfast or $40 with dinner and breakfast. You can also camp; an unpowered site is $5 a single, plus an extra $3 for power, with use of shower facilities. You can also have a meal and a cool beer under the mango trees.

The *Ang-Gnarra Aboriginal Corporation Caravan Park* (☎ (070) 60 3214), on the main north-south road, has camp sites for $3 per person.

On the main north-south road, opposite the caravan park, is the *Laura Cafe*, which sells fuel, a few groceries and takeaways. You can also get cooked breakfasts, reasonable burgers and more substantial meals like steaks, chicken or fish dishes – mains range from $5.50 to $11. They open from 7 am to 10 pm, and accept major credit cards and good old cash.

LAURA TO MUSGRAVE (136 km)

The road continues to be well-formed dirt as it heads north from Laura. Most of the creek crossings are dry, but early in the dry season some may have water in them. Some of these creek and river crossings provide a welcome spot to stop and camp. The Little Laura River, 12 km north of Laura, and the Kennedy River, 32 km north, are two such spots.

On the banks of the Hann River, 75 km north of Laura, is the *Hann River Roadhouse* (☎ (070) 60 3242). This is another pleasant place to stop at. The roadhouse sells fuel and does minor repairs, has limited food supplies, takeaways, a bar and a restaurant with a good selection of main meals from $8 to $13. It even has its own airstrip. The combination of a camping ground with all amenities, including powered sites, and the nearby permanent water and fishing make it a pleasant spot to camp. Camp sites cost $4 per person. The roadhouse is open from 7 am to 10 pm every day.

From here to Musgrave it is 60 km of corrugated dirt road that in sections winds through some hilly country. A few bad creek crossings and nasty dips will keep your speed down. About the only spot worth camping at is the **Morehead River**, 28 km north of the Hann River.

Musgrave

There is only one main building in Musgrave – the historic *Musgrave Telegraph Station* (☎ (070) 60 3229), built in 1887. It sells fuel (unleaded, super and diesel), a few groceries, meals, takeaway food and cold beer. Accommodation is available for $20/30 a single/double and breakfast can be arranged. It is also possible to camp at Musgrave, and although there is no fee for this, it does cost $2 to use the showers.

An airstrip runs beside the station, and aviation fuel can be organised if you notify

Barramundi, prized fish of the Far North

the station at least one week before you intend flying in.

From near here, tracks run east to the Lakefield National Park or west to Edward River and the Pormpuraaw Aboriginal Community.

MUSGRAVE TO COEN (107 km)

The road for the next 110 km to Coen is little different to what you have experienced before. There may be a few more bull dust patches which can play hell with a motorcycle rider or a low-slung conventional car, but if you've got this far you'll probably make it to Weipa.

About 65 km north of Musgrave you meet a road junction. The better, newer road leads left to Coen, while the older, rougher road swings right, crossing the **Stewart River** twice before reaching Coen. With little traffic, the first crossing of the Stewart River makes a fine camp site.

The old road also gives access to the road to **Port Stewart** on the east coast of the Cape (reasonable camping and good fishing) and *Silver Plains Homestead* (☎ (070) 60 3228) where you can camp or be accommodated. Fishing and hunting trips to nearby rivers or to the close reefs of the Great Barrier Reef can also be organised.

Coen

Coen is the 'capital' of the Cape, and unless you take the turn off into Weipa, it is the biggest town you'll see north of Cooktown. People have some funny times in this place, all of course in and around the pub, the social heart of any country town.

There is a choice of places where you can buy food and fuel and even a couple of places offering accommodation, although that doesn't include the police station with its lock-up, or the hospital.

Facilities *Clark's General Store & Garage* (☎ (070) 60 1144) has a mini-supermarket with a good range of groceries, and supplies fuel, gas refills for camping bottles, mechanical repairs and welding. The store is open

Cape York Track: Coen to the Tip

Unsealed roads can vary from excellent to impassable, depending on many factors.

0   25   50 km

daily from 7.30 am to 6 pm (less frequently during the Wet) but the workshop is not usually open on Sunday. They accept major credit cards and Ampol cards.

Ambrust & Co General Store (☎ (070) 60 1134) also has a good range of groceries, and doubles as the post office with a Commonwealth Bank agency. There is also a fax facility. Fuel and camping gas are available. They also open daily from 7.30 am to 6 pm (during the Wet, from 9 am to 5 pm on weekdays and from 9 am to 11 am on Saturday). It is also the agent for aviation fuel, although you will need to contact them beforehand to arrange supply and fuelling. The store runs a camping ground with most amenities for $5 a night per person for an unpowered site (power is $1 extra); there are special rates for children and families. Dogs are allowed, under control.

The Coen Aerodrome (☎ (070) 60 1136) is 24 km north of Coen on the Peninsula Developmental Road.

The QNP&WS ranger's office (☎ (070) 60 1137) is worth visiting if you require any information about Cape York's national parks.

Places to Stay & Eat The *Exchange Hotel* (☎ (070) 60 1133), or the Sexchange Hotel as it likes to be known, has basic pub rooms with shared bathrooms costing $25/35/45 for singles/doubles/triples, or motel rooms for $35/45/55. All the rooms are air-conditioned, but there are no phones or TVs. The pub's bistro serves lunches and dinners, with main meals in the $10 to $14 range, or you can have three courses for $18.

Just down from the pub is the *Homestead Guest House* (☎ (070) 60 1157), run by a delightful elderly lady called Irene Taylor. The guesthouse has simple, comfortable rooms with ceiling fans and shared bathroom facilities. Singles/doubles cost $30/40. Home-cooked meals are also available, with breakfasts costing from $6 to $10, lunches around $10 and a three-course dinner (soup, roast and dessert) $15. This place is also the local Westpac Bank agency.

COEN TO ARCHER RIVER (66 km)
About three km north of Coen, the main road north parallels the **Coen River** for a short distance. There is some good camping along the river, and while it is a popular spot, there is generally no problem in finding a place to throw down the swag or erect a tent. Toilet facilities are provided.

For the first 23 km north of Coen the road is very well maintained, but once you have passed the Coen Aerodrome the road quickly returns to its former standard. About two km past the airfield you reach the main access track to **Rokeby National Park**. This park straddles the Archer River and its tributaries, taking in much of the country from the western edge of the Great Dividing Range almost to the boundary of the Archer Bend National Park.

Rokeby National Park has excellent camping on a number of lagoons and along the banks of the Archer River. Access to the more remote **Archer Bend National Park** is only by rarely given permit. No facilities are provided. The ranger station is about 70 km west from the Peninsula Developmental Road at Rokeby Homestead, or see the district ranger based in Coen.

Further north, the main road continues as before, until about 50 km north of Coen the road is more like a roller coaster.

Archer River
The *Archer River Roadhouse* (☎ (070) 60 3266), 65 north of Coen, is a great place to stop and enjoy a cold beer and friendly company, along with the famous Archer Burger. General food supplies, takeaway food, snacks, books and maps can be purchased, along with fuel. Limited repairs can also be carried out. They accept major credit cards, and are open from 7 am to 10 pm.

Campers can pitch their tent in the camping ground with the use of all amenities, for $5 per person per night, $2 for children. They also have four good, clean units that sleep up to four people and cost $20 per person ($40 for a single). The units share bathroom and laundry facilities.

There is an airstrip near the roadhouse and

aviation fuel can be supplied, but only if you give them plenty of warning to get fuel flown in.

Just down the hill from the roadhouse is the magnificent Archer River. During the Dry this river is normally just a pleasant stream bordered by a wide, tree-lined, sandy bed. It is an ideal spot to camp, although at times space is at a premium. As with many of the permanent streams on the Cape, the banks are lined with varieties of paperbarks, or melaleucas. Growing to more than 40 metres they offer shade for passing travellers and, when in flower, food for hordes of birds and fruit bats that love the heavy, sweet-smelling nectar.

The Archer River crossing used to be a real terror, but now, with its concrete causeway, is quite easy. However, any heavy rain in the catchment will quickly send the water over the bridge, cutting access to Weipa and places further north.

ARCHER RIVER TO IRON RANGE NATIONAL PARK (128 km)

For the first 15 km past the Archer River crossing, the road can be corrugated. The main road to Portland Roads, Chili Beach and Iron Range National Park turns east off the main road, 20 km north of the Archer, and crosses the Wenlock River, close to the old goldfield of Batavia. Many old relics can still be seen here.

Iron Range National Park is probably the greatest tropical rainforest park in Australia. Forget what you've heard about the Daintree; this place is better and wilder, with more endemic animals and plants. There is a rich variety of vegetation, from heathland to dense rainforest.

The rare and vivid eclectus parrot, large palm cockatoo, shy fawn-breasted bowerbird, small red-bellied pitta and giant cassowary are some of the birds of the forest.

The spotted and the grey cuscus and the rufous spiny bandicoot are three of the mammals found in the park, which are also found in the forests of Papua New Guinea. One animal that is commonly seen here is the northern native cat. This striking mammal, a

small predator, sometimes wanders into camps and houses in the region looking for something to eat. If you're lucky enough to see one you won't forget the encounter – they are beautiful!

Be Sure and Tell 'Em Toots Sent You

In the car park in front of the Archer River Roadhouse is a memorial stone to 'Toots' Holzheimer, a truckie who drove her way into the Cape York history books. Toots, one of the Cape's transport pioneers, was killed in a loading accident in February 1992. She is fondly remembered by locals as one of the legends of Cape York, someone who frequently battled flooded roads, cyclones and other hazards to deliver her loads. One of her fellow truckies tells of the time he drove past and saw a very pregnant-looking Toots rolling 40-gallon barrels onto her truck – a couple of days later, he heard she had given birth to her second daughter.

Reading about Toots, I couldn't help but notice some uncanny parallels between her story and a sequence out of Pee Wee Herman's weird first film *Pee Wee's Big Adventure*. Lost in the midst of a dark and foggy night, Pee Wee is picked up by a female truckie who appears out of nowhere. When she drops him at a roadhouse, she utters the immortal words; 'Be sure and tell 'em Large Marge sent you'. Pee Wee does just that, but is horrified when the locals tell him that Large Marge was killed in a traffic accident 10 years earlier, on that very night. Large Marge may have died in the crash, but her spirit lived on, driving her enormous rig up and down the highway and watching over lost and lonely travellers... ■

Some 10% of Australia's butterflies also reside in this park, including 25 species found no further south, with the park being their stronghold.

There are only a couple of camping grounds in this park. Near the East Claudie River and Gordon Creek is the Rainforest camping ground. The other is at Chili Beach, but this is hardly in the rainforest. Other small camp sites are dotted on or near streams along the road. The QNP&WS ranger (☎ (070) 60 7170) is based at King Park Homestead.

Portland Roads is a small fishing port with no facilities for the traveller, except a telephone. The fishing off shore, if you have a small boat, is excellent.

Chili Beach is just a few km south of Portland Roads and is where all the travellers camp. Pit toilets are provided. It is now part of the Iron Range National Park and a camping permit is required: available from the ranger based at King Park Homestead or the QNP&WS headquarters in Cairns. While it is a nice spot, it would be even better if the wind would stop blowing – which it does occasionally late in the season. A small boat will give you access to the islands just off shore and to some good fishing.

Visitors to the **Lockhart River Aboriginal Community**, 40 km south of Portland Roads, are welcome to stop for fuel and supplies, but are asked to respect the community's privacy. Use of cameras and videos is not permitted. There is also a police station and a hospital. A permit is not required to enter the community. You can contact the Lockhart River Community Council on ☎ (070) 60 7144.

The *General Store* (☎ (070) 60 7192) can supply most food items, including meat, fruit and vegetables, as well as fuel (which is expensive). It also has a post office with a Commonwealth Bank agency (☎ (070) 60 7138). Lockhart River Airfield (☎ (070) 60 7121) is approximately five km from the community.

There are no camping facilities, but accommodation is available at the *guesthouse* (☎ (070) 60 7139) and it is best to book ahead. The house is self contained, but you need to supply your own linen. It costs $30 per person per day.

ARCHER RIVER TO WEIPA

There are two main routes leading into Weipa, known respectively as the Southern Access Route and the Northern Access Route. Both routes are described below.

Weipa via the Southern Access Route (145 km)

The most direct route to Weipa is the continuation of the Peninsula Developmental Road, which stops following the route of the Overland Telegraph Line 44 km north of the Archer. The road has been realigned and greatly improved. It is as good as a dirt road gets!

Just over halfway, at the 74-km mark, a track which left the Telegraph Track at Batavia Downs, south of the Wenlock River, joins up with the Peninsula Developmental Road at Sudley, 71 km east of Weipa. This track between Batavia Downs and Sudley is often chopped up and a couple of the creek crossings are muddy early in the Dry. This route gives people another option to leave or join the route to the Top.

As you get closer to Weipa, the mining activities increase and the road improves. Heed all the warning signs, especially where the road crosses the mine haulage ways.

Weipa via the Northern Access Route (169 km)

Heading north out of Weipa, this route goes via Stones Crossing, over the Wenlock River, to Agnew and eastwards to the Telegraph Track, south of Bertiehaugh.

This track crosses private land and, depending on the owner, access across Bertiehaugh is sometimes open, sometimes closed! This is a good run and well worth the effort, so ask other travellers at each end of the route for the latest advice.

Stones Crossing is 57 km north-east of Weipa. First, take the Old Mapoon Road and at the 28-km mark veer right at the major Y-junction. The road swings east for 20 km before turning north for the last nine km to

CAPE YORK PENINSULA

the crossing of the Wenlock River. This is a magic spot to camp, but remember that the river is tidal as far as the crossing itself and is inhabited by estuarine crocodiles.

From the river, the track deteriorates and heads north for 31 km before turning east. **Agnew** was once a wartime airstrip that is now dominated by tall termite mounds. You drive down the edge of the old airstrip before turning eastwards. From here you continue on a sandy, rough track for 50 km before coming to a track junction. Keep to the right and after 11 km you will meet the Telegraph Track, 26 km north of the Wenlock River.

WEIPA (pop 2500)

Weipa is a modern mining town which works the world's largest deposits of bauxite (the ore from which aluminium is processed). It offers an interesting glimpse of what life is like in a remote mining community. The mining company, Comalco, runs tours of its operations, and the town has a wide range of facilities including a hotel/motel and a camping ground. In the vicinity, there's interesting country to explore, good fishing and some pleasant camp sites.

History

The Aboriginal people lived in this area for thousands of years before the arrival of the Europeans. Beside many of the rivers around Weipa are enormous midden heaps, consisting mainly of cockle shells – these sites are protected under the Aboriginal Relics Preservation Act.

The first European to sight this coast was the Dutch explorer Willem Jansz, who sailed into the Gulf in 1606. In 1802, during his historic circumnavigation of the Australian coastline, Matthew Flinders sailed the *Investigator* into Albatross Bay, naming Duyfken Point in honour of Jansz's ship.

In 1955 a geologist, Harry Evans, led an expedition to Cape York in search of oil. Almost by chance, he discovered a large outcrop of bauxite near Weipa. He collected a number of ore samples which were later analysed and found to be high grade, and within a few years Comalco commenced mining operations. Their first trial shipment of bauxite was sent to Japan in 1961.

Information

Weipa is the largest town on the Cape, and because it is a mining town, all facilities are available. These include a Commonwealth Bank (with full banking facilities), a post office, a chemist, a hospital, a large supermarket in the suburb of Nanum, and numerous mechanical service centres.

Things to See & Do

Around Weipa itself and the areas north there are some excellent fishing places. Weipa River Safaris (☎ (070) 69 7597) operates fishing safaris out of Weipa, or you can hire a boat yourself from the Weipa Snack Shack & Boat Hire Service (☎ (070) 69 7495), at the Evans Landing wharf. It has 13-foot aluminium boats, and it's best to ring and pre-book a boat during the tourist season. Cost is $60/40 per day/half day. The Shack also sells bait and fishing accessories and can give you information on the best spots to fish.

Cambell's Coach Tours (☎ (070) 69 7871) runs 2½-hour tours of Comalco's mining operations every day (at 9 am and 1 pm) during the tourist season. The tours costs $12 for adults, $6 for children, and pick-ups and bookings can be made at the camping ground.

Weipa even has its own golf course. The Carpentaria Golf Club (☎ (070) 69 7332) is open to the general public – green fees are $7, and you can hire clubs for another $5.

Places to Stay & Eat

The only camping area is the *Pax Haven Caravan & Camping Ground* (☎ (070) 69 7871) which has tent sites for $12 a double or powered sites for $14 a double.

The *Albatross Hotel-Motel* (☎ (070) 69 7314) has motel rooms from $85/110 for singles/doubles, or they have basic bungalows with shared bathrooms at $50 a double or $80 for a family. The pub's bistro serves meals in the $10 to $12 range, or there's a

Weipa

0   0.5   1 km
Approximate Scale

To Andoom Mine,
Marpuna (Mapoon)
Aboriginal Community,
Port Musgrave &
Stones Crossing

Mission River

Uningan
Nature
Reserve

Rocky Point

Hospital
Police

Kumrunja
Beach

Albatross
Hotel-Motel

Golf
Club

Wallaby
Island

Wanum Beach

Trunding Creek

Shopping
Centre

Pax Haven
Caravan &
Camping
Ground

Post Office
& Shops

Hibberd
Point

Lake
Mcleod

Lake
Patricia

Weipa
Rent-a-Car

Weipa River
Safaris

Weipa Snack Shack
& Boat Hire

Evans
Landing

Comalco
Workshop &
Stores Area

Tourist
Information

Lorim Point

Home Creek

To Airport &
Archer River
Roadhouse

Embley River

Napranum
Local
Authority
(Weipa South)

Point
Jessica

more expensive à la carte restaurant. The *Weipa River View Cabins* (☎ (070) 69 9159), down near Evans Landing, has basic cabins with shared bathrooms from $38 a double.

Getting There & Away

Air Ansett (☎ 13 1300) has a daily flight from Cairns to Weipa. The one-way fare is $219, although discounted fares are often available.

Skytrans (☎ (070) 69 7248), based in Weipa, has flights on Wednesday and Saturday from Weipa to Bamaga ($142 one way) and Thursday Island ($158).

Bus Cape York Coaches (☎ (070) 93 0176), based at 21 Vievers Dve in Kuranda, operates a twice-weekly service from Cairns to Weipa, departing from Cairns on Tuesday and Friday and from Weipa on Wednesday and Saturday. The trip takes about 15 hours. The fare is $235 return, or $198 if you book seven days in advance. Bookings can also be made through Skytrans in Weipa (see Air).

Sea Gulf Freight Services runs a popular barge service between Weipa and Karumba, which means you can sit on the boat for a couple of days instead of retracing your wheel ruts. See the Sea section in Getting There & Away at the start of this chapter for details.

Getting Around

Weipa Rent-A-Car (☎ (070) 69 7311), at Evans Landing, has 4WD vehicles available for touring around Weipa and for going to the Top, from $130 to $165 a day.

ARCHER RIVER TO WENLOCK RIVER (117 km)

After the turn off to Weipa, which is 44 km north of the Archer River, the road heading north quickly deteriorates and becomes more of a track, although it's still reasonably well maintained.

On the left of the road is **Batavia Downs Station**, which marks the second major turn off to Weipa, 50 km north of the first, southernmost one. The final 23 km to the Wenlock

River is along a road that is sandy and rough in places.

The **Wenlock River** is the first major water challenge you meet on your way north to the Cape. It looks surprisingly easy, but it is astonishing how many people come to grief here. Early or late in the dry season, the river may be running high because of rains in the ranges to the east.

A base of rocks has been put down in the riverbed at the crossing point, and provided it hasn't been washed away in the last Wet, you shouldn't have too much trouble. If you do bog down, don't despair, you're not the first.

The north bank of the Wenlock River is a popular spot to camp and at times it does get crowded. Toilets are provided, as is a telephone. A small store is open sometimes and sells drinks, souvenirs and the like, and provides information and minor mechanical and welding repairs.

Just north of the Wenlock is the old Moreton Telegraph Station, which is now used as a research station.

WENLOCK RIVER TO JARDINE RIVER (155 km)
The Telegraph Track

The 155 km from the Wenlock River to the Jardine River is the best part of the trip, with some great creek crossings and excellent camp sites. Take your time and enjoy all the delights the Cape has to offer.

The challenge of following the rough track along the historic Overland Telegraph Line means that the trip will take at least a very long day, even if all goes well. A newer and easier route, known as the DCS Road or the 'main' Cairns Road, bypasses much of the Telegraph Track and avoids most of the creeks and rivers between the Wenlock and Jardine rivers. This route is covered later in the section on Bypass Roads.

Most of the major creek crossings have water in them; however, it's not the water that is the problem but the banks on each side. Take care. Washaways elsewhere demand you keep your speed down.

Amongst the scattered timber and blanket

of grass you can see zamia, or cycad palms. In places they form quite dense stands, and as they come in male and female forms they must be having quite a party! Aborigines once used the palm nuts as a food source. The nuts are poisonous when raw and need special preparation and cooking before they are safe to eat.

The track improves after 10 km and is reasonable until the first of the bypass roads leaves the old track.

The turn offs to **Bramwell Station** and **Bertiehaugh Station** are 26 km north of the Wenlock River. *Bramwell Station* (☎ (070) 60 3237) is on the east side of the road and offers very pleasant accommodation and camping. There are 14 rooms in transportable cabins near the homestead which cost $15 per person twin share, or you can camp here for $7 a head. Breakfasts range from $8 for continental to $12 for cooked.

The route westwards through Bertiehaugh leads to Stones Crossing and then onwards to Weipa (see the Weipa via the Northern Access Route section earlier).

Rocky Creek, 39 km north of the Wenlock River, can be a minor challenge to cross.

The first of the major bypass roads, the **Southern Bypass Road**, turns off the Telegraph Track 40 km north of the Wenlock. This route keeps to the high country, staying well away from the many creek crossings the Telegraph Track makes. See the section on Bypass Roads that follows for more details.

Palm Creek, 43 km north of the Wenlock, is followed by Ducie Creek, South Alice Creek and North Alice Creek, before you reach the **Dulhunty River**, 70 km north of the Wenlock. This is a popular spot to camp. There are also some lovely places to swim, and the falls beside the road make a pleasant natural spa.

After crossing another major stream, a road leaves the Telegraph Track two km north of the Dulhunty and heads for **Heathlands Station**, the base for the ranger for Jardine River National Park. This road also bypasses the **Gunshot Creek** crossing. This crossing, just 15 km past the track junction, is one of the hardest and most daunting

on the route north and has a number of drops into the creek. The experience of other travellers and the nature of the previous wet season will determine the route you take. Many travellers backtrack to the road junction and take the safer, but longer, way around via Heathlands Station. You can rejoin the Telegraph Track just north of Gunshot Creek after a diversion of 27 km.

The vegetation changes again. No longer is it dominated by straggly eucalypts such as ironbarks and bloodwoods, but instead the country is covered in tall heathland. Take a close look and you'll be surprised at the flowers you can find. The open plains are dominated by grevilleas, hibbertias and small melaleucas, to name just a few, while the creek banks and wetter areas are clothed in banksias and baeceas.

One of the plants that observant nature lovers will find is the pitcher plant. These are found along the banks of the narrow creeks, Gunshot Creek being a prime spot for them. These special plants trap insects in the liquid at the bottom of the 'pitcher', where their nutrients are absorbed by the plant. It's an adaptation to living in an area that is poor in plant food.

After Gunshot Creek the track is sandy until you come to the **Cockatoo Creek** crossing, 93 km north of the Wenlock River. Once again the actual riverbed is no drama; it's the banks that are the problem. In this case it is the north bank which often has a long haul of soft sand. A little speed makes a big difference here, as does lower tyre pressures. The Injinoo people have a permanent camp set up at Cockatoo Creek.

For the next 24 km the road improves slightly. A couple more creek crossings follow and 14 km past Cockatoo Creek the Southern Bypass Road joins up with the Telegraph Track. Just 10 km further on, the second major bypass, the **Northern Bypass Road**, heads west away from the Telegraph Track to the ferry that crosses the Jardine River. Stick to the Telegraph Track at this point and keep heading north, even though the track north does deteriorate a little. There are other tracks that lead back to the Northern

Bypass Road and the ferry, if you don't want to drive across the Jardine River.

Within a few hundred metres a track heads off to the east, taking travellers to **Fruit Bat Falls**. Camping is not allowed here but it is a good spot to stop, have lunch and enjoy the waters of **Eliot Creek**. If you have a canoe, this is a good place to put it in for an easy paddle downstream to the camping ground at **Indian Head Falls**, one of the places not to miss on a trip to Cape York. The paddle between Fruit Bat Falls and Indian Head Falls is easy with a good, steady current pushing you all the way. The total distance is less than 10 km and is very enjoyable. At Indian Head Falls you will need to take your canoe out and portage, even if you are paddling further downstream.

The turn off to **Indian Head Falls** and **Twin Falls** is 6.5 km north of the previous track junction to Fruit Bat Falls. The track leads less than two km to an excellent camping ground. On one side is Canal Creek and the delightful Twin Falls, while on the other is the wider Eliot Creek and Indian Head Falls which drop into a small, sheer-sided ravine.

Pit toilets and showers are set up within the camping ground and the ranger from Heathlands keeps the place in good condition, with your help. This is the most popular camping spot on the trip north, and although it gets crowded, it is still very enjoyable. A camping permit is required and a small camping fee payable.

You can spend an enjoyable few days camped here, doing not much else but swimming and lazing in the creeks between lunch and dinner. If you have a mask and snorkel, the water is clear enough for a paddle and there are fish and turtles to watch; or walk around and enjoy some birdwatching.

Back on the Telegraph Track, over the next eight km there are Canal, Sam, Mistake, Cannibal and Cypress creeks to cross. All offer their own sweet challenge. Just south of **Mistake Creek** a track heads west to join up with the Northern Bypass Road, which leads to the ferry across the Jardine River. If you're having fun crossing the creeks, keep

heading north at this point, but if you have had enough, it may pay to take the track out to the Northern Bypass Road and the ferry.

From Cypress Creek it is a 7.5 km run to **Logan Creek**. From here the road is badly chopped up and often flooded in places. You are now passing through the heart of an area the early pioneers called the 'Wet Desert' because of the abundance of water but lack of feed for their stock.

Five km further on is **Bridge Creek**, or Nolan's Brook, which once had a bridge, and when you get to it you'll know why. It is an interesting crossing, and though it is short it does demand a lot of care. Less than two km north of here the last track to the ferry heads west, while just 4.5 km past this junction the main track veers away from the original telegraph line route to the right and winds through tall open forest to the Jardine River.

Jardine River

The Jardine River has some magical camping sites along its southern bank, west of the vehicle ford. There are no facilities here, and because you are in a national park, a camping permit is required from the ranger at Heathlands Station.

The river is wide and sandy. If you want to swim, stick to the shallows where the sandbars are wide. Crocs don't like such open territory but may be lurking in the deep, dark, lily-covered holes that line sections of the river.

Fishing upstream of the crossing is not allowed as you are in a national park. Downstream from this point there is no problem and at times the fishing can be good, although closer to the mouth is better again.

The current makes paddling a canoe upstream a real chore, although in a boat you will be plagued with shallow water.

Jardine River Vehicle Ford In recent times the QNP&WS and the Injinoo Aboriginal Community have asked that all travellers use the ferry crossing and do not drive across the river at the vehicle ford. See the Jardine River Ferry section later on for more information on the ferry.

The vehicle ford leads out across the wide, sandy bed of the fast-flowing Jardine River. Midway across the river is a steep-sided tongue of sand that constantly changes its position, up and down the river. This tongue of soft sand often causes vehicles to bog in the middle of the stream. The water slowly gets deeper and is at its deepest, generally over a metre deep, within a few metres of the trees on the northern bank. The shallow exit point runs between a corridor of trees. There are some old timbers in this dark water between the trees which can easily stub a toe or hang up a vehicle, so be careful.

Never underestimate this crossing, even if it looks shallow. The 170 metres between entrance and exit is a long way – certainly most winch cables can't reach you if you stop mid-stream!

Remember, the Jardine River is inhabited by estuarine crocodiles, and although you might not be able to see them they are definitely there. In December 1993 a man was killed by a crocodile while he was swimming to the ferry at the ferry crossing, not far downstream from the vehicle ford.

Bypass Roads

As an alternative to sticking to the old Telegraph Track, there are several bypass roads which avoid most of the creeks and rivers between the Wenlock and Jardine rivers. This route is also called the DCS Road or the 'main' Cairns Road.

Both sections of this road are corrugated and people travel too fast on them. In 1993, 21 head-on accidents occurred in the first two months of the Dry, most of those on the Southern Bypass Road. Be careful!

The Southern Bypass This road leaves the Telegraph Track 40 km north of the Wenlock River crossing and heads east and then north. The turn off east to Shelburne Station is 24 km north of the junction, while another 35 km will find you at the junction of Heathlands ranger station, 14 km to the west.

When you reach a large patch of rainforest, 11 km north of the Heathlands turn off, the bypass road swings north-west, while a track to Captain Billy Landing, on the east coast, continues straight ahead. Keep on the bypass road for the next 45 km to rejoin the Telegraph Track 14 km north of Cockatoo Creek.

The Northern Bypass This road leaves the Telegraph Track 10 km north of where the Southern Bypass Road rejoins the Telegraph Track, north of Cockatoo Creek.

This route heads west away from the Telegraph Track and for 50 km winds through tropical savannah woodland to the ferry across the Jardine River. At the 18-km and 30-km marks, tracks head east to the Telegraph Track.

Jardine River Ferry

The Jardine River ferry (☎ (070) 69 1369) normally operates seven days a week during the Dry from 8 am to 5 pm. A fee (currently an expensive $40 one way or $80 return) is charged to use the ferry, which also gets you a permit and allows you to camp in the area north of the Jardine, including at Pajinka. The *Jardine River Roadhouse*, on the south bank of the river, supplies fuel and has a basic camping ground. Contact the Injinoo Community Council (☎ (070) 69 3252) for further details.

JARDINE RIVER TO CAPE YORK (79 km)

From the ferry crossing to the Top it is less than 80 km and for most of the way the track is in good condition. Once you have crossed the Jardine, the track swings to the east, joining up with the old Telegraph Track after about 10 km, before heading north to the Top.

If you crossed the Jardine at the vehicle ford, it is less than 70 km to the Top. The track, once out of the trees bordering the Jardine River, swings to the west and rejoins the Telegraph Track. Turning right, or northwards, will lead to the main road to the north, while turning left will take you back to the river and the ferry point.

A number of minor tracks in this area lead back down to the river and some reasonable

CAPE YORK PENINSULA

camp sites. The best camp site is on the northern bank where the telegraph line crosses the river; an old linesman's hut marks the spot. The sandy beach here is a pleasant swimming place – keep to the shallows – popular with travellers and locals alike.

Following the old line north brings you to a major crossroad, less than two km from the exit point on the Jardine. Ignore the Telegraph Track that leads away directly north – this is unused and leads into the heart of the swamp. The main road heading off to the west leads to the ferry crossing of the river. Turning right, or eastwards, will take you to Bamaga.

At the next T-junction, 22 km north of where you came onto this major dirt road, turn right. Left will lead to the coast at the old wartime port of **Mutee Heads**, just north of the Jardine River.

Just over seven km further on there is a small car park beside a fenced area that encloses the remains of an **aeroplane wreck**. Watch out for the fence posts as you drive through – they're surprisingly close together. Dating back to WW II, these remains are of a DC-3 which ploughed in on its return from New Guinea. This is the easiest aeroplane wreck to see in the area but there are a few more scattered around the main airfield, which is just a stone's throw away.

A couple of hundred metres past the car park there is a second T-junction. Right will lead to the main airfield, while left will lead to Bamaga.

Less than five km from the second T-junction, a signposted road heads off to the right leading to Cape York, Somerset and places close to the Tip. This is the road you will require, but most travellers will need fuel and other supplies, and will continue straight ahead to Bamaga.

Bamaga

Bamaga is the largest Islander community on the northern Cape and is a spread-out town with all the facilities most travellers need. There is a hospital, police station, general store and service station. There is no camping ground at Bamaga, these being located at Seisia (Red Island Point) and Pajinka Wilderness Lodge at the Tip. The Bamaga Annual Show is run in August or September each year and features rodeo events, horse races, carnival stalls and an amusement fair.

Facilities The *Bamaga Service Centre* (☎ (070) 69 3275) has fuel available and can provide mechanical repairs, along with ice and camping-gas refills. It is open from Monday to Friday, and Saturday and Sunday mornings, and accepts major credit cards.

A reasonably well-stocked *supermarket* (☎ (070) 69 3186) is open seven days a week during the tourist season, with limited trading hours on the weekend. There is also a National Australia Bank agency within the store (passbook only accepted).

The post office (☎ (070) 69 3126) is also the Commonwealth Bank agency (again passbook only).

Beer and wine can be purchased from the *Bamaga Canteen*, fresh bread from the bakery, and ice from the ice works. There is also a snack bar and newsagency.

Seisia

The Islander settlement of Seisia, five km north-west of Bamaga, is an idyllic spot for the weary traveller to relax after the long journey to the Top. There is an excellent foreshore camping ground, a kiosk and service station, and the nearby jetty is a great place for the family to fish.

Information The Seisia Camping Ground (see Places to Stay & Eat) is definitely the place to go to learn about what is happening in and around the top end of Cape York. It is the booking agent for all tours, the ferry service, taxi service, and anything else that is available. You can get up-to-date fishing information and maps, along with general tourist information.

Facilities Seisia Marine Engineering (☎ (070) 69 3321) provides general fabrication and engineering, gas refills for camping bottles, aluminium welding, boat repairs, trailer and suspension repairs, and radiator clean-outs and repairs. Major credit cards are accepted.

Top End Motors (☎ (070) 69 3182), Tradesmans Way, is the place to go for all mechanical and welding repairs to your vehicle, along with batteries, tyres, oils and a range of spare parts.

The Seisia Palms Service Station (☎ (070) 69 3172) is Australia's northernmost service station and can supply super, unleaded and diesel fuel, outboard oils and marine products.

Activities Red Island Point jetty is one of the top fishing spots in Australia, and Gebadi's Tackle Shop (☎ (070) 69 3279) can supply anything you need. A number of tour operators work from Seisia offering a wide range of tours, including birdwatching, nature tours, fishing and hunting safaris. Contact the Seisia Camping Ground (☎ (070) 69 3243) for details.

Places to Stay & Eat The *Seisia Camping Ground* (☎ (070) 69 3243) overlooks the islands of Torres Strait and features palm-thatched picnic shelters, hot showers, washing machines and calm-water boating. Camping fees are $6 per person per night. Dogs are allowed. During the tourist season the Seisia Island Dancers give regular performances. Also in the camping ground is the new *Seisia Seaview Lodge*, with units for $30 a single.

The *Seisia Kiosk* (☎ (070) 69 3285), next to the camping ground, is open seven days a week. Hot food and meals are served in the restaurant, and snacks and takeaway food are available.

Getting There & Away Peddell's Ferry & Tourist Service runs regular ferries between Seisia and Thursday Island – see the Thursday Island section for details.

Getting Around Seisia Hire Cars (☎ (070) 69 3368) operates from Seisia and has 4WDs available from $100 a day for daily or weekly

hire. Visitors can use the vehicles to explore the surrounding area, including the Tip, Bamaga and areas north of the Jardine River. It is advisable to ring and book ahead to ensure a vehicle is available.

Injinoo Aboriginal Community
The small township of Injinoo is eight km south-west of Bamaga. It has a general store, Commonwealth Bank agency, fuel and mechanical repair facilities. For information, phone the Injinoo Community Council (☎ (070) 69 3252).

New Mapoon
New Mapoon is midway between Bamaga and Seisia. Facilities are limited at this small settlement, with only general food items and ice available. However, a new camping ground is proposed in the area with beach frontage. For further information, contact the New Mapoon Community Council (☎ (070) 69 3277).

Umagico
Limited facilities, including a general food store and canteen, are available from this small community. For more details, contact the Umagico Community Council (☎ (070) 69 3251).

Bamaga to Cape York
From Bamaga, turn north towards the Tip along a well-formed dirt road. The ruins of Jardine's outstation, **Lockerbie**, are 16 km north, close to the right-hand side of the road. While the galvanised iron and timber building is a more recent residence, built by the Holland family in 1946. Nearby you will find mango trees and pathways established by Frank Jardine. There is usually a small store at the Lockerbie site and visitors are welcome to stop for refreshments, souvenirs and information.

Just north of Lockerbie a track heads west to **Punsand Bay**, about 11 bumpy, sandy km away. A few km later and the main track north begins to pass through an area of rainforest called the **Lockerbie Scrub**. This small patch of rainforest, only 25 km long and between one and five km wide, is the northernmost rainforest in Australia.

Seven km from Lockerbie a Y-junction in the middle of the jungle gives you a choice of veering right for Somerset or left for the top of Australia. Less than three km from this point on the way to the Top, a track on the left will lead you seven km to the **Punsand Bay Private Reserve** – see that section later for details.

Seven km further on will bring you to the **Pajinka Wilderness Lodge** and the camping ground. There is a small kiosk to service the camping ground. From near the kiosk, a walking track leads through the forest bordering the camping ground at Pajinka to the beach near the boat ramp. A scattering of mangroves lines part of the beach as they do on most of the beaches on the Cape, and sometimes it is almost imperceptible where forest ends and mangroves begin. From the beach you can head overland on the marked trail, or, when the tide is low, you can head around the coast to the northern tip. Both routes are relatively easy walks of an hour or so, depending on how long you dabble your feet in the briny.

The islands of Torres Strait are just a stone's throw away and dot the turquoise sea all the way to New Guinea, just over the horizon. Swimming is not recommended here as the tidal stream never seems to stop running one way or the other. The fishing, though, can be pretty good. Have your photo taken near the sign proudly proclaiming you have made it all the way to Australia's northernmost point.

Pajinka Wilderness Lodge

The *Pajinka Wilderness Lodge* (☎ (070) 31 3988) is run by the Injinoo Aboriginal Community and is only 400 metres from the northernmost tip of Australia. This is a great place to reward yourself with a little luxury for making it to the top. There are 24 cabin-style rooms in groups of four, a swimming pool, an open-sided restaurant and a bar. The rooms are simple and airy with a tropical feel, with their own bathroom and a little

verandah. The standard nightly tariffs range from $180 per person over summer to $250 per person during the tourist season, which includes all meals. There are often cheaper stand-by rates available for self-drive guests. The lodge also has a range of packages available from Cairns which include return airfares and transfers, all meals and accommodation. The three-night packages cost $925/1239 per person in the low/high season; seven nights costs $1499/2099. For bookings or further information, contact the Cairns agent toll free on ☎ 1800 802 968.

The lodge also has its own *Camping Ground*, with unpowered sites costing $5 per person per night. Normal amenities are provided for campers, and a licensed kiosk supplies limited stores, takeaway food and ice.

The lodge has a resident naturalist and fishing guide, and can organise a variety of tours – fishing trips, 4WD safaris, bird-watching tours and bushwalks. There are dinghies and mountain bikes for hire. If you're flying in, they can pick you up from the airfield.

There is a regular ferry service from Pajinka to Thursday Island – see the Thursday Island section for details.

Punsand Bay

Punsand Bay, on a north-facing beach just a few km west from the tip of Cape York, is one of the best and most scenic spots on the Cape. The *Punsand Bay Private Reserve* (☎ (070) 69 1722) is very well set up, with a camping ground, on-site tents, cabins, a kiosk and dining room, hot showers and a laundry. Activities include night walks and tours to Cape York and the surrounding area. There is also a resident fishing guide.

Those with a tent can camp, an unpowered site costing $7 per person per night, or $5 extra per site will get you power. Accommodation is also available in on-site tents with beds, and cabins, for $65 and $95 per person per night, including all meals.

There is a regular ferry service from the reserve to Thursday Island – see the Thursday Island section for details.

Thursday Island & the Torres Strait

There are a number of islands scattered across the reef-strewn waters of Torres Strait, running like stepping stones from the top of Cape York to the south coast of Papua New Guinea, about 150 km north of the Australian mainland. The islands are politically part of Australia, although some of them are only a few km from Papua New Guinea. The islands exhibit a surprising variety in form and function. There are three main types: the rocky, mountain-top extension of the Great Dividing Range makes up the western group that includes Thursday Island and Prince of Wales Island; the central group of islands that dot the waters east of the Great Barrier Reef are little more than coral cays; while the third type of islands are volcanic in origin and are in the far east of the strait, at the very northern end of the Great Barrier Reef. These Murray Islands are some of the most spectacular and picturesque in the area.

While Thursday Island (or TI as it's often known) is the 'capital' of Torres Strait, there are 17 inhabited islands, the northernmost being Saibai and Boigu islands, a couple of km from the New Guinea coast. The population of the islands is about 9000 and the people are Melanesians, racially related to the peoples of Papua New Guinea.

History

Despite the islands being likened to a stepping stone between Papua New Guinea and Australia, there seems to have been remarkably little movement across the straits and the dramatic differences between development in Papua New Guinea and amongst the Aboriginals of Australia is of great scientific interest.

In 1606 two European explorers became the first Westerners to pass through Torres Strait, although they were unaware of each other's presence at the time. The Dutchman Willem Jansz sighted the west coast of Cape York from his ship the *Duyfken*. He led a party ashore and could have claimed the honour of being the first European to set foot on Australia, except that he thought he was still on Papua New Guinea. Meanwhile Spanish explorer Luiz Vaez de Torres was approaching the strait from the eastern side with his ship the *San Pedrico*. He had set out from Peru as part of an expedition led by Pedro Fernandez de Quiros to search for *Terra Australis Incognita*, the Great South Land, but the two ships were separated.

While Quiros sailed back to Mexico, Torres continued east and was swept through the straits by the prevailing winds and current. He landed on several islands before continuing around Papua New Guinea, eventually reaching the Phillipines.

The Spanish, however, did not reveal Torres' historic discovery and for the next two centuries the straits remained a rumour until Captain Cook confirmed their existence in 1770. After his involuntary halt at Cooktown to repair his damaged vessel Cook continued north and then, like Torres, was carried through the straits by the prevailing winds and current. He paused long enough at Possession Island to claim the whole east coast of Australia for King George III.

In 1802 Matthew Flinders, during his epic circumnavigation of Australia, made the most systematic survey yet of the islands and channels of the straits and also named the straits after Torres.

When pearl shell was discovered in the waters of the strait during the 1860s, it led to an invasion of boats and crews in search of this new form of wealth. It was a wild and savage industry with 'blackbirding', a form of kidnapping for sale into slavery, and killing being common. Being on the very edge of the frontier, the strait and all those who worked in it and plundered its resources were out of reach of the law.

Around the same time, the missionaries arrived and they were obviously successful, as the Islanders are still one of the most church-going populations in Australia.

During the first half of this century the pearling industry was the lifeblood of the area. It was a dangerous job as there was little knowledge of the physiological aspects of deep diving, and death from the 'bends', or decompression sickness, was common. Poor equipment and the odd storm or cyclone were also perils that the divers and crews faced. In fact, it was a cyclone in March 1899 that caused the biggest loss of life and devastated the industry. That cyclone struck Bathurst Bay where 45 boats from the TI pearling fleet were anchored, and in the following hours only one boat survived and over 300 men were killed.

While a number of nationalities made up the working population, the Japanese were considered by many to make the best divers. The price they paid for their expertise is evident in the TI cemetery where over 500 were prematurely buried.

In WW II Torres Strait and the islands were part of Australia's front line in the battle against the Japanese. Horn Island, in essence TI's airport, was bombed a number of times in 1942, but TI never had a bomb dropped on it. Some say that was due to the legend that a Japanese princess was buried on the island, but it was more than likely the fact that there was a large population of Japanese living on TI.

After the war, plastics took over where pearl shell left off. A number of cultured pearl bases still operate around the waters of TI, but the 100 or more boats that once worked the beds have long since disappeared.

In 1975 Papua New Guinea became independent. Though there was some dispute over international boundaries, all the islands up to two km off the New Guinea coast remained Australian.

Today much of the wealth of the area still comes from the sea in the form of prawns from the Gulf, for which TI is a major port, and crayfish from the reefs of the strait. Tourism is also playing its part in this region of Australia that is so vastly different to the mainland.

THURSDAY ISLAND (pop 2600)

No visit to the top of the Cape would be complete without a visit to TI. TI can be a fascinating place to visit, although it's a long way removed from the resort islands down along the Queensland coast. It's a working island, and life here can be somewhat tough and uncompromising.

The island is little more than three sq km in area, with the town of TI being located on its southern shore.

There are a few stores, including a general store, chemist, takeaways, a post office (with a Commonwealth Bank agency) and a branch of the National Bank (with full banking facilities). There are also four hotels, three with accommodation (as well as cold beer). There is intense but friendly rivalry between the hotels, with each supporting a local Rugby League football club. TI also has a police station (☎ (070) 69 1520) and a hospital (☎ (070) 69 1109).

Things to See

The **Quetta Memorial Church** was built in 1893 in memory of the *Quetta*, wrecked three years earlier with 133 lives lost. The TI **cemetery**, with its Japanese graves and the more recent Japanese Pearl Memorial for those who lost their lives diving for shell, is a poignant place. **Green Hill Fort**, on the west side of town, was built in 1891 when the Russians were thought to be coming.

While there some other historic buildings and places of interest around TI, it is the atmosphere of the island and the people that set it apart from the rest of Australia.

Festivals

The Torres Strait Cultural Festival (☎ (070) 69 1698) is held on the island every May and numerous activities are organised such as art exhibitions, traditional singing, ceremonial dancing and cooking, along with a colourful procession. Visitors can also wander through the many stalls set up during the festival, many of which have local art and craft displayed.

Places to Stay

The *Jumula Dubbins Hostel* (☎ (070) 69 2122), on Victoria Pde, is a modern hostel which mainly caters for Aboriginals and

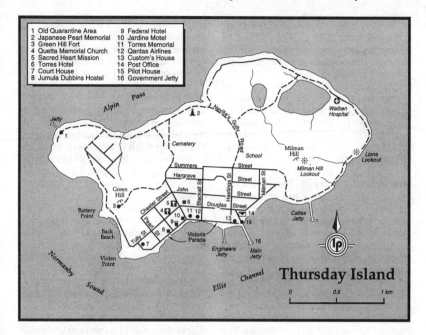

Thursday Island

Map key:
1 Old Quarantine Area
2 Japanese Pearl Memorial
3 Green Hill Fort
4 Quetta Memorial Church
5 Sacred Heart Mission
6 Torres Hotel
7 Court House
8 Jumula Dubbins Hostel
9 Federal Hotel
10 Jardine Motel
11 Torres Memorial
12 Qantas Airlines
13 Custom's House
14 Post Office
15 Pilot House
16 Government Jetty

Islanders, but also takes in travellers. Accommodation is in basic twin-share rooms costing $23.05 per person per night, which includes breakfast, lunch and dinner. There's another hostel, the *Mura Mudh Hostel* (☎ (070) 69 1708), in Douglas St, which operates on a similar basis and has room-only at $20 per person or full board for $45.

The *Federal Hotel* (☎ (070) 69 1569), also on Victoria Pde, has air-con motel rooms with attached bathrooms at $55/80 for singles/doubles and hotel rooms for $40 a single plus $20 for each extra person. The *Torres Hotel* (☎ (070) 69 1141), on the corner of Douglas and Normanby Sts, costs $30/50 for singles/doubles.

The *Jardine Motel* (☎ (070) 69 1555) has a pool, bar and restaurant, and air-con motel rooms cost $120/150 for singles/doubles.

Places to Eat

The various hotels have counter meals from Monday to Saturday while there's often a barbecue on Sunday. The *Torres Hotel* claims to have the most comprehensive menu on TI, with *Pics Cafe* serving lunches and dinners. At the *Federal Hotel* there's the *Pearl Lugger Restaurant* for evening meals, and the beer garden out the back serves counter meals. The *Somerset Restaurant* at the Jardine Motel specialises in seafood and beef dishes.

Ronies, *Tropics* and *K&B Snackbar* have ice creams, snacks and takeaways.

Getting There & Away

Air The TI Airport is actually on neighbouring Horn Island, so if you fly you will also be up for a ferry ride across the 1.5-km-wide Ellis Channel (see Getting Around later).

Sunstate/Qantas Airlines have regular flights between Cairns and Thursday Island. The one-way fare is $307 and the flight takes two hours direct, longer if it goes via Weipa or Bamaga. On TI the Qantas Airlines office

CAPE YORK PENINSULA

(☎ (070) 69 1264) is on the corner of Victoria Pde and Blackall St. Flight West (☎ (070) 69 1325) also flies from Cairns to TI for $307, although cheaper fares are often available with both airlines.

A number of smaller airlines operate flights and charter services around the islands of the Torres Strait. These include Air Cairns (bookings through Flight West), Uzu Air (☎ (070) 69 2377) Falcon Airlines (☎ (070) 69 2777) and Reef Helicopters (☎ (070) 69 1473).

Sea Peddell's Ferry & Tourist Service (☎ (070) 69 1551) runs two regular ferry services to Thursday Island, both of which operate Monday to Saturday during the peak tourist season (June to October). Their first service leaves the jetty at Seisia at 8 am and returns from Thursday Island at 2 pm; the one-way/return fares are $35/58. The second service leaves from Pajinka Wilderness Lodge at 7 am and from Punsand Bay at 8 am and returns from Thursday Island at 2 pm; the one-way/return fares are $40/50 from Punsand Bay and $45/65 from Pajinka. The return fare only applies if you return on the same day. Bookings are essential and can be made through Peddell's direct or at the Seisia Camping Ground, Punsand Bay or Pajinka Lodge. Peddell's also operates a bus tour of Thursday Island in conjunction with the ferry service.

The cruise ships SV *Atlantic Clipper* and the *Kangaroo Explorer* operate regularly Cairns-Thursday Island-Cairns. Although most passengers take the round trip cruise you can also travel one way. See the Organised Tours section at the start of this chapter for details.

Intrepid travellers have, in the past, continued on from the Torres Strait Islands to Papua New Guinea by finding a fishing boat across the straits to Daru, from where you can fly or ship to Port Moresby. These days you will probably run into severe visa problems if you try this since Papua New Guinea officials frown on this unconventional entry point.

The Torres Strait's south-east trade wind is the strongest and longest lasting trade wind in the world. Combine this with numerous reefs and islands plus fickle tides and currents and it's easy to see why this is frequently not an easy area to sail through.

Getting Around

NETS (☎ (070) 69 2132) operates a regular ferry service between Thursday Island and Horn Island, where the TI airport is located. The fare for locals is $4 one way, but airline passengers pay $30 return which includes the ferry and bus transport. Ferries operate hourly Monday to Saturday, less frequently on Sunday.

To see the island, you can grab a local taxi (☎ (070) 69 1666) or join any of the tours that generally meet the ferry from the mainland, such as Peddell's Wongai Isle Bus Tours (☎ (070) 69 1551) and Willie Nelson's TI Tours (☎ (070) 69 1588).

Alternatively, you can hire a car from TI Travel (☎ (070) 69 1264), or R&F Rent-a-Car (☎ (070) 69 1173) opposite the post office rent Daihatsu Charades for $22 an hour or $65 a day. TI is small enough to walk around quite easily.

OTHER ISLANDS

The other inhabited islands of the strait are isolated communities wresting a living from the surrounding reef-strewn sea. The Islanders who inhabit them are fiercely proud of their heritage, with a separate identity to the Aborigines.

Outside of TI the largest group of people are found on Boigu, close to the New Guinea coast, where the population numbers less than 400. Most of the inhabited islands have populations between 100 and 200 people, while Booby Island in the far west of the strait is home to just a couple of families who look after the lighthouse.

Getting around and staying on the other islands of Torres Strait is really for the adventurous traveller. To visit any of the islands other than TI or Horn Island, you usually need a permit or permission from the island's council. Permits are issued by the local council and may not be easy to get. Contact the Islanders Community Council (☎ (070) 69 1446), at the office in Summers St, Thursday Island.

Places to Stay & Eat

Accommodation on these islands is very limited. The community on Yorke Island, 110 km north-east of TI, runs a small, self-contained *guesthouse*. The cost is $25 a single or $30 with meals. Intending visitors should first write to the community council stating details of their visit. It will then be put before the chairperson for approval. For further details, contact the Yorke Island Community Council on ☎ (070) 69 4128.

Accommodation is also available on Horn Island. The *Gateway Torres Strait Resort* (☎ (070) 69 1902) has motel-style rooms at $85/100 for singles/doubles, and the *Wongai Tavern* (☎ (070) 69 1683) has rooms from $65 a night.

Getting There & Away

Once you have a permit you have a choice of flying or chartering a boat. Flying may be quicker and easier, but the essence of Torres Strait is somehow lost. Air Cairns and Falcon Airlines operate regular flights servicing the islands. For further information and reservations, contact the Air Cairns agent on TI at the Flight West office (☎ (070) 69 1325), or Falcon Airlines at its Horn Island office (☎ (070) 69 2777) or in Cairns (☎ (070) 35 9359), or Uzu Air on ☎ (070) 69 2377).

Gulf Savannah

The Gulf Savannah is a vast, flat and empty landscape of bushland, saltpans and savannah grasslands, all cut by a huge number of tidal creeks and rivers which feed into the Gulf of Carpentaria. It's a remote, hot, tough region with excellent fishing and a large crocodile population.

The actual coastline of the Gulf is mainly mangrove swamps which is why there is so little habitation – only a few thousand people live in the area, scattered amongst a handful of small towns, isolated cattle stations, lonely pubs and roadhouses, and Aboriginal communities.

The Gulf's two major natural attractions are at opposite ends of the region: the Lawn Hill National Park is a virtual oasis in the midst of the arid north-west, a stunning river gorge which harbours a verdant remnant of rainforest; and the spectacular Undara Lava Tubes, a collection of ancient and enormous volcanic lava tubes, are near the east end of the Gulf Developmental Rd.

The Gulf's main towns – Burketown, Normanton and Karumba – still have the feel of frontier settlements. There are plenty of interesting fossicking areas in the area, including the rich gemfields and old mining towns around Croydon, Georgetown and Mt Surprise.

During the Wet (December to March), the dirt roads turn to mud and even the surfaced roads can be flooded, so April to September is the safest time to visit this area.

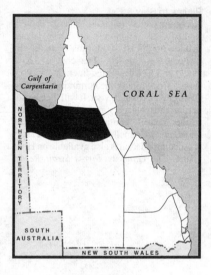

History

The coastline of the Gulf of Carpentaria was charted by Dutch explorers long before Cook's visit to Australia. Willem Jansz sailed the *Duyfken* into the Gulf in 1606; in 1644 Abel Tasman named it the Gulf of Carpentaria after the then-governor of Batavia.

In 1802 Matthew Flinders sailed into the Gulf during his historic circumnavigation of the Australian continent, stopping at Sweers Island (amongst other places) where he is said to have dug a well.

The first European to pass through this area was Ludwig Leichhardt, the eccentric Prussian explorer who skirted around the Gulf on his 1844 trek from Brisbane to the newly settled Port Essington (near Darwin). After Leichhardt came the ill-fated Burke and Wills expedition. Burke, Wills, King and Gray camped a little way west of Normanton in February 1861. Because of the thick mangrove swamps which line the coast here, they didn't actually manage to reach the sea, but knew they were close to it because of the tidal movement on the rivers.

After their disappearance, a number of other explorers came looking for them, including the intrepid William Landsborough, who was responsible for opening up much of the Gulf region. Landsborough's enthusiastic reports of the

Gulf's potential as fine pastoral land motivated many settlers to come to the area in the 1860s with herds of sheep and cattle.

Two of the settlements in the region, Burketown and Normanton, were founded in the 1860s, before better-known places on the Pacific coast like Cairns and Cooktown came into existence. Burketown, founded in 1865, was nearly wiped out by a fever brought by a ship from Java a year later, and the remaining population was evacuated off shore to Sweers Island. Many of them moved to the new settlement of Normanton in 1867 and Burketown has been the smaller place ever since.

An overland telegraph line from Cardwell, north of Townsville, to Normanton was opened in 1872. Queenslanders hoped that Normanton rather than Darwin would be the landing point for the new telegraph line to Australia from London, but by the time that line reached Australia later in 1872, the Adelaide-Darwin line was also ready. Thus Darwin, not Normanton, became the main town on Australia's north coast.

When gold was discovered near Croydon in the 1880s, the ensuing rush brought thousands of hopefuls into the region. Croydon developed into a major town, and at one time had more than 30 pubs. At the height of the rush, a railway line was constructed from Normanton to Croydon to link the goldfields to the nearest port town. Nowadays the anachronistic *Gulflander* train trip along this short route is one of the region's most popular attractions.

Geography & Climate

The majority of the Gulf Savannah is made up of the vast, empty plains and saltpans from which it takes its name. The plains are cut by an intricate network of creeks and rivers, which during the Wet fill up and frequently flood, at times turning parts of the region into an immense inland lake. In the north-west region, the escarpments of the Barkly Tableland rise – in the centre of this area are the spectacular Lawn Hill National Park and unique fossil fields of Riversleigh.

Travel is not recommended in the region between the beginning of December and the end of March, when extreme heat and humidity make conditions uncomfortable or even dangerous. Apart from that, heavy rain at this time can close the roads for lengthy periods. The most pleasant time to visit the Gulf is during the winter months, when you will encounter cool mornings, warm days and balmy evenings.

Maps

The best road guide to use is Sunmap's *Gulf Savannah* Tourist Map (1:1,750,000). It is produced by Queensland's Department of Geographic Information and is available from most newsagencies and tourist information centres.

Radio Frequencies

The Gulf is serviced by the Mt Isa RFDS base (call sign VJI – Victor Juliet India), which can be contacted on 2020 and 5110 kHz during office hours (8 am to 5 pm Monday to Friday). For after-hours emergency calls, use 5110 kHz. Ring the base (☎ (077) 432 800) for an update on services.

Activities

Most travellers to the Gulf come with a sense of adventure; prospectors searching for gold or gemstones, 4WD adventurers and anglers make up the majority of visitors.

The fishing here is nothing short of sensational. Inshore, there are barramundi, salmon and mudcrabs, while out in the Gulf mackerel, tuna, cod and red emperor are all abundant. A number of places have been set up especially to cater for people who have become addicted to barramundi fishing.

The Gulf is also a birdwatcher's paradise, particularly during the Wet.

Organised Tours

Savannah Guides The Savannah Guides are a network of professional guides who staff guide posts at strategic locations throughout the Gulf, including the Undara Lava Tubes, the Tallaroo Hot Springs, Lawn

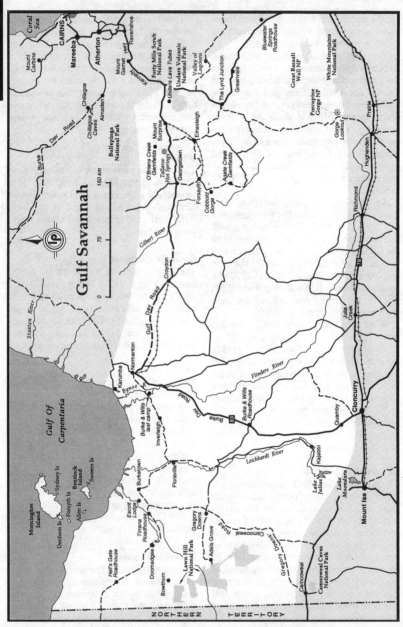

Hills National Park and Hell's Gate Roadhouse. They act as interpreters and protectors of the local environment, as well as tour guides, and can cater for anything from day trips to organising major expeditions. They are people with good knowledge of the local environment and conditions, and can take visitors to some of the Gulf's most interesting and remote points of interest, many of which are on private property and would be difficult to visit unaccompanied. For more information, contact their head office (☎ (070) 31 7933), at 57 McLeod St in Cairns.

Getting There & Away

Air Flight West Airlines (☎ (077) 43 9333) has flights from Cairns to various places in the Gulf, including Burketown ($345 one way, Mondays only), Bamaga ($279, daily), Normanton ($262, daily except Tuesday and Sunday) and Karumba ($285, daily except Tuesday and Sunday).

Flight West also has flights from Cairns to Mt Isa, and from Mt Isa to the Gulf – see the Outback chapter for details of these.

Bus Campbell's Coaches (☎ (077) 43 2006) has a weekly bus service between Mt Isa, Normanton and Karumba (see Mt Isa in the Outback chapter for details).

Cairns-Karumba Coachline (☎ (070) 35 1853) has a service three times a week between Cairns and Karumba, which takes almost 12 hours and costs $116 one way. Stops en route from Cairns include Undara ($40 one way), Georgetown ($61), Croydon ($83) and Normanton ($105). Departures are from Cairns on Monday, Wednesday and Thursday, and from Karumba on Tuesday, Thursday and Friday.

Getting Around

Train While there are no direct rail services *into* the Gulf, there are two short services *within* the Gulf which are very popular with travellers.

The famous *Gulflander* runs just once weekly in each direction between Croydon and Normanton, alongside the last stretch of the Gulf Developmental Road. There are connecting bus services from Cairns and Mt Isa to Croydon and Normanton. See the Normanton section for details of the *Gulflander*.

The *Savannahlander* is a new train service which runs between Mt Surprise and Forsayth twice weekly. Again, there are connecting bus services and packaged tours from Cairns. See the Mt Surprise section for details.

Car & Motorcycle This chapter is divided into sections which basically follow the routes of the major roads through the Gulf.

From Queensland's east coast, the Gulf Developmental road takes you from the Kennedy Hwy, south of the Atherton Tableland, across to Normanton and Karumba. If you're coming from the Northern Territory, the unsealed Gulf Track takes you across the top of the Gulf country to Burketown, and on to Normanton. From Burketown you have two options if you're heading south; the unsealed road to Camooweal, via Gregory Downs and the Lawn Hill National Park; or the Nardoo-Burketown Rd, which cuts across to meet the Burke Developmental Rd at the Burke & Wills Roadhouse.

The other major route is the Burke Developmental Rd, a good sealed highway which takes you south from Normanton to the Burke & Wills Roadhouse. From here, you can continue south to Cloncurry, or head south-east to Julia Creek.

There aren't too many options apart from these major routes, particularly if you don't have a 4WD. Even if you do, remember that this is remote country and the going can be rough once you get off the beaten track. If you're thinking of attempting other routes, such as the continuation of the Burke Developmental Rd, which takes you east from between Normanton and Karumba to Mareeba, via Chillagoe, you'll need to be well prepared and carrying good maps, plenty of water, and preferably a radio.

Eastern Gulf Region

The Gulf Developmental Rd is the main route into the Gulf from the east. It leaves the Kennedy Hwy 66 km south of Mt Garnet, passing through the towns of Georgetown and Croydon en route to Normanton. The first section of the highway is paved and in reasonably good condition. About 110 km past Georgetown the surface changes to unsealed dirt, and the rest of the route alternates between sections of sealed and unsealed highway. The unsealed sections are corrugated dirt and quite bumpy, although you can usually sit on 80 to 90 km/h. This section of the route is sometimes impassible during the Wet – check on road conditions before heading out.

The region crossed by this road has many ruined gold mines and settlements, and still attracts some gem fossickers.

UNDARA LAVA TUBES

Just 17 km past the start of the Gulf Developmental Rd is the turn off to the Undara Lava Tubes, one of inland Queensland's most fascinating natural attractions. An impressive tourist complex has been built here to cater for visitors. Guided tours of the tubes and the surrounding countryside are offered, and you can camp or stay overnight in restored railway carriages.

These massive lava tubes were formed around 190,000 years ago following the eruption of a single shield volcano. The eruption continued for three months. The huge lava flows drained towards the sea, following the routes of ancient river beds, and as the lava cooled it formed a surface crust – just like skin on a cooling custard. The hot lava continued to flow through the centre of the tubes, eventually leaving these huge hollow basalt chambers.

Organised Tours

You can only visit the tubes as part of a guided tour. The Undara Lava Lodge's resident Savannah Guides run three different

Entrance to one of the Undara Lava Tubes

tours of the lava tubes: full-day tours depart daily at 9 am and cost $70 for adults and $35 for kids; half-day tours depart at 8.30 and 9.30 am and at 1 pm and cost $52/26. These prices all include lunch. There's also 1½-hour tours, which depart at 8, 9, 10, and 11 am and 12.45 and 3.45 pm, and cost $18/12. Note that these departure times are for the main tourist season (April to September) – at other times, tours are less frequent and it's worth ringing ahead to book and check times.

The lodge also organises a variety of activities for its guests, including scenic flights, walking tours, 4WD safaris and trips to the Tallaroo Mineral Hot Springs.

Places to Stay & Eat

The *Undara Lava Lodge* (☎ (070) 97 1411) is a unique tourist complex with three levels of guest accommodation. There are plenty of camping or caravan sites costing $8 for adults or $4 for kids, with good facilities including barbecues, hot showers and laundries. Then there are the 'camp-o-tels', semi-permanent tents with beds and lights which cost $14 per person, or $56 per person with breakfast, lunch and dinner included. Top of the range are the collection of charmingly restored old railway carriages, which make rather quaint and comfortable sleeping quarters; these have shared bathroom facilities. The nightly cost is $98 per adult or $48 per child, which includes breakfast, lunch and dinner.

The lodge has a souvenir shop, a bar and a restaurant, but note that there are no shops or kiosks and you can't buy groceries or takeaway meals here, so if you're wanting to self-cater you'll have to stock up on supplies before you come.

The lodge's restaurant is also housed in restored railway carriages and has an open-air courtyard. If you're not taking the option of the meals package, breakfast and lunch both cost $15 per person, and for dinner you can have a main course for $15, two courses from $20 or three courses for $25. Meal times are scheduled to fit around the tour times.

Getting There & Away

By car, the lodge and lava tubes are 15 km of corrugated dirt road off the main highway.

The lodge has its own airstrip, and organises regular flights from Cairns – ring their Cairns office (☎ (070) 31 7933) for details.

Cairns-Karumba Coachlines (☎ (070) 35 1853) has services three times a week from Cairns to Undara (continuing on to Karumba). The one-way fare is $40 for adults, $20 for children. (See Organised Tours in the Cairns section for details of tours to Undara.)

MT SURPRISE

Back on the Gulf Developmental Road, 39 km past the Undara turn off, is the small township of Mt Surprise, which has a pub, a railway station and two roadhouses. In the centre of rich cattle country, the town was founded in 1864 by Ezra Firth, a stonemason and gold-miner turned sheep farmer. You can read his strange story in the cafe at the Shell Roadhouse.

O'Brien's Creek Gemfields, 42 km north-west of town, is one of Australia's best topaz fields.

The **Old Post Office Curiosity Museum** has a small and quirky display of local history items.

The *Mobil Service Station & General Store* (☎ (070) 62 3115) sells groceries and takeaway meals. It does welding and most mechanical repairs, and has a towing service. It's also the local agent for the Post Office and the Commonwealth and Westpac banks (passbook accounts only). By the time you read this they should also have EFTPOS facilities.

The *Shell Roadhouse & Caravan Park* (☎ (070) 62 3153) has tent sites at $5 per person and on-site vans for $30. The cafe next door serves a good range of meals including excellent burgers, and has a couple of information books full of interesting details on what to see in the area, yarns and local history, as well as mud maps of the fossicking fields around Mt Surprise.

The *Mt Surprise Hotel* (☎ (070) 62 3118) has basic pub-style rooms upstairs costing $20 per person, or $10 if you stay more than one night. They also serve meals any time the pub is open, from sandwiches to steaks and seafood dishes. There's a small beer garden beside the pub.

Getting There & Away

You can get to Mt Surprise from Cairns with Cairns-Karumba Coachlines (☎ (070) 35 1853); several of their services connect with the *Savannahlander* (see the following section). The one-way fare is $48 for adults and $24 for children.

THE SAVANNAHLANDER

Mt Surprise is connected to Forsayth, 120 km south-west, by the *Savannahlander*. This new train service is an abbreviated version of the old Cairns-Forsayth service which was discontinued (somewhat controversially) in 1995.

The *Savannahlander* runs twice weekly, departing from Mt Surprise every Monday and Thursday at 12.30 pm and returning from Forsayth every Tuesday and Friday at 7.30 am (most people stay overnight in Forsayth, returning the next day). The trip takes five hours, with several stops along the way, and the one-way fares are $35 for adults and $18 for children.

You can connect with the *Savannahlander* by bus from Cairns (see the previous Getting There & Away section); there are also several companies which offer tours from Cairns which package the *Savannahlander* trip with other places including the Undara Lava Tubes, Tallaroo Hot Springs and Cobbold Gorge.

EINASLEIGH & FORSAYTH

Thirty-two km west of Mt Surprise, you can take an interesting if somewhat slow detour off the highway through the old mining townships of Einasleigh and Forsayth. Both towns are on the old Cairns-Forsayth railway line, so you can also visit them on the *Savannahlander* train (see the previous section).

The turn off to Einasleigh from the Gulf Developmental Rd is poorly marked and easy to miss. It's a 150-km loop from here back to Georgetown, and the going is quite slow and bumpy. The road is unsealed and fairly rough in sections, but is passable for normal vehicles during the dry season. You can also cut across to Einasleigh from The Lynd Junction on the Kennedy Developmental Rd, via 76 km of unsealed dirt road.

Einasleigh, a former copper-mining centre and railway siding, has a population of about 35. Set in a rugged landscape of low, flat-topped hills, it's a sprawling, ramshackle town with a collection of mostly derelict tin and timber buildings. The *Central Hotel* (☎ (070) 62 5222) on Daintree St has pub-style accommodation at $20/30 for singles/doubles. It sells pies, but doesn't do bistro meals apart from the occasional Friday night fry-up. Across the road from the pub, the

Einasleigh Gorge is a good swimming spot. The **Kidston goldmine**, the largest open-cut goldmine in the country, is 45 km south of Einasleigh off the Einasleigh-Lynd Junction road.

Forsayth is 67 km further west. This place isn't much bigger than Einasleigh, although it is perhaps a little more alive, and has a railway station, a post office and a phone booth. The *Goldfields Hotel* (☎ (070) 62 5374) has basic accommodation in dongas, with rooms with air-con and shared bathrooms costing $45 per person including breakfast and dinner. (If you don't want meals, you can negotiate a bed-only price). They serve a set menu each night, with meals ranging from $7 to $9. The pub also sells fuel and a few groceries.

There are a couple of operators who offer tours in the local area: Forsayth Gold Fossicking Tours (☎ (070) 62 5374) has a half-day tour of a mining lease 15 minutes from town, which includes a lesson on gold panning and detecting. The cost is $45 per person and you can book through the pub. See the following section for details of tours to Cobbold Gorge.

You can also drive from Forsayth to the **Agate Creek Gemfields**, which are 75 km south-west, although the road conditions are fairly rough and you'll need a good map (or ask at the pub for directions).

If you're driving from Forsayth on to Georgetown, be sure to turn right just *before* the pub. Believe me, it's quite easy to miss the sign to Georgetown and end up in the middle of nowhere, opening and closing cattle gates as the sun slowly sets...

COBBOLD GORGE

The Lovely Cobbold Gorge was discovered a couple of years ago on a cattle station 45 km south of Forsayth. It's a scenic oasis, with a swimming hole, rugged cliffs and gorges, and an abundance of wildlife, and you can camp nearby and take a tour of the gorge.

The *Cobbold Camping Village* (☎ (070) 62 5470) has toilets, showers and barbecue facilities: sites cost $5 per adult and $4 per child. There are full-day tours of the gorge, departing daily at 8.30 am and costing $75 for adults and $30 for children, or half-day tours, departing daily at 12.30 pm and costing $45/20. Tours depart from the camping ground, although if you're travelling on the *Savannahlander* the operators will pick you up from Forsayth.

MT SURPRISE TO GEORGETOWN

Back on the Gulf Developmental Rd, 40 km west of Mt Surprise is the turn off to the **Tallaroo Hot Springs**, where you can soak in one of five naturally terraced hot springs. The springs are open every day from 8 am to 5 pm between Easter and the end of September. Admission costs $8 for adults and $4 for kids, which includes a tour of the property. Meals are available from a kiosk here.

GEORGETOWN (pop 310)

Georgetown has three roadhouses, a pub, a post office and two cafes. During the days of the Etheridge River gold rush, Georgetown was a bustling commercial centre, but things are much quieter and a lot less exciting nowadays and, unless you need fuel, food or sleep, there aren't too many reasons to linger here.

Places to Stay & Eat

The *Midway Caravan Park & Service Station* (☎ (070) 62 1219), on the highway, has camp sites for $9.50 and on-site vans for $25. It also has a cafe and takeaway section, and has EFTPOS facilities and takes major credit cards.

The *Wenaru Hotel* (☎ (070) 62 1208), on the corner of St George and Normanton Sts, has simple but clean pub rooms with shared bathrooms at $25/40 for singles/doubles.

The *Latara Resort Motel* (☎ (070) 62 1190), on the highway one km west of Georgetown, is by far the best place to stay. They have small, modern motel units with air-con, TV and a pool, with singles/doubles at $45/55. There's also a very pleasant dining room with home-cooked evening meals and

main courses around $16. Breakfast will set you back $6 (continental) or $12 (cooked). The *Travellers Tavern*, at the Ampol service station, has a small supermarket and does takeaway meals. It also has EFTPOS facilities.

CROYDON (pop 220)

Connected to Normanton by the curious-looking *Gulflander* train, this old gold-mining town was once the biggest in the Gulf. Gold was discovered here in 1885 by J W Aldridge, and within a couple of years there were 8000 diggers living here. It's reckoned there were once 5000 gold mines in the area and reminders of them are scattered all around the countryside. The goldfields were spread over an area 36 km wide and 180 km long, and Croydon was surrounded by more than 30 satellite townships. Such was the prosperity of the town that it had its own aerated water factory, gas street lamps, a foundry and coach-builders, and more than 30 pubs.

The town's boom years were during the 1890s, but by the end of WW I the gold had run out and the town became little more than a ghost town. There is still a handful of interesting historic buildings here to remind passers-by of the days of yore: the old **Shire Hall** on Samwell St is a great old timber building topped by a clock tower – inside there are several interesting and large murals painted on hessian by Steve Johns. The **Old Courthouse**, the **Mining Warden's Office**, the **General Store**, the **old butcher shop** and the **Club Hotel** also date back to the mining days.

The *Gulflander* train arrives in town every Wednesday and returns to Normanton every Thursday – see the following section for more details.

Facilities

The *Croydon General Store* (☎ (077) 45 6163) is the local RACQ depot. It sells fuel, does most repairs and has a 24-hour towing service. The general store sells takeaway meals and groceries, and has a small museum next door, with a collection of photos, tools, rocks and records, all fairly well hidden under an even more impressive collection of dust and cobwebs.

On the eastern outskirts of town is the *Gulf Gate Roadhouse*, a Caltex service station with a cafe.

Organised Tours

Chris Weirman is the local tour guide. He has lived in the town for most of his life, and knows a fair bit about local history and sights around Croydon. Chris conducts walking tours of Croydon's historic precinct according to demand – he can usually be contacted at the Shire Hall or by phoning ☎ (077) 45 6125.

Eddie and Eva from the Club Hotel also organise tours to some of the old mining areas by horse-drawn cart. The tour takes four hours and costs $18 per person – contact them at the pub for details.

Places to Stay & Eat

The *Golden Picdewehousma Caravan Park,* on the corner of Brown and Alldridge Sts, is a bleak little camping ground run by the local council.

The *Club Hotel* (☎ (077) 45 6184), on the corner of Brown and Sircom Sts, has accommodation upstairs. The rooms are pretty basic but have plenty of character, with their bare timber floors and corrugated iron walls. You can stay in a single bed on the enclosed verandah for $8, or have a room to yourself for $20/35 for singles/doubles. Next to the pub are a couple of air-con motel-style units with communal bathrooms – these cost $28/43. The pub has an excellent swimming pool.

You can get the usual takeaway food at either of the cafes, although don't expect anything more inspiring than burgers and Chico rolls. The pub serves a small selection of counter meals at night with main courses ranging from $7 to $10, and on Wednesday when the train comes in they put on a smorgasbord lunch.

THE GULFLANDER

The Normanton to Croydon railway line was completed in 1891 with the aim of linking the booming gold-mining centre with the port town at Normanton.

Normanton's Railway Station is a lovely old Victorian-era building with well-kept gardens, a small souvenir shop and a railway museum. When it's not running, the *Gulflander*, a weird-looking, snub-nosed little train, is housed here under the arch-roofed platform.

The *Gulflander* travels the 153 km from Normanton to Croydon and back once a week, leaving Normanton on Wednesday at 8.30 am and returning from Croydon on Thursday at 8.30 am. The trip takes a leisurely four hours, with a couple of stops at points of interest along the way. It's one of the Gulf's most popular attractions – if you have the time, don't miss it. Most people stay overnight in Croydon at the Club Hotel, returning to Normanton the next day. The return fare is $52 for adults and $25 for children.

From mid-June to mid-September, the *Gulflander* also does a two-hour 'tea and damper' trip every Saturday at 9.30 am. The cost is $20 for adults – children ride for free. For bookings, phone the station on ☎ (077) 45 1391.

NORMANTON (pop 1190)

Normanton, the Gulf's major town, was established on the banks of the Norman River back in 1868. The town's boom years were during the 1890s, when it acted as the port town for the gold rush around the Croydon goldfields.

Since the heady days of gold ended, the town has existed as a major supply point for the surrounding cattle stations, and as the shire centre. Today more and more travellers pass through Normanton on their way to the Gulf or Cape York.

It's a busy little town with three pubs, a motel and a caravan park, as well as several roadhouses, fuel outlets and two supermarkets. Some of the historic buildings still in use; these include the **Shire Offices** and the large **Burns Philp & Co Ltd store**, down

Top: Einasleigh Gorge, Gulf Savannah
Middle: Birdsville Hotel
Bottom: Cattle on the 'Long Paddock', North of Winton

Red Sandhill near Windorah, Outback

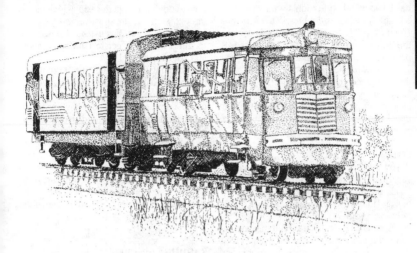

The snub-nosed *Gulflander*

towards the river end of the town; the **Westpac Bank**; and the simple **Normanton Railway Station**.

Travellers may also be interested in the Normanton Rodeo & Gymkhana held in June, the area's biggest social and sporting event of the year. In August the Normanton Races and a ball take place.

As a base for fishing, Normanton is hard to beat, with the Norman River producing some magic-size barramundi. From here it's just a hop, step and jump across the plains to the Gulf port of Karumba.

Facilities

The *Gulf Service Station* (☎ (077) 45 1221), on Landsborough St is the local RACQ depot, and does repairs, welding and 24-hour towing. It sells fuel and a range of auto accessories.

The Shire Offices (☎ (077) 45 1166), on the corner of Haig and Landsborough Sts, have a small information section with brochures and a collection of old photos.

Normanton's post office has a Commonwealth Bank agency, and there's a Westpac Bank on the corner of Landsborough and Little Brown Sts.

Organised Tours

Len Taylor, the manager of the caravan park, runs various day trips to places like Burke and Wills' last camp site, the Inverleigh cattle station and to an old stagecoach crossing on the Norman River. The tours take a couple of hours and cost around $10 a head. Contact Len at the park or phone ☎ (077) 45 1121 for details.

Places to Stay

The *Normanton Caravan Park* (☎ (077) 45 1121), in Brown St, has tent sites for $10 and two on-site vans (one with air-con) for $30 a double. It also has a 25-metre pool.

The *Albion Hotel/Motel* (☎ (077) 45 1218), on Haig St just off the main road, is a friendly little place with good motel-style rooms with air-con for $50. They also have three simple singles in transportable miners' huts at $15 a bed, although these are often booked out by workers.

The *Central Hotel* (☎ (077) 45 1215), on the corner of Haig and Landsborough Sts, has basic motel-style rooms with air-con at $30/40 for singles/doubles. The *National Hotel* (☎ (077) 45 1324), widely known as the Purple Pub, has pub-style rooms at $18 per person and motel units at $40/50.

The *Gulfland Motel* (☎ (077) 45 1290), the first place you see as you drive in from Croydon, is a well-kept motel with good air-con singles/doubles for $50/60. The motel has its own licensed restaurant and a good swimming pool.

Places to Eat

If you need to buy supplies, there are two supermarkets in town – *Normanton Traders* inside the historic Burns Philp & Co building, and the *Stop Shop* one block south of the railway crossing.

There are several cafes and takeaways along the main street, with the usual selection of burgers, sandwiches, fried chicken and fish & chips.

The *Albion Hotel* serves good meals in the $5 to $10 range, and there's a shady balcony next to the bar. The *Central Hotel* also has counter meals, and their fish & chips nights on Friday are supposedly great value and very popular.

Getting There & Away

Flight West Airlines has regular flights from Mt Isa to Normanton ($248) and from Cairns to Normanton ($270). There are also regular bus services from Mt Isa and Cairns to Karumba, via Normanton – see the Karumba section for details.

NORMANTON TO KARUMBA (72 km)

Heading out of town, the Burke Developmental Road soon crosses the Norman River and, less than 29 km up the road, a major tributary of the river, Walker Creek. At the 30-km mark from the centre of town, you come to a major intersection. Veer left here, sticking to the bitumen, and the road quickly swings almost due west. If you continued straight on, the unsealed Burke Developmental Rd would eventually take you all the way across to Cairns, via Chillagoe and Mareeba. You need a 4WD and plenty of

preparation to attempt this trip, which passes through some of the most remote and isolated parts of north Queensland. There are no facilities until you get to Chillagoe, about 600 km east of here!

Traversing these great plains, it is not hard to imagine that during the torrential rains of the wet season, this area becomes one huge lake. At times, with king tides backing up the waters of the rivers, the floods isolate towns like Normanton for weeks at a time.

The birdlife is rich and varied – this region is the best in Australia to see the stately brolga and the very similar sarus crane – a recent natural invader from South-East Asia. Another large bird which you'll see is the magpie-coloured jabiru, certainly one of the most majestic birds of the tropics.

KARUMBA (pop 700)

Karumba, 70 km north of Normanton, lies at the point where the Norman River meets the Gulf of Carpentaria. The town actually has two separate sections – Karumba itself is on the banks of the Norman River, while Karumba Point is a couple of km north (as the crow flies) on the shores of the Gulf.

Originally established as a telegraph station in the 1870s, it became a stopover for the flying boats of the Empire Mail Service in the 1930s. The discovery of prawns in the Gulf in the 1960s brought Karumba alive, and today the prawning and barramundi industries keep the town humming. You certainly can't miss seeing the boats as they sit beside the jetty, draped with nets, just a stone's throw from the pub and the centre of town.

Karumba has a pub, a couple of caravan parks and a number of holiday units, all of which mainly cater for fishing people. The pub can really be jumping when the boats come in for a short break or for resupply. There is also a new tavern being constructed at Karumba Point, which should be open by the time you read this.

The town lives and breathes fish and fishing, prawns and prawning. If you aren't interested in these things, you won't stay long. Sure, you can actually get to the sea at Karumba Point, but once you've done that, had a look around town and enjoyed a prawn or two at the pub, there is not much else to hold your attention. Of course you could always fly to Mornington or Sweers islands out in the Gulf, but once again, these are favoured fishing haunts and you need to love fishing to fully appreciate these wild, remote places.

Note that while the beach at Karumba Point may look rather inviting, don't even *think* about having a swim in the Gulf – if the sharks don't get you, the crocs will.

Facilities
B & B Supermarket (☎ (077) 45 9188), on Yappar St, has just about everything you may need, and its Westpac EFTPOS machine handles all credit cards.

The Westpac Bank, in Yappar St, is open only on Tuesday and Thursday, and there is a Commonwealth Bank agency at the post office.

Boat Hire
If you don't have your own boat, there are several places where you can hire one: Karumba Boat Hire (☎ (077) 45 9393), at Karumba Point, has a variety of dinghies at $45 for a half day or $60 a full day; and Gulf Hire Boats (☎ (077) 45 9274), in Yappar St, has dinghies from $45 a day.

Cruises & Tours
The Ferryman (☎ (077) 45 9155), operating from the Karumba boat ramp, runs a couple of different cruises along the Norman River. His 2½-hour morning birdwatching cruise costs $25 for adults and $12 for children; his 2½-hour sunset cruise costs $25/12; and his 1½-hour sunset cruise costs $18/8.

There are also a number of boating and fishing tours run from Karumba.

Air Karumba (☎ (077) 45 9354) has flights to Mornington and Sweers islands, as well as further afield around the Gulf to places including Lawn Hill National Park, Escott Lodge and Dorunda Station.

Festivals
Festivals held during the year include the Snake Creek Turnout (in July), the Barra Ball (in November) and the Fisherman's Ball (in December).

Places to Stay
The *Gulf Country Caravan Park* (☎ (077) 45 9148), in Yappar St, has tent sites at $10 and on-site units at $40 a double. Also in Yappar St is *Matilda's End Holiday Units* (☎ (077) 45 9368). These are old and plain holiday units, some with kitchens, all with air-con and TVs. They sleep from two to eight people and cost from $40/50 for singles/doubles plus $10 for extras.

The *Karumba Lodge Hotel* (☎ (077) 45 9143) has motel-style units overlooking the Norman River, costing $55/65 for singles/doubles.

There are also two caravan parks and several holiday units out at Karumba Point. The best of these is *Ashley's Holiday Units* (☎ (077) 45 9132), on the corner of Palmer and Ward Sts. The self-contained units sleep up to six people and cost $50 a night for up to four, plus $10 for each extra person. There's a good pool and a kiosk selling meals, tackle and bait.

Places to Eat
The *Karumba Cafe*, in Yappar St next to the B&B Supermarket, sells fresh fish, fish & chips, burgers and pizzas. The *Karumba Lodge Hotel* has a bistro with lunches and dinners, and a restaurant which opens most nights.

The *Karumba Recreation Club*, which is about three km east of Karumba, is a good alternative to the pub if you're looking for a quieter atmosphere. It has a small bar and bistro, with meals from Wednesday to Saturday nights. It also has a four-hole golf course, and sometimes has live entertainment on weekends.

Getting There & Away
Air Flight West has regular flights from Cairns to Karumba ($294) and from Mt Isa to Karumba ($243).

Boat Gulf Freight Services (☎ (077) 45 9333) has regular weekly barge services from Karumba to Weipa on the Cape York Peninsula, transporting freight, people and vehicles. See Getting There and Away at the start of the Cape York Peninsula chapter for more details.

Bus Cairns-Karumba Coachlines (☎ (070) 35 1853) has services from Cairns to Karumba three times a week. Campbell's Coaches (☎ (077) 43 2006) has a weekly service from Mt Isa to Karumba. See Getting There & Away at the start of this chapter for details.

Western Gulf Region

NORTHERN TERRITORY BORDER TO BURKETOWN (228 km)

This route is part of the historic Gulf Track, which stretches from Roper Bar in the Northern Territory's Top End to Normanton. The entire route is along unsealed roads, although a 4WD vehicle isn't normally required during the dry season unless you plan to take the track that leads to the coast from Hell's Gate. Traffic along this route varies from none in summer to an average of about 30 vehicles a day at the height of the winter tourist season. Travel isn't recommended between the beginning of December and March, when extreme heat and humidity make conditions uncomfortable or even dangerous. Heavy rains at this time can also close the roads for lengthy periods.

This section of road was one of the worst in Australia until 1993, when the horrendous bull dust holes on the Queensland side were covered with gravel. Now you can safely sit on 100 km/h most of the way – unless, of course, a big Wet has destroyed the government's good work. The country has little going for it in the way of scenery, being mainly flat and covered with scrubby vegetation. In fact, apart from Hell's Gate and the Gregory River, there is little reason to linger on this section.

Hell's Gate

Fifty-two km east of the border you arrive at the *Hell's Gate Roadhouse* (☎ (077) 45 8258), located among low outcrops of grey conglomerate that rise from the surrounding bush. In the droving days the police from Turn-Off Lagoon, on the Nicholson River, escorted westbound travellers as far as these rocks, after which they were on their own.

The roadhouse has four air-conditioned, two-bed rooms, with B&B costing $25 per person with a tropical breakfast, $35 with a cooked meal. It also has camp sites at $10 each, and a good licensed restaurant that serves breakfast, lunch and dinner – the Sunday night barbecue shouldn't be missed if you're in the area. Avgas is available. The roadhouse is open daily from 7 am to 10 pm (or later). Bookings are recommended for accommodation.

Hells' Gate is also a Savannah Guide Station. Bill Olive, the owner of the roadhouse, runs half-day and full-day 4WD tours for groups of five or more, taking in spectacular escarpment landscapes and lagoons rich in birdlife. Bookings are preferred and prices are available on application.

Kingfisher Camp & Bowthorn Homestead

Between Hell's Gate and Doomadgee there's a signposted turn off to *Kingfisher Camp* (☎ (077) 45 8212), a good camping ground beside a long hole on the banks of the Nicholson River. The facilities here are new and include hot showers, toilets and laundry, and firewood is supplied. There's a small kiosk selling basic supplies. It costs $5 per person to camp here.

It's about another 70 km south-west from here to *Bowthorn Homestead* (☎ (077) 45 8132), a working cattle station with a large homestead which takes in travellers. This is a chance to glimpse life on a big outback station; there are seven beds in three rooms, with shared bathrooms, and the nightly cost is $75 per person including meals. The owners can arrange sightseeing trips, and there are some spectacular bushwalks with plenty of birdlife in the area. The homestead has several airstrips, or if you're in a 4WD you can also get up here from Lawn Hill. Advance bookings are necessary.

Doomadgee

Other than patches of open forest along occasional creek lines, there is little break in the mallee and paperbark scrub that lines the Track for the 80 km between Hell's Gate and the Doomadgee turn off. Doomadgee is an Aboriginal community of about 1300 residents. While you are welcome to shop at the store, camping on the community's land is subject to permission being obtained from the council.

The well-stocked *Doomadgee Retail Store* sells fuel, meat, groceries, limited hardware items, Aboriginal art and a good range of motoring accessories. It's open from 8.30 am to 5 pm Monday to Friday and from 8.30 to 11.30 am on Saturday.

Doomadgee to Burketown

Four km past Doomadgee you arrive at the **Nicholson River** crossing, which is the longest and least attractive of all the Track's fords. The river is about 600 metres across, and in the dry season its bed of solid rock presents a desolate picture. Scattered small water holes and low trees do little to gladden the eye – a swim would be nice but signs on the bank warn of saltwater crocodiles.

In remarkable contrast, the **Gregory River**, 57 km further on, presents a lush picture of running water crowded by tropical vegetation. Herons stalk the shallows, and the milky water holds promise of feasts of yabbies. However, motorists must exercise extreme care here, as the single-lane concrete crossing has a sharp bend in it and you can't see the other side. If you're towing a caravan, it would be wise to stop before the causeway and send someone across (it's only 200 metres from bank to bank) to warn any oncoming traffic of your approach.

On the other side, the little *Tirranna Roadhouse* sells fuel, ice, sit-down or takeaway meals and a few groceries (including meat, milk and bread). They can also handle minor mechanical repairs. There's also a pleasant

little camping ground out the back with shade trees and lawn, where sites cost $5 per vehicle per night. Free bush camping is available along the river.

Escott Lodge Five km before you reach Burketown, there's a turn off to *Escott Lodge* (☎ (077) 48 5577). It's another 12 km northwest from the turn off to the lodge. The lodge is a working cattle station on the Nicholson River, and has a range of accommodation for travellers. You can camp on the attractive property for $5 per person, or there's a collection of fairly basic flats and cottages which cost $45/75 for singles/doubles plus $25 for each extra person. The lodge has its own restaurant, and also offers meals-and-accommodation packages. Bed, breakfast, lunch and dinner costs $85/155 for singles/doubles. You can fish for barramundi here, and the lodge organises various other activities for its guests, including joy flights, 4WD safaris, croc-spotting cruises and clay-target shooting.

BURKETOWN (pop 230)

For many, Burketown is 'on the Gulf', but in reality it is over 30 km from the actual waters of the Gulf of Carpentaria. Even so, it sits precariously on the very flat plains that border the waters of the Gulf, just a few metres above the high-tide mark. Just a stone's throw from the waters of the Albert River, Burketown operated as a port with ships coming up the muddy waters of the river to service the town and the hinterland.

The river was first sighted by Captain John Stokes on the 1841 survey by the HMS *Beagle*. He was enthusiastic about what he thought was a rich region to the south, imagining English villages and church towers dotting the land which he called the 'Plains of Promise'.

While Burketown was named after the Burke and Wills exploration party of 1860, Burke and his party were really a long way east; other, more successful explorers came closer to Burketown and the Albert River. Then again, they didn't die!

Founded in 1865, Burketown almost came to a premature end a year later when a fever wiped out most of the residents. Then, in 1887, an extremely big tidal surge almost carried the town away, and while nothing so dramatic has occurred since, the township is often cut off from the rest of Australia by floods.

Once (by all accounts) the wildest township in Australia, Burketown today is much more peaceful and friendly. Not only is it the administrative centre for a vast region dotted with huge cattle properties, it is also a major supply centre for travellers heading to, from, or along the Gulf. Being such an important centre, it can supply all your normal requirements and, while perhaps not pretty to look at, is a good base from which to explore the surrounding area, take in a little fishing or fly out to any of the islands in the Gulf.

There are a few **historic sites** to see around the place: the old wharves, the boiling-down works (where meat, hooves and hides were processed) and, not far away, the tree emblazoned by the explorer Landsborough. Landsborough had been sent out to try and find the Burke and Wills expedition and had set up a base on the Albert River before pushing south. Like many historic sites, this one is fast decaying under the onslaught of the weather and the white ants. Soon there will be nothing here but a fence around an old tree stump. The cemetery is also interesting.

Burketown is also home to the phenomenon known as 'Morning Glory' – weird tubular cloud formations, extending the full length of the horizon, which roll out of the Gulf in the early morning, often in lines of three or four. This only happens from September to November.

Facilities
The post office on Beames St has a Commonwealth Bank agency (passbook accounts only). *Nowland's Engineering* (☎ (077) 45 5107), the Shell roadhouse next to the post office, has a Westpac agency (again, passbook accounts only).

The *Burketown General Store* (☎ (077) 45

5101), on Beames St, also sells fuel and has a supermarket, a licensed restaurant and a takeaway food section.

Organised Tours
The Burketown Pub (☎ (077) 45 5104) organises a three-hour boat trip along the Albert River on demand. The tour costs $120 for up to three people, plus another $30 for each extra person. Fuel is an additional charge.

The pub also organises a range of flying tours, as do Savannah Aviation (☎ (077) 45 5177). These include visits to Sweers Island, Lawn Hill Gorge and to Normanton to meet up with the *Gulflander*.

Festivals
Burketown hosts a number of events throughout the year. A barramundi fishing competition is held over Easter, the Burketown Rodeo is held on the second week in July, and the famous Variety Club Bash car rally comes through town in May.

Places to Stay & Eat
The *Burketown Caravan Park* (☎ (077) 45 5101), on Sloman St, has tent sites for $9.50 a double and powered sites for $12. Bookings can be made at the general store.

The *Burketown Pub* (☎ (077) 45 5104) (formerly the Albert Hotel) is the heart and soul of Burketown. Originally built as the local customs house, it's the oldest building in town – all its contemporaries have been blown over or washed away! It's a well-run outback pub and definitely worth a visit – you never know who you'll meet in the bar. It's also a good source of local information, and has a souvenir shop with Aboriginal artwork. The pub has very simple accommodation upstairs. The external rooms have air-con and cost $30/45 for singles/doubles, and the internal rooms have ceiling fans and go for $25/40. They sometimes also have backpacker beds out on the verandah, although these aren't always available. Next to the pub are four semi-permanent motel-type units with air-con, TVs and fridges – these go for $50/70.

The pub also has a small dining room and serves a good range of meals, anything from a burger for $3.50 to a $50 seafood platter for two. Steaks, roasts and barramundi dishes are regulars on the menu.

Getting There & Away
Flight West has regular flights to Burketown from Mt Isa and Cairns.

BURKETOWN TO NORMANTON (233 km)
From Burketown the Track improves as it sweeps across the flat plains of the Gulf to Normanton. The road, which follows the original coach route between Darwin and Port Douglas, was known as the Great Top Road.

Heading south out of Burketown, you'll pass the 100-year-old artesian bore on the right, just on the outskirts of town. At Harris Creek, 15 km from the centre of town, the dirt begins, and while the bitumen was pleasant, you should be used to the corrugations and the bull dust by now. If you're not, you have another few hundred km to relish the idea. Talking of bull dust, you'll find that on these vast, flat plains, it is finer, deeper and seemingly more enveloping than anywhere else in Australia. The dust hides suspension-wrenching potholes, and if you think it is bad in an air-conditioned 4WD, it is dynamite on a motorcycle!

This route is also open to conventional vehicles throughout the dry season, and shouldn't present too many problems if you take it easy. As you head south on the Burketown Road, most of the creek crossings of any note have been upgraded to a bitumen causeway-type affair. How bad the road is depends on when the graders have been out and how bad the preceding wet season has been – sometimes it can be little better than a track, while at other times it is a wide, graded road interspersed with a few corrugations, potholes and stretches of bull dust.

Floraville Station
The turn off to Floraville Station is found at the 73-km mark, on the right. A 'Historic Site' sign indicates that this is more than a station track, and it is worth the 1.3-km diversion to check the plaque and monument to Frederick Walker, who died here in 1866. He was a wild lad in his time, but a fine explorer, who had been sent out to find Burke and Wills. While he didn't find them, he did discover their Camp 119, from which they made their final push to the Gulf.

Walker's monument is found through the gate, heading towards the station. Keep left at the first track junction, about 400 metres from the road, and turn left again a short time later. By now you should be able to see the monument, down the rise a little, across a narrow creek. The station people and the homestead just a short distance away should be left alone – they are trying to run a business and, though they are friendly enough, being continually interrupted doesn't make for a productive day.

Leichhardt Falls
Just one km after the turn off to Floraville, the road drops down the sandy bank of the Leichhardt River and winds its way across the rock bar that makes up the wide bed of the river here. A narrow, short bridge crosses the stream in one spot.

The best place to pull up for a short wander, and probably the best camp on the run between Burketown and Normanton, is at the small, sandy, tree-covered island on the left, about halfway across the river's rocky bed, just past the narrow bridge. From here it is only a short walk downstream to the spectacular Leichhardt Falls. There are pools of water to cool off in (don't swim in the big stretch of water above the road crossing – there are crocs!), the trees offer plenty of shade and the birdlife is rich and varied, although the noisy corellas number in the thousands and definitely dominate the scene.

History has it that the Falls was a spot where a number of the early explorers camped on their trips through this harsh land. Both McKinlay and Landsborough camped here in 1861 in their separate expeditions to find Burke and Wills, blazing trees in the vicinity of the falls.

In a big flood, there is so much water

coming down the river that the falls are barely a ripple. Those sorts of floods occur every 10 years or so, and looking down into the gorge below the falls, you realise that once-large trees are now just sticks jutting out of the sand. It would be spectacular to fly over the falls when the river was in flood.

The owners of Floraville, who found Walker's grave and erected the monument to him, are also responsible for the thought-provoking sign near the road crossing in the middle of the riverbed. 'God Is' is all that it says. There are no facilities here, although at times the local shire puts in a couple of rubbish bins. Really, it's better to take your rubbish with you.

Leichhardt Falls to Normanton

Once you have climbed the eastern bank of the Leichhardt River, the road winds a short distance and crosses a causeway before reaching a road junction, which can be easy to miss. You are less than four km from the Floraville Station turn off, less than two km from the eastern bank of the Leichhardt and a total of 77 km from Burketown. You need to turn left here for Normanton. Heading south on the better-looking road will take you to the Burke & Wills Roadhouse, 146 km away on the Burke Developmental Road.

Turn left at the junction, go through a gate (leave it as you found it – it could be closed), and 500 metres later you will begin crossing the rough – very rough – bed of the **Alexandra River**.

After the Alexandra, the road continues in a north-easterly direction, crossing the occasional creek (some have a causeway) and ploughing through bull dust and across corrugations. The turn off to **Wernadinga station** is 16 km from the Alexandra River crossing, while the track into Inverleigh station is 84 km from the river (85 km from the road junction).

You cross the **Flinders River** 28 km past the Inverleigh turn off, and then three km later the Big Bynoe River. The Little Bynoe River is crossed 2.5 km further east. Just up the top of the eastern bank, 500 metres from

the river, is a track heading south (right); it leads less than two km to Burke and Wills' **Camp 119**. This is a good spot to have a brew, and if you want to camp, a track leads a short distance back to the edge of the **Little Bynoe**, where you can pitch a tent.

Camp 119 was the northernmost camp of the Burke and Wills expedition. Leaving their companions, Gray and King, to mind the camels and their equipment at Cooper Creek (near present-day Innamincka in South Australia), Burke and Wills pushed north across the wet and flooded country to try and reach the waters of the Gulf. It was 11 February 1861. While the water was salty and they observed a rise and fall in the tide, they were disappointed that the barrier of mangroves and mud kept them from seeing waves lapping on the shore.

Returning to Camp 119, they planned their dash back to Cooper Creek. No longer was it an exploratory expedition with mapping and observing a prime consideration, but a dash south for survival. In the end, only King survived.

Camp 119 is marked by a ring of trees and a centre one blazed by Burke and Wills. A couple of monuments also mark the spot.

All the rivers previously mentioned are home to estuarine crocodiles, so swimming is not advisable. A huge number of cattle use these places for drinking and cooling off, so unless the river is flowing, it's not recommended for drinking either.

Continuing eastwards you reach the bitumen at a road junction 32 km east of the turn off to Camp 119. Turn left here, and five km later you are in Normanton.

BURKETOWN TO CAMOOWEAL (334 km)

The road from Burketown to Camooweal via Gregory Downs is the most direct approach road for people heading for the Lawn Hill National Park, although for conventional vehicles the longer route via the Burke & Wills Roadhouse route provides much easier access, as the road is sealed for most of the route. This road is unsealed dirt all the way, and while there are no major river crossings to negotiate, the road is quite rough in patches and a 4WD vehicle is recommended. Having said all that, it is *possible* to drive this route in a conventional vehicle, particularly if the road has been recently graded. On the other hand, conditions can quickly deteriorate after heavy rain, so either way it's important to check on local conditions before heading out here.

From Burketown it's 117 km south to Gregory Downs, which is the main turn off to Lawn Hill. Gregory Downs consists of a pub and a couple of other buildings on the other side of the road. The *Gregory Downs Hotel* (☎ (077) 48 5566) has four motel units with air-con which cost $46/57 for singles/ doubles, or you can camp behind the pub on the river bank. The pub sells fuel and can handle emergency repairs, towing, welding and tyre-fitting. Meal hours are fairly inflexible here – lunch is served from noon to 1 pm, dinner from 6.30 to 8 pm. Selections include sausages ($8), T-bone steaks ($13) and fishermen's baskets ($14). At other times you can get a pie or a sausage roll.

Every Labour Day weekend in May, the pub hosts the famous Gregory River Canoe Races – a great event, and not to be missed if you're around at this time of year.

Opposite the pub is a small craft shop called YankOzzie. Housed in the old police station, it has a collection of local crafts and a few grocery items on sale. Behind the shop is the old jail, which looks like it's about to fall over. Maybe it has by now.

From Gregory Downs, it's another 217 km to Camooweal. About 40 km south the road turns from dirt to gravel as you start to move into a series of low hills. This section gets pretty bumpy, with stoney patches and sand drifts competing for your attention, and the occasional (and sudden) sharp dip to keep you on your toes, so it pays to keep your speed down along here. Sixty-nine km south of Gregory Downs, you pass the second turn off to Lawn Hill – this route is only open to 4WD vehicles.

The next section of the road resembles a dirt rollercoaster, and it's a real boneshaker in sections. One hundred and twenty-six km south of Gregory Downs the road splits in two. The left-hand branch heads south for another 58 km before meeting the Barkly Hwy, and this is the route you'll take if you're heading for Mt Isa. The right-hand branch continues south-west for another 91 km, meeting the Barkly Hwy two km west of Camooweal.

LAWN HILL NATIONAL PARK

Amid arid country 100 km west of Gregory Downs and the Camooweal to Burketown road, the Lawn Hill gorge is an oasis of gorges, creeks, ponds and tropical vegetation which the Aborigines have enjoyed for perhaps 30,000 years. Their paintings and old camping sites abound. Two rock-art sites have been made accessible to visitors.

The gorge was formed by the waters of the Lawn Hill Creek, which is fed by a network of springs in the limestone plateaus west of the park. The creek is surrounded by an abundance of plant life including cabbage palms, Leichhardt pines, figs, river red gums and pandanus palms. There are freshwater crocodiles – the inoffensive variety – in the creek, as well as short-necked tortoises and various freshwater fish. Also in the park are extensive and virtually unexplored limestone formations.

Getting there is the problem – it's a beautiful, pristine place that's miles from anywhere or anybody. There are a couple of different ways of getting there, and, as mentioned above, the easiest route for conventional vehicles is to come via the Burke & Wills Roadhouse. If you're coming along the Camooweal to Burketown road, 4WD vehicles are recommended, though they are not always necessary in the dry season.

There's a camping ground with showers and toilets beside the Lawn Hill Creek. Sites can be booked with the park rangers (☎ (077) 48 5572) or through the QNP&WS in Mt Isa (☎ (077) 43 2055).

There are 20 km of walking tracks alongside and around the gorge, providing access to places like the Island Stack, Duwadarri Water hole, a limestone dam, a two-metre waterfall and a natural spa. You can also

GULF SAVANNAH

explore the gorge in a canoe or inflatable raft – if you don't have your own, these can be hired from the kiosk at Adel's Grove.

There's a Savannah Guide Post at Adel's Grove, 10 km east of the entrance to the park. The *Adel's Grove Kiosk* (☎ (077) 48 5502) has a camping ground with tent and caravan sites, running water and hot showers. It costs $4 per person to camp here. They also have four pre-erected tents with beds and linen which cost $13 per person. There's a small kiosk here that sells basic food supplies, fuel, ice and cold drinks. The kiosk also rents out canoes from here or at the gorge, costing $6 an hour. There's an airstrip nearby.

CLONCURRY TO NORMANTON (375 km)

The major road into the Gulf from the south is the Burke Developmental Rd, which runs from Cloncurry to Normanton. This is the last section of the route known as the Matilda Hwy, which starts way down south at Cunnamulla near the Queensland/New South Wales border. The highway is bitumen all the way and in excellent condition.

Quamby, 43 km north of Cloncurry, was once a Cobb & Co coach stop and a centre for the gold mining that helped develop the region. Quamby now has nothing but the historic *Quamby Hotel* (☎ (077) 42 5952). The pub has simple accommodation with air-con costing $20 a room, and an in-ground pool. It serves breakfast, lunch and dinner, from burgers and pies to steaks and schnitzels. The pub's owner also does horse-drawn stagecoach tours, and was planning to start offering overnight trips from Quamby to Kajabbi and back – check with him for the latest. Fuel is also available here.

Continuing north across the rolling hills dotted with low, spindly gums, you reach the turn off to **Kajabbi** 29 km north of Quamby. Once the focus of the area, Kajabbi has been all but forgotten. The town was once the railhead for this part of the Gulf's cattle industry and the nearby copper mines, but all that has long since disappeared. The *Kalkadoon Hotel* (☎ (077) 42 5979) is the focal point for locals and visitors alike. From here there is much to explore, including the

Mt Cuthbert Mine site, and Battle Mountain, the site of the last stand of the local warlike Kalkadoon people, who resisted the White invasion in bloody battles during the 1880s.

Just before you get to the Burke & Wills Roadhouse along the Burke Developmental Road, 180 km north of Cloncurry, the Wills Developmental Road from Julia Creek joins the road you are on from the right.

Nearly everyone stops at the *Burke & Wills Roadhouse* (☎ (077) 42 5909) where there's a little shade, some greenery at any time of the year, ice creams to buy from the well-stocked store and, if you really need it, fuel. You can camp here for $3.50 per person, and there are four air-con rooms at $30/40 for singles/doubles.

From the roadhouse you can strike northwest along the Wills Developmental Road to the fabulous Gregory River and the equally famous *Gregory Downs Hotel* (see the Burketown to Camooweal section). From there the reasonable dirt road leads to Burketown.

For those travelling on to Normanton, the route continues in a more northerly direction towards the Gulf. The country remains reasonably flat, but once you get to **Bang Bang Jump-up** and descend the 40-odd metres to the Gulf plains proper, you really know what 'flat' means. This near-sheer escarpment vividly marks where the high country ends, 80 km north of the roadhouse.

From this point the road stretches across vast, billiard-table-flat plains covered in deep grass, which in the Dry is the colour of gold. Dotted here and there are clumps of trees, and wherever there is permanent water or shade there are cattle. In this country the cattle stand out – during the day. At night, as everywhere in outback Queensland, they can make driving on the roads very hazardous. If you have to drive, do so with extreme care; if you make a habit of it, invest in a good set of driving lights.

GULF ISLANDS

There are numerous islands scattered in the Gulf of Carpentaria north of Burketown, most of which are Aboriginal communities and are not open to visitors. There are, however, a couple of places set up specifically to cater to people wanting to fish the abundant waters of the Gulf. Reef fish such as coral trout, sweetlip, cod, and red emperor, as well as mackerel and tuna, are all plentiful.

Mornington Island

The largest of the Gulf Islands, Mornington Island has an Aboriginal community administered from Gununa, on the south-west coast.

On the north-west coast of the island is the *Birri Fishing Resort* (☎ (077) 45 7277), a remote lodge which caters for anglers. The lodge is open from the last week in March to the end of October; the cost is $220 per person per day, including meals, accommodation, fishing guides and all tackle and boat hire.

There are regular flights to the island from Karumba, and you can also fly to the island from Burketown – see those sections for details.

Sweers Island

The smaller Sweers Island, midway between Burketown and Mornington Island, became the headquarters of the Gulf district after an outbreak of fever in Burketown in 1865, but because of its remoteness Normanton later took over as the administrative centre. Today, Sweers Island also has its own fishing resort.

The *Sweers Island Resort* (☎ (077) 48 5544) has cabin-style accommodation with shared bathroom facilities and caters for families and anglers. The nightly tariff is $155 per person per night, which includes all meals, boat hire, fuel, bait and handlines. You'll need to book during the peak Spanish mackerel season (June to August).

You can also camp at the resort – there are showers, toilets and a laundry, and you can cook for yourself or eat at the resort's dining area. Lunch costs $10, dinner $25.

There are flights to the island from Karumba and Burketown; Savannah Aviation (☎ (077) 45 5177) also has day trips to the resort from Burketown for $65 per person.

Outback Queensland

This chapter covers Queensland's vast outback region. Stretching westward beyond the mountains of the Great Dividing Range, the mythical outback is truly, in the well-worn words of Dorothea Mackellar, '...a sunburnt country, a land of sweeping plains, of rugged mountain ranges, of droughts and flooding rains...'.

The outback has some outstanding attractions, including the Australian Workers Heritage Centre in Barcaldine, the Stockman's Hall of Fame & Outback Heritage Centre in Longreach, and the Birdsville Working Museum. But the outback isn't really about attractions or sights, it's essentially about experiences – the characters you meet in pubs and roadhouses; the sense of exhilaration from being in the middle of nowhere in the shimmering heat, surrounded by silence, spinifex and sand; the acute boredom of sitting behind the wheel watching the unchanging landscape for hour after hour...

There are plenty of reminders of the outback's unique history out here, from the old stone and timber buildings bleached by the suns of a hundred summers to the fascinating tales of the early explorers and pioneers who opened up the region to white settlement.

Remember that this is harsh, unforgiving country – as the locals say, you should never underestimate the outback. No matter how safe you feel sitting in your air-conditioned cruiser, expect the unexpected. The combination of the extreme temperatures, scarcity of water and isolation make it one of the few places in the world where your survival is in your hands – there is no replacement for good preparation.

History

Ludwig Leichhardt crossed the outback's Western Plains on his way to Port Essington in the Northern Territory in 1844. Over the next 20 years, some of Australia's greatest explorers, including Thomas Mitchell (later

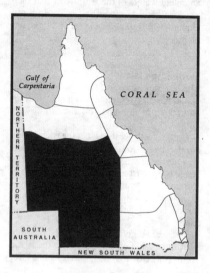

knighted for his exploration achievements), Burke and Wills, William Landsborough, Augustus Gregory and John McKinlay, crisscrossed the vast plains and the low rugged ranges of outback Queensland. In the process they opened up this land to the sheep and cattle graziers who quickly followed.

Geography

The area 'out back' of the Great Dividing Range is a vast, semi-arid region known as the Western Plains. Beneath these endless grassy plains lies the Great Artesian Basin, an enormous underground water supply that supports the outback's sheep and cattle stations. The arid south-west corner of the state, known as the Channel Country, is cut by innumerable rivers and creeks that remain dry all year until they are filled to overflowing by waters flowing down from the north of the state during the Wet.

The outback isn't all flat land – there are several low mountain ranges in the region including the ancient Selwyn Range east of Mt Isa, the Aramac Range north of Barcaldine, and the Grey Range which stretches from near Blackall down to the New South Wales border.

The outback's major river systems include the Diamantina, Thomson, Barcoo, Bulloo and Warrego rivers.

Climate
Summer isn't a great time to visit the outback. Average temperatures are over 35°C and frequently soar towards 50°C, and travelling in such extreme temperatures can be hazardous. Summer is also the time of the Wet, when the monsoonal rains in the north of the state fill the region's hundreds of rivers and creeks, flooding vast areas of the Channel Country and cutting many of the outback roads.

Conditions are much more favourable in the cooler months between April and October, with generally mild to warm days and temperatures seldom topping 30°C, although it can be bitterly cold at night in winter when temperatures below freezing are not uncommon.

Rain is a rare occurrence in the outback, with the southern areas averaging around 150 mm a year. Rainfall is slightly heavier north of the Tropic of Capricorn, particularly in the summer months, but you still won't find many uses for an umbrella out here, apart from as a sun shade.

Getting There & Away
Air The major towns of the outback are serviced by Flight West Airlines, which flies between Brisbane and Birdsville via Charleville, Quilpie and Windorah; from Brisbane and Townsville to Longreach and Winton; and from Cairns and Townsville to Cloncurry and Mt Isa.

Ansett also flies to Mt Isa from Cairns and Brisbane. Augusta Airways flies from Port Augusta in South Australia to Birdsville, Bedourie and Boulia on Saturday, and back on Sunday.

Bus There are three major bus routes through the outback – from Townsville to Mt Isa via Hughenden, from Rockhampton to Longreach via Emerald, and from Brisbane to Mt Isa via Roma and Longreach. All three routes are serviced by both Greyhound Pioneer Australia and McCafferty's. Buses continue from Mt Isa to Three Ways in the Northern Territory, from where you can head north to Darwin or south to Alice Springs.

Train Similarly, there are three train services from the coast to the outback, all running twice-weekly: the *Spirit of the Outback* runs from Brisbane to Longreach via Rockhampton, with connecting bus services continuing on to Winton; the *Westlander* runs from Brisbane to Charleville, with connecting bus services to Cunnamulla and Quilpie; and the *Inlander* runs from Townsville to Mt Isa.

Car & Motorcycle The outback, although sparsely settled, is well serviced by major roads – the Flinders Hwy connects northern Queensland with the Northern Territory, meeting the Barkly Hwy at Cloncurry, the Capricorn Hwy runs along the Tropic of Capricorn from Rockhampton to Longreach, while the Landsborough and Mitchell highways run from the New South Wales border south of Cunnamulla right up to Mt Isa.

Once off these major arteries however, road conditions deteriorate rapidly, services are extremely limited and you need to be fully self-sufficient, carrying spare parts, fuel and water. With the correct preparation, it's possible to make the great outback journeys down the tracks which connect Queensland with South Australia – the Strzelecki and Birdsville tracks.

Charters Towers to Camooweal – the Flinders & Barkly Hwys

The Flinders Hwy, which stretches for almost 770 km from Townsville to Cloncurry, is the major route across the top of outback Queensland. From Cloncurry, the

Barkly Hwy picks up where the Flinders Hwy leaves off and takes you on to Mt Isa, Camooweal and into the Northern Territory.

As a scenic drive, this is probably the most boring route in Queensland, although there are a few minor points of interest along the way to break the monotony. Apart from the Charters Towers to Torrens Creek section, which passes through the Great Dividing Range, the terrain is flat as a pancake and features a seemingly endless landscape of dry, grassy plains. There is little visual relief until you pass Cloncurry and reach the low red hills that surround Mt Isa.

The highway is paved all the way and is generally in better condition than much of the coastal Bruce Hwy. The inland railway line runs beside the highway for the majority of the route.

Greyhound Pioneer Australia and McCafferty's operate daily services along the Townsville to Mt Isa route and on to the Northern Territory. The *Inlander* train follows an almost identical route twice weekly, with stops at most towns along the way.

CHARTERS TOWERS TO HUGHENDEN (243 km)

It's 243 km from Charters Towers to Hughenden. This route is a former Cobb & Co stage run, and along its length are a series of tiny townships which were originally established as stopovers for the coaches. The theory is that the towns are evenly spaced – with roughly a day's run for the Cobb & Co horses between each one.

The first section of the route, from Charters Towers to Torrens Creek, passes through the hills of the Great Dividing Range. Beyond Torrens Creek, the land soon starts to become flatter and drier, trees start to become a rarity and the flat grassy plains begin.

The small settlement of **Pentland**, 105 km west of Charters Towers, has a small art gallery and craft store, the *Pentland Hotel-Motel*, a Shell service station, a general store and a caravan park.

Another 50 km on is **Torrens Creek**. The *Exchange Hotel* (☎ (077) 41 7342) has grassy camp sites beside the pub which cost $4 per person, one on-site van at $25 a

The Art of the Drive-By Wave

Driving along these long, remote roads of the outback certainly gives you plenty of time to contemplate life, loneliness and the transient nature of contemporary existence. In the days of yore when the pace of the world was much gentler, travellers would have the time to stop and chat with those riding or walking the other way and exchange news and information, such as which inns had the softest beds, the best meals, the coldest beer etc. Nowadays all of this has been compressed into a split-second greeting as we zoom past each other on smooth black-topped highways, encased in our metal contraptions, at collective speeds of over 200 km an hour.

The incidence of the drive-by wave rises in direct proportion to the remoteness of the road being travelled. Closer to the coast and larger cities, hardly anyone acknowledges other drivers, but as you head into the outback you'll start to notice passing drivers waving at you. At first you might think all these waves are identical, but a closer study will reveal subtle but significant variations in the wave.

The most common method is the four-finger version, in which the thumb remains hooked around the steering wheel while the four fingers of the right hand are raised in an abrupt, Nazi-style salute. This is widely recognised as the state of the art drive-by wave. Variations include the nonchalant one or two finger-wave – this is usually practiced by seasoned outback travellers, although an imitative version is often attempted by novices attempting to be incredibly cool. At the other extreme is the full-hand wave, where the right hand actually leaves the steering wheel. Those employing this potentially dangerous method are probably deeply lonely, insecure people, desperate for a fleeting moment of on-the-road acceptance that they can never hope to achieve back in urban society. ∎

Outback Queensland

double, and pub-style rooms at $20/30 for singles/doubles. The pub serves bistro meals, sells fuel and has its own 9-hole bush golf course.

South of Torrens Creek, Cheltenham (☎ (077) 41 7306) is a 10,000 hectare working cattle station with rustic accommodation in the former shearers' quarters. The daily tariff is $90 per person, which includes all meals and station activities.

It's another 44 km to the aptly-named town of **Prairie**, which consists of a small cluster of houses around a railway station and a hotel. The *Prairie Hotel* (☎ (077) 41

5121) is an interesting old pub. It was first licensed in 1884, but operated for about a dozen years before that as a Cobb & Co coach stop – you can still see the old rounding yard out in the backyard. The pub is run by a friendly couple, and has a good collection of old artefacts, tools, riding gear and photos. It even has its own ghost (you can read about him in the pub). Travellers can camp out the back of the pub and use the facilities for $5. There are also two basic pub rooms at $15/30, and two simple units with their own bathrooms at $30/40. Meals are served every day and night except Sunday.

Next to the pub is the *Prairie Cafe*, where you can buy fuel and takeaway meals.

HUGHENDEN (pop 1600)

Hughenden is on the banks of the Flinders River, in the same spot where explorer William Landsborough camped in 1862 during his fruitless search for survivors from the Burke and Wills expedition. Today Hughenden is a busy commercial centre that services the surrounding cattle, wool and grain industries. It's also the junction of the railway line which heads south to Winton and Longreach.

The town bills itself as the home of beauty and the beast. The 'beauty' is the Porcupine Gorge National Park, 65 km north of town; the 'beast' is imprisoned in the **Dinosaur Display Centre**, a large tin shed on Gray St.

Inside the display centre is a replica of the skeleton of *Muttaburrasaurus*, one of the largest and most complete dinosaur skeletons ever found in Australia. It was found by a grazier in 1961 in a cattle holding yard at Muttaburra, 206 km south of Hughenden. The University of Queensland reconstructed the skeleton based on similar finds in Europe, and donated a replica to the town some years ago. *Muttaburrasaurus* was an enormous plant-eating dinosaur and dates back 100 million years – the skeleton is seven metres long and three metres high. The centre also has a few locally found fossils and other historic relics on display.

Information

Tourist Information The Hughenden Garden Centre (☎ (077) 41 1493), near the Dinosaur Display Centre, at 33 Gray St, acts as a local tourist information centre. It is open on weekdays from 10 am to 4 pm and Saturday from 10 am to noon.

Post & Money Hughenden has a Commonwealth Bank and a National Bank, both on Brodie St, and an ANZ Bank and a post office, which are both on the corner of Gray and Brodie Sts.

Fuel & Services Close Auto Sales (☎ (077) 41 1311), the BP service station on the Richmond side of town, is the local RACQ depot. The Shell Top of the Hill Roadhouse, two km west of town, is open 24 hours. It accepts all credit cards but doesn't have EFTPOS facilities.

Places to Stay & Eat

The *Allan Terry Caravan Park* (☎ (077) 41 1190), on the Winton road and opposite the railway station, has tent sites for $8 and on-site vans from $20. The town swimming pool is next door, although the railway yard opposite is a bit noisy.

On the corner of Gray and Stanfield Sts is the *Grand Hotel* (☎ (077) 41 1588), a classic old two-storey timber pub which was built in 1912. The upstairs rooms are timber-lined and fairly basic but well presented. Singles/doubles cost $15/30, or $40 with air-con. There's a big old dining room downstairs that serves country-style tucker on Friday and Saturday nights, with main meals ranging from $9 to $15. The family that runs the pub are country-music fans, and they have a barbecue dinner with live music here every second Saturday night.

The *Rest Easi Motel* (☎ (077) 41 1633), on the highway on the western outskirts, is a neat little motel with a pool and motel units at $45/55, as well as camp sites for $11 and powered sites for $13.

There are a couple of eateries along Brodie St: the *White Swan Cafe*, at No 55, has passable toasted sandwiches, as well as burgers and the like; *Chang's Chinese Restaurant* is at No 31; and the *Hughenden Coffee Lounge* is at No 27.

PORCUPINE GORGE NATIONAL PARK

If the weather has been dry, and you're not in a hurry and have a vehicle, take a trip out to Porcupine Gorge National Park. Known locally as 'Australia's Little Grand Canyon', it's an oasis in the dry country north of Hughenden off the mostly unpaved, often corrugated Kennedy Developmental Road.

The best spot to drive to is **Pyramid Lookout**, about 70 km north of Hughenden.

You can camp here and it's an easy 30-minute walk down into the gorge, with some fine rock formations and a permanently running creek. Few people come here and there's a fair bit of wildlife. The Kennedy Developmental Road would eventually take you to the Atherton Tableland, but it would be a pretty rough trip, particularly during the wet season.

RICHMOND (pop 630)
Like most of the towns out here, Richmond exists primarily to service the local cattle and sheep industries. The town is set on the Flinders River and last century, before the railway line was built, was one of the major stopovers for Cobb & Co coaches. There's a restored **Cobb & Co mail coach** in a cage beside the main intersection – it's worth stopping here and considering what it would have been like travelling in one of these things, drawn by feisty horses over unpaved roads through the heat and dust. Makes the hours you've just spent sitting in your air-conditioned car or bus a lot less agonising, doesn't it?

The area around Richmond is abundant in sandalwood, and a factory in the town processes the wood for export to Asia, where it is used for incense and joss sticks.

Information
Fuel & Services The Midway Motel Roadhouse (☎ (077) 41 3192), an Ampol service station on the east side of town, is open 24 hours. It has EFTPOS facilities and takes all major credit cards. Richmond Panel Repairs (☎ (077) 41 3258) is the local RACQ depot and handles towing and repairs.

Places to Stay & Eat
The *Richmond Caravan Park* (☎ (077) 41 2772), on the eastern outskirts, is a tiny council-run caravan park with tent sites at $5 and powered sites at $10. It's about as basic as they come, and features a few trees, a white water tower and toilet blocks.

There are two pubs on Goldring St which do meals and accommodation. The friendly *Federal Palace Hotel* (☎ (077) 41 3463), at 64 Goldring St, has pub-style rooms, some opening up onto the balcony, with shared bathrooms. Singles/doubles cost $19/34. They also serve a good range of bistro meals, with most mains costing $6 to $10. Judging by my T-bone steak, it's good, basic pub grub – nothing flashy, but it'll fill you up and keep you going. Like most pubs out here, there are no meals on Sunday.

Nearby, the *Mud Hut Hotel-Motel* (☎ (077) 41 3223) has a choice of pub-style rooms at $15/25 or motel units with air-con at $35/45. This place also has bistro meals at similar prices. The pub was built in the 1890s from flagstones and adobe mud. Unfortunately the original walls have been covered over, but you can see some sections of the old walls inside the pub.

The *Midway Motel Roadhouse* (☎ (077) 41 3192), on the east side of town, also has air-con motel units at $32/42.

JULIA CREEK (pop 570)
It's another flat and featureless 144 km from Richmond to Julia Creek, a small pastoral centre which specialises in selling and transporting cattle.

Four km west of Julia Creek, the sealed Wills Developmental Rd leaves the highway and heads north to the *Burke & Wills Roadhouse* (235 km). From the roadhouse you can continue north to Normanton and Karumba; you can also reach Burketown this way. See the Gulf Savannah chapter for more details.

Places to Stay
The *Julia Creek Caravan Park* (☎ (077) 46 7305), at the end of Julia St, has tent sites from $8 a double – the town's swimming pool is nearby.

In the centre of town is the *Gannon Hotel-Motel* (☎ (077) 46 7103), a typical little country pub with yellow weatherboards, a tin roof and a verandah. Motel-style units here go for $35/45 for singles/doubles. The *Julia Creek Motel* (☎ (077) 46 7305), on the highway on the west side of town, has rooms with air-con from $48/56.

Places to Eat

Julia Creek has a pretty limited range of eating options. There are a couple of cafes and takeaways, including the *Oasis Coffee Lounge*. If you want a sit-down meal you could try the pub, or the *Town & Country Club*, on the highway just west of the centre, which also serves bistro meals in the $8 to $10 range. It opens for lunch and dinner from Monday to Saturday.

JULIA CREEK TO CLONCURRY (134 km)

Terrain-wise, it's more of the same for this 134-km stretch of the highway – which means more of those flat, treeless plains you've grown to love by now, and not much to see apart from the cattle which frequently graze along the side of the highway. They can be quite a hazard to drivers as they often wander onto and across the road – stay alert!

CLONCURRY (pop 2310)

The centre for a copper boom in the last century, Cloncurry was the largest copper producer in the British empire in 1916. Today it's a busy little pastoral centre with four pubs, several service stations and a couple of attractions for passing tourists.

The town's major claim to fame is as the birthplace of the Royal Flying Doctor Service. The **John Flynn Place Museum & Art Gallery**, on the corner of Daintree and King Sts, is a well set up museum, with interesting exhibits on the Flying Doctor Service, the School of the Air and mining. Displays include the first Traegar pedal wireless, an automatic Morse keyboard, a one-third-scale model of the single-engine Victory DH50 in which the flying doctor service began, informative signboards, old photos and documents, and a good art gallery. The museum is open on weekdays from 7 am to 4 pm and, from May to October, on weekends from 9 am to 3 pm. Entry costs $4 for adults, $2 for children or $10 for a

family. If you're feeling the heat, the town's **swimming pool** is opposite the museum.

Cloncurry's **Mary Kathleen Park & Museum**, just off the highway on the eastern side of town, is partly housed in buildings transported from the former uranium-mining town of Mary Kathleen. The collection includes relics of the Burke and Wills expedition and a big collection of local rocks and minerals. You can see steam engines outside for free. Opening hours and admission prices are the same as for the John Flynn Place Museum.

The Burke Developmental Road, which takes you north from Cloncurry, is paved all the way to Normanton (375 km) and Karumba (449 km) near the Gulf of Carpentaria. Burketown is 443 km from Cloncurry. See the Gulf Savannah chapter for details of these routes.

Information

Post & Money Cloncurry has a National Bank and a post office with a Commonwealth Bank agency, both on Sheaffe St, and a Westpac Bank on Ramsay St.

Fuel & Services Nev's Auto (☎ (077) 42 1243), on the corner of Ramsay and Sheaffe Sts, is the local RACQ agent and does all mechanical repairs and 24-hour towing.

John Flynn – Founder of the Royal Flying Doctor Service

OUTBACK QUEENSLAND

Places to Stay & Eat

The *Cloncurry Caravan Park* (☎ (077) 42 1313) opposite the museum has tent sites for $10 or you can take an on-site van for $28 a double. On the corner of Sheaffe and Scarr Sts, the *Central Hotel* (☎ (077) 42 1418) has basic pub rooms, some with air-con, at $15/30 for singles/doubles.

There are two motels here. The cheapest option, the *Wagon Wheel Motel* (☎ (077) 42 1866) at 54 Ramsay St, has budget singles/doubles at $35/45 and newer units at $55. The motel is fronted by a historic building which houses a restaurant and motel reception. The restaurant opens nightly for dinner and serves basic country tucker with main meals ranging from $8 to $16. There is an interesting collection of old B&W photos on display.

The best of Cloncurry's accommodation options is the *Gilbert Park Cabins* (☎ (077) 42 2300), a set of 20 modern units on the highway on the eastern edge of town. The units sleep up to five people, have air-con and are self-contained. Singles/doubles cost $42/48 without linen or a hefty $50/55 with linen supplied, plus $6 for each additional person. I guess they hate doing the laundry as much as the rest of us.

CLONCURRY TO MT ISA (124 km)

After Cloncurry, the terrain finally starts to change as you leave behind the prairies and pass into the low, rocky, scrub-scattered red hills that surrounds Mt Isa.

This 124-km stretch of the Flinders Hwy has a number of interesting stops. Beside the **Corella River**, 41 km west of Cloncurry, there's a memorial cairn to the Burke and Wills expedition, which passed here in 1861. Another km down the road is the **Kalkadoon & Mitakoodi Memorial**, which marks an old

Last Stand of the Kalkadoons

Before the coming of the Europeans, the arid and rocky hill country to the north-west of Mt Isa was home to the Kalkadoons, one of the fiercest and most warlike of the Aboriginal tribes. The Kalkadoons, who had lived in this rugged and inhospitable area for many generations, were one of the last tribes to resist white settlement, and from the mid-1870s fought an ongoing battle against the pastoralists and the Native Police.

They were a formidable and feared opponent, often using guerilla tactics to attack settlers and troops. Warriors decorated themselves with body-paint and feathers, and used pole clubs and razor-sharp tomahawks and knives made from local stone for weapons. Hudson Fysh describes a Kalkadoon tribesman in his book *Taming the North: The Story of Alexander Kennedy and Other Queensland Pathfinders*: 'When a big member of the Kalkadoon tribe, standing over six feet high and broad in proportion, was done up ready for a ceremonial corroboree he was a fearsome object indeed. With several large emu or eaglehawk feathers decorating his head, his already tall stature is increased. His broad face, stretched wide open in a resounding yell, is banded around with minute white feathers stuck on with dried blood'.

In 1884 the authorities sent Frederic Urquhart, the Sub-Inspector of Police, to the region to take command, but the Kalkadoons continued to ambush and attack the invaders. In September of that year, Urquhart gathered his troops and local squatters and, heavily armed, they rode to the rocky hill which came to be known as Battle Mountain.

When they saw the mounted troops, the Kalkadoons formed themselves into ranks and made a series of disciplined but suicidal charges down the hill. With only their spears for weapons, they stood no chance against the carbines of the troopers, and were mowed down in waves until they were all but wiped out. Only a handful of tribesmen survived, and the massacre marked the end of Aboriginal resistance in the region.

A memorial beside the Barkly Highway, 42 km west of Cloncurry, is inscribed with the words: *'You who pass by are now entering the ancient tribal lands of the Kalkadoon/Mitakoodi, dispossessed by the European. Honour their name, be brother and sister to their descendants.'* ■

Aboriginal tribal boundary. When I was last there the monument had been defaced by redneck graffiti morons, but it's still worth stopping here. Each side of the stone wall is inscribed with dedications to the Kalkadoon and Mitakoodi people, with brass plaques bearing poems dedicated to them.

Nine km further on you pass the (unmarked) former site of **Mary Kathleen**, a uranium-mining town from the 1950s to 1982. It has been completely demolished.

The turning to **Lake Julius**, Mt Isa's reserve water supply, is 36 km beyond Mary Kathleen. It's 90 km of unsealed road from the highway to the lake, which is on the Leichhardt River. This is a good spot for fishing, canoeing, sailing and water-skiing, and a popular day trip from Mt Isa.

One km from the dam is the *Lake Julius Recreation Camp* (☎ (077) 42 5998), an accommodation complex run by the Department of Tourism, Sport & Racing. You have a choice of camp sites ($2.60 per person) or dormitory beds ($5.50 per person), or there are seven self-contained units with air-con that sleep from five to eight people and cost $32.60 a night for up to four people plus $6.30 for each extra adult.

North-east of Lake Julius is the tiny town of **Kajabbi**, a former mining settlement on the banks of the Leichhardt River. There are about 25 people still living in the town, and you can stay at the historic *Kalkadoon Hotel* (☎ (077) 42 5979), a turn-of-the-century pub which was moved here from the mining town of Mt Cuthbert in 1938. The pub is renowned for its character, and Trevor the guitar-playing, singing publican hosts barbecues every Saturday night and the Kajabbi Yabby Races every April. The pub has basic rooms for $15 a bed, plus a couple of units at $22 per person. It serves breakfasts and dinners, and lunches by request.

From Kajabbi you can explore several abandoned copper-mining towns such as Dobbyn and Mt Cuthbert.

South of Kajabbi is **Battle Mountain**, which was the scene of the last stand of the Kalkadoon people in 1884, a rare pitched battle between Aborigines and Europeans.

MT ISA (pop 23,400)
The mining town of Mt Isa owes its existence to an immensely rich copper, silver, lead and zinc mine, and the skyline is dominated by the massive 270-metre-high exhaust stack from the lead smelter. 'The Isa', as the town is known locally, is inland Queensland's major town and also lays claim to being the largest city in the world since the area administered by its city council stretches 188 km west as far as Camooweal and covers nearly 41,000 sq km (which is about the same size as Switzerland).

It's a rough-and-ready though prosperous town, and the job opportunities here have attracted people from about 60 different ethnic groups. There are plenty of low-cost accommodation options for travellers stopping over, and you can tour the mine.

The first Mt Isa deposits were discovered in 1923 by a prospector called John Campbell Miles who gave Mt Isa its name – a corruption of Mt Ida, a goldfield in Western Australia. Since the ore deposits were large and low grade, working them required the sort of investment only a company could make. Mt Isa Mines was founded in 1924. Life was predicably rough and tough in Mt Isa's early days and the Isa Hotel had a 'bullring' in its backyard where men could sort out their differences without disturbing others. It was during and after WW II that Mt Isa really took off and today it's the Western world's biggest silver and lead producer, and ranks in the top 10 for production of copper and zinc. Virtually the whole town is run by Mt Isa Mines, and the ore is railed 900 km to Townsville on the coast.

Orientation
Mt Isa is divided in two by the Leichhardt River, which runs north-south through the centre of the town. The Barkly Hwy is the main route in from the east, taking you past the tourist information centre and through the centre of town, before crossing the river and heading north. The town centre, a fairly compact area bordered by Grace, West, Isa and Simpson Sts, is immediately east of the

Leichhardt River. Across on the west side of the river are the mine itself, the railway station and the bus terminal.

Information

Tourist Information The tourist information office (☎ (077) 43 7966), on Marian St (the Barkly Hwy), has recently been redeveloped to incorporate the Riversleigh Interpretive Centre, and will feature a collection of fossils which were found at Riversleigh Station, 250 km north-west of Mt Isa. The centre is open Monday to Friday from 8 am to 5 pm, plus Saturday and Sunday (between April and September) from 8.30 am to 1.30 pm.

Post & Money Mt Isa's main post office is on Isa St near the corner of Camooweal St, and is open on weekdays from 9 am to 5 pm. All the major banks have branches in the city centre; the ANZ, National and Commonwealth banks are in Miles St, and the Westpac Bank is in West St.

Useful Organisations The RACQ has an office (☎ (077) 43 2542), at 15 Simpson St. The Queensland National Parks & Wildlife Service (QNP&WS) district office (☎ (077) 43 2055), on the corner of Hilary and Butler Sts, is open on weekdays from 9 am to 5 pm, and can provide info on all the national parks in the area including Lawn Hill and Camooweal Caves. The QNP&WS also has an information section in the Riversleigh Interpretive Centre next to the tourist office.

Bookshop The Crusade Bookshop, at 11 Simpson St, is the best between Townsville and Darwin.

Laundry The City Laundromat is right in the centre of things at 12 Miles St.

Outdoor Gear Curly Dan's Outdoor World, on Simpson St, stocks a good range of camping and fishing gear.

The Mine

The mine is the town's major attraction and there are two tours available.

The three-hour underground tour, for which you don a hard hat and a miner's suit, takes you down into some of the 4600 km of tunnels. Since only nine people are allowed on each tour, it's advisable to book as far ahead as possible by phoning the visitors centre (☎ (077) 44 2104). You also have to be over 16 years of age to take this tour. Tours leave at 8 and 11.45 am Monday to Friday and cost $25.

The two-hour surface tours (by bus) are run by Campbell's Coaches (☎ (077) 43 2006) – they depart from their terminal at 27 Barkly Hwy, or they can pick you up from your accommodation if there are more than four people. Between April and September, tours depart at 9 am and 1 pm on weekdays and at 9 am on weekends; from October to March, they only depart at 9 am on weekdays. The cost is $12 for adults and $6 for kids. It's well worth the money, especially as the bus takes you right through the major workshops and the mine site, and the price includes a visit to the company's mining display and visitors centre. You need to be wearing enclosed shoes to take this tour.

John Middlin Mining Display & Visitors Centre

This visitors centre, on Church St near the town centre, has various displays which teach you about the mining operations. They include informative photograph display boards, ore and mineral samples, an audio-visual programme, and even a 'simulated underground experience'. Between April and October, the centre is open on weekdays from 9 am to 4 pm and on weekends from 9 am to 2 pm. During the rest of the year it is open from 9 am to noon and from 1 to 4 pm on weekdays, and from 10 am to noon on weekends. Entry costs $4 for adults and $2 for kids.

Other Attractions

The **Frank Aston Museum** is a partially underground complex on a hill close to the town centre at the corner of Shackleton and Marian Sts. This rambling place has a diverse and interesting collection ranging

OUTBACK QUEENSLAND

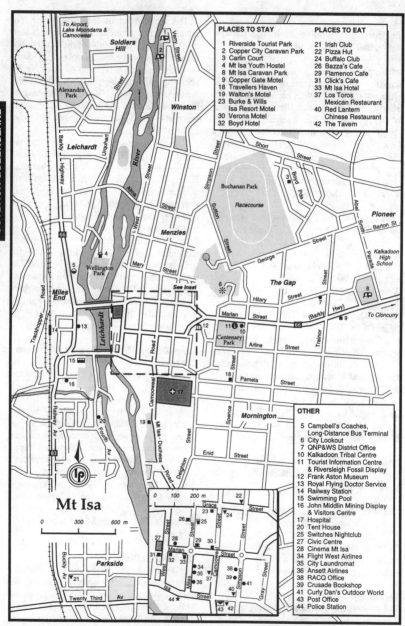

PLACES TO STAY

1 Riverside Tourist Park
2 Copper City Caravan Park
3 Carlin Court
4 Mt Isa Youth Hostel
8 Mt Isa Caravan Park
9 Copper Gate Motel
18 Travellers Haven
19 Walton's Motel
23 Burke & Wills
   Isa Resort Motel
30 Verona Motel
32 Boyd Hotel

PLACES TO EAT

21 Irish Club
22 Pizza Hut
24 Buffalo Club
26 Bazza's Cafe
29 Flamenco Cafe
31 Click's Cafe
33 Mt Isa Hotel
37 Los Toros
   Mexican Restaurant
40 Red Lantern
   Chinese Restaurant
42 The Tavern

OTHER

5 Campbell's Coaches,
  Long-Distance Bus Terminal
6 City Lookout
7 QNP&WS District Office
10 Kalkadoon Tribal Centre
11 Tourist Information Centre
   & Riversleigh Fossil Display
12 Frank Aston Museum
13 Royal Flying Doctor Service
14 Railway Station
15 Swimming Pool
16 John Middlin Mining Display
   & Visitors Centre
17 Hospital
20 Tent House
25 Switches Nightclub
27 Civic Centre
28 Cinema Mt Isa
34 Flight West Airlines
35 City Laundromat
36 Ansett Airlines
38 RACQ Office
39 Crusade Bookshop
43 Curly Dan's Outdoor World
43 Post Office
44 Police Station

Mt Isa

from old mining gear to ageing flying doctor radios, and displays on the Lardil Aborigines of Mornington Island in the Gulf of Carpentaria and the Kalkadoon people from the Mt Isa area. It is open every day from 10 am to 3 pm and costs $4. The museum is closed during summer.

It is possible to visit the **Royal Flying Doctor Service** base, on the Barkly Hwy, on weekdays from 9 am to 5 pm and on weekends from 10 am to 2 pm. The $2.50 admission includes a film.

The **School of the Air**, which brings education by radio to children in remote places, is based at the Kalkadoon High School on Abel Smith Pde. It's open for public tours at 10 and 11 am on school days; the tours cost $2.

The National-Trust-classified **Tent House**, at 16 Fourth Ave, is one of the last surviving houses typical of the early days of Mt Isa. About 200 of these half-house, half-tents, were built during the 1930s specifically to suit the Mt Isa climate. The interior of the house features furniture, fittings and displays from the 1930s. It is open weekdays from 9 am to 3 pm.

The **Kalkadoon Tribal Centre & Culture-Keeping Place**, on Marian St next to the tourist office, is open most weekdays (admission $1). It's partly a museum and you can see some artefacts.

A short drive or climb off Hilary St is the **City Lookout** – coming up here certainly puts things into perspective. You can see virtually the whole town, sprawled out across a flat valley, backed by a series of low hills and watched over by the huge, dark, brooding mine. There's also a white signboard up here, with pointers to Melbourne, Rome, the South Pole and all sorts of other places.

Mt Isa has a big, clean **swimming pool** on Isa St, just over the river and next to the tennis courts. Entry costs $1, and the pool opens daily at 7 am from May to August, and at 10 am (noon on Monday) for the rest of the year.

Lake Moondarra, 16 km north of town, is a popular spot for swimming, boating, water-skiing, fishing and birdwatching. There are barbecue facilities at the lake and at Warrina Park, which is just below the dam wall.

Organised Tours

Between April and September, Campbell's Coaches (☎ (077) 43 2006) offers a couple of different tours from Mt Isa. Their one-day outback trip, which visits Aboriginal rock paintings, an old copper mine and Mary Kathleen, costs $50 for adults and $25 for children. The three-day camping safari to Lawn Hill National Park and the Riversleigh fossil sites costs $290 per person including all meals and camping gear. Air Mt Isa (☎ (077) 43 2844), the local mail run operator, will take tourists along on its twice-weekly flights to the more remote reaches of Queensland and the Northern Territory. On Wednesday the flights take in the Gulf area, with stops including Gregory Downs, Lawn Hill Station, Burketown and Augustus Downs Station. On Friday the mail run covers the Queensland-Northern Territory border, with stops at stations including Barkly Downs, Austral Downs and Manners Creek. Flights depart at 9 am, return at 4 pm and cost around $180 per person. Air Mt Isa is also available for charter flights for up to 11 people to various places including Lawn Hill National Park.

Festivals

The Mt Isa Rotary Rodeo, held every year in August, is the biggest in Australia with $100,000 in prize money up for grabs. The rodeo is held at Kalkadoon Park on the Barkly Hwy.

The town also holds a traditional Oktoberfest each year in, you guessed it, October.

Places to Stay

Camping Mt Isa has a string of caravan parks, some along the Barkly Hwy going east, others in the north of town, and all about two km from the centre. The *Mt Isa Caravan Park* (☎ (077) 43 3252), at 112 Marion St (the Barkly Hwy), is pretty basic and has tent sites from $11.

Two km north of the centre are two

caravan parks backing onto the Leichhardt River. The *Riverside Tourist Park* (☎ (077) 43 3904), at 195 West St, and the *Copper City Caravan Park* (☎ (077) 43 4676), at 185 West St, have swimming pools, tent sites for around $12 and on-site vans from $30.

If you have transport, one of the best camping spots is the *Moondarra Caravan Park* (☎ (077) 43 9780). There's a good pool and shady camp sites by the river bank costing $5 per person. To get there, follow the Barkly Hwy north of town for six km and take the turn off to Lake Moondarra. You'll soon see the park on your left (it's another 15 km from here to the lake).

Hostels The *Travellers Haven* (☎ (077) 43 0313), about a half a km from the centre on the corner of Spence and Pamela Sts, is a well set up backpackers' hostel. All the rooms are twin share and have air-con, with bunk beds costing $11 and singles/doubles from $22/26. The owner of this place is a good source of information on what to see and places to visit in the local area, and can supply maps if you want to get off the main routes. The hostel has a good pool, bikes for hire ($10 a day), and its courtesy coach does pick-ups.

Mt Isa's 28-bed youth hostel (☎ (077) 43 5557), in the shadow of the mines at Wellington Park Rd, costs $10 ($11 nonmembers). It's very basic, and unless Travellers Haven is full it's hard to think of any good reason for walking the two km.

Hotels & Motels The *Boyd Hotel* (☎ (077) 43 3000), on the corner of West and Marian Sts, has basic pub rooms at $20 per person.

At 23 Camooweal St, *Walton's Motel* (☎ (077) 43 2377) is one of the cheapest central motels, with air-con singles/doubles at $40/50 and a small pool. *Carlin Court* (☎ (077) 43 2019), at 11 Boyd Parade, has clean self-contained units with kitchenettes and air-con from $30/40 for singles/doubles – if you're staying longer, their weekly rates are very good value. The *Copper Gate Motel* (☎ (077) 43 3233), which is at 97 Marian St (the Barkly Hwy), has singles/doubles from $42/54.

If you're looking for something more expensive, the three-star *Burke & Wills Isa Resort Motel* (☎ (077) 43 8000), on the corner of Grace and Camooweal Sts, is an impressive modern motel with spas, water beds, a pool and its own licensed restaurant – rooms here range from $85 to $100 a night.

The *Verona Motel* (☎ (077) 43 3024), on the corner of Marian and Camooweal Sts, is a four-star three-storey motel that dates back to the 1960s. The rooms have all been refurbished, with standard rooms starting from $90 and executive rooms from $105. The motel has a pool and a good licensed restaurant (see Places to Eat).

Places to Eat

There are a number of centrally located pizzerias, cafes and snack bars, including *Clicks*, on West St, and *Bazza's Cafe*, on Miles St, which both offer a variety of burgers and sandwiches. *Flamenco Cafe*, on Marian St near the corner of Miles St, also has burgers, sandwiches and 20 flavours of ice cream.

If you've just stepped off an early morning bus, the *Mt Isa Hotel*, on the corner of Marian and Miles Sts, serves good breakfasts in their upstairs restaurant from 6.30 to 8.30 am, which cost from $5 to $10.

Mt Isa's clubs are amongst the best places to eat. In the south of town, the *Irish Club*, on the corner of Buckley and Nineteenth Aves, has a restaurant with two sections: the buffet has excellent smorgasbords at $6.50 for lunch and $12.50 for dinner; and the bistro has roasts, burgers, seafood, grills, pasta and chicken dishes, all in the $4 to $10 range. The club specialises in big, old-fashioned servings – you won't go home hungry. On the corner of Camooweal and Grace Sts, the *Buffalo Club* also has good bistro meals (and excellent steaks!) ranging from $7 to $12. Visitors to the clubs sign in as honorary buffaloes or Irish persons, and dress regulations apply.

The Tavern, on Isa St, has excellent

counter meals at lunch times and evenings. You'll pay about $5 to $10 in the public bar, and meals in the bistro range upwards from $10. At the Boyd Hotel, *Someplace to Eat* serves good bistro meals in the $8 to $15 range.

Los Toros Mexican Restaurant (☎ (077) 43 7718), at 79 Camooweal St, is deservedly one of the most popular places in town. It's a lively cantina-style Mexican eatery with main meals in the $10 to $14 range, good sangria and an incredibly spicy chorizo sausage. The restaurant also brews its own beer, although it usually sells out straight away. You'll probably need to book, especially on weekends.

For Chinese food, try the *Red Lantern* on the corner of Isa and Simpson Sts. It's a spacious place with all the usual suspects on the menu, and main meals ranging from $12 to $16.

There's also a very good licensed restaurant at the *Verona Motel*, on the corner of Marian and Camooweal Sts. It's an elegant dining room which specialises in Italian cuisine and seafood, with pastas from $10 and other main courses in the $20 to $30 range.

Entertainment

The recently opened *Switches Nightclub*, on Miles St, is a huge, up-market nightclub which features both live music and DJs, and has a restaurant section upstairs. The club is open from Wednesday to Saturday nights until 3 am. There's a cover charge of $5 and a 'no-jeans' dress code here.

There are usually live bands in the *Boyd Hotel* on weekend evenings. Also popular are the *Kave* nightclub in the Mt Isa Hotel and the *Buffalo Club* on Grace St. The *Irish Club* has a good entertainment programme, including free video nights on Monday and Tuesday, and a mixture of live music, a disco and karaoke on weekends – it's worth ringing to find out what's on.

The *Cinema Mt Isa* (☎ (077) 43 2043), on Marion St between West and Miles Sts, screens the latest releases. Mt Isa's Civic Centre (☎ (077) 44 4244), on West St, which

includes a theatre and a 1000-seat auditorium, is the town's major venue for live performances and hosts a variety of concerts, plays, balls and events throughout the year.

Getting There & Away

Air Ansett has an office at 8 Miles St, and Flight West Airlines (☎ (077) 43 9333) is at 14 Miles St.

Ansett has nonstop flights daily to Brisbane ($393 one way), on Sunday to Alice Springs or Ayers Rock ($227) and on Saturday and Sunday to Cairns ($254).

Flight West also flies daily to Cairns ($331 one way), as well as to Townsville ($280), Normanton ($240), Karumba ($235) and various places along the Flinders Hwy.

Air Mt Isa takes passengers along on its twice-weekly mail run – see the Organised Tours sections for details.

Bus Greyhound Pioneer Australia and McCafferty's (☎ (077) 43 3685) both operate from the Campbell's Coaches terminal (☎ (077) 43 2006), at 27 Barkly Hwy.

Both bus companies run daily services between Townsville and Tennant Creek, passing through Mt Isa. Townsville to Mt Isa takes 11 hours and costs around $80, while the trip on to Tennant Creek takes another six or seven hours ($70). Both companies have connections at Tennant Creek for Alice Springs ($120) and Darwin ($130).

Greyhound Pioneer Australia and McCafferty's also operate daily to Brisbane ($120, about 24 hours) by the inland route through Winton ($45) and Longreach ($50).

Campbell's Coaches (☎ (077) 43 2006) go to Normanton ($64) and Karumba ($70) once a week, leaving each Tuesday at 11 am.

Train The air-con *Inlander* operates twice weekly between Townsville and Mt Isa, via Charters Towers, Hughenden and Cloncurry. The full journey takes about 18 hours and costs $95 for an economy seat. It's another $30 for an economy sleeper, or another $50 in 1st class.

Getting Around

There are no local bus services. If you want a taxi, call ☎ (077) 43 2333.

There are several car hire firms in Isa, including Avis (☎ (077) 43 3733), Hertz (☎ (077) 43 4142) and Thrifty (☎ (077) 43 2911). Rent-a-Ute (☎ (077) 43 3355) may be a little cheaper than the national operators.

CAMOOWEAL (pop 230)

Camooweal, 13 km east of the Northern Territory border, is either your first or last chance to get fuel or food in Queensland – depending on which way you're headed.

The town was established in 1884 as a service centre for the vast cattle stations of the Barkly Tablelands. It has a couple of semi-historic buildings – the **Shire Hall** (1922), and **Freckleton's General Store**, an old corrugated tin building which also acts as an informal tourist information centre – and is the turn off for the Camooweal Caves National Park. You can also turn off here for Lawn Hill National Park, Gregory Downs and Burketown (see the Gulf Savannah chapter for details).

Information

Fuel & Services The Shell Camooweal Roadhouse (☎ (077) 48 2155), on the west side of town, is the local RACQ depot. It is open from 6 am to 10 pm daily, does minor repairs and has a 24-hour towing service. There is also the BP Camooweal Driveway, which is open from 7 am to 9.30 pm – both of these places have EFTPOS facilities and take major credit cards.

Places to Stay & Eat

The *Shell Camooweal Roadhouse* (☎ (077) 48 2155) has a camping ground ($3 per person, coin-operated showers 60c), as well as six old but cleanish motel-units with air-con and TV costing $45/50 for singles/doubles. They have a cafe that does takeaways or you can dine in – my cheese and bacon burger was pretty good.

The *Post Office Hotel* (☎ (077) 48 2124) in the centre of town has a tin roof and a wrap-around verandah. It has eight basic pub-style rooms at $20/40 for singles/doubles, and four motel units at $40/50 – all the rooms have air-con. If you're after a pub meal, the bistro serves lunches and dinners every day except Sunday. Offerings include a pie & chips or a steak sandwich for $5, or a T-bone or a seafood basket for $12.

There are two general stores here if you need to stock up on groceries – Freckleton's, and the *Camooweal General Store* next to the BP service station.

CAMOOWEAL CAVES NATIONAL PARK

Beneath the surface of this small national park is a network of unusual caves and caverns with sinkhole openings. The largest of these, the Great Nowranie Cave, is 70 metres deep and almost 300 metres long. The caves can be explored, but only if you're an experienced caver and have all the right equipment – the entrance to Great Nowranie, for example, is an 18-metre drop from the surface. For the average punter, the park can be a dangerous place to wander around, and it's extremely isolated. If you are planning to visit, check with the local police and the QNP&WS office in Mt Isa (☎ (077) 43 2055) first. The caves are usually flooded during the wet season, so the middle of the year is the best time to visit – at other times you can expect extreme high temperatures.

The entrance to the national park is eight km south of Camooweal along a rough, unsealed road. There are several creek crossings and the road is usually impassable after rain. There are no facilities here, apart from a self-registration camping ground with toilets.

CAMOOWEAL TO THREEWAYS (460 km)

There's nothing much for the whole 460 km from Camooweal to the Threeways junction in the Northern Territory. West of Camooweal, the next service station (and the most expensive petrol anywhere between Townsville and Darwin) is 270 km along at *Barkly Homestead* (☎ (089) 64 4549). You can camp here for $3.50 per person. Motel rooms are $62/72.

Cloncurry to Cunnamulla – the Matilda Highway

The Matilda Hwy is the best and most popular north-south route through outback Queensland. This all-bitumen highway starts at the Queensland/New South Wales border south of Cloncurry and runs north for over 1700 km, ending in Karumba on the Gulf of Carpentaria.

The Matilda Hwy takes you through most of the outback's major towns and to some of its best tourist attractions, including the Australian Workers' Heritage Centre in Barcaldine, the Stockman's Hall of Fame in Longreach and the historic Woolscour in Blackall.

The Matilda Hwy is in fact the name given to a route made up of a number of roads and highways. Sections of the Mitchell Hwy, the Landsborough Hwy and the Burke Developmental Road make up what is now called the Matilda Hwy. The Cloncurry to Cunnamulla section is covered in this chapter – see the Gulf Savannah chapter for details of the northern section of the route.

Books & Maps

The Queensland Tourist & Travel Corporation has produced the excellent book *The Matilda Highway*, which is readily available in good book/map shops or from branches of the automobile clubs in each state. The Queensland state mapping authority has also produced a map called *The Matilda Highway*, which can be purchased from Sunmap centres or agencies, as well as from good book/map shops.

CLONCURRY TO WINTON (343 km)

Fourteen km east of Cloncurry, the narrow Landsborough Hwy turns off the Flinders Hwy and heads south-east to Winton via the one-pub towns of McKinlay and Kynuna.

The first section of this route, from Cloncurry to McKinlay, passes through a rugged and rocky landscape of low, craggy hills before gradually giving way to the flat plains that characterise most of the outback region.

McKinlay (pop 20)

McKinlay is a tiny settlement which would probably have been doomed to eternal insignificance were it not for the fact this is the location of the *Walkabout Creek Hotel* (☎ (077) 46 8424), which featured in the amazingly successful Paul Hogan movie *Crocodile Dundee*. Photos from the film and other memorabilia clutter the walls of the pub.

Buses travelling between Mt Isa and Brisbane via Longreach make a refreshment stop here, and if you want to hang around for a while there are clean and simple rooms with air-con at $30/40 for singles/doubles, or the *Crocodile Dundee Van Park* out the back of the pub has tent sites at $10 and powered sites at $12.

The pub serves breakfasts, lunches and dinner, and sells super, unleaded and diesel fuel.

Kynuna (pop 30)

Kynuna, another 74 km south-east, isn't much bigger than McKinlay. The 107-year-old *Blue Heeler Hotel* (☎ (077) 46 8650) is another renowned old outback pub, which for some reason has its own surf life-saving club! The pub serves meals all day every day between 7 am and 9.30 pm and has hotel rooms from $30 and motel rooms from $45, all with air-con, as well as a caravan park with tent sites at $6 and powered sites at $12.

Every year in September, the Blue Heeler hosts its own surf life-saving carnival. The nearest beach may be almost 1000 km away, but in true outback tradition the locals improvise by carrying a surf boat up and down the main street.

The festival also features surfboard relays, a tug of war and an evening beach party with a live band. You can't miss the pub at night

– it's the place with the blue neon dog with a flashing red tongue on the roof.

The *Kynuna Roadhouse & Caravan Park* (☎ (077) 46 8683) has tent sites, powered van sites, one on-site van and four cabins, and a licensed restaurant. The roadhouse is open daily from 6 am to 9 pm; there's a night bell if you need after-hours fuel.

Kynuna to Winton

The turn off to the **Combo Water Hole**, which Banjo Paterson is said to have visited in 1895 before he wrote *Waltzing Matilda*, is signposted off the highway about 12 km east of Kynuna. The water hole is on Dagworth Station.

WINTON (pop 1160)

Winton is a sheep-raising centre and also the railhead from which sheep and cattle are transported after being brought from the Channel Country by road train. The road north to Cloncurry is fully paved, but still gets washed out during a really bad wet season.

On the main street, there's a *Jolly Swagman* statue and the Qantilda Museum, which commemorates two local claims to fame: the founding of Qantas airlines at Winton in 1920 and the regionally inspired poetry of one of Australia's most famous poets, Banjo Paterson. An annual bush-verse competition, the Bronze Swagman Award, attracts entries from all over Australia, keeping alive the Banjo Paterson tradition and celebrating its influence on Australian literature.

The Waltzing Matilda Centenary festival, held in April 1995, celebrated the centenary of the first public performance of *Waltzing Matilda* at the North Gregory Hotel. The festival was a great success, attracting thousands of visitors from around the country and placing Winton on the map as an outback destination.

The town isn't exactly stunning, but it's a friendly, laid-back place with some interesting attractions and characters, and if you're not in a hurry it's a good place for a stopover.

The town centre is spread along Elderslie St,

a broad street, divided by a central plantation, with three pubs, three cafes and a couple of well-stocked general stores, as well as an open-air cinema – not to be missed!

Information

Tourist Information The Gift & Gem Centre (☎ (076) 57 1296), on Elderslie St, acts as the local information centre.

Post & Money The post office, Westpac and National banks are all along Elderslie St.

Fuel & Services Winton Fuel & Tyre Service (☎ (076) 57 1305), the BP roadhouse on the corner of Elderslie and Oondooroo Sts, is the local RACQ depot. They are open daily from 7 am to 8 pm, but also do emergency after-hours towing. They have EFTPOS facilities and take all major credit cards.

Things to See & Do

The **Qantilda Museum**, on Elderslie St beside the post office, is well worth a look with a good collection of memorabilia including Qantas and Waltzing Matilda displays and a number of historic cottages and buildings. It is open daily from 9 am to 4 pm; entry costs $5 for adults, $3 for students and is free for children accompanied by adults.

Across the road from the museum is the bronze **Jolly Swagman** statue, a tribute to Banjo Paterson and the unknown swagmen who lie in unmarked graves in the area. Behind the statue is the **Winton Swimming Pool** – just the place for a cooling dip.

The National-Trust-classified **Corfield & Fitzmaurice Building**, a former general store in the centre of town, has been lovingly restored to house a craft co-operative centre, with art exhibitions and a dinosaur display.

The **North Gregory Hotel** is said to be the place where Banjo Paterson's song *Waltzing Matilda* was first performed on 6 April 1895. The original pub has burned down, as have several subsequent constructions, and the present pub is a solid brick building built in 1955.

The **Royal Theatre**, out the back of the Stopover Cafe on Elderslie St in the centre of town, is a wonderful open-air theatre with canvas-slung chairs, corrugated tin walls and a star-studded ceiling – the outback's version of *Cinema Paradiso*. Films are screened every Saturday and also on Wednesday between April and September. Saturday nights features two mainstream films, Wednesday feature old favourites like Abbott & Costello or Laurel & Hardy, news-reels and sing-alongs, with tea and damper served afterwards. Tickets cost $7 on Saturday and $5.50 on Wednesday; kids pay somewhere between $3 and $6 – it sort of depends on their height, age etc.

Organised Tours

Diamantina Outback Tours (☎ (076) 57 1514) offers day trips to the Lark Quarry Environmental Park, costing $75 for adults and $35 for children with lunch included.

OUTBACK QUEENSLAND

100 Years of Waltzing our Matildas

Written back in 1895 by the 'bard of the bush' Banjo Paterson, *Waltzing Matilda* is widely regarded as Australia's unofficial national anthem. While not many people can sing *Advance Australia Fair* without a lyric sheet, just about every Aussie knows the words to the strange ditty about a jolly swagman who jumped into a billabong and drowned himself rather than be arrested for stealing a jumbuck (a sheep). But what the hell does it mean, if anything?

The Waltzing Matilda Centenary festival, held in Winton in April 1995, created a raging controversy amongst local historians over the origins and meaning of the famous tune as first Winton, and then Kynuna, claimed to be the true 'birthplace' of *Waltzing Matilda*.

To understand the origins of the song, it has to be seen in the political context of the time in which it was written. The 1890s was a period of social upheaval and political change in Queensland. Along with nationalistic calls for the Australian states to amalgamate and form a federation, the decade was dominated by an economic crisis, mass unemployment and severe droughts. An ongoing battle between the pastoralists and the shearers led to a series of strikes which divided the state and led to the formation of the Australian Labor Party to represent workers' interests.

In 1895, Paterson visited his fiance in Winton, and together they travelled to Dagworth Station south of Kynuna, where they met Christina McPherson. During their stay they went on a picnic to the Combo Waterhole, a series of billabongs on the Diamantina River, where Paterson heard stories about the violent 1894 shearer's strike on Dagworth Station. During the strike, rebel shearers had burned seven woolsheds to the ground, leading the police to declare martial law and place a reward of £1000 on the head of their leader, Samuel Hofmeister. Rather than allow himself to be captured, Hofmeister had drowned himself in a billabong near the Combo Waterhole.

Paterson later wrote the words to *Waltzing Matilda* to accompany a tune played on a zither by Christina McPherson. While there is no direct proof that he was writing allegorically about Hofmeister and the shearers' strikes, a number of prominent historians have supported the theory and claimed the song was a political statement. Others maintain that it is just an innocent but catchy tune about a hungry vagabond, but the song's undeniable anti-authoritarianism and the fact that it was adopted as an anthem by the rebel shearers weigh in heavily in favour of the former theory.

One hundred years later, *Waltzing Matilda* and the events surrounding the country's unofficial anthem take on even greater significance as the calls for Australia to become a republic by the turn of the century grow louder. ■

You can also take a day trip to Carisbrook Station – see the South of Winton section for details.

Festivals

Winton's major festival is the nine-day Outback Festival, held every second year (odd numbers) during the September school holidays. The festival features crayfish races, a dunny derby, iron man and woman competitions, country music, bush bands and buskers. A highlight of the festival is the presentation of the Bronze Swagman Award for bush poetry.

Another regular event, the Boulder Opal Auctions, is held in the Royal Theatre every year over weekends in May and August and attracts buyers from around the country.

Places to Stay

The *Matilda Country Caravan Park* (☎ (076) 57 1607), at 43 Chirnside St, has a pool, a kiosk, tent sites from $10, powered sites from $14 and on-site vans from $25 ($29 with linen). They also have good cabins with air-con and TVs from $45 ($50 with linen), and backpackers can stay in an on-site van here for $12.50 per person. The park is on the Longreach side of town, near the junction of the Landsborough Hwy and the Kennedy Developmental Rd.

The *North Gregory Hotel* (☎ (076) 57 1375), at 67 Elderslie St, has clean budget rooms with air-con at $20 a head.

Banjo's Overnight Family Motel & Cabins (☎ (076) 57 1213), on the corner of Manuka and Bostock Sts on the Longreach side of town, has self-contained units from $35/40. Across the road from the Qantilda Museum, the *Matilda Motel* (☎ (076) 57 1433) has units from $42/47.

Places to Eat

The *North Gregory Hotel*, at 67 Elderslie St, has good bistro meals. You can eat in the bar or the dining room next door, or there's a beer garden out the back with an open-air chargrill and plate-sized steaks. Across the road, *Tanya's Cafe* is a typical country town cafe with a spacious dining area, and does the regular eats – burgers, sandwiches, roast chicken and lots of deep-fried things, as well as pizzas.

There's another cafe at the front of the BP Roadhouse, on the corner of Elderslie and Oondooroo Sts, with a fruit and vegie shop next door.

You can also have a meal in the Qantas Board Room Lounge at the *Winton Club*, where the first board meeting of the Queensland and Northern Territory Aerial Service was held back in 1921. The club is one block back from the town centre on the corner of

Water pumps dot the horizon

Oondooroo and Vindex Sts, and is open for lunch and dinner from Monday to Saturday.

Getting There & Away

Winton is on the main Brisbane to Mt Isa bus route, and you can get here with either Greyhound Pioneer Australia or McCafferty's.

There are also connecting bus services between Winton and Longreach that meet up with the twice-weekly *Spirit of the Outback* train.

SOUTH OF WINTON

The country around Winton is rough and rugged, with much wildlife, notably brolgas. There are also Aboriginal sites with paintings, carvings and artefacts.

At **Lark Quarry Environmental Park**, 115 km south-west of Winton, dinosaur footprints 100 million years old have been perfectly preserved in limestone. It takes around two hours to drive from Winton to Lark Quarry in a conventional vehicle but the dirt road is impassable in wet weather. There are no facilities other than a toilet and a rainwater tank. Well signposted from Winton, the site now sports a raised walkway and a sheltering tin roof to protect this unique find from the elements and from people. Contact the Winton Shire Council (☎ (076) 57 1188), at 78 Vindex St, for more information.

Carisbrooke Station (☎ (076) 57 3885), set amidst spectacular escarpment country 85 km south-west of Winton, has a wildlife sanctuary, an old opal mine, Aboriginal paintings and bora rings (circular ceremonial grounds). The station offers day tours from Winton for $60 per person (children under 12 free), and has self-contained accommodation for up to 16 people from $20 per person.

The **Opalton Mining Field**, 115 km south of Winton, is a remote gemfield where the unique boulder opals can be found. Unlike opals from places like Lightning Ridge and Coober Pedy, which are found in clay, boulder opals are attached to a host rock which has to be ground away to free the opal. The name relates more to the host rocks than to the size of the opals. There are no facilities here, apart from a phone box, and the road is unsealed and slow going.

WINTON TO LONGREACH (173 km)

This is a long, lonely and dull stretch of highway with nothing much to see, apart from endless flat plains punctuated by the occasional tree and the odd windmill.

Fifty km south-east of Winton is the turn off to *Lorainne Station* (☎ (076) 57 1693); it's another six unsealed km from the highway to the resort. This huge sheep and cattle station has a canteen serving breakfast, lunch and dinner, and a range of accommodation for tourists. Tent or caravan sites cost $10 each, and facilities include showers, laundry and barbecues. They also have guest units which cost $60 per person for dinner, B&B, or $95 per person with all meals and

The Origins of Qantas

Qantas, the Queensland & Northern Territory Aerial Service, had humble beginnings as a joy flight and air taxi service in Queensland's outback – and at times it seems like every second town in the outback has claims to being the birthplace of Australia's major airline.

The idea to establish the airline came about when two former Flying Corps airmen, Hudson Fysh and Paul McGuinness, travelled through outback Queensland to prepare the route for the famous London to Melbourne Air Race. Together, they saw the potential for an air service to link the remote outback centres, and with the financial backing of a number of local pastoralists, they established an airline.

The fledgling company was registered for business at Winton on 16 November 1920, and the first official meeting was held in the Winton Club. Soon after it was decided to move the company headquarters to Longreach, where the first office was opened in Duck St. Qantas' first regular air service, begun on 22 November 1922, was between Cloncurry and Charleville; Longreach remained the headquarters of the airline until it was moved to Brisbane in 1930. ■

activities like horse riding and property tours included. If you're flying, the station has its own airstrip.

LONGREACH (pop 3610)

This prosperous outback town was the home of Qantas earlier this century, but these days it's just as famous for the Australian Stockman's Hall of Fame & Outback Heritage Centre, probably the biggest attraction in outback Queensland.

Longreach's human population is vastly outnumbered by the sheep, which number over a million; there are a fair few cattle too.

It was here that the Queensland & Northern Territory Aerial Service, better known as Qantas, was based in its early days in the 1920s. The original Qantas hangar, which still stands at Longreach Airport (almost opposite the Hall of Fame), was also the first aircraft 'factory' in Australia – six DH-50 biplanes were assembled here in 1926. There are plans to build an aviation museum alongside the original hangar, but in the meantime there's a 'preview' display housed in the Longreach tourist office, itself a replica of the first Qantas booking office.

Information

Tourist Information The tourist information office (☎ (076) 583 555) is on the corner of Duck and Eagle Sts in the centre of town. It is open daily from 9 am to 5 pm; hours are shorter during the off season.

Post & Money The post office is on the corner of Eagle and Duck Sts. All the major banks have branches in Longreach – ANZ, Commonwealth, National and Westpac.

Fuel & Services The local RACQ depot is Mobil Midtown Service Station (☎ (076) 58 1747) on Swan St.

Laundry There's a 24-hour laundrette in a little shed on Galah St, opposite the police station.

Captain Starlight

Longreach was also the starting point for one of Queensland's most colourful early crimes when, in 1870, Harry Redford and two accomplices stole 1000 head of cattle from Mt Cornish, north of Longreach, and drove them down the Thomson River and its continuation, Cooper Creek, to the present site of Innamincka. From there he followed the Strzelecki Creek south, finally selling his ill-gotten gains to a station owner north of Adelaide. His exploit opened up a new stock route south, and when he was finally brought to justice, in Roma in 1873, he was found not guilty by the adoring public! Rolf Boldrewood's novel *Robbery Under Arms* later immortalised Redford as 'Captain Starlight'. ■

Stockman's Hall of Fame & Outback Heritage Centre

The centre is housed in a beautifully conceived building, two km east of town along the road to Barcaldine. The excellent displays are divided into periods from the first White settlement through to today; and these deal with all aspects of the pioneering pastoral days. The centre was built as a tribute to the early explorers and stockmen, and it also commemorates the crucial roles played by the pioneer women, Aboriginal stockmen and Aboriginal women.

It's well worth visiting the Hall of Fame, as it gives a fascinating insight into this side of the European development of Australia. A 12-minute film introduces visitors to the centre, and there are dozens of static exhibits featuring the stories of the characters of the outback, as well as some excellent audio visual displays like the **Talking Drover**, a computerised recreation of a stockman's bush camp at dusk, with an old drover reminiscing. You can also watch the 40-minute 'Back to the Bush' show featuring a stockman demonstrating yard and paddock teamwork with his horses and dogs.

There is a good bookshop, plus a souvenir shop and a cafe. Admission is $15 for adults, $12 for concession card holders, $10 for all students, $7 for children and $35 for a family ticket. The centre is open daily (except Christmas Day) from 9 am to 5 pm. Allow yourself half a day to take it all in. Greyhound Pioneer Australia and McCafferty's both operate daily services from the terminal on Eagle St for $3 (free with Greyhound Pioneer Australia if you have an Aussie Pass). Otherwise it's a half-hour walk, or a taxi from the centre will cost you about $5.50.

Other Attractions

Apart from the Hall of Fame, Longreach doesn't have terribly much up its sleeve, although there are some interesting tours on offer from here – see the following section.

At the Longreach tourist information office, on the corner of Duck and Eagle Sts, there is a small preview display of the proposed **aviation museum**. There isn't much to see at this stage, and apart from the half-hour film on the history of Qantas it's not worth the admission fee of $3 for adults and $1.50 for kids. The office is open daily from 9 am to 5 pm, although hours are shorter during the off season.

If you want to go for a swim, the inviting-looking **Longreach Memorial Pool** is across the railway line in Eagle St.

Organised Tours

Day Tours The number of tours available is surprising, and most of them can be booked through the Outback Travel Centre (☎ (076) 58 1776), at 115 Eagle St. They offer a one-day tour of the town which includes visits to the Hall of Fame and an outback station and a dinner cruise along the Thomson River at $80 for adults, $45 for children. Other day trips on offer include tours to Winton ($60 adults, $30 children), Lorraine Station ($60/30), Barcaldine and the Australian Workers Heritage Centre ($79/50), half-day tours to Ilfracombe ($28/18), and a combined day trip to Winton, the Lark Quarry Environmental Park and Carisbrooke Station (Monday and Friday, $99/59).

Cattle farming dominates the outback

River Cruises Yellowbelly Express (☎ (076) 58 1919) does popular river trips on the nearby Thomson River.

Longreach Billabong Boat Cruises offers three-hour 'sunset and stars' dinner cruises along a water hole on the Thomson River with live entertainment, a barbecue or camp oven meal, and billy tea and damper. Costs are $20 for adults and $5 for children.

Outback Stations You can also make a visit to one or more of the sheep stations in the area. They include: Toobrack (☎ (076) 58 9158), 68 km south; Longway (☎ (076) 58 2191), 17 km north; and Avington (☎ (076) 57 5952), 75 km west of Blackall. Some of these places are only open for day trips while others offer accommodation and a range of activities. Avington, for example, has beds in its shearers' quarters for $15 as well as rooms in its homestead for $50/90, including B&B and dinner. Activities include horse riding, trail-bike riding, canoeing and barge cruises. For any visit to a sheep station you'll need to ring before you arrive.

Scenic Flights Queensland Helicopters offers scenic flights in a helicopter from the Longreach Aerodrome costing $20 for adults and $10 for children.

Festivals

A number of events are held in Longreach

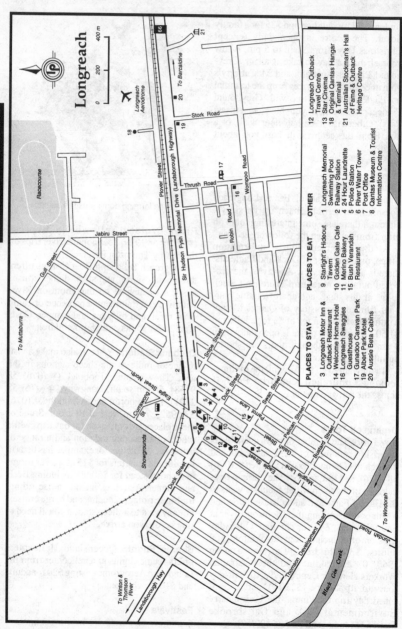

Longreach

OUTBACK QUEENSLAND

PLACES TO STAY

3 Longreach Motor Inn &
  Outback Restaurant
14 Welcome Home Hotel
16 Longreach Swaggies
  Guesthouse
17 Gunadoo Caravan Park
19 Albert Park Motel
20 Aussie Beta Cabins

PLACES TO EAT

9 Starlight's Hideout
  Tavern
10 Golden Gate Cafe
11 Merino Bakery
15 Bush Verandah
  Restaurant

OTHER

1 Longreach Memorial
  Swimming Pool
2 Railway Station
4 24 Hour Laundrette
5 Police Station
6 River Water Tower
7 Post Office
8 Qantas Museum & Tourist
  Information Centre
12 Longreach Outback
  Travel Centre
13 Star Cinema
18 Original Qantas Hangar
  & Terminal
21 Australian Stockman's Hall
  of Fame & Outback
  Heritage Centre

during the year. The Thomson River Campdraft and the annual Show take place in May, and during July there are the Diamond Shears and South Pacific Shearing Championships, as well as the Stockman's Hall of Fame Endurance Ride, run between Winton and Longreach. In September of every even-numbered year the Starlight Stampede Festival is held.

Places to Stay
Caravan Park The *Gunnadoo Caravan Park* (☎ (076) 58 1781), east of town on the corner of the highway and Thrush Rd, has a shop and two pools, with tent sites at $10, on-site vans at $28 and a long row of new self-contained timber cabins from $45.

Hostel The *Longreach Swaggies Guesthouse* (☎ (076) 58 3777) is on the corner of Robin and Thrush Rds, about one km east of the centre. It's pretty basic but quite well set up, with cooking and laundry facilities and a TV lounge. Dorm beds cost $14 and singles/doubles are $25/40, and it does pickups from the train and bus terminals if you ring. This place has recently changed hands, and the new owners are planning to make improvements and to supply evening meals for around $5.

Pubs There's a choice of at least four pubs on Eagle St, including the *Welcome Home Hotel* (☎ (076) 58 1361) with air-con pub rooms for $20/35.

Motels & Cabins At 84 Galah St, the *Longreach Motor Inn* (☎ (076) 58 2322) is quite central and has a licensed restaurant (see Places to Eat), a pool and good motel rooms from $60/70, plus $7 for each extra person – their rooms sleep up to six people.

If you're looking for somewhere self-contained, the *Aussie Beta Cabins* (☎ (076) 58 3811), out on the highway about 100 metres west of the Hall of Fame, is a complex of 16 new timber cabins that sleep up to five people and have cooking facilities and air-con. The tariff is $50/55 for singles/doubles plus $5 for each extra person.

Nearby on the corner of the highway and Stork Rd, the *Albert Park Motel* (☎ (076) 58 2411) is a large modern motel with a good pool, a spa and a licensed restaurant. Singles/doubles are $56/66.

Places to Eat
There are several cafes and takeaways along Eagle St, including the *Golden Gate Cafe* and the *Coffee Shop*, both of which have OK sandwiches, pies etc. You could also try the *Merino Bakery*, on the corner of Eagle and Swan Sts.

Starlight's Hideout Tavern, also on Eagle St, has a cavernous bistro out the back with good meals in the $8.50 to $11.50 range.

The licensed *Outback Restaurant* at the Longreach Motor Inn, on Galah St, opens nightly for dinner. It's quite formal and up-market, with international cuisine in the $14 to $18 range and a few vegetarian dishes in the $8 to $10 range.

On the corner of Galah and Swan Sts, the *Bush Verandah Restaurant* is a cosy little BYO with a rustic décor and good country cooking.

Entertainment
The *Star Cinema* (☎ (076) 58 1357), at 117 Eagle St, screens latest-release movies on Friday, Saturday and Sunday, and sometimes on Wednesday.

Getting There & Away
Air Flight West has daily flights from Longreach to Brisbane ($303), and also flies twice a week to Winton ($85) and Townsville ($216).

Bus Greyhound Pioneer Australia and McCafferty's both have daily services to Winton (two hours, $20), Mt Isa (7½ hours, $53) and Brisbane (17 hours, $83). McCafferty's also operates three times a week to Rockhampton (nine hours, $51).

McCafferty's buses stop at Transwest Tours (☎ (076) 58 1155), at 113 Eagle St, and Greyhound Pioneer Australia's buses stop at the Outback Travel Centre (☎ (076) 58 1776), at 115A Eagle St.

Train The twice-weekly *Spirit of the Outback* connects Longreach with Rockhampton (14 hours, $72 in economy, $102 for an economy sleeper and $165 for a 1st-class sleeper); there are connecting bus services between Longreach and Winton.

LONGREACH TO WINDORAH – THE THOMSON DEVELOPMENTAL ROAD (310 km)

The Thomson Developmental Rd, which roughly follows the route of the Thomson River from Longreach to Windorah, is the most direct route for people wanting to cut across to Birdsville (the Diamantina Development Rd) from Longreach. The first half of the route, from Longreach to Stonehenge (150 km), is over a narrow sealed road; the second leg, from Stonehenge to Windorah (160 km), is over unsealed roads of dirt and gravel, and then soft red sand – this section is slower going and is often closed during the Wet.

Four km off the main road, **Stonehenge** is a tiny settlement in the midst of a dry, dusty and rocky landscape, with half a dozen tin houses and a pub. The *Stonehenge Hotel* (☎ (076) 58 5944) has rooms at $15 a head, or $40 with three meals a day. The pub sells fuel – super, unleaded and diesel – and you can get a sandwich ($2.50), a burger ($3.50) or something more substantial like a T-bone or rump steak ($9). Stonehenge has a bush race meeting every year in March and a rodeo every year in mid to late-August.

Sixty five km south of the Stonehenge turn off is **Jundah**, a neat little township which acts as the little administrative base for the Barcoo Shire council. The town's general store sells super, unleaded and diesel fuel; it is open daily from 8 am to 7 pm, but closes at 2 pm on Sunday in summer. The *Jundah Hotel-Motel* (☎ (076) 58 6166) is a low and little two-room pub with an accommodation block next door with clean, tidy rooms with shared bathrooms and air-con at $20/35 for singles/doubles. Counter meals are served every day – lamb chops or a seafood basket cost around $9. The council-run *caravan*

park in Miles St is a small, treeless block of land with an amenities block.

It's another 95 km from Jundah to Windorah. Another unsealed road which heads south out of Jundah also meets the Diamantina Developmental Rd, about 50 km east of Windorah.

See the Channel Country section later for details of Windorah.

LONGREACH TO BARCALDINE (108 km)
Ilfracombe (pop 150)
This tiny little township 28 km east of Longreach modestly calls itself 'the Hub of the West', and boasts a railway station, a general store, a swimming pool, a golf course and a good pub.

The **Ilfracombe Folk Museum**, scattered along the north side of the highway through the centre of town, features an impressive collection of old tractors and farm machinery, carts and buggies, and several historic buildings with period furniture displays and memorabilia. The museum is always open, and entry is free.

Places to Stay & Eat The *Teamster's Rest Caravan Park* (☎ (076) 58 2295), on the highway, is a straightforward little park with tent sites at $8 and a couple of on-site vans at $22.

The *Wellshot Hotel* (☎ (076) 58 2106) is a charming and historic little pub with a row of clean, simple rooms with shared bathroom facilities out the back. Singles/doubles cost $20/35 and family rooms range from $45 to $55. Breakfast, lunch and dinner are served every day, with bistro meals in the $5 to $9 range. Run by former TV journo Warren Clarke and his wife Kerrin, this friendly pub is a good place for a stopover, and features numerous reminders of the town's history as the railhead for Wellshot Station. The 'Public Baa' has an aquarium and a great display of old stockmen's hats and cattle brands; the dining room features a bar made from old wool presses, walls lined with stencilled wool-packs, and a whole wall covered with a long poem called *The Wellshot & The Bush*

Pub's Hall of Fame by Robert Raftery: 'She has heard the creak of wagons and the snort of tethered beasts, Fortified their flinty drivers for their prospects further east...'.

BARCALDINE (pop 1530)

Barcaldine lies at the junction of the Landsborough and Capricorn highways, 575 km west of Rockhampton via Emerald, surrounded by sheep and cattle stations. It's known as the 'Garden City of the West', with good supplies of artesian water nourishing orchards of citrus fruits – Barcaldine was the first town in Australia to realise its underground bounty, in 1887.

Established in 1886 when the railway arrived, Barcaldine gained a place in Australian history in 1891 when it became the headquarters of the historic shearers' strike during which over 1000 men camped in and around the town. That confrontation saw troops called in, and the formation of the Australian Workers' Party, the forerunner of today's Australian Labor Party. The **Tree of Knowledge**, a ghost gumtree near the railway station, was the meeting place of the organisers, and still stands as a monument to workers and their rights.

The Australian Workers Heritage Centre is one of the outback's major attractions, and although it gets nowhere near the publicity generated by Longreach's Hall of Fame, it is equally impressive in its own way.

Beside the centre is **The Artesian Memorial**, a giant windmill dedicated to the pioneers who explored the Artesian Basin.

Note that, unless you want to get into a fight, Barcaldine is pronounced Bar-*call*-din – *not* Barcal-*dean* or Barcal-*dine*.

Information

Tourist Information Barcaldine's tourist information centre (☎ (076) 51 1724) is in a small railway carriage next to the railway station on Oak St.

Fuel & Services The Mobil service station, in front of the Homestead Caravan Park (☎ (076) 51 1308), on Box St, opens daily from 6 am to 10 pm; there's a night bell in the driveway if you need fuel after hours. The local RACQ depot is Barcaldine Engineering Works (☎ (076) 511 337) on Dale St.

The Australian Workers Heritage Centre

This centre, built to commemorate the role played by workers in the formation of Australian social, political and industrial movements, was opened during the Labor Party's centenary celebrations in Barcaldine in 1991. Set in landscaped grounds around a central billabong, the centre includes the impressive **Australian Bicentennial Theatre**, a huge circular big-top tent which toured Australia in 1988 as part of the Bicentennial celebrations. A theatre inside screens the film *Celebration of a Nation* every half hour between 9 am and 4.30 pm, and there is an interesting display here tracing the history of the shearers' strike.

Another notable feature is the **One Teacher School**, the old Torrens Creek schoolhouse which takes you back in time to an old-fashioned school room with timber desks, slates, learners and an original school bell, as well as the classic 'Good Manners' poster, which instructed students to 'Be Honest, Truthful and Pure', 'Never be rude to anybody' and 'Do not Bully; only Cowards Do This'.

Other displays include a replica of an **Old Hospital Ward**, a **Power House** contrasting the old generators that supplied Quilpie's power with the power supplies of the future, a replica of Queensland's Legislative Assembly, and the **Workers Wall**, a photographic montage of prominent members of the Labor Party.

This centre is a major achievement and offers a fascinating look into Australian history. It is open Monday to Saturday from 9 am to 5 pm and Sunday from 10 am to 5 pm. Entry costs $5 for adults, $4 for students and children under 15 get in for free.

Other Attractions

The **Barcaldine & District Folk Museum**, on the corner of Gidyea and Beech Sts, is an old timber Queenslander crammed with a

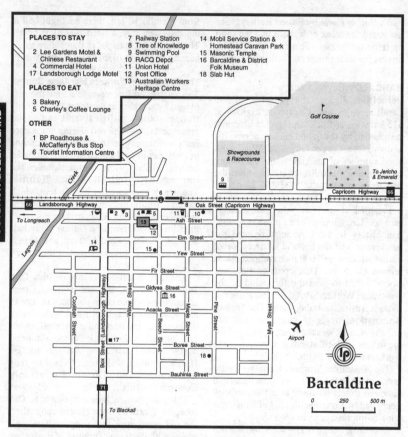

PLACES TO STAY

2 Lee Gardens Motel & Chinese Restaurant
4 Commercial Hotel
17 Landsborough Lodge Motel

PLACES TO EAT

3 Bakery
5 Charley's Coffee Lounge

OTHER

1 BP Roadhouse & McCafferty's Bus Stop
6 Tourist Information Centre

7 Railway Station
8 Tree of Knowledge
9 Swimming Pool
10 RACQ Depot
11 Union Hotel
12 Post Office
13 Australian Workers Heritage Centre

14 Mobil Service Station & Homestead Caravan Park
15 Masonic Temple
16 Barcaldine & District Folk Museum
18 Slab Hut

Golf Course

Showgrounds & Racecourse

To Jericho & Emerald

Capricorn Highway

Barcaldine

0   250   500 m

fascinating collection of memorabilia including old photos, clocks, tools, cash registers, horse-drawn buggies and farming equipment. It is open every day from 7 am to 5 pm; entry costs $2.

On the corner of Pine and Bauhinia Sts is the **Slab Hut**, run by Mad Mick and his artist wife Wanita. Also known as the **Beta Farm Outback Heritage & Wildlife centre**, it's a wonderfully ramshackle, cluttered farmlet with a collection of historic buildings, art studios, shearers quarters and dray sheds, and a small fauna park with emus, possums, peacocks and wallabies. Pop in for some

billy tea and damper – Mick takes kids for rides in his old T-Model Ford, Wanita's art is on display, and there are wool spinning demonstrations. The complex is open most days between April and September; entry costs $7 for adults and $5 for kids.

Organised Tours

Barcaldine Town & Country Tours (☎ (076) 51 1308) (based at the Homestead Caravan Park) offers a couple of day tours: their 'Town & Country' tour takes in the Tree of Knowledge, the Australian Workers Heritage Centre, the Slab Hut, an outback station and a deer farm; and their 'Country Spectacular' tour visits several outback stations, Australia's biggest shearing shed on Kerry Packer's Isis Downs Station, and a bush pub. Both tours cost $79 for adults and $39 for children.

Places To Stay

The *Homestead Caravan Park* (☎ (076) 51 1308), behind the Mobil service station on Box St, has tent sites from $10, powered sites from $12, on-site vans from $28 and new timber cabins from $28/32. The owners of this place are helpful with information on the area, and run tours of the town and surrounds (see Organised Tours).

At 67 Oak St is the *Commercial Hotel* (☎ (076) 51 1242), a green and white two-storey pub that was built in the 1920s. It's a friendly place with good meals and clean, simple rooms upstairs opening out onto a broad verandah; the beds are comfortable, but the lack of ceiling fans or air-con is a drawback in the heat. Singles/doubles cost $15/30. Up on the corner of Oak and Maple Sts, the *Union Hotel* (☎ (076) 51 2269) has basic and clean pub-style rooms with air-con at $25/35 for singles/doubles and $45 for a family room sleeping up to five people.

The best of the four motels is the *Landsborough Lodge Motel* (☎ (076) 51 1100), south of the centre on the corner of Box St (the Landsborough Hwy) and Boree St. It's a modern colonial-style place with motel units at $55/68 for singles/doubles and self-contained suites that sleep up to six people and range from $100 to $120. The *Lee Garden Motel* (☎ (076) 51 1488), on the corner of Oak and Box Sts, has units from $50.

Places to Eat

The *Barcaldine Bakery* on Oak St sells good pies, pastries and cakes, and there's a *Foodstore Supermarket* next door if you need to buy supplies.

Head to the *Commercial Hotel* for a good pub feed – bistro meals are in the $7 to $10 range, and they also have light lunches for around $4. Next door, the friendly *Charley's Coffee Lounge* is a good cafe with a comfy

dine-in section. They do everything from sandwiches and home-made quiches, pies and cakes to cooked meals in the $8 to $10 range; the cafe is open daily between 7 am and 9 pm (2 pm on Saturday). The *Witch's Kitchen*, the bistro inside the Union Hotel on the corner of Oak and Maple Sts, also has good meals ranging from $7.50 to $10.50. Beside the Lee Gardens Motel on Oak St, the *Lee Gardens Chinese Restaurant* is a simple little place serving eat-in or takeaway Chinese meals.

Getting There & Away

Bus Barcaldine is on the main Brisbane-Mt Isa bus route, and both of the major bus companies have daily services. One-way fares from Barcaldine are $68 to Brisbane, $13 to Longreach and $65 to Mt Isa. You can also get to Rockhampton three times a week with McCafferty's; the one-way fare is $50.

McCafferty's buses stop at the BP Roadhouse which is at the intersection of the Landsborough and Capricorn Hwys, and Greyhound Pioneer Australia's buses stop at the newsagency at 89 Oak St.

Train The *Spirit of the Outback* between Rockhampton and Longreach stops in Barcaldine twice weekly.

BARCALDINE TO HUGHENDEN (357 km)

From Barcaldine you can head north through the small but interesting towns of **Aramac** and **Muttaburra** to Hughenden, 357 km north of Barcaldine. The unsealed road from Muttaburra to Hughenden passes through flat country and can be a bit rough in places, but is usually quite manageable in a conventional vehicle with sufficient ground clearance, driven with care.

BARCALDINE TO ALPHA – THE CAPRICORN HIGHWAY (136 km)

The Capricorn Hwy starts in Barcaldine and runs all the way across to Rockhampton on the coast.

North Delta Station (☎ (076) 51 1634), 32 km east of Barcaldine, is a working sheep and cattle station that is open to visitors for shearing demonstrations, property tours and lunches, and has budget accommodation for up to eight people – ring and let them know you're coming.

Midway between Barcaldine and Alpha is the small township of **Jericho**, with a railway station, a pub and a cafe. There's a strange, interesting sculpture called *The Crystal Trumpeters* in the centre of town opposite the old town hall. Dedicated to the trumpeters who blew down the walls of Jericho, it's an abstract work of large clay trumpets surrounded by obelisk-like boulders.

The *Jordon Valley Hotel* has budget accommodation, and you can get a bite to eat at the *Jordan Cafe*. Pearce's Garage (☎ (076) 51 4237) is the local RACQ depot.

ALPHA (pop 450)
Alpha, 136 km east of Barcaldine, has an interesting and growing collection of wall murals which were started by a group of local artists in 1991. The murals are on a number of public buildings along Shakespeare St, the main street, including the hardware shop, art gallery, railway station and school. There are also murals inside both pubs – there's even a great bush camping scene on the toilet block in front of the rail yards.

From Alpha you can turn off south to Tambo (163 km) or north-east to Clermont (184 km). Both of these routes are along unsealed roads for the majority of the way – they can be tackled in a conventional vehicle, with care, but might be impassable during the Wet.

Information
Fuel & Services The Ampol Service Station (☎ (079) 85 1287), in the centre of town, opens daily from 6.30 am to 11.30 pm, but you can phone them if you need fuel after hours.

Tilston's Garage (☎ (079) 85 1131), the Shell service station, is the local RACQ depot.

Places to Stay & Eat
There are two caravan parks in town. The *Jolly Swagman Caravan Park* (☎ (079) 85 1156), on the Clermont road just across the railway line, has tent sites from $7 and on-site vans from $20.

In Shakespeare St, the *Criterion Hotel* (☎ (079) 85 1215) is a traditional old two-storey verandah-fronted pub with simple rooms at $18/30/36 for singles/doubles/triples. The pub serves bistro meals from Monday to Saturday evenings. Next door, the *Alpha Hotel-Motel* (☎ (079) 85 1311), a low cream brick pub from the 1960s, has a set of neat motel units out the back which cost $40/48 for singles/doubles.

Also on Shakespeare St, the *Cafe Elite* is good country cafe which sells everything from pies and toasted sandwiches to a mixed grill ($10) or fish, chips and salad ($8). It opens daily until around 8.30 pm.

ALPHA TO ROCKHAMPTON (430 km)
See the Capricorn Coast chapter for information on the rest of the Capricorn Hwy route across to the coast from here.

BLACKALL (pop 1600)
Blackall claims to be the site of the mythical black stump – according to outback mythology, anywhere west of Blackall was considered to be 'beyond the black stump'.

Gazetted in 1868, Blackall is named after the second governor of Queensland, Samuel Blackall. The town is a pleasant spot to stop on trips north or south along the Matilda Hwy, and fuel and supplies are available from a good range of outlets.

The town prides itself on the fact that it was near here, at Alice Downs station, that the legendary shearer Jackie Howe set his world record of shearing 321 sheep in less than eight hours, with a set of hand shears! Established in 1892, the record still stands today – it was not even beaten by shearers using machine-powered shears until 1950. Acclaimed as the greatest 'gun' (the best in the shed) shearer in the world, Jackie's name lives on in the working man's blue singlet which he made popular. After his shearing days were over, he ran one of the hotels in Blackall, and is buried there.

Blackall is also famous for being the site of the first artesian well to be drilled in Queensland, although the well didn't strike water at first and when it did the product was undrinkable. After you use the bore water for washing or whatever, you'll probably agree with most travellers and say it stinks a little. Locals say it's got a bit of 'body'.

Information
Tourist Information The Blackall Historic Woolscour & Tourist Office (☎ (076) 57 4637), on Short St, is open on weekdays from 8.30 am to 5 pm and weekends from 9 am to 3 pm.

Money Banks represented in Blackall are the Commonwealth, National and Westpac.

Fuel & Services The local RACQ depot is Wood's Mechanical Repairs (☎ (076) 57 4100) on Rose St.

Things to See & Do
The **Blackall Woolscour**, the only steam-driven scour (wool-cleaner) left in Queensland, is four km north-east of Blackall. Built in 1908, it operated up until 1978 and all of the machinery is intact and still in working order. The complex incorporates a shearing shed, a wool-washing plant and a pond fed by an artesian bore, and opens daily for personalised tours from 8 am to 4 pm; entry costs $5 for adults and $2 for children.

The bronze **Jackie Howe Memorial Statue** has pride of place in the centre of town on the corner of Short and Shamrock Sts. When Jack retired from shearing in 1900, he bought Blackall's Universal Hotel. The original pub was demolished in the 1950s, but the facade of the **New Universal Garden Centre & Gallery**, built on the original site at 53 Shamrock St, reflects the design of the old pub. The gallery houses a great collection of Jackie Howe memorabilia and souvenirs, as well as works by local artists.

A number of local properties and dairies open for public tours – check with the tourist office.

About 130 km east of Blackall is **Black's Palace**, an Aboriginal site with burial caves and impressive rock paintings. It's on private property but can be visited with the permission of the warden (☎ (076) 57 4455/4663).

Festivals
Annual events in Blackall include the Claypan Bogie Country Music Festival (in March), the Show (in May) and the Jackie Howe Run shearing competition (in October). In September or October every even-numbered year, the Barcoo Rush Festival takes place. It's a 10-day town festival with a street parade, fireworks displays, barbecues and a ball.

Places to Stay
The *Blackall Caravan Park* (☎ (076) 57 4816), just off the highway east of the centre at 53 Garden St, has tent sites from $9, on-site vans from $16 and three cabins from $30.

There are three pubs along Shamrock St (the main street) and all have budget accommodation: the *Barcoo Hotel* (☎ (076) 57 4197) is at No 95, the *Prince of Wales Hotel* (☎ (076) 57 4731) is at No 63, and the *Bushman's Hotel* (☎ (076) 57 4143) is at No 166.

The *Blackall Motel* (☎ (076) 57 4491), on the corner of Shamrock and Myrtle Sts, has good motel units with singles/doubles at $40/50.

ISISFORD (pop 120)
A small historic township 90 km south of Ilfracombe and 125 km west of Blackall, Isisford was established in 1877 by the Whitman brothers, two travelling hawkers who broke an axle on their wagon while crossing the Barcoo River and decided to stay. They built a small settlement which today has a population of around 150. Kerry Packer's Isis Downs Station, with the largest

shearing shed in Australia, is 20 km east of Isisford.

Clancy's Overflow Hotel (☎ (076) 58 8210), built in 1875, has budget accommodation downstairs at $20 a room and more comfortable rooms upstairs at $30/35 for singles/doubles. The pub serves breakfast, lunch and dinner every day, and the publican, Jim Kilby, runs 4WD expeditions to the Grey Ranges which cost $85 per person per day.

IDALIA NATIONAL PARK

This remote national park, off the Blackall-Emmet road 112 km south-east of Blackall, is only accessible for 4WD vehicles. In the rugged escarpment county of the Gowan Ranges, the park includes the headwaters of the Bulloo River and its numerous tributaries, with a predominantly mulga scrub landscape.

There are no facilities here, and visitors need to be totally self-sufficient. Camping permits are required in advance; contact the park office (☎ (076) 57 5033) or the QNP&WS in Longreach (☎ (076) 58 1761) for more information.

BLACKALL TO CHARLEVILLE (300 km)
Barcoo River

Continuing south-east along the Landsborough Hwy, the Barcoo River is crossed 42 km south of Blackall, and there is an excellent spot to stop and camp on the east side of the road. You can even get back a bit off the road, away from the traffic noise.

The Barcoo is one of the great rivers of western Queensland, and must be the only river in the world that in its lower reaches becomes a creek! The Barcoo flows northwest past Blackall, then swings south-west through Isisford and into the Channel Country of south-western Queensland, where it becomes Cooper Creek, probably the most famous of Australia's inland rivers.

While Mitchell had waxed lyrical about this river in 1846, thinking it was a route to the Gulf, it was left to his second-in-command Edmund Kennedy (later of Cape York fame) to discover the real course of the river and to call it the Barcoo in 1847.

Both Banjo Paterson and Henry Lawson mention the Barcoo in their writings. The name has also entered the Australian idiom, appearing in the *Macquarie Dictionary* in such terms as 'Barcoo rot' (basically scurvy), the 'Barcoo salute' (the waving about of hands to keep flies away from the face) and the 'Barcoo spews' (vomiting caused by the heat).

Tambo (pop 350)

On the banks of the Barcoo River, Tambo is surrounded by perhaps the best grazing land in western Queensland, and this small hamlet also has some of the earliest historic buildings in the region. In the main street are timber houses that date back to the town's earliest days, in the 1860s, while the 'new' post office has been operating since 1904. The **'old' post office**, built in 1876, and at that time the main repeating station for south-west Queensland, is now a museum.

The information centre is at the shire council chambers (☎ (076) 54 6133). There's a National Australia Bank branch in Arthur St.

The town promotes itself as 'the friendly town of the west', and each year races are held at the local track, a tradition dating back to the formation of the Great Western Downs Jockey Club in 1865.

From Tambo you continue southwards on the Matilda Hwy, but for a good excursion, there is access to the **Salvator Rosa** section of Carnarvon National Park. The Salvator Rosa park is 120 km east of Tambo and is accessed via the Dawson Developmental Road and Cungelella station, generally a 4WD route. See the Capricorn Coast chapter for more information on the Carnarvon National Park.

Places to Stay The *Tambo Caravan Park* (☎ (076) 54 6463), on the highway west of the centre, caters for campers with tent sites at $8 and powered sites at $10.

The *Royal Carrangarra Hotel* (☎ (076) 54 6127) has basic pub-style rooms at $15/25 for singles/doubles, and the *Club Hotel-*

Motel (☎ (076) 54 6109) has budget rooms or motel-style units from $28/36. The *Tambo Mill Motel* (☎ (076) 54 6466) has a swimming pool and good motel rooms from $48/58.

Augathella (pop 430)
The town of Augathella is 116 km south of Tambo is the town of Augathella. It lies five km south of the junction of the Mitchell and Longreach Hwys. South-east Queensland travellers heading north to Mt Isa, the Gulf or the Northern Territory often join the Matilda at this junction.

Surveyed in 1880, Augathella began as a bullock team camp beside the Warrego River. Today it services the sheep properties that dot the surrounding countryside.

Information This small country town has one hotel, one motel and a caravan park, with fuel and supplies from the shops in town. Tourist information can be obtained from Russell's Roadhouse (☎ (076) 54 5255). There is a branch of the National Australia Bank in Main St.

Places to Stay Travellers can stay at the *Augathella Motel & Caravan Park* (☎ (076) 54 5177), which has tent sites at $8 and motel units at $45/55.

CHARLEVILLE (pop 3510)
About 800 km from the coast, Charleville is at the junction of the Mitchell Hwy, the Warrego Hwy and the Diamantina Developmental Rd. Set on the Warrego River, Charleville is something of an oasis and one of the major centres in outback Queensland.

History
Edmund Kennedy passed this way in 1847, and the town was gazetted in 1868, six years after the first settlers had arrived. By the turn of the century the town was an important centre for the outlying sheep and cattle stations, a role it still carries out today.

Cobb & Co began building coaches here in 1893, and these coaches, especially designed for Australian conditions, were built here until 1920. Charleville is also linked to the origins of Qantas; the airline's first regular route was between Charleville and Cloncurry in 1922.

The floods of 1990 devastated large areas of the Channel Country, and Charleville was one of the hardest hit towns. As the Warrego River rose the flood waters swept through the town at around 70 km an hour, carrying away houses like toys, and the streets literally opened up and swallowed cars. There are photos and books on the floods in the town's tourist office, and a red line almost two metres up the wall shows the high water mark.

Information
Tourist Information The tourist information

The Meteorologist and the Drought-Buster Guns
Charleville is the site of one of the more bizarre episodes in meteorological history. In 1902, meteorologist Clement Wragge proposed importing six Stiger Vortex guns from Germany in an attempt to break the 'great drought', which since 1896 had devastated large areas of Queensland. Wragge had seen wine-makers in northern Italy firing the guns at storm clouds to try and reduce hailstones into raindrops, and he theorised that the guns could be used in the outback as sure-fire drought-busters.

When they arrived, the conical, five-metre high guns were assembled and installed around the town. On 26 September 1902, Wragge poured gunpowder into the guns and detonated them with fuses. Horses bolted at the deafening noise, and two of the guns exploded into pieces. Fortunately no-one was injured. Rain continued not to fall. Wragge left town the next day.

You can see two of the original guns on display at the front of Bicentennial Park in Sturt St. ■

centre (☎ (076) 54 3057), on the corner of Wills and Edward Sts, is a good source of information on Charleville and the surrounding region. Between March and September the office is open daily from 9 am to 6 pm; over the quieter summer months, hours vary according to demand. There are several cattle stations in the district that open to visitors at different times of year – check with Trish if you're interested.

National Parks The QNP&WS has an office (☎ (076) 54 1255) at the end of Park St, just off the highway and across the railway line; opening hours are weekdays from 8.30 am to 4.30 pm.

Fuel & Services The Shell Roadhouse, at 50 Wills St, is open daily from 7 am to 9 pm (to 10 pm on Friday and Saturday); they take all credit cards and have EFTPOS facilities. The local RACQ depot is Bert's Body Shop (☎ (076) 54 1733) on Sturt St.

Post & Money There are Westpac and National banks in Wills St, and a Commonwealth Bank in Alfred St beside the post office.

Laundry The Golden West Laundromat is down an arcade on Alfred St, between the supermarket and the Historic House Museum.

Things to See & Do
The **Historic House Museum**, at 91-93 Alfred St, is an old timber Queenslander that was originally built as the Queensland Bank, and later became a private residence and then a guesthouse. Nowadays it's a folk museum with an impressive collection of memorabilia; entry costs $2 for adults and 20c for kids.

The QNP&WS office (see the Information section) operates a captive breeding programme and has a **bird aviary** and a **fauna display** where you can see several endangered species – the rare yellow-footed rock wallaby and the bridled nail-tail wallaby, and the bilby (sometimes called the rabbit-eared bandicoot) – in small enclosures.

At the front of a small park in Sturt St, you can see 1½ of the **Stiger Vortex Rainmaker Guns** that were used in a futile drought-breaking attempt on 26 September 1902. The half gun exploded during testing.

The **Skywatch** observatory at the Meteorological Bureau (four km south of the centre off Airport Drive), has high-powered telescopes which you can gaze through in the evenings. It opens every night (unless it's cloudy) between March and October; the sessions start at 6.30 pm from May to August and at 7 pm at other times, and run for 1½ to two hours. You need to book in advance at the tourist office or by phoning ☎ (076) 54 1260. The cost is $8 for adults, $5 for children and $20 for a family.

The office of the **Meteorological Bureau** also opens for free guided tours, and interested people can visit the vital facilities at the **Royal Flying Doctor Service base** (☎ (076) 54 1341) and the **School of the Air** (now called the School of Distance Education) – check with the information office.

On the corner of Parry and Warrego Sts, the **Murweh Shire Memorial Pool** is a good Olympic-sized swimming pool.

Places to Stay
Caravan Parks The best of the two caravan parks here is the *Bailey Bar Caravan Park* (☎ (076) 54 1744), at 196 King St. It's a well-kept park with lots of grass and eucalypt trees; tent sites cost $10, powered sites $12, on-site vans $25 and self-contained cabins $44.

Pubs On the corner of Wills and Galatea Sts, *Corones Hotel* (☎ (076) 54 1022) is one of Queensland's grand old country pubs. It doesn't look much from the outside, but the interior is a monument to nostalgia, from the huge public bar with its lovely, simple leadlight windows to the honey-coloured timber lounge with its central staircase, old club lounge chairs, open fire and colonial furnishings. There are literally dozens of rooms upstairs. Simple pub-style rooms cost

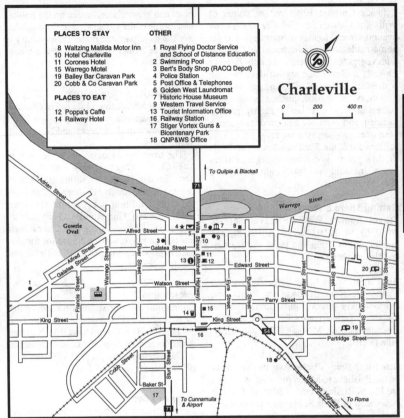

PLACES TO STAY

8 Waltzing Matilda Motor Inn
10 Hotel Charleville
11 Corones Hotel
15 Warrego Motel
19 Bailey Bar Caravan Park
20 Cobb & Co Caravan Park

PLACES TO EAT

12 Poppa's Caffe
14 Railway Hotel

OTHER

1 Royal Flying Doctor Service
   and School of Distance Education
2 Swimming Pool
3 Bert's Body Shop (RACQ Depot)
4 Police Station
5 Post Office & Telephones
6 Golden West Laundromat
7 Historic House Museum
9 Western Travel Service
13 Tourist Information Office
16 Railway Station
17 Stiger Vortex Guns &
   Bicentenary Park
18 QNP&WS Office

Charleville

0   200   400 m

OUTBACK QUEENSLAND

\$15/22 for singles doubles, or \$25/35 with a private bathroom, or you can have a charmingly restored heritage-style room with an original bathroom, TV and air-con for \$30/40 – great value! There are also motel units out the back at \$35/45. Breakfasts range from \$4 to \$10.

The *Hotel Charleville* (☎ (076) 54 1076), on the corner of Wills and Alfred Sts, has basic pub-style rooms at \$15/30.

Motels Charleville has three motels. The *Waltzing Matilda Motor Inn* (☎ (076) 54 1720), at 125 Alfred St, is a straightforward

little timber motel with a pool, spa and units around a central courtyard – singles/doubles go for \$35/40. The *Warrego Motel* (☎ (076) 54 1299), at 77 Wills St, has better units at \$55/65.

Places to Eat

The *Railway Hotel*, on the corner of Wills and King Sts, has good-value bistro meals, with \$3.50 lunches from Monday to Saturday, barbecues on Friday nights, and a carvery on Saturday costing \$5 for adults and \$2 for children. Other meals range from \$7 to \$12, and kids' meals are \$4.

Inside Corones Hotel on the corner of Wills and Galatea Sts, *The Carvery* is open evenings from Monday to Saturday – you get home-made soup, garlic bread and a roast with vegies for $11. Beside the pub, *Poppa's Caffe* is a classy and stylish daytime cafe with excellent food – filled and grilled sandwiches, hot roast rolls, quiches, lasagna, real coffee and great cakes – highly recommended, and certainly a notch or two above your average country town cafe.

The cafe at the *Shell roadhouse*, on Wills St, has pretty good breakfasts and takeaways, including very tasty club sandwiches ($4.25).

Getting There & Away

Travel Agents Western Travel Service (☎ (076) 54 1260), at 94 Alfred St, can handle all bus, train and plane reservations and ticket sales.

Air Flight West have daily flights into Charleville from Brisbane via Roma, and twice-weekly direct flights from Brisbane. One-way fares from Charleville include Brisbane ($226), Mt Isa ($298) and Birdsville ($210).

Bus McCafferty's buses pass through daily on the Brisbane to Mt Isa run. One-way fares are $52 to Brisbane and $120 to Mt Isa. The buses stop in Wills St opposite the newsagency.

Train The twice-weekly *Westlander* runs from Brisbane to Charleville; one-way fares are $77 for an economy seat, $107 for an economy sleeper and $172 for a 1st-class sleeper. There are connecting bus services continuing on to Cunnamulla and Quilpie.

CHARLEVILLE TO CUNNAMULLA (199 km)

This section of the Mitchell Hwy parallels the Warrego River (which is off to the west). The old railway line follows a similar route northwards, and a couple of railway sidings, the odd station homestead and the small community of **Wyandra**, with the obligatory

hotel and general store, make up the habitation profile of the 197-km trip to Cunnamulla. For the most part, the mainly flat country is clothed in mulga, a low tree of the wattle family.

CUNNAMULLA (pop 1650)

The southernmost town in western Queensland, Cunnamulla is on the Warrego River 120 km north of the Queensland/New South Wales border.

The town was gazetted in 1868, and in 1879 Cobb & Co established a coach station here. In the 1880s, an influx of farmers opened up the country to sheep farming and today two million sheep graze the open plains around Cunnamulla. The railway arrived in 1898, and since then Cunnamulla has been a major service centre for the district; in good years it is Queensland's biggest wool-loading rail yard.

Information

Cunnamulla's tourist information centre (☎ (076) 55 2121) is based in the Shire Hall on Jane St. The Commonwealth, National Australia and Westpac banks have branches in Cunnamulla. The local RACQ depot is Bill's Auto (☎ (076) 55 1407).

Things to See

For sightseers, there's the **Historical Society Display** on John St, telling the story of the pioneers of the district, and the **Robber's Tree** at the southern end of Stockyard St, a reminder of a robbery that was bungled back in the 1880s. Another tree at the civic centre takes some importance from the fact that it is a yapunyah tree, floral emblem of the Paroo Shire – and this one was planted by royalty!

Festivals

In late August the town celebrates the Cunnamulla-Eulo Festival of the Opal, a week-long festival with arts & crafts, a parade and ball. Another major event is the annual show, held in May.

Places to Stay
The *Jack Tonkin Caravan Park* (☎ (076) 55 1421), on Watson St, has tent sites from $9, powered sites from $12 and four cabins from $25 a double.

The *Warrego Hotel-Motel* (☎ (076) 55 1737), at 9 Louise St, has pub rooms at $25/35 and motel units at $45/55. The *Corella Motor Inn* (☎ (076) 55 1593), on the corner of Emma and Wicks Sts, has units at $40/50.

Getting There & Away
There are bus services connecting Cunnamulla with the twice-weekly *Westlander* train service from Charleville to Brisbane.

WEST OF CUNNAMULLA
See the Channel Country section for details of the westward route from Cunnamulla.

The Channel Country

The remote and sparsely populated south-western corner of Queensland, bordering the Northern Territory, South Australia and New South Wales, takes its name from the myriad channels which crisscross the area. In this inhospitable region it hardly ever rains, but water from the summer monsoons further north pours into the Channel Country along the Georgina, Hamilton and Diamantina rivers and Cooper Creek. Flooding towards the great depression of Lake Eyre in South Australia, the mass of water arrives on this huge plain, eventually drying up in water holes or salt pans.

Only on rare occasions (the early '70s and in 1989) has the vast amount of water actually reached Lake Eyre and filled it. For a short period after each wet season, however, the Channel Country does become fertile, and cattle are grazed here.

Getting There & Around
Some roads from the east and north to the fringes of the Channel Country are paved,

but during the October to May wet season even these can be cut – and the dirt roads become quagmires. In addition, the summer heat is unbearable so a visit is best made in the cooler winter from May to September. Visiting this area requires a sturdy vehicle (4WD if you want to get off the beaten track) and some experience of outback driving. If you're travelling anywhere west of Cunnamulla or Quilpie, always carry plenty of petrol and drinking water and notify the police, so that if you don't turn up at the next town, the necessary steps can be taken.

The main road through the Channel Country is the Diamantina Developmental Road that runs south from Mt Isa through Boulia to Bedourie and then turns east through Windorah and Quilpie to Charleville. In all, it's a long and lonely 1340 km, a little over half of which is surfaced.

The Kennedy Developmental Road runs from Winton to Boulia and, for the most part, is surfaced with a couple of fuel and accommodation stops on the way.

MT ISA TO BOULIA (295 km)
This section of the Diamantina Developmental Rd is the northern access route into the Channel Country. This first section is over narrow, sealed bitumen. The only facilities along the route are at **Dajarra**, a small railway siding 150 km south of Mt Isa. The *Dajarra Hotel* (☎ (077) 48 4955) has budget accommodation at $15 per person, and there's a roadhouse here selling super, unleaded and diesel fuel.

BOULIA (pop 280)
Boulia is the 'capital' of the Channel Country. Burke and Wills passed through here on their long trek, and there's a museum in a restored 1888 stone house in the little town. Near Boulia, the mysterious Min Min Light, a sort of earthbound UFO, is sometimes seen. It's said to resemble the headlights of a car and can hover a metre or two above the ground before vanishing and reappearing in a different place.

Boulia has the *Australian Motel/Hotel*

(☎ (077) 46 3144), on Herbert St, with pub-style rooms at $27/32 for singles/doubles and motel units at $40/50. There's also the council-run *Boulia Caravan Park* (☎ (077) 46 3134), on the Winton road, with tent sites at $6 and powered sites at $12.

The Shell Roadhouse (☎ (077) 46 3131), on Herbert St, is the local RACQ depot and it is open Monday to Saturday from 8 am to 9 pm and Sunday from 8.30 am to 8.30 pm. If you need emergency fuel after hours, knock on the door of the house behind the roadhouse.

BOULIA TO WINTON (360 km)
The Kennedy Developmental Rd links Boulia with Winton. The only fuel stop along this route is 192 km east of Boulia at **Middleton**, which started out as staging post for Cobb & Co coaches. The *Middleton Hotel* (☎ (076) 57 3980) sells super, unleaded and diesel fuel, serves meals daily and has two caravans which it rents out for $20 a night.

BEDOURIE (pop 60)
Almost 200 km south of Boulia is Bedourie. First settled in 1880 as a depot for Cobb & Co coaches, Bedourie is now the administrative centre for the huge Diamantina Shire council. The town's water supply is supplied by an artesian bore.

The old *Royal Hotel* (☎ (077) 46 1201) hasn't changed much since it was built in 1880. The pub has budget accommodation at $25/30 for singles/doubles, sells fuel and acts as a post office agency. There's also a general store selling fuel and groceries and takeaway meals.

Bedourie's newest development is the impressive *Simpson Desert Roadhouse* (☎ (077) 46 1291) on the northern side of town. The roadhouse sells super, unleaded and diesel fuel, as well as having a general store and a restaurant, and it's open daily from 9 am to 9 pm; there's a night bell for emergency fuel. The development also includes a motel with modern units from $45/57 for singles/doubles plus $12 for each

extra person, and a caravan park across the road with tent sites and powered sites.

You can get tourist information from the Shire Council offices (☎ (077) 46 1202), where there's a good rest stop with a shaded picnic and barbecue area and toilets. The council-run caravan park is signposted off the highway.

Bedourie hosts a race meeting on the second weekend in September.

BIRDSVILLE (pop 100)
This tiny settlement is the most remote place in Queensland and possesses one of Australia's most famous pubs – the *Birdsville Hotel*.

Birdsville, only 12 km from the South Australian border, is at the northern end of the 481-km Birdsville Track which leads down to Marree in South Australia. In the late 19th century, Birdsville was quite a busy place as cattle were driven south to South Australia and a customs charge was made on each head of cattle leaving Queensland. With Federation, the charge was abolished and Birdsville became almost ghost-like, although in recent years the growing tourism industry has revitalised the town. Its big moment today is the annual Birdsville Races on the first weekend in September, when as many as 6000 racing and boozing enthusiasts make the trip to Birdsville.

Birdsville gets its water from a 1219-metre-deep artesian well which delivers the water at over 100°C.

Information
Post & Money The only banking facilities are at the Commonwealth Bank agency at the post office, although both service stations have EFTPOS facilities.

Fuel & Services Birdsville Auto (☎ (076) 56 3226) (the Shell roadhouse) is open daily from 8 am to 6 pm. This place is the local RACQ depot and can handle towing, all mechanical repairs and has a limited range of spare parts. There's also a Mobil service station opposite the pub. Both of these places sell super, unleaded and diesel (the most expensive fuel in Queensland!), have EFTPOS facilities and take all major credit cards, and will also open for after-hours fuel.

Supplies The historic *Brookland's Store*, the ubiquitous general store, sells groceries and a bit of everything else. They are generally open from 8.30 am until 5 or 5.30 pm, and close at lunch time for a couple of hours.

Things to See & Do
One of Birdsville's highlights is a visit to the **Birdsville Working Museum**. From the outside it just looks like a big tin shed, but inside is one of the most impressive private museums you'll ever see. This well-presented collection includes an amazing array of...well, stuff. Old tobacco tins and road signs, petrol bowsers and gas drums, farm machinery, drover's gear, shearing equipment, wool presses, an art gallery, mule-driven rounding yards out the back, and lots more. Just about everything is in working order, and the owner, John Menzies, will take you on a private tour complete with demonstrations. The museum is open daily from 8.30 am to 8.30 pm; entry is good value at $5 for adults and $3 for kids.

Birdsville's **cemetery** has a grim, desolate setting amongst sand dunes and spinifex, with several small clusters of headstones – some marble, others just scraps of wood or tin with roughly tattooed epitaphs to those whose 'earthly race is run'. To get there, take the road towards Big Red and the Simpson Desert and turn right after one km – a rocky, sandy track leads 1.5 km to the cemetery.

Opposite the pub are two **stone memorials** to several expeditions which crossed the Simpson Desert with camels in the 1930s.

In the main street are the stone ruins of the **Royal Hotel** (1883), which was also the town's first hospital. Nearby, the **Frontier Services Hospital** welcomes visitors and will show you around. They have a few souvenirs on sale – T-shirts, mugs, tea towels etc – and while there's no entry fee, donations are gratefully accepted. You can also join in their thrice-weekly aerobics session

(free), and the Flying Doctor visits once a month.

The famous **Birdsville Cup Race Meeting** is held on the first weekend in September every year. The Birdsville races are part of a circuit, with races in Bedourie and then Betoota on consecutive weekends.

The races are a fairly wild and woolly event, with up to 6000 visitors driving or flying into town, many of them arriving in light aircraft. Horse races are held on the Friday and Saturday, and Fred Brophy's travelling boxing troupe provides entertainment at nights. You'll need to book a long way in advance to secure any sort of accommodation. Otherwise, the council provides temporary showers and toilets – most of the fly-ins just pitch a tent beside their planes.

Places to Stay & Eat
The *Birdsville Caravan Park* (☎ (076) 56 3214), behind the Shell roadhouse, backs onto a billabong on the Diamantina River. The park has recently been revamped and has new amenities blocks, hot showers, laundries and coin-operated barbecues, although the park is fairly barren and there isn't much shade. Powered sites cost $5 per person and tent sites cost $5 for two people or $10 for three or more – there are no on-site vans or cabins here.

The *Birdsville Hotel* (☎ (076) 56 3244) dates from 1884 but has been tastefully and impressively renovated inside, with slate floors and whitewashed walls. The public bar has a collection of old photos, road signs and battered old bushmen's hats (the hats, not the bushmen...), and there are several other bars and a separate dining room. This is one of the great Australian pubs, full of outback history and characters – definitely not to be missed. Behind the pub is a row of 10 modern, motel-style units with air-con and bathrooms, but no phones or TVs. Singles/doubles cost $42/64, triples/quads $75/84. Another nine units are being built in the near future. Breakfast, lunch and dinner are served in the dining room – you'll need to book during the high season – or there are cheaper meals in the public bar. The pub is open from 10 am until around midnight; hours are limited on Sunday, usually from 11 am to 7 pm, and the pub closes between 1 and 5 pm on Sunday in summer.

Getting There & Away

Air Birdsville has its own sealed airstrip. Avgas, jet fuel and petrol are available through the hotel.

Two airlines have regular flights to Birdsville. Augusta Airways (☎ (086) 42 3100) has a weekly mail-run service between Port Augusta in South Australia and Birdsville, arriving in Birdsville on Saturday and leaving on Sunday. The one-way fare is $205.

Flight West Airlines (☎ 13 2392 within Queensland or toll-free 1800 777 879 from elsewhere in Australia) has a twice-weekly service between Brisbane and Birdsville via Charleville, Quilpie and Windorah; the one-way fare is $392. Flight West Airlines also has a twice-weekly service between Mt Isa and Birdsville via Boulia and Bedourie; the one-way fare is $211.

Bus There are no regular bus services to Birdsville.

Car & Motorcycle There are two roads into Birdsville from Queensland – the north-south Eyre Developmental Rd from Bedourie and Boulia, and the east-west Birdsville Developmental Rd from Windorah and Betoota.

Both of these routes are rough and unsealed, and while both are drivable in conventional vehicles you'd be much better off in a 4WD. The surfaces vary from gravel and dirt to soft red sand, with frequent cattle grids and creek crossings. You need to watch out for the sudden dips at dry creek beds, particularly in a conventional vehicle – it's easy to bottom out and come to grief if you go too fast through these natural 'speed bumps'. Apart from the potholes, bull dust patches, dips and crests, another hazard are the sharp rocks, and it's advisable to carry at least two spare tyres, as well as plenty of drinking water and spare parts.

AROUND BIRDSVILLE

Off the Simpson Desert Rd about 40 km west of Birdsville is **Big Red**, a massive wave-like sandhill which is a popular destination for 4WD travellers. Off the road to Bedourie, about 15 km north of Birdsville, is a patch of rare **Waddi trees** which grow nowhere else in the world apart from central Australia.

Birdsville Track

To the south, the Birdsville Track passes between the Simpson Desert to the west and Sturt Stony Desert to the east. The first stretch from Birdsville has two alternative routes. Ask local advice about which is better. The Inner Track – marked 'not recommended' on most maps – crosses the Goyder Lagoon (the 'end' of the Diamantina River) and a big Wet will sometimes cut this route.

The longer, more easterly Outside Track crosses sandy country at the edge of the desert where it is sometimes difficult to find the track.

While it is no longer necessary to register with the Birdsville police before tackling the track, it's a good idea to keep friends or relatives informed of your movements so they can notify the authorities should you fail to report in on time. You can contact the Birdsville police (☎ (076) 56 3220) for advice on road conditions.

Simpson Desert National Park

The waterless Simpson Desert occupies a massive 200,000 sq km of central Australia, and stretches across the Queensland, Northern Territory and South Australian borders. The Queensland section of the desert, in the far south-west corner of the state, is protected as the Simpson Desert National Park and adjoins South Australia's Simpson Desert Conservation Park and Simpson Desert Regional Reserve.

The park is a remote, arid region with a landscape of long, high sand dunes, and limited vegetation of spinifex, canegrass and various shrubs.

While conventional cars can tackle the

Birdsville Track quite easily, the Simpson crossing requires a 4WD and far more preparation. Official advice is that crossings should only be tackled by parties of at least two 4WD vehicles and that you should have an HF radio to call for help if necessary. Temperatures are extreme, ranging from over 35°C in summer to freezing on some winter mornings. Travel in the summer months is not recommended.

There are no facilities, so you need to be totally self-sufficient and equipped with adequate supplies of water, food, fuel and spare parts. The park boundary is 80 km west of Birdsville; from the boundary, it's another 70 km to Poepple Corner, the intersection of the three states.

Permits are required before you can traverse the park, and you should advise the Birdsville police of your intended movements. Permits are available from the police station in Birdsville or from QNP&WS offices. For more information, contact the QNP&WS offices in Longreach (☎ (076) 58 1761), Emerald (☎ (079) 82 2246) or Charleville (☎ (076) 54 1255).

You also need a permit to travel into the South Australian sections of the park – these are available through the South Australian National Parks & Wildlife Service (☎ (086) 48 4244) in Hawker, South Australia.

BETOOTA (pop 1)

Betoota, 164 km east of Birdsville, isn't exactly a town. It consists of a couple of old tin buildings, a phone booth and a fairly run-down pub, and has an official population of one – old Simon, the publican, who's been keeping the flies company out here for a quarter of a century.

The *Betoota Hotel* (☎ (076) 56 4963), open Monday through Saturday from 10 am to 10 pm, sells fuel, drinks and potato chips. If you want to hang around, there are a couple of rooms out the back, although they're not exactly flash and at $30 a head they're not particularly good value either.

Betoota hosts its own race meeting on the third weekend in September.

WINDORAH (pop 70)

Windorah is either very dry or very wet and has a pub, a general store and a caravan park.

Gordon's General Store (☎ (076) 56 3145), open weekdays from 8 am to 6 pm and weekends from 8.30 am to 1.30 pm and from 4 to 6 pm, although they will open at any time if you need fuel. They sell super, unleaded and diesel, plus a range of groceries and takeaway meals, and take all major credit cards and have EFTPOS facilities.

Across the road, the *Western Star Hotel* (☎ (076) 56 3166) is a cute colonial-style pub fronted by three tall eucalypts, with nine good rooms with air-con at $25/35. They serve bistro meals on Friday nights, and can do evening meals other nights if you ring in advance and let them know you're coming.

The *Windorah Caravan Park* is a small fenced-in block on the west side of town, with a couple of trees and an amenities block.

QUILPIE (pop 620)

Quilpie is an opal-mining town and the railhead from which cattle, grazed here during the fertile wet season, are railed to the coast. It has two pubs with rooms, a motel and a good swimming pool. The **Quilpie Memorial Swimming Pool** is in Brolga St, east of the centre.

The name Quilpie comes from the Aboriginal word for stone curlew, and all but one of the town's streets are named after birds.

Information

Fuel & Services The local RACQ agent is John Crawley (☎ (076) 56 1344), at the Ampol service station on the corner of Chulungra and Boonkai Sts. You can also get fuel from the Mobil service station on Brolga St and from the Quilpie Cafe, which is open daily from 8 am to 9 pm.

Places to Stay & Eat

The *LR McManus Caravan Park* (☎ (076) 56 1371), in Chipu St 100 metres off the highway, has tent sites at $10 and powered sites at $12.

The modern *Imperial Hotel-Motel*

(☎ (076) 56 1300), on the corner of Brolga and Buln Buln Sts, has average motel-style rooms in transportable units at $45/50 for singles/doubles, and serves bistro meals.

The *Quilpie Motor Inn* (☎ (076) 56 1277), on Brolga St 100 metres west of the centre, has good units from $45/50. If you're interested in staying on a cattle station in this area, the owner of this motel can book you in and take you out to one of five properties on his books – ring him and ask what's available.

The *Quilpie Bakery* opposite the Imperial Hotel is a good lunch spot, with pies, pastries, salad rolls, roast chicken and pizzas – there's a small eat-in section.

In an old verandah-fronted building at 34 Brolga St, *Redgums Restaurant* has hearty home-style cooking with meals like pork chops, spaghetti and meatballs and shepherd's pie. Their set menus range from $8 to $12; they open for lunch Tuesday to Friday and dinner Tuesday to Saturday, and are BYO.

Getting There & Away
There are bus services connecting Quilpie with the twice-weekly *Westlander* train service from Charleville to Brisbane.

QUILPIE TO CHARLEVILLE (210 km)
There are a couple of small townships along this section of the Diamantina Developmental Rd: **Cheepie**, 76 km east of Quilpie, has a railway station and a phone booth, and 45 km further east **Cooladdi** has a motel and general store that has emergency fuel. See the earlier Matilda Highway section for details of the Charleville region.

CUNNAMULLA TO INNAMINCKA (640 km)
Heading west from Cunnamulla, the all-bitumen Bulloo Developmental Rd takes you through the small settlements of Eulo, Thargomindah and Noccundra. You can take a northern detour to the Yowah opalfields, and if you have a 4WD you can continue west from Noccundra to the town of Innamincka, on the Strzelecki Track in South Australia.

Eulo (pop 60)
Eulo, 68 km west of Cunnamulla, is on the Paroo River close to the Yowah opalfields. In late August/early September the town hosts the World Lizard Racing Championships, beside the Eulo Queen Hotel and the **Destructo Cockroach Monument**. Erected in memory of a racing cockroach who died when a punter stood on it, this granite plinth must be the only cockroach memorial in the world. Don't let this, or the lizard-racing competition, put you off visiting Eulo – the people are really quite friendly.

The *Eulo Queen Hotel* (☎ (076) 55 4867) has air-con pub rooms at $15/25 for singles/twins, or there's the *Eulo Caravan Park* (☎ (076) 55 4890). The Eulo Store sells fuel and supplies.

Yowah (pop 40)
Yowah is an opal-mining settlement about 90 km north-west of Eulo – the road is good bitumen most of the way with 23 km of gravel at the final section. It's a popular fossicking field where boulder opals are found.

Yowah has a caravan park, a general store, a motel and a museum, and a couple of the mines open up for visitors.

About 100 km further north from Yowah are the **Duck Creek opalfields**.

Thargomindah (pop 300)
On the banks of the Bulloo River, Thargomindah is almost 200 km south of Quilpie and almost 200 km west of Cunnamulla. The road from Cunnamulla is good sealed bitumen; the majority of the route to Quilpie is unsealed. The town was gazetted back in 1874, and camel trains used to cross from here to Bourke in New South Wales.

The *Bulloo River Hotel* (☎ (076) 55 3125) has six air-con rooms at $30/40 for singles/doubles, and the *Oasis Motel* (☎ (076) 55 3155) has units from $40/45. There's also a council-run caravan park (☎ (076) 55 3133) with tent sites at $7 and powered sites at $10.

The pub serves bistro meals, and there's a

cafe and restaurant at the *Oasis Motel*. Baxy's General Store sells fuel, as does the BP service station.

Contact the Shire Council offices (☎ (076) 55 3133) for further information.

Noccundra (pop 8)

Noccundra, 145 km further west on the Wilson River, was once a busy little community. It now has just a hotel and a population of eight. The *Noccundra Hotel* (☎ (076) 55 4317), a sandstone building which dates back to 1882, serves breakfasts and evening meals every day, and has a small guesthouse with air-con rooms at $15/25 for singles/ twins and $35 for a double. The pub also sells super, unleaded and diesel fuel, and can handle some emergency repairs. They can also supply avgas with advance notice. If you're after a meal or need a bed, it's best to ring in advance and let them know you're coming – you might miss out if you just blow in.

Continuing on from Noccundra, head 20 km north back to the Bulloo Developmental Rd, which continues west for another 75 km through the Jackson Oil Field to the Naccowlah Oil Field. The sealed road ends here, but you can continue across to Innamincka on the Strzelecki Track in South Australia, via the site of the **Dig Tree**, of Burke and Wills fame, on Nappa Merrie Station on the Cooper Creek, near the Queensland/South Australia border (see History section Facts about Queensland chapter). This route is particularly rough and stony with frequent creek crossings, and is only recommended for 4WD vehicles; the road is usually closed during the Wet. If you are heading this way, check at the pub for directions – the signs tend to go missing along this route.

OUTBACK QUEENSLAND

Glossary

amber fluid – beer
ankle-biter – small child, *tacker, rug rat*
arvo – afternoon
avagoyermug – traditional rallying call, especially at cricket matches
award wage – minimum pay rate

back o' Bourke – back of beyond, middle of nowhere
backblocks – *bush* or other remote area far from the city
bail out – leave
bail up – hold up, rob, earbash
Balmain bug – see *Moreton Bay bug*
banana bender – resident of Queensland
banker – a river almost overflowing its banks (as in 'the Cooper is running a banker')
barbie – barbecue (BBQ)
barra – barramundi (prized fish of the north)
barrack – cheer on team at sporting event, support (as in 'who do you barrack for?')
bastard – general term of address which can mean many things. While mostly used as a good-natured form of greeting ('*G'day,* you old bastard!'), it can also denote the highest level of praise or respect ('He's the bravest bastard I know!') or it can be the most dire of insults ('You lousy, lying copper bastard!')
bathers – swimming costume (Victoria)
battler – hard trier, struggler (the outback is full of 'great Aussie battlers')
beaut, *beauty, bewdie* – great, fantastic
big bikkies – a lot of money, expensive
big mobs – a large amount, heaps
bikies – motorcyclists
billabong – waterhole in dried-up riverbed, more correctly an ox-bow bend cut off in the dry season by receding waters
billy – tin container used to boil tea in the bush
bitumen – asphalt, surfaced road
black stump – where the *back o' Bourke* begins
blaze – (a blaze in a tree) a mark in a tree trunk made by cutting away bark, indicating a path or reference point; also 'to blaze'

bloke – man
blowies – blowflies, bluebottles
bludger – lazy person, one who won't work and lives off other people's money (originally, a prostitute's pimp)
blue heeler – cattle dog
blue (ie *have a blue*) – to have an argument or fight
bluey – *swag*; also nickname for a red-haired person
bonzer – great, *ripper*
boomer – very big; a particularly large male kangaroo
boomerang – a curved flat wooden instrument used by Aborigines for hunting
booze bus – police van used for random breath testing for alcohol
boozer – pub
bottleshop – liquor shop
bottle – 750 ml bottle of beer
bottlo – bottleshop
bowser – fuel pump at a service station (named after the US inventor S F Bowser)
brumby – wild horse
bruss – brother, *mate* (used by central Australian Aborigines)
Buckley's, *Buckley's chance* – no chance at all ('Across the Tanami? They've got *Buckley's* in that *shitbox*'). The origin of this term is unclear. Maybe it derives from the Melbourne department store of Buckley's & Nunn; or from the escaped convict William Buckley, whose chances of survival were considered negligible but who ended up living with Aborigines for 20 years; or from the Sydney escapologist Buckley, who had himself chained-up in a coffin and thrown into Sydney Harbour, with dire results
bug – see *Moreton Bay bug*
Bulamakanka – place even beyond the *back o' Bourke*, way beyond the *black stump* (see *never-never*)
bull bar – outsize front bumper on car or truck as ultimate barrier against animals on the road
bull dust – fine, powdery and sometimes

deep dust on outback roads, often hiding deep holes and ruts that you normally wouldn't drive into; also bullshit

bunfight – a quarrel over a frivolous issue or one that gets blown out of proportion

bungarra – any large (1.5-metre-plus) goanna, but specifically an Aboriginal name for Gould's goanna, prized as food

bunyip – mythical bush spirit said to inhabit Australia's swamps

burl – have a try (as in 'give it a burl')

bush tucker – food available naturally

bush (ie *go bush*) – go back to the land

bush – country, anywhere away from the city; *scrub*

bushbash – to force your way through pathless bush

bushranger – Australia's equivalent of the outlaws of the American Wild West (some goodies, some baddies) – the helmeted Ned Kelly was the most famous

BYO – Bring Your Own (booze to a restaurant, meat to a barbecue etc)

caaarn! – come on, traditional rallying call, especially at football games, as in 'Caaarn the Bombers!'

cackle-berries – eggs; also 'hen-fruit', 'chook-nuts' and 'bum-nuts'

camp draft – Australian rodeo, testing horse rider's skills in separating cattle or sheep from a herd or flock

camp oven – large, cast-iron pot with lid, used for cooking in an open fire

cask – wine box (a great Australian invention)

Chiko roll – vile Australian junk food

chocka – completely full (from 'chock-a-block')

chook – chicken

chuck a U-ey – do a U-turn

chunder – vomit, technicolour yawn, pavement pizza, curbside quiche, liquid laugh, drive the porcelain bus, call Bluey

clobber – clothes

cobber – mate (archaic)

cocky – small-scale farmer; cockatoo

come good – turn out all right

compo – compensation such as workers' compensation

cooee – long, loud call used in the bush to

attract attention; also, shouting distance (to be within cooee of...)

cop, *copper* – policeperson (not uniquely strine but very common nevertheless); see *walloper*

counter meal, *countery* – pub meal

cow cocky – small-scale cattle farmer

cozzie – swimming costume (New South Wales)

crook – ill, badly made, substandard

crow eater – resident of South Australia

culvert – channel or pipe under road for rainwater drainage

cut lunch – sandwiches

cut snake – see *mad as a...*

dag, *daggy* – dirty lump of wool at back end of a sheep; also an affectionate or mildly abusive term for a socially inept person

daks – trousers

damper – bush loaf made from flour and water and cooked in a *camp oven*

Darwin stubby – two-litre bottle of beer sold to tourists in Darwin

dead horse – tomato sauce

deli – delicatessen

didgeridoo – cylindrical wooden musical instrument played by Aboriginal men

digger – Australian or New Zealand soldier or veteran (originally, a miner); also a generic form of address assuming respect, mainly used for soldiers/veterans but sometimes also between friends

dill – fool

dingo – indigenous wild dog

dink – carry a second person on a bicycle or horse

dinkum, *fair dinkum* – honest, genuine ('fair dinkum?' – really?)

dinky-di – the real thing

distillate – diesel fuel

divvy van – police divisional van

dob in – to tell on someone

dodgy – false, unreliable

dog fence – the world's longest fence, erected to keep dingoes out of south-eastern Australia

don't come the raw prawn – don't try and fool me

donga – small transportable hut; also the

bush, from the name for a shallow, eroded gully, found in areas where it doesn't rain often, so people don't go there

donk – car or boat engine

down south – the rest of Australia, according to anyone north of Brisbane

drongo – worthless person

droving – moving livestock a considerable distance

Dry, the – the dry season in the north

duco – car paint

duffing – stealing cattle (literally: altering the brand on the 'duff', or rump)

dunny budgies – *blowies*

dunny – outdoor lavatory

earbash – talk nonstop

eastern states – the rest of Australia viewed from Western Australia

Esky – trademark name for a portable ice box used for keeping beer etc cold

fair crack of the whip! – *fair go!*

fair go! – give us a break!

feeding the ants – being in a very deceased condition out in the *donga*

FJ – most revered Holden car

flagon – two-litre bottle (of wine, port etc)

flake – shark meat, often used in fish & chips down south

floater – meat pie floating in pea soup – yuk

flog – steal; sell; whip

fluke – undeserved good luck ('they had three flat tyres, no spare, no puncture kit, no water, but they fluked a lift into town on the monthly mail truck. Otherwise they'd still be there *feeding the ants'*)

fossick – hunt for gems or semiprecious stones

from arsehole to breakfast – all over the place

furphy – a misleading statement, rumour or fictitious story, named after Joseph Furphy, who wrote a famous Australian novel, *Such is Life,* then reviewed the book for a literary journal of the time and criticised it; the public bought it by the ton. Or maybe this is a furphy and the term instead derives from the water or sewerage carrier made by his brother's company in Shepparton, Victoria;

in WW I these carriers were places where the troops met, swapped yarns and information, and no doubt construed a few furphies

g'day – good day, traditional Australian greeting

galah – noisy parrot, thus noisy idiot

game – brave (as in 'game as Ned Kelly')

gander – look (as in 'have a gander')

garbo – person who collects your garbage

gibber – Aboriginal word for stone or boulder; gibber plain – stony desert

gidgee – a type of small acacia

give it away – give up

good on ya – well done

grade – (to grade a road) to level a road, usually by means of a bulldozer fitted with a 'blade' that scrapes off the top layer and pushes it to the side

grazier – large-scale sheep or cattle farmer

Green, the – term used in the Kimberley for the wet season

grog – general term for alcoholic drinks

grouse – very good, unreal

gun shearer – the best shearer in any shearing shed

homestead – the residence of a *station* owner or manager

hoon – idiot, hooligan, *yahoo;* also 'to hoon' or 'hooning around', often in a vehicle – to show off in a noisy fashion with little regard for others

how are ya? – standard greeting – expected answer: 'Good, thanks, how are *you?'*

how ya goin'? – *how are ya?*

HQ – second-most revered Australian car

Hughie – the god of rain and surf ('Send her down, Hughie!', 'Send 'em up, Hughie!'); also God when things go wrong ('It's up to Hughie now')

humpy – Aboriginal bark hut ('it was so cold, it would freeze the walls off a bark humpy')

icy-pole – frozen *lolly water* or ice cream on a stick

jackaroo – young male trainee on a *station*

jaffle – sealed toasted sandwich

jerky – dried meat

jillaroo – young female trainee on a *station*

jocks – men's underpants

joey – young kangaroo or wallaby

journo – journalist

jumbuck – young sheep

jump-up – escarpment

jumped-up – arrogant, full of self-importance (a 'jumped-up petty Hitler')

kiwi – (also 'kay-one-double-you-one') New Zealander

knackered – exhausted, very tired

knock – criticise, deride

knocker – one who *knocks*

Koori – Aborigine (mostly south of the Murray River)

lair – layabout, ruffian

lairising – acting like a *lair*

lamington – square of sponge cake covered in chocolate icing and coconut

larrikin – a bit like a *lair;* rascal

lay-by – put a deposit on an article so the shop will hold it for you

lean-to – a temporary shelter, usually bark or tin placed diagonally against a tree trunk

lemonade – Australian Seven-Up

lock-up – *watch house*

lollies – sweets, candy

lolly water – soft drink made from syrup and water

lurk – a scheme

mad as a cut snake – insane, crazy; also insane with anger

mallee – low, shrubby, multi-stemmed eucalypt. Also 'the mallee' – the *bush*

manchester – household linen

March fly – horsefly, gadfly

mate – general term of familiarity, whether you know the person or not (but don't use it too often with total strangers)

Matilda – *swag*

Mexican – to a Queenslander, anyone from south of the border

middy – 285 ml beer glass (New South Wales)

milk bar – general store

milko – milkman

mob – a herd of cattle or flock of sheep while *droving;* any bunch of people (group, club, company)

Moreton Bay bug – (also known as *bug* or *Balmain bug)* an estuarine horseshoe crab closely related to the shovel-nosed lobster (good *tuckerwith an unfortunate name)*

mozzies – mosquitoes

mud map – map drawn on the ground with a stick, thus any rough map drawn by hand

mulga – arid-zone acacia; the *bush*, away from civilisation (as in 'he's gone up the mulga')

Murri – Aborigine (mostly in Queensland)

muster – round up livestock

mystery-bags – sausages

never-never – a place even more remote than *back o' Bourke*

no worries – *she'll be right*, that's OK

no-hoper – hopeless case

north island – mainland Australia, viewed from Tasmania

northern summer – summer in the northern hemisphere

nulla-nulla – wooden club used by Aborigines

O-S – overseas (as in 'he's gone O-S')

ocker – an uncultivated or boorish Australian

ocky strap – octopus strap: elastic strap with hooks for tying down gear and generally keeping things in place

off-sider – assistant or partner

on the piss – drinking alcohol ('they're on the piss tonight')

outback – remote part of the bush, back o' Bourke

outstation – an outlying *station* separate from the main one on a large property

OYO – own your own (flat or apartment)

Oz – Australia

pad – animal track ('cattle pad')

paddock – a fenced area of land, usually intended for livestock (paddocks can be huge in Australia)

pal – *mate*

pastoralist – large-scale *grazier*

pavlova – traditional Australian meringue and cream dessert, named after the Russian ballerina Anna Pavlova

perve – to gaze with lust

pineapple, rough end of – *stick, sharp end of*

piss turn – boozy party

piss – beer

pissed off – annoyed

pissed – drunk

plonk – cheap wine

pocamelo – camel polo

pokies – poker machines, found in clubs, mainly in New South Wales

pom – English person

pommy's towel – a notoriously dry object ('the Simpson Desert is as dry as a pommy's towel')

possie – advantageous position (pronounced 'pozzy')

postie – mailman or -woman

pot – 285 ml beer glass (Victoria, Queensland)

push – group or gang of people, such as shearers

Queenslander – dwellings which are generally square in shape and raised off the ground by stumps or poles, with a high-pitched iron roofs and broad, shady verandahs on at least two, and often four sides. They are a distinctive aspect of Queensland architecture

QNP&WS – Queensland National Park & Wildlife Service

quid – literally: a pound, $2. Still a common term in the *bush* for a non-specified amount of money, as in 'can you lend me a quid?' (enough money to last me until I'm not *skint*)

RACQ – Royal Automobile Club of Queensland

rapt – delighted, enraptured

rat's coffin – meat pie of dubious quality

ratbag – friendly term of abuse (friendly trouble-maker)

ratshit (R-S) – lousy

razoo – a coin of very little value, a subdivision of a rupee ('he spent every last razoo'). Counterfeit razoos made of brass circulated in the goldfields during *two-up* sessions, hence 'it's not worth a brass razoo'

reckon! – you bet!, absolutely!

rego – registration (as in 'car rego')

ridgy-didge – original, genuine, *dinky-di*

ripper – good, great (also 'little ripper')

road train – *semi-trailer*-trailer-trailer

roo bar – *bull bar*

root – have sexual intercourse

rooted – tired

ropable – very bad-tempered or angry

rubbish (ie *to rubbish*) – deride, tease

rug rat – small child, *ankle-biter, tacker*

salvo – member of the Salvation Army

sandgroper – resident of Western Australia

sanger – sandwich

scallops – fried potato cakes (Queensland), the edible muscle of certain molluscs (north Queensland), shellfish (elsewhere)

schooner – a 425 ml beer glass in New South Wales, or a 285 ml glass in South Australia (where a 425 ml glass is called a 'pint')

scrub – stunted trees and bushes in a dry area; a remote, uninhabited area

sea wasp – box jellyfish

sealed road – tarred road

sedan – a closed car seating four to six people

see you in the soup – see you around

seismic line – *shotline*

semi-trailer – articulated truck

septic tanks – (also 'septics') rhyming slang for Yanks

session – lengthy period of heavy drinking

shanty – pub, usually unlicensed (proliferated in gold-rush areas)

she'll be right – *no worries*, it'll be OK

sheila – woman, sometimes derogatory

shellacking – comprehensive defeat

shitbox – neglected, worn-out, useless vehicle

shonky – unreliable

shoot through – leave in a hurry

shotline – straight trail through the bush, often kilometres long and leading nowhere, built by a mining company for seismic research

shout – buy round of drinks (as in 'it's your shout')

sickie – day off work through illness or lack of motivation

singlet – sleeveless shirt

skint – the state of being *quidless*

slab – package containing four six-packs of *tinnies or stubbies*, usually encased in plastic on a carboard base; also called a 'carton' when packaged in a box (Victoria)

sleep-out – a covered verandah or shed, usually fairly open

sling off – criticise

smoke-oh – tea break

snag – sausage

sport – *mate*

spunky – good looking, attractive (as in 'what a spunk')

squatter – pioneer farmer who occupied land as a tenant of the government

squattocracy – Australian 'old money' folk, who made it by being first on the scene and grabbing the land

squiz – a look (as in 'take a squiz')

station – large sheep or cattle farm

stick, sharp end of – the worse deal

stickybeak – nosy person

stinger – box jellyfish

stoush – fist fight, brawl (also verbal)

stretcher – camp bed

strides – *daks*

strine – Australian slang (from how an *ocker* would pronounce the word 'Australian')

Stubbies – trademark name for rugged short shorts

stubby – 375 ml bottle of beer

sunbake – sunbathe (well, the sun's hot in Australia)

super – superannuation (contributory pension)

surfaced road – tarred road

surfies – surfing fanatics

swag – canvas-covered bed roll used in the outback; also a large amount

swaggie, swagman – itinerant worker carrying his possessions in a *swag* (see *waltzing Matilda*)

ta – thanks

table drain – rainwater run-off area, usually quite deep and wide, along the side of a dirt road

tacker – small child, *ankle-biter, rug rat*

takeaway – fast food, or a shop that sells it

tall poppies – achievers (*knockers* like to cut them down)

Taswegian – resident of Tasmania

tea – evening meal

terrorist – tourist

thingo – thing, whatchamacallit, hooza meebob, dooverlacky, thingamajig

thirst you could paint a picture of – the desire to drink a large quantity of foaming, ice-cold, nut-brown ale

thongs – flip-flops

tinny – 375 ml can of beer; also a small aluminium fishing dinghy

Tip, the – the top of Cape York

togs – swimming costume (Queensland, Victoria)

too right! – absolutely!

Top End – northern part of the Northern Territory, sometimes also Cape York

Top, the – the tip of Cape York

Troopie – Toyota Landcruiser Troopcarrier (seats up to 11 people)

trucky – truck driver

true blue – *dinkum*

tucker – food

two-pot screamer – person unable to hold their drink

two-up – traditional heads/tails gambling game

uni – university

up north – New South Wales and Queensland when viewed from Victoria

ute – utility, pickup truck

vegies – vegetables

waddy – wooden club used by Aborigines

wag – to play truant ('to wag school')

wagon – station wagon, estate car

walkabout – lengthy walk away from it all

wallaby track, on the – to wander from place to place seeking work (archaic)

walloper – policeperson (from 'wallop', to hit something with a stick)

waltzing Matilda – to wander with one's

swag seeking work or a place to settle down (archaic)

washaway – washout: heavy erosion caused by running water across road or track

watch house – temporary prison at a police station

weatherboard house – wooden house clad with long, narrow planks

Wet, the – rainy season in the north

wharfie – dockworker

whinge – complain, moan

willy-willy – whirlwind, dust storm

wobbly boot – (as in 'to put on the wobbly boot') to have consumed too much alcohol

wobbly – disturbing, unpredictable behaviour (as in 'throw a wobbly')

woof wood – petrol used to start a fire

woolly rocks – sheep

woomera – stick used by Aborigines for throwing spears

wowser – spoilsport, puritan

yabby, to – to catch yabbies, a relaxed activity often involving *mates* and a *slab* or two ('they're going yabbying this *arvo*')

yabby, *yabbie* – small freshwater crayfish

yahoo – noisy and unruly person, *hoon*

yakka – work (from an Aboriginal language)

yobbo – uncouth, aggressive person

yonks – ages, a long time

youse – plural of you (pronounced 'yooz')

yowie – Australia's yeti or bigfoot

Index

MAPS

Airlie Beach 380

Barcaldine 630
Bowen 398
Brisbane 136
  Brisbane & Moreton Bay 132
  Central Brisbane 144
  Brisbane River & Inner Suburbs 138
  Fortitude Valley, New Farm & Kangaroo Point 156
  Southern Inner Suburbs 160
Broadbeach & Mermaid Beach 224
Bundaberg 308
Burleigh Heads 228

Cairns 466
  Around Cairns 489
  Central Cairns 475
Caloundra 242
Cape York Peninsula 551
Cape York Track: Cairns to Coen 559
Cape York Track: Coen to the Tip 566
Capricorn Coast 314
Central Maryborough 293
Central Toowoomba 275
Charleville 637
Charters Towers 432
Chillagoe 499
Cooktown 539
Coolangatta & Tweed Heads 230

Darling Downs 263

Far North Queensland 457
Fraser Coast 287
Fraser Island 303

Gladstone 318
Gold Coast & Hinterland 210
Gold Coast Locator Map 213
Great Keppel Island 342
Gulf Savannah 586
Gympie 289

Hamilton Island 392
Hervey Bay 296
Hinchinbrook Island 442

Innisfail 461

Kuranda 493

Longreach 626

Mackay 360
  Central Mackay 362
Magnetic Island 422
  Magnetic Island – Picnic Bay, Nelly Bay & Arcadia 425
Main Beach & Southport 216
Maroochydore, Alexandra Headland & Mooloolaba 244
Mission Beach Area 449
Mt Isa 614

Noosa Heads 249
North Coast 403

Outback Queensland 607

Peregian Beach & Coolum Beach 247
Petrie Terrace & Paddington 159
Point Lookout 202
Port Douglas 509
  Central Port Douglas 514

Queensland 12, 13
Queensland Airfares 118
Queensland Chapters 15
Relative Size of Queensland 31

Rockhampton 329
  Central Rockhampton 331
Roma 280

Spring Hill 154
Stanthorpe 270
Sunshine Coast 238
Surfers Paradise 220

Thursday Island 581
Townsville 407
  Around Townsville 412
  Central Townsville 414

Warwick 266
Weipa 571
Whitsunday Coast 357

TEXT

Map references are in **bold** type.

Aboriginal art 192
Aboriginal tours 295
accommodation 91-96
Agnes Water 315-317
Agnew 569-570
air travel 104-117
  discount tickets 104-108
  domestic flights 111
  flying yourself 111-112
  to/from Africa & South America 108
  to/from Asia 108
  to/from New Zealand 107-108
  to/from North America 105, 107
  to/from the UK 105
  air travel glossary 106-107
Airlie Beach 379-387, **380**
Alexandra Headland 243, **244**
Alexandra Range 528
Alexandria Bay 250
Allen, Davida 48
Allora 268
Alma Park Zoo 151

Almaden 498
Alpha 632
Alva Beach 405
Amity Point 201
Anakie 351-352
Annan River Gorge 538
Anu, Christine 51
apartments, serviced 96
Araluen Falls 372
Aramac 631
Arcadia 423
Archer Bend National Park 567
Armanno, Verano 49

arts 46-51
  architecture 49-50
  cinema 47
  literature 48-49
  music 51
  painting 47
Astley, Thea 49
Atherton 500-501
Augathella 635
Australian Institute of Marine
  Sciences 405
Australian Republic 43
Australian Workers Heritage
  Centre 629
automobile associations 62-63
Awoonga Dam 319
Ayr 404-405
Ayton 535

B&Bs 95
Babinda 462-463
Babinda Boulders 463
backpackers' hostels 93
backpacking 94
Balancing Rock 498
Bald Rock Point 341
Balloon Cave 352
Bamaga 576
Banana 338, 354
Bang Bang Jump-up 602
Banks, Joseph 19, 544
Baralaba 338
Barcaldine 27, 629-631, 630
Barcoo River 634
bareboat charters 374
Bargara 311
Barkly Homestead 618
Barney Point Beach 319
barramundi 40
Barren Island 342
Bartle Frere 491
Batavia Downs 569
Batavia Downs Station 572
Battle Camp 538, 560
Battle Camp Station 560
Battle Mountain 612
Baralaba 338
Beaudesert 236
Bedarra Island 453
Bedourie 640
beer 99
Beerburrum 240
Beerwah 240
Bellara 207
Bellenden Ker 491
Bellenden Ker Range 31
Benaraby 321
Berserker Range 335-336
Bertiehaugh 569

Betoota 643
bicycle travel 87, 127-128
Big Red 642
Biloela 354-355
birds of prey 39
Birdsville 640-642
Birdsville Track 642
Bizant 562
Bjelke-Petersen, Sir Joh 29-30, 51-52
Black Mountain 538
Black's Beach 367
black-necked stork 38
Blackall 632-633
Blackall Mountains 259
Blackdown Tableland National
  Park 346
Blackwater 346-347
Blair Athol Mine 349
Bli Bli 243
Bloomfield River 535
Bloomfield Track 534
Blue Lagoon 545
Bluff Point 340
boat travel 115-130
  cargo ships 116
  crewing on yachts 115-116
Boigu Island 582
Boldrewood, Rolf 48
Bongaree 208
Booby Island 582
books 71-74
  Aborigines 71-72
  children's 74
  history 72-73
  politics 73
  travel guides 73
Boreen Point 256-257
Bouldercombe 336
Bouldercombe Gorge 336
Boulia 639
Bowen 397-401, 398
box jellyfish 81-82
Brampton Island 368-369
Bramston Beach 462
Bribie Island 207-208
Bridge Creek 574
Brighton 199
Brisbane 131-208, 132, 136,
  138, 144, 156, 160
  activities 157
  City Botanic Gardens 147
  entertainment 184-191
  festivals 163
  foreign consulates 135
  galleries 142
  gay & lesbian accommodation
    168
  historic houses 147
  markets 193-194

museums 141-142
  places to eat 174-184
  places to stay 164-174
  Queensland Cultural Centre 147-
    148
  river cruises 162
  South Bank Parklands 148-149
  tourist offices 133-134
  walks 140-141
Brisbane Biennial International
  Music Festival 51
Brisbane Forest Park 150-151
Brisk Island 437
Broadbeach 224-226, 224
Broken River 372-373
Brolga 39
Brook Islands Group 445
Bucasia 368
Bulcock Beach 241
Bulwer 205
Bundaberg 306-311, 308
  beaches 311, 312
  diving 309
  whale watching 309
bungy jumping 89
Bunya Mountains National Park
  282
Burke and Wills 21-22, 584, 611
  Dig Tree 645
Burke & Wills Roadhouse 602
Burketown 597-599
Burleigh Heads 226-229, 228
Burleigh Heads National Park
  226
bus travel 112-118
bushfires 84
bushwalking 86
business hours 66
Bustard Beach 317
Bustard Head 316
Byfield 339-340
Byfield National Park 340
Byfield State Forest 339

Caboolture 239
Cairns 464-488, 466, 475,
  489
Calliope 321
Caloundra 241-243, 242
Camooweal 618
Camooweal Caves National
  Park 618
'Camp 119' 22, 600
camping 91-92
cane toads 41
Cania Gorge National Park 285
canoeing 87, 470
Canungra 234-235
Cape Flattery 547, 560

Cape Hillsborough National
   Park 369, 370
Cape Kimberley Beach 528
Cape Melville National Park 560
Cape Palmerston National Park
   345-346
Cape Richards 441
Cape Tribulation 525-534
Cape Tribulation National Park
   527
Cape York Aboriginal Dance
   Festival 556
Cape York Peninsula 549-583,
   551, 559, 566
Capella 348
Capricorn Coast 313-355, **314**
Captain Billy Landing 575
Cook, Captain James 18-19,
   315, 544, 550, 579
Captain Starlight 624
car travel 115-126
   buying a car 123-124
   car rental 124-126
   drive-by wave 606
   outback travel 121-123
   road rules 120-121
   4WD travel 122, 557
caravanning 91-92
Cardwell 437-441
Carlisle Island 369-370
Carlo Sandblow 290
Carmila 345
Carnarvon National Park 352-
   353, 634
Carstensz, Jan 18
Cassowaries 528
Cathedral Beach 301
Cathedral Cave 352
Cato, Nancy 49
Causeway Lake 340
Cedar Bay National Park 535
Cedar Creek Falls 388
Cedar Creek National Park 233
Channel Country 639-645
Charleville 635-638, **637**
Charlevue Lookout 346
Charters Towers 430-434, **432**
Charters Towers Goldfields 25
Cheepie 644
Childers 304-305
Chili Beach 569
Chillagoe 498-500, **499**
Chillagoe-Mungana Caves
   National Park 498
Chinchilla 278
Chinese in Queensland 25
Cid Harbour 397
Cinema 99
Clairview 345

Cleveland 200-1
Clifton Beach 507
climate 32-33
   climate chart 32
Cloncurry 610-611
Cockatoo Creek 573
cockatoos 38
Cockermouth Island 370
Cockle Bay 423
Cockroach Monument 644
Coen 565-567
colleges 95
Collinsville 401
Combo Water Hole 620
Condon, Matthew 49
Considine Beach 344
Conway Beach 388
Conway National Park 387-388
Coochiemudlo Island 207
Cooee Bay 340
Cook's Look 546
Cooktown 538-544, **539**
Coolabahs 34
Cooladdi 644
Coolangatta 229-232, **230**
Cooloola Coast 256-257
Cooloola National Park 257-290
Coolum Beach 246, **247**
Coppabella 349
Cow Bay 528
Cowan Cowan 205
cricket 101
Crocodile Dundee 619
crocodiles 39-40, 82
Croydon 591-592
Crystal Cascades 469
cultural events 66-67
culture 46-51
   alternative lifestyles 51
Cunnamulla 638-639
Cunningham, Allan 20
Curacao Island 437
Currumbin Sanctuary 227
Currumbin Valley 227-229
Curtis Island 321
customs 56-57

Daintree 522-524
Dajarra 639
Dalby 278
Dalrymple, George
   Elphingstone 23
Danbulla Forest Drive 500-501
Dandabah 282
dangers & annoyances 80-84
Darling Downs 262-285, **263**
Davies Creek National Park 495
Dawson, Andrew 27
Daydream Island 390-391

Deepwater National Park 317
Demidenko, Helen 49
De Quiros, Pedro Fernandez 579
Dig Tree 22, 645
Dimbulah 496
Dingo 346
Dingo Beach 397
dingoes 38
disabled travellers 64-65
dive courses 469-470, 512
diving 86-87, 309, 374, 381
diving 86-87, 309, 374, 381
documents 56
Dolphin Heads 367
Doomadgee 597
Double Head 340
Double Island 508
Double Island Point 290
Ducie Creek 573
Duck Creek Opalfields 644
Dulhunty 573
Dululu 338
Dundubara 301
Dunk Island 451-453
Dunwich 201

Eagle Islet 547
Earlando 397
Earlystreet Historical Village
   147
Eastern Gulf Region 588
echidnas 38
Eclipse Island 437
economy 43-44
ecotourism 50
Eddie Mabo 18
Edmonton 464
Edmund Kennedy National Park
   439
Eidsvold 284-285
Eimeo 368
Einasleigh 590
El Arish 454
Elanda Point 257
Eliot Creek 574
Ellis Beach 508-509
embassies 55-56
Emerald 347-348
emergency 84
Emu Park 340-341
emus 38
Endeavour River 558
entertainment 99-101
environmental groups
Erskine Island 326
Esk Island 437
Eulo 644
Eumundi 258
Eungella 372
Eungella National Park 363, 371

Eurimbula National Park 316-317
Eurong 301
Expo '88 30

Facing Island 321
Fairweather, Ian 48
Falcon Island 437
Fantome Island 437
Far North Queensland 456-548, **457**
farm & station stays 95
fauna 36-40
  birds 38-39
  fish 40
  introduced species 40
  mammals 37-38
  reptiles 39-40
fax 70
ferals 51
Fig Tree Point 257
Finch Hatton 371
Finch Hatton Gorge 371
Fisher, Andrew 28
Fishermans Beach 341
fishing 89, 296, 374
Fitzroy Island 490
Fleay's Wildlife Park 227
Flinders, Matthew 579, 584
Flinders River 600
flora 33-36
  Acacias 34
  botanic gardens 33
  bottle trees 35
  Bunya Pine 35
  Eucalypts 33-34
  jacarandas 35
  mangroves 34
  Moreton Bay Fig 35
  poincianas 35
  rainforest 34-35
  saltbush 36
  spinifex 35-36
  weeds 36
  wildflowers 36
Floraville Station 599
Flying Doctor Service 28, 48
Flying Fish Point 460
Flynn, John 28
food 96-98
  fruits & nuts 97
Forrest Beach 436
Forsayth 590
Fortitude Valley 153
Forty Mile Scrub National Park 506
fossicking 89-90
Four Mile Beach 512
Frankland Islands 490-491

Fraser Coast 286 - 312, **287**
Fraser Island 300-304, **303**
Freshwater 257
Fruit Bat Falls 574
Fysh, Hudson 623

galleries 142
Garden Island 445
Garnet, Darkie 350
gay & lesbian travellers 80
Gayndah 284
gemfields 349-352
geography 30-32
George Point 441
Georgetown 591
Ghost Gum 34
Gin Gin 306
Girraween National Park 272
Gladstone 317-321, **318**
Gladstone Harbour Islands 321
Glass House Mountains 240-241
Glass House Mountains township 240
Gliding 88-89
Gloucester Island 397
Go Betweens 51
Gold Coast 209-236, **210**
Gold Coast Hinterland 232-236
Goldfield Track 463
Goldsborough Valley State Forest Park 463
Goldsmith Island 370
Gondwana Rainforest Sanctuary 148
Gondwanaland 33
Goold Island 445
Goondiwindi 273-274
Gordonvale 463
government 42-43
Granite Belt Wineries 271-272
Granite Gorge 496
Grassy Island 397
Great Barrier Reef 324-325
Great Barrier Reef Wonderland 409
Great Dividing Range 31
Great Keppel Island 341-344, **342**
Great Palm Island 437
Green Dragon Museum 207
Green Island 488-490
Gregory, Augustus 23
Gregory River 597
guesthouses 95
Gulflander 592
Gulf Savannah 584-603, **585**
Gunshot Creek 573
Gympie 286-290, **289**

Halfway 344-345
Hall, Rodney 49
Hamilton Island 391-394, **392**
hang-gliding 88-89
Hann Crossing 562
Hann, William 23, 25
Happy Valley 301
Harbour Beach 362
Harris Creek 599
Harry's Hut 257
Havannah Island 437
Hayman Island 394-395
health 76-80
  basic rules 77-78
  medical kit 76-77
  precautions 77
  problems 78-80
  travel insurance 76
  women 80
Heathlands Station 573
Helenvale 525, 535, 538
Hell's Gate 538, 596
Henning Island 396
Herberton 491, 504-505
Heron Island 326
Hervey Bay 293-300, **296**
Hibiscus Beach 545
Hideaway Bay 397
Higgins Field 550
highlights 90-91
Hinchinbrook Island 441-445, **442**
Hinkler, Bert 28-29
history 15-30
  Aborigines 15-18
  convicts & European settlement 19-20
  European exploration 18-19, 20-23
  gold & mining 25
  labour vs capital 26-27
  Moreton Bay Penal Colony 20
  separation & growth 23-24
  sugar & the plantation economy 25-26
  transport & communications 24-25
  20th century 27-30
hitching 128-129
holiday flats 96
holidays 66
Holloway's Beach 506
Holzheimer, Toots 568
Home Hill 404
Homebush 359
Hook Island 389-390
Hopevale Aboriginal Community 558
Hopevale Show & Rodeo 556

Horn Island 582
Horse Riding 89, 471, 530
Horseshoe Bay 423
Horseshoe Lookout 346
hotels 96
Howe, Jackie 632
Hughenden 608
Humpy 344-345
Humpybong 199

Idalia National Park 634
Idriess, Ion 48
Ilfracombe 628
Illawong Beach 362
Illawong Fauna Sanctuary 361
Indian Head Falls 574
Indycarnival 67
Ingham 435-436
Inglewood 273
Injinoo Aboriginal Community 577
Injune 353
Innisfail 459-460, **461**
Innot Hot Springs 505
Inskip Point 290
Ipswich 264
Iron Range National Park 568
Irvinebank 497
Isabella Falls 560
Isisford 633
Isla Gorge Lookout 354
Isla Gorge National Park 354

Jabiru 38
Jacky Jacky 550
Jansz, Willem 18, 550, 579, 584
Jardine family 23
Jardine, Frank 550
Jardine River 574-575
Jardine River Ferry 575
Jericho 632
Jondaryan 277-278
Jospehine Falls 462
Jourama Falls National Park 435
Jundah 628

Ka Ka Mundi 353
Kajabbi 612
Kalkadoons 611
Kanakas 26
kangaroos 37
Karnak Playhouse 522
Karragarra Island 207
Karumba 594-596
Kenilworth 261
Kennedy, Edmund 21, 550
Kidman, Sydney 48
Killarney 268
King Park Homestead 569

King Reef 454
Kingaroy 282-283
koalas 38
Kondaparinga Station 496-497
Kondilla Falls National Park 260
kookaburras 38
Kooringal 205
Kuranda 492-495, **493**
Kurrimine Beach 454
Kynuna 619

Lady Elliot Island 307, 319, 321-322
Lady Musgrave Island 307, 315, 322, 326
Laguna Lookout 250
Laguna Quays 378
Lake Awoonga 321
Lake Baroon 259
Lake Barrine 491, 502-503
Lake Cooroibah 256
Lake Cootharaba 257
Lake Eacham 492
Lake Euramoo 501
Lake Julius 612
Lake Maraboon 348
Lake Moondarra 615
Lake Tinaroo 491, 501
Lakefield National Park 560-561
Lakeland 537-538, 562
Lakes Eacham 502-503
Lamb Island 207
Lamington National Park 235-236
Lammermoor Beach 340
language 53
    Aboriginal language 53
Landsborough, William 22, 584
Lark Quarry Environmental Park 623
Laura 562-564
Laura River 560
Lawler, Ray 48
Lawn Hill National Park 601-602
Lawson, Henry 48
Leichhardt Falls 599
Leichhardt, Ludwig 16, 20-21, 48-49, 354, 550, 584
Leslie, Patrick 20
Lindeman Island 395-396
Lizard Island 544
Lizard Island Research Station 546-547
lizards 39
local transport 129
Lockerbie 577
Lockhart River Aboriginal Community 569
Logan Creek 574

Lone Pine Koala Sanctuary 151-152
Long Beach 341
Long Island 388-389
Longreach 624-628, **626**
Low Isles 513-514
Low Lake 562
Lucinda 436
Lunn, Hugh 49
Lumholtz National Park 439
Lungfish 40
Lyrebirds 38

Machans Beach 506
Mackay 359-367, **360**, **362**
Macleay Island 207
Macrozamia Grove National Park 232
Magnetic Island 421-429, **422, 425**
magpies 38
Maiala National Park 151
Main Beach 215-217, **216**
Malanda 503
Maleny 259-260
Maleny Folk Festival 259
Maleny-Woodford Folk Festival 51
Mallee 34
Mooloolaba 246
Malouf, David 49
Manly 199-200
Manorina Bush Camp 150
Mapleton 261
Mapleton Falls National Park 261
Mareeba 495-496
Margate 199
Marian 371
Marina Plains Station 562
Marlborough 345
Maroochydore 243, **244**
Mary Kathleen 612
Maryborough 292-293, **293**
Masthead Island 316, 322, 326
Maud Bay 423
Maytown 537
McGahan, Andrew 49
McGuinness, Paul 623
McKinlay 619
McPherson Ranges 31
media 74-75
medical services 139
melomies 531
Mermaid Beach 224-226, **224**
Miall Island 344
Middle Island 341, 344-345
Middleton 640
Miegunyah Folk Museum 147

Miles 278-279, 354
Millaa Millaa 462, 504
Mimosa Creek 346
Mirani 371
Miriam Vale 315-316
Mission Beach 446-451, **449**
Mistake Creek 574
Mitchell 281
Mitchell, Major Thomas 21
mobile homes 92
Mon Repos Beach 311
money 57-59
    costs 59
    credit cards 58
    tipping 59
    travellers' cheques 57-58
Monkey Beach 341
Monto 285
Montville 260-261
Mooloolaba 243
Moore Park 311
Moranbah 349
Morehead River 562, 565
Moreton Bay 199-208
Moreton Island 205-206
Mornington Island 603
Morven 281
Mossman 520
Mossman Gorge 514, 520-521
motels 96
motorcycle travel 115, 126-
    127
Moura 353
Mourilyan 454
Mt Barney National Park 236
Mt Bartle Frere 31, 462
Mt Beerwah 240
Mt Carbine 536
Mt Castletower National Park
    321
Mt Cook National Park 541
Mt Coonowrin 240
Mt Cooroora 258
Mt Coot-tha Park 149-150
Mt Cougal National Park 227
Mt Elliot National Park 406
Mt Etna National Park 336
Mt Garnet 505
Mt Glorious 150-151
Mt Hypipamee National Park
    504
Mt Isa 612-618, **614**
Mt Larcom 319
Mt Lindesay Highway 236
Mt Mellum 260
Mt Moffatt 353
Mt Molloy 521, 536
Mt Morgan 25, 336-337
Mt Mulligan 496-497

Mt Mulligan Mining Disaster
    497
Mt Nebo 150
Mt Ngungun 240
Mt Spec National Park 434
Mt Surprise 589
Mt Tempest 205
Mt Tibrogargan 240
Mt Zamia 352
Muckadilla 281
Mud Crabs 40
Mulga 34
Mulgrave Rambler 463
Mulligan, James Venture 497
Mundubbera 284
Murgon 283-284
Murray Falls 439
Musgrave 565
Mutee Heads 576
Muttaburra 631
Muttaburrasaurus 608
mystery craters 307

Nambour 259
Nanango 283
national parks 40-42
    permits 42
    National Parks & Wildlife
    Service (QNP&WS) 41, 63
National Trust 65
Native Title Act 18
Natural Bridge 234
Nebo 349
Nelly Bay 423
New Farm 152-153
New Laura Homestead 560
New Mapoon 577
Newell Beach 522
Newry Island 371
Nicklin, George 29-30
Noccundra 645
Noosa Heads 248-255, **249**
Noosa National Park 250
Noosa/Lake Weyba National
    Park 247
Normanton 592-594
North Alice Creek 573
North Coast 402 - 455, **403**
North Direction Island 547
North Kennedy River 562
North Molle Island 396
North Stradbroke Island 201-205
North Stradbroke Island
    Historical Museum 202
North West Island 322, 327
Nymph Island 548

Olsen's Capricorn Caves
    335-336

Oodgeroo Noonuccal (Kath
    Walker) 49
Opalton Mining Field 623
Orchid Beach 441
Orchid Valley 463
Orpheus Island 436-437
Osprey Island 547
outback festival 622
outback Queensland 604 - 645,
    607
outback survival 84-85
Outer Newry Island 371
Overland Telegraph Line 550
Oxley, John 20

Paddington 153-155, **159**
Pajinka 575
Palfrey Island 545, 547
Pallarenda 410
Palm Cove 507-508
Palm Creek 573
Palmer River 536
Palmer River Gold Rush 25
Palmerston, Christie 465
Palmerville 537
Palmwoods 261
Paluma 434-435
paragliding 88-89
parrots 38
Paterson, A B ('Banjo') 48, 620
Peak Range Mountains 349
Pebbly Beach 545
Peeramon 503
Pelorus Island 437
Pentland 606
Peregian Beach 246-248, **247**
Peregrine Lookout 346
Performing Arts Complex 148
Petford 497
Petrie Terrace 153-155, **159**
Photography 75-76
Pialba 294
Picnic Bay 423
Pinnacle Point 340
Pioneer Valley 371
platypuses 38
Poepple Corner 643
Point Lookout 201, **200**
Point Vernon 294
Pomona 258
population & people 44
Porcupine Gorge National Park
    608-609
Pormpuraaw Aboriginal Commu-
    nity 565
Port Curtis 319
Port Douglas 509-520, **509, 514**
Port Essington 584
Portland Roads 569

Port Stewart 565
Possession Island 550, 579
possums 37
Postal Services 67-68
Prairie 607
prickly pear 36
Prince of Wales Island 579
Princess Charlotte Bay 558
Proserpine 378-379
pubs 95-96, 98
Pumicestone National Park 207
Pumpkin Island 344-345
Punsand Bay 577, 578
Putney Beach 341

Qantas 25, 28, 623-624
Quamby 602
Queensland **12, 13**
Queensland airfares **118**
Queensland Art Gallery 148
Queensland Cultural Centre
    147-148
Queensland Dairy Industry
    Museum 283
Queensland Government Travel
    Centre 134
Queensland Museum 148
Queensland Relative Size **31**
Queensland Shearers' Union 27
Queenslanders 50
Quilpie 643-644
Quinkan Art 563
Quoin Island 321

Rabbit Island 371
Radical Bay 423
Radio Frequencies 553, 585
Rainbow Beach 257, 290-291
Rainbow Falls 346
Ramsay Bay 441
Ravenshoe 505
Ravenswood 429-430
Red Beach 341
Red Ted, *see* Theodore, Edward
Redcliffe 199
Redcliffe Peninsula 199
reef cruises 375-376
Reef Trips 513, 529
Rees, Lloyd 48
Religion 52-53
resorts 96
Richmond 609
River Red Gums 34
Rivers, Godfrey 48
Riversleigh Station 613
Robinson, Bill 48
rockclimbing 89
Rockhampton 327-335, **329, 331**
Rocky Bay 423

Rocky Islet 547
Rokeby National Park 567
Rolleston 352
Roma 279-281, **280**
Rosedale 317
Rosslyn Bay 322
Rosslyn Bay Harbour 340
Rossville 535
Round Hill Creek 315-317
Rowes Bay 413
Rubyvale 350-351
Rudd, Steele 48
Russell Island 207
Ryan, T J 28

Saddleback Island 397
Safety 80-84
sailing 88
Saltwater Creek 562
Salvator Rosa 353
Sanctuary Cove 215
Sandgate 199
Sapphire 351
Sarina 358
Sarina Beach 358-359
Savannahlander 589-590
Scarborough 199
Scarness 294
Scawfell Island 370
sea-kayaking 87, 470
Seabird Islet 545, 547
Seisia 576-577
Seventeen Seventy 315-317
Shapcott, Thomas 49
Shearers' Strike 27
shopping, *see* thing to buy
Shute, Neville 48
Simpson Desert National Park
    642-643
Skase, Christopher 510
skydiving 89
Slade Point 367
Smith, Charles Kingsford 28
Smithfield 465
Snakes 39
Snapper Island 528, 530
Snorkelling 86-87
South Alice Creek 573
South Burnett Region 281-285
South Direction Island 547
South Island 545, 547
South Molle Island 391
South Stradbroke Island 217-218
Southern Reef Islands 319, 322-
    325, 327
Southport 215-217, **216**
spectator sports 100-101
Split Rock Galleries 562
Spring Hill 152, **154**

Springbrook 233-234
Springbrook Plateau 233-234
Springsure 352
St George 274
St Helena Island 206-207
Stanage Bay 345
Stanthorpe 269-271, **270**
Starke National Park 560
State Forests 42
State Library 148
Stewart River 565
Stingers, See Box Jellyfish 81
Stockman's Hall of Fame &
    Outback Heritage Centre 624-
    625
Stonehenge 628
Stony Creek Falls 346
Sudley 569
Sundown National Park 273
Sunset Beach 545
Sunset Lookout 346
Sunshine Coast 237 - 261, **238**
Surfers Paradise 218-224, **220**
surfing 87-88
Sweers Island 584, 603
swimming 88

Tallaroo Hot Springs 591
Tambo 634-635
Tamborine Mountain 232-233
Tangalooma 205
Taroom 354
Tarzali 504
Tasman, Abel 550, 584
Telephone 68-70
Tewantin 255-256
Texas 273
Thargomindah 644-645
The Moss Garden 352
The Northern Bypass 575
The Saints 51
The Southern Bypass 575
The Telegraph Track 572-574
The Thorsborne Trail 443
theme parks 214-215
Theodore 354
Theodore, Edward 28
things to buy 101-102
Thornton Beach 528, 531
Thorsborne Trail 441
Thursday Island 579-582, **581**
time zones 70
Tin Can Bay 291-292
Tinaroo Falls 501
Tinaroo Falls Dam 501
Tolga 500
Toowoomba 274-277, **275**
Torilla Peninsula 345
Torquay 294

Torrens Creek 606
Torres Strait Cultural Festival 556
Torresian Imperial Pigeons 445
Total Fire Ban, See Bushfires 84
tourist offices 61-62
tours 129-130
Town Beach 362
Townsville 406, **407**, **412**, **414**
Traditional Aboriginal Culture 44-45
Traeger,Alfred 28
train travel 114-115, 118-120
    passes 120
    rail services 119
Tree of Knowledge 629
Trekking 89
Trinity Beach 506-507
Tropical Winery 307
Tryon Island 322, 327
Tully 32, 446
Tumoulin 505
Turner Hospital, Janet 49
Turtle Bay 441
Turtle Rookery 311-312
Tweed Heads 229, **230**
Twin Falls 574
Two Mile Falls 346

Umagico 577
Undara Lava Tubes 588-589
University Of Queensland 155-157
Upper Stoney Dam 339
Urangan 294

Vaez De Torres, Luiz 579

Vincent Gair 29
Virgin Rock 352
Visas 55-56
    Extensions 56
    Tourist Visas 55

Waddy Point 301
Wait-a-While 534
Walk-About Creek 150
Walker's Monument 599
Walkerston 359
Wallaby Track 29
Wallaman Falls National Park 435
Walsh's Pyramid 463
Waltzing Matilda 51, 621
Wandoan 354
Wanggoolba Creek 301
Ward's Canyon 352
Warwick 264-268, **266**
Waterfalls Circuit 504
Waterpark Creek Forest Park 340
Watson, Judy 48-610
Watson, Mary 545
Weipa 570, **571**
Wenlock River 568, 572
Wernadinga Station 600
Westgrove Station 353
Whale Watching 295-296, 309
White-Water Rafting 87, 470
Whitehaven Beach 396
Whitsunday Coast 356 - 401, **357**
Whitsunday Island 396
Whitsundays Area 373-377
Wildhorse Mountain Lookout 240
Willows Gemfields 352

Wilson Island 319, 326
Windorah 643
Wine 99
    Granite Belt 271-272
Winton 620-623
Witches Falls National Park 232
Wombats 37-38
Womblebank Station 353
Women's Organisations 135
Women Travellers 80
Wonga Beach 522
Woodford 259
Woodgate 305-306
Woodgate National Park 306
Woody Point 199
Woorim 207
Work 85
World Heritage List 41
Wowan 338
Wragge, Clement 635
Wujal Wujal Aboriginal Community 525, 535
Wyandra 638
Wynnum 199-200

Yandina 258
Yarrabah Aboriginal Community 463-464
Yeppoon 338-339
Yongala 511
Yorkeys Knob 506
Yothu Yindi 51
youth hostels 92-93
Yowah 644
Yungaburra 463, 501-502

Zoe Bay 441

LONELY PLANET TV SERIES & VIDEOS

Lonely Planet travel guides have been brought to life on television screens around the world. Like our guides, the programmes are based on the joy of independent travel, and look honestly at some of the most exciting, picturesque and frustrating places in the world. Each show is presented by one of three travellers from Australia, England or the USA and combines an innovative mixture of video, Super-8 film, atmospheric soundscapes and original music.

Videos of each episode – containing additional footage not shown on television – are available from good book and video shops, but the availability of individual videos varies with regional screening schedules.

Video destinations include:
Alaska; Australia (Southeast); Brazil; Ecuador & the Galapagos Islands; Indonesia; Israel & the Sinai Desert; Japan; La Ruta Maya (Yucatan, Guatemala & Belize); Morocco; North India (Varanasi to the Himalaya); Pacific Islands; Vietnam; Zimbabwe, Botswana & Namibia.

Coming in 1996:
The Arctic (Norway & Finland); Baja California; Chile & Easter Island; China (Southeast); Costa Rica; East Africa (Tanzania & Zanzibar); Great Barrier Reef (Australia); Jamaica; Papua New Guinea; the Rockies (USA); Syria & Jordan; Turkey.

The Lonely Planet television series is produced by:
Pilot Productions
Duke of Sussex Studios
44 Uxbridge St
London W8 7TG
United Kingdom

Lonely Planet videos are distributed by:
IVN Communications Inc
2246 Camino Ramon, San Ramon
California 94583, USA

107 Power Road, Chiswick
London W4 5PL, UK

For further information on both the television series and the availability of individual videos please contact Lonely Planet.

PLANET TALK
Lonely Planet's FREE quarterly newsletter

We love hearing from you and think you'd like to hear from us.

When...is the right time to see reindeer in Finland?
Where...can you hear the best palm-wine music in Ghana?
How...do you get from Asunción to Areguá by steam train?
What...is the best way to see India?

For the answer to these and many other questions read PLANET TALK.

Every issue is packed with up-to-date travel news and advice including:

- *a letter from Lonely Planet founders Tony and Maureen Wheeler*
- *travel diary from a Lonely Planet author - find out what it's really like out on the road*
- *feature article on an important and topical travel issue*
- *a selection of recent letters from our readers*
- *the latest travel news from all over the world*
- *details on Lonely Planet's new and forthcoming releases*

To join our mailing list contact any Lonely Planet office.

Also available: Lonely Planet T-shirts. 100% heavyweight cotton (S, M, L, XL)

LONELY PLANET PUBLICATIONS
Australia: PO Box 617, Hawthorn 3122, Victoria
tel: (03) 9819 1877 fax: (03) 9819 6459 e-mail: talk2us@lonelyplanet.com.au

USA: Embarcadero West, 155 Filbert St, Suite 251, Oakland, CA 94607
tel: (510) 893 8555 TOLL FREE: 800 275-8555 fax: (510) 893 8563
e-mail: info@lonelyplanet.com

UK: 10 Barley Mow Passage, Chiswick, London W4 4PH
tel: (0181) 742 3161 fax: (0181) 742 2772 e-mail: 100413.3551@compuserve.com

France: 71 bis rue du Cardinal Lemoine – 75005 Paris
tel: 1 46 34 00 58 fax: 1 46 34 72 55 e-mail: 100560.415@compuserve.com

World Wide Web: http://www.lonelyplanet.com/

Guides to the Pacific

Australia – a travel survival kit
The complete low-down on Down Under – home of Ayers Rock, the Great Barrier Reef, extraordinary animals, cosmopolitan cities, rainforests, beaches ... and Lonely Planet!

Bushwalking in Australia
Two experienced and respected walkers give details of the best walks in every state, covering many different terrains and climates.

Bushwalking in Papua New Guinea
The best way to get to know Papua New Guinea is from the ground up – and bushwalking is the best way to travel around the rugged and varied landscape of this island.

Islands of Australia's Great Barrier Reef – Australia guide
The Great Barrier Reef is one of the wonders of the world – and one of the great travel destinations! Whether you're looking for the best snorkelling, the liveliest nightlife or a secluded island hideaway, this guide has all the facts you'll need.

Melbourne – city guide
From historic houses to fascinating churches and from glorious parks to tapas bars, cafés and bistros, Melbourne is a dream for gourmets and a paradise for sightseers.

New South Wales & the ACT – Australia guide
Ancient aboriginal sites, pristine surf beaches, kangaroos bounding across desert dunes, lyre-birds dancing in rainforest, picturesque country pubs, weather-beaten drovers and friendly small-town people, along with Australia's largest and liveliest metropolis (and the host city of the year 2000 Olympic Games) – all this and more can be found in New South Wales and the ACT.

Sydney – city guide
From the Opera House to the surf; all you need to know in a handy pocket-sized format.

Outback Australia – Australia guide
The outback conjures up images of endless stretches of dead straight roads, the rich red of the desert, and the resourcefulness and resilience of the inhabitants. A visit to Australia would not be complete without visiting the outback to see the beauty and vastness of this ancient country.

Victoria – Australia guide
From old gold rush towns to cosmopolitan Melbourne and from remote mountains to the most popular surf beaches, Victoria is packed with attractions and activities for everyone.

Fiji – a travel survival kit
Whether you prefer to stay in camping grounds, international hotels, or something in-between, this comprehensive guide will help you to enjoy the beautiful Fijian archipelago.

Hawaii – a travel survival kit
Share in the delights of this island paradise – and avoid some of its high prices – with this practical guide. It covers all of Hawaii's well-known attractions, plus plenty of uncrowded sights and activities.

Micronesia – a travel survival kit
The glorious beaches, lagoons and reefs of these 2100 islands would dazzle even the most jaded traveller. This guide has all the details on island-hopping across the Micronesian archipelago.

New Caledonia – a travel survival kit
This guide shows how to discover all that the idyllic islands of New Caledonia have to offer – from French colonial culture to traditional Melanesian life.

New Zealand – a travel survival kit
This practical guide will help you discover the very best New Zealand has to offer: Maori dances and feasts, some of the most spectacular scenery in the world, and every outdoor activity imaginable.

Tramping in New Zealand
Call it tramping, hiking, walking, bushwalking or trekking – travelling by foot is the best way to explore New Zealand's natural beauty. Detailed descriptions of over 40 walks of varying length and difficulty.

Papua New Guinea – a travel survival kit
With its coastal cities, villages perched beside mighty rivers, palm-fringed beaches and rushing mountain streams, Papua New Guinea promises memorable travel.

Rarotonga & the Cook Islands – a travel survival kit
Rarotonga and the Cook Islands have history, beauty and magic to rival the better-known islands of Hawaii and Tahiti, but the world has virtually passed them by.

Samoa – a travel survival kit
Two remarkably different countries, Western Samoa and American Samoa offer some wonderful island escapes, and Polynesian culture at its best.

Solomon Islands – a travel survival kit
The Solomon Islands are the best-kept secret of the Pacific. Discover remote tropical islands, jungle-covered volcanoes and traditional Melanesian villages with this detailed guide.

Tahiti & French Polynesia – a travel survival kit
Tahiti's idyllic beauty has seduced sailors, artists and travellers for generations. The latest edition of this book provides full details on the main island of Tahiti, the Tuamotos, Marquesas and other island groups. Invaluable information for independent travellers and package tourists alike.

Tonga – a travel survival kit
The only South Pacific country never to be colonised by Europeans, Tonga has also been ignored by tourists. The people of this far-flung island group offer some of the most sincere and unconditional hospitality in the world.

Vanuatu – a travel survival kit
Discover superb beaches, lush rainforests, dazzling coral reefs and traditional Melanesian customs in this glorious Pacific Ocean archipelago.

Western Australia – Australia guide
This is the most detailed and practical guidebook to Australia's largest state. It's full of down-to-earth information and reliable advice for every budget. Whether you've got a spare weekend or a month, there are hundreds of tips to help you make the most of your trip.

Also available:
Australian phrasebook, **Fijian** phrasebook, & **Pidgin** phrasebook.

Lonely Planet Guidebooks

Lonely Planet guidebooks cover every accessible part of Asia as well as Australia, the Pacific, South America, Africa, the Middle East, Europe and parts of North America. There are six series: *travel survival kits*, covering a country for a range of budgets; *shoestring guides* with compact information for low-budget travel in a major region; *walking guides*; *city guides*, *travel atlases* and *phrasebooks*.

Australia & the Pacific
Australia
Australian phrasebook
Bushwalking in Australia
Islands of Australia's Great Barrier Reef
Outback Australia
Fiji
Fijian phrasebook
Melbourne city guide
Micronesia
New Caledonia
New South Wales
New Zealand
Tramping in New Zealand
Papua New Guinea
Queensland
Bushwalking in Papua New Guinea
Papua New Guinea phrasebook
Rarotonga & the Cook Islands
Samoa
Solomon Islands
Sydney city guide
Tahiti & French Polynesia
Tonga
Vanuatu
Victoria
Western Australia

North-East Asia
Beijing city guide
China
Cantonese phrasebook
Mandarin Chinese phrasebook
Hong Kong, Macau & Canton
Japan
Japanese phrasebook
Korea
Korean phrasebook
Mongolia
Mongolian phrasebook
North-East Asia on a shoestring
Seoul city guide
Taiwan
Tibet
Tibet phrasebook
Tokyo city guide

South-East Asia
Bali & Lombok
Bangkok city guide
Cambodia
Indonesia
Ho Chi Minh City city guide
Indonesian phrasebook
Jakarta city guide
Java
Laos
Lao phrasebook
Malaysia, Singapore & Brunei
Myanmar (Burma)
Burmese phrasebook
Philippines
Pilipino phrasebook
Singapore city guide
South-East Asia on a shoestring
Thailand
Thailand travel atlas
Thai phrasebook
Thai Hill Tribes phrasebook
Vietnam
Vietnamese phrasebook

Middle East
Arab Gulf States
Egypt & the Sudan
Arabic (Egyptian) phrasebook
Iran
Israel
Jordan & Syria
Middle East
Turkey
Turkish phrasebook
Trekking in Turkey
Yemen

Africa
Africa on a shoestring
Central Africa
East Africa
Trekking in East Africa
Kenya
Swahili phrasebook
Morocco
Arabic (Moroccan) phrasebook
North Africa
South Africa, Lesotho & Swaziland
West Africa
Zimbabwe, Botswana & Namibia

Mail Order

Lonely Planet guidebooks are distributed worldwide. They are also available by mail order from Lonely Planet, so if you have difficulty finding a title please write to us. US and Canadian residents should write to Embarcadero West, 155 Filbert St, Suite 251, Oakland CA 94607, USA ; European residents should write to 10 Barley Mow Passage, Chiswick, London W4 4PH; and residents of other countries to PO Box 617, Hawthorn, Victoria 3122, Australia.

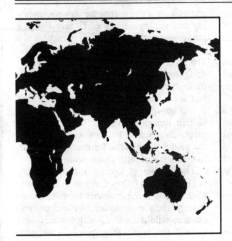

Indian Subcontinent
Bangladesh
India
India travel atlas
Hindi/Urdu phrasebook
Trekking in the Indian Himalaya
Karakoram Highway
Kashmir, Ladakh & Zanskar
Nepal
Trekking in the Nepal Himalaya
Nepali phrasebook
Pakistan
Sri Lanka
Sri Lanka phrasebook

Central America & the Caribbean
Baja California
Central America on a shoestring
Costa Rica
Eastern Caribbean
Guatemala, Belize & Yucatán: La Ruta Maya
Mexico

North America
Alaska
Backpacking in Alaska
Canada
Hawaii
Honolulu city guide
Pacific Northwest USA
Rocky Mountain States
Southwest USA
USA phrasebook

Europe
Baltic States & Kaliningrad
Baltics States phrasebook
Britain
Central Europe on a shoestring
Central Europe phrasebook
Czech & Slovak Republics
Dublin city guide
Eastern Europe on a shoestring
Eastern Europe phrasebook
Finland
France
Greece
Greek phrasebook
Hungary
Iceland, Greenland & the Faroe Islands
Ireland
Italy
Mediterranean Europe on a shoestring
Mediterranean Europe phrasebook
Poland
Prague city guide
Scandinavian & Baltic Europe on a shoestring
Scandinavian Europe phrasebook
Slovenia
Switzerland
Trekking in Greece
Trekking in Spain
USSR
Russian phrasebook
Vienna city guide
Western Europe on a shoestring
Western Europe phrasebook

South America
Argentina, Uruguay & Paraguay
Bolivia
Brazil
Brazilian phrasebook
Chile & Easter Island
Colombia
Ecuador & the Galápagos Islands
Latin American Spanish phrasebook
Peru
Quechua phrasebook
Rio de Janeiro city guide
South America on a shoestring
Trekking in the Patagonian Andes
Venezuela

Indian Ocean
Madagascar & Comoros
Maldives & Islands of the East Indian Ocean
Mauritius, Réunion & Seychelles

The Lonely Planet Story

Lonely Planet published its first book in 1973 in response to the numerous 'How did you do it?' questions Maureen and Tony Wheeler were asked after driving, bussing, hitching, sailing and railing their way from England to Australia.

Written at a kitchen table and hand collated, trimmed and stapled, *Across Asia on the Cheap* became an instant local bestseller, inspiring thoughts of another book.

Eighteen months in South-East Asia resulted in their second guide, *South-East Asia on a shoestring*, which they put together in a backstreet Chinese hotel in Singapore in 1975. The 'yellow bible' as it quickly became known to backpackers around the world, soon became *the* guide to the region. It has sold well over half a million copies and is now in its 8th edition, still retaining its familiar yellow cover.

Today there are over 140 Lonely Planet titles in print – books that have that same adventurous approach to travel as those early guides; books that 'assume you know how to get your luggage off the carousel' as one reviewer put it.

Although Lonely Planet initially specialised in guides to Asia, they now cover most regions of the world, including the Pacific, South America, Africa, the Middle East and Europe. The list of *walking guides* and *phrasebooks* (for 'unusual' languages such as Quechua, Swahili, Nepali and Egyptian Arabic) is also growing rapidly.

The emphasis continues to be on travel for independent travellers. Tony and Maureen still travel for several months of each year and play an active part in the writing, updating and quality control of Lonely Planet's guides.

They have been joined by over 50 authors, 110 staff – mainly editors, cartographers & designers – at our office in Melbourne, Australia, at our US office in Oakland, California and at our European office in Paris; another five at our office in London handle sales for Britain, Europe and Africa. Travellers themselves also make a valuable contribution to the guides through the feedback we receive in thousands of letters each year.

The people at Lonely Planet strongly believe that travellers can make a positive contribution to the countries they visit, both through their appreciation of the countries' culture, wildlife and natural features, and through the money they spend. In addition, the company makes a direct contribution to the countries and regions it covers. Since 1986 a percentage of the income from each book has been donated to ventures such as famine relief in Africa; aid projects in India; agricultural projects in Central America; Greenpeace's efforts to halt French nuclear testing in the Pacific; and Amnesty International.

Lonely Planet's basic travel philosophy is summed up in Tony Wheeler's comment, 'Don't worry about whether your trip will work out. Just go!'